Visual Basic 5

Professional Reference Edition

Rob Thayer

with Michael D. Amundsen, John W. Charlesworth, John D. Conley III, Ashton Hobbs, Dan Horsefield, Paul Kimmel, Anthony Mann, Lowell Mauer, Mike McMillan, and Mark Spenik

SAMS

201 West 103rd Street
Indianapolis, IN 46290

Visual Basic 5 Unleashed, Professional Reference Edition

International Standard Book Number: 0-672-31297-2

Library of Congress Catalog Card Number: 97-81341

First Printing: May, 1998

00 99 98 4 3 2 1

Composed in AGaramond and MCPdigital

Printed in the United States of America

Executive Editor
Christopher Denny

Acquisitions Editor
Sharon Cox

Development Editor
Richard Alvey

Technical Editors
Shelley Powers
Jeff Perkins

Managing Editor
Jodi Jensen

Software Development Specialists
John Warriner
Andrea Duvall

Project Editor
Susan Ross Moore

Copy Editors
Geneil Breeze
Theresa Mathias

Indexers
Christine Nelsen
Erika Millen

Production
Michael Henry
Linda Knose
Tim Osborn
Staci Somers
Mark Walchle

Cover Designer
Aren Howell

Book Designer
Gary Adair

Contents at a Glance

Contents

50 Third-Party Controls 997

Dedication

This book is dedicated to my mother and father, who have never failed to provide me with an incredible amount of love and support. They've always been there for me when I needed them, and I owe them a debt that can never be repaid.

Acknowledgments

It takes a lot of work to finish a book like this one, far more than one person could ever handle. The single name on the cover is misleading, because all books require the efforts of a great number of people. This one is certainly no exception.

I'd like to sincerely thank Sharon Cox, the Acquisitions Editor for this project, for all of her help and terrific patience. Thanks also to Rich Alvey, Chris Denny, and everyone else who was involved in getting this book on the shelf. Heartfelt appreciation also goes to Valda Hilley, whose guidance and insight have been invaluable to me.

Last but not least, a great big "thank you" is due to all of my wonderful friends who have offered their unwavering support during this long project. Peter Stutsman, Joe Miano, Chuck Seifert, and Keith Lopaty have all played instrumental roles in making this book happen. In particular, I'd like to thank David and Ellen Adams. Their dear friendship and assistance has helped me in ways that cannot be expressed in words. Good friends, I couldn't have done it without you.

Rob Thayer

About the Author

Robert Thayer is the president of Thayer Technologies, Inc., a Phoenix-based company that specializes in the design and creation of Windows applications and client/server systems. He can be reached at `rob@thayertech.com` or via TTI's Web site at `http://www.thayertech.com`.

Part I

Development Fundamentals You Should Never Forget or Take for Granted

IN THIS PART

CHAPTER 1

Working with Arrays

IN THIS CHAPTER

One of the most fundamental data structures in Visual Basic is the array. Arrays are used in many computer programs because they are easy to implement and very efficient. Arrays are also fundamental because they resemble how memory is structured in virtually all computer systems.

Many computer applications, such as databases and spreadsheets, are conceptually based on the array. A database table, for example, can be thought of as an array of rows and columns. The rows are the field names of the database, and the columns are where the data that goes in the fields is stored.

A spreadsheet is an even more direct representation of an array. The rows and columns of a spreadsheet correspond directly to the rows and columns that make up a multidimensional array.

Arrays are used primarily to store data of a like kind and to perform operations on that data. An example of this is matrix mathematics. A *matrix* is, quite simply, a multidimensional array that stores related data (numbers). The matrix is then used as a basis to perform operations for calculating statistics, for example. One operation often performed on a matrix is a matrix transpose. A *transpose* of a matrix is performed by writing the columns of a matrix as rows. If you have a small matrix A defined as

```
1 2 3
4 5 6
7 8 9
```

The transpose of matrix A is

```
1 4 7
2 5 8
3 6 9
```

At the end of this chapter, you will develop a program that can perform the transpose of a matrix.

An Overview of Arrays

An *array* is a set of values, stored contiguously in memory, of the same data type. Because an array holds values of the same data type, you have to declare its data type when you create the array. An array can be declared as any legal data type; you can even have an array of user-defined types or an array of objects. If you declare an array to be of type `Variant`, each item in the array can be any legal data type.

NOTE

Even though a `Variant` can store any data type, it is itself a single data type. An array declared as a `Variant` can store any and all data types because that is the definition of `Variant`. Many newcomers to Visual Basic are confused by this concept because they are used to only being able to store one type of data in an array.

Figure 1.1 shows three arrays storing different data types: `Integer`, `String`, and `Variant`.

FIGURE 1.1.
Three arrays of different data types.

```
(0  1  2  3  4  5  6  7  8  9)
```

An array of integers

```
("Visual Basic", "Word", "Excel", "Power Point")
```

An array of strings

```
(1, "Visual Basic", 2, "Word", 3.125, "Excel")
```

An array of variants

The two kinds of arrays are fixed size and dynamic. As its name implies, a *fixed-size array* cannot change its size after it has been created. A *dynamic array*, on the other hand, can change in size after it has been created. I will discuss dynamic arrays later in this chapter.

Fixed-Size Arrays

Arrays can be declared as `Public` or `Private`. To make an array `Public`, declare it in the `Declarations` section of a module. To declare an array at the module level, declare it as `Private` in the `Declarations` section of a module. To create a local array, declare it as `Private` in any procedure.

A public array can be accessed from anywhere in the project. A private array can only be accessed from the module in which the array is declared. For example, if in the code section of `Form1` you declare a private array, the array cannot be accessed from any other forms or modules. However, if you declare a public array in a code module, code from any form in the project can successfully access the array.

Arrays can also be declared by using `Dim` or `Static`. Arrays, like other variables, have a lifetime during which they retain their value. Arrays declared with `Public` have a lifetime that lasts as long as the application is running. Arrays declared with `Dim` within a procedure have a lifetime that lasts only as long as the procedure is running. When the procedure quits, the array declared with `Dim` loses its values. To make a locally declared array retain its value throughout the life of an application, declare it with the `Static` keyword. The array will then retain its value until the application quits, just as if it had been declared as `Public` in a code module.

After declaring the scope of an array, you must assign a fixed-size array a size, or number of elements it will hold. This number is called the array's upper bound, and the number can never exceed the range of a `Long` integer (–2,147,483,647 to 2,147,483,647). An array that is `Public` and holds 20 integer elements is declared in this way:

```
Public Items(19) As Integer 'A global array of 20 integers
```

Other array declarations for different data types and sizes are described in the following lines:

```
Private Items(49) As String 'A local array of 50 strings
Static Items(29) As Variant 'A local array of 30 variants
Dim Items(9) As Double      'A local array of 10 double precision numbers
```

Notice that the numbers declared as the upper bound are one less than the number of items you actually want in the array. In Visual Basic, the array index starts numbering at zero.

NOTE

If you don't want the array index to start at zero, you can do one of two things:

- Include the statement `Option Base 1` in the `Declarations` section of the global module.
- Explicitly declare the lower bound of the array.

The first option sets the lower bound for all arrays in the project to 1. Do this if you never want an array index to start with 0.

You can explicitly declare the lower bound of an array by using the `To` keyword. An array declaration with an explicit lower bound looks like this:

```
Dim Items(1 To 20) As Integer
```

When explicitly declaring the lower bound of an array, you are not required to set the bound at 1. You can use any integer. If you want the `Items` array to start at 10, for example, you can write

```
Private Items(10 To 20) As Integer
```

The only limitation on setting the lower bound is that the number for the lower bound must be less than or equal to the number for the upper bound. This means that it's perfectly legal to declare an array in this way:

```
Dim Items(20 To 20) as Integer
```

Only one item is in this array, and its index is `20`, but you can assign a value to it and treat it the same as if it were a part of a large group of elements.

Now that I have covered all the details of declaring arrays, here is the formal syntax for declaring an array:

```
(Dim, Static, Public, Private) arrayname([subscripts]) [As datatype]
```

The interpretation of this syntax for the array is as follows:

- An array must be declared as either `Dim`, `Static`, `Public`, or `Private`.
- An array must be given a name, although the choice of the name is strictly up to the developer.
- An array can have a set of subscripts, such as `(10,10)`, but if the array is a dynamic array, it is declared with empty parentheses.
- An array can be declared as a data type if it is not a dynamic array.

Initial Values of Array Items

When you declare an array at any level, the items of the array are initially given a value according to the data type of the array:

- A numeric array variable is initialized to 0.
- A variable-length string array variable is initialized to a zero-length string ("").
- A fixed-length string array variable is initialized to `Empty`.
- An array of variants is initialized to `Empty`.
- Each element of a user-defined type array variable is initialized according to its data type.

Assigning Values to Array Elements

In other computer languages, such as C, you can assign values to an array when the array is first declared. You cannot do this in Visual Basic. The declaration must be done first, followed later in the program with a statement or programming construct that assigns values to the array.

There are two ways to assign values to the individual elements of an array. One way is to explicitly assign them with an assignment statement. For example, if you have declared a string array called `Item`, you can assign a value to the first element of the array in this way:

```
Item(0) = "Chair"
```

Other elements of the array can be assigned values at the same time or anywhere else in the body of a procedure. However, if you know the values to be assigned to the array elements in advance, it is good programming practice to place the assignment statements at the beginning of a procedure. Placing all your array element assignment statements together makes your code easier to read and makes it clear exactly where to look to find what value was assigned to an array element initially.

The other way to assign values to array elements is to use some sort of looping structure to loop through the array, assigning values to array elements as you go. For example, if you have an array (`MultOfFive`) that will contain multiples of 5 from 5 to 100, you can write code like this to initialize the array:

```
Dim MultOfFive(1 To 100) As Integer
Dim intArrayVal As Integer
Dim intArrayLoop As Integer

intArrayVal = 5
For intArrayLoop = 1 To 100
    MultOfFive(intArrayLoop) = intArrayVal
    intArrayVal = intArrayVal + 5
Next intArrayLoop
```

NOTE

If you're not familiar with the `For...Next` loop, you can read about it in Chapter 2, "Controlling Program Flow."

Another example of initializing an array is to fill an array with up to 50 items from the contents of a ListBox. The code to initialize the array involves looping through the items of the ListBox, assigning an item to an element of the array until no more items are in the ListBox. Here is an example:

```
Dim ListItems(49) As String
Dim intArrayLoop As Integer

For intArrayLoop = 0 To lstAList.ListCount
   If intArrayLoop < 50 Then
       ListItems(intArrayLoop) = lstAList.List(intArrayLoop)
   End If
Next intArrayLoop
```

Extracting Data from an Array

Loops play an important role in array processing. You have seen how to use loops to put data into arrays; loops are also important for extracting data from arrays. For example, here is a code fragment that takes items out of an array (`Item`) and puts them into a ListBox:

```
Dim intArrayLoop As Integer

For intArrayLoop = 0 To 20
   lstAList.AddItem Item(intArrayLoop)
Next intArrayLoop
```

Multidimensional Arrays

Up to this point, I have discussed arrays that only have one dimension. Not every problem, however, fits into just one dimension. Take the classic example of a course gradebook. One dimension of a course gradebook is the list of students taking the course. The other dimension of the gradebook is the grade the student receives for the course. To store a course grade for each student in the course, you cannot use a single-dimensional array; you have to use a multidimensional array.

A multidimensional array is declared in this way:

```
Dim Algebra(19,19) As String
```

This statement creates an array with 20 rows and 20 columns, or enough storage space to hold the names of 20 students and 20 course grades.

As with single-dimensional arrays, you can explicitly declare the lower bound of multidimensional arrays:

```
Dim Algebra(1 To 20, 1 To 20) As String
```

You are not limited to only two dimensions. You can expand the `Algebra` array to three dimensions by declaring the array as follows:

```
Dim Algebra(19,19,19)
```

The total number of elements that can be stored in this array is 20 times 20 times 20, or 8000 elements. An array can be declared with up to 60 dimensions (as if you would ever need one), but keep in mind that every new dimension that is added to an array multiplies the amount of memory needed to hold the array by the number of elements in the new dimension. Multidimensional arrays can hog up memory quickly.

Initializing Multidimensional Arrays

Multidimensional arrays are initialized in much the same way as single-dimensional arrays. However, two loops are usually used because there are two dimensions to initialize. Here is a code fragment to initialize a two-dimensional array that stores the multiples of 2 through 200:

```
Dim MultOfTwo(1 To 10, 1 To 10) As Integer
Dim intArrayVal As Integer
Dim intLoopX As Integer
Dim intLoopY As Integer

intArrayVal = 1

For intLoopX = 1 To 10
    For intLoopY = 1 To 10
        intArrayVal = intArrayVal + 2
        MultOfTwo(intLoopX, intLoopY) = intArrayVal
    Next intLoopY
Next intLoopX
```

Notice how the two loops are used. This is called a nested `For` loop. For each value of `intLoopX`, the program loops through `intLoopY` 10 times. The end result is a table of values like the array shown in Figure 1.2.

FIGURE 1.2.
A multidimensional array of the multiples of 2 to 200.

2	4	6	8	10	12	14	16	18	20
22	24	26	28	30	32	34	36	38	40
42	44	46	48	50	52	54	56	58	60
62	64	66	68	70	72	74	76	78	80
82	84	86	88	90	92	94	96	98	100
102	104	106	108	110	112	114	116	118	120
122	124	126	128	130	132	134	136	138	140
142	144	146	148	150	152	154	156	158	160
162	164	166	168	170	172	174	176	178	180
182	184	186	188	190	192	194	196	198	200

Arrays Made Up of Other Arrays

Arrays can hold any data type as long as it is the same data type throughout the array. This requirement is loosened a little when the elements of an array are other arrays. A simple example will make this concept clear.

First, create an array of integers and assign values to some of the elements of the array:

```
Dim SomeInts(20) As Integer
SomeInts(0) = 25
SomeInts(1) = 30
SomeInts(2) = 20
SomeInts(3) = 15
```

Now declare a string array and put some values into it:

```
Dim SomeStrs(20) As String
SomeStrs(0) = "Chair"
SomeStrs(1) = "Couch"
SomeStrs(2) = "Bookshelf"
SomeStrs(3) = "Bed"
```

Finally, you need to declare a `Variant` array that will consist of these other two arrays:

```
Dim CombinedArrays(2) As Variant
CombinedArrays(0) = SomeInts()
CombinedArrays(1) = SomeStrs()
```

To display an element from each array, you can write

```
MsgBox CombinedArrays (0) (1) 'Displays "30"
MsgBox CombinedArrays(1) (2)  'Displays "Bookshelf"
```

This method works because the `CombineArrays` array is a `Variant` and can consist of elements of any data type, even other arrays. With a little imagination, you can see how working with arrays of different data types can solve problems that couldn't be solved if you weren't allowed to mix array types within another array.

Dynamic Arrays

Sometimes when working with arrays, you either won't know the maximum size of an array or you won't want to declare an upper bound and perhaps arbitrarily limit the size of an array. In cases such as these, a fixed-size array does not work because when an upper bound is declared in a fixed-size array, that size cannot be changed. Visual Basic provides a useful data structure to deal with this situation, the dynamic array.

Declaring Dynamic Arrays

A dynamic array is an array that can be resized any time after it is declared. To declare a dynamic array, you can use a `Public` statement or a `Dim` statement at the module level, or use a `Private`, `Dim`, or `Static` statement if you want the array to be local to a procedure. The syntax for declaring a dynamic array is

```
Dim Items() As String
```

`Dim` can be replaced with any of the other scope-setting keywords I mentioned. Notice that there is an empty dimension list after the array name. This tells Visual Basic that the array is dynamic and will be dimensioned later.

To allocate storage space to the array, use the `ReDim` statement. You can only use this statement in a procedure because, unlike the `Dim` and `Static` statements, the `ReDim` statement is executable, meaning that `ReDim` makes the application execute the action of resizing the array at runtime.

To give the array an initial set of elements for storage, you can write

```
ReDim Items(20)
```

You do not have to mention the data type because you have already declared it.

Lower and Upper Bounds of Dynamic Arrays

The syntax that fixed-size arrays follow concerning their lower and upper bounds also applies to dynamic arrays. Every time you redimension an array, you can change the number of elements and the upper and lower bounds of each dimension:

```
Dim Items() As String
    .
    .
    .
ReDim Items(20)
    .
    .
    .
ReDim Items(10)
```

or

```
Dim Items() As String
     .
     .
     .
ReDim Items(5,5)
     .
     .
     .
ReDim Items(10,10)
```

However, the following code is illegal:

```
ReDim Items(5,5,5)
```

Only the number of elements and the lower and upper bounds of each dimension can be changed. The total number of dimensions of a dynamic array cannot be changed.

Preserving the Contents of Dynamic Arrays When Resizing

The `ReDim` statement, when executed, erases all the current values in a dynamic array. The values are set to the default initialization for the array's data type. For many applications, such as when you want to prepare the array to accept new data or you want to conserve memory, erasing the contents of an array is exactly what you want to do. For other applications, however, the last thing you want to do is lose the values already in the array. You can save the current values of an array before you resize it by using the `Preserve` keyword with the `ReDim` statement.

Here is a code fragment that puts three items into a dynamic string array:

```
ReDim Items(2)
Items(0) = "Chair"
Items(1) = "Couch"
Items(2) = "Bed"
```

You can increase the size of the array by writing the following statement:

```
ReDim Preserve Items(UBound(Items) + 10)
```

This statement takes the upper bound of `Items`, adds 10 to it, and resets the upper bound to that number, which is 13. Also, the elements in `Items(0)`, `Items(1)`, and `Items(2)` will remain unchanged. Had you not used the `Preserve` keyword, each element would have been set to either `Empty` or the empty string, depending on whether the array was declared as a fixed-length string type or a variable-length string type.

Redimensioning Multidimensional Arrays

The contents of multidimensional arrays can also be retained using the `Preserve` keyword. However, when resizing a multidimensional array, you can change only the upper bound of the last dimension. If you try to change any of the other dimensions, or if you try to change the lower bound of the last dimension, you get a runtime error.

Look at a sample code fragment to see why this is so:

```
Dim Algebra() As String
ReDim Algebra(5,1)
Algebra(0,0) = "Johnny Smith"
Algebra(0,1) = "B"
Algebra(1,0) = "Betty Doe"
Algebra(1,1) = "A"
ReDim Preserve Algebra(2 To 7,2) ' This generates a runtime error
```

The last statement generates a runtime error because by trying to set the lower bound of the first dimension to 2, Visual Basic wants to erase the array elements with a first dimension of 0 or 1 (see Figures 1.3 and 1.4). Because you used the `Preserve` keyword to save the contents of the array, Visual Basic detects a conflict and issues a runtime error.

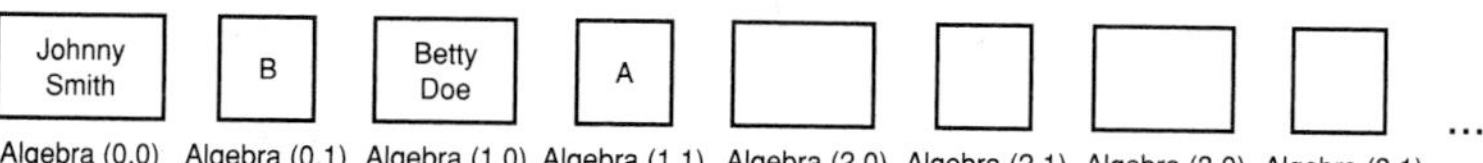

FIGURE 1.3.
The `Algebra` *array before redimensioning by using the* `Preserve` *keyword.*

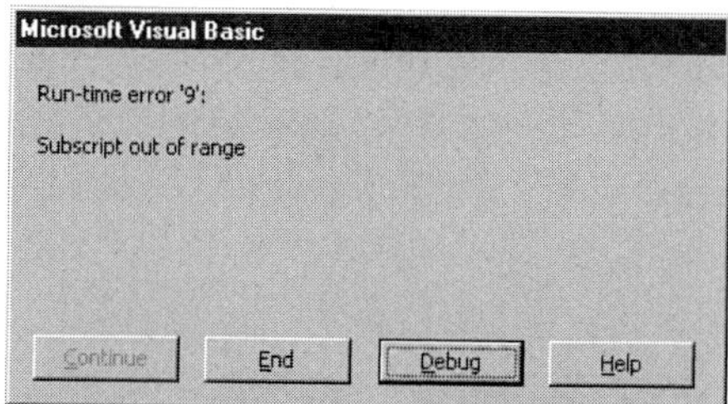

FIGURE 1.4.
The error message generated from an attempt to redimension an array using `Preserve` *outside the bounds of stored data in the array.*

Passing Arrays as Arguments to Functions and Subprocedures

Arrays can serve one more purpose as a data structure. When you need the values of the elements of an array in a function or subroutine, you can pass the whole array as an argument. You can then have access to the elements of the array in the normal way.

You pass an array to a function or subroutine in the same way you pass any other argument, except that an array always must be passed by reference as opposed to by value.

NOTE

By reference (`ByRef`) indicates that the memory address and not the actual value of the argument is passed. When an address is passed, the argument's value can be changed by the function or subroutine. If an argument is passed by value (`ByVal`), then a copy of the argument's value is passed and the actual value cannot be changed. By default, arguments are passed by reference in Visual Basic.

Look at an example of passing an array to a function. First, set up the array:

```
Dim Ints(10) As Integer
Dim intLoop As Integer

For intLoop = 0 To UBound(Ints) - 1
   Ints(intLoop) = intLoop
Next intLoop
```

Here's the code for the function:

```
Private Function GetElement(ByRef intArray() as Integer, _
   intArrayElement as Integer) As Integer

   GetElement = intArray(intArrayElement)

End Function

Private Sub Command1_Click()

   Dim strMessage As String
   Dim strTitle As String
   Dim strDefault As String
   Dim strSomeElement As String
   Dim intTheNumber As Integer

   strMessage = "Enter an element number: "
   strTitle = "Passing an Array to a Function as an Argument"
   strDefault = "1"
   strSomeElement = InputBox(strMessage, strTitle, strDefault)
   intTheNumber = GetElement(Ints(), Val(strSomeElement))
   MsgBox "The value of element " & strSomeElement & " is " & _
     intTheNumber

End Sub
```

This sample code passes the array and an element number to the function `GetElement`. The value of `GetElement` is simply the element located in the position of the number passed to the function.

Versions of Visual Basic before Version 4 could not pass arrays as arguments to functions and subprocedures. Being able to pass arrays as arguments to functions and subprocedures is another example of how newer versions of Visual Basic have increased the expressive power of the language.

Transposing a Matrix

As mentioned in the introduction to this chapter, one use of arrays is storing data in a matrix. A matrix is a row-and-column representation of a set of data. In economics, for example, you can use a matrix to store data for a simple puzzle.

Suppose that you are writing a puzzle program that stores the numbers zero through nine in a 3-by-3 matrix. The numbers in each column of the matrix add up to 13, and the numbers in each row also add up to 13. Such a matrix might look like this:

```
7    5    1
4    0    9
2    8    3
```

In the puzzle program, you may need to transpose the matrix so that the columns become the rows and vice versa. To do this, you must set up the matrix as an array and then perform a series of loops that exchange the rows and columns. Listing 1.1 contains the program.

Listing 1.1. Transposing a matrix.

```
Dim intMatrix(2, 2) As Integer
Dim intRow As Integer
Dim intCol As Integer
Dim intTemp As Integer

intMatrix(0, 0) = 7: intMatrix(0, 1) = 5: intMatrix(0, 2) = 1
intMatrix(1, 0) = 4: intMatrix(1, 1) = 0: intMatrix(1, 2) = 9
intMatrix(2, 0) = 2: intMatrix(2, 1) = 8: intMatrix(2, 2) = 3

For intRow = LBound(intMatrix, 1) To (UBound(intMatrix, 1) - 1)
    For intCol = (intRow + 1) To (UBound(intMatrix, 2))
        intTemp = intMatrix(intRow, intCol)
        intMatrix(intRow, intCol) = intMatrix(intCol, intRow)
        intMatrix(intCol, intRow) = intTemp
    Next intCol
Next intRow
```

The interesting thing about the preceding code is that it does not require another array to transpose the original array. It simply moves the array elements in such a fashion that it never overwrites an element unless it has already been moved to another array element. The code only works for arrays that have identical dimensions—that is, the same number of columns and rows.

If you run the preceding program, it will transpose the puzzle matrix so that its columns become its rows and vice versa. The new matrix (which is stored in the array `intMatrix`) will then look like this:

```
7    4    2
5    0    8
1    9    3
```

As you can see, the numbers in the columns and rows still add up to 13, indicating that the transpose worked correctly.

Summary

The array is a powerful data structure, fundamental to the capability to solve problems in Visual Basic. Some of the more powerful features of arrays include

- Using loops to initialize arrays
- Conserving array contents in dynamic arrays with the `Preserve` keyword
- Passing arrays as arguments to functions and subprocedures

CHAPTER 2

Controlling Program Flow

IN THIS CHAPTER

Programs in Visual Basic are never conceived to be executed in a purely linear manner, where statements are executed one after the other in sequence. Usually, as you write a program to solve a problem, you make decisions based on the data the program receives, and depending on the data, a certain set of statements is executed. This mode of program execution relies on the capability of Visual Basic to make decisions and control the flow of the program as new data is received. This chapter reviews several sets of statements available for decision making and controlling program flow.

Programming constructs that control program flow depend on a set of operators that determine what course a control flow statement takes. For example, one of the basic control flow constructs in Visual Basic is the `If...Then` construct. `If...Then` works by making a comparison:

```
If (A > B) Then Debug.Print "A is greater than B"
```

The greater-than sign is one of the comparison operators that are a necessary part of making decisions and controlling program flow in Visual Basic. This chapter explains two sets of operators: comparison operators (such as < and >) and logical operators (such as `And`, `Or`, and `Not`).

Making Comparisons and Combining Comparisons

Control flow constructs in Visual Basic (and all computer languages, for that matter) operate by making comparisons between items of data. The comparison is the basis for how the program changes its flow of execution. Comparisons are made using a set of operators called *comparison operators.* Sometimes, for more complex decisions, two or more comparisons must be made at the same time. To do this, comparison operators must be joined using another set of operators called *logical operators.* Together, these operators actually make the decisions that the control flow constructs use to determine which set of program statements is executed.

Comparison Operators

Comparison operators are used to determine the relationship between two objects. You can use comparison operators in three ways, which can be explained by showing the possible syntactical forms of comparison expressions:

```
result = expression1 comparisonoperator expression2
result = object1 Is object2
result = string Like pattern
```

Every comparison expression returns a result, either `True` or `False`. The value of the comparison expression is placed in the `result` variable. Later in this chapter, you will see that with control flow constructs, the value of the comparison expression, instead of being assigned to the `result` variable, is used to determine how the control flow construct executes.

In the first comparison expression, two expressions are compared using a comparison operator. In the second expression, one object is compared to another object to see whether the first object `Is` the same type of object as the second object. The third expression compares a string to a particular pattern of characters to see whether the string matches the pattern in some way. This type of comparison will become clearer when you see an example.

When comparing two data items, a comparison expression can result in one of three values, `True`, `False`, or `Null`, depending on the type of comparison being made. Table 2.1 shows the list of comparison operators and the conditions that determine their resulting values.

Table 2.1. The comparison operators and their conditions.

Operator	`True` *when*	`False` *when*	`Null` *when*
< (Less than)	*expression1* < *expression2*	*expression1* >= *expression2*	*expression1* or *expression2* = Null
<= (Less than or equal to)	*expression1* <= *expression2*	*expression1* > *expression2*	*expression1* or *expression2* = Null
> (Greater than)	*expression1* > *expression2*	*expression1* <= *expression2*	*expression1* or *expression2* = Null
>= (Greater than or equal to)	*expression1* >= *expression2*	*expression1* < *expression2*	*expression1* or *expression2* = Null
= (Equal to)	*expression1* = *expression2*	*expression1* <> *expression2*	*expression1* or *expression2* = Null
<> (Not equal to)	*expression1* <> *expression2*	*expression1* = *expression2*	*expression1* or *expression2* = Null

The `Is` and `Like` operators follow different rules from the other comparison operators. In comparing two objects, `Is` evaluates to `True` if *`object1`* and *`object2`* are the same object. The following code fragment demonstrates the `Is` operator:

```
Dim objTestA As Object
Dim objTestB As Object
Dim objTestC As Object
Dim booResult As Boolean                ' Either True or False

Set objTestA = Controls!txtTextBox1
Set objTestB = objTestA
Set objTestC = Controls!txtTextBox2

booResult = objTestB Is objTestA        ' They are the same
Debug.Print booResult                   ' Prints True

booResult = objTestC Is objTestB        ' They are different
Debug.Print booResult                   ' Prints False
```

The `Like` operator is more complicated because it is used to test whether *expression1* is matched by a pattern defined in *expression2*. Pattern matching can get complicated, but if you start out by learning the basic rules, you can quickly learn how to match complex patterns without too much trouble.

The best way to learn pattern matching is to first learn the basic pattern-matching characters. The following shows the characters used in pattern matching and the patterns they match:

`?`	Matches any single character
`*`	Matches zero or more characters
`#`	Matches any single digit
`[`*charlist*`]`	Matches any single character in *charlist*
`[!`*charlist*`]`	Matches any single character not in *charlist*

The following code shows some examples of how the pattern-matching characters work. By studying these simple examples, you will find it easier to design more complex pattern-matching expressions:

```
booResult = "Visual Basic" Like "V*"              ' booResult = True
booResult = "Visual Basic" Like "V???????????"    ' booResult = True
booResult = "VISUAL" Like "v*"                    ' booResult = False
booResult = "Visual Basic 5" Like "*#"            ' booResult = True
booResult = "V" Like "!?"                         ' booResult = False
booResult = "1" Like "#"                          ' booResult = True
booResult = "Vi" Like "V[a-z]"                    ' booResult = True
booResult = "VB" Like "V[a-z]"                    ' booResult = False
```

The sort order for strings relies on the internal binary representations of the characters in Microsoft Windows. The default sort order is `A < B ... < E ... < Z < a < b ... < e ... < z < 0`. This is also the default sort order for Visual Basic and is reflected in the `Option Compare Binary` statement, which tells Visual Basic to do binary sorting. You will only use this statement if you have previously changed the sort order with the `Option Compare Text` statement.

You can change the sort order by issuing the following statement in a code module: `Option Compare Text`. This changes the sort order to a case-insensitive order represented by the following sort order `(A=a) < (B=b) ... < (E=e) ... < (Z=z) < 0`.

Logical Operators

For more complex decisions, you can combine comparison operators, as in `(A > B) And (B > C)` or other such expressions. The connecting operator that compares the comparison expressions is called a logical operator. The two logical operators used most often are `Or` and `And`. You use `Or` to perform a logical disjunction on two expressions; in other words, `Or` returns `True` if either one of two expressions evaluates to true and returns `False` if both expressions evaluate to false. A simple code fragment illustrates how `Or` works:

```
Dim intTest1 As Integer
Dim intTest2 As Integer
Dim booResult As Boolean
```

```
intTest1 = 12
intTest2 = 10
booResult = (intTest1 > intTest2) Or (intTest2 > intTest1)
Debug.Print booResult        ' Prints True
```

This code fragment displays `True` in the Debug window because the first expression in the comparison (`intTest1 > intTest2`) is true. Here is another code fragment to illustrate how the `Or` operator works:

```
Dim intTest1 As Integer
Dim intTest2 As Integer
Dim booResult As Boolean

intTest1 = 10
intTest2 = 10
booResult = (intTest1 > intTest2) Or (intTest2 > intTest1)
Debug.Print booResult        ' Prints False
```

This code fragment displays `False` in the Debug window because neither the first expression (`intTest1 > intTest2`) nor the second expression (`intTest2 > intTest1`) is true.

The second logical operator, `And`, performs a logical conjunction on the two expressions; in other words, `And` returns `True` if both expressions evaluate to true and returns `False` if either expression evaluates to false. Here is an example:

```
Dim intTest1 As Integer
Dim intTest2 As Integer
Dim intTest3 As Integer
Dim booResult As Boolean

intTest1 = 10
intTest2 = 14
intTest3 = 9
booResult = (intTest1 < intTest2) And (intTest2 > intTest3)
Debug.Print booResult        ' Prints True
```

This code fragment displays `True` in the Debug window because both the first expression (`intTest1 < intTest2`) and the second expression (`intTest2 > intTest3`) are true. Here is another example:

```
Dim intTest1 As Integer
Dim intTest2 As Integer
Dim intTest3 As Integer
Dim booResult As Boolean

intTest1 = 10
intTest2 = 14
intTest3 = 9
booResult = (intTest1 > intTest2) And (intTest2 > intTest3)
Debug.Print booResult        ' Prints False
```

This code fragment displays `False` in the Debug window because the first expression (`intTest1 > intTest2`) is false, even though the second expression is true.

For both `Or` and `And`, if either expression evaluates to `Null`, then the result of the comparison is `Null`.

Another logical operator is XOR, which is not used as often as Or or And but can be used for certain types of comparisons. You use the XOR operator for logical exclusion, meaning that XOR returns False if both of the expressions are true and returns True if one of the expressions evaluates to true and the other one evaluates to false. The following code fragment illustrates the use of XOR:

```
Dim intTest1 As Integer
Dim intTest2 As Integer
Dim intTest3 As Integer
Dim booResult As Boolean

intTest1 = 10
intTest2 = 14
intTest3 = 9
booResult = (intTest1 < intTest2) Xor (intTest3 > intTest2)
Debug.Print booResult
```

This code fragment displays True in the Debug window because only one of the expressions (intTest1 < intTest2) is true. Here is another example of XOR:

```
Dim A As Integer
Dim B As Integer
Dim C As Integer
Dim MyResult As Boolean
A = 10
B = 14
C = 9
MyResult = (A < B) XOR (C < B)
Debug.Print MyResult
```

This code fragment displays False in the Debug window because, in this case, both expressions are true and XOR is checking for exclusion, not inclusion.

Figure 2.1 shows the XOR evaluation rules.

FIGURE 2.1.
XOR *evaluation rules.*

Expression 1 evaluates to	Expression 2 evaluates to	The result is
True	True	False
True	False	True
False	True	True
False	False	False

An operator similar to XOR is Eqv, which is the logical equivalence operator. Whereas XOR returns True if either but not both of the expressions evaluates to true, Eqv returns True if both of the expressions are true or false and returns False if one expression is true and the other expression is false. A sample code fragment illustrates how to use Eqv:

```
Dim intTest1 As Integer
Dim intTest2 As Integer
Dim intTest3 As Integer
Dim booResult As Boolean
```

```
intTest1 = 10
intTest2 = 14
intTest3 = 9
booResult = (intTest1 < intTest2) Eqv (intTest2 < intTest3)
Debug.Print booResult          ' Prints True
```

This code fragment displays `True` in the Debug window because both expressions are true. Here is another example:

```
Dim intTest1 As Integer
Dim intTest2 As Integer
Dim intTest3 As Integer
Dim booResult As Boolean

intTest1 = 10
intTest2 = 14
intTest3 = 9
booResult = (intTest1 < intTest2) Eqv (intTest2 < intTest3)
Debug.Print booResult          ' Prints False
```

This code fragment displays `False` in the Debug window because the second expression is false.

If either of the expressions in a `XOR` or `Eqv` comparison is `Null`, then the result of the comparison is `Null` also.

Figure 2.2 outlines the `Eqv` evaluation rules.

FIGURE 2.2.
`Eqv` *evaluation rules.*

Expression 1 evaluates to	Expression 2 evaluates to	The result is
True	True	True
True	False	False
False	True	False
False	False	True

Bitwise Operators

Visual Basic has the capability to work with the individual bits that make up the values stored in memory. You can use `Or`, `And`, `XOR`, and `Eqv` to manipulate the bits of the contents of an expression.

Before you can understand the rules of the bitwise operators, you need to understand how Visual Basic stores values in memory. Most people know that computers store information in terms of zeros and ones—the two digits that make up the binary system. Eight binary digits (bits) make up a byte, which is the unit of storage most characters, numbers, strings, and so on are described in. For example, an integer value takes 2 bytes (16 bits) of storage space. In the computer, the integer 2 is represented by the following binary number: 0000000000000010. The integer 4 is written in binary as 0000000000000100.

Now you are ready to see how you can use the bitwise operators to manipulate bits. First, look at the bitwise OR. The rules for the bitwise OR look much like the rules for the logical Or, but you are working with bits rather than expressions (see Figure 2.3).

FIGURE 2.3.
Bitwise OR evaluation rules.

Bit in expression 1 is	Bit in expression 2 is	Result is
0	0	0
0	1	1
1	0	1
1	1	1

Now look at a code fragment that uses the bitwise OR:

```
Dim intTest1 As Integer
Dim intTest2 As Integer
Dim intResult As Integer

intTest1 = 5
intTest2 = 3
intResult = intTest1 Or intTest2
Debug.Print intResult
```

This code fragment displays 7 in the Debug window. Figure 2.4 shows the values of A and B in binary form and the result of the bitwise OR.

FIGURE 2.4.
Bitwise OR performed on binary 5 and binary 3.

```
 5 = 0101
 3 = 0011
---------
or = 0111
```

Now that you understand how to make comparisons between different data values, you are ready to learn how to use these comparisons with the different program flow constructs Visual Basic provides to change the execution flow of your programs.

Making Decisions

All computer programs, whether written in Visual Basic or some other language, must be able to make decisions about how to deal with data processed during the execution of a program. Making decisions becomes a matter of choosing a course to take by evaluating the data. Visual Basic provides a set of decision structures and functions that can test data and perform different operations based on the outcome of the test. These decision structures and functions are

- If...Then
- If...Then...Else
- Select Case
- Switch
- Choose

If...Then

You use the `If...Then` structure to execute one or more statements based on a condition or set of conditions. You can write an `If...Then` as a statement on one line, or you can write it as a structure using block syntax, where you put each statement to be executed on a separate line. The syntax for an `If...Then` statement is

```
If condition Then statement
```

The syntax for the `If...Then` structure is

```
If condition Then
    statement-1
    statement-2
    statement-n
End If
```

NOTE

It is standard programming practice to indent the statements within a control flow structure. There are many different ways to indent statements, but the most popular way is to tab over once so that each statement is one tab space to the right of the control structure. Keep in mind, however, that Visual Basic doesn't require you to indent your code, and this is done just to make your code easier to read.

Of course, you can execute just one statement in the `If...Then` structure. You may want to do so anyway to make your code more readable.

The *`condition`* part of the `If...Then` structure usually consists of one or more comparison expressions, although it can be any expression that evaluates to a numeric value. The *`condition`* evaluated by Visual Basic must be either `True` or `False`. An expression that evaluates to zero is considered `False`, whereas any non-zero expression is considered `True`.

In an `If...Then` statement, if the *`condition`* evaluates to `True`, the statement following `Then` is executed. If the *`condition`* evaluates to `False`, nothing happens, and the program control reverts to the line of code after the `If...Then`.

In an `If...Then` structure, if the *`condition`* evaluates to `True`, the statements below the `If...Then` line are executed. If the *`condition`* evaluates to `False`, then the program control reverts to the line of code immediately following the `End If`.

Here is an example of an `If...Then` statement:

```
If curAccountBalance < 0 Then booOverdrawn = True
```

Here is the equivalent statement written in an `If...Then` structure:

```
If curAccountBalance < 0 Then
    booOverDrawn = True
End If
```

If you want to execute more than one statement when *condition* evaluates to True, then you must use the If...Then structure:

```
If curAccountBalance < 0 Then
    booOverDrawn = True
    txtMessage = "Insufficient Funds"
End If
```

If...Then...Else

For more complex decision making, you use the If...Then...Else decision structure. This structure allows you to execute one of many different blocks of statements. The syntax of the If...Then...Else structure looks like this:

```
If condition1 Then
    [statement block 1]
[ElseIf condition2 Then
    [statement block 2]]
[Else
    [statement block 3]]
End If
```

The flow of the If...Then...Else structure proceeds as follows. Visual Basic tests *condition1*. If it is false, the program tests *condition2*. This process repeats until a true condition is found. When a true condition is found, Visual Basic executes the block of statements under the true condition, and program control reverts to the statement following the End If. If no condition evaluates to True, Visual Basic simply transfers program control to the statement after the End If. However, you can include an optional Else statement at the end of the structure so that Visual Basic executes the corresponding statement block if all the preceding conditions are false.

It is important to note that you can have one, many, or no ElseIf clauses in an If...Then...Else. The following examples will make using If...Then...Else easier to understand:

```
If curAccountBalance < 0 Then
    booOverDrawn = True
ElseIf curAccountBalance <= 1000 Then
    booOverDrawn = False
    booServiceCharge = True
Else
    booOverDrawn = False
    booServiceCharge = False
End If
```

You can include as many ElseIf clauses in an If...Then...Else as you want, but beware that using more than a few ElseIf clauses makes your code more difficult to read. A more readable way to check many conditions is to use the Select Case structure, which is discussed later in this chapter.

Nested If...Thens

You can nest If...Then structures for more complex decision making. When you have more than two or three If...Then structures nested together, however, you can usually rewrite that section of code using `If...Then...Else` or `Select Case`. The following code fragment shows an example of a nested `If...Then`:

```
If curAccountBalance > 0 Then
    If curAmtToWithdraw > curAccountBalance Then
        txtMessage = "Insufficient funds for withdrawal"
    End If
    booOverDrawn = False
End If
```

Select Case

An alternative to the `If...Then...Else` structure for selecting one of many conditions is the `Select Case` structure. `Select Case` provides the same functionality as the `If...Then...Else`, but it makes your code more readable when there are several choices.

First, take a look at the syntax of the `Select Case` structure:

```
Select Case testexpression
    [Case expressionlist1
        [statement block 1]]
    [Case expressionlist2
        [statement block 2]]
    .
    .
    .
    [Case Else
        [statement block n]]
End Select
```

`Select Case` works by first evaluating *`testexpression`*. The result of this evaluation is then tested against each `Case` clause in the structure. If a match is found, each of the statements in the statement block of the `Case` is executed. You can also add the `Case Else` clause to execute a block of statements if none of the other `Case` clauses is successfully matched. After a statement block is executed, program control reverts to the line of code after `End Select`.

The *`expressionlist`* can be one or more values with multiple values separated by commas. Each statement block has zero or more statements. If more than one `Case` clause matches the *`testexpression`*, the program executes the statement block of the first `Case` that matches, and then control immediately reverts to the line of code after `End Select`.

The following `Select Case` structure implements a basic ATM transaction system:

```
Private Sub mnuATM_Click(Index As Integer)

   Select Case Index
      Case 0      ' Withdrawal
         Call Withdrawal
      Case 1      ' Deposit
         Call DispenseEnvelope
      Case 2      ' Account Balance
         Call DisplayAccountBalance
      Case 3      ' Transfer
         Call TransferChoice
```

```
        Case Else
            Call InvalidChoice
    End Select

End Sub
```

Although you can use a `Select Case` structure in place of an `If...Then...Else` structure, `Select Case` acts differently than `If...Then...Else`. A `Select...Case` structure can only compare a single data item, whereas an `If...Then...Else` structure can make multiple comparisons on different data items in each `ElseIf` clause. For example, the `Select Case` structure shown previously only evaluates one data item, `Index` (which was one of the function's arguments). It makes several comparisons to that data item (Is it 0?, Is it 1?, and so on), but all the comparisons relate to the same data item.

Switch

The previous decision-making examples you have seen are structures. `Switch` is a function that returns a value or expression based on the evaluation of a test expression.

The syntax of the `Switch` function is

```
Switch(expr-1, value-1[,expr-2, value-2, ...[,expr-n,value-n]])
```

The two parts to the `Switch` function are the expression part and the value part. The expression part is a `Variant` expression that evaluates to either `True` or `False`. If the expression evaluates to `True`, the value associated with the expression is returned as the value of the function. If the first expression evaluates to `False` and there are more expressions to test, each expression is evaluated in turn, and the value associated with the first expression that evaluates to `True` is returned. If no expression evaluates to `True`, `Switch` returns a `Null` value.

NOTE

Be careful of undesirable side effects in a `Switch` function. If an expression evaluation leads to a runtime error, even if it is evaluated after an expression evaluates to `True`, the error condition is still flagged.

Here is an example of the `Switch` function:

```
Function SetATMMessage(curAcctBalance As Currency, _
    curAmtToWithdraw As Currency) As String

    SetATMMessage = Switch(curAcctBalance < 0, _
        "Account overdrawn", _
        curAcctBalance > 0 And curAmtToWithdraw > curAmtToWithdraw, _
        "Insufficient funds", _
        curAcctBalance > curAmtToWithdraw, _
        "Please take your money")

End Function
```

Choose

A variation of the `Switch` function is the `Choose` function. Whereas `Switch` can test on many expressions, `Choose` returns a value based on the value of an index that is passed to it. Here is the syntax for the `Choose` function:

```
Choose(index, choice-1[,choice-2,...[,choice-n]])
```

`Choose` returns a choice from the list of *`choice-1`*, *`choice-2`*, ... *`choice-n`* based on the value of *`index`*. If the *`index`* is `1`, *`choice-1`* is returned; if the *`index`* is `2`, the value returned is *`choice-2`*; and so on.

The index should be a whole number; if the index is not a whole number, it is rounded to the nearest whole number before it is evaluated.

Here is an example of the `Choose` function:

```
Function GetChoice(intChoice As Integer) As String

    GetChoice = Choose(intChoice, "User chose #1", _
        "User chose #2", "User chose #3")

End Function
```

If `Ind` is `2`, then `GetChoice` is equal to the string `"User chose #2"`.

If the value of `intChoice` is less than `1` or greater than the number of choices, `Choose` returns `Null`.

Program Flow Constructs

As I mentioned at the beginning of this chapter, computer programs rarely proceed in a sequential order. Usually, you need to be able to make your programs execute certain lines of code more than once in response to some condition. Other times, you need to be able to move from one place in the program to someplace else to perform a set of instructions. Visual Basic provides two programming constructs to allow control over how programs flow:

- Looping structures
- Branching structures

Looping Structures

Looping structures give you the capability to execute one or more lines of code repetitively. If you don't know how many times you want to execute a set of statements, the `Do...Loop` structure is usually the best to use. If you want to process a set of statements a specific number of times, then the `For...Next` structure is what you want. When you want to perform a set of operations on a set of data that are grouped together as an array or object, then Visual Basic offers the `For Each...Next` structure.

Do...Loop

To execute a block of statements an indefinite number of times, use a `Do...Loop`. The `Do...Loop` structure evaluates a numeric condition in deciding whether to continue executing. The condition must be able to evaluate to `True` (nonzero) or `False` (zero).

The four variations of the `Do...Loop` structure can be divided into two groups:

- `Do...Loops` that execute as long as the condition is `True`
- `Do...Loops` that execute as long as the condition is `False`

Do While...Loop

`Do While...Loop` and its variation, `Do...Loop While`, execute when the condition evaluates to `True`. Here is the syntax of the `Do While...Loop` structure:

```
Do While condition
    statements
Loop
```

When a Visual Basic program encounters a `Do While` *`condition`* statement, it first evaluates *`condition`*. If *`condition`* is `True`, the statements immediately following the *`condition`* are executed. After the last statement is executed, the `Loop` statement is encountered. Visual Basic then returns to the `Do While` *`condition`* line and reevaluates *`condition`*. As long as *`condition`* is `True`, the statements are executed. However, if and when *`condition`* evaluates to `False`, the program jumps to the line of code immediately following the `Loop` statement and continues executing the rest of the program.

The following procedure allows someone to make withdrawals from an ATM as long as he has enough money in his account:

```
Private Sub MakeWithdrawal(curAcctBalance As Currency)

    Dim curWithdrawalAmt As Currency

    Do While curAcctBalance > 0
        curWithdrawalAmt = InputBox "Enter an amount to withdraw: "
        If curWithdrawalAmt > curAcctBalance Then
            curAcctBalance = curAcctBalance - curWithdrawalAmt
        Else
            MsgBox "Insufficient funds for this transaction. _
                Enter a smaller amount."
        End If
    Loop
    MsgBox "Your account balance is zero."

End Sub
```

If the `curAcctBalance` is zero or less, the program prints an `"Insufficient Funds"` message and the `Do` loop does not execute; otherwise, the `Do` loop executes until `curAcctBalance` is equal to or less than zero.

A variation of the `Do While...Loop` structure is `Do...Loop While`. The `Do` loop guarantees that the block of statements inside the loop executes at least once. The following code fragment shows the preceding example rewritten with a `Do...Loop While` structure:

```
Private Sub MakeWithdrawal(curAcctBalance As Currency)

    Dim curWithdrawalAmt As Currency

    Do
        curWithdrawalAmt = InputBox "Enter an amount to withdraw: "
        If curWithdrawalAmt > curAcctBalance Then
            curAcctBalance = curAcctBalance - curWithdrawalAmt
        Else
            MsgBox "Insuffcient funds for this transaction. _
                Enter a smaller amount."
        End If
    Loop While (curAcctBalance > 0)
    MsgBox "Your account balance is zero."

End Sub
```


Do Until...Loop

The second group of `Do` loops executes the block of statements within the loop as long as the condition is `False`. As with the `Do While...Loop` structure, the two variations are `Do Until...Loop` and `Do...Loop Until`. Look at the ATM withdrawal example using a `Do Until...Loop` structure:

```
Private Sub MakeWithdrawal(curAcctBalance As Currency)

    Dim curWithdrawalAmt As Currency

    Do Until curAcctBalance <= 0
        curWithdrawalAmt = InputBox "Enter an amount to withdraw: "
        If curWithdrawalAmt > curAcctBalance Then
            curAcctBalance = curAcctBalance - curWithdrawalAmt
        Else
            MsgBox "Insufficient funds for this transaction. _
                Enter a smaller amount."
        End If
    Loop
    MsgBox "Your account balance is zero."

End Sub
```

In this example, the `MakeWithdrawal` procedure is executed as long as `curAcctBalance` doesn't fall to zero or less. If `curAcctBalance` does become zero or less, the loop ends, and the program displays the message `"Your account balance is zero."`

Here is the same example again using the `Do...Loop Until` variation:

```
Private Sub MakeWithdrawal(curAcctBalance As Currency)

    Dim curWithdrawalAmt As Currency

    Do
```

```
        curWithdrawalAmt = InputBox ("Enter an amount to withdraw: ")
        If curWithdrawalAmt <= curAcctBalance Then
            curAcctBalance = curAcctBalance - curWithdrawalAmt
        Else
            MsgBox "Insufficient funds for this transaction. _
                Enter a smaller amount."
        End If
    Loop Until (curAcctBalance <= 0)
    MsgBox "Your account balance is zero."

End Sub
```

Using this structure guarantees that the code within the loop executes at least one time. If you don't want that to happen, be sure to put the test condition at the top of the loop by using a `Do Until...Loop` structure.

`While...Wend` Loops

An alternative to the `Do` loop is the `While...Wend` looping structure. The syntax for the `While...Wend` structure is

```
While condition
    statements
Wend
```

Quite simply, in a `While...Wend` loop, a statement or block of statements is executed while *`condition`* is `True`, and when *`condition`* becomes `False`, program control reverts to the line after the `Wend` statement.

The following `While...Wend` loop increments a variable until the variable reaches a certain number:

```
Dim intValue As Integer

intValue = 0
While intValue < 100
    intValue = intValue + 1
Wend
```

`For...Next` Loops

When you don't know how many times you need to execute a block of statements, the `Do` loop structures are the best to use. When you do know how many times a block of statements should execute, however, the `For...Next` structure is a better choice. Using a counter, a `For...Next` structure executes a block of statements a number of times.

Look at the syntax of the `For...Next` structure to get a better idea of how it works:

```
For counter = start To end [Step increment]
    statements
Next
```

The `For...Next` loop takes three arguments, *`counter`*, *`start`*, and *`end`*, and one optional argument, *`increment`*. Each of these arguments must be numeric, either a number or a variable with a numeric value.

Here is a simple For...Next loop that prints the contents of an array:

```
Private Sub cmdDisplayArray_Click()

    Dim MyArray(100) As Integer
    Dim intLoop As Integer

    For intLoop = 0 To UBound(MyArray)
        Debug.Print MyArray(intLoop)
    Next intLoop

End Sub
```

To execute the preceding For...Next loop, Visual Basic performs the following steps:

1. Set intLoop (*counter*) equal to 0 (*start*).
2. Test to see whether intLoop is greater than the upper bound of MyArray (*end*).
3. If intLoop isn't greater than *end*, execute the Debug.Print command. If intLoop is greater than *end*, revert execution to the line of code after Next intLoop.
4. Increment intLoop by one because the default for *step* is one.
5. Repeat steps 2 through 4 until intLoop is greater than *end*.

You can change the increment amount of the loop by including the Step clause. By using the preceding example, if you want to print every other element of the array, you can write the new For...Next loop fragment in this way:

```
For intLoop = 0 To UBound(MyArray) Step 2
    Debug.Print MyArray(intLoop)
Next intLoop
```

Another variation on the preceding example is to move backwards through the array, printing the last items first. Here is the code fragment to do this:

```
For intLoop = UBound(MyArray) To 0 Step -1
    Debug.Print MyArray(intLoop)
Next intLoop
```

In this example, the counter moves in a negative direction, starting at the upper bound of the array and moving to the first element index of the array, 0.

For Each...Next Loops

For many applications, you need to be able to loop through all the elements of a group of data, such as an array or an object. Calculating the upper bound of the array or the total number of members in an object unnecessarily adds an extra operation to the program. Visual Basic provides a special For...Next structure to simplify this kind of looping, the For Each...Next structure.

The syntax for the For Each...Next structure looks like this:

```
For Each element In group
    statements
Next element
```

The following sample code fragment loops through all the elements of an array:

```
Dim varElement As Variant

For Each varElement In MyArray()
    Debug.Print varElement
Next varElement
```

A `For Each...Next` loop can operate on any object in your Visual Basic program. For example, you can loop through the `Controls` collection that groups together all the controls situated on a form using a `For Each...Next` loop. Here is an example where the `Enabled` property on all the controls on a form is set to `False`:

```
Private Sub DisableControls(frmWork As Form)

    Dim WorkControl As Control

    For Each WorkControl In frmWork.Controls
        frmWork.WorkControl.Enabled = False
    Next WorkControl

End Sub
```

There are three rules to follow when using `For Each...Next` loops:

- The *`element`* in a `For Each...Next` loop that accesses a collection can only be a `Variant` variable, a generic `Object` variable, or an object listed in the Object Browser.
- The *`element`* in a `For Each...Next` loop that accesses an array can only be a `Variant` variable.
- You cannot access an array of user-defined types with a `For Each...Next` loop because a `Variant` cannot contain a user-defined type.

Exiting Loops

Sometimes in your programs, a condition arises that necessitates exiting a loop early, before the loop ends naturally. Visual Basic provides the `Exit` statement for exiting loops. You can use the `Exit` statement with all types of loops, `Sub` procedures, and `Function` procedures.

The following code shows an example of using an `Exit` statement in a `Do` loop:

```
Private Sub MakeWithdrawal(curAcctBalance As Currency)

    Dim curWithdrawalAmt As Currency

    Do
        curWithdrawalAmt = InputBox "Enter an amount to withdraw or 0 to end: "
        If curWithdrawalAmt = 0 Then
            Exit Do
        Else
            If curWithdrawalAmt > curAcctBalance Then
                MsgBox "Insufficient funds for this transaction. _
                     Enter a smaller amount."
            Else
                curAcctBalance = curAcctBalance - curWithdrawalAmt
```

```
            End If
        End If
    Loop While (curAcctBalance > 0)
    MsgBox "Thank you!"

End Sub
```

In this variation of the `MakeWithdrawal` routine from earlier in this chapter, the user can continue making withdrawals until he enters a zero as the withdrawal amount or the balance of his account dips to zero or less. If the user enters a zero as the withdrawal amount, an `Exit Do` statement transfers control of the program to the line of code immediately following the `Loop While` statement.

You can use this general form of the `Exit` statement for the other loop types and `Sub` and `Function` procedures.

With

In an object-oriented programming environment such as Visual Basic, much of what a program does involves checking and setting the properties of objects. For example, based on how a user interacts with a form in your program, the size and location of the controls on the form might have to change. For each control, the set of properties that need to change must be changed through a block of assignment statements such as

```
txtUserName.Height = 2500
txtUserName.Width = 2500
txtUserName.Left = 2040
txtUserName.Top = 960
```

Each property is prefaced, quite appropriately, with the name of the control. Fully naming each control, however, can become tedious if you must set the properties of many controls during the course of your program. Visual Basic provides a shortcut method that allows you to use the control's name only once, the `With` statement.

The `With` statement allows you to perform a set of operations on a given object without requalifying (using the name of) the object for each operation. The syntax for the `With` statement is

```
With object
    statements
End With
```

You can rewrite the preceding example using the `With` statement in this way:

```
With txtUserName
    .Height = 2500
    .Width = 2500
    .Left = 2040
    .Top = 960
End With
```

CAUTION

When using the `With` statement, once you start a `With` block, the object being referenced cannot change. This means that you cannot use one `With` statement with a number of different objects.

You can nest `With` statements, but if you do and you want to reference a member of the object of an outer `With` block in an inner `With` block, you must use a fully qualified reference to that member (the object's name). Here is an example of nesting `With` statements:

```
With OuterObject
    .Height = 200
    .Left = 200
    With InnerObject
        .Height = 300
        .Top = 1000
        OuterObject.Caption = "Outer Object"
        .Caption = "Inner Object"
    End With
End With
```

Do not allow your program to jump into or out of a `With` block. If a statement in a `With` block is executed, but neither the `With` nor `End With` statement is executed, your program might generate a runtime error or exhibit some sort of unpredictable behavior.

Branching Statements and Structures

In the ancient days of programming, before BASIC became a structured language, the language had a set of statements that transferred (or branched) program control from one part of a program to another. The most famous of these, the `GoTo` statement, has been vilified in computer programming textbooks for many years now. The problem with branching statements and structures is that in large programs, code that constantly branches from one part of a program to another part and back again quickly becomes difficult to read and maintain. As structured programming concepts became more widely taught and practiced, the use of branching constructs became less common.

Today, of course, Visual Basic is a completely structured programming language and has all the modern constructs that generally preclude the necessity of using branching statements and structures. There are, however, certain situations when the use of a branching statement or structure is preferred, and for this reason, combined with the need to stay compatible with other versions of BASIC, Visual Basic retains these branching constructs.

GoTo Statement

The most famous of the branching constructs is the `GoTo` statement. I already mentioned the problems with `GoTo`, but in small programs, `GoTo` can be easier to use than other, more structured constructs. Another, more complicated example of when `GoTo` might be useful is when you are in a nested loop of some sort and you want to exit all loops at once. A GoTo can take you anywhere in a program you want to go. Programmer, beware!

The GoTo statement transfers control of the program unconditionally to a specified line number or label within a procedure. The syntax of the GoTo is simple:

```
GoTo line
```

The following simple example shows how you can use GoTo to branch from one part of a program to another:

```
Sub cmdCheckNumber_Click()

    Dim intNumber As Integer

    intNumber = 1
    If intNumber = 1 Then
        GoTo NumberIsOne
    Else
        GoTo NumberIsSomethingElse
    End If

NumberIsOne:
    txtStatus = "Number equals 1"
    GoTo EndRoutine

NumberIsSomethingElse:
    txtStatus = "Number does not equal 1"

EndRoutine:
    Debug.Print "End of routine"

End Sub
```

In this procedure, because intNumber equals 1, the statement immediately following the NumberIsOne line label is executed, and txtStatus gets the string "Number equals 1". Then, another GoTo executes, and the statement after the ExitRoutine label executes.

GoTo statements are almost always unnecessary. The danger of using GoTos comes into play in large programs where trying to follow the logic of many GoTos can be difficult for the programmer and anyone else who must read the program code. It has also been shown that using the GoTo statement results in programs with more bugs than programs written with more structured programming constructs.

GoSub...Return Structure

In the early days of BASIC, the language did not have the capability to call functions and subprocedures. Instead, a BASIC programmer had to create subroutines within his program by using the GoSub...Return structure. The syntax of the GoSub...Return structure is

```
GoSub line

line
    statements
    Return
```

The GoSub statement transfers control of the program to the line label used as its argument. A statement or block of statements is executed until the program encounters the Return statement. Control of the program then reverts immediately to the line following the GoSub statement.

The following code fragment shows an example of the GoSub...Return structure:

```
Sub cmdTestNumber_Click()

    Dim intNumber As Integer

    intNumber = 2
    If intNumber > 0 Then GoSub ShowStatus
    Debug.Print "Number is: "; Str$(intNumber)
    Exit Sub

ShowStatus:
    Debug.Print "Number is greater than zero."
    Return

End Sub
```

NOTE

A GoSub...Return structure can have more than one Return statement, but the first Return encountered causes the program to transfer control to the line immediately following the GoSub statement.

Although the GoSub...Return structure is perfectly legal to use, in almost every case, you can replace it with a function or subprocedure to ensure more readable code.

The On...GoSub and On...GoTo Structures

The On...GoSub and On...GoTo structures are alternatives to the GoSub...Return and GoTo constructs. You use them when the branching decision must have multiple choices. The syntax for these two structures is

On *expression* GoSub *destinationlist*

On *expression* GoTo *destinationlist*

expression must evaluate to a whole number between 0 and 255, and *destinationlist* is a set of line numbers or line labels separated by commas. If *expression* evaluates to 1, then the first line label or line number is where control transfers; if *expression* evaluates to 2, then control transfers to the second line number or line label; and so on. If you use the On...GoSub structure, a Return statement transfers control of the program to the line immediately following the On...GoSub. On...GoTo cannot use a Return statement.

Here is an example of `On...GoSub`:

```
Sub cmdTestNumber_Click()

    Dim intNumber As Integer

    intNumber = 2
    On intNumber GoSub NumOne, NumTwo, NumThree
    Debug.Print intNumber
    Exit Sub

NumOne:
    Debug.Print "Number equals one."
    Return

NumTwo:
    Debug.Print "Number equals two."
    Return

NumThree:
    Debug.Print "Number equals three."
    Return

End Sub
```


Here is the same example using `On...GoTo`:

```
Sub cmdTestNumber_Click()

    Dim intNumber As Integer

    intNumber = 2
    On intNumber GoTo NumOne, NumTwo, NumThree
    Debug.Print "Number is not one, two, or three."
    GoTo EndRoutine

NumOne:
    Debug.Print "Number equals one."
    GoTo EndRoutine

NumTwo:
    Debug.Print "Number equals two."
    GoTo EndRoutine

NumThree:
    Debug.Print "Number equals three."

EndRoutine:

End Sub
```

Four things can happen if *`expression`* evaluates to a number not represented in *`destinationlist`*:

- If *`expression`* evaluates to `0`, program control reverts to the statement following `On...GoSub` or `On...GoTo`.
- If *`expression`* evaluates to a number greater than the number of items in *`destinationlist`*, program control reverts to the statement following `On...GoSub` or `On...GoTo`.

- If *`expression`* is negative, an error is generated.
- If *`expression`* is greater than `255`, an error is generated.

For situations where an `On...GoSub` or `On...GoTo` seems called for, the `Select Case` structure can provide a more structured way of doing multiple branching.

Summary

All computer programs must have constructs that allow decision making and program control transfer. The decision-making constructs you reviewed include the following:

- `If...Then`
- `If...Then...Else`
- `Select Case`
- `Switch`
- `Choose`

The different kinds of structures and statements you learned for transferring program control include the following:

- `Do While...Loop`
- `Do Until...Loop`
- `While...Wend`
- `For...Next`
- `For Each...Next`
- `With`
- `GoTo`
- `GoSub...Return`
- `On...GoSub`
- `On...GoTo`

An important focus of this chapter was how to use decision-making and program control transfer in the course of following structured programming techniques. Although some statements and structures that do not promote good structured programming practices were included, they should be avoided at all costs.

CHAPTER

Handling Errors

IN THIS CHAPTER

This chapter covers an important aspect of programming—handling runtime errors. Although you should always work to make sure that your program can anticipate any problems that might occur while users run your software, you can't account for every possibility. That's why every good program should have a solid error-handling system.

In this chapter, you'll learn just what an error handler is and why error handlers are so important. You'll also learn about some of the inner workings of Visual Basic and how that affects error handling.

You'll learn about the difference between local error-handling methods and global error-handling methods, as well as the advantages and disadvantages of each method. You'll see the various types of errors your programs will likely encounter and some guidelines on how to handle each error type.

You'll learn about the `Err` object and the `Errors` collection and how to use these objects to improve the accuracy of error reporting within your application. You'll also find out how to use the `Raise` method of the `Err` object to flag errors within custom controls or OLE server objects.

You'll learn how to create error logs to keep track of errors that occur in your program and how to create a trace log to analyze your programs. You'll also discover how you can write your programs to turn these features on or off without rewriting program code.

Finally, you'll build an OLE server DLL that contains an improved error handler, an error-logging facility, and a module trace routine. You can use this new OLE server in all your future VBA-compliant programming projects.

Error Handling in General

Error handling is an essential part of any program. No program is complete unless it has good error handling. It's important to write your programs in a way that reduces the chances that errors will occur, but you can't think of everything. Errors do happen! Well-designed programs don't necessarily have fewer errors—they just handle them better.

Writing error handlers isn't difficult. In fact, you can add consistent error handling to your program by adding only a few lines of code to each module. The difficult part of writing good error handlers is knowing what to expect and how to handle the unexpected. You'll learn how to do both in this chapter.

Adding error handling to your program makes your program seem much more polished and friendly to your users. Nothing is more annoying—or frightening—to users than seeing the screen freeze up, hearing a startling beep, or watching the program (and any file your users had been working on) suddenly disappear from the screen entirely. This needs to happen only a few times before your users vow never to use your program again.

Error Handling in Visual Basic

Writing error handlers in Visual Basic is a bit trickier than in most computer languages, for several reasons:

- Visual Basic is an *event-driven* language model, rather than *procedure-driven* like most computer languages.
- Visual Basic uses a call stack method that isolates local variables. When you exit the routine, you can lose track of the values of internal variables, which can make resuming execution after error handling difficult.
- In Visual Basic, all errors are local. If an error occurs, it's best to handle it in the routine in which the error occurred, which means you must write a short error handler for each routine in your Visual Basic program.

NOTE

Technically, Visual Basic allows the use of a global error handler. After Visual Basic travels up the procedure stack to locate the error handler, however, it can't travel back down the stack to resume execution after the error is corrected. (This is typical of most object-oriented languages.) For this reason, I highly recommend using local error handlers in your Visual Basic programs.

The Built-In Visual Basic Error Objects

Visual Basic 5.0 has two built-in objects that you can use to track and report errors at runtime. The `Err` object is a built-in object that exists in all Visual Basic programs. This object contains several properties and two methods. Each time an error occurs in the program, the `Err` object properties are filled with information that you can use within your program.

The second built-in object that helps in tracking errors is the `Error` object and `Errors` collection, available to any VB5 program that has loaded one Microsoft data-access object library. The `Error` object is a child object of the `DBEngine`. You can use the `Error` object to get additional details on the nature of the database errors that occur in your program.

CAUTION

The `Error` object is available only if you've loaded a Microsoft data-access object library. If you attempt to access the `Error` object from a Visual Basic program that doesn't have a Microsoft data-access object library loaded, you receive an error.

The advantage of the `Error` object over the `Err` object is that the `Error` object contains more information about the database-related errors. In some cases, back-end database servers return several error messages to your Visual Basic application. The `Err` object reports only the last error received from the back-end server. The `Errors` collection, however, can report all errors received. For this reason, it's always a good idea to use the `Error` object when you're working with Visual Basic database applications.

Working with the `Err` Object

VB5's built-in `Err` object has all the information about the most recent error that occurred within the running application space.

CAUTION

There's a bit of confusion regarding the `Err` keyword in Visual Basic. VB5 still supports the outdated `Err` and `Error` functions, but I don't advise using them in your programs. In some rare cases, the values reported by these functions aren't the same as those reported by the `Err` object. Throughout this chapter, when I mention `Err`, I am referring to the `Err` object, not the `Err` function.

The `Err` object has several important properties. Table 3.1 lists these properties and explains their use.

Table 3.1. The properties of the `Err` object.

Property	*Type*	*Value*
`Number`	`Long`	The actual internal error number returned by Visual Basic.
`Source`	`String`	Name of the current Visual Basic file in which the error occurred. This could be an `.EXE`, `.DLL`, or `.OCX` file.
`Description`	`String`	An error description that corresponds to the error number returned in the `Number` property. If no corresponding description exists, an application-defined or object-defined error is returned.
`HelpFile`	`String`	The fully qualified drive, path, and filename of the help file. You can call this help file to support the reported errors.
`HelpContext`	`Long`	The help file context (topic) ID in the help file indicated by the `HelpFile` property.
`LastDLLError`	`Long`	The error code for the last call to a dynamic-link library (DLL). This is available only on 32-bit Microsoft platforms.

When an error occurs in your Visual Basic program, the `Err` object properties are populated with the details of the error. You can inspect these values during your program execution and, if possible, use Visual Basic code to correct the error and continue the program.

For example, when an error occurs, you can inspect the properties of the object with the following code:

```
Msgbox "<" & CStr(Err.Number) & "> " _
   & Err.Description & "[" & Err.Source & "]"
```

When the error occurs and the `Err` object properties are updated, the `Err` object values don't change until another error is reported or the error-handling system is re-initialized.

NOTE

The error-handling system is re-initialized each time a procedure exit or end occurs or when the special error-handling keywords `Resume` or `On Error` are executed. You'll learn more about these keywords later in the section "Using `Resume` to Exit the Error Handler."

If the reported error has an associated help file and help context ID, these properties are also filled in. You can use the `Err` object's `HelpFile` and `HelpContext` properties to display an online help topic to explain the error condition to users.

If your application calls a dynamic-link library (DLL), you might be able to use the `LastDLLError` property of the `Err` object to get additional information about an error that occurred in a DLL. This property is available only on the 32-bit platform and might not be supported by the DLL you're calling.

Working with the `Error` Object and the `Errors` Collection

In addition to the built-in `Err` object, VB5 also has a built-in `Error` object for database errors. This object is a child object of the `DBEngine` object. For this reason, you can access the `Error` object only if you loaded a Microsoft data-access object library (choose Project | References from the menu).

The primary advantage of the `Error` object is that it can report additional error information not included in the standard `Err` object mentioned earlier. Many times, your database application will need to depend on external processes, such as ODBC data connections or OLE server modules. When an error occurs in these external processes, they may report more than one error code back to your Visual Basic application.

The `Err` object can remember only the most recent error reported. However, the `Error` object (and its associated `Errors` collection) can remember all the errors reported by external processes. That's why using the `Error` object for reporting errors in all your Visual Basic database programs is a good idea.

The properties of the Microsoft data-access `Error` object are almost identical to the properties of the Visual Basic `Err` object. The only difference is that the `Error` object doesn't have the optional `LastDLLError` property. Therefore, the calling convention for the `Error` object is basically the same as that for the `Err` object:

```
Msgbox "<" & CStr(Error.Number) & "> " & _
  Error.Description & "[" & Error.Source & "]"
```

Although the `Error` and `Err` objects are quite similar, one major difference is worth noting. The `Err` object stands alone, but the Microsoft data access `Error` object belongs to the `Errors` collection. This difference is very important when dealing with back-end database servers, especially when your Visual Basic program is connected to databases via the Open Database Connectivity (ODBC) interface. When an error occurs during an ODBC transaction, the `Err` object always returns the same error message: `ODBC failed`. However, the `Errors` collection often contains more than one error message that can tell you a great deal more about the nature of the problem. You can retrieve all the error information by enumerating all the `Error` objects in the `Errors` collection. Listing 3.1 shows how that can be done.

Listing 3.1. Enumerating the `Errors` collection.

```
Dim objTempErr as Object
Dim strMsg as String
For Each objTempErr In Errors
   strMsg = "<" & CStr(objTempErr.Number) & "> "
   strMsg = strMsg & objTempErr.Description
   strMsg = strMsg & " in [" & objTempErr.Source & "]" & vbCrLf
Next
Msgbox strMsg
```

The code in Listing 3.1 creates a single line of text (`strMsg`) that contains all the error messages reported by the back-end database server. You'll learn more about using the `Err` and `Error` objects in the next section.

Creating Your Own Error Handlers

Before getting into the details of using the `Err` and `Error` objects in your Visual Basic programs, look at a basic error handler in Visual Basic. Error handlers in Visual Basic have three main parts:

- The `On Error GoTo` statement
- The error-handling code
- The exit statement

The `On Error GoTo` statement appears at the beginning of the sub or function. This line tells Visual Basic what to do when an error occurs, as in the following example:

```
On Error GoTo LocalErrHandler
```

In the preceding code line, every time an error occurs in this sub or function, the program immediately jumps to the LocalErrHandler label in the routine and executes the error-handling code. The error-handling code can be as simple or as complex as needed to handle the error. A very simple error handler just reports the error number and error message:

```
LocalErrHandler:
   MsgBox CStr(Err.Number) & " - " & Err.Description
```

In the preceding code example, as soon as the error occurs, Visual Basic reports the error number (Err.Number) and the error message (Err.Description) in a message box.

The third and final part of a Visual Basic error handler is the exit statement. This line tells Visual Basic where to go after the error handler is done with its work. You can exit an error-handling routine in four ways:

- To re-execute the same instruction, use the Resume keyword to return to the location in the program that caused the error.
- Use the Resume Next keywords to resume execution at the Visual Basic code line immediately following the line that caused the error.
- Use the Resume *label* keywords to resume execution at a specified location within the routine that caused the error. This location could be anywhere within the routine, before or after the line that caused the error.
- Use the Exit Sub or Exit Function keywords to immediately exit the routine in which the error occurred.

Which exit method you use depends on the type of error that occurred and the error-handling strategy you use throughout your program.

Now that you have the basics of error handling covered, you can write some error-handling routines.

Creating a Simple Error Handler

To start, write a simple error-handling routine to see how Visual Basic behaves when errors occur. Start a new Standard EXE project in VB5. Add a single CommandButton control to the default form. Set its Name property to cmdSimpleErr and its Caption property to Simple. Now add the code in Listing 3.2 to cmdSimpleErr's Click event.

Listing 3.2. A simple error handler.

```
Private Sub cmdSimpleErr_Click()

    ' a simple error handler demonstration
    On Error GoTo LocalErr   ' turn on error handling

    Dim intValue As Integer ' declare integer
    Dim strMsg As String    ' declare string
```

continues

Listing 3.2. continued

```
    intValue = 10000000        ' create overflow error
    GoTo LocalExit             ' exit if no error

    ' local error handler

LocalErr:
   strMsg = CStr(Err.Number) & " - " & Err.Description ' make message
   MsgBox strMsg, vbCritical, "cmdSimpleErr_Click"     ' show message
   Resume Next  ' continue on

   ' routine exit
LocalExit:

End Sub
```

Save the form as `BASICERR.FRM` and the project as `BASICERR.VBP`. Then execute the program and click the command button. You'll see the error message onscreen (see Figure 3.1).

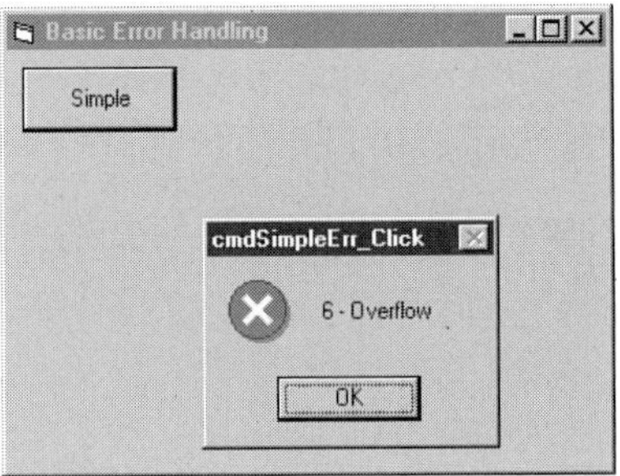

FIGURE 3.1.
Displaying the results of a simple error handler.

The example in Listing 3.2 exhibits all the parts of a good error handler. The first line in the routine tells Visual Basic what to do in case of an error. Notice that the name for the error-handling code is given as `LocalErr` (every local error handler written in this chapter is named `LocalErr`). Next, the routine declares an integer variable and then purposely loads that variable with an illegal value. This causes the error routine to kick in.

The error routine is very simple. It constructs a message that contains the error number and the associated error description. The routine then displays that message along with the warning symbol and the name of the routine reporting the error.

The next line tells Visual Basic what to do after the error is handled. In this case, Visual Basic resumes execution with the line of program code that immediately follows the line that caused the error (`Resume` at the `Next` line).

When Visual Basic resumes execution, the routine hits the line that tells Visual Basic to go to the exit routine (`GoTo LocalExit`). Notice again the naming convention for the exit routine; all exit jump labels in this chapter are named `LocalExit`.

Handling Cascading Errors

What happens if you get an error within your error routine? Although it's not fun to think about, it can happen. When an error occurs inside the error-handling routine, Visual Basic looks for the next declared error routine—an error routine started in the previous calling routine using the `On Error GoTo label` statement. If no error routine is available, Visual Basic halts the program with a fatal error.

For example, add a new button to the `BASICERR` project. Set the button's `Name` property to `cmdCascadeErr` and its `Caption` property to `Cascade`. First, create a new subprocedure named `CreateErr`. Then enter the code from Listing 3.3 that, when executed, creates a cascading error condition.

Listing 3.3. The `CreateErr` routine.

```
Public Sub CreateErr()

    ' create an internal error

    On Error GoTo LocalErr

    Dim strMsg As String
    Dim intValue As Integer

    intValue = 900000 ' create an error
    GoTo LocalExit    ' all done

LocalErr:
    strMsg = CStr(Err.Number) & " - " & Err.Description
    MsgBox strMsg, vbCritical, "CreateErr"

    Open "junk.txt" For Input As 1 ' create another error
    Resume Next

LocalExit:

End Sub
```

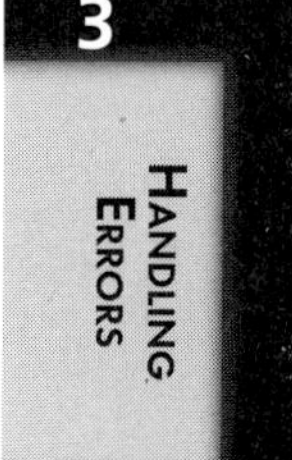

Notice that this routine is quite similar to the code from Listing 3.2. The biggest difference is in the lines of code in the error-handling portion of the subroutine. Notice that Visual Basic attempts to open a text file for input. Because this file doesn't currently exist, this causes an error.

Now add the code from Listing 3.4 to the `cmdCascadeErr_Click` event. This is the code that calls the `CreateErr` routine.

Listing 3.4. The `cmdCascadeErr` routine.

```
Private Sub cmdCascadeErr_Click()

    ' create an error cascade

    On Error GoTo LocalErr

    Dim strMsg As String

    CreateErr       ' call another routine
    GoTo LocalExit  ' all done

LocalErr:
    strMsg = CStr(Err.Number) & " - " & Err.Description
    MsgBox strMsg, vbCritical, "cmdCascadeErr"
    Resume Next

LocalExit:

End Sub
```

Save the program and run it to see the results. When you first click the Cascade button, you see the error message that announces the overflow error. Notice that the title of the message box indicates that the error is reported by the `CreateErr` routine (see Figure 3.2).

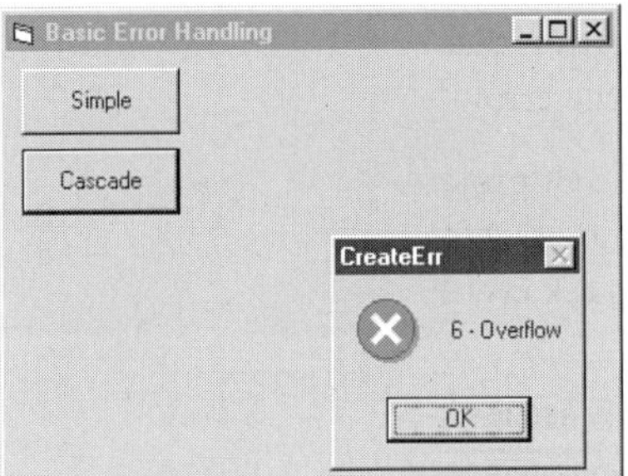

FIGURE 3.2.
Reporting the error from `CreateErr`.

When you click OK in the message box, you'll see another error message (see Figure 3.3). This one reports a `53 - File not found` error message, which occurred when `CreateErr` tried to open the nonexistent file.

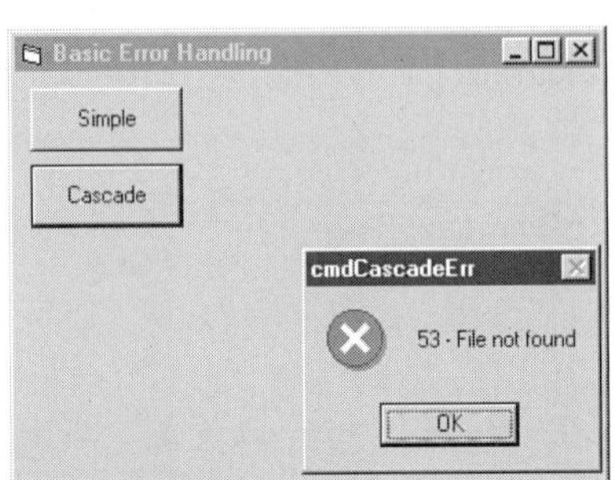

FIGURE 3.3.
Reporting the `File not found` *error.*

Here's the important point. Notice that the second error message box tells you that the error is reported from the cmdCascadeErr routine—even though the error occurred in the CreateErr routine! The error that occurred in CreateErr error-handling routine couldn't be handled locally, and Visual Basic searched upward in the call stack to find the next available error handler to invoke. This action by Visual Basic can be a blessing—and a curse. It's good to know that Visual Basic uses the next available error-handling routine when things like this happen, but it's also likely to cause confusion for you and your users if you aren't careful. For all you can tell in this example, an error occurred in cmdCascadeErr. You must keep this in mind when you're debugging Visual Basic error reports.

It's also worth mentioning that if you use the Resume Next keyword (see the section "Using Resume Next to Exit the Error Handler"), the execution begins *after* the call to CreateErr and not where the error actually occurred. This can be very confusing and, in some cases, may actually compound the error by executing invalid code in some other routine.

Using Resume to Exit the Error Handler

The simplest method for exiting an error handler is the Resume method. When you exit an error handler with the Resume keyword, Visual Basic returns to the line of code that caused the error and attempts to run that line again. The Resume keyword is useful when you encounter an error that users can easily correct, such as attempting to read a disk drive when they forget to insert a disk or close the drive door. You can use the Resume keyword whenever you're confident that the situation that caused the error has been remedied, and you want to retry the action that caused the error.

Modify the BASICERR project by adding a new button to the project. Set its Name property to cmdResumeErr and its Caption property to Resume. Now add the code in Listing 3.5 to cmdResumeErr's Click event.

Listing 3.5. Using the Resume keyword.

```
Private Sub cmdResumeErr_Click()

    ' show resume keyword

    On Error GoTo LocalErr

    Dim intValue As Integer
    Dim strMsg As String

    intValue = InputBox("Enter an integer:")
    GoTo LocalExit

LocalErr:
    strMsg = CStr(Err.Number) & " - " & Err.Description
    MsgBox strMsg, vbCritical, "cmdResumeErr"
    Resume ' try it again

LocalExit:

End Sub
```

Save and run the project. When you click the Resume button, you're prompted to enter an integer value. If you simply click Cancel or OK without entering data (or if you enter a value greater than 32,767), you invoke the error handler and receive an error message from Visual Basic (see Figure 3.4).

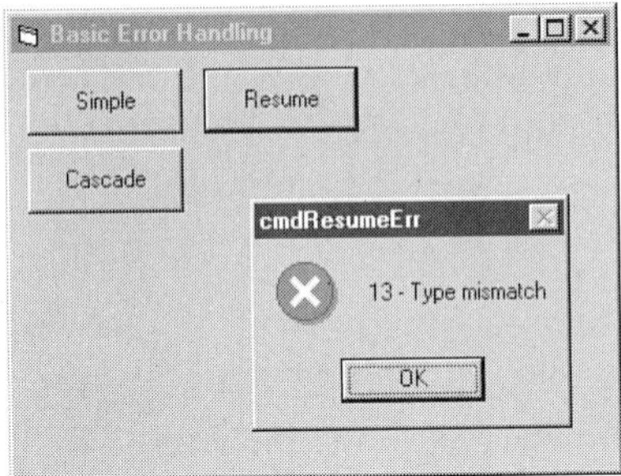

FIGURE 3.4.
Reporting an error message from the input box.

When you click OK, Visual Basic redisplays the input prompt and waits for your reply. If you enter another invalid value, you see the error message, and then you see the prompt again. This is the `Resume` exit method in action. You can't get beyond this screen until you enter a valid value.

This can be very frustrating for your users. What if they don't know what value to enter here? Are they stuck in this terrible error handler forever? Whenever you use the `Resume` keyword, you should give your users an option to ignore the error and move on or cancel the action completely.

Using Resume Next to Exit the Error Handler

Using the `Resume Next` method to exit an error handler allows users to get past a problem spot in the program as though no error had occurred. This is useful when you use code within the error handler to fix the problem or when you think the program can go on even though an error is reported.

Deciding whether to continue the program even though an error is reported is sometimes a tough call. It's usually not a good idea to assume that your program will work fine even though an error is reported. This is especially true if the error that occurs is related to physical devices (such as a missing disk or lost communications connection) or file errors (such as missing, corrupted, or locked data files). The `Resume Next` keywords are used usually in error-handling routines that fix any reported error before continuing.

To illustrate the use of `Resume Next`, add a new command button to the project. Set its `Name` property to `cmdResumeNext` and its `Caption` property to `Next`. Now enter the code in Listing 3.6 to `cmdResumeNextErr`'s `Click` event.

Listing 3.6. Using the `Resume Next` keywords.

```
Private Sub cmdResumeNextErr_Click()

    ' show use of resume next

    On Error GoTo LocalErr

    Dim intValue As Integer
    Dim strMsg As String
    Dim lngReturn As Long

    intValue = InputBox("Enter a valid Integer")
    MsgBox "intValue has been set to " + CStr(intValue)
    GoTo LocalExit

LocalErr:
    If Err.Number = 6 Or Err.Number = 13 Then ' was it a type-mismatch or overflow?
strMsg = "You have entered an invalid integer value." & vbCrLf
        strMsg = strMsg & "The program will now set the value to 0 for you." &
           ➥ vbCrLf
        strMsg = strMsg & "Select YES to set the value to 0 and continue." & vbCrLf
        strMsg = strMsg & "Select NO to return to enter a new value."

        lngReturn = MsgBox(strMsg, vbCritical + vbYesNo, "cmdResumeNextErr")
        If lngReturn = vbYes Then
            intValue = 0
            Resume Next
        Else
            Resume
        End If
    Else ' must have been some other error(!)
        strMsg = CStr(Err.Number) & " - " & Err.Description
        MsgBox strMsg, vbCritical, "cmdResumeNext"
        Resume
    End If

LocalExit:

End Sub
```

In Listing 3.6, you added a section of code to the error handler that tests for the anticipated overflow error. You explain the options to users and then give them a choice of how to proceed. This is a good general model for error handling that involves user interaction: tell users the problem, explain the options, and let users decide how to go forward.

Notice also that this routine includes a general error trap for those cases when the error isn't caused by an integer overflow. Even when you think you've covered all the possible error conditions, you should always include a general error trap.

Save and run this project. When you click the Next button and enter an invalid value (that is, any number greater than 32,767), you see the error message that explains your options (see Figure 3.5).

FIGURE 3.5.
An error message that asks for user input.

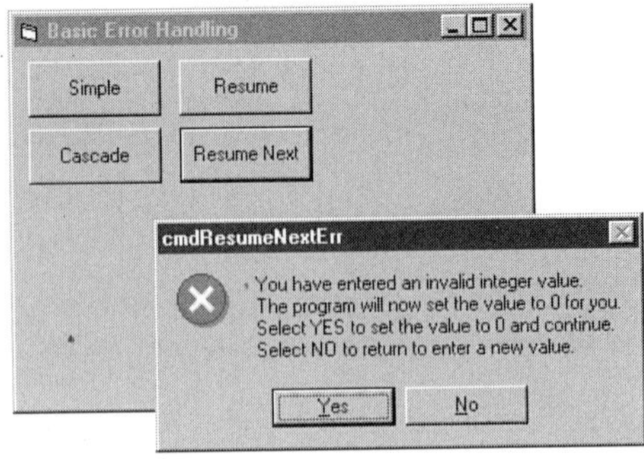

Using `Resume` *`label`* to Exit an Error Handler

Sometimes you need your program to return to another spot within the routine to fix an error that occurs. For example, if you ask users to enter two numbers that you'll use to perform a division operation and it results in a divide-by-zero error, you want to ask users to enter both numbers again. You might not be able to simply use the `Resume` statement after you handle the error.

When you need to force the program to return to a specific point in the routine, you can use the `Resume` *`label`* exit method, which lets you return to any place within the current procedure. You can't use `Resume` *`label`* to jump to another sub or function within the project.

Modify the `BASICERR` project to include an example of `Resume` *`label`*. Add a new command button to the project. Set its `Name` property to `cmdResumeLabelErr` and its `Caption` property to `Resume` *`label`*. Now, add the code in Listing 3.7 to `cmdResumeLabelErr`'s `Click` event.

Listing 3.7. Using the `Resume` *`label`* keywords.

```
Private Sub cmdResumeLabelErr_Click()

    ' show resume label version

    On Error GoTo LocalErr

    Dim intX As Integer
    Dim intY As Integer
    Dim intZ As Integer

LabelInput:
    intX = InputBox("Enter a Divisor:", "Input Box #1")
    intY = InputBox("Enter a Dividend:", "Input Box #2")
    intZ = intX / intY
    MsgBox "The Quotient is: " + Str(intZ), vbInformation, "Results"
    GoTo LocalExit

LocalErr:
    If Err = 11 Then       ' divide by zero error
        MsgBox CStr(Err.Number) & " - " & Err.Description, _
          vbCritical, "cmdResumeLabelErr"
```

```
        Resume LabelInput ' back for more
    Else
        MsgBox CStr(Err.Number) & " - " & Err.Description, vbCritical, _
        "cmdResumeLabelErr"
        Resume
    End If

LocalExit:

End Sub
```

Save and run the project. Enter **13** at the first input box and **0** at the second input box. This causes a divide-by-zero error, and the error handler takes over from there. You see the error message shown in Figure 3.6 and then you're returned to the line that starts the input process.

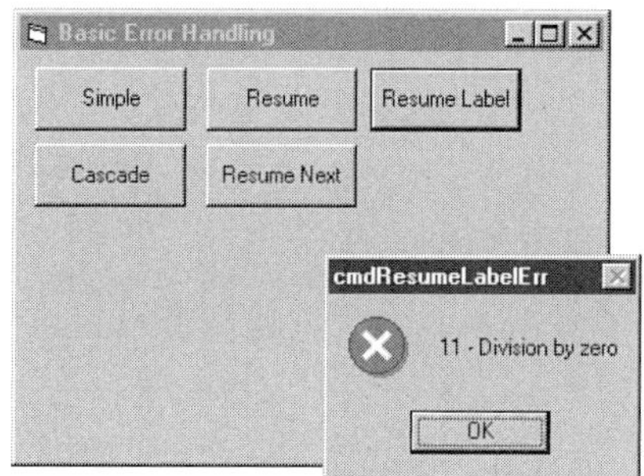

FIGURE 3.6.
Viewing the divide-by-zero error message.

Using the `Exit` or End Method to Exit an Error Handler

Sometimes an error occurs, and there's no good way to return to the program. A good example of this error type can occur when the program tries to open files on a network file server and users forgot to log on to the server. In this case, you need to exit the routine and return to the calling procedure, or exit the program completely. Exiting to a calling routine can work if you write your program to anticipate these critical errors. Usually, it's difficult to do that. Most of the time, critical errors of this type mean you should end the program and let users fix the problem before restarting the program.

Add one more button to the `BASICERR` project. Set its `Caption` property to `End` and its `Name` property to `cmdEndErr`. Enter the code in Listing 3.8 to `cmdEndErr`'s `Click` event.

Listing 3.8. Using the `End` keyword.

```
Private Sub cmdEndErr_Click()

    ' use End to exit handler

    On Error GoTo LocalErr
```

continues

Listing 3.8. continued

```
    Dim strMsg As String
    Open "junk.txt" For Input As 1
    GoTo LocalExit

LocalErr:
   If Err.Number = 53 Then
      strMsg = "Unable to open JUNK.TXT" & vbCrLf
      strMsg = strMsg & "Exit the program and check your INI file" & vbCrLf
      strMsg = strMsg & "to make sure the JUNKFILE setting is correct."
      MsgBox strMsg, vbCritical, "cmdEndErr"
      Unload Me
   Else
      MsgBox CStr(Err.Number) & " - " & Err.Description, vbCritical, "cmdEndErr"
      Resume Next
   End If

LocalExit:

End Sub
```

Listing 3.8 adds a check in the error handler for the anticipated `File not found` error. It gives users some helpful information and then tells them that the program is closing (it's always a good idea to tell users when you're about to exit the program). Notice that you didn't use the Visual Basic `End` keyword; you used `Unload Me`. Remember that `End` stops all program execution immediately. Using `Unload Me` causes Visual Basic to execute any code placed in the `Unload` event of the form. This event should contain any file-closing routine needed to safely exit the program.

Save and run the project. When you click the End button, you see a message box explaining the problem and suggesting a solution (see Figure 3.7). When you click OK, Visual Basic ends the program.

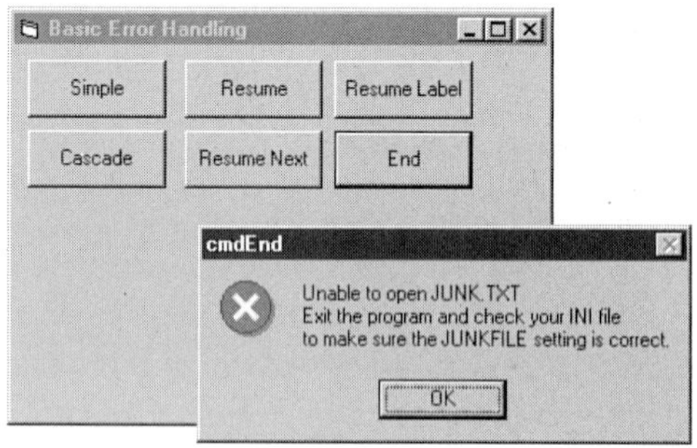

FIGURE 3.7.
Showing the error message before exiting the program.

Using the `Err.Raise` Method to Create Your Own Error Conditions

Many times it's not practical or desirable to display an error message when an error occurs. Other times, you might want to use VB5's error-handling capabilities to your own advantage by creating your own error codes and messages. You can do this by using the `Err` object's `Raise` method. Using the `Raise` method allows you to alert users (or other calling applications) that an error has occurred but gives you and users additional flexibility on how the error is handled.

The `Raise` method takes up to five parameters:

- `ErrorNumber` is a unique number identifying the error that just occurred.
- `ErrorSource` is the code module that generated the error.
- `ErrorDescription` is the text message associated with the error.
- `HelpFile` is the help file that contains support information on the error.
- `HelpContextID` is the ID number of the help topic associated with this error.

When you raise your own errors, you're required to report an error number. This number can be any unique value you want. If you use a number already defined as a Visual Basic error, you'll automatically get the `ErrorDescription` and any associated `HelpFile` and `HelpContextID` information as well. If you generate your own unique number, you can fill in the other parameters yourself. It's recommended that you use the `vbObjectError` constant as a base number for your own error codes, to guarantee that your error number won't conflict with any Visual Basic errors.

The following is a typical call to use the `Err.Raise` method:

```
'
LocalErr:
    ' trouble with file stuff!
    Err.Raise vbObjectError + 1, "errHandler.LogError", _
    "Can't write log file [" & errLogFileName & "]"
    '
End Sub
```

It's especially important to use this method for marking errors when you're coding ActiveX DLL servers. Because servers can run at a remote location on the network, you can't be sure that users will ever see any error dialog box you display. Also, remember that even if the DLL is running on the local PC, error dialog boxes are application-modal. No other processing occurs until the dialog box is dismissed. You'll learn to use the `Err.Raise` method when you create your `errHandler` object library later in the section "Creating Your Error-Handing OLE Server."

So far, you've seen how to build a simple error handler and the different ways to exit error handlers. Now you need to learn about the different types of errors that you'll encounter in your Visual Basic programs and how to plan for them in advance.

Types of Errors

To make writing error handlers easier and more efficient, you can group errors into typical types. These error types can usually be handled in a similar manner. When you get an idea of the types of errors you can encounter, you can begin to write error handlers that take care of more than one error. You can write handlers that take care of error types.

There are four types of Visual Basic errors:

- *General file errors* are ones you encounter when you're attempting to open, read, or write simple files. This type of error doesn't include errors related to internal database operations (read/write table records).
- *Physical media errors* are caused by problems with physical devices—errors such as unresponsive communications ports or printers and low-level disk errors (`Unable To Read Sector` and so on).
- *Program code errors* appear in your programs due to problems with your code. Errors include `Division by zero`, `Invalid Property`, and others that can be corrected only by changing the Visual Basic code in your programs.
- *Database errors* occur during database operations, usually during data read/write or data object create/delete operations.

Each error type needs to be handled differently within your Visual Basic programs. You'll learn general rules for handling these errors in the following sections.

General File Errors

General file errors occur due to invalid data file information, such as a bad filename, data path, or device name. Usually users can fix these errors, and the program can continue from the point of failure. The basic approach to handling general file errors is to create an error handler that reports the problem to users and asks for additional information to complete or retry the operation.

The error handler is called when the program in Listing 3.9 attempts to open a control file called `CONTROL.TXT`. The error handler then prompts users for the proper file location and continues processing. Start a new Standard EXE project (`ERRTYPES.VBP`) and add a command button to the form. Set its `Caption` property to `Control` and its `Name` property to `cmdControl`. Also, add a CommonDialog control to the project and change its name to `dlgFileOpen`. Finally, enter the code in Listing 3.9 into the `cmdControl_Click` event.

NOTE

If the CommonDialog control isn't already in your toolbox, choose Project | References from VB's menu. Select the Microsoft Common Dialog Control 5.0 check box and then click OK to add the new control to your toolbox.

Listing 3.9. The `cmdControl_Click` event.

```
Private Sub cmdControl_Click()

    ' show general file errors

    On Error GoTo LocalErr

   Dim strFile As String
   Dim strMsg As String
   Dim lngReturn As Long

   strFile = "control.txt"

   Open strFile For Input As 1
   MsgBox "Control File Opened"
   GoTo LocalExit

LocalErr:
   If Err.Number = 53 Then ' file not found?
      strMsg = "Unable to Open CONTROL.TXT" & vbCrLf
      strMsg = strMsg & "Select OK to locate CONTROL.TXT" & vbCrLf
      strMsg = strMsg & "Select CANCEL to exit program."

      lngReturn = MsgBox(strMsg, vbCritical + vbOKCancel, "cmdControl")

      If lngReturn = vbOK Then
         dlgFileOpen.filename = strFile
         dlgFileOpen.DefaultExt = ".txt"
         dlgFileOpen.ShowOpen
         Resume
      Else
         Unload Me
      End If
   Else
      MsgBox CStr(Err.Number) & " - " & Err.Description
      Resume Next
   End If

LocalExit:

End Sub
```

Save the form as `ERRTYPES.FRM` and the project as `ERRTYPES.VBP`. Now run this project. When you click the Control button, the program tries to open the `CONTROL.TXT` file. If it can't be found, you see the error message (see Figure 3.8).

If users select OK, the program calls the `dlgFileOpen` CommonDialog control and prompts them to locate the `CONTROL.TXT` file. It can be found in the same folder that contains the source code for this chapter (see Figure 3.9).

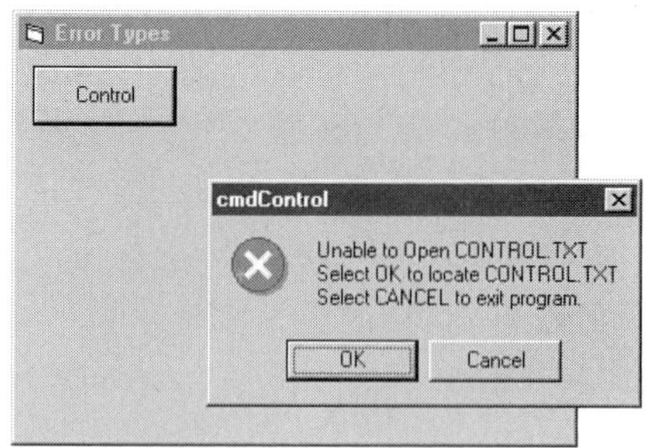

FIGURE 3.8.
Displaying a `File not found` *error.*

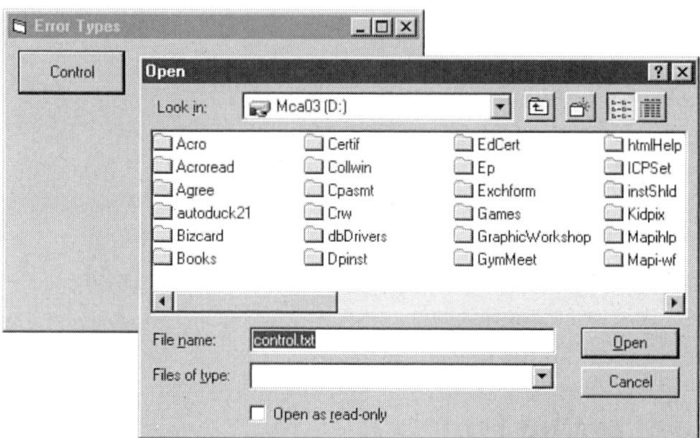

FIGURE 3.9.
Attempting to locate the `CONTROL.TXT` *file.*

TIP

Notice the use of the CommonDialog control to open the file. Whenever you need to prompt users for file-related action (such as open, create, or save), you should use this control. This dialog box is familiar for your users and handles all the dirty work of scrolling, searching, and so on.

Table 3.2 lists errors similar to the `File not found` error used in Listing 3.9. Errors of this type usually involve giving users a chance to re-enter the filename or reset some value. Most often, you can write an error trap that anticipates these errors, prompts users to supply the corrected information, and then retries the operation that caused the error.

Table 3.2. Common general file errors.

Error Code	*Error Message*
52	`Bad filename or number`
53	`File not found`
54	`Bad file mode`

Error Code	Error Message
55	`File already open`
58	`File already exists`
59	`Bad record length`
61	`Disk full`
62	`Input past end of file`
63	`Bad record number`
64	`Bad filename`
67	`Too many files`
74	`Can't rename with different drive`
75	`Path/File access error`
76	`Path not found`

In cases when it's not practical to prompt users for additional information (such as during initial startup of the program), it's usually best to report the error in a message box. Then give users some ideas about how to fix the problem before exiting the program safely.

Physical Media Errors

Another group of common errors is caused by problems with physical media. Unresponsive printers, disk drives that don't contain disks, and downed communications ports are the most common examples of physical media errors. These errors might, or might not, be easily fixed by your users. Usually, you can report the error, wait for users to fix the problem, and then continue with the process. For example, if the printer is jammed with paper, all you need to do is report the error to users and then wait for them to click OK to continue.

Add another button to the `ERRTYPES.VBP` project to display an example of physical media error handling. Add a new command button to the project. Set its `Caption` property to `Media` and its `Name` property to `cmdMedia`. Enter the code in Listing 3.10 into the `cmdMedia_Click` event.

Listing 3.10. Trapping media errors.

```
Private Sub cmdMedia_Click()

    ' show handling of media errors

    On Error GoTo LocalErr
    Dim strMsg As String
    Dim lngReturn As Long

   ' open a file on the a drive
   ' an error will occur if there
   ' is no diskette in the drive
```

continues

Listing 3.10. continued

```
   Open "a:\junk.txt" For Input As 1
   Close #1
   GoTo LocalExit

LocalErr:
   If Err.Number = 71 Then
      strMsg = "The disk drive is not ready." & vbCrLf
      strMsg = strMsg & "Please make sure there is a diskette" & vbCrLf
      strMsg = strMsg & "in the drive and the drive door is closed."

      lngReturn = MsgBox(strMsg, vbCritical + vbRetryCancel, "cmdMedia")

      If lngReturn = vbRetry Then
         Resume
      Else
         Resume Next
      End If
   Else
      MsgBox CStr(Err.Number) & " - " & Err.Description
      Resume Next
   End If

LocalExit:

End Sub
```

The code in Listing 3.10 attempts to open a file on a disk drive that has no disk (or has an open drive door). The error handler prompts users to correct the problem and allows them to try the operation again. If all goes well the second time, the program continues. Users also have the option of canceling the operation.

Save and run the project. When you click the Media button, you should get results that look like those in Figure 3.10.

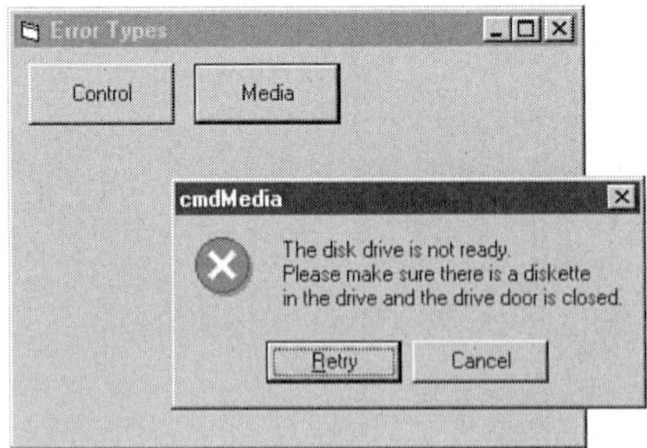

FIGURE 3.10.
The results of a physical media error.

Program Code Errors

Another common error type is the program code error. These errors occur as part of the Visual Basic code. Users can't fix errors of this type; the errors are usually due to unanticipated conditions within the code itself. Error messages such as `Variable not found`, `Invalid object`, and so on are a mystery to most of your users. The best way to handle errors of this type is to tell users to report the message to the programmer and close the program safely.

Database Errors with the Data Control

A common type of error that occurs in database applications is the data-related error. These errors include those that deal with data-type or field-size problems, table-access restrictions (including read-only access), locked tables due to other users, and so on. Database errors fall into two groups:

- The most common errors caused by attempting to read or write invalid data to or from tables, including data integrity errors
- Errors caused by locked tables, restricted access, or multiuser conflicts

In most cases, all you need to do is trap for the error, report it to users, and allow users to return to the data-entry screen to fix the problem. If you use the Visual Basic data control in your data forms, you can take advantage of the automatic database error reporting built into the data control. For example, put together a simple data entry form to illustrate some common data entry-oriented database errors.

To see how common database errors occur, start a new Visual Basic Standard EXE project. Add a data control, two bound input controls, and two label controls. (Use Table 3.3 as a reference for adding the controls to the form and changing their properties, and Figure 3.11 as a guide for placing the controls.)

> **NOTE**
>
> You can find the database used by this program (`ERRORDB.MDB`) on the CD-ROM that accompanies this book. Before you begin creating the program, copy the database to your working directory so that it will be accessible when the program is executed.

Table 3.3. Controls for the `frmDataErr` form.

Property	*Setting*
	Form control
`Name`	`frmDataErr`
`Caption`	`Data Error Demo`
`Height`	`1740`
`Width`	`4665`
`StartUpPosition`	`3 - Windows Default`

continues

Table 3.3. continued

Property	*Setting*
	Data control
Name	datErrorDB
Align	2 - Align Bottom
Caption	datErrorDB
Connect	Access
DatabaseName	errordb.mdb
Height	360
RecordSource	Table1
	CommandButton control
Name	cmdAdd
Caption	&Add
Height	375
Left	3300
Top	60
Width	1215
	TextBox control
Name	txtName
DataSource	datErrorDB
DataField	Name
Height	315
Left	1500
Text	(nothing)
Top	540
Width	3015
	Second TextBox control
Name	txtKeyField
DataSource	datErrorDB
DataField	KeyField
Height	315
Left	1500
Text	(nothing)
Top	60
Width	1515

Property	Setting
	Label control for first TextBox control
Name	lblName
Caption	Name
Height	255
Left	120
Top	540
Width	1215
	Second Label control for second TextBox control
Name	lblKeyField
Caption	Key Field
Height	255
Left	120
Top	120
Width	1215

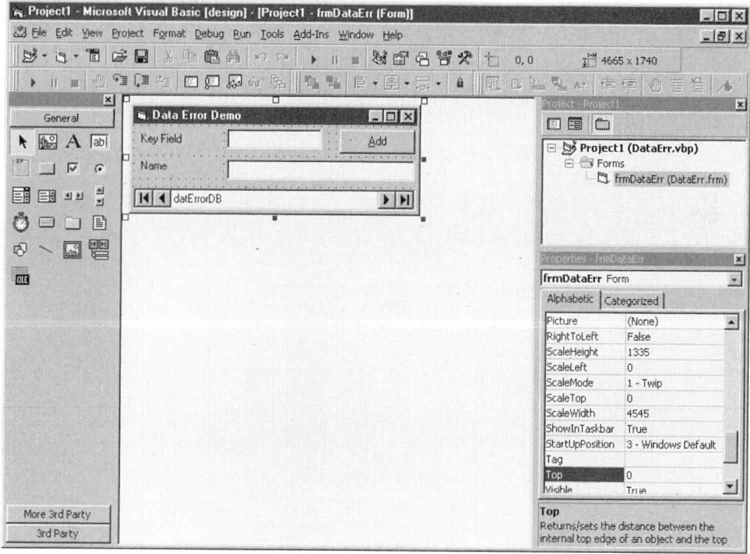

FIGURE 3.11.
Laying out the `frmDataErr` *form.*

The only code you need to add to this form is a single line behind the Add button. Place the following code in the `cmdAdd_Click` event:

```
Private Sub cmdAdd_Click()
   datErrorDB.Recordset.AddNew
End Sub
```

Now save the new form as DATAERR.FRM and the project as DATAERR.VBP. When you run the project, you can test the built-in error trapping for data controls by adding a new duplicate record to the table. Click the Add button, enter **KF009** in the Key Field text box, and then click an arrow on the data control to force it to save the record. You should see a database error message like the one in Figure 3.12.

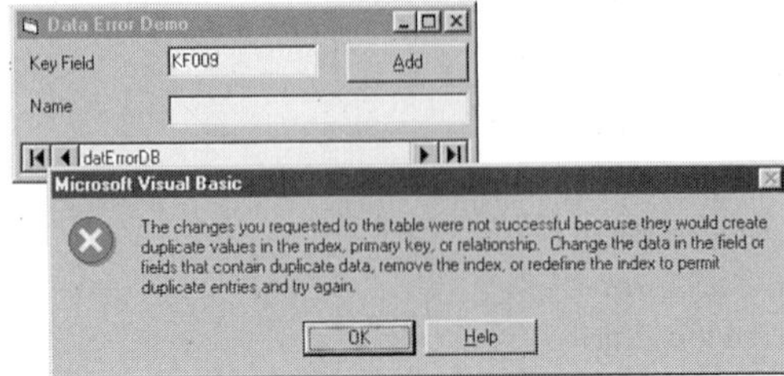

FIGURE 3.12.
A sample Microsoft data control error message.

Are you surprised? You didn't add an error trap to the data entry form, but you still have a complete database error message! The Visual Basic data control is kind enough to provide complete database error reporting, even if you have no error handlers in your Visual Basic program. Along with the automatic errors, the data control also has the Error event. Each time a data-related error occurs, this event occurs. You can add code in the datErrorDB_Error event to automatically fix errors, display better error messages, and so on.

Modify the program a bit to show you how you can use the datErrorDB_Error event. First, add a CommonDialog control to your form and call it dlgDatabaseError. Then edit the DatabaseName property of the data control to read C:\ERRORDB.MDB. Next, add the code from Listing 3.11 to the datErrorDB_Error event.

Listing 3.11. The datErrorDB_Error event.

```
Private Sub datErrorDB_Error(DataErr As Integer, Response As Integer)

    ' add error-trapping for data errors

    Dim strFileName As String

    Select Case DataErr
        Case 3024 ' database not found
            MsgBox "Unable to locate data file", _
            vbExclamation, "Database Missing"

            dlgDatabaseError.DialogTitle = "Locate ERRORDB.MDB"
            dlgDatabaseError.filename = "ERRORDB.MDB"
            dlgDatabaseError.Filter = "*.mdb"
            dlgDatabaseError.ShowOpen
            datErrorDB.DatabaseName = dlgDatabaseError.filename

            Response = vbCancel ' cancel auto-message
    End Select

End Sub
```

Notice that the code in Listing 3.11 checks to see whether the error code is 3024. This error number corresponds to the "database missing" message. If the 3024 code is reported, users see a short message and then the file open dialog box, ready to locate and load the database. Finally, notice the line that sets the `Response` parameter to `vbCancel`. This step tells Visual Basic not to display the default message.

TIP

Usually, trying to override the default error handling of the data control with your own database errors isn't a good idea. As long as you use the Visual Basic data control, you don't need to add database error-trapping routines to your data-entry forms. The only time you need to add error-related code is when you want to perform special actions in the `Error` event of the data control.

You need to add one more little bit of code to complete this error trap. Add the following code to the `Form_Activate` event:

```
Private Sub Form_Activate()
    datErrorDB.Refresh
End Sub
```

This code ensures that the data-entry fields on the form are updated with the most recent data from the database.

Now save and run the project. You'll first see a message telling you that the database is missing (see Figure 3.13). Next, you'll see the open file dialog box wait for you to locate and load the requested database (see Figure 3.14). Finally, after you load the database, the data-entry screen opens ready for your input.

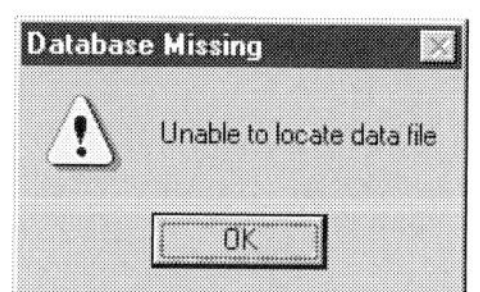

FIGURE 3.13.
A custom error message in the `datErrorDB_Error` *event.*

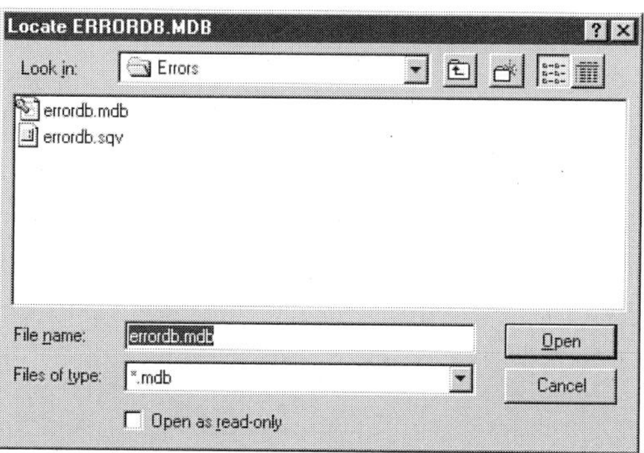

FIGURE 3.14.
Locating the requested database.

Database Errors with Microsoft Data Access Objects

If you use Microsoft data-access objects instead of the Visual Basic data control, you need to add error-handling routines to your project. For example, if you want to create a dynaset with Visual Basic code, you need to trap for any error that might occur along the way.

Add the code in Listing 3.12 to the `Form_Load` event of `frmDataErr`. This code opens the database and creates a dynaset to stuff into the data control that already exists on the form. Before you enter the code, however, make sure that you set `datErrorDB`'s `DatabaseName` property back to the correct path for the `ERROR.MDB` database.

Listing 3.12. The `Form_Load` event.

```
Private Sub Form_Load()

    ' create recordset using DAO

    On Error GoTo LocalErr

    Dim ws As Workspace
    Dim db As Database
    Dim rs As Recordset
    Dim strSQL As String

    strSQL = "SELECT * FROM Table2"
    Set ws = DBEngine.Workspaces(0)
    Set db = ws.OpenDatabase(datErrorDB.DatabaseName)
    Set rs = db.OpenRecordset(strSQL, dbOpenDynaset)
    Exit Sub

LocalErr:
    MsgBox "<" & CStr(Errors(0).Number) & "> " & _
      Errors(0).Description, vbCritical, "Form_Load Error"
    Unload Me

End Sub
```

The code in Listing 3.12 establishes some variables and then opens the database and creates a new dynaset from a data table named `Table2`.

NOTE

Instead of the Visual Basic `Err` object, the DAO `Errors` collection is used to retrieve the most recent database error. The `Errors` collection is available only if you have the Microsoft DAO library loaded by using the Project | References option from the main Visual Basic 5.0 menu.

Because there's no `Table2` in `ERRORDB.MDB`, you see a database error when the program runs. The error message is displayed and then the form is unloaded completely (see Figure 3.15).

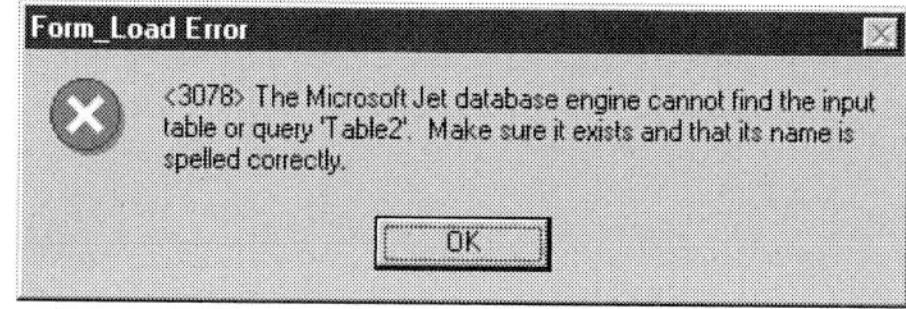

FIGURE 3.15.
Displaying an error message from the `Form_Load` *event.*

It's a good idea to open any data tables or files that you need for a data-entry form during the `Form_Load` event. That way, if problems occur, you can catch them before data entry begins.

Creating Your Error-Handling OLE Server

In the previous sections, you created several error handlers, each tuned to handle a special set of problems. Although this approach works for small projects, it can be tedious and burdensome if you have to put together a large application. Also, after you write an error handler that works well for one type of error, you can use that error handler in every other program that might have the same error. Why write it more than once?

Although Visual Basic requires error traps to be set for each subroutine or function, you can still create a generic approach to error handling that takes advantage of code you've already written. In the following sections, you'll write a set of routines—the error-handling OLE server—that you can install in all your Visual Basic programs. This OLE server will offer some generic error-handling capabilities as well as the capability to log these errors to a disk file and to keep track of the procedure call stack. These last two services can be very valuable when you encounter a vexing bug in your program and need to get additional information on the exact subroutines and functions executed before the error occurred.

To build the new error-handling OLE server, you need to start a new Visual Basic ActiveX DLL project. Name the default class module `errHandler` and set the project name to `prjErrHandler`. You also need to add a `.BAS` module, which holds a new user-defined type and some API definitions that are used with the customized error dialog box.

Building the `errHandler` Class

Building the `errHandler` class involves several steps. First, add the code in Listing 3.13 to the general declaration section of the `Class` object.

Listing 3.13. Code for the declaration section of the `errHandler` class.

```
Option Explicit

' error types
Enum errType
    errItem = 0
    errColl = 1
End Enum
```

continues

Listing 3.13. continued

```
' return/option values
Enum errReturn
    errExit = 0
    errResume = 1
    errNext = 2
    errSelect = 3
End Enum

' handler storage
Private errDefRtn As errReturn
Private errDefType As errType
```

The first two items in the declaration section define enumerated types. This special kind of user-defined type is a mix between a standard user-defined type and a public constant. Enumerated types make it easy to write well-documented code. Along with the enumerated types, you see two private variables declared for local use.

Next, you need to add some declaration code to the `.BAS` module in your DLL project. This code defines a special custom data type that you can use to control the display of your custom error dialog box. The `errHandler` DLL also allows you to access any possible help topics associated with the error messages. For this reason, the `.BAS` module contains the `WinHelp` API declaration, which is used on the custom dialog box. Open the `.BAS` module, set its `Name` property to `modErrHandler`, and enter the code in Listing 3.14 into the general declaration section of the module.

Listing 3.14. Code for the general declaration section of the `modErrHandler` `.BAS` module.

```
Option Explicit

' define dialog data type
Public Type errDialog
    Message As String
    Buttons As Variant
    Title As String
    HelpFile As String
    HelpID As Long
    Return As Long
End Type

Public udtErrDialog As errDialog

' declare winHelp API
Declare Function WinHelp Lib "user32" Alias "WinHelpA" (ByVal hwnd As Long, _
  ByVal lpHelpFile As String, _
  ByVal wCommand As Long, _
  ByVal dwData As Long) As Long

Public Const HELP_CONTEXT = &H1
Public Const HELP_QUIT = &H2
```

That's all you need to add to `modErrHandler`. Next, you need to add code to the `Initialize` event of the `errHandler` class module. Add the code from Listing 3.15 to the `Class_Initialize` event.

Listing 3.15. The `Class_Initialize` event of the `errHandler` class.

```
Private Sub Class_Initialize()

    ' set starting values
    errDefRtn = errExit
    errDefType = errItem

    udtErrDialog.Buttons = ""
    udtErrDialog.HelpFile = ""
    udtErrDialog.HelpID = -1
    udtErrDialog.Message = ""
    udtErrDialog.Return = -1
    udtErrDialog.Title = ""

End Sub
```

This `errHandler` class has two public properties: `DefaultAction` and `DefaultType`. These defaults were set in the `Initialize` event and can be overridden by setting the properties at runtime. Create the `DefaultAction` property (choose Tools | Add Procedure) and add the code from Listing 3.16 into the `Property Let` and `Property Get` routines.

3
HANDLING ERRORS

Listing 3.16. Defining the `Property Let` and `Property Get` routines for the `DefaultAction` property.

```
Public Property Get DefaultAction() As errReturn
    '
    ' return default
    '
    DefaultAction = errDefRtn
    '
End Property

Public Property Let DefaultAction(ByVal vNewValue As errReturn)
    '
    ' verify parm and store
    '
    If vNewValue >= errExit Or vNewValue <= errSelect Then
        errDefRtn = vNewValue
    End If
    '
End Property
```

NOTE

The data type for the property is `errReturn`, an enumerated type defined in the declaration section of the class module.

Next, create the `Property Let` and `Property Get` routines for the `DefaultType` property and enter the code from Listing 3.17 into the project.

Listing 3.17. Defining the `Property Let` and `Property Get` routines for the `DefaultType` property.

```
Public Property Get DefaultType() As errType
    '
    DefaultType = errDefType
    '
End Property

Public Property Let DefaultType(ByVal vNewValue As errType)
    '
    If vNewValue >= errColl Or vNewValue <= errItem Then
        errDefType = vNewValue
    End If
    '
End Property
```

You're now ready to write the main error-handling method, which you can call from any VBA-compliant program. You pass the Visual Basic `Err` object (or database `Errors` collection) along with a few optional parameters that can control the behavior of the message dialog box. After the method is finished, a value is returned. You can use this value to control program flow and error recovery. Create a new function method named `errHandler` in your class module and enter the code in Listing 3.18.

Listing 3.18. The `errHandler` function.

```
Public Function errHandler(objErrColl As Variant, _
     Optional intType As errType, Optional errOption As errReturn, _
     Optional errRefName As String) As errReturn
    ' ------------------------------------------------
    ' produce msg and prompt for response
    '
    ' inputs:
    '   objErrColl  - DAO collection -OR- VBA Err object
    '   intType     - errType enum that describes objErrColl (coll or item)
    '   errOption   - errReturn enum sets dialog behavior
    '   errRefName  - string to reference caller
    '
    ' returns:
    '   errExit     - end program
    '   errResume   - try again
    '   errNext     - skip to next line
    ' ------------------------------------------------

    Dim strMsg As String
    Dim strTitle As String
    Dim rtnValue As errReturn

    ' retrieve action option
    If IsMissing(errOption) Then
        errOption = errDefRtn
    End If
```

```
    ' retrieve reference name
    If IsMissing(errRefName) Then
        errRefName = ""
    Else
        errRefName = " from " & errRefName
    End If

    ' build full message
    strMsg = errMsg(objErrColl, intType)

    ' evaluate things
    Select Case errOption
        Case errExit
            udtErrDialog.Title = "Exiting Program"
            udtErrDialog.Message = strMsg
            udtErrDialog.Buttons = Array("&Exit")
            frmErrDialog.Show vbModal
            rtnValue = errExit

        Case errResume, errNext
            udtErrDialog.Title = "Error Message" & errRefName
            udtErrDialog.Message = strMsg
            udtErrDialog.Buttons = Array("&OK")
            frmErrDialog.Show vbModal
            rtnValue = errOption

        Case Else
            udtErrDialog.Title = "Error Message" & errRefName
            udtErrDialog.Message = strMsg
            udtErrDialog.Buttons = Array("&Cancel", "&Retry", "&Ignore")
            frmErrDialog.Show vbModal
            rtnValue = udtErrDialog.Return
    End Select

    ' give it back
    errHandler = rtnValue

End Function
```

The code in Listing 3.18 calls a support function (`errMsg`) and a dialog box (`frmErrDialog`). You need to code these two remaining objects before you can test your error handler. Create a new function (`errMsg`) in the class module and enter the code in Listing 3.19 into the project.

Listing 3.19. The `errMsg` support function.

```
Public Function errMsg(objErrColl As Variant, intType As errType) As String

    ' build and return complete error msg

    Dim strMsg As String
    Dim vntItem As Variant

    strMsg = ""
```

continues

Listing 3.19. continued

```
    If intType = errColl Then
        For Each vntItem In objErrColl
            strMsg = strMsg & "<" & CStr(vntItem.Number) & "> "
            strMsg = strMsg & vntItem.Description
            strMsg = strMsg & " (in " & vntItem.Source & ")." & vbCrLf
        Next
    Else ' intType= errItem
        strMsg = "<" & objErrColl.Number & "> "
        strMsg = strMsg & objErrColl.Description
        strMsg = strMsg & " (in " & objErrColl.Source & ")"

        udtErrDialog.HelpFile = objErrColl.HelpFile
        udtErrDialog.HelpID = objErrColl.HelpContext
    End If

    errMsg = strMsg

End Function
```

The main job of the `errMsg` routine is to build a complete error message for users. To do this, `errMsg` needs to know whether the passed object was a single VBA `Err` object or the DAO `Errors` collection. That's why the `errType` parameter is included in the call.

Also note that the `errMsg` method is declared as a `Public` method. You can call this method from your Visual Basic 5.0 programs, too. That way, even if you don't want to perform all the error-handling operations, you can use `errMsg` to get a improved error message for your users.

Coding the `frmErrDialog` Form

The last main piece of the `errHandler` class is a custom dialog box to display the error message and get input from users. Often, you want to do more than just display the message and let users click OK. You can ask them to retry the same process, or ask whether they want to ignore the error and continue. This dialog box not only displays the message and gives you an opportunity to get a user response, but it also lets you provide an optional Help button so users can get greater support to see how to resolve the encountered error.

With the `prjErrHandler` project still open, add a form to the project. Use Table 3.4 and Figure 3.16 as a guide in laying out the form.

Table 3.4. Control table for the `frmErrDialog` form.

Property	*Setting*
	Form control
`Name`	`frmErrDialog`
`BorderStyle`	`3 - Fixed Dialog`
`Caption`	`Error Report`

Property	Setting
	Form control
Height	2115
Left	45
Top	330
Width	5460
ControlBox	0 - False
MaxButton	0 - False
MinButton	0 - False
ShowInTaskbar	0 - False
StartUpPosition	2 - CenterScreen
	TextBox control
Name	txtErrMsg
BackColor	&H80000000&
Height	1035
Left	900
Locked	-1 - True
MultiLine	-1 - True
ScrollBars	2 - Vertical
Top	120
Width	4395
	CommandButton control
Name	cmdBtn
Caption	&Help
Height	315
Index	3
Left	4080
Top	1320
Visible	0 - False
Width	1215
	Second CommandButton control
Name	cmdBtn
Caption	&Ignore

continues

Table 3.4. continued

Property	*Setting*
	Second CommandButton control
Height	315
Index	2
Left	2760
Top	1320
Visible	0 - False
Width	1215
	Third CommandButton control
Name	cmdBtn
Caption	&Retry
Height	315
Index	1
Left	1440
Top	1320
Visible	0 - False
Width	1215
	Fourth CommandButton control
Name	cmdBtn
Caption	&OK
Height	315
Index	0
Left	120
Top	1320
Visible	0 - False
Width	1215
	Image control
Name	imgNo
Height	600
Left	120
Picture	intl_no.bmp
Stretch	-1 - True
Top	120
Width	600

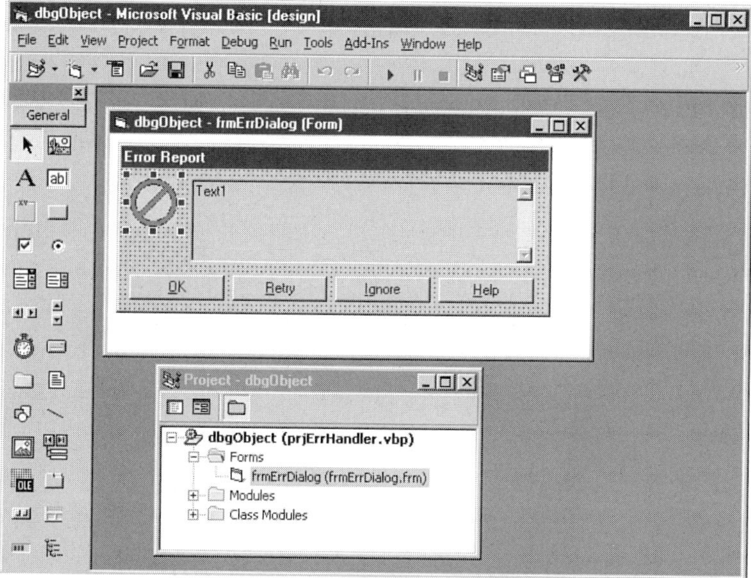

FIGURE 3.16.
Laying out the `frmErrDialog` *form.*

> **NOTE**
>
> You can find the `INTL_NO.BMP` image used by the Image control on VB5's CD-ROM.

Be sure to build the command buttons as a control array and to set their `Visible` properties to `False`. You'll write code to arrange and enable these buttons as needed at runtime.

You need to code only two events for this form. The `Form_Load` event handles most of the dirty work. Listing 3.20 shows the code that you should add to the `Form_Load` event.

Listing 3.20. The `Form_Load` event of the `frmErrDialog` form.

```
Private Sub Form_Load()

    Dim intBtns As Integer
    Dim intLoop As Integer

    txtErrMsg = udtErrDialog.Message
    Me.Caption = udtErrDialog.Title

    intBtns = UBound(udtErrDialog.Buttons)
    For intLoop = 0 To intBtns
        cmdBtn(intLoop).Caption = udtErrDialog.Buttons(intLoop)
        cmdBtn(intLoop).Visible = True
        cmdBtn(intLoop).Top = Me.ScaleHeight - 420
        cmdBtn(intLoop).Left = 120 + (1300 * intLoop)
    Next
```

continues

Listing 3.20. continued

```
    ' check for help file
    If udtErrDialog.HelpFile <> "" Then
        cmdBtn(3).Visible = True
        cmdBtn(3).Top = Me.ScaleHeight - 420
        cmdBtn(3).Left = 120 + (1300 * 3)
    End If

End Sub
```

The code in Listing 3.20 first sets the dialog box caption and message box. Then, based on the properties of the `udtErrDialog` type, the buttons are arranged on the form. The only other code that you need to add to this form is the code that goes behind the command button array. Place the code from Listing 3.21 in the `cmdBtn_Click` event of the form.

Listing 3.21. The `cmdBtn_Click` event.

```
Private Sub cmdBtn_Click(Index As Integer)

    ' return user selection

    Dim lngReturn As Long

    Select Case Index
        Case 0
            udtErrDialog.Return = errExit
            lngReturn = WinHelp(Me.hWnd, udtErrDialog.HelpFile, HELP_QUIT, &H0)
            Unload Me
        Case 1
            udtErrDialog.Return = errResume
            lngReturn = WinHelp(Me.hWnd, udtErrDialog.HelpFile, HELP_QUIT, &H0)
            Unload Me
        Case 2
            udtErrDialog.Return = errNext
            lngReturn = WinHelp(Me.hWnd, udtErrDialog.HelpFile, HELP_QUIT, &H0)
            Unload Me
        Case 3
            lngReturn = WinHelp(Me.hWnd, udtErrDialog.HelpFile, _
            HELP_CONTEXT, udtErrDialog.HelpID)
    End Select

End Sub
```

The code in Listing 3.21 allows users to select the command button appropriate for the moment. If users click the Help button, the properties from the `udtErrDialog` type are used to fill in the parameters of the WinHelp API call.

That's all the code you need to create your `errHandler` ActiveX DLL. Save the project as `prjErrHandler` and then compile it (with File | Make prjErrHandler.dll). If it compiles without error, you're all set for a quick test!

Testing the ErrHandler Object Library

Start a new Visual Basic 5.0 Standard EXE project. Set the form name to `frmTest` and the project name to `prjTest`. Add a data control and a command button to the form. Use Figure 3.17 as a reference for laying out the form.

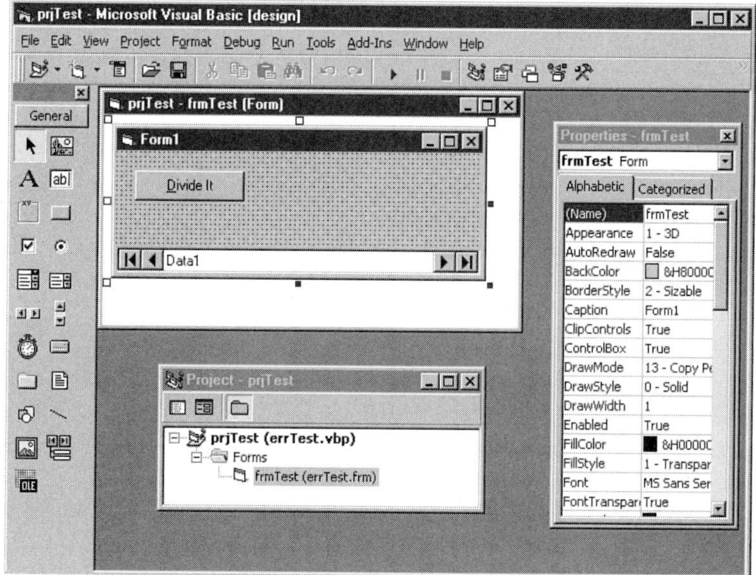

FIGURE 3.17.
Laying out the `frmTest` form.

Next, you need to add a reference to the error-handler object library to your project. Choose Project | References and locate and add the `prjErrHandler` DLL (see Figure 3.18).

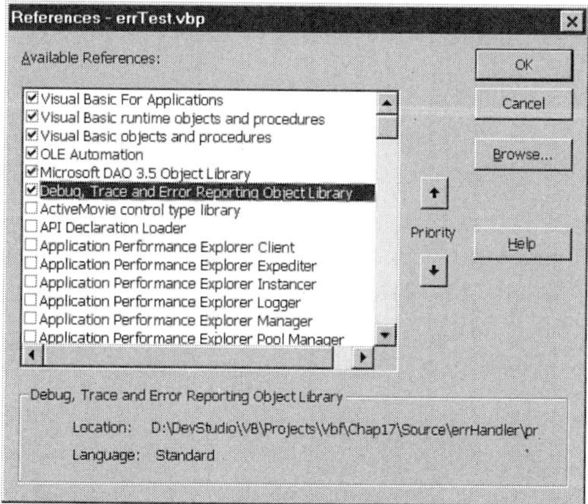

FIGURE 3.18.
Adding the error-handler object library to the project.

Now you can add a bit of code to the form that sets up the error handler and then causes an error to be handled. First, add the following code to the general declaration section of the form, to declare the object that contains the error handler:

```
Option Explicit

Public objErr As Object
```

Next, add the code from Listing 3.22 to the `Form_Load` event of the project.

Listing 3.22. The `Form_Load` event.

```
Private Sub Form_Load()

    Data1.DatabaseName = "junk"
    Set objErr = New errHandler

End Sub
```

The code in Listing 3.22 creates the new error-handler object and then sets up the data control with a bogus database name. Now add the code from Listing 3.23 to the `Data1_Error` event. This code intercepts the database error and displays the new custom dialog box.

Listing 3.23. Trapping the data-control error.

```
Private Sub Data1_Error(DataErr As Integer, Response As Integer)

    Dim rtn As Long

    Response = 0
    rtn = objErr.errHandler(Errors, errColl)

End Sub
```

Save the form (`FRMTEST.FRM`) and the project (`PRJTEST.VBP`) and run the code. You should see your new object library error dialog box telling you about the database error (see Figure 3.19).

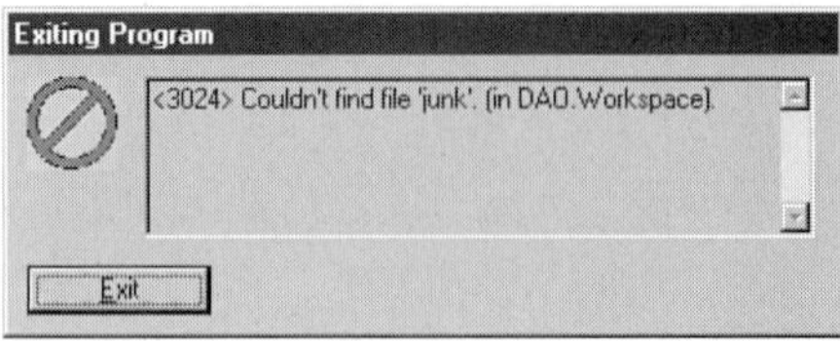

FIGURE 3.19.
The new `Error` *object library in action.*

Add some code behind the `Command1_Click` event that creates a divide-by-zero error. The code in Listing 3.24 does just that.

Listing 3.24. Creating a divide-by-zero error in code.

```
Private Sub Command1_Click()

    On Error GoTo Localerr
    Dim rtn as Long

    Print 6 / 0

    Exit Sub

Localerr:
    rtn = objErr.errHandler(Err, errItem, errResume, _
      "prjTest.Form1.Command1_Click")
    Resume Next

End Sub
```

When you save and run this code, click the command button to see the new error report. You should see that the Help button is active. Click the button to see Visual Basic 5.0 help on dealing with the divide-by-zero error (see Figure 3.20).

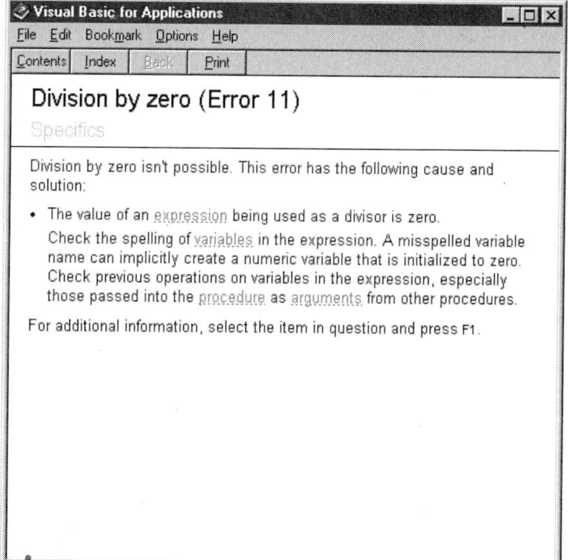

FIGURE 3.20.
Viewing help on the divide-by-zero error.

Now add an option that creates an error report file whenever the error handler is activated.

Adding Error Logs to the Error Handler

When errors occur, users often don't remember details that appear in the error messages. It's more useful to create an error log on disk whenever errors occur, so programmers or system administrators can review the logs and see the error messages without sitting right next to users when the error occurs.

To build error-logging features into the existing `errHandler` class, you need to declare two new properties (`LogFileName` and `WriteLogFlag`), create a `LogError` method to write the errors to a disk file, add some code to the general declarations area and the `Class_Initialize` and `Class_Terminate` events, and add a few lines to the `errHandler` method to call the `LogError` method.

First, restart the `errHandler` DLL project and add the following code to the General Declarations section of the `errHandler` class module:

```
' logging storage
Private errLogFileName As String
Private errLogFlag As Boolean
```

These code lines appear at the end of the section. They declare local storage space for the new properties. Now choose Tools | Add Procedure to add two new public properties to the class: `LogFileName` and `WriteLogFlag`. Listing 3.25 shows the code you need to add to the `Property Let` and `Property Get` statements for these two new properties.

Listing 3.25. The `Property Let/Get` statements for the `LogFileName` and `LogFlag` properties.

```
Public Property Get LogFileName() As String

    LogFileName = errLogFileName

End Property

Public Property Let LogFileName(ByVal vNewValue As String)

    errLogFileName = vNewValue

End Property

Public Property Get WriteLogFlag() As Boolean

    WriteLogFlag = errLogFlag

End Property

Public Property Let WriteLogFlag(ByVal vNewValue As Boolean)

    errLogFlag = vNewValue

End Property
```

The `LogFileName` property holds the name of the disk file that holds the log records. The `LogFlag` property controls the status of the error logging. If the `LogFlag` property is set to `True`, log records are created. Add the following code to the end of the `Class_Initialize` event to set the default values for the two new properties:

```
errLogFileName = App.EXEName & ".err"
errLogFlag = False
```

Now create a new private sub method named `LogError` and enter the code from Listing 3.26 into the routine. This code actually creates the log entries.

Listing 3.26. The `LogError` method.

```
Private Sub LogError(strErrMsg As String)

    ' write error to disk file
    On Error GoTo LocalErr

    Dim intChFile As Integer

    intChFile = FreeFile
    Open errLogFileName For Append As intChFile
        Print #intChFile, Format(Now, "general date")
        Print #intChFile, strErrMsg
        Print #intChFile, ""
    Close intChFile

    Exit Sub

LocalErr:
    ' trouble with file stuff!
    Err.Raise vbObjectError + 1, "errHandler.LogError", _
      "Can't write log file [" & errLogFileName & "]"

End Sub
```


Notice that you added an error handler in this routine. Because you're about to perform disk operations, you need to be ready for errors here, too. Notice also that the internal error isn't displayed in a message box. Instead, the `Raise` method of the `Err` object generates a unique error number and description, which are sent back to the calling application for handling.

TIP

The Visual Basic `FreeFile()` function returns a number that represents the first available file channel Visual Basic uses to open the data file. Using `FreeFile()` guarantees that you don't select a file channel that Visual Basic is already using for another file.

All you need to do is add a call to the `LogError` method from the public `errHandler` method. Listing 3.27 shows the code you need to add in the routine. Make sure that you add these lines of code right after the call to the `errMsg` function and just before the start of the `Select Case` statement.

Listing 3.27. Updating the `errHandler` method.

```
' build full message
strMsg = errMsg(objErrColl, intType)

' write it out, if allowed           '<<< new code
If errLogFlag = True Then            '<<< new code
    LogError strMsg                  '<<< new code
End If                               '<<< new code

' evaluate things
Select Case errOption
```

That's the end of the code to add logging to the error handler. Save the project and compile the ActiveX DLL. When the DLL is successfully compiled, close this project and open the test project you built earlier.

Open the `Form_Load` event of the `frmTest` form and add two lines to set the `LogFileName` and `WriteLogFlag` properties of the `errHandler` object. Listing 3.28 shows how to modify the code.

Listing 3.28. Modifying the `Form_Load` event to include error logging.

```
Private Sub Form_Load()

    Data1.DatabaseName = "junk"
    Set objErr = New errHandler

    objErr.WriteLogFlag = True
    objErr.LogFileName = App.Path & "\" & App.EXEName & ".log"

End Sub
```

When you run the project, each error is logged to a file with the same name as the application in the same folder as the application. In the previous example, a file called `ERRTEST.LOG` was created in the default folder. Listing 3.29 shows the contents of this error log file.

Listing 3.29. The `ERRTEST.LOG` file.

```
05-Feb-97 5:27:01 AM
<3024> Couldn't find file 'junk'. (in DAO.Workspace).
05-Feb-97 5:27:08 AM
<11> Division by zero (in prjTest)
```

You can easily modify the layout and even the contents of the log reports by changing only a few lines of code in the `LogError` method.

Adding a Module Trace to the Error Handler

The final touch to add to your error-handler library is the option to track and print a *module trace*, which keeps track of all the modules called and the order in which they're invoked. A module trace can be very valuable when you're debugging programs. Often, a routine works just fine when it's called from one module but reports errors if called from another module. When errors occur, it's handy to have a module trace to help find the source of your problems.

You'll implement the module trace routines as a new `objclass` object in the `prjErrHandler` project. Reload the ActiveX DLL project and add a new class module to the project. Set its `Name` property to `TraceObject` and keep its `Instancing` property to the default `5 - MultiUse`.

You need two new properties for this object (`TraceFileName` and `TraceFlag`) and a handful of new public methods:

- `Push` adds a sub or function name to the call list.
- `Pop` removes a sub or function name from the list.
- `List` returns an array of all the names on the call list.
- `Dump` writes the complete call list to a disk file.
- `Show` displays the complete call list in a message box.
- `Clear` resets the call list.

First, add the code in Listing 3.30 to the general declarations area of the class module.

Listing 3.30. Declaring the `TraceObject` variables.

```
Option Explicit

' local property storage
Private strFileName As String
Private booFlag As Boolean

' internal variables
Private strStack() As String
Private lngPointer As Long
```

Next, create the two new public properties, `TraceFile` and `TraceFlag`, and enter the code in Listing 3.31 into the `Property Let` and `Get` statements for these two new properties.

Listing 3.31. The `Property Let/Get` statements for the `TraceFile` and `TraceLog` properties.

```
Public Property Get TraceFileName() As String

    TraceFileName = strFileName

End Property

Public Property Let TraceFileName(ByVal vNewValue As String)

    strFileName = vNewValue

End Property
```

continues

Listing 3.31. continued

```
Public Property Get TraceFlag() As Boolean

    TraceFlag = booFlag

End Property

Public Property Let TraceFlag(ByVal vNewValue As Boolean)

    booFlag = vNewValue

End Property
```

Now add the code from Listing 3.32 to the `Class_Initialize` event. This code sets the default values for the two public properties.

Listing 3.32. The `Class_Initialize` event.

```
Private Sub Class_Initialize()

    ' startup stuff
    strFileName = App.EXEName & ".trc"
    booFlag = False

End Sub
```

It's time to code the various methods you need to manage call tracing in VB5. First, create the `Public` sub methods `Push` and `Pop`, which handle the details of keeping track of each function or sub as it's executed. Listing 3.33 shows the code for these two methods.

Listing 3.33. The `Push` and `Pop` methods of `TraceObject`.

```
Public Sub Push(ProcName As String)

    ' push a proc onto the stack
    lngPointer = lngPointer + 1
    ReDim Preserve strStack(lngPointer)
    strStack(lngPointer) = ProcName

End Sub

Public Sub Pop()

    ' pop a proc off the stack
    If lngPointer <> 0 Then
        lngPointer = lngPointer - 1
        ReDim Preserve strStack(lngPointer)
    End If

End Sub
```

Create another Public sub method Clear and a Public function method List. Add the code from Listing 3.34 to the class.

Listing 3.34. The List and Clear methods of TraceObject.

```
Public Function List() As Variant

    ' return an array of the trace log
    List = strStack

End Function

Public Sub Clear()

    ' clear off the stack
    lngPointer = 0
    ReDim Preserve strStack(0)

End Sub
```

TIP

Using the Variant data type to return an array of items is a very efficient way to pass array data among Visual Basic methods.

Create a new Public sub called Dump. This writes the trace list to a disk file. Fill in the method with the code from Listing 3.35.

Listing 3.35. The Dump method of the TraceObject.

```
Public Sub Dump()

    ' write trace log to file
    Dim intFile As Integer
    Dim intLoop As Integer

    intFile = FreeFile
    Open strFileName For Append As intFile
        Print #intFile, "***TRACE STACK DUMP***"
        Print #intFile, "***DATE: " & Format(Now(), "general date")
        Print #intFile, ""

        For intLoop = lngPointer To 1 Step -1
            Print #intFile, vbTab & Format(intLoop, "000") & _
            ": " & strStack(intLoop)
        Next

        Print #intFile, ""
        Print #intFile, "***EOF"
    Close #intFile
```

continues

Listing 3.35. continued

```
    Exit Sub

LocalErr:
    Err.Raise vbObjectError + 3, "Trace.Dump", _
    "Can't write trace file [" & strFileName & "]"

End Sub
```

Finally, create the `Public` sub method called `Show` and enter the code from Listing 3.36.

Listing 3.36. The `Show` method of the `TraceObject`.

```
Public Sub Show()

    ' show trace log in dialog

    Dim intLoop As Integer
    Dim strMsg As String

    strMsg = ""
    For intLoop = lngPointer To 1 Step -1
        strMsg = strMsg & Format(intLoop, "000")
        strMsg = strMsg & ": "
        strMsg = strMsg & Trim(strStack(intLoop))
        strMsg = strMsg & vbCrLf
    Next

    MsgBox strMsg, vbInformation, "Trace Stack"

End Sub
```

Notice that the code in Listing 3.36 prints the call array in *reverse* order. This is the conventional way to print trace lists. The top entry shows the most recently executed routine; the bottom entry shows the first routine in this trace.

After adding this last code, save and compile the ActiveX DLL and then load your `errTest` project. After you load the `frmTest` form, add the following line of code to the general declarations area of the form:

```
Public objTrace As Object
```

Next, update the `Form_Load` event as shown in Listing 3.37 to add use of the trace module to the project.

Listing 3.37. Updating the `Form_Load` event to include module tracing.

```
Private Sub Form_Load()

    Data1.DatabaseName = "junk"

    Set objErr = New errHandler
```

```
    Set objTrace = New TraceObject

    objTrace.Push "Form_Load"

    objErr.WriteLogFlag = True
    objErr.LogFileName = App.Path & "\" & App.EXEName & ".log"

    objTrace.Pop

End Sub
```

Notice the use of `objTrace.Push` to add the name of the method to the trace stack. You should do this as soon as possible in the method code. The `objTrace.Pop` line at the very end of the method removes the name of the method from the stack just as the method is completed.

Add trace coding to the `Command1_Click` event. Update your form's `Command1_Click` event to match the one in Listing 3.38.

Listing 3.38. Updating the `Command1_Click` event to use module tracing.

```
Private Sub Command1_Click()

    On Error GoTo LocalErr
    Dim varList As Variant
    Dim rtn As Long

    objTrace.Push "Command1_Click"

    Print 6 / 0

    Exit Sub

LocalErr:

    rtn = objErr.errHandler(Err, errItem, errResume, _
    "prjTest.Form1.Command1_Click")

    objTrace.Show
    objTrace.Pop
    Resume Next

End Sub
```

Save this code and run the project. When you click the command button, you get a trace report onscreen (see Figure 3.21).

To add module tracing to a project, you need to add only a `.Push` line at the start of the routine and a `.Pop` line at the end of the routine. That's all you need to do to update the procedure stack for the program. For this to be really valuable, however, you have to do this for every routine you want to track.

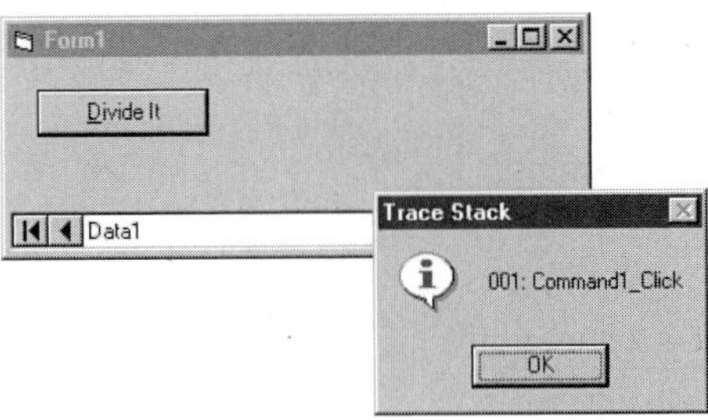

FIGURE 3.21.
Viewing the trace message.

In a real application environment, you don't want to show the procedure stack each time an error is reported. The best place for a stack dump is at exit time due to a fatal error. You should use the `TraceFile` option to write the stack to disk rather than display it to users.

Other Error-Handling Options

Now that you have the basics of error handling under your belt, you can continue to add features to the generic error handler. As you add these features, your programs take on a more professional look and feel. Also, using options such as error report logs and procedure stack logs makes it easier to debug and maintain your applications.

Features that you can add to your error handler include the following:

- Add the name of the user or workstation address to the reports.
- If you created an error trap for common errors, such as error 53, `File not found`, add that recovery code to your generic handler. Now you can count on consistent handling of common errors without adding code to every project.

Summary

This chapter covers all the basics of creating your own error-handling routines for Visual Basic applications. You learned that an error handler has three basic parts:

- The `On Error GoTo` statement
- The body of the error-handler code
- The error-handler exit

You learned that an error handler has four possible exits:

- `Resume` re-executes the code that caused the error.
- `Resume Next` continues processing at the line immediately following the code line that caused the error.
- `Resume label` continues processing at the location identified by the `label`.
- `Exit` ends processing for the current routine, and `End` exits the program completely.

You learned how to use the `Err.Raise` method to flag errors without resorting to modal dialog boxes.

You learned about the major types of errors that you're likely to encounter in your program:

- *General file errors* include errors such as `File not found` and `Invalid path`. Errors of this type usually can be fixed by users and then re-attempted. Use `Resume` as an exit for these types of errors.
- *Database errors* include errors related to data-entry mistakes, integrity violations, and multiuser-related errors, such as locked records. Errors of this type are best handled by allowing users to correct the data and attempt the operation again. If you use the Visual Basic data control, you don't have to write error handlers—the data control handles them for you. For operations that don't use the data control, you need to write your own error-handling routines.
- *Physical media errors* relate to device problems, such as unresponsive printers and downed communications ports. Sometimes users can fix the problems and continue (such as refilling the paper tray of the printer). Other times, users can't fix the problem without first exiting the program. It's a good idea to give users an option of exiting the program safely when errors of these types are reported.
- *Program code errors* occur due to problems within the Visual Basic code itself. Examples of program code errors include `Object variable not set` and `For loop not initialized`. Usually, users can't do anything to fix errors of this type. It's best to encourage users to report the error to the system administrator and then exit the program safely.

You also learned that you can declare a global error handler or a local error handler. The advantage of the global error handler is that it allows you to create a single module that handles all expected errors. The disadvantage is that because of the way Visual Basic keeps track of running routines, you can't resume processing at the point the error occurred once you arrive at the global error handler. The advantage of the local error handler is that you can always use `Resume`, `Resume Next`, or `Resume` *`label`* to continue processing at the point the error occurred. The disadvantage of the local error handler is that you need to add error-handling code to every routine in your program.

Finally, you learned how to create an error-handler object library that combines local error trapping with global error messages and responses. The error-handler object library also contains modules to keep track of the procedures running at the time of the error, a process for printing procedure stack dumps to the screen and to a file, and a process that creates an error log file for later review.

CHAPTER

Debugging and Testing Techniques

IN THIS CHAPTER

Two of the most unpleasant phases of application development are debugging and testing. Unfortunately, there is no getting around them; they have to be done. Even the most accomplished programmer is likely to have bugs creep into his code now and then or fail to account for situations that may make his program act in unexpected ways.

Recent versions of Visual Basic have come a long way in preventing obvious coding errors. With features like Auto Syntax Check, Auto List Members, Auto Quick Info, and ToolTips, common programming mistakes such as syntax errors are often "nipped in the bud." On the other hand, problems such as logic errors are not so apparent and are far more difficult to find and debug. Hunting them down requires a firm grasp of debugging and testing techniques. This chapter details such techniques and how you can use some of VB's powerful program debugging features to your benefit.

Starting at the Beginning

The best way to take care of program errors is to prevent them from occurring in the first place. Easier said than done, of course, but there are some simple things you can do that will decrease the likelihood of a serious coding error.

The first and most important thing you can do to prevent errors is to design your program thoroughly before you write a single line of code. Many errors occur simply because not enough thought was given to how the program will work and how it will react to unusual situations. For example, a program that accepts some form of input from users may not take the proper precautions to ensure that the data entered is valid. The program may crash when an unexpected data value is encountered. The culprit behind the error is not poor coding but poor planning. If more attention had been paid during the program's design phase, it's likely that such a situation would have been accounted for. The code would reflect this by trapping for such a situation.

Of course, there are times when even the most diligent design and planning efforts leave some circumstance unaccounted for, causing an error to pop up unexpectedly. It happens to everyone from time to time; no one is perfect. But proper design tenets should be followed to keep such errors at a minimum.

Object-oriented programming (OOP) techniques also lend themselves to the prevention of errors. OOP makes it possible to write and thoroughly test code once and then use it again and again. By not having to "reinvent the wheel," the likelihood of errors occurring in reusable objects is reduced.

Design and object-oriented programming methods are beyond the scope of this chapter. However, you can find more information on those subjects in Part II of this book, "Object-Oriented Programming: What It Means to You."

Error Handling

In the old days of BASIC programming, lines of code were prefixed with numbers. Error messages would specify the number of the line of code that generated the error, so debugging was somewhat simplified. Unfortunately, Visual Basic is not nearly as specific when reporting errors. When an error does occur in a VB program, little information is provided as to its source or even in which module it occurred. To make things worse, error messages are often cryptic. The same error message may signify a variety of problems, leaving the programmer with only a vague idea of what the actual problem might be.

The fact that VB offers little in the way of error reporting makes the implementation of error trapping all the more important. By adding even simple error trapping code to all the routines in your programs, you can greatly enhance the information produced when an error occurs. You can also use the error trapper to take care of any last-minute chores that need to be completed before the program ends. For example, you may want to save any data that the user entered. Errors are never easy to take (especially for end users), but they're even worse when their effect is a loss in productivity.

When creating an error handling routine, try to design it in a way that will facilitate debugging efforts. Display as much information as possible as to where the error occurred, such as the name of the Sub or Function. A little thing like that can cut down substantially on your debugging time.

Chapter 3, "Handling Errors," provides more information on effective error handling techniques.

Avoiding Program Errors

Some of the most common program errors can be avoided by simply adding a few lines of code to your program modules. The `Option Explicit` and `Option Base` statements are two easy additions to your program code that may help you find errors.

The `Option Explicit` is used at module level (add it to your form or module's General Declarations section) and ensures that you do not use variables that have not been specifically declared. How many times have you mistyped the name of a variable somewhere in your code, resulting in a runtime error or, more often, a hard-to-find logic error? Under normal circumstances, Visual Basic assumes that any undeclared variable names are of the `Variant` type. So if you define the variable `intCounter` as an `Integer` but mistype the variable name in your code as `intCoutner`, Visual Basic will mistakenly assume that `intCoutner` is a new `Variant` variable.

Adding an `Option Explicit` statement to your code prevents errors like that. If the VB compiler detects an undeclared variable name, it generates an error and won't let the program run until you fix it.

The `Option Base` statement is useful for preventing errors pertaining to array variables. By default, arrays in Visual Basic are zero-based, meaning that their first (base) element is number 0. So if you define a string array as `strItems(25)`, the individual elements are numbered from 0 to 24. Being humans, we don't naturally tend to think that way. Instead, we think of `strItems(25)` as being an array of items from 1 to 25. Experienced programmers are more likely to remember that arrays are zero-based by default and compensate for that fact in their code. But even experienced programmers slip up once in a while and assume that an array is one-based instead of zero-based.

Adding an `Option Base 1` statement to your code changes the default for declared arrays from zero-based to the more natural one-based. If you find yourself consistently falling into the zero-based array trap, use `Option Base` to change VB's default array attitude.

Perhaps a review of the `Option Explicit` and `Option Base` statements is elementary, but they are important tools in thwarting errors and improving the code's readability. Of course, they can't catch every error—if only it were that simple. In many cases, a solid understanding of debugging techniques is necessary for tracking down errors. The next section will tell you what you need to know to become an effective bug killer.

Debugging Programs in Visual Basic

Visual Basic programmers are fortunate. Many program debugging and testing features are included within VB's design environment, which means that programs can be fully debugged before they are compiled into executable code and distributed. Although you may have a basic understanding of debugging in Visual Basic, you may not be aware of all of VB's built-in debugging tools.

This section will introduce you to VB's debugging options and tools. These are split into two categories: those that let you control program flow by stepping through lines of code, and those that display information in special windows.

Stepping Through Code

When you need to flesh out a program bug, the best way is often to step through your code line by line. Fortunately, Visual Basic provides a way to do this while the program is running.

To begin, make sure that the Debug toolbar is displayed. Choose View | Toolbars to show which menus are currently being displayed. If there is no check mark next to the Debug option, click on Debug to highlight it. A toolbar like the one shown in Figure 4.1 will be added to VB's toolbar area. If you don't like its placement, you can grab its "handle" (the two vertical bars at the far left of the toolbar) and drag it to another part of the toolbar area, or you can make it free-floating by moving it away from the toolbar area.

FIGURE 4.1.
The Debug toolbar.

The Debug toolbar contains icons that allow you to perform certain debugging tasks, such as stepping through lines of code. It also allows you to display special windows that can be used to assist in your debugging efforts. Many of these icons have a corresponding hotkey, as shown in Table 4.1. The purpose of each icon (and its hotkey) will be discussed in a moment.

Table 4.1. The icons on the Debug toolbar and their corresponding hotkeys.

Icon	*Hotkey*
Start	F5
Break	Ctrl+Break
End	
Toggle Breakpoint	F9
Step Into	F8
Step Over	Shift+F8
Step Out	Ctrl+Shift+F8
Locals Window	
Immediate Window	Ctrl+G
Watches Window	
Quick Watch	Shift+F9
Call Stack	Ctrl+L

All the debugging options (plus a few more) can also be found on VB's Debug, Run, and View menus. However, the icons and the hotkeys are usually the best way to go because they require fewer mouse clicks or keystrokes.

You're undoubtedly already aware of the Start, Break, and End icons because they are also displayed on VB's Standard toolbar. In fact, you probably use these icons to start and stop your programs. Therefore, there's little reason to talk about them other than to say that Start compiles and runs a program, Break halts program execution temporarily, and End terminates a program. These options are used to switch between a project's three modes: design time, runtime, and break mode. The current mode is always shown (enclosed in brackets) on VB's title bar.

You're probably also be aware of the Toggle Breakpoint (F9) and Step Into (F8) options. Toggle Breakpoint lets you specify that program execution is to stop before a certain line of code is executed. To use it, you need only position the cursor on the line of code before which you want execution to stop and then click the icon or press F9. The line will be highlighted in reverse video (white on red), and a red dot will appear in the gray area to the left of the line of code. Certain lines, such as `Dim` statements, cannot be set as breakpoints. Visual Basic will let you know if you try to set an invalid breakpoint. To clear all breakpoints, press Ctrl+Shift+F9.

You can also have the program execute up to (but excluding) the line of code where the cursor is located without having to set a breakpoint. Choose Debug | Run to Cursor, or press Ctrl+F8.

The Step Into option lets you step through code line by line. A small yellow arrow appears to the left of the line of code that will be executed next. You can also change the code line that will be executed next by dragging the yellow icon to point to a new line.

When you're stepping through code using Step Into, you may come upon a line of code that calls a procedure, such as a Sub or Function. If you are sure that the procedure's code is working correctly, you can use the Step Over option. It will execute the entire procedure and then stop at the line of code immediately following the procedure call.

If you find yourself stepping through a procedure that you know is working properly, you can use the Step Out option to execute the rest of the procedure and then stop at the line immediately following the procedure call.

While you are stepping through program code, you can instantly find out the value of a variable by moving the cursor to a variable or property name. After about a second, the value of the variable or property will be displayed in a small "balloon."

Special Debugging Windows

Visual Basic also has several special windows that can be used specifically for debugging. They are the Locals, Immediate, and Watches windows.

The Immediate window is probably the best known of the three. It allows you to enter Visual Basic code to be executed immediately while the program is in break mode. Typically, the Immediate window is used to display the value of a variable or property. For example, the following line of code entered into the Immediate window would display the value of `Form1`'s `Width` property:

```
print Form1.Width
```

Although the Immediate window is used primarily to enter simple statements such as the preceding one, it can execute just about any valid line of Visual Basic code. You can also display results in the Immediate window by adding a line of code to your program, such as

```
Debug.Print Form1.Width
```

The Locals window (see Figure 4.2) shows a list of every property and variable within the scope of the current procedure. It also shows each property or variable's value and type.

Locals

Project1.Form1.Command1_Click

Expression	Value	Type
PaletteMode	0	Integer
⊞ Picture		Picture/Picture
RightToLeft	False	Boolean
ScaleHeight	3195	Single
ScaleLeft	0	Single
ScaleMode	1	Integer
ScaleTop	0	Single
ScaleWidth	4680	Single
ShowInTaskbar	True	Boolean

FIGURE 4.2.
The Locals window, which shows all the variables and properties within the current procedure's scope.

The Watches window (see Figure 4.3) can be used to monitor certain variables or properties. It can also be used to halt the program when a given expression becomes true.

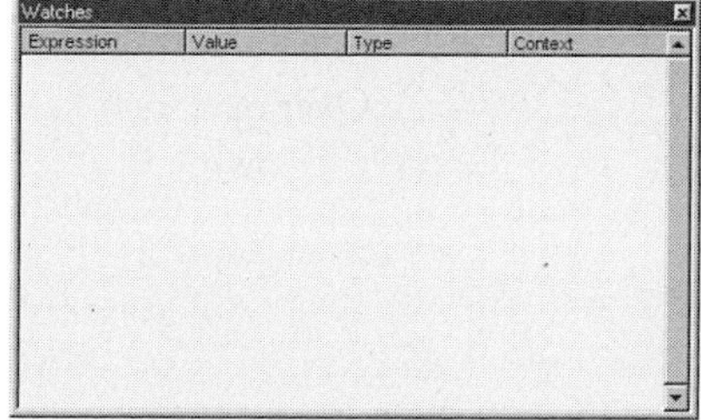

FIGURE 4.3.
The Watch window, which can be used to monitor variables and properties or to break when expressions become true.

To add a new watch expression, right-click the Watches window. From the pop-up menu, select the Add Watch option. You will then see the Add Watch dialog box shown in Figure 4.4.

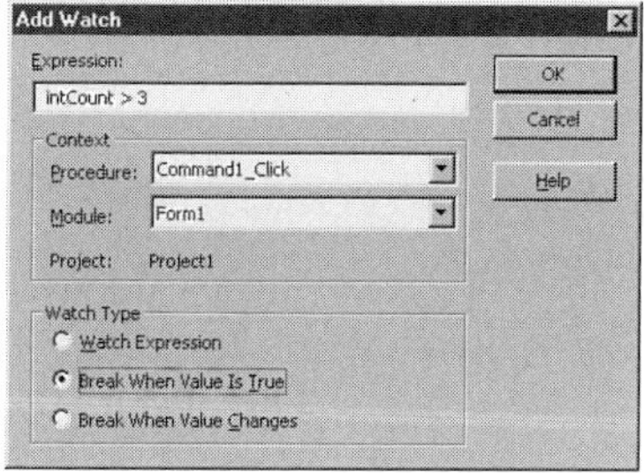

FIGURE 4.4.
The Add Watch dialog box, where new or existing watch expressions are edited.

To monitor a variable or property, enter its name in the Add Watch dialog box's Expression text box; then set the Watch Type to either Watch Expression or Break When Value Changes. If you set the Watch Type to Watch Expression, the property or variable (and its value, type, and context) will be displayed in the Watches window. If you choose Break When Value Changes, the property or variable will still be displayed in the Watches window, but you can run the program and have execution stop automatically whenever the property or variable's value changes.

You can also enter any valid expression into the Expression text box and have its value displayed in the Watches window. For example, you might want to enter a formula, such as

```
(intYearRate / 12) * 1.1
```

into the Expression text box and then choose the Watch Expression option. Then you will always see the value of that expression in the Watches window. Alternatively, you can choose the Break When Value Changes just as you would to monitor a property or variable. When the program runs, a change in the value of the `intYearRate` variable would cause the program to halt because that would affect the expression's value.

You can enter an expression and have program execution halt when the expression becomes True. For example, the expression

```
(intYearRate / 12) * 1.1 > .05
```

could be specified, and the Break When Value Is True option selected. The program can then run and be automatically halted when the expression becomes True.

When you enter a Watch expression, you can also specify its context. You can have the Watch only performed within certain procedures, or you can specify that it be performed throughout the program. By being able to define an expression's scope, you can add Watch expressions for two variables that have the same name but exist in different procedures.

You can add as many Watch expressions as you like to the Watches window, but you should always try to keep it to the smallest number necessary. Otherwise, things become too complicated. To edit or delete a Watch expression, simply right-click the expression in the Watches window and choose Edit Watch or Delete Watch from the pop-up menu.

Another way to add a watch is to move the cursor to a variable or property name (or highlight an expression) and select the Quick Watch icon (or press Shift+F9). You will then see the Quick Watch dialog box (see Figure 4.5), which shows the variable, property, or expression's value and context. If you want to add the watch to the Watches window, click the Add button; otherwise, click Cancel.

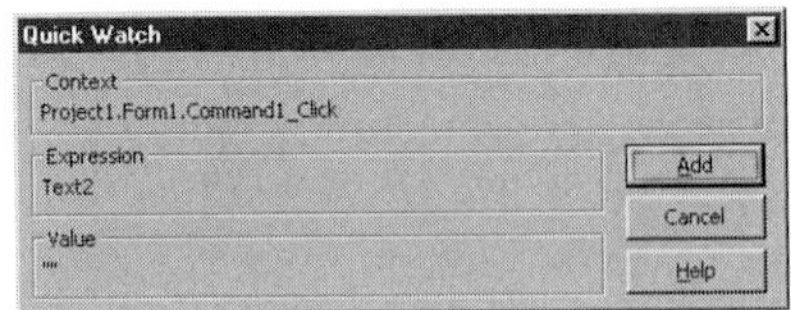

FIGURE 4.5.
The Quick Watch dialog box, which can be used to view expressions or add them to the Watches window.

Another handy debugging tool is the Call Stack dialog box, which can be displayed by clicking on the Call Stack icon or by pressing Ctrl+L. The Call Stack dialog box lists all the active procedure calls. Take, for example, the following section of code:

```
Private Sub Procedure1()

Dim intValue As Integer
intValue = Procedure2(5)

End Sub

Private Function Procedure2(intMult As Integer) As Integer

Dim intProduct As Integer
intProduct = intMult * intMult
Procedure3(intProduct)

End Function

Private Sub Procedure3(intNumber As Integer)

Dim intCalc As Integer
intCalc = intNumber * 2

End Sub
```

Here you have three procedures, where each one calls another. The first procedure (Procedure1) is called when a command button is clicked. When debugging this kind of code, things can get confusing pretty quickly. If you were to place a breakpoint in the first line of code in Procedure3, you could then display the Call Stack dialog box to see which procedures have been called (see Figure 4.6).

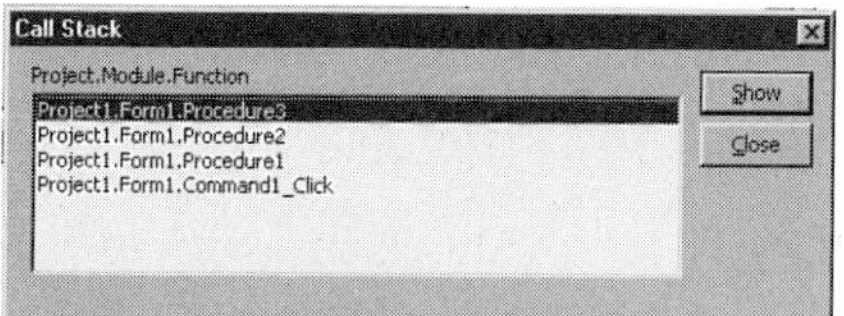

FIGURE 4.6.
The Call Stack box, which shows the procedures that have been called.

The current procedure is listed first, followed by the procedure that called it, then the one that called the second procedure, and finally the command button's `Click` event that called the first procedure. By displaying the Call Stack dialog box, you can see at a glance how the program's code arrived at the current procedure.

If you want to go directly to one of the procedures listed in the Call Stack, simply select the procedure name and click the Show button. You will then be taken to the last line of code that was executed in that procedure.

As you can see, Visual Basic has a host of tools and options that facilitate program testing and debugging from within its development environment. Knowing what they are and how to use them will make you much more efficient at combatting bugs.

Summary

The best way to ease your debugging efforts is to prevent bugs from happening in the first place. There are several easy things you can do towards this goal, though it is impossible to eliminate bugs altogether.

When more intensive debugging techniques are in order, Visual Basic has an arsenal of built-in tools for that phase of program development. They allow you to step through code and monitor important information concerning a running program.

This chapter introduced you to the tools you'll need to become a more effective program debugger. After you understand the tools, you'll be better equipped to handle comprehensive program testing and debugging.

CHAPTER

Using Windows API Functions

IN THIS CHAPTER

The Visual Basic programming environment is a very powerful platform for creating Windows applications. Sometimes, however, you will want to extend the features of Visual Basic to do things that are possible in the Windows environment but are not directly supported by Visual Basic.

An example of extending Visual Basic is printing angled, or slanted, text. In the Visual Basic environment, all text is displayed horizontally, usually within the confines of a text box or some other control. If you want to display text at any other angle than 45 degrees—and you don't have an ActiveX control that will do it for you—you have to call a Windows function that is located in the Windows Application Programming Interface (API).

The Windows API is a set of several hundred functions and subroutines that are located in a set of files called dynamic link libraries (DLLs). You can make a function from the Windows API available to your Visual Basic program by "declaring" the function to be callable from your program. You can then use the Windows API function as you would any built-in Visual Basic function or a function you have written yourself. Once you master the use of the Windows API, you'll have a powerful new tool that will allow you to break out of the confines of Visual Basic and extend your programs in ways you may not have thought were possible.

This chapter covers the following topics concerning using the Windows API:

- The set of dynamic link libraries and what they are used for
- How to include Windows API functions in your programs—the `Declare` statement
- The syntax and data types of the `Declare` statement
- How to use the API Text Viewer program
- Examples of using Windows API functions in your applications
- How to use Windows API callbacks

The Windows API Library Files

The Dynamic Link Library (DLL) files that make up the Windows API are commonly located in the Windows `SYSTEM` subdirectory. These files are found on every PC that is running Windows, so you don't have to worry about including them if you create a set of setup disks for distribution.

The three major Windows DLLs are `USER32.DLL`, `KERNEL32.DLL`, and `GDI32.DLL`. Several smaller DLLs are known as extension DLLs and provide functions in addition to those found in the three major DLLs. Some useful extension DLLs include the following:

```
COMDLG.DLL

DLLLZ32.DLL

VERSION.DLL

APIGID.DLL
```

COMCTL32.DLL

MAPI32.DLL

NETAPI32.DLL

ODBC32.DLL

WINMM.DLL

Figure 5.1 details the relationship between the three major DLLs and the Windows operating system.

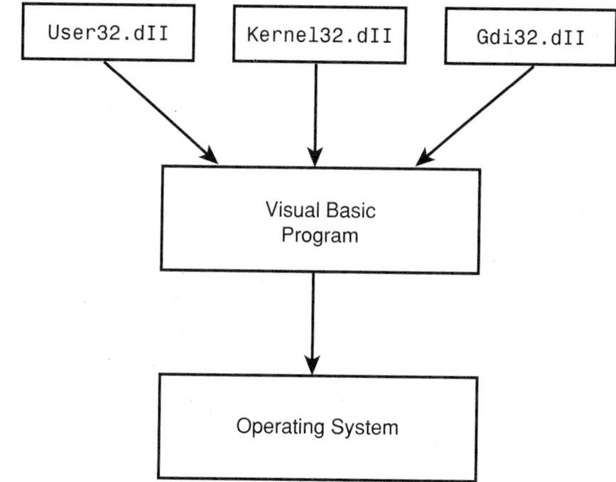

FIGURE 5.1.
The relationship of the major DLLs to the Windows operating system.

The following sections discuss in some detail the primary purposes of each DLL as well as some examples of the functions they provide.

USER32.DLL

The `USER32.DLL` library file contains functions that relate to managing the Windows environment, such as

- Handling messages between windows
- Managing cursors
- Managing menus
- Handling other non-display functions

The following list outlines some of the functions of the `USER32` library:

`GetCursorPos&` returns the cursor's screen position in X and Y coordinates.

`SetWindowPos&` sets a window's position, size, state, and Z-order.

`GetParent&` returns the handle of a parent window.

`GetActiveWindow&` returns the handle of the active window.

`SendMessage&` sends a message to a window, triggering an event for that window or telling it to perform some action.

GDI32.DLL

The `GDI32.DLL` library file (the Graphics Device Interface library) contains functions that help manage output to different devices, especially the screen. Following are some of the functions in `GDI32`:

`BitBlt&` copies a bitmap image between two device contexts.

`DeleteObject&` deletes a GDI object (that is, fonts or bitmaps) from memory.

`RoundRect&` draws a rectangle with rounded corners.

`SelectObject&` selects a graphics object into a device context.

`StretchBlt&` stretches and manipulates a bitmap image as it copies it from one device context to another.

KERNEL32.DLL

The `KERNEL32.DLL` library contains functions that manage the low-level operating system functions. These functions include

- Memory management
- Task management
- Resource handling
- File and directory management
- Module management

Here are some of the functions in the `KERNEL32` library:

`GetSystemDirectory&` returns the full path of the Windows system directory.

`GetTempFileName&` returns the path and name of a temporary file that can be used by an application.

`GetModuleFileName&` returns the full path name for a module (that is, DLL or application) that is loaded into memory.

`GetVersionEx&` returns the versions of DOS and Windows currently running on the system.

The Extension DLL Libraries

The extension DLLs are libraries added to Windows when the functionality of Windows has changed in some way, usually with the addition of new features to the operating system. Instead of completely rewriting the operating system whenever a new feature is added, a new DLL is added to the system that includes the functions that add the new feature to the operating system. For example, when Microsoft added multimedia capabilities to Windows, it created a new DLL that includes the multimedia functions, `WINMM.DLL`.

The major extension libraries that are a part of Windows are

- `COMCTL32.DLL` adds the new Windows common controls that are part of Windows 95 and Windows NT 4.0. Examples of these include the ToolBar and TreeView controls.
- `MAPI32.DLL` implements the functions that let any application work with electronic mail.
- `NETAPI32.DLL` adds a set of functions that let applications access and control networks.
- `ODBC32.DLL` implements a set of functions that let applications work with databases that are ODBC-compliant. ODBC stands for Open Database Connectivity.
- `WINMM.DLL` implements a set of functions that access the operating system's multimedia capabilities, such as playback of sound and video.

These are the library files and extensions to the Windows operating system you will call when you write programs that access the Windows API. Once you learn how to call these libraries from your Visual Basic applications (the subject of the next section), you can tap the full power of the Windows environment.

Declaring a Windows API Function

You include a Windows API function in your Visual Basic programs by using the `Declare` statement to "declare" the function to be a part of your program. The `Declare` statement is added to the General Declarations section of either a standard module or a form. If the `Declare` statement is added to a standard module, the function is considered `Public` and can be called from anywhere in your application. If the `Declare` statement is added to the General Declarations section of a form, the function is local to that form and can only be called from within that form. In the latter case, you must precede the declaration with the `Private` keyword.

The syntax of the `Declare` statement depends on whether the procedure you call returns a value. If the procedure does return a value, you use the `Function` form of the `Declare` statement:

```
[Public ¦ Private] Declare Function publicname Lib "libname" [Alias "alias"] _
 [([[ByVal ¦ ByRef] argument [As Type] [,[ByVal ¦ ByRef] argument [As Type]]...])]
[As Type]
```

If the procedure does not return a value, you use the `Sub` form of the `Declare` statement:

```
[Public ¦ Private] Declare Sub publicname Lib "libname" [Alias "alias"] _
 [([[ByVal ¦ ByRef] argument [As Type] _
 [,[ByVal ¦ ByRef] argument [As Type]] ...])]
```

This may look pretty complicated, but it isn't when you break it down into its separate parts. The `Public` and `Private` options define the scope of the function and determine whether it can be used outside of the module in which it is declared. The name of the function is defined by the `publicname` parameter, and the DLL library in which it is located is specified by the `libname` parameter.

> **NOTE**
>
> Although API routines that return a value are defined as Functions and those that do not are defined as Subs, the word "function" is typically used to indicate either case. So whenever you see the word "function" used in the text of this chapter, take it to mean "a Windows API routine."

Some functions have aliases, or alternate names by which they can be called. For example, the `SetFocus` function has an alias of `SetFocusAPI`. Without the alias, the function would not be useable from within Visual Basic because its name conflicts with the `SetFocus` method. The use of aliases will be discussed in more detail later in this chapter.

The next part of the `Declare` statement is an optional list of arguments. Arguments can be passed to the function by reference (the default), or by value using the `ByVal` keyword. You'll learn more about this in the next section.

Finally, in the case of a Function (and not a Sub) you may need to define the type of value that is returned by the function using the optional `As Type` construct. The only difference between subs and functions is that functions return a value and subs do not. The majority of the Windows API is made up of functions, and they typically return a `LONG` integer value that indicates the success or failure of the function. You can either define the type of return value using the `As Type` construct, or you can simply append an identifier to the function name itself. For example, `BitBlt&` indicates that the `BitBlt` function returns a `LONG` integer.

Here is an example of calling a Windows API function using the `Function` form of the `Declare` statement from a standard module. This function returns the handle of the currently active window on a desktop:

```
Declare Function GetActiveWindow Lib "User32" () As Long
```

Here is an example of calling a Windows API function using the sub form of the `Declare` statement from the General Declarations section of a form. This Windows API function moves the referenced window and changes its size:

```
Private Declare FunctionSub MoveWindow& Lib "User32" (ByVal hWnd As _
   Long, ByVal X As Long, ByVal Y As Long, ByVal _
   nWidth As Long, ByVal nHeight As Long, ByVal _
   bRepaint As Long)
```

The two sample Windows API function calls only had `LONG` integer argument types. However, many more data types are used in calling Windows API functions. Some of these data types are standard Visual Basic data types, but some are based on C data types and can be tricky to use for a programmer who doesn't have experience in C. The following sections cover in more detail the structure of the `Declare` statement's arguments, including how the arguments are passed to the Windows API and the legal data types for `Declare` statement arguments.

Passing Arguments by Value and by Reference

You can pass arguments to a function by value or by reference. Passing an argument by value means that a copy of the argument is sent to the function. Passing arguments by value means that the function cannot change the value of the actual argument because it is only working with a copy of the argument.

Passing an argument by reference means that the function is actually passing a 32-bit pointer to the memory address where the value of the argument is stored. When an argument is passed to a function by reference, it is possible for the function to actually change the value of the argument because the function is working with the actual memory address where the argument's value is stored and not just a copy of the argument's value.

With Windows API functions, the passing of arguments by value or by reference is not simply a matter of choice by the programmer. The functions that make up the Windows API expect its arguments to be passed either by value or by reference. It is up to you, the programmer, to know the proper way to pass arguments to a particular function. If you pass an argument by value when the function expects the argument to be passed by reference, or vice versa, the function will receive the wrong type of data and will probably not work correctly. And when you're dealing with system-level functions, the results can be very unpredictable indeed.

Visual Basic, by default, passes arguments to functions by reference. It is not necessary then, when writing a `Declare` statement, to explicitly pass an argument to the function using the `ByRef` keyword. When passing arguments by value, however, you must explicitly use the `ByVal` keyword.

Some Windows API functions that require more than one argument might have some arguments that must be passed by value and some arguments that are passed by reference. In this case, you have to use `ByVal` for the arguments passed by value, but you can use the `ByRef` keyword or leave it out for arguments passed by reference.

The following code shows an example of a `Declare` statement that declares a function that requires some arguments to be passed by value and some to be passed by reference:

```
Declare Function CreateIcon& Lib "user32" (ByVal hInstance As Long, _
   ByVal nWidth As Long, ByVal nPlanes As Byte, ByVal nBitsPixel As Byte, _
   lpANDbits As Byte, lpXORbits As Byte)
```

Two of the arguments to this function, `lpANDbits` and `lpXORbits`, are passed by reference (the default), whereas the other arguments are passed by value.

Declare Statement Argument Data Types

The functions that make up the Windows API are written in C. The data types that C accepts are often similar to the data types of Visual Basic, but in some cases, there are significant differences between the data types of the two languages. Not having a clear understanding of these differences can lead to Windows API function calls that don't work properly or don't work at all in some cases. The following sections discuss the most common data types the different Windows API functions expect and how they are declared in Visual Basic.

INTEGER

The `INTEGER` data type is used for 16-bit numeric arguments that correspond to the C data types `short`, `unsigned short`, and `WORD`. Arguments of the `INTEGER` data type are passed by value, and are typically written as `(ByVal *argument* As Integer)` or `(ByVal *argument%*)`.

LONG

The `LONG` data type is used for 32-bit numeric arguments that correspond to the C data types `int`, `unsigned int`, `unsigned long`, `BOOL`, `DWORD`, and `LONG`. `LONG` data type arguments are passed by value, and are typically written as `(ByVal *argument* As Long)` or `(ByVal *argument&*)`. This is the most common data type used with Windows API functions.

STRING

The Windows API functions expect the `LPSTR` C data type, which is a memory pointer to characters (in C, a string is an array of characters). `STRING` data type arguments are passed by value and are typically written as `(ByVal *argument* As String)` or `(ByVal *argument$*)`. When a string parameter is passed to a Windows API function, the string is supposed to be passed as a pointer to a null-terminated string, which is a string with a last character with the ASCII value 0. Visual Basic automatically converts a string passed by value to this type of string by adding a null termination character.

STRUCTURE

Some Windows API functions expect their arguments to be a `STRUCTURE` type. A `STRUCTURE` in C is the equivalent to a user-defined type (UDT) in Visual Basic. UDT data type arguments are passed by reference, and are typically written as `(*argument* As UDT)`. For example, an argument as shown in `(myRect As RECT)`, where `RECT` is a UDT that defines a rectangle structure which is very common in controlling windows with the Windows API. Before declaring and calling API functions that use `STRUCTURE` argument types, you must be sure to define the structure first in your program using a `Type...End Type` construct.

NOTE

The file WIN32API.TXT that comes with Visual Basic contains `Type...End Type` constructs for all of the `STRUCTURE`s used by the Windows API functions. It can usually be found in VB5's `WINAPI` subdirectory. You can cut and paste what you need from that file, or you can use the API Text Viewer tool that also comes with Visual Basic. That program is discussed in more detail in the next section.

ANY

Some Windows API functions accept more than one data type for the same argument. If you want to be able to pass more than one data type with the argument, use the `ANY` data type. The `ANY` data type is passed by reference and are typically written as `(argument As Any)`.

These are the major data types you will encounter when calling Windows API functions. But before you look at some examples of actually using the Windows API in a program, some other aspects of the `Declare` statement need to be discussed.

Using Aliases

Some Windows API functions are named using characters that are illegal in Visual Basic. A very common example is the underscore, as in `_lopen`. Trying to reference this name in Visual Basic generates an error because of the underscore character. The way around this is to "alias" the name in the `Declare` statement. For example, to use the `_lopen` function, the following `Declare` statement will work:

```
Declare Function lopen Lib "kernel32" Alias "_lopen" _
(ByVal lpPathname As String, ByVal ireadWrite As Long) As Long
```

The Windows API function `_lopen` is renamed `lopen` so that it is recognized as a legal name in Visual Basic. The `Alias` keyword lets Visual Basic know that the function it is really working with is `_lopen`.

Another use of the `Alias` keyword is to change the name of a function, usually for readability. For example, the `GetRgnBox&` function might be renamed `GetRegionBox&` through the use of the `Alias` keyword so its purpose is more apparent.

Using Ordinal Numbers as Function Names

Sometimes a Windows API function can be named with its ordinal number rather than a more descriptive text name. Using an ordinal number requires less system resources, so it is slightly more efficient than using a text name.

If you want to refer to a function by its ordinal number, use the `Alias` keyword to refer to the number, as in

```
Declare Function GetWindowsDirectory Lib "kernel32" Alias "#432" _
 (ByVal lpBuffer As String, ByVal nSize As Long) As Long
```

NOTE

To find the ordinal number of a Windows API function, you must use a utility program such as `Dumpbin.exe`, which is included with Microsoft Visual C++.

The API Text Viewer

As you have probably surmised by now, creating a `Declare` statement that gets the right Windows API function and declares it using the proper syntax and data types can be a little tricky. Starting with Visual Basic 4, Microsoft included with the Visual Basic distribution a utility program to help with finding the right API function and declaring it legally and properly within an application—the API Text Viewer. The API Text Viewer, or just the API Viewer, separates three different aspects of calling API functions—constants, declares, and types—into groups that can be viewed together. You can then select an item from the group, and the proper syntactical form is displayed in the API Viewer. You can then take the form and cut and paste it directly into your application. This helps ensure that you do not have a mistake in a `Declare` statement or a `Constant` declaration.

The API Viewer is usually found in the same program group as Visual Basic. Figure 5.2 shows the API Viewer in all its glory.

FIGURE 5.2.
The API Viewer form.

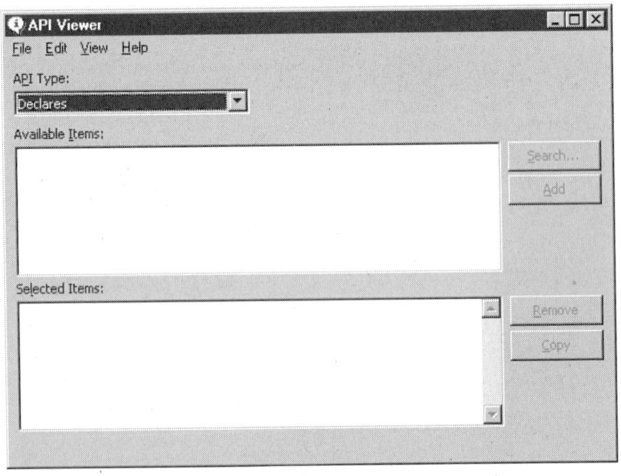

The API Type ComboBox allows you to select the type of API information you'd like to view. There are three types available:

- Declares
- Constants
- Types

These three API types are stored in a text file called `Win32api.txt`. When you select one of the types from the API Type listbox, that section of the `Win32api` text files is displayed.

To load the text file, select File | Load Text File from the API Viewer menu. Then select the `Win32api` file from the dialog box that appears. This is a pretty big file, so it make take a few moments to load in. Figure 5.3 shows the API Viewer form after the `Win32api` text file is loaded.

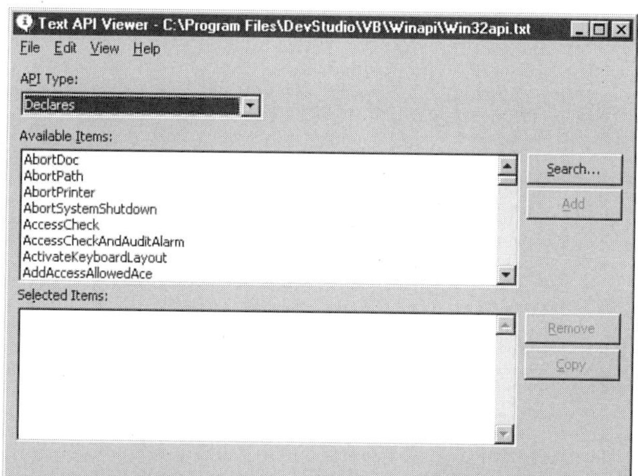

FIGURE 5.3.
The API Viewer form displaying Declare API types from the `Win32api` *text file.*

NOTE

After the `Win32api` text file loads, a dialog box may pop up asking if you want to convert the text file to a database (`.MDB`) file. Converting the text file to a database file enables the API types to load faster. Once you do this, you select Load Database File instead of Load Text File from the File menu.

All of the API functions are displayed in the Available Items ListBox in alphabetical order. To select a function to view, double-click the item. It is then added to the Selected Items ListBox. Figure 5.4 shows the `GetWindowTextLength` function displayed in the Selected Items ListBox.

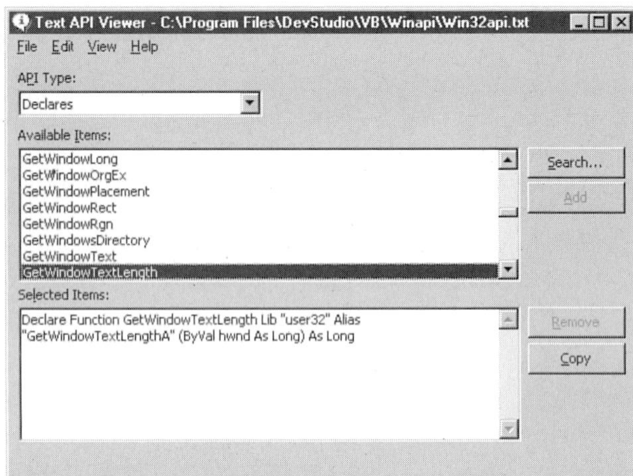

FIGURE 5.4.
The `GetWindowTextLength` *function displayed in the API Viewer.*

NOTE

If you're not seeing the entire `Declare` statement in the Selected Items ListBox as shown in Figure 5.4, select Full Text from the API Viewer's View menu.

After you select a `Declare` statement to view, you can copy it to the Clipboard by clicking the Copy button located to the right of the Selected Items ListBox. After the text is on the Clipboard, you can easily paste it into your Visual Basic application.

You can also copy `Type` structures and constants that are used by the Win32 API functions by selecting either Types or Constants in the API Type ListBox, then repeating the same steps that you did for copying `Declare` statements. Of course, you will need to know which constants and `Type` structures your API functions use. You can find this information in an API reference, such as Dan Appleman's *Visual Basic 5.0 Programmer's Guide to the Win32 API.*

When trying to locate a particular item, you can click the Search button to the right of the Available Items ListBox. A dialog box opens and you can enter part or all of the name of the item you wish to find. Figure 5.5 shows the Search dialog box and a search string entered into the ListBox.

When you click OK, if the function you are searching for is found, it is highlighted in the Available Items ListBox. You can then double-click the item to add it to the Selected Items ListBox, or you can click the Add button. The `Declare` statement is then added to the Selected Items ListBox and you can then copy it to the Clipboard.

FIGURE 5.5.
The Search dialog box.

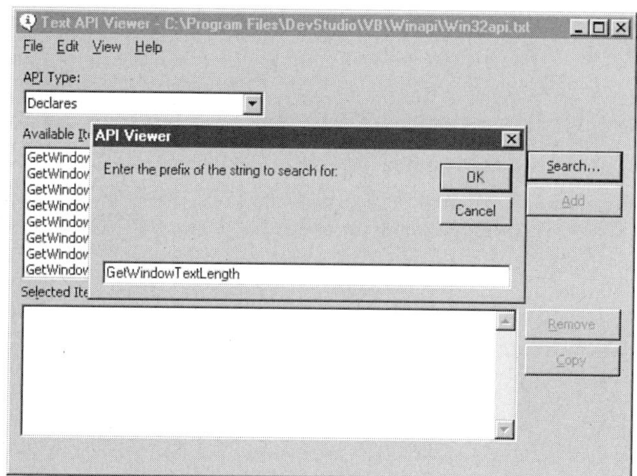

Using Windows API Functions in Your Applications

There are many ways to use the Windows API functions in your applications. One set of API functions you will use often when you start writing advanced Windows applications are the API functions that deal with getting information about a window or set of windows.

Every window in the Windows operating system is identified by a handle. The desktop window has a handle, a Visual Basic form displayed in an application has a handle, and even the controls on a form, which are themselves actually windows, have handles. You can gather a lot of information about the windows in your application once you get the handle of the window that interests you.

To get the handle of the active window on your desktop, you need to use the function `GetActiveWindow`. This function returns the handle of the active window. To use this function in your application, add the following line to a standard module:

```
Declare Function GetActiveWindow Lib "user32" () As Long
```

With this function declared, you can now add code to your application to call the function. For example, to use this function in a simple application, create a form with one command button on it. Add the following code to the command button's `Click` event:

```
Dim lonHwnd As Long
lonHwnd = GetActiveWindow&
MsgBox "Active Window Handle: " & Str$(lonHwnd)
```

When you run this application and click the command button, you see the message box shown in Figure 5.6.

FIGURE 5.6.
Getting the handle of the active window.

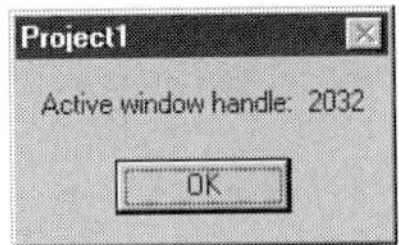

After you get the handle of a window, you can use that information to do other things with the windows on your desktop using the Windows API. For example, to make a window the active window, you can pass its handle to the `SetActiveWindow&` function, which makes active the window associated with whichever handle it is passed.

The `Declare` statement for `SetActiveWindow&` is

```
Declare Function SetActiveWindow Lib "user32" (ByVal hWnd As Long) As Long
```

You can add this function to your code to make a window the active window:

```
Dim lonStatus as Long
lonStatus = SetActiveWindow(lonHwnd)
```

The argument `lonHwnd` is the handle of a window, which was acquired through another Windows API function such as `GetActiveWindow&`. The variable `lonStatus` is used because the `SetActiveWindow&` function returns a `Long` integer that represents the handle of the previously active window.

NOTE

Most of the ActiveX controls in Visual Basic have an `hWnd` property that you can use for obtaining its handle.

The preceding examples give only a hint of the power of the Windows API functions. Every aspect of the Windows environment, from the Windows environment to handling hardware such as printers and disk drives, can be controlled to a greater or lesser extent using Windows API functions. Taking the time to learn these functions can help you gain greater control over your applications' environment, and you can often achieve significant efficiency gains using the API functions in your applications. Chapter 53, "Useful API Functions," details many more handy API functions and provides examples of how to use them.

NOTE

When writing Windows API functions, be sure to save your work often because it is easy to crash your system and lose your work if one of your API functions goes awry. In fact, many programmers set up their Visual Basic environment to prompt them to save the project every time they run it.

How to Use Windows API Callbacks

The Windows API includes several functions called enumeration functions. An example of a Windows API enumeration function is `EnumWindows`. `EnumWindows` provides a list of the handles of all parent windows in the Windows environment. It does this by sending the list to a user-defined function that handles the list in some way, say by adding the handles to a ListBox control. For this to work, Visual Basic must be able to call the user-defined function *from within* the Windows API function—in this case, `EnumWindows`. The technique for doing so is called a callback.

To perform a callback, a function pointer that points to the memory address where the function is stored must be in the argument list of the Windows API function. Previous versions of Visual Basic did not have a feature to facilitate this, but Visual Basic 5.0 has the `AddressOf` operator. `AddressOf` can provide an API function with the memory address of the function it is associated with. The `AddressOf` operator is used this way:

```
AddressOf functionname
```

`functionname` is the name of the function `AddressOf` points to. To see a callback in action, try out the following program. It uses the `EnumWindows` function to compile a list of all current parent windows and displays them in a ListBox.

Create a project with one form and one module. Add a ListBox control to the form, and call it `lstWinHandles`. Then add the following code to the `Form_Load` event:

```
Private Sub Form_Load()

   Module1.GetWinHandles

End Sub
```

Type the following code into the module you added earlier:

```
Declare Function EnumWindows& Lib "user32" (ByVal lpEnumFunc As Long, _
    ByVal lParam As Long)

Public Sub GetWinHandles()

    Dim lonStatus As Long
    Dim lonDummy As Long

    lonStatus = EnumWindows&(AddressOf EnumWindowsProc, lonDummy)

End Sub

Function EnumWindowsProc (ByVal AddhWnd As Long, ByVal OptParam As Long) As Long

    Form1.lstWinHandles.AddItem Str$(AddhWnd&)
    EnumWindowsProc = True

End Function
```

The first thing that happens when you run this program is that the `ListWinHandles` subroutine in `Module1` is called. This subroutine in turn calls the Windows API function `EnumWindows`, passing to it the memory address of our own `EnumWindowsProc` function and a dummy parameter value.

The `EnumWindowsProc` function is very simple. It takes the information that was passed from the `EnumWindows` API function (`AddhWnd&`) and adds it to the `lstWinHandles` ListBox. The second parameter passed to `EnumWindowsProc` (`OptParam&`) is not used. Note that `EnumWindowsProc` may be called several times, once for each parent window that is found by the `EnumWindows` API function.

The `AddressOf` operator is used to determine the memory address of the `EnumWindowsProc` function, which will act as the callback function in this example. Therefore, when the `EnumWindows` API function executes, it will send information to the `EnumWindowsProc` function (more about this in just a moment). Although it's not used in this example, the `lonDummy` argument is also passed to the `EnumWindowsProc`. This optional parameter gives the programmer some additional control as to how the callback function will work. For example, the argument could be changed from a `Long` integer to a ListBox so the name of the ListBox that is used to hold the windows handles obtained by the `EnumWindows` API function could be specified at runtime. As it is now, the ListBox `lstWinHandles` is hard-coded into the `EnumWindowsProc` function, so that ListBox is used every time the function is called.

In the example, the API function (`EnumWindows`) passes two arguments to the callback function (`EnumWindowsProc`). The first is a window handle (remember, the whole purpose of the `EnumWindows` API function is to get the handles of all current parent windows). The last argument is of our own design, and it can be any type we define it to be.

Other API functions pass different arguments to the callback function. If you want to try implementing callbacks with other API functions, you'll have to do some research to find out which arguments they will pass to your callback function.

This example sends the enumerated windows handle list to a procedure `ListProc`, which handles the list in some way. This function returns a `Long` value, which is non-zero if the function is successful or zero if the function is not successful. The argument `aVal` can be any `Long` value of the programmer's choosing, which does nothing but fill out the argument list for the function.

Summary

The Windows API function library provides the Visual Basic programmer with all the power available from the Windows platform. Every aspect of Windows, from the desktop environment to the hardware environment, can be controlled with one or more API functions. However, using the API functions can be tricky for a number of reasons, most of which revolve around the fact that the functions themselves are written in C and are not always compatible with Visual Basic. Many Visual Basic programmers are afraid to use the API functions because of this difficulty. However, by spending the time to learn the syntax of the API functions you want to call, you can avoid the unexpected results and system crashes that have given the Windows API a bad name in Visual Basic circles. Using the API Text Viewer program can also help you get a handle on the complexity of the API functions.

Part II

Object-Oriented Programming: What It Means to You

IN THIS PART

CHAPTER

Reviewing Object-Oriented Concepts

IN THIS CHAPTER

Object-oriented programming (OOP) is the process of developing *code* (one to many lines of programming instructions) based on well-defined design models. A *design model* is a graphical illustration that represents different views of objects, their parents (from which they derive functions and property variables), and their interaction with each other. For instance, a class model would be a static design model because it gives you a view only of relationships among classes, with no illustration of behavior. A *sequence diagram* is a dynamic model, as it shows how objects communicate with each other to carry out some system behavior expected by the user (or human actor).

With all the hoopla surrounding the emergence and increasing acceptance of object-oriented programming—in a technological world still dominated by older technologies and concepts that struggle against this emergence—you might be saying to yourself, "Oh, boy!" Every week, it seems, some new technology pronounces itself the guardian of true object orientation: Java/CORBA, C++/Visual Basic/ActiveX/MFC, and so on. Databases are becoming more object-relational, and even the Internet is moving away from CGI (Common Gateway Interface) services to more robust distributed object architectures that use CORBA, Java Servlets, ActiveX Server Pages, and Oracle Web Application Server cartridges. Seasoned object-oriented practitioners merely fold useful technologies into their minds with little learning curve. But if you aren't accustomed to object technology (and all its children) and your skills still depend on more classical predecessor technologies, the steady rise of object-oriented programming is a frightening, unknown menace, threatening to overturn the status quo. "What does this all mean?" you might ask.

Significant shifts in technology always seem to increase fear. Yet when you stop to think about this, the fear is usually derived from not knowing the technology from the ground up. Many books explain OOP very well, but new groups of professionals aren't aware of some of these other books. Many OOP novices are trying to learn OOP through Visual Basic. The aim of this chapter is to help you, the OOP apprentice, understand Visual Basic and OOP properly. Looking at the term *properly*, you shouldn't necessarily infer that other books and periodicals have done a poor job. In fact, the idea here is that because OOP is relatively new for the Visual Basic (VB) community—OOP has been around since the 1960s—many newcomers to VB, and some seasoned VB developers, haven't had the opportunity to understand OOP and object technology in general.

Coping with Old Programming Practices

To understand how to use object-oriented programming, you need to re-evaluate past programming habits. (If you're very experienced in OOP, you should still read this section because it could give you information to pass to other programmers trying to migrate to OOP.) Without a proper object-oriented background, many novices to OOP in Visual Basic have taken their old on-the-fly, VB3-style code; wrapped it in generic, vague class modules (if class modules are used at all); and considered themselves OOP experts. When it comes time to reuse such "classes," the "expert" has to re-engineer the class code all over again from scratch.

Further, other enterprise development teams usually find they can't use such classes because of poorly defined class interfaces, which are the public functions (methods) and state variables (properties) of each class. (Interfaces and protocols are discussed later in the section "Understanding How Objects Talk to Each Other.")

On-the-fly programming (OTFP) is the easiest, most popular, and worst programming style that ever mutated in the software development community. In OTFP, almost every function or sub is public and global, with hardly any concern for the arguments in the argument list. At least with structured analysis and structured design (SA/SD) methods, there's some thought in creating well-defined functions and subs (although SA/SD isn't recommended either). OTFP is a horrid mutation that evolved as a knee-jerk reaction by programmers responding to the high-pressure deadlines placed on them by sometimes unreasonable project schedules, which themselves are creatures of OTFP and chaotic project planning.

Even in small, cozy environments where everyone knows your name, OTFP tends to waste money in the long run because the resulting program depends extremely on both the original programmer and the technology it uses at a point in time. This means two things:

- If the programmer dies or quits, the often-undocumented program will have to be rewritten, and the person who rewrites it will likely use OTFP.
- If the technology becomes extinct or greatly changes (which happens very often), the programmer will have to surf through the entire code base to find every reference to members of that technology (API calls, object references, and so on).

OTFP generally leads to what's commonly referred to as *spaghetti code*. In OTFP, all code is perfect to the original programmer, but beauty is in the eyes of the beholder. Developers working in a small, informal environment can get away with OTFP because it takes far less analysis and design, and it may provide increased job security for them (but provides little benefit to their clients). But they still face the risk of changes in technology and user requirements now and in the future. In OTFP, they'll have to change every line of code (which can be hundreds or thousands of lines of code) to accommodate such changes, whereas in OOP they would simply go to the object responsible for that technology or behavior.

What's more, OTFP doesn't lend itself at all to team development. The common response to this statement is, "Well, there are only two developers: Frank and I. We know each other well, and we just get together and hammer out our differences." This seldom (if at all) works because this represents on-the-fly design (OTFD), on which no program architecture is based. Without some organized methodology for the programming process, one person's spaghetti-code style takes precedence over that of the other programmer. This is especially damaging where that other programmer is timid and non-confrontational, which is a prevalent behavior in the programming community. More often than not, one of these programmers usually quits or in some way is removed from the project when things go wrong (and with OTFP, they very, very often do).

Going from OTFP to OOP

OOP—and the entire object-oriented process—provides much better and longer-lasting benefits to every project stakeholder (programmer, manager, end user, and so forth). Visual Basic 5 offers enough features to ease the implementation of object technology and formal object-oriented analysis and design methodologies. Team development is also easier in VB5, and facilitates the creation of projects that incorporate each developer's individual talents. The VB project, in any corporate enterprise, also reflects the competence of its team members. In this context, a project represents a group of people who have as a common goal the development of an application or suite of applications to carry out some business process.

OOP lends itself well to project team development because of the capability to break down a complex system into simpler *abstractions* (understandable portions). Each abstraction, then, can be more easily assigned to team members for better definition and construction (application design and programming). Without an OOP background, VB novices tend to revert to traditional waterfall techniques (if that much) as soon as the first problem comes up in the project. This chapter will help you avoid these mistakes by helping you embrace OOP.

Understanding Classes

Please read the following carefully. (You may want to read it twice if you're still grappling with some OOP terms.) Some real-world explanations follow: A *class* is an *abstract entity* (a "thing" that carries out a subset of your user's requirements) with *behavior* (a set of functions or methods) and *attributes* (variables or properties that identify the class).

You might say that a class is a template. Some people call classes *cookie cutters* because they can be *instantiated* (brought into your computer's memory) into real-world, *concrete* objects (with which you can interact in your application). Although this is true of *concrete classes*, this isn't completely true of *every* class. This might help you grasp the concept of classes: They define the behavior and identity of objects. Some classes can also define the behavior and identity of other classes. Such classes are called *base classes*. Base classes that can't be instantiated into concrete objects are called *abstract classes*. Objects implement (provide runtime code logic for) the behavior of concrete classes. Because VB isn't as object-oriented as C++ (not C) or SmallTalk, your classes will generally be concrete or *pure virtual* (its child class must implement every one of its methods).

The Visual Basic Class

The structure of a class is physically deployed differently in different programming languages, although the structure itself remains the same. For instance, in C++ the class is usually separated into a header file and an implementation file. The header file contains the definitions of the class itself, including its methods and properties (attributes). The implementation file shows how each member (method or property) of the class is used in a particular domain. In Visual Basic there's no such distinction—at least not quite (more on this in a moment).

The Visual Basic class module is virtually the same as the familiar form module, which, unfortunately, has led to some confusion over the difference between the graphical user interface form object and the class module. For example, a form module and a class module can implement the interface of another class. To *implement* an interface means that the implementing class assumes the public responsibilities of the supplier class and executes them for its clients. You can add properties and methods to both form and class modules. Both have a constructor and destructor. For the form, the constructor would be `Form_Load` and the destructor would be `Form_Unload`. For the class, the constructor would be `Class_Initialize` and the destructor would be `Class_Terminate`. As a result, many VB developers place lots of business logic code into forms that make it very difficult to try to reuse such code, much less partition the application into packages that can then be assigned to individual developers on a team.

Figure 6.1 shows what a typical class module looks like.

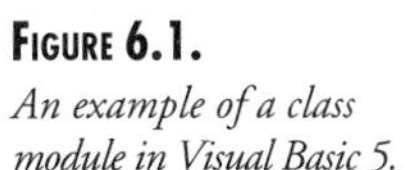

FIGURE 6.1.
An example of a class module in Visual Basic 5.

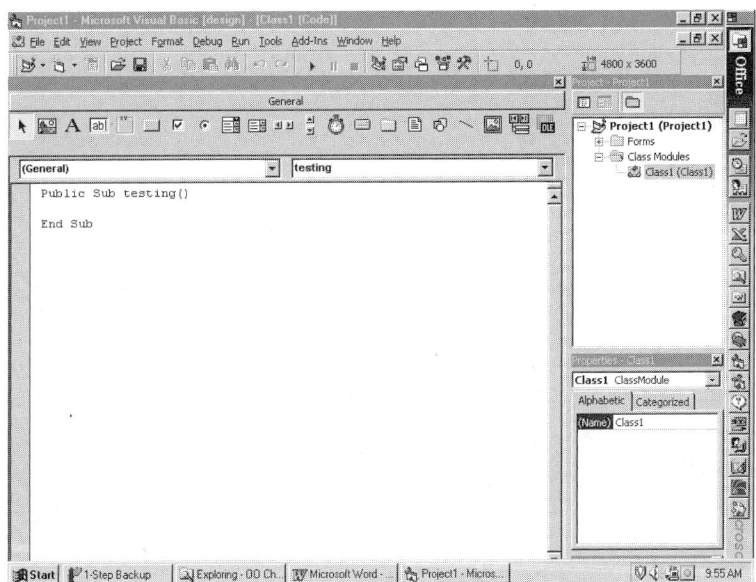

A class module consists of the definition and implementation of class members. These class members are methods (functions or subs) and properties (variables that hold information about an object whose type is defined by a class). You define the name and return type (if any) of the methods as well as the data types of the properties. The members of a class can be defined as *public*, *private*, or *friend*.

The keyword `Public` means that the member is accessible to all modules within the project and in external projects. If you don't want any members to be public outside the project, you can insert the following line of code in the general declarations section of the class module:

```
Option Private
```

The keyword `Private` means that the member is accessible only by other members within the class module. This doesn't mean that you can't pass the value of the private property to an external module via a public property or method, however. Suppose that you have a class called `CheckingAccount` with the members in Listing 6.1.

Listing 6.1. Class members for the class `CheckingAccount`.

```
'General Declarations
Private mstrAccountNumber As String

Public Property Get pAccountNumber() As String
    pAccountNumber = mstrAccountNumber
End Property

Public Property Let pAccountNumber(ByVal strNewAccountNumber As String)
    mstrAccountNumber = strNewAccountNumber
End Property
```

Because the property `pAccountNumber` is publicly available, the value of the private module-level variable `mstrAccountNumber` is also publicly available, even though the variable `mstrAccountNumber` itself isn't.

Like a `Public` member, a member defined using the `Friend` keyword can be used by all of the modules in the member's project. It cannot, however, be used by modules outside of its project.

An Example of Class Identities

Now for some interesting illustrations to help you remember the object-oriented concepts just discussed. The automotive industry provides one of the best analogies for understanding OOP. Think of Chrysler, for example, as a base class for the Sebring class of cars. When you go to the Chrysler dealer, you don't actually buy a Sebring; you buy an instance of a Sebring. The instance you buy is the actual Sebring object because you can interact with it by driving it. The Sebring class, then, is a concrete class because with it, the assembly plant knows how to make real-world cars (objects) based on the Sebring class specification (behavior and attributes).

The Sebring class has methods (ways of operating), such as ignite the engine, turn the wheels, go in reverse, open doors, adjust speed, and so on. Its properties (or variables or attributes) would be color of car, current speed, maximum speed, light status (off or on), wheel base, wheel size, window tint, cabin style (sunroof, convertible, hardtop), retail price, and so on. When you instantiate a Sebring class into an actual Sebring car, these properties will be filled in by an *actor* (a human who interacts with a system, such as the automotive engineer or assembly person in this example). Thus, the color might be red, window tint might be dark smoke, wheel size might be 15 inches, price might be $25,000, and so on. These values, taken together, represent the current *state* of the object.

Did you notice something interesting about the Sebring class? Some of its methods and properties have something in common with other cars Chrysler makes. For instance, all Chrysler cars ignite engines, turn wheels, go in reverse, open doors, adjust speed…you get the idea. They also each have color, wheel size, wheel base, and so on. So rather than re-create these methods and properties for each subclassed car (*subclass* means child class), Chrysler created abstract classes such as the H-Body cars, among others.

This is a good example of what an abstract class means—that is, you can't go to the Chrysler dealer and pay for an H-Body car itself. The dealer, instead, will recommend H-Body car classes, such as the Sebring. The point is that H-Body is abstract (and actually might be pure abstract because certain behavior might be implemented at a finer level for certain subclasses). The Sebring class implements the H-Body abstract class. These entities are more important to the automotive engineer and repair technician than the buyer (end user). The actual Sebring car is the object that you, the end user, buys.

Creating VB Classes

By now, you should be fairly comfortable with the idea of classes and objects and their interrelationships. Let's revisit the Visual Basic development environment, where you'll actually create a class and observe simple class behaviors at runtime.

There are four ways (also known as *development processes*) to create classes in Visual Basic:

- Add class module
- Add class from template
- Create class in Class Builder
- Create class in modeling tool

In the Learning, Professional, and Enterprise Editions of Visual Basic, you can simply add a new class module from the standard menu or the right-click pop-up menu, or by adding a new class module based on an existing class template in the `\VB\TEMPLATE` folder. In the Professional and Enterprise Editions, you can use the Class Builder to create a new class, or use a modeling tool such as Rational Rose/VB or Microsoft Visual Modeler. Because these tools are principally for automating the design phase/iteration of the object-oriented software engineering life cycle, they are discussed in more detail in Chapter 8, "Creating Your Own Objects." For this chapter, you'll concentrate on the first three development processes.

NOTE

In Chapter 8, you'll learn how to elaborate the requirements, which are embodied in use cases, into a robust set of design models. These design models will provide the foundation for your programming code.

By far the easiest way to add a new class to a Visual Basic project is simply to add a new class module from the menu. Two implementations of this process support this menu-driven approach:

- Choose Project | Add Class Module from Visual Basic's menu bar. A dialog box like the one in Figure 6.2 appears. Double-click the Class Module icon to add a new class module with the default name `Class1` to your project.

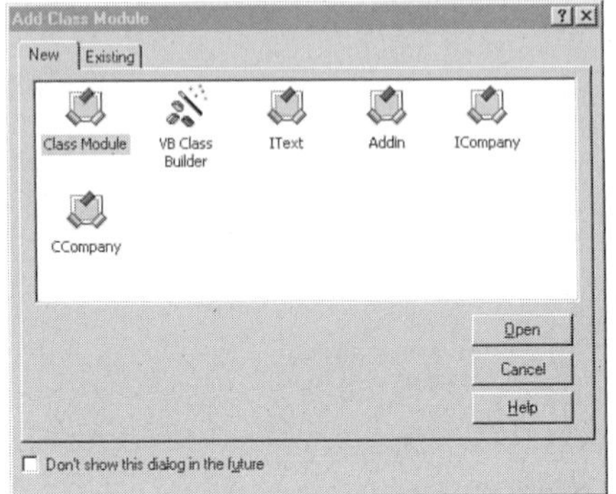

FIGURE 6.2.
The Add Class Module dialog box lets you add a new class from scratch or create a new one based on one of the class templates shown.

- Right-click in the Project browser on the right side of the Visual Basic IDE. From the pop-up menu, choose Add Class Module. At this point, you'll also see the Add Class Module dialog box (refer to Figure 6.2). Double-click a Class Module icon, or double-click an existing class template icon.

Building Classes with the Class Builder

If you have the Professional or Enterprise Edition of Visual Basic 5, you can create classes from scratch by using the helpful Class Builder. This utility is a distant cousin of Rational Rose/VB and Microsoft Visual Modeler in that it lets you build classes automatically.

If you haven't done so already, make sure that Class Builder is available in the Add-In Manager. To make it available, choose Add-Ins | Add-In Manager from the menu. You should see the Add-In Manager dialog box (see Figure 6.3). Select the VB Class Builder Utility by clicking the checkbox associated with this item. Click OK.

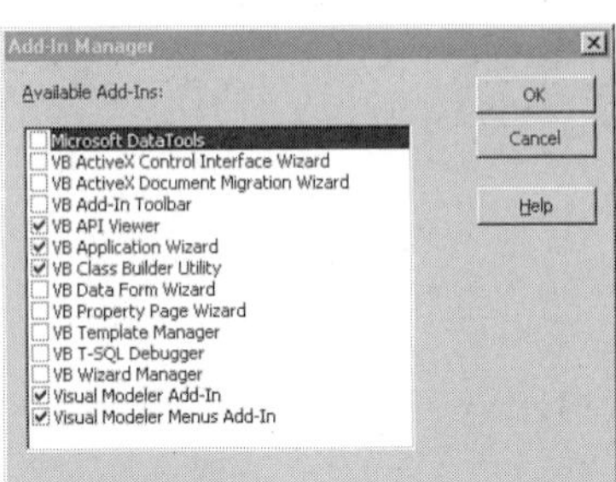

FIGURE 6.3.
The Add-In Manager dialog box.

NOTE

You can also access the Class Builder when you add a new class module to a project. Simply double-click the VB Class Builder icon from the Add Class Module dialog box.

Now you're ready to work with Class Builder. To start this utility, choose Add-Ins | Class Builder from the menu. You should see the Class Builder utility applet, as illustrated in Figure 6.4.

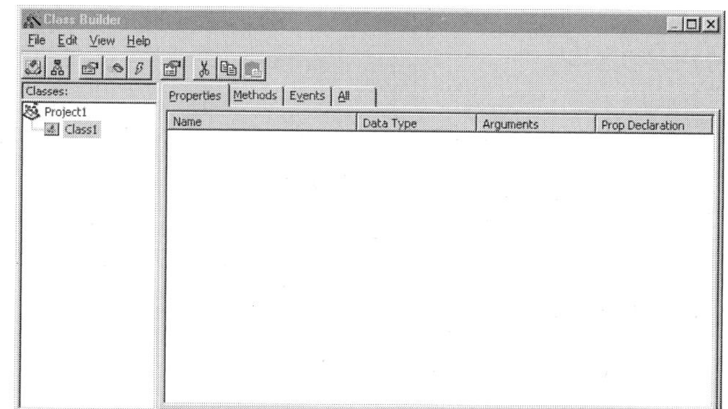

FIGURE 6.4.
Class Builder automates the process of creating classes in Visual Basic 5 Professional or Enterprise Edition.

NOTE

If you've already added a class module to the existing project with Class Builder, you'll get an informational dialog box telling you that the hierarchy of the classes created outside Class Builder can be incorporated into Class Builder. You also can't edit or delete members of that class; if you get this dialog box, just click OK. You can always edit existing classes manually or in design tools such as Rational Rose/VB or Microsoft Visual Modeler.

Not only does Class Builder automate the process of creating classes, it also tracks the hierarchy of all your classes and collections. Class Builder also generates the skeleton code you'll need to implement the classes and collections, including the properties, methods, and events of each class.

NOTE

An event is similar to a method or function but is triggered by a human actor or an external system action. VB Forms have built-in events; however, you can raise your own events as well by using the `RaiseEvent` keyword. Events are particularly useful in ActiveX controls,

continues

continues

where you can allow programmers who use your controls to execute code for your control's event. Thus, when your control's event occurs, your programmer/user can insert code that handles further processing.

On examining the Class Builder utility environment, notice the Windows Explorer-style visual representation. The standard menu and toolbar reside at the top. Below these two is the Object Model pane on the left and the Properties, Methods, and Events pane on the right.

The Object Model pane visually displays the hierarchy of the classes and collections in your project. If you click a class in this pane, you make it available for editing in the Properties, Methods, and Events pane. In turn, if you click a method, property, or event in the Properties, Methods, and Events pane, that class member becomes available for editing.

Classes and collections that existed in previous sessions of the Class Builder can't be edited or deleted in later Class Builder sessions. Therefore, you must manually edit or delete unwanted members that survived (or persisted) beyond a previous Class Builder session.

You also can modify classes by using drag-and-drop features to, for instance, copy a property from one class to another.

The Menus

The Class Builder menus are pretty standard. The File menu offers these commands:

- If you choose New, you have the option of adding a new class, collection, property, method, or event.
- Delete deletes the currently selected class, collection, or class member.
- Rename allows you to rename the currently selected class, collection, or class member.
- Update Project immediately updates your current Visual Basic project with the new or modified class and collection information.
- Exit closes Class Builder after saving current changes not previously updated.

The Edit menu's commands are as follows:

- Cut and Copy work in the same manner as in any other Windows application. You can cut or copy the currently selected item.
- Choosing Properties displays an edit dialog box for the currently selected class or class member.

The View menu seems insignificant at first:

- Choosing Toolbar toggles the display of the toolbar on (displayed) and off (not displayed). Simple enough.

- Then there's the Options command. Choosing Options brings up the unimposing, yet far-reaching, Class Builder Options dialog box (see Figure 6.5).

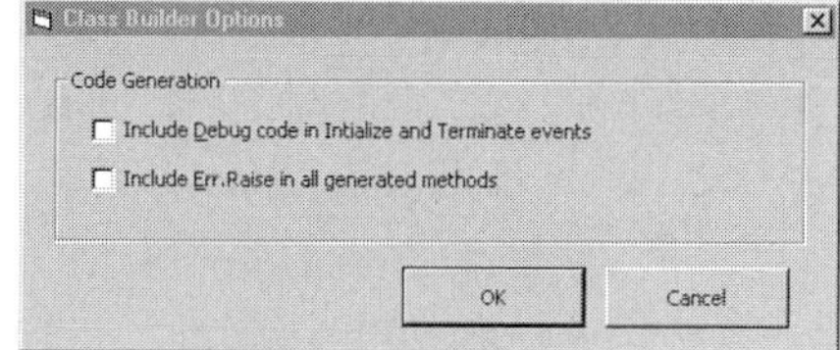

FIGURE 6.5.
The Class Builder Options dialog box has far-reaching implications for your Visual Basic project.

The Class Builder Options dialog box gives you two code-generation options:

- Include Debug Code in Initialize and Terminate Events
- Include Err.Raise in All Generated Methods

Because these two options are tightly coupled with development processes related to the design phase/iteration of the project life cycle, detailed discussions of them will be taken up in Chapter 8. For now, suffice it to say that these options let you track the creation and destruction of objects at runtime, as well as trap and raise errors in each object's methods at runtime. Keep in mind that objects are runtime copies (or instances) of classes.

The Help menu is pretty straightforward, allowing you to access information about the Class Builder utility. The toolbar contains shortcut buttons for operations already available in the menu.

The Properties, Methods, and Events Pane

In the Properties, Methods, and Events pane on the right, you see an index tab control with four tabs: Properties, Methods, Events, and All.

The Properties page shows all the properties of the currently selected class (see Figure 6.6). With this page, you can add, edit, and delete properties from the currently selected class. The container area is broken into four columns: Name, Data Type, Arguments, and Prop Declaration. The Name column shows the name of a given property in the class. The Data Type column shows the data type for each property. The Arguments column lists the arguments that the property method accepts (remember that properties in VB can be implemented as property methods). Finally, the Prop Declaration column indicates what type of operation the property method performs on the property.

In the Prop Declaration column, the Get type allows clients (other modules needing a value or service) to access the current value or object reference of the property. The Let type allows other modules to change the value of the property. The Set type is similar to the Let type, but other modules can change only the object reference (assuming that the class property was declared as `Variant` or `Object`). If you right-click anywhere in the tab container area, a pop-up menu lets you add a new property, delete a property, perform cut and copy operations, rename the property, or display the detailed specification of each property. Figure 6.7 shows a detailed specification, which is housed in the Property Builder dialog box (double-clicking the tab container area also brings up this dialog box).

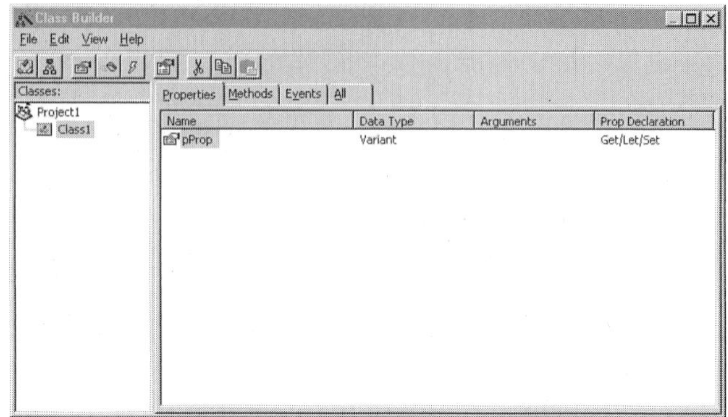

FIGURE 6.6.
The Properties page allows you to add, edit, and delete properties from the currently selected class.

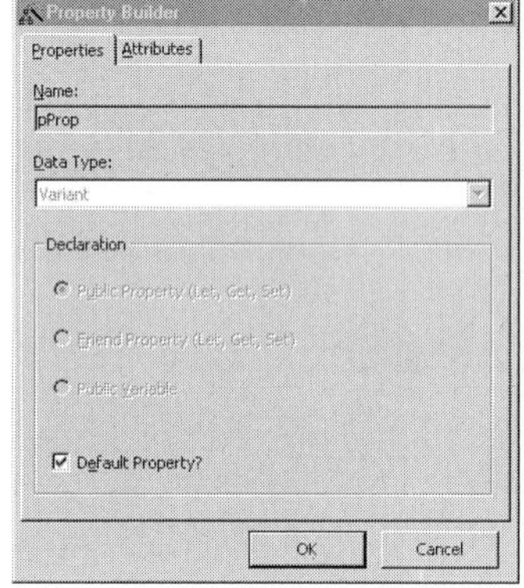

FIGURE 6.7.
The Property Builder dialog box allows you to view and modify information about each property.

By using the Property Builder, you can specify a name and data type for the property, as well as declare its scope (`Public Property`, `Friend`, or `Public Variable`). You also can specify that one of the properties is the default property of the class. This way, when you use the class variable in code like any other variable, the value of the default property is set or returned.

Similar to the Properties page is the Methods page, which displays the methods of the currently selected class or collection. You access the Method Builder the same way you access the Property Builder. By using the Method Builder, you can perform the same maintenance operations as with the Property Builder (see Figure 6.8). The key differences are these:

- You can specify a return value. The absence of a return value means that the method is a `Sub`; otherwise, it's a `Function`.
- You can specify that the method is a `Friend`, meaning that it's available to all modules in the project, but not to modules outside the project.

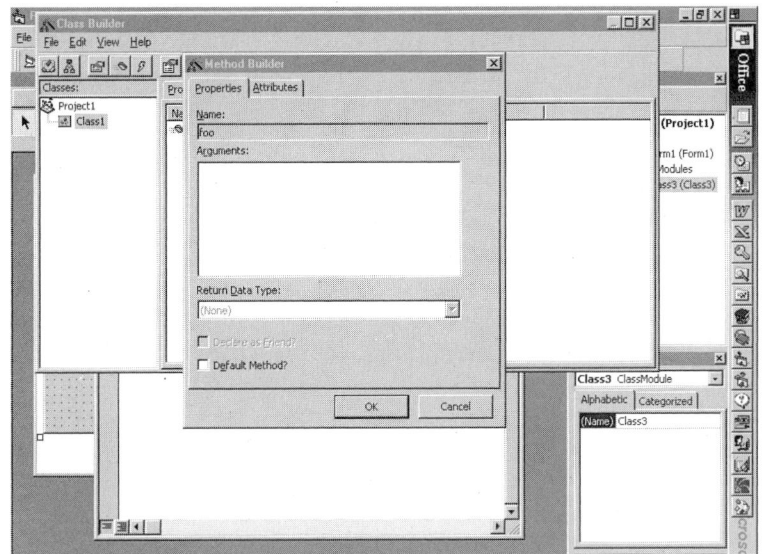

FIGURE 6.8.
The Method Builder dialog box.

- You can specify whether the current method should be the default method. Therefore, if you used the class variable in code as you would a function or a sub, the VB compiler would use the default method to provide the requested service.
- There's no Prop Declaration column.

The Events page in the Class Builder shows all the events associated with the current class or collection. Because the creation and maintenance of events is essentially the same as that of methods, selecting New Event... from the pop-up menu that appears when you right-click the Events page brings up the Event Builder, which is very similar to the Method Builder. The only difference between a method and event, as far as Class Builder is concerned, is that an event doesn't require a data type.

Finally, the All page combines the specifications for every member of the current class into one convenient list.

NOTE

To convert a class in the Object Model pane into a collection, right-click the class and choose Set As Collection. To convert back to a class, right-click the collection and choose Set As Class.

Understanding the Difference Between Collections and Aggregations of Objects

In the earlier discussion of Class Builder, you came across the word *collection* and probably wondered what it meant. *Collection* is synonymous with the expression *object collection*, which is, well, a collection of objects. It's a list of objects, you might say. By that, you should understand that a collection is, itself, an object. This object holds references to other objects and has methods for adding, accessing, and deleting objects within it. An *aggregation* of objects is an object that contains other objects, but not in the sense of a collection. In VB, a collection is a nice object mechanism for manipulating the similarly named methods and properties of objects.

There's no sense of context (the purpose for using objects in the collection) other than for bundling them into a collection for easy access. With aggregation, though, there is a reason that the aggregate object owns other objects. That is, the subordinate object (contained object) serves the aggregate object. This means that the contained object's lifetime depends on the lifetime of the aggregate and, in particular, when the aggregate needs to use the contained object. Whew! Let's look at the Sebring example again.

On further examination, have you noticed that the Sebring is actually composed of other objects? These objects would include tires, the steering wheel, the door, the window, brakes, headlights, and so forth. You can say that the Sebring is actually an aggregate of all these objects. A collection of objects—sometimes hard to identify in the real world—might include the fuse box under the dashboard (another object) or under the hood (another object). Each fuse is an object and the fuse box is a collection of fuse objects. A key method of each fuse would be to shut down a car's electrical system to avoid major problems.

Understanding How Objects Talk to Each Other

Objects talk to each other via their *interfaces* and the *protocols* set forth by the designer for carrying out this communication. Together, the public methods and properties of an object are the object's *interface*. This interface implements the protocol of the object. A *protocol* is the way two objects communicate with each other to properly carry out some goal. One object's interface, then, dispatches a message (a value, an object, or a pointer to a method) to another object's interface. Again, the Sebring class will help you understand the interface.

In the fuse box collection, you find that the fuses all interact with the same interface to relay electrical information to the engine (another object) and, in particular, the engine's computer (another object, which means the engine is also an aggregate). The fuse box itself has an interface to each electrical component in the Sebring. The protocol—I hope I'm not stretching this one—is based on each component expecting a particular voltage of electricity from the fuse to shut itself down when a problem is encountered. (By *problem*, I mean the state of the car. The subsequent activities related to this state would be the *scenario* for defining how these objects interact.) If the voltage isn't the one the component expects, the electrical message is ignored.

In case that wasn't pretty straightforward, look at another example: the automatic transmission as an object. The usual methods for an automatic transmission are park, drive on normal roads, drive on slight incline, drive on steep incline, drive in reverse, and free the transmission (neutral). Together, these selections (which would be modeled as methods in your models) represent the interface to the transmission. The protocol (gulp!) would involve the nasty details of the stick interaction with the gears, among others.

Let's try another one to be safe. The air conditioner (AC) is an object whose behavior is to supply cool air when the weather is hot. Of course, you don't simply tell the AC to turn itself on and adjust itself to your favorite temperature (but that technology isn't far off). The high-level protocol calls for you to push some buttons and slide some levers. These buttons and levers are the interface to the AC. When you push the On button, this event (pushing the button) causes the button's internal methods to send an electrical message to the AC to power-up. Another way of explaining this power-up process is that the AC initializes itself to default (factory) settings or your previous settings. Other real-world objects have interfaces as well, such as your thermostat in your home, your microwave, and your television. In turn, these objects interface with the object that supplies electricity. Because the real world operates with classes, objects, and their interfaces, why not use the same paradigm in software development?

Understanding Subsystems

Now that you've become familiar with the nature of classes and objects, it's time to introduce another concept. In the real world—or, at least, in theory—every object is made up of smaller objects. For instance, humans are made up of organs. In turn, these organs are made up of atoms. Likewise, a well-developed object-oriented application is made up of *subsystems* (categories or packages), which are then made up of classes (or sometimes other subsystems).

Understanding Application Subsystems

A *subsystem* is a portion of the application/system that carries out a particular behavior of the entire application/system. This portion can consist of classes as well as other subsystems. For instance, you may design one portion of an application to manage all database retrieval and storage (database subsystem), another to handle the display of data in and retrieval of data from GUI objects (GUI subsystem), and yet another to handle printing and reporting (printing and reporting subsystem).

Returning to the Sebring example, the portion of the car (synonymous with application for these purposes) that handles the movement energy is the engine. The portion that handles stopping is the braking mechanism. The portion that handles air flow and temperature control is the AC. The engine *subsystem* (or portion), in turn, consists of different classes of nuts and bolts, as well as other subsystems, such as timing, cooling, starting (ignition), and so on. On another front, your house would be like an application, and it, too, has portions. Your house contains the AC subsystem (with some abstract similarities to the car's AC), the plumbing subsystem, the electrical subsystem, and so forth. Get the idea? The class, then, would be the atomic unit (assuming that it didn't contain other objects).

Understanding How Subsystems Talk to Each Other

Subsystems (or categories) communicate with each other through classes that play the role of subsystem brokers or subsystem interfaces. If you think of subsystems as themselves being big classes, a class within one would act as an agent on behalf of the subsystem. You might also view this agent class as a diplomat or an ambassador. When two subsystems need to communicate, one dispatches an ambassador's envoy (a message) to the other's ambassador. The hosting ambassador validates the message (making sure that it's not a package bomb that might blow up and crash your system). If the ambassador feels the message has come to the right place, it passes the message to the proper "authorities" (some delegated class) for further processing.

Suppose that a user of your application enters some personal information such as name, address, and the like, and clicks a button to save the data to the database. At a high level this is simple: Just save it to the database straight from the form (or dialog box, for you C++ transplants). However, in OOP, the process is more method-based and organized. The form actually sends a message (packed with the data) to the GUI subsystem, which in turn separates the data from the form objects (for example, the text box, list box, and so on) and sends it to a business layer class. This business layer class places each data value to its attributes (or properties), does some business rule processing, and, if all is okay, sends this data to the database subsystem, which then saves this data to the database. (This process of saving class property values to the database is called *persistence*, because the data persists beyond the current application session.) When you finish reading this book, you should be able to think your applications through in this manner. The idea of breaking an application down into subsystems (or packages) is the core of object-oriented methods.

Summary

In this chapter, you learned about the fundamentals of object-oriented programming. At the center of this evolving technology is the class and its runtime equivalent, the object. A class is a design-time template that determines the behavior of objects based on it. Visual Basic 5 lets you perform OOP with the class module and the Class Builder utility.

The fundamental idea to keep in mind in OOP is that the Visual Basic project must be viewed as a round trip (or cyclical), evolving process, meaning that the artifacts of the analysis phase need to be synchronized with the design and construction phases. Without this periodic synchronization process, you lose the ability to trace the classes you create from the analysis phase down to the construction phase. This is where novice object-oriented programmers—sometimes bent on being impatient—get confused and discouraged. When requirements need to be revisited, novice OO programmers can't tell what class corresponds to what entity in the analysis and design models. Traceability, then, is of fundamental importance to object-oriented programming.

Chapter 7, "Using Objects in Your Applications," shows how to discover and evolve class identities from user requirements (even if you'll be the primary user) into a use-case model that's the foundation for the class model. Chapter 8, "Creating Your Own Objects," shows how to iterate or evolve from the analysis phase to the design phase—meaning that you'll learn how to evolve your project from the use-case model to the class and object models. Design tools such as Class Builder, Rational Rose/VB, and Microsoft Visual Modeler are discussed. Finally, Chapter 9, "Implementing Polymorphism for Your Objects," teaches you how to make classes and subsystems (class packages) communicate with each other properly. This communication-building process is also associated with the software development (or construction or programming) phase of the project life cycle.

CHAPTER 7

Using Objects in Your Applications

IN THIS CHAPTER

For many, many years, programmers have gone through each project life cycle with that enduring and possibly natural enmity toward the analysis process. The standard thinking is that users don't know how to tell programmers what they want. There's some real-world precedence for this. Before business management gurus Edward Deming and Peter Drucker came on the scene, most companies tended to ignore their customers' wishes. (For that matter, monopolies have a natural tendency to ignore customers; just look at your utility monopolies' response to your billing complaints.) Then Deming and Drucker came along and led the corporate world toward more customer- and employee-oriented management styles.

Likewise, the three leading figures of the object-oriented software development paradigm shift—Jacobson, Booch, and Rumbaugh—have also led the software development community toward not just object-oriented styles of programming, but also toward user-oriented project-planning. The central idea behind object-oriented systems is that objects respond to stimuli (events or messages) from human users at some point in the execution of a business process. The response of the objects can incorporate issuing client requests to other external systems, which would make the client system an actor as well (more on actors in a moment).

The important thing to understand about the analysis process is that you must be able to effectively translate the initial set of user requirements into a model or foundation on which your design models can be implemented properly.

Realizing the Importance of Using Analysis Methods

Now that you've gone through the object-oriented programming aspects well enough (and there will be plenty more on OOP later), step back a bit and look at analysis. You might think that analysis is a waste of time. Most newcomers to OOP bring this attitude with them from the procedural, non-OOP world, where most application logic is hammered out in the isolated world of programmers. Many programmers favor this approach because they each decide for themselves how the application will work and avoid getting caught up in "analysis paralysis." If there's a team of developers, each programmer simply splits the user requirements document up, codes in isolation, and returns to the team to argue over who's wrong or right, what should be hacked out of the current release, and so on. As complex as user requirements are, such an approach is prone to errors, and users usually end up with a system they didn't really ask for or want. To get along with (or out of sympathy for) the developers—who probably stayed up all night for a whole week—users say something like, "Yeah, this looks okay. I guess I can do my work with this." Then a month later, the application is seldom used or is full of major bugs, and users return to the manual way of doing business.

The same thing applies when you try to implement OOP without doing the necessary analysis. In general, *analysis* is the process of bringing a discovered solution to a business problem from being a dream in someone's head to being a high-level, often user-friendly, model that can evolve into an application. Using a *methodology* (an organized, disciplined system for doing something) or carrying out some goal(s) to cultivate this evolutionary process is crucial. Perhaps the most widely used methodology for this process is the objectory method introduced by Ivar Jacobson. It's also generally known as object-oriented software engineering (OOSE). With it, you initiate a process of identifying what the current problem is, and then help users identify how they see themselves using the proposed application.

Building the Foundation for Object-Oriented Analysis

To effectively use OOA to create a solid, easily extensible system with Visual Basic, you should understand the overall approach to the project. This means that every activity you expect to undertake in creating a Visual Basic application really should be reasonably thought out beforehand. That is, you as a Visual Basic developer must concede that you usually (but not quite always) wear many hats on a typical development project, and these hats (or roles) should be identified and specified. Further, in performing these roles, you perform tasks related to each role. These tasks, too, must be identified and quantified. The roles you'll be concerned about in this chapter are *requirements gatherer*, *object-oriented analyst*, and *architect*.

The Requirements Gatherer

As a requirements gatherer, you typically interrogate end users, business managers (or domain experts), project managers, or anyone else who had the misfortune of getting in your way. Usually, there's no predefined method for gathering requirements; you simply draft an almost ad hoc list of questions centered around mouse clicks instead of business processes executed by users. A requirements model is never generated. However, as a requirements gatherer, that's exactly what you want to do. A requirements model captures all the ways users will use the Visual Basic system you're developing. Figure 7.1 shows what a typical requirements model might look like.

In gathering requirements, you ask yourself and users how the system will be used. Initial requirements-gathering activities should shy away from inquiries such as, "When you click such and such a button onscreen, what happens next?" In this respect, you're forcing users to think like a machine rather than like a business process user. Requirements gathering centered on graphical user interface (GUI) objects tends to focus on the semantics of clicking controls and moving a mouse as opposed to the business tasks to be accomplished by users. When centered on GUI objects, requirements gathering misses the big picture, and the foundation for further analysis activities becomes inefficient as the project evolves.

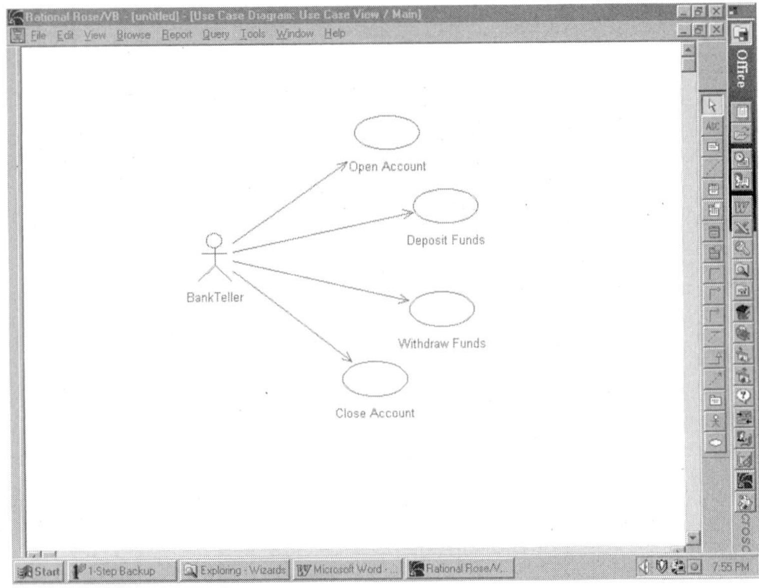

FIGURE 7.1.
A requirements model (the initial use-case model) visually illustrates how end users will use your system from a business processing perspective.

The Object-Oriented Analyst

As analysts in traditional projects, some developers are probably driven by a simplified focus of just making the gathered requirements fit into the Visual Basic project. They may have quickly come up with a list of global or form-level functions that seem to roughly provide the expected system behavior; analysis is over in a heartbeat. Analysis is really design, if that. Then, VB developers grab some programming tips and tricks books and start forcing this analysis and design model of functions to incorporate their ideas of how the system should work. This fly-by-the-seat-of-your-pants development is also known as *programming by chaos.*

Quoting noted object-oriented methodologist Jim Rumbaugh, analysis "is the careful examination of the requirements for a system with the intent of understanding them, exploring their implications, and removing inconsistencies and omissions." Effective analysis builds on the mature (or evolved) requirements model by evolving an ideal structure that endures throughout the life cycle of the proposed system under development. At this stage—which can and should be revisited throughout the project lifetime—you don't want to try to come up with a detailed list of low-level functions that you want to rush out the door without a concern for how users use the system and how the system responds to those uses. You should understand *low-level* to mean that you don't want to worry about which database you're using, which neat trick you want to incorporate to make a MAPI or Windows API call, or similar notions. This is important because changes in vendors, for instance, may necessitate changes in tools or even operating systems. Also, by avoiding the detailed design stuff early in the analysis iteration, you can better concentrate on the activities of the business process user because the analysis model is far simpler than the design model(s).

A mature design model provides direct guidance to your programming activities, whereas an analysis model provides a solid foundation for your design model(s). Figure 7.2 gives you an example of a simple analysis model. Note how it's focused only on high-level business objects when initially created. In the User Services layer of the proposed system (on the left), a Teller Interface class encapsulates your understanding of the interaction between users and the system. Don't worry about button clicks or mouse movements. Also, there are Checking Account and Savings Account classes to encapsulate your knowledge of each account type. You could have easily had one class called Account at this stage; it just depends on your particular environment. Finally, a Persistence class is responsible for storing and retrieving information created or modified in your application, as well as getting rid of information users want destroyed. In the analysis model, it's called *persistence* rather than *database management* because you don't know whether the data repository will be a database or a flat file (regular text or binary file you store anywhere on your hard disk). That kind of detail is left to your design model.

FIGURE 7.2.
A service model.

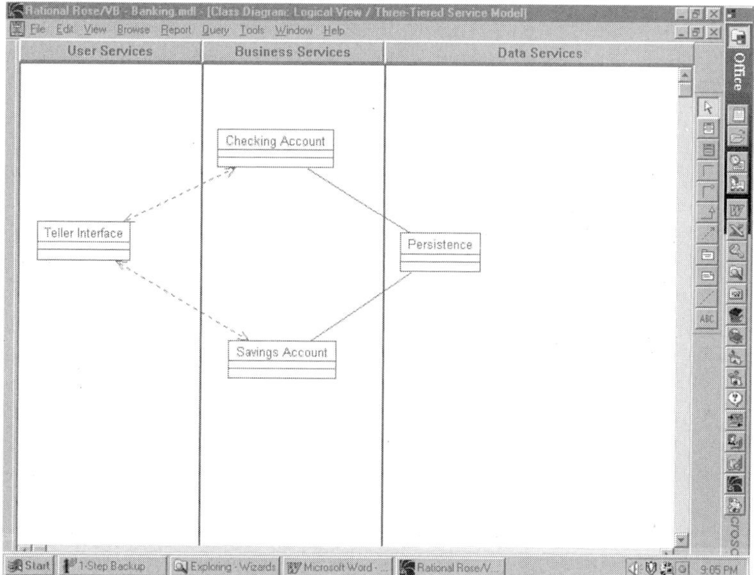

The Architect

As pseudo-architects in a traditional shop, developers actually do what you might call detailed analysis, but it's really ad hoc design. Such developers take the list of functions and manipulate each one to communicate with another. Often, the code for some functions is hidden behind GUI control events (for example, `Command1_Click`) for the sake of convenience (ad hoc spaghetti architecting). Such architecting makes it extremely difficult to trace application behavior back to the requirements and analysis models.

Object-oriented architects work with analysts—and sometimes are the analysts—to ensure that project team members can trace the names of business objects between the requirements and analysis models. (Architects also work with designers and developers, but your concern is analysis here.) In traditional analysis, end users and managers assumed that programmer-analysts had a near perfect understanding of the problem domain (the business functionality being addressed by the proposed system under development). This inevitably led to a decreased emphasis on analysis and more emphasis on construction activities. Because the actual gap in knowledge between the users and developers isn't adequately addressed in the beginning, all members and beneficiaries of the project teams (also known as *stakeholders*) experience higher-than-necessary levels of stress as the project approaches its deadline.

The driving assumption behind object-oriented analysis, on the other hand, is that the analyst doesn't have anywhere near a perfect knowledge of the problem domain. That is, a gap in knowledge is acknowledged between the users ordering the application being developed and the manufacturers of that system. Hence, all stakeholders in the project tend to depend on the round-trip development process offered by object-oriented technology to help bridge this gap over time. Given that, the benefits to Visual Basic developers of the object-oriented analysis approach become quite clear.

Implementing the Use-Case Methodology for Your Environment

When Microsoft released version 5 of Visual Basic, the Visual Basic language moved into the ballpark of object-oriented languages (though only as a "pinch hitter" perhaps, but close enough). The capability to create classes whose interfaces can be implemented by other classes and the capability to create complex ActiveX components have really made Visual Basic a serious commercial development tool. Added to that is the automation of the design process with the help of Microsoft Visual Modeler. However, Visual Basic doesn't help with the discovery and identification of classes, actors (human and external system), and use cases. To compound this situation, the vast majority of VB programmers don't have object-oriented backgrounds, which leaves them resorting to traditional, familiar ways of developing software.

The reality is that solid system architectures and class structures never evolve or mature properly when programmers don't know how to discover use cases and classes. As a result, Visual Basic 5.0, which is actually a very strong development tool for implementing object technology, will continue to be maligned as you try to pour new wine into old wineskins. The rest of this chapter explains how to use object-oriented analysis techniques—specifically, use-case identification and modeling—to help you successfully initiate the analysis process and give Visual Basic a better name in the development community.

The Problem Statement

Figure 7.1 showed what a simple use-case model looks like. Of course, the elements within a use-case model don't appear out of thin air. As an analyst, you would have asked users, "In what ways do you want to use the system?" Users, who are tellers within your development context, respond that they want to be able to open an account, close an account, deposit new funds, and withdraw funds. Notice how each phrase includes important verbs, such as *open*, *close*, *deposit*, and *withdraw*. These verb phrases, as I'll call them, taken together with the actor (the teller in this case) performing these verbs, provide the context for your system. When formally written down, these phrases become the core verbiage in what's called the *problem statement*. In other words, a problem statement provides the formal boundaries (or context) for the foundation of your Visual Basic application. Figure 7.3 gives you an idea of what a problem statement might resemble.

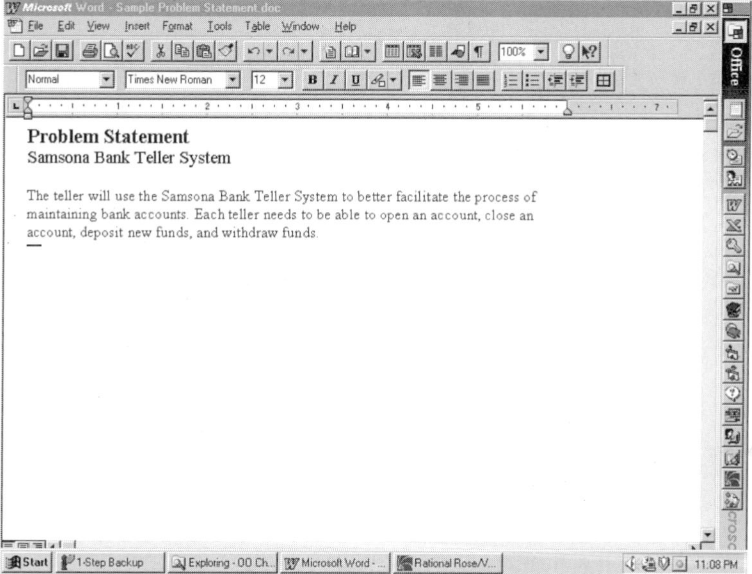

FIGURE 7.3.
By using a word processor such as Microsoft Word, you can document a plain-English, high-level description of how users will use the system you'll be developing with Visual Basic.

After the problem statement matures over one or more sessions with domain experts (users knowledgeable about a particular area of concern), you'll want to peruse this document to identify key nouns and verbs. The list of nouns actually becomes a list of candidate actors or classes, whereas the list of verbs (and sometimes *gerunds*—nouns that are verbs ending with *-ing*) provides a candidate list of business processes carried out by actors (human users of your system or external systems that interact with your system) or methods that are members of a candidate class. By *candidate* I mean that these nouns and verbs require further analysis to determine whether they're truly actors, classes, business processes (or use cases), or methods.

Based on your problem statement, the following list represents candidate classes and actors:

teller

Samsona Bank Teller System

process

bank accounts

account

funds

In analyzing each actor/class candidate, you or your team determines whether each item is meaningful in the context of the business processes being addressed by your system. By *meaningful*, I mean something that represents a role performed by users or external system, helps users produce a product or service that's valuable to the business, and isn't too vaguely defined within the context of your proposed system. For instance, the word *funds* is too vague for your system because the tellers don't actually create the funds or place the funds into your system. They merely accept funds from customers or give funds to them. Therefore, funds would be eliminated from your list of candidates.

If you're a beginning or intermediate object-oriented practitioner (an architect, analyst, designer, programmer, and tester), you might wonder why customers aren't mentioned in the problem statement. Answer: Customers aren't in the context of your system (your problem domain). The exchange of cash or information between tellers and customers is outside the scope of the Samsona Bank Teller System. Recall from the problem statement that your system helps tellers "better facilitate the process of maintaining bank accounts." Tellers interface with their customers in one context and then interface with your system in another. Your problem domain is concerned only with the second context. Business process engineering (designing and modeling of business tasks/responsibilities and events at the enterprise or workgroup level) would likely be concerned with the first context.

Going back to your list of candidate actors/classes, you'll notice that *teller* is obviously an important noun because this is the main actor who will use your system. Therefore, you now have your first actor. The noun *Samsona Bank Teller System* is actually the name of your system and, at this point, you assume that you don't have a compelling reason to model it as an actor or a class; therefore, it's no longer a viable candidate.

NOTE

In general, you wouldn't model your application as an actor or class. However, it can be modeled as a subsystem or package if it's part of a suite of applications.

The noun *process* actually describes the act of maintaining accounts and is too vague to be anything more than a description to help express the problem statement more fully for system developers. It, too, is no longer a viable candidate.

The noun *bank accounts* is a collection of accounts. Within the sentence that mentions bank accounts, you see that they're the main objects that tellers manage and, hence, as a collection, would be a strong candidate for a class (or more specifically, a collection class).

TIP

If you discover pluralized nouns in your problem statement that are significant to your system, make a design note to yourself that such nouns might be a collection class, which Visual Basic supports. An example of pluralized nouns are nouns with an s at the end that imply more than one of something.

Along similar lines, the noun *account* is also a strong candidate for a class. Again, the noun *funds* doesn't fit within your context, and is therefore not a viable candidate. Now you have a more streamlined, definitive list of actors and candidates that resembles Table 7.1.

Table 7.1. Strong candidate actors and classes.

Noun	*Type*
Teller	Actor
Bank Accounts	Class
Account	Class

You may also want to journal the reasons for rejecting a candidate. This list becomes an artifact that might help future stakeholders on this project or other enterprise projects so that even the process of analyzing requirements and use cases can be reused throughout the company.

Your candidate list of verbs and verb phrases would include

use

facilitate

maintain bank accounts

needs

open an account

close an account

deposit new funds

withdraw funds

Again, you want to model only meaningful verbs that provide value to the problem domain. This list of verbs and verb phrases eventually provides the context for a use-case model (which is roughly similar to the functional model of the Object Modeling Technique, or OMT), a class model, and an object model. (The class model and sequence diagram are discussed in Chapters 8, "Creating Your Own Objects," and 9, "Implementing Polymorphism for Your Objects.") Some verbs in your list of candidate verbs will be superfluous. Identifying such verbs might appear to be an elusive goal to beginners, but with only a few practice runs you should get a good feel for the process.

The verb *use* is too generic. It simply restates what you already know—that users will use your system. Hence, you would discard this verb from the list. The verb *facilitate* is also used merely as an expression of how users use the system; it doesn't convey any behavior that's meaningful for the actor (teller) or the system.

Maintain bank accounts sounds meaningful because, within the context of your system, tellers will do something with bank accounts, which at first glance might include some sort of management of such accounts. So let's keep it.

The verb *needs* conveys only that the following information is a requirement. Therefore, while the information that follows could very well pass from candidate to real verb, the verb *needs* by itself doesn't mean anything to the behavior of the system. So let's discard this verb.

Open an account, close an account, deposit new funds, and *withdraw funds* each sound like something tellers need to do with your system. A normal part of a teller's business processes is to open and close accounts, as well as deposit and withdraw funds. Let's keep this one.

IDENTIFYING TRUE ACTORS

Keep in mind that within the requirements context of your system, human tellers use your system, not customers. If it were customers, each teller would need to be an automated teller machine, and therefore opening and closing accounts wouldn't be meaningful to your system for logistical and legal reasons.

This is your list of verb phrases:

maintain bank accounts
open an account
close an account
deposit new funds
withdraw funds

Now comes a gray area for most OOP novices. At this point, you could continue on to the use-case model and then on to design. However, the trained practitioner will notice that there's a potential conflict or overlapping of verbs. That is, you've just identified that your actor, the teller, can maintain accounts, as well as open and close accounts, and withdraw and deposit funds. Therefore, a question arises: Exactly what does *maintain bank accounts* mean? Is it not the operation (within your context) of opening and closing accounts and withdrawing and depositing funds? The intermediate object-oriented practitioner might say it is and proceed to eliminate the verb-like noun phrase *maintain bank accounts* from your list of system uses. However, the advanced practitioner might say that *maintain bank accounts* can be a high-level description of the grouping of operations represented as open account, close account, withdraw funds, and deposit funds. The assessment you choose is entirely up to you; however, for the sake of simplicity, discard *maintain bank accounts*, as it's a grouping of the other verbs. Now your list looks more like this:

open an account

close an account

deposit new funds

withdraw funds

The Use-Case Model

The use-case model captures the verbs you discovered to be meaningful with the actor and business domain classes that support each use case. A *use case* is an identified use by the actor of the system under development. In its simplest form, a use case is a description of one of many ways users use your system. These *ways* are also called *transactions*. Users (or human actors) perform a sequence of steps (or events) from beginning to end; that is what a use case captures. A use case can be *customized* (or instantiated) to capture how users execute the use case for a given scenario.

For instance, tellers can open an account (a use case), but how do they open an account when a customer wants to open it with more than $10,000 cash? As you might know, in this situation the bank must file paperwork with the federal government to comply with laws that govern bank transactions involving cash amounts in excess of $10,000. This scenario, then, is a different instance (or customization) of the use case *open account*. It's certainly different from opening an account with less than $10,000 in cash. Use-case scenarios (and their corresponding sequence diagrams) describe each path (or instantiation) the use case can take.

Now re-examine the use-case model in Figure 7.1. This use-case model is the end result (or artifact) of your initial analysis process. At this point, you'd be proud to have your first use-case model complete. You're so proud, in fact, that you race off to display your stroke of genius with your domain experts (expert users or managers) who own the business process(es) behind this model.

At first, the experts are pleasantly surprised and impressed. They brag about you to an actual teller who will use the system being developed. The teller is pleased that progress is being made but notices something missing. He needs to be able to look up the customer's account information before closing it to make sure that the customer doesn't owe money to the bank and to make sure that the person is authorized to close the account. Also, he may just want to view the account information to answer a customer's questions.

In the traditional analysis process, you would have to restructure the data-flow diagrams in various places and redo the program code (because you probably already started coding the requirements). This rework usually involves patching in the new functionality, meaning new global functions were inserted in some module somewhere, or the code was tucked behind a button on a form. Some programmers aren't even this nice; they might growl that the requested feature wasn't in the original specs and therefore can't be incorporated.

With the object-oriented analysis approach, such crucial change requests are easily incorporated, provided they fit naturally within the context of your problem domain. Clearly, the viewing of account information is a mission-critical feature (as agreed by each stakeholder in the project) and as such needs to be added to your use-case model. Because you've done no coding, the only time needed is to insert another use case into your model and update the problem statement (another often-overlooked step). Figure 7.4 shows your updated problem statement; Figure 7.5 represents the updated use-case model.

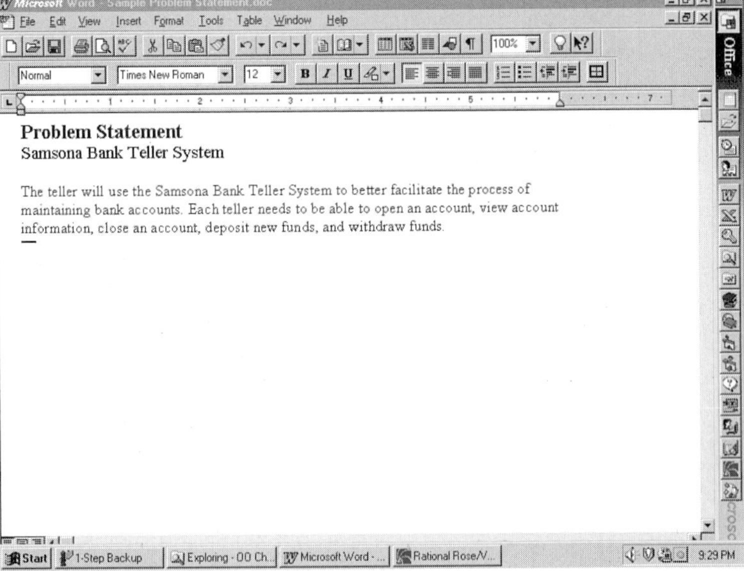

FIGURE 7.4.
The updated problem statement.

FIGURE 7.5.
The updated use-case model.

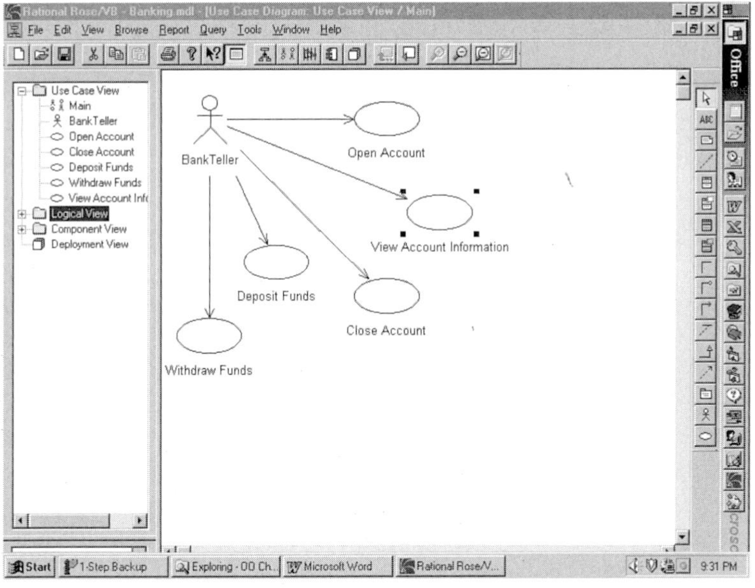

The Sequence Diagram

As alluded to earlier, a sequence diagram (also known as an *interaction diagram* or *event trace diagram*) is a diagrammatic representation of a specific instance of a use case. This specific use-case instance is called a *scenario*. There are two types of scenarios: normal and abnormal.

The *normal scenario* captures the normal interaction between the actor and the system. At the analysis level, the system is represented by the main domain object that's the object affected by the actor's activities. You don't care about forms, buttons, or interfaces at this point; these objects are exposed during the design iteration (or phase). In diagramming a normal scenario, you're asking yourself and your project stakeholders what actions the actor will normally carry out when there are no anomalies or error conditions.

A normal scenario can take alternate paths, each of which is still normal. For instance, the use case *open account* could have at least two alternate normal scenarios: *open savings account* and *open checking account*.

Abnormal scenarios capture use-case paths that take into consideration anomalies and error conditions. For instance, an abnormal path for *close account* might be this: The account being closed doesn't exist. Also, for the *withdraw funds* use case, you'll have a scenario that deals with the situation where there aren't enough funds to withdraw.

To build a list of normal and abnormal scenarios to illustrate in your sequence diagrams, you'll need to interview domain experts and end users. Assuming that this was accomplished, the current scenarios are listed in Table 7.2.

Table 7.2. Use cases and their respective scenarios.

Use Case	*Scenario*
Open an Account	The customer is new with no previous accounts and has the minimum required balance. The customer has an existing account that's active. The customer has an existing account that's inactive. The customer is new but doesn't have the minimum required balance. The customer is new with no previous accounts but wants to deposit more than $10,000 in cash.
Close an Account	An active account exists and the customer is authorized to close it. The account being closed is inactive. The customer isn't authorized to close the account. The customer is authorized to close the account, but the account is deficient or the customer owes money to the bank.
Deposit New Funds	An active account exists and the customer is authorized to deposit money in it. The customer isn't authorized to deposit money in the account. The amount being deposited exceeds $10,000 in cash.
Withdraw Funds	An active account exists and the customer is authorized to withdraw money from it. The customer isn't authorized to withdraw money from the account. The teller tries to withdraw more money at the customer's request than is available.

For simplicity's sake, you'll concentrate on the first sequence diagram for the *Open an Account* use case. Assume that you had a use-case meeting with the users and domain experts, who then elaborated on the steps involved.

The First Sequence Diagram

As noted in Table 7.2, the first scenario is the normal path that reads "The customer is new with no previous accounts and has the minimum required balance." Before diagramming this scenario, you should elaborate on the steps involved. A good format for proceeding would be to identify the scenario that belongs to the use case. You could assign a unique identifier to the use case as well as the scenario as follows:

> Use Case 001: Open an Account.
>
> Scenario 01: The customer is new with no previous accounts and has the minimum required balance.
>
> Step 1: The Teller provides the customer information to the system.
>
> Step 2: The Teller wants to check the customer's checking history with Telecheck.
>
> Step 3: Once the Teller sees that the customer has a good checking history, the Teller provides the opening deposit balance to the system.
>
> Step 4: The Teller prints out the new account information.

Notice that in elaborating on the steps involved in this use case, you've actually uncovered some more significant nouns and verbs, as follows:

Nouns	*Verbs*
customer information	provide the customer information to the system
customer	check the customer's checking history
system	provide the opening deposit balance to the system
checking history	print out the new account information
Telecheck	
opening deposit balance	
account information	

Before creating the sequence diagram, you must again determine which nouns and verbs are significant and which aren't.

The nouns *customer information* and *account information* each have a word in them that provides strong clues as to its importance in your proposed system: *information.* Words such as *customer information* or *account information* almost always imply properties (or attributes) of classes in your system. They certainly imply relational database tables. Because the words *customer* and *account* are so pivotal in your domain, the architects, analysts, and lead designers agree that these should be nominal domain classes. Let's keep them.

The noun *customer* is just another representation of *customer information.* You already decided to incorporate a nominal class named *customer*, so this is repetition. You can discard it.

The noun *system* is a more generic reference to your application name, which is Samsona Bank Teller System. If you want the analysis-view use case to remain generic enough to be reused across your enterprise, it's probably best to leave it as *system.* However, if you decide that the actual application name is more meaningful, by all means use the full system name. Because you already have identified the system as the Samsona Bank Teller System, use the full name. Thus, you've just replaced the word *system* with *Samsona Bank Teller System*.

The noun *checking history* is rather interesting. For simplicity's sake, you've left out that there's more than one kind of account in banking systems. Furthermore, in your domain (or context), the domain experts and users didn't mention any particular type of account. After a quick meeting with these stakeholders, you agreed that for this release of the system, you won't consider the various kinds of accounts. Therefore, *checking history* becomes a nominal class, but not a specialization of the `Account` class you already identified in your earlier analysis.

NOTE

Many object-oriented novices miss this very important point entirely. Don't create classes and actors simply because it seems logical. Stick to the project plan. Such deviations, although thoughtful, usually slow down the object-oriented process, which then leads many to sarcastically exaggerate the length of time object-oriented projects typically take. (In many ways, this negative impression is similar to the impression others have of VB: It's slow. However, it seems slow because of the competence level of the professionals using it.) You can speed up object-oriented projects by not adding unnecessary or uncalled-for features and objects to the project.

The noun *Telecheck* is, in the familiar English composition sense, an indirect object in that it's on the receiving end of the action initiated by the Teller. However, you don't know exactly what Telecheck means, so you ask the experts. They tell us that it's a vendor who provides research services to the bank. The Teller views the information supplied by Telecheck to determine whether the customer can establish an account. On further investigation, you discover that an electronic interface exists between the bank teller's machine and the vendor. Through this interface, the Teller sends customer information to Telecheck for verification and research. The results of the research are returned directly to the terminal screen in the current system.

Based on this behavior, you've concluded that Telecheck is an actor that you could stereotype as an *external system*. Therefore, you promote it from a noun to an actor and have to update your use-case model. Figure 7.6 shows what your new use-case model looks like.

The noun *opening deposit balance* is a monetary amount. You might be tempted to model it as a class, but does it really exhibit behavior or have attributes? If it were a candidate class, it would have only one attribute (or property): `Value`. Identifying classes and members of classes (properties and methods) isn't always an easy process, and even the very best object technologists admit that sometimes they don't always immediately identify classes correctly the first time. So, on further analysis, you discover that *opening deposit balance* is actually a property of your `Account` class. How did you gather this? The adjective *opening* provides a big clue—it implies that something other than the object *balance* is going to fluctuate at some point in time. Balances fluctuate, but so do accounts. Then you remember that when you get a monthly account statement from your bank, there's a beginning balance and an ending balance. And because the account statement is merely a snapshot (or instance) of your account information, you've finally decided that `Balance` is an attribute of the `Account` class. In general, a good rule of thumb to use (loosely) is that if a candidate class has only one property (or attribute) and no methods, it might actually be a property of a larger class.

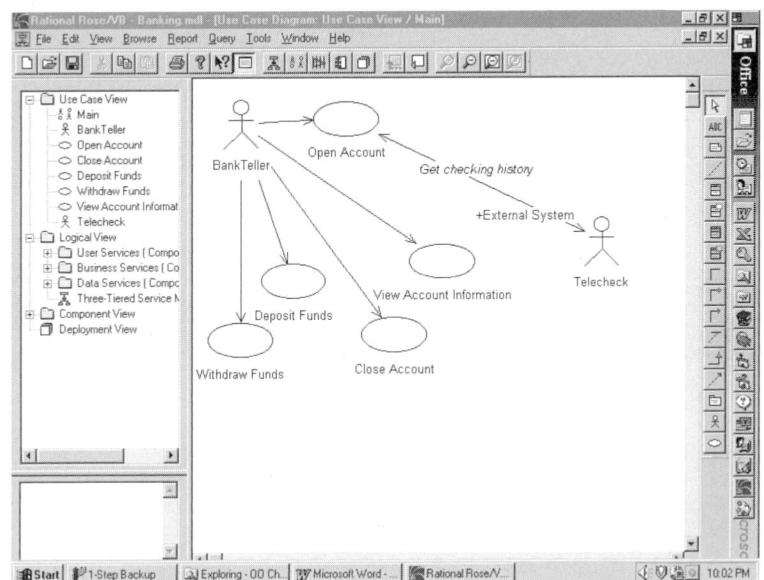

FIGURE 7.6.
The actor Telecheck is incorporated into your use-case model.

The verb phrase *provide the customer information to the system* (*system* now being *Samsona Bank Teller System*) indicates an action taken by the Teller against the system. This action is also known as an *event*. You've decided that this event is valid and, therefore, will incorporate this verb phrase into your sequence diagram.

The verb phrase *check the customer's checking history* is an action the Teller carries out by using the interface to the Telecheck system. Therefore, you should incorporate it into your sequence diagram.

The verb phrase *provide the opening deposit balance to the system* (*system* now being *Samsona Bank Teller System*) specifies information about the new account being supplied by the Teller. Thus, you should incorporate it into your sequence diagram.

The verb phrase *print out the new account information* is also an event initiated by the Teller against the system. Therefore, you should incorporate it into your sequence diagram.

NOTE

Because the Teller is specifying that account information be printed out, this suggests that *print* is a possible method for your `Account` class. This is true of each verb and verb phrase; they become possible methods for the class indicated in the indirect object part of the sentence or phrase.

Now you're ready to create your sequence diagram. Samsona Bank Teller System will be represented by some class that implements one of its behaviors. Your nominal noun and verb phrases list looks like this:

Nouns	*Verbs*
customer	provides the customer information to the Samsona Bank Teller System
Samsona Bank Teller System	checks the customer's checking history
checking history	provides the opening deposit balance to the Samsona Bank Teller System
Telecheck	prints out the new account information
account (property: Balance)	

Figure 7.7 shows what your sequence diagram looks like. The stick figures are the Jacobson symbols for actors. Although Telecheck is a machine-based system, you still model it as a stick-figure actor. The lines with the arrow at one end represent events and actions being carried out by actors and domain class instances (or objects). The rectangle preceding each line is called the *focus of control bar*. These bars indicate that each line protruding from it is part of the same event or action. For instance, the Teller-initiated event `Provide Info` is the only event in the Teller's focus of control (or duration of a single event or action). However, both Check lines, as well as the Supply History and Display History lines, are all part of the Check History event initiated by the Teller.

NOTE

Rational Rose/VB allows you to do this type of modeling automatically. Rational Rose/VB, based on the Unified Modeling Language (UML), is available for a hefty price from Rational Corporation (`www.rational.com`). If you don't have the resources to purchase Rational Rose, simply do it by hand. According to some rumors, Visio's latest version offers features for the Unified Modeling Language.

At Microsoft's Web site (`www.microsoft.com`), Visual Modeler is available free to owners of Visual Basic 5.0 Enterprise Edition. It doesn't incorporate use cases, however, so you can't do sequence diagrams in it.

FIGURE 7.7.
The sequence diagram shows the stimuli being sent from one object to another. The main actor, the Teller, initiates the events and is therefore the first object on the left.

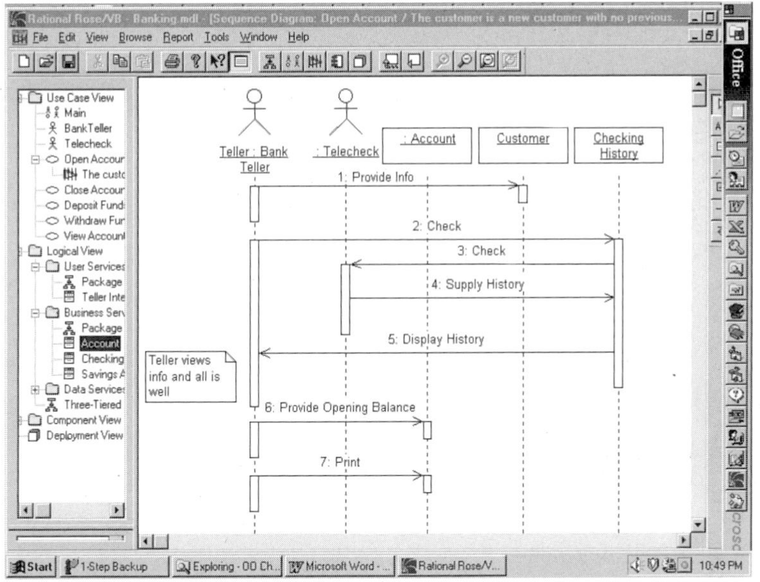

The Analysis Class Model

By now, you've identified a collection class (`BankAccounts`) and several classes (`Account`, `Customer`, `CheckingHistory`). The initial class model will have these three classes as model items. Figure 7.8 shows what this model looks like.

FIGURE 7.8.
The initial class model.

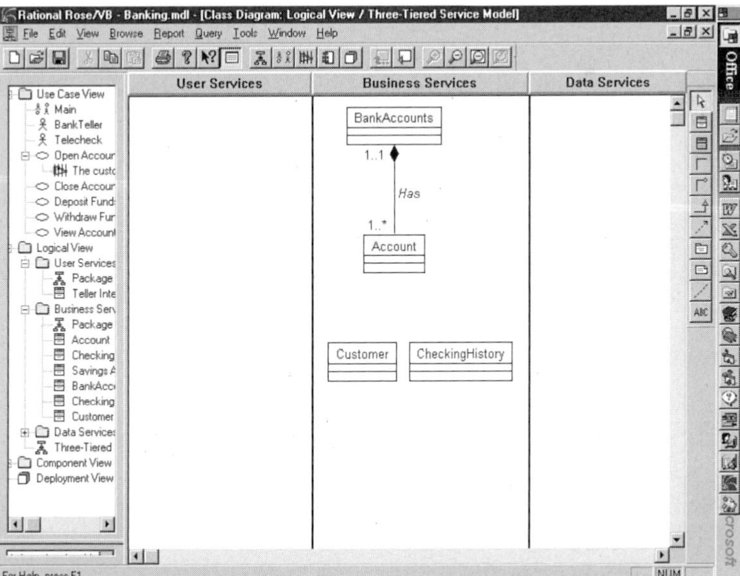

Notice that the collection class `BankAccounts` contains many `Account` class instances (or objects). The black diamond indicates this relationship, which in Visual Basic would be represented as `ByVal` (as opposed to just `ByRef`). This relationship is named *Has*, which is another way of saying that `BankAccounts` contains many `Account` objects. The notation 1..1 and 1..* together is known as the relationship's *cardinality*. Because there's only one `BankAccounts` object, its cardinality is 1..1; because you can have one to an unlimited number of `Account` objects in your collection, `Account`'s cardinality in the relationship is 1..*. The asterisk (*) represents an unlimited number. The `Customer` and `CheckingHistory` classes are relationships that have meaning only with respect to the actors in your system. You can formalize these actors' events in your system through *control objects*, a subject you'll examine in Chapter 8.

Summary

In this chapter, you should have gained not only a better understanding of the role of analysis in object-oriented system development, but a lasting appreciation of it. There can be no effective object-oriented programming in Visual Basic without a thorough and iterative analysis process. Analysis should never be confused with design or programming; doing so leads to a flawed system architecture and *hacking* (or disorganized, haphazard programming). Using a *methodology* to cultivate this evolutionary process is crucial. An analysis methodology centered on how users expect to use the proposed system is absolutely necessary. Ivar Jacobson provides perhaps the best methodology for capturing these expected uses. This methodology is part of the overall objectory method and gives birth to the use-case modeling technique.

The three primary roles usually involved in the use-case identification process are the requirements gatherer, the object-oriented analyst, and the architect. The requirements gatherer typically interrogates end users, business managers (or domain experts), and project managers to draft a problem statement and, optionally, an initial requirements model. The object-oriented analyst carefully examines the requirements model to understand the requirements and elaborates on the requirements model, assesses the implications of each requirement, and removes inconsistencies and requirements discovered to no longer be valid. Object-oriented architects work with analysts and designers to ensure that project team members can trace the names of business objects between the list of requirements, analysis models, and design models. Architects sometimes perform the roles of analyst and designer; otherwise, the architect is a mediator and final decision-maker with regard to the system architecture. With the advent of the software reuse structure of the business organization, these roles will become more specialized (partitioned into smaller roles).

The problem statement is used to capture, in plain English, how users see the system helping them complete their business processes. From this problem statement, the analyst and architect identify and list meaningful nouns and verbs, which helps technicians identify potential actors, classes, class behavior, and use cases. When a list of these objects is drafted, the superfluous or vague items are discarded in favor of those with stronger meaning to the current problem domain (or business context). The main artifacts of the analysis process are the problem statement, the use-case model, and an analysis class model.

In Chapter 8 you'll learn how to take the artifacts of the analysis process and create a more refined design class model, design-view scenario diagrams, and other design artifacts.

Creating Your Own Objects

IN THIS CHAPTER

As with analysis, design is usually a whirlwind "quickie" process for many developers, in which decisions about the detail architecture of the proposed system under development are made for the most part on an ad hoc basis. Such crucial decisions are usually made in isolated settings, where one individual uses his or her thought processes from a previous whirlwind design process to dictate the design process for the current domain. Typically, fellow developers, analysts (if any), and domain experts don't provide a healthy "sanity check" (or organized feedback).

This isn't entirely the programmer's fault, however. Executives and managers, accustomed to the mainframe application development processes, have seldom established their IS and IT departments as they would other business groups. There's no separation between a designer role and the programmer role. They apply pressure to programmers to double as designers (and sometimes analysts, architects, testers, documenters, and so on). Such a variety of roles, coupled with the typical unreasonable deadline, would cause anyone undue stress.

System design should be a very careful, methodical process. It's during the design phase where you want to pursue different coding strategies based on the initial architecture exposed by the analysis phase. Architectural flaws discovered during design are far less costly than architectural flaws discovered during the actual development phase because during design, no coding is done (except for evolving a prototype as a sanity check for proof of concept). The artifacts of design are non-programming models, meaning that when logic flaws are discovered, those flaws can be corrected easily by modifying the corresponding document. Correcting these flaws while the system is still a model on paper is less costly compared to the cost of having to hunt down these same architectural flaws while you're halfway into the process of programming the system. You might even realize a tenfold development cost savings when flaws are detected and corrected on paper. When you skip or skim past design, the inevitable flaws you'll encounter during programming will cost you in terms of

- Many extra hours of overtime
- Unnecessarily increased levels of stress
- Abnormally high levels of impatience among users and managers
- Personnel turnover
- Faulty programmer assumptions about the system made in isolation
- Excessive cost overruns
- An abnormally high increase in the risk of project failure

Programmers who've never tried implementing design in their software development repertoire criticize this phase as wasteful, time-consuming, and pointless. Usually, such believers are novices or have never given thought to the historical problems of the software development process. Unfortunately, many of these programmers hail out of the Visual Basic camp because VB makes development work seem intuitively simple and straightforward. However, it must be stressed time and time again that the design phase is absolutely critical to the development of high-quality software. Incorporating object-oriented design principles in your development efforts pays off in the long run in terms of

- Increased productivity
- Lower project costs on average
- Greater respect for your productive abilities among your peers and managers

This chapter will help you on your way toward these ends.

Understanding Object-Oriented Design

Implementing object-oriented design helps you identify classes and objects you've discovered in the analysis phase, as well as those not yet discovered. During design, you also elaborate on the architecture of the system, including the identification of possible design patterns and frameworks. Design patterns, in simple terms, are repeated ways that objects communicate with each other to carry out some system goal.

NOTE

Although you'll look at design patterns in the last section of this chapter, not enough space is available to discuss all the design patterns discovered thus far. You can find more information at `http://st-www.cs.uiuc.edu/users/patterns/DPBook/DPBook.html` (it's mainly for C++, but some patterns can be translated for VB).

When you finish with the last design iteration (there can be many iterations through the design phase, depending on the complexity of your proposed system), you'll have enough of a detailed system specification to develop the system without having to make assumptions about the system architecture or user motivations. The problems discovered during the actual development phase should be minor, and they should require minor iterations through the design phase to update the corresponding models. At the same time, minor updates in design models should lead to very minor updates in the analysis models, such as changes in the name of a class or class member or the addition of an argument to a private method.

Major changes—such as drastic changes in the way objects communicate, the addition of a new subsystem or package, changes to the graphical user interface, or changes to interfaces between systems—shouldn't occur during the development phase. If such changes weren't addressed during design before development, this might suggest inadequate skill sets among domain experts, analysts, architects, or designers. In any event, such modifications should be deferred to a future release of the system, if possible. If it's not possible, the development phase must be postponed while the design flaws are revisited.

The object-oriented community has many flavors of object-oriented design these days. The following sections briefly introduce the most pervasive ones:

- Object-oriented software engineering (Objectory)
- Object Modeling Technique (OMT)
- Booch

Object-Oriented Software Engineering (Objectory)

Noted object-oriented methodologist Ivar Jacobson is the brains behind the Objectory method. Because of its ease of use and powerful effectiveness in accurate document and model requirements (via the use-case model), it has become the foundation behind object-oriented design efforts in general. However, Jacobson also offers the object-oriented software engineering (OOSE) approach to software construction (or design and programming).

The OOSE design approach models the behavior of the system as documented by the use cases into logical parts, also known as *classes.* At the core of the design model in OOSE are three types of classes, whose instances are objects:

- Entity
- Interface
- Control

Entity Classes

Entity classes represent the type of objects whose data needs to be stored persistently beyond the lifetime of the application session. This persistent storage is usually realized in the form of a database or flat file. Because you're not always sure which storage approach a project will incorporate, you want to logically refer to these storage media as *information repositories* or *information persistence.* Thus, as storage media changes over time, your project artifacts (models and documentation) can better stand the test of time and be reusable for future projects.

An example of an entity class is in order. Suppose that a Visual Basic entity class is structured as follows:

Class: `SavingsAccount`

Properties: `Number`

`CurrentBalance`

`DepositAmount`

`WithdrawalAmount`

`InterestRate`

Methods: `depositFunds`

`withdrawFunds`

`viewTransactionHistory`

As part of your domain-specified requirements, you may need to persistently store the savings account number, current balance, deposit amount, withdrawal amount, and interest rate. Alternatively, you might feel that the current balance is a derived property value, meaning that a cumulative query of your persistent storage media would give you the current balance.

Derived properties are typically borderline issues that must be taken up on a case-by-case basis. Nevertheless, you should understand what an entity class is. Entity classes are usually the first types of classes discovered during the earliest stages of analysis. For instance, if you're developing a system for a defense contracting firm, you might discover a class called `ProcurementRuleEnforcement` or `GovernmentCustomer`. If your client is a bank, a key entity class would be `Account` or `Customer`. Many times, such entity classes become subsystems (or packages). Use cases provide the justification for entity classes. Any entity class not addressed in a use-case model should be eliminated to avoid *scope creep*, where projects get off track and behind schedule.

Interface Classes

Interface classes represent the type of objects that allow actors (humans or external systems) to interact with your proposed system. As Jacobson mentions in several books and magazine articles, object instances of interface classes convert inputs from actors into events and method invocations within your system. For instance, one of the use cases for the Samsona Bank Teller System is `Open a new account`. After several design reviews with users, you find that you need to have a GUI button captioned Open New Account. That button is an interface object with an associated `Click` event, among others. In turn, the `Click` event may trigger the invocation of several class methods. Because these method invocations can become quite complex, it's not unusual to have a control object handle the details of invoking the proper methods.

Control Classes

Control classes represent the type of objects that don't easily fit into entity or interface classes. More complex systems (and, hence, more complex use cases) require the inclusion of control objects in your domain. Control classes may translate user inputs into method invocations on more than one entity class. For instance, if your users need the capability of canceling an in-process request for checking account and credit history information for a particular banking customer, they would click a Cancel button. This would call a control object, possibly named `CustomerVerification`, that would then invoke the appropriate methods on entity objects named `CheckingAccountHistoryInfo`, `CreditHistoryInfo`, `Account`, and `Customer` (among possibly many others). Control objects control the flow of events for complex use cases.

OMT

Jim Rumbaugh developed the Object Modeling Technique (OMT) to help developers capture the design specification of a proposed system. OMT is primarily based on entity/relationship modeling (Rumbaugh has a database design background) with emphasis on modeling classes, inheritance, and encapsulated behavior. The cornerstone of the OMT process includes the following:

- Analysis
- System design
- Object design
- Coding
- Testing

The analysis phase is pretty much similar to what you learned in Chapter 7, "Using Objects in Your Applications." System design is concerned with the initial versions of the Object model, the Dynamic model, and the Functional model. The *Object model* shows the relationships (or links) between classes. The *Dynamic model* elaborates on states of objects and events that are associated with changes in state. The *Functional model* shows how the invoking of methods (or class operations) generate resulting values from a set of input values. The object design phase is an elaboration of the system design phase. Coding and testing aren't unlike what you'll learn about in Chapter 9, "Implementing Polymorphism for Your Objects." Much of OMT's notation has been captured in the Unified Modeling Language, which you explore later in this chapter.

Booch

The Booch method, fathered by Grady Booch, poses questions for designers to use in the elaboration of class structures and relationships. The questions follow the following formats:

- Candidate Class A "is a" type of Class B
- Candidate Class A "has a" Class B type of object
- Candidate Class A "uses" Class B

The "is a" relationship suggests that A is everything that B represents (and possibly more). This is called *inheritance* (albeit, implementation inheritance is restricted in Visual Basic 5). For instance, a checking account *is a* type of account.

The "has a" relationship suggests that A owns B for its own purpose, meaning that the lifetime of B depends on the lifetime of A. There has been much heated discussion on this topic in the OOP community. Essentially, the idea is that, for instance, a bank customer *has* several accounts with the bank. When the customer stops being a customer of the bank, these accounts also cease as the customer closes them (at least, in most cases).

The "uses" relationship suggests that A uses B for a particular task or activity but doesn't own B. For instance, in the Samsona Bank Teller System, the `Account` class might use the `CheckingAccountHistoryInfo` class to verify the customer's checking account history before opening a new account. The `Account` class doesn't own `CheckingAccountHistoryInfo`; `Account` just uses it for this verification process. In Visual Basic, a uses relationship might look like the following:

```
cmdVerifyCheckAccountHistory_Click()
     theAccount.verifyCheckAccountHistory(SomeCustomerSSN)
End Sub
```

In the `Account` class, this method call would then have the following uses relationship:

```
Public Sub verifyCheckAccountHistory(SomeCustomerSSN)
     theCheckingAccountHistoryInfo.verify(SomeCustomerSSN)
End Sub
```

In most cases, the uses relationship resembles delegation, where an object delegates one or all of its responsibilities to another object.

The Booch method is primarily concerned with discovering the chief *abstractions* (areas of specialized focus) of classes and objects as parts of the overall system in your problem domain. The identification process looks at the vocabulary of the business domain, much the way OOSE does. Booch also looks at the contextual meaning of these classes and objects and how they're used by others. Grasping the meaning of classes and objects is by no means an easy process and involves many iterations through design and analysis to fully realize. Thus, domain experts become critical stakeholders in producing analysis and design models and other artifacts.

Finally, Booch breaks the system down into several views and models. Among the views are the Logical View and the Physical View, the basis of Microsoft's Visual Modeler. The Logical View encompasses the structure of and relationships between classes and objects. The Physical View encompasses the actual file location of the classes in the Logical View.

UML

UML (Unified Modeling Language) represents the combination of the most important object-oriented methodologies in the software development community today. The three top methodologists—Ivar Jacobson, Jim Rumbaugh, and Grady Booch—are the chief architects behind UML. The UML creation process began in late 1994 when Booch and Rumbaugh collaborated to unify their respective methodologies. Jacobson joined them shortly thereafter.

The UML doesn't really represent an elimination of OOSE, the OMT, or the Booch method, as some have suggested. Instead, it represents a unified way of modeling elements in each. Of course, the UML creation process has led to some version upgrades in the top three methodologies, but the UML represents only a standard way to express each one.

The UML is wholly encapsulated within the Rational Rose automation tool. This shouldn't be surprising, because Jacobson, Booch, and Rumbaugh are the joint chiefs of Rational Corporation. Because UML and Rational Rose 4.0 are so tightly intertwined, you'll learn more details of the UML in the section on Rational Rose later in this chapter. For now, remember that the UML incorporates four views of the system:

- The Use Case View encompasses all the use-case models, including the actors.
- The Logical View encompasses the classes and objects needed to support the use-case models.
- The Component View, like Booch's Physical View, shows the actual location of the files for each class and component (that is, ActiveX controls and other third-party tools).
- The Deployment View encompasses the physical locations of key processors and hardware devices in your system domain.

You'll see examples of these later in this chapter.

Using Rational Rose/VB and Microsoft Visual Modeler

As seasoned software developers will tell you (if you don't know already), having automation tools that help ease the process of developing sophisticated software is a must in today's technology-intensive environment. Two tools stand out in this arena: Rational Rose/VB and Microsoft Visual Modeler.

Similarities and Differences

Some of you may be saying, "Hey, these tools look alike." This is because Microsoft, the masters of the graphical user interface, and Rational, the rulers of automated object-oriented software development, joined forces to provide a much-needed facelift to Rational Rose. (If you remember the previous versions of Rose, you're probably pretty glad the GUI was brought up to speed.)

Although a number of similarities exist between Visual Modeler and Rose/VB, using both will quickly bring to light the obvious differences. The following are the obvious similarities:

- Both tools support Microsoft's three-tier (or partition) approach to application architecture. The three tiers are User Services (GUI-centered objects), Business Services (rules and entity objects), and Data Services (database objects, recordset objects, flat-file interfaces, and so forth).
- Both tools support the Logical and Physical Views of the application.

The key difference is that Rose/VB supports the Use Case View, whereas Visual Modeler doesn't, possibly due to licensing restrictions negotiated by Rational. Whatever the reason, the lack of the Use Case View in Visual Modeler makes it more difficult to enforce traceability from the use cases to the detail design class models. Thus, project risks must be assessed appropriately and allocated to this situation.

Common Activities

The most important project activity you engage in with Rose/VB or Visual Modeler is the creation of architecture models, diagrams, and documentation. You also can create the necessary class modules and class utilities (or general code modules) to support the evolving system architecture as you iterate and increment through the various project phases. With either tool, you can also reverse-engineer an existing Visual Basic project, thereby creating a model automatically.

The Importance of Traceability

Traceability is that attribute of a project artifact wherein business-related entity classes can be followed from the actual code to the lowest class models, up to the high analysis models, and to the project documentation itself. Master test cases and test scripts also refer to the same class, object, and actor names as other artifacts of the project life cycle.

Unfortunately, too many projects give little attention to the necessity of traceability. It might seem like extra work, but be sure to keep all artifacts (documents, models, diagrams, and code files) in sync when it comes to business domain terminology. Failing to do so very often results in unnecessary confusion and stress down the road.

The Design-View Class Model

When you get into modeling your classes in the design phase, the resulting models become more detailed with each iteration. Figure 8.1 shows what the class model from the analysis phase now looks like. Notice that traceability is still evident.

As you can see, two more classes have been added to the class model: `CheckingAccountHistoryInfo` and `CreditHistoryInfo`. For the sake of simplicity, these classes each have a method called `verify` to handle customer information processing. That both classes can have a method with the same name but different implementations is an example of a form of polymorphism.

POLYMORPHISM

Polymorphism literally means "many forms." In languages that support full interface and implementation inheritance, such as Java, many different subclasses that inherit from a single common base class can customize the abstract class methods for specialized

continues

continued

purposes. The language compiler resolves which method between the parent class and child class is invoked. VB now supports only interface inheritance, and even then true inheritance polymorphism can't be implemented because the class that implements an interface class must implement every public method and property. But classes in a collection that have methods with the same name can contribute to that collection exhibiting polymorphic behavior.

Consider a collection class named `colAccountHistoryInfo`. It has two objects: `CheckingAccountHistoryInfo` and `CreditHistoryInfo`. The following code would use this collection's implied polymorphic behavior:

```
For Each AccountHistoryObject In colAccountHistoryInfo
    AccountHistoryObject.verify
Next
```

The method name `verify` is the same for both objects in the collection, but the respective classes of each object do different things when their `verify` methods are invoked.

Some would argue that this still doesn't qualify as polymorphism, and given the mix of existing definitions, this argument may have some merits. Generally speaking, polymorphism was mainly aimed at getting rid of large, complex `If...Then` statements and other condition-branching mechanisms. The common understanding in the object-oriented community is that if your code has an `If...Then` or `Select` statement whose processing is based on an object type, it's a red flag that polymorphic behavior wasn't a factor in your design. Late binding of object types, where the type of the object isn't known until the object is needed at runtime, is crucial ingredient for implementing polymorphism.

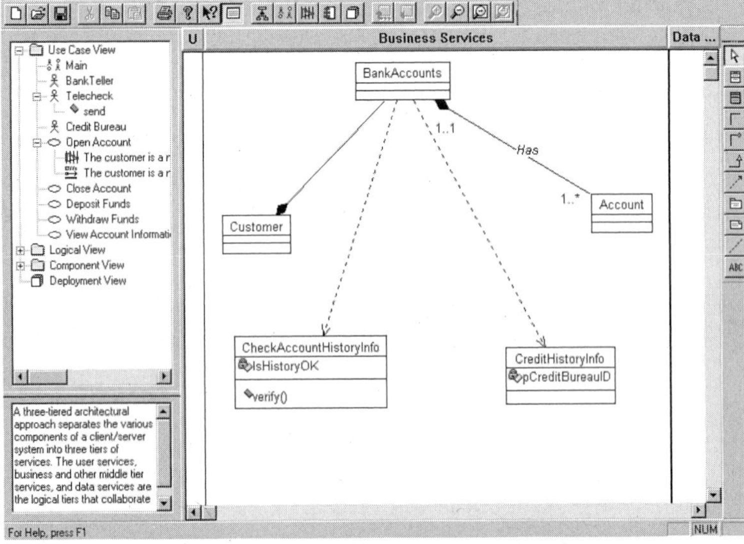

FIGURE 8.1.
The updated class model has two more classes due to new discoveries about the domain.

The modeling tools (Visual Modeler and Rational Rose/VB) let you show the methods for each class. Figure 8.2 shows each class with its methods and properties displayed. Note that in most cases, you don't want to show more class members than necessary to explain a particular scenario. Otherwise, the models become cluttered with model elements and become almost unreadable.

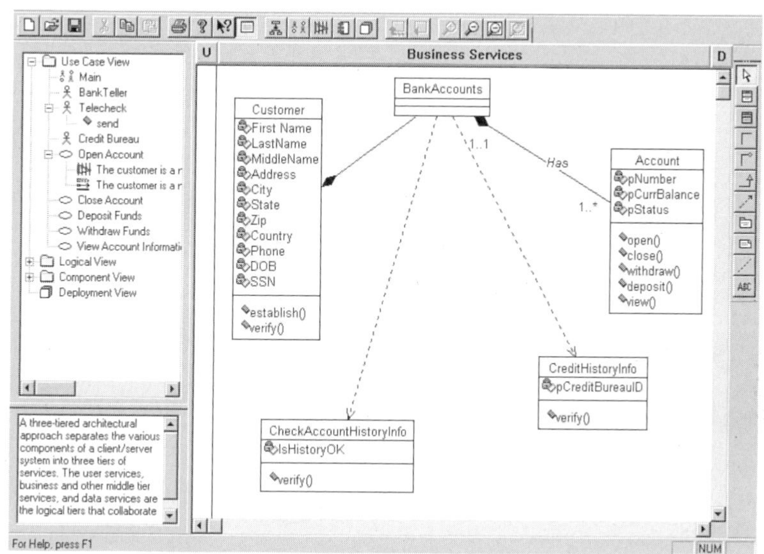

FIGURE 8.2.
Now the class diagram has more expressive classes with properties and methods.

The lack of clutter in models is important because readability is one of the obvious benefits of object-oriented models. Certain scenarios call for different views of the class model. Breaking a complex model into simpler models with different views is ideal. For instance, if you have a scenario that deals with the opening of an account where the customer has a valid Social Security number and has a good credit and checking account history, your class model view would show only the members of the `Account` and `Customer` classes. All other classes would display only a name and possibly a single method that's meaningful to the context (if at all).

Sequence Diagrams

Sequence diagrams literally show a sequence of interactions between actors and objects in your system. In the analysis phase in Chapter 7, you saw an illustration of such a diagram. Many novices to OOP immediately associate sequence diagrams to data flow diagrams (DFDs). They aren't the same. DFDs show only dimly defined paths of function calls. Sequence diagrams show the interaction between actors and objects for a given scenario, with focus on state changes and timing issues.

Figure 8.3 shows the sequence diagram from Chapter 7 updated to include the two new classes (`CheckingAccountHistoryInfo` and `CreditHistoryInfo`). If you don't have Rational Rose/VB, you can just as easily create sequence diagrams by hand.

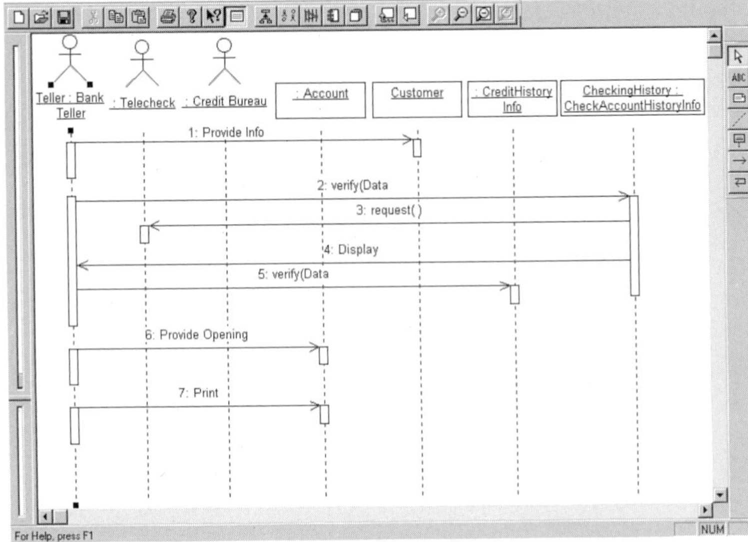

FIGURE 8.3.
The sequence diagram has been updated to incorporate the new classes.

Collaboration Diagrams

Collaboration diagrams are similar to sequence diagrams, except they don't look as sequential and structured. Figure 8.4 shows what the sequence diagram would look like as a collaboration diagram.

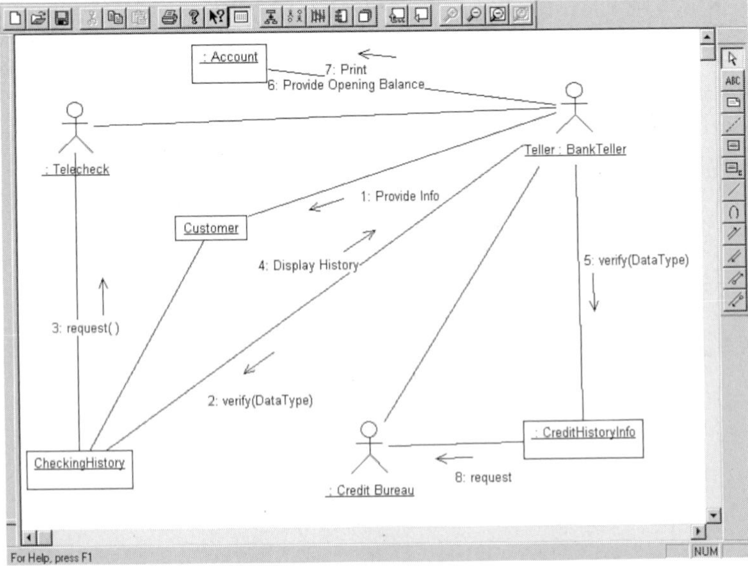

FIGURE 8.4.
The sequence diagram as a collaboration diagram.

Collaboration diagrams aren't as popular with some OOP camps as the sequence diagram. Nevertheless, in some situations, the collaboration diagram captures views of the system that better show method invocations on objects. Generally speaking, the choice is really more a matter of taste than science.

Breaking a Proposed VB Application into Subsystem Packages

As if the concept of classes and objects wasn't already difficult enough, you must also become familiar with the idea of breaking your applications into logical subapplications or subsystems. A *subsystem* consists of one-to-many classes whose object instances interact with each other to carry out a common application behavior. Groupings of classes are also called *packages*. For example, you have a subsystem that handles communications between the data repository (database, flat file, and so on) and the application.

There's no sense in having every form need to communicate directly with the data repository, as has become the idiom in the Visual Basic development community. This leads to flattening the system architecture and graying the lines between the User, Business, and Data Services layers, and thus can cause spaghetti code. What's more, it's next to impossible to hope for code reuse when all the layers of the application code are embedded within forms. Delegating key functionality to subsystems not only helps avoid spaghetti code, but greatly increases the code's readability and the capability of assigning parts of the application to each member of a team of developers.

WHAT ABOUT DATA CONTROLS?

It's okay to have data controls (although not advisable in most cases), as long as you have a central subsystem that handles the actual communication with the database. This is done by passing the data control to the database subsystem, which then "dresses up" the control, as required, to display and save data. For advanced OOP experts, the idea of dressing up the data control is similar to the Visitor design pattern.

Naming Subsystem Packages, Classes, and Objects

Naming and coding standards aren't very pervasive among newcomers to programming (and sometimes among seasoned developers who have managed to skirt the issue of implementing such standards). Microsoft's naming suggestions, of course, are fine, but I'll mention the ones that apply to classes and objects:

- Class names might start with a capital `C` (`CAccount`), as is the case with Microsoft Visual C++. Or you can opt to capitalize the first letter of the class, as in `Account`. Class names should be in the form of a noun, and they should adequately and briefly describe the types of functionality and attributes the class will encapsulate. The same naming convention holds true for subsystems (or packages), which also are classes that are aggregates of one-to-many classes.
- Object names start with `cls` (`clsAccount`). Or you might choose to prefix object names with `the` or `rep`—for example, `theAccount` or `repAccount`.
- Methods start with lowercase verbs (`openAccount`). Avoid using nouns as the name of a method because you might confuse it with a property. Method names with verb forms also accurately convey that an action will be carried out by the class (which is a noun).
- Class properties start with lowercase `p` (`pName`), unless you can differentiate between methods and properties (which is possible with the suggestion on naming methods).
- Implementation variables at the module level start with a lowercase `m` or `m_`. Class Builder prefixes implementation property variables with `mvar`. Implementation variables are just variables used internally within a class.

A multitude of books have been written on coding standards (including those by Jacobson, Booch, and Rumbaugh). At a high level, you'll use a mix of limited inheritance and delegation to express "is a," "has a," and "uses" relationships (discussed earlier in the section "Booch"), where delegation would be the default in your Visual Basic design models. You'll want to develop your interfaces (or protocols) so that they don't change; only the implementation changes.

You can have newer versions of an interface, which means that during some overlapping period, you'll support the old and new interfaces for compatibility (but compatibility isn't your immediate concern). You'll want to break your application model into nice categories (or subsystems) so that each developer has an island of classes with which to work. The idea here is that while these categories are being worked on, no two developers need to try to develop together. Only when the interfaces of each category are developed well will the two come together for integration (which shouldn't take too much time, depending on the complexity of the behavior being carried out). If one finishes before the other, the slower developer (for lack of a better term) could check out the category with which to work.

Understanding Advanced Design Issues: Design Patterns

Although identifying patterns isn't a new science, the concept of design patterns has been gaining rapid popularity in the object-oriented software development community over the last several years. The purpose of design patterns within the object-oriented community is to make available a repository of problems and solutions to help software overcome common issues that repeat themselves. Identifying design patterns facilitates the communication of in-depth knowledge and experience about these recurring problems and points out how best to implement solutions. Having this at the disposal of developers, especially VB developers, helps them evolve well-structured system architectures that provide rapid reuse for the client and understandability among fellow developers.

The idea of object-oriented design patterns is very complex and is for intermediate-to-advanced object technologists. The premier book on design patterns is *Design Patterns: Elements of Reusable Object-Oriented Software* by Erich Gamma, Richard Helm, Ralph Johnson, and John Vlissides. Several others exist. It's advisable that you acquire such books to familiarize yourself with the idea of design patterns. Be forewarned, however, that current design pattern books are written with C++ in mind because many design patterns deal with inheritance, an area in which VB isn't yet capable.

Christopher Alexander, a noted scientist and building architect/theorist, describes a *pattern* as

> ...a three-part rule, which expresses a relation between a certain context, a problem, and a solution. The pattern is, in short, at the same time a thing, which happens in the world, and the rule which tells us how to create that thing, and when we must create it. It's both a process and a thing; both a description of a thing which is alive, and a description of the process which will generate that thing.

NOTE

Because the term *design pattern* has become immensely popular to the point of being a buzzword, too many vanity patterns have entered the community that really aren't solutions, but merely vain attempts at seeking glory by the pattern author/discoverer.

When to Use Design Patterns in Your Project

Because design patterns are a somewhat advanced topic, you might not want to delve into them until at least one of the following is true:

- You have access to an OOP mentor or architect who is knowledgeable about implementing design patterns.
- Time is allocated toward the end of the first release of the project—or sometime thereafter—to examine the need and implementation of design patterns.

Attempting to learn both OOP and design patterns can be overwhelming, so pace yourself. Meanwhile, the next two sections provide examples of design patterns that you can use in your Visual Basic code.

The Singleton Pattern Example

If you've had any experience with Visual Basic 3 programming, you probably remember how difficult it was to allow users to start only one instance of your application. Or if you've been doing a little object-oriented programming, you may have come to the point where you needed to make sure that only one instance of a particular object was in memory. The Singleton design pattern is quite analogous to the first situation, and it's a solution to the second one.

The Singleton pattern makes sure that only one instance of an object is available to prospective client objects. The enforcement of one object instance can be quite important if that object is global within your application, and even more so if that object is global to other applications within an enterprise or across several enterprises. An example of a Singleton object would be a reporting object that resides on a server and is the broker for all requests for reporting services. Another example in the Samsona Bank Teller System might be the `Customer` class, because the teller user (for simplicity's sake) can handle account transactions for only one customer at a time.

Assuming that the `Customer` class needs to make sure that only one instance of it can be in memory, the Singleton class would look like Listing 8.1. Note that this listing shows the actual contents of the class module file rather than the code as it would look when viewed in Visual Basic.

Listing 8.1. The Singleton `Customer` class.

```
VERSION 1.0 CLASS
BEGIN
  MultiUse = -1  'True
END
Attribute VB_Name = "Customer"
Attribute VB_GlobalNameSpace = False
Attribute VB_Creatable = True
Attribute VB_PredeclaredId = False
Attribute VB_Exposed = False
Attribute VB_Ext_KEY = "SavedWithClassBuilder" ,"Yes"
Attribute VB_Ext_KEY = "Top_Level" ,"Yes"
'local variable(s) to hold property value(s)
'Private mvarpSoleInstance As Customer  'local copy
Private mvarpSoleInstance As Object     'local copy

Friend Property Set pSoleInstance(ByVal vData As Object)

'used when assigning an Object to the property, on the left side of a Set
statement.
'Syntax: Set x.pSoleInstance = Form1
    Set mvarpSoleInstance = vData

End Property

Friend Property Get pSoleInstance() As Object

'used when retrieving value of a property, on the right side of an assignment.
'Syntax: Debug.Print X.pSoleInstance
    Set pSoleInstance = mvarpSoleInstance
```

```
End Property

Public Static Function createSoleInstance() As Customer

Attribute createSoleInstance.VB_UserMemId = 0
If TypeName(mvarpSoleInstance) = "Customer" Then
        MsgBox "Only one instance allowed"
        Exit Function
    End If

    Set mvarpSoleInstance = New Customer
    MsgBox "New Customer object created"

End Function

Private Sub Class_Initialize()

End Sub
```

The property `pSoleInstance` was declared as `Friend` so that only those objects within the project can access the `Customer` class instance. The `createSoleInstance` method is the key enforcer in the class. In it, you allow only one instance of the `Customer` class via the `Set...New` syntax. Of course, you can create more than one instance of `Customer` outside the class, which means that the one instance that's created (in this case, `theCustomer`) must be mutually agreed to be the only broker for creating instances of the `Customer` class. Nevertheless, you could have designed this method as in Listing 8.2. Again, this listing reflects the contents of a class module file.

Listing 8.2. The modified `createSoleInstance` method.

```
Public Static Function createSoleInstance() As Customer

Attribute createSoleInstance.VB_UserMemId = 0
    Dim m_InstanceCount As Byte  'local copy
    If m_InstanceCount = 1 Then
        MsgBox "Only one instance allowed"
        Exit Function
    End If

    Set mvarpSoleInstance = New Customer
    MsgBox "New Customer object created"
    m_InstanceCount = 1

End Function
```

In the `createSoleInstance` method in Listing 8.1, the `TypeName` method is used to test whether the late-bound object is of the type `Customer`. When the class is first initialized, it's of the type `Object`. Thus, the check for the `TypeName` method is `False` on the first invocation of `createSoleInstance`. However, because it's the first time, the object will be set to something other than `Object`—namely, `Customer`. Thus, when a second `Set...New Customer` is encountered, the `TypeName` test becomes `True`, meaning that additional instances can't be allowed. In Listing 8.2, on the other hand, a `Static` instance counter is used to limit the instance count to 1. Either pattern is effective for ensuring that only one instance exists.

Gearing Up for Code Implementation

The main complaint about the entire object-oriented development process is that it takes too long to move a project from inception to production. Critics also ignore that most projects end disastrously or achieve hardly any of their initial goals, for numerous reasons. No doubt, your first object-oriented project will be slow because you're actually forced to think about the proposed system from the user's point of view.

In traditional environments, programmers placed themselves on the same pedestal as users (sometimes higher than that!). This often led to products that had to satisfy user and programmer equally, and compromises left users dissatisfied. If a programmer's attitude was boisterous enough, users were bullied into accepting the application, and then a month or two later, abandoned its use. Because programmers typically aren't around to see this long-term end result, they're left with the erroneous perception that the project was successful.

With true object-oriented development, the foundation of the system is constructed with only user needs in mind. Note the word *true* in the previous sentence. Many newcomers to OOP bring their previous traditions with them into the process. This untrue OOP process leads to faulty use cases and, thus, foundations that have cracks everywhere. Only the end users and domain experts can provide the concrete for the foundation. It's your job to fashion and mold it into a stable, long-lasting slab. Just as with building a real house, laying a solid foundation consumes the bulk of the time it takes to develop the entire system. If you try to take shortcuts to produce a foundation in record time, your foundation will inevitably crack and, just as with building contractors, you may be held liable for the damages. If you're an independent consultant, you'll want to take your time to develop the system's foundation properly.

When the foundation is nicely laid, the rest of the process becomes quicker than you ever expected. Future projects that overlap with the first object-oriented project become that much faster because you can reuse code and documentation. With each successive project with similar requirements, the project deadlines become easily met, with time to spare. Time-to-market is thus minimal. But be patient! It may take up to three years before you reach the point where a project benefits from full reuse, much shorter if you hire a consultant with reusable class libraries and libraries of standard use cases. Because software is a capital asset of a company, it's wise to consider the three years or less as the initial investment period of the asset.

Summary

In this chapter, you gained a better understanding of the object-oriented design process. You became familiar with the Objectory design process introduced by Ivar Jacobson, the Object Modeling Technique by Jim Rumbaugh, and the Booch method by Grady Booch. You learned about the importance of traceability from one model and diagram to another, as well as the design-view class model.

You were introduced to two software development automation tools: Rational Rose/VB and Microsoft Visual Modeler. You learned some reasons you might want to use them and explored the differences and similarities between them. You also learned how to break a proposed Visual Basic application into subsystem packages and how to name subsystem packages, classes, and objects.

Finally, you became familiar with an advanced issue in object-oriented design—design patterns. Examples of the Singleton and Adapter patterns were provided in the form of `Customer` class. Chapter 9, "Implementing Polymorphism for Your Objects," rounds out the fundamental concepts of OOP with lots of sample code and explanations following the Samsona Bank Teller System example.

CHAPTER 9

Implementing Polymorphism for Your Objects

IN THIS CHAPTER

In Chapter 6, "Reviewing Object-Oriented Concepts," you learned about the fundamentals of object-oriented programming and which OOP pillars Visual Basic supports. In this chapter, you take your learning a step further. You learn how to construct actual Visual Basic code from the simple Rational Rose/VB sequence diagrams you created in the previous chapter. You could have also created these diagrams by hand.

Identifying Technical Constraints of the Implementation Environment

Because Visual Basic 5 still doesn't allow you to fully implement every pillar of object-oriented programming, you need to keep some notions in mind. Along with these notions, this chapter offers some solutions.

Visual Basic doesn't support *implementation inheritance*, which means that the private members of class A can't be inherited by class B. However, Visual Basic does support *limited interface inheritance,* which means that class B can inherit the public members of class A. It's *limited* because class B can't inherit the public members that class A inherits from another class.

The inheritance of public members in Visual Basic is done via the `Implements` keyword. The keyword `Implements` doesn't imply implementation inheritance, however—it facilitates interface inheritance. *Interface inheritance* is when a subclass inherits the public methods and attributes of a superclass. *Implementation inheritance* is when a subclass inherits both the public and private methods and attributes of a superclass.

In any event, you can replace the use of implementation inheritance in most cases with *delegation.* Whole books have been written about delegation, but the idea (as explained briefly in Chapter 6) is that object A delegates some or all of its behavior to object B. Although you may not have noticed it, delegation was also used in Chapter 8, "Creating Your Own Objects." The `Account` class used the `CheckingAccountHistoryInfo` class to verify a customer's checking account history. Hence, the `Account` class instance (`theAccount`) used the `CheckingAccountHistoryInfo` class instance (`theCheckingAccountHistoryInfo`) as follows:

```
Public Sub verifyCheckAccountHistory(SomeCustomerSSN)
     theCheckingAccountHistoryInfo.verify(SomeCustomerSSN)
End Sub
```

The concept of delegation is synonymous with the uses relationship defined in the Unified Modeling Language.

Visual Basic also doesn't support the kind of polymorphism associated with inheritance lattices. In other words, assume the following: a superclass named `theSuperClass` has a method called `print`; a subclass of `theSuperClass`, `theSubclass`, also has a specialized (or customized) method called `print`; and a subclass of the `theSubclass` has a specialized method named `print`. The compiler would use the specialized method of the class instance being used for a given context (or section of code).

With the absence of implementation and full interface inheritance, this kind of polymorphism is practically nonexistent. (Of course, a class's interface can be inherited one level down as though it were a pure virtual base class, but Visual Basic expects the public methods and properties to be implemented by the client class.)

Visual Basic supports the other kind of polymorphism, where a collection of objects with one or more methods of the same name will have varying behaviors when iterated. In the Samsona Bank Teller System example, you have two collections of history verification objects: `theCheckingAccountHistoryInfo` and `theCreditHistoryInfo`. As you saw in Chapter 8, each of these objects has a method called `verify`. To create a collection object called `HistoryVerifiers`, follow these steps:

1. Start a new project in Visual Basic.
2. Create a class called `CheckingAccountHistoryInfo` and one called `CreditHistoryInfo`. If you're using Rational Rose/VB or Visual Modeler, you can generate the classes by choosing Tools | Code Generation Wizard from either application's menu.

Working with Design Models

To fully benefit from the object-oriented features in Visual Basic 5, you need some effective way to capture the attributes and behaviors of classes, as well as how they interact with one another at runtime as objects. Toward this end, the class diagram and scenario diagrams provide you with the capability of modeling these elements.

A class diagram shows the unique identity of one or more classes and their behaviors, as well as any inheritance, delegation, or aggregation relationships. Scenario diagrams (along with collaboration diagrams) capture how the instances of these classes interact at runtime to carry out some system behavior. Because of the easy-to-follow nature of these model types, you can break down complex systems into simpler abstractions. Together, they provide the architectural expression of the proposed system.

The Importance of Not Deviating from the Architecture

The requirements for the proposed system expressed by end users and domain experts to project technicians must be directly translated into a use-case model, which then must be translated into the architecture of the system. Requirements not adequately expressed by users before the evolution of the system's architecture winds down will lead to a very lopsided architecture that will crack at the foundation during system construction. The causes of inadequate expression of user requirements—and, thus, architecture deviation—can be many, but the most common appear to be the following:

- Lack of executive sponsorship of a project
- Inexperienced system architects or business analysts
- Impatient software developers/programmers
- Uncooperative users

Lack of Executive Sponsorship of a Project

Lack of executive sponsorship is the single biggest risk to any Visual Basic project. It's usually the result of competition between executives for a particular fiefdom in an aging, antiquated corporate environment. During the inception phase of the project (the one that rarely involves any technical experts), many managers and executives seem to make big political promises to employees and shareholders with such sloganeering as "Change is constant" and "The new system will satisfy all your needs." However, when the project moves past the inception phase into the iterative elaboration phase—after they seal the campaign victory—these same managers and executives disappear, vanishing into the political black holes found in most companies.

Executives seldom want to sponsor fledgling software projects because if one fails (and a high probability of failure exists), they'll look bad or—worse—be demoted or fired. Thus, the reality is that many executives make big promises and then quickly back out of the limelight, secretly hoping against hope that the project will somehow succeed.

Other executives take more drastic measures by hiring a scapegoat project manager to hold the sole responsibility for a project. In some cases, these project managers don't have the right skill sets to ensure the project's success. For instance, the typical characteristics of project managers for object-oriented client/server projects are that they are middle-aged, have a long background exclusively in mainframe software development (without a clear development methodology), and secretly prefer the security of the mainframe versus the rapidly evolving technology of object-oriented client/server projects. Project managers typically are non-combative, meaning that whatever executives want them to do is what they'll do.

How does this relate to architecture deviation? It's the most prevalent cause of failed projects that no one wants to discuss. Experienced architects, in giving architectural advisories to project managers and executives, typically run into subtle hostility, jealousy, and brick walls. That is, project managers are prone to treat the object-oriented project much the way they treated legacy software development: minimize the analysis and maximize the programming, at any cost, with little or no attention paid to methodology. This leads to architectural foundations built on sand, where new requirements that lie outside the scope of the project are added with reckless abandon to satisfy demanding users. Because the core of the system was never designed in a methodical way, these additions almost always put undue stress on the project and the system architecture (if you can call it that).

Executive sponsorship is to the project what the use-case model is to the system architecture: the absolute foundation that determines the success or failure of the project. Lack of executive sponsorship can lead to inadequate use cases, which then leads to inadequate system architectures.

Inexperienced System Architects or Business Analysts

Inexperience among the top echelon of a project's technical staff can have a devastating effect on the project's outcome and use cases. Proper executive sponsorship of a project can increase the chance of finding and hiring the right technical architects and business analysts, but it can't give 100 percent assurance of this. Inexperienced technical leaders may not know how to adjust a given object-oriented methodology to the dynamics of user and executive behavior. This alone leads to inadequate use cases (if any) and faulty system architectures. Other factors include the inability to make a transition of a project from one iteration to another, to give technical advisories to less-experienced stakeholders in the project, and to manage the artifacts of the project.

Impatient Software Developers/Programmers

Assume that you have reasonably proper executive sponsorship, knowledgeable project managers, and proactive user involvement in conveying use cases, and thus could develop a sound architecture for the system. Because many VB programmers haven't embraced object-oriented programming, the chances of hiring impatient developers are high. This is important because many programmers believe that OOP minimizes individualistic efforts, a threat to programmer creativity. Many others feel that reading project artifacts and spending time to follow design models are useless activities. Of course, such sentiments couldn't be further from the truth, yet they persist.

Impatient developers have a tendency to take shortcuts, resorting to the disorganized spaghetti-style coding prevalent among many developers. User input is minimized in order to maximize programmer satisfaction. Such developers frown on anything resembling a use case, thus increasing the risk of the system's architecture being faulty, to say the least.

Uncooperative Users

To put it bluntly, the more your users are uncooperative, the greater the risk of project failure. Non-participation by users is usually a symptom of the existence of one or more of three problems listed previously, but not always. If users don't actively participate in the early architectural design of the system, you may as well update your résumé. Not only will the architecture of the system be completely faulty, division and strife will creep up over time among the project stakeholders, programmers will have to work around the clock to help the project manager save face, and everyone will experience unnecessarily high levels of stress.

Programming solutions just seem to appear out of thin air. Users determine the system behavior, and without their participation, there is no architecture and thus no scope, which leads to architecture deviation.

Code Generation in Rational Rose/VB and Visual Modeler

Automating the process of creating object-oriented programming code considerably reduces the normal risks associated with software development projects. Such risks include the obvious human error factor in coding, the risk of not making a proper transition from a model to the actual code base, the risk of not properly documenting code, and so on. Rational Rose/VB 4.0 and Microsoft Visual Modeler offer automated code engineering and reverse code engineering to drastically reduce these risks. Because Rational Rose/VB is used for the use cases in Chapter 7, "Using Objects in Your Applications," and class modeling in Chapter 8, this chapter uses Microsoft Visual Modeler.

> **NOTE**
>
> The process of creating code from models and reverse-engineering existing code are exactly the same in both products, so you can use the following steps in either tool.

If you own Visual Basic 5 Professional or Enterprise Edition, you can go to `www.microsoft.com/vbasic`, register in the Owners' Area as a licensed user, and download Visual Modeler for free. Otherwise, you need to go to `www.rational.com` and make arrangements to pay for Rational Rose/VB.

Generating Code for the Samsona Bank Teller System Example

You create the code for the ongoing Samsona Bank Teller System example in this chapter. To do so, you need to launch Visual Basic 5, if you haven't already done so.

> **CAUTION**
>
> Make sure that you have plenty of hardware capacity when running VB 5 and Visual Modeler simultaneously. I work with these tools on a P133 with 32MB of RAM and 5GB of disk space (with the maximum recommended virtual memory setting). Otherwise, these tools may suffer serious performance degradation and could crash your machine.

With VB running, follow these steps:

1. Start Visual Modeler.
2. In the browser window, right-click the package folder named Logical and choose New Class. A class icon appears in the browser window.
3. With the default class `NewClass` highlighted, enter **`Customer`**.
4. Double-click the Customer class icon you just created. The Class Specification for Customer dialog box appears.
5. Notice the Methods and Properties tabbed pages. On each page is a big white box. Right-click this box and choose Insert to add the methods and properties for the `Customer` class.

Repeat these steps for the other classes except for the `BankAccounts` collection. Instructions for creating this collection class follow the class listings.

Class: `Customer`

Properties: `FirstName`
`LastName`
`MiddleName`
`Address`
`City`
`State`
`Zip`
`Country`
`Phone`
`DOB`
`SSN`

Methods: `establish`
`verify`

Class: `BankAccounts` (`Collection` class)

Class: `Account`

Properties: `Number`
`CurrBalance`
`Status`

Methods: `open`
`close`
`withdraw`
`deposit`
`view`

Class: `CreditHistoryInfo`

Properties: `CreditBureauID`

Methods: `verify`

Class: `CheckingAccountHistoryInfo`

Properties: `IsHistoryOK`

Methods: `verify`

Class: `Teller_Interface`

Methods:
```
closeAccount(argAcctNum As String)
depositFunds(argAmount As Currency)
openAccount(argSSN As String)
queryCheckingHistory(argSSN As String)
queryCreditHistory(argSSN As String)
Private: verifyExistingAccount(Optional argSSN,
Optional argAcctNum)
withdrawFunds(argAmount As Currency)
```

Notice that `BankAccounts` is a collection class that you'll implement in Visual Basic. You can manually put in the standard methods and properties that collections typically have. Or you can automate the process of creating collection classes by following these steps:

1. Choose Tools | Class Builder Utility from the menu. If you've used VB5 before reading this chapter or read Chapter 6, you'll recognize the familiar Class Builder window.
2. Choose File | New Collection from the Class Builder's menu. The Collection Builder dialog box appears.
3. By default, the name suggested for the new collection is `Collection1`; change this to `BankAccounts`. (Delete the `BankAccounts` class from the model if you're going to continue with this process; otherwise, add the typical collection properties and methods to the existing `BankAccounts` class in the model and don't proceed with the remaining steps.)

   Leave the Based On: drop-down list box alone because you're creating a new collection.
4. In the Collection Of section, choose New Class to trick the utility into letting you proceed (you won't need the class it creates). Click OK.
5. Choose File | Update Project from Class Builder's menu (VB needs to be running).
6. Exit Class Builder.

7. The Reverse Engineering Wizard welcome dialog box appears. Because you're creating the `BankAccounts` collection class first with the Class Builder utility within Visual Modeler, you must reverse-engineer it into your current model. Click the Next button.
8. You don't need to select a component, so click Next again.
9. Assign the new collection class to a Logical View Package. The standard packages are User, Business, and Data Services:
   - User Services includes the class associated with graphical user interface processes.
   - Business Services has those classes associated with real-world entities in the client's environment.
   - Data Services houses the classes that facilitate saving precious business information from an application session to a persistent information repository, such as a database or a flat file.

   The `BankAccounts` collection class is a business domain class, so it belongs in the Business Services package. Drag it to the Business Services package folder and click the Next button.
10. The Wizard copies the collection class to your current model. Click the Finish button.
11. Click the Close button.

Now to generate the code, choose Tools | Code Generation Wizard from Visual Modeler's menu. The Code Generation Wizard dialog box appears. For this simple exercise, click the Next button in each dialog box that displays until you see the Finish button. Then click the Finish button.

NOTE

Although this sample exercise made navigating through the code-generation steps easy, in the real world, you should give serious thought to the decisions in each step, such as error-raising options and debug information insertion. Failure to properly consider these decisions might result in improperly developed code.

NOTE

If you didn't have VB running during the code-generation process, Visual Modeler would have notified you that VB must be running to generate code.

To see your newly generated code, switch to your current Visual Basic session. You should see several cascaded code windows for each class created.

Putting On the Finishing Touches

Although Visual Modeler is a pretty smart tool, it's still not smart enough to provide all the logic necessary to make your code work the way your client wants the system to work. If it did, you would probably be out of a job!

For your newly generated code to work, you have to re-examine the use cases to further determine what users want. This activity may prompt several more use-case iterations with the users to ensure that every requirement for the current release of the system is in place and that there are no discrepancies. It's far cheaper in terms of time and money to verify use cases before coding than afterward, so be patient with this process. The use cases will also guide you in developing the components of the graphical user interface, because they generally tell you how users will use the proposed system.

On the CD-ROM accompanying this book is an example of how you might implement the Samsona Bank Teller System example (see Listing 9.1, which shows the actual contents of the various program modules that compose the sample project). Your coding style will no doubt vary, but the general goal is to keep your code style and syntax as simple and clear as possible. Resist the individualistic signature and artistic flair too many developers hope to instill in their code. Traceability among all the artifacts of the development process, including the use cases and code, is important. This is particularly true to future evolutionary activities, such as maintenance and enhancements.

Listing 9.1. An example of the Samsona Bank Teller System.

```
VERSION 1.0 CLASS
BEGIN
  MultiUse = -1  'True
END
Attribute VB_Name = "BankAccounts"
Attribute VB_GlobalNameSpace = False
Attribute VB_Creatable = True
Attribute VB_PredeclaredId = False
Attribute VB_Exposed = False
Attribute VB_Ext_KEY = "ClassBuilderProperty" ,""
Attribute VB_Ext_KEY = "SavedWithClassBuilder" ,"Yes"
Attribute VB_Ext_KEY = "Collection" ,"Class1"
Attribute VB_Ext_KEY = "Member0" ,"Class1"
Attribute VB_Ext_KEY = "Top_Level" ,"Yes"
Attribute VB_Ext_KEY = "RVB_UniqueId" ,"340AE45103CA"
'
Option Base 0

'local variable to hold collection
'##ModelId=340AE4540186
Private mCol As Collection
```

```
'##ModelId=340AE5030142
Public theCustomer As Customer

'##ModelId=340AE50403CC
Public theAccount As Collection
'##ModelId=340AE45402D0
Public Function Add(Key As String, Optional sKey As String) As Class1
    'create a new object
    Dim objNewMember As Class1
    Set objNewMember = New Class1

    'set the properties passed into the method
    objNewMember.Key = Key

    If Len(sKey) = 0 Then
        mCol.Add objNewMember
    Else
        mCol.Add objNewMember, sKey
    End If

    'return the object created
    Set Add = objNewMember
    Set objNewMember = Nothing

End Function

'##ModelId=340AE4560136
Public Property Get Item(vntIndexKey As Variant) As Class1
Attribute Item.VB_UserMemId = 0
    'used when referencing an element in the collection
    'vntIndexKey contains either the Index or Key to the collection,
    'this is why it is declared as a Variant
    'Syntax: Set foo = x.Item(xyz) or Set foo = x.Item(5)
  Set Item = mCol(vntIndexKey)
End Property

'##ModelId=340AE4570208
Public Property Get Count() As Long
    'used when retrieving the number of elements in the
    'collection. Syntax: Debug.Print x.Count
    Count = mCol.Count
End Property

'##ModelId=340AE45800E6
Public Sub Remove(vntIndexKey As Variant)
    'used when removing an element from the collection
    'vntIndexKey contains either the Index or Key, which is why
    'it is declared as a Variant
    'Syntax: x.Remove(xyz)

    mCol.Remove vntIndexKey
End Sub

'##ModelId=340AE459010E
Public Property Get NewEnum() As IUnknown
Attribute NewEnum.VB_UserMemId = -4
    'this property allows you to enumerate
    'this collection with the For...Each syntax
```


continues

Listing 9.1. continued

```
    Set NewEnum = mCol.[_NewEnum]
End Property

'##ModelId=340AE45903A2
Private Sub Class_Initialize()
    'creates the collection when this class is created
    Set mCol = New Collection
End Sub

'##ModelId=340AE45A024E
Private Sub Class_Terminate()
    'destroys collection when this class is terminated
    Set mCol = Nothing
End Sub

VERSION 1.0 CLASS
BEGIN
  MultiUse = -1  'True
END
Attribute VB_Name = "Account"
Attribute VB_GlobalNameSpace = False
Attribute VB_Creatable = True
Attribute VB_PredeclaredId = FalseAttribute VB_Exposed = False
Attribute VB_Ext_KEY = "RVB_UniqueId" ,"33D412D90352"
Attribute VB_Ext_KEY = "SavedWithClassBuilder" ,"Yes"
Attribute VB_Ext_KEY = "Top_Level" ,"Yes"
'
Option Base 0

'set this to 0 to disable debug code in this class
#Const DebugMode = 1
#If DebugMode Then
    'local variable to hold the serialized class ID that
    'was created in Class_Initialize
    '##ModelId=340B72E600A0
    Private mmlClassDebugID As Long
#End If

'##ModelId=33E6AE1D02BC
Public pNumber As Variant

'##ModelId=33E6AE2302E4
Public pCurrBalance As Variant

'##ModelId=33E6AE2E0186
Public pStatus As Variant

'##ModelId=33D8246C00FA
Public theVariant As Variant

'##ModelId=340AE50403CB
Public theBankAccounts As BankAccounts

'##ModelId=33E6AE060276
Public Sub closeAccount()
    On Error GoTo closeErr

    'your code goes here...
```

```
    MsgBox "Account will be closed..."
    Exit Sub
closeErr:
    Call RaiseError(MyUnhandledError, "Account:close Method")
End Sub

'##ModelId=33E6AE00035C
Public Sub openAccount()
    On Error GoTo openErr

    'your code goes here...
    If theCustomer.establish Then
        pNumber = "0001" 'example purpose only
        MsgBox "Account Established"
    End If
    Exit Sub
openErr:
    Call RaiseError(MyUnhandledError, "Account:open Method")
End Sub

'##ModelId=33E6AE060276
Public Sub close()
    On Error GoTo closeErr

    'your code goes here...

    Exit Sub
closeErr:
    Call RaiseError(MyUnhandledError, "Account:close Method")
End Sub

'##ModelId=33E6AE00035C
Public Sub open()
    On Error GoTo openErr

    'your code goes here...

    Exit Sub
openErr:
    Call RaiseError(MyUnhandledError, "Account:open Method")
End Sub

'##ModelId=33E6AE060276
Public Sub close()
    On Error GoTo closeErr

    'your code goes here...

    Exit Sub
closeErr:
    Call RaiseError(MyUnhandledError, "Account:close Method")
End Sub

'##ModelId=33E6AE00035C
Public Sub open()
    On Error GoTo openErr

    'your code goes here...
```


continues

Listing 9.1. continued

```
    Exit Sub
openErr:
    Call RaiseError(MyUnhandledError, "Account:open Method")
End Sub

'##ModelId=340B89570168
Public Property Get mlClassDebugID() As Long
   Let mlClassDebugID = mmlClassDebugID
End Property

'##ModelId=340B89550226
Public Property Let mlClassDebugID(Value As Long)
   Let mmlClassDebugID = Value
End Property

'##ModelId=340B72E90190
Private Sub Class_Terminate()
    #If DebugMode Then
    'the class is being destroyed
        Debug.Print "'" & TypeName(Me) & "' instance " & CStr(mlClassDebugID) _
          & " is terminating"
    #End If
End Sub

'##ModelId=340B72E802E4
Private Sub Class_Initialize()
    #If DebugMode Then
        'get the next available class ID, and print out
        'that the class was created successfully
        mlClassDebugID = GetNextClassDebugID()
        Debug.Print "'" & TypeName(Me) & "' instance " & CStr(mlClassDebugID) _
          & " created"
    #End If
End Sub

'##ModelId=33E6AE0A03CA
Public Sub withdraw(argTransAmt As Currency, _
argOptionCtrl As OptionButton)
    On Error GoTo withdrawErr

    'your code goes here...
    'pCurrBalance>0 assumes no overdraft protection, otherwise
    'insert a variable for overdraft in place of 0, thus giving
    'pCurrBalance > pCurrBalance - mc_OverdraftAmt
    If argOptionCtrl(eTransOption.withdraw) And pCurrBalance > 0 Then
        pCurrBalance = pCurrBalance - argTransAmt
    End If

    Exit Sub
withdrawErr:
    Call RaiseError(MyUnhandledError, "Account:withdraw Method")
End Sub

'##ModelId=33E6AE100050
Public Sub deposit(argTransAmt As Currency, _
argOptionCtrl As OptionButton)
```

```
    On Error GoTo depositErr

    'your code goes here...
    If argOptionCtrl(eTransOption.deposit) Then
        pCurrBalance = pCurrBalance + argTransAmt
    End If
    Exit Sub
depositErr:
    Call RaiseError(MyUnhandledError, "Account:deposit Method")
End Sub

'##ModelId=33E6AE170032
Public Sub view()
    On Error GoTo viewErr

    'your code goes here...

    Exit Sub
viewErr:
    Call RaiseError(MyUnhandledError, "Account:view Method")
End Sub

#If DebugMode Then
    '##ModelId=340B72E6028A
    Public Property Get ClassDebugID() As Long
        'if we are in debug mode, surface this property that consumers can query
        ClassDebugID = mlClassDebugID
    End Property
#End If

Public Sub processTrans(argTransAmt As Currency, _
argOptionCtrl As OptionButton)
    If TypeOf argOptionCtrl Is OptionButton Then
        'Only one method invocation will work
        deposit argTransAmt, argOptionCtrl
        withdraw argTransAmt, argOptionCtrl
    End If
End Sub

VERSION 1.0 CLASS
BEGIN
  MultiUse = -1  'True
END
Attribute VB_Name = "CheckingAccountHistoryInfo"
Attribute VB_GlobalNameSpace = False
Attribute VB_Creatable = True
Attribute VB_PredeclaredId = False
Attribute VB_Exposed = False
Attribute VB_Ext_KEY = "RVB_UniqueId" ,"33E6A47F01F4"
Attribute VB_Ext_KEY = "SavedWithClassBuilder" ,"Yes"
Attribute VB_Ext_KEY = "Top_Level" ,"Yes"
'
Option Base 0

'set this to 0 to disable debug code in this class
#Const DebugMode = 1
#If DebugMode Then
```

continues

Listing 9.1. continued

```
    'local variable to hold the serialized class ID that
    'was created in Class_Initialize
    '##ModelId=340B72FD003C
    Public mlClassDebugID As Long
#End If

'##ModelId=33E6AD6B00F0
Private mIsHistoryOK As Variant

'##ModelId=33E6A50C03A2
Public theVariant As Variant

'##ModelId=340B89600398
Public Property Get IsHistoryOK() As Variant
   If IsObject(mIsHistoryOK) Then
      Set IsHistoryOK = mIsHistoryOK
   Else
      Let IsHistoryOK = mIsHistoryOK
   End If
End Property

'##ModelId=340B895F01B8
Public Property Let IsHistoryOK(Value As Variant)
   Let mIsHistoryOK = Value
End Property

'##ModelId=340B72FF00C8
Private Sub Class_Terminate()
    #If DebugMode Then
    'the class is being destroyed
        Debug.Print "'" & TypeName(Me) & "' instance " & CStr(mlClassDebugID) _
          & " is terminating"
    #End If
End Sub

'##ModelId=340B72FE0258
Private Sub Class_Initialize()
    #If DebugMode Then
        'get the next available class ID, and print out
        'that the class was created successfully
        mlClassDebugID = GetNextClassDebugID()
        Debug.Print "'" & TypeName(Me) & "' instance " & CStr(mlClassDebugID) _
          & " created"
    #End If
End Sub

'##ModelId=33E6AD9A03CA
Public Sub verify(argCustomerSSN As DataType)
'History of customer is returned

End Sub

#If DebugMode Then
    '##ModelId=340B72FD0186
    Public Property Get ClassDebugID() As Long
        'if we are in debug mode, surface this property that consumers can query
        ClassDebugID = mlClassDebugID
```

```
    End Property
#End If
VERSION 1.0 CLASS
BEGIN
  MultiUse = -1  'True
END
Attribute VB_Name = "CreditHistoryInfo"
Attribute VB_GlobalNameSpace = False
Attribute VB_Creatable = True
Attribute VB_PredeclaredId = False
Attribute VB_Exposed = False
Attribute VB_Ext_KEY = "RVB_UniqueId" ,"33E6A495019A"
Attribute VB_Ext_KEY = "SavedWithClassBuilder" ,"Yes"
Attribute VB_Ext_KEY = "Top_Level" ,"Yes"
'
Option Base 0

'set this to 0 to disable debug code in this class
#Const DebugMode = 1
#If DebugMode Then
    'local variable to hold the serialized class ID that
    'was created in Class_Initialize
    '##ModelId=340B73000352
    Public mlClassDebugID As Long
#End If

'##ModelId=33E6ACEE00E6
Private mpCreditBureauID As Variant

'##ModelId=340B8994003C
Public Property Get pCreditBureauID() As Variant
   If IsObject(mpCreditBureauID) Then
      Set pCreditBureauID = mpCreditBureauID
   Else
      Let pCreditBureauID = mpCreditBureauID
   End If
End Property

'##ModelId=340B89920316
Public Property Let pCreditBureauID(Value As Variant)
   Let mpCreditBureauID = Value
End Property

'##ModelId=340B73020226
Private Sub Class_Terminate()
    #If DebugMode Then
    'the class is being destroyed        Debug.Print "'" & TypeName(Me) & "'
instance " & CStr(mlClassDebugID) _
          & " is terminating"
    #End If
End Sub

'##ModelId=340B730103B6
Private Sub Class_Initialize()
    #If DebugMode Then
        'get the next available class ID, and print out
        'that the class was created successfully
```

continues

Listing 9.1. continued

```
        mlClassDebugID = GetNextClassDebugID()
        Debug.Print "'" & TypeName(Me) & "' instance " & CStr(mlClassDebugID) _
          & " created"
    #End If
End Sub

'##ModelId=33E6ACAB014A
Public Sub verify(argCustomerSSN As DataType)
'History of customer is returned

End Sub

#If DebugMode Then
    '##ModelId=340B73010046
    Public Property Get ClassDebugID() As Long
        'if we are in debug mode, surface this property that consumers can query
        ClassDebugID = mlClassDebugID
    End Property
#End If
VERSION 1.0 CLASS
BEGIN
  MultiUse = -1  'True
END
Attribute VB_Name = "Customer"
Attribute VB_GlobalNameSpace = False
Attribute VB_Creatable = True
Attribute VB_PredeclaredId = False
Attribute VB_Exposed = False
Attribute VB_Ext_KEY = "RVB_UniqueId" ,"33D825080316"
Attribute VB_Ext_KEY = "SavedWithClassBuilder" ,"Yes"
Attribute VB_Ext_KEY = "Top_Level" ,"Yes"
'
Option Base 0

'set this to 0 to disable debug code in this class
#Const DebugMode = 1
#If DebugMode Then
    'local variable to hold the serialized class ID that
    'was created in Class_Initialize
    '##ModelId=340B72F7023A
    Private mlClassDebugID As Long
#End If

'##ModelId=33E6AEB601F4
Private mFirst_Name As Variant

'##ModelId=33E6AEBF01FE
Private mLastName As Variant

'##ModelId=33E6AEC300F0
Private mMiddleName As Variant
Public Function attributesHaveValues()
    attributesHaveValues = (First_Name <> "")
    attributesHaveValues = (LastName <> "")
    attributesHaveValues = (Address <> "")
    attributesHaveValues = (City <> "")
    attributesHaveValues = (Country <> "")
```

```
    attributesHaveValues = (DOB <> "")
    attributesHaveValues = (MiddleName <> "")
    attributesHaveValues = (State <> "")
    attributesHaveValues = (Phone <> "")
    attributesHaveValues = (Zip <> "")
    attributesHaveValues = (SSN <> "")
End Function

'##ModelId=33E6AECC01D6
Private mAddress As Variant

'##ModelId=33E6AED00140
Private mCity As Variant

'##ModelId=33E6AED40140
Private mState As Variant

'##ModelId=33E6AED90032
Private mZip As Variant

'##ModelId=33E6AEDC037A
Private mCountry As Variant

'##ModelId=33E6AEE00384
Private mPhone As Variant

'##ModelId=33E6AEE6037A
Private mDOB As Variant

'##ModelId=33E6AEEA023A
Private mSSN As Variant

'##ModelId=33E6A4E003AC
Public theVariant As Variant

'##ModelId=340AE5030141
Public theBankAccounts As BankAccounts

'##ModelId=340B89850154
Public Property Get SSN() As Variant
   If IsObject(mSSN) Then
      Set SSN = mSSN
   Else
      Let SSN = mSSN
   End If
End Property

'##ModelId=340B8983019A
Public Property Let SSN(Value As Variant)
   Let mSSN = Value
End Property

'##ModelId=340B898200D2
Public Property Get DOB() As Variant
   If IsObject(mDOB) Then
      Set DOB = mDOB
   Else
```


continues

Listing 9.1. continued

```
      Let DOB = mDOB
   End If
End Property

'##ModelId=340B89800118
Public Property Let DOB(Value As Variant)
   Let mDOB = Value
End Property

'##ModelId=340B897F0082
Public Property Get Phone() As Variant
   If IsObject(mPhone) Then
      Set Phone = mPhone
   Else
      Let Phone = mPhone
   End If
End Property

'##ModelId=340B897D0140
Public Property Let Phone(Value As Variant)
   Let mPhone = Value
End Property

'##ModelId=340B897C0032
Public Property Get Country() As Variant
   If IsObject(mCountry) Then
      Set Country = mCountry
   Else
      Let Country = mCountry
   End If
End Property

'##ModelId=340B897A00F0
Public Property Let Country(Value As Variant)
   Let mCountry = Value
End Property

'##ModelId=340B897900FA
Public Property Get Zip() As Variant
   If IsObject(mZip) Then
      Set Zip = mZip
   Else
      Let Zip = mZip
   End If
End Property

'##ModelId=340B897701EA
Public Property Let Zip(Value As Variant)
   Let mZip = Value
End Property

'##ModelId=340B89760190
Public Property Get State() As Variant
   If IsObject(mState) Then
      Set State = mState
   Else
```

```
      Let State = mState
   End If
End Property

'##ModelId=340B89740280
Public Property Let State(Value As Variant)
   Let mState = Value
End Property

'##ModelId=340B8973024E
Public Property Get City() As Variant
   If IsObject(mCity) Then
      Set City = mCity
   Else
      Let City = mCity
   End If
End Property

'##ModelId=340B8971037A
Public Property Let City(Value As Variant)
   Let mCity = Value
End Property

'##ModelId=340B89700384
Public Property Get Address() As Variant
   If IsObject(mAddress) Then
      Set Address = mAddress
   Else
      Let Address = mAddress
   End If
End Property

'##ModelId=340B896F0136
Public Property Let Address(Value As Variant)
   Let mAddress = Value
End Property

'##ModelId=340B896E0140
Public Property Get MiddleName() As Variant
   If IsObject(mMiddleName) Then
      Set MiddleName = mMiddleName
   Else
      Let MiddleName = mMiddleName
   End If
End Property

'##ModelId=340B896C02DA
Public Property Let MiddleName(Value As Variant)
   Let mMiddleName = Value
End Property

'##ModelId=340B896B0320
Public Property Get LastName() As Variant
   If IsObject(mLastName) Then
      Set LastName = mLastName
   Else
      Let LastName = mLastName
```


continues

Listing 9.1. continued

```
   End If
End Property

'##ModelId=340B896A0136
Public Property Let LastName(Value As Variant)
   Let mLastName = Value
End Property

'##ModelId=340B896901AE
Public Property Get First_Name() As Variant
   If IsObject(mFirst_Name) Then
      Set First_Name = mFirst_Name
   Else
      Let First_Name = mFirst_Name
   End If
End Property

'##ModelId=340B89670384
Public Property Let First_Name(Value As Variant)
   Let mFirst_Name = Value
End Property

'##ModelId=340B72FA03CA
Private Sub Class_Terminate()
    #If DebugMode Then
    'the class is being destroyed
        Debug.Print "'" & TypeName(Me) & "' instance " & CStr(mlClassDebugID) _
          & " is terminating"
    #End If
End Sub

'##ModelId=340B72FA0172
Private Sub Class_Initialize()
    #If DebugMode Then
        'get the next available class ID, and print out
        'that the class was created successfully
        mlClassDebugID = GetNextClassDebugID()
        Debug.Print "'" & TypeName(Me) & "' instance " & CStr(mlClassDebugID) _
          & " created"
    #End If
End Sub

'##ModelId=33E6AE4C0294
Public Function establish()
    On Error GoTo establishErr

    'your code goes here...
    If attributesHaveValues Then
        establish = True
    End If
    Exit Function
establishErr:
    Call RaiseError(MyUnhandledError, "Customer:establish Method")
End Function

'##ModelId=33E6AE68030C
```

```
Public Sub verify()
    On Error GoTo verifyErr

    'your code goes here...

    Exit Sub
verifyErr:
    Call RaiseError(MyUnhandledError, "Customer:verify Method")
End Sub

#If DebugMode Then
    '##ModelId=340B72F703B6
    Public Property Get ClassDebugID() As Long
        'if we are in debug mode, surface this property that consumers can query
        ClassDebugID = mlClassDebugID
    End Property
#End If
VERSION 5.00
Begin VB.Form frmTellerSystem
   BorderStyle     =   3  'Fixed Dialog
   Caption         =   "Samsona Bank Teller System"
   ClientHeight    =   5670
   ClientLeft      =   45
   ClientTop       =   330
   ClientWidth     =   9300
   LinkTopic       =   "Form1"
   MaxButton       =   0   'False
   MinButton       =   0   'False
   ScaleHeight     =   5670
   ScaleWidth      =   9300
   ShowInTaskbar   =   0   'False
   StartUpPosition =   3   'Windows Default
   Begin VB.CommandButton cmdClose
      Caption         =   "Close Account"
      Height          =   375
      Left            =   2400
      TabIndex        =   36
      Top             =   5040
      Width           =   1215
   End
   Begin VB.CommandButton cmdOpen
      Caption         =   "Open Account"
      Height          =   375
      Left            =   120
      TabIndex        =   35
      Top             =   5040
      Width           =   1215
   End
   Begin VB.CommandButton cmdProcessTrans
      Caption         =   "Do Transaction"
      Height          =   375
      Left            =   5040
      TabIndex        =   34
      Top             =   5040
      Width           =   1215
   End
   Begin VB.CommandButton cmdDone
      Caption         =   "Done"
```


continues

Listing 9.1. continued

```
      Height          =   375
      Left            =   7560
      TabIndex        =   33
      Top             =   5040
      Width           =   1215
   End
   Begin VB.Frame Frame1
      Caption         =   "Account Information"
      Height          =   1215
      Index           =   1
      Left            =   120
      TabIndex        =   21
      Top             =   3720
      Width           =   8655
      Begin VB.Frame Frame2
         Height          =   975
         Left            =   5280
         TabIndex        =   28
         Top             =   120
         Width           =   3135
         Begin VB.OptionButton optTransactionType
            Caption         =   "Deposit"
            Height          =   255
            Index           =   1
            Left            =   1680
            TabIndex        =   32
            Top             =   630
            Width           =   1215
         End
         Begin VB.OptionButton optTransactionType
            Caption         =   "Withdrawal"
            Height          =   255
            Index           =   0
            Left            =   1680
            TabIndex        =   31
            Top             =   360
            Width           =   1335
         End
         Begin VB.TextBox txtNewAccount
            Height          =   375
            Index           =   14
            Left            =   120
            TabIndex        =   29
            Top             =   480
            Width           =   1455
         End
         Begin VB.Label lblNewAccount
            Caption         =   "Transaction Amount"
            Height          =   255
            Index           =   16
            Left            =   120
            TabIndex        =   30
            Top             =   240
            Width           =   1455
         End
      End
```

```
      Begin VB.TextBox txtNewAccount
         Height          =   375
         Index           =   11
         Left            =   240
         TabIndex        =   24
         Top             =   600
         Width           =   1815
      End
      Begin VB.TextBox txtNewAccount
         Height          =   375
         Index           =   12
         Left            =   2160
         TabIndex        =   23
         Top             =   600
         Width           =   1455
      End
      Begin VB.TextBox txtNewAccount
         Height          =   375
         Index           =   13
         Left            =   3840
         TabIndex        =   22
         Top             =   600
         Width           =   1335
      End
      Begin VB.Label lblNewAccount
         Caption         =   "Account Number"
         Height          =   255
         Index           =   19
         Left            =   240
         TabIndex        =   27
         Top             =   360
         Width           =   1815
      End
      Begin VB.Label lblNewAccount
         Caption         =   "Account Status"
         Height          =   255
         Index           =   18
         Left            =   2280
         TabIndex        =   26
         Top             =   360
         Width           =   1215
      End
      Begin VB.Label lblNewAccount
         Caption         =   "Current Balance"
         Height          =   255
         Index           =   17
         Left            =   3840
         TabIndex        =   25
         Top             =   360
         Width           =   1215
      End
   End
   Begin VB.Frame Frame1
      Caption         =   "Customer Information"
      Height          =   3495
      Index           =   0
      Left            =   120
      TabIndex        =   0
```


continues

Listing 9.1. continued

```
Top                 =   120
Width               =   8655
Begin VB.TextBox txtNewAccount
   Height           =   375
   Index            =   10
   Left             =   5880
   TabIndex         =   37
   Top              =   1440
   Width            =   2295
End
Begin VB.TextBox txtNewAccount
   Height           =   375
   Index            =   9
   Left             =   3600
   TabIndex         =   19
   Top              =   2880
   Width            =   3135
End
Begin VB.TextBox txtNewAccount
   Height           =   375
   Index            =   8
   Left             =   240
   TabIndex         =   9
   Top              =   2880
   Width            =   3135
End
Begin VB.TextBox txtNewAccount
   Height           =   375
   Index            =   7
   Left             =   4800
   TabIndex         =   8
   Top              =   2160
   Width            =   975
End
Begin VB.TextBox txtNewAccount
   Height           =   375
   Index            =   6
   Left             =   3600
   TabIndex         =   7
   Top              =   2160
   Width            =   975
End
Begin VB.TextBox txtNewAccount
   Height           =   375
   Index            =   5
   Left             =   240
   TabIndex         =   6
   Top              =   2160
   Width            =   3135
End
Begin VB.TextBox txtNewAccount
   Height           =   375
   Index            =   4
   Left             =   240
   TabIndex         =   5
   Top              =   1440
   Width            =   4935
```

```
End
Begin VB.TextBox txtNewAccount
   Height          =   375
   Index           =   3
   Left            =   6720
   TabIndex        =   4
   Top             =   600
   Width           =   1455
End
Begin VB.TextBox txtNewAccount
   Height          =   375
   Index           =   2
   Left            =   4080
   TabIndex        =   3
   Top             =   600
   Width           =   2535
End
Begin VB.TextBox txtNewAccount
   Height          =   375
   Index           =   1
   Left            =   2160
   TabIndex        =   2
   Top             =   600
   Width           =   1815
End
Begin VB.TextBox txtNewAccount
   Height          =   375
   Index           =   0
   Left            =   240
   TabIndex        =   1
   Top             =   600
   Width           =   1815
End
Begin VB.Label lblNewAccount
   Caption         =   "Social Security Number"
   Height          =   255
   Index           =   10
   Left            =   5880
   TabIndex        =   38
   Top             =   1200
   Width           =   2295
End
Begin VB.Label lblNewAccount
   Caption         =   "Phone"
   Height          =   255
   Index           =   9
   Left            =   3600
   TabIndex        =   20
   Top             =   2640
   Width           =   1095
End
Begin VB.Label lblNewAccount
   Caption         =   "Country"
   Height          =   255
   Index           =   8
   Left            =   240
   TabIndex        =   18
```


continues

Listing 9.1. continued

```
      Top             =   2640
      Width           =   1095
   End
   Begin VB.Label lblNewAccount
      Caption         =   "Zip Code"
      Height          =   255
      Index           =   7
      Left            =   4800
      TabIndex        =   17
      Top             =   1920
      Width           =   975
   End
   Begin VB.Label lblNewAccount
      Caption         =   "State"
      Height          =   255
      Index           =   6
      Left            =   3600
      TabIndex        =   16
      Top             =   1920
      Width           =   855
   End
   Begin VB.Label lblNewAccount
      Caption         =   "City"
      Height          =   255
      Index           =   5
      Left            =   240
      TabIndex        =   15
      Top             =   1920
      Width           =   1095
   End
   Begin VB.Label lblNewAccount
      Caption         =   "Address"
      Height          =   255
      Index           =   4
      Left            =   240
      TabIndex        =   14
      Top             =   1200
      Width           =   1095
   End
   Begin VB.Label lblNewAccount
      Caption         =   "Date of Birth"
      Height          =   255
      Index           =   3
      Left            =   6720
      TabIndex        =   13
      Top             =   360
      Width           =   1455
   End
   Begin VB.Label lblNewAccount
      Caption         =   "Last Name"
      Height          =   255
      Index           =   2
      Left            =   4080
      TabIndex        =   12
      Top             =   360
      Width           =   1215
   End
```

```
        Begin VB.Label lblNewAccount
           Caption         =   "Middle Name"
           Height          =   255
           Index           =   1
           Left            =   2160
           TabIndex        =   11
           Top             =   360
           Width           =   1215
        End
        Begin VB.Label lblNewAccount
           Caption         =   "First Name"
           Height          =   255
           Index           =   0
           Left            =   240
           TabIndex        =   10
           Top             =   360
           Width           =   1095
        End
     End
  End
  Attribute VB_Name = "frmTellerSystem"
  Attribute VB_GlobalNameSpace = False
  Attribute VB_Creatable = False
  Attribute VB_PredeclaredId = True
  Attribute VB_Exposed = False
  Private Sub cmdClose_Click()
      theAccount.closeAccount
  End Sub

  Private Sub cmdDone_Click()
      End
  End Sub

  Private Sub cmdOpen_Click()
      theAccount.openAccount
  End Sub

  Private Sub cmdProcessTrans_Click()
      theAccount.processTrans txtNewAccount(14), optTransactionType
  End Sub

  Private Sub Command1_Click()

  End Sub

  Private Sub lblNewAccount_Click(Index As Integer)

  End Sub

  Private Sub txtNewAccount_Change(Index As Integer)
      theCustomer.First_Name = txtNewAccount(0)
      theCustomer.MiddleName = txtNewAccount(1)
      theCustomer.LastName = txtNewAccount(2)
      theCustomer.DOB = txtNewAccount(3)
      theCustomer.Address = txtNewAccount(4)
      theCustomer.SSN = txtNewAccount(10)
      theCustomer.City = txtNewAccount(5)
      theCustomer.State = txtNewAccount(6)
```

continues

Listing 9.1. continued

```
    theCustomer.Zip = txtNewAccount(7)
    theCustomer.Country = txtNewAccount(8)
    theCustomer.Phone = txtNewAccount(9)

    theAccount.pNumber = txtNewAccount(11)
    theAccount.pStatus = txtNewAccount(12)
    theAccount.pCurrBalance = txtNewAccount(13)
    theAccount = txtNewAccount(14)
End Sub

Attribute VB_Name = "modClasses"
Global theAccount As Account
Global allBankAccounts As BankAccounts
Global theCheckingAccountHistoryInfo As CheckingAccountHistoryInfo
Global theCreditHistoryInfo As CreditHistoryInfo
Global theCustomer As Customer
Global theTellerInterface As Teller_Interface

Public Enum eTransOption
    deposit
    withdrawal
End Enum
```

As you may have noticed, more code is added to the example than previously anticipated. That's normal. When you're elaborating on the body of code, you'll add code to make the system work smoothly. The idea is to add the code in an object-oriented way: methods belong to classes that make sense, there is very little use of global variables (preferably none at all), there are edit checks for required fields, and there are sanity checks for significant business processes (such as closing accounts).

CAUTION

The references to model numbers are for Visual Modeler. Don't mess with these values; otherwise, your model won't work properly.

Summary

In this chapter, you learned the essence of object-oriented programming in Visual Basic 5. In other words, you learned how to make classes communicate with each other to carry out a behavior or set of behaviors for a proposed system. You also became familiar with design models and the importance of not deviating from the architecture of the system. You received some background on generating code in Rational Rose and Visual Modeler and on identifying the known technical constraints of Visual Basic. After you generated some example code, you got an idea of how to put the finishing touches on the application and saw a sample listing.

Data Structures, Collections, and Enumerations

IN THIS CHAPTER

One of the keys to efficient programming is to organize your data in such a way that makes performing operations on it easier. Just as structuring programs in a modular fashion helps you create programs that are easier to understand, structuring data in a modular fashion helps you control the complexity of the problem you are trying to solve.

Although programmers sometimes deal with singular data objects that exist on their own with no relation to other data, they typically work with compound data objects made up of several different data types. For example, a human resources system tracks data associated with a company's employees. The kinds of data associated with employee records include items such as name, Social Security number, department, salary, years of employment, date of hire, and so on. This single data object, the employee record, consists of several data types—strings, dates, integers, and currency. These kinds of data are best structured as a group of data types combined into one, larger compound data type. Visual Basic provides the *user-defined type (UDT)* to create this data structure.

Other kinds of data are best stored as a higher-level group. For example, the employees in the human resources system can all be grouped together and dealt with as a collection of employees. You can then reference each employee individually without knowing that employee's name. For example, to implement an across-the-board pay increase, a procedure can access the collection of employees and deal with them as a whole. The *collection* structure in Visual Basic allows the programmer to create this type of grouping.

Sometimes you want to give particular names to data that actually mean something else. For example, if you need to track the days of the week by number, it is easier for someone maintaining a piece of code to see the days named Monday, Tuesday, Wednesday, and so on, rather than 1, 2, 3, 4.... Visual Basic's special data type for this kind of data is the *enumeration*.

User-Defined Types

Most of the data objects programmers manipulate in their programs are compound in nature. An accounts receivable program tracks customer accounts that consist of many parts—customer name, account balance, terms of payment, address, and so on. If each part of the customer account was kept in a separate variable, keeping track of all the variables of a medium- to large-size project would soon become a nightmare. Visual Basic provides a powerful way to create and work with compound data objects—the user-defined type (UDT).

Creating a User-Defined Type

A UDT is created by using the `Type...End Type` statement. In the following example, several elements of different data types (strings, integers, and currency) combine to form a new data type called `udtCustomerRecord`:

```
Public Type udtCustomerRecord
    strName As String
    strAddress1 As String
```

```
    strAddress2 As String
    strCity As String
    strState As String
    strZip As String
    intDiscountPercent As Integer
    intGracePeriodDays As Integer
    curAccountBalance As Currency
    curYTDPurchases As Currency
    strTerms as String
End Type
```

UDTs are defined in the `Declarations` section of a module, and they can be either `Public` or `Private` in scope. All of Visual Basic's data types can be used as elements of a UDT. You can even use an array as a UDT element. This UDT definition acts as a kind of "blueprint" with which you can declare one or more UDT variables:

```
Dim udtCust01 as udtCustomerRecord
```

To add actual data to the elements of a UDT, you use a form called dotted notation. This means that to access an individual element of the UDT, you preface its name with that of the name of the variable you've defined as a UDT, plus a period:

```
udtCust01.strName = "John Smith"
udtCust01.strAddress1 = "3234 W. 25th Street"
udtCust01.curAccountBalance = 325.37
udtCust01.curInvoiceTotal = 1425.28
```

Using UDTs

The individual elements of a UDT can be treated the same way as any other variable. For example, you could use the `curAccountBalance` element of the UDT defined earlier in an equation, such as:

```
curTotalOfAllAccounts = curTotalOfAllAccounts + udtCust01.curAccountBalance
```

Or, you could transfer the value of a UDT element to another variable of the same data type:

```
strCustomerName = udtCust01.strName
```

In some cases, you can also use the UDT variable as a whole. If you have two variables that have each been declared as the same user-defined type, you can assign the values of one UDT to another:

```
udtCust02 = udtCust01
```

The data elements of `udtCust02` now contain the same values as the elements of `udtCust01`. If `udtCust01.Name` had the value of "John Smith," then `udtCust02.Name` would now equal "John Smith," and so on.

Finally, you can create an array of a user-defined type:

```
Dim udtCustomers(100) as udtCustomerRecord
```

You would then refer to the udtCustomers array just as you would any other array. For example, to assign values to the Name and Address1 data elements of the first element in the array, you would use code similar to the following:

```
udtCustomers(0).Name = "John Smith"
udtCustomers(0).Address1 = "3234 W. 25th Street"
```

Enumerations

A second type of data structure provided by Visual Basic is the enumeration. The best way to define an enumeration is by providing an example of one. Suppose that you are writing a program that needs to track the day of the week. Many decision points in the program key off of which day of the week it is. The first scheme you imagine is to simply use numbers to represent the days of the week: 1, 2, 3, 4, 5, 6, and 7. This works fine for a small program. For a large, complex program, however, it becomes more difficult for the programmer who wrote the code, or for a programmer who comes in later to maintain the code, to understand what all the 1s and 3s and 5s mean.

A better solution to this problem is to use the names of the days of the week:

```
If intDayOfWeek = Friday Then
   txtGreeting.Text = "Thank Goodness!"
End If
```

There can be no confusion over what the variable represents. Providing a way to name numerical values used in a program is an important tool in the battle of code complexity.

The Enum Statement

The statement used to create an enumeration data type is the Enum statement. Here is the syntax:

```
[Public¦Private] Enum name
   membername [= constantexpression]
   membername [= constantexpression]
   ...
End Enum
```

The optional Public and Private declarations define the scope of the enumeration type (by default, enumerations are Public). The *name* parameter is required to give a name to the enumeration type.

One or more *membername* identifiers specify the constituents of the enumeration type. Each identifier can also be assigned an optional value (*constantexpression*). If no value is given, the identifier is assigned a value of one greater than its preceding identifier in the enumeration type. If the identifier is the first item in the Enum and no value is given, it is assigned a value of zero.

Enum types are always defined at the module level, and they can never be empty.

Here is an enum statement where the *membernames* are assigned values explicitly in the code:

```
Public Enum ColdMonths
   January = 1
   February = 2
   November = 11
   December = 12
End Enum
```

If no values were assigned to the enumeration's identifiers, such as in the following code:

```
Public Enum ColdMonths
   January
   February
   November
   December
End Enum
```

January is assigned a value of 0, February is 1, November is 2, and December is 3. This is the normal behavior of the Enum statement. As you can see, it may be necessary to assign values to the identifiers of the enumerated type to get the results you really want. There are some shortcuts, however. The ColdMonths enumeration can be defined in this way:

```
Public Enum ColdMonths
   January = 1
   February
   November = 11
   December
End Enum
```

This accomplishes the exact same thing as the first sample Enum statement. January is assigned a value of 1. Because February does not have a value assigned to it, it gets one more than January (2). November gets a value of 11, and December gets one more than that (12).

If you want to use more than one word in your identifier name, enclose the name in brackets.

```
Public Enum ColdMonths
    [No Month Selected] = 0
    January = 1
    February
    November = 11
    December
End Enum
```

After you've defined an enumeration type, you can assign it to a variable. For example:

```
Public PickAMonth As ColdMonths
```

Although you can still assign any value to the PickAMonth variable, you do get a helpful pop-up window listing the identifiers in the ColdMonths enumeration type whenever you assign a value to PickAMonth in design mode (see Figure 10.1).

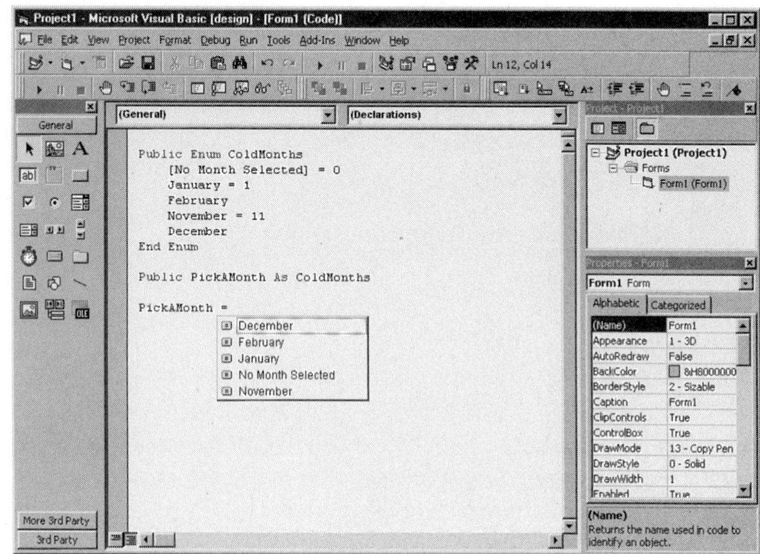

FIGURE 10.1.
A pop-up window appears when you assign a value to an enumerated variable in design mode.

Enumerations really come in handy when you're creating a list of possible values for an ActiveX control property. Chapter 19, "Advanced ActiveX Control Creation," shows examples of using enumerations for that purpose.

Collections

Another advanced data structure provided by Visual Basic is the collection. A collection is an ordered set of items that can be referenced as one unit. The Visual Basic programming environment has several collections that are used to organize its many elements. For example, all the controls on a form make up the Controls collection. Likewise, all the forms loaded into memory are contained in the Forms collection.

Because collections are ordered, you can refer to the individual members of the collection by number. You may already be aware that each control on a form has an `Index` property, but you may not know that that property actually indicates the location of the control in the form's Controls collection. Therefore, if you have a CommandButton control on the form called `cmdClickMe` and its `Index` property is `3`, you can change its `Caption` property using the following line of code:

```
Controls(3).Caption = "Click Here"
```

Although this is a rather simple example, it does show how a collection's member can be referred to by its index number. You may think that collections are similar to arrays, and in this way they are. But as you'll see later in this chapter, there are some important differences between collections and arrays.

NOTE

Collections can be either *zero-based* or *one-based*. If the indexing of a collection's members begins with zero, it is zero-based; if it begins with one, it is one-based. Although any collections that you define yourself will be one-based, some of those that are built into Visual Basic may be zero-based. For example, the `Forms` and `Controls` collections are both zero-based.

Collection Properties

Actually, collections only have one property—`Count`. This read-only property returns a long integer number of the total members in a collection. Knowing the `Count` of a collection is useful when you want to perform an operation on all the members in a collection, but you aren't sure exactly how many there are.

For example, if you wanted to move every control on a form to the leftmost side, you could use the following code:

```
Dim lonColIndex As Long

For lonColIndex = 0 To frmMain.Controls.Count - 1
   frmMain.Controls(lonColIndex).Left = 0
Next lonColIndex
```

Note that with the preceding code, the number of controls on the form is irrelevant—it could be one, or it could be a hundred. The code will work just as well in either case.

A more efficient variation of the `For...Next` loop is the `For Each...Next` loop. Use a `For Each...Next` loop with collections when you want to iterate through each and every item in the collection. To use this loop, create a variable of type Variant that will hold each collection object as the loop progresses through the collection. The actual processing is performed on the variable, acting as a proxy for the collection object. Here is a program that adds the name of the font of each control in `frmMain`'s Controls collection into a ListBox called `lstFontNames`:

```
Dim varTempControl As Variant

For Each varTempControl In frmMain.Controls
   lstFontNames.AddItem varTempControl.Font
Next
```

When processing collections using a `For...Next` or `For Each...Next` loop, you can be more selective about which controls you want to include with the `TypeOf` keyword. For example, if you wanted to modify the preceding program so that only those controls of type CommandButton have their font names added to the ListBox, you could use the `TypeOf` keyword as shown here:

```
Dim varTempControl As Variant
```

```
For Each varTempControl In frmMain.Controls
   If varTempControl TypeOf CommandButton Then
      lstFontNames.AddItem varTempControl.Font
   End If
Next
```

Collection Methods

Visual Basic provides three methods to add, remove, and reference the members in a collection. These properties are `Add`, `Remove`, and `Item`.

The Add Method

To add a member to a collection, use the `Add` method, which has the following syntax:

`object``.Add (`*`item, [, key][, before][, after])`*

The various components of the `Add` method's syntax are described in Table 10.1.

Table 10.1. The components of the Add method's syntax.

Component	*Description*	*Example*
`object`	The name of a Visual Basic collection or the name of a collection created by the programmer.	`colContacts`
`item`	The name of the object that will be added to the collection.	`objSalesperson`
`key`	A unique string that can be used later to identify the item being added. Optional.	`"ECampbell"`
`before`	Specifies the collection member (either by index or by key) before which the item is to be inserted. Optional.	`5` `"Jones"`
`after`	Specifies the collection member (either by index or by key) after which the item is to be inserted. Optional.	`3` `"Smith"`

If you want to add a single object called `objSalesperson` to a collection of objects called `colContacts`, you might use the following line of code:

```
colContacts.Add objSalesperson
```

Actually, the object itself is not added to the collection, but instead a *reference* to the object is added. Collections don't actually store objects; they store references. When you remove an object from a collection (by using the `Remove` method, as you'll see in just a moment), you are really only destroying the reference to the object.

The `Remove` Method

To delete an item from a collection, use the `Remove` method, which has the following syntax (detailed in Table 10.2):

```
object.Remove index
```

Table 10.2. The components of the `Remove` method's syntax.

Component	*Description*	*Example*
`object`	The name of a Visual Basic collection or the name of a collection created by the programmer.	`colContacts`
`index`	The index number or key of the collection member that is to be removed.	`12` `"FNewkirk"`

As stated in the previous section, removing an object from a collection only destroys the collection's reference to that object; it does not destroy the object itself. Of course, if no other reference to the object exists, the object is for all intents and purposes destroyed.

You must be careful when removing items from a collection because Visual Basic will give you an error if you attempt to use an invalid index. If you don't have the proper error handling to trap for this error, your program will crash.

The `Item` Method

To reference a specific item of a collection, use the `Item` method, which has the following syntax (detailed in Table 10.3):

```
object.Item(index)
```

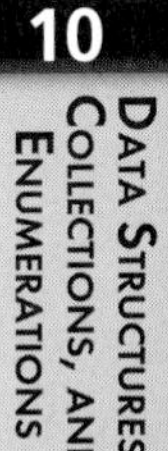

Table 10.3. The components of the `Item` method's syntax.

Component	*Description*	*Example*
`object`	The name of a Visual Basic collection or the name of a collection created by the programmer.	`colContacts`
`index`	The index number or key of the collection member that is to be referenced.	`7` `"GSmith"`

`Item` is the default method of a collection, so you do not have to use it when you want to reference an item in the collection, as in

```
Set objContact = colContacts(1)
```

This code assigns the first object member in the collection (position 1) to the `objContact` object. Another way of coding the same thing is

```
Set objContact = colContacts.Item(1)
```

Adding and Removing from a Collection

The following sample program (`Ch1001`) illustrates adding objects to and removing objects from collections. It uses a collection of employees (`colEmployees`) that consists of objects of the `clsEmployeeInfo` class, a simple user-defined class that has three properties: `FirstName`, `LastName`, and `SSN` (Social Security number).

The top portion of the program's form facilitates the creation of new `clsEmployeeInfo` objects and their addition to the `colEmployees` collection. The bottom portion of the form contains a ListBox that lists all the objects in `colEmployees`. These objects can be selected from the ListBox and, with the click of a button, removed from the collection.

Table 10.4 lists the various properties for the form and the controls that make up the sample program's interface. First create a new project and change the form's properties to those shown in the table. Then add the controls to the form and change their properties so that they correspond to what is shown in Table 10.4. When you're finished, the program's interface should look something like the one shown in Figure 10.2.

Table 10.4. The controls and properties that make up program `Ch1001`'s user interface.

Control Type	*Property*	*Value*
Form	`Name`	`frmMain`
	`Caption`	`Collections Demo - Chapter 10`

Control Type	*Property*	*Value*
	`Height`	`4605`
	`StartUpPosition`	`2 - CenterScreen`
	`Width`	`8685`
Label	`Name`	`lblEmployeeName`
	`Caption`	`Employee Name:`
	`Font`	`MS Sans Serif 12pt`
	`Height`	`315`
	`Left`	`240`
	`Top`	`450`
	`Width`	`2085`
Label	`Name`	`lblFirstName`
	`Caption`	`First`
	`Height`	`255`
	`Left`	`255`
	`Top`	`870`
	`Width`	`330`
TextBox	`Name`	`txtFirstName`
	`Height`	`285`
	`Left`	`780`
	`Text`	(Nothing)
	`Top`	`825`
	`Width`	`1965`
Label	`Name`	`lblLastName`
	`Caption`	`Last`
	`Height`	`255`
	`Left`	`2970`
	`Top`	`870`
	`Width`	`330`
TextBox	`Name`	`txtLastName`
	`Height`	`285`
	`Left`	`3450`
	`Text`	(Nothing)
	`Top`	`825`
	`Width`	`1860`

continues

Table 10.4. continued

Control Type	*Property*	*Value*
Label	`Name`	`lblSSN`
	`Caption`	`Social Security Number:`
	`Font`	`MS Sans Serif 12pt`
	`Height`	`315`
	`Left`	`225`
	`Top`	`1290`
	`Width`	`2895`
TextBox	`Name`	`txtSSN`
	`Height`	`285`
	`Left`	`3450`
	`Text`	(Nothing)
	`Top`	`1290`
	`Width`	`1860`
CommandButton	`Name`	`cmdAddEmployee`
	`Caption`	`Add Employee`
	`Height`	`375`
	`Left`	`6075`
	`Top`	`810`
	`Width`	`1770`
Line	`Name`	`linDivider`
	`X1`	`240`
	`X2`	`8475`
	`Y1`	`2025`
	`Y2`	`2025`
ListBox	`Name`	`lstEmployeeNames`
	`Font`	`Courier 10pt`
	`Height`	`1620`
	`Left`	`240`
	`Top`	`2520`
	`Width`	`5085`
Label	`Name`	`lblCollectionName`
	`Alignment`	`1 - Right Justify`
	`Caption`	`Name`
	`Height`	`255`
	`Left`	`5535`
	`Top`	`2565`
	`Width`	`435`

Control Type	Property	Value
TextBox	Name	txtCollectionName
	Enabled	False
	Height	285
	Left	6060
	Text	(Nothing)
	Top	2535
	Width	2400
Label	Name	lblCollectionSSN
	Alignment	1 - Right Justify
	Caption	SSN
	Height	255
	Left	5520
	Top	2985
	Width	435
TextBox	Name	txtCollectionSSN
	Enabled	False
	Height	285
	Left	6060
	Text	(Nothing)
	Top	2925
	Width	2400
Label	Name	lblCollectionKey
	Alignment	1 - Right Justify
	Caption	Key
	Height	255
	Left	5520
	Top	3375
	Width	435
TextBox	Name	txtCollectionKey
	Enabled	False
	Height	285
	Left	6060
	Text	(Nothing)
	Top	3330
	Width	2400
CommandButton	Name	cmdDeleteEmployee
	Caption	Delete Employee
	Height	330
	Left	6075
	Top	3750
	Width	2370

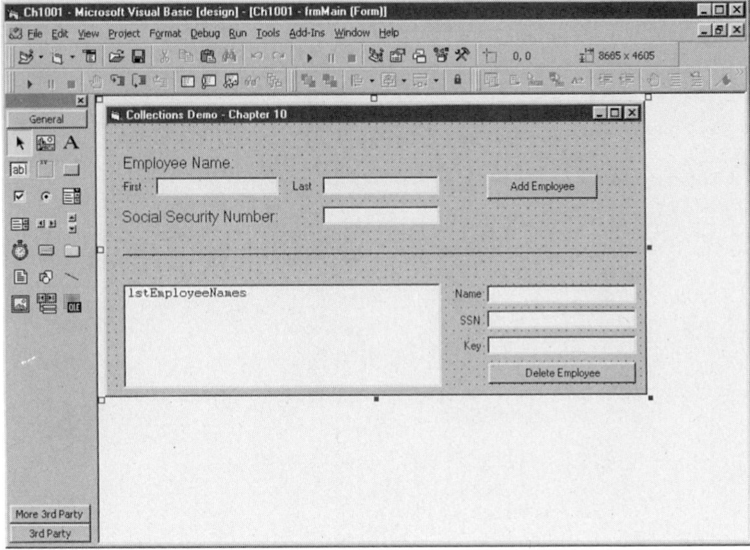

FIGURE 10.2.
Program `Ch1001`'s interface.

After the program's interface is completed, you can start adding its code. Listing 10.1 shows all the code for the `Ch1001` program.

Listing 10.1. Code for the Ch1001 program, which illustrates adding and removing objects from a collection.

```
Public Enum OrderOptions
    LastNameFirst = 1
    FirstNameFirst = 2
End Enum

Public OrderFlag As OrderOptions
Public colEmployees As New Collection


Private Sub cmdAddEmployee_Click()

Dim strEmployeeName As String
Dim strListItem As String
Dim strUniqueKey As String

' Set OrderFlag, which indicates how the employee's
' name will be shown in the ListBox.
OrderFlag = FirstNameFirst

' Verify that all of the information has been
' entered.
If txtFirstName.Text = "" Or txtLastName.Text = "" Then
    MsgBox "Please enter a first and last name."
    Exit Sub
End If
```

```
If txtSSN.Text = "" Then
    MsgBox "Please enter a Social Security number."
    Exit Sub
End If

' Create a unique key for the employee that consists
' of his/her last and first names.
strUniqueKey = Left$(txtFirstName.Text, 1) _
    + Left$(txtLastName.Text, 1) _
    + Right$("0000" + Right$(txtSSN.Text, 4), 4)

Set objEmployee = New clsEmployeeInfo

' Move the newly-entered employee information to
' the properties of the objEmployee object.
objEmployee.FirstName = txtFirstName.Text
objEmployee.LastName = txtLastName.Text
objEmployee.SSN = txtSSN.Text

' Add the employee name (in the order specified by
' OrderFlag) to the ListBox.
strListItem = strUniqueKey + Space$(2)
If OrderFlag = LastNameFirst Then
    strListItem = strListItem _
        + RTrim$(txtLastName.Text) + ", " _
        + txtFirstName.Text
Else
    strListItem = strListItem _
        + RTrim$(txtFirstName.Text) + "," _
        + txtLastName.Text
End If
lstEmployeeNames.AddItem strListItem

' Add the objEmployee object and the unique key
' to the colEmployees collection.
colEmployees.Add objEmployee, strUniqueKey

' Blank out the input fields so more employees
' can be entered and set the focus back to the
' first input field.
txtFirstName.Text = ""
txtLastName.Text = ""
txtSSN.Text = ""
txtFirstName.SetFocus

End Sub


Private Sub cmdDeleteEmployee_Click()

Dim strUniqueKey As String

' Make sure the user has selected an employee from
' the ListBox.
If lstEmployeeNames.ListIndex = -1 Then
    MsgBox "Please select an employee to delete."
    Exit Sub
End If
```


continues

Listing 10.1. continued

```
' Get the unique key from the ListBox, then use it
' to remove the member from the collection.
strUniqueKey = Left$(lstEmployeeNames.List(lstEmployeeNames.ListIndex), 6)
colEmployees.Remove strUniqueKey

' Remove the key from the ListBox, too. Then
' update (refresh) the ListBox.
lstEmployeeNames.RemoveItem (lstEmployeeNames.ListIndex)
lstEmployeeNames.Refresh

' Finally, clear out the information in the display
' fields.
txtCollectionName.Text = ""
txtCollectionSSN.Text = ""
txtCollectionKey.Text = ""

End Sub


Private Sub lstEmployeeNames_Click()

Dim objThisEmployee As New clsEmployeeInfo
Dim strUniqueKey As String

' Get the unique key from the ListBox, then use it
' to retrieve the member from the collection.
strUniqueKey = Left$(lstEmployeeNames.List(lstEmployeeNames.ListIndex), 6)
Set objThisEmployee = colEmployees.Item(strUniqueKey)

' Fill in the TextBox objects that are used to
' display the employee information.
txtCollectionName.Text = objThisEmployee.FirstName _
    + Space$(1) + objThisEmployee.LastName
txtCollectionSSN.Text = objThisEmployee.SSN
txtCollectionKey.Text = strUniqueKey

End Sub
```

The only thing left to do is create the `clsEmployeeInfo` class. This requires the addition of a class module to the project. Choose Project | Add Class Module from VB's menu. Double-click the Class Module icon, and you'll see the new class (`Class1`) added to the Project Explorer window. Change the name of the class by clicking on `Class1` in the Project Explorer and then changing the `Name` property in the Properties window to `clsEmployeeInfo`.

Finally, add the code in Listing 10.2 to `clsEmployeeInfo`'s `General Declarations` section. These few lines will define the properties (`FirstName`, `LastName`, and `SSN`) for the new class.

Listing 10.2. Code for `clsEmployeeInfo`'s `General Declarations` section.

```
Public FirstName As String
Public LastName As String
Public SSN As String
```

Now would be a good time to save the project. Use `CH1001.VBP` for the project, `CH1001.FRM` for the form, and `EMPLOYEEINFO.CLS` for the class module.

Run the program and try entering a few employees (see Figure 10.3). When you click the Add Employee button, you should see a new entry in the ListBox at the bottom of the form. The first six characters of each ListBox entry is the unique key for the newly added object. It is created by taking the leftmost characters of the employee's first and last names plus the last four digits of the employee's Social Security number.

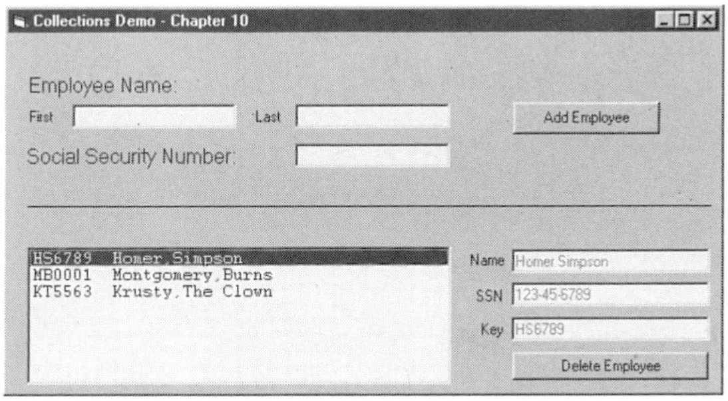

FIGURE 10.3.

The `Ch1001` *program in action: the contents of the* `colEmployees` *collection can be seen in the ListBox at the bottom of the form.*

If you click one of the entries in the ListBox, you'll see that employee's name and Social Security number displayed in the TextBoxes to the right of the ListBox. You'll also see the unique key for the object that was selected. If you click the Delete Employee button, the currently selected object will be removed from the ListBox (and from the `colEmployees` collection).

So how does it work? We'll go through it piece by piece.

Before the code for the various functions and procedures, an `OrderOptions` enumeration is defined. This enumeration contains the two values that can be selected to specify whether employees' names should be display last name first (`LastNameFirst`) or the other way around (`FirstNameFirst`). The `OrderFlag` variable is then declared as the `OrderOptions` enumeration type, indicating that only the two values defined in the enumeration can be stored in `OrderFlag`. Finally, the `colEmployees` collection, which will be used throughout the sample program, is defined as a new collection.

The first section of code is for the `cmdAddEmployee_Click` event. After checking to make sure that some data has really been entered, a unique key is created by using elements from the input values. Next, a new object of the `clsEmployeeInfo` class is created. The properties for this new object are assigned from the corresponding TextBox controls, and a new entry (consisting of the unique key, a few spaces, and the employee's last and first names) is added to the ListBox (`lstEmployeeNames`). The object and its unique key are then added to the `colEmployees` collection using the `Add` method. Finally, the TextBox controls used for input are cleared, and focus is set back to the first TextBox, making the program ready to accept more employees.

The next section of code is for the cmdDeleteEmployee_Click event. It checks to see that an entry has been selected from the ListBox (lstEmployeeNames) and then retrieves the object's unique key from the ListBox entry (remember, the first six characters of each ListBox entry is the unique key). The object is removed from the collection by passing the unique key (temporarily stored in strUniqueKey) to the collection's Remove method. The entry is also removed from the ListBox, and the TextBoxes used to display the employee object's information are cleared.

The final section of code is for the lstEmployeeNames_Click event, which is fired when the user selects an entry from the ListBox (lstEmployeeNames). After retrieving the object's unique key from the ListBox entry and storing it in strUniqueKey, a new object (objThisEmployee) is created. The collection object corresponding to the ListBox entry is referenced using the Item method and is copied to the new objThisEmployee object. The properties of the new object are then copied to the TextBoxes that display the employee information.

Note that in the last section of code, it is not really necessary to create a new object and copy the selected collection object to it. The lstEmployeeNames_Click event could be replaced with this bit of code:

```
Private Sub lstEmployeeNames_Click()

Dim strUniqueKey As String

' Get the unique key from the ListBox.
strUniqueKey = Left$(lstEmployeeNames.List(lstEmployeeNames.ListIndex), 6)

' Fill in the TextBox objects that are used to
' display the employee information.
txtCollectionName.Text = colEmployees(strUniqueKey).FirstName _
    + Space$(1) + colEmployees(strUniqueKey).LastName
txtCollectionSSN.Text = colEmployees(strUniqueKey).SSN
txtCollectionKey.Text = strUniqueKey

End Sub
```

Here, the objThisEmployee object is not defined or used at all. Instead, the properties are read directly from the object in the collection. Although this way of coding is shorter, it does have one drawback: the collection's Item method is invoked three times rather than just once.

Granted, this is a simple program. It doesn't trap for errors, such as the entry of the same employee information twice. But it does show the addition and removal of objects in a collection.

Collections Versus Arrays

Because the objects in a collection can be referenced by an index number, you may think that collections are similar to arrays. In some ways, they are. But don't think of a collection as a glorified array because there are some important differences.

For one thing, whereas arrays can store any kind of Visual Basic variable type (integers, strings, variants, user-defined types, and so on), collections can only contain objects (or, to be more specific, references to objects). In this way, arrays are much easier to work with and are more flexible than collections.

Collections, on the other hand, have something that arrays do not: keyed members. The members of a collection can be designated with a unique key, making retrieval of the collection member quick and easy. Arrays, however, must be looped through sequentially to find a given element and provide no easy way of indexing (a hash table can be used for large arrays, but that requires some coding overhead and takes up a fair amount of memory).

Collections can also be reordered much easier than arrays. When adding an object to a collection, you can specify exactly which position it should occupy. On the flip side, adding an element to the middle of an array requires some extra coding and may be time-consuming and inefficient.

Collections and arrays are different animals, and they should be treated as such. Each has its own strengths and weaknesses, and each serves a different purpose.

Using the Object Browser to View Data Structures

Visual Basic provides a handy utility for viewing the data structures you create in your programs through user-defined types and enumerations. This utility is called the Object Browser, and you can invoke it by choosing View | Object Browser from VB's menu or by pressing the F2 key.

When the Object Browser dialog box is initially displayed, the Project/Library ComboBox defaults to `<All Libraries>`, as shown in Figure 10.4.

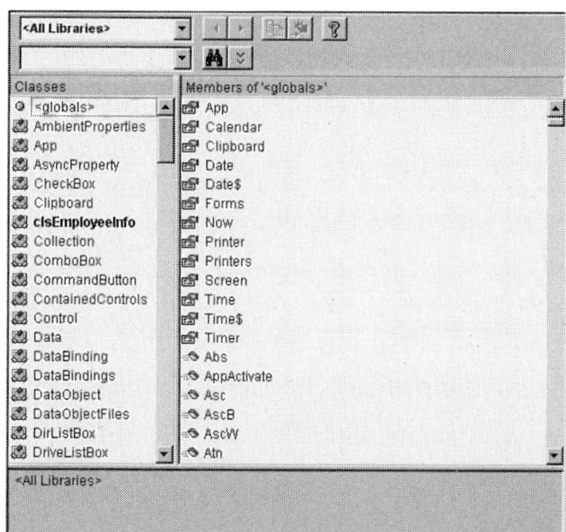

FIGURE 10.4.
The Object Browser's default view.

Below the ComboBoxes are two ListBoxes. The ListBox on the left shows the names of all the classes in the selected library. The ListBox on the right shows the members of the selected class.

By highlighting a class or object type, you can view the properties, methods, and events (the members) of that object. Of course, each type of object (such as a ListBox control or a Printer object) has a different set of properties, methods, and events available to it. Nevertheless, any class or object type available through Visual Basic is visible in the Object Browser.

The default Project/Library selection is `<All Libraries>`, but you can narrow your view by selecting a new value from the Project/Library ComboBox. Figure 10.5 shows the selections available in this example, including `Ch1001`, the sample project from this chapter.

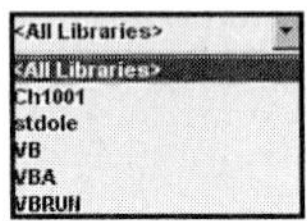

FIGURE 10.5.
Selecting a library to view.

The other selections in the ListBox include

`stdole`	Standard OLE controls and object types
`VB`	Classes and object types in the Visual Basic environment
`VBA`	Classes and object types in the Visual Basic for Applications environment
`VBRUN`	Classes and object types in the Visual Basic runtime environment

Because we are mostly concerned with the objects that have been defined in our project, we'll select `Ch1001` for this example. Figure 10.6 shows that four classes have been defined so far in `Ch1001`:

`<globals>`	
`clsEmployeeInfo`	A user-defined class
`frmMain`	The project's main form
`OrderOptions`	An enumeration type

The Members ListBox shows the properties, methods, events, and identifiers that have been defined as members for the object that is highlighted in the `Classes` ListBox. Notice that the members of the `<globals>` object look familiar. They are the identifiers from the enumeration type `OrderOptions`, which, as you may remember, were defined in the `Global Declarations` section of the same project.

This is where things get pretty neat. Select one of the items in the `Members` ListBox, and you'll see some information about the item appear in the gray area beneath the two ListBoxes. For example, if you click on the `FirstNameFirst` identifier (a member of the `<global>` object), you'll see that it is a member of `Ch1001.frmMain.OrderOptions` (our enumeration type), and that it's a constant (`Const`), and its value is `2`. Try clicking on members from other classes, and you'll quickly see that the Object Browser is an extremely useful tool for examining objects.

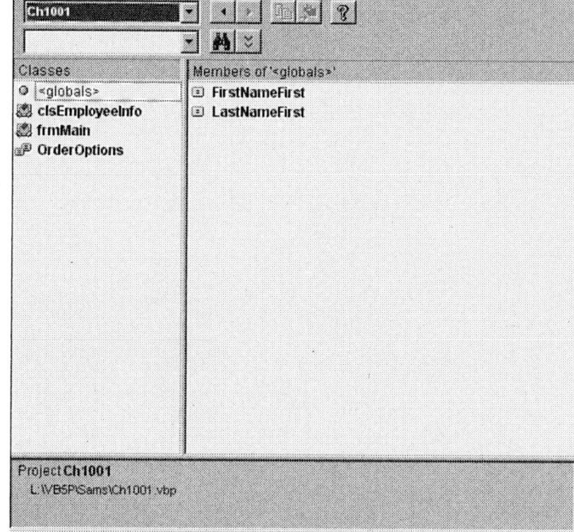

FIGURE 10.6.
The Object Browser displaying classes and objects from the `Ch1001` *project.*

You can go directly from the Object Browser to the code that defines the object by double-clicking the object. If you're unsure of where in your project an object is being defined, this is a handy way of finding out.

Another way to move to the definition of the object in the code is to position the cursor on the object you want to find and then right-click the mouse. You'll see a floating menu like the one shown in Figure 10.7. Choose the View Definition option, and you'll be whisked away to the proper section of code.

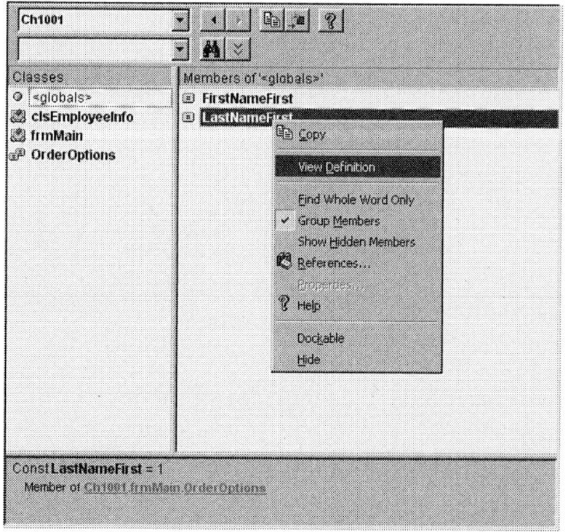

FIGURE 10.7.
The Object Browser floating menu. Choose View Definition to go directly to the object's definition in the Code window.

There is even a third way of viewing an object's definition in the code. Select a member and click the View Definition button (to the left of the question mark button for Help).

Two other important selections from the floating menu are Group Members and Show Hidden Members. When Group Members is checked, the list of members is sorted so that the properties of an object are grouped together, the methods of an object are grouped together, and the events of an object are grouped together. If Group Members is not checked (the default), the properties, methods, and events of an object are displayed in alphabetical order.

When Show Hidden Members is checked, information marked as hidden in the type library is displayed. These items are displayed in light gray type.

Summary

Visual Basic 5 provides strong support for creating data structures for your programming requirements. Providing support for data structures is important because the capability to create easy-to-understand data structures to solve complex programming problems is the key to successful computer programming.

Visual Basic provides three major data structures for the programmer:

- User-defined types
- Collections
- Enumerations

This chapter showed how you can use these data structures to organize complex data into simple structures that can then be used to solve the problem at hand.

11 Reusing and Sharing Components Using the Template Manager and Templates

IN THIS CHAPTER

In previous versions of Visual Basic, it was a hassle to create customized projects and add regularly used classes and code modules. For customized projects, you had to manually edit the sole default project template file, adding the references to components (OCX and DLL files) and other application files used repeatedly for a particular application architecture. If this architecture changed, you had to reconfigure the file for the new files. In the situation where you always added the same class, module, or form to a project, you had to do a file lookup in the File dialog box, browsing through every directory tree until you found it. With the template services provided in Visual Basic 5, this reuse process is better automated.

What Are Templates?

Templates are groups of components saved to a predefined directory structure in the `\VB` directory when you install your VB environment. You might refer to them as *frameworks*. For instance, an automobile maker would have different car frames (templates) for different classes of cars. Whenever an automobile manufacturer makes a car that is made up of a frame H, the automobile maker simply grabs that frame from its supply of body frames and runs it through the assembly line for that car class. Likewise, templates in VB provide a way for you to reuse components and add them to projects. *Component*, in this case, refers not only to OCX controls, but also to the physical file itself. In other words, the physical representation of every object in our application persists beyond the application in the form of files (otherwise known as components). This clarification may seem trivial, but when you use Visual Modeler (which now ships with Visual Studio Enterprise and the Enterprise Edition of Visual Basic 5), this definition becomes helpful when designing component models that show the mapping of application objects to the physical file system.

The Benefits of Using Templates

It's probably a well-known fact that Visual Basic 5 still does not support inheritance in the classic sense of object-oriented inheritance (if that much). Although you can accomplish the benefits of inheritance through delegation (where a method on a client object simply calls a method of a server object to carry out all its own implementation), using VB templates provides a mechanism for simply inserting whole frameworks of classes into a new project. In addition, Microsoft ships the Template Manager to help you with additional automated template reuse for general code, controls, and menus.

Why is reuse so important? Many companies have found that projects developed independently of other enterprise projects seem to cost the company more in the long run. What's more, it costs companies more money than it's worth to try to dig through tons of code in search of salvageable, freestanding functions. This code mining process doubles where the code is spaghetti code. *Spaghetti code* is a body of programming code that lacks structure and organization and is only understandable to the programmer who created it. Spaghetti code is the most prevalent artifact of the programming process today and has led to many failed projects and monetary waste as a result of the inability to reuse such code. With well-designed class modules, menu controls, and projects readily available in the \TEMPLATE subdirectory, your managers and clients will enjoy the increased productivity and lower costs that such reuse practices bring about. Each successive project becomes more productive and less costly because reusable classes, components, and projects have been identified and more effectively archived for easier access.

Using Templates for the First Time

It's easy to use templates. The first thing you should do is become familiar with the \TEMPLATE subdirectory of Visual Basic. Figure 11.1 shows a typical directory structure you get when you install Visual Basic (except for CODE, MENUS, and CONTROLS, which we'll discuss later).

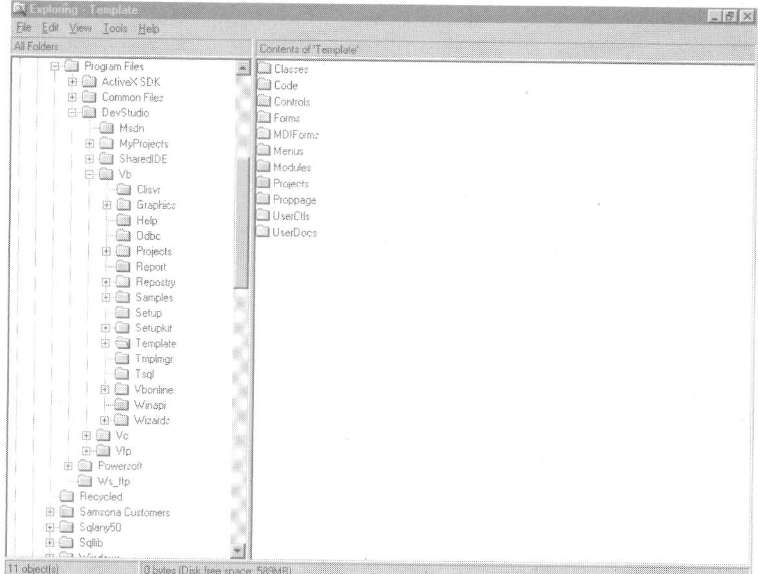

FIGURE 11.1.
For each type of template supported by Visual Basic, there is a corresponding folder (or subdirectory) under \VB\TEMPLATE.

The Template Folders

Each folder under \TEMPLATE is, in a sense, a type of template you can implement. Thus, the following types of templates are part of your reuse arsenal:

- Class
- Code
- Forms
- MDI forms
- Modules
- Projects
- Proppage (a property page template for your ActiveX controls)

- User controls
- User documents

A View of Templates in VB

When you run Visual Basic, the Projects list of templates displays on the screen by default (see Figure 11.2).

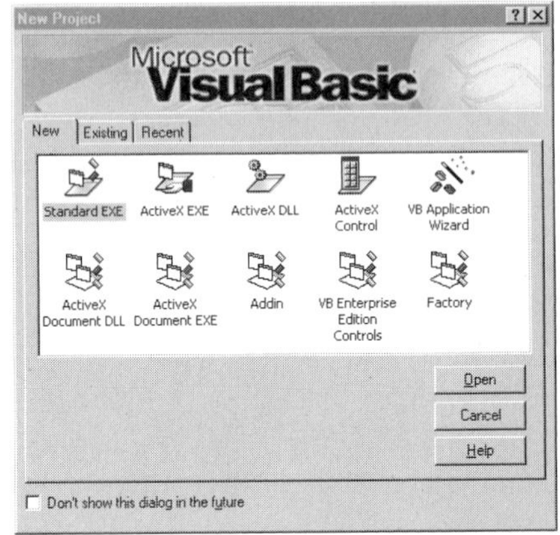

FIGURE 11.2.
A list of project templates displays when you first run Visual Basic.

To view this list, simply run Visual Basic the way you normally run it. The New Project dialog box displays. Notice the series of project template icons. Now click the Cancel button. We're going to add our own project template using one of the sample projects provided in Visual Basic. Go to the main Visual Basic directory and navigate to the `\SAMPLES\COMPTOOL\DIALER` subdirectory. Copy the files `DIALER.VBP` and `DIALER.FRM` to the `\TEMPLATE\PROJECTS` subdirectory. From the Visual Basic IDE menu, choose File | New. You should see an icon for Dialer, as illustrated in Figure 11.3.

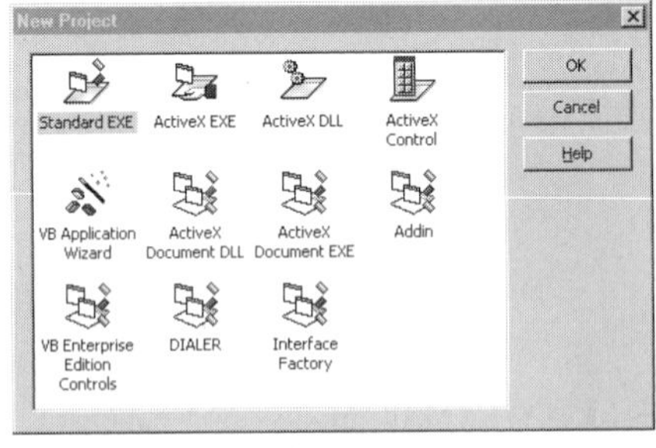

FIGURE 11.3.
After you add the Dialer project to the `PROJECTS` *folder, you can reuse it as a template for future projects.*

Double-click the Dialer icon. The Dialer project has now been instantiated into your current VB session. See how easy that is?

If you decide that you don't necessarily need every template type available, you can turn off the ones you don't want. To do so, choose Tools | Options from the menu. This brings up the Options dialog box. Select the Environment tab. You should see the dialog box shown in Figure 11.4.

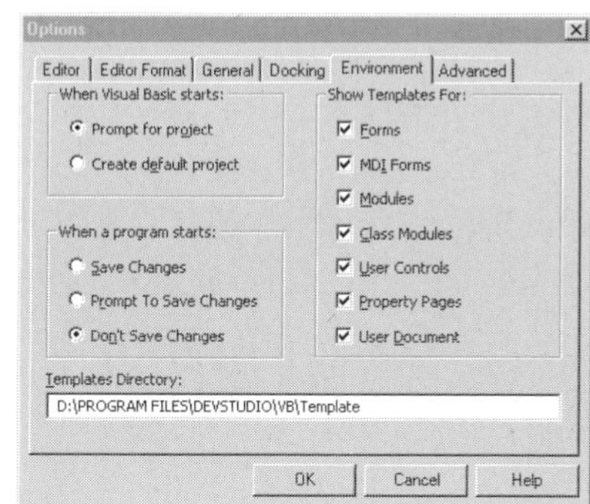

FIGURE 11.4.
You use the Environment tab to choose which types of templates to reuse.

Notice the frame titled Show Templates For: on the right. Every template type is checked, meaning that by default, they are all available. Simply uncheck the ones you don't use and click OK. You might ask why this is important. It really depends on how often you reuse certain types of Visual Basic template items. For instance, if you usually add to your projects new code modules as opposed to existing ones, uncheck the Modules option. That way, when you choose Project Add Module from the menu or right-click the Project list box, you bypass the Add Module dialog box, and a module is added by default. If you normally add new ones and reuse existing ones, leave the Module option checked.

Becoming Familiar with the Template Manager

In addition to the regular template services provided by the Visual Basic development environment, Microsoft ships an unsupported add-in called the Template Manager. This add-in helps facilitate the reuse of snippets of code, menus that you commonly use, and controls that you often use in forms, user documents, and user controls. After you install Template Manager, a subdirectory under the `\TEMPLATE` directory is created for `CODE`, `MENUS`, and `CONTROLS`. Any code you may have implemented for the menus and controls is preserved, as are the code snippets. When you first install Visual Basic 5, you're not made aware of the Template Manager. In fact, you'd have to browse the installation CD carefully to find it.

Installing the Template Manager

The version of the Template Manager that comes with Visual Basic 5 is the first implementation of the software, and therefore is labeled as "unsupported" by Microsoft. It also lacks a setup program, so you'll have to follow a few steps to get it installed and working with Visual Basic.

The good news is that Microsoft has released a newer version of the Template Manager that includes a setup program, which makes installation much easier. The bad news is that you'll have to download the updated version from the VB Owners Area of Microsoft's Web site. If you do obtain the new version—and I highly recommend that you do—then run the setup program just as you would for any other program. Follow the onscreen instructions and skip to the section "Using the Template Manager" later in this chapter. However, if you decide to use the version of the Template Manager included on the VB5 CD, follow the instructions in the next section.

Installing the Template Manager from the VB5 CD

Although using the Template Manager adds more productivity to your enterprise projects, installing the version that is included on the VB5 CD is rather clumsy. And if your licensed copy of Visual Basic was installed by a member of your company's network or software administration team, you'll have to hunt that person down to add the Template Manager. If you reuse menus and controls often, though, it might be worth the hassle.

CAUTION

Installation of this version of the Template Manager involves several steps, and it is best left to someone experienced with Windows 95. You are advised to read through the rest of this chapter carefully before proceeding to make sure that you are comfortable with the installation process.

Locating the Template Manager

The first step in installing this add-in is to get your Visual Basic CD. (If you really need to use Template Manager but don't want to wait several days or weeks before getting the CD from your software administrator, you might be able to get the TEMPMGR.DLL file from a colleague in the same environment who already has it. This assumes that both of you have licenses for Visual Basic 5.) With the CD in your CD-ROM drive, browse to TOOLS\UNSUPPRT\TMPLMGR using Windows Explorer. The directory structure you see should resemble that in Figure 11.5.

Copy the TEMPLATE folder and the TEMPMGR.DLL file to the Visual Basic root directory (where you installed VB). By default, the VB directory is \PROGRAM FILES\VB. Copying the template folder to the \VB subdirectory adds the CODE, MENUS, and CONTROLS folders to the existing template folders. The TEMPMGR.DLL file is just inserted into the VB directory.

Registering the Template Manager

The next installation step involves registering the add-in. For this, you'll need to use the REGSVR32.EXE file. You can find a copy of it in the \TOOLS\REGUTILS directory on your VB5 CD. To make the registration process as simple as possible, copy this executable to the VB directory. Now bring up the MS-DOS prompt. If you're not familiar with this, click the Start button on the Windows 95 taskbar, move the mouse cursor to Programs, and then move the mouse cursor to and click the MS-DOS Prompt. You should see a dialog box that resembles Figure 11.6.

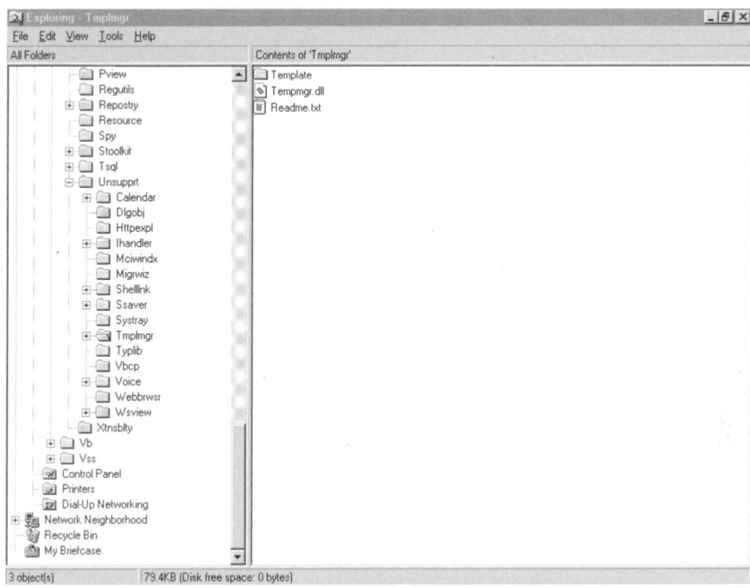

FIGURE 11.5.
The folder that contains the Template Manager add-in files is not exactly easy to find but will have the `TEMPMGR.DLL` *file and the* `TEMPLATE` *folder.*

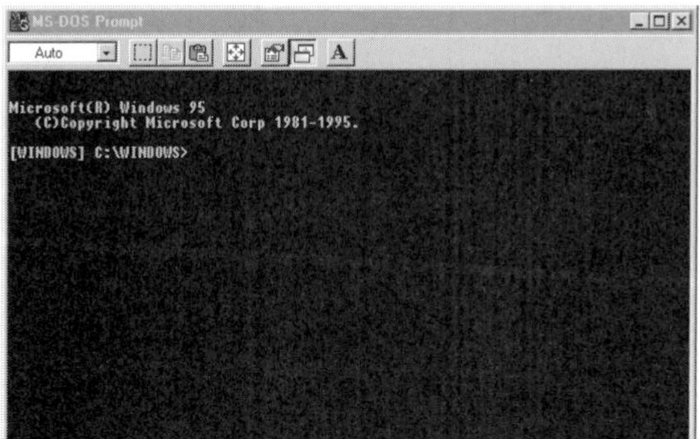

FIGURE 11.6.
Use the MS-DOS Prompt dialog box to register your Template Manager add-in.

Make sure that the current directory shows the path to your Visual Basic root directory, where you just copied the `TEMPLMGR.DLL` file. If it does not, you'll need to use the change directory DOS syntax `CD` *`DRIVE LETTER`*`:\`*`DIRECTORY`* to point to the proper directory. After you have the right path, you can issue the registration command. At the command line in the dialog box, type the following:

```
regsvr32 tempmgr.dll
```

and press the Enter key. You'll hear your computer cranking away, and then it should display a dialog box informing you that the registration process was successful (see Figure 11.7).

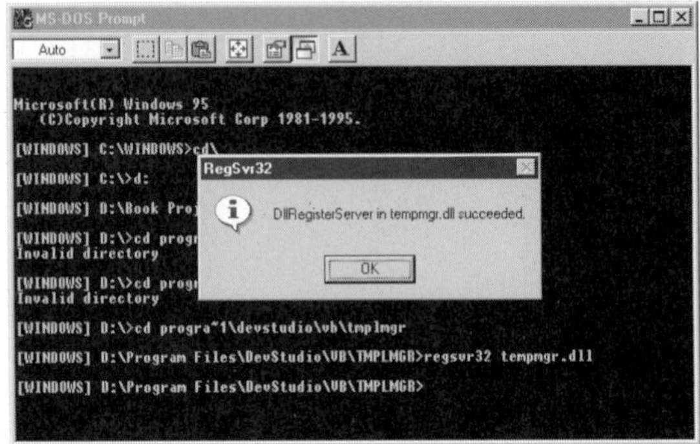

FIGURE 11.7.
After you enter the command to register the Template Manager add-in, the system will inform you that the process was successful.

Troubleshooting Installation Problems

If you were not successful, check for common grammatical mistakes that can occur when entering characters on the command line. After you've corrected the mistakes, try the command again. If you're still not successful, you might try reinstalling Visual Basic or recopying the Template Manager files from your CD. The Template Manager is not supported, so Microsoft may not provide assistance. You might try one of the Visual Basic newsgroups at `WWW.MICROSOFT.COM\VB` or browse to the numerous Web sites that have Visual Basic content, such as `WWW.SAMSONA.COM`.

If that were not awkward enough, you're going to have to manually modify your `VBADDIN.INI` file in the `\WINDOWS` directory (or wherever you installed your Windows 95 operating system files). If you're not comfortable with modifying initialization files and settings, find someone capable of doing it or simply don't use Template Manager.

The VBADDIN.INI File

The information contained in the `VBADDIN.INI` file helps Visual Basic load the add-ins supported by (or registered for) the Visual Basic development environment. To modify the `VBADDIN.INI` file, use a text file editor such as Notepad or WordPad. Because of the extra information inserted by more robust word processors, you should not use Word to edit this file. At the end of the file, add the following line:

```
TempMgr.Connect=0
```

Save the revised `VBADDIN.INI` file and close the text file editor. Now you're ready to use the Template Manager. If you already had Visual Basic running, save any existing projects, exit, and restart it.

CAUTION

Using Template Manager may consume much of your memory and cause your Visual Basic session to become corrupt. Before using Template Manager, save any work you have opened in other applications and then close them.

Using the Template Manager

To run the Template Manager, you first must run Visual Basic. Then from the menu, choose Add-Ins | Add-In Manager. The Add-In Manager dialog box is displayed (see Figure 11.8).

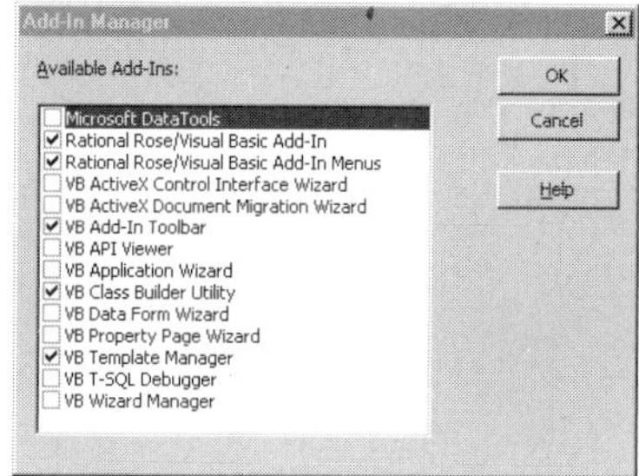

FIGURE 11.8.
The Add-In Manager dialog box facilitates the use of standard and custom add-ins such as the Template Manager.

All the add-ins are listed in alphabetical order, where VB Template Manager is closer to the bottom. Check it by clicking the check box next to VB Template Manager. Click OK.

Where Are the Template Manager Services?

Your first temptation might be to choose Add-Ins from the menu to see the Template Manager. Not so fast there, partner. You won't find Template Manager features there. To find the Template Manager services, choose Tools from the menu, leaving the pop-up menu list intact. The Tools submenu pop-up should have items labeled Add Code Snippet, Add Menu, and Add Control Set.

NOTE

You can use wizard files (with the `.VBZ` extension) in the Template Manager. Just place the wizard files into one of the following directories:

- `\TEMPLATE\CODE`
- `\TEMPLATE\MENUS`
- `\TEMPLATE\CONTROLS`

Template Manager will automatically run the corresponding wizard.

Using the set of Template Manager tools is easy. If you have a favorite code module you want to reuse, you can add it to the `\TEMPLATE\CODE` directory. Then choose Tools | Add Code Snippet. Of course, you can achieve the same thing with the already existent `\MODULES` directory. Just add your code module to the `\TEMPLATE\MODULES` directory. That's why you probably won't get much value out of the Add Code Snippet service.

The Add Control Set Service

The Add Control Set service allows you to add commonly used control sets to your forms (see Figure 11.9). *Control sets* refers to a group of controls that commonly work together in some fashion.

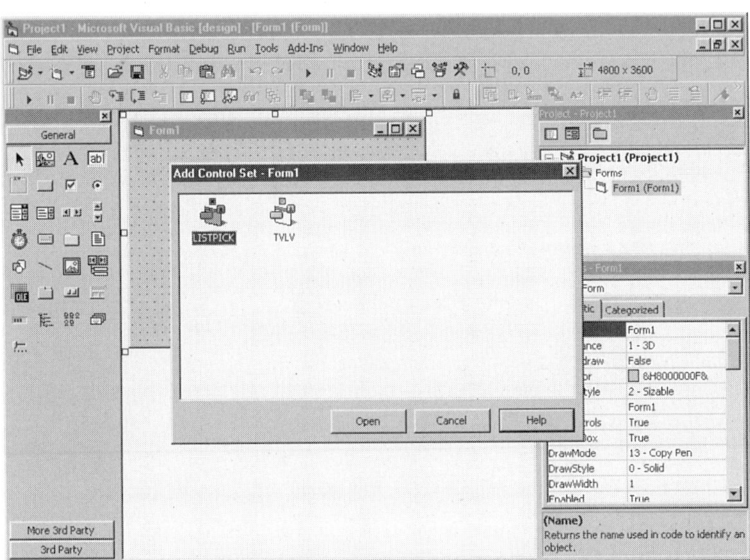

FIGURE 11.9.
The Template Manager's Add Control Set service comes with a few control sets that you can use right away. You can also add your own.

For example, the `LISTPICK` control set contains a few Label controls, two ListBox controls, and several CommandButton controls. Together, they make up a system by which users can choose items from one ListBox and add them to or remove them from another ListBox (see Figure 11.10). You've no doubt seen this kind of setup before, especially in installation programs where you are asked to choose the options you want to include or exclude. If you wanted to implement this kind of functionality in your programs, it would probably take you a significant amount of time to place the controls and code them so that they work together properly. But with the Template Manager's Add Control Set service, you can add the same functionality in just a few seconds.

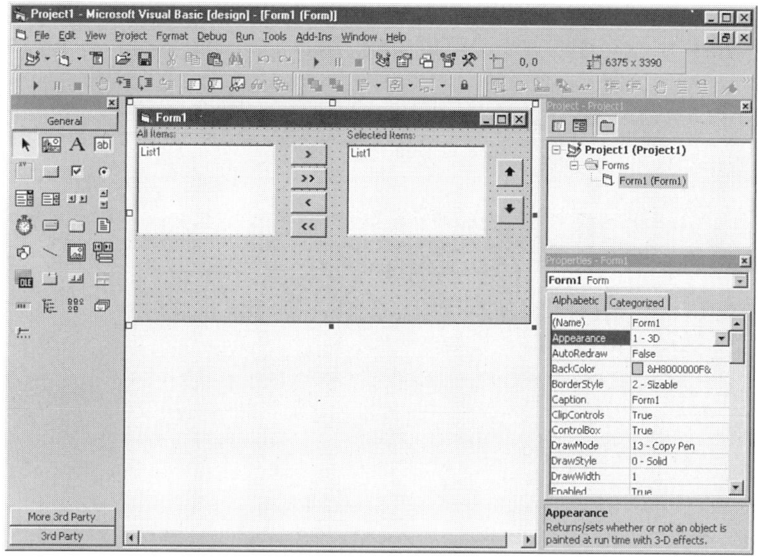

FIGURE 11.10.
The `LISTPICK` *control set provides a system by which users can add to or remove items from one ListBox or another.*

If you want to add your own control sets to the Template Manager, doing so is easy. Simply create a blank form, add the controls and any necessary code, and then copy the `.FRM` file and its corresponding `.FRX` file to VB's `\TEMPLATE\CONTROLS` directory.

The Add Menu Service

Perhaps the most beneficial Template Manager service is the Add Menu service. Of course, if you often reuse the same form that has the menu you want, you can simply place this form in the `\TEMPLATE\FORMS` directory. However, if you don't reuse the form but do reuse the menu on the form, save the menu onto a blank form and save this form to the `\TEMPLATE\MENUS` directory. Be sure to have some code in each menu item. If you don't and you subsequently try to insert a custom menu template onto a new form, you will get an error. If you do get this error, you can usually click OK and ignore it, but you'll get this annoying error every time you try to use your custom menus. To use this service, choose Tools | Add Menu from the Visual Basic menu. Figure 11.11 shows the Add Menu dialog box you should see.

NOTE

Sometimes when you use the Template Manager, you might receive an error stating that no templates could be found. A helpful trick (prescribed by Microsoft) is to choose Tools | Options from the menu. A dialog box appears. Simply click OK. This forces an update to the Registry.

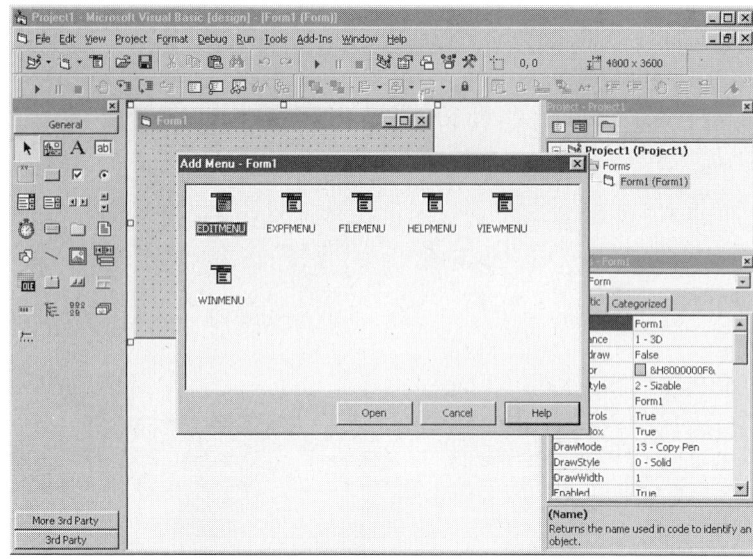

FIGURE 11.11.
Using the Add Menu feature to add a reusable menu component to your target form.

Understanding Effective Component Reuse Strategies and Standard Interfaces

The Visual Basic environment provides helpful facilities for reusing many types of custom-developed components (for example, menus, code modules, and controls), as mentioned earlier. However, such reuse implementations are of no use if the components being developed are not properly planned and documented. Such planning does not occur magically overnight but takes time.

If you are a developer in a corporate enterprise environment, you won't have nearly as good a list of candidates for reuse on the first project as you will on subsequent projects. Trying to find reusable components during the first project is almost like trying to find the lowest common denominator between several fractions when you only have one fraction. It takes at least two projects to find suitable candidates for reuse, and with each subsequent project, your list of candidates will become finer, focusing on more obvious components that can be reused. A seasoned developer will likely have standard, reusable components in his or her arsenal because such a developer will have already identified reusable components after having worked on many projects. These components will usually be small, specialized components as opposed to bloated, unwieldy, and therefore ineffective components.

In addition to identifying candidates for reuse, you should also spend ample time designing a proper interface on the components that support interfaces. Such components include class modules as well as subs and functions in code modules, form modules, and ActiveX controls.

An *interface* is the set of public methods (that is, subs and functions) and properties supported by a module. This is different from a module's accompanying *implementation*, which refers to a module's internal way of executing the service offered by the interface. So if you have a method called `displayMessage`, it might have the following interface:

```
Public Sub displayMessage(argString As String)

End Sub
```

and the following implementation:

```
Public Sub displayMessage(argString As String)
    MsgBox argString
End Sub
```

The interface is the name of the sub, `displayMessage`, as well as its argument (`argString`). The single line of code is the implementation. The outside world (that is, those other parts of your application that call this method) does not care how you implement the `displayMessage` interface. It only cares that the sub exists and is functional. So if you change the line of code to read

```
MsgBox "This is great"
```

that is okay, so long as the client expected to see this message. But if you change the name of the method from `displayMessage` to `showMessage`, the client users of the interface won't be too happy (and may take their business elsewhere). That is, when you change your interface, you will lose compatibility with existing applications that still call `displayMessage`. This becomes especially important when, after you have made a great revision to the newer method, you try to use it in a previous application that still references the old interface. None of the template services in Visual Basic can help you in designing reusable components. The key to reusability, then, is consistency, backward compatibility, and sufficient documentation so that others on a project team can also benefit from reuse.

Summary

In this chapter, you have learned what Visual Basic templates are and how they are implemented in the Visual Basic development environment. You have seen the directory structure of the various types of templates and read some of the key benefits of using templates. You have been introduced to the Template Manager, an important (but unsupported) template service add-in that supplements the standard Visual Basic templates. You have learned how to add menus, controls, and project and class templates. Finally, you have learned the importance of planning components for reuse and why building well-defined, consistent interfaces is the key to successful component reuse.

IN THIS PART

PART

The ListView, TreeView, and ImageList Controls

IN THIS CHAPTER

The ListView, TreeView, and ImageList controls are all part of the Windows Common Controls library. These controls allow you to organize data in the same type of format as the Windows Explorer. In this chapter, you will be creating samples of both ListView and TreeView projects. The projects will show you some of the features of these controls and allow you to understand how they work. Finally, you will combine both controls to create a simple address book application.

When using the ListView and TreeView controls, you will need to have a list of bitmaps available for them to access. You accomplish this by using the ImageList control. The ImageList control is used by several different controls as a repository of icons or bitmaps that will be used in the application.

What Are the ListView, TreeView, and ImageList Controls?

The ListView and TreeView controls are related in that they both give you a way of displaying data as items in a relational format. The ListView control will display the items in one of four different views. You can arrange the data into columns with or without column headings, and you can also display icons and text with the items. Using the ListView control, you can organize the list data items into one of the following views:

- Large icons (standard)
- Small icons
- List view
- Report view

By comparison, a TreeView control displays the data items in a hierarchical list of objects called *nodes*. This control is typically used to display entries in an index, the files or directories on a disk, or any other information that would fit into a hierarchical view. The most common use of both the TreeView and ListView controls can be seen in the Windows 95 Explorer window (see Figure 12.1).

An ImageList control contains a collection of `Image` objects, each of which can be referred to by its index or key. The ImageList control is not meant to be used alone but as a central repository to conveniently supply other controls with images. You can use the ImageList control with any control that assigns a `Picture` object to a `Picture` property. The ImageList control can be used to supply images for the following controls using certain properties:

- ListView control
- TreeView control
- Toolbar control
- Tabstrip control

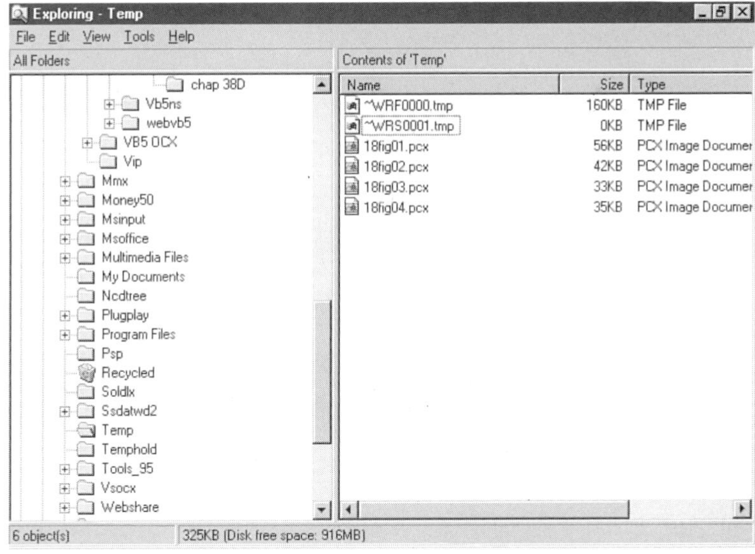

FIGURE 12.1.
The TreeView and ListView common controls are both used in the Windows Explorer interface. The left pane uses the TreeView, and the right pane uses the ListView.

You should populate the ImageList control with images before you associate it with another control.

Understanding the ListView Control

The ListView control is similar to a ListBox, but with enhanced features that allow you to associate icons with list items in the control.The ListView control also allows you to choose from four different views to display the list items.

Because the ListView control displays images (or icons) associated with the various items contained in its list, it often enlists the use of one or two ImageList controls. The ListView control has two properties, `Icons` and `SmallIcons`, that need to be set to appropriate ImageList controls for the images to be displayed. As you can probably guess, the `Icons` property is set to the ImageList control that contains the large icons, and the `SmallIcons` property is set to the ImageList control that contains the small icons. In either case, the images can be of only two file types, `.ICO` or `.BMP`.

> **CAUTION**
>
> If you don't set the `Icons` or `SmallIcons` properties correctly, the associated list graphics will not appear.

Remember also that if you want to have a report view with resizable column headings, you must create and configure a `ColumnHeaders` object to be set to the `ColumnHeaders` properties of the ListView. You'll see how to do so later in this chapter.

Building the ListView Project

The ListView control allows you to display a window that contains a list of information. To illustrate the concepts of using the ListView control, you will create a new Visual Basic project called `CH1201.VBP`. This project shows you how to display a small list of names and their associated phone numbers in a ListView control.

To begin the creation of the project, start a new Standard EXE project in Visual Basic and save it as `CH1201.VBP`. Next, change the name of the default form to `frmAddrBook` and save the form as `CH1201.FRM`.

> **NOTE**
>
> The sample projects in this chapter require that the Microsoft Common Controls (ListView, TreeView, and ImageList) be included in your toolbox. If they are not, select Project | Components from VB's menu; then check the box next to Microsoft Windows Common Controls 5.0. Click OK to close the Components dialog box, and the three controls will be added to your toolbox.

Add two ImageList controls and a ListView control to the form as shown in Figure 12.2. Name the ImageList controls `ilsLargeIcons` and `ilsSmallIcons`, and name the ListView control `lvwAddresses`. The ListView control will be used to display the addresses (and their corresponding icons), and the ImageList controls will store the large and small icons.

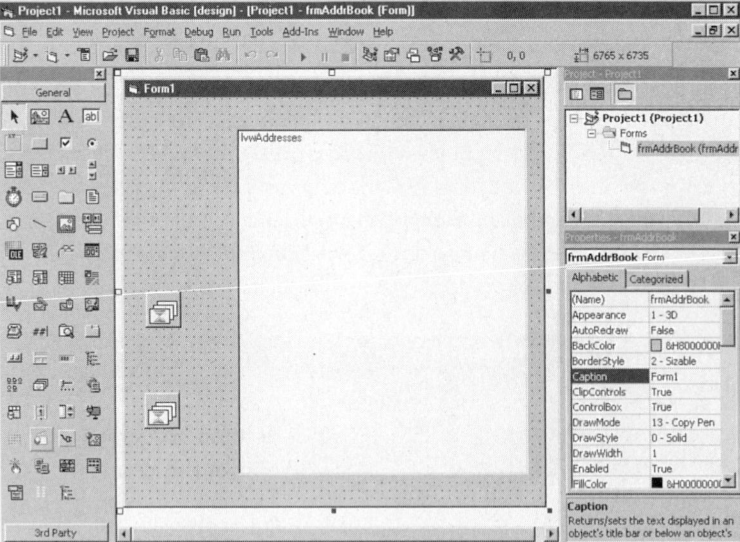

FIGURE 12.2.
The ListView and ImageList controls after being added to the new form in Visual Basic.

Setting the Properties of the ListView Control

There are two ways that you can set up the ListView control: by using the properties window and property pages or by adding code to the `Form_Load` routine to set these properties. If you want to set up the ListView while you are in the design environment, you can use the custom property pages shown in Figure 12.3. You can access the property pages by right-clicking the ListView control and then selecting Properties from the pop-up menu.

Note that the property settings for the sample program are set in the code included in this chapter, so you don't have to use the property pages if you don't want. However, it may be a good idea to take a look at the property pages to familiarize yourself with them. In any case, three key properties need to be set.

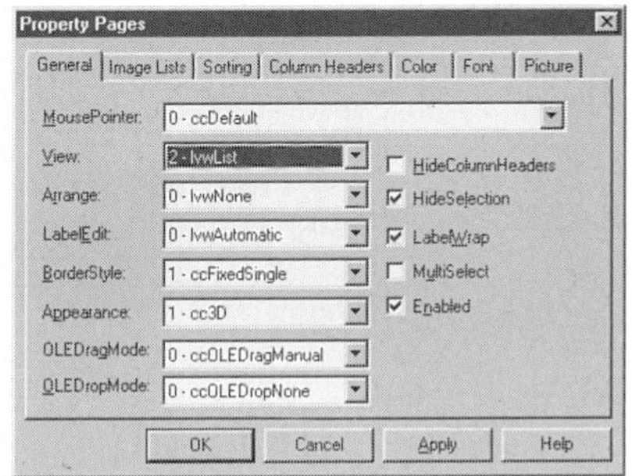

FIGURE 12.3.
The Property Pages dialog box lets you set the ListView control properties.

The first property that needs to be set is the `View` property. This property determines how the list will present information to the user. The `View` property has four possible values: `Icon`, `SmallIcon`, `List`, and `Report`. This project will have its `View` property set to `Report` as its default property rather than the normal default value of `List`.

The next properties you will need to set for the ListView control are the `Icon` and `SmallIcons` properties to indicate which ImageList controls will contain the pictures for the large and small icons shown in the list. If you are using the property pages, you can select the ImageList controls from the drop-down ListBoxes on the Image Lists tab. These ListBoxes will contain all the ImageList controls on your form. Assign the `ilsLargeIcons` control to the `Icon` property and the `ilsSmallIcons` control to the `SmallIcons` property. The ImageList controls will be discussed in more detail later in this chapter.

When displaying the data as a report, you need to set column headers to label each column of the report. This can be done by either by using the Column Headers tab on the ListView property sheet (see Figure 12.4) or by defining a column header object and then adding items to that object, as shown in Listing 12.1. The syntax of this command is

```
Set ColObject = ListView1.ColumnHeaders.Add(,,"Header Text")
```

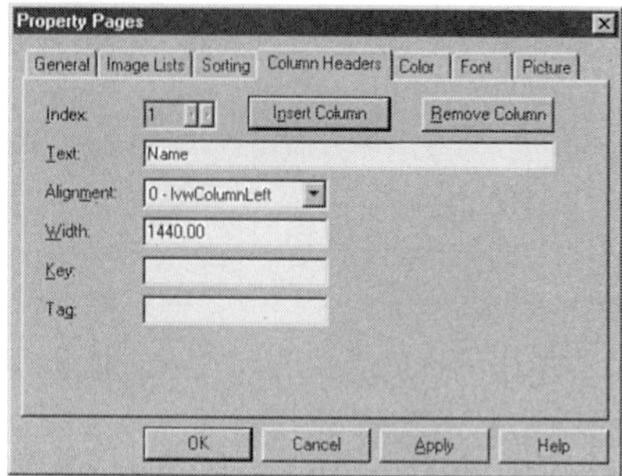

FIGURE 12.4.
Use the Column Headers tab to set the column header labels to be used in the Report view.

You can also set the properties of the ListView control using code when the form is loaded. In the sample project, you will use the code method to set these properties. This will allow you to better understand the process. To set these properties, insert the code in Listing 12.1 into the `Load` event for the `frmAddrBook` form.

Listing 12.1. Using the Load event to set up the ListView control.

```
Private Sub Form_Load()

    ' Create object variables for the ColumnHeader object and
    ' the ListItem object.
    Dim hdrAddresses As ColumnHeader
    Dim itmAddress As ListItem

    ' Set the size and position of the ListView
    ' control (lvwAddresses).
    lvwAddresses.Width = ScaleWidth
    lvwAddresses.Height = ScaleHeight
    lvwAddresses.Top = ScaleTop
    lvwAddresses.Left = ScaleLeft

    ' Set the ListView control's Icons and SmallIcons properties
    ' to the ImageList controls.
    lvwAddresses.Icons = ilsLargeIcons
    lvwAddresses.SmallIcons = ilsSmallIcons

    ' Add ColumnHeaders.  The width of the columns is the width
    ' of the control divided by the number of ColumnHeader objects.
    Set hdrAddresses = lvwAddresses.ColumnHeaders.Add(, , "Name")
    Set hdrAddresses = lvwAddresses.ColumnHeaders.Add(, , "Phone #1")
    Set hdrAddresses = lvwAddresses.ColumnHeaders.Add(, , "Phone #2")

    ' Add some data to the ListItem (itmAddress)
    ' The first name - Microsoft
    Set itmAddress = lvwAddresses.ListItems.Add(, , "Microsoft", 1, 1)       'Name
    itmAddress.SubItems(1) = "206-555-1212"    ' Phone #1.
    itmAddress.SubItems(2) = "206-444-1212"    ' Phone #2.
    ' The second name - Que Publishing
    Set itmAddress = lvwAddresses.ListItems.Add(, , "Que Publishing", 1, 1)  'Name
    itmAddress.SubItems(1) = "317-555-1212"    ' Phone #1.
    itmAddress.SubItems(2) = "317-444-1345"    ' Phone #2.
    ' The third name - Sams Publishing
```

```
    Set itmAddress = lvwAddresses.ListItems.Add(, , "Sams Publishing", 1, 1)  'Name
    itmAddress.SubItems(1) = "407-555-1212"    ' Phone #1.
    itmAddress.SubItems(2) = "407-123-4455"    ' Phone #2.

    lvwAddresses.View = lvwReport              ' Set View property to Report.

End Sub
```

If you looked carefully at the code in Listing 12.1, you might have noticed that the code not only set up the properties of the ListView control but also added to the list the items to be viewed. Using code is the only way to set up the list of items. This list is not accessible from the design environment.

The last line in the code for the `Load` event sets the `View` property of the ListView control to the constant `lvwReport`, which indicates that the Report-format view mode should be used. There are a total of four defined constants for this property:

- *`lvwIcon`*—Displays each item in the list using a large icon and a simple text description.
- *`lvwSmallIcon`*—Displays each item in the list using a small icon and a simple text description. The items are listed horizontally.
- *`lvwList`*—Similar to the small icon view, except that items are arranged in a single vertical column.
- *`lvwReport`*—Displays each item with a small icon, a text description, and detail information, if it is provided. As with the list view, items are arranged in vertical columns.

Perform the following steps to add list items to a ListView control:

1. Create a `ListItem` object that will be used to add items to the ListView control. Use the following syntax:

   ```
   Dim MyListItem as ListItem
   ```

2. Using the `Set` statement, add the object to the ListView's `ListItems` collection:

   ```
   Set MyListItem = ListView1.ListItems.Add(1, "First Name", "Microsoft", 1, 1)
   ```

The syntax for a `ListItems Add` method is as follows:

```
object.Add(index, key, text, icon, smallIcon)
```

Here are the components of this syntax:

- *`object`*—Refers to the `ListItems` collection of the `ListItem` object. This is a required parameter.
- *`index`*—A number used to specify the position in which the `ListItem` object will be inserted into the `ListItems` collection. If you don't set this argument to a value, the `ListItem` is added to the end of the collection. This is an optional parameter.

- *key*—Used to assign a label to the `ListItem` for easier access. This is also an optional parameter.
- *text*—This is the string that you want the `ListItem` to display in the ListView window. It is an optional parameter. This argument should not be confused with the *key* argument.
- *icon*—The index number of the image within the ImageList that has been assigned to the `Icons` property of the ListView control. An ImageList can hold many images. Use this number to select the one you want. This argument is optional.
- *smallIcon*—Similar to the previous argument, *icon*, it is the index number of the image within the ImageList that has been assigned to the `SmallIcons` property of the ListView control. It is optional. Again, be careful!

CAUTION

Remember that for both large icons and small icons, if you forget to fill in a value, no icon will appear in the ListView's Icons, Small Icons, List, or Report views.

If you want to add additional information, such as file creation date or file size, to the newly created `ListItem` object, `MyListItem`, you would manipulate the object's `SubItems(Index)` property. Subitems are arrays of strings representing the `ListItem` object's data that are displayed in Report view. For example, you could show the file size and the date last modified for a file. A `ListItem` object can have any number of associated item data strings (subitems), but each `ListItem` object must have the same number of subitems.

Setting Up the ImageList Controls

To provide the icons for the ListView control, you will need to add ImageList controls to your form. In the earlier section "Building the ListView Project," you added the two ImageList controls needed. All that remains is to add images to the list. To do this, right-click the first ImageList control, `ilsLargeIcons`, to display a pop-up menu. Select the Properties item at the bottom of the menu list. This will display the property sheet for the ImageList control. Select the Image tab and click the Insert Picture button. Choose the bitmap file `SAVE.BMP` that comes with Visual Basic in `GRAPHICS\BITMAPS\OFFCTLBR\LARGE\COLOR`. The bitmap is now inserted in `ilsLargeIcons` as the first image, as shown in Figure 12.5.

Although the sample program only uses one bitmap, you could repeat this process for each additional bitmap you wanted to add to the ImageList. To add the bitmaps to use as small icons, repeat the appropriate steps for the second ImageList, `ilsSmallIcons`. This time, use the `SAVE.BMP` file located in the `GRAPHICS\BITMAP\OFFCTLBR\SMALL\COLOR` directory.

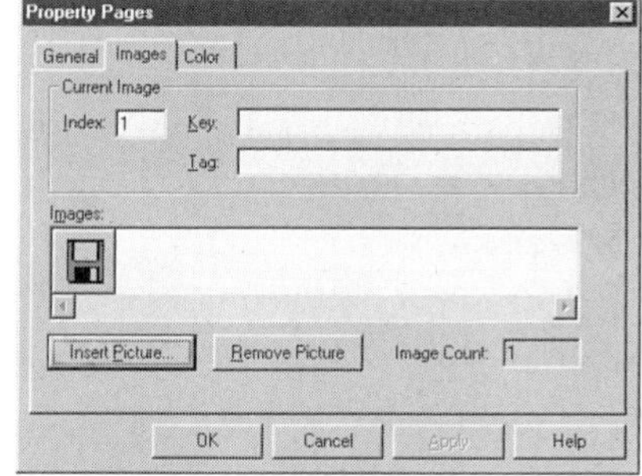

FIGURE 12.5.
Inserting the bitmap `SAVE.BMP` *as the first image in* `ilsLargeIcons`.

Adding a Menu to the ListView Project

To make it easy for you to select different list views of the sample program, you will need to create a menu for the program. Use the Menu Editor to add the menu items shown in Figure 12.6.

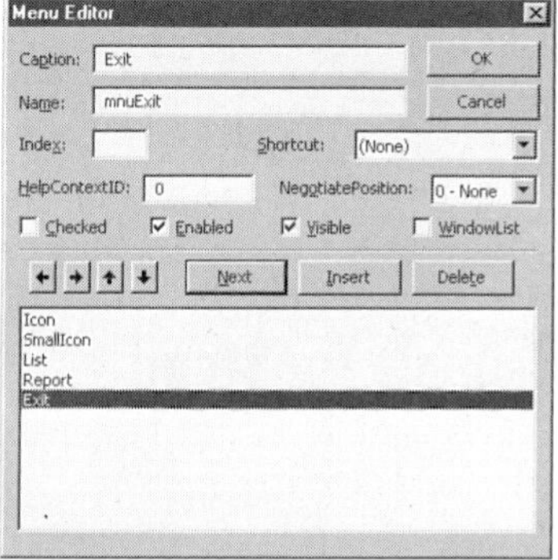

FIGURE 12.6.
The menu for `FRMADDRBOOK.FRM`*, as shown in the Menu Editor.*

After exiting the Menu Editor, you will need to add code to each menu item to perform the required action. In this case, the menu items are designed to change the view mode for the ListView control, so the code you'll be adding will set the control's `View` property according to the menu option that was selected. Listing 12.2 shows the code that needs to be added to the `Click` events for the menu items.

Listing 12.2. The menu `Click` events.

```
Private Sub mnuIcon_Click()

    ' Change the ListView control's view mode to Icon mode.
    lvwAddresses.View = lvwIcon

End Sub
```

continues

Listing 12.2. continued

```
Private Sub mnuSmallIcon_Click()

     ' Change the ListView control's view mode to Small Icon mode.
     lvwAddresses.View = lvwSmallIcon

End Sub

Private Sub mnuList_Click()

     ' Change the ListView control's view mode to List mode.
     lvwAddresses.View = lvwList

End Sub

Private Sub mnuReport_Click()

     ' Change the ListView control's view mode to Report mode.
     lvwAddresses.View = lvwReport

End Sub

Private Sub mnuExit_Click()

     ' End the program.
     End

End Sub
```

Executing the Sample Program

At this point, you are ready to run the program. Figure 12.7 shows the running program using the Icon view mode.

FIGURE 12.7.
The Icon view mode is one of the options in the program.

When the project starts, the program initializes the size and location of the ListView control to fill the client area of the form in the `Form_Load` event. In addition, the `ListItem` objects (names, home phone numbers, and work phone numbers) for the ListView's `ListItem` collection are created and added. As each `ListItem` is added to the `ListItems` collection, values are assigned to `SubItems(1)`, (the `Phone #1` column), and `SubItems(2)`, (the `Phone #2` column), of the `ListItem` object, `itmAddress`.

After the program is running, test the different views of the `ListView` control by selecting from the different options on the program's menu. You can see that the Report view is the only view option that displays the subitem information.

Understanding the TreeView Control

The TreeView control is similar to a ListView control because it displays items with a combination of text and graphics. However, the TreeView control does so by showing items within a tree hierarchy. Given the hierarchical nature of the control, *root*, *parent*, and *child* are fundamental concepts that must be understood to work with this control. In addition, the TreeView control uses the `Node` object extensively. Understanding the `Node` object is a must for effective use of the TreeView control.

Understanding Nodes

Nodes are the positions within a tree hierarchy. All TreeView controls have nodes just as all real-life trees have branches. Normally this would seem simple enough. But with TreeView controls, it can be a bit confusing. This is because `Nodes` is both a property of a TreeView control and an object all by itself.

Consider the following analogy. If a tree (this is an analogy, remember) has branches and all branches of a tree collectively are considered a single property of the tree, the property might be called `Branches`. The tree may have other properties associated with it:

- *`Type`*—For example, oak or maple
- *`Height`*—For example, the tree is as tall as my house
- *`Location`*—For example, the tree is in my backyard

Each of these characteristics is a single property of the tree. Just because a tree has lots of branches does *not* mean that it has lots of `Branch` properties. It has only one property, `Branches`. The property `Branches` has a value that is a collection of individual branches.

Just as a tree has a property `Branches`, a TreeView control has a property `Nodes`. The TreeView control has only one `Nodes` property, which has a collection of nodes as its value.

Understanding the Root Property

In a real-life tree, roots exist at the bottom, and the tree grows up from them. The `Root` property, however, is the top node of any tree hierarchy. In the Windows Explorer hierarchy, the Desktop is the root. A root is that from which everything descends.

Working with the Parent Property

A *parent* is an object that has children. A parent node is a node that has child nodes, much like a real-life tree has a branch that contains other branches.

All nodes have parents, but not all nodes are parents. The `Parent` property of a given `Node` object indicates the parent node for that particular `Node` object. For instance, the value of the `Parent` property for the node Pontiac is General Motors. The `Parent` property does not report whether a given node *is* a parent, only if it *has* a parent.

Working with the Children Property

The `Children` property returns the total number of children a given node has. To find out whether a node is a parent, you query the `Children` property using code similar to that shown in Listing 12.3. If the value of the `Children` property is greater than 0, the node is a parent. For example, if you ask me how many children I have and I report none, then you know that I am not a parent.

Listing 12.3. Determining a parent node.

```
Private Sub TreeView1_NodeClick(ByVal MyNode As Node)

    If MyNode.Children = 0 Then
        MsgBox "I have no children; therefore, I am not a parent."
    End If

End Sub
```

Working with the Child Property

The `Child` property returns the value of the first of the given parent node's descendants (or children). Common sense would say that the `Child` property should report whether a node is a child. Well, it doesn't. In the node family there is only one `Child`, and that is the first descending `Node`. All the other nodes that share the child's parent are considered `Next` or `Previous` nodes. However, among all the nodes that share the same value for their `Parent` property, there is a `FirstSibling` and `LastSibling`.

For example, the nodes Pontiac, Chevrolet, Oldsmobile, Buick, and Cadillac share the same `Parent` value, General Motors (which is also a node).

> The `Child` of General Motors is Pontiac.
>
> The `Next` is Chevrolet.

The Next from Chevrolet is Oldsmobile.

The Next from Oldsmobile is Buick.

The Next from Buick is Cadillac.

The Previous from Buick is Oldsmobile.

The FirstSibling is Pontiac.

The LastSibling is Cadillac.

NOTE

Granted, grasping the concepts of trees, nodes, parents, and children can be confusing. One of the best ways to understand nodes is to see the node program code in action. Using the sample code included with the online help information for the TreeView control is the best way to see how everything operates.

Building the TreeView Project

The TreeView control lets you display hierarchical data in a treelike format. The only difference in the analogy is that the root of the TreeView control is shown at the top of the list (unlike a real tree, which starts at the bottom and works its way up). To illustrate the concepts of the TreeView control, you will create a new Visual Basic project that will show you how to display data in the tree format.

To begin the creation of the project, start a new project in Visual Basic and save it as CH1202.VBP. Next, change the default form name to frmTreeBook and save it as CH1202.FRM.

If your toolbox doesn't already include the ListView, TreeView, and ImageList controls, add them by choosing Project | Components and selecting Windows Common Controls from the list of components.

After you have added the controls to the toolbox, you can add them to your form. First, add a TreeView control to the form and change its name to treAddrBook. Next, add an ImageList control and change its name to ilsAddrIcons. This ImageList control will contain the bitmaps that the TreeView control will use when displaying the data.

Finally, use the Menu Editor to add a menu item to allow you to exit the application. Give it the Caption Exit and the name it mnuExit. Figure 12.8 gives you an idea of how your form should look at this point. Now you are ready to start setting the properties of the control.

Creating the Code to Set Up the TreeView Control

As was the case in the ListView project, most of the setup for the TreeView control is easier to accomplish through code. However, a few properties can be set in the custom Properties window (see Figure 12.9).

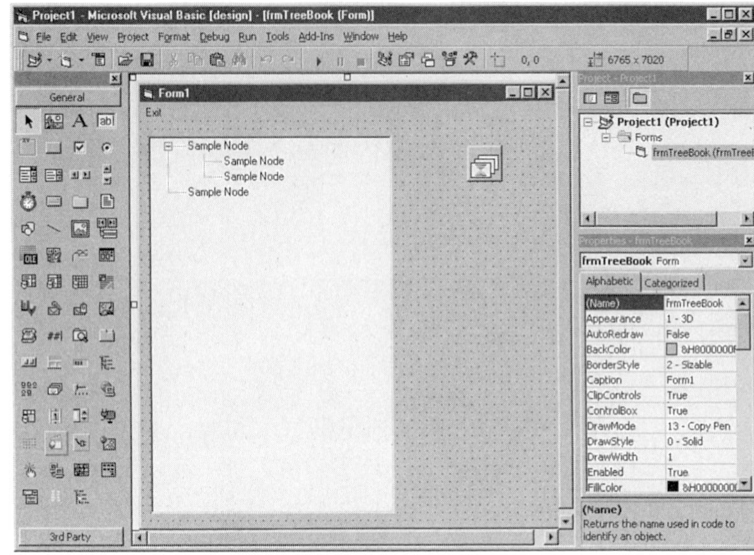

FIGURE 12.8.
The TreeView and ImageList controls after being added to the new form in Visual Basic.

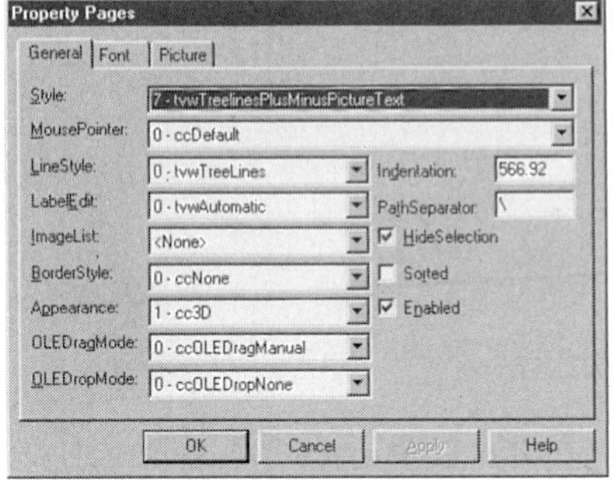

FIGURE 12.9.
The Property Pages dialog box lets you set the TreeView control properties.

The `Style` property determines how the tree information will be displayed. These are the available values:

Value	*Description*
`0-tvwTextOnly`	Text only
`1-tvwPictureText`	Image and text
`2-tvwPlusMinusText`	Plus/minus and text
`3-tvwPlusPictureText`	Plus/minus, image, and text
`4-tvwLinesText`	Lines and text
`5-tvwLinesPictureText`	Lines, image, and text
`6-tvwLinesPlusMinusText`	Lines, plus/minus, and text
`7-tvwLinesPlusMinusPictureText`	(Default) Lines, plus/minus, image, and text

The `LineStyle` property lets you set whether you want the root lines displayed (see Figure 12.10).

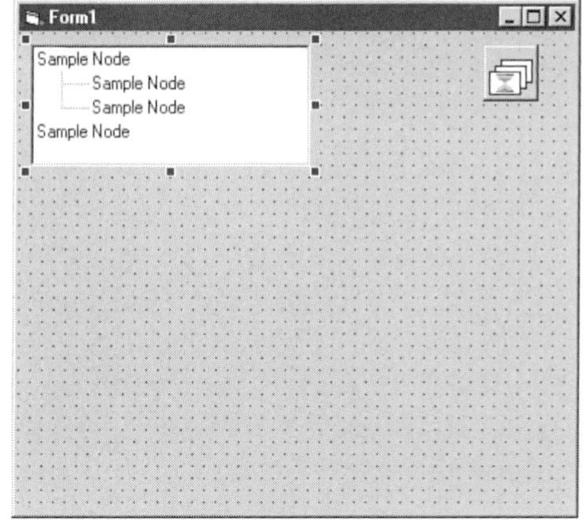

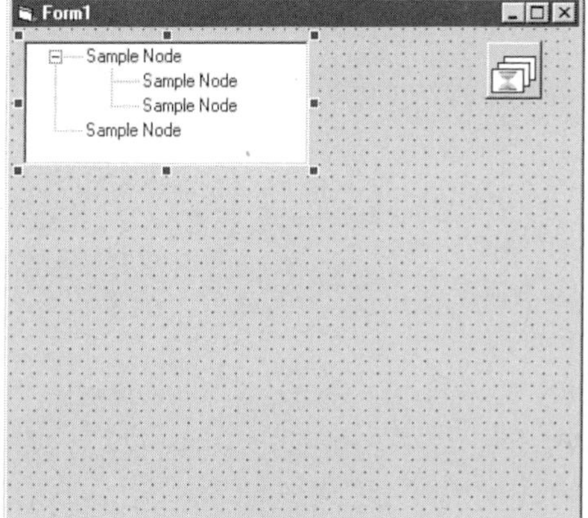

FIGURE 12.10.
Line styles displayed without and with root lines.

Finally, you need to set the `ImageList` property to `ilsAddrIcons`, the name of the ImageList control that you had previously added to the form. Before it can be used, however, the ImageList control needs to have an image assigned to it. Add a small icon or bitmap to the control via its custom Property page, just as you did with the ImageList controls used in the previous sample program. The `SPELL.BMP` file in the `GRAPHICS\BITMAPS\OFFCTLBR\SMALL\COLOR` subdirectory on the VB5 CD is a suitable choice.

The initialization code for the General Motors company TreeView is shown in Listing 12.4. This listing needs to be added your form as a procedure.

Listing 12.4. The `SetCompany` procedure displays address book information in the TreeView control.

```
Public Sub SetCompany(treWork As TreeView)

    '*********************************
    'The sub takes a TreeView as an argument and sets that
    'control to show the Address Books available
    '*********************************

    Dim MyNode As Node

    ' Clean out the TreeView control
    treWork.Nodes.Clear

    ' Set the Address Book
    Set MyNode = treWork.Nodes.Add(, , "A", "Address Book", 1)

    ' Set the Book Types
    Set MyNode = treWork.Nodes.Add("A", tvwChild, "P", "Personal", 1)
    Set MyNode = treWork.Nodes.Add("A", tvwChild, "B", "Business", 1)
    MyNode.EnsureVisible

    'Set the Letter Tabs for the Personal Address Book
    Set MyNode = treWork.Nodes.Add("P", tvwChild, "P1", "ABC")
    Set MyNode = treWork.Nodes.Add("P", tvwChild, "P2", "DEFG")
    Set MyNode = treWork.Nodes.Add("P", tvwChild, "P3", "HIJK")
    Set MyNode = treWork.Nodes.Add("P", tvwChild, "P4", "LMNOP")
    Set MyNode = treWork.Nodes.Add("P", tvwChild, "P5", "QRST")
    Set MyNode = treWork.Nodes.Add("P", tvwChild, "P6", "UVW")
    Set MyNode = treWork.Nodes.Add("P", tvwChild, "P7", "XYZ")
    MyNode.EnsureVisible

    ' Set the Letter Tabs for the Business Address Book
    Set MyNode = treWork.Nodes.Add("B", tvwChild, "B1", "ABC")
    Set MyNode = treWork.Nodes.Add("B", tvwChild, "B2", "DEFG")
    Set MyNode = treWork.Nodes.Add("B", tvwChild, "B3", "HIJK")
    Set MyNode = treWork.Nodes.Add("B", tvwChild, "B4", "LMNOP")
    Set MyNode = treWork.Nodes.Add("B", tvwChild, "B5", "QRST")
    Set MyNode = treWork.Nodes.Add("B", tvwChild, "B6", "UVW")
    Set MyNode = treWork.Nodes.Add("B", tvwChild, "B7", "XYZ")
    MyNode.EnsureVisible

    treWork.Style = tvwTreelinesPictureText ' Style 4.
    treWork.BorderStyle = vbFixedSingle
    treWork.Height = 4455
    treWork.Width = 4575

End Sub
```

Perform the following command to add tree nodes to the TreeView control. The syntax of the command is as follows:

```
Set MyNode = TreeView1.Nodes.Add("A", tvwChild, "P", "Personal")
```

The syntax for a node's `Add` method is as follows:

```
object.Add(relative, relationship, key, text, image, selectedimage)
```

Here are the components of this syntax:

- *`object`*—Refers to the `nodes` collection of the `TreeView` object. This is a required parameter.
- *`relative`*—This is the key or index number of a preexisting `Node` object. The relationship between the new node and this preexisting node is found in the next argument, *`relationship`*. This is an optional parameter.
- *`relationship`*—This specifies the relative placement of the `Node` object. This is an optional parameter.
- *`key`*—Used to assign a label to the node for easier access. This is also an optional parameter.
- *`text`*—The text that appears in the node. This argument is required.
- *`image`*—The index number of the image in an associated ImageList control. This is also an optional parameter.
- *`selectedimage`*—The index number of the image in an associated ImageList control that is shown when the node is selected. This is also an optional parameter.

The settings to use for the relationship parameter are

Value	*Description*
`0-tvwFirst`	The node is placed before all the other nodes at the same level of the node named in *`relative`*.
`1-tvwLast`	The node is placed after all other nodes at the same level of the node named in *`relative`*.
`2-tvwNext`	The node is placed after the node named in *`relative`*. This is the default.
`3-tvwPrevious`	The node is placed before the node named in *`relative`*.
`4-tvwChild`	The node becomes a child node of the node named in *`relative`*.

NOTE

If you do not name a `Node` object in the relative position, the node is placed in the last position of the top node hierarchy.

For the `SetCompany` procedure to execute, it should be called when the program starts running. Add the following line of code to the `Form_Load` event:

```
Call SetCompany(treAddrBook)
```

The final line of code that needs to be added is for Exit, the single menu item. Add the following line of code to the mnuExit_Click event:

```
End
```

Executing the Sample Program

At this point, you are ready to run the program. Figure 12.11 shows the running program with the TreeView control visible.

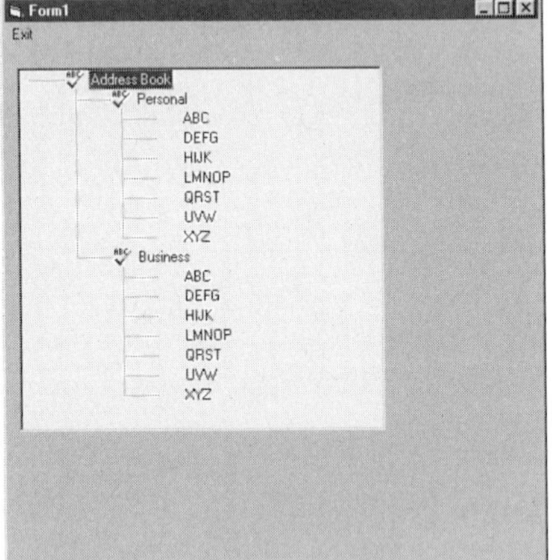

FIGURE 12.11.
Using TreeView to display structured information.

When the project starts, the program initializes the TreeView control by calling the routine you added that sets the nodes in the tree. After the program is running, test the way the TreeView allows you to expand and collapse the different levels of the tree information.

Understanding How the Application Works

The crux of the project CH1202.VBP is the procedure SetCompany. When the procedure is called, the TreeView control treAddrBook is passed as an argument (treWork). The procedure configures and displays information for treAddrBook.

First the procedure creates a node for the different phone books:

```
Set MyNode = treWork.Nodes.Add("A", tvwChild, "P", "Personal")
```

The constant tvwChild tells the application to make this new node a child of the node "A".

Then to each phone book node the groups of letters are added as a group node:

```
Set MyNode = treWork.Nodes.Add("P", tvwChild, "P1", "ABC")
```

Notice that the first argument in the `Add` method is now `"P"`, which is the unique key of the node of the personal phone book. This is how the `"P1"` node, (which displays `"ABC"`) knows that it is a child of the personal phone book.

Next, the entire phone book node and its children are told to remain expanded (TreeView nodes can be expanded and collapsed) in the line:

```
MyNode.EnsureVisible
```

You can see that little code is needed to use a TreeView control (except, of course, for the code required to populate the tree with data).

Enhancing Visual Basic Applications Using the TreeView and the ListView Controls Together

In this section, you will combine both the TreeView and the ListView controls into a single application. This application will allow you to choose from two phone books using the TreeView control and displaying the name and phone numbers for the selected book using the ListView control. You will be able to create this application using the techniques you have learned so far in this chapter.

The controls used in this application are the TreeView, ListView, and ImageList controls. There will actually be two ListView controls, one for each phone book, and three ImageList controls, one for the TreeView control and two for the ListView controls. In addition, you will add several sections of code to initialize the controls and display the appropriate ListView control based on which book node is selected in the TreeView control.

Building the Application

By using the TreeView control's methods and events, you will be able to switch the ListView control that is visible to the user. To begin the creation of the project, start a new project in Visual Basic and save it as `CH1203.VBP`. Next, change the name of the default form to `frmPhoneBook` and save the form as `CH1203.FRM`.

After you have created and saved the form and project files, you will need to add the controls to your form. For this project, we'll be using three ImageList controls, two ListView controls, and one TreeView control. Use Table 12.1 and Figure 12.12 as a guide for placing the controls on the form and changing their properties.

Table 12.1. Property settings for the form and the controls.

Control Type	Property	Value
Form	Name	frmPhoneBook
	Caption	Phone Book (Ch1203)
	Windowstate	vbMaximized
TreeView	Name	treIndex
	Height	1395
	Left	120
	Style	1 - tvwPictureText
	Top	495
	Width	2385
ImageList	Name	ilsTreeIcons
	Left	5145
	Top	3660
ImageList	Name	ilsLgListIcons
	Left	5145
	Top	600
ImageList	Name	ilsSmListIcons
	Left	5145
	Top	2130
ListView	Name	lvwPersonal
	Height	1425
	Left	2775
	Top	495
	Width	2025
	View	3 - lvwReport
	Visible	False
ListView	Name	lvwBusiness
	Height	1425
	Left	2775
	Top	2040
	Width	2025
	View	3 - lvwReport
	Visible	False

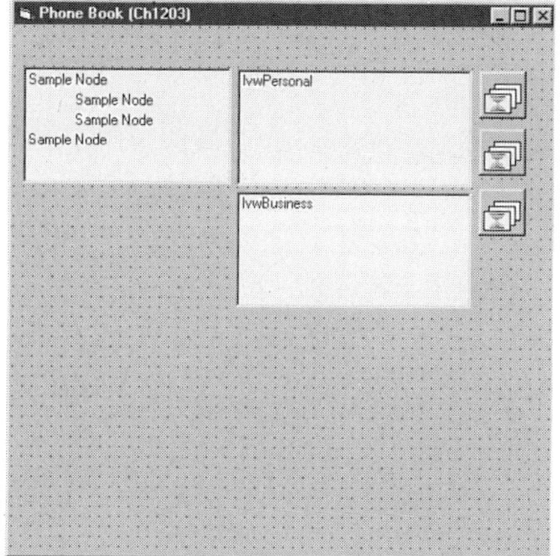

FIGURE 12.12.
Adding the controls to the form.

Setting the Custom Properties

As you're probably aware by now, the ImageList controls need to have images or icons added to them. Display the custom Property page for each of the three ImageList controls and add to them the following bitmaps:

`ilsTreeIcons`	`SMALL\COLOR\SPELL.BMP`
	`SMALL\COLOR\NEW.BMP`
`ilsLgListIcons`	`LARGE\COLOR\SAVE.BMP`
`ilsSmListIcons`	`SMALL\COLOR\SAVE.BMP`

The preceding bitmaps can be found starting from the `\VB\GRAPHICS\BITMAPS\OFFCTLBR\` subdirectory on the Visual Basic CD.

Adding the Program Logic

Much of the code needed for this program will be placed in the `Form_Load` event. To begin with, this is where the program's interface needs to be set up. The TreeView and ListView controls are positioned and sized accordingly. Next, some of the control properties that couldn't be set at design time (`Icons` and `SmallIcons` for the two ListView controls and ImageList for the TreeView control) are assigned. The column headers for the two ListView controls are also set, and a few phone book entries (each with Name, Phone #1, and Phone #2) for each control are added. Finally, the subroutine that sets up the TreeView control (`SetTreeview`) is called. Listing 12.5 shows the code that needs to be added to the `Form_Load` event.

Listing 12.5. The `Form_Load` event for project `CH1203.VBP`.

```
Private Sub Form_Load()

    ' Create object variables for the ColumnHeader object and
    ' the ListItem object.
    Dim hdrPhonebook As ColumnHeader
    Dim itmBookItem As ListItem

    ' Set the size and position of the TreeView
    ' control.
    treIndex.Top = 600
    treIndex.Left = 30
    treIndex.Height = Screen.Height * 0.75
    treIndex.Width = Screen.Width * 0.25

    ' Set the size and position of the first ListView
    ' control (lvwBusiness)...
    lvwBusiness.Top = 600
    lvwBusiness.Left = treIndex.Width + 90
    lvwBusiness.Height = treIndex.Height
    lvwBusiness.Width = Screen.Width * 0.5

    ' ... and use the same settings for the second
    ' ListView control (lvwPersonal).
    lvwPersonal.Top = lvwBusiness.Top
    lvwPersonal.Left = lvwBusiness.Left
    lvwPersonal.Height = lvwBusiness.Height
    lvwPersonal.Width = lvwBusiness.Width

    ' Use the ImageList controls ilsLgListIcons and
    ' ilsSmListIcons for the Icons and SmallIcons
    ' properties of both ListView controls.
    lvwBusiness.Icons = ilsLgListIcons
    lvwBusiness.SmallIcons = ilsSmListIcons
    lvwPersonal.Icons = ilsLgListIcons
    lvwPersonal.SmallIcons = ilsSmListIcons

    ' Use the ImageList control ilsTreeIcons for the
    ' ImageList property of the TreeView control.
    treIndex.ImageList = ilsTreeIcons

    ' Add ColumnHeaders for the lvwBusiness ListView
    ' control.
    Set hdrPhonebook = lvwBusiness.ColumnHeaders.Add(, , "Name")
    Set hdrPhonebook = lvwBusiness.ColumnHeaders.Add(, , "Phone #1")
    Set hdrPhonebook = lvwBusiness.ColumnHeaders.Add(, , "Phone #2")

    ' Add ColumnHeaders for the lvwPersonal ListView
    ' control.
    Set hdrPhonebook = lvwPersonal.ColumnHeaders.Add(, , "Name")
    Set hdrPhonebook = lvwPersonal.ColumnHeaders.Add(, , "Phone #1")
    Set hdrPhonebook = lvwPersonal.ColumnHeaders.Add(, , "Phone #2")

    ' Add some items to the lvwBusiness ListView
    ' control (via the itmBookItem object)
    ' -- ABC Advertising
    Set itmBookItem = lvwBusiness.ListItems.Add(, , _
        "ABC Advertising", 1, 1)   ' Name
```

```
    itmBookItem.SubItems(1) = "800-555-5555"    ' Phone #1.
    itmBookItem.SubItems(2) = "317-555-5555"    ' Phone #2.
    ' -- Cooper's Copying Service
    Set itmBookItem = lvwBusiness.ListItems.Add(, , _
        "Cooper's Copying Service", 1, 1)  ' Name
    itmBookItem.SubItems(1) = "800-444-4444"    ' Phone #1.
    itmBookItem.SubItems(2) = "213-444-4444"    ' Phone #2.
    ' -- Smith & Jones Law Offices
    Set itmBookItem = lvwBusiness.ListItems.Add(, , _
        "Smith & Jones Law Offices", 1, 1) ' Name
    itmBookItem.SubItems(1) = "888-333-3333"    ' Phone #1.
    itmBookItem.SubItems(2) = "602-333-3333"    ' Phone #2.

    ' Add some items to the lvwPersonal ListView
    ' control (via the itmBookItem object)
    ' -- Fred Flintstone
    Set itmBookItem = lvwPersonal.ListItems.Add(, , _
        "Flintstone, Fred", 1, 1)               ' Name
    itmBookItem.SubItems(1) = "908-123-4567"    ' Phone #1.
    itmBookItem.SubItems(2) = "908-123-9999"    ' Phone #2.
    ' -- Hank Hill
    Set itmBookItem = lvwPersonal.ListItems.Add(, , _
        "Hill, Hank", 1, 1)                     ' Name
    itmBookItem.SubItems(1) = "609-555-1234"    ' Phone #1.
    itmBookItem.SubItems(2) = "609-555-4321"    ' Phone #2.
    ' -- Homer Simpson
    Set itmBookItem = lvwPersonal.ListItems.Add(, , _
        "Simpson, Homer", 1, 1)                 ' Name
    itmBookItem.SubItems(1) = "595-999-9999"    ' Phone #1.
    itmBookItem.SubItems(2) = "595-998-8888"    ' Phone #2.

    ' Call the routine that sets up the TreeView
    ' control.
    Call SetTreeview(treIndex)

End Sub
```

The last line of code in the `Form_Load` event calls the `SetTreeview` routine, which sets up the nodes of the TreeView control (`treIndex`). This code is almost identical to the code in Listing 12.4, with only two exceptions: the subroutine name has been changed to `SetTreeview`, and the last two lines that set the TreeView controls `Height` and `Width` properties have been removed. Listing 12.6 shows the new `SetTreeview` routine, which sets up the nodes for the TreeView control.

Listing 12.6. The `SetTreeview` routine for project `CH1203.VBP`.

```
Public Sub SetTreeview(treWork As TreeView)

    '*********************************
    'The sub takes a TreeView as an argument and sets that
    'control to show the Address Books available
    '*********************************
```

continues

Listing 12.6. continued

```
    Dim MyNode As Node

    ' Clean out the TreeView control
    treWork.Nodes.Clear

    ' Set the Address Book
    Set MyNode = treWork.Nodes.Add(, , "A", "Address Book", 1)

    ' Set the Book Types
    Set MyNode = treWork.Nodes.Add("A", tvwChild, "P", "Personal", 2)
    Set MyNode = treWork.Nodes.Add("A", tvwChild, "B", "Business", 2)
    MyNode.EnsureVisible

    'Set the Letter Tabs for the Personal Address Book
    Set MyNode = treWork.Nodes.Add("P", tvwChild, "P1", "ABC")
    Set MyNode = treWork.Nodes.Add("P", tvwChild, "P2", "DEFG")
    Set MyNode = treWork.Nodes.Add("P", tvwChild, "P3", "HIJK")
    Set MyNode = treWork.Nodes.Add("P", tvwChild, "P4", "LMNOP")
    Set MyNode = treWork.Nodes.Add("P", tvwChild, "P5", "QRST")
    Set MyNode = treWork.Nodes.Add("P", tvwChild, "P6", "UVW")
    Set MyNode = treWork.Nodes.Add("P", tvwChild, "P7", "XYZ")
    MyNode.EnsureVisible

    ' Set the Letter Tabs for the Business Address Book
    Set MyNode = treWork.Nodes.Add("B", tvwChild, "B1", "ABC")
    Set MyNode = treWork.Nodes.Add("B", tvwChild, "B2", "DEFG")
    Set MyNode = treWork.Nodes.Add("B", tvwChild, "B3", "HIJK")
    Set MyNode = treWork.Nodes.Add("B", tvwChild, "B4", "LMNOP")
    Set MyNode = treWork.Nodes.Add("B", tvwChild, "B5", "QRST")
    Set MyNode = treWork.Nodes.Add("B", tvwChild, "B6", "UVW")
    Set MyNode = treWork.Nodes.Add("B", tvwChild, "B7", "XYZ")
    MyNode.EnsureVisible

    treWork.Style = tvwTreelinesPictureText ' Style 4.
    treWork.BorderStyle = vbFixedSingle
End Sub
```

Next, if you want to be able to change the ListView display style, you must create the menu options shown in Figure 12.6 and add the code for their `Click` events as shown in Listing 12.7. These menu items are used to alter the view mode for the project's ListView controls.

Listing 12.7. The code for the menu items' `Click` events.

```
Private Sub mnuIcon_Click()

    ' Change both ListView controls' view mode to
    ' Icon mode.
    lvwBusiness.View = lvwIcon
    lvwPersonal.View = lvwIcon

End Sub

Private Sub mnuSmallIcon_Click()
```

```
        ' Change both ListView controls' view mode to
        ' Small Icon mode.
        lvwBusiness.View = lvwSmallIcon
        lvwPersonal.View = lvwSmallIcon

End Sub

Private Sub mnuList_Click()

        ' Change both ListView controls' view mode to
        ' List mode.
        lvwBusiness.View = lvwList
        lvwPersonal.View = lvwList

End Sub

Private Sub mnuReport_Click()

        ' Change both ListView controls' view mode to
        ' Report mode.
        lvwBusiness.View = lvwReport
        lvwPersonal.View = lvwReport

End Sub

Private Sub mnuExit_Click()

        ' End the program.
        End

End Sub
```


You've probably noticed that the code in Listing 12.7 is similar to the code in Listing 12.2. The only difference is that we are now setting the `View` properties of both ListView controls because we are uncertain which ListView control is currently visible.

The last section of code that is needed is the piece that will check which phone book is selected in the TreeView control and then make the appropriate ListView control visible. This is done by using the `Click` event for the `Node` object. When a node is clicked, you can check the parent for that node to see which phone book should be displayed and then which group is selected. You can then set the properties and the position of the appropriate ListView control. Listing 12.8 contains the code that performs the described actions:

Listing 12.8. The `treIndex_Click` event, which determines the ListView control to display.

```
Private Sub treIndex_Click()

        ' If the user clicks on the "Personal" node,
        ' show the lvwPersonal ListView. If the user
        ' clicks on the "Business" node, show the
        ' lvwBusiness ListView. If the "Address Book"
        ' node is clicked, hide both ListView controls.
```

continues

Listing 12.8. continued

```
    If treIndex.SelectedItem.Text = "Personal" Then
        lvwPersonal.Visible = True
        lvwBusiness.Visible = False
    ElseIf treIndex.SelectedItem.Text = "Business" Then
        lvwPersonal.Visible = False
        lvwBusiness.Visible = True
    ElseIf treIndex.SelectedItem.Text = "Address Book" Then
        lvwPersonal.Visible = False
        lvwBusiness.Visible = False
    End If

End Sub
```

Executing the Program

You are now ready to execute this program. After the program starts, try changing the display of the ListView, and then in the TreeView, select different groups or the other phone book node. Figure 12.13 shows what the working program should look like.

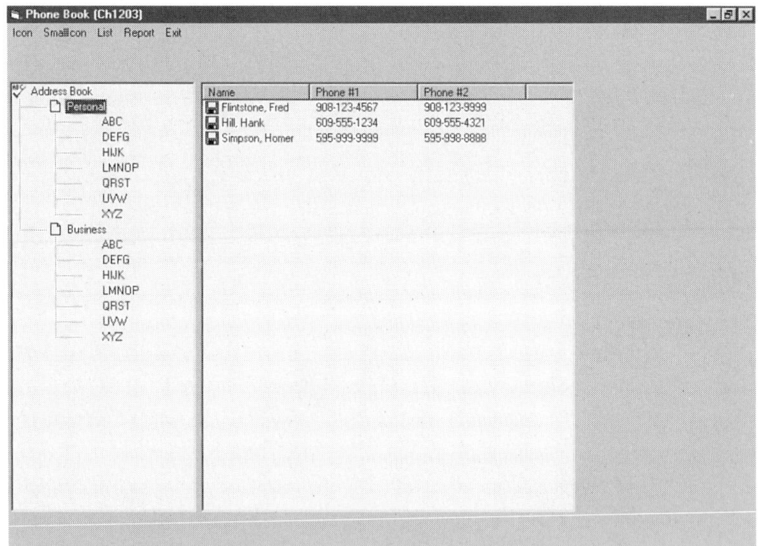

FIGURE 12.13.
The `CH1203.VBP` *project in action, with TreeView, ListView, and ImageList controls all working together.*

You can see that with a little more enhancing, you have a working phone book to use on your computer. By adding database access to add and retrieve the names and phone numbers to display in the list, this program would be complete. A completed copy of this application is included on the CD-ROM that comes with this book.

Summary

This chapter covered how to make use of the ListView and TreeView controls from the Windows common controls. In addition, you have seen how the ImageList control is used to store the bitmaps that will be used with both the TreeView and ListView controls. You have also seen how to incorporate both of these controls into a Visual Basic application to allow the user to select the information he needs using a format that he is familiar with (because it is just like the Windows Explorer).

Leveraging Windows: Using the Common Dialog Creation Control

IN THIS CHAPTER

In this chapter, you'll learn how to use one of most versatile controls in your Visual Basic 5 toolbox—the Common Dialog control. This control gives you access to the most commonly used services of the Windows operating system. You'll learn how you can use this single control to provide users access to their own font and color selections and give them the capability to print and perform printer setups and installations. You'll also learn how to use the Common Dialog control to easily open and save files from any available device, or access the built-in help services on the workstation—including the capability to link help files to the various dialog boxes.

Throughout this chapter, you'll build a sample Visual Basic 5 application that will demonstrate each of the dialog boxes available to you when you use the Common Dialog control. Each example focuses on a single dialog box service (fonts, colors, and so on) and is divided into three parts. The first part of the example shows you the basics of how to access the dialog box and get results. The second part shows how, with a little added coding, you can greatly enhance the efficiency and effectiveness of each of the dialog boxes. The third part of the example shows you how to add advanced options to your dialog boxes to customize them for your needs.

When you are finished with this chapter, you'll know how to unleash the power of one of the most useful controls in your programmer's toolkit. You'll know how to add customized fonts and colors to your dialog boxes, to provide access to printers, to easily add File Open and Save dialog boxes to your applications, and to help users get additional information about your program through the help services available through the Common Dialog control.

What Is the Common Dialog Control?

The Common Dialog control was one of the first controls developed by Microsoft. It was intended to be a single source for all the common services required by every good Windows program. Microsoft wanted to encourage programmers to make all their programs adhere to the Windows look and feel. The company reasoned that one of the best ways to encourage the common interface was to provide ready-made dialog boxes that handled the most commonly requested services: opening and saving files, setting the fonts and colors, handling printing, and gaining access to online help. To do this, Microsoft created a single control object that contained all these services—the Common Dialog control.

It's Not Like the Others

The Common Dialog control does not behave like most of the other controls that ship with Microsoft Visual Basic. First, it is not an intrinsic control; that is, it is not a built-in part of Visual Basic as are the TextBox, Label, and other basic controls. When you use the Common Dialog control, you are adding disk and memory requirements to your project.

NOTE

Including the Common Dialog control in your project will actually result in two additional disk files in your installation package: `COMDLG32.OCX` and `COMMMDLG.DLL`.

Because the Common Dialog control is not a built-in control, you can use it only after you have added it to your current project by using the Project | Components menu option (see Figure 13.1).

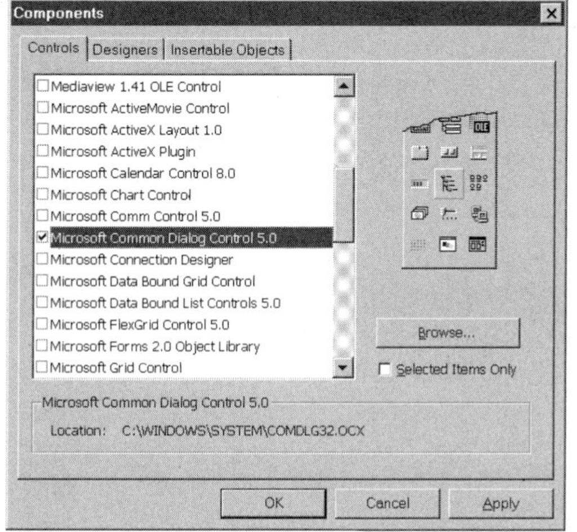

FIGURE 13.1.
Adding the Common Dialog control to the current project.

CAUTION

You will not be able to access any of the Common Dialog control's methods or properties unless you first add the component to your current project.

Another unusual thing about the Common Dialog control is that it is invisible at runtime. Even though you see it on your form at design time, you cannot see it when the program is actually running. You can't resize the Common Dialog control on the form, either, but because it is invisible while the program is running, its size and location on the form are of no significance.

Finally, unlike most other controls that have a single purpose (text input, picture display, and so on), the Common Dialog control actually provides several services. Instead of having a control for fonts, another control for colors, and so on, you can use the Common Dialog control to handle multiple chores. Although this is handy for programmers, it means that learning to understand and use the Common Dialog control can be more difficult than learning the other controls. Many of the same properties are used differently depending on the service you are requesting. And some of the properties are ignored completely for one service, but for another service that same property might be required!

You'll learn more about how each service uses the Common Dialog control properties later in this chapter. First, let's take a quick tour of all the methods and properties of the Common Dialog control.

The Methods of the Common Dialog Control

The Common Dialog control has only a handful of built-in methods. Table 13.1 lists these methods, along with a short description.

Table 13.1. The Common Dialog control methods.

Method	*Description*
`AboutBox`	Displays the About box for this control. Not needed for most programs.
`ShowColor`	Displays the Color selection dialog box. Used to allow users to select a color for painting forms, setting foreground or background colors for controls, and so on.
`ShowFont`	Displays the Font selection dialog box. Used to allow users to select font type, style, and size, and, optionally, to indicate underlines, strikethrough, and/or font color.
`ShowPrinter`	Displays the Printer dialog box. Used to allow users to select and install printers, indicate the number of copies to print, specify the starting and ending pages, and so on.
`ShowOpen`	Displays a File Open dialog box. Used to allow users to navigate any available device and locate and select one or more file objects to load, print, process, and so on.
`ShowSave`	Displays a File Save dialog box. Used to allow users to indicate the final save name of a file object.
`ShowHelp`	Provides access to several Windows Help dialog boxes, including displaying online help text, search dialog boxes, and other help services.

As you can see from the table, each method gives you access to one of the basic Windows operating-system services. In the sections that follow, you'll learn how to use each of these methods to provide easy access to the desired dialog box.

The Properties of the Common Dialog Control

Along with the seven methods shown previously, the Common Dialog control has 36 properties. The property list for the Common Dialog control is a bit daunting at first glance but is not really as difficult as it appears. First, ten of the properties are dialog box specific; in other words, they are used by only one (in a few cases by two) of the dialog box services. Another seven of the properties are part of the standard ActiveX control properties (`Name`, `Index`, `Tag`, and so on). Also, one of the properties (`Action`) is no longer in use in the current version of the Common Dialog control but is included for compatibility with earlier versions. That accounts for about half the properties in the list. The other half, however, presents a bit of a challenge. These properties are used by more than one dialog box and, in some cases, actually have a different meaning depending on the dialog box in service.

Finally, one property is very versatile: the `Flags` property. This single value is probably the most-used property of all. It is used to set various control flags that affect the behavior and appearance of the requested dialog box. And there are almost 70 different flag values! You'll learn about the various flag values as you learn about each dialog box service. For now, review Table 13.2 to get a quick summary of the Common Dialog control's properties and their descriptions. You'll also see a column that indicates the data type for the property and another that shows which dialog box method uses the property. The Basic designation in the Methods column indicates that the property is a basic ActiveX control property—one that appears for almost all the ActiveX controls.

Table 13.2. The properties of the Common Dialog control.

Property	*Valid Methods*	*Type*	*Description*
`Action`	All	`Integer`	Used to request a dialog box. Valid values for this property are `0`—No Action. `1`—Displays the Open dialog box. `2`—Displays the Save As dialog box. `3`—Displays the Color dialog box. `4`—Displays the Font dialog box. `5`—Displays the Printer dialog box. `6`—Runs `WINHLP32.EXE` (Help).

continues

Table 13.2. continued

Property	*Valid Methods*	*Type*	*Description*
			Note: This property is no longer in use and is only included for compatibility with earlier versions of the Common Dialog control. Its use is not recommended.
`CancelError`	All	`Boolean`	A value indicating whether an error is generated when the user clicks the Cancel button. If the value is set to `True`, an error code (`32755`) is returned when the user clicks the Cancel button on the dialog box.
`Color`	`ShowFont` `ShowColor`	`Long`	Returns or sets the selected color. This long integer can be set using the built-in `RGB()` or `QBColor()` function. You must set the `Flag` property to `cdlCFEffects` to include the `Color` property in the Font dialog box.
`Copies`	`ShowPrinter`	`Integer`	Indicates the number of copies that should be printed. This value may be ignored by some printer drivers.
`DefaultExt`	`ShowOpen` `ShowSave`	`String`	Used to set the default extension for reading and writing files—for example, `TXT` or `MDB`. The value in this property should *not* contain the dot (.).
`DialogTitle`	All except `ShowHelp`	`String`	This string is displayed at the top of the requested dialog box.

Property	*Valid Methods*	*Type*	*Description*
`FileName`	`ShowOpen` `ShowSave`	`String`	Returns or sets the complete name (device, folder, and filename) of the file to write or read. Can be set prior to calling the dialog box to act as a default value.
`FileTitle`	`ShowOpen` `ShowSave`	`String`	Returns the name of the file (without the device and folder) to read or write. Only works if the property is not set with `cdlOFNNoValidate`.
`Filter`	`ShowOpen` `ShowSave`	`String`	Used to set the list of file types displayed in the dialog box. Valid format is *`description¦mask`*, where *`description`* is a friendly string, and *`mask`* is the file filter to use (for example, `"TEXTFILES¦*.TXT"`). You can string multiple *`description|mask`* pairs (such as `"TEXT¦*.TXT¦ASCII¦*.ASC"`). Use the `FilterIndex` to set the property pair to display as the default selection.
`FilterIndex`	`ShowOpen` `ShowSave`	`Integer`	A value that indicates which of the *`description¦mask`* pairs in the `Filter` property should be used as the default set upon opening the dialog box. The first valid value is `1`, not `0`.

continues

Table 13.2. continued

Property	Valid Methods	Type	Description
`Flags`	All	`Long`	Contains one or more control values that alter the look and behavior of the requested dialog box. There are close to 70 different valid values depending on the requested dialog box. Detailed lists that apply to each dialog box are included in later sections of this chapter.
`FontBold` `FontItalic` `FontUnderline` `FontStrikethru`	`ShowFont`	`Boolean`	Boolean values that indicate whether the font effect is turned on (`True`) or off (`False`). You must set the `Flags` property to `cdlCFEffects` to use the `FontStrikethru` and `FontUnderline` properties.
`FontName`	`ShowFont`	`String`	Used to return or set the name of the selected font.
`FontSize`	`ShowFont`	`Integer`	Used to return or set the size of the selected font. The selected font determines valid values. The absolute maximum value is `2160`.
`FromPage` `ToPage`	`ShowPrinter`	`Integer`	Used to set or return the starting and ending page numbers to send to the printer. The `Flag` property must be set to `cdlPDPageNums` for these properties to be valid.
`hDC`	`ShowPrinter`	`Long`	Contains the device context handle of the selected printer. This value can be used in conjunction with Windows API calls.

Property	*Valid Methods*	*Type*	*Description*
`HelpCommand`	`ShowHelp`	`Long`	Indicates the type of help service you are requesting. There are 12 valid values for this property. See the section "The Help Services," later in this chapter, for details on how to use this property.
`HelpContext`	All	`Long`	A number indicating the help topic to display. Valid numbers are supplied by the author of the help file.
`HelpKey`	`ShowHelp`	`String`	A string indicating the keyword to search for and display in the help file. If an exact match is found, the help topic will be displayed. If more than one topic contains the selected keyword, a list of topics is displayed. If no topic contains the keyword, the keyword list is displayed with the closest match highlighted.
`Index`	Basic	`Integer`	Returns the index value that identifies this control in a control array.
`InitDir`	`ShowOpen` `ShowSave`	`String`	Used to indicate the default directory to use when displaying the Open or Save dialog box. If this value is empty, the current directory is used.
`Left, Top`	Basic	`Long`	Used to indicate the location of the control on the parent object (usually the form).

continues

Table 13.2. continued

Property	*Valid Methods*	*Type*	*Description*
`Max`, `Min`	`ShowFont` `ShowPrinter`	`Integer` `Integer`	For the `ShowFonts` method, used to indicate the maximum and minimum font size allowable. For the `ShowPrinter` method, used to indicate the maximum and minimum pages allowed in the `FromPage` and `ToPage` properties. If these values are used for the `ShowFont` method, the `Flags` property must be set to `cdlCFLimitSize`.
`MaxFileSize`	`ShowOpen`	`Integer`	Used to set the maximum size of the filename allowed in the `ShowOpen` dialog box. Default value is `256`. Minimum value is `1`; the maximum is 32,000 MB. If the `Flag` property is set to `cdlOFNAllowMultiSelect`, it is advisable to set this value higher than the 256-byte default.
`Name`	Basic	`String`	The internal name of the control object.
`Object`	Basic	`Object`	Used for OLE Automation services.
`Parent`	Basic	`Object`	Contains the name of the object on which the Common Dialog control resides (usually a form).
`PrinterDefault`	`ShowPrinter`	`Boolean`	Indicates whether the user's settings in the `ShowPrinter` dialog box are saved to the Registry. The default value is `True`.

Property	*Valid Methods*	*Type*	*Description*
`Tag`	Basic	`String`	Free-form storage space. Can be used for any type of information required.

As you can see from the table, the Common Dialog control has quite a collection of properties to work with. One of the real challenges of working with the Common Dialog control is learning to use these properties to create effective dialog boxes. In the sections that follow you'll learn how each dialog box can be modified and improved through the use of the proper collection of property settings.

Building the Common Dialog Control Sample Form

Before jumping into the Common Dialog control sample code, let's build a simple input form. This form will act as the test bed for the various Common Dialog control methods by simulating most of the common operations that every Visual Basic application must deal with and helping you learn how to use the Common Dialog control to provide real-life solutions to common programming challenges.

Laying Out the `cdlSample` Form

First, start a new Visual Basic 5 Standard EXE project. Set the project's `Name` property to `prjCDLSample` and set the default form's `Name` property to `frmCDLSample`. Next, select Project | Components from the main menu of Visual Basic 5 and select Microsoft Common Dialog Control 5.0 from the list of available components that appears (see Figure 13.1).

After the Common Dialog control has been added to your project, lay out the `cdlSample` form using Table 13.3 and Figure 13.2 as a guide.

TIP

You'll notice that several controls have their `Index` property set. This indicates that these are control arrays. The easiest way to build a control array is to add one control to the form, set all its properties (including the `Index` property), and then use Copy and Paste to add additional controls. This will cut down on typographical errors and speed up the form design process.

FIGURE 13.2.
Laying out the `cdlSample` *form.*

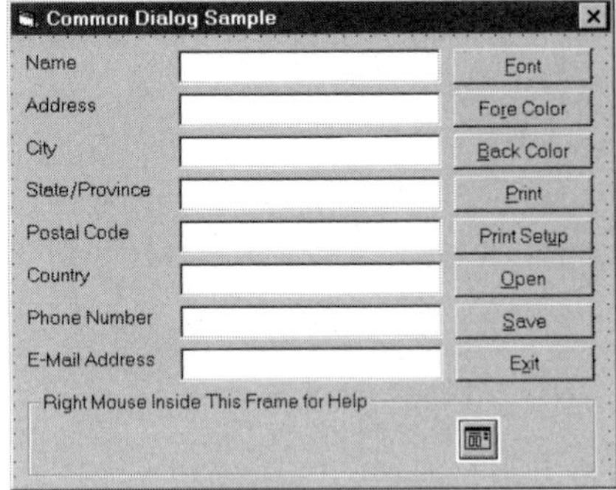

Table 13.3. The configuration of the controls for the `frmCDLSample` form.

Control	*Property*	*Setting*
Form	`Name`	`frmCDLSample`
	`BorderStyle`	`3 - Fixed Dialog`
	`Caption`	`Common Dialog Sample`
	`Height`	`3816`
	`Left`	`36`
	`Top`	`324`
	`Width`	`5208`
CommonDialog	`Name`	`cdlSample`
	`Left`	`3840`
	`Top`	`3240`
Frame	`Name`	`fraHelp`
	`Caption`	`Right Mouse Inside This Frame for Help`
	`Height`	`732`
	`Left`	`120`
	`Top`	`3000`
	`Width`	`4932`
TextBox	`Name`	`txtField`
	`Height`	`288`
	`Index`	`7`
	`Left`	`1440`
	`Tag`	`E-Mail`
	`Text`	(Nothing)

Control	Property	Setting
	Top	2640
	Width	2292
CommandButton	Name	cmdDialog
	Caption	E&xit
	Height	300
	Index	7
	Left	3840
	Top	2640
	Width	1200
TextBox	Name	txtField
	Height	288
	Index	6
	Left	1440
	Tag	Phone
	Text	(Nothing)
	Top	2280
	Width	2292
CommandButton	Name	cmdDialog
	Caption	&Save
	Height	300
	Index	6
	Left	3840
	Top	2280
	Width	1200
CommandButton	Name	cmdDialog
	Caption	&Open
	Height	300
	Index	5
	Left	3840
	Top	1920
	Width	1200

continues

Table 13.3. continued

Control	*Property*	*Setting*
TextBox	Name	txtField
	Height	288
	Index	5
	Left	1440
	Tag	Country
	Text	(Nothing)
	Top	1920
	Width	2292
CommandButton	Name	cmdDialog
	Caption	Print Set&up
	Height	300
	Index	4
	Left	3840
	Top	1560
	Width	1200
CommandButton	Name	cmdDialog
	Caption	&Print
	Height	300
	Index	3
	Left	3840
	Top	1200
	Width	1200
CommandButton	Name	cmdDialog
	Caption	&Back Color
	Height	300
	Index	2
	Left	3840
	Top	840
	Width	1200

Control	*Property*	*Setting*
CommandButton	Name	cmdDialog
	Caption	Fo&re Color
	Height	300
	Index	1
	Left	3840
	Top	480
	Width	1200
CommandButton	Name	cmdDialog
	Caption	&Font
	Height	300
	Index	0
	Left	3840
	Top	120
	Width	1200
TextBox	Name	txtField
	Height	288
	Index	4
	Left	1440
	Tag	Postal Code
	Text	(Nothing)
	Top	1560
	Width	2292
TextBox	Name	txtField
	Height	288
	Index	3
	Left	1440
	Tag	State/Province
	Text	(Nothing)
	Top	1200
	Width	2292

continues

Table 13.3. continued

Control	Property	Setting
TextBox	Name	txtField
	Height	288
	Index	2
	Left	1440
	Tag	City
	Text	(Nothing)
	Top	840
	Width	2292
TextBox	Name	txtField
	Height	288
	Index	1
	Left	1440
	Tag	Address
	Text	(Nothing)
	Top	480
	Width	2292
TextBox	Name	txtField
	Height	288
	Index	0
	Left	1440
	Tag	Name
	Text	(Nothing)
	Top	120
	Width	2292
Label	Name	lblField
	Caption	E-Mail Address
	Height	252
	Index	7
	Left	120
	Top	2640
	Width	1212

Control	Property	Setting
Label	Name	lblField
	Caption	Phone Number
	Height	252
	Index	6
	Left	120
	Top	2280
	Width	1212
Label	Name	lblField
	Caption	Country
	Height	252
	Index	5
	Left	120
	Top	1920
	Width	1212
Label	Name	lblField
	Caption	Postal Code
	Height	252
	Index	4
	Left	120
	Top	1560
	Width	1212
Label	Name	lblField
	Caption	State/Province
	Height	252
	Index	3
	Left	120
	Top	1200
	Width	1212
Label	Name	lblField
	Caption	City
	Height	252

continues

Table 13.3. continued

Control	*Property*	*Setting*
	`Index`	`2`
	`Left`	`120`
	`Top`	`840`
	`Width`	`1212`
Label	`Name`	`lblField`
	`Caption`	`Address`
	`Height`	`252`
	`Index`	`1`
	`Left`	`120`
	`Top`	`480`
	`Width`	`1212`
Label	`Name`	`lblField`
	`Caption`	`Name`
	`Height`	`252`
	`Index`	`0`
	`Left`	`120`
	`Top`	`120`
	`Width`	`1212`
Menu	`Name`	`mnuHelp`
	`Caption`	`&Help`
	`Visible`	`0 - False`
Menu	`Name`	`mnuHelpItem`
	`Caption`	`&Contents`
	`Index`	`0`
Menu	`Name`	`mnuHelpItem`
	`Caption`	`&Index...`
	`Index`	`1`
Menu	`Name`	`mnuHelpItem`
	`Caption`	`&Help on Help`
	`Index`	`2`

Control	*Property*	*Setting*
Menu	`Name`	`mnuHelpItem`
	`Caption`	`&Key Word`
	`Index`	`3`
Menu	`Name`	`mnuHelpItem`
	`Caption`	`Help Partial Key`
	`Index`	`4`
Menu	`Name`	`mnuHelpItem`
	`Caption`	`Help Macro`
	`Index`	`5`

You'll notice that the control list contains a set of menu array controls. It's easy to build menu arrays. Simply set the `Name` property to the same name as another control and increment the `Index` property each time you add a new copy of the control (see Figure 13.3).

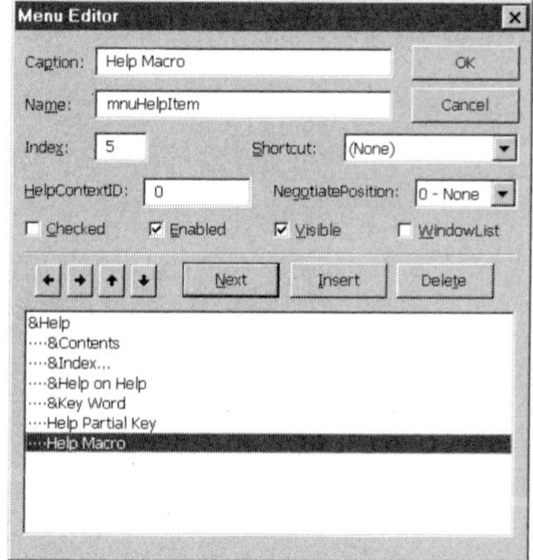

FIGURE 13.3.
Building the `cdlSample` *menu.*

You might also note that the top-level menu control (`mnuHelp`) has its `Visible` property set to `False`. That is because you are building a pop-up menu for the form. Pop-up menus do not always appear on the form itself until the user performs the correct sequence of mouse clicks and keystrokes in the right place on the form. In this example, the user will be able to click the right mouse button while the cursor is hovering over the `fraCDLSample` frame to make the pop-up menu appear.

Also be sure to enter the information in the `Tag` properties of the text box controls. You'll need that data when you code the `ShowSave` and `ShowOpen` dialogs.

After building the Common Dialog control sample form, save the project (`PRJCDLSAMPLE.VBP`) and the form (`FRMCDLSAMPLE.FRM`) before going on to the next section.

Coding the `frmCDLSample` Form

Before coding the specific examples, you need to add a bit of code to help the form work correctly. First, add the code in Listing 13.1 to the General Declarations section of the form.

Listing 13.1. Coding the General Declarations section of the form.

```
Option Explicit

' color flags
Enum clrType
    clrFore = 0
    clrBack = 1
End Enum

' form-level vars
Dim strHelpFile As String

' help context ids for dialogs
Private Const Select_a_Font = 10
Private Const Select_a_Foreground_Color = 11
Private Const Select_A_Background_Color = 12
Private Const Print_the_Data = 13
Private Const Perform_Print_Setup = 14
Private Const Open_the_Data_File = 15
Private Const Save_the_Data_File = 16
```

The enumerated type (`clrType`) will be used to indicate whether the user wants to apply the color selection as the foreground or the background, the `strHelpFile` string will be used throughout the project to access and display Help files, and the list of private constants is settings that point to specific topics in the help file.

Now add the code from Listing 13.2 to the `Form_Load` event of the form.

Listing 13.2. Coding the `Form_Load` event.

```
Private Sub Form_Load()

    ' point to sample help file
    strHelpFile = App.Path & "\Help\cdlSample.hlp"

End Sub
```

The code in Listing 13.2 sets the `strHelpFile` variable to the location of the `CDLSAMPLE.HLP` help file. You will need to adjust this setting if the `CDLSAMPLE.HLP` is stored somewhere else on your machine.

NOTE

The `CDLSAMPLE.HLP` document is a compiled Windows help file. It was built using a help compiler tool in conjunction with Microsoft Word 97. Although the MS Help Compiler ships with Visual Basic 5, creating Windows help files is not covered in this chapter. The Help folder contains all the source code for the help file. If you know how to use the MS Help Compiler, you can use these source code files to create your own custom help files.

Now add the code from Listing 13.3. This is the code that will pop up the Help menu each time the user clicks the right mouse button inside the frame control at the bottom of the form.

Listing 13.3. Coding the Help menu's PopUp event.

```
Private Sub fraHelp_MouseDown(Button As Integer, Shift As Integer,
   X As Single, Y As Single)

    ' respond to right mouse over form

    If Button = vbRightButton Then
        PopupMenu mnuHelp
    End If

End Sub
```


Next, you need to add several custom methods to the form. In this first stage, you'll add the new methods, but you will not add any Visual Basic code to them. This creates a set of stub methods that you will fill in later.

TIP

Stub methods are short entries that declare the methods but contain no working code. Stub methods are great for building large systems where you don't have all the details worked out but need to have the method declared so that other routines work without errors.

To add new methods to the form, select Tools | Add Procedure from the menu bar, fill in the method name in the dialog box and click OK (see Figure 13.4).

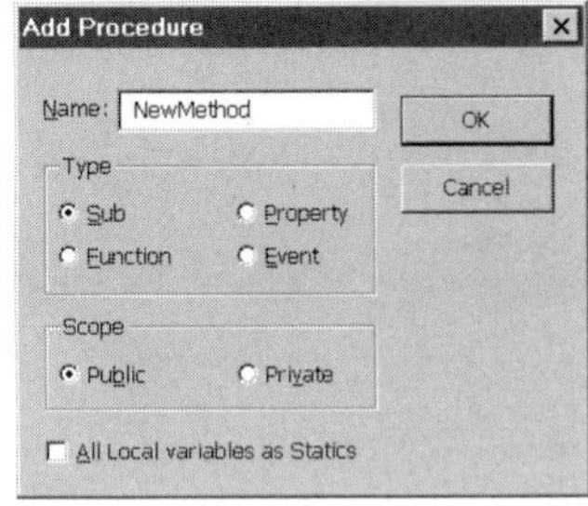

FIGURE 13.4.
Adding a new method to the form.

Using the information in Table 13.4, create the six methods needed for the `cdlSample` project.

Table 13.4. Adding custom methods to the form.

Method Name	*Parameters*
`SetFont`	
`SetColor`	`clrFlag as clrType`
`SetPrint`	
`SetPrintSetup`	
`ReadData`	
`SaveData`	

After adding the methods, you need to locate the `SetColor` method and add the parameter declaration to the method. When you're finished, it should look like the following code sample:

```
Public Sub SetColor(clrFlag As clrType)
End Sub
```

The last set of code you need to add to the basic form is shown in Listing 13.4. This is the code that translates the command-button clicks into code that executes the proper custom methods.

Listing 13.4. Coding the `cmdDialog_Click` event.

```
Private Sub cmdDialog_Click(Index As Integer)

    ' handle cdl selections

    Select Case Index
        Case 0 ' font
            Call SetFont
        Case 1 ' fore color
            Call SetColor(clrFore)
        Case 2 ' back color
            Call SetColor(clrBack)
        Case 3 ' print
            Call SetPrint
```

```
        Case 4 ' print setup
            Call SetPrintSetup
        Case 5 ' open
            Call ReadData
        Case 6 ' save
            Call SaveData
        Case 7 ' exit
            Unload Me
    End Select

End Sub
```

That's all the setup code you need to add. Now you're ready to start coding the Common Dialog control's demonstration routines. Be sure to save the form (`FRMCDLSAMPLE.FRM`) and the project (`PRJCDLSAMPLE.VBP`) before you continue with the chapter.

The Font Dialog Box

The first Common Dialog control demonstration routine you'll create is the one that shows how you can add custom font selections to your projects. In this example, you'll add some code to the `SetFont` custom method. This code will execute the `ShowFont` method of the Common Dialog control and then use the information from the dialog box to alter the fonts on the demonstration form.

The Basic ShowFont Example

Locate the `SetFont` custom method you created earlier and enter the code from Listing 13.5. This will set up the Common Dialog control to handle a call to the `ShowFont` method and then use the resulting selections to alter the fonts used on the sample form.

Listing 13.5. Coding the basic ShowFont example.

```
Public Sub SetFont()

    ' set font for entire screen


    ' in case control does not support the property
    On Error Resume Next

    ' for local loop
    Dim ctlTemp As Control
    Dim lngFlags As Long

    ' ignore user cancels
    cdlSample.CancelError = False

    ' set some flag values
```

continues

Listing 13.5. continued

```
    lngFlags = lngFlags + cdlCFBoth ' use both screen and printer fonts
    cdlSample.Flags = lngFlags       ' move to property

    ' show font screen
    cdlSample.ShowFont

    ' set all controls to user selection
    For Each ctlTemp In Me.Controls
        ctlTemp.FontName = cdlSample.FontName
        ctlTemp.FontSize = cdlSample.FontSize
        ctlTemp.FontBold = cdlSample.FontBold
        ctlTemp.FontItalic = cdlSample.FontItalic
        ctlTemp.FontUnderline = cdlSample.FontUnderline
        ctlTemp.FontStrikethru = cdlSample.FontStrikethru
        ctlTemp.ForeColor = cdlSample.Color
    Next

End Sub
```

The code in Listing 13.5 sets the `CancelError` property to `False` so that you won't get an error message if the user clicks the Cancel button on the dialog box. The next section of code sets the `Flag` property to indicate that you want to see both screen and printer fonts in the list of available fonts. Then it executes the call for the `ShowFonts` dialog box.

The next section of code does not execute until the user closes the Fonts dialog box. This code takes the settings from the dialog box and copies them to every control on the form.

Save and execute the project. When you click the Font button, you should see a dialog box that looks like the one in Figure 13.5.

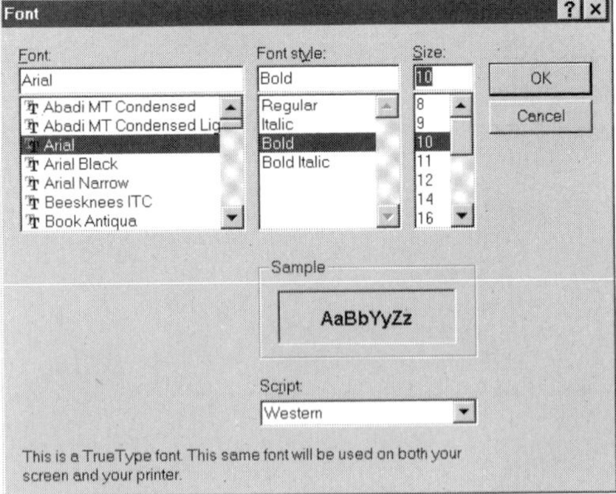

FIGURE 13.5.
Viewing the Font dialog box.

Some Added Settings for the Font Dialog Box

You might have noticed that the code in Listing 13.5 copies the `Underline`, `Strikethru`, and `Color` properties from the Common Dialog control to the controls on the form, but the Font dialog box has no options displayed for these features. To see these added special font effects, you need to include additional values in the `Flag` property.

In fact, there are several possible values for the flag that can be useful in creating an effective Font dialog box. Modify the code for the `SetFont` method so that it matches the code shown in Listing 13.6.

Listing 13.6. Some added settings for the Font dialog box.

```
Public Sub SetFont()

    ' set font for entire screen


    ' in case control does not support the property
    On Error Resume Next

    ' for local loop
    Dim ctlTemp As Control
    Dim lngFlags As Long

    ' ignore user cancels
    cdlSample.CancelError = False
    cdlSample.Min = 8  ' minimum font size
    cdlSample.Max = 12 ' maximum font size

    ' set some flag values
    lngFlags = cdlCFApply                         ' add apply button
    lngFlags = lngFlags + cdlCFHelpButton         ' show help button
    lngFlags = lngFlags + cdlCFEffects            ' allow colors/underline/strikethru
    lngFlags = lngFlags + cdlCFBoth               ' use both screen and printer fonts
    lngFlags = lngFlags + cdlCFForceFontExist     ' must select an available font
    lngFlags = lngFlags + cdlCFLimitSize          ' control min/max size
    cdlSample.Flags = lngFlags                    ' move to property

    ' show font screen
    cdlSample.ShowFont

    ' set all controls to user selection
    For Each ctlTemp In Me.Controls
        ctlTemp.FontName = cdlSample.FontName
        ctlTemp.FontSize = cdlSample.FontSize
        ctlTemp.FontBold = cdlSample.FontBold
        ctlTemp.FontItalic = cdlSample.FontItalic
        ctlTemp.FontUnderline = cdlSample.FontUnderline
        ctlTemp.FontStrikethru = cdlSample.FontStrikethru
        ctlTemp.ForeColor = cdlSample.Color
    Next

End Sub
```

Note the addition of a number of new `Flag` settings and the inclusion of the `Min` and `Max` properties to limit the size of the fonts available to the user. Save and run the project. When you click the Font button, you should see something like the dialog box shown in Figure 13.6.

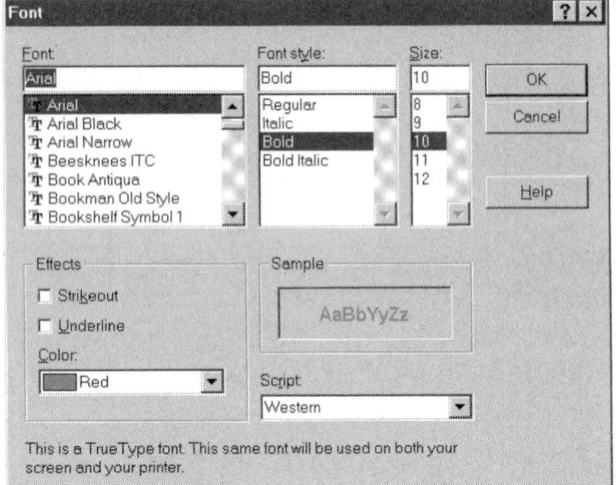

FIGURE 13.6.
Viewing the modified Font dialog box.

The Font Dialog Box's Flag Settings

The flag settings you see in Listing 13.6 are not all the possible settings. Because the Font dialog box can be used to set both screen and printer fonts, there are a number of flag settings you can use to limit the types of fonts shown in the dialog box. Table 13.5 lists all the valid values for the `Flag` property when you are calling the `ShowFont` method of the Common Dialog control.

Table 13.5. Valid `Flag` values for the `ShowFont` method.

Constant	*Value*	*Description*
`cdlCFANSIOnly`	`&H400`	Specifies that the dialog box allows only those fonts that use the Windows character set. If this flag is set, the user won't be able to select a font that contains only symbols.
`cdlCFApply`	`&H200`	Enables the Apply button in the dialog box.
`cdlCFBoth`	`&H3`	Causes the dialog box to list the available printer and screen fonts. The `hDC` property identifies the device context associated with the printer.
`cdlCFEffects`	`&H100`	Specifies that the dialog box enables strikethrough, underline, and color effects.
`cdlCFFixedPitchOnly`	`&H4000`	Specifies that the dialog box selects only fixed-pitch fonts.

Constant	*Value*	*Description*
`cdlCFForceFontExist`	`&H10000`	Specifies that an error message box is displayed if the user attempts to select a font or style that doesn't exist.
`cdlCFHelpButton`	`&H4`	Causes the dialog box to display a Help button.
`cdlCFLimitSize`	`&H2000`	Specifies that the dialog box selects only font sizes within the range specified by the `Min` and `Max` properties.
`cdlCFNoFaceSel`	`&H80000`	Indicates that no font name has been selected.
`cdlCFNoSimulations`	`&H1000`	Specifies that the dialog box doesn't allow graphic device interface (GDI) font simulations.
`cdlCFNoSizeSel`	`&H200000`	Indicates that no font size was selected.
`cdlCFNoStyleSel`	`&H100000`	Indicates that no style was selected.
`cdlCFNoVectorFonts`	`&H800`	Specifies that the dialog box doesn't allow vector-font selections.
`cdlCFPrinterFonts`	`&H2`	Causes the dialog box to list only the fonts supported by the printer, as specified by the `hDC` property.
`cdlCFScalableOnly`	`&H20000`	Specifies that the dialog box allows only the selection of fonts that can be scaled.
`CdlCFScreenFonts`	`&H1`	Causes the dialog box to list only the screen fonts supported by the system.
`cdlCFTTOnly`	`&H40000`	Specifies that the dialog box allows only the selection of TrueType fonts.
`cdlCFWYSIWYG`	`&H8000`	Specifies that the dialog box allows only the selection of fonts that are available both on the printer and onscreen. If this flag is set, the `cdlCFBoth` and `cdlCFScalableOnly` flags should also be set.

Many of the `Flag` values are mutually exclusive, and some work in partnership. You can experiment with the various values to arrive at a Font dialog box that fits your needs.

An Advanced Font Dialog Box

When you ran the last example, you might have noticed that clicking the new Help button on the Font dialog box did not result in any helpful information. This is because you, as the programmer, must supply the help information for the button. Setting some of the help-related properties of the Common Dialog control before you execute the `ShowFonts` method does this.

The code in Listing 13.7 shows the `SetFont` method with additional code that sets the help values and allows the user to get customized help information when the Help button is clicked. Change your `SetFont` code to match the code in Listing 13.7 and then save and run your project.

Listing 13.7. Adding custom help to the Font dialog box.

```
Public Sub SetFont()

    ' set font for entire screen


    ' in case control does not support the property
    On Error Resume Next

    ' for local loop
    Dim ctlTemp As Control
    Dim lngFlags As Long

    ' ignore user cancels
    cdlSample.CancelError = False
    cdlSample.Min = 8  ' minimum font size
    cdlSample.Max = 12 ' maximum font size

    ' set some flag values
    lngFlags = cdlCFApply                       ' add apply button
    lngFlags = lngFlags + cdlCFHelpButton       ' show help button
    lngFlags = lngFlags + cdlCFEffects          ' allow colors/underline/
                                                ' strikethru
    lngFlags = lngFlags + cdlCFBoth             ' use both screen and printer
                                                ' fonts
    lngFlags = lngFlags + cdlCFForceFontExist   ' must select an available font
    lngFlags = lngFlags + cdlCFLimitSize        ' control min/max size
    cdlSample.Flags = lngFlags                  ' move to property

    ' set help topic for button
    cdlSample.HelpFile = strHelpFile
    cdlSample.HelpCommand = cdlHelpContext
    cdlSample.HelpContext = Select_a_Font

    ' show font screen
    cdlSample.ShowFont

    ' set all controls to user selection
    For Each ctlTemp In Me.Controls
        ctlTemp.FontName = cdlSample.FontName
        ctlTemp.FontSize = cdlSample.FontSize
```

```
        ctlTemp.FontBold = cdlSample.FontBold
        ctlTemp.FontItalic = cdlSample.FontItalic
        ctlTemp.FontUnderline = cdlSample.FontUnderline
        ctlTemp.FontStrikethru = cdlSample.FontStrikethru
        ctlTemp.ForeColor = cdlSample.Color
    Next

End Sub
```

Now when you run the project, you can click the Help button and see customized help on how to use the control (see Figure 13.7).

FIGURE 13.7.
Viewing the Font dialog box's Help information.

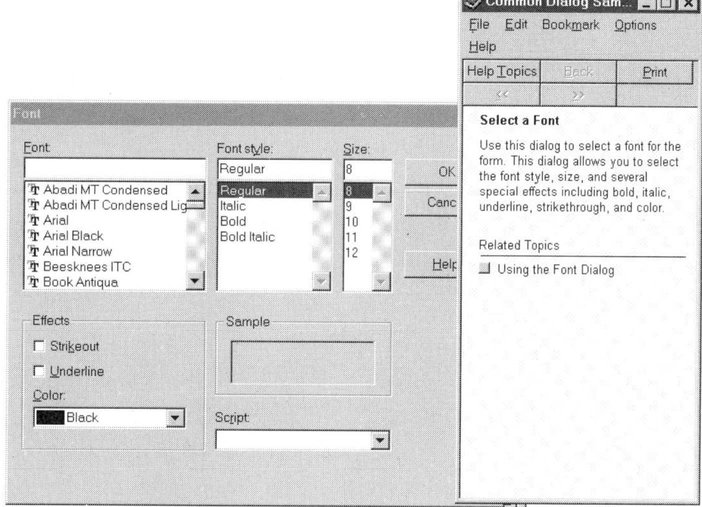

Now that you've completed the Font dialog box example, you're ready to move on to the next Common Dialog control dialog box: the Color dialog box.

The Color Dialog Box

The Color dialog box is used to collect information about color selections from the user. You can use this information to set the foreground or background color of any control, including any lines you might draw or the background of the form itself. In this example, you'll add code that will reset either the foreground or background colors of all the controls on the form.

The Basic Color Dialog Box Example

Locate the `SetColor` method you added earlier and enter the code shown in Listing 13.8. This code simply starts the Color dialog box and, on return, copies the selected color to either the `ForeColor` or `BackColor` property of the form's controls.

Listing 13.8. Coding the basic Color dialog box example.

```
Public Sub SetColor(clrFlag As clrType)

    ' set color for entire form



    ' in case object does not support colors
    On Error Resume Next

    ' for local loop
    Dim ctlTemp As Control
    Dim lngFlags As Long

    ' ignore user cancel
    cdlSample.CancelError = False

    ' show color set
    cdlSample.ShowColor

    ' set all controls w/ user selection
    For Each ctlTemp In Me.Controls
        If clrFlag = clrFore Then
            ctlTemp.ForeColor = cdlSample.Color
        Else
            If TypeOf ctlTemp Is TextBox Then
                ctlTemp.BackColor = vbWhite          ' force inputs to white
            Else
                ctlTemp.BackColor = cdlSample.Color ' use selected color
            End If
        End If
    Next

    ' set form w/ user selection
    If clrFlag = clrFore Then
        Me.ForeColor = cdlSample.Color
    Else
        Me.BackColor = cdlSample.Color
    End If

End Sub
```

After adding this code, save and run your project. When you click the ForeColor or BackColor button, you should see a dialog box that looks like the one in Figure 13.8.

Some Added Settings for the Color Dialog Box

You can add a few `Flag` values to improve the Color dialog box. Modify your `SetColor` code to match the code in Listing 13.9.

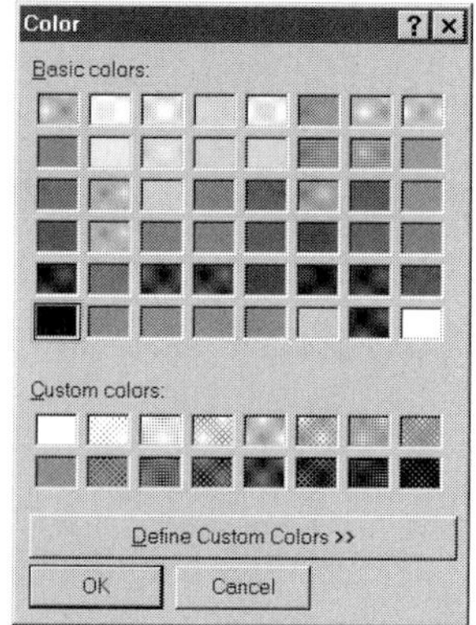

FIGURE 13.8.
Viewing the basic Color dialog box.

Listing 13.9. Some added settings for the Color dialog box.

```
Public Sub SetColor(clrFlag As clrType)

    ' set color for entire form



    ' in case object does not support colors
    On Error Resume Next

    ' for local loop
    Dim ctlTemp As Control
    Dim lngFlags As Long

    ' ignore user cancel
    cdlSample.CancelError = False
    lngFlags = cdlCCFullOpen                    ' show full color palette
    lngFlags = lngFlags + cdlCCHelpButton       ' display help button
    lngFlags = lngFlags + cdlCCRGBInit          ' preset the color
    cdlSample.Flags = lngFlags                  ' move to property

    ' set starting color
    If clrFlag = clrFore Then
        cdlSample.Color = Me.ForeColor
    Else
        cdlSample.Color = Me.BackColor
    End If

    ' show color set
    cdlSample.ShowColor

    ' set all controls w/ user selection
    For Each ctlTemp In Me.Controls
        If clrFlag = clrFore Then
            ctlTemp.ForeColor = cdlSample.Color
```

continues

Listing 13.9. continued

```
        Else
            If TypeOf ctlTemp Is TextBox Then
                ctlTemp.BackColor = vbWhite             ' force inputs to white
            Else
                ctlTemp.BackColor = cdlSample.Color     ' use selected color
            End If
        End If
    Next

    ' set form w/ user selection
    If clrFlag = clrFore Then
        Me.ForeColor = cdlSample.Color
    Else
        Me.BackColor = cdlSample.Color
    End If

End Sub
```

Notice that, along with new `Flag` property settings, the code in Listing 13.9 also copies the current color (foreground or background) into the `Color` property *before* executing the `ShowColor` method.

When you save and run the project this time, you'll see an expanded Color dialog box when you click the ForeColor or BackColor button (see Figure 13.9).

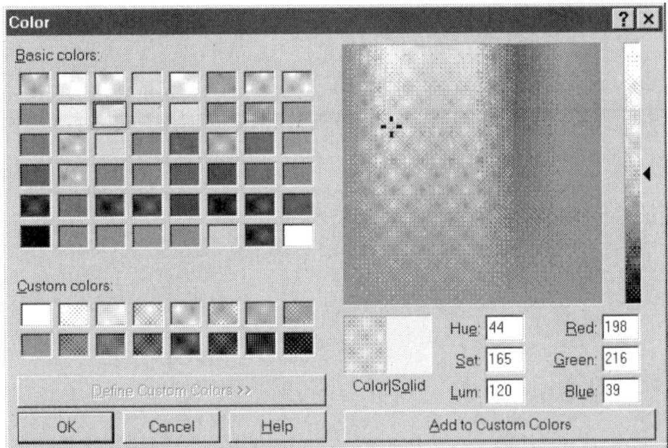

FIGURE 13.9.
Viewing the expanded Color dialog box.

The Color Dialog Box Flag Settings

There are only four possible `Flag` property settings for the Color dialog box (see Table 13.6).

Table 13.6. Valid Flag settings for the Color dialog box.

Constant	Value	Description
cdlCCFullOpen	&H2	Entire dialog box is displayed, including the Define Custom Colors section.
cdlCCHelpButton	&H8	Causes the dialog box to display a Help button.
cdlCCPreventFullOpen	&H4	Disables the Define Custom Colors command button and prevents the user from defining custom colors.
cdlCCRGBInit	&H1	Sets the initial color value for the dialog box.

CAUTION

Due to a typographical error, the help file that ships with some copies of Visual Basic 5 incorrectly identifies the cdlCCFullOpen constant as cdCClFullOpen and the cdlHelpButton constant as cldShowHelp. Be sure to use the correct constants when setting the Flag value.

Adding Help to the Color Dialog Box

Finally, you can use the help-related properties to establish a custom help topic for the Help button that appears on the Color form. Modify your SetColor method to match the code in Listing 13.10 and then save and run the project.

Listing 13.10. Adding help to the Color dialog box.

```
Public Sub SetColor(clrFlag As clrType)

    ' set color for entire form



    ' in case object does not support colors
    On Error Resume Next

    ' for local loop
    Dim ctlTemp As Control
    Dim lngFlags As Long

    ' ignore user cancel
    cdlSample.CancelError = False
```

continues

Listing 13.10. continued

```
    lngFlags = cdlCCFullOpen                          ' show full color palette
    lngFlags = lngFlags + cdlCCHelpButton             ' display help button
    lngFlags = lngFlags + cdlCCRGBInit                ' preset the color
    cdlSample.Flags = lngFlags                        ' move to property

    ' set starting color
    If clrFlag = clrFore Then
        cdlSample.Color = Me.ForeColor
    Else
        cdlSample.Color = Me.BackColor
    End If

    ' set help topic for button
    cdlSample.HelpFile = strHelpFile
    cdlSample.HelpCommand = cdlHelpContext
    If clrFlag = clrFore Then
        cdlSample.HelpContext = Select_a_Foreground_Color
    Else
        cdlSample.HelpContext = Select_A_Background_Color
    End If

    ' show color set
    cdlSample.ShowColor

    ' set all controls w/ user selection
    For Each ctlTemp In Me.Controls
        If clrFlag = clrFore Then
            ctlTemp.ForeColor = cdlSample.Color
        Else
            If TypeOf ctlTemp Is TextBox Then
                ctlTemp.BackColor = vbWhite               ' force inputs to white
            Else
                ctlTemp.BackColor = cdlSample.Color   ' use selected color
            End If
        End If
    Next

    ' set form w/ user selection
    If clrFlag = clrFore Then
        Me.ForeColor = cdlSample.Color
    Else
        Me.BackColor = cdlSample.Color
    End If

End Sub
```

Notice that the `SetColor` method sets the help topic to match either the foreground or background color change request.

Be sure to save your form (`FRMCDLSAMPLE.FRM`) and project (`PRJCDLSAMPLE.VBP`) before continuing.

The Print Dialog Box

You can use the ShowPrinter method to display the Print dialog box. This dialog box allows users to select (or install) a printer and set the print range, the number of copies, and the collate option. You can also allow (or remove) a Print To File check box. In this example, you'll display the dialog box and then, using the selected settings, send data to the printer for output.

The Basic Print Dialog Box

Locate the SetPrint method you built earlier and add the code from Listing 13.11 to it. This code gets the user's selections and then sends a copy of the data to the attached default printer.

Listing 13.11. Coding the basic Print dialog box.

```
Public Sub SetPrint()

    ' handle call for a print run

    On Error GoTo SetPrintErr       ' trap for errors

    ' some local  vars
    Dim ctlTemp As Control
    Dim lngFlags As Long            ' use to hold control flags

    ' don't ignore user cancel
    cdlSample.CancelError = True

    ' show print selection dialog
    cdlSample.ShowPrinter

    ' send header to the print device
    Printer.Print "Common Dialog Sample Printout"      ' title
    Printer.Print Now()                                ' date
    Printer.Print ""                                   ' empty line

    ' print data
    For Each ctlTemp In Me.Controls                        ' loop through controls
        If TypeOf ctlTemp Is TextBox Then                  ' text box?
            Printer.Print ctlTemp.Tag; "="; ctlTemp.Text   ' write it out
        End If                                             ' ctlTemp=Textbox
    Next                                                   ' ctlTemp

    Printer.EndDoc                                         ' end of job
    Exit Sub

SetPrintErr:

End Sub
```

Notice in the code that the CancelError property has been set to True for the first time. When sending data to another device (printer, disk drive, FTP location, and so on), it's best to allow the user to cancel the job if he wants.

When you save and run the project and click the Print button, you'll see a dialog box that looks like the one in Figure 13.10.

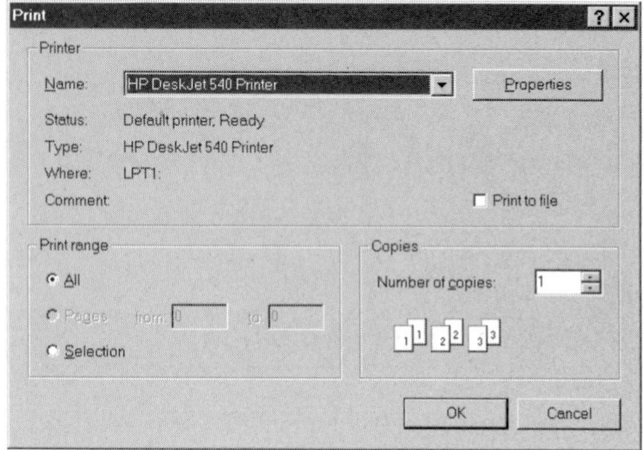

FIGURE 13.10.
Viewing the basic Print dialog box.

Some Added Settings for the Print Dialog Box

You can greatly improve the Print dialog box by including some additional settings for the Common Dialog control properties. Modify your version of the `SetPrint` example to match the one shown in Listing 13.12.

Listing 13.12. Some added settings for the Print dialog box.

```
Public Sub SetPrint()

    ' handle call for a print run

    On Error GoTo SetPrintErr                   ' trap for errors

    ' some local  vars
    Dim ctlTemp As Control
    Dim lngFlags As Long                        ' use to hold control flags

    ' don't ignore user cancel
    cdlSample.CancelError = True

    ' handle various flag options
    ' let printer decide if multi-copies are allowed
    lngFlags = cdlPDUseDevModeCopies            ' let printer decide if
    lngFlags = lngFlags + cdlPDHelpButton       ' show help button for user
    lngFlags = lngFlags + cdlPDPageNums         ' allow page num option
    lngFlags = lngFlags + cdlPDNoSelection      ' disallow selection option
    lngFlags = lngFlags + cdlPDHidePrintToFile  ' hide print to file flag
    cdlSample.Flags = lngFlags                  ' move flags to cdl property

    ' show print selection dialog
    cdlSample.ShowPrinter

    ' send header to the print device
```

```
    Printer.Print "Common Dialog Sample Printout" ' title
    Printer.Print Now()                           ' date
    Printer.Print ""                              ' empty line

    ' print data
    For Each ctlTemp In Me.Controls                        ' loop through controls
        If TypeOf ctlTemp Is TextBox Then                  ' text box?
            Printer.Print ctlTemp.Tag; "="; ctlTemp.Text   ' write it out
        End If                                             ' ctlTemp=Textbox
    Next                                                   ' ctlTemp

    Printer.EndDoc                                         ' end of job
    Exit Sub

SetPrintErr:

End Sub
```

The `cdlDevModeCopies` setting will check the printer to see whether it supports multiple-copy printing. If it does, the Number of copies spinner is displayed. If the printer does not support multiple copies, the spinner control is removed from the form.

When you save and run your example and click the Print button, you should see a dialog box like the one in Figure 13.11.

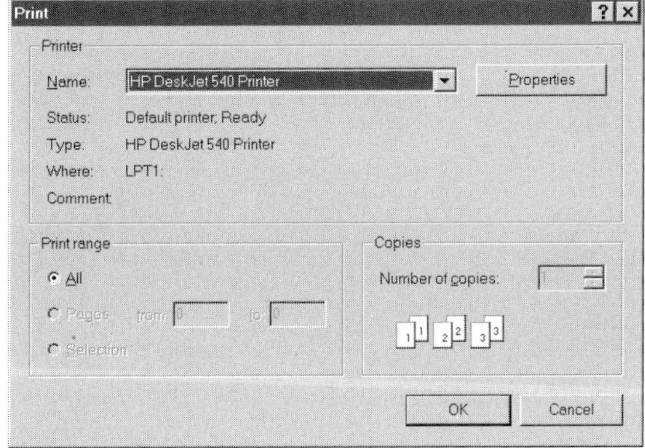

FIGURE 13.11.
Viewing the modified Print dialog box.

Notice that the Print to file, Number of copies, and Collate items have been disabled or removed completely. This was done using the `Flags` settings.

Be sure to save your work before continuing.

The `Flag` Settings for the Print Dialog Box

The Print dialog box has many valid `Flag` property settings. Study Table 13.7 for a review of the valid values.

Table 13.7. The `Flag` settings for the Print dialog box.

Constant	*Value*	*Description*
`cdlPDAllPages`	`&H0`	Returns or sets the state of the All Pages option button.
`cdlPDCollate`	`&H10`	Returns or sets the state of the Collate check box.
`cdlPDDisablePrintToFile`	`&H80000`	Disables the Print To File check box.
`cdlPDHelpButton`	`&H800`	Causes the dialog box to display the Help button.
`cdlPDHidePrintToFile`	`&H100000`	Hides the Print To File check box.
`cdlPDNoPageNums`	`&H8`	Disables the Pages option button and the associated edit control.
`cdlPDNoSelection`	`&H4`	Disables the Selection option button.
`cdlPDNoWarning`	`&H80`	Prevents a warning message from being displayed when there is no default printer.
`cdlPDPageNums`	`&H2`	Returns or sets the state of the Pages option button.
`cdlPDPrintSetup`	`&H40`	Causes the system to display the Print Setup dialog box rather than the Print dialog box.
`cdlPDPrintToFile`	`&H20`	Returns or sets the state of the Print To File check box.
`cdlPDReturnDC`	`&H100`	Returns a device context for the printer selection made in the dialog box. The device context is returned in the dialog box's `hDC` property.
`cdlPDReturnDefault`	`&H400`	Returns the default printer name.
`cdlPDReturnIC`	`&H200`	Returns an information context for the printer selection made in the dialog box. (An information context provides a fast way to get information about the device without creating a device context.) The information context is returned in the dialog box's `hDC` property.

Constant	Value	Description
cdlPDSelection	&H1	Returns or sets the state of the Selection option button. If neither cdlPDPageNums nor cdlPDSelection is specified, the All option button is in the selected state.
cdlPDUseDevModeCopies	&H40000	If a printer driver doesn't support multiple copies, setting this flag disables the Number of copies spinner control in the Print dialog box. If a driver does support multiple copies, setting this flag indicates that the dialog box stores the requested number of copies in the Copies property.

Accessing the Print Setup Dialog Box

You can use one of the Flag settings to force the ShowPrinter method to display only the Print Setup options. This is a great way to add support for the Print Setup menu options you see in almost all programs.

Locate and select the SetPrintSetup method you added earlier and enter the code from Listing 13.13.

Listing 13.13. Coding the SetPrintSetup routine.

```
Public Sub SetPrintSetup()

    ' handle print setup dialog


    ' set some properties
    cdlSample.CancelError = False
    cdlSample.Flags = cdlPDPrintSetup

    ' set help topic for button
    cdlSample.HelpFile = strHelpFile
    cdlSample.HelpCommand = cdlHelpContext
    cdlSample.HelpContext = Perform_Print_Setup

    ' show the dialog
    cdlSample.ShowPrinter

End Sub
```

After adding this code, save and run your project. When you click the Print Setup button, you should see a dialog box that looks like the one in Figure 13.12.

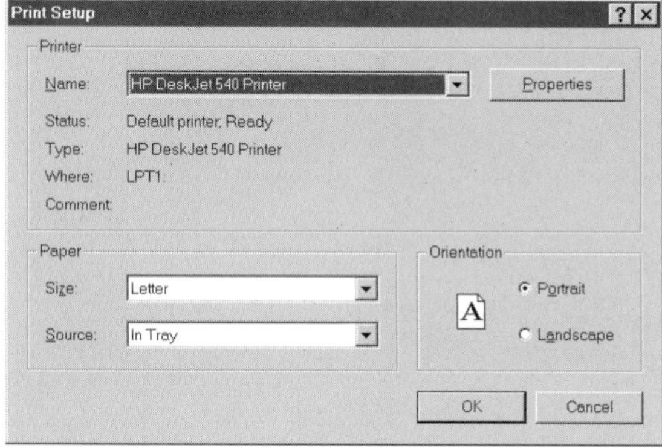

FIGURE 13.12.
Viewing the Print Setup dialog box.

The File Save and File Open Dialog Boxes

The File Save dialog box and its counterpart, the File Open dialog box, are probably the two most frequently used services of the Common Dialog control. Like the `ShowPrint` method, the `ShowOpen` and `ShowSave` methods do not actually perform the requested file operation. Their only role is to present an efficient dialog box for collecting the filename to use when reading and writing data files.

In this example, you'll first create a routine that uses the File Save dialog box to collect a filename and then save data from the input controls on the form to the selected file. Then you'll build a routine that uses the File Open dialog box to collect a filename and then read the stored data into the form's input controls.

Using the File Save Dialog Box

The File Save dialog box is used to prompt the user for a location and name of the file to use as the target in a data-saving operation. It is important to remember that the File Save dialog box does not actually save any data—it just prompts the user for a valid filename. Your program must handle the actual saving of the data. The techniques used to save data to the disk are as varied as the number of data formats you can find on your machine. In this example, you'll be saving simple text data. For this you can use a few built-in Visual Basic keywords to open and write to (and read from) the file.

The Basic File Save Dialog Box

Unlike the previous dialog boxes, a number of properties should be set for this dialog box *before* you invoke the `ShowSave` method. These properties will allow you to assist the user in determining the default location, file type, and other key parameters needed to safely save the data to disk.

One of the more important of these properties is the `Filter` property. This property establishes the suggested file types to use when displaying information in the File Save dialog box. The `File` property is a string that has the following format:

description¦*mask*

description represents a friendly word or phrase that describes the type of file—for example, `Text Files` or `Bitmaps`. *mask* represents the actual filter used when selecting files from the current directory for display in the dialog box list. For example, to force the dialog box to display only text files, you would set the *mask* portion of the string to "`*.TXT`". To display only bitmap files, the mask would be set to `"*.BMP"`.

The code in Listing 13.14 shows a basic example of the File Save Common Dialog control operation. Locate the `SaveData` method you built earlier and add this code to the method.

Listing 13.14. Coding the basic File Save example.

```
Public Sub SaveData()

    ' save the data from the form to a file


    On Error Resume Next                        ' ignore errors

    Dim ctlTemp As Control                      ' for reading text boxes
    Dim lngFlags As Long                        ' for dialog flags
    Dim strFileName As String                   ' for filename to write

    ' set dialog properties
    cdlSample.CancelError = False
    cdlSample.DialogTitle = "Save Data Dialog"
    cdlSample.DefaultExt = "txt"
    cdlSample.InitDir = App.Path                ' start looking in the application's path
    cdlSample.Filter = "ASCII File(*.asc)¦*.asc¦Comma Separated
Values(*.csv)¦*.csv¦Text File(*.txt)¦*.txt"
    cdlSample.FilterIndex = 3                   ' which item to show

    strFileName = ""
    cdlSample.ShowSave                          ' show the save dialog
    strFileName = cdlSample.filename            ' get returned filename

    ' if it's a good name, write the data as requested
    If Len(strFileName) <> 0 Then                         ' a good file?
        Open strFileName For Output As #1                 ' open the file
        For Each ctlTemp In Me.Controls                   ' loop through controls
            If TypeOf ctlTemp Is TextBox Then             ' a text box?
                Print #1, ctlTemp.Tag&; ","; ctlTemp.Text
            End If                                        ' ctlTemp=TextBox
        Next ' ctlTemp
        Close #1                                          ' close open file
    End If

End Sub
```

13 LEVERAGING WINDOWS

Note the use of the `Filter` and `FilterIndex` properties. This will force the dialog box to display only the files that have `.TXT`, `.ASC`, or `.CSV` as their file extension. Which files are displayed is determined by the `FilterIndex` property. Because `FilterIndex` is set to `3`, only the `.TXT` files will be displayed when the dialog box starts. Users can use the drop-down list box to change the `FilterIndex` (see Figure 13.13).

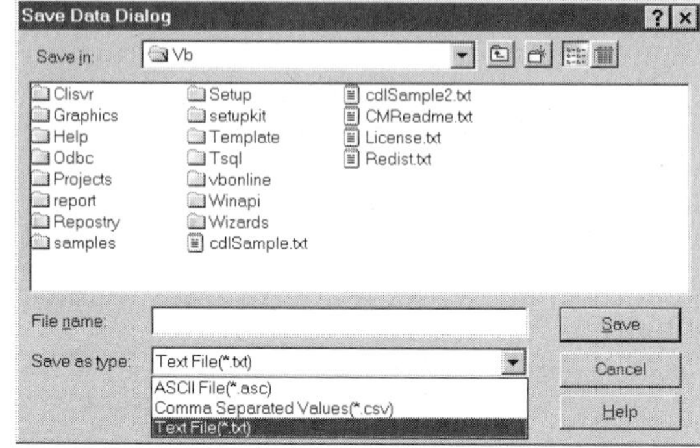

FIGURE 13.13.
Modifying the `FilterIndex` *property of the ShowSave dialog box.*

Now save and run the project. Fill in each of the fields on the form with some data and then click the Save button. You'll see a dialog box pop up, much like the one shown in Figure 13.13. Enter a filename and click Save. This will copy the data from the form into the file you selected.

NOTE

A sample file called `CDLSAMPLE.TXT` is included with the sample code on the CD-ROM. You can read this file with Windows `NOTEPAD.EXE` to see how it looks. You can compare this file with the one you wrote to make sure that your program is working properly.

Some Added Settings for the File Save Dialog Box

There are a number of `Flag` values you can use with the File Save and File Open dialog boxes. The code in Listing 13.15 shows the most useful flags for the File Save dialog box. Modify your code to match this listing.

Listing 13.15. Some added settings for the File Save dialog box.

```
Public Sub SaveData()

    ' save the data from the form to a file
```

```
    On Error Resume Next            ' ignore errors

    Dim ctlTemp As Control          ' for reading text boxes
    Dim lngFlags As Long            ' for dialog flags
    Dim strFileName As String       ' for filename to write

    ' set dialog properties
    cdlSample.CancelError = False
    cdlSample.DialogTitle = "Save Data Dialog"
    cdlSample.DefaultExt = "txt"
    cdlSample.Filter = "ASCII File(*.asc)¦*.asc¦Comma Separated Values(*.csv) _
     ¦*.csv¦Text File(*.txt)¦*.txt"
    cdlSample.FilterIndex = 3 ' which item to show

    ' set some flag values
    lngFlags = cdlOFNHelpButton                 ' add help button
    lngFlags = lngFlags + cdlOFNCreatePrompt    ' confirm file creates
    lngFlags = lngFlags + cdlOFNHideReadOnly    ' don't show read-only check
    lngFlags = lngFlags + cdlOFNOverwritePrompt ' confirm overwriting existing file
    lngFlags = lngFlags + cdlOFNPathMustExist   ' confirm valid path
    cdlSample.Flags = lngFlags

    strFileName = ""
    cdlSample.ShowSave                          ' show the save dialog
    strFileName = cdlSample.filename            ' get returned filename

    ' if it's a good name, write the data as requested
    If Len(strFileName) <> 0 Then               ' a good file?
        Open strFileName For Output As #1       ' open the file
        For Each ctlTemp In Me.Controls         ' loop through controls
            If TypeOf ctlTemp Is TextBox Then   ' a text box?
                Print #1, ctlTemp.Tag&; ","; ctlTemp.Text ' write tag and value
            End If                              ' ctlTemp=TextBox
        Next                                    ' ctlTemp
        Close #1                                ' close open file
    End If

End Sub
```

You'll notice that the `Flag` settings have been added to force the dialog box to automatically do a number of handy things:

- Confirm the creation of a new file
- Hide the Read-Only check box
- Confirm file overwrites
- Make sure that the entered path (folder) already exists

Now when you save and run the project, you'll see a much friendlier dialog box that confirms your selection.

Adding Help to the File Save Dialog Box

The code in Listing 13.16 shows you how to add help support for the File Save dialog box. Keep in mind that you need to have the custom help file already built, and you must also have the exact context ID value for the topic that relates to the File Save dialog box. Of course, your program might call the File Save dialog box in more than one place. You can create as many custom help topics as you need, and link the Common Dialog control to the help topic appropriate for the current file-save operation.

Listing 13.16. Adding custom help to the File Save dialog box.

```
Public Sub SaveData()

    ' save the data from the form to a file


    On Error Resume Next                ' ignore errors

    Dim ctlTemp As Control              ' for reading text boxes
    Dim lngFlags As Long                ' for dialog flags
    Dim strFileName As String           ' for filename to write

    ' set dialog properties
    cdlSample.CancelError = False
    cdlSample.DialogTitle = "Save Data Dialog"
    cdlSample.DefaultExt = "txt"
    cdlSample.Filter = "ASCII File(*.asc)¦*.asc¦Comma Separated Values(*.csv) _
      ¦*.csv¦Text File(*.txt)¦*.txt"
    cdlSample.FilterIndex = 3           ' which item to show

    ' set some flag values
    lngFlags = cdlOFNHelpButton                ' add help button
    lngFlags = lngFlags + cdlOFNCreatePrompt   ' confirm file creates
    lngFlags = lngFlags + cdlOFNHideReadOnly   ' don't show read-only check
    lngFlags = lngFlags + cdlOFNOverwritePrompt ' confirm overwriting existing file
    lngFlags = lngFlags + cdlOFNPathMustExist  ' confirm valid path
    cdlSample.Flags = lngFlags

    ' set help topic for button
    cdlSample.HelpFile = strHelpFile
    cdlSample.HelpCommand = cdlHelpContext
    cdlSample.HelpContext = Save_the_Data_File

    strFileName = ""
    cdlSample.ShowSave                  ' show the save dialog
    strFileName = cdlSample.filename    ' get returned filename

    ' if it's a good name, write the data as requested
    If Len(strFileName) <> 0 Then                         ' a good file?
        Open strFileName For Output As #1                 ' open the file
        For Each ctlTemp In Me.Controls                   ' loop through controls
            If TypeOf ctlTemp Is TextBox Then             ' a text box?
                Print #1, ctlTemp.Tag&; ","; ctlTemp.Text ' write tag and value
            End If                                        ' ctlTemp=TextBox
        Next                                              ' ctlTemp
        Close #1                                          ' close open file
    End If

End Sub
```

Using the File Open Dialog Box

The code for the File Open dialog box is almost identical to the code you used for the File Save dialog box. In fact, you could easily use one dialog box to perform both tasks because you are only retrieving a filename in each case. However, the File Open dialog box's default button has a caption of `Open`, whereas the default button for the File Save dialog box is set to `Save`.

NOTE

Although you can customize almost every aspect of the File Save and File Open dialog boxes (dialog titles, and so on), you cannot change the captions of the command buttons in the dialog boxes.

In this section, you'll create a routine that can read the data created in the `SaveData` method and copy it into the form to display.

The Basic File Open Dialog Box

Listing 13.17 shows the basic form of the File Open dialog box. Just as you did with the File Save dialog box, you need to set a few parameters before starting the dialog box. Locate the `ReadData` method you created earlier and add the code shown in Listing 13.17.

Listing 13.17. Coding the basic File Open dialog box.

```
Public Sub ReadData()

    ' read data from file and load form


    On Error Resume Next                ' ignore errors

    Dim ctlTemp As Control              ' for text boxes
    Dim strField As String              ' for field tag
    Dim strValue As String              ' for field value
    Dim lngFlags As Long                ' for dialog flags
    Dim strFileName As String           ' for read filename

    ' set dialog properties
    cdlSample.CancelError = False
    cdlSample.DialogTitle = "Read Data Dialog"
    cdlSample.DefaultExt = "txt"
    cdlSample.Filter = "ASCII File(*.asc)¦*.asc¦Comma Separated Values(*.csv) _
     ¦*.csv¦Text File(*.txt)¦*.txt"
    cdlSample.FilterIndex = 3           ' which item to show

    ' do the dialog action
    strFileName = ""
```

continues

Listing 13.17. continued

```
    cdlSample.ShowOpen                    ' show dialog
    strFileName = cdlSample.filename      ' get selected file

    ' if it's a good name, load the data
    If Len(strFileName) <> 0 Then
        Open strFileName For Input As #1           ' open the file
            Do Until EOF(1)                        ' read until no more records
            Input #1, strField, strValue           ' read a line
            For Each ctlTemp In Me.Controls        ' loop thru controls
                If ctlTemp.Tag = strField Then     ' a match?
                    ctlTemp.Text = strValue        ' fill it in
                    Exit For                       ' skip the rest
                End If                             ' if tag=strfield
            Next                                   ' next ctlTemp
        Loop                                       ' until EOF(1)
        Close #1                                   ' close the open file
    End If

End Sub
```

By this time, most of this code should look familiar. You can see that the `DialogTitle` property has been changed, but all the rest of the Common Dialog control-related code is identical to the File Save dialog box request.

Save and run the project, and then click the Open button. You'll see a dialog box that waits for you to select a file to read (see Figure 13.14).

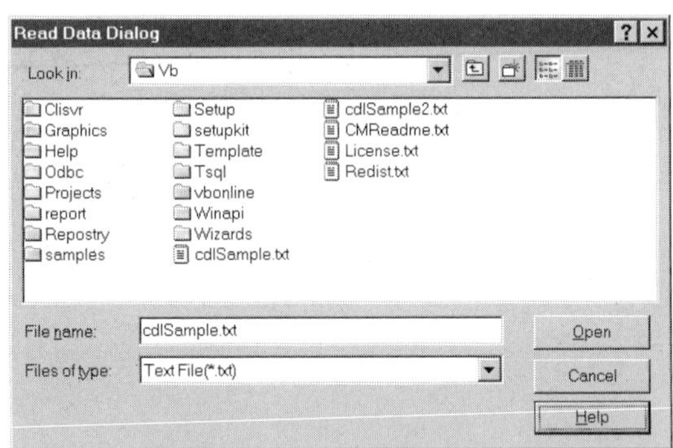

FIGURE 13.14.
Using the File Open dialog box.

Some Added Settings for the File Open Dialog Box

The real difference between the File Save and File Open dialog boxes is in the `Flag` settings. Whereas the `Flag` settings for the File Save dialog box are focused on confirming the overwrite of an existing file, the File Open dialog box has settings that will automatically confirm that the file actually exists.

Alter your `ReadData` method to match the code in Listing 13.18. Then save and run the project to test the effects of the new flag settings.

Listing 13.18. Some added settings for the File Open dialog box.

```
Public Sub ReadData()

    ' read data from file and load form


    On Error Resume Next            ' ignore errors

    Dim ctlTemp As Control          ' for text boxes
    Dim strField As String          ' for field tag
    Dim strValue As String          ' for field value
    Dim lngFlags As Long            ' for dialog flags
    Dim strFileName As String       ' for read filename

    ' set dialog properties
    cdlSample.CancelError = False
    cdlSample.DialogTitle = "Read Data Dialog"
    cdlSample.DefaultExt = "txt"
    cdlSample.Filter = "ASCII File(*.asc)¦*.asc¦Comma Separated Values(*.csv) _
     ¦*.csv¦Text File(*.txt)¦*.txt"
    cdlSample.FilterIndex = 3       ' which item to show

    ' set some flag properties
    lngFlags = cdlOFNHelpButton                      ' show help button
    lngFlags = lngFlags + cdlOFNFileMustExist        ' must be a real file
    lngFlags = lngFlags + cdlOFNHideReadOnly         ' don't show read-only box
    lngFlags = lngFlags + cdlOFNLongNames            ' allow long filenames
    lngFlags = lngFlags + cdlOFNPathMustExist        ' path must already exist
    cdlSample.Flags = lngFlags                       ' move it into the property

    ' do the dialog action
    strFileName = ""
    cdlSample.ShowOpen                  ' show dialog
    strFileName = cdlSample.filename    ' get selected file

    ' if it's a good name, load the data
    If Len(strFileName) <> 0 Then
        Open strFileName For Input As #1            ' open the file
            Do Until EOF(1)                         ' read until no more records
            Input #1, strField, strValue            ' read a line
            For Each ctlTemp In Me.Controls         ' loop thru controls
                If ctlTemp.Tag = strField Then      ' a match?
                    ctlTemp.Text = strValue         ' fill it in
                    Exit For                        ' skip the rest
                End If                              ' if tag=strfield
            Next                                    ' next ctlTemp
        Loop                                        ' until EOF(1)
        Close #1                                    ' close the open file
    End If

End Sub
```

Adding Help to the File Open Dialog Box

As with all the other dialog boxes, you can easily add a custom help topic to the File Open dialog box, too. Listing 13.19 shows how this can be done.

Listing 13.19. Adding custom help to the File Open dialog box.

```
Public Sub ReadData()

    ' read data from file and load form


    On Error Resume Next            ' ignore errors

    Dim ctlTemp As Control          ' for text boxes
    Dim strField As String          ' for field tag
    Dim strValue As String          ' for field value
    Dim lngFlags As Long            ' for dialog flags
    Dim strFileName As String       ' for read filename

    ' set dialog properties
    cdlSample.CancelError = False
    cdlSample.DialogTitle = "Read Data Dialog"
    cdlSample.DefaultExt = "txt"
    cdlSample.Filter = "ASCII File(*.asc)¦*.asc¦Comma Separated Values(*.csv) _
     ¦*.csv¦Text File(*.txt)¦*.txt"
    cdlSample.FilterIndex = 3       ' which item to show

    ' set some flag properties
    lngFlags = cdlOFNHelpButton                    ' show help button
    lngFlags = lngFlags + cdlOFNFileMustExist      ' must be a real file
    lngFlags = lngFlags + cdlOFNHideReadOnly       ' don't show read-only box
    lngFlags = lngFlags + cdlOFNLongNames          ' allow long filenames
    lngFlags = lngFlags + cdlOFNPathMustExist      ' path must already exist
    cdlSample.Flags = lngFlags                     ' move it into the property

    ' set help topic for button
    cdlSample.HelpFile = strHelpFile
    cdlSample.HelpCommand = cdlHelpContext
    cdlSample.HelpContext = Open_the_Data_File

    ' do the dialog action
    strFileName = ""
    cdlSample.ShowOpen                   ' show dialog
    strFileName = cdlSample.filename     ' get selected file

    ' if it's a good name, load the data
    If Len(strFileName) <> 0 Then
        Open strFileName For Input As #1           ' open the file
            Do Until EOF(1)                        ' read until no more records
            Input #1, strField, strValue           ' read a line
```

```
            For Each ctlTemp In Me.Controls              ' loop thru controls
                If ctlTemp.Tag = strField Then           ' a match?
                    ctlTemp.Text = strValue              ' fill it in
                    Exit For                             ' skip the rest
                End If                                   ' if tag=strfield
            Next                                         ' next ctlTemp
        Loop                                             ' until EOF(1)
        Close #1                                         ' close the open file
    End If

End Sub
```

After modifying your `ReadData` method, save and run the project. Now when you click the Open button and then click the Help button, you'll see online help on how to use the Open button of the form (see Figure 13.15).

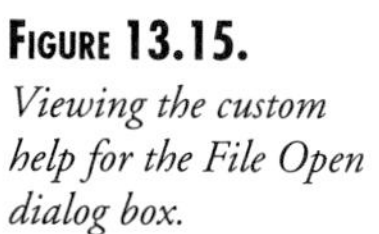

FIGURE 13.15.
Viewing the custom help for the File Open dialog box.

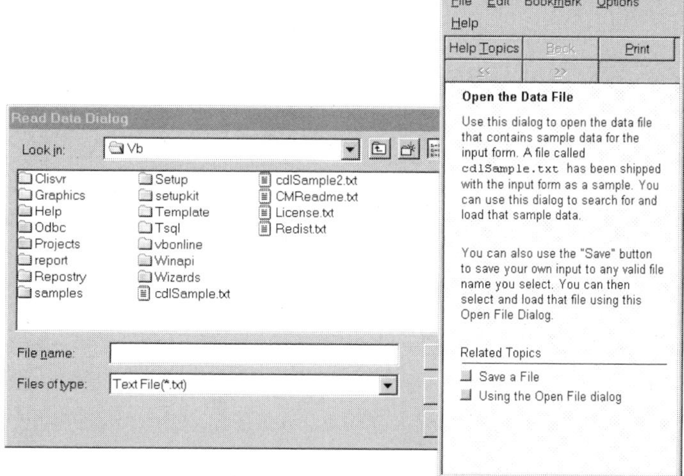

The Flag Settings for the File Open and File Save Dialog Boxes

As mentioned earlier, there are many possible values for the `Flag` property when you are requesting the `ShowOpen` or `ShowSave` method of the Common Dialog control. Table 13.8 lists the possible values, their types, and their descriptions.

Table 13.8. Valid `Flag` values for the File Open and File Save dialog boxes.

Constant	*Value*	*Description*
`cdlOFNAllowMultiselect`	`&H200`	Specifies that the File Name list box allows multiple selections. The user can select more than one file at runtime by pressing the Shift key and using the up-arrow and down-arrow keys to select the desired files. When this is done, the `FileName` property returns a string containing the names of all selected files. The names in the string are delimited by spaces.
`cdlOFNCreatePrompt`	`&H2000`	Specifies that the dialog box prompts the user to create a file that doesn't currently exist. This flag automatically sets the `cdlOFNPathMustExist` and `cdlOFNFileMustExist` flags.
`cdlOFNExplorer`	`&H80000`	Use the Explorer-like Open A File dialog box template. Works with Windows 95 and Windows NT 4.0.
`cdlOFNExtensionDifferent`	`&H400`	Indicates that the extension of the returned filename is different from the extension specified by the `DefaultExt` property. This flag isn't set if the `DefaultExt` property is `Null`, if the extensions match, or if the file has no extension. This flag value can be checked when closing the dialog box.
`cdlOFNFileMustExist`	`&H1000`	Specifies that the user can enter only names of existing files in the File Name text box. If this flag is set and the user enters an invalid filename, a warning is displayed. This flag automatically sets the `cdlOFNPathMustExist` flag.
`cdlOFNHelpButton`	`&H10`	Causes the dialog box to display the Help button.
`cdlOFNHideReadOnly`	`&H4`	Hides the Read Only check box.

Constant	Value	Description
cdlOFNLongNames	&H200000	Indicates that long filenames are valid.
cdlOFNNoChangeDir	&H8	Forces the dialog box to set the current directory to what it was when the dialog box was opened.
cdlOFNNoDereferenceLinks	&H100000	Specifies to not dereference shell links (also known as shortcuts). By default, choosing a shell link causes it to be dereferenced by the shell.
cdlOFNNoLongNames	&H40000	Indicates that long filenames are *not* valid.
cdlOFNNoReadOnlyReturn	&H8000	Specifies that the returned file won't have the Read Only attribute set and won't be in a write-protected directory.
cdlOFNNoValidate	&H100	Specifies that the common dialog box allows invalid characters in the returned filename.
cdlOFNOverwritePrompt	&H2	Causes the Save As dialog box to generate a message box if the selected file already exists. The user must confirm whether to overwrite the file.
cdlOFNPathMustExist	&H800	Specifies that the user can enter only valid paths. If this flag is set and the user enters an invalid path, a warning message is displayed.
cdlOFNReadOnly	&H1	Causes the Read Only check box to be initially checked when the dialog box is created. This flag also indicates the state of the Read Only check box when the dialog box is closed.
cdlOFNShareAware	&H4000	Specifies that sharing-violation errors will be ignored.

That's all there is to the File Open and File Save dialog boxes. Be sure to save your project (PRJCDLSAMPLE.VBP) and form (FRMCDLSAMPLE.FRM) before you move on to the last coding section in this chapter.

The Help Services

The last type of service that the Common Dialog control provides to programmers is access to the Windows Help system. If you've been working through the previous examples in this chapter, you know that several properties can be used to attach help files and specific topics to a dialog box. However, these same properties (along with a few others) can be used to make direct calls to the Windows Help system. You can use these calls to display a help topic, a search dialog box, a help contents page, or other help-related services.

In this section, you'll learn how to use the Common Dialog control to gain easy access to help files and the functions of the Windows Help system.

Demonstrating Common Dialog Control Help Services

The process of gaining access to the Windows Help system involves one more step than the other Common Dialog control services. Along with the call to the `ShowHelp` method, you also need to set the `HelpCommand` property to tell the Common Dialog control which form of Help service you would like to access.

The code in Listing 13.20 shows the most common help service requests. Locate the `mnuHelpItem_Click` event and add the code from Listing 13.20 to your form.

Listing 13.20. Coding the Common Dialog control help example.

```
Private Sub mnuHelpItem_Click(Index As Integer)

    ' handle help requests

    Dim strPartialKey As String

    cdlSample.HelpFile = strHelpFile

    Select Case Index
        Case 0 ' contents page
            cdlSample.HelpCommand = cdlHelpContents
        Case 1 ' index page
            cdlSample.HelpCommand = cdlHelpIndex
        Case 2 ' help on help
            cdlSample.HelpCommand = cdlHelpHelpOnHelp
        Case 3 ' helpkey
            cdlSample.HelpCommand = cdlHelpKey
            cdlSample.HelpKey = "font"
        Case 4 ' helppartialkey
            strPartialKey = InputBox("Enter a search word:", _
             "Help Partial Key", "font")
            cdlSample.HelpCommand = cdlHelpPartialKey
            cdlSample.HelpKey = strPartialKey
        Case 5 ' help command (macro)
```

```
            cdlSample.HelpCommand = cdlHelpCommandHelp
            cdlSample.HelpKey = "about()"
    End Select

    cdlSample.ShowHelp

End Sub
```

As you can see from Listing 13.20, there are several possible service options for the `ShowHelp` method. `cdlHelpContents` and `cdlHelpIndex` both return the default contents page of the associated help file. The `cdlHelpHelpOnHelp` setting provides an online tutorial on how to use the help system. `cdlHelpKey` and `cdlHelpPartialKey` each make calls to the search capabilities of the Windows Help engine. The last request (`cdlHelpCommandHelp`) actually allows you to run a help macro from within your Visual Basic program. In this example, you are calling the `about()` macro, which will display the Windows Help About screen.

After entering the code from Listing 13.20, save and run the project. To test the help features of the Common Dialog control, click the right (alternate) mouse button over the frame at the bottom of the form. You'll see a menu pop up. Select an item from the menu to see the related help service (see Figure 13.16).

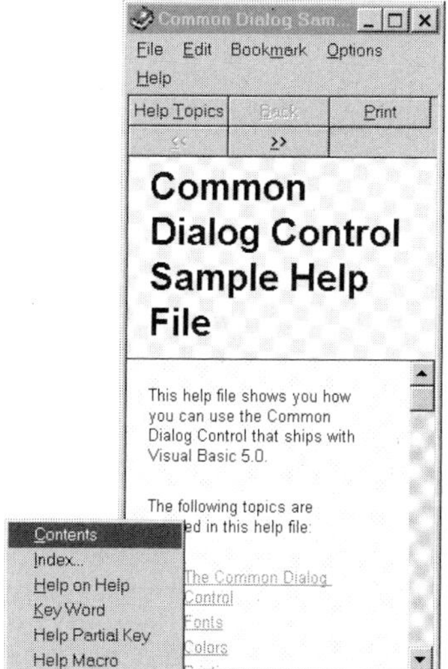

FIGURE 13.16.
Viewing the pop-up Help menu.

The Flag Settings for the ShowHelp Method

Even though the `ShowHelp` method does not present a consistent dialog box as do the other Common Dialog control methods, you can still have some control over how the help services are presented by modifying the `HelpCommand` property of the Common Dialog control.

CAUTION

It is important to remember that the constants that control the behavior of the help services are not applied to the `Flags` property. All help-related settings are passed in the `HelpCommand` property.

Table 13.9 shows all the possible values for the `HelpCommand` property of the Common Dialog control.

Table 13.9. Valid values for the `HelpCommand` property.

Constant	*Value*	*Description*
`cdlHelpCommandHelp`	`&H102`	Executes a Help macro
`cdlHelpContents`	`&H3`	Displays the Contents topic in the current Help file
`cdlHelpContext`	`&H1`	Displays help for a particular topic
`cdlHelpContextPopup`	`&H8`	Displays a topic identified by a context number
`cdlHelpForceFile`	`&H9`	Creates a help file that displays text in only one font
`cdlHelpHelpOnHelp`	`&H4`	Displays help for using the Help application itself
`cdlHelpIndex`	`&H3`	Displays the index of the specified Help file (same as `cdlHelpContents`)
`cdlHelpKey`	`&H101`	Displays Help for a particular keyword
`cdlHelpPartialKey`	`&H105`	Calls the search engine in Windows Help
`cdlHelpQuit`	`&H2`	Notifies the Help application that the specified Help file is no longer in use
`cdlHelpSetContents`	`&H5`	Designates a specific topic as the Contents topic
`cdlHelpSetIndex`	`&H5`	Sets the current index for multi-index Help

Summary

In this chapter, you learned how to add the Common Dialog control to your Visual Basic 5 projects and how to use that control to gain access to common Windows services, including

- `ShowColor`, which displays the Color Selection dialog box
- `ShowFont`, which displays the Font Selection dialog box

- `ShowPrinter`, which displays the Printer dialog box
- `ShowOpen`, which displays a File Open dialog box
- `ShowSave`, which displays a File Save dialog box
- `ShowHelp`, which provides access to several Windows Help dialog boxes

You also learned that there are many properties of the control and many special `Flag` values that you can use to improve the effectiveness of the program.

CHAPTER 14

Dynamic Control Creation and Indexing

IN THIS CHAPTER

The ability to add objects and controls to your Windows applications at runtime can be a very powerful tool, ultimately allowing programs to become truly dynamic in their design. Although most programs can be designed with a static, unchanging user interface, there are times when more flexibility is necessary. An extreme example of dynamic program design can be found in Visual Basic itself. Once VB has been loaded, the user is free to add or remove controls to facilitate the creation of new programs. This flexibility allows programs of almost any kind to be designed. Your programs may not need to be as dynamic as Visual Basic, but there may be times when controls or objects need to be created on-the-fly at runtime instead of design time. The question of how to create objects programmatically will be answered in this chapter.

Another important aspect of control creation is the definition of control arrays. By grouping together similar controls into an array (much like arrays that hold strings or some other data type), you can cut down on the amount of code in your program. Since all of the controls in the array share event handlers (for example, there is only one Click event for an array of CommandButton controls no matter how many controls are in the array), you do not have to duplicate event code for each individual control. As you'll see later in this chapter, the savings in terms of program code can be significant.

Combining dynamic controls with control arrays offers the best of both worlds. Dynamic controls enable your program to do a little jig in step with your end users' needs; the control array enables you to easily manage the pool of dynamically created controls. In this chapter, you will learn how to create and use dynamic controls and control arrays by reading and referring to the following topics:

- The mechanics of defining control arrays.
- Determining when a control array is best and how to maximize it.
- How to use control array properties and methods.
- Examples of creating forms on the fly.

If you have never created control arrays or dynamic controls, this chapter is a must-read. If you are an old hand at Visual Basic programming, you may find examples and demonstrations in this chapter that will help you hone your skills.

Creating Control Arrays

A control array, like any other array, groups together a number of like items. Some arrays group together integer numbers, and some group together strings. Control arrays group together controls. They can be CommandButtons, ListBoxes, or just about any kind of control in the Visual Basic toolbox. The controls in a control array do have to be like controls: all CommandButtons or all ListBoxes, for example. You cannot have a control array that contains some CommandButtons and some ListBoxes, just like you can't have an array that contains some integers and some strings (unless, of course, it's an array of Variants).

You may have noticed that all controls in Visual Basic have an Index property. This property indicates the control's position in a control array. To add a control to a control array at design time, you need only set the Name property of one or more like controls to the same name. When you try to give the second control the same Name property as the first control, Visual Basic will automatically ask you if you want to create a control array (see Figure 14.1). When it was created, the first control was assigned an Index number of 0. The second control, now part of the control array, is assigned an Index number of 1. If you add yet another control with the same Name property as the first two, it automatically becomes a part of the control array and is given the next sequential Index number (3).

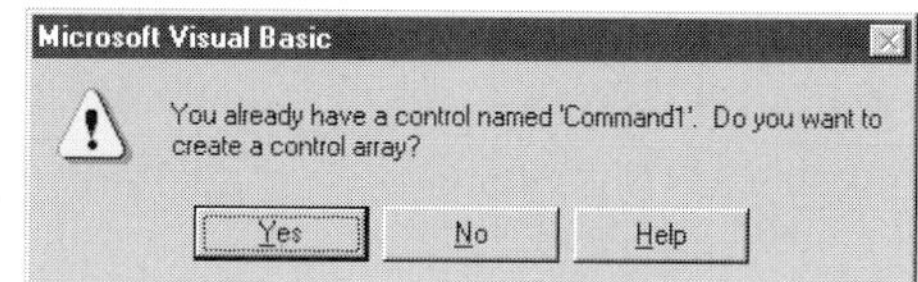

FIGURE 14.1.
The dialog box that asks whether you want to create a control array.

Another way to quickly create a control array is to create one control, then copy it to the Clipboard by right-clicking on the control and choosing the Copy command from the pop-up menu (or Edit | Paste from VB's menu). Then choose Edit | Paste from VB's menu and you'll see the prompt shown in Figure 14.1. If you continue pasting controls onto your form, they will all become part of the control array.

Try this simple example. Open Visual Basic 5. Select View | Toolbox if the toolbox is not showing. Double-click the CommandButton in the Toolbox. While the newly created CommandButton control is still selected—denoted by the solid squares surrounding the button—select Edit | Copy, followed by Edit | Paste. The dialog box shown in Figure 14.1 will be displayed. Clicking Yes will create a control array with two CommandButtons in the array.

Pros and Cons of Using Control Arrays

A control array can significantly reduce the amount of code you have to write if several controls of the same type utilize the same or similar code routines. For example, consider a slide viewer program that displays multiple thumbnail images (in Image controls) onscreen and allows the user to click an image to show it at full size. Without using a control array, the code for displaying each image in full size would have to be coded into each Image control's DblClick event. Putting all of the Image controls into a control array, however, requires coding only one Click event for the entire control array. Since the index number of the actual control that was clicked on is passed to the Click event, you can easily determine exactly which thumbnail image was selected and tailor your code to display that image in full size.

Determining whether or not the use of a control array makes sense is easy. If multiple objects share the same or similar function (such as in the preceding example), it would probably be worth creating a control array. However, if individual controls have different functions and you would have to make exceptions in your code for them, a control array probably is not a good idea.

TIP

If you find it necessary to add a significant amount of code to an event procedure because a single control in the array requires some exceptional processing, it's a good idea to place that code in a separate Function or Sub and call it from the event procedure. This will give your code a greater degree of modularity and readability.

When using control arrays, you can reduce the amount of code necessary by a factor of however many controls are in your array. For example, if there are a dozen controls in your array, you may reduce the amount of code in your program to roughly a twelfth of what it would have been if you had to add the code for each control separately. There may be some overhead in the way of determining which control in the array to act on (by examining the control index), but that is usually minimal.

Using a Control Array

To illustrate how powerful the effective use of control arrays can be, let's go back to the slide show example that was mentioned in the previous section. Create a new project and then use Table 14.1 as a guide for adding controls and changing their properties.

Table 14.1. Controls and their properties for the slide show example program.

Control Type	*Property*	*Value*
Form	`Name`	`frmSlideShow`
	`Caption`	`Control Array Example`
	`Height`	`6255`
	`Width`	`6540`
Image	`Name`	`imgThumbnail`
	`BorderStyle`	`1 - Fixed Single`
	`Index`	`3`
	`Height`	`1305`
	`Left`	`4860`
	`Stretch`	`True`
	`Top`	`135`
	`Width`	`1485`
Image	`Name`	`imgThumbnail`
	`BorderStyle`	`1 - Fixed Single`
	`Index`	`2`

Control Type	Property	Value
	Height	1305
	Left	3285
	Stretch	True
	Top	135
	Width	1485
Image	Name	imgThumbnail
	BorderStyle	1 - Fixed Single
	Index	1
	Height	1305
	Left	1710
	Stretch	True
	Top	135
	Width	1485
Image	Name	imgThumbnail
	BorderStyle	1 - Fixed Single
	Index	0
	Height	1305
	Left	120
	Stretch	True
	Top	135
	Width	1485
Image	Name	imgFullSize
	BorderStyle	1 - Fixed Single
	Height	4575
	Left	120
	Stretch	True
	Top	1560
	Width	6240

For the Picture property of the Image controls in the imgThumbnail control array, use any bitmap images you may have on your system. Since Visual Basic now supports .JPG and .GIF images, finding some sample images shouldn't be too difficult—anything will do.

NOTE

In Table 14.1, the Image controls in the imgThumbnail array are given in reverse order so Visual Basic does not prompt you to create a control array. When you add the first Image control and assign it an Index number of 3, Visual Basic knows the control is part of a control array.

This sample program is very straightforward. In fact, would you believe that it only has one line of code? It's true, and it's a testament to the power of using control arrays. Listing 14.1 shows the line of code that needs to be added to the Click event for the imgThumbnail control array. You can bring up the code window for this event by double-clicking any of the imgThumbnail Image controls.

Listing 14.1. A bitmap slide viewer using one event for an arbitrary number of bitmaps.

```
Private Sub imgThumbnail_Click(Index As Integer)

    imgFullSize = imgThumbnail(Index)

End Sub
```

Listing 14.1 uses the Index argument of this one event handler to distinguish which control in the array of Images was clicked and assigns that Image to the larger imgFullSize Image. It is evident that the amount of code saved is proportionate to the number of controls in the array.

When you're done adding the code, save the form as `CH1401.FRM` and the project as `CH1401.VBP`; then run the program.

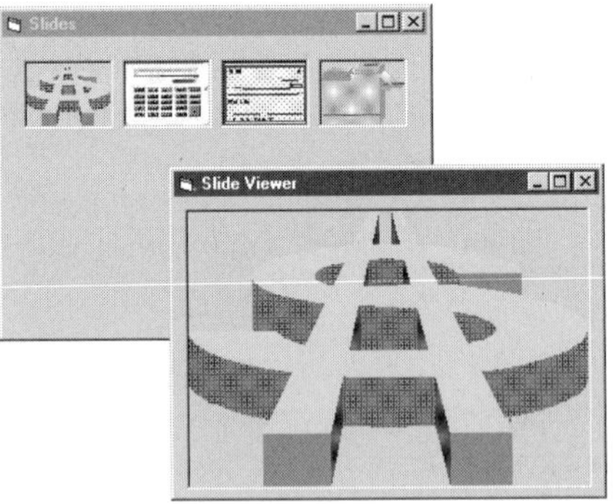

FIGURE 14.2.
A bitmap slide viewer created with an Image control array.

Control arrays are powerful, but they have the potential of convoluting program code when used improperly. If some controls in the array have wildly different functions than the others, you have to make exceptions for those controls in your event procedure code. This can make your programs hard to decipher. Remember to only group together controls of similar or the same function and exclude those that require additional processing. The next section examines event handling for control arrays more closely.

NOTE

A good demo program illustrating the use of control arrays is included with Visual Basic and can be found in VB's `SAMPLES\VISDATA` subdirectory. In the program, an array of `Toolbar` controls is used.

Designing Event Handlers for Control Arrays

Event handlers are generally associated with a single control. The importance of this is that when you are writing code for a control, the event handler provides the context. For example, there is clearly a distinction between the Click event for a form and one for a PictureBox control. The naming convention used—*`controlname_eventname`*—for event handlers also suggests the owner of the control. Hence, context determines which control originated the event. For control array events, the only way to determine the originator is by examining the Index argument. Consider the slight differences between a Click event handler for a PictureBox control and one for a PictureBox control array:

```
' Click for a PictureBox array
Private Sub Picture1_Click(Index As Integer)

End Sub

' Click for PictureBox that is not in an array
Private Sub Picture2_Click()

End Sub
```

The obvious distinction between the two events shown above is that in the Picture1_Click event, the argument Index (an integer value) is passed to the event. Only events for control arrays will have this argument. The Index argument is crucial for determing which control in the array actually raised the event.

The last section contained an example of using the Index argument passed to the event procedure directly. The code for all of the controls in the array was identical, and the Index argument was used to refer to the control that generated the event. Event processing may not always be so cut and dry, however. In some cases, you will need to take different action based on which control generated the event. If the control array consists of two or three controls, you may decide to use an `If...Then` construct, such as in the following example:

```
Private Sub cmdEditOptions_Click(Index As Integer)

   If Index = 0 Then
      CutText
```

```
    ElseIf Index = 1 Then
        CopyText
    Else
        PasteText
    EndIf

End Sub
```

The code shown above tests the Index argument to see which subroutine should be called. If the first control in the cmdEditOptions control array raised the event (Index = 0), then the CutText subroutine is called. If the second control raised the event, the CopyText subroutine is called. In all other cases, the PasteText subroutine is called.

Using an `If...Then` construct is fine if you have a limited number of controls in your array, but a `Select...Case` construct is best for larger control arrays. In fact, because `Select...Case` statements are easier to read, you may opt to use them no matter how many controls are in the array. They also make it easier to code if you add additional controls to the array. Consider the following example:

```
Private Sub cmdEditOptions_Click(Index As Integer)

    Select Case Index
        Case 0
            CutText
        Case 1
            CopyText
        Case 2
            PasteText
        Case Else
            ' Do nothing
    End Select

End Sub
```

The `Select...Case` construct above does essentially the same thing as the previous example, but it's considerably easier to read and can be expanded on with minimal effort. It also allows you to provide for an Index number that is unexpected with the `Case Else` statement.

When using a `Select...Case` construct, it's a good idea to keep the code under each `Case` statement to a minimum. If more than one or two lines of code are needed for processing the event for a given control, put the code into a Function or Sub and call it from the `Case` statement. The example above calls three Subs (CutText, CopyText, and PasteText) rather than include the code within the `Select...Case` construct.

You know how to create control arrays at design time and associate event handlers with arrayed controls. In the next section, you will see examples demonstrating how to create controls at runtime, reasons why you might want to do so, and how predefined event handlers are associated with dynamic control arrays.

Creating Controls Dynamically

There are two ways to create controls: at design time and at runtime. The former is by far the more commonly used. When you are designing a program in Visual Basic and select a control from the Toolbox then add it to a form, you have created a design-time instance of the control. Obviously, this is how most Visual Basic programs are conceived.

Runtime control creation, on the other hand, refers to adding a control to an existing form programmatically while the compiled program is running. This is seldom done, usually because a static user interface (with all controls added at design time) is all that is necessary. Some programs do need to be more flexible, however, and that is where runtime control creation comes in handy.

In some cases, you may want to dynamically add one or more additional controls to an existing control array. Visual Basic makes it extremely easy to do so. Listing 14.2 shows a Click event that dynamically adds clones a control (`cmdTest`) and adds it to a control array every time it is invoked. Note that the original control, `cmdTest`, must have its Index property set to 0 (indicating that it is part of a control array) before the event can work properly.

Listing 14.2. Adding controls on-the-fly is as straightforward as this example.

```
Private Sub cmdTest_Click(Index As Integer)

    Static intArrayPtr As Integer

    intArrayPtr = intArrayPtr + 1
    Load cmdTest(intArrayPtr)
    cmdTest(intArrayPtr).Left = cmdTest(intArrayPtr - 1).Left + 150
    cmdTest(intArrayPtr).Top = cmdTest(intArrayPtr - 1).Top + 150
    cmdTest(intArrayPtr).Caption = "Clone" & Str$(intArrayPtr)
    cmdTest(intArrayPtr).Visible = True
    cmdTest(intArrayPtr).ZOrder (0)

End Sub
```

The static variable intArrayPtr is used to keep track of the next available Index number for the control array and is incremented by one every time the event procedure is invoked. The Load statement is used to dynamically load (add) the new control into memory. The next four lines set the new control's Left, Top, Caption, and Visible properties. Figure 14.3 shows how a form might look if the event procedure in Listing 14.2 was triggered five times, causing five new CommandButton controls to be dynamically created.

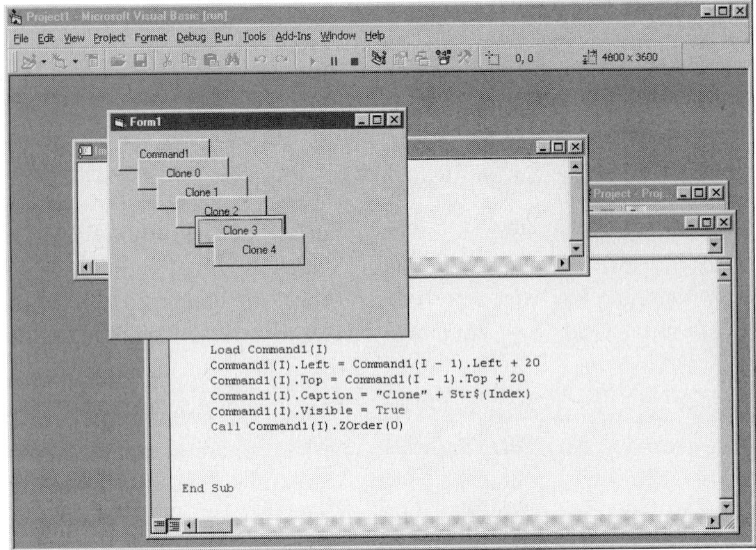
Form1
Command1
Clone 0
Clone 1
Clone 2
Clone 3
Clone 4
Load Command1(I)
Command1(I).Left = Command1(I - 1).Left + 20
Command1(I).Top = Command1(I - 1).Top + 20
Command1(I).Caption = "Clone" + Str$(Index)
Command1(I).Visible = True
Call Command1(I).ZOrder(0)
End Sub

FIGURE 14.3.
Command buttons added dynamically demonstrate the steps required to add controls.

Instantiating Forms at Runtime

A special kind of control that can be created dynamically is the MDI (or multiple-document interface) style document. Software applications such as spreadsheets use MDI to share the code from one form among many instances. Consider Microsoft Excel's spreadsheet document. The cells and related code that make Excel work are the same among all worksheets, regardless of the number of worksheets in use. The only difference is the data in the sheets. Setting the MDIChild property of a form to `True` enables you to designate a child as an MDI document.

The implication is that you may have many copies of the same form open, and they will all behave differently except for the data that is placed in them. MDI child forms are ideal candidates for control arrays. The array structure enables you to centrally manage the forms, regardless of the number of forms in use.

A classic example of an MDI application is provided with Visual Basic in VB's `SAMPLES\PGUIDE\MDI` subdirectory. The sample project, `MDINOTE.VBP`, illustrates the dynamic creation of MDI child forms, as shown in Figure 14.4.

Prior to MDI and Windows, text editors and word processors were designed to display one text document at a time. The `MDINOTE.VBP` example demonstrates how easy it is to use MDI and how easy it is to manage MDI child documents using a control array. The MDI child itself is a form with a TextBox control (see Figure 14.5). In addition to the TextBox control, the form has its own menu, which because it is an MDI child form, will be merged with the MDI form, or the parent form.

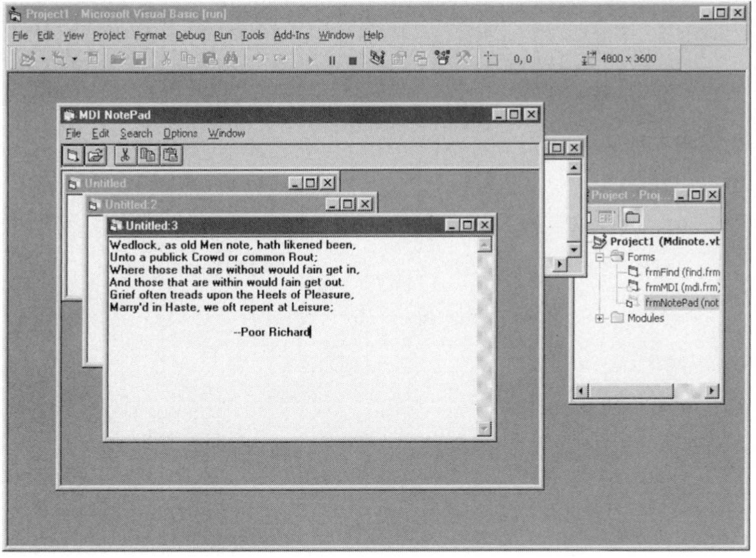

FIGURE 14.4.
The `MDINOTE.VBP` *project provided with Visual Basic 5 demonstrates how to use a control array with MDI child forms.*

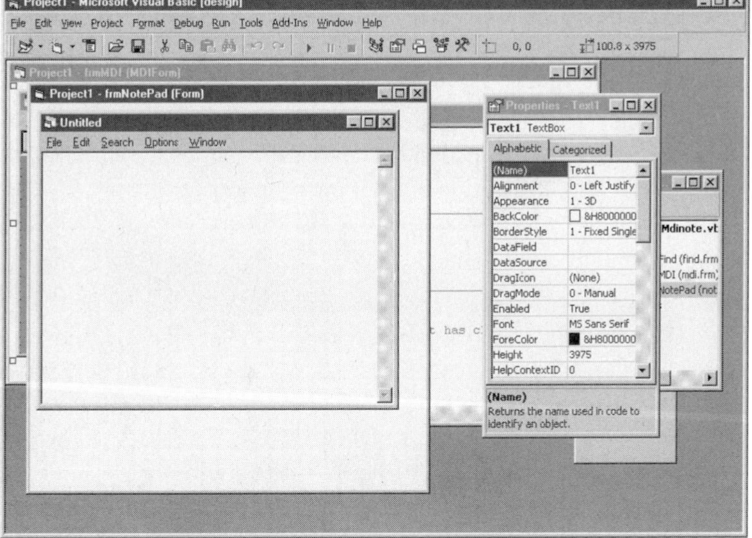

FIGURE 14.5.
`notepad.frm` *is the MDI child form that is capable of having multiple instances.*

The module `mdinote.bas` contains the code that has the form array, which in turn manages all the child forms. The program looks simple, but there is a significant amount of code involved. That code would be greater if it were not for control arrays and MDI. Browse the brief fragment in Listing 14.3, which is followed by an explanation.

Listing 14.3. MDINOTE.VBP demonstrates form control arrays and MDI document applications.

```
Public Document() As New frmNotePad      ' Array of child form objects

Sub FileNew()

   Dim fIndex As Integer

   ' Find the next available index and show the child form.
   fIndex = FindFreeIndex()
   Document(fIndex).Tag = fIndex
   Document(fIndex).Caption = "Untitled:" & fIndex
   Document(fIndex).Show
   ' Make sure the toolbar edit buttons are visible.
   frmMDI.imgCutButton.Visible = True
   frmMDI.imgCopyButton.Visible = True
   frmMDI.imgPasteButton.Visible = True

End Sub
```

The first line in Listing 14.3 declares a new control array of child forms called Document, all of which will have the characteristics of the previously defined frmNotePad form. The subroutine, FileNew, contains the code to add a new instance of a form to the Document control array. Note that a form is considered to be a control and can be stored in a control array just like other controls can.

The FileNew subroutine uses the variable fIndex to indicate the index number of the form that will be added to the array. Instead of simply incrementing fIndex by one, the FindFreeIndex function is called. This function, which is also a part of the `MDINOTE.VBP` sample project, finds and returns the first available index number in a control array. Remember that a child form can be closed by the user, leaving gaps in the Document array. Therefore, simply incrementing the fIndex variable is not sufficient.

The next two lines in the FileNew subroutine set the properties for the dynamically added form, Document(fIndex). Then the new form's Show method is invoked so the form is displayed on the screen. Finally, the Cut, Copy, and Paste buttons on the parent MDI form are made visible.

Using Control Array Properties

Control arrays can access four properties that can be used in facilitating the processing of the array: `Count`, `Item`, `LBound`, and `UBound`. The `Count` property indicates the total number of controls in the array. The `Item` property is used to refer to specific controls in the array. The `LBound` and `UBound` properties are used to determine the lower and upper bounds of the array, respectively. All of these properties will be discussed in more detail in this section.

The Count Property

The Count property returns an integer number indicating the number of items that are in a control array. You can use the Count property for loop control. For example, the following code fragment demonstrates how you might iterate through all controls in a control array named datTestDB:

```
Dim intLoop As Integer

For intLoop = 0 to datTestDB.Count - 1

    ' Shows all record sets in the datTestDB control array
    MsgBox datTestDB(intLoop).RecordSet

Next intLoop
```

Note that the loop starts at zero and ends at the value returned by the Count property minus one. Remember that all control arrays are zero-based; that is, the first Index number in the array is always zero. You cannot change this, even if you include an Option Base 1 statement in your code.

The Item Property

The Item property is the default property. Item enables you to refer to a specific item in the control array by specifying its index number. Since it is the default property, both

```
Command1.Item(number)
```

and

```
Command1(number)
```

refer to the same object. For all intents and purposes, these two lines of code are identical in their function.

The LBound and UBound Properties

The LBound and UBound—lower bound and upper bound, respectively—are included because you cannot use the functions with the same name to perform these tests. For example, given an array of integers

```
Dim intNumbers(10) As Integer
```

testing it with either UBound or LBound in the following manner

```
If LBound(intNumbers) < 0 Or UBound(intNumbers) > 10 Then
    ' Perform some action
End If
```

is syntactically correct. The same test cannot be performed on a control error. Hence this:

```
' The following section of code results in a syntax error.
If UBound(cmdOptions) > 5 Then
    ' Perform some action
End If
```

where `cmdOptions` is defined as a control array, is syntactically incorrect. The correct way to perform the equivalent test for either the lower or upper bound is

```
cmdOptions.LBound
```

or

```
cmdOptions.UBound
```

provided that `cmdOptions` is a control array. In this context, the control array name refers to all of the controls in an array. Note that because control arrays are always zero-based, the `LBound` property will always return 0.

Creating Data Controls Dynamically

You may write dynamic and extensible database programs by using what you have learned thus far and applying it to the `Data` control. The `Data` control can also be designated as a control array.

Dynamic `Data` controls can have many applications. Suppose you want to manage several recordsets at once. A `Data` control array is a great way to do it. Consider the scenario where you want to queue any users' most frequent dynamic SQL queries. Combining a `Data` control array with a `DBGrid` control makes it a snap. Listing 14.4 shows a portion of a program that inserts a new `Data` control into a control array named datCustomerDB. Figure 14.6 shows how such a program might look onscreen.

Listing 14.4. A `Data` control array.

```
Public Sub AddNew()

    Const SQL = "Select CustomerID From Customers"
    Dim intDataPtr As Integer

    intDataPtr = datCustomerDB.Count
    dbgCustGrid.ClearFields
    Load datCustomerDB(intDataPtr)
    Set datCustomerDB(0).Recordset = datCustomerDB(0).Database.OpenRecordset(SQL)
    dbgCustGrid.ReBind

End Sub

Private Sub AddDataSourceMenu_Click()

    Call AddNew

End Sub
```

Listing 14.4 provides another example of a control array. Each time the user clicks Query | Add Datasource in the sample program, the same SQL statement is pushed to the front of the control array.

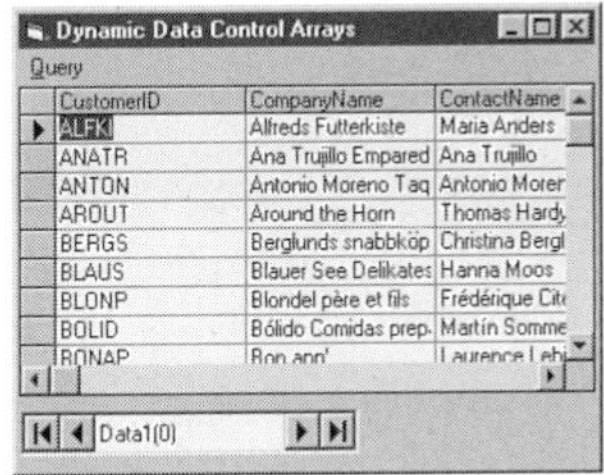

FIGURE 14.6.
A short program demonstrating a control array of `Data` *controls.*

One important aspect of the code in Listing 14.4 is the `Load` statement. As with other control arrays, `Load` creates the control referred to by the index. On the following line, the 0th element is set to an open recordset; the statement used is roughly the same for any `Data` control whose recordset you want to change at runtime. For the sample program, `DBGrid` was used. The line `dbgCustGrid.ClearFields` resets the Microsoft Databound Grid Control to its default of two empty columns. The `Set` statement binds the fields in the current record, causing the correct number of columns to be displayed.

Summary

Using control arrays is a means by which you can share code among many like controls. You have learned that given an event handler for a control array, all controls in the array share the same code. Dynamic control creation also enables you to easily make your programs more flexible and extensible by offering your users a way to add controls during the execution and life cycle of their programs.

There are many supporting topics that make using control arrays and dynamic control creation possible. To learn about related topics, read the following chapters:

- Chapter 1, "Working with Arrays," gives you ample opportunity to become an expert in using arrays.
- Chapter 10, "Data Structures, Collections, and Enumerations," offers additional opportunities to experiment with other data structures.

Implementing OLE Drag-and-Drop Capabilities into Controls

IN THIS CHAPTER

Almost every Windows application on your PC has drag-and-drop functionality. Whether you are using a word processor to move (drag) a letter, word, or sentence to another location or using Explorer to copy a file to another folder, you are using drag and drop.

OLE drag and drop is an advanced version of the simple drag-and-drop functionality. Instead of dragging one object to another to invoke a section of code, you are moving *data* from one control or application to another. For example, dragging a text file from Windows Explorer into an open Notepad window uses OLE drag-and-drop operations.

In fact, when Microsoft developed the standards for Windows 95, it included OLE drag and drop as one of the features that defines a Windows 95-compliant product. These standards are used to determine whether a new product meets the requirements to be able to display the Windows 95 logo on its packaging and documentation.

In this chapter, you will see what OLE drag and drop is, how it works, and more important, how to use it in a Visual Basic application. You will see how to use OLE drag and drop for something that is useful in an actual application.

What Is OLE Drag and Drop?

OLE drag and drop is probably the most powerful and useful feature available to a Visual Basic programmer by adding the capability to drag text or graphics from one control to another, from a control to another Windows application, or from a Windows application to a control. The new feature of OLE drag and drop allows you to add this functionality to your application.

If you have been coding in Visual Basic for a while, you should be familiar with the standard drag-and-drop capabilities of the controls within a Windows application. All the concepts you learned to use the drag-and-drop functions still pertain to the new OLE drag-and-drop functions. The difference is that the OLE drag-and-drop features open your Visual Basic application to any other application that the user has on his PC.

NOTE

Although OLE drag and drop is new to Visual Basic 5, it is already available in most current ActiveX-compliant controls, such as the RichTextBox control.

Most Visual Basic controls support OLE drag and drop in some fashion. Depending on the control, you can use OLE drag and drop without any code, or you might need to write some sections of code to support the function you need. The following list outlines the standard and ActiveX controls included in the Professional and Enterprise editions of Visual Basic along with the level of OLE drag-and-drop support that they have.

The first group provides full support for the automatic OLE drag-and-drop capabilities. These controls are

- Apex data-bound grid
- Image
- Masked edit box
- Picture box
- Rich text box
- Text box

The second group supports only automatic drag functions. If you need any drop functionality, you must code for it. These controls are

- Combo box
- Data-bound combo box
- Data-bound list box
- Directory list box
- File list box
- List box
- List view
- Tree view

The final group supports only manual OLE drag and drop. This requires you to write the code needed to support any drag-and-drop functionality. These controls are

- Data
- Drive list box
- Check box
- Command button
- Frame
- Label
- Option button

TIP

The easiest way to see what OLE drag-and-drop capabilities an ActiveX control has is to load the control and check the properties list. If `OLEDragMode` and `OLEDropMode` are listed, then the control supports automatic or manual processing.

How Does OLE Drag and Drop Work?

Certain events are triggered whenever an OLE drag-and-drop operation is performed. The events for source control are always generated for both automatic and manual processing. However, events for the target control are only generated during a manual drop operation. Table 15.1 shows which events occur on the drag source and which occur on the drop target.

Table 15.1. OLE source and target events.

Source	*Target*
`OLEStartDrag`	`OLEDragDrop`
`OLESetData`	`OLEDragOver`
`OLEGiveFeedback`	
`OLECompleteDrag`	

Depending on how you want OLE drag and drop to perform, you generate code for only those events that you want to respond to. For example, you can create an application with a text box that allows the user to automatically drag data from another application into the text box. To do this, you simply set the text box's `OLEDropMode` property to `Automatic`. If you want to allow the user to drag the data from the text box control as well, you just set its `OLEDragMode` property to `Automatic`.

If you want to change the mouse cursors or perform different functions based on the button that was clicked or the Shift key that was pressed, you need to manually respond to the source and target events. Also, if you want to analyze or change the data before it's dropped into the control, you need to use manual OLE drag-and-drop operations. This gives you full control of the drag-and-drop process.

Because you can drag and drop data into many different Visual Basic controls and Windows applications, implementing OLE drag and drop can range in difficulty from straightforward to complex. The easiest method, of course, is dragging and dropping between two automatic objects, whether the object is a Word document or a control in your application that is set to `Automatic`.

NOTE

Even though many controls support OLE drag and drop, the examples used in this chapter use the text box control. The text box control is the simplest control with which to learn drag-and-drop concepts.

Beginning the Drag

A manual OLE drag-and-drop operation in your Visual Basic application starts when the user drags data from an OLE drag source (such as a text box control) by selecting and then holding down the left mouse button. The `OLEStartDrag` event is triggered, and you can then either store the data or simply specify the formats that the source supports. You also need to specify whether copying or moving the data or both is allowed by the source.

Going Over the Target

As the user drags the data over the target, the target's `OLEDragOver` event is triggered. You can specify what the target will do if the data is dropped there. The three choices are copy, move, or refuse the data. The default is generally set to move, but it could just as easily be set to copy.

After the drop effect is set, the `OLEGiveFeedback` event is triggered. You use the `OLEGiveFeedback` event to give the user feedback on what action is taken when the data is dropped (that is, the mouse pointer changes to indicate a copy, move, or "no drop" action). Figure 15.1 shows the three different mouse pointer icons that come with Visual Basic.

FIGURE 15.1.
Default mouse icons for the OLE drag-and-drop process.

Completing the Drag

When the user drops the data onto the target, the target's `OLEDragDrop` event is triggered. The target checks the data from the source object to see whether it is the proper data type for the intended target. Depending on the outcome of that check, it either retrieves or rejects the data.

If the data was stored when the drag started, the `GetData` method retrieves the data. If the data wasn't stored when the drag started, the source's `OLESetData` event is triggered, and the `SetData` method retrieves the data.

When the data is accepted or rejected, the `OLECompleteDrag` event is triggered, and the source can then perform the necessary clean-up. If the data is accepted and a move was requested, the source deletes the data.

Automatic or Manual Processing?

Deciding whether to use automatic or manual OLE drag and drop really depends on the type of functionality you allow the user to perform with your application.

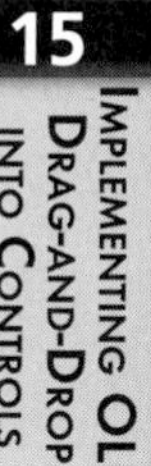

With automatic drag and drop, all operations are controlled by Windows and the internal Visual Basic process. You can drag text from one text box control to another by simply setting the `OLEDragMode` and `OLEDropMode` properties of these controls to `Automatic`. No code is required to respond to any of the OLE drag-and-drop events. When you drag a range of cells from Excel into a Word document, you perform an automatic drag-and-drop operation. Depending on how a given control or application supports OLE drag and drop and what type of data is dragged, automatically dragging and dropping data may be the best and simplest method.

When using manual drag and drop, you manually handle one or more of the OLE drag-and-drop events. Manual implementation of OLE drag and drop may be the better method when you need greater control over each step in the process or you need to provide the user with customized visual feedback. Manual implementation is the only option when a control does not support automatic drag and drop.

It is useful to know the terms for discussing OLE drag-and-drop operations. In a drag-and-drop operation, the object from which data is dragged is called the *source*. The object into which the data is dropped is called the *target*. Visual Basic provides the properties, events, and method to control and respond to actions affecting both the source and the target. Remember that the source and the target may be in different applications, in the same application, or even in the same control. Depending on your requirements, you might need to write code for either the source or target or both.

Using Automatic OLE Drag and Drop

If the controls you want to use support automatic drag and drop, you can activate the features by setting the control's `OLEDragMode` or `OLEDropMode` properties to `Automatic`. To see how this works, you are going to create a Visual Basic application that accepts text from a Word document and also allows you to drag text from the application into the Word document. To create this application, follow these steps:

1. Start Visual Basic and open a new project.
2. Place two text boxes on the form and name them `txtDrag` and `txtDrop`.
3. Add two labels, one for each text box. Enter **`Drag from Me`** in the caption for one label and place it next to the `txtDrag` text box. Enter **`Drop on Me`** in the label caption for the other text box.
4. Place a command button, `cmdQuit`, on the form and set its caption to `Quit`.

   Your completed form should look like the form displayed in Figure 15.2.
5. In the `cmdQuit_click` routine, enter **`END`** to terminate the application.
6. To allow data to be dragged from the `txtDrag` text box, set its `OLEDragMode` property to `Automatic`.
7. To allow data to be dropped into the `txtDrop` text box, set its `OLEDropMode` property to `Automatic`.

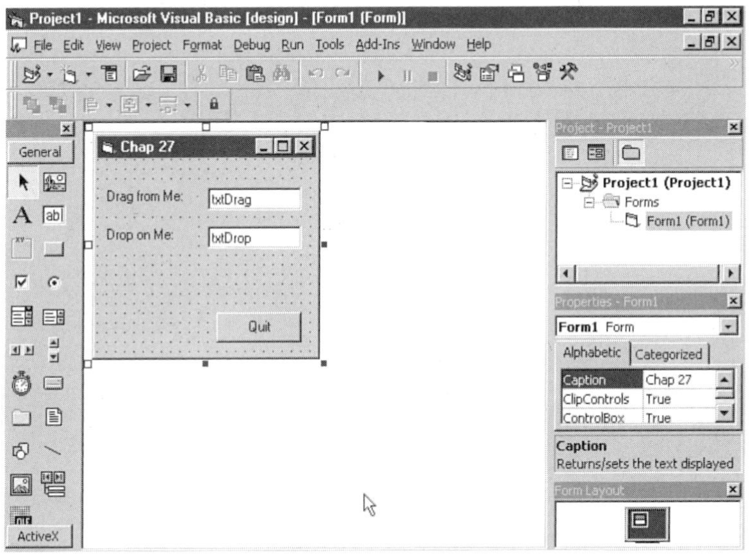

FIGURE 15.2.
An automatic drag-and-drop form.

8. Start the new application and then start Word.
9. In Word, enter some text. Select it and drag it into the Drop on Me text box (see Figure 15.3).
10. Enter some text in the Drag from Me text box. Select this text and then drag it into the Word document.

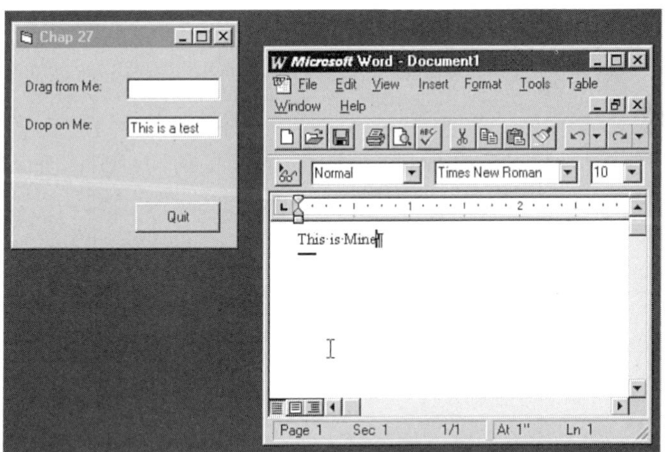

FIGURE 15.3.
An application after drag-and-drop operations.

By default, when you drag text from the text box into a Word document, it is moved rather than copied into the document. To copy the text rather than move it, you can hold down the Ctrl key while you are dragging the text. This is the default behavior for all objects or applications

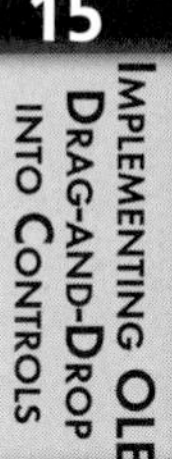

that support OLE drag and drop. To change this default, you need to use the manual drag-and-drop techniques rather than the automatic process.

Automatic support does have some limitations; some limitations are derived from the controls themselves. For example, if you move text from a Word document into a text box, all the rich text formatting in the Word document is stripped out because the standard text box control doesn't support this formatting. Similar limitations exist for most controls. The `RichTextBox` control is the correct control to use for this particular situation.

Modify the previous example by adding a `RichTextBox` control to the form and set its `OLEDropMode` property to `Automatic`. In the Word document, format some text and then drag it into both the standard text box and the `RichTextBox`.

NOTE

When dragging data, you might notice that the mouse pointer shows whether the control it is currently on supports OLE drag and drop for the type of data you are dragging. If it does, the "drop" pointer is displayed; if it doesn't, a "no drop" pointer is displayed.

Controlling the Manual Process

If you want to specify which data formats or drop effects (copy, move, or no drop) are supported, or if the control you want to drag from doesn't support the automatic drag operation, you need to make your OLE drag operation manual.

Starting a manual drag-and-drop operation is done by calling the `OLEDrag` method. At that time, you can set the allowed drop effects and supported data formats, and if necessary, you can place data into the `DataObject` object.

You use the `OLEDrag` method to manually start the drag operation and the `OLEStartDrag` event to specify the allowed effects and the supported data formats.

Manual OLE drag and drop works the same way as the simple event-driven drag-and-drop manual operations. With OLE drag and drop, you're not dragging one control to another control to invoke some code; you're moving *data* from one control or application to another control or application. An example of this is when the user drags a range of cells from Excel into the `DBGrid` control in your application.

The `DataObject` Object

When working with the simple, event-driven drag and drop, you were always sure of where the data came from. Because it was within the same application, the code could reference the `Source` variable in the event routine at runtime to access the information. However, when using OLE drag and drop, you do not always know where the data is coming from. The code process must work whether the data is within the same application or from another application, such as Word or Excel. To facilitate this process, Visual Basic provides an object to contain the data being moved, no matter where it comes from.

The `DataObject` object is the way Visual Basic moves data from the source to the target. It does this by providing the methods needed to store, retrieve, and analyze the data. Table 15.2 lists the property and methods used by the `DataObject` object.

Table 15.2. `DataObject` properties and methods.

Category	*Item*	*Description*
Property	`Files`	Holds the names of files dragged to or from the Windows Explorer.
Methods	`Clear`	Clears the content of the `DataObject` object.
	`GetData`	Retrieves data from the `DataObject` object.
	`GetFormat`	Determines whether a specified data format is available in the `DataObject` object.
	`SetData`	Places data into the `DataObject` object or sets a specified format.

These methods allow you to manage data in the `DataObject` object only for controls contained in your Visual Basic application. The `Clear` method allows you to empty the `DataObject` before setting the object with new information. The `Files` property allows you to send a list of filenames that can be dropped into a target.

Finally, the `SetData` and `GetData` methods use the *`data`* and *`format`* arguments to put or get data stored in the `DataObject` object.

NOTE

Visual Basic can detect only a few data types. If the data being dragged is a bitmap, metafile, enhanced metafile, or text, Visual Basic sets the format. All other formats must be specified explicitly, or an error will occur.

Table 15.3 outlines the constants used to specify the format of the data.

Table 15.3. Data type constants.

Constant	*Value*	*Meaning*
vbCFText	1	Text
vbCFBitmap	2	Bitmap (.BMP)
vbCFMetafile	3	Metafile (.WMF)
vbCFEMetafile	14	Enhanced metafile (.EMF)
vbCFDIB	8	Device-independent bitmap (.DIB or .BMP)
vbCFPalette	9	Color palette
vbCFFiles	15	List of files
vbCFRTF	-16639	Rich text format (.RTF)

The `SetData`, `GetData`, and `GetFormat` methods use the *`data`* and *`format`* arguments either to return the type of data in the `DataObject` object or to retrieve the data itself if the format is compatible with the target. In following code, data in a text box was selected, and the *`format`* was specified as text (`vbCFText`). This information is stored in the `DataObject` to allow the target control (wherever it is) to retrieve the data:

```
Private Sub txtSource_OLEStartDrag(Data As DataObject, _
    AllowedEffects As Long)

    Data.SetData txtSource.SelText, vbCFText

End Sub
```

The OLEDrag Method

Just like a simple drag and drop, the `OLEDrag` method is called from an object's `MouseMove` event when data is selected by clicking and holding down the left mouse button to drag the data.

The `OLEDrag` method's primary purpose is to initiate a manual drag and then allow the `OLEStartDrag` event to set the conditions of the drag operation.

You must set the `OLEDragMode` property to `Manual` and then use the `OLEDrag` method to have manual control over the drag operation. If the control supports manual but not automatic OLE drag, it will not have the `OLEDragMode` property; however, it will still support the `OLEDrag` method and the OLE drag-and-drop events.

The OLEStartDrag Event

When the `OLEDrag` method is called, the control's `OLEStartDrag` event is triggered. This event is used to specify what drop effects and data formats the source will support.

The `OLEStartDrag` event uses two arguments to set the supported data formats and indicate whether the data can be copied or moved when the data is dropped.

CAUTION

If no drop effects or data formats are specified in the `OLEStartDrag` event, the manual drag will not start.

The `AllowedEffects` argument specifies which drop effects the drag source supports. Listing 15.1 specifies that a move or a copy can be performed when the data is dragged. This argument can be checked in the target control's `OLEDragDrop` event, and the program can respond based on the settings.

To specify which data formats the source control supports, the `format` argument is set in the `OLEStartDrag` event. The `SetData` method is used to set the format of the data. Listing 15.1 also assigns the data format of the `DataObject` to both text and rich text data.

Listing 15.1. Code to modify the start drag process.

```
Private Sub rtbSource_OLEStartDrag(Data As _
    DataObject, AllowedEffects As Long)

    AllowedEffects = vbDropEffectMove Or vbDropEffectCopy
    Data.SetData , vbCFText
    Data.SetData , vbCFRTF

End Sub
```

Placing Data into the `DataObject` Object

Data is usually placed into the `DataObject` object when you begin a drag operation by using the `SetData` method in the `OLEStartDrag` event:

```
Private Sub txtSource_OLEStartDrag(Data As DataObject, _
    AllowedEffects As Long)

    Data.Clear
    Data.SetData txtSource.SelText, vbCFText

End Sub
```

The preceding code clears the default data formats from the `DataObject`, specifies the data format of the selected data, and then places that data into the `DataObject` object.

The `OLEDragOver` Event

The `OLEDragOver` event is triggered whenever data is dragged over a control. Two important arguments in the `OLEDragOver` event are the `Effect` and `State` arguments. These inform the program of the exact properties and status of the data being dropped.

The `Effect` argument of the `OLEDragOver` event is used to specify what action is taken if the object is dropped. Whenever the effect value is changed, the source's `OLEGiveFeedback` event is triggered. The `OLEGiveFeedback` event contains its own `Effect` argument, which is used to provide visual feedback to the user. (The mouse pointer is changed to indicate a copy, move, or "no drop" action.) Table 15.4 shows the constants used by the `Effect` argument of the `OLEDragOver` event.

Table 15.4. `Effect` constants.

Constant	*Value*	*Meaning*
`vbDropEffectNone`	`0`	Drop target cannot accept the data.
`vbDropEffectCopy`	`1`	Drop results in a copy. The original data is untouched by the drag source.
`VbDropEffectMove`	`2`	Drag source removes the data.
`VbDropEffectScroll`	`&H80000000&`	Scrolling is about to start or is currently occurring in the target.

The `State` argument of the `OLEDragOver` event allows you to respond to the source data entering, passing over, and leaving the target control. For example, when the source data enters the target control, the `State` argument is set to `vbEnter`.

The `State` argument of the `OLEDragOver` event specifies when the data enters, passes over, and leaves the target control by using the constants in Table 15.5.

Table 15.5. `State` constants.

Constant	*Value*	*Meaning*
`vbEnter`	`0`	Data was dragged within the range of a target.
`vbLeave`	`1`	Data was dragged out of the range of a target.
`vbOver`	`2`	Data is still within the range of a target, and either the mouse has moved, a mouse or keyboard button has changed, or a certain system-determined amount of time has elapsed.

The following code checks the `DataObject` object for a data format compatible with the target control. If the data is compatible, the `Effect` argument tells the source that a move is requested if the data is dropped. If the data is not compatible, the source is informed, and a "no drop" mouse pointer is shown.

```
Private Sub txtTarget_OLEDragOver(Data As _
    DataObject, Effect As Long, Button As _
    Integer, Shift As Integer, X As Single, _
    Y As Single, State As Integer)

    If Data.GetFormat(vbCFText) Then
        Effect = vbDropEffectMove And Effect
    Else
        Effect = vbDropEffectNone
    End If

End Sub
```

Providing Customized Visual Feedback

To modify the default visual behavior of the mouse in an OLE drag-and-drop operation, you can insert code in the `OLEDragOver` event for the target or the `OLEGiveFeedback` event for the source.

OLE drag and drop provides automatic visual feedback during a drag-and-drop operation. For example, when you start a drag, the mouse pointer changes to indicate that a drag has been initiated. When you pass over objects that do not support OLE drop, the mouse pointer changes to the “no drop” cursor.

The `OLEGiveFeedback` Event

The source’s `OLEGiveFeedback` event is triggered automatically whenever the `Effect` argument of the `OLEDragOver` event is changed. In this event, you can change the default behavior of the mouse pointer based on the `Effect` argument. The `OLEGiveFeedback` event contains the `Effect` and the `DefaultCursors` arguments. These allow you to check the effects allowed and then modify the default mouse pointers as needed.

The `Effect` argument, like the other OLE drag-and-drop events, specifies whether data is to be copied, moved, or rejected. The purpose of this argument in the `OLEGiveFeedback` event is to allow you to provide customized feedback to the user by changing the mouse pointer to indicate these actions.

The `DefaultCursors` argument specifies whether the default OLE cursor set is used. Setting this argument to `False` allows you to specify your own cursors using the `Screen.MousePointer` property of the `Screen` object.

TIP

Specifying custom mouse pointers is unnecessary because the default behavior of the mouse is handled by OLE.

CAUTION

If you decide to specify custom mouse pointers using the `OLEGiveFeedback` event, you need to account for every possible effect, including scrolling.

The following code example shows how to specify custom cursors (`.ICO` or `.CUR` files) for the copy, move, and scroll effects by setting the `MousePointer` and `MouseIcon` properties of the `Screen` object:

```
Private Sub TxtSource_OLEGiveFeedback(Effect As Long, _
    DefaultCursors As Boolean)

    DefaultCursors = False
    If Effect = vbDropEffectNone Then
        Screen.MousePointer = vbNoDrop
    ElseIf Effect = vbDropEffectCopy Then
        Screen.MousePointer = vbCustom
        Screen.MouseIcon = _
          LoadPicture("c:\Program Files\devstudio\vb\icons\copy.ico")
    ElseIf Effect = (vbDropEffectCopy Or _
     vbDropEffectScroll) Then
        Screen.MousePointer = vbCustom
        Screen.MouseIcon = _
          LoadPicture("c:\Program Files\devstudio\vb\icons\copyscrl.ico")
    ElseIf Effect = vbDropEffectMove Then
        Screen.MousePointer = vbCustom
        Screen.MouseIcon = LoadPicture("c:\Program
           Files\devstudio\vb\icons\move.ico")
    ElseIf Effect = (vbDropEffectMove Or _
      vbDropEffectScroll) Then
        Screen.MousePointer = vbCustom
        Screen.MouseIcon = _
          LoadPicture("c:\Program Files\devstudio\vb\icons\movescrl.ico")
    Else
        DefaultCursors = True
    End If

End Sub
```

CAUTION

Always reset the mouse pointer in the `OLECompleteDrag` event if you specify a custom mouse pointer in the `OLEGiveFeedback` event.

The OLEDragDrop Event

The `OLEDragDrop` event is triggered whenever the user drops the data onto the target. If data was placed into the `DataObject` object, it can be retrieved when the `OLEDragDrop` event is triggered by using the GetData method. The following example retrieves data from the DataObject and places it into the target control. The dragged data is retrieved using the GetData method.

```
Private Sub txtTarget_OLEDragDrop(Data As _
    DataObject, Effect As Long, Button As _
    Integer, Shift As Integer, X As Single, _
    Y As Single)

    txtTarget.Text = Data.GetData(vbCFText)

End Sub
```

You might need to query the DataObject object for the data type that is dropped onto the target. You use the GetFormat method to check whether the data being dropped is compatible with the target. If it is, the drop action is completed.

The following code shows how to perform this action using an If...Then statement to choose which format to process:

```
Private Sub txtTarget_OLEDragDrop(Data As _
    DataObject, Effect As Long, Button As _
    Integer, Shift As Integer, X As Single, _
    Y As Single)

    If Data.GetFormat(vbCFText) Then
       txtTarget.Text = Data.GetData(vbCFText)
    End If

End Sub
```

If the data was not placed into the DataObject object when the OLEStartDrag event occurred, the OLESetData event is triggered when the target uses the GetData method to retrieve source data. The OLESetData event allows the source to respond to only one request for a given format of data.

The following code shows the OLESetData event responding only to text data:

```
Private Sub txtSource_OLESetData(Data As _
    DataObject, DataFormat As Integer)

    If DataFormat = vbCFText Then
        Data.SetData txtSource.SelText, vbCfText
    End If

End Sub
```

The Effect argument of the OLEDragDrop event specifies how the data was moved to the target when the data was dropped. Whenever this argument is changed, the OLECompleteDrag event is triggered for the source control. The source control can then take the appropriate action in its event routine.

The OLECompleteDrag event is also triggered if the OLE drag-and-drop operation was canceled. The OLECompleteDrag is the last event in the drag-and-drop operation.

The OLECompleteDrag Event

The OLECompleteDrag event contains only one argument (Effect), which is used to inform the source of the action that was taken when the data is dropped onto the target.

If a move is specified and the data is dropped into the target, the following code deletes the data from the source control and resets the default mouse pointer:

```
Private Sub txtSource_OLECompleteDrag(Effect As Long)

   If Effect = vbDropEffectMove Then
       txtSource.SelText = ""
   End If
   Screen.MousePointer = vbDefault

End Sub
```

The Button and Shift arguments can respond to the state of the mouse buttons and the Shift, Ctrl, and Alt keys. For example, when dragging data into a control, you can allow the user to specify a copy operation by pressing the Ctrl key when dragging the data.

In the following code, the Ctrl argument of the OLEDragDrop event is used to determine whether the Ctrl key is pressed when the data is dropped. If it is, a copy is performed. If it is not, a move is performed.

```
Private Sub txtTarget_OLEDragDrop(Data As _
    DataObject, Effect As Long, Button As _
    Integer, Shift As Integer, X As Single, _
    Y As Single)

    If Shift And vbCtrlMask Then
        txtTarget.Text = Data.GetData(vbCFText)
        Effect = vbDropEffectCopy
    Else
        txtTarget.Text = Data.GetData(vbCFText)
        Effect = vbDropEffectMove
    End If

End Sub
```

You can use the Button argument to respond to the various mouse button states. For instance, you might want to let the user move the data by clicking the right mouse button.

Enhancing Visual Basic Applications with OLE Drag and Drop

Now that you have seen what OLE drag and drop is and what it can do, you will create a small Visual Basic application that allows you to drag a text file from Windows Explorer into a text box.

The following application uses a text box control and the `OLEDragOver` and `OLEDragDrop` events to open a single text file using the `Files` property and the `vbCFFiles` data format of the `DataObject` object.

To create this application, follow these steps:

1. Start a new project in Visual Basic.
2. Add a text box control to the form. Set its `OLEDropMode` property to `Manual`. Set its `MultiLine` property to `True` and clear the `Text` property. Then set its `ScrollBars` property to `Vertical`.
3. Add an Exit menu item that will end the application and call it `mnuExit`. Your application form should look the same as the one in Figure 15.4.

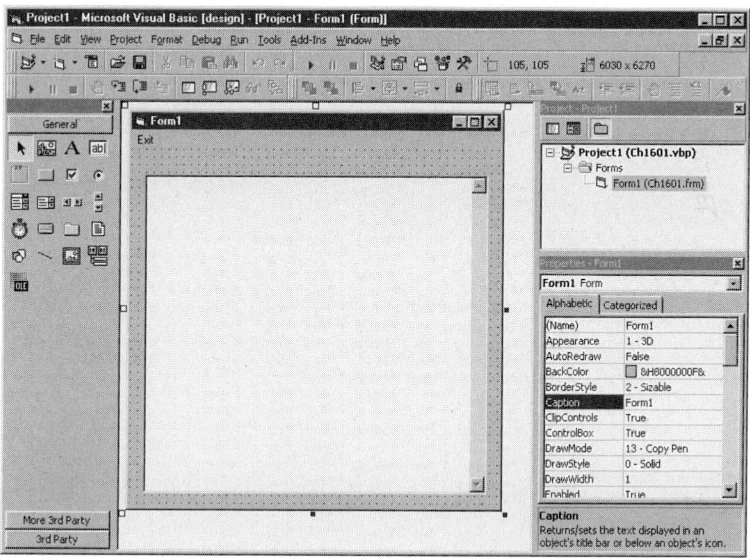

FIGURE 15.4.
Text box control example with properties set.

4. Add the following code to open the selected file and move the text into the text box in your application:

```
Sub DropFile(ByVal txtDropBox As TextBox, ByVal strFilename As String)

    Dim intFile As Integer
    Dim strDataIn As String
    Dim strLineIn As String

    ' Open the filename that is passed to this
    ' routine in the strFilename argument, and
    ' read it in line by line.
    intFile = FreeFile
    Open strFilename For Input As #intFile
```

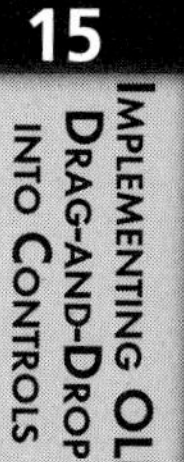

```
    While Not EOF(intFile) And Len(strDataIn) <= 32000
        Line Input #intFile, strLineIn
        If strDataIn <> "" Then
            strDataIn = strDataIn + vbCrLf
        End If
        strDataIn = strDataIn & strLineIn
    Wend
    Close #intFile
    ' Add the contents of the file just read in
    ' (stored in strDataIn) to the end of the
    ' TextBox passed as an argument to this
    ' routine (txtDropBox).
    txtDropBox.SelStart = Len(txtDropBox)
    txtDropBox.SelLength = 0
    txtDropBox.SelText = strDataIn

End Sub
```

5. Add the following procedure to the `OLEDragOver` event. The `GetFormat` method is used to test for a compatible data format (`vbCFFiles`):

```
Private Sub Text1_OLEDragOver(Data As DataObject, Effect As Long, _
    Button As Integer, Shift As Integer, X As Single, Y As Single, _
    State As Integer)

    ' Check to see if the file to be dragged
    ' is in the right format. If it is, set the
    ' Effect to show that the file can be dropped.
    ' If the file is an invalid format, set the
    ' Effect to show no drop is possible.
    If Data.GetFormat(vbCFFiles) Then
        Effect = vbDropEffectCopy And Effect
    Else
        Effect = vbDropEffectNone
    End If

End Sub
```

6. Add the following code to the `OLEDragDrop` event:

```
Private Sub Text1_OLEDragDrop(Data As DataObject, Effect As Long, _
Button As Integer, Shift As Integer, X As Single, Y As Single)

    ' If the file format is acceptable, then
    ' pass its filename to the DropFile routine,
    ' which adds the file's contents to the
    ' Text1 control.
    If Data.GetFormat(vbCFFiles) Then
        If Data.Files(1) <> "" Then
            DropFile Text1, Data.Files(1)
        End If
    End If

End Sub
```

7. Finally, add the following code to the `Click` event for the `mnuExit` menu item:

```
    Private Sub mnuExit_Click()

    ' End the program.
    End

End Sub
```

8. Run the application, open the Windows Explorer, highlight a text file, and drop it into the text box control. The final outcome should look like Figure 15.5.

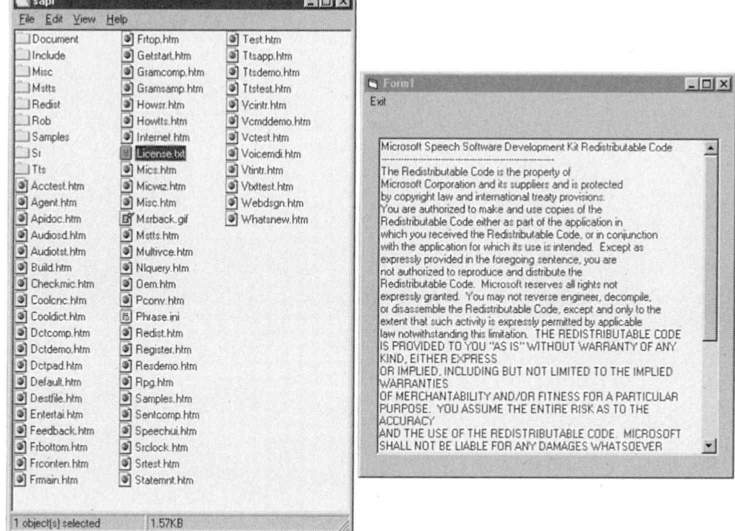

FIGURE 15.5.
A text box application showing a dragged text file.

Summary

This chapter showed you how versatile OLE drag and drop really is. By using this feature of Visual Basic, you can use many different applications' data and allow your application to get data from and send data to anywhere.

You have seen that the OLE techniques are almost the same as the simple, event-driven techniques for drag and drop. The examples in this chapter have shown you only one useful way of using the OLE drag-and-drop features. By understanding how these examples work, you can take the techniques and extend them into your applications.

IN THIS PART

IV
PART

Energizing Your Applications with ActiveX

CHAPTER

ActiveX and DCOM

IN THIS CHAPTER

In Redmond, Washington, on July 26, 1996, Microsoft Corporation announced a lofty plan to fulfill its vision of open channels for ActiveX. To achieve this vision, Microsoft executives announced that they would transition the ActiveX specifications and the underlying technology to an industry-standards body. To do this, they selected an independent group to assist with establishing a meeting where interested industry spokespeople would gather and determine how the transition would take place.

Understanding ActiveX's Independence

To the uninitiated, Microsoft's announcement was another boring press release, but it inspired Internet service providers, information technology professionals, server system vendors, desktop operating system vendors, computer manufacturers, and many program developers interested in the new technology. They saw an opportunity to jump on a successful bandwagon with a booming growth market. This announcement meant that major corporations could embrace the new technology, knowing it would be supported by a cross-segment of interested vendors of software and hardware technology and tools.

If this cross-segment of vendors of hardware and software could work out the details, new standards would provide a solution to many compatibility and efficiency problems plaguing their industries. Many barriers would fall by the wayside. A group consisting of customers, independent software vendors (ISVs), and operating system vendors would convene to determine the process for transitioning ActiveX technology to an independent organization. The group of professionals, referred to as the Working Group, later appointed a smaller group of professionals, the Open Group, to work out the details.

The Working Group, led by Microsoft and other customer-driven companies, would develop a way for everyone to share the benefits of interactive content. ActiveX would become an open, cross-platform set of technologies used to integrate distributed computing with components over all networks, including the Internet. Microsoft's contribution to the process of inspiring the formation of an independent ActiveX Group would be three-fold. Microsoft announced commitment to the following:

- Providing source-code reference implementations on multiple platforms including UNIX, Macintosh, and Windows. Key implementations of ActiveX, by using COM (Component Object Model) and DCOM (Distributed Component Object Model), would be included to help vendors create their own solutions incorporating the new technology.
- Unveiling the technology and specifications behind COM, which had become a popular and widely used technology. COM would assist in the implementation of a language that would allow various components to work together in one application. Now the requirement for licensing COM would become more relaxed.
- Exposing DCOM, the key new technology that made ActiveX so attractive. DCOM would assist in the implementation of a language that would allow the various

components to work together over networks, especially the Internet. DCOM implementation would "bind" objects (application components and applications) residing on different platforms at various locations.

- Providing the necessary specifications used in the technology.
- Granting appropriate rights to ActiveX trademarks.

Looking at Cross-Platform Vendor-Neutral Standards

Microsoft took another step toward transforming ActiveX component architecture from a proprietary specification to an industry standard. A large task group met and voted to name the Open Group as an outside arbiter to head up the effort of transitioning ActiveX to an independent body. A majority of representatives from more than 100 companies voted at the task group's first meeting on October 1, 1996, to turn over licensing, branding, and management of the ActiveX specification to the Open Group.

The Open Group is an industry consortium experienced in promoting other cross-platform technologies. The meeting brought together a cross-section of the industry to form a group that Microsoft referred to as *ActiveX stakeholders*. At the meeting, 63 votes were cast in support of handing over ActiveX to the Open Group, which would, in turn, organize a subgroup called the Active Group. The Active Group would handle licensing, branding, and validation of ActiveX technologies.

At that October meeting, Microsoft identified the following items that the company would turn over to the Open Group for use by the Active Group. These topics comprise the ActiveX technologies, according to Microsoft:

- Reference implementations of ActiveX on Windows (Win32), Macintosh, and UNIX platforms
- Specifications for ActiveX core technologies:
  - *Component Object Model (COM)*
  - *Distributed Component Object Model (DCOM)* Microsoft indicated that COM and DCOM are the underlying architecture "object models" for ActiveX. See "Learning How ActiveX Works" later in this chapter for details about COM and DCOM and how they enable ActiveX computing.
  - *Microsoft Remote Procedure Call (MS-RPC)* This compatible implementation of DCE RPC is also known as *Object Remote Procedure Call (ORPC)*. It provides scalability, marshaling, and privacy support. DCE (Distributed Computing Environment) is an older cross-platform architecture already supported by multiple vendors. DCE is managed and promoted by the Open Group.

- *Standard Security Provider Interface (SSPI)* NT LAN Manager (NTLM) SSPI allows secure invocation of components. NTLM is the security protocol of Windows NT.
- *Structured Storage of COM components* A rich, transaction-based hierarchical file format. The hierarchical file format allows applications to share files across application and platforms.
- *The COM registry* Similar to the Windows 95 Registry, this provides a database of COM components and their configuration information.
- *Monikers* Monikers provide for persistent, intelligent names.
- *Automation* OLE Automation allows objects to expose functionality to high-level programming languages and scripting environments.

In summary, ActiveX is a relatively new set of client/server technologies that represent a major rework of earlier technologies. The new technology initially was created and controlled exclusively by Microsoft. The cross-platform set of technologies was widely adopted by information technology professionals, managers of information systems, technical directors, communications architects, network architecture professionals, corporate solutions providers, and information services groups.

Exploring System Interoperability

Interoperability became a buzzword in 1996. All Microsoft executives used the word to describe a new way of computing with distributed components over the Internet. The term might best be defined as the means by which different computer applications, various computer languages, and various operating system platforms could share *common threads* over a diverse network. The threads they would share have come to be known as ActiveX controls and the underlying code that makes them work. *ActiveX controls* are computer components (objects) enabled for use on the Internet.

All computer users can share ActiveX controls residing on Internet sites only if interoperability is in place. Interoperability requires the incorporation of a few groups of technologies being used by Microsoft and others for distributed computing. These technologies, including COM and OLE, are the basic building blocks making interoperability a reality over all networks, including the Internet. DCOM is Microsoft's *definition* (suggested standard or specification) regarding how this interoperability should be implemented on various platforms. A standard is necessary so that ActiveX controls will be accessible and functional for all users.

Understanding DCOM and Platform Compatibility

The popularity and flexibility of the Java programming language has helped inspire rapid growth on the Internet. Java lets you launch independent applets within other programs over a network. The vision of DCOM and its primary benefits are explained in the following text. Some of the information is condensed from *DCOM: A Business Overview* (`dcombus.exe`), which you can download from `http://www.microsoft.com/ntserver/guide/pdcwp.asp`.

Information technology managers consider the ramifications of Java technology and its evolving impact on the Internet to be of critical importance to the future of computing as we know it today. One key technology in this evolution is distributed component computing over a network. The basis of this technology includes DCE (Distributed Computing Environment) and DCOM (Distributed Component Object Model).

DCE, an older architecture already supported by some vendors, enables cross-platform computing. DCOM is Microsoft's specification for a cross-platform, client/server computing environment. It supports the use of components (applets) over existing networks.

NOTE

Think of *components* as ActiveX controls containing useful visual objects such as command buttons, input boxes, checkboxes, marquees, animated objects, image controls, and the like.

DCOM is paving the way for widespread use of component software technology over networks. With this technology, you can break large, complex software applications into a series of flexible, prefabricated software modules. One logical conclusion to be drawn from this new technology's popularity is that prefabricated ActiveX controls will affect the computing industry just as prefabricated home components did in the residential and commercial construction industries almost a decade ago.

Similar to the modules found in the COM (Component Object Model) technology, the controls can be easily developed, understood, and modified. These applets (including ActiveX controls) are the means of delivering software solutions more quickly and at a lower cost. The goal of the new technology is to achieve economies of scale for software deployment across multiple platforms and networks. (*Economies of scale* means that programs of widely varied sizes, purposes, and complexities can be written and deployed to various systems and still take advantage of the same core benefits.) This new component architecture for building software applications promotes fast, affordable, and flexible applications because of the following benefits:

- *Faster development* As a programmer, you can build solutions more quickly and create software by assembling prebuilt parts.
- *Lower integration costs* You can create a common set of interfaces (Netscape Navigator and Internet Explorer, for example) for software programs from specialized software vendors. The interfaces reduce the custom work required to integrate components into complete solutions.

- *Programming flexibility* Many of the new DCOM interfaces are programmable, as are almost all third-party ActiveX components based on DCOM. They feature built-in support for plug-ins, or the distributors of the software offer the source code for modification and reuse.
- *Deployment flexibility* COM makes it easier to customize a specific software solution for different divisions of a company by simply changing *some* of the components in the overall application.
- *Lower maintenance costs* Software functions are isolated into discrete components, providing a low-cost, more efficient mechanism to upgrade a component. This eliminates the necessity of retrofitting an entire application.

DCOM Architecture

A distributed component architecture provides unique benefits for multiuser, multiplatform applications:

- *COM support* DCOM is based on the most widely used component technology today: COM. DCOM has been characterized very simply as "COM with a longer wire"—a low-level extension of the Component Object Model, which is the core object technology within Microsoft ActiveX.
- *Ready-made tools* Major development tools vendors—including Microsoft, Borland, Sybase/Powersoft, Symantec, Oracle, IBM, and Micro Focus—already sell software-development tools that produce ActiveX components. These tools and the applications they produce automatically support DCOM, providing the broadest possible industry support.
- *Native to the Internet* DCOM is an ActiveX technology that works natively with Internet technologies such as TCP/IP protocol, the Java language, and the HTTP network protocol. It's the key link that allows business applications to work on the Internet.

Businesses can realize the benefits of a modern component application architecture without having to replace investments in existing systems, staff, and infrastructure. Why? Consider these three factors: the largest installed base, native support for Internet protocols, and open support for multiple platforms.

DCOM enables distributed Java today without requiring any communications-specific code or add-on schemes such as remote classes. DCOM is an open technology that runs on several popular platforms. The ActiveX Working Group (the Active Group) is openly licensing DCOM technology to software companies to run on all the major operating systems, including multiple implementations of UNIX-based systems.

Software AG has DCOM running on the Solaris-based operating system today. Also, Microsoft broke ground in 1996 by working with the Internet standards bodies, including the Internet

Engineering Task Force (IETF) and the World Wide Web Consortium (W3C), to promote DCOM as a public Internet technology.

NOTE

A technical publication that contains a publicly available description of the DCOM network protocol can be found at `http://www.microsoft.com/oledev/olecom/draft-brown-dcom-v1-spec-01.txt`.

Object Technology

Component-based development is established today as a mainstream business technology on the desktop. DCOM has its roots in Microsoft's object technology. Let's briefly look at the evolution of this technology:

- The first big evolutionary step the past decade was from DDE (dynamic data exchange) to OLE (object linking and embedding). DDE is a form of messaging between Windows-based programs. OLE provides a means for embedding visual links between programs within an application.
- OLE then evolved into COM, which is used as the basis for all object binding. By opening, binding to, and later closing objects, remote calls to these objects can add functionality to a client application.
- The latest step in the evolutionary chain is ActiveX (COM enabled for the Internet). ActiveX gets its power from DCOM, which uses an enhancement to the network protocol DCE RPC.

The evolution of this technology shares a common theme: Each iteration reduces the complexity of building large applications while allowing the delivery of progressively improved functionality for end users.

This process lowers application development costs because you can *leverage* prebuilt components and their interfaces without having to spend as much time testing and integrating the work of many people. It is common knowledge that applications built from components are simply easier to generate and debug than large, monolithic applications.

Examples of Present and Future Benefits

Many of you have read and reviewed the problems regarding the year 2000 and its impact on legacy-based applications. Almost all large organizations, including financial institutions, are scrambling to resolve this potential fiasco. In two years, when computer clocks begin using the year 2000 with data and applications that don't support numbers beyond 1999 (or, in some cases, 99), the predicted outcome is data integrity failure. To avoid failure when the date changes to the new millennium requires an application design solution. This isn't simply a date problem—it's a problem brought by a lack of foresight in the design of many software programs. Databases and production systems are very vulnerable to potential disaster.

If legacy applications were written with a common date component, the fix would be easy to isolate and inexpensive to repair. That's what DCOM is bringing to the future of computing. An accurate time control source is now available on the Internet, courtesy of the National Institute of Standards and Technology.

Suppose that everyone used a common dataset for their date information. A standards body maintains redundant sites with this dataset and computers automatically synchronize with the dataset at regular intervals—minutes, days, weeks or years. Because everyone synchronizes with the single dataset, when the year 2000 arrives, all clients of the dataset would face the same problem and the same patch would work for everybody.

This would be a single date component or mini-application. A relatively simple upgrade to this single theoretical Internet-based component would be all that's necessary to avoid pending catastrophe for thousands of companies.

If this dataset had been designed 100 years ago and the technology was available then, we wouldn't be facing the Year 2000 problem. Most Windows developers understand DCOM's benefits and are already using the ActiveX component architecture, even if they don't call it ActiveX. Remember, this is just the next step in an evolution of Microsoft's object technology. Because DCOM is included as part of Microsoft's most recent operating systems, it has eliminated the need to acquire third-party Object Request Broker (ORB) software.

Another appropriate example of how this new technology makes programs easier to generate and debug is a modern stock ticker running in a Web browser window. You can use a single database to run all the tickers used on numerous Web pages across the Internet. With DCOM, all the individual desktop applications update their respective ticker like this:

1. A single query to a database of ticker information runs on the server.
2. A new current dataset is created with the latest figures for the ticker.
3. The individual desktop PCs linked to the Internet would run a "personalized" query against that single dataset when they update their ticker.

You can see how much computing work this would eliminate. It also permits customization because the desktop query can request only information needed from the dataset.

Widespread Acceptance of DCOM

That the DCOM technology has been turned over to a vendor-neutral standards body for distribution and standardization doesn't mean every computer program developer will embrace and use it. According to Microsoft, however, more than 3 million programmers are trained on ActiveX and its technologies—OLE, COM, and DCOM. Hundreds of independent software companies are shipping thousands of prebuilt software components.

You can use Microsoft Visual Basic, PowerBuilder, Micro Focus Visual Object, COBOL, and other popular tools to manipulate these commercial software controls, utilities, interfaces, and full-featured applications. The key business benefits of ActiveX on the desktop extend to DCOM across the network: Because ActiveX is language-neutral, you can build ActiveX components from any language. ActiveX components built in COBOL can work with components built in Java, Visual Basic, VBScript, and so on.

The logical boundary for component applications is no longer on a single platform, such as a Windows-based IBM-compatible PC. Shared applications on multiple machines are now available because of ActiveX and related technologies. These programs are referred to as *n-tier applications*, because *tiers* of application logic, presentation services, business services, information retrieval and management services are broken into different components that can communicate directly with each other across a network.

Each tier of service would reside on a computer system other than the system where users interact with the program. A three-tier application, for example, may be a very basic PC application that features extensive functionality, because it draws on resources from three tiers available on three sophisticated computer systems.

To end users, these applications appear as a seamless extension of their existing desktop or mainframe environment. For the information technology or information systems manager, these applications represent the opportunity to apply the economics and flexibility of desktop development across a broader set of challenges. For example, a business can deploy a new personnel management system based on a multitier application design by using components. The application includes different data-entry components, each designed for a separate department or division.

These components all use a common, single payroll income tax calculation component that runs on a server. As income-tax laws change, the company must change only the tax component located on the server, without retrofitting the components for each department or division. ActiveX technology, when used to save money, permits downsizing of computer software.

DCOM is an ideal technology solution for three-tier applications because it allows ActiveX components to work across networks. You can easily build complex systems that escape single-machine boundaries. For example, you can achieve number crunching on a large mainframe server and use the resulting data on a PC with more limited processing capability. This way, you can integrate the components without having to worry about network programming, system compatibility, and integration of various components that were built with different languages.

DCOM is popular because it allows the millions of existing ActiveX programmers to build server components that interoperate with desktop counterparts, thereby broadening the target audience and user base for the application. Companies can assign the same developers to client and server applications, therefore reducing training costs, the number of tools purchased, and support costs. DCOM was designed initially to run on Windows 95 and Windows NT, but also works on Macintosh, UNIX, and legacy operating systems. This way, platform designers have a basis for a *common application infrastructure*, which can broaden the entire computing environment, thus lowering integration costs while reducing integration complexities.

Complying with Earlier Technologies

DCOM is layered on the Open Group's Distributed Computing Environment Remote Procedure Call mechanism (DCE RPC), a network communications protocol developed and endorsed by IBM, Sun Microsystems, Hewlett-Packard, and DEC.

Because a source code implementation of DCOM is available free from the Open Group, additional computer vendors will be incorporating it. Examples of the additional object-related extensions to the DCE RPC required by DCOM are contained within a text file available at `http://www.microsoft.com/oledev/olecom/draft-brown-dcom-v1-spec-01.txt`.

Businesses will use the new Internet protocols and ActiveX technology to link component-based applications across public and private networks, projecting a presence of their business systems onto the World Wide Web. The simplicity, ubiquity, and industry momentum of standard Internet protocols such as HTTP make DCOM an ideal technology for linking components together in applications that require more than just a desktop PC to function.

HTTP is easy to use, is inherently cross-platform, and supports an accessible, universal naming service. Much of the excitement generated by the Java language derives from its potential as a mechanism to build distributed component applications on the Internet. For example, many companies have built investment portfolio management systems that rely on Internet-based data streams, such as PointCast, for stock information. PCQuote is enlisting programmers to develop spreadsheet-based stock analysis data streams. Many others are developing these kinds of Internet services and capabilities, using ActiveX, DCOM, and related technologies.

Using DCOM and ActiveX Development

Integrating existing services and applications into in-house solutions by using browsers and Web technology is the new norm. You can simply plug in the services of a remote server component that's already communicating with many clients over the Internet to provide a low-cost—sometimes free—way to enhance the functionality of an in-house software offering.

DCOM is ideally positioned to become a mainstream Internet technology for business applications because it's considered *transport neutral*. This means that it doesn't matter what protocols the client and server are using to communicate. DCOM supports connection-oriented (analog, satellite, and the like) and "connectionless" transport (cabled or wired LAN) including TCP/IP, UDP/IP, IPX/SPX, AppleTalk, and HTTP protocols.

Because you can embed ActiveX components into browser-based applications, DCOM allows a rich application infrastructure for distributed Internet applications that leverage the latest browser technology. Today's browsers use DCOM's efficiency, network recovery, and security offerings. DCOM supports security by integrating Internet certificate-based security with an even richer level of Windows NT-based security, combining the best of both worlds.

As distributed applications built from simple components and Internet protocols emerge, a new set of enterprise platform services for component applications will be required. Some are already emerging. Likewise, computer users can benefit from new advances in technology through HTML (Hypertext Markup Language) anchors that point to sources of upgrades and allow users to automatically upgrade their systems with ActiveX components. These components can be in the form of `.cab` files that automatically update the operating system registry as the browser downloads the software.

A key goal of any component software architecture is to separate business logic (how a tax component calculates tax rates, for example) from execution logic (whether the tax component runs in a browser or on a multiprocessor server). DCOM extends the separation of business logic and execution logic even further because the same components can communicate with each other across processes in a single machine or across the Internet via HTTP. Components by themselves don't solve all the issues of enterprise application complexity, such as exception handling, system failures, network outages, and performance load peaks.

To address the enterprise requirements for a distributed component architecture without sacrificing rapid development and cost effectiveness, Microsoft is integrating DCOM into the ActiveX Server Framework, a series of technology services that speed deployment of component-based applications across the Internet and corporate intranets. Some of the ActiveX Server Framework services include

- Transactions, a term that describes rollback and recovery for component-based applications in the event of system failure.
- Queuing, which represents the integration of component communication with reliable store-and-then-forward spooling queues. These queues allow component applications to operate on occasionally or frequently unavailable networks.
- Server scripting, which refers to the easy integration of components by using a programming language within HTML files. Scripting works with browser pages and browser-compatible application interfaces referred to as *active documents.*
- The integration of component applications with legacy production systems, including mainframe systems running CICS and IMS.

The ActiveX Server Framework technologies were built with publicly available Internet protocols and began to appear in 1996. DCOM first shipped with Windows NT Server 4.0 and Windows NT Workstation 4.0 in mid-1996. On September 18, 1996, Microsoft released the DCOM for Windows 95 Developer Beta at no charge to Windows developers and Windows 95 customers.

DCOM for the Macintosh was offered on the Internet at the beginning of 1997. DCOM for Solaris was available for download on the Internet in late 1996. Additional implementations of DCOM on other Internet and enterprise platforms are emerging now. For the latest information on Windows NT Server, go to `http://backoffice.microsoft.com/`.

Working with Third-Party Controls

The emergence of controls other than those packaged with ActiveX Control Pad and offered at no charge by Microsoft quickly gained popularity among developers in the third quarter of 1996. The list of available controls is expanding at a rapid pace.

Some of the popular new controls are offered at no charge or for less than 20 dollars, but others sell for 1,000 dollars or more. You can add some controls to the ActiveX Control Pad toolbox utility, whereas some have limited functionality in Control Pad. More than 1,000 of these independent controls—some of them merely variations of the existing controls—were being offered by dozens of software vendors by the first quarter of 1997. Some appeared to have some significant sophistication and usefulness for developers. Some even required monthly fees to acquire.

> **NOTE**
>
> Chapter 51, "Third-Party Add-Ins," describes many of the more popular third-party ActiveX controls that are available for use in Visual Basic.

Dozens of small, medium, and large software companies are creating the controls, including Borland, Oracle, and Sybase/Powersoft. Some of these companies also offer development tools to build ActiveX controls. Many companies that create Web design and development tools have built ActiveX support into their products, allowing their customers to create and use the controls in their programs.

The ActiveX standard is now supported on operating systems other than Windows. Mainsoft Corporation has developed an ActiveX support system for UNIX platforms, and other companies have announced products that provide ActiveX support for other platforms. Because of these efforts, ActiveX controls will have one of the broadest computer markets of any software being distributed. This move to ActiveX cross-platform compatibility could inspire a seriously radical trend in software marketing. If ActiveX is supported universally, the controls will obviously have more appeal with a wider customer base.

It's important to remember that ActiveX involves both client and server technologies. Its elements include

- *The ActiveX controls* Interactive objects in a Web page or application that provide interactive and user-controllable functions
- *ActiveX documents* Technology that lets users view non-HTML documents such as Microsoft Excel or Word files in a Web browser window
- *Active Scripting* A language used to control the integrated behavior of several ActiveX controls or Java applets from the browser or server

- *Java Virtual Machine* The code that allows the browser to run Java applets and integrate applets with ActiveX controls
- *ActiveX Server Framework* A framework that provides a number of Web server-based functions, such as security, database access, and others

You can find an ActiveX Web site at `http://www.microsoft.com/activex/gallery/`. This commercial Web site promotes the sale and use of free and proprietary ActiveX controls (and interfaces). Full-featured programming environments used to build specific types of controls, such as interactive animated movies, are also offered.

Learning How ActiveX Works

At the heart of ActiveX technology is a method for allowing an object, otherwise known as a *component* or *control*, to dynamically call on external resources to carry out its intended function. Most of you are familiar with dynamic links of this nature. DDE is a phenomenon of significant importance in distributed computing. It allows an object to remain small while the functionality of the object is less restrained. How these objects bind to the code segments they depend on is what sets ActiveX technology ahead. The reliable binding of objects over a very diverse network is what makes ActiveX unique.

Most of you understand how DLLs and OLE work. DLLs are organized code segments or code snippets used by an application. More than one part of the program can call on different parts of the DLL to carry out a function. OLE files are linked or embedded and act as visual placeholders in a document or program. They help keep the code small by not duplicating each instance of the file.

COM is a first cousin to DLLs and OLE files. COM distributes computing that uses computer program components. These components, to put it simply, are prebuilt code shells that serve specific purposes. A text box, for example, is a COM object shell for ASCII data. By using this COM object, you can assign certain properties, methods, and events to the COM object to determine how users can use the shell and generate an action.

Each COM component has something in common with all the other COM components: They rely on the same underlying code to function. The underlying code is a sort of a common headquarters or base of operations. With ActiveX, the common headquarters scenario is more complex. The base of the code can be local or remote. Ordinary COM objects rely on this base of operations to function. Each COM object in a program *seems* to be an independent program module, but really the COM objects are very dependent. Their illusion of independence is necessary to make the COM objects simple to build, change, deploy, organize, and launch.

COM allows you to build complex applications faster and at a lower cost because the "common" code that the objects rely on doesn't have to be duplicated for each object. You can think of COM objects as prefabricated walls. The walls have different shapes, thickness, and colors, but each has common features including the lumber, drywall, nails, and paint. You take the basic shell of a wall and fabricate it to specification without having to know much about the rest of the building. You don't have to know details about the rooms in the building that your wall will eventually become a part of.

DCOM is a closely related technology with additional features. It takes care of the task of conforming to network and platform differences. DCOM's purpose is less specific than COM. DCOM uses a fairly complex networking technology that takes into account variances in protocols and operating systems. It's technically a sophisticated network protocol. A basic introduction to how DCOM and distributed computing works is a prerequisite for learning how ActiveX works.

To get a basic understanding of DCOM without studying DCOM specifications and network architectures in detail, let's try to draw on some simple analogies. Think of DCOM as the electrical current in a network of independent appliances in a laundry business. This laundry is an unmanned store where people go to wash and dry their clothes. Picture the laundry as the Internet. Without DCOM (the electricity), the laundry can't carry out its function. The laundry depends on DCOM.

To illustrate how ActiveX controls work, I'll refer to ActiveX controls as COM objects. The COM objects in the laundry are the individual appliances—the washers and dryers. Each COM object has a function. The appliances in this laundry come in different colors, sizes, and shapes. That's the nature of the Internet—diversity. Each COM object is like a washer or dryer because each has different capacities, cycles, timers, pumps, heating elements, and the like. These differences—including the COM object's visual representation, its purpose, its properties, events, and methods—are what make the controls unique. On the other hand, they're similar enough to each other to be programmed by using a single programming interface such as Visual Basic.

All the COM objects have a common purpose. The purpose of each control isn't much different from the purpose of programs two decades ago—to allow a user to create an input and then generate an output. The actual inputs and outputs are much different, however, than what was seen in those early days of computing. The appliances in the laundry analogy, like COM objects, must work together reliably to consistently get the clothes from their dirty state to a clean state.

The washers come in different brands and configurations. Think of an Apple Macintosh COM object as one brand, a UNIX workstation COM object as another brand, and an IBM-compatible PC COM object as a third brand. DCOM must conform to each platform's needs so that everything will work together. It does this behind the scenes by using "transformers" that allow the electrical current to be conditioned for each unique platform. The development of these transformers is considered "work in progress" for some computer platform manufacturers.

In 1996, Microsoft released code source implementations of DCOM on various platforms. DCOM was already running on the Solaris platform in addition to 32-bit Windows platforms. In 1997, some new DCOM-compatible platforms and operating systems emerged. Perhaps in the future almost all platforms will feature interoperability using DCOM.

To understand ActiveX a little better, consider that each appliance has its own configuration. The Java applet appliance, for example, works differently from the Brand X ActiveX control appliance. The two appliances are related, however, because they're both objects that rely on DCOM and DCOM's underlying technologies for interoperability. They can work together in the same application just as the washers and dryers work together in the laundry.

DCOM allows distributed Java without requiring any communications-specific code or add-ins. Remote classes aren't required for Java to work under DCOM. This may be one reason Microsoft has embraced Java and made significant efforts to incorporate Java's functionality into its own technology fold. Whether DCOM or Java arrived on the scene first is a moot point; the important point from your perspective is that they can coexist.

COM, a scaled-down version of DCOM, was originally intended for DDE in desktop applications. In some cases, a network that uses a particular protocol to sustain the dynamic links is used with COM. For example, in a peer-to-peer local area network (LAN), a drive mapping would allow COM to work over the network. If the network fails, the COM link typically fails and the program can crash. DCOM is a technology that allows this dynamic link to be stronger and more versatile by standardizing the method of binding and sustaining the link. The intent is to make the link more reliable when differences are encountered or when the network fails.

COM and DCOM support the use of components. The most commonly used components of this nature today are COM objects. Think of COM objects as *common* objects—they're common in use and have common functionality. When you consider the analogy of COM objects to appliances, picture these appliances with a model number (class ID) and a serial number (filename). Each appliance has an ID and serial number so that the platform can interpret the code to generate the desired results. Each COM object has a unique function but belongs to a class of similar objects.

Microsoft, Borland, Sybase/Powersoft, Symantec, Oracle, IBM, and Micro Focus already sell software-development tools used to produce ActiveX components. This broad industry support is what has made DCOM the distributed computing technology of choice. Because a few thousand ActiveX controls are already built with these tools, the use of DCOM in the marketplace is becoming prevalent. This is true despite some developers not really understanding the details of how DCOM works.

Since Microsoft openly licensed DCOM in 1996 and then agreed to transition the technology to a third-party task force to make the technology independent, the implementation of DCOM on various platforms continues to expand. In 1996, DCOM was running on a Solaris-based system, and other implementations were on a number of UNIX systems. By the end of 1996, Macintosh was offering DCOM functionality. Some platform vendors complained that DCOM was a technology better suited for a Windows environment than for their platform, but DCOM really is just an application of existing Internet technologies that were founded on network protocols, programming languages, and platforms from various vendors, including Microsoft.

DCOM protocol works hand in hand with TCP/IP and HTTP, the primary protocols used for Internet traffic. In technical terms, DCOM is *layered* on—and therefore compatible with—the Distributed Computing Environment. It's also layered on TCP/IP and HTTP. You could see this phenomenon as technology borrowing from other technologies, because it's not to anyone's advantage to rewrite standards that already have been proven to work.

Compatibility and multiplatform usefulness means that companies can build applications by using existing investments in networks, programs, objects, databases, and platforms. One major benefit of interoperability and the way ActiveX works is the availability of remote components for use in local applications. For example, a company selling financial services can use Object Remote Procedure Calls built into DCOM (based on RPC and borrowed from DCE) to acquire data from a database that contains stock data. In this way, each company can create its own unique stock ticker while using a common data source, dramatically decreasing the cost of providing timely stock data to users.

Interoperability will continue to boost the use of browsers in the future because ActiveX components can be embedded into browser-based applications. DCOM provides an application infrastructure for distributed Internet applications that make efficient use of the latest browser technology.

Some organizations other than Microsoft are tackling the issues of standardizing this interoperability. You can find one such organization, Object Management Group, at `http://www.omg.org`. OMG has devised its own implementation for Distributed Object Computing called CORBA, which competes with Microsoft's DCOM standard. However, CORBA-DCOM interoperability is supposed to be in the works.

You can find another standards group, the ECTF (Enterprise Computer Telephony Forum), at `http://www.ectf.org`. This group has a more specialized interest in standardizing the interoperability of a particular computing environment. If you're interested in the standards associated with interoperability in general or for specific types of computing, search the Internet with the keyword **`interoperability`**.

Handling Necessary Network Tasks

DCOM helps you handle the authentication, authorization, and message integrity capabilities of DCE's Remote Procedure Call. A DCOM implementation may support any level of DCE RPC security. You can make any connection or call as secure or as insecure as the client application dictates. The client and the server negotiate this level of security. Developers commonly make the mistake of getting the proverbial cart before the horse when trying to use this authentication and authorization process for the first time. The key to avoiding this pitfall is to make sure that the first step (authentication) is completed before attempting the second step (authorization). Servers don't always respond quickly enough with these calls to permit you to attempt this with two lines of code. There has to be code between the authentication and authorization calls that checks to see whether the processing of the first call is complete before proceeding with another call.

DCOM uses universally unique identification (UUID) to determine and handle different interface versions. During remote procedure calls by objects (ORPC), the object's ID field (contained in the invocation header) sends an IPID to the server being called. (An IPID, or *interface pointer identifier*, is a 128-bit identifier.) The IPID specifies a particular interface on a particular object in a particular server. The IPID is located in the object ID fields of a remote procedure call. The static type of IPID is really a UUID, but you have to make a distinction between the two; IPIDs and UUIDs are different birds.

IPIDs are relative to the server process that originally allocated them. In other words, they aren't global or universal in scope. IPIDs don't necessarily use the standard UUID allocation algorithm. They may use a machine-specific algorithm that organizes how the data is dispatched. This is one key to successful interoperability. To put it another way, the identifier is "machine-dependent." When it comes time to process the object, the server determines how the data is dispatched.

The interface ID field of the RPC header specifies the identification of the object and the arguments found in the body of the object. RPC normally works this way. When viewed from the DCOM perspective, however, an additional first argument is always present that isn't part of the COM interface specification. It's placed as the first identifier in the body of the request Protocol Data Unit (PDU, a packet of data that's passed across a network). This special type of argument, known technically as `ORPCTHIS`, assists the machine in generating an 8-byte alignment of arguments. The `ORPCTHIS` is padded with bytes of zeros, if necessary, to achieve this alignment for the remaining arguments.

The replies to the ORPC—output or feedback to the client—has a corresponding additional return value not found in COM. This value, technically known as `ORPCTHAT`, is also placed in the body of the PDU (in this case, the response PDU) before the normal return values.

ORPC calls might summon a method on an interface that isn't supported by that interface. The method number is, in technical terms, beyond the number of methods the server recognizes for that interface. In DCOM, this generates a fault. When a fault is encountered, the `ORPCTHAT` is placed in specific locations in the response packet. The locations depend on whether the call was connectionless (non-network) or connection-oriented (network). This form of error-trapping, unique to DCOM, prevents crashes. The client can handle the fault PDU with an error message such as `Method Not Supported`. `ORPCTHIS` and `ORPCTHAT` are necessary to retain the 8-byte alignment necessary for evaluation by the client and server on all platforms.

When ActiveX uses remote objects and procedures, the DCOM protocol or DCE RPC is used to control the traffic. This traffic control relies on OXID resolvers (formerly referred to as `IObjectExporter`) on the client and server. In the earlier laundry analogy, a transformer is needed to make sure that the appliances will work together despite their differences. These transformers are the OXID resolvers.

Transforming Information and Binding

Here is how the transformation of information works: An OXID resolver on the server receives a call from an object. Packaged with the object's call arguments and other identification, described previously, is a packet of information that informs the server regarding the type of binding being requested. This information doesn't contain any data regarding how to bind to the desired objects or dispatch the data. If it did, the code would be bulky and would have to take into account too many variations in operating systems. Instead, this data, known as an *identifier*, defines the type of binding being sought by the client. This information is carried in a 64-bit value called an *object exporter identifier*. The object exporter identifier has recently been renamed OXID.

The server evaluates the OXID to create the necessary binding work on the server's end. To evaluate the OXID requires the OXID resolver that was referred to previously as a transformer. This resolver (one per machine, per protocol) is located at specific ports on the server's network, depending on the type of protocol being used for communication. These ports are known in DCOM terminology as *endpoints*.

The important thing about OXID resolvers is that they work strategically to keep the binding active and carry out the actual invocation of the binding. This work opens the door for two-way communication with objects and keeps the objects "alive," so to speak. The resolver also keeps the client and server in constant communication despite any inactivity on either end while the interaction work is under way. In this way, the binding exchanges can be frequent or infrequent, and bulky processing work can take place on the server or the client without losing the link.

An OXID resolver is on the client as well. This OXID resolver can cache information about the response OXIDs so that repeated calls to the server for this information aren't needed.

To draw on another analogy, think of this two-way communication as a telephone call to Japan. Japanese and U.S. citizens in a room in America are on a conference call with Japanese and U.S. citizens in a room in Japan. Interpreters are in both rooms. Sometimes, during the interpretation work, one interpreter might have to explain that he's still listening to a lengthy explanation and isn't ready to give the translation yet. Another interpreter might have to indicate that he's still waiting for a response or reaction from the other room. In DCOM and other network protocols, this communication negotiation is achieved with *pings*, simply bursts of data between the client and server that inform each other they're standing by, waiting for the other party to send. The OXID resolvers are the translators in this analogy, and they ping each other to keep the communication alive during periods of inactivity.

You can think of an OXID as the *scope of implementation* sought by the object. This is the general description of the assignment that the object carries to the server for processing. It can refer to a given process, a thread within a process, or a whole machine. The scope of implementation doesn't affect the protocol itself. DCOM's resolvers take the scope of the task into account and react accordingly. Meanwhile, the data structure of the program that exported the object's call or response keeps track of the IPIDs (128-bit interface pointer identifiers).

The actual OXID resolver is a DCE RPC interface. One OXID service on a given machine keeps track of all the OXIDs, and there may be several at any given moment. The OXID resolver does its work by caching the mapping information used to create and maintain the bindings for dynamic exchange of data. When a destination application receives an object reference (an OXID), it checks to see whether it recognizes it. If it doesn't, the OXID resolver is queried for the translation, and the resolver saves the resulting set of string bindings in a local table that maps OXIDs to string bindings.

Each OXID is associated with an OXID COM object that depends on a COM interface (`IRemUnknown`) to manage reference counts and requests. Interface references are a new data type that can be marshaled. DCOM extends the Network Data Representation (NDR) by defining these interface references to an object. This is the only extension to NDR made by the DCOM protocol. In technical terms, an `OBJREF` is the data type used to represent an actual marshaled object reference. This `OBJREF` can be empty (Null) or assume one of three variations (Standard, Custom, or Handler). Which variation the `OBJREF` assumes depends on the degree to which the object being marshaled uses the hook architecture in the marshaling infrastructure.

`OBJREF` contains a *switch flag* (determines type) and then the appropriate data. The `OBJREF` variations are as follows:

- *Null* points out that there's no object.
- *Standard* contains one interface of an object marshaled in standard form. This means it contains a standard reference and a set of protocol sequences and network addresses that can be used to bind to an OXID resolver. The standard variation contains several items:
  - An IPID (interface pointer) that uniquely specifies the interface and object.
  - An object ID (OID), which uniquely specifies the unique object on which the IPID is found (depending on the OXID with which the object is associated).
  - An OXID.
  - A reference count, indicating the number of references to this IPID being conveyed. This count, typically a value of 1, can be 0, 1, or more.
  - Any pertinent flags useful for identification of state.

  The OXID resolver can translate the OXID in the `STDOBJREF`. This is useful when using (marshaling) a proxy (go-between) to give to another machine. The first machine (marshaling machine) identifies the `saResAddr` for the OXID resolver on the server machine. This eliminates a need for the "unmarshaler" to call the go-between back to get this information. The first machine doesn't need to keep the OXID in its cache to satisfy requests from clients that it just gave the `OBJREF` to. Table 16.1 lists the members of the `OBJREF` standard variation.
- *Custom* contains a class ID (`CLSID`) and class-specific information. The custom variation gives an object control over references to itself. For example, an immutable

object might be passed by value, in which case the class-specific information would contain the object's immutable data. Table 16.2 lists the members of the custom variation.

- *Handler* specifies that the object requires handler marshaling. For example, an object is to be represented in client address spaces by a proxy object that caches state. The class-specific information in this variation is a standard reference to an interface pointer that the proxy object (handler) uses to communicate with the original object. Table 16.3 lists members of the `OBJREF` handler variation.

Table 16.1. The `OBJREF` standard variation members.

Member	*Data Type*	*Semantic Description*
signature	`unsigned long`	Must be `OBJREF_SIGNATURE`
flags	`unsigned long`	`OBJREF` flags
GUID	`iid`	Interface identifier
std	`STDOBJREF`	A standard object reference used to connect to the source object
SaResAddr	`STRINGARRAY`	The resolver address

Table 16.2. The `OBJREF` custom variation members.

Member	*Data Type*	*Semantic Description*
signature	`unsigned long`	Must be `OBJREF_SIGNATURE`.
flags	`unsigned long`	`OBJREF` flags.
GUID	`iid`	Interface identifier.
clsid	`CLSID`	The `CLSID` of the object to create in the destination client.
cbExtension	`unsigned long`	The size of the extension data.
size	`unsigned long`	The size of the marshaled data provided by the source object, plus the size of the extension data, and passed in `pData`.
pData	`byte`	The data bytes that should be passed to `IMarshal::UnmarshalInterface` on encountering a new instance of class `clsid` to initialize it and complete the unmarshal process (class-specific data). The first `cbExtension` bytes are reserved for future extensions to the DCOM protocol and shouldn't be passed into the custom unmarshaler.

Table 16.3. The OBJREF handler variation members.

Member	*Data Type*	*Semantic Description*
signature	`unsigned long`	Must be `OBJREF_SIGNATURE`
flags	`unsigned long`	`OBJREF` flags
GUID	`iid`	Interface identifier
std	`STDOBJREF`	A standard object reference used to connect to the source object
clsid	`CLSID`	The `CLSID` of handler to create in the destination client
SaResAddr	`STRINGARRAY`	The resolver address

Developing Network Architectures

A key part of keeping networked computing intact on such a diverse hierarchy of clients and servers requires some creative thinking with respect to network architectures and how to make protocols work with these architectures. In response to this challenge, DCOM's authors arrived at some network architecture conclusions that led to some unique thinking.

For example, in the DCOM protocol, remote reference counting is conducted and each interface pointer represents a count of 1. The actual increment and decrement calls are carried out by using `RemAddRef` and `RemRelease`. These methods are part of a COM interface known as `IRemUnknown` found on the `OXID` object associated with each OXID. The interface pointer for the OXID is returned by the function `IOXIDResolver::ResolveOxid`.

What's important about DCOM's handling of the resolver is that a single call can increment or decrement numerous interface pointers, improving network efficiency. Also, on the client, the actual remote release of all interfaces on an object is typically deferred until all local references to all interfaces on that object are released.

DCOM allows for secure releases and secure transmission of data to avoid snooping and to keep virus programs from maliciously trashing a program by disrupting the bindings being used. This is achieved only when a client or host application requests secure references. This method isn't as efficient and requires additional communication. It works like this:

1. The application must call `RemAddRef` (and later `RemRelease`) securely and request private references. Private references are stored by client identity, so one client can't release another client's references.
2. DCOM requires that each client make a call to get its own secure references. The clients can't receive a secure reference transmission belonging to another client.

DCOM shines when you consider the thought behind the creation of a new way of keeping object bindings alive without cluttering bandwidth with redundant pings. Abnormal termination of a program can disrupt the reference-counting scheme; telephone transmission interference, a system malfunction, or an electrical outage breaks the connection between the client and server. Periodic pings have always been used to detect abnormal termination in all the primary protocols used on the Internet and on connection-oriented networks.

The older DCE RPC architecture used context handles to deal with abnormal program termination. Context handles aren't incorporated into DCOM, however, because of the expense of redundant pings. DCOM's authors believed that naïve use of RPC context handles would result in per-object per-client process pings being sent to the server, resulting in an overtaxed communication bandwidth. The DCOM protocol uses a pinging infrastructure that significantly reduces network traffic by relying on the client's OXID resolver (the OXID implementation) to conduct local management of this phenomenon.

The pings are sent only on a machine-to-machine basis, are used on a per-object level (per OID), and aren't associated with the individual interface pointers. Each exported object (exported OID) gets a `pingPeriod` time value assignment on the server. An additional counter value, `numPingsToTimeOut`, works with the `pingPeriod` value to determine the overall amount of time that must elapse before expiration of the remote references (the *ping period*). If the ping period expires before receiving a ping on that OID, all the remote references to IPIDs associated with that OID expire.

After the remote references expire, the interfaces can be reclaimed on the basis of "local knowledge." The time to reclaim the interface is implementation-specific and depends on the server. If the server's COM infrastructure delegates what's commonly called *garbage collection* tasks in this situation (perhaps because it has local references keeping the interface pointer alive) and it later receives a ping, it can recover based on the indication that a network partition recovered. This recovery is known in network architecture terms as a *partition healing*. Now the resolver can consider the remote references to be reactivated and can continue remote operations.

When interface pointers are conveyed from one client to another (incoming or outgoing parameters to a call), the interface pointer is marshaled in one client and unmarshaled in the other. This is done by incrementing one reference count and decrementing another reference count. To successfully unmarshal the interface, the destination client must obtain at least one reference count on the interface, which is usually accomplished by passing in the marshaled interface `STDOBJREF` a `cPublicRefs` of one or more. The destination client then takes ownership of that many (more) reference counts to the indicated IPID, and the source client then owns that many fewer reference counts on the IPID.

If the destination client is also the object's server (local processing on the client), special processing is required by the destination client. This is necessary because the remote references have to be removed as the references are converted to local references. The reference counts present in the `STDOBJREF` are decremented from the remote reference count for the IPID in question.

Because of the manner in which some objects are used, some instances don't require any pings at all. These objects are identified by the presence of a flag in a standard `STDOBJREF` to an interface on the object. Objects that aren't pinged don't need reference counts. For all other objects, assuming that the ping period is a positive number, it's the responsibility of the holder of an interface reference on some object to assure that pings reach the server frequently enough to prevent expiration of the object.

Increasing Networking Efficiency

There's a method to customize the manner in which the pings are handled so that clients and servers can be more compatible and more efficient in terms of communication. The frequency used by a client depends on the ping period, the reliability of the channel between the client and the server, and the probability of failure on the network. If no pings get through, the client may not tolerate the disruption and may not recover. The ping packet or its reply may request changes to the ping period. Through this mechanism, network traffic can actually be reduced. With slow links to busy servers, the pings can be infrequent and the ping periods high without losing the link.

DCOM uses something called the *Delta Mechanism* to further reduce ping traffic. In some scenarios, ping messages can be unwieldy. For example, if a desktop PC held 1,024 remote object references (OIDs) on a server in an adjoining state, the client would send about 16K of byte ping messages. This could be annoying and not very efficient if the set of remote objects was relatively stable and the ping messages were identical from ping to ping. The Delta Mechanism reduces the size of ping messages, using a ping-set interface that allows the pinging of a single set to replace the pinging of multiple OIDs. Rather than ping each OID, the client defines a set. Then each ping contains only the set ID and a list of additions and subtractions to be made to the set.

DCOM uses the `IRemUnknown` interface to handle more than one task. The interface, as well as conduct the reference-counting activity, handles `QueryInterface` calls for remote clients for interface pointers managed by that object exporter. In other words, the `IRemUnknown` interface is optimized for network access by being able to retrieve multiple interfaces at once.

DCOM goes beyond the older DCE RPC technology in several areas. For example, DCOM requires the object ID field of the header to contain the IPID (interface pointer ID). Because Object RPC sits on top of DCE RPC, this kind of variation is necessary. Also, the interface ID of the RPC header must contain the IID, even though it's not needed because there's an IPID. This is what permits ORPC to sit on top of DCE RPC.

When the DCE packet header is formatted this way, an unmodified DCE RPC implementation will still correctly dispatch data based on IID and IPID. An optimized RPC may dispatch data based solely on the IPID. An IPID uniquely identifies a particular interface on a particular object on a machine. The opposite is not true—a particular interface on a particular object may be represented by *multiple* IPIDs. IPIDs are unique on their OXID; they may be reused, but this reuse of IPIDs is discouraged. Datagram broadcasts aren't allowed in ORPC.

Avoiding Network Failures

Some other requirements of DCOM that go beyond the DCE RPC standards include the requirement that faults are returned in the stub fault field of the DCE RPC fault packet. Any 32-bit value may be returned. Only `RPC_E_VERSION_MISMATCH` is prespecified. DCE RPC cancel is supported. All interface version numbers must be 0.0.

The COM network protocol is built on several fundamental data types and structures. These types are illustrated in the DCOM specification that can be found at `http://www.microsoft.com/oledev/olecom/draft-brown-dcom-v1-spec-01.txt`.

DCOM uses ORPC flags referred to as `ORPCINFOFLAGS`, which Table 16.4 describes.

Table 16.4. Various `ORPCINFOFLAGS` in the DCOM specification.

Flag	*Meaning*
`ORPCF_NUL`	This isn't a real flag; it's really just a defined constant that acts as a placeholder indicating the absence of any flag values.
`ORPCF_LOCAL`	The destination of this call is on the same machine on which it originates. This value cannot be specified in remote calls. This flag indicates that network protocol work isn't necessary.
`ORPCF_RESERVED1`	If `ORPCF_LOCAL` is set, this flag indicates that it's reserved for local use (locked). Otherwise, it's reserved for future use.
`ORPCF_RESERVED2`	If `ORPCF_LOCAL` is set, this flag indicates that it's reserved for local use. Otherwise, it's reserved for future use.
`ORPCF_RESERVED3`	If `ORPCF_LOCAL` is set, this flag indicates that it's reserved for local use. Otherwise, it's reserved for future use.
`ORPCF_RESERVED4`	If `ORPCF_LOCAL` is set, this flag indicates that it's reserved for local use. Otherwise, it's reserved for future use.

DCOM implementations may use the local and reserved flags to indicate any extra information needed for local calls. The inclusion of the last four flags in the DCOM protocol gives developers flexibility to set flags for specific uses of the DCOM protocol that they define.

NOTE

If the `ORPCF_LOCAL` bit isn't set and any of the other bits are set, the receiver should return a fault.

The keyword `comversion` is used to set the version number of the COM protocol used to make the particular ORPC. The initial value will be 5.1. Each packet contains the sender's major and minor ORPC version numbers. The client's and server's major version numbers must be equivalent. Backward-compatible changes in the protocol are, of course, indicated by higher minor version numbers. Therefore, a server's minor version must be greater than or equal to the client's.

On the other hand, if the server's minor version exceeds the client's minor version, it must return the client's minor version and restrict its use of the protocol to the minor version specified by the client. Protocol version mismatches cause the `RPC_E_VERSION_MISMATCH` ORPC.

DCOM uses *body extensions* to convey additional information regarding invocations. These extensions are UUID-tagged blocks of data useful for conveying out-of-band information on incoming invocations (within `ORPCTHIS`) and in replies (within `ORPCTHAT`).

Any implementations of the DCOM protocol may define its own extensions with their own UUIDs. Implementations should skip over extensions that they don't recognize or don't want to support. Body extensions are marshaled as an array of bytes with initial 8-byte alignment. There are several existing body extensions, including the debugging extension and the extended error extension. You can find details regarding these extensions with error-description tables in the DCOM specification found at `http://www.microsoft.com/oledev/olecom/draft-brown-dcom-v1-spec-01.txt`. Generally, the errors are very semantically intuitive. An invalid argument will generate an error with the words `Invalid` and `Argument`.

Another DCOM improvement over DCE RPC conserves resources when numerous protocols are used. In a homogeneous network, all machines communicate via the same protocol sequence. In a heterogeneous network, machines may support multiple protocol sequences. Because it's often expensive in terms of resources to allocate endpoints (`RpcServerUseProtseq`) for all available protocols, ORPC provides a mechanism where they can be allocated on demand. To implement this extension, changes in the server are needed. If these optional changes aren't made, ORPC will still work, but not as efficiently on a heterogeneous network.

In DCOM, the server may or may not implement *lazy protocol registration*, where the implementation of `ResolveOxid` is modified slightly. When the client OXID resolver calls the server OXID resolver, it passes the requested protocol's *sequence vector*. If none of the requested protocol sequences have endpoints allocated in the server, the server OXID resolver allocates them according to its own endpoint allocation mechanisms.

If the server doesn't use lazy protocol registration, all protocol sequences are registered by the server at server initialization time. When registering protocol sequences, the server registers endpoints and its string bindings will contain the complete endpoints. If the server doesn't register endpoints when it registers protocol sequences, a mapping process is used to forward the call to the server.

Summary

ActiveX was solely controlled by Microsoft until July 1996, when Microsoft announced plans to transition the technology to an independent standards body. In October 1996, a group voted to move the technology into the hands of the Open Group, an experienced organization with roots in distributed computing.

Vendor-neutral standards and their impact opened up ActiveX so that rapid improvements in various lucrative fields could be made without having to pay Microsoft to use the technology each time.

Enhancing and enabling system interoperability was the goal of creating the DCOM protocol. ActiveX uses the protocol to allow COM objects to run and interact on different types of computers.

ActiveX objects (COM objects) use DCOM as an Object Request Broker (ORB) to control the traffic between client and server portions of an application.

Third-party controls quickly gained popularity even before Microsoft released all the technology, and the new independent standards helped boost the technology for several reasons, including that Microsoft won't require any major fees to use it.

CHAPTER 17

Creating and Using ActiveX Controls

IN THIS CHAPTER

Although Visual Basic 5 allows you to create ActiveX controls, doing so requires a thorough understanding of the VB language. However, there is an easier way to create and use simple ActiveX controls on Web pages without a lot of coding. The ActiveX Control Pad from Microsoft makes it simple.

The Control Pad can be downloaded from Microsoft's Site Builder Network Web site (HTTP://WWW.MICROSOFT.COM/SITEBUILDER/). You must become a Site Builder member before you can download the program, but membership is free and well worth signing up for.

The Control Pad includes a useful HTML layout interface for creating customized sections of a window filled with various controls. Control Pad gives HTML layout files the .ALX extension, to identify each file as a control containing a group of one or more controls. Files with the .OCX extension are installed on the client computer and contain the code that makes the interactive controls functional.

In this chapter, you'll explore a real-life example of using the controls with a fill-out form designed for an Internet Web site. You'll use an HTML layout to build the ActiveX page in ActiveX Control Pad.

NOTE

The newest version of Internet Explorer, IE4, now supports other methods of implementing ActiveX controls on Web pages other than using the control layout forms discussed in this chapter. However, layout forms are still supported to maintain backward compatibility, and they will work on both IE3 and IE4 browsers.

Building a Control with ActiveX Control Pad

Imagine this assignment: You're told by your supervisor that you need to create a Web page that must include an interactive form. The form should contain input text fields and buttons that visitors to your company's Web site will activate by clicking. They click the buttons to indicate what types of materials they want your company to send.

These visitors use the online form to request company-specific information. The information entered in the form is forwarded automatically to the sales manager's electronic mailbox at your company when visitors click a Submit button. The information referenced on this form should include

- A product catalog
- A distributor's information packet
- A company prospectus
- A business profile for the company

The form also can be used by an existing customer to request a call from a customer service representative, or by a new customer to request a call from a sales representative. Above the form, you need to include a simple scrolling marquee showing your company's toll-free telephone number on the Web page. You won't use Control Pad to create the marquee because you can create the marquee with a simple line of HTML text.

The order form also must include text box areas for your visitors to fill in information regarding where the materials they request can be sent.

The CEO of your company wants to review the fill-out form on the company's Web site tomorrow. It's a good thing for you that you have a few basic Web-building tools installed on your computer.

What the boss and your supervisor don't realize is that it will take about an hour to create the form, integrate ActiveX controls with it, and deploy it at the Web site. Now for the crash course on how to pull it off. Here is a list of tools you've loaded on your computer:

- ActiveX Control Pad.
- An HTML editor such as Microsoft FrontPage (optional).
- Internet Explorer 3.01 (or newer).
- `WS_FTP_LE(3).EXE`. Also known as `WS_FTP`, this program uploads and downloads Web files to and from an FTP site. It's freeware that you can download from `HTTP://WWW.SHAREPAPER.COM/APPS/REVIEWS/WS_FTP.HTML` and from various other Internet sources.

To set up the Control Pad interface so that it resembles the Visual Basic interface you're familiar with, follow these steps:

1. Launch ActiveX Control Pad; a page of tags for a blank HTML Web page appears. The HTML tags are simple to learn, but you don't need to do anything to this template yet.
2. Maximize your window so that you'll have some work space onscreen.
3. Choose File | New HTML Layout from the menu to open a window called Layout1. This HTML Layout control is a child window that you can simply think of as the *control window*. Technically, this is the HTML Layout Editor window.

   You'll also see a toolbox with a few tools in it. Don't worry how many tools appear; you can customize the toolbox and add tools as you go.

   Figure 17.1 shows how your screen should appear at this point.
4. Maximize the HTML Layout Editor window so that it fits the screen instead of extending beyond the bottom of the window.
5. Drag the toolbox as far to the right and to the bottom of the window as it will go.

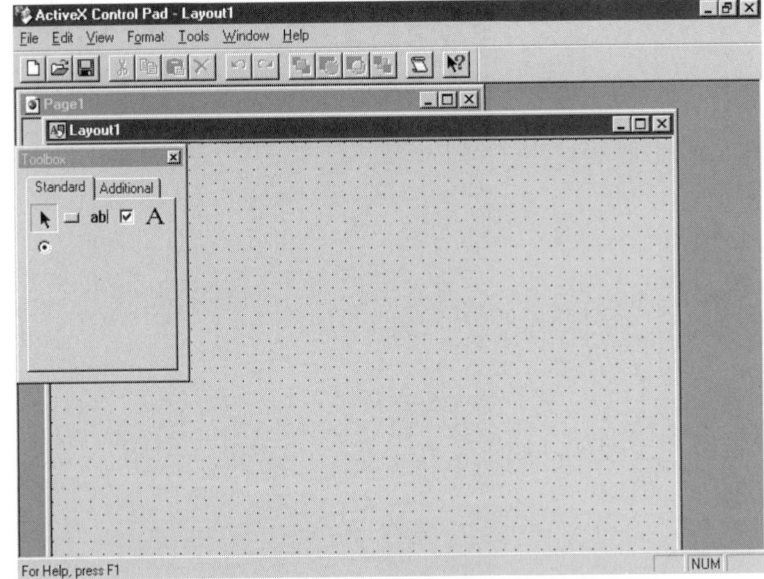

FIGURE 17.1.
Launching ActiveX Control Pad opens a default window called Page1 (representing the HTML Web page) and a window representing the HTML Layout control you're planning to construct.

TIP

As you add controls, you can view their properties in an associated Properties window. Double-click a control to view its properties. Drag the window containing the table of properties to the far right and above the toolbox. When using the Properties window, you may find it to your advantage to stretch the box as tall as possible so that you can see as many properties as possible without having to scroll.

NOTE

This interface is familiar to Visual Basic programmers. The HTML Layout Editor uses a WYSIWYG (What You See Is What You Get) window that acts as a container for all controls placed in it. When you complete an HTML layout, it's saved as a text document with an `.ALX` extension. This file is associated with your Web page and run by the browser when the Web page is loaded.

6. To decrease the height of the Layout1 window, right-click it and choose Properties. Click the word `Height`. The value for `Height` may be 293, 300, or larger. This number now also appears in the text box at the top of your layout properties chart. Highlight the number in the text box to the right of the Apply button. Overwrite the value with the value 175. Press Enter or click Apply. You now have a long horizontal window. Close the Properties window.

Drawing Your Controls

You will place all your ActiveX controls in the HTML Layout Editor window. To create a small ActiveX control in which users can click a button to request an item of information, follow these steps:

1. To add a new tool to the toolbox, right-click an empty area in the toolbox and choose Additional Controls. Scroll down to the Microsoft Forms 2.0 `OptionButton` selection and mark its check box. Click OK.

TIP

Placing your mouse pointer over the radio button in the toolbox displays a text description of the tool (`OptionButton`). This way, you can verify that you've placed the correct tool you were seeking in the toolbox.

2. Click the new OptionButton tool. In the upper-left corner of the window, click and drag a long horizontal rectangle down two grid marks and to the right far enough so that the box can contain a long sentence. (In Control Pad, the corner of your rectangle will snap to the grid dots unless you turn off the Snap option.)

TIP

Always make the rectangle wider than needed so that browsers with larger fonts can still display the entire text. A text line generally appears to be longer in the browser window than in Control Pad.

   A radio button automatically appears on the left, and the default text `OptionButton1` appears on the right. The text represents the `Caption` property of the OptionButton control you just created. `OptionButton1` also is the control's default `ID` property—that is, the object's name—and doesn't need to be modified unless you want to rename the object.

   If the rectangle isn't large enough for the text, click it and drag one of its handles to reshape it. If you move the mouse pointer over the edge of the highlight, you can click and drag the whole rectangle to reposition it when the pointer changes to an arrow shape.

3. Save the project under the filename `RFINFO.ALX` (your request for info control).
4. Right-click `OptionButton1` and choose Properties to display the Properties window. You'll see the default properties for this object, including `Caption`, `ID`, `GroupName`, and `Value`.

5. In the Properties window, select the `Caption` property and then type **PLEASE SEND A PRODUCT CATALOG** in the input box at the top to the right of the Apply button. Then click Apply to set the value.

> **TIP**
>
> You also can change the `Caption` property by typing directly over the default text in the `OptionButton1` control. Click the text to highlight it, overwrite it with the new text, and then click outside the control.

6. For the next property to change, select `GroupName`. Set this property to `Group1`.

   You won't assign this group name to any other objects you might place in the request for info control. That means `Group1` will be "independent" of any other object in the control and can be turned on or off without having any effect on the other option buttons.

   At runtime, users can select only one option button in each group. If you don't understand how these groups work, you will by the time you've created the rest of your control and tested it.

7. In the Properties window, scroll to the `Value` property and select it. Type **False** in the text box at the top and click the Apply button. This setting deselects the radio button control to the left of your text line.

   Figure 17.2 shows how the control should appear at this time.

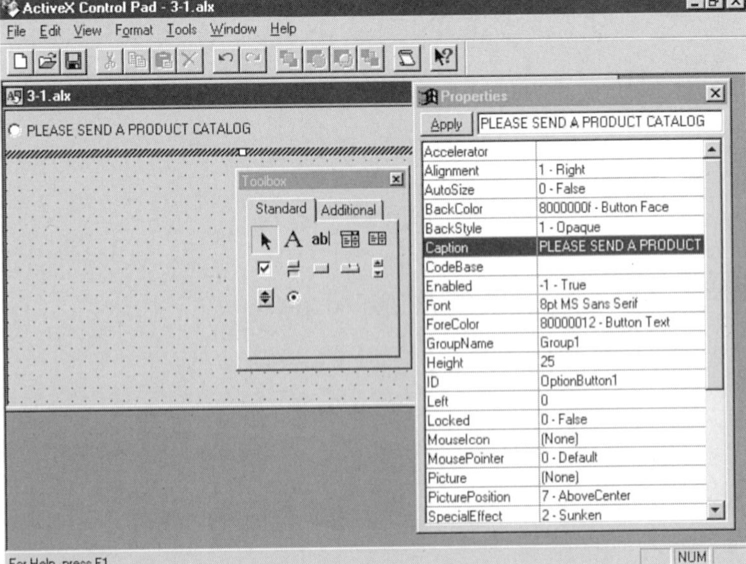

FIGURE 17.2.
Notice in the Properties window the text box that you use to revise properties.

8. Click the `OptionButton1` object, press Ctrl+C to copy it, and then press Ctrl+V to paste it. Drag the pasted control so that it's immediately below the first. Continue copying and pasting until you have six controls stacked vertically. (Don't worry about the captions; you'll change those soon.)

You now should have six identical rectangles with radio buttons on the left and text to the right. Now would be a good time to resave the project.

Altering Properties Quickly

Copying the control copied all the property settings assigned to it except for the `ID` setting; each pasted object received a new default `ID` (`OptionButton2`, `OptionButton3`, and so on).

To modify these properties, click the second OptionButton from the top. Its property settings appear in the Properties window. Change the caption to read `PLEASE SEND DISTRIBUTOR MATERIALS` and then click the Apply button. In the same manner, change the `GroupName` property to `Group2`. For `OptionButton3`, change the caption to read `PLEASE SEND INVESTOR'S PROSPECTUS` and change `GroupName` to `Group3`. `OptionButton4` gets a caption that reads `PLEASE SEND A BUSINESS PROFILE` and change `GroupName` to `Group4`. `OptionButton5` gets a caption reading `HAVE A CUSTOMER SVC. REP. CALL`, and the `GroupName` property is changed to `Group5`.

On the sixth option button, change the caption to read `HAVE A SALES REPRESENTATIVE CALL`. But rather than change the `GroupName` property to `Group6`, you will join this control's interactivity with the `OptionButton5` radio button by changing `OptionButton6`'s `GroupName` property to `Group5`. Now if a user clicks `OptionButton5` at runtime, the `OptionButton5` radio button turns black (and the corresponding value for the button changes from `False` to `True`).

Now, when users click `OptionButton6`, `OptionButton6` is selected (`True` is assigned to the `Value` property), and `OptionButton5` is deselected (assigned `False`). The way the buttons work in `Group5` is inherent to these intrinsic ActiveX controls. You don't have to add code to make them act as a group; simply give them the same `GroupName` property. If users again click `OptionButton5`, `OptionButton5` is selected again, and `OptionButton6` is deselected. Because these two objects have the same `GroupName` property, they function as a group, and only one in the group can be selected at any time. Therefore, users can select any or all of the first four buttons, but only one of the last two buttons in the HTML layout. Save your file again.

TIP

The value property for all the controls should already be set to `False`. To change a property for several controls at once, drag a window around the controls to select them and then change the property in the Properties window.

Adding Functionality to Your Control

Now you have a slight problem to overcome. The controls you created are still bare; they require functionality. At runtime, users can click the first four buttons to select them. If users make a mistake and select one but then try to deselect it by clicking again, the button remains selected.

Perhaps the easiest way to program a workaround is to use ActiveX Control Pad's CommandButton tool to create another button and then insert a few simple lines of code in the Script Wizard. Click the CommandButton tool (it looks like a rectangle in the toolbox) and place a button immediately to the right of your OptionButtons, slightly overlapping them. Center the button vertically between `OptionButton3` and `OptionButton4` (vertical center of the control). Change `CommandButton1`'s `Caption` property to read `Clear Buttons At Left` and then save your file again.

The HTML Layout Editor window is larger than you need it to be because you maximized it before creating the HTML Layout control. You can resize the window by dragging the edges until your controls fit loosely in the window.

Save your file. Figure 17.3 shows how your finished controls should look in ActiveX Control Pad.

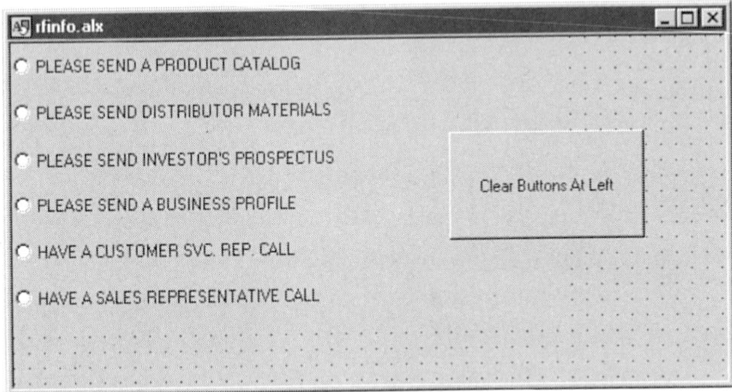

FIGURE 17.3.
The HTML Layout control `RFINFO.ALX`*, after adjusting the height and width of the control.*

Open the `RFINFO.ALX` file in a text editor and scroll through the code lines to get a feel for the syntax associated with these objects' properties. The object descriptions appear in the same order as you placed the controls on the page. At the top of the code window, you'll add a few code lines to add functionality to your command button to solve the problem with the radio buttons.

At runtime, you want users to click the command button object to deselect all six radio buttons at left and return their values to `False`. To program this functionality, right-click `OptionButton1` and choose Script Wizard (or click the toolbar icon that looks like a scroll). You now see an event pane on the left, an action pane on the right, and a script pane with two different view options at the bottom. In the left event pane, click the plus sign near

CommandButton1 to view the available events that can be programmed. Find and highlight the Click event.

Click the Code View selection button in the script pane at the bottom of the window. In the action pane on the right, click the plus sign near OptionButton1 and double-click the action item Value to paste a code line in the code view at the bottom. Modify this code line to read OptionButton1.Value=False. Copy and paste this code line in the Code View window for each option button. Remember to change the OptionButton *names* in the code view to OptionButton2, OptionButton3, and so on. (You don't need to end your subroutine with an End Sub because the Script Wizard is going to add this for you.)

Click OK. Once again, save the file. You can open the file in a text editor again and view the code lines. The VB Scripting Edition code lines will appear at the top of the file. Your HTML Layout control file RFINFO.ALX is complete and should resemble the lines that appear in Listing 17.1.

Listing 17.1. The minimal code generated when you created the HTML layout file.

```
<SCRIPT LANGUAGE="VBScript">
<!--
Sub CommandButton1_Click()
OptionButton1.Value=False
OptionButton2.Value=False
OptionButton3.Value=False
OptionButton4.Value=False
OptionButton5.Value=False
OptionButton6.Value=False
end sub
-->
</SCRIPT>
<DIV ID="Layout1" STYLE="LAYOUT:FIXED;WIDTH:390pt;HEIGHT:184pt;">
<OBJECT ID="OptionButton1"
CLASSID="CLSID:8BD21D50-EC42-11CE-9E0D-00AA006002F3"
STYLE="TOP:0pt;LEFT:0pt;WIDTH:305pt;HEIGHT:25pt;TABINDEX:0;ZINDEX:0;">
<PARAM NAME="BackColor" VALUE="2147483663">
<PARAM NAME="ForeColor" VALUE="2147483666">
<PARAM NAME="DisplayStyle" VALUE="5">
<PARAM NAME="Size" VALUE="10760;882">
<PARAM NAME="Value" VALUE="False">
<PARAM NAME="Caption" VALUE="PLEASE SEND A PRODUCT CATALOG">
<PARAM NAME="GroupName" VALUE="Group1">
<PARAM NAME="FontCharSet" VALUE="0">
<PARAM NAME="FontPitchAndFamily" VALUE="2">
<PARAM NAME="FontWeight" VALUE="0">
</OBJECT>
<OBJECT ID="OptionButton2"
CLASSID="CLSID:8BD21D50-EC42-11CE-9E0D-00AA006002F3"
STYLE="TOP:25pt;LEFT:0pt;WIDTH:305pt;HEIGHT:25pt;TABINDEX:1;ZINDEX:1;">
<PARAM NAME="BackColor" VALUE="2147483663">
<PARAM NAME="ForeColor" VALUE="2147483666">
<PARAM NAME="DisplayStyle" VALUE="5">
```

continues

Listing 17.1. continued

```
<PARAM NAME="Size" VALUE="10760;882">
<PARAM NAME="Value" VALUE="False">
<PARAM NAME="Caption" VALUE="PLEASE SEND DISTRIBUTOR MATERIALS">
<PARAM NAME="GroupName" VALUE="Group2">
<PARAM NAME="FontCharSet" VALUE="0">
<PARAM NAME="FontPitchAndFamily" VALUE="2">
<PARAM NAME="FontWeight" VALUE="0">
</OBJECT>
<OBJECT ID="OptionButton3"
CLASSID="CLSID:8BD21D50-EC42-11CE-9E0D-00AA006002F3" _
STYLE="TOP:50pt;LEFT:0pt;WIDTH:305pt;HEIGHT:25pt;TABINDEX:2;ZINDEX:2;">
<PARAM NAME="BackColor" VALUE="2147483663">
<PARAM NAME="ForeColor" VALUE="2147483666">
<PARAM NAME="DisplayStyle" VALUE="5">
<PARAM NAME="Size" VALUE="10760;882">
<PARAM NAME="Value" VALUE="False">
<PARAM NAME="Caption" VALUE="PLEASE SEND INVESTOR'S PROSPECTUS">
<PARAM NAME="GroupName" VALUE="Group3">
<PARAM NAME="FontCharSet" VALUE="0">
<PARAM NAME="FontPitchAndFamily" VALUE="2">
<PARAM NAME="FontWeight" VALUE="0">
</OBJECT>
<OBJECT ID="OptionButton4"
CLASSID="CLSID:8BD21D50-EC42-11CE-9E0D-00AA006002F3" _
STYLE="TOP:74pt;LEFT:0pt;WIDTH:305pt;HEIGHT:25pt;TABINDEX:3;ZINDEX:3;">
<PARAM NAME="BackColor" VALUE="2147483663">
<PARAM NAME="ForeColor" VALUE="2147483666">
<PARAM NAME="DisplayStyle" VALUE="5">
<PARAM NAME="Size" VALUE="10760;882">
<PARAM NAME="Value" VALUE="False">
<PARAM NAME="Caption" VALUE="PLEASE SEND A BUSINESS PROFILE">
<PARAM NAME="GroupName" VALUE="Group4">
<PARAM NAME="FontCharSet" VALUE="0">
<PARAM NAME="FontPitchAndFamily" VALUE="2">
<PARAM NAME="FontWeight" VALUE="0">
</OBJECT>
<OBJECT ID="OptionButton5"
CLASSID="CLSID:8BD21D50-EC42-11CE-9E0D-00AA006002F3" _
STYLE="TOP:99pt;LEFT:0pt;WIDTH:305pt;HEIGHT:25pt;TABINDEX:4;ZINDEX:4;">
<PARAM NAME="BackColor" VALUE="2147483663">
<PARAM NAME="ForeColor" VALUE="2147483666">
<PARAM NAME="DisplayStyle" VALUE="5">
<PARAM NAME="Size" VALUE="10760;882">
<PARAM NAME="Value" VALUE="False">
<PARAM NAME="Caption" VALUE="HAVE A CUSTOMER SVC. REP. CALL">
<PARAM NAME="GroupName" VALUE="Group5">
<PARAM NAME="FontCharSet" VALUE="0">
<PARAM NAME="FontPitchAndFamily" VALUE="2">
<PARAM NAME="FontWeight" VALUE="0">
</OBJECT>
<OBJECT ID="OptionButton6"
CLASSID="CLSID:8BD21D50-EC42-11CE-9E0D-00AA006002F3" _
STYLE="TOP:124pt;LEFT:0pt;WIDTH:305pt;HEIGHT:25pt;TABINDEX:5;ZINDEX:5;">
<PARAM NAME="BackColor" VALUE="2147483663">
<PARAM NAME="ForeColor" VALUE="2147483666">
<PARAM NAME="DisplayStyle" VALUE="5">
```

```
<PARAM NAME="Size" VALUE="10760;882">
<PARAM NAME="Value" VALUE="False">
<PARAM NAME="Caption" VALUE="HAVE A SALES REPRESENTATIVE CALL">
<PARAM NAME="GroupName" VALUE="Group5">
<PARAM NAME="FontCharSet" VALUE="0">
<PARAM NAME="FontPitchAndFamily" VALUE="2">
<PARAM NAME="FontWeight" VALUE="0">
</OBJECT>
<OBJECT ID="CommandButton1"
CLASSID="CLSID:D7053240-CE69-11CD-A777-00DD01143C57" _
STYLE="TOP:50pt;LEFT:239pt;WIDTH:107pt;HEIGHT:58pt;TABINDEX:6;ZINDEX:6;">
<PARAM NAME="Caption" VALUE="Clear Buttons At Left">
<PARAM NAME="Size" VALUE="3784;2046">
<PARAM NAME="FontCharSet" VALUE="0">
<PARAM NAME="FontPitchAndFamily" VALUE="2">
<PARAM NAME="ParagraphAlign" VALUE="3">
<PARAM NAME="FontWeight" VALUE="0">
</OBJECT>
</DIV>
```


Now it's time to test your code. To test the code, you need to create an HTML file—a simple Web page—and add the control to it. Then you add a few code lines to make the form on the Web page communicate its data to an email mailbox.

Creating a Simple Web Page

Create a simple HTML file with your HTML editor or a text editor. ActiveX Control Pad is great for editing Web pages when you're inserting or programming controls, but it's not intended to be used as a full-featured HTML editor. If you have an HTML editor such as Microsoft FrontPage 2.0, most of the code lines you'll be adding don't need to be typed; you can pick a tool from the toolbar, click the page, view the code to see the properties for the HTML tags, and so on.

> **NOTE**
>
> The instructions for creating the test HTML page are geared towards those who have Microsoft FrontPage. If you don't have FrontPage, use a text editor such as Notepad or WordPad and type in the code in Listing 17.2.

In the FrontPage editor, open a new file, choose Insert | Marquee from the menu, and type **`Call 1-800-`*`YOUR NUMBER GOES HERE`*** in the dialog box. If you view the source code for the HTML page, you will see a simple line of code. In a text editor, you can add `<marquee>Call 1-800-`*`YOUR NUMBER GOES HERE`*`</marquee>` to your HTML file for the same effect. Now create an HTML form and assign the form the action URL `HTTP://WWW.MYWEBSITE.COM/CGI-BIN/MAILIT.CGI`. In this form, create a simple two-column table and then insert the `RFINFO.ALX` file object as shown in Figure 17.4.

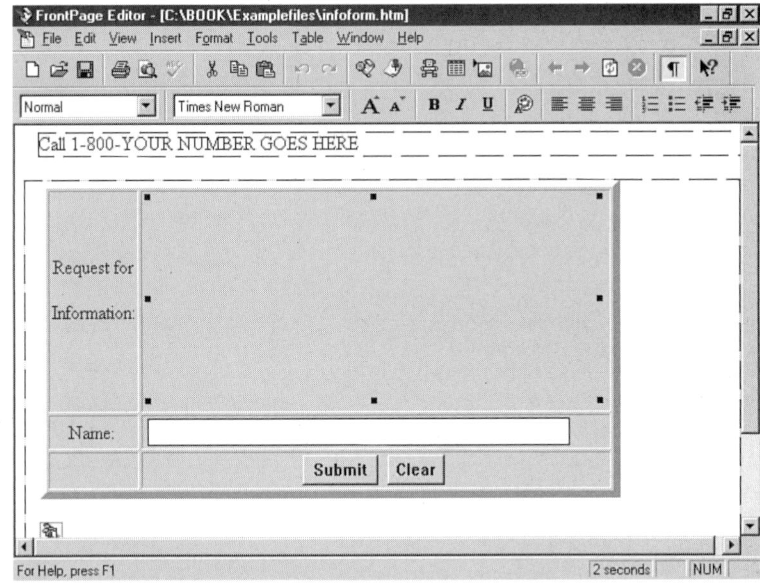

FIGURE 17.4.
This shows where you'll place the `RFINFO.ALX` *file in the table in FrontPage Editor.*

> **CAUTION**
>
> Open and save the file in the same directory. If you save to a remote directory, your reference to objects, such as the control `RFINFO.ALX`, will be assigned a full pathname to the file. You want the reference to be to a local file.

The control file here is being placed in the second column of the first row. Place the text line `Request for Information` in the first cell of the first row. Then add a form element—a text input box (`<input type ="text" name="FirstName">`)—in the second column of the second row and enter **`Name:`** in the first cell of the row. (If you are using a text editor and aren't familiar with using HTML to place an input box, refer to the code example in Listing 17.2.) Now add a Submit button and a Clear button below the table. Give the HTML file the title `Request for Information Form`.

Now the code for your HTML file should look something like Listing 17.2. You're getting close to having a working form. Save your file as `INFOFORM.HTM`. This code is generated by your HTML editor. It isn't the finished file; the file will be complete after you add the script to bind data from the control to the form.

Listing 17.2. The code for `INFOFORM.HTM`.

```
<!DOCTYPE HTML PUBLIC "-//IETF//DTD HTML//EN">
<html>
<head>
<meta http-equiv="Content-Type"
```

```
content="text/html; charset=iso-8859-1">
<meta name="GENERATOR" content="Microsoft FrontPage 2.0">
<title>REQUEST FOR INFORMATION FORM</title>
</head>
<body bgcolor="#FFFFFF" text="#000000" link="#663333"
vlink="#000000" topmargin="6" leftmargin="20" language="VBSCRIPT">
<p align="center"><marquee bgcolor="#FFFFFF">Call 1-800-YOUR
NUMBER GOES HERE</marquee></p>
<form action="http://www.myWebsite.com/cgi-bin/mailit.cgi"
method="POST" name="MainForm">
<div align="left"><table border="6" cellpadding="2"
bgcolor="#C0C0C0">
<tr>
  <td align="center">Request for<p>Information:</p>
</td>
<td><object id="rfinfo_alx"
classid="clsid:812AE312-8B8E-11CF-93C8-00AA00C08FDF"
align="baseline" border="0" vspace="12" width="390"
height="151"><param name="ALXPATH" value="rfinfo.alx"></object>
              </td>
</tr>
<tr>
<td align="center">Name: </td>
<td valign="top"><input type="text" size="40"
name="FirstName"> </td>
</tr>
<tr>
<td align="center"> </td>
<td align="center"><input type="submit" name="Send"
value="Submit"> <input type="reset" name="Clear"
value="Clear"> </td>
</tr>
</table>
</form>
</body>
</html>
```

Open the new HTML file in your ActiveX-enabled browser. Make sure that the RFINFO.ALX file is in the same directory as INFOFORM.HTM. Experiment with the control buttons. You'll get an error or no response if you try using the Submit button because you haven't finished adding functionality to it. You may have noticed that you placed the ActiveX control in the right-hand cell of a two-column table within INFOFORM.HTM. You can add the rest of the form fields for text input to the simple HTML file now.

The first input box code (FirstName) is shown in Listing 17.2. The others will be similar. You'll merely substitute LastName for FirstName, and so on, as you add these input boxes. You may want to add input boxes for Address1, Address2, City, State, Zipcode, Email, and Phone, as well as another large text box for anything not listed on the form that users may want to request. Listing 17.3 shows a sample of the updated HTML file. Use it as a guide for making changes, or put your HTML coding skills to work and complete the interface yourself. However, for the sake of simplicity, the rest of the examples in this book will use the version of the INFOFORM.HTM file shown in Listing 17.2.

Listing 17.3. An updated version of INFOFORM.HTM, with additional input boxes for customer information.

```
<!DOCTYPE HTML PUBLIC "-//IETF//DTD HTML//EN">
<html>
<head>
<meta http-equiv="Content-Type" content="text/html; charset=iso-8859-1">
<meta name="GENERATOR" content="Microsoft FrontPage 2.0">
<title>REQUEST FOR INFORMATION FORM</title>
</head>
<body bgcolor="#FFFFFF" text="#000000" link="#663333"
  vlink="#000000" topmargin="6" leftmargin="20" language="VBSCRIPT">
<p align="center"><marquee bgcolor="#FFFFFF">Call 1-800-YOUR NUMBER GOES HERE</
marquee></p>
<form action="http://www.mywebsite.com/cgi-bin/mailit.cgi" method="POST"
name="MainForm">
<div align="left"><table border="6" cellpadding="2" bgcolor="#C0C0C0">
<tr>
  <td align="center">Request for<p>Information:</p>
</td>
<td><object id="rfinfo_alx"
  classid="clsid:812AE312-8B8E-11CF-93C8-00AA00C08FDF"
  align="baseline" border="0" vspace="12" width="390"
  height="151"><param name="ALXPATH" value="rfinfo.alx"></object>
</td>
</tr>
<tr>
<td align="center">First Name: </td>
<td align="top"><input type="text" size="40" name="FirstName"> </td>
</tr>
<tr>
<td align="center">Last Name: </td>
<td align="top"><input type="text" size="40" name="LastName"> </td>
</tr>
<tr>
<td align="center">Address 1: </td>
<td align="top"><input type="text" size="40" name="Address1"> </td>
</tr>
<tr>
<td align="center">Address 2: </td>
<td align="top"><input type="text" size="40" name="Address2"> </td>
</tr>
<tr>
<td align="center">City: </td>
<td align="top"><input type="text" size="25" name="City">
 State: <input type="text" size="2" name="State">
 Zip: <input type="text" size="10" name="Zipcode"> </td>
</tr>
<tr>
<td align="center">E-mail: </td>
<td align="top"><input type="text" size="40" name="Email"> </td>
</tr>
<tr>
<td align="center">Phone: </td>
<td align="top"><input type="text" size="40" name="Phone"> </td>
</tr>
<tr>
<td align="center">Comments: </td>
<td align="top"><input type="text" size="60" name="Comments"> </td>
```

```
</tr>
<tr>
<td align="center"> </td>
<td align="center"><input type="submit" name="Send"
  value="Submit"> <input type="reset" name="Clear"
  value="Clear"> </td>
</tr>
</table>
</form>
</body>
</html>
```


You'll add validation to your file later to make sure that the correct boxes contain input. You can validate by ensuring that numbers (as opposed to alpha characters) appear in the Zip Code or Phone Number text box. A functioning INFOFORM.HTM is on the CD-ROM accompanying this book. The file must be modified to reflect the correct URL path to the CGI script it calls. Also, you can find a similar HTML file with validation code at HTTP://WWW.LASERUSA.COM/RFQ.HTM.

Adding the Form Submission Script

Now you need a custom script to *bind* (append) the data from the ActiveX HTML Layout control RFINFO.ALX to the form data generated by the text input boxes. Then you submit the whole data package by using the MAILIT.CGI script referred to by the Action property when you created the form.

To add your custom script, open the INFOFORM.HTM file on the CD-ROM and paste the code lines shown in Listing 17.4. These lines should follow the last form tag, </form>, and be above the </body> and </HTML> tags to maintain integrity of the form and the file.

Listing 17.4. The code to bind data from the OptionButtons to the data from one of the form's input boxes.

```
</div>
<script language="VBScript">
<!--
Function MainForm_OnSubmit()
Title="Request for Information"
Set TheForm=MainForm
dim x()
x1=TheForm.rfinfo_alx.optionbutton1.value
x2=TheForm.rfinfo_alx.optionbutton2.value
x3=TheForm.rfinfo_alx.optionbutton3.value
x4=TheForm.rfinfo_alx.optionbutton4.value
TheForm.FirstName.Value=TheForm.FirstName.Value & "Catalog=" & x1 _
 & " DistributorInfo=" & x2 & " Prospectus=" & x3 & " Profile=" & x4 _
 & " Cust Svc Call=" & x5 & " Sales Rep Call=" & x6
End Function
-->
</script><p align="left"> </p>
```

Make sure that the last few tags, `</body>` and `</html>`, are in your file and save the `INFOFORM.HTM` file again.

Writing a Simple CGI Script

The following simple CGI script is compatible with many commercial Web servers. The Internet service provider (ISP) that maintains the Web server you'll be using can suggest changes to the lines in this simple script that might point to an incorrect path for the SendMail program.

Remember, this script is being called by the following HTML code in your `INFOFORM.HTM` file:

```
<form action="http://www.myWebsite.com/cgi-bin/mailit.cgi"
method="POST" name="MainForm">
```

You need to modify this line to point to the actual URL where this CGI script resides on the server. This URL can be relative, as in `MAILIT.CGI`, if the CGI file resides in the same directory as the Web page.

> **TIP**
>
> Your Internet service provider may suggest where the CGI script file should reside. It's a good idea to talk to your ISP because location of this file may help prevent anyone from tampering with the script, depending on the server security used by your ISP.

You can temporarily place the file in the same directory as the `INFOFORM.HTM` file for testing purposes. Make sure that the HTML tag points to the file in the same directory (`action="mailit.cgi"`). This script invokes a SendMail program on the server, assigns all the name-value pairs from the form to a simple email message area, and submits the mail message to the specified email address.

This script was derived from a similar script made public on the Web. You can search for other similar shared public CGI script files on the Web by using `CGI` and `MAILTO` as keywords. At the end of the file are a few simple HTML lines that generate confirmation text in a simple HTML window so that users know the form has been submitted correctly.

Confirming the Submission

This confirmation should contain a hyperlink back to the form or to the URL where the company's Web site home page resides. Use a full-path URL—`HTTP://WWW.`*`MYWEBSITE`*`.COM/`*`INDEX.HTML`*—where *`MYWEBSITE`* is your company's domain and *`INDEX.HTML`* is the home page filename. You don't have to use a CGI script like the simple one in Listing 17.5 to send the email, but this simple method gets the data forwarded automatically as soon as the form is submitted.

Listing 17.5. The simple CGI script that launches a SendMail program to forward the Web form's data to a specified email address.

```
#!/usr/bin/perl
# Down and dirty Web form processing script.  Emails the data
# to the recipient.
$mailprog = '/usr/sbin/sendmail';
$recipient = 'yourpobox@yourdomain.com';
# Print out a content-type for HTTP/1.0 compatibility
print "Content-type:text/html\n\n";
# Get the input and shape it into something legible
read(STDIN, $buffer, $ENV{'CONTENT_LENGTH'});
$postinput = $buffer;
$postinput =~ s/&/\n/g;
$postinput =~ s/\+/ /g;
$postinput =~ s/%([\da-f]{1,2})/pack(C,hex($1))/eig;
# Now send mail to $recipient
open (MAIL, "¦$mailprog $recipient") ¦¦ die "Sorry, can't open $mailprog!\n";
print MAIL "Subject: Request for Information Form Data\n\n";
print MAIL $postinput;
print MAIL "\n\n";
print MAIL "Server protocol: $ENV{'SERVER_PROTOCOL'}\n";
print MAIL "HTTP From: $ENV{'HTTP_FROM'}\n";
print MAIL "Remote host: $ENV{'REMOTE_HOST'}\n";
print MAIL "Remote IP address: $ENV{'REMOTE_ADDR'}\n";
close (MAIL);
# Print a thank-you page
print <<EndHTML;
print "
<html>
<head>
<Title>THANKS</Title>
</Head>
<body>
<H2>Thank you for this opportunity to provide you with more information!</H2>
Return to our <a href="http://www.myWebsite.com/index.htm">home page</a>.<p>
</body>
</html>
EndHTML
;
# the end
```

Uploading the Files to Your Web Site

Assuming that you have a functioning Web site that's maintained offsite with a dial-up connection to an FTP server, this procedure uploads your files after you test everything but the email submit function. Open `WS_FTP_LE.EXE` and configure the login and password for your Web site. Make sure that your dial-up connection logs you in with the correct login and password. If your server requires Passive Transfer Mode, set it under the options in `WS_FTP_LE.EXE` if you aren't having any luck.

Work with your ISP until you get the login to open automatically to the remote directory you'll be loading your files into. Click the Connect button. When you see a directory listing in the host window, click the ASCII selection button. Change your local directory window to show the contents of the directory where your `RFINFO.ALX`, `INFOFORM.HTM`, and `MAILIT.CGI` files reside.

Ctrl+click each file to select them and then click the Transfer button. Your status window indicates the status of each transfer. You can scroll this window back or simply view the updated directory listing in the host window. You may need to refresh the host window manually to see your files.

When the files are there, you can minimize `WS_FTP` and launch Internet Explorer. Navigate to the Web site and add the filename `INFOFORM.HTM` at the end of the Web site URL. The HTML file and the form should load first. The status window in IE 3.01 indicates `Done`, the `RFINFO.ALX` file loads into the browser, and your ActiveX controls are visible.

TIP

If the HTML file loads but the `.ALX` file doesn't, check the HTML source code by choosing View | Source from Internet Explorer's menu. Make sure that the path points to the file. If you change the path in Notepad or a similar editor, be sure to resave the file to your local directory to overwrite the old file and then maximize `WS_FTP` and retransfer the file to the Web site.

You can continue to work in ActiveX Control Pad, FrontPage Editor, and `WS_FTP` until everything is working correctly.

Assuming that you have access and authority to modify the Web site's home page (or other page where a link would be appropriate), you can now add a simple anchor (hyperlink) on the page. The hyperlink will point to the new `INFOFORM.HTM` file that you created. When users click the hyperlink, your form and the controls load.

Suppose that your company's home page is at `HTTP://WWW.PENCAPITAL.COM/INDEX.HTM`. Open a copy of `INDEX.HTM` in FrontPage Editor or similar HTML editor window. Go to where you want the link and place a line of text that reads

> If you would like more information or specific company materials available, visit our Request For Information page.

Now select the `Request For Information` text and choose Insert | Hyperlink from the menu. In the dialog box, place the local path to the `INFOFORM.HTM` file.

You can also do this by adding a similar code to your Web's home page HTML file:

```
Click here to see our <font color="#FF0000">[</font>
<a href=" http://www.pencapital.com/infoform.htm">
<font color="#FF0000" size="3">Request For Information Form</font></a>
<font color="#FF0000" size="3">]
```

You can add this code to your existing `INFOFORM.HTM` file and substitute the word `INFOFORM.HTM` after `href=` to reload the page when you click the link.

Figure 17.5 shows how your finished Web page should look in Internet Explorer 3.01. The `RFINFO.ALX` file must reside in the same directory.

FIGURE 17.5.
This is how the finished Web page looks in Internet Explorer 3.01.

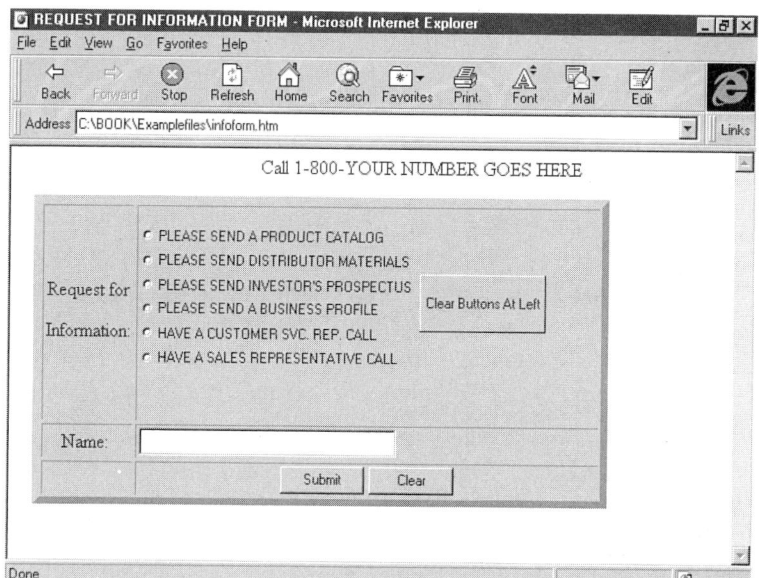

Summary

Creating HTML pages, HTML Layout controls, and other ActiveX controls is simple. You can create these items by using available free tools.

In this chapter, you learned how to create a simple Web page, create and insert a simple control, add functionality to an object in the control with a script, create a form, and create a way for the form's information to be submitted to an email address. You also explored a method to move these files onto a remote Web site.

The process has numerous steps, but you can complete the work quickly with the tools used for the examples.

ActiveX Control Creation

IN THIS CHAPTER

Now that you've been introduced to DCOM and some of the design considerations important to ActiveX control creation, it's time to get down to business and start developing some ActiveX controls. In this chapter, you'll create a versatile but simple control that you can use in your own applications or on your own Web pages.

The first part of this chapter discusses the importance of good design techniques. You'll learn how to design your own controls so that they will be flexible but sturdy. We'll also plan the details of the sample control.

The second part of this chapter will begin to guide you through the creation of the sample control while easing you into the finer details of ActiveX control creation. In later chapters, we'll expand on the sample control until it fits all the specifications that are a part of its original design.

Think First, Code Later

If you're like most programmers (myself included), you're tempted to dive into a programming project without giving much thought to design. An astonishing number of programs have been created with the idea that they will "design themselves" as they are being developed. As new features are added to the program, code gets rewritten and changed around until it bears only a vague resemblance to its original concept. The worst part is that bad design (or *no* design) often leads to the programmer being burdened with supporting a tangled mess of code that is difficult for him to comprehend—even when he is the original author! Be honest—how many times have you decided to rewrite some or all of a program after having to make modifications to it long after the programming was supposedly "done"?

Many programming problems are the result of poor design caused by little thought being put into the entire project from start to finish. When creating ActiveX controls, good design is an even bigger issue than when creating applications. Not only are you designing a component that should work with the project it was initially designed for, you should also be thinking ahead to the future when your control may be needed again. And if you're creating something that will be distributed to other programmers for their own use, your control needs to be even more flexible. After all, you never know what kind of crazy functionality *other* programmers may require!

To put it another way, what would the chapter of this book be like if it was written with no predefined outline of instruction in mind? First off, it's a sure bet that Sams would never have let me write it! But if they did, it's doubtful that you would read very far into it, and it probably wouldn't be much use to you. Instead of following a fairly straight path that attempts to gradually guide you through the finer points of control design, it would be filled with random thoughts and ideas. You would likely be so confused that you would give up in disgust before finishing the first chapter. Luckily, some thought was put into assembling a complete and orderly flow of information, and I've tried to cover all the issues important to the topic of creating ActiveX controls.

It's difficult to overestimate the virtues of good design techniques. Just a bit of foresight and careful thought before coding can save you literally hours of programming time later. As the old saying goes, "an ounce of prevention is worth a pound of cure." Nowhere is that adage truer than in computer programming—Visual Basic programming included!

The Power of ActiveX Controls

ActiveX controls can be powerful—provided that they're designed correctly. Generally, the hottest-selling third-party controls all have two important things in common. They are all flexible, and they all have good interfaces. Great care was taken in their creation, and it paid off handsomely for their developers. It can pay off for you, too.

To illustrate just how powerful a control can be, take a look at Microsoft's Internet Explorer Web browser. Would you believe that entire program consists primarily of two ActiveX controls? It's true, and you can use the same controls (`SHDOCVW.OCX` and `HTMLCTL.OCX`) to implement a fully functional Web browser (complete with support for VBScript, JavaScript, and all the rest of IE's goodies) into your own applications. Now *that's* power!

Another important factor of good design is standardization. Certain standards for interface elements—properties, events, and methods—are often desired if not expected. It is in the control designer's best interest to have as many interface elements as possible follow certain standards. For example, the background color of an object is best represented by a property named `BackColor` rather than `BGColor`, `Background`, or `BkgrndColor`. Programmers are already familiar with the `BackColor` property because it is used in many other controls. If your control adheres to certain standards, it will be easier and more intuitive to use.

Like properties, there are certain methods and events that your control may be expected to provide, depending on its type. For example, if your control is some mutation of the standard `CommandButton`, it would be downright bizarre if it didn't include a `Click` event or a `Move` method.

The Birth of an ActiveX Control

Controls start out as an idea. You probably have several ideas for ActiveX controls already floating around in your head. If so, that's great! But give them a little time to mature before trying to crank out some code.

In this chapter, we're going to build a new ActiveX control from start to finish. Without further ado, here's the start: an idea of what the control will do and how it will look.

Our sample control will look similar to the standard Label control (and will use that control in its construction), but it will act more like a CommandButton. The idea is to have a button that will automatically "light up" whenever the cursor is on it. When the cursor is moved off it, the button "darkens" to its original state. Most likely, it will be used as part of an array of controls that present a menu of options that give the user a visual cue (the control lighting up) as to when an option is ready to be selected. It's a simple but versatile control that can be used again and again in all kinds of applications.

Of course, the first impulse is to fire up Visual Basic and get down to coding the thing. But let's hang on for just a minute and think about this just a little longer.

One good way to generate some ideas for expanding on the original idea is to visualize the control—or similar controls—being used in many different applications. Think about the neatest CD-ROM program you've ever seen. How could its developers have used the control? And what would they have added to it to make it fit in with the rest of their program? The goal here is not to make your control the end-all be-all of controls but to think up ways its functionality can be increased with some simple tweaks and maybe a little extra coding time.

The current version of our sample control would be versatile, but admittedly it wouldn't exactly knock your socks off in terms of visual appeal. Really snazzy programs would probably have a high-res graphic for their option buttons that would change to another high-res graphic when selected, or "on." Wait a minute…we could do that with our control. We wouldn't want to scrap the original idea though because there are times when high-res graphics are either not appropriate or just aren't desired. To make the control really flexible, we'll offer the developer (that is, the person using it in her application) two options: one for a quick-and-dirty text-only implementation and one where images can be specified.

Using the first option, the developer need only specify a caption and some colors (or use the defaults), and the control will be ready to go. The second option would require the creation of some graphic images, but it would look much slicker. For example, the "unselected" image could be a beveled picture with some text centered on it, and the "selected" image could be the same thing with the text "glowing." When the user moves the cursor on the image, the text appears to glow—a neat effect with absolutely no programming required by the developer.

The beauty of all this is that adding the support for the graphic images option would be minimal in terms of coding the control. The meat of the control will be in determining whether the cursor is on it, which will be the exact same no matter which of the two options is used. With a few extra lines of code, an otherwise good control can often become a potentially great control.

We undoubtedly could add many other features to our sample control to beef it up. Maybe you have a few of your own already. But for the sake of brevity, we're going to move along and start thinking about the design of the control's interface. Under other circumstances, a lot more thought would definitely be a good idea.

Here are a few other ways to get your brain neurons firing and come up with some ideas of how you can enhance your control:

- Get away from the computer for a while and do something else. Sometimes ideas will come from out of nowhere even when you're not consciously thinking about the control.

- Look at other similar controls. There's no use in programming an exact copy of a control that's already available somewhere else because you would probably be better off just buying or downloading a copy of it. Instead, look at the features that other controls provide (or don't provide). Maybe you'll see something that can be improved upon.
- Sleep on it. You may wake up with some new ideas.
- Draw your control on paper. Actually seeing what the control will look like may make you realize that it's lacking something. It's better to realize it now than after you've spent a lot of time getting the control to look "just so."

The Three Paths of Control Creation

There are three ways you can go about creating a new control. But no matter which path you decide to take in designing your control, you will always start out with a `UserControl` object. Just as you start designing an application with a blank `Form` object, you start designing a control with a blank `UserControl` object. You can then use one of the three basic design methods detailed in the following paragraphs to expand on the `UserControl` object.

The first method involves expanding on an already existing control. For example, you could take VB's PictureBox control, add a few new properties and methods to it, and you would have a whole new control class. However, there may be some ethical (and legal) considerations involved in doing so. You couldn't, for example, purchase a third-party control, make a few changes to it, and remarket it as your own. You could, however, make modifications to the control for use in your own application—provided, of course, that you've purchased the control.

The second method of control creation is similar to the first: using one or more other controls (such as those in VB's toolbox) to build your own control. For example, you could use the TextBox control together with a few CommandButton controls to create something of a mini word processor. This is the easiest way to create a new control because it's almost like building a small application. It's also the method we'll use to create our sample control.

The final method is to start completely from scratch. If you have something in mind that is completely unlike any other control you've ever seen before, this is the method you'll use to create it. Because you have to draw the control entirely on your own, controls created in this fashion are referred to as *user-drawn controls*. Obviously, this is the most difficult way to create a control because you're not using prewritten objects to build it—you have to do everything yourself. On the other side of the coin, this method gives you the most freedom in design.

Whichever method you select for creating your controls is entirely up to you. Of course, it will also depend in a large part on the type of control you're creating.

Using Constituent Controls

Preexisting controls used to build your new control are called *constituent controls*. Although this is the fastest path to creating controls, you need to watch out for some pitfalls. For example, this method requires some overhead in terms of distributing your control because you also need to distribute copies of any constituent controls. In terms of difficulty, this is not too large of an issue because you can use the Setup Wizard to quickly create a setup program for your control that will seamlessly handle the installation (and registration) of all constituent controls. A bigger problem comes in the form of licensing issues. If you have licensed third-party components that you use as constituent controls, whomever you distribute your new control to must also have licenses for those components.

The good news is that you have carte blanche for using many of the objects in VB's toolbox as constituent controls. Some of the control objects included in the Professional Edition of Visual Basic, however, may need to be licensed by the end-user before being used on his or her system. The list of "safe" VB controls include (but are not limited to) the following: CheckBox, ComboBox, CommandButton, Data, DirListBox, DriveListBox, FileListBox, Frame, HScrollBar, Image, Label, Line, ListBox, OptionButton, PictureBox, Shape, TextBox, Timer, and VScrollBar.

Licensing of controls may seem like a nuisance, but it is required to protect the developers of controls—which may in fact be you, if you're planning to market your control to other VB programmers. For example, say that you create a new control called SuperWidget and sell it to Joe for use in his own applications. Joe in turn uses the control as a constituent control for his own ActiveX control, MegaWidget. If he sells or gives away copies of MegaWidget, he would also be indirectly selling or giving away copies of the SuperWidget control. Pretty soon, many programmers would have a working copy of SuperWidget, and it's doubtful that they would want to buy another copy of it from you. Thus, licensing is important for protecting developers.

We're not going to be using any constituent controls that are affected by licensing issues in our sample control. Using only the standard VB control objects, you can still create an incredible number of unique and interesting ActiveX controls.

Passing Along Properties

When using constituent controls, you can often "pass along" the properties of those controls to the interface of the new control. For example, because we'll be using the Label control as one of the constituent controls in our sample control, we can utilize several of its properties when creating the new control's interface, including its `ForeColor` and `Font` properties. When the developer using the new control changes its `Font` property, he is in effect changing the `Font` property of the Label constituent control. This is all transparent to him, but the code for our sample control is simplified because the addition of a new `Font` property (and all the code that it would require) is not needed—it's already provided by the Label control.

One of the first things you want to do when designing your control's interface is determine which constituent control properties you want to make available to developers (that is, the users of your control, including yourself). After all, there's no use in reinventing the wheel, so you might as well utilize as much of the power of your constituent controls as you can.

The same thing goes for events and methods. You can pass along the events of constituent controls using the `RaiseEvent` statement, and you can of course call the methods of other controls quite easily within the methods of your control that you make available to developers. Events and methods are discussed in more detail in Chapter 19, "Advanced ActiveX Control Creation."

Down to the Basics

As I stated earlier, developers will expect certain basics or standards from your control. If your control has some text or a caption of some sort, they will instinctively use the `ForeColor` property to change the color of that text. And when they click the cursor on your control, they will expect it to raise a `Click` event. By following certain guidelines, you can make your control as intuitive as possible.

If at all possible (and applicable), your control should provide the properties in Table 18.1 as a part of its interface. Note that some of these properties are automatically provided by the control's container object. More information is available in the following section, "Control Containers."

Table 18.1. Standard properties that should be included in a control's interface, if applicable.

Property	*Used to Specify*
`BackColor`	The color of the control's background
`BackStyle`	The opaqueness or transparency of the control's background (if applicable)
`BorderStyle`	The type of border around the control (if any)
`Caption`	The text on a button or label (if applicable)
`Enabled`	The availability of a control for receiving focus
`Font`	The text or caption's font type, attributes, and size
`ForeColor`	The color of any foreground objects, including text
`Height`	The vertical size of the control
`Left`	The X coordinate of the control on the screen
`Name`	The name by which the control is referenced
`Text`	The text in a text box (if applicable)
`Top`	The Y coordinate of the control on the screen
`Visible`	The visual state of the control on the screen
`Width`	The horizontal size of the control

Like properties, certain standard events also should be included in your control's interface. They are listed in Table 18.2.

Table 18.2. Standard events that should be included in a control's interface, if applicable.

Event	*Triggered When*
`Click`	The user clicks the mouse cursor on the control.
`DblClick`	The user double-clicks the mouse cursor on the control.
`KeyDown`	The user holds down a key on the keyboard.
`KeyPress`	The user presses (and releases) a key on the keyboard.
`KeyUp`	The user releases a key on the keyboard that was held down.
`MouseDown`	The user holds down the mouse button.
`MouseMove`	The user moves the mouse cursor within the control.
`MouseUp`	The user releases the mouse button.

Note that the `KeyDown`, `KeyPress`, and `KeyUp` events are only triggered for the control if it has the focus.

Last but not least, your control's interface should include certain methods. They are listed in Table 18.3. Some of them are automatically provided for you by the control's container, which we'll talk about in just a moment.

Table 18.3. Standard methods that should be included in a control's interface, if applicable.

Method	*Does the Following*
`Move`	Changes the position of the control on the screen
`Refresh`	Redraws the control if it is visible on the screen

Control Containers

Certain properties, methods, and events are provided by the control's *container.* A control cannot exist by itself and must always be contained by some other object. If you're going to use the control in an application, the container is likely to be a form. If you're using the control on an HTML page, the container is the page itself.

The properties furnished by the container object are called *extender properties* because the container "extends" them to the control. A control's `Top` and `Left` properties are actually extender properties because they relate to the control's position within its container. There is no way that you could code the `Top` and `Left` properties in your control because you have no idea where (or on what kind of container) the control will be used. Even if you did attempt to add a `Top` or `Left` property, the extender properties of the same name would take precedence over your custom properties. If the developer sets the `Left` property of your control using conventional methods, only the extender property would be altered.

The `Left`, `Name`, `Top`, and `Visible` properties are all provided by the container, which means that you don't have to add any code to include those properties in your control's interface. This is certainly good news because it helps shave off some of the time it takes to develop a control.

You may be wondering why the `Name` property would originate from the container rather than the control itself. You could set the name of your control (for example, `UltraWingding`) in the control's code, but then every instance of your control will have the same name—which is, of course, unacceptable. Instead, the container automatically assigns a name to a control instance using its class name and a sequential number: `UltraWingding1`, `UltraWingding2`, and so on.

If you want, your control can also function as a container. You don't need to do anything special to add this capability, only set the `UserControl`'s `ControlContainer` property to `True`. Your control would then automatically provide extender properties to its constituent controls.

Ambient Objects

There may be times when your control will require some information about its container. Certain properties, such as its background and foreground colors, are furnished by the `Ambient` object, and they are appropriately referred to as *ambient properties*. If, for example, you want the font used by your control to match that of its container object, your control can do so by checking the Ambient object's `Font` property and then setting its own `Font` property to match it.

Other commonly used ambient properties include `LocaleID` (or LCID), which is used to determine the version of Visual Basic that the object was compiled in, allowing controls to be *localized*, or modified on-the-fly for different international flavors of VB; `DisplayName`, which can be used in design time error-trapping routines to indicate exactly which instance of the control caused the error; and `DisplayAsDefault`, which indicates to your control whether it is the default button for the container object.

Another important ambient property is `UserMode`. By checking the `UserMode` property, your control can determine whether it is being used at design time or runtime. This comes in handy if you want to disable certain properties or functionality from a runtime instance of your control. We'll use the `UserMode` property in the development of our sample control later in this chapter.

If any ambient properties change, the `UserControl`'s `AmbientChanged` event is triggered. If you use ambient properties in some way to alter your control's appearance, you'll want to add code in that event to automatically have any changes applied to your control also.

Putting It All Together: The Interface

The properties, events, and methods that your control exposes to developers make up its interface. When designing a control's interface, your main goal is to get it right the first time. After the interface is defined, it's set in stone and should not be changed. This is one of the major stipulations of ActiveX controls: Control interfaces must not change. If you do need to make some changes to an interface (perhaps due to some additional functionality being added to the control), you need to define a new interface and still maintain all the properties, events, and methods of the old one. Your control will then contain multiple interfaces and will still maintain compatibility with applications that rely on the previous interface.

This is why good design is so important when it comes to the creation of ActiveX controls. If great care isn't taken in designing the control, it's likely that some important element of its interface will be missing. You simply cannot make a change—even a minor one—to the interface of a control that has been distributed or used in other applications. If you do, you risk the likely possibility of someone receiving a new copy of the control that suddenly won't work with applications that relied on its previous interface.

Before we get into the actual coding of our sample control, it would be a good idea to list all the properties, events, and methods that will comprise its interface. Table 18.4 lists each element, including its type (property, event, or method) and its source (the control itself or extender properties). Properties also show value type (Long integer, String, and so on) and default value.

Table 18.4. The elements that will make up the sample control's interface.

Element	*Type*	*Source*	*Value Type*	*Default Value*
`BackColor`	Property	Control	`OLE_COLOR`	`&H00FFFFFF`
`BorderStyle`	Property	Control	`Integer`	`1`
`ButtonMode`	Property	Control	`Integer`	`0`
`Caption`	Property	Control	`String`	`Control Name`
`Enabled`	Property	Control	`Boolean`	`True`
`Font`	Property	Control	`StdFont`	`Arial Bold 20 point`
`ForeColor`	Property	Control	`OLE_COLOR`	`&H80000008`
`Height`	Property	Control	`Long`	Varies
`Left`	Property	Extender	`Long`	Varies
`Name`	Property	Extender	`String`	Assigned by container
`Picture`	Property	Control	`StdPicture`	None
`SelColor`	Property	Control	`OLE_COLOR`	`&H0080FFFF`

Element	Type	Source	Value Type	Default Value
`SelPicture`	Property	Control	`StdPicture`	None
`Top`	Property	Extender	`Long`	Varies
`Visible`	Property	Extender	`Boolean`	`True`
`Width`	Property	Control	`Long`	Varies
`Click`	Event	Control		
`DblClick`	Event	Control		
`KeyDown`	Event	Control		
`KeyPress`	Event	Control		
`KeyUp`	Event	Control		
`MouseDown`	Event	Control		
`MouseMove`	Event	Control		
`MouseUp`	Event	Control		
`Move`	Method	Extender		
`Refresh`	Method	Control		

You may notice that certain properties listed as "standard" in Table 18.1 have been omitted from this list. For example, the `BackStyle` property is not applicable because if the background were transparent, we would never know whether the control was selected. Remember that the control will be changing the background color to indicate a "lighted" (or selected) condition. A transparent background would always be the same, so by default the `BackStyle` property *must* be set to 0 - Opaque.

Four new properties have also been added to the list: `ButtonMode`, `Picture`, `SelPicture`, and `SelColor`. `ButtonMode` will be used to specify which of the control's modes should be used (text-only or images). `Picture` and `SelPicture` will specify which graphic images to use for the button's selected or deselected states (these two properties will be ignored if the control is in text-only mode). The `SelColor` property indicates which color to use for the background when the control is selected.

The control will also have several additional events that are not listed because they are hidden from the user of the control. These events are specific to the `UserControl` object and are used to read and set property values and so on.

Now that the control's interface has been completely planned, we're finally ready to start coding. So bring up Visual Basic 5 and let's get started!

Creating the Control

Our sample control will be called `LightButton` because it "lights up" whenever the cursor is on it. Rather than present you with all the code for the control at one time, I'll give it to you a little at a time. First, we'll create a basic version that will only support the text-only mode. Then we'll add to the control little by little until it is built up into the final product. As new sections of code are added and existing parts are modified, you'll learn more about the details of creating ActiveX controls.

Assembling the Control

When you start up Visual Basic 5, you're presented with a screen similar to the one shown in Figure 18.1. You are given many different project types from which to choose. To create a new ActiveX control, double-click the ActiveX Control icon.

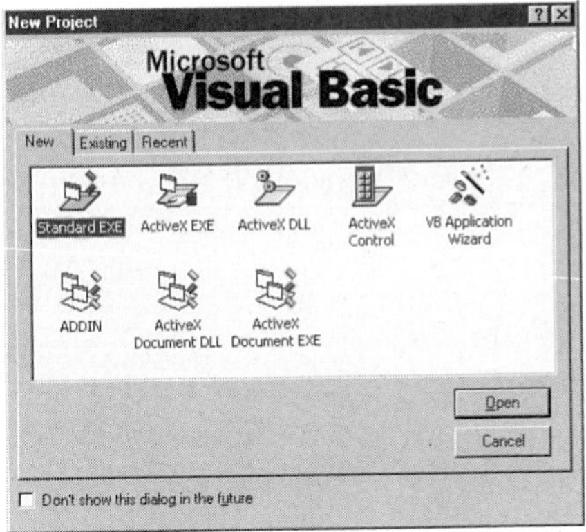

FIGURE 18.1.
Visual Basic 5 prompts you to select a project type when it starts up.

After Visual Basic loads in a few components, you'll see a blank Design window (see Figure 18.2). Although this looks suspiciously like a standard VB form, it's not. It's actually an instance of a `UserControl` object, which is the basis for designing controls in Visual Basic.

When you resize the `UserControl` object, you're changing the default size of your control. The default size specifies how big new instances of the control will be when they are first created, so you don't want it any bigger than necessary. To resize the control, simply use its drag handles to make it smaller or larger. Notice that the left and top sides of the `UserControl` object are flush against the Design window, and that the sizing handles on those sides are hollow. You can resize the `UserControl`, but you cannot *move* it. You really don't need to. Remember, it's not a form. Screen position is not relevant with `UserControl` objects at this point because their true positions will not be known until they are placed on their container objects.

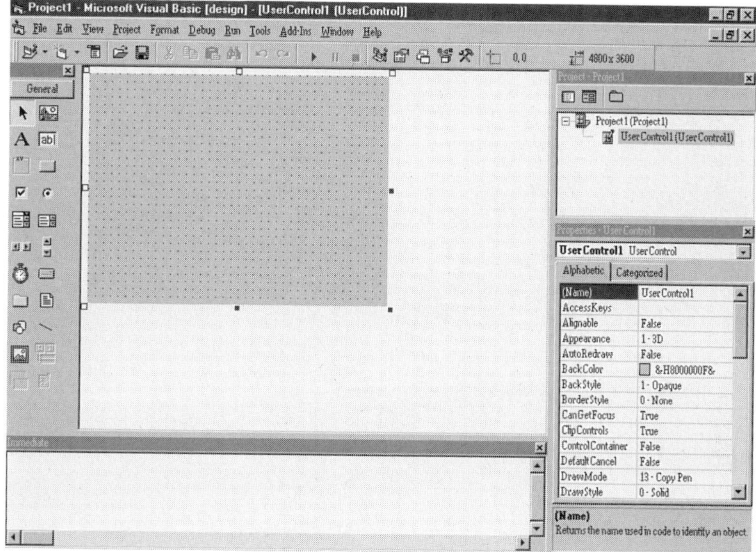

FIGURE 18.2.
A blank ActiveX Control project.

The top of VB's IDE window shows the project name (currently, the default name of `Project1`), the name of the control (`UserControl1`), and the control's class name (`UserControl`). The class name will always be the same, even after you've changed the name of the control. No matter what kind or how many changes you make to the control, it is still an instance of the `UserControl` class while you're in design mode. But when the control is in run mode, it becomes a class of its own. We'll talk more about the state of a control's class later in this chapter.

The first thing we want to do in the creation of our control is give it a name. In the Properties window, change `UserControl1`'s `Name` property to `LightButton`. As soon as you make the change, you'll see that the name of the control has been changed at the top of the IDE window. By changing the control's name, you've also changed the name of its class, although this won't be apparent until later.

NOTE

The use of the words *object* and *control* can be confusing because an object can be a control, and a control is always an object. To simplify things, I'll always refer to `LightButton` as a control, and other components (such as those from VB's toolbox) as objects or "constituent controls."

Several other changes need to be made to the `UserControl` (now called `LightButton`) control's properties. Make the changes to the properties listed in Table 18.5 by altering the corresponding values in the Properties window.

Table 18.5. The properties that need to be changed for the `UserControl` object.

Property	*Change to*
`Appearance`	`0 - Flat`
`BackColor`	`&H00FFFFFF&`
`BorderStyle`	`1 - Fixed Single`

Now we need to add two objects from VB's toolbox to the `LightButton` control. These are the constituent controls that will be used to build our new control. Add a `Label` object and a `Timer` object to the `LightButton` control, as shown in Figure 18.3. The exact sizes of the objects are not important because the `Label` object's size and position will be modified in the control's code, and the `Timer` object is invisible anyway. But try to make your control look similar to the one shown in Figure 18.3.

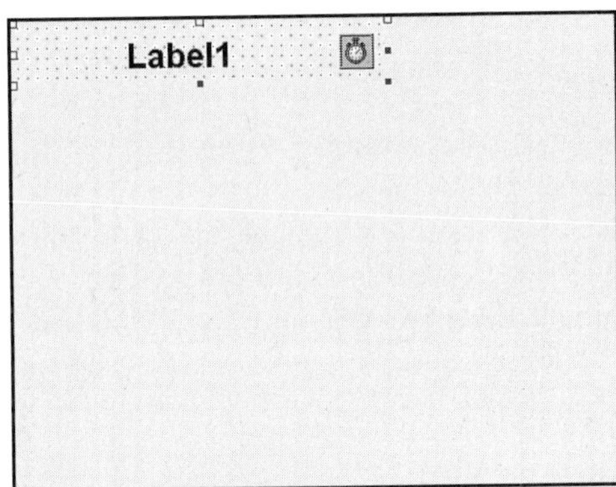

FIGURE 18.3.
A `Label` object and a `Timer` object are added to the control.

Change the property values for the `Label` object (`Label1`) to those listed in Table 18.6. Then change the property values for the `Timer` object (`Timer1`) to those in Table 18.7.

Table 18.6. The properties that need to be changed for the `Label` object.

Property	*Change to*
`Alignment`	`2 - Center`
`Appearance`	`0 - Flat`
`AutoSize`	`True`
`BackStyle`	`0 - Transparent`
`Font`	`Arial Bold 20 point`
`ForeColor`	`&H80000008&`
`Name`	`lblCaption`

Table 18.7. The properties that need to be changed for the `Timer` object.

Property	*Change to*
`Interval`	`250`
`Name`	`tmrChkStatus`

> **NOTE**
>
> Throughout this chapter, the names of objects from VB's toolbox will be prefixed with a three-character mnemonic indicating a class type: `txt` for objects of the `TextBox` class, `pic` for objects of the `PictureBox` class, and so on. Using such mnemonics is a good programming practice because it makes it easy to tell the type of object being referenced in your code.

Adding the Code

Now that the control's external appearance is finished, it's time to fill in the code that will bring the control to life. We need to declare some Windows API functions, and that requires a global code module. To add one to the current project, choose Project | Add Module from the menu. This will bring up the Add Module dialog box. Double-click the Module icon to add a new module to the project. The Project Explorer window should now show that `Project1` contains two parts: `LightButton` (the control itself) and `Module1` (the global code module you just added).

Bring up the Code window for `Module1` by double-clicking its name in the Project Explorer window. Add the code in Listing 18.1 to the `General Declarations` section.

Listing 18.1. Code that should be added to `Module1`'s `General Declarations` section.

```
Type POINTAPI
     X As Long
     Y As Long
End Type

Declare Function GetCursorPos& Lib "user32" (lpPoint As POINTAPI)
Declare Function WindowFromPoint& Lib "user32" (ByVal lpPointX As Long, _
     ByVal lpPointY As Long)
```

To know whether the cursor is on the control, two Windows API functions (`GetCursorPos` and `WindowFromPoint`) are required. The purpose of those two functions will be explained shortly.

Next, add the code in Listing 18.2 to `LightButton`'s `General Declarations` section.

Listing 18.2. Code that should be added to UserControl's General Declarations section.

```
Private mbooButtonLighted As Boolean
Private molcBackColor As OLE_COLOR
Private mpoiCursorPos As POINTAPI
```

The two Private statements declare variables that will be used later. By declaring them as Private variables, they are not exposed outside the control but can be used in any subroutine or function of the LightButton control.

You may think the names used for these variables look a little strange because they are prefixed with mnemonics "mboo" and "mpoi". However, there is a method behind the madness. The naming convention used (both here and throughout the rest of this chapter) allows the name to relay some basic information about the variable. The first character ("m") signifies that the variable is defined as module-level as opposed to procedure-level. The next three characters indicate the variable type: "boo" for Boolean and "poi" for the POINTAPI structure. When these variable names are used in the control's code, you can instantly tell their type.

The next section of code that needs to be added will go into UserControl's Initialize event. The Initialize event is triggered whenever an instance of the control is created. Add the code in Listing 18.3 to UserControl's Initialize event.

Listing 18.3. Code that should be added to UserControl's Initialize event.

```
Private Sub UserControl_Initialize()

    ' When the control initializes, the button is
    ' not "lighted".
    mbooButtonLighted = False

    ' Since UserControl's BackColor property will
    ' be changed if the control is "selected", its
    ' initial value must be stored in a temporary
    ' variable.
    molcBackColor = UserControl.BackColor

End Sub
```

The first thing that the control needs to do when it is initialized is set the ButtonLighted flag to False, indicating that the button is not currently selected. It also needs to keep the default value of the control's BackColor property because that property will change later when the control is selected, and its original value will be lost. The default color is what the control's background will be changed back to if the control is unselected.

Note that even though the name of the UserControl object was changed to LightButton, the control's event procedure names still reference it as UserControl. Like the events for Form objects, a UserControl's event procedure names do not change and will always reference the control as UserControl no matter what its name is. When referencing the control's properties and methods, the same rule applies. Listing 18.4 includes several references to UserControl's properties.

The next section of code goes into `tmrChkStatus`'s `Timer` event. This is where all the real work is done. The `Timer` event (which is triggered approximately four times a second) determines whether the cursor is on the control and takes the appropriate action to indicate the control's status. Add the code in Listing 18.4 to `tmrChkStatus`'s `Timer` event.

Listing 18.4. Code that should be added to `tmrChkStatus`'s `Timer` event.

```
Private Sub tmrChkStatus_Timer()

    ' This event will fire about 4 times per second,
    ' and is used to see if the control's status
    ' changes from selected ("lighted") to
    ' un-selected, and vice-versa.

    Dim plonCStat As Long
    Dim plonCurrhWnd As Long

    ' Disable the timer temporarily.
    tmrChkStatus.Enabled = False

    ' Using two Windows API functions, determine the
    ' handle of the window that the cursor is
    ' currently positioned on.
    plonCStat = GetCursorPos&(mpoiCursorPos)
    plonCurrhWnd = WindowFromPoint(mpoiCursorPos.X, mpoiCursorPos.Y)

    If mbooButtonLighted = False Then
        ' If the control is not currently "lighted",
        ' and it matches the handle of the window that
        ' the cursor is on, light it up.
        If plonCurrhWnd = UserControl.hWnd Then
            mbooButtonLighted = True
            UserControl.BackColor = &H0080FFFF
        End If
    Else
        ' If the control is "lit", and it no longer
        ' matches the handle of the window that the
        ' cursor is on, un-light it.
        If plonCurrhWnd <> UserControl.hWnd Then
            mbooButtonLighted = False
            UserControl.BackColor = molcBackColor
        End If
    End If

    ' Re-enable the timer.
    tmrChkStatus.Enabled = True

End Sub
```

The `Timer` event uses the two Windows API functions we defined earlier to check on the status of the mouse cursor. In a nutshell, this is accomplished by comparing the control's handle with the handle of whatever object the cursor is currently on. If the two handles match, then the cursor is on the control.

Just about every object that you see on the screen has its own handle, a unique number that is used to identify the object to the Windows operating system. Our control is no exception, and every instance of the control is assigned its own handle when it's created.

The `Timer` event is, as stated earlier, triggered about four times each second (you can shorten or lengthen the amount of time between firings by changing `tmrChkStatus`'s `Interval` property). When the event is triggered, it calls the `GetCursorPos` API function to fetch the mouse cursor's X and Y coordinates. Those coordinates are then fed into the `WindowFromPoint` API function, which returns the handle (hWnd) of whichever window (or object) currently occupies those coordinates. By comparing the value returned by the `WindowFromPoint` function with the handle of our control (`UserControl.hWnd`), we can tell whether the cursor is currently on it. It's a simple but effective method.

You may be wondering why we didn't simply use `UserControl`'s `MouseMove` event to determine whether the cursor was on the control. The `MouseMove` event is triggered only when the cursor is within the boundaries of the control. When the cursor moves off the object, the `MouseMove` event is no longer triggered. Unfortunately, `MouseMove` can only do half the job for us, and that's just not enough.

There's only one more section of code to add before we can try out the control, and it will be added to `UserControl`'s `Resize` event (see Listing 18.5). The control needs to reposition the `Label` object whenever it is resized so that it will always be centered. Because the `Resize` event is triggered when a new instance of the control is created, there's no need to duplicate this code in `UserControl`'s `Initialize` event.

Listing 18.5. Code that should be added to `UserControl`'s `Resize` event.

```
Private Sub UserControl_Resize()

    lblCaption.Top = (Height - lblCaption.Height) / 2
    lblCaption.Left = (Width - lblCaption.Width) / 2

End Sub
```

Because the `Label` object's `AutoSize` property is set to `True`, it will automatically be set to the smallest size possible whenever its `Caption` or `Font` properties change. Therefore, all that needs to be done in the `Resize` event is to center the `Label` object on the control.

There is a slight problem with the `Resize` event. If the `Label` object is larger than the size of `UserControl`, it will still be centered, but its left and right sides will be truncated. Under other circumstances, it would probably be a good idea to change the size of `UserControl` to match the size of the `Label` object. However, that would not be feasible here. Keep in mind that the control will offer the capability of displaying graphic images to indicate a selected or unselected state. In that case, the developer using the control will undoubtedly set its `Height` and `Width` properties to match the exact size of the graphic images. Changing the `Height` and `Width` of the control to accommodate the entire `Label` object would then cause a gap between the images and the control's border—and that would be unsightly. It's better to just truncate the `Label` caption.

Now that all the code has been added, it would be a good idea to save the control project. Choose File | Save Project As from the menu. You will be asked for the names of each file in the project. Use the information in Table 18.8 as a guide for naming the project files.

Table 18.8. The names that should be given to the project files when they are being saved.

Project File	*Save As...*	*Save As Type*
`Module1`	`LightButton`	Basic Files (*.BAS)
`LightButton`	`LightButton`	User Defined Control Files (*.CTL)
`Project1`	`TestControl1`	Project Files (*.VBP)

You're probably eager to try out the sample control, but there's still one step left. Because controls cannot run by themselves, we need a test form that will act as a container for the control. We can't simply add a form to the `TestControl1` project because the form would become a part of the control, which would put us back to square one. Instead, we need to create a whole new project that will act as the testing grounds for the new control.

To add a new project, choose File | Add Project from the menu. This will bring up the Add Project dialog box. Double-click the Standard Exe icon to create the kind of project that we can use for testing purposes.

If you look in the Project Explorer window, you should see that `Project2` has been added, as shown in Figure 18.4. One of the neat new features of VB5 is the capability to work on more than one project simultaneously in the Visual Basic environment. This allows you to test out controls without having to compile them—an incredible time-saver. If you could work on only one project at a time (as previous versions of Visual Basic mandated), you would have to edit your control, save it, compile it, load in a test project, test the control, and then load in the control project again to make any necessary changes. The entire edit-and-test process would then begin anew. With VB5, you can easily switch between project modules by double-clicking their names in the Project Explorer window or by choosing a module name from VB's Window menu.

NOTE

If your Project Explorer window doesn't look like the one in Figure 18.4, try clicking the small icon that looks like a folder at the top of the Project Explorer. This toggles between the two different project views.

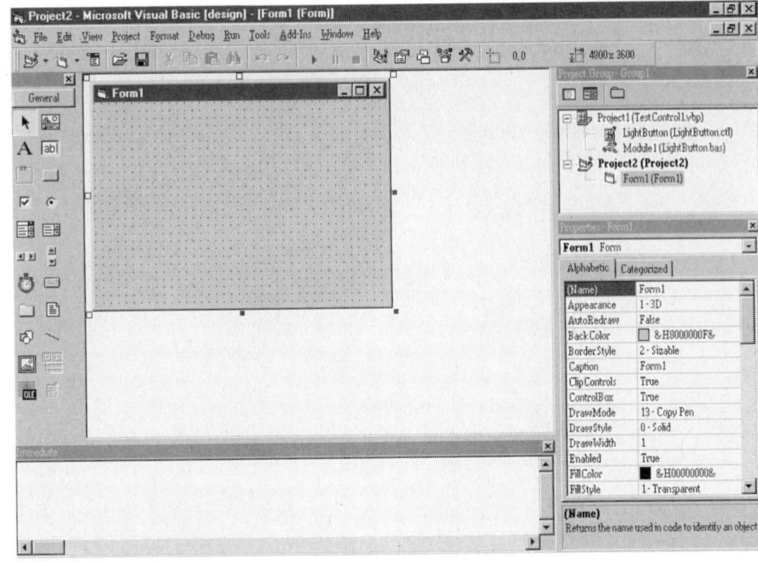

FIGURE 18.4.
The Project Explorer window, which shows that two projects (`LightButton` and `Project2`) are being worked on simultaneously.

With the new project (`Project2`) added, you now have a test form on which you can try out the control. Because a control cannot be run by itself, `Project2` automatically becomes the Startup project for the current *project group*. Its name appears in bold in the Project Explorer window, indicating its status as Startup project.

The test form is ready to go, but how do you create an instance of the control on the form? After all, there is no icon for it in the toolbox. That's true, but it's only because the control is still in design mode. For it to be available for use in other projects, it has to be taken out of design mode and put into run mode.

To put the control into run mode, go back to the control by double-clicking its name (`LightButton`) in the Project Explorer window. You should then see the `LightButton` control's Design window. By closing its Design window, you immediately switch the control from design mode to run mode. To close the Design window, click on the "Close Window" icon (as indicated in Figure 18.5).

As soon as `LightButton`'s Design window is closed, VB switches back to the next project in the project group, which happens to be `Project2`—the test project. An icon for the `LightButton` control also appears in the toolbox, as shown in Figure 18.6. If you position the mouse cursor on the icon, a tooltip window will appear with the name of the control: `LightButton`.

Double-click the `LightButton` control icon to create an instance of it on the test form. Note that its size is the exact same as it was in `LightButton`'s Design window. Remember, whatever size you make the control in the Design window will be its default size. The test form should now look similar to the one shown in Figure 18.6.

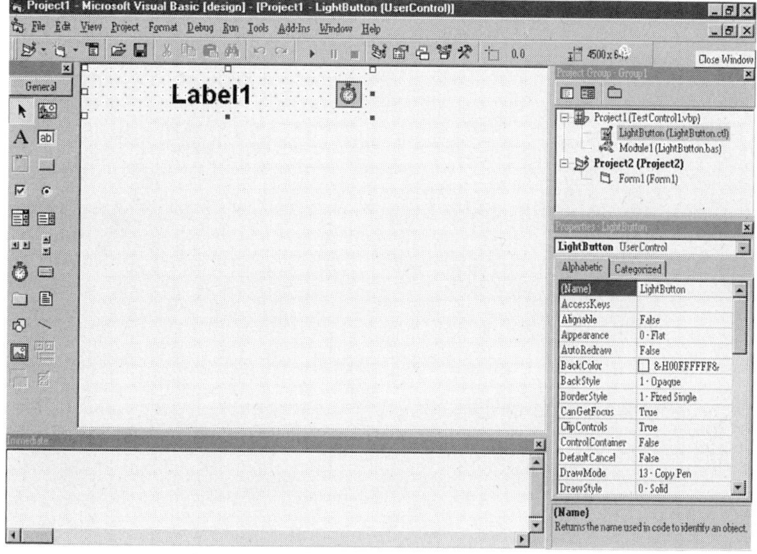

FIGURE 18.5.
The Close Window icon, which closes the Design window, is located at the top right of the Visual Basic IDE.

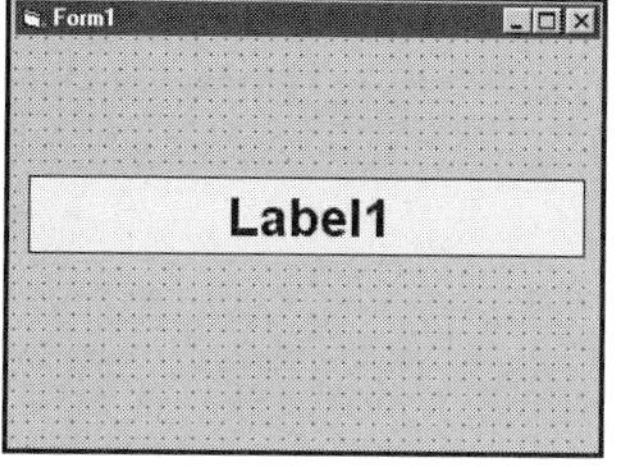

FIGURE 18.6.
The test form, complete with a new instance of the `LightButton` *control.*

Now for the neat part. Position the cursor anywhere on the control. When you do, the control's background changes from white to yellow. Move the cursor off the control, and the background color changes back to white. Congratulations, you've just created your first working control!

Try resizing the control. When you do, its caption (currently, "`Label1`") is automatically centered. This is because of the code we added to the control's `Resize` event.

Select the control by clicking it, then look at the Properties window. You'll notice that the name of this instance of the control has appropriately been named `LightButton1`. That name originated from the control's container, which in this case is `Project2`'s `Form1`. As stated earlier in this chapter in the section titled "Control Containers," the container uses a control's class name and a sequential number to name instances of a control. Thus, we get `LightButton1` as the default name for our control.

Look at the properties for `LightButton1`. As you can see, there aren't many available. In fact, all the properties listed have been automatically provided by the control's container (`Form1`).

When you create a control, you have a great deal of power over which properties it will expose; that's the good news. The bad news is that you have to add code to accommodate each property that is to be exposed. We'll add several properties to the sample control later in this chapter. But before we do, we'll take a look at the runtime version of our control to see whether there are any immediate ways in which it can be improved.

A Few Problems with the `LightButton` Control

You may have already noticed that VB's title bar has developed something of a "twitch." This is caused by `LightButton`'s `Timer` event, which is triggering four times each second. To prevent this, we should disable `LightButton`'s `Timer` object if the control's container is in design mode and only enable it when the container has been put into run mode.

Another problem is that the default caption for the control is `Label1`, which is derived from the default name of `LightButton`'s `Label` object. A better default caption would be the name assigned to the instance of the `LightButton` control, which in this case would be `LightButton1`.

To make these changes, the `LightButton` control has to be switched back into design mode. To do so, double-click `LightButton`'s name in the Project Explorer window. Note that when `LightButton` returns to design mode, its icon is disabled in the toolbox. Because the control is no longer in run mode, it is not currently available for use in other projects.

To verify this, double-click `Project2`'s `Form1` in the Project Explorer window. When the form appears, you should see its instance of the `LightButton` control filled with diagonal lines (see Figure 18.7). This indicates that the control cannot be displayed because it is not in run mode. Double-click `LightButton`'s name again in the Project Explorer window to switch back to the control project.

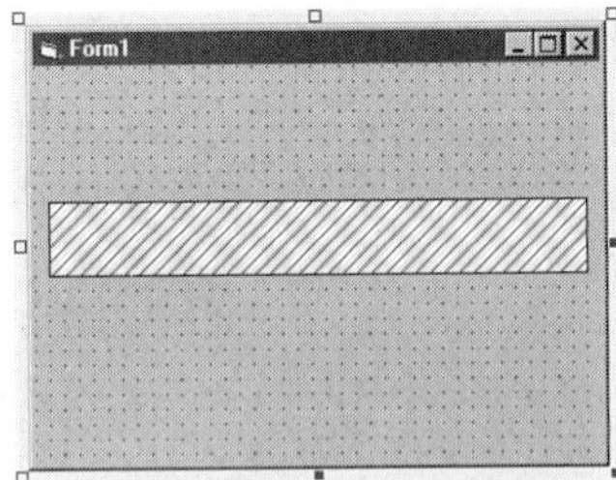

FIGURE 18.7.
`Form1`'s instance of the `LightButton` control cannot be displayed when the control is in design mode.

To take care of the first problem (the `Timer` event triggering while its container, the test form, is still in design mode), modify `UserControl`'s `InitProperties` and `ReadProperties` events, as shown in Listing 18.6.

Listing 18.6. Modifications to the `InitProperties` and `ReadProperties` events need to be made to disable the control's `Timer` when its container is in design mode.

```
Private Sub UserControl_InitProperties()

    ' If the control's container is in design mode,
    ' disable the Timer, which causes the control to
    ' not function.
    tmrChkStatus.Enabled = Ambient.UserMode

    ' Set the default values for some properties.

    ' The Caption property defaults to the name
    ' assigned to the control by its container.
    Caption = Ambient.DisplayName


End Sub


Private Sub UserControl_ReadProperties(PropBag As PropertyBag)

    ' If the control's container is in design mode,
    ' disable the Timer, which causes the control to
    ' not function.
    tmrChkStatus.Enabled = Ambient.UserMode

End Sub
```


The `InitProperties` event contains a line of code that assigns a default value to the `Caption` property that we'll be adding in just a moment. Right now, we're more concerned with the line that sets `tmrChkStatus`'s `Enabled` property.

If you're wondering why the same line of code was added to both the `InitProperties` event and the `ReadProperties` event, that will become apparent when you understand the sequence of events triggered for `UserControl` objects. That topic will be discussed in just a moment. For now, just add the same line of code to both events.

You may also be wondering why `tmrChkStatus`'s `Enabled` property was changed in the `InitProperties` event rather than the `Initialize` event. There's a good reason for this. Ambient properties and extender properties cannot be referenced in a control's `Initialize` event because at that point, the control has not yet been *sited* on its container. That is, the control has no idea what container it is in until it has already been initialized. `Ambient` and `Extender` objects are examples of *late bound* objects, meaning that any information about them is not available when the control is compiled. On the other hand, an *early bound* object—for example, the `Label` object that was used in the creation of the sample control—has all information about it available to the control when the control is compiled.

The second problem (the caption not accurately reflecting the name assigned to the control as a default) is best solved by adding a `Caption` property to the control. Make sure that the control's Code window is displayed; then choose Tools | Add Procedure from the menu. This will bring up the Add Procedure dialog box. For the Name, enter **`Caption`**. Make sure that `Property` is selected as the procedure `Type`, and `Public` is selected for `Scope`. Click OK to add the necessary property procedures.

Two new empty procedures have been added to `UserControl`'s Code window: one that retrieves the value of the property (the `Get` procedure), and one that stores the value of the property (the `Let` procedure). The procedures should appear as they do in Listing 18.7. These procedures are provided only as a starting point and require some modifications before they will work properly.

Listing 18.7. Two new `Property` procedures are added to expose the control's `Caption` property.

```
Public Property Get Caption() As Variant

End Property


Public Property Let Caption(ByVal vNewValue As Variant)

End Property
```

The first thing that needs to be changed is the type of variable used by these procedures to reference the property. By default, the `Variant` variable type is used because it can accommodate any kind of value. Even though the procedures could be used as-is, using `Variant` variable types is inefficient. Because the `Caption` property is a string, all variable types should be changed from `Variant` to `String`. Some code also needs to be added to each procedure to facilitate the actual storing or retrieving of the property's value. Use Listing 18.8 as a guide for modifying the two `Property` procedures.

Listing 18.8. Adding code to the `Property` procedures handles the storing and retrieving of the control's `Caption` property.

```
Public Property Get Caption() As String

    ' The Caption property comes directly from
    ' lblCaption's Caption property.
    Caption = lblCaption.Caption

End Property


Public Property Let Caption(ByVal NewValue As String)

    ' Caption's new value is passed directly to
    ' lblCaption's Caption property.
```

```
    lblCaption.Caption = NewValue
    UserControl.PropertyChanged "Caption"

End Property
```

Property procedures are similar to Sub or Function procedures. A Property Get procedure returns a value when it is called, much like a Function. The value returned is the value of the property. A Property Let procedure, on the other hand, does not return a value but instead requires that a value be passed to it. The value passed to it indicates what the property should be changed to.

For example, the following line of code would cause the Property Get Caption procedure to be triggered:

```
TestCaption = LightButton1.Caption
```

When the procedure is triggered, the value for Caption (a string variable) is obtained from lblCaption's Caption property.

The Property Let Caption procedure would be triggered with a line of code such as the following:

```
LightButton1.Caption = "Put Cursor Here"
```

When the Property Let procedure is triggered, the string "Put Cursor Here" is passed to the routine in its NewValue argument. That string is in turn stored in the lblCaption object's Caption property.

When the control is initialized, the Caption property receives the default value of the Ambient object's DisplayName for the control. This has already been taken care of in UserControl's InitProperties event (refer to Listing 18.6).

NOTE

Some properties have a Property Set procedure rather than a Property Let procedure. The two work in the same way, except that Property Set is used for properties that reference objects rather than variables. For example, a property that references a string value (a variable) such as the Caption property above would have a Property Let procedure. A property that references a picture (an object) would have a Property Set procedure.

Property Let or Property Set procedures should call UserControl's PropertyChanged if any changes are made to the property, as shown earlier in Listing 18.8. The name of the property is passed to PropertyChanged so that the event can tell exactly which property has been modified. Calling PropertyChanged is not mandatory, but it is a good idea because it lets Visual Basic know that the property has been changed.

In the preceding `Property Get` and `Property Let` procedures, the `lblCaption` object's `Caption` property is passed to `LightButton`'s `Caption` property, and vice versa. This is an example of passing a control's properties directly to and from constituent controls. In this case, the `Caption` property that is exposed by the `LightButton` control is really nothing more than a middleman for changing and reading the `lblCaption` object's `Caption` property.

The Property Bag

We're not out of the woods just yet. We still need a way of saving and retrieving the `Caption` property to and from memory. But why do we need to this? After all, the control's caption value is stored in the `lblCaption` object's `Caption` property, right? Yes, that's true, but we still need a way to save the value between instances of the control. Remember, control instances have a violent life and get destroyed and re-created again and again (as you'll soon see).

The saving and retrieving of property values is done in `UserControl`'s `WriteProperties` and `ReadProperties` events. Add the code to those events as shown in Listing 18.9.

Listing 18.9. The code that needs to be added to `UserControl`'s `WriteProperties` and `ReadProperties` events to save and retrieve the `Caption` property from memory.

```
Private Sub UserControl_WriteProperties(PropBag As PropertyBag)

    PropBag.WriteProperty "Caption", Caption, Ambient.DisplayName

End Sub


Private Sub UserControl_ReadProperties(PropBag As PropertyBag)

    tmrChkStatus.Enabled = Ambient.UserMode
    Caption = PropBag.ReadProperty("Caption", Ambient.DisplayName)

End Sub
```

To facilitate the easy saving and retrieving of property values, Visual Basic provides a nifty little item called the *property bag*. The property bag is a phantom spot in memory that temporarily stores property values. You can put property values into the bag, and you can take them out of the bag by using property bag's methods `WriteProperty` and `ReadProperty`, respectively. This is exactly what we've done in the preceding events.

When you call the `WriteProperty` method to put a value into the property bag, you need to specify the property name (in this case, `"Caption"`), the variable name (`Caption`), and a default name. It seems odd to specify a default name when storing a value, but Visual Basic uses the default to see whether the value needs to be saved. If the current property value is the same as the default value, VB won't save it in the property bag because it doesn't need to.

When retrieving properties with the `ReadProperty` method, you must specify the property name (again, `"Caption"`) and the default value. If you try to read a property value that is not in the property bag, the `ReadProperty` method returns the default value.

Every reference to a property by the `WriteProperty` method invokes the property's `Property Let` (or `Property Set`) procedure. Likewise, a reference to a property by the `ReadProperty` method invokes the property's `Property Get` procedure.

There is actually a simple way of adding properties to controls with only a single line of code. Consider the following line of code:

```
Public EasyProperty As String
```

That single line of code, placed into `UserControl`'s `General Declarations` section, is enough to create a property called `EasyProperty` that can be set from within other objects (such as a form). The property does not need to be written to the property bag, and it does not require a `Property Get` or `Property Let` procedure. So why bother with all the overhead of `Property Get`, `Property Let`, `WriteProperties`, and `ReadProperties`?

Even though this method is easy to use, it has some serious drawbacks. For one, it gives you absolutely no control over validation of property values—using a `Property Let` (or `Property Set`) procedure does. Using a public variable, any value that can be stored by the variable's value type can be assigned to the property. You also have no control over whether the property will be read-only or write-only. All Public variables can be read or changed freely.

Another problem is that there is no way to notify Visual Basic that the property has been changed, as you can by calling `UserControl`'s `PropertyChanged` event in a `Property Let` or `Property Set` procedure. If the property is to be passed to a constituent control, you must use `Property` procedures so that you are aware of when the property changes.

If you want to implement a property that does not affect constituent controls and can accept any value for its type, you can use this shortcut method if you want. However, I recommend sticking with the `Property Get`/`Property Let`/`ReadProperties`/`WriteProperties` combination. It means a little more work, but it's worth it for the extra control that you get over your properties.

In a nutshell, for every property that you include in your control's interface, you'll follow these four basic steps:

1. Add a `Property Get` procedure. Modify the procedure's declaration statement to reflect the type of value or object that the property references. Add code to the procedure to assign the property's value to the variable or object indicated in the procedure's declaration. *This step does not need to be done if the property is write-only; that is, it can be changed but not read. Write-only properties are rarely used.*
2. Add a `Property Let` (or `Property Set`) procedure. Modify the procedure's declaration statement to reflect the type of value or object that the property references. Add code to the procedure to check the value that was passed to the procedure to ensure that it is valid. If it is, assign that value to whatever variable, object, or property is being used to hold the property's value; then call `UserControl`'s `PropertyChanged` event. If it is not, raise an error indicating that an invalid property value was specified. *This step does not need to be done if the property is read-only and should not be modified.*

3. Add a call to the property bag's `ReadProperty` method in `UserControl`'s `ReadProperties` event. *If no* `Property Get` *procedure was included (indicating a write-only property), this step can be skipped.*
4. Add a call to the property bag's `WriteProperty` method in `UserControl`'s `WriteProperties` event. *If no* `Property Let` *or* `Property Set` *procedure was included (indicating a read-only property), this step can be skipped.*

Don't worry, it sounds like much more work than it really is. Many properties can be added in just minutes by using the Add Property dialog box, making some minor modifications to the `Property` procedure declarations, and adding a few lines of code. It gets much easier with only a little bit of practice.

Trying Out the `LightButton` Control... Again

It's time to try out the changes that have been made to the `LightButton` control. But first, make sure that you save all the files in the project group by choosing File | Save Project Group from the menu. You'll be prompted for the names of the files in `Project2` as well as the name of the project group. Use the information in Table 18.9 as a guide for naming the files.

Table 18.9. The names that should be given to the new project groups files when they are being saved.

Project File	*Save As...*	*Save As Type*
`Form1`	`LBTestForm`	Form files (*.FRM)
`Project2`	`LBTestProj`	Project files (*.VBP)
`LightButton`	`LBTest`	Project Group files (*.VBG)

Now switch the control back into run mode by closing its Code window and its Design window. When both windows have been closed, the icon for the `LightButton` control will reappear in the toolbox, and you'll see the test form with an instance of the sample control on it.

Move the cursor onto the control. It no longer lights up because the test project (and the test form) are still in design mode. If you run the test project by pressing F5 or clicking the Run button in Visual Basic's toolbar, you'll see that the control now functions as expected. That's because the test form (the control's container) is in run mode. The `LightButton` control's `Ambient.UserMode` property is now `True`, which enables the `Timer` object that allows the control to do its thing.

When you stop the test project, an interesting thing happens. The `Ambient.UserMode` property changes to `False`, and the `Timer` object is disabled. But how can this happen when the code to change the `Timer` object's `Enabled` property is in the `InitProperties` and `ReadProperties` events? These events happen at the beginning of a control instance's lifetime, not at the end. So why are those events triggered again, causing the `Timer` object to be disabled based on the new status of the `Ambient.UserMode` property?

When the test project stops running, the instance of the `LightButton` control on the test form is destroyed and a new one is created in its place, thereby triggering the `ReadProperties` event again. Objects—especially controls—are constantly being destroyed and re-created. The sequence of events that occur during a control's lifetime may seem a little strange, but they must be understood if you are to go any further in designing controls.

The Life of a Control Instance

A control can be thought of as having two different modes *in regards to its container object*: design-time and runtime. *Design time* begins when you place an instance of the control on the container object. *Runtime* begins when you run the project that contains the control's container object, either from within Visual Basic or as a compiled executable file that runs outside VB. To better illustrate just what happens to an instance of a control when it is in these different modes, I'll list the exact sequence of events for each.

As stated before, design-time mode occurs when an instance of the control is placed on a container object (usually a form). A control is also in design-time mode when changes are being made to the control's project or to the control itself. Design-time mode only happens within the Visual Basic environment.

When changes are made to a control and the *control* is taken out of design mode, its *container* is still in design-time mode. Any instances of a control on the container are destroyed and immediately re-created when the control is put into run mode. This occurs all the time, though there is no obvious indication that it is happening.

The following list shows the sequence of events that occur when a design-time instance of a control is created:

```
Initialize
InitProperties
Resize/Paint
```

Note that this is the only time that the `InitProperties` event is ever triggered, with one important exception that will be covered in a moment. The `InitProperties` event sets all the control instance's properties to their default values.

The `Resize` and `Paint` events may or may not be triggered, depending on how the control itself was created. If the control utilizes constituent controls, then the `Resize` event will occur so that the size and locations of any constituent controls can be adjusted based on the control's default property settings (which, of course, were just initialized in the `InitProperties` event). In this case, the `Paint` event will not occur.

If, however, the control was created from scratch and does not use constituent controls (that is, it's a user-drawn control), then the `Paint` event is triggered, but the `Resize` event is not. User-drawn controls always re-create their appearance in their `Paint` event rather than in their `Resize` event.

Either the `Resize` event or the `Paint` event is also triggered when the size of the control instance is altered, either from within code or by dragging its grab handles. These events do not occur when the control instance is moved on the form because the actual appearance of the instance does not change.

When a container that includes an instance of a control is run from within the Visual Basic environment, the design-time instance of the control is destroyed, and a runtime instance is created in its place. But before the design-time instance is destroyed, two events occur:

```
WriteProperties
Terminate
```

The `WriteProperties` event gives the design-time instance of the control a chance to save any changes that were made to its properties. They are saved to the copy of the form that is in memory but not to the `.FRM` file that is saved on disk.

By the time the `Terminate` event is triggered, the control instance is no longer displayed on the form. This is the last step before the instance is destroyed completely.

Now, a new runtime instance of the control is created. The events that occur at this point are similar to the sequence of events that occurred when the design-time instance was first created:

```
Initialize
ReadProperties
Resize/Paint
```

The only difference is that the `InitProperties` event has been replaced with the `ReadProperties` event. Because it's likely that changes were made to the control instance's properties during design time, triggering the `InitProperties` event and resetting all the instance's default property values wouldn't make much sense—the control would lose all its changes. Instead, the `ReadProperties` event occurs, so any property changes that were made (and that were recently saved in memory using the `WriteProperties` event) can be restored and applied to the new instance of the control.

Note also that the `Resize` and `Paint` events follow the same rules as they did earlier, with the `Resize` event only occurring for controls that utilize constituent controls and the `Paint` event only occurring for user-drawn controls.

When the project stops running, the runtime instance of the control is destroyed, and a new design-time instance is created. Control instances are constantly getting destroyed and re-created!

The only event that occurs before creating a new design-time instance is the `Terminate` event. You may be wondering why the `WriteProperties` event doesn't also get triggered. It's because runtime changes to properties are never saved. When the design-time instance is re-created, you want its properties to be exactly the same as the last design-time instance you were working on. Otherwise, things would really get confusing.

Now the new design-time instance of the control is ready to be created. The events that occur are the same as they were for the previous runtime instance:

```
Initialize
ReadProperties
Resize/Paint
```

The design-time instance's properties have been restored, and the control instance has been redisplayed. `Resize` and `Paint` are still following the rules mentioned earlier.

Going back to the changes made to the sample control earlier in this chapter, remember that we had to check the `Ambient` object's `UserMode` property (to enable or disable the control's `Timer` event) in both the `InitProperties` event and the `ReadProperties` event. Remember also that we couldn't check the `UserMode` property in the control's `Initialize` event because the `Ambient` object's properties are not yet available during that event. When the control instance is created on the form for the first time, the `InitProperties` event is triggered, but the `ReadProperties` event is not. And when a new design-time instance is created, the `ReadProperties` event is triggered, but the `InitProperties` event is not. Therefore, the `UserMode` check has to be in both to cover all the bases.

Event sequences are tricky when using controls within the Visual Basic environment because controls are constantly alternating between design-time and runtime modes. But when a control is executed as part of an executable (`.EXE`) file or is included on a Web page, things get much simpler. Here's what happens when a control instance is used as part of a compiled application:

```
Initialize
ReadProperties
Resize/Paint
- Other events -
Terminate
```

Again, note that the `Resize` event only occurs for controls that use constituent controls, and the `Paint` event only occurs for user-drawn controls.

The `Terminate` event does not occur until the container housing the instance of the control is unloaded or destroyed. Also, several other events are likely to happen between the initial `Resize` or `Paint` event and the `Terminate` event: `GotFocus`, `LostFocus`, `Click`, `DblClick`, and so on.

You may notice that there is no `WriteProperties` event. That's because there is nowhere for the control to write its properties. It can't modify the contents of the executable file to save the properties, nor would you want it to—then the control's properties would not be properly initialized the next time the application was run. Any changes to a control's properties during runtime are lost, just as they were when the runtime instance was destroyed to create a new design-time instance of the control in our previous example.

Controls used on Web pages act a little differently from those used in applications. This is because HTML pages have no way of saving property values. Because the controls exist on their own and not as a part of a form, an HTML page acts as if the control instance is being created for the first time no matter how many times the page is loaded and displayed:

```
Initialize

InitProperties

Resize/Paint

* Other events *

Terminate
```

The sequence of events is basically the same as it is for a control used in an executable file, but the `ReadProperties` event has been replaced with our old friend, the `InitProperties` event. Because there is no form from which it can read property settings, they are instead initialized to their default values every time the Web page is loaded. However, property values *can* be changed using the `<PARAM>` tag that is part of HTML's `<OBJECT>` tag. Implementing ActiveX controls on Web pages is discussed in Chapter 20, "Trying Out the Control." For now, it's important to understand the basic sequence of events that occur in the life of a control instance, no matter what mode it may happen to be in.

Adding More Properties to the `LightButton` Control

Part one of the `LightButton` control is working pretty well, but we still need to add the capability to use graphic images to indicate a selected or deselected button status. To do that, we're going to need to add some properties.

But before adding more properties, a few variables, types, and objects need to be defined in `UserControl`'s `General Declarations` section. Change that section to reflect the code shown in Listing 18.10.

Listing 18.10. Changes to `UserControl`'s `General Declarations` section.

```
Public Enum ModeTypes
     TextOnlyMode = 0
     ImageMode
End Enum

Public Enum BorderStyleTypes
     None = 0
     FixedSingle
End Enum

Private mbooButtonLighted As Boolean
Private mfonFont As StdFont
Private mmodButtonMode As ModeTypes
Private molcBackColor As OLE_COLOR
Private molcSelColor As OLE_COLOR
Private mpicPicture As New StdPicture
Private mpicSelPicture As New StdPicture
Private mpoiCursorPos As POINTAPI
```

You can either type in the code in Listing 18.11 verbatim, complete with the `Property` procedure declarations, or you can choose Tools | Add Procedure from the menu as a shortcut. If you use the second method, add all the procedures listed in Table 18.10, making sure that you type the name of the procedure in the Name box, select `Property` for Type, and select `Public` for Scope. Then use Listing 18.11 to add the code for each `Property` procedure.

No matter which method you decide to use, be sure that the code in your sample control matches the code in Listing 18.11. Be careful—there are some subtle differences in the `Property` procedure declaration lines that vary from procedure to procedure. For example, note that although most properties use a `Property Let` declaration, the `Picture` property uses a `Property Set` declaration instead.

Table 18.10. Add `Property` procedures for the following properties.

Property Name	*Type*	*Scope*
`BackColor`	Property	`Public`
`BorderStyle`	Property	`Public`
`ButtonMode`	Property	`Public`
`Font`	Property	`Public`
`ForeColor`	Property	`Public`
`Picture`	Property	`Public`
`SelColor`	Property	`Public`
`SelPicture`	Property	`Public`

Listing 18.11. Adding the following `Property` procedures code to your control, making sure that you pay close attention to details.

```
Public Property Get BackColor() As OLE_COLOR

    ' The control's BackColor property is "stored" in
    ' the UserControl object's BackColor property.
    BackColor = UserControl.BackColor

End Property


Public Property Let BackColor(ByVal NewValue As OLE_COLOR)

    ' The control's new BackColor value is passed
    ' directly to the UserControl object's BackColor
    ' property.
    UserControl.BackColor = NewValue
    UserControl.PropertyChanged "BackColor"

    ' Store the new BackColor value in a "holding"
```

continues

Listing 18.11. continued

```
    ' variable for later use.
    molcBackColor = NewValue

End Property


Public Property Get BorderStyle() As BorderStyleTypes

    ' The control's BorderStyle property is "stored" in
    ' the UserControl object's BorderStyle property.
    BorderStyle = UserControl.BorderStyle

End Property


Public Property Let BorderStyle(ByVal NewValue As BorderStyleTypes)

    ' Make sure that the value being assigned to the
    ' BorderStyle property is valid.
    If NewValue = None Or NewValue = FixedSingle Then
        ' The control's new BorderStyle value is passed
        ' directly to the UserControl object's BorderStyle
        ' property.
        UserControl.BorderStyle = NewValue
        UserControl.PropertyChanged "BorderStyle"
    Else
        ' Invalid BorderStyle value - raise an error.
        Err.Raise Number:=vbObjectError + 32112, _
            Description:="Invalid BorderStyle value (0 or 1 only)"
    End If

End Property


Public Property Get ButtonMode() As ModeTypes

    ' The ButtonMode property is stored in a "holding"
    ' variable, mmodButtonMode.
    ButtonMode = mmodButtonMode

End Property


Public Property Let ButtonMode(ByVal NewValue As ModeTypes)

    ' Don't let a new value be assigned to
    ' mmodButtonMode (ButtonMode's "holding" variable)
    ' unless it is valid.
    If NewValue = TextOnlyMode Or NewValue = ImageMode Then
        mmodButtonMode = NewValue
        ' If ButtonMode is TextOnlyMode (0), show
        ' the lblCaption object. If ButtonMode is
        ' ImageMode (1), hide the lblCaption object.
        If mmodButtonMode = TextOnlyMode Then lblCaption.Visible = True
        If mmodButtonMode = ImageMode Then lblCaption.Visible = False
        UserControl.PropertyChanged "ButtonMode"
    Else
```

```
            ' Invalid ButtonMode value - raise an error.
            Err.Raise Number:=vbObjectError + 32113, _
                Description:="Invalid ButtonMode value (0 or 1 only)"
        End If

End Property


Public Property Get Font() As StdFont

    ' The value for the control's Font property is
    ' "stored" in the lblCaption object's Font property.
    Set Font = lblCaption.Font

End Property


Public Property Set Font(ByVal NewValue As StdFont)

    ' Store the control's new Font value in the
    ' lblCaption object's Font property.
    Set lblCaption.Font = NewValue
    UserControl.PropertyChanged "Font"

End Property


Public Property Get ForeColor() As OLE_COLOR

    ' The control's ForeColor property is "stored" in
    ' lblCaption's ForeColor property.
    ForeColor = lblCaption.ForeColor

End Property


Public Property Let ForeColor(ByVal NewValue As OLE_COLOR)

    ' The control's new ForeColor value is passed
    ' directly to lblCaption's ForeColor property.
    lblCaption.ForeColor = NewValue
    UserControl.PropertyChanged "ForeColor"

End Property


Public Property Get Picture() As StdPicture

    ' The control's Picture property is passed directly
    ' to the UserControl object's Picture property.
    Set Picture = UserControl.Picture

End Property


Public Property Set Picture(ByVal NewValue As StdPicture)

    ' First, change UserControl's Picture property to
    ' display the image selected.
```


continues

Listing 18.11. continued

```
    Set UserControl.Picture = NewValue

    ' Then store the new image in a "holding" picture
    ' object.
    Set mpicPicture = NewValue

    ' If Picture's image is Nothing, set the ButtonMode
    ' property back to TextOnlyMode (0). If Picture
    ' does contain an image, set the ButtonMode
    ' property to ImageMode (1).
    If NewValue Is Nothing Then
        ButtonMode = TextOnlyMode
    Else
        ButtonMode = ImageMode
    End If

    UserControl.PropertyChanged "Picture"

End Property


Public Property Get SelColor() As OLE_COLOR

    ' The control's SelColor property is stored in a
    ' "holding" variable, molcSelColor.
    SelColor = molcSelColor

End Property


Public Property Let SelColor(ByVal NewValue As OLE_COLOR)

    ' Store SelColor's new value in a "holding"
    ' variable, molcSelColor.
    molcSelColor = NewValue
    UserControl.PropertyChanged "SelColor"

End Property


Public Property Get SelPicture() As StdPicture

    ' SelPicture's image is retrieved from a "holding"
    ' picture object, mpicSelPicture.
    Set SelPicture = mpicSelPicture

End Property


Public Property Set SelPicture(ByVal NewValue As StdPicture)

    ' Store SelPicture's new value in a "holding"
    ' picture object, mpicSelPicture.
    Set mpicSelPicture = NewValue
    UserControl.PropertyChanged "SelPicture"

End Property
```

There are many things going on in these `Property` procedures, so I'll go through them on a property-by-property basis and explain what's happening.

BackColor

`BackColor` is used just like any other control's `BackColor` property: it specifies the control's background color.

Because the `lblCaption` object is transparent (as defined earlier), changing the `UserControl` object's `BackColor` property essentially changes the background color of the control as a whole. Thus, we can store the control's `BackColor` property value directly in `UserControl`'s `BackColor` property.

Whenever the `BackColor` property changes (and its `Property Let` procedure is invoked), the new value is passed directly to `UserControl.BackColor`, which creates an immediate change in the control's appearance. The new value is also stored in a "holding" variable because `UserControl`'s `BackColor` property will change when the control is selected, and its original contents will be lost. The holding variable, `molcBackColor`, is used to save the original value.

Properties such as `BackColor` that specify color values use `OLE_COLOR` in their procedure declarations.

BorderStyle

The `BorderStyle` property is another example of passing values directly to other objects. `UserControl`'s `BorderStyle` property is used to store `BorderStyle`'s value. Changing `UserControl.BorderStyle` also modifies the appearance of the control.

The `BorderStyle` property is defined as `BorderStyleTypes`, an enumeration that was added to `UserControl`'s `General Declarations` section. The items in the enumeration (`None` and `FixedSingle`) will become the options that can be selected for the `BorderStyle` property in the Properties window for an instance of the `LightButton` control.

`BorderStyle`'s `Property Let` procedure keeps values other than those in the enumeration from being assigned to the property. If an invalid value is detected, an error is raised.

ButtonMode

The `ButtonMode` property cannot be directly passed to another object's property because no other object has a `ButtonMode` property—we made it up! If you remember correctly, `ButtonMode` specifies how the control will work. If it's set to `TextOnlyMode (0)`, the control uses a "text-only" display and changes its background color to indicate a selected or unselected state. If it's set to `ImageMode (1)`, images (specified by the `Picture` and `SelPicture` properties) will be used instead.

In `ButtonMode`'s case, a module-level integer variable (`mmodButtonMode`) is used to hold its value. Note that code has been added to `ButtonMode`'s `Property Let` procedure to ensure that only the values `TextOnlyMode (0)` and `ImageMode (1)` will be accepted. If anything other than `0` or `1` is passed to the `Property Let` procedure, an error message is displayed.

After the property's value has been validated, `lblCaption`'s `Visible` property is set accordingly. If the control is in `TextOnlyMode` (`ButtonMode = 0`), then the label should be displayed. However, if the control is in `ImageMode` (`ButtonMode = 1`), the label is hidden so that it doesn't display on top of the images.

Font

Here's another example of passing values directly to constituent controls. The `Font` property is stored (and retrieved from) `lblCaption.Font`. Thus, whenever the `Font` property is modified, the change is automatically reflected in the control's appearance.

`Font` properties use `StdFont` in their procedure declarations. `StdFont` is a special object type that contains the font type, size, and attributes in one package. And because the `Font` property refers to an object (`StdFont`), it uses a `Property Set` procedure rather than a `Property Let` procedure.

ForeColor

`ForeColor` works similarly to the `BackColor` property and is passed directly to the `lblCaption` object. However, a copy of `ForeColor`'s value does not need to be copied to a "holding" variable because the control's `ForeColor` property does not change when the control goes from a selected to a nonselected state and vice versa.

Because the `ForeColor` property specifies a color, it also uses `OLE_COLOR` in its procedure declarations.

Picture

The `Picture` property is used to specify the image that should be displayed if the control is in a nonselected state. This image is also used as the default image; that is, the image that will be showing when the control is initially displayed.

Any value passed to the `Picture` property goes directly into `UserControl`'s `Picture` property, altering the appearance of the control. But the value also goes into a "holding" object, `mpicPicture`. But why both?

Consider what happens when the control changes from a nonselected to a selected state. The image that currently resides in `UserControl.Picture` will be replaced with the image (specified by the `SelPicture` property) that indicates that the control is selected. The original image would be lost. Therefore, a copy of it is stored in `mpicPicture` just in case it needs to be recalled later.

The value assigned to the `Picture` property is in the form of a `StdPicture` object. The `StdPicture` object dictates that the property uses a `Property Set` procedure rather than a `Property Let` procedure. Also, notice that whenever values are assigned to the `Picture` property (or its holding object, `mpicPicture`), Visual Basic's `Set` command must be used. The rule is that if the property requires a `Set` command to assign it a value, a `Property Set` procedure must be used in lieu of `Property Let`.

If the control's `Picture` property is altered, the `Property Set` procedure also modifies the value of the `ButtonMode` property. After all, if an image is specified for the `Picture` property, the control should automatically switch out of `TextOnlyMode` into `ImageMode` (`ButtonMode = 1`). However, a little extra logic is needed to determine whether the `Picture` property's new value is indeed an image. This is done by checking to see whether the new value is `Nothing`.

If `NewValue` is anything other than `Nothing`, `NewValue` should contain an image, and the `ButtonMode` property can be switched to `ImageMode (1)`. If it is `Nothing`, then `NewValue` does not contain an image, and the `ButtonMode` property should be set back to `TextOnlyMode (0)`.

SelColor

The `SelColor` property is used to specify which color the control's background will be changed to in order to indicate a selected state for the control. This property is really meaningless unless the control is in `TextOnlyMode` (`ButtonMode = 0`).

`SelColor`'s value is stored in `molcSelColor`, a module-level variable defined as type `OLE_COLOR`.

SelPicture

The `SelPicture` property specifies the image that will be used to indicate a selected state for the control when it is in image mode (`ButtonMode = 1`). Like the `Picture` property, it is of the `StdPicture` type and requires a `Property Set` procedure rather than a `Property Let` procedure.

Initializing, Reading, and Writing Properties

Even though we've added several new properties that influence how the control looks or works, they wouldn't do much good if they couldn't be stored and retrieved as instances of the control are destroyed or re-created. Also, some properties need to be assigned default values when the control is initially created. To accomplish the initialization, reading, and writing of properties, we need to make some modifications to `UserControl`'s `InitProperties`, `ReadProperties`, and `WriteProperties` events. Use Listing 18.12 as a guide to making changes to those events.

Listing 18.12. Changes that need to be made to `UserControl`'s `InitProperties`, `ReadProperties`, and `WriteProperties` events so that the control's properties can be initialized, stored, and retrieved.

```
Private Sub UserControl_InitProperties()

    ' If the control's container is in design mode,
    ' disable the Timer, which causes the control to
    ' not function.
    tmrChkStatus.Enabled = Ambient.UserMode

    ' Set the default values for some properties.

    ' The Caption property defaults to the name
    ' assigned to the control by its container.
    Caption = Ambient.DisplayName

    ' The SelColor property defaults to the color
    ' yellow.
```

continues

Listing 18.12. continued

```
    SelColor = &H80FFFF

    ' The ButtonMode property defaults to
    ' TextOnlyMode (0).
    ButtonMode = TextOnlyMode

End Sub


Private Sub UserControl_ReadProperties(PropBag As PropertyBag)

    ' If the control's container is in design mode,
    ' disable the Timer, which causes the control to
    ' not function.
    tmrChkStatus.Enabled = Ambient.UserMode

    ' Read the stored values of the control's
    ' properties from the property bag.
    BackColor = PropBag.ReadProperty("BackColor", &HFFFFFF)
    BorderStyle = PropBag.ReadProperty("BorderStyle", 1)
    ButtonMode = PropBag.ReadProperty("ButtonMode", mmodButtonMode)
    Caption = PropBag.ReadProperty("Caption", Ambient.DisplayName)
    ForeColor = PropBag.ReadProperty("ForeColor", &H80000008)
    SelColor = PropBag.ReadProperty("SelColor", &H80FFFF)

    Set Font = PropBag.ReadProperty("Font", mfonFont)
    Set Picture = PropBag.ReadProperty("Picture", Nothing)
    Set SelPicture = PropBag.ReadProperty("SelPicture", Nothing)

End Sub


Private Sub UserControl_WriteProperties(PropBag As PropertyBag)

    ' Store the control's property values in the container's
    ' property bag.
    PropBag.WriteProperty "BackColor", BackColor, &HFFFFFF
    PropBag.WriteProperty "BorderStyle", BorderStyle, 1
    PropBag.WriteProperty "ButtonMode", ButtonMode, mmodButtonMode
    PropBag.WriteProperty "Caption", Caption, Ambient.DisplayName
    PropBag.WriteProperty "ForeColor", ForeColor, &H80000008
    PropBag.WriteProperty "SelColor", SelColor, &H80FFFF

    PropBag.WriteProperty "Font", Font, mfonFont
    PropBag.WriteProperty "Picture", Picture, Nothing
    PropBag.WriteProperty "SelPicture", SelPicture, Nothing

End Sub
```

Code has been added to the `InitProperties` event to assign default values to the `SelColor` and `ButtonMode` properties, neither of which are held in the properties of constituent controls.

The ReadProperties and WriteProperties events now contain all the code necessary to read and write the control's new properties from and to the property bag. Any values that are assigned to the properties will now "stick" as new instances of the control are created (and old ones are destroyed).

You may be wondering exactly how to go about determining what a property's default value should be for the WriteProperty and ReadProperty methods. As a rule of thumb, it should be whatever value the property initially contains when a new instance of the control is created. And you must make sure that the default value used in the WriteProperty method is the same as the one used in the ReadProperty method. Otherwise, you may get unpredictable results.

Only one more change needs to be made before the control can be tested again. Right now, the tmrChkStatus object's Timer event is only set up to change the background color. But because the ButtonMode property has been added and the control can be in either TextOnlyMode or ImageMode, the Timer event has to differentiate between the two modes and take the appropriate action.

Listing 18.13 shows the new tmrChkStatus_Timer event. The only part that needs to be changed is the large If...End If block at the end of the event's code. However, the entire section of code has been included here to avoid any confusion about the changes that need to be made.

Listing 18.13. The new tmrChkStatus_Timer event code.

```
Private Sub tmrChkStatus_Timer()

    ' This event will fire about 4 times per second,
    ' and is used to see if the control's status
    ' changes from selected ("lighted") to
    ' un-selected, and vice-versa.

    Dim plonCStat As Long
    Dim plonCurrhWnd As Long

    ' Disable the timer temporarily.
    tmrChkStatus.Enabled = False

    ' Using two Windows API functions, determine the
    ' handle of the window that the cursor is
    ' currently positioned on.
    plonCStat = GetCursorPos&(mpoiCursorPos)
    plonCurrhWnd = WindowFromPoint(mpoiCursorPos.X, mpoiCursorPos.Y)

    If mbooButtonLighted = False Then
        ' If the control is not currently "lighted",
        ' and it matches the handle of the window that
        ' the cursor is on, either light it up (if
        ' ButtonMode = TextOnlyMode) or switch its
        ' background image to the one that indicates
        ' that the button is selected.
        If plonCurrhWnd = UserControl.hWnd Then
            mbooButtonLighted = True
```

continues

Listing 18.13. continued

```
                If mmodButtonMode = TextOnlyMode Then
                    UserControl.BackColor = molcSelColor
                Else
                    Set UserControl.Picture = mpicSelPicture
                End If
            End If
        Else
            ' If the control is "lit", and it no longer
            ' matches the handle of the window that the
            ' cursor is on, either un-light it (if
            ' ButtonMode = TextOnlyMode) or switch its
            ' background image to the one that indicates
            ' that the button is not selected.
            If plonCurrhWnd <> UserControl.hWnd Then
                mbooButtonLighted = False
                If mmodButtonMode = TextOnlyMode Then
                    UserControl.BackColor = molcBackColor
                Else
                    Set UserControl.Picture = mpicPicture
                End If
            End If
        End If

        ' Re-enable the timer.
        tmrChkStatus.Enabled = True

End Sub
```

All Systems Go!

Now that all the proper changes have been made to the control, it's finally time to test it again. Save your changes to the Project Group and then switch back to the test project.

Delete the previous instance of the `LightButton` control and create a new one. It should appear labeled as "`LightButton1`".

In the control's Properties window, you'll see all the new properties that we've added: `BackColor`, `ButtonMode`, `Caption`, `Font`, `ForeColor`, `Picture`, `SelColor`, and `SelPicture`. Experiment by changing any of the properties, and you'll see that they work just like the properties of any other control. Don't change the `Picture` or `SelPicture` properties just yet because we're going to try them out in a moment.

Try running `Project2` and moving the cursor on and off the control. When the cursor is on the control, the background color should change to whatever color was specified by the `SelColor` property. When the cursor is off the control, the background color should be whatever the `BackColor` property specifies. Stop the program so that you can make some more changes to the control's properties.

Try setting the control's `Width` property to 3000 and its `Height` property to 900. Then use the two image files (`TEST-OFF.BMP` and `TEST-ON.BMP` located in the `\SOURCE\CHAP18` directory) that are included on the CD-ROM as the values for the `Picture` and `SelPicture` properties, respectively. Notice that when a picture value is assigned to the `Picture` property, `ButtonMode` automatically switches to `ImageMode`.

Run `Project2` again to try the control in `ImageMode`. When the control is initially displayed, it shows the `TEST-OFF.BMP` image (see Figure 18.8) as the default. When the cursor is moved onto the control, the `TEST-ON.BMP` image is displayed (see Figure 18.9), and the text appears to "light up" to indicate a selected status. Because any two images can be used with the `LightButton` control, the possibilities for what it can do are endless!

FIGURE 18.8.
The `LightButton` *control, running in* `ImageMode`, *initially shows the* `TEST-OFF.BMP` *image.*

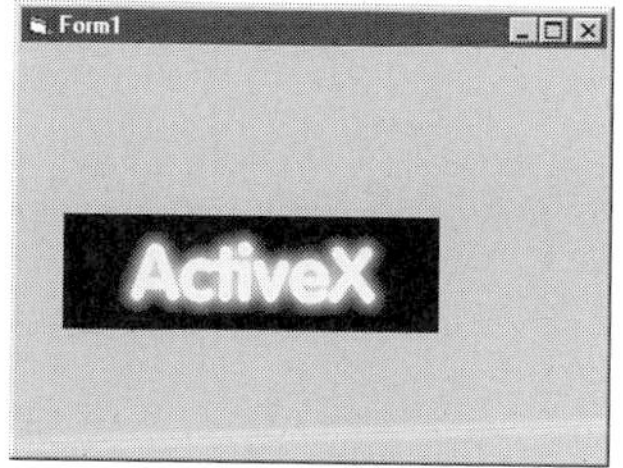

FIGURE 18.9.
The `LightButton` *control shows the* `TEST-ON.BMP` *image to indicate a selected state.*

One More Thing

One more property needs to be added to the `LightButton` control: the `Enabled` property. Some special considerations need to be taken with this property, so I wanted to discuss it separately from the rest.

To begin with, the `Property Get` and `Property Let` statements can be added for the `Enabled` property just like any of the others. Get back into the control's design mode and add the `Property` procedures shown in Listing 18.14.

Listing 18.14. The `Property` procedures for the `Enabled` property.

```
Public Property Get Enabled() As Boolean
     Enabled = UserControl.Enabled
End Property


Public Property Let Enabled(ByVal NewValue As Boolean)
     UserControl.Enabled = NewValue
     UserControl.PropertyChanged "Enabled"
End Property
```

Next, add the following line of code to `UserControl`'s `WriteProperties` event:

```
PropBag.WriteProperty "Enabled", Enabled, True
```

Finally, add the following line to `UserControl`'s `ReadProperties` event:

```
Enabled = PropBag.ReadProperty("Enabled", True)
```

Nothing new here. Any new value assigned to the `Enabled` property is passed directly to the `UserControl` object's `Enabled` property, and any time the `Enabled` property's value is read, it is taken directly from `UserControl.Enabled`. Also, the `WriteProperty` and `ReadProperty` events don't look any different from those of the other properties. So what's the big deal?

The `Enabled` property will not work correctly as it is. If the control's container becomes disabled, it is supposed to disable all the controls that it contains; that is, none of the controls can have their events triggered. However, the controls still need to be able to redraw themselves if required. Therefore, the control needs to *think* it's enabled when in fact it is not.

There is a way to get around this quirky problem, but to do so the container needs to know the *procedure ID* of the control's `Enabled` property. If it knows the procedure ID, the container can set the `Enabled` property of the control to `False` without actually calling the `Enabled` property procedures.

Assigning the correct procedure ID to the control's `Enabled` property is done using the Procedure Attributes dialog box. To access it, choose Tools | Procedure Attributes from the menu. This will bring up a dialog box similar to the one shown in Figure 18.10.

FIGURE 18.10.
The Procedure Attributes dialog box, which is used to set the `Enabled` *property's procedure ID.*

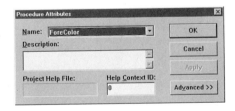

In the Name box, select the `Enabled` property. Click the Advanced button, and then select `Enabled` in the Procedure ID box. Click OK.

That's all there is to it. The `Enabled` property should now work correctly.

Summary

In this chapter, you learned to create a control from start to finish, starting with the most important step: designing the control thoroughly.

After a solid design was created and the control's interface was mapped out, the control was built piece by piece. Several properties were added to the control to increase its functionality.

In the chapters that follow, the `LightButton` control's interface will be completed by adding its events and methods. Finally, the control will be compiled and used on a Web page.

CHAPTER 19

Advanced ActiveX Control Creation

IN THIS CHAPTER

In Chapter 18, "ActiveX Control Creation," you learned how to build a control from the ground up, starting with designing its interface, then actually creating the control in Visual Basic, and finally adding properties to the control as specified by its interface design. In this chapter, we'll expand on the `LightButton` sample control even further by adding events and methods to the control's interface. We'll also take care of some odds and ends that will make the control truly complete.

Expanding on the Control's Interface

Now that all the properties defined in the control's interface have been added, it's time to add the events and methods that were also a part of the interface. Table 19.1 shows the elements of the control's interface that still need to be implemented.

Table 19.1. The events and methods defined in the `LightButton` control's interface that have not yet been implemented.

Element	*Type*
`Click`	Event
`DblClick`	Event
`KeyDown`	Event
`KeyPress`	Event
`KeyUp`	Event
`MouseDown`	Event
`MouseMove`	Event
`MouseUp`	Event
`StatusChanged`	Event
`Flash`	Method
`Refresh`	Method

If you compare Table 19.1 to the table in Chapter 18 that lists all the control's interface elements, you'll see that several methods (`Drag`, `Move`, `SetFocus`, `ShowWhatsThis`, and `ZOrder`) have been omitted from this list. They're still a part of the control's interface, but they have already been implemented—furnished automatically by the control's container object. Remember, certain elements that appear to be part of a control are actually provided for and controlled by the container itself. The same thing goes for properties. Many are automatically provided by the control's container or the `Ambient` object, including `DragIcon`, `DragMode`, `Height`, `HelpContextID`, `Index`, `Left`, `Object`, `Parent`, `TabIndex`, `TabStop`, `Tag`, `ToolTipText`, `Top`, `WhatsThisHelpID`, and `Width`. As you can see, much of a control's base functionality is already built in.

Four events (DragDrop, DragOver, GotFocus, and LostFocus) are also missing from Table 19.1 because they too are provided by the control's container. So right off the bat, your control has four events, five methods, and more than 15 different properties that are a part of its interface but don't require a single line of code on your part. Not bad!

Almost all the events and methods listed in Table 19.1 that *will* require some coding will originate from the control's UserControl object. Just as the properties of constituent controls can be "passed" to the control's interface, so it goes with events and methods. There's no need to reinvent the wheel; the functionality required is already provided by the constituent controls.

Only one event (StatusChanged) and one method (Flash) will need to be custom created. Don't worry, adding events and methods (even custom ones) is easy to do, as you'll see in the next few pages.

Adding Events to the Sample Control

We'll begin by adding the events that originate from the control's UserControl object: Click, DblClick, KeyDown, KeyPress, KeyUp, MouseDown, MouseMove, and MouseUp.

Events raised by a control's constituent controls or the UserControl object give you, the control's developer, an opportunity to react to those events and, if desired, expose them as a part of your control's interface. However, the events of constituent controls are unavailable to the user of the control unless the events have been purposely exposed. For example, if the user clicks the mouse cursor on an instance of the LightButton control, the UserControl object's Click event will be raised. You might also expect that LightButton's Click event would also be raised automatically, but it is not. You need to *expose* UserControl's Click event *as* LightButton's Click event. The developer using the control won't know the difference—just as he would be unaware that LightButton's Caption property is in reality the same thing as the Caption property of LightButton's constituent control lblCaption.

To expose a constituent control's event, only two lines of code are needed. The first line needs to be added to the end of UserControl's General Declarations section as follows:

```
Public Event Click()
```

As you've probably already surmised, this adds a public Click event to the control. Declaring the event as public *exposes* it, allowing it to be available to other objects.

The other line of code required to expose UserControl's Click event appropriately goes into UserControl_Click:

```
RaiseEvent Click
```

This will raise LightButton's Click event (which was defined by the Public Event statement earlier) whenever UserControl's Click event is triggered. If you want, you could also include code in UserControl_Click to do something special (such as making a "clicking" sound) before raising the control's Click event. The developer using the control can in turn put his own code in the LightButton_Click event, which has now been made available to him.

As you can see, exposing the events of constituent controls is easy. With only two lines of code required, it makes sense to expose as many events as possible to provide your control with the greatest functionality.

To expose the rest of `UserControl`'s events, first use Listing 19.1 as a guide for making changes to `LightButton`'s General Declarations section. Then use Listing 19.2 to make the necessary changes to the appropriate `UserControl` event procedures.

Listing 19.1. `LightButton`'s General Declarations section, with lines added to facilitate the exposure of the `UserControl` object's events.

```
Public Enum ModeTypes
     TextOnlyMode = 0
End Enum

Public Enum BorderStyleTypes
     None = 0
     FixedSingle
End Enum

' Expose the control's events as a part of its
' interface.
Public Event Click()
Public Event DblClick()
Public Event KeyDown(KeyCode As Integer, Shift As Integer)
Public Event KeyPress(KeyAscii As Integer)
Public Event KeyUp(KeyCode As Integer, Shift As Integer)
Public Event MouseDown(Button As Integer, Shift As Integer, _
     X As Single, Y As Single)
Public Event MouseMove(Button As Integer, Shift As Integer, _
     X As Single, Y As Single)
Public Event MouseUp(Button As Integer, Shift As Integer, _
     X As Single, Y As Single)

Private mbooButtonLighted As Boolean
Private mfonFont As StdFont
Private mmodButtonMode As ModeTypes
Private molcBackColor As OLE_COLOR
Private molcSelColor As OLE_COLOR
Private mpicPicture As New StdPicture
Private mpicSelPicture As New StdPicture
Private mpoiCursorPos As POINTAPI
```

Listing 19.2. `UserControl`'s event procedures, which, when triggered, raise the `LightButton` events defined in the General Declarations section.

```
Private Sub UserControl_Click()

     ' If UserControl's Click event is triggered,
     ' LightButton's Click event is in turn raised.
     RaiseEvent Click

End Sub
```

```
Private Sub UserControl_DblClick()

     ' If UserControl's DblClick event is triggered,
     ' LightButton's DblClick event is in turn raised.
     RaiseEvent DblClick

End Sub


Private Sub UserControl_KeyDown(KeyCode As Integer, _
     Shift As Integer)

     ' If UserControl's KeyDown event is triggered,
     ' LightButton's KeyDown event is in turn raised,
     ' and the KeyCode and Shift arguments are passed
     ' to that event.
     RaiseEvent KeyDown(KeyCode, Shift)

End Sub


Private Sub UserControl_KeyPress(KeyAscii As Integer)

     ' If UserControl's KeyPress event is triggered,
     ' LightButton's KeyPress event is in turn raised,
     ' and the KeyAscii argument is passed to that
     ' event.
     RaiseEvent KeyPress(KeyAscii)

End Sub


Private Sub UserControl_KeyUp(KeyCode As Integer, _
     Shift As Integer)

     ' If UserControl's KeyUp event is triggered,
     ' LightButton's KeyUp event is in turn raised,
     ' and the KeyCode and Shift arguments are
     ' passed to that event.
     RaiseEvent KeyUp(KeyCode, Shift)

End Sub


Private Sub UserControl_MouseDown(Button As Integer, _
     Shift As Integer, X As Single, Y As Single)

     ' If UserControl's MouseDown event is triggered,
     ' LightButton's MouseDown event is in turn raised,
     ' and the Button, Shift, X and Y arguments are
     ' passed to that event.
     RaiseEvent MouseDown(Button, Shift, X, Y)

End Sub


Private Sub UserControl_MouseMove(Button As Integer, _
     Shift As Integer, X As Single, Y As Single)
```

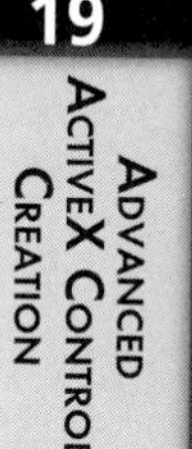

continues

Listing 19.2. continued

```
    ' If UserControl's MouseMove event is triggered,
    ' LightButton's MouseMove event is in turn raised,
    ' and the Button, Shift, X and Y arguments are
    ' passed to that event.
    RaiseEvent MouseMove(Button, Shift, X, Y)

End Sub


Private Sub UserControl_MouseUp(Button As Integer, _
    Shift As Integer, X As Single, Y As Single)

    ' If UserControl's MouseUp event is triggered,
    ' LightButton's MouseUp event is in turn raised,
    ' and the Button, Shift, X and Y arguments are
    ' passed to that event.
    RaiseEvent MouseUp(Button, Shift, X, Y)

End Sub
```

Although the `Click` and `DblClick` events are straightforward, the others require that information obtained when the original event is triggered be passed along when the corresponding control event is raised. This requires declaring the types of arguments for the event in its `Public Event` declaration and listing the arguments in the appropriate `RaiseEvent` command, as you can see in Listings 19.1 and 19.2.

If you want to test the passing of events from constituent controls to the `LightButton` control, here's a simple test. Add two `Label` objects (`Label1` and `Label2`) to the test form of the project started in Chapter 18. Then add the following lines of code to the `LightButton1_MouseMove` event:

```
Label1.Caption = Str$(X)
Label2.Caption = Str$(Y)
```

Now run the test project. When you move the mouse cursor anywhere on the `LightButton` control, its coordinates will be displayed in `Label1` and `Label2` (and, of course, the control will indicate a "selected" state). When you move the cursor off the control, the cursor's coordinates are no longer updated. That's because the `MouseMove` event, which actually originated as `UserControl_MouseMove`, only fires when the cursor is on the control (or, more specifically, when it is on the `UserControl` object). When you're finished with this test, remove the code from the `LightButton1_MouseMove` event and delete the two `Label` objects.

Creating Custom Events

There isn't much difference between using the events of constituent controls and creating events of your own design. You still need to declare the event using a `Public Event` statement just as you did before. And you need to add a `RaiseEvent` statement just like the ones that you added to the constituent controls' event procedures. The only difference is that now you need to decide *where* to put the RaiseEvent statement or statements so that the event will be properly triggered.

The last event that needs to be implemented in LightButton's interface is the StatusChanged event. It is to be triggered whenever a change occurs to the status of the LightButton control. Therefore, the event will be raised when the control becomes selected and when it becomes deselected. This gives the developer using the control the opportunity to take some action when the control's state changes. For instance, he may want to pop up a small help window when the cursor is on the control and then remove it when the control becomes unselected. By using LightButton's StatusChanged event, he can do just that.

To add the StatusChanged event, it first needs to be declared with the Public Event command. Add the following line of code to the rest of the Public Event declarations in LightButton's General Declarations section:

```
Public Event StatusChanged(NewStatus As Integer)
```

This will add the StatusChanged event to the control's interface. The event uses a single argument, which will indicate the control's new status (0 = Not selected, 1 = Selected).

Now, to actually raise the StatusChanged event, change the code in the tmrChkStatus_Timer event to what is shown in Listing 19.3. Pay close attention to the position of the two newly added RaiseEvent commands.

Listing 19.3. The tmrChkStatus_Timer event, with two new lines of code added to raise the control's StatusChanged event at the appropriate times.

```
Private Sub tmrChkStatus_Timer()

    ' This event will fire about 4 times per second,
    ' and is used to see if the control's status
    ' changes from selected ("lighted") to
    ' unselected, and vice versa.

    Dim plonCStat As Long
    Dim plonCurrhWnd As Long

    ' Disable the timer temporarily.
    tmrChkStatus.Enabled = False

    ' Using two Windows API functions, determine the
    ' handle of the window that the cursor is
    ' currently positioned on.
    plonCStat = GetCursorPos&(mpoiCursorPos)
    plonCurrhWnd = WindowFromPoint(mpoiCursorPos.X, mpoiCursorPos.Y)

    If mbooButtonLighted = False Then
        ' If the control is not currently "lighted",
        ' and it matches the handle of the window that
        ' the cursor is on, either light it up (if
        ' ButtonMode = TextOnlyMode) or switch its
```

continues

Listing 19.3. continued

```
        ' background image to the one that indicates
        ' that the button is selected.
        If plonCurrhWnd = UserControl.hWnd Then
            mbooButtonLighted = True
            If mmodButtonMode = TextOnlyMode Then
                UserControl.BackColor = molcSelColor
            Else
                Set UserControl.Picture = mpicSelPicture
            End If
            RaiseEvent StatusChanged(1)
        End If
    Else
        ' If the control is "lit", and it no longer
        ' matches the handle of the window that the
        ' cursor is on, either un-light it (if
        ' ButtonMode = TextOnlyMode) or switch its
        ' background image to the one that indicates
        ' that the button is not selected.
        If plonCurrhWnd <> UserControl.hWnd Then
            mbooButtonLighted = False
            If mmodButtonMode = TextOnlyMode Then
                UserControl.BackColor = molcBackColor
            Else
                Set UserControl.Picture = mpicPicture
            End If
            RaiseEvent StatusChanged(0)
        End If
    End If

    ' Re-enable the timer.
    tmrChkStatus.Enabled = True

End Sub
```

The two `RaiseEvent` commands have been strategically placed to trigger the `StatusChanged` event only when the control's status actually changes. You must be careful not to place a `RaiseEvent` command where it will be constantly triggered—unless, of course, that is your intent. Also, in most cases you will want to handle any special processing *before* raising the event. In Listing 19.3, you can see that the `StatusChanged` event is raised only *after* the appearance of the control has been changed.

When the control changes from an unselected to a selected state, the `RaiseEvent` is called with a 1 as its argument. When the reverse happens and the control's state changes from selected to unselected, `RaiseEvent` uses a 0 as its argument. The value of the argument can be tested by code added to `LightButton`'s `StatusChanged` event to see what the control's new status is.

There is still one more place where a `RaiseEvent` statement should be added. It makes sense that whenever the control's status changes, the `StatusChanged` event should be triggered. But it also stands to reason that the event should also fire whenever the control's status is initialized. The status is initialized (appropriately enough) in `UserControl`'s `Initialize` event, so that's where the last RaiseEvent statement needs to be added. Change UserControl_Initialize as shown in Listing 19.4.

Listing 19.4. The last RaiseEvent command needs to be added to the UserControl_Initialize event, where the control's status is initialized.

```
Private Sub UserControl_Initialize()

    ' When the control initializes, the button is
    ' not "lighted".
    mbooButtonLighted = False

    ' Since the control's status has just been
    ' initialized, the StatusChanged event should
    ' be raised.
    RaiseEvent StatusChanged(0)

    ' Since UserControl's BackColor property will
    ' be changed if the control is "selected", its
    ' initial value must be stored in a temporary
    ' variable.
    molcBackColor = UserControl.BackColor

End Sub
```

The StatusChanged event is initially raised to indicate an unselected state because that is the control's default status.

As you can see, adding events to your controls is simple. When you design your control's interface and determine all the custom events that you would like to include, you may want to keep them in mind when you are working out the logic of your control's code. That way, it will be easier to figure out exactly where and when you should raise the events.

A Few Last Words on Events

It's important that you choose a descriptive name for your custom events. For example, the StatusChanged event name clearly indicates when and why the event is triggered. If you choose cryptic names for your events, developers that use them may not be aware of their exact function. If, for example, the name StatChg were used rather than StatusChanged, would you have known right away what event it was supposed to represent? It's unlikely that you would.

Another little frill that you may want to include in your control is the selection of a default event—the event that will be shown when you double-click an instance of the control in VB's design mode. For example, when you double-click an instance of a CommandButton control, the CommandButton_Click event appears, ready to be edited. This makes sense because that is the event that will most likely be modified for that particular object class.

To make the StatusChanged event the default event for the LightButton control, you'll need to bring up the Procedure Attributes dialog box—the same tool that was used to change the Enabled property's Procedure ID in Chapter 18.

To display the Procedures Attribute dialog box, choose Tools | Procedure Attributes from VB's menu. Make sure that the `StatusChanged` event is selected in the Name box; then click the Advanced button. Click the User Interface Default box so that it is checked; then click OK. The `StatusChanged` event will now be the control's default event.

Adding Methods to the Sample Control

If adding events to a control is easy, then adding methods is even easier. Basically, methods are Public procedures that can be called from outside the control. In this section, we will add two new methods (`Refresh` and `Flash`) to the `LightButton` control.

The `Refresh` Method

Unless your control is of the invisible kind (for example, a variation on the `Timer` object), it is wise to include a `Refresh` method. The `Refresh` method redraws the control whenever requested. Actually, all you need to add to the control's `Refresh` method is a call to `UserControl.Refresh`, so all the work is already done for you!

Add the procedure shown in Listing 19.5 to the `LightButton` control's code.

Listing 19.5. `LightButton`'s `Refresh` method, a public procedure, which consists of a call to `UserControl.Refresh`.

```
Public Sub Refresh()

    UserControl.Refresh

End Sub
```

It doesn't get much easier than that! If your control is of the user-drawn variety, `UserControl.Refresh` will in turn raise `UserControl`'s `Paint` event so that the control is redrawn. If your control uses constituent controls, each control's `Resize` event will be raised by `UserControl.Refresh`. Either way, all bases will be covered, and you don't have to worry about adding complex code to redraw your control.

Adding the `Refresh` method is simple. Adding the `Flash` method takes only marginally more effort.

The `Flash` Method

The `Flash` method is, to be honest, nothing more than a frill added to the `LightButton` control to illustrate the addition of custom methods. It does serve a function, however, by letting the developer "flash" the control (that is, quickly switch it from a selected to an unselected state) a specified number of times. Among other things, the `Flash` method could be used to draw attention to the control.

Like the `Refresh` method, the `Flash` method consists of a single public procedure that is added to the `LightButton` control's code. Use Listing 19.6 to add that procedure.

Listing 19.6. The public procedure that facilitates the `Flash` method.

```
Public Sub Flash(NumTimes As Integer)

     Dim pbooButtonLighted As Boolean
     Dim pintFlashLoop As Integer
     Dim psinOldTimer As Single

     ' If an invalid argument was passed to the
     ' method, exit now.
     If NumTimes <= 0 Then Exit Sub

     pbooButtonLighted = mbooButtonLighted

     For pintFlashLoop = 1 To (NumTimes * 2)
          ' Switch the button's status.
          pbooButtonLighted = Not pbooButtonLighted
          If pbooButtonLighted = True Then
               ' Change the control's background color or
               ' image to reflect a "selected" state.
               If mmodButtonMode = TextOnlyMode Then
                    UserControl.BackColor = molcSelColor
               Else
                    Set UserControl.Picture = mpicSelPicture
               End If
          Else
               ' Change the control's background color or
               ' image to reflect an "unselected" state.
               If mmodButtonMode = TextOnlyMode Then
                    UserControl.BackColor = molcBackColor
               Else
                    Set UserControl.Picture = mpicPicture
               End If
          End If
          ' Wait a short amount of time before changing the
          ' control's status again.
          psinOldTimer = Timer
          Do
               DoEvents
          Loop Until (Timer >= psinOldTimer + 0.5)
     Next pintFlashLoop

End Sub
```


The `Flash` method first checks to make sure that it was not passed an invalid argument. Although anything greater than zero will be considered valid as the code is now, you may want to specify an upper range for the `NumTimes` argument as well. For example, to make sure that the control flashes no more than ten times, change the method's first `If...Then` statement to the following:

```
If NumTimes <= 0 Or NumTimes > 10 Then Exit Sub
```

Of course, you can change the validation process for the `NumTimes` argument to use whatever rules you want.

After the `NumTimes` argument has been tested, the current value of `mbooButtonLighted` (the Boolean variable that keeps track of the control's selected or unselected status) is stored in `pbooButtonLighted`. A `For...Next` loop is then performed twice as many times as indicated by the `NumTimes` argument—one time to select the control and another time to unselect it, although not necessarily in that order.

Every time the loop is executed, the control's status is "flip-flopped," or changed from a selected to an unselected status or vice versa. This is easily accomplished by the following line of code:

```
pbooButtonLighted = Not pbooButtonLighted
```

Because the `pbooButtonLighted` variable is of type Boolean, its value is changed to its opposite whenever this statement is executed. Thus, it changes from True to False, or from False to True.

The same code that was used in `tmrChkStatus`'s `Timer` event is used in the `For...Next` loop to change the control's appearance. But before the next pass through the loop, a short period of time must pass; otherwise, the flashing will happen too quickly. A few lines of code have been added to pause for half a second—though you can change the amount of time from .5 second to whatever you think is appropriate. A `DoEvents` statement is executed again and again until the allotted amount of time has passed because we wouldn't want to tie up the system while the control is busy flashing.

When the `For...Next` loop is finished, the control's status will have been switched back to whatever it was before the `Flash` method was called because the loop always executes an even number of times.

So there you have it—two new methods added to the `LightButton` control, accomplished using nothing more than two `Public` procedures. The control's interface can now be called complete. However, you can still add a few more things to the `LightButton` control that will help to round it out, as you'll see in the next section.

Odds and Ends

When you've completed all the design and coding for your control, there are a few odds and ends that you can take care of to give it more of a professional look. For example, you may want to add an About box to your control to relay copyright or author information, especially if you plan on distributing the control to other developers.

Other frills that you can add to your control include assigning it a toolbox bitmap to replace the standard `UserControl` icon. Believe me, if you create several ActiveX controls in Visual Basic and add them to the toolbox, you'll be unable to tell one from the other if they all use the same icon!

You can also group your control's properties together by type (appearance, font, and so on) and add short descriptions of their use. Doing so is easy and requires absolutely no coding, but it may be helpful to any developers who use your control—including yourself!

None of these odds and ends are really necessary, and you do not need to add them to your controls if you don't want to. But if you plan on distributing your controls to other developers, your goal should be to make them as easy to use as possible. Taking a few minutes to add these last few polishes will help advance you toward that goal.

Adding an About Box

Adding an About box to your control allows you to convey important information about the control to the developer using it. It can show the control's copyright notice, an email address for support, or even your company's logo. You can put whatever you want in your control's About box.

The first step in adding an About box is to add a form to the control's project. Make sure that the control is selected in the Project Explorer window; then choose Project|Add Form from VB's menu. You'll then see a blank form—which is, in actuality, going to be your About box.

You are free to change the form however you want. You can add objects from the toolbox to the form, change its properties, or even assign a bitmap image to the form's `Picture` property to display a custom-created graphic as the About box. Just remember that anything you add to the form will increase the size of your control—an important consideration when implementing controls on the Internet. My advice is to keep it as simple as possible while still conveying all the information desired.

For the `LightButton` control's About box, I came up with the layout shown in Figure 19.1. The entire thing consists of four `Label` objects (`lblAbout1`, `lblAbout2`, `lblAbout3`, and `lblAbout4`) and one `CommandButton` object (`cmdDone`).

FIGURE 19.1.
The `LightButton` *control's About box.*

I also changed several of the form's properties to get rid of its title bar. The properties that I changed are listed in Table 19.2.

Table 19.2. The About box form's properties that were changed.

Property	*Value*
BackColor	&H00FFFFFF&
BorderStyle	3 - Fixed Dialog
ControlBox	False
MaxButton	False
MinButton	False
Moveable	False

Adding an About box does require a little coding, but it's not much. To begin with, a public procedure needs to be added to `LightButton`'s code (*not* the form's code) to actually display the About box when it is called for. Listing 19.7 shows such a procedure.

Listing 19.7. A public procedure that will display the About box form when requested. The procedure should be added to the `LightButton` control's code, not to the form's code.

```
Public Sub DisplayAboutBox()

     frmAbout.Show vbModal

End Sub
```

In Listing 19.7, the procedure is named `DisplayAboutBox`, but you can call it whatever you like.

Next, we need to hide the form (and clear it out of memory) when its Done button is clicked. The code to do that goes into the `Click` event of the Form's `CommandButton` object. I called the `CommandButton` on my AboutBox `cmdDone`, which is reflected in Listing 19.8.

Listing 19.8. The About box form is unloaded and removed from memory when its Done button is clicked.

```
Private Sub cmdDone_Click()

     Unload frmAbout
     Set frmAbout = Nothing

End Sub
```

The only thing left to do is to use our old friend, the Procedure Attributes dialog box, to assign the `DisplayAboutBox` procedure to the correct Procedure ID. To bring up the dialog box, make sure that the `LightButton` control is displayed in the Design window and that the `UserControl` object is selected. Then choose Tools | Procedure Attributes from the menu.

Select the `DisplayAboutBox` procedure (or whatever you called it) in the Name box; then click the Advanced button. Select AboutBox in the Procedure ID box; then click OK. That's all there is to it!

Before testing the About box, be sure to close the form's Design and Code windows. Also close the `LightButton` control's Design and Code windows, if necessary. Then display the test form by double-clicking its name in the Project Explorer window.

Click once on the instance of the `LightButton` control so that its properties are displayed in the Properties window. Click the About property; then click on the ... button. The About box that you created should pop up. When you're finished viewing it, click the "Done" button and the box will disappear.

Your About box forms do not need to be like the one shown here, with only a few lines of text and a Done button. You can get as creative as you want.

Property Grouping and Descriptions

The Procedure Attributes dialog box is also used to group properties into general categories and add short descriptions. You can put your control's properties into one of the default categories (Appearance, Behavior, Data, DDE, Font, List, Misc, Position, Scale, and Text), or you can add your own category.

Admittedly, the process of describing properties and grouping them into categories can be tedious. Thankfully, it doesn't take too long—and it is worth the effort.

To call up the Procedure Attributes dialog box, first make sure that the control's Code or Design window is displayed. Then choose Tools | Procedure Attributes from VB's menu. Click the dialog box's Advanced button to display the advanced options.

Select a property in the Name box. To add a description to the selected property, simply type in as much or as little text as you want in the Description box.

To select a category for the property, choose one from the Property Category drop-down list box. If you want to add the property to a category other than those provided in the list box, type in the category name in the Property Category text box. When you've finished making changes to the property, click the Apply button.

To maintain consistency, it's a good idea to group properties into the categories that they would be assigned to in other controls. A list of the standard properties often included in the interfaces of custom controls is shown in Table 19.3, along with the category that they are usually assigned to. You can use this table as a guide for grouping properties into categories.

Table 19.3. The categories that the standard properties are usually assigned to.

Property	*Category*
`BackColor`	Appearance
`BorderStyle`	Appearance
`Caption`	Appearance
`DragIcon`	Behavior
`DragMode`	Behavior
`Enabled`	Behavior
`Font`	Font
`ForeColor`	Appearance
`Height`	Location
`HelpContextID`	Misc
`Index`	Misc
`Left`	Location
`Name`	Misc
`Picture`	Appearance
`TabIndex`	Behavior
`TabStop`	Behavior
`Tag`	Misc
`ToolTipText`	Misc
`Top`	Location
`Visible`	Behavior
`WhatsThisHelpID`	Misc
`Width`	Location

Group the `SelPicture` and `SelColor` properties into the Appearance category, and the `ButtonMode` property into the Misc category. If you're not sure which group a property should belong to, put it in the Miscellaneous (Misc) category.

After the properties have been assigned categories, it's time to give them descriptions. The good news is that many of your control's properties will already have default descriptions assigned to them. This includes any properties provided by the control's container or `Ambient` object. Only the properties that have been added to the control with the `Property Get`/`Property Let` procedures will require descriptions. For the `LightButton` control, this leaves only the `BackColor`, `BorderStyle`, `ButtonMode`, `Caption`, `Font`, `ForeColor`, `Picture`, `SelColor`, and `SelPicture` properties left to describe.

If you want to skip the assigning of descriptions to all the remaining properties, that's okay. But I suggest that you add descriptions for the `BackColor`, `ButtonMode`, `Picture`, `SelColor`, and `SelPicture` properties. Some of those properties are unique to the `LightButton` control, and their uses may not be readily transparent. Also, the `BackColor` and `Picture` properties are used slightly differently than they are in other controls. This should be pointed out to whomever uses the `LightButton` control.

Table 19.4 lists the descriptions that I used for the remaining properties. You can use the same ones, or you can come up with your own descriptions.

Table 19.4. The descriptions given to each of `LightButton`'s properties.

Property	*Description*
`BackColor`	Specifies the control's background color. Only used if the `ButtonMode` property is set to `TextOnlyMode (0)`.
`BorderStyle`	Specifies the type of border the control should have (0=None, 1=Fixed Single).
`ButtonMode`	Determines how the control will function. `TextOnlyMode (0)` uses the background color to indicate the control's state, and `ImageMode (1)` uses images to indicate state.
`Caption`	The text that is displayed on the control. Only used if the `ButtonMode` property is set to `TextOnlyMode (0)`.
`Font`	The font used to display the control's caption.
`ForeColor`	The color of the control's caption. Only used if the `ButtonMode` property is set to `TextOnlyMode (0)`.
`Picture`	The image displayed when the control is in an unselected state. Only used if the `ButtonMode` property is set to `ImageMode (1)`.
`SelColor`	The background color used to indicate that the control is in a selected state. Only used if the `ButtonMode` property is set to `TextOnlyMode (0)`.
`SelPicture`	The image displayed when the control is in a selected state. Only used if the `ButtonMode` property is set to `ImageMode (1)`.

You may notice when you're adding the property descriptions that the control's events and methods are also listed in the Name box. You can add descriptions to them, too. If you do, they will be displayed in the Object Browser when the control's class is viewed. If you have added any events or methods unique to your control, I suggest that you assign short descriptions to them.

Because the `StatusChanged` event and the `Flash` method are unique to the `LightButton` control, I've added descriptions to them, too. The descriptions I used are listed in Table 19.5.

Table 19.5. Descriptions for the `LightButton` control's `StatusChanged` event and `Flash` method.

Event/Method	*Description*
`StatusChanged`	Triggered if the control's status changes from selected to unselected, or vice versa.
`Flash`	Used to "flash" the control (switch it from a selected to an unselected state) a specified number of times.

Now that descriptions have been added to the `LightButton` control's properties, events, and methods, and the properties have been grouped into the proper categories, there's only one thing left to do until the control can be finally considered done, and that's to assign it a unique toolbox icon.

Changing the Control's Toolbox Icon

This is one of the easiest things you can do when designing controls, but it does take some graphics skills. Create a bitmap graphic 16 pixels wide by 15 pixels high and then assign that image to `UserControl`'s `ToolboxBitmap` property.

You don't have to use a bitmap that is 16 × 15 pixels. But if you use a larger image, it will be scaled down to the correct size, and it may look odd after being scaled. Your best bet is to create an image that is exactly 16 × 15 pixels so that you don't get any surprises.

On the CD-ROM, you'll find a bitmap graphic for the `LightButton` control called `LB.BMP`. If you want to use that graphic to assign to the `ToolboxBitmap` property, feel free to do so. Or, you can create your own bitmap. You don't need a super-powerful graphics package to create the image. Windows 95's Paint program will do just fine.

Summary

This chapter put the finishing touches on the `LightButton` control. If you've come this far, you should know how to create your own controls from start to finish. You should also have all the code necessary for a fully functioning ActiveX control that, once compiled, can be added to your Visual Basic applications or Web pages.

In the next chapter, you'll compile the control into an `.OCX` file. Finally, you'll add the control to a Web page and try it in Internet Explorer.

Trying Out the Control

IN THIS CHAPTER

Now that the LightButton control has been designed and coded, it needs to be compiled into an .OCX file. After the .OCX file has been created, the control can be used in Visual Basic applications, on World Wide Web pages, or in ActiveX documents. It can even be permanently added to VB5's toolbox if you want.

In this chapter, the LightButton control will be compiled and used first in a Visual Basic application and then on a Web page. It will be "put through its paces" and tested under many different circumstances.

Compiling the Control

When you compile an ActiveX control into an .OCX file using Visual Basic 5, you are presented with a substantial number of options. You can choose to optimize the control for speed or size, or to favor the Pentium Pro processor. You can also add documentation directly to the .OCX file, which will be displayed when the control is viewed with the Object Browser. The following section documents the options available to you when compiling controls.

Creating an .OCX File

You may think that you need to remove the test form from the LightButton control project group before the control can be compiled, but that isn't necessary. The control project (Project1) is completely separate from the test project (Project2), and it can be compiled separately.

Before attempting to compile the control, you have to make sure that it is not in run mode. To do so, double-click on LightButton's name in the Project Explorer window. You should then see the control's Design window, indicating that the control is in design mode.

To compile the control, choose File | Make TestControl1.ocx from the menu. You should see a Make Project dialog box like the one shown in Figure 20.1.

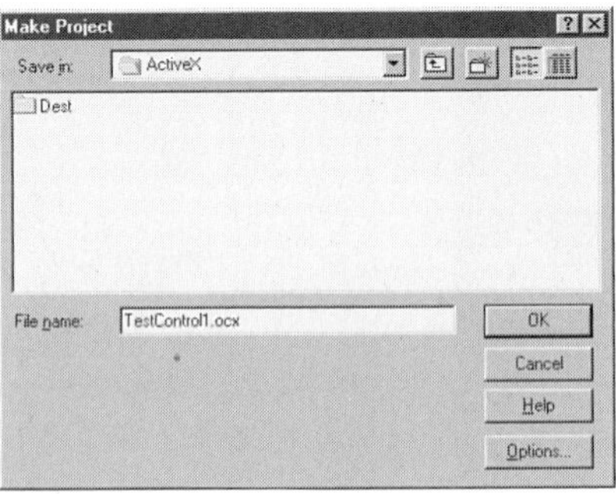

FIGURE 20.1.
The Make Project dialog box.

The default name given to the .OCX file is the same as the name of the control's project (in this case, TestControl1). It would make more sense to use the name of the control instead, so change the value in the File name text box from TestControl1 to LightButton.

If you click OK at this point, the control will be compiled into native code and optimized for speed rather than size. Instead of compiling right now, click the Options button. You'll be given the opportunity to change the compiler options and add some documentation to the control. Figure 20.2 shows the Project Properties dialog box that appears after clicking the Options button.

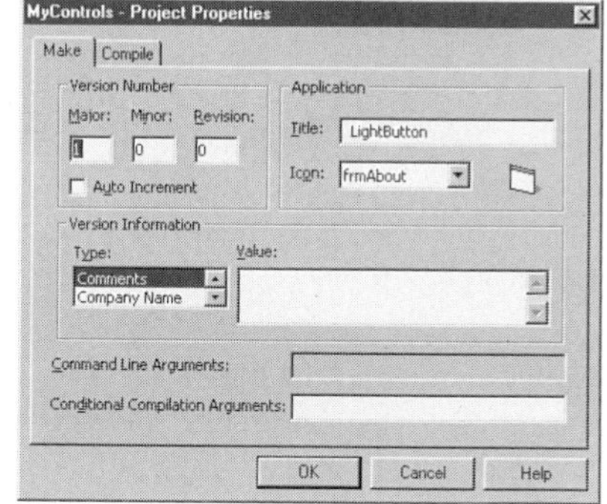

FIGURE 20.2.
The Project Properties dialog box.

The Project Properties dialog box has two tabs, Make and Compile. The Make tab lets you add documentation and a version number to the control. The Compile tab lets you set the compiler's optimization options, as well as whether the control will be compiled into native code or P-code.

On the Make tab, you can change the control's three-part version number. Because this is the first compilation of the `LightButton` control, it will receive the default version number of 1.0.0 (which breaks down as Major.Minor.Revision). If you check the Auto Increment box, the Revision number will be automatically incremented by one every time the control is compiled. The Revision number indicates only slight changes made to a control. If substantial changes are made, you'll need to manually change the Major or Minor version numbers and reset the Revision number to zero. I suggest changing the Major version number any time you make changes to the control's interface.

The Make tab also gives you the opportunity to add short descriptions for version-related information such as Company Name, File Description, Legal Copyright, Legal Trademarks, Product Name, and general Comments. For example, you might use the Comments description to document any changes that have been made to the control since its last Revision. This information will be displayed when a user views the executable file's properties in Windows (by right-clicking the program icon and selecting Properties). Because adding descriptions is not necessary, you can skip it and leave them all blank.

The Application section of the Make tab is not really used when compiling controls and applies mostly to application compilation, allowing a title and an icon to be assigned to the application.

The Command Line Arguments box also applies to application compilation, letting you pass command line arguments to an application when it is being run from within Visual Basic. Because controls cannot run by themselves and must be placed on a container of some sort, they obviously cannot accept command line arguments. Leave the Command Line Arguments box empty.

The Conditional Compilation Arguments box allows you to specify certain constant declarations that determine how certain parts of the control (or application) will be compiled. This is only used if there are `#If...Then` and `#End If` statements in the control or application's code. The compiler processes the `#If...Then/#End If` statements to determine what code it should include in its compilation. For example, imagine that you designed a control that consisted of several `TextBox` objects, each with a descriptive caption below it. If you wanted the captions to be available in three different languages (English, Spanish, and French), you can use conditional compilation to specify the language desired at compile time. By setting a constant in the Conditional Compilation Arguments box, a set of `#If...Then/#End If` statements could selectively assign different string values to the captions based on the value of the constant. Using the conditional compilation method in this way, you can create an English, Spanish, or French version of the control without having to change its code each time it is compiled.

Because the `LightButton` control does not require the use of conditional compilation, the Conditional Compilation Arguments box can be left empty.

The Project Properties dialog box's Compile tab gives you the capability to select either a P-code (pseudo-code) or native code compilation. P-code is not as fast as native code, but it doesn't take as long to compile. When compiling your controls for distribution, always select the native code option.

When compiling a control into native code, you are given your choice of optimization methods. You can choose to have the compiler optimize the control's code for fastest running speed or smallest `.OCX` size. If the control is going to be used primarily on systems that use Pentium Pro processors, you can choose to have the compiler factor that in also when optimizing the control's code.

When compiling controls that are going to be distributed via the Internet, it would make sense to have the compiler optimize the control to be the smallest size possible. Because Internet-based controls need to be downloaded by users before they can be used on a Web page, the smaller the control the better. But you may want to try optimizing the control for size and then for speed and compare the size of the resulting `.OCX` files. Often, the size difference between the two is only a few thousand bytes, which translates to only a few extra seconds of download time. In cases where the size of a speed-optimized `.OCX` file is only marginally larger than a size-optimized `.OCX`, I suggest optimizing for speed. As a general rule, you'll find that there is less difference in file size between speed- and size-optimized `.OCX` files for controls that don't have a lot of code. More sophisticated and complex controls that require a lot of code may benefit from size-optimization.

Table 20.1 shows the file sizes of three `.OCX` files compiled for the `LightButton` control. Each was compiled using a different optimization method. As you can see, there is only a 1,536 byte difference in size between the speed- and size-optimized `.OCX` files. The `LightButton` control's code is not very long or complex, so the difference is only marginal. Even when using no optimization at all, the difference is slight. For this compilation of the `LightButton` control, select the Optimize for Fast Code option.

Table 20.1. `.OCX` file sizes for the `LightButton` control, each compiled using a different optimization method.

Optimization Method	*File Size*
Speed	35,328 bytes
Size	33,792 bytes
No optimization	37,888 bytes

NOTE

If you compile the `LightButton` control using the different optimization options listed in Table 20.1, you may get slightly larger or smaller `.OCX` file sizes.

No matter which optimization method you choose (speed, size, or none), you can also specify that the compiled code favor the Pentium Pro processor. Native code compiled with this option will still run on other processors, but it may be somewhat sluggish. When compiling controls for distribution on the Internet, never select the Favor Pentium Pro option. After all, you have no idea what kind of processors your Internet users will have in their systems, and it's a sure bet that many won't have a Pentium Pro.

If you have CodeView or a similar debugger, you can also choose to have the compiler generate debugging information by checking the Create Symbolic Debug Info option. In addition to the executable file normally output by the compiler, you'll also get a `.PDB` file that contains the debugging information. Utilities such as CodeView are used primarily for complex projects that require advanced debugging features over and above those that are offered by Visual Basic. We won't be doing any CodeView debugging, so make sure that this option is unchecked for now.

The Project Properties dialog box's Compile tab also lets you set a DLL base address (where in memory the compiled program loads) and change some advanced optimization switches. We won't use either of those options when compiling the `LightButton` control or any of the other controls in this book.

You should now have the compiler ready to compile version 1.0.0 of the `LightButton` control in native code, optimized for speed. Click OK to exit the Project Properties dialog box; then click the Make Project box's OK button to compile the control. The status of the compilation process will be displayed on Visual Basic's toolbar.

At this point, you should have a file called `LIGHTBUTTON.OCX` in whichever directory you stored the control's project files.

Using the Control in Visual Basic

To use the `LightButton` control in your Visual Basic programs, you need only add it to the Toolbox using the Components option from VB's Project menu. Simply find the name of the control in the list, make sure that its check box is checked, and then click OK. The control will be added to the toolbox, and you can use it just like you would use any other ActiveX control.

Using the Control on a Web Page

There are two ways to include your ActiveX controls on Web pages. The first way is to use the `.OCX` file directly and add the control to the Web page using the HTML `<OBJECT>` tag (examples of how to use the `<OBJECT>` tag are shown in Chapter 17, "Creating and Using ActiveX Controls"). The other way is to package your control as a compressed `.CAB` file and add the `.CAB` to the Web page using the `<OBJECT>` tag. The latter method is preferred because it verifies that the system on which the control will be used already has any necessary support files, such as the Visual Basic runtime file. If any support files are missing, the `.CAB` file includes pointers to locations on the Internet where they can be found and downloaded. The whole process is transparent to the user.

Another benefit of using `.CAB` files is that they are compressed. This won't make much difference if your control is small and simple but can be beneficial when dealing with larger, more complex controls.

The good news is that `.CAB` files are easy to create using the Setup Wizard included with Visual Basic. The rest of this chapter includes detailed instructions for using the Setup Wizard to create distributable `.CAB` files for your ActiveX controls.

Using the Setup Wizard

The best way to package your ActiveX controls for delivery to users via the World Wide Web is using `.CAB` files. `.CAB` (short for "CABinet") files are Microsoft's way of bundling together and compressing program and data files so that they can be installed on a user's machine. Almost all the install files on the Windows 95 CD-ROM are in `.CAB` format.

`.CAB` files can also be used to send and install ActiveX controls through the Web. Because they are compressed, download time is shorter. They can also contain any support files that the control requires. When a `.CAB` file is transferred to a user's system, it automatically uncompresses and installs itself—all of which is done seamlessly, with little or no intervention required on the part of the user.

Thankfully, Microsoft provides an easy way to create Internet-specific `.CAB` files by way of the Application Setup Wizard. This is the same wizard that is used to generate quick and easy setup programs for Visual Basic applications. In VB5, it has been enhanced with an option for creating Internet Download Setup files.

The Setup Wizard is one of the applications in the VB5 program group. Run it now to create a `.CAB` file for the `LightButton` control.

When the Setup Wizard starts, you may see an Introduction page. If you do, click the Next button to proceed to the next page.

The Setup Wizard: Select Project and Options

The first page (after the Introduction) is the Select Project and Options page, which should look similar to Figure 20.3.

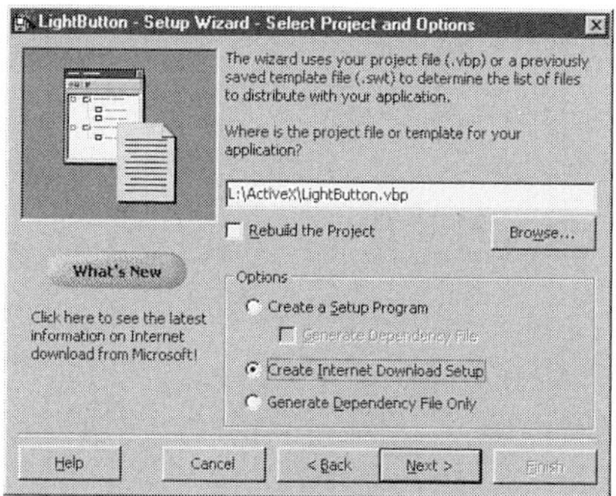

FIGURE 20.3.
The Application Setup Wizard's Select Project and Options page.

On this page, you need to specify the location of the ActiveX control for which you want to create the `.CAB` file. But first, make sure that the Create Internet Download Setup option is checked and that the Rebuild the Project option is unchecked.

If you click the What's New icon, you'll be sent to one of Microsoft's Web pages. If you want to find out the latest on the exciting world of Internet file downloading, give it a click. Just make sure that you have established a connection to the Internet first, if necessary.

On with the setup! Either type in the location and name of the `LIGHTBUTTON.OCX` file in the text box at the top of the Select Project page or click the Browse button to search for it. When you're finished and the correct file location is displayed, click the Next button to go to the next step.

The Setup Wizard: Internet Distribution Location

The Internet Distribution Location page (see Figure 20.4) is a little misleading. Supposedly, it allows you to indicate where on your system the control's `.CAB` file should be placed. This information will be included in a mock HTML file that is also created by the Setup Wizard.

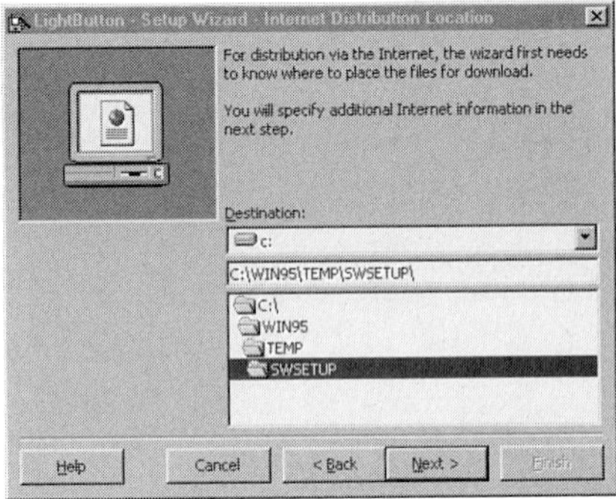

FIGURE 20.4.
The Setup Wizard's Internet Distribution Location page.

However, unless your system functions as a Web server or is somehow directly connected to a Web server, you will have to transfer the .CAB file to the proper location on your Web server after it has been created. For many, Internet access is accomplished via a dial-up modem connection. The Web server is often a completely different entity than the system on which we develop Web pages or ActiveX controls.

If you do have direct access to the directory from which you want your users to download the control's .CAB file, then by all means specify that directory here. But if you must transfer the .CAB file to the Web server later, I suggest creating a temporary subdirectory below the directory that contains the control's .OCX file (the Setup Wizard won't let you use the same directory, so don't even try it). I usually create a subdirectory called "Dist"—short for "Distribution."

After you specify the directory that will contain the control's .CAB files (as well as a few other files), click the Next button to go to the next page.

The Setup Wizard: Internet Package

Unfortunately, all VB5-created ActiveX controls require one or more runtime support files. If the user of your ActiveX control does not have the necessary support files, they must be downloaded and installed on the user's system prior to receiving your control. However, it is likely that the user will already have the required support files.

The Setup Wizard's Internet Package page (see Figure 20.5) allows you to specify the Internet location of the support files. You can either choose a location on your own system (again, which is only valid if your system functions as a Web server), or you can specify that Microsoft's Web site be used. The latter is the best option because you can be sure that Microsoft will have the most up-to-date versions of the support files.

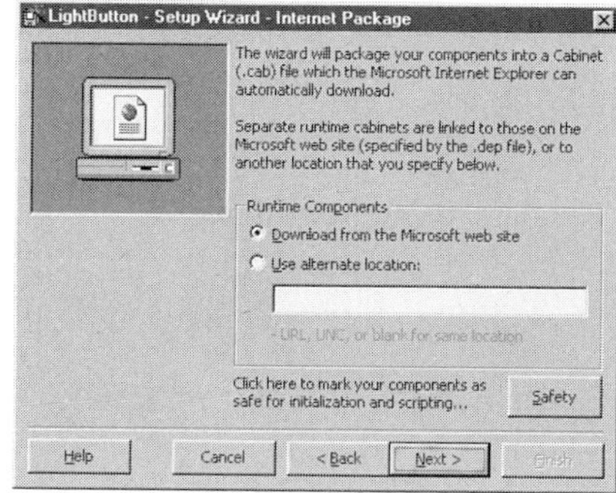

FIGURE 20.5.
The Setup Wizard's Internet Package page.

Remember, the specification of the support files' location is included just in case the user does not already have the necessary files. This is a good thing because the support files are real whoppers! The Visual Basic 5 VM `.DLL` (required to run VB5-built controls) is itself more than 1 MB in size. If, by chance, the user does not have the files needed—or has an older version of any of those files—they will be automatically downloaded before your control is installed. So, theoretically, your 15 KB control could require that several megabytes of support files be downloaded first. Just consider it the price you have to pay for being a pioneer.

Also included on the Internet Package page is an option for marking your control as safe for initialization and safe for scripting. Click the Safety button to display the Safety dialog box (see Figure 20.6).

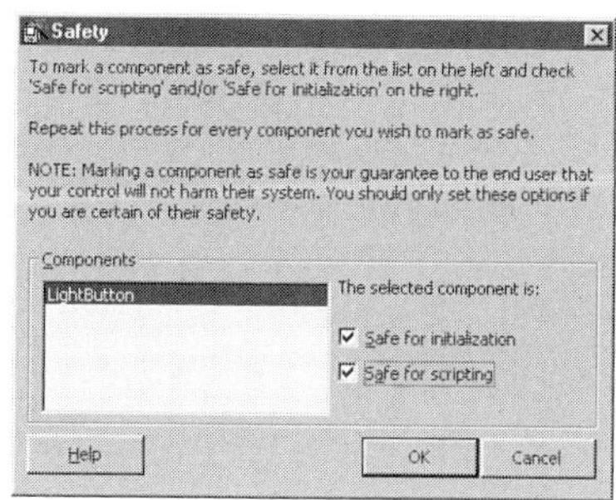

FIGURE 20.6.
The Setup Wizard's Safety dialog box, which allows a control to be marked as safe for initialization or safe for scripting.

As you can imagine, using ActiveX controls poses certain safety concerns. ActiveX controls can be powerful—in some ways, *too* powerful. It wouldn't be very difficult at all to create a control that completely wipes out a user's hard drive (but please don't do it!).

Of course, controls may not be purposely malicious. A bug can sometimes cause serious consequences, depending on the operation being performed. If the proper precautions aren't taken to ensure that a control is "bullet-proof," it could easily crash a user's system—or worse.

Because ActiveX controls can be potential troublemakers, there are several levels of "guarantees" that can be assigned to a control. The simplest of these is the safe for initialization and safe for scripting guarantee. If you decide to check either of these safety options, you are personally guaranteeing that your control is, on a basic level, "safe."

By declaring a control as safe for scripting, you are essentially stating that the control cannot do anything wrong no matter what VBScript or JavaScript code is used to implement it. The focus here is not so much on minor problems or bugs as it is on major, system-corrupting problems (though any bugs or loose ends are considered unacceptable). If, for example, your control allows VBScript or JavaScript to indirectly manipulate the user's System Registry in some way via the setting of the control's properties, you must be absolutely certain that it won't accidentally corrupt that file by altering critical Registry entries. Doing so would cause serious harm to the user's system, even to the point of requiring a complete reinstall of Windows 95. If you mark your control as safe for scripting and it does cause harm to a user's system, you can be held legally responsible.

Because VBScript or JavaScript code can also directly call a control's methods (and sometimes pass arguments to them), you must also be sure that the method's code will not cause problems. If an invalid argument is passed to the method, will the control do unpredicatable things? If so, then it cannot be declared safe for scripting.

Safe for initialization is similar to safe for scripting. Marking a control as safe for initialization guarantees that no matter which property settings (or combination of settings) are used when the control is initialized, they will not cause problems. This is one reason that it is so important to use `Property Let`/`Property Set` procedures to validate property values.

You may be wondering why you should even bother to declare a control as safe for scripting or safe for initialization. Why incur possible legal liabilities just to put a control on a Web page? Think of it this way: If you were accessing a Web page that uses ActiveX controls that were *not* marked as safe for scripting or safe for initialization, would you choose to download and use them, knowing full well that they could cause serious damage to your system?

Under most circumstances, the issue of declaring a control as "safe" is straightforward. Most ActiveX controls don't manipulate System Registry entries or perform other possibly detrimental operations. In the case of simple controls like `LightButton`, not much can really go wrong. Although it's entirely possible that a bug could occur or an invalid property setting could cause the control to crash, it's unlikely that any serious harm would be the result. This is not to say that bugs are okay or acceptable, but personally I'll take a bug that crashes Internet Explorer over a corrupt System Registry any day.

The decision of marking the `LightButton` control as safe for scripting and safe for initialization is entirely up to you. Either way, click OK when you're finished with the Safety dialog box to return to the Internet Package page. Then click the Next button to proceed to the next page.

The Setup Wizard: ActiveX Server Components

If a control requires any additional ActiveX components to run properly, they can be specified on the ActiveX Server Components page (see Figure 20.7). The `LightButton` control does not require any additional components, so click the Next button to skip this step.

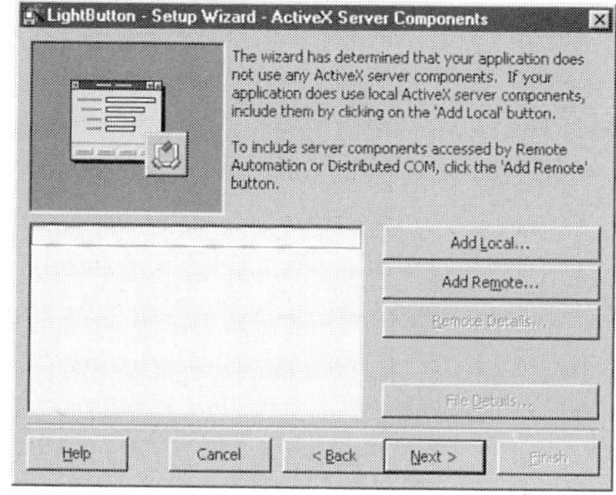

FIGURE 20.7.
The Application Setup Wizard's ActiveX Server Components page allows you to specify any additional ActiveX components required to use the control.

The Setup Wizard: File Summary

Before the Setup Wizard finishes, it will provide you with a list that shows all the files that will be included in the `.CAB` file on the File Summary page (see Figure 20.8). You may find a few surprises here because ActiveX controls created in Visual Basic often require support files that you may not have been aware of. As you can see in Figure 20.8, the `LightButton .CAB` file will include a total of five files: `MSVBVM50.DLL`, `ASYCFILT.DLL`, `LIGHTBUTTON.OCX`, `LIGHTBUTTON.VBL`, and `MSSTKPRP.DLL`.

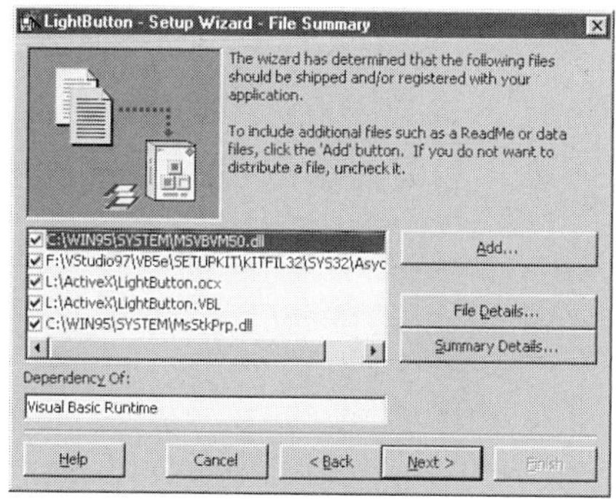

FIGURE 20.8.
The Setup Wizard's File Summary page, which lists all the files that will be included in the `.CAB` file.

If you're not sure what role each file plays, you can click its name to see what component it is a dependency of. For example, if you clicked the filenames for the `LightButton` control's `.CAB` file, you would find that the `MSVBVM50.DLL` and `ASYCFILT.DLL` files are Visual Basic runtime files, and that the `LIGHTBUTTON.VBL` and `MSSTKPRP.DLL` files are both dependencies of `LIGHTBUTTON.OCX`.

If you want even more information about any of the files, make sure that the file's name is highlighted; then click the File Details button. A window will pop up that shows the file's date and time stamp, version number, copyright, size, description, and other details.

Note that not all the files shown on the File Summary page will actually be included in the .CAB file. The .CAB file includes an .INF file that details the components of the .CAB as well as the Internet locations of those components. The MSVBVM50.DLL runtime file, for example, will not be included in the .CAB but will have a pointer to its location in the .CAB file's .INF file. When the .CAB file is installed, the .INF file is accessed to determine the name of each component file and its version. The user's system is checked to see whether it already contains the same or a newer version of the file. If it does, then the file does not need to be transferred. However, if the user's system does not have the required file, or if the file it does have is an older version, a new copy of the file will be downloaded based on the Internet location specified in the .INF file. This process is completely transparent to the user.

The .INF file is nothing more than a text file, and it can be viewed with any text browser, such as Notepad. A copy of the file will be placed in the SUPPORT subdirectory off of the directory you specified earlier as the location in which the Setup Wizard should place the .CAB file.

Before going on to the next page of the Setup Wizard, click the Summary Details button. You'll see a window like the one shown in Figure 20.9 that tells you the total bytes of the .CAB file's contents. As you can see, it shows the size of the LIGHTBUTTON.CAB file components as totaling just under 2 MB. This is misleading, however, because not all the components will actually be included in the .CAB file. The actual size of the compressed LIGHTBUTTON.CAB file is only about 20 KB.

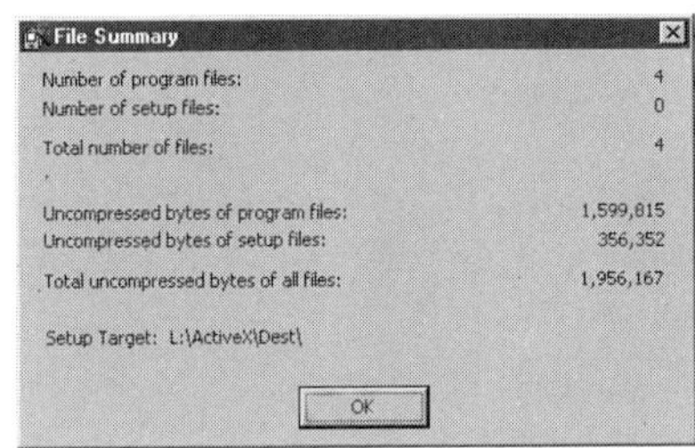

FIGURE 20.9.
The File Summary dialog box provides useful file size information.

When you're finished viewing the file summary, click OK. Then click the Next button to proceed to the next page in the setup.

The Setup Wizard: Finished!

At this point, the Setup Wizard will actually create the .CAB file. It may take a while, especially if you had specified earlier that the .OCX file be recompiled. When it's finished, you'll see the Finished! page (see Figure 20.10).

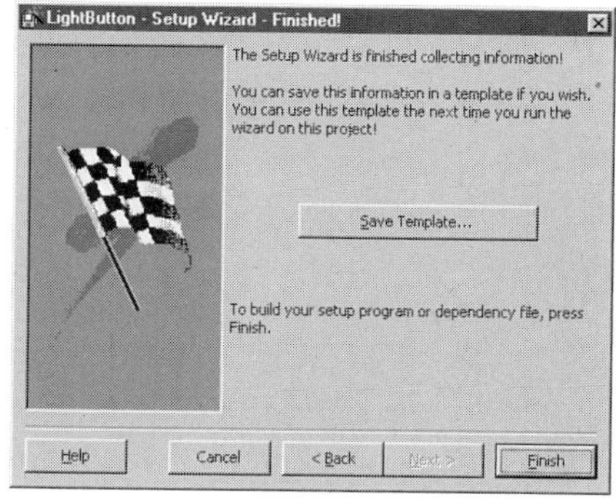

FIGURE 20.10.
The Setup Wizard's Finished! page—a welcome sight.

If you think you'll need to create a `.CAB` file for your project again, you may want to create a template file by clicking the Save Template button. The template file will contain all the options you had selected during your session with the Setup Wizard, saving you from having to repeat the process for the same control.

Now that you're finished, click the Finish button. You'll see one final page (see Figure 20.11) that confirms that everything is done and your `.CAB` file has been created successfully.

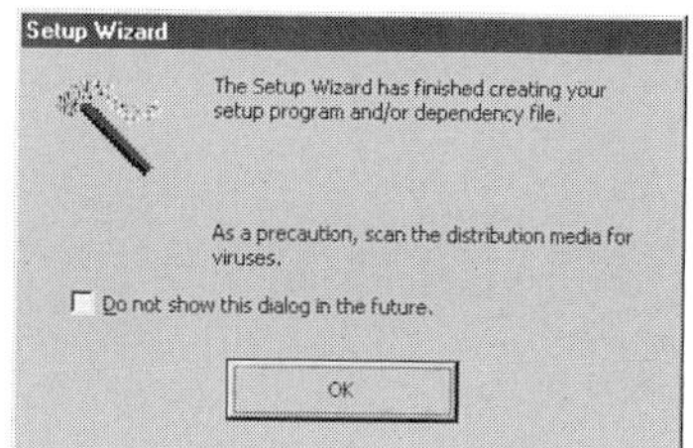

FIGURE 20.11.
The Setup Wizard indicates that it is completely done.

Trying Out the .CAB File

If you want to use the newly created `.CAB` file on a Web page, you can use the `<OBJECT>` tag to insert the `.CAB` file object. Chapter 22, "ActiveX Project Management," discusses how to use the `<OBJECT>` tag and the ActiveX Control Pad program to insert ActiveX controls into Web pages.

If you're anxious to see a quick sample of how the `.CAB` file is used on a Web page, you're in luck. The Setup Wizard creates a down-and-dirty Web page that includes the `.CAB` file. It can be found in the same directory that you specified as the location for the new `.CAB` file, and its name will be the same as the `.CAB` file with an extension of `.HTM` rather than `.CAB`. For example, the Setup Wizard should have created a `LIGHTBUTTON.HTM` file for you during the sample session detailed in this chapter.

Figure 20.12 shows the sample Web page in Internet Explorer. There's not much to it, but it does include a working sample of the `LIGHTBUTTON.OCX` control, and that's the most important.

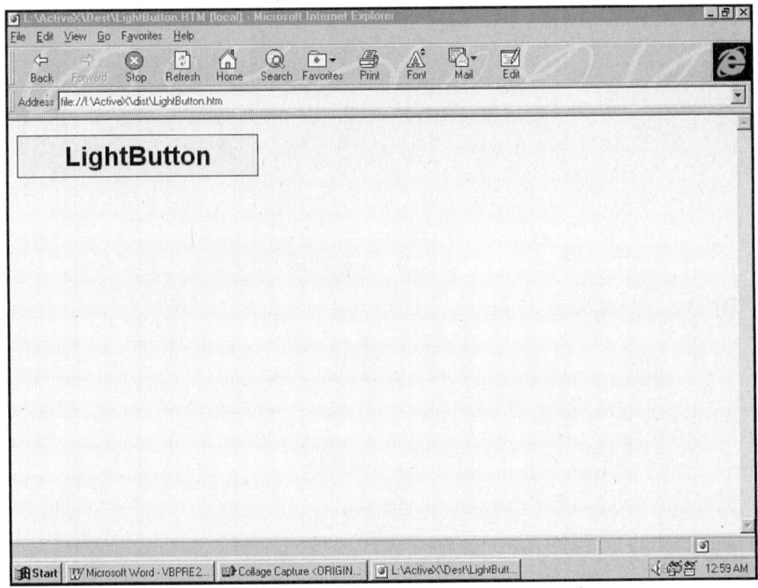

FIGURE 20.12.
The light button's ready to go on your Web page.

Summary

After an ActiveX control project has been compiled into an `.OCX` file, it can be used in Visual Basic programs or on Web pages. The best way to include ActiveX controls is by compressing them into `.CAB` files, which can also include any support files required by the control. The Application Setup Wizard that comes with Visual Basic provides an easy way to create `.CAB` files.

CHAPTER 21

ActiveX Scripting with Visual Basic Script

IN THIS CHAPTER

The creation of Web scripting languages has redirected the work of processing data to the desktop PC. Web scripting was formerly confined to server-side processing. Common Gateway Interface (CGI) scripts, also sometimes referred to as CGI programs, were simple text files that included source code that could be translated and processed on a server.

CGI scripts are stored on the server, triggered when the browser file is loaded, and processed on the server. Output is ported back to the Web browser on the desktop, courtesy of the server.

The CGI method of processing data is still valuable. In many cases, a CGI script may be more appropriate because the designer of the interaction may require server processing. CGI scripts are no longer the only choice. CGI languages such as Perl are losing ground to a newer method of processing, *ActiveX scripting*. This processing method requires embedding ActiveX scripting directly into the client-side HTML files. By using standard HTML tags (text commands), the browser locates a server's HTML Web page file and the client computer executes script written directly into the HTML file. The browser no longer has to wait for the server to process the CGI script and return its output to the browser. Instead, the browser merely loads the internal script as the page loads, binding the internal objects, and executes the user interaction (clicks, keystrokes, and mouse moves) with simple scripting calls.

The function calls aren't traditional. You don't place a line of code beginning with `Go Sub`. Instead, you write the HTML manually or with a scripting wizard utility. The resulting code includes a reference to the function or subroutine call.

Understanding Scripting

ActiveX scripting is based on a general language dataset that includes JavaScript programming language (JScript in Internet Explorer) and Visual Basic Script (VBScript). JavaScript, based on the Java language that has come into vogue in the last few years, preceded the advent of the full ActiveX experience.

Microsoft knew that many programmers would embrace Visual Basic scripting because of the popularity of VB development programs it had sold and continued to support in the marketplace. But because Netscape's Navigator browser already supports client/server applications that use Java and JavaScript, Microsoft engineered Internet Explorer to accommodate both Java and VBScript. That way, Microsoft promoted Internet Explorer as a more compatible browser—one of the pivotal points that led users to scramble for compatibility. Everyone knew VBScript and Java would both be used on the Internet.

When Internet Explorer was introduced, an ActiveX layout control (`.ALX`) would appear in the new browser's window, ready for user interaction. The file, embedded by reference in an HTML file, wouldn't appear in the browser window when viewed with Netscape Navigator. Netscape does not natively support ActiveX controls, but it can be extended with a plug-in from NCompass Labs that adds support for ActiveX controls and VBScript.

Using Control Pad

ActiveX Control Pad and scripting are primarily used today for creating lightweight OLE-style controls on pages suitable for a PC or the Internet. Control Pad's features allow you to design an independent window (group of controls) by using its visual interface.

In this window, you place and program events for numerous ActiveX control objects. This programmed window (the window itself becomes an ActiveX control) is an *HTML Layout* control. A reference to each HTML Layout is typed in an HTML file (`.HTM` or `.HTML`). When the HTML file is loaded in Internet Explorer, each HTML Layout referenced in the file appears as a rectangle with no borders within the Web page defined by the HTML code. With an HTML Layout, users can't view the code unless they have access to a stored copy of the `.ALX` file.

ActiveX Control Pad features an HTML Layout tool, which is technically an ActiveX control container for other controls (the tool creates an HTML Layout window). The HTML Layout editing tool is launched by choosing File | New HTML Layout.

Control Pad isn't required to create ActiveX content in a Web page, but it makes it much easier. To insert a single control without an HTML file, you launch Control Pad, choose Edit | Insert ActiveX Control, and select the control from a list box. This method requires manual code scripting in the HTML editor window or in another HTML editor.

Programming in VBScript

VBScript, a subset of the Visual Basic language, is intended to make programming easier without permitting access to low-level Windows functions, including access to the user's API.

VBScript is designed to work within the Internet Explorer environment. This chapter provides some important points and examples. For a comprehensive listing reference for VBScript, go to `HTTP://WWW.MICROSOFT.COM/VBSCRIPT/US/DOWNLOAD/VBSDOC.EXE`.

The default data type for VBScript is `Variant`. To convert the `Variant` data type to a type that matches your object's data type, use the following conversions:

- Use `Asc(`*`string`*`)` to return the ASCII code for the first letter of a string expression.
- Use `CBool(`*`expression`*`)` to return the value of a Boolean expression (`True` or `False`). If zero is the expression, `False` is returned. If other than zero, `True` is returned.
- Use `CByte(`*`expression`*`)` to force byte arithmetic in cases where currency, single-precision, double-precision, or integer arithmetic normally would occur.
- Use `CCur(`*`expression`*`)` to return the value of the expression converted into currency.
- Use `CDate(`*`expression`*`)` to return the value of the expression converted into a `Date` datatype. You can use time literals and numbers that fall within the range of acceptable dates. When a number is converted to a date, the whole number portion is

converted to a date. Any fractional part of the number is converted to a time of day, starting at midnight.

- Use `CDbl(expression)` to return a `double` datatype.
- Use `Chr(expression)` to return the character string equivalent to the ASCII value (0–31) of a non-printable character. `Chr(10)` would return a linefeed, for example.
- Use `CInt(expression)` to return an integer value and force integer arithmetic where double-precision or other type arithmetic would otherwise be used.
- `CLng(expression)` converts the expression to the `Long` datatype.
- Use `CSng(expression)` to return a `Single` number datatype.
- `CStr(expression)` converts a variant expression, such as a number, to a `String` datatype, which can be printed or displayed.
- The `Hex(expression)` function converts a number to the hexadecimal equivalent for the number. If a whole number isn't used, the number is rounded to the nearest whole number before evaluation.
- Use `Oct(expression)` to return the octal value of an expression.

For more information on the use or definitions of the various datatypes, download the `VBSDOC.EXE` file from `HTTP://WWW.MICROSOFT.COM/VBSCRIPT/`. This self-extracting file includes a comprehensive collection of HTML files that will be installed on launching `VBSDOC.EXE`. Both 16- and 32-bit versions of the documentation are available at the Web site. Click the Free Downloads link and look for the VBScript Documentation icon.

Using Loops

`Do...Loops` are useful tools and similar to `For...Next` loops. You don't necessarily have to know how many loops are going to be needed. In the following example, the variable `y` is assigned to 32:

```
y = 15
x = 1
Do
    x = x + 1
    ComboBox1.AddItem CStr(x)
Loop Until (x = y)
```

To propagate a ComboBox with this script, create a ComboBox and then a CommandButton. Program the `Click` event for the CommandButton to execute this script.

`If...Then...Else` statements are used for conditional testing. In the following example, if CommandButton5 is clicked, you get a warning that tells you the `y` counter is at 5. The message appears two more times as the counter increments to 7.

```
<SCRIPT LANGUAGE="VBScript">
<!--
Sub CommandButton5_Click()

y = 1
```

```
For i = 1 to 7
    y = y + 1
    If y > 5 Then
        MsgBox "We're at 5", 16, "Warning"
    End if
Next i

End Sub
-->
</SCRIPT>
```

`Elseif` syntax allows two tests within the `If` loop. This reduces the code by one line each time it's used because `Elseif` doesn't have to be terminated with an `End if` each time the test is performed.

```
If y > 5 Then
    MsgBox "We're at 5", 16, "Warning"
ElseIf y > 7
    MsgBox "We're at 7", 16, "Warning"
End if
```

`exit` is a VBScript statement that forces a subroutine or function to terminate execution. It can be used with an `If` statement within a loop to terminate the loop before the count reaches the specified number of loops. In the following example, a loop is used to propagate a ComboBox, but the box goes only from 1 to 30 because of the `exit` statement:

```
For I = 1 To 99
    y = I + 1
    ComboBox1.AddItem CStr(y)
    If y = 30 Then Exit Sub

Next I
```

Most programmers are familiar with `For...Next` loops. These loops can be nested. The syntax is very basic. The following example would increment the variable `c` 5,000 times.

```
c = 1

For x = 1 To 500
    For y = 1 To 10
        c = c + 1
    Next y
Next x
```

To step the incrementation by units not equal to 1, use the following syntax:

```
For x = 1 To 500 Step .2
```

`Select Case` is used as an alternative structure for `If...End If` statements. It's used primarily when several options are available. ActiveX OptionButtons use this type of structure within their groups:

```
x = InputBox ("Enter a number between 1 and 4")

Select Case x
    Case 1
        MsgBox "You selected 1."
```

```
    Case 2
        MsgBox "You selected 2."
    Case 3
        MsgBox "You selected 3."
    Case 4
        MsgBox "You selected 4."
End Select
```

CAUTION

The use of variables within the `Select Case` selection isn't supported. Use literals.

`While...Wend` is like the `For...Next` loops with an important distinction: The `While...Wend` (While End) structure keeps looping as long as a specified condition remains true. For example, if you want the loop to continue until a counter reaches 1,000, try this:

```
x = 1

While x < 1000
    x = x + 1
    MsgBox x
Wend
```

Using Functions

`Abs()` is a rather rare function that returns a variable of the same type, but if the value was previously negative, it becomes positive. For example, if `i` equals –10, `Abs(i)` returns the value 10 and `MsgBox Abs(i)` prints 10.

`Alert()` is a VBScript function similar to `MsgBox` and can be substituted for `MsgBox` in the code.

The `Cos()`function gives the cosine of an angle in radians:

```
x = Cos(.8)
returns 0.9999025240093
```

The `DateSerial()` function converts year, month, day, and time into a serial number.

The `DateValue()` function converts a `String` expression into a date/time serial number.

The `Day()` function extracts the day of the month from a serial number created by the previous functions or by the `Now` function, which gets the current computer date/time serial number.

`Exp()` is a mathematical function that calculates the exponential value of a variable or a literal number:

```
Exp (3)
```

`Function` is a type of statement used to return something to the location from which the function was called. In the following example, zero would be returned when the `Validate` function is called, if the input box called TextBox1 contains no data. This in turn would generate a message box informing users of the omission.

```
Sub CommandButton1_Click()

If Validate(TextBox1.Value) <> 0 Then
    Submit
    Exit SubEnd If
MsgBox "You forgot to enter data in TextBox1.", 16, "Warning"

End Sub

Function Validate(y)

Set MyForm = Document.MainForm
If MyForm.y.Value = "" Then x = 0
End FunctionHex()
```

`Hex()` is a function that returns the hexadecimal value of a numeric value, but the value returned is a `text` string data type. The following example would generate the hex equivalent, `F`, in a message box when run in Internet Explorer:

```
<SCRIPT LANGUAGE="VBScript">
<!--
Sub CommandButton3_Click()

n = Hex(15)
MsgBox n, 16, "ActiveX Testing Hex 15"

End Sub
-->
</SCRIPT>
```

The `Hour()` function tells users the hour based on a serial number that VBScript generates when functions such as `Now` are used. The hour is returned in military value, with 0 equivalent to 12 a.m. and 23 equivalent to 11 p.m. For example,

```
n = Hour(Cdbl(Now))
MsgBox n, 16, "ActiveX Testing Hex 15"
```

`InputBox()` is a VBScript function that launches a pop-up box and pauses for user input to be assigned to a variable. The following example launches the box, prompts users for input with the text message, and waits for users to confirm that the input is complete. Then the input is stored in variable `m`.

```
m = InputBox ("Please enter your age.")
```

`Instr()` isolates a part of a string (parsing) and returns the number corresponding to the position where the first character of the string was encountered (if it's encountered). In the following examples, the returned value in the message box is 10. The first example begins with the default starting position, 1, because a starting position isn't specified. The second example starts at 3.

```
x = Instr("ABCDEFGHIJKLMNO", "J")
MsgBox x, 16, "VBScript Testing"
```

Or

```
x = Instr(3, "ABCDEFGHIJKLMNO", "J")
MsgBox x, 16, "VBScript Testing"
```

TIP

You might want to convert a character string to lowercase before using `InStr()` so that case matching won't deter your efforts. See the `Lcase()` function in the following paragraphs.

`Int()` rounds off a number that contains a fraction, deleting the fraction portion of the number. To round to the nearest whole number, use `Int(N+.5)`. Then if the fraction is .5 or higher, the next whole number is reached and the proper value is returned. If the fraction is less than .5, the fraction will be dropped.

The `IsArray()`, `IsDate()`, `IsEmpty()`, `IsError()`, `IsNumeric()`, and `IsObject()` functions are used to test the data type of a variable. Generally, these functions are used with `If...Then` statements:

```
y = InputBox ("Enter a Date")
If IsDate(y) Then
    MsgBox CStr(y) & "is the date."
End if
```

`LBound()` reveals the lower boundary of an array's index. Normal use of `LBound()` in VBScript returns zero because all arrays will begin with 0:

```
Dim y(50)

x = LBound(y)
MsgBox y
```

`Lcase()` forces lowercase character strings. The following example returns a lowercase string `Howdy Do...` in a message box:

```
x = "Howdy Do..."
y = Lcase(x)
MsgBox y
```

`Left()` in VBScript strips the left side of the string beginning with the character identified by number in the `Left()` function statement. To strip the word *Howdy* from `Howdy Do...`, use this example:

```
x = "Howdy Do..."
y = Left(x,6)
MsgBox y
```

`Len()` in VBScript measures the length of string. The following returns the number 17 and stores it in the `x` variable:

```
y = "JUST ABOUT ENOUGH"
x = Len(y)
MsgBox x
```

`Log()` is a math function that returns the natural logarithm of a number. In the following example, the result 3.0910245335832 is displayed in a message box:

```
x = Log(22)
MsgBox x
```

`Ltrim()` removes leading spaces from a string being evaluated. The following example generates the string `Howdy, howdy!` in a message box:

```
x = "    Howdy, howdy!"
y = Ltrim(x)
MsgBox y
```

`Mid()` extracts a portion of text from a string. You must specify the starting position from which to begin gathering data and enter the number corresponding to how many digits you want to extract, plus 1. In this example, `I'm Howdy` is extracted from the text string:

```
x = "Howdy, I'm Howdy Do. How Do You Do"
y = Mid(x, 7, 10)
MsgBox y
```

`Minute()` is used primarily to extract the current time in minutes, derived from using the `Now` function:

```
MsgBox Minute(Now)
```

`Month()` provides the month of the year and is generally used to provide an accurate date from January 1, 100 to December 31, 9999. It's used primarily with the `Now` function to return the current month identified by the PC's time/date clock:

```
MsgBox Month(Now)
```

`Now` is a function that translates an internal PC clock's serial number into a `string` expression equivalent to the current `Month()`, `Day()`, `Year()`, `Hour()`, `Minute()`, and `Second()`. See the discussions on these functions for examples of use.

`Oct()` is a math function that converts a numeral into a string representation of the octal value of the numeral. It's not used much today.

`Right()` strips (returns) a portion of text from the end of a string expression. This code displays `bored` in a message box:

```
x = "Labored"
y = Right(x, 5)
MsgBox y
```

`Rtrim()` is used to remove trailing spaces from a string expression. See `Ltrim()` for syntax.

`Second()` is a function that returns the value in seconds for the current time when used with the `Now` statement:

```
x = Second(Now)
```

`Sgn()` evaluates a numeric variable to determine whether it's positive, negative, or zero. It returns the numeral 1 if the number is positive, 0 if it's zero, and –1 if it's negative.

`Sin()` is a function that evaluates a numeric expression and returns the sine of an angle expressed in radians. Its syntax is similar to `Atn()`, `Cos()`, and `Tan()`. For example,

```
x = Sin(.8)
```

`Sqr()` is a function that provides the square root of any positive number:

```
x = 9
y = Sqr(9)
```

`StrComp()` is a function that compares string expressions to determine which is alphabetically lower (A <B <C <D, and so on). For example,

```
x = StrComp(Y,Z)
If x < 0 Then     MsgBox "Y is less than Z"
End If
If x = 0 Then
    MsgBox "Y is equal to Z"
End If
If x > 0 Then
    MsgBox "Y is greater than Z"
End If
```

`String()` is a simple function used to generate a number of instances of a specific character. Specify how many, and then the character enclosed in quotes:

```
x = String(35,"/")
MsgBox x
```

`Tan()` returns the tangent of an angle expressed in radians:

```
x = 5.2
y = Tan(x)
```

`Time()` is used to call the same information as the `time` command in DOS. You can assign the time to a variable as follows:

```
x = Time
```

`TimeSerial()` converts a time expressed in hours, minutes, and seconds to a unique serial number equivalent to one of 86,400 seconds in a day:

```
x = TimeSerial(11,30,59)
MsgBox x
```

`TimeValue()` performs the same conversion as `TimeSerial`, but you input the time as a string value:

```
x = TimeValue("11:30:59")
MsgBox x
```

`Trim()` is a function that removes any blank spaces from either end of a string. Refer to `Ltrim()` and `Rtrim()`.

`VarType()` is a function used to determine the variable subtype of a variable.

`Weekday()` is a function that returns a numeral in the range 1–7, which equates with a day of the week. Sunday is assigned 1 in the range; Saturday is 7.

```
x = Weekday(Now)
If x = 1 Then
    MsgBox "Sunday"
End If
```

`Year()` is a function that reveals the year, based on a unique serial number for a specific point in time. `Year()` is commonly used with the `Now` function:

```
x = Year(Now)
MsgBox x
```

To try out some of the code examples and variations of these code examples in ActiveX Control Pad, you can load the `arrayit.alx` file and click the command buttons. Use the Script Wizard and compare the contents of the `Click` events programmed for the command buttons. The file isn't particularly a pretty one, but it was used to test many of the code samples in the text examples listed here.

Using Miscellaneous Statements

Arrays are variables clustered into theoretical rows and columns. In this dimension statement, `x` would equate to column one and `12` would create 12 rows within the column:

```
Dim x(12)
```

This creates 12 placeholders in the column to which data can be assigned. The same could be created by assigning the space with 12 lines of code that look like this:

```
x(1) = ""
x(2) = ""
```

`Clear` is a VBScript method that resets the `Err` object. Use `Err.Clear` to clear the error so debugging won't repeat the appropriate error message.

Concatenation is achieved by using the ampersand. To get the words *Jack And Jill*, use this code snippet:

```
j = "Jack " & "And" & "Jill"
MsgBox j
```

`Erase` is a statement used to work one of two ways. The statement will reset all cells in a static array to zero, if they're numeric and blank for variables.

The `Erase` statement completely removes a dynamic array. Here's an example of how an `Erase` statement is used:

```
Dim x(2)
x(1) = 100
x(2) = 200
MsgBox CStr(x(1)) & " " & CStr (x(2))
Erase x
MsgBox CStr(x(1)) & " " & CStr (x(2))
```

Place the code in a CommandButton's `Click` event and load it in Explorer. Click the CommandButton, and the first message box contains the `X(1)` and `X(2)` array values. The second message box displays nothing because the array was erased.

`Err` is a VBScript object that uses an error code system to help developers locate an error's origin at runtime. `Err` can report an internal scripting error or an OLE object's runtime error. Use of `Err` evaluates `Err` for a non-zero value. If the value is zero, no error was encountered in the code.

TIP

Use `Err` in an `If` statement to trap the error and assist users in resolving the problem.

In the following example, users are asked to input a number for the day of the week when they want you to call. The first `If` statement checks the value entered for the day of the week to make sure that it's not 8 or greater. The second `If` statement uses the `cInt()` function and `Err` to check to see whether a character other than a number was entered. The day of the week is represented by the InputBox variable `q`.

```
<SCRIPT LANGUAGE="VBScript">
<!--
Sub CommandButton8_Click()

On Error Resume Next
q = InputBox ("Please enter a number for the day of the week for us to call.")
If q => 8 Then
    MsgBox "Please try again. The numeral you selected for day was " & q
    Exit Sub
End if
If q <= 0 Then
    MsgBox "Please try again. The value you selected for day was " & q
    Exit Sub
End if
q = CInt(q)
If Err Then
    MsgBox "Please try again. The value you selected for day was " & q
End if
```

```
End Sub
-->
</SCRIPT>
```

`Imp` is a logical operator that compares two expressions to determine their relationship. Technically, the `Imp` operator performs a bitwise comparison of identically positioned bits in two numeric expressions and sets the corresponding bit. See the *VBScript Reference* documentation for tables that indicate the outcome of using this operator.

`MsgBox x` displays a pop-up box with a message designed by the programmer and waits for the user to click OK.

The `TypeOf...Is` statement evaluates the object to determine what action to perform on the object:

```
If TypeOf Object1 Is ComboBox Then
    Object1.AddItem "Next Item . . ."
End if
```

`Let` is a statement that historically has been used to assign a value to a variable. It has been retained to retain functionality with older code segments:

```
Let MyName = "Tex Reed"
```

`MOD` provides you with the remainder of a numeric division. This is useful in generating hexadecimal conversion programs and the like. This code example returns the number 4 in a message box:

```
x = 40 MOD 12
MsgBox x
```

`Not` is a Boolean operator that lets you reverse the logic of a test. For example, `x = Not False` would return `True` to the `x` variable. With bit logic, 0 would become 1, or 1 would become 0.

`OnLoad` is a VBScript event that equates to when a file is loaded in a program. The `OnLoad` code runs in a subroutine during initial loading and without any user interaction.

`Option Explicit`, which forces dimensioning of variables, is a command used at the top of a script on a separate command line.

Parentheses are used to avoid confusion with the precedence of operators such as mathematical multiplication and addition. On a line that adds 3 to 5 and then multiplies by 10, the result would be 53 if no parentheses are used. The following example returns 35 to variable `x`. The items in the parentheses are evaluated first:

```
x = (5 + 3) * 10
```

You can invoke property changes with VBScript in connection with ActiveX controls. Many examples are used in the previous section of the chapter. ActiveX control properties are manipulated with event procedures. The following line changes the text in TextBox1 during runtime:

```
TextBox1.Value = "This is the new text."
```

Procedures are subroutines and functions. See the discussion on functions earlier in the section "Using Functions." Many functions are built into VBScript. They're addressed by their command names.

`Raise` is a method useful for simulating an error and testing the interaction when an error is encountered:

```
Err.Raise 35
```

`Randomize` is a statement used to allow the script to provide truly random numbers each time it runs. Each time the script is parsed (refreshed or loaded), a new and unique series of random numbers is available. Use `Randomize` on a separate line as the first command in the script.

`ReDim` allocates space to temporarily hold an array during a procedure's executions. Use between `Sub...End Sub` or between `Function...End Function`.

`Rem` is used to create a remark on a line in the script. Everything on the current line following `Rem` will be ignored.

`Rnd` is used to generate random numbers. Specify the range 1 to 75 with the first code line; specify a range of 0 to 75 with the second code line:

```
x = Int(Rnd * 75 + 1)
y = Int(Rnd * 75)
```

The `Set` statement is used to assign an object a variable name. By using `Dim` to assign the variable and then `Set`, you can shorten the object name and reduce script typing. For example, you could continue to assign property changes with less typing in this code, which changes the CommandButton's `BackColor` property to red and displays a message box:

```
Dim x
Set x = CommandButton15
x.BackColor = 255
MsgBox "Do you like red?"
```

`UBound()` returns the upper boundary value of an array's index. Refer to `LBound()` for syntax.

`UCase()` forces all the characters of a string to be uppercase:

```
x = "HOWDY, HOWDY"
y = UCase(x)
MsgBox y
```

`Xor` is an operator used in encryption. You can use it with letters and numbers other than zeros:

```
Letter1 = "A"
Letter2 = "B"
Key1 = "N"
Key2 = "N"
x = Asc(Letter1) Xor Asc(Key1)
y = Asc(Letter2) Xor Asc(Key2)
```

```
x = Chr(x)
y = Chr(y)
MsgBox x & y
```

To decrypt the example, substitute the values in the message box for A and B in the code example. Run the script again. The letters toggle back to their original values.

Summary

In this chapter, you learned how ActiveX scripting languages are different from CGI scripts, because the work is done on the client computer and doesn't rely on the bandwidth speed restrictions to process the interactive events being programmed. You also learned why VBScript was created and explored most of the commonly used loops, functions, and statements and their syntax. The simple examples can be easily programmed and tested in HTML files.

CHAPTER 22

ActiveX Project Management

IN THIS CHAPTER

Visual Basic's use of project files for organizing an application is an efficient way to prepare for packaging and distributing a final executable program, prototyping an Internet-enabled application, or creating a user control. Think of a project file as a collection of files that contain the data necessary to carry out the functionality of the executable program, control, or control group being programmed. Most file handling is done behind the scenes; you, as the programmer, don't have to pick apart the files themselves.

Using a Structured Project Approach

Start each new project, even if you're building a small ActiveX control, with a checklist for creation. This will be your wish list because all programmers who complete a project *wish* they had made more decisions *before* the programming rather than *during* the programming. Planning saves literally hours of fighting a renegade program. Poorly planned programs lead to hours of debugging to remedy data type mismatches, invalid object references, calls to nonexistent methods, misspellings of variable names, reuse of the same common variable names, confusion regarding variables and constants, and so on.

Study the list before preparing the application for distribution to help determine whether the program should be optimized for performance or for file size. This optimization is occasionally necessary with programs that intensively use algorithms or are large in terms of file size. Preparing this list as a first step also helps you focus on the consistent use of conventional name assignments for variables, constants, objects, forms, and so on. One easy way to achieve consistency in your programming is by assigning prefixes to variable and object names, as discussed in Chapter 44, "Object and Variable Naming Conventions."

All items on this wish list are factors you eventually have to study, analyze, or at least think about. In other words, you have to generate all the names on the list, write all the procedures, and so on. By first tackling the issues on paper (or, more conveniently, in a typed text file), you have a handy reference list to build from and a focused goal to achieve. This list doesn't need to be perfect; it requires only notation-style entries that you'll understand later in the process.

For example, an entry on the list might read *Input for company name,* `strCompName`*, check for null validation (*`NulChk`*), prompt Enter Company Name:*. In this example, you would need a line of code that uses an input box to gather company name data, assigns the value to a string variable named `strCompName`, and then calls a procedure that tests to make sure that something is entered in the input box when the user clicks OK.

NOTE

The term `NulChk` is simply the name of the validation procedure that performs this check for a null value. Validation routines are frequently required to make sure that the program segment can access all the data input required to perform its task.

It's difficult to imagine each instance of when you'll need a variable for counting, for example. By having a list, however, you can compare the new variable name you plan to use with other items on the list. That way, you can create a unique assignment for a variable name and compare the associated purpose of the variable with items on the list. The comparison can be helpful because if the purpose of the item is similar to another purpose on the list, you probably can write the code snippet and reuse it in another part of the program (perhaps with a simple modification to the variable name and code comments, if necessary).

Your wish list should be designed to accommodate user needs. It's beneficial to encourage users (or the supervisor of a group of users) to help define exactly what the program must do to achieve basic functionality before you start building. Incorporate all functionality into your list so that subsequent embellishment of the program is limited to improving existing functionality and appearance. This can be done by using notes about what users want and placing a check mark next to items as they're added to your programming wish list.

When developing the visual interface and before proceeding with difficult parts of the code, get some feedback from a user, supervisor, or colleague regarding the appearance and planned events for the objects in the program that users will interact with.

If you didn't plan your last application from a checklist, think of the last application you personally worked on and imagine how fast you could have completed the work if you had had such a list. Also, think about the list in terms of group development. If everyone in a group developing an application has a similar list, much of the initial confusion and wasted conversation about which party is doing what can be eliminated. The list will outline the appropriate responsibilities. Developers working on one part of the program can share code snippets that need only minor modifications for use by other programmers working on other parts of the project. The list will help programmers know whom to coordinate with.

The following list is to be taken as a general guideline or template for creation of your wish list. Modify the list items to suit your unique application and personal programming style. If your project includes any of the items mentioned, make sure that you document where you can easily find them:

1. A list of visual objects (user controls) that allow users to manipulate, organize, locate, and view the necessary data:
   - Visual controls for the input of data.
   - Visual controls for user interaction to manipulate the data.
   - Visual controls for arranging data output.
   - Visual controls for displaying data or images as output.
   - Visual ActiveX controls—generally a *group of* visual controls—that can be reused in the program or other programs. (These are referred to as *user controls* in VB.)
   - Visual messages to users containing output, instructions, message notifications, alerts, warnings, and so on.

2. A simple flow chart showing the outcome of each step in the input-output cycle to be used in the program. This may require numerous pages of simple sketches. For example, each looping routine with a test (`If...Then`) would be shown on the chart as a box containing the name of the test and two arrows indicating whether the expression evaluates as true or false. After the arrows are the next steps taken by the program, depending on the outcome of the test.
3. A hierarchy list of the classes of objects to be used in the project (thorough detail in the creation of classes reduces the length and complexity of a program):
   - Name and purpose of each class
   - Name and purpose of members of the classes
   - Subclasses of the class, if applicable
4. Actions that will be activated on input of data:
   - Dimensioning (declaring) of variables and data arrays. Keep notes regarding variable scope: Will they be global variables accessible from all modules, module-level public variables available to a specific module, or procedure-level variables that are created and terminated with each call to the procedure?
   - Declaration of array variables. Sometimes, especially with two-dimensional arrays (three dimensions and beyond are rarely used), making a simple sketch of rows and columns helps keep a visual representation in mind regarding how the data will be arranged. Some people have a knack for understanding rows and columns, but others might benefit from placing sample data on an Excel worksheet page or a Microsoft Access table to mimic the arrays to be used. If calculations based on data in specific locations in the array are required, this spreadsheet approach can be helpful, especially if the logic to be used with the array isn't easily understood.
   - Assignment of data to named variables. Special attention to naming variables with respect to the scope and specific data types that will be used is required here. For example, use `gstrCusName` as a global variable name for the input from a text box that will accept a user's name (`gstr` denotes the global scope and string data type associated with the variable). Use `intCountA` as the variable name for a counter in a procedure that uses integers to increment and decrement (`int` denotes that the data type Integer is associated with the variable, and the absence of a scope prefix indicates that the variable is procedure level). Use `vntXsites` as the variable name for an item that will be a string value containing numbers (`vnt` denotes the data type Variant). See Chapter 44.
   - Purpose and name of all validation routines to be used to check the integrity or validity of the data. Use notes such as *Check for null characters in* `strFirstName` *field,* `Private Sub CheckForNull()` or *Check for alpha in numeric* `strTelPhone` *input field,* `Private Sub CheckForNum()`.

5. A list of data types for each object or control variable to be used. This listing requires logical (conventional) naming to keep variable types organized, as noted earlier:
   - Property data types (Boolean, Integer, String, and so on)
   - Developer's hidden variable types (Integer, long, string, values used for comparisons, counters, control name condensations [name shortcuts], and so on)
6. A list of methods to be used for data manipulation:
   - Functions that return (pass) data values and calls that receive the data.
   - Subroutine procedures (branches) that manipulate data and return to the next line of code during program execution. These should be listed separately so that optimization considerations are easier to evaluate before distribution.
   - Counting routines.
   - Sorting routines.
   - Routines for creating concatenations or parsing of values.
7. A property value list:
   - Name, purpose, and scope of property value retrievals (`Property Get` statements)
   - Name, purpose, and scope of property value declarations (`Property Let` statements)
   - Name and purpose of property value groups (Property Bags and Property Pages to be created)

Using Containers in Your Program

You need a separate section of the wish list to top off the project with logical names for the major parts of the program (this part of the list can be created before or after the individual items listed in the previous section):

1. *Project modules*—The name, filename, and purpose of particular projects (`.VBP` files). Keep the projects concise in terms of function. Include the existing project modules you'll be reusing from a previous program at the top of the list. (If you're reusing a project, give it a unique name and filename immediately to prevent overwriting the existing project.) Evaluate the existing (reused) projects from the standpoint of removing extraneous portions first; then check for potential variable name conflicts by comparing with your planned list of variable names. The next step requires you to organize the modules as follows:
   - Assign unique names to your forms and MDI child window forms. Make sure that you give them unique filenames immediately to avoid overwriting your existing forms. Modify them for use in your project.
   - Assign unique names for your control modules. Give any existing control project a unique filename immediately after loading the project to avoid overwriting a control's file or installed registration data (OCX).

2. *For project groups*—Assign a unique group name to be used for the project group, if used. Use `group` or `grp` as part of the filename to avoid confusing groups with the individual projects.

When the list of notes about the programming to be performed is completed, review it for any confusing variable names that might be similar. If there are any, give them unique names. Review the list to see whether it addresses the predetermined needed user functionality.

Before starting Visual Basic, create a directory (or directories) to store the project files, forms, controls, and control groups. Usually, this is a single directory, unless a group of developers is working on the project. Multiple directories can be useful if the project is significant in size because it might be desirable—on encountering significant problems—to start over with a new approach and delete an entire directory of files that are no longer needed.

Another reason for using subdirectories involves the naming of the forms, user controls, and project files. If you want to change a filename, you might need to change every name in the subdirectory. Deleting or renaming these files will be more difficult to achieve if several controls, projects, and forms all appear in a single directory. Remember, before testing and debugging the program, you can create a new comprehensive directory containing all files and place copies of all parts from the various subdirectories in the comprehensive directory. This creates original file backups during the debugging work. When a program change is made, save the changes to this comprehensive directory and also to the particular subdirectory where the repaired file should reside.

As you open existing projects in VB5, remember to save the project immediately under a new filename in a different subdirectory to avoid overwriting the existing file. The same goes for user controls. It's imperative that a user control doesn't have the same OCX file created twice because duplication can lead to confusion. If the user control will be used as is with no modifications, there's no reason to re-create the OCX.

CAUTION

When creating an OCX file with the same filename as one previously used (overwriting an OCX), it's usually necessary to terminate Internet Explorer first because it can interfere with updating the OCX. Even though the current browser address and the current page loaded don't directly use the existing OCX, the browser apparently retains a link to the OCX. This access by IE prevents the old OCX with the same name from being overwritten and generates an error.

It's also a good idea to terminate ActiveX Control Pad before re-creating the OCX (if Control Pad's toolbox contains the custom user control associated with the OCX). The old tool in Control Pad must be removed, and the new OCX custom tool must be added before the user control can be drawn in Control Pad. Any HTML layouts using the old (previous) OCX will no longer be valid. The script associated with the HTML layout is still valid, but the user control must be redrawn in the HTML Layout Editor.

At this juncture, you have all the tools needed to begin designing the application. The organization work is done. When you design a project, Visual Basic is so easy to use that it facilitates programming of complex interfaces. To take advantage of the ease of the environment to speed development, follow this process:

1. Create your visual ActiveX user controls, which will contain the reusable groupings of objects including text boxes, labels, list boxes, combo boxes, command buttons, check boxes, option buttons, images, and so forth. (Don't confuse these controls with ordinary form controls.)

   These user controls, unlike the form controls, must be placed precisely where they need to appear in the final application. Draw, resize, and assign properties to each control before adding the code. Again, try to use identical or similar name and caption properties for each individual object to speed up programming.
2. When all controls have their properties assigned and are sized and arranged properly in the control window, double-click them and add the procedures and methods that will allow messaging between application modules and the user control. A typical user control project will consist primarily of simple procedures and property assignments.

NOTE

When you're finished adding code, don't create the OCX yet. You'll need to see the control's code when you add the next project.

3. Add a project that contains at least one form on which the user control will later be drawn. This time, you don't have to be particular about object size and positioning. Place the objects vertically on the form and program each one, beginning at the top, to facilitate completing the code for each. Leave the layout of the objects on the form for later. It's easy to move the objects without having any impact on the code; these objects can be resized and moved into position as a last step.
4. When you think you've finished adding code for the first procedure call that will perform messaging functions by using the user control (typically referenced by the name `UserControl1` when you later draw it on the form), save the project under a unique filename and then remove it from the group.
5. With the user control project visible as the only project group, create your OCX. Choose File | Make *xxx*.OCX, where *xxx* is the name of your control.
6. Add the project with the form you just saved. Your toolbox now contains the new tool representing the OCX you just saved.
7. Click the new tool and draw your user control on your form.
8. Choose Run | Start to test the code for the first messaging function.

9. Debug as necessary before proceeding. There's a good chance that the code will need to be refined if this is the first user control you've tried to design and access by using the messaging method.

After the control methods and the first messaging function appear to be working properly, program the other objects on your form, one at a time. Test each before proceeding with the rest of the project group. Using message boxes after each important step in the project can assist with troubleshooting and speed up debugging. Although the debugging tools generally highlight the offending code, sometimes it's helpful to know immediately how far the execution of logic has traveled before an error or unexpected event occurs. Unexpected events don't necessarily generate a debugging error, so use a message box to display the current value of the variables being used in the code segment; sometimes it will give a clue regarding the cause of the problem. You also can use message boxes to announce the state of the objects as the program proceeds.

NOTE

When designing a networked program (commonly referred to as a *client/server application*), be sure not to overburden the messaging between the client part of the application and an instance of the user control residing on the server. Try to keep all storage functions on the local client unless a central database or data object is used. If a central data access object is used, it most likely will reside on the server, and that's a special case.

When you're using data access objects on a server, the data ordinarily must be manipulated or queried with Structured Query Language (SQL) statements. Try to achieve the processing of these queries on the server and temporarily store the results on the server. Refine the resulting set with additional queries by using messaging until only the required data remains and then return only this data—the final output of all queries—to the client application. This technique isn't always available if the remote data object resides on a server that the developer can't maintain. In that scenario, depending on the workload created by the application, it might be appropriate to work with the people maintaining the server's data so that server-side programs can be installed to handle this work and reduce the amount of data being returned over the network.

Keeping Ergonomic Considerations in Mind

Most developers create fantastic programs without really noticing that some people might spend hours at a stretch looking at and using their application. Other developers will make the programs ergonomic without even having to think about why they've designed a form the way they have.

Force yourself to think about the ergonomics that will have an impact on the individuals who will use the program. Assume that you have a command button that changes what's displayed in a list box. To improve the program, place the command button close to the box to reduce the distance the user's eyes must travel when bouncing back and forth between the mouse pointer and the list box.

When possible, attempt to place the cursor at a ready position (selected state) in any text box that will be used routinely for keyboard input. If users will key in data every time a command button is activated, for example, design the procedure to resume focus to the box with a blinking cursor and a blank area to type the next segment of data. If users leave the text box and enter the next input in another text box, use the tab order properties. Likewise, if tabs and carriage returns aren't used in a specific text box to enter the data, program the "lost focus" event handler to activate any necessary procedure when a tab or carriage return is typed.

Try to avoid the need for scrolling when using an MDI form. If you're programming an HTML Web page, automatic scrolling jumps are handled by using links to bookmarks on the page to skip down to the area where the next task needs to be achieved.

If you're using Windows-style menus, be sure to use unique keyboard shortcuts for most or all menu selections, especially those that will be accessed frequently, by using the ampersand (`&`) symbol in the name of the menu selection. For example, use the menu name `&Edit` to make the E key the shortcut key for the Edit menu. Taking a little time to create these shortcuts might save users a significant amount of time when using the program. The best commercially available programs on the market accommodate users who prefer mouse moves as well as accomplished typists who prefer keyboard shortcuts.

Although gray forms aren't used much anymore, using background patterns and images creates a new set of challenges for programmers. When you use labels, for example, use colors that aren't too dark to display small text characters. Likewise, textures must have small patterns so that they don't interfere with text displayed directly on the background. Remember that not all users will have total control over their monitor settings in a work environment. If the monitor is set to display the text very small, even if the resolution is set very high, dark colors with black text will blend together, making the text hard to read and causing undue eye strain.

Pay attention to tab order. When a text box that's part of a group of text boxes being used for data entry is relocated on a form during design work, be sure to correct the tab order so that typists can tab sequentially across the page and down the page without using the mouse. Without this attention to detail, you can create a serious aversion to your program for accomplished typists.

Most Web page input boxes automatically feature a correct tab order as they're placed in the HTML code. With ActiveX Control Pad and VB5 forms, this tab order must be addressed in the properties dialog boxes. As the boxes are added, the next available tab number is assigned automatically. If you delete or move boxes, the tab ordering number values accompanying a box's tab property don't change automatically.

Don't place text too tightly in user controls such as labels and option buttons. Also avoid placing controls too close to each other. If your application will be used on the Internet, it won't necessarily be displayed the same way on every system, and you must accommodate for the difference by leaving room for larger display fonts and inaccuracies caused by differences in operating systems.

Dressing Up Your Application

If your file uses many forms and takes a bit of time to load when it's first launched, you can make the application look more professional by creating a splash screen (not to be confused with *Flash animations*, which were called *Splash movies* when the software was formerly known as FutureSplash Animator). The *splash screen* is simply a separate form that loads when an application starts and displays simple graphics with information about the application (name, version, and purpose are typically illustrated). When you launch VB5, notice that Microsoft's splash screen displays information about Visual Basic while the various forms load in the background.

Here's the simple way to create a splash screen: Create a form called `frmMySplash` and set the `StartupPosition` property to `2 - Center Screen`. You can select a bitmap for the `Picture` property or just add a text box with the text `Picture Appears Here`. Then add labels with the information about your program on this form. Size the form so that it doesn't cover the whole screen. Leave the `BorderStyle` property set to `1 - Fixed Single`, or the code won't work. Change the property setting for `ControlBox` to `False` to make the bar at the top disappear.

Rather than have a startup form, you need to create a separate subroutine in a separate module. Choose Project | Add Module. The code window automatically opens. Call the subroutine `Private Sub Main()`. Assuming that you have an MDI parent form called `MDIForm1`, the first functioning form in your program is a child form called `frmEnter`, and your splash screen with the bitmap and information about your program is called `frmMySplash`. Your code would look like this:

```
Private Sub Main()

    ' Load the splash screen form
    frmMySplash.Show
    MsgBox "Your splash screen should be centered here"

    ' Place your "on-load" loading code here so it_
    ' is achieved in the background while the splash screen has focus.

    ' Now load the child form frmEnter
    frmEnter.Show
    MsgBox "Loading frmEnter"

    ' Now unload the splash screen form
    Unload frmMySplash

End Sub
```

Now in the Project Explorer, right-click the icon for your project and choose the option Project1 Properties. At the right, you'll see a drop-down box for the startup object. Click the down arrow and select `Sub Main`. This code will execute first when your program begins to load. Choose

Start | Run to view how the forms load onscreen. Later, remove the MsgBox entries and choose Start | Run to see how the code will manipulate the appearance of your application at runtime.

Distributing Applications from VBA

Although the bulk of this chapter so far has focused on regular Visual Basic, I can't ignore the diversity of applications that you can create using Visual Basic for Applications. VBA has three primary functions that yield different styles of applications:

- VBA 5.0 is an ActiveX (OLE) control container. The ActiveX controls are placed in VBA forms in this scenario.
- VBA 5.0 is an automation controller. Objects provided by the host (server) application, objects exposed by ActiveX controls, and objects exposed by other applications running on the client system can be accessed by VBA.
- VBA 5.0 is an Automation server. You can use the VBA object models for creating forms and a development environment. The bulk of this work will be done by using special software packages provided by Microsoft and VBA licensees. For example, Microsoft Office 97 has a Developer's Edition that facilitates custom-designing applications that use the basic functionality of Microsoft Word, Access, PowerPoint, and Excel.

In general, you'll simply choose File | Make *xxx*.EXE, where *xxx* is the name of your project, to compile your code into an executable. To select options for how your program is optimized and compiled, right-click the project icon and select Project*xxx* properties, where *xxx* is the name for your project. Click the Compile tab and then check the appropriate check boxes and option buttons to set your compiler preferences. Click OK. Use the Application Setup Wizard to make a distribution setup file.

VB5's Enterprise and Professional Editions contain a native code compiler, but the default method of compiling programs into executable programs uses interpreters (p-code). Using the interpreter option is generally required for all OCX-style controls that will be deployed on the Internet because the OCX must be interpreted by the particular client platform that will install the OCX and use its code.

For executables designed to run on the Windows platform (generally, Windows 95 and Windows NT), the native compiler can yield some reasonable improvements in speed, especially if lengthy algorithms are required. The binary compiled code executes faster when this number-crunching work is a significant part of a program. Testing by Microsoft has suggested that the bulk of most programs in use today don't require this kind of number crunching, so don't expect miracle gains in the performance of an application due to use of the native code compiler.

You might be able to recall that native code is what we started with when we began using computers. We used binary data for everything. If you take into account how the computing platforms have changed since the days of exclusive use of binary compiled machine language, you'll understand that these gains are really minimal for most programs.

With regret, I feel compelled to dispel the myth surrounding the market appeal of a native code compiler. Despite the hype, Microsoft estimates that typically only 5 percent of an application's time to execute is actually spent executing p-code. Most of the time is spent loading DLLs and forms. This means that even if the native compiler executed instantaneously, the highest performance gain for a typical program would be less than 5 percent. What this really means is that unless you're building a program such as a computer-aided drafting (CAD) application, a fractal generation program, or a function that transfers bits and bytes and heavily depends on number crunching and loops, don't expect more than a 3–4 percent performance gain.

This might be a shock to those who have read the Web claims about 5,000 percent performance gains that could be realized by using VB5 and a native code compiler. I believe it's unlikely that any *major* VB applications could realize anything exceeding a 100 percent performance gain unless the program is purely mathematical bits-and-bytes manipulation. That includes VB4 programs converted to VB5 and compiled with the native compiler.

Microsoft has indicated that the native code compiler still requires the distribution of the VB5 runtime dynamic link library. Loading this library alone may be a source of irritation to those who misunderstood the meaning of a native code compiler. Just because the code is compiled in the processor's native language doesn't mean that the code can be implemented without the runtime library. The library file `MSVBVM50.DLL`, the virtual machine library used to run the programs, is still required for all Visual Basic projects.

Native commands understood by the processor chip can be included in the compiled application. These low-level instructions are in the chip's native machine language if you select the Compile to Native Code option. This might speed up loops and calls to services from the virtual machine DLL, but the impact may be less than dramatic. To set this option, right-click the Project1 icon in the Project Explorer and select Project1 Properties. Click the Compile tab and then the appropriate option button. Click OK.

Services provided by the virtual machine DLL file include startup and shutdown tasks, presentation of intrinsic controls, handling the functionality of forms, and initiating the execution of runtime functions.

Summary

This chapter showed how to organize an ActiveX project by using a structured approach to avoid common potential obstacles to smooth program development.

This chapter also evaluated the final touches an application may require and explored some basic distribution issues so that your Visual Basic application can be deployed efficiently to users.

V PART

IN THIS PART

Database Tools and Techniques

23

Creating Forms with the Data Form Wizard

IN THIS CHAPTER

One of the most time-consuming tasks in Visual Basic programming is designing forms. You need to consider so many things—from how to place controls on the form to programming the many possible events—that a project with several forms can overwhelm you. Visual Basic 5 provides the Data Form Wizard to automate many of the more routine tasks involved in designing forms that are used to access and display information from a database.

An Overview of the Data Form Wizard

The Data Form Wizard is used to generate Visual Basic forms that are made up of bound controls and the procedures necessary to work with data coming from database tables or queries that pull data from those database tables. The Data Form Wizard can design three different form types:

- *A single-record form,* based on a single database table or a query on a single database table
- *A grid (datasheet) form,* based on multiple selections from a single database table or query
- *A master/detail form,* based on a complex query joining two or more tables in a one-to-many data relationship

A single-record form displays on a form only those fields you specify to the wizard, one record per screen. The grid form displays a group of data on the form at the same time in a spreadsheet view using the DBGrid control. The master/detail form displays the master record source in a single record format and the detail record source in a spreadsheet view, again using the DBGrid control.

The Data Form Wizard provides users with many other options to choose from as it designs the form. These options include

- Database type
- Database name
- Column to sort by
- Controls to appear on the form
- Name of the form

As you use the Data Form Wizard to create a form, you'll see just how flexible and time-saving this wizard can be in the initial prototyping of a Visual Basic application.

Installing the Data Form Wizard

The Data Form Wizard comes with Visual Basic 5 as one of the add-in options available from the Add-In Manager. This means that it has to be installed to be used. The good news is that installing the Data Form Wizard involves nothing more than checking it off in the options box in the Add-In Manager.

NOTE

The Data Form Wizard comes with the Professional and Enterprise Editions of Visual Basic but is not included in the Learning Edition.

To install the Data Form Wizard, choose Add-Ins | Add-In Manager from the Visual Basic menu. Figure 23.1 shows the Add-In Manager dialog box listing the available add-ins. To install the Data Form Wizard, check the box beside it and then click OK to add the Data Form Wizard to the Add-Ins menu. Now when you want to use the Data Form Wizard, you can select it directly from that menu (see Figure 23.2).

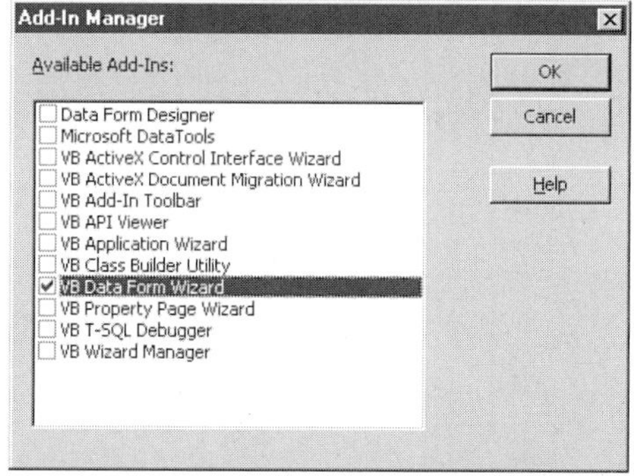

FIGURE 23.1.
Selecting the Data Form Wizard add-in.

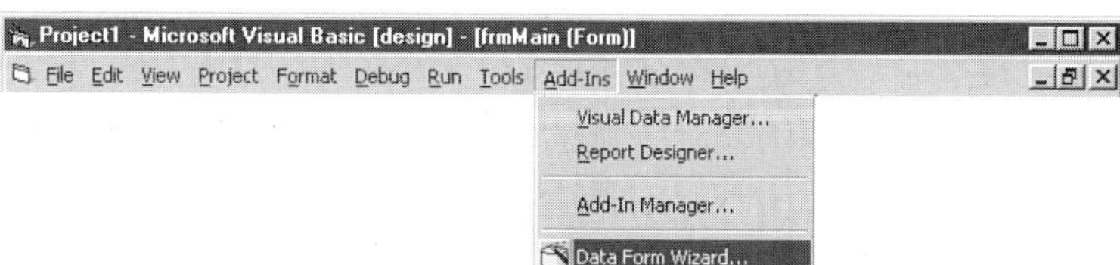

FIGURE 23.2.
The Data Form Wizard is added to the Add-Ins menu.

NOTE

If you want to uninstall the Data Form Wizard later, just go through the same procedure, except remove the check mark for the wizard in the Available Add-Ins list and click OK.

Creating a Single-Record Form with the Data Form Wizard

The first type of form you can create with the Data Form Wizard is the *single-record form.* For many applications, such as a program that browses a database's contents, this type of form will be exactly what you need. As you'll see, selecting this form lets you place some or all of the fields from the database table you select onto one form so that they can be viewed at the same time. You'll also be able to control which actions users can perform on the form, such as adding records to the database table, deleting records from the table, and so on. You'll also have control over where the fields and controls will be placed on the form.

First, choose Add-Ins | Data Form Wizard from the menu. (If you can't find the wizard on the menu, return to the preceding section and follow the procedure to install it.)

The Data Form Wizard - Introduction Dialog Box

When you launch the Data Form Wizard, you'll first see the wizard's Introduction dialog box (see Figure 23.3).

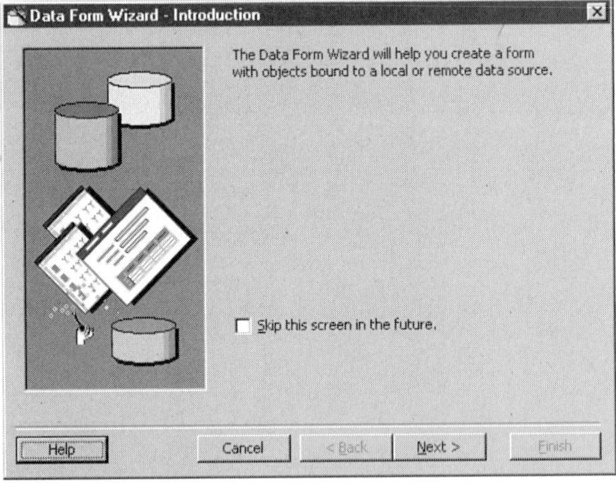

FIGURE 23.3.
The Introduction dialog box of the Data Form Wizard.

This dialog box merely points out that this wizard is used to create a form with controls that are bound to a local or remote database. There's also a check box that, when selected, prevents this Introduction dialog box from being displayed in subsequent sessions with the Data Form Wizard. At the bottom of the dialog box are five command buttons:

- *Help*—Opens the Help window for the Introduction step. Pressing F1 also displays the Help window.
- *Cancel*—Cancels all work done in this session and closes the Data Form Wizard.

- *Back*—Moves you to the previous dialog box in the wizard. This button isn't available in the Introduction dialog box because it's the first step in the Data Form Wizard. In future dialog boxes, you can go back.
- *Next*—Moves to the next dialog box in the wizard.
- *Finish*—Accepts default selections for all remaining unchosen options and builds the data form. This button isn't available if you haven't made enough choices to build an appropriate data form.

The Data Form Wizard - Database Type Dialog Box

To continue with the Data Form Wizard, click the Next button. The Data Form Wizard - Database Type dialog box appears (see Figure 23.4).

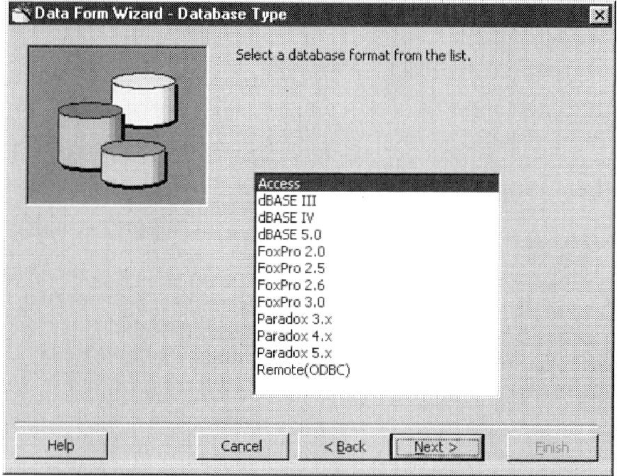

FIGURE 23.4.
The Data Form Wizard - Database Type dialog box, showing available database types.

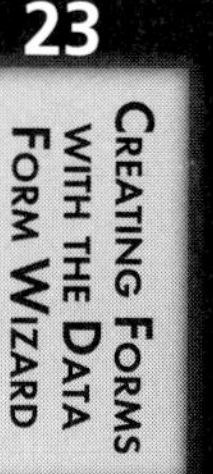

This dialog box lists the five main database types that the wizard supports. You can select one of the following from the list box:

- *Microsoft Access*—Any version of the Jet (`.MDB`) engine
- *dBASE*—dBASE III, dBASE IV, or dBASE 5.0
- *Microsoft FoxPro*—FoxPro versions 2.0, 2.5, 2.6, or 3.0
- *Borland Paradox*—Paradox versions 3.*x*, 4.*x*, or 5.*x*
- *Remote (ODBC)*—Any ODBC-compliant database driver (for example, Microsoft SQL Server, Oracle, or Sybase)

Select the database type you want by highlighting it in the list box and clicking the Next button.

The Data Form Wizard - Database Dialog Box

If you don't select an ODBC database, the next dialog box you'll see is Data Form Wizard - Database. In this dialog box, you enter the database name you're connecting to and whether your record source will come from the tables associated with the database (or, if you're connecting to Microsoft Access, queries associated with the database).

To select a database, enter the full path to the database you're wanting to connect to in the text box. If you aren't sure of the full path, you can use the Browse button to find the database. If the database is an Access database, you can select tables and queries in the Record Sources group box; otherwise, you can select only tables. Figure 23.5 shows the full path to the `Biblio` database from Visual Basic 5, which is the database being used in this chapter.

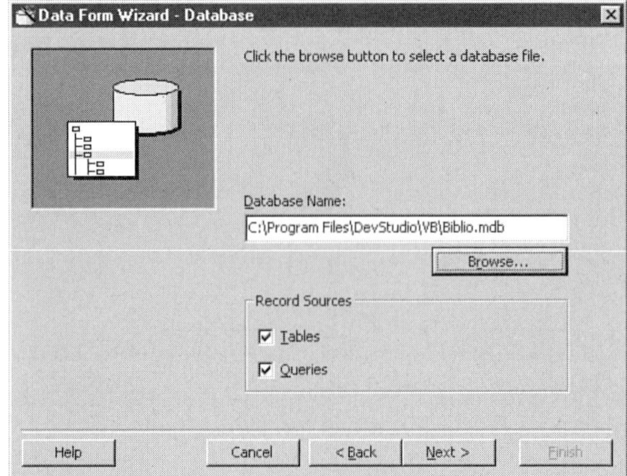

FIGURE 23.5.
The Database dialog box after a database is selected.

After you enter the full path to the database and select the appropriate record sources, click Next to move to the next step.

The Data Form Wizard - Form Dialog Box

The Data Form Wizard - Form dialog box allows you to select which layout type to use on the form:

- Single record
- Grid (datasheet)
- Master/detail

Figure 23.6 shows the Data Form Wizard - Form dialog box with the Single record form type selected. Notice also that in the upper-left portion of the dialog box is a representation of what a Single record form layout looks like. Figure 23.7 shows the Form dialog box with the Grid form type selected; Figure 23.8 shows the Form dialog box with the Master/Detail form type selected.

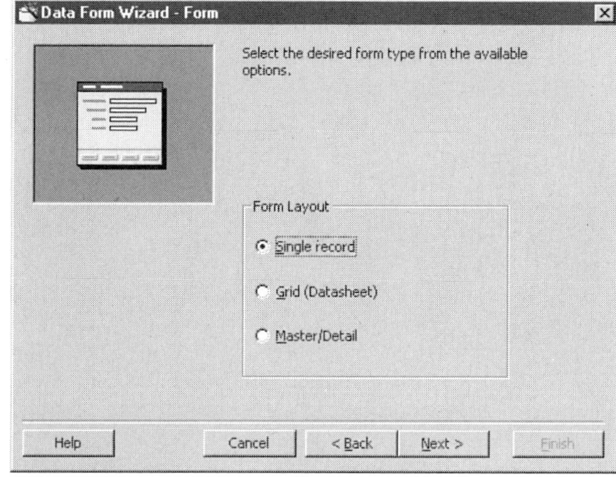

FIGURE 23.6.
The Form dialog box with Single record layout selected.

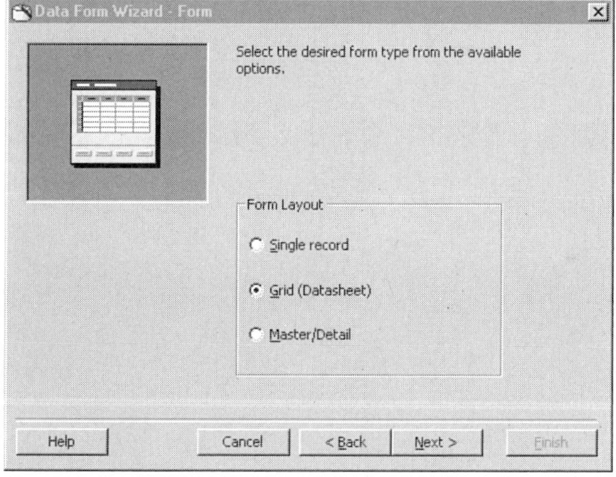

FIGURE 23.7.
The Form dialog box with Grid layout selected.

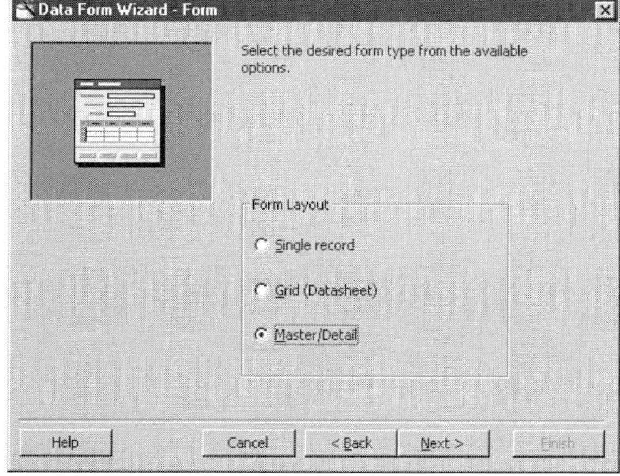

FIGURE 23.8.
The Form dialog box with Master/Detail selected.

The thumbnail samples of the various form layouts give you a better idea of which option you should select. In this example, we are going to create a single record form, so choose the first option. Then click Next to proceed to the next dialog box.

The Data Form Wizard - Record Source Dialog Box

The Data Form Wizard - Record Source dialog box lets you select the record source for the data that will appear on the form and the fields that will be placed on the form (see Figure 23.9).

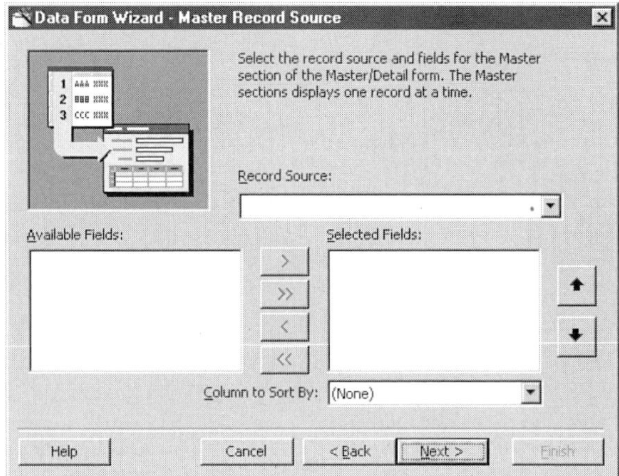

FIGURE 23.9.
The Record Source dialog box.

First, select the record source that will provide data to your form from the Record Source combo box. If the database is an Access database, the available tables and queries will appear in the combo box; otherwise, only table names will appear. You make a selection by clicking the highlighted table or query you want.

After a record source is selected, the available fields appear in the Available Fields list box. To select a field to add to the form, highlight it in the list box and click the > button to move it to the Selected Fields list box. Continue doing this until you have all the fields you want on the form listed in the Selected Fields list box.

> **TIP**
>
> To select all the fields at one time, click the >> button.

While selecting fields, or after you select them all, you can change the order in which the fields will appear on the form by highlighting a field in the Selected Fields box and clicking the up- or down-arrow button. Finally, if you want the data to be displayed in sorted order, select a field to sort on in the Column to Sort By combo box. This sort is a descending-order sort.

The Record Source dialog box shown in Figure 23.10 is configured with the Titles table from the `Biblio` database as the record source, and the selected fields are Title, ISBN, Description, Subject, and Comments. The Title field has been selected as the sort field.

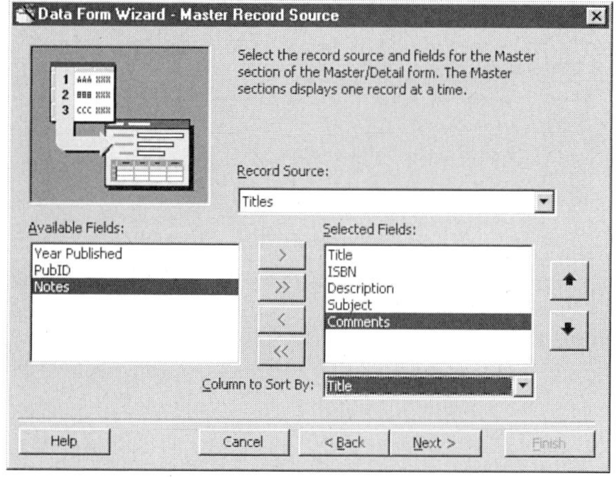

FIGURE 23.10.
The Record Source dialog box, completely configured.

You can click the Finish button at this point to accept the defaults for the rest of the dialog boxes and complete the Data Form Wizard process. However, the next dialog box lets you decide which controls to place on the form, so click the Next button.

The Data Form Wizard - Control Selection Dialog Box

The Control Selection dialog box presents the different control buttons that you can place on the form. As shown in Figure 23.11, all control buttons are initially selected by default.

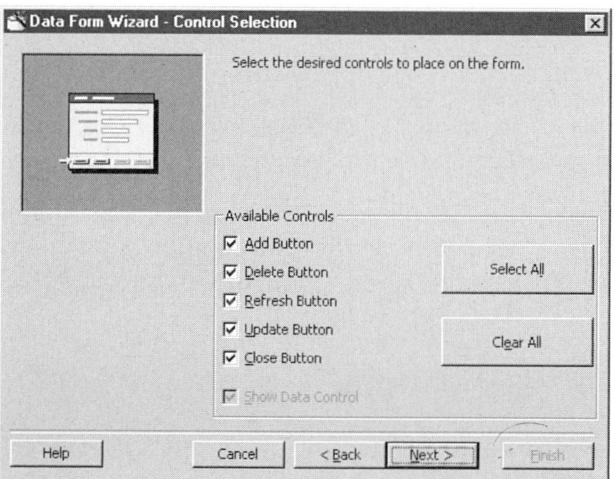

FIGURE 23.11.
The initial Control Selection dialog box.

You can choose the following buttons from this dialog box:

- *Add*—Places an Add button on the form to allow the addition of new records to the database.
- *Delete*—Places a Delete button on the form to allow the deletion of records from the database.
- *Refresh*—Places a Refresh button on the form to refresh the displayed data from a database.
- *Update*—Places an Update button on the form to update the currently displayed record in the database.
- *Close*—Places a Close button on the form to close the form.
- *Show Data Control*—Makes the Data control visible on the form (default).

You can choose any combination of controls. If you don't want the wizard to add any controls, click Clear All. If you change your mind and want the wizard to add all the controls, click Select All. For this example, make sure that all the controls will be added to the form.

You can click Finish at this step and accept the defaults for the final dialog box. However, if you want to change the name of the form or save your selections for future uses of the Data Form Wizard, click Next to continue.

The Data Form Wizard - Finished! Dialog Box

The last step in the Data Form Wizard is the Finished! dialog box. As Figure 23.12 shows, a default title made from the table chosen earlier is displayed in the text box. If you don't like the default name, type over it.

FIGURE 23.12.
The Finished! dialog box, with the default form name displayed.

Below the text box is the Save Current Settings as Default check box, which you can select if you want to use the selections you made in this session of the Data Form Wizard in future sessions. For example, if you think you'll always choose a Grid style layout for your forms and you made that selection this time, select this check box to ensure that the wizard selects the Grid layout style as the default. If you don't select this check box, the wizard will display the system defaults as you go through the dialog boxes.

Finally, click the Finish button. (Notice that the Next button is now disabled because no more steps are left to create a data form.) A confirmation box appears to tell you that your form has been added to the current project (see Figure 23.13). If you don't want to see this confirmation box in future sessions with the Data Form Wizard, click the check box titled Don't Show This Dialog in the Future. Click OK to display your data form (see Figure 23.14).

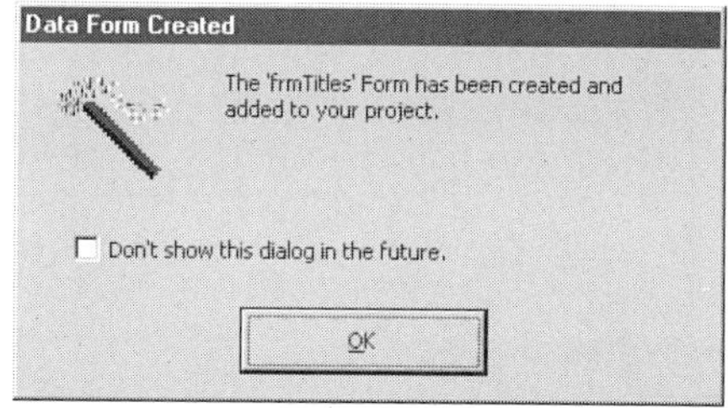

FIGURE 23.13.
The Data Form Created confirmation box.

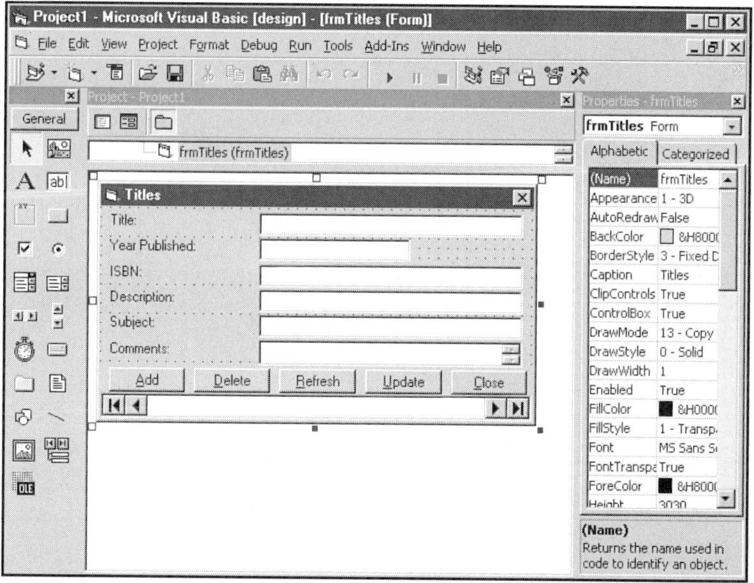

FIGURE 23.14.
The finished data form.

At this point, the form is ready to be run. Of course, if you don't like the way the controls were placed on the form by the Data Form Wizard, you can change them any way you like. You can change the properties of the controls to change the font size, the alignment of the control, and so on. However, if you change any of the properties that specify how the control is bound to the Data control and the database, you might change what data, if any, is displayed in the control. So be careful when changing control properties!

If you like the way everything is placed on the form, you can run the form to see how it works. Figure 23.15 shows the single-record form I created, displaying data from the `Biblio` database.

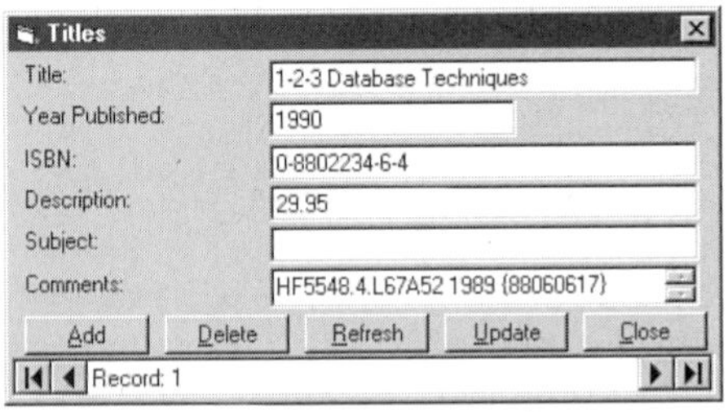

FIGURE 23.15.
A single-record form created with the Data Form Wizard.

> **TIP**
>
> Make sure that the form created with the Data Form Wizard is the startup form; otherwise, you'll have to add code to the startup form to make sure that it displays the new data form.

All the controls on the form are those that were selected in the Data Form Wizard except one, the Data control, which is the bottom control on the form. The wizard adds this control automatically because Visual Basic requires it to be on the form before any bound controls can be placed on the form.

> **NOTE**
>
> In the Data Form Wizard - Control Selection dialog box, the Data control is disabled because it can't be removed from the form if the controls placed on the form are to be bound to the database.

If you're not familiar with the Data control, you should know that it performs two main functions on the data form. First, through some of its properties (discussed in Chapter 24, "Binding Controls to Your Database"), the Data control connects the database to the tables or queries used as the record source.

The control's second function is to provide some basic navigational tools for moving around the database. On either side of the Data control are a pair of buttons. Clicking the right-arrow button moves the display one record forward in the database table. Clicking the left-arrow button moves the display one record backward in the database table. The right arrow/bar button moves the display to the last record in the database table; the left arrow/bar button moves the display to the first record in the database table.

Creating a Grid Data Form

A second form type that you can create with the Data Form Wizard is the grid (datasheet) form. A *grid form* displays data from a database table in a spreadsheet-type layout by using the DBGrid control.

To create a grid data form, click the Grid radio button in the Data Form Wizard - Form dialog box. (The other dialog boxes and choices are the same as for the single-record form.) When you click the Finish button in the Finished! dialog box, the Data Form Wizard generates a grid form like the one in Figure 23.16.

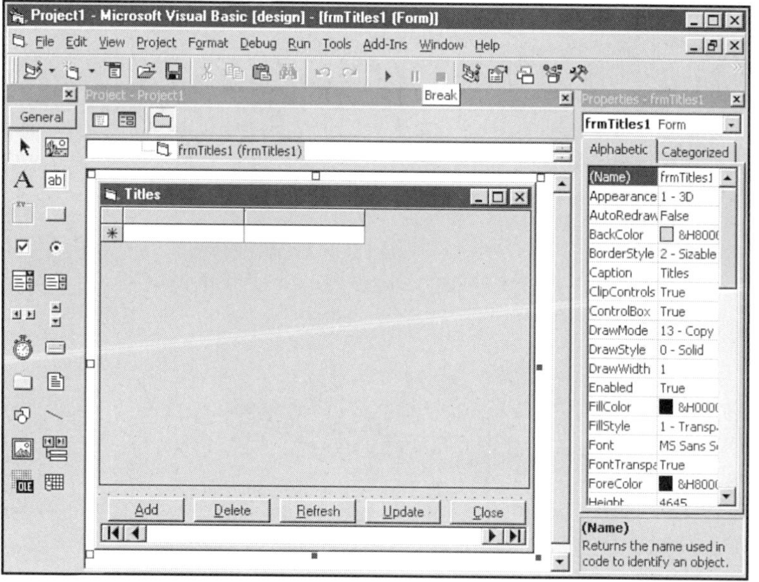

FIGURE 23.16.
A grid form generated by the Data Form Wizard.

The grid form has the same control buttons that were placed on the single-record form, and the Data control is also located at the bottom of the form. Instead of the text boxes and label controls that were added to the single-record form, however, the grid form has an empty DBGrid control. To get a better view of how the data will be presented on this form, you'll need to run the program, which results in the form shown in Figure 23.17.

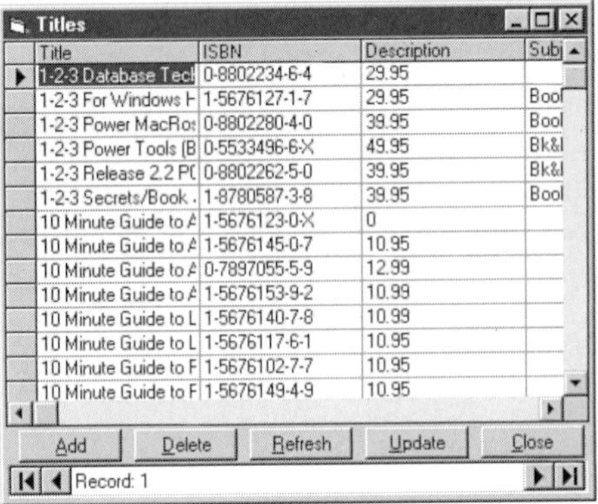
Titles

Title	ISBN	Description	Subj
1-2-3 Database Tec	0-8802234-6-4	29.95	
1-2-3 For Windows H	1-5676127-1-7	29.95	Boo
1-2-3 Power MacRo	0-8802280-4-0	39.95	Bool
1-2-3 Power Tools (B	0-5533496-6-X	49.95	Bk&I
1-2-3 Release 2.2 P(	0-8802262-5-0	39.95	Bk&I
1-2-3 Secrets/Book .	1-8780587-3-8	39.95	Bool
10 Minute Guide to A	1-5676123-0-X	0	
10 Minute Guide to A	1-5676145-0-7	10.95	
10 Minute Guide to A	0-7897055-5-9	12.99	
10 Minute Guide to A	1-5676153-9-2	10.99	
10 Minute Guide to L	1-5676140-7-8	10.99	
10 Minute Guide to L	1-5676117-6-1	10.95	
10 Minute Guide to F	1-5676102-7-7	10.95	
10 Minute Guide to F	1-5676149-4-9	10.95	

FIGURE 23.17.
The grid form, presenting data from the `Biblio` *database.*

To make more of the form's columns visible, you can resize the form by dragging its corners or sides. To make more of the rows visible, drag the top or the bottom of the form.

Just like with the single-record form, you can add, delete, and update data on the table by using the command buttons at the bottom of the form. You can navigate through the table by using the arrow buttons on the Data control.

Creating a Master/Detail Data Form

The third form type available with the Data Form Wizard is the *master/detail form.* This form allows you to create a form based on the data from more than one table, usually by joining two tables based on a field common to both tables.

For an example from the `Biblio` database, we'll try creating a form that lists all book titles published by a particular publisher. This type of form requires the creation of a master/detail form, with the Publisher table providing the master data and the Titles table providing the detail data.

To create the form, click the Master/Detail radio button on the Data Form Wizard - Form dialog box and then click the Next button. Figure 23.18 shows the Data Form Wizard - Master Record Source dialog box.

This dialog box asks which record source you want to use as the master record for the form. This data will be displayed one record at a time on the form. For the Titles by Publisher example, select the Publishers table as the master record source.

Choosing Publishers in the Record Source combo box brings up a listing of fields from the Publishers table in the Available Fields list box. You can select as many of these fields as are needed to display and add them to the Selected Fields list. Figure 23.19 shows the choices made for this example.

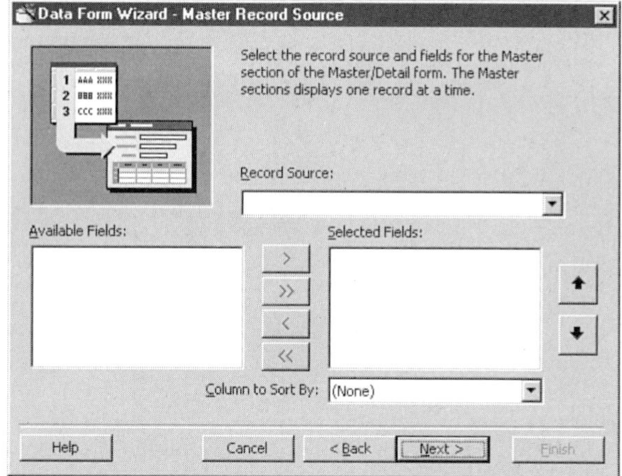

FIGURE 23.18.
The Master Record Source dialog box.

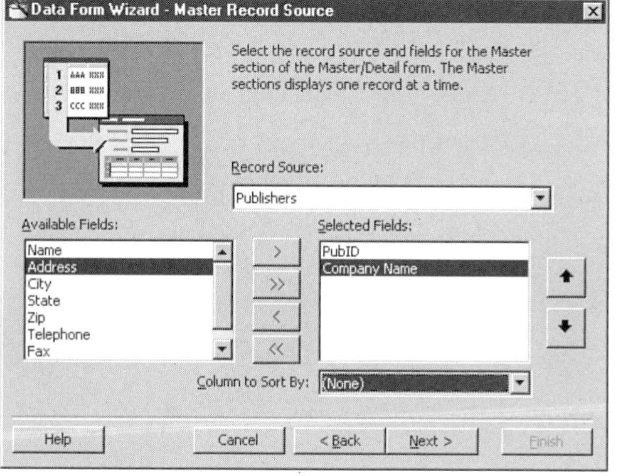

FIGURE 23.19.
Making selections for the master record source.

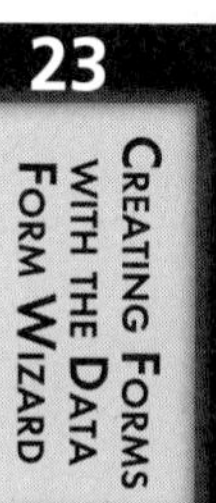

One field in the Selected Fields list deserves special attention. Because book titles in the Titles table are being linked to publishers in the Publishers table, a link between the two tables needs to be created. Often, a common field, called a *key field*, is used to create this link. For the Titles and Publishers tables, the key field is PubID, which is present in both tables. Although this field doesn't have to be one of the Selected Fields to appear on the form, it has been selected to appear in this example to illustrate its importance in providing a link between the two tables.

After all selections are made for the Master Record Source, click the Next button to move to the next step: selecting a Detail record source. The Detail Record Source dialog box looks similar to the Master Record Source dialog box. The table that will provide detail data for this master/detail form is the Titles table. As with the Master Record Source dialog box, you can select the fields you want displayed in the detail section of the form from the available fields in the Titles table. For this example, we want to see the book titles sorted in alphabetical order, so the Title field in the Column to Sort By combo box should be selected. Figure 23.20 shows the final selections for the Detail Record Source dialog box.

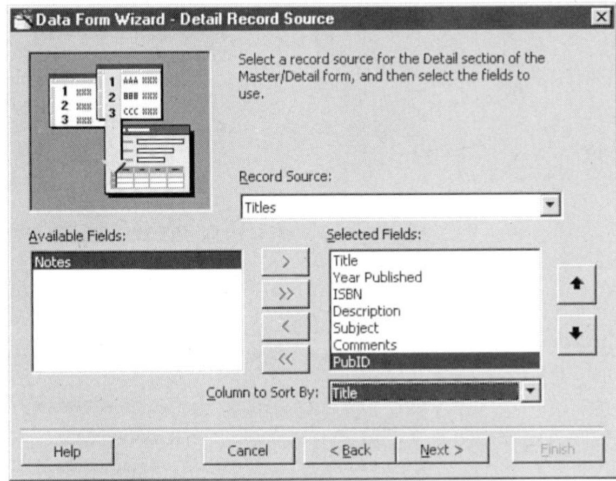

FIGURE 23.20.
Making selections for the Detail Record Source dialog box.

Click the Next button to move to the next step. Now you see a dialog box you haven't seen before: the Data Form Wizard - Record Source Relation dialog box, which asks you to select a field from both the master record source (the Titles table) and the detail record source (the Publishers table) that can be used to link together the two record sources. Once again, the PubID field is the linking, or key, field in this example. Highlight the PubID field in each list box (see Figure 23.21) and then click Next to move to the next step.

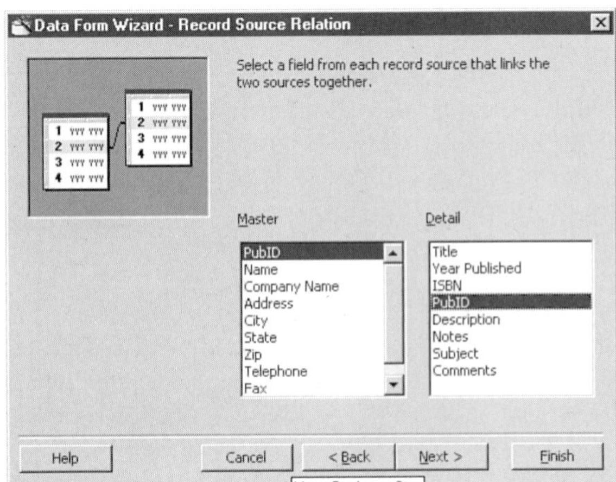

FIGURE 23.21.
Selecting the key field in the Record Source Relation dialog box.

The rest of the steps to create a master/detail data form are just like the steps for creating the other two types of data forms. Select the controls you want on the Control Selection dialog box and, finally, name the form in the Finished! dialog box. When you're done, the Data Form Wizard generates a master/detail form like the one shown in Figure 23.22.

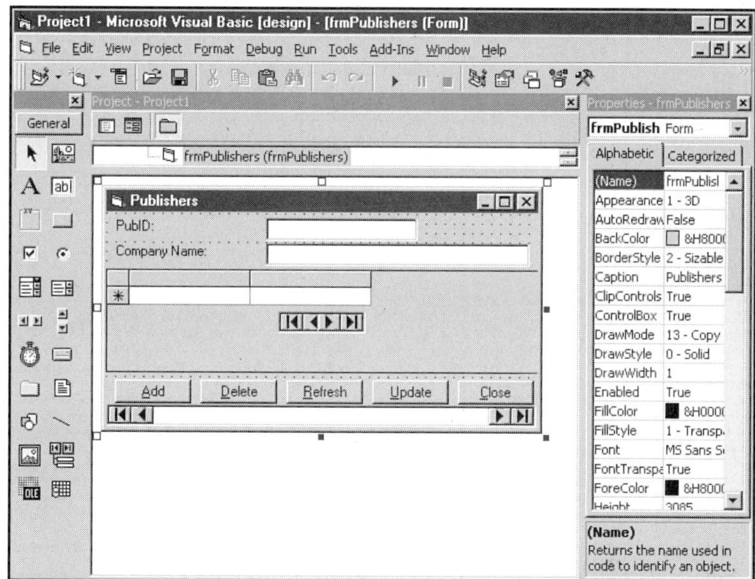

FIGURE 23.22.
The master/detail form generated by the Data Form Wizard.

The top part of the form displays the labels PubID and Company Name, which make up the master section of the form. The detail section of the form contains an empty DBGrid control, which will contain the detail data when the program is run. Notice that below the DBGrid control is a Data control. A master/detail form needs two Data controls to allow navigating through the master and detail sections. The Data control below the DBGrid is for the detail section; the Data control for the master section is at the bottom of the form. Figure 23.23 shows what the master/detail form looks like when the program is running.

Publishers

PubID: 721

Company Name: Sams Publications

Title	Year Published	ISBN	Description	Subject
10 Minute Guide to C	1991	0-6722283-2-7	0	
10 Minute Guide to C	1991	0-6723003-5-4	10.95	
32-Bit Programming	1995	0-6723076-2-6	49.99	
3D Madness!/Book,	1994	0-6723049-2-9	45	Bk Cd&Ds
Absolute Beginner's I	1993	0-6723036-6-3	16.95	
Absolute Beginner's I	1994	0-6723051-0-0	22	2nd
Absolute Beginner's I	1994	0-6723034-1-8	0	2nd

Add Delete Refresh Update Close

Record: 721

FIGURE 23.23.
The master/detail form in the running program.

Each title associated with Sams Publications is shown in the detail section. You can navigate through the grid with the up- and down-arrow keys to the right of the grid. To change publishers, click the left or right arrow on the Data control at the bottom of the form.

Connecting to an ODBC Database

If you're accessing data from a database that doesn't reside on your PC, you'll probably connect to the database by using ODBC. I won't cover the details of setting up your PC to connect via ODBC (that comes in a later chapter), but I will show you the one different step the Data Form Wizard takes when you select a Remote (ODBC) database in the Data Form Wizard - Database Type dialog box.

When you select a remote database as the database type, the Data Form Wizard takes you to the Data Form Wizard - Connect Information dialog box, in which you provide some information concerning your ODBC setup. Again, I won't provide the details of setting up ODBC, but I will show you the Connect Information dialog box so that you can see what information it wants (see Figure 23.24).

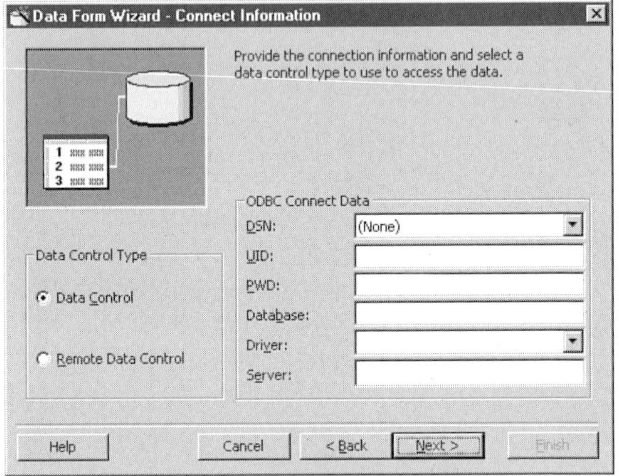

FIGURE 23.24.
The Data Wizard Form - Connect Information dialog box.

The first text box wants the DSN (Data Source Name) for your ODBC connection to the database. This information is located in the 32-bit ODBC program of your PC's Control Panel, if it has already been set up. If it hasn't been set up (or if you're not sure), have your system administrator check it for you. He or she can tell you how to set it up, or, if it has been set up and you can't tell what the DSN is supposed to be, he or she can tell you what the correct DSN is for the database to which you want to connect.

The second and third text boxes want a UID (user ID) and a PWD (password) for the data source. Again, your system administrator can tell you what these are.

The last text box wants the name of the database to which you're connecting. You can enter the database name here, or you can check with your system administrator to find out the proper name of the database.

Finally, on the left side of the dialog box are two radio buttons: Data Control and Remote Data Control. If you're not using the Enterprise Edition of Visual Basic, you don't have the Remote Data Control available to you, and you must select Data Control. If you're using the Enterprise Edition, you can select the Remote Data Control only if it has already been registered.

Summary

Using the Data Form Wizard to create forms bound to database tables or queries can be a time-saving tool in prototyping a new application. The Data Form Wizard can generate three types of forms:

- Single-record layout
- Grid (datasheet) layout
- Master/detail layout

This chapter highlighted the flexibility the Data Form Wizard provides in selecting

- A database type
- The form type
- What tables or queries will be used to generate data
- The fields that will be displayed on the form and how they're displayed
- What controls will be displayed on the form
- A name for the form

CHAPTER 24

Binding Controls to Your Database

IN THIS CHAPTER

One of Visual Basic's most powerful features is its capability to access data from a database while requiring little or no code to do so. The Data control, one of Visual Basic's standard controls, provides all the back-end processing necessary to create powerful database front ends that can add, display, edit, and delete data from many different kinds of databases. You do nothing more than place some controls on a form and set the right properties to provide access to the database. This chapter provides detailed instructions on how to design and implement these powerful database front ends.

Using the Data Control

The single most important element for creating a database front end in Visual Basic is the Data control, a standard Visual Basic control found in the Toolbox. In Visual Basic 5, the Data control is in the bottom-right corner of the standard controls found in the Toolbox when Visual Basic first loads (see Figure 24.1).

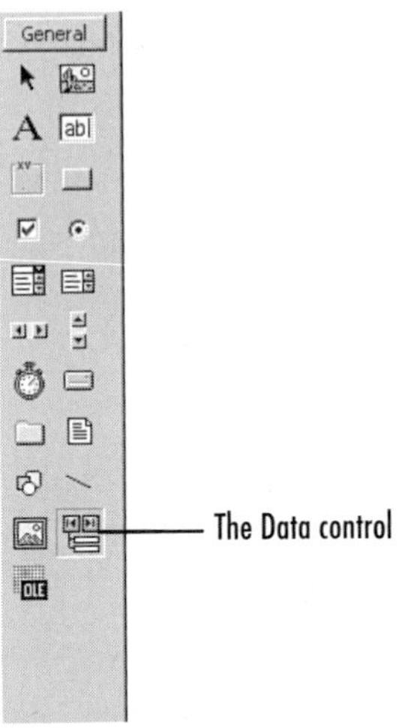

FIGURE 24.1.
The Data control in the Toolbox.

The Data control has a set of properties that let you establish a connection with a database, a database table, and the fields (columns) in a table. Double-clicking the Data control places it on the form (see Figure 24.2).

The Data control provides four buttons for navigating through a database table:

- The right-arrow button moves one record forward in the table.
- The right-arrow/bar button moves to the last record of the table.
- The left-arrow button moves one record backward in the table.
- The left-arrow/bar button moves to the first record of the table.

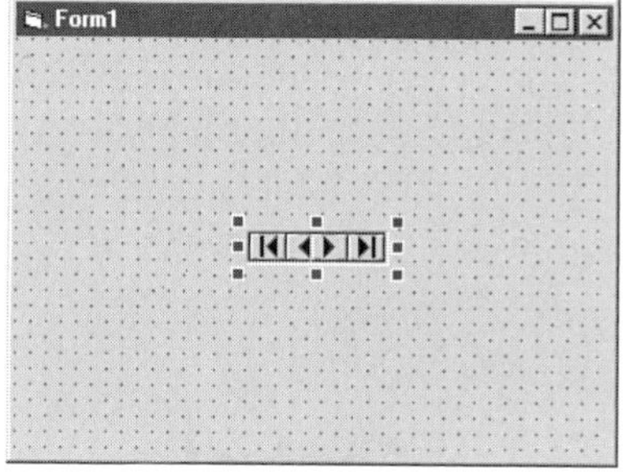

FIGURE 24.2.
The Data control on a form.

Like any other control, the Data control can be resized after it's placed on a form. If you widen the control, you can see that between the two sets of navigational buttons is the control's caption (see Figure 24.3). This caption can have any descriptive title you want to give it, or you can leave it with its default caption. However, just as with other controls, giving the Data control a logical name will help make your code easier to read, especially if you add other Data controls to the form later.

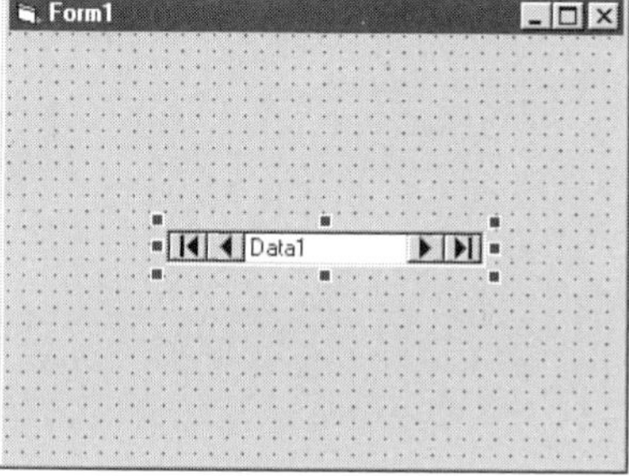

FIGURE 24.3.
The caption of the Data control.

Setting the Data Access Properties of the Data Control

After you place the Data control on a form, you need to connect it to a database. Connecting it to a database involves describing the database you're wanting to access at three levels:

- The database type, such as a Microsoft Access database
- The name of the database
- The name of the table that has the data you want to access

The Data control uses three properties to set these access levels:

- `Connect`, to identify the type of database
- `DatabaseName`, to identify the database name
- `RecordSource`, to identify the database table

The first property to set is `Connect`, which tells Visual Basic what type of database you're connecting to. The standard Data control allows connections to the following types of databases:

- Microsoft Access (all versions)
- dBASE III, IV, and 5.0
- Excel 3.0, 4.0, 5.0, and 8.0
- FoxPro 2.0, 2.5, 2.6, and 3.0
- Lotus WK1, WK3, and WK4
- Paradox 3.x, 4.x, and 5.x
- Text

Notice that three of the database types aren't databases at all; two are spreadsheets (Excel and Lotus) and one is plain text. As long as the data within these file types is organized in a row/column format, the Data control can read it like a database table.

NOTE

Of the database types listed here, only the Microsoft products provide access to the internal structure of the database, spreadsheet, or text file.

Figure 24.4 shows the properties associated with a Data control that has been placed on a form. The `Connect` property by default is set to `Access`. If you're connecting to this type of database, you don't have to do anything else with this property. If you want one of the other database types, however, click the `Connect` property, and a drop-down button will appear at the right of the property. Clicking the drop-down button lists the other database types that you can connect to (see Figure 24.5). Simply select your choice to place the database type in the `Connect` property's box.

After you select the database type, you're ready to select the name of the database you're connecting to by setting the `DatabaseName` property, which is right below the `Connect` property. Clicking the `DatabaseName` property brings up a Browse button to the right of the property setting box (see Figure 24.6).

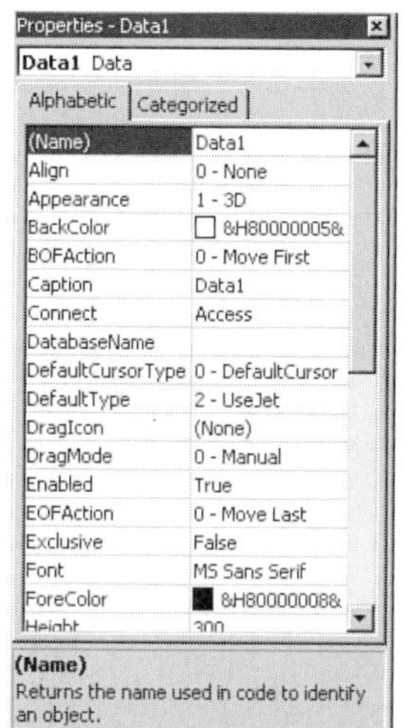

FIGURE 24.4.
The `Connect` *property in the Properties window of the Data control.*

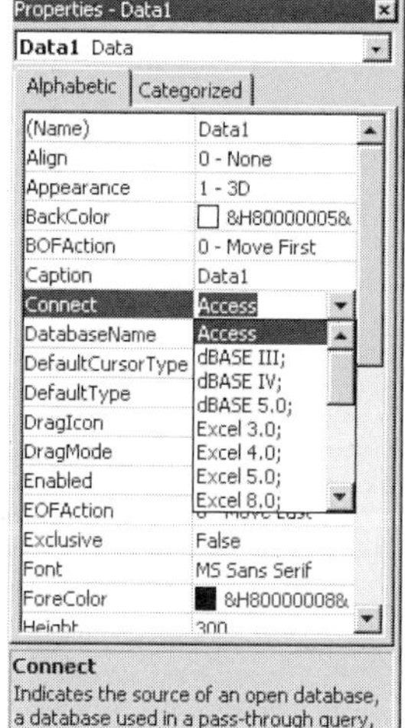

FIGURE 24.5.
A drop-down list of the database types for selection in the `Connect` *property.*

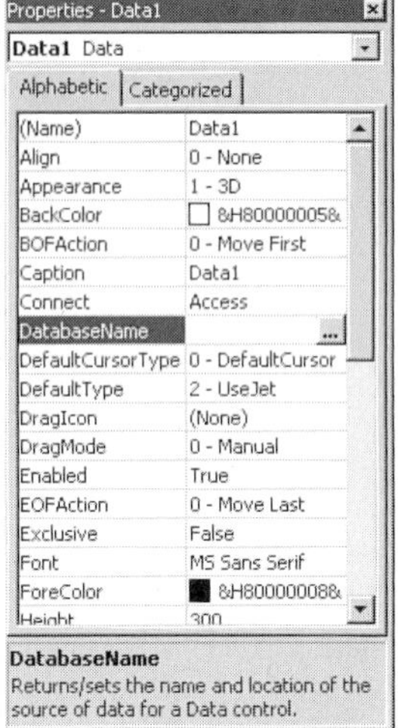

FIGURE 24.6.
Preparing to browse to select a database name.

When you click the Browse button, a dialog box appears to allow you to find the database that you want to connect to. Figure 24.7 shows the `BIBLIO.MDB` database being selected for the `DatabaseName` property. Clicking the Open button places the full file path to the database into the `DatabaseName` property box, as shown in Figure 24.8.

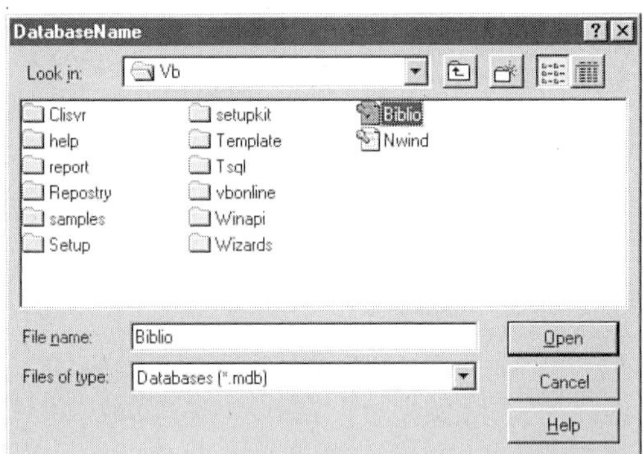

FIGURE 24.7.
Selecting the `BIBLIO.MDB` *database.*

With a database type and a database name selected, you're ready to select which table in the database you want to access by setting the `RecordSource` property. Clicking the `RecordSource` property displays a drop-down button like the one you saw with the `Connect` property. Clicking this button gives you a list of the different tables in the `Biblio` database that you can access (see Figure 24.9). Select the table you want by clicking it, and the table name will be added to the `RecordSource` property box (see Figure 24.10).

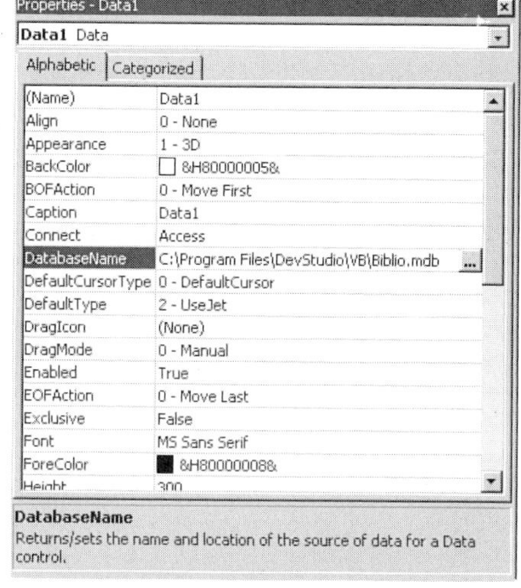

FIGURE 24.8.
The `DatabaseName` *property, set to access a database.*

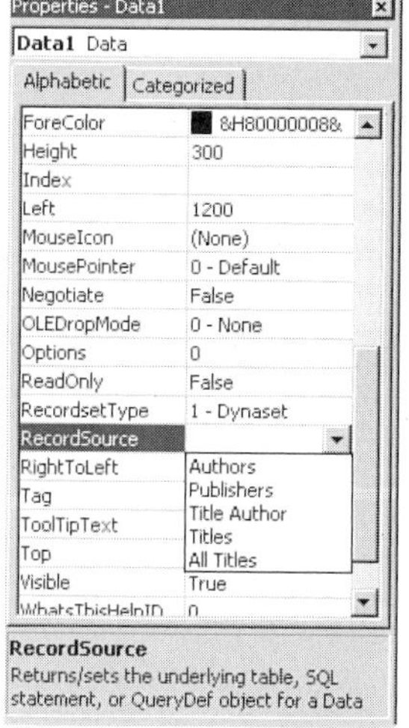

FIGURE 24.9.
Viewing the list of tables in the `Biblio` *database.*

You're now ready to add controls to your form to display data from the database you're accessing.

Binding Controls to a Database

After the Data control properties are properly set to connect to a database type, a particular database, and a specific database table, you next need to add controls to a form to display the data. Initially, you're going to create a form that displays data in text boxes, although later in the chapter you'll use some advanced Visual Basic data-bound controls that allow more complex views of database information.

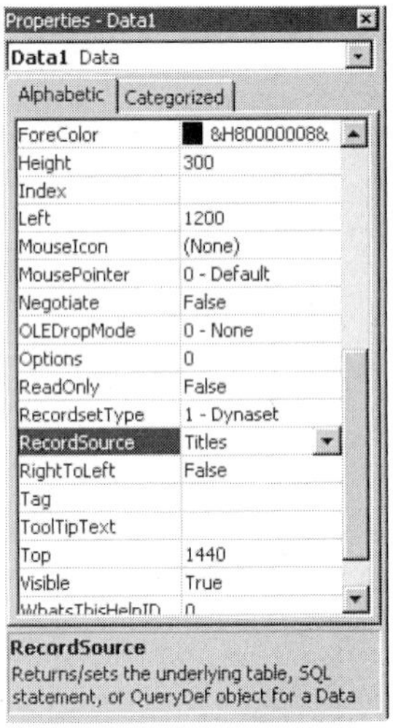

FIGURE 24.10.
Selecting a table name for the `RecordSource` *property.*

When the controls on a Visual Basic form are associated with a database table, the process of selecting the database, the table, and the record source is called *binding the control.* Visual Basic provides properties in each control to help with binding the control to a database table. After these properties are set, whenever the form is activated it displays data from the chosen database table and record source. This process is particularly useful because it doesn't involve writing any code, just setting the right properties.

Designing a Database Front-End Form

As in the design of any Visual Basic form, putting a little forethought into the design of the database front-end form helps make the form visually pleasing and more functional.

The information you'll display in the following example comes from the Titles table of the `Biblio` database that comes with Visual Basic. The Titles table has the following fields:

Title	Description
Year Published	Notes
ISBN	Subject
PubID	Comments

For this example, let's start with a basic form design. Each field has a label to display the field name and a text box to hold the data associated with the field. Figure 24.11 shows the example form, `frmTitles`. Add the Data, Label, and TextBox controls to the form as shown. Use Table 24.1 as a guide for changing the controls' properties.

Table 24.1. The properties for the form and the controls that make up the sample program.

Control Type	*Property*	*Value*
Form	`Name`	`frmTitles`
	`Caption`	`Titles Table`
	`Height`	`4605`
	`Width`	`6375`
Data	`Name`	`datTitles`
	`Height`	`345`
	`Left`	`105`
	`Top`	`4230`
	`Width`	`6165`
Label	`Name`	`lblTitle`
	`Caption`	`Title`
	`Height`	`240`
	`Left`	`150`
	`Top`	`210`
	`Width`	`1830`
Label	`Name`	`lblYearPub`
	`Caption`	`Year Published`
	`Height`	`240`
	`Left`	`150`
	`Top`	`570`
	`Width`	`1830`
Label	`Name`	`lblISBN`
	`Caption`	`ISBN`
	`Height`	`240`
	`Left`	`150`
	`Top`	`930`
	`Width`	`1830`
Label	`Name`	`lblPubID`
	`Caption`	`PubID`
	`Height`	`240`

continues

Table 24.1. continued

Control Type	*Property*	*Value*
	`Left`	`150`
	`Top`	`1290`
	`Width`	`1830`
Label	`Name`	`lblDescription`
	`Caption`	`Description`
	`Height`	`240`
	`Left`	`150`
	`Top`	`1650`
	`Width`	`1830`
Label	`Name`	`lblNotes`
	`Caption`	`Notes`
	`Height`	`240`
	`Left`	`135`
	`Top`	`2010`
	`Width`	`1830`
Label	`Name`	`lblSubject`
	`Caption`	`Subject`
	`Height`	`240`
	`Left`	`135`
	`Top`	`2370`
	`Width`	`1830`
Label	`Name`	`lblCommand`
	`Caption`	`Comments`
	`Height`	`240`
	`Left`	`135`
	`Top`	`2730`
	`Width`	`1830`
TextBox	`Name`	`txtTitle`
	`Text`	(Blank)
	`Height`	`285`
	`Left`	`2115`
	`Top`	`135`
	`Width`	`3720`

Control Type	*Property*	*Value*
TextBox	`Name`	`txtYearPub`
	`Text`	(Blank)
	`Height`	`285`
	`Left`	`2115`
	`Top`	`495`
	`Width`	`1305`
TextBox	`Name`	`txtISBN`
	`Text`	(Blank)
	`Height`	`285`
	`Left`	`2115`
	`Top`	`855`
	`Width`	`3720`
TextBox	`Name`	`txtPubID`
	`Text`	(Blank)
	`Height`	`285`
	`Left`	`2115`
	`Top`	`1215`
	`Width`	`1305`
TextBox	`Name`	`txtDescription`
	`Text`	(Blank)
	`Height`	`285`
	`Left`	`2115`
	`Top`	`1575`
	`Width`	`3720`
TextBox	`Name`	`txtNotes`
	`Text`	(Blank)
	`Height`	`285`
	`Left`	`2115`
	`Top`	`1935`
	`Width`	`3720`
TextBox	`Name`	`txtSubject`
	`Text`	(Blank)

continues

Table 24.1. continued

Control Type	Property	Value
	`Height`	285
	`Left`	2115
	`Top`	2295
	`Width`	3720
TextBox	`Name`	`txtComments`
	`Text`	(Blank)
	`Height`	285
	`Left`	2115
	`Top`	2655
	`Width`	3720

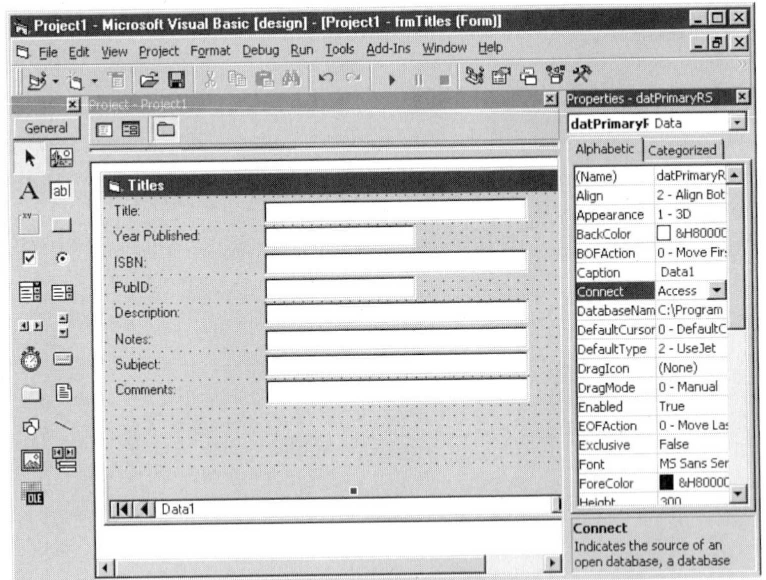

FIGURE 24.11.
The `frmTitles` *form will display data from the* `Biblio` *database table.*

After you place the controls on the form, you're ready to bind them to the database. You'll actually bind each control to its associated field in the Titles table. Notice in Figure 24.11 that the Data control, `datTitles`, is at the bottom of the form. Remember, you can't bind any controls on a form to a database until the Data control is placed on the form and has its data access properties set. Therefore, the next step in building the sample program is to set the properties for the `datTitles` control. Set its `Connect` property to `Access`, its `DatabaseName` property to the path of the `Biblio` database on your system, and its `RecordSource` property to `Titles`.

Now you're ready to bind your first field to the database. The top TextBox on the form is labeled Title. To bind the TextBox, `txtTitle`, to the Title field of the Titles table, you have to set two properties: `DataField` and `DataSource`.

You first need to set the `DataSource` property to the name of the Data control on the form. In this example, the Data control is named `datTitles`, so that's what you enter for the `DataSource` property. When you click the `DataSource` property, a drop-down button appears. Clicking the button will pop up the name of the Data control. Click the name, and the `DataSource` property will be set to `datTitles`.

Next, set the `DataField` property, which associates a field in the table with a control on the form. Because the TextBox associated with the Title label will hold book titles, you want to associate it with the Title field on the Titles table. Click the `DataField` property, and a drop-down button appears. Click it, and all the fields from the Titles table pop up (see Figure 24.12). Click the Title name, and the `DataField` property will be set to `Title`.

FIGURE 24.12.
Listing the fields from the Titles table.

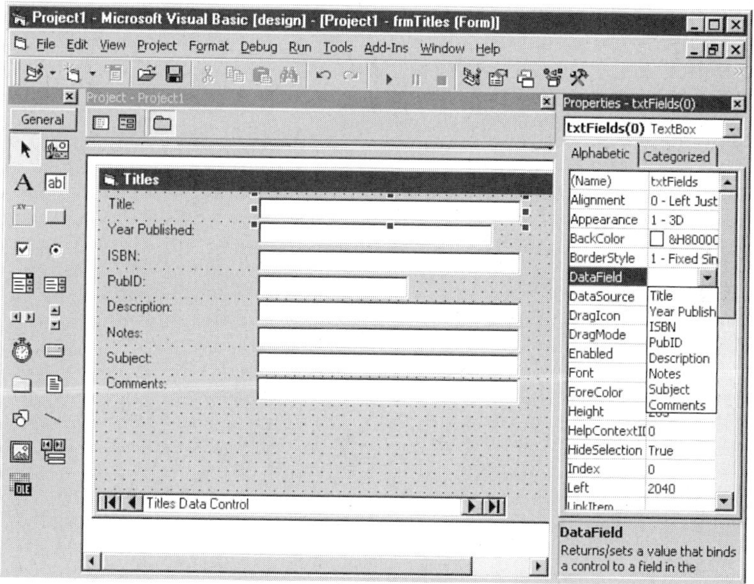

The other controls on the form are set in the same manner. When the `DataSource` and `DataField` properties are set for each text box, you're ready to run the project to display data from the Titles table. The first record in the table, with its data displayed in the newly created front end, is shown in Figure 24.13.

To move forward through the table, click the right-arrow button on the Data control. To move to the last record, click the right-arrow/bar button. To move backward, click the left-arrow button. To move to the first record, click the left-arrow/bar button.

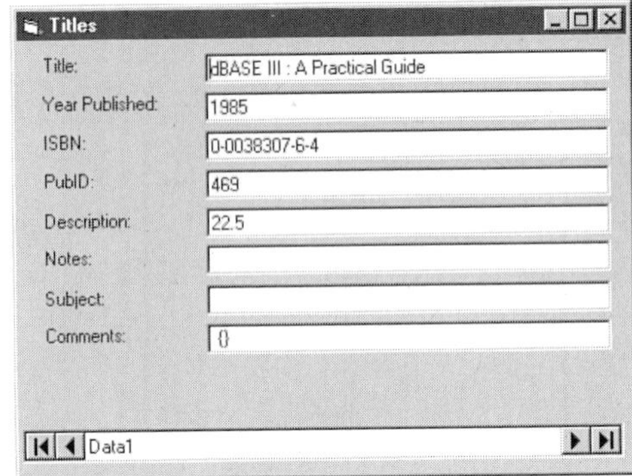

FIGURE 24.13.
The front end to the Titles table.

You now have a fully functional database front end that can be used to browse the Biblio table, and you created it without writing a single line of Visual Basic code. Of course, if you want to add any additional functionality to the program (such as adding new records, deleting records, or editing existing records), you'll have to write code to provide these functions. Still, you can create a functional database browser by doing nothing more than placing some controls on a form and setting a few properties.

Using the Data-Bound Controls

Although using text boxes to display data from a database table is adequate for simple database browsing, some applications require more complex views of the data in a database. One example is a *lookup table*, which lets you select a particular item and then displays all the other data associated with that item. The most direct way to implement a lookup table is to create a list box that's filled with table data. However, to do this by using a standard Visual Basic ListBox control requires writing code to add items to the list.

Another example is displaying data from a database table in a spreadsheet view so that users can edit a record while viewing other records in the table. The standard Grid control can be made to do this, but only after writing a lot of code to add the functionality not found in the Grid control.

Visual Basic 5 provides three data-bound controls so that you can create programs like the preceding examples:

- DBList for a data-bound list box
- DBCombo for a data-bound combo box
- DBGrid for a data-bound grid control

These controls have a set of properties that let you connect them to database tables through the Data control to provide access to multiple records in the table. You can also use the data-bound list controls for a lookup table application, such as the one I just mentioned. For example, in the `Biblio` database, one DBList control can provide a list of publishers from the Publishers table that you can select from to access a list of the book titles in another DBList control on the same form.

Loading the Data-Bound Controls

The data-bound controls aren't part of the Toolbox that's loaded when you first start Visual Basic; you have to add them to a project manually. To do this, choose Project | Toolbox from the menu or press Ctrl+T. The Components dialog box appears (see Figure 24.14).

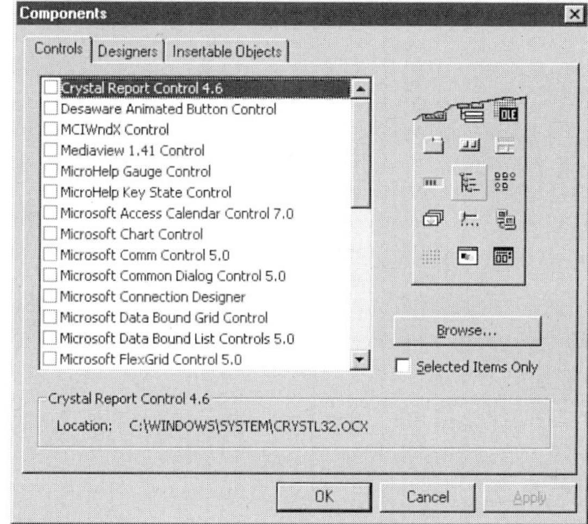

FIGURE 24.14.
The Components dialog box.

To add the data-bound controls to a project, simply click the check boxes next to Microsoft Data Bound Grid Control and Microsoft Data Bound List Controls 5.0. Click OK to add these controls to the bottom of the Toolbox (see Figure 24.15).

FIGURE 24.15.
The Toolbox with the data-bound controls added.

Working with the Data-Bound List Box (DBList)

The DBList control acts like a standard ListBox control except in the way data is added to the list. With the standard ListBox, to add data to the list you have to write code by using the `AddItem` method. With the DBList control, the list is filled simply by setting the right properties to connect a Data control on the form with the DBList control. As with binding a text box, the DBList control has a set of properties that you set to specify which Data control to attach to and which field is its source of data.

The following properties must be set to bind the DBList control to a database table and a particular field:

- Set `DataSource` to the name of the Data control.
- Set `RowSource` to the name of the Data control used as a source of items for the DBList control.
- Set `ListField` to the name of the field in the table specified by `RowSource` that's used to fill the list.

After these properties are set, you can use the DBList control to pull data from a database table. The DBList control is filled with publisher names from the Publishers table in the `Biblio` database. Of course, before attempting to use the DBList control, you must first make sure that the Data control that you are using has its `Connect`, `DatabaseName`, and `RecordSource` properties set accordingly.

Creating a Lookup Table

In many programming applications, you'll want to present users with a list of choices to make and another list of alternatives based on the first set of choices. For example, by using the scenario briefly discussed in the preceding section, one list will include the list of book publishers and the second list will include the book titles published by that publisher. By using just standard list boxes, creating a lookup table like this would require a lot of code to synchronize the lists. By using the DBList control, however, creating a lookup table involves nothing more than setting the right properties.

To illustrate that one DBList control can be used to determine the contents of another DBList control, we'll create another sample program. It will contain two DBList controls and two Data controls. Use Table 24.2 and Figure 24.16 as guides for building the program's interface.

Table 24.2. The controls and their properties for the sample program that links two DBList controls together.

Control Type	*Property*	*Value*
Form	`Name`	`frmDBListSample`
	`Caption`	`DBList Sample`

Control Type	Property	Value
	Height	5460
	Width	6600
Label	Name	lblPublishers
	Caption	Publishers
	Height	240
	Left	630
	Top	600
	Width	2055
Label	Name	lblTitles
	Caption	Titles
	Height	240
	Left	3960
	Top	600
	Width	2055
DBList	Name	dblPublishers
	Height	3570
	Left	165
	Top	1005
	Width	2955
DBList	Name	dblTitles
	Height	3570
	Left	3495
	Top	1005
	Width	2955
Data	Name	datPublishers
	Caption	Publishers
	Height	315
	Left	165
	Top	4635
	Width	2955
Data	Name	datTitles
	Caption	Titles

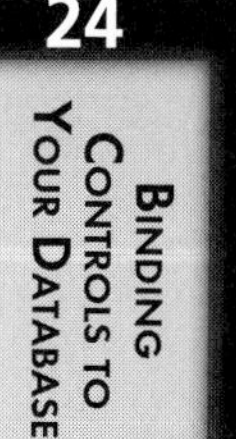

continues

Table 24.2. continued

Control Type	Property	Value
	`Height`	315
	`Left`	3495
	`Top`	4635
	`Width`	2955

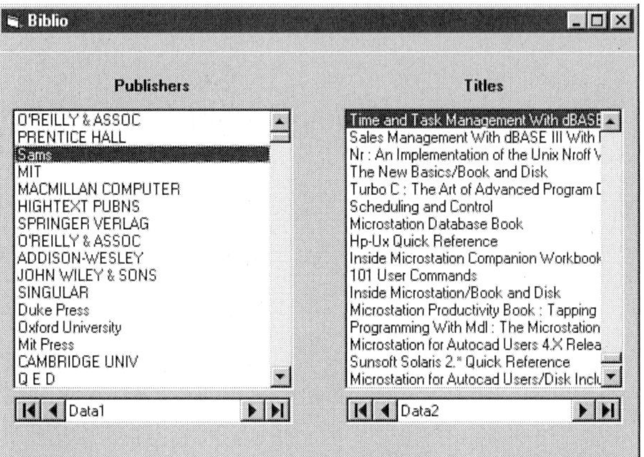

FIGURE 24.16.
The lookup table form.

To create the lookup table of publishers and book titles, continue working with the DBList control that you've already set up. Recall that to fill the list with the names of the publishers, you had to set these properties: `DataSource`, `RowSource`, and `ListField`. To create a lookup table, you have to set some additional properties.

A lookup table works by having the DBList control with the "lookup" data (a term or phrase such as *Sams*) pass a key field to the second DBList control that has the data you're looking for. In the example, the Publishers and Titles tables are linked by the PubID field, which is common to both tables. Through this link, when you select a publisher, the DBList control passes the value of that publisher's PubID field to the second DBList control, which displays the Titles table data. The second DBList control takes the PubID value, passes it to its Data control, matches it with a PubID field in its table, and displays the list of related book titles. If there isn't a match, nothing will happen. Before you can bind the DBList controls to the proper fields, you'll have to set the properties for the two Data controls. Both Data controls should have their `Connect` properties set to `Access` and their `DatabaseName` properties set to the path for the `Biblio` database on your system. The first Data control, `datPublishers`, should have its `RecordSource` property set to `Publishers`. The `RecordSource` property for the second Data control, `datTitles`, should be set to `Titles`.

Now you're ready to set the database properties for the two DBList controls, `dblPublishers` and `dblTitles`. The `dblPublishers` control should have its `DataSource` and `RowSource` properties set to `datPublishers`, the Data control being used to access the Publishers table in the `Biblio` database. The `DataSource` and `RowSource` properties of the `dblTitles` control should both be set to the other Data control, `datTitles`.

The `ListField` property of the `dblPublishers` control can now be set to the field in the Publishers table that it will represent. We want to show a list of the publisher names in this DBList control, so `ListField` should be set to `Company Name`. The other DBList control, `dblTitles`, will contain a list of book titles, so its `ListField` property should be set to Title, a field in the Titles table.

The two DBList controls will be linked by a common field: PubID. Therefore, the `DataField` and `BoundColumn` properties for both controls must be set to `PubID`.

Finally, a few lines of code need to be added to get the `dblTitles` control to display the correct titles whenever a new publisher is selected from the `dblPublishers` control. Add the code in Listing 24.1 to the form.

Listing 24.1. The code needed to update the `dblTitles` control whenever a new publisher is selected in the `dblPublishers` control.

```
Private Sub dblPublishers_Click()

Dim sql As String

sql = "SELECT * FROM TITLES WHERE PubID=" & dblPublishers.BoundText
datTitles.RecordSource = sql
datTitles.Refresh

End Sub
```

When the `dblPublishers` DBList control is clicked, a SQL statement is issued to the `datTitles` Data control, to which `dblTitles` is bound. This creates a `Recordset` for the Data control of only those titles that match the selected PubID (`dblPublishers.BoundText`).

The DBList control on the left displays the names of book publishers from the Publishers table of the `Biblio` database. The DBList control on the right displays the list of book titles from the Titles table published by a publisher based on the value of the PubID field that's common between the record from the Publishers table and the record from the Titles table. The two DBList controls are linked so that as you move from one publisher to the next in the left DBList control, the list of book titles changes in the right DBList control.

Working with the Data-Bound Combo Box (DBCombo)

Another way to present a list of data bound to a database is with the DBCombo control. The main difference between the DBCombo control and the DBList control is that the DBList control presents the whole list, whereas the DBCombo control presents a text box with the selected item from the list in it and a drop-down list box containing the rest of the list.

The DBCombo control is bound to a database in the same way the DBList control is bound to a database. The following properties have to be set to bind the DBCombo control to a database table and a field:

- Set `DataSource` to the name of the Data control.
- Set `RowSource` to the name of the Data control used as a source of items for the DBCombo control.
- Set `ListField` to the name of the field in the table specified by `RowSource` that's used to fill the list.

Also, three styles are associated with the DBCombo control, just like with the standard Combo control. The style type determines what information will display in the selected text box and how the list of items bound to the control will be displayed. The styles are `dbcDropDownCombo`, `dbcSimpleCombo`, and `dbcDropDownList`.

dbcDropDownCombo

Figure 24.17 shows a DBCombo control bound to the Titles table in the `Biblio` database. This DBCombo control uses style 0: `dbcDropDownCombo`.

FIGURE 24.17.
The `dbcDropDownCombo` *style.*

With this DBCombo style, the caption of the control appears in the selected text box. As with a standard Combo control, clicking the down arrow displays the list of items that can be selected from the list (see Figure 24.18).

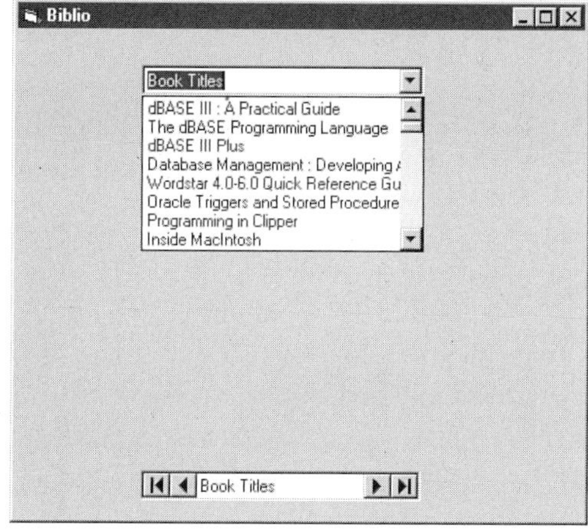

FIGURE 24.18.
Using the `dbcDropDownCombo` *style DBCombo control.*

You can now scroll through the list and select an item by clicking it; the selected item will be displayed in the text box. If you know the item you're looking for, you can type it into the text box, and the control will use a Soundex search to find the item in the list. Visual Basic performs a Soundex search by trying to perform a match as you type characters. Typing **`Sa`** is like searching for the pattern Sa*, with Visual Basic doing the searching while you type. Figure 24.19 shows a partial book title typed into the Selected text box.

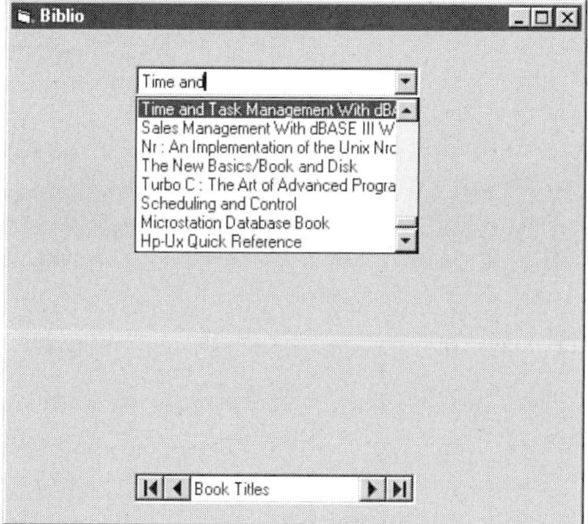

FIGURE 24.19.
Doing a Soundex search in a DBCombo control.

dbcSimpleCombo

Figure 24.20 shows a DBCombo control in the `dbcSimpleCombo` style. The control caption is displayed in the text box, and the items in the list are shown one at a time, using the spin button to scroll through the list. When you click an item in the list, it's displayed in the text box. You also can type in the text box if you want to search for a specific item.

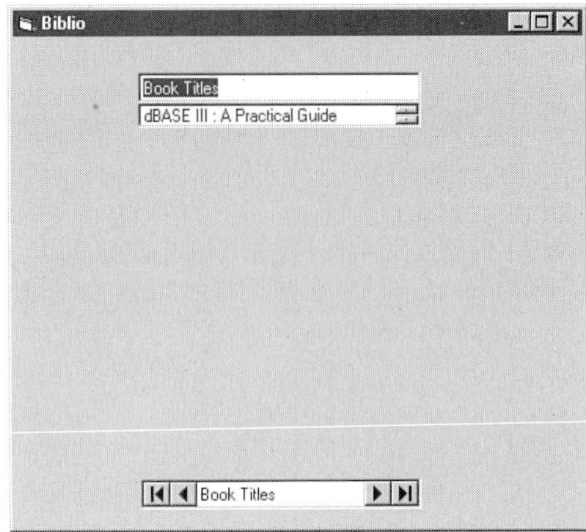

FIGURE 24.20.
The `dbcSimpleCombo` *style.*

`dbcDropDownList`

The `dbcDropDownList` style displays an empty text box (see Figure 24.21). Clicking the drop-down button pops up the list of items to select. When you click an item, it's displayed in the text box. Unlike with the other two DBCombo styles, you can't do a Soundex search with this control.

FIGURE 24.21.
The `dbcDropDownList` *style.*

Working with the Data-Bound Grid Control (DBGrid)

The DBGrid control lets you present data from a database in a spreadsheet view, much like you can do with the standard Grid control. Unlike the standard Grid control, however, the DBGrid control automatically fills its rows and columns with data because it's linked to a Data control. From the `Recordset` object of the Data control, the DBGrid control can create and place column headers in the grid, as well as the data records themselves. These features make the DBGrid control highly preferable to the standard Grid control for a spreadsheet view of data from a database.

Setting the Data Access Properties of the DBGrid Control

The following properties must be set on the DBGrid control to allow access to a database:

- Set `DataMode` to `Bound` (to link to a Data control).
- Set `DataSource` to the name of the Data control.

The DBGrid control is less flexible than the data-bound list controls. The DBGrid control is designed to display data from a database and not from a customized `RowSource`, such as a SQL statement. However, the DBGrid control does have some functionality not found in the data-bound list controls; this functionality is discussed in the following section.

Using the DBGrid Control

The DBGrid control can be used to edit data as well as display it. Figure 24.22 shows a DBGrid control bound to the Titles table of the `Biblio` database. The DBGrid control, with data in its rows and columns, looks like the standard Grid control. Because some of the column cells aren't wide enough to display all the data in the field, you can drag the right edge of a column cell in the column heading to make it wider (see Figure 24.23).

FIGURE 24.22.
The DBGrid control.

Biblio

Title	Year Published	ISBN	PubID	Descripti
dBASE Programming	1986	0-0038307-6-4	472	22.5
The dBASE Programmi	1986	0-0038326-7-8	469	29.5
dBASE III Plus	1996	0-0038337-8-X	469	29.5
Database Managemen	1989	0-0131985-2-1	715	54
Wordstar 4.0-6.0 Quick	1990	0-0133656-1-4	460	14.95
Oracle Triggers and St	1996	0-0134436-3-1	715	0
Programming in Clipper	1988	0-0201145-8-3	9	0
Inside MacIntosh	1994	0-0201406-7-3	9	99.01
Omni Online Database	1983	0-0207992-0-9	156	0
Structured C for Engine	1995	0-0230081-2-1	715	54
An Introduction to Asse	1995	0-0230362-0-6	715	60
Applied Calculus With I	1995	0-0230650-8-7	119	70.67
Information Systems Lit	1991	0-0230942-1-4	156	48
Information Systems Lit	1991	0-0230942-8-1	156	14
Information Systems Lit	1991	0-0230943-1-1	156	30
Information Systems Lit	1993	0-0230948-1-8	156	40
Information Systems Lit	1993	0-0230949-1-5	156	8

Book Titles

You can use the scrollbar at the bottom of the control to scroll across the fields on a row and the scrollbar at the right of the control to scroll through the rows. Of course, you also can scroll through the rows by using the arrow buttons on the Data control.

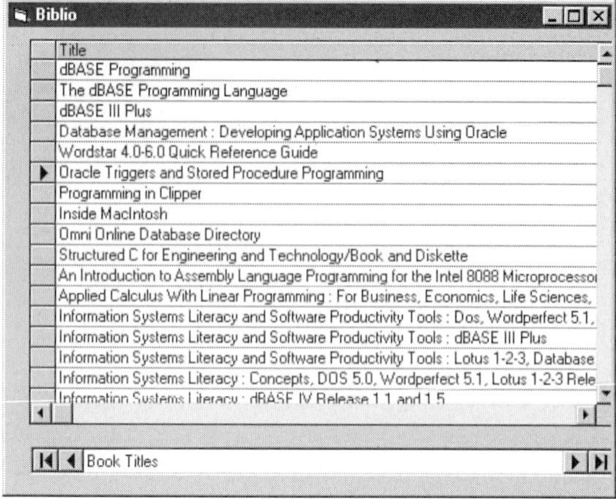

FIGURE 24.23.
A widened column in the DBGrid control.

Summary

Binding controls to a database provides an easy yet powerful way to create database front-end browsing programs. By learning how to set the right properties, you can create controls on a form to display, add, edit, and delete data on a database without writing any code at all.

Visual Basic also provides a set of data-bound controls that provide views of multiple data records at one time. To create these views with the standard Visual Basic controls would take many lines of code.

CHAPTER 25

Managing Your Databases with the Visual Data Manager

IN THIS CHAPTER

One of Visual Basic 5's improvements over Visual Basic 4 is the Visual Data Manager (called the Data Manager in Visual Basic 4). The Data Manager in Visual Basic 4 was a database-access tool that let you perform basic operations on a database. Data Manager's major capabilities included

- Creating a new database
- Opening an existing database
- Repairing a Jet database
- Compacting a Jet database
- Adding, editing, and deleting fields in a table
- Creating indexes on a table
- Attaching Access tables to SQL Server tables

As powerful as Visual Basic 4's Data Manager seemed to be, Visual Basic 5's new Visual Data Manager has many more powerful tools for managing databases within the Visual Basic environment.

This chapter covers using the Visual Data Manager to perform many aspects of database management from within Visual Basic 5:

- Creating a new database
- Editing an existing database
- Managing the database environment
- Building database queries with the Query Builder
- Creating and testing SQL statements

The Visual Data Manager, also called VisData, is an application that can help you manage your databases while working within the Visual Basic IDE. VisData is actually written in Visual Basic as an example of Visual Basic's powerful database-access features. It's installed as an add-in to the Visual Basic IDE and is loaded from the Add-Ins menu. If you have the Professional or Enterprise Edition of Visual Basic 5, you can find the source code for VisData in the `\SAMPLES` directory.

VisData is a powerful data manager. From VisData, you can perform most of the operations on a database that you can from within the database's own development environment. This means that many administrative tasks that in the past forced you to leave the Visual Basic IDE can now be done in VisData. This is a major convenience because many times in the development of an application you'll need to make some sort of change to the database, such as changing a field name or adjusting a field length. Being able to do these types of database administration tasks in VisData saves a lot of time and doesn't require you to be an expert database administrator (not that anything is wrong with that).

Understanding the VisData Environment

When you choose Add-Ins | Visual Data Manager from the menu, you'll see the form shown in Figure 25.1.

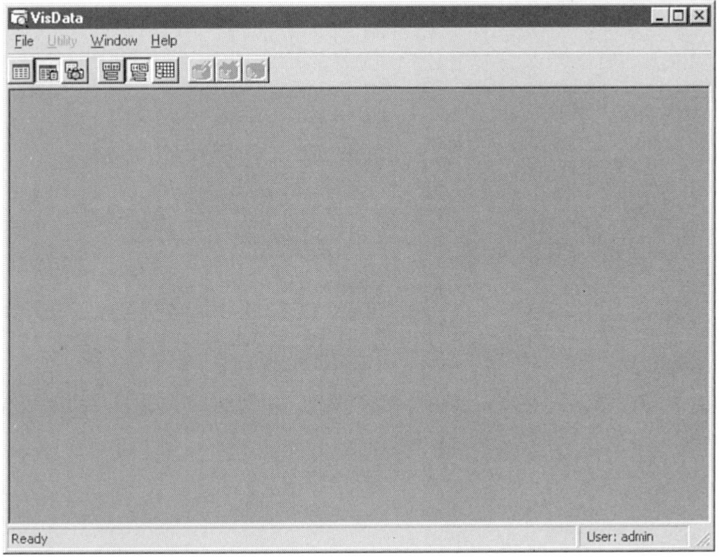

FIGURE 25.1.
VisData's opening form.

At this initial stage, the File menu has the following choices:

Open DataBase...
New...
Workspace...
Errors...
Compact MDB...
Repair MDB...
Exit

Figure 25.2 shows the File menu when first loading VisData.

To work with some data during this overview, open an existing database. Choose File | Open DataBase from the menu and then click Microsoft Access to open a database. In the dialog box that appears, double-click `BIBLIO.MDB` to load the `Biblio` database. You'll see two MDI forms: Database Window and SQL Statement (see Figure 25.3).

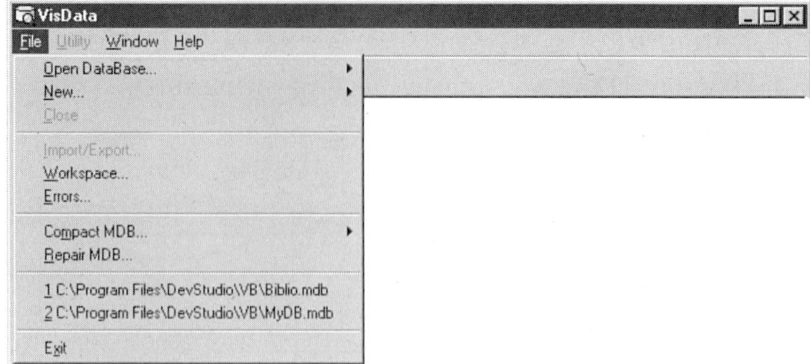

FIGURE 25.2.
The File menu in VisData.

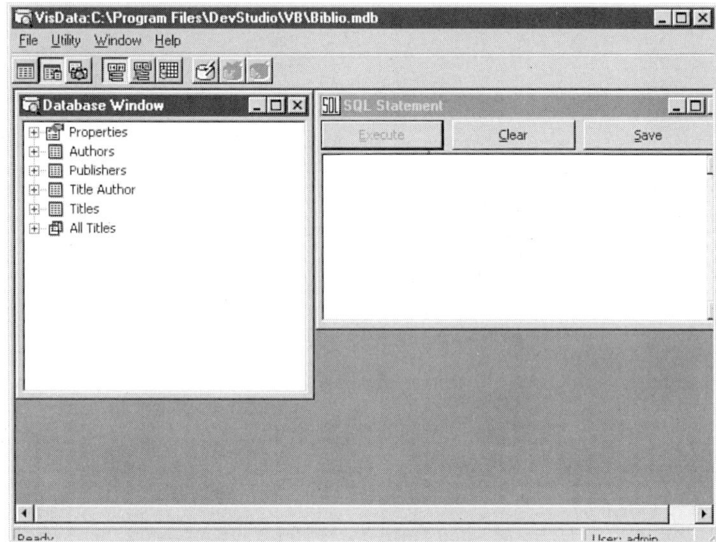

FIGURE 25.3.
The Database Window and SQL Statement forms.

The Utility menu is enabled now that there's a database loaded that the utilities can work with. Table 25.1 shows the utilities VisData provides.

Table 25.1. VisData's utilities.

Utility	*What It Does*
Query Builder	Builds a search expression
Data Form Designer	Builds a database-access form
Global Replace	Builds a SQL statement to update a field for all records in a selected table
Attachments	Lists all attached tables and their connect strings
Groups/Users	Modifies groups, users, permissions, and owners

Utility	What It Does
System.MD?	Creates different SYSTEM.MDA files and sets up security for each one from the same application
Preferences	Sets a login timeout value, the last database loaded as the default, and a default query timeout value

The Database Window is an Explorer-like tree view that displays the structure of the tables of the database. The Properties setting in the Database Window holds the following settings for the Biblio database:

```
Name=
Connect=
Transactions=
Updatable=
CollatingOrder=
QueryTimeout=
Version=
RecordsAffected=
ReplicaID=
DesignMasterID=
Connection=
AccessVersion=
Build=
```

Of course, each property will have a value, if any, based on your particular installation of Microsoft Access. Figure 25.4 shows a partial view of the properties of my Biblio database.

FIGURE 25.4.
Partial view of author's Biblio *properties.*

For each table in the database selected, you can view the following in the Database Window:

- *Fields*—Each field in the table
- *Indexes*—Each index defined in the table
- *Properties*—Property settings for the table

You can view the following properties for each table:

```
Name=
Updatable=
DateCreated=
LastUpdated=
Connect=
Attributes=
SourceTableName=
RecordCount=
ValidationRule=
ValidationText=
ConflictTable=
ReplicaFilter=
OrderByOn=
```

Again, the property settings for each table depend on your specific configuration. Figure 25.5 displays the property settings for the Authors table in the `Biblio` database based on my configuration.

FIGURE 25.5.
A partial view of the Authors table's properties.

Working with Tables in the Database Window Form

In addition to providing you with a view of the structure and properties of a database, the Database Window form lets you open a table and change a table design from within the form. By highlighting one of the tables in the Database Window and clicking the right mouse button, you can perform the following operations on the table:

- *Open*—Opens a table for editing
- *Design*—Opens a table to change the table design
- *Rename*—Renames the table
- *Delete*—Deletes the table
- *Copy Structure*—Copies the structure of the table to another table
- *Refresh List*—Redisplays the table list

- *New Table*—Creates a new table
- *New Query*—Uses the Query Builder to create a new query

Opening a Table in the Database Window

To open the Authors table, highlight it in the tree and click the right mouse button. Clicking Open brings up the Dynaset:Authors window (see Figure 25.6).

FIGURE 25.6.
The Dynaset:Authors window.

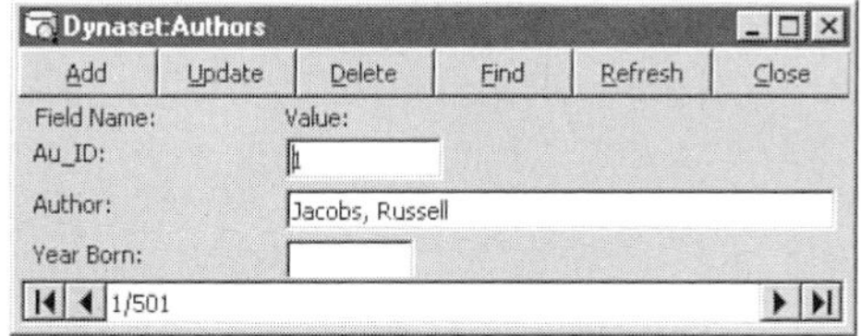

This window is called Dynaset:Authors because the type of *recordset* you're working with is a dynaset, which is the default in the Visual Data Manager. You can also show table-type and snapshot-type recordsets by clicking on their icons in Visual Data Manager's toolbar before opening the recordset.

A *dynaset* is a dynamic set of records that contains the records from a database table or the results of a query. A dynaset is considered dynamic because you can add, edit, and delete records in a dynaset, which you can't do with a snapshot-type recordset.

NOTE

Remember that a snapshot-type recordset is read only and won't allow any changes to be made to the table.

Under the title bar of the Dynaset:Authors window are six buttons that provide functionality:

- *Add*—Adds a new record to the table
- *Update*—Updates the table
- *Delete*—Deletes a record from the table
- *Find*—Finds a record in the table
- *Refresh*—Regenerates the data in the table
- *Close*—Closes the form

Clicking Add brings up a new record with an autogenerated Au_ID field, a blank Author field, and a default Year Born date of `0`. Also, the Add button changes to Cancel so users can cancel adding the record if necessary (see Figure 25.7).

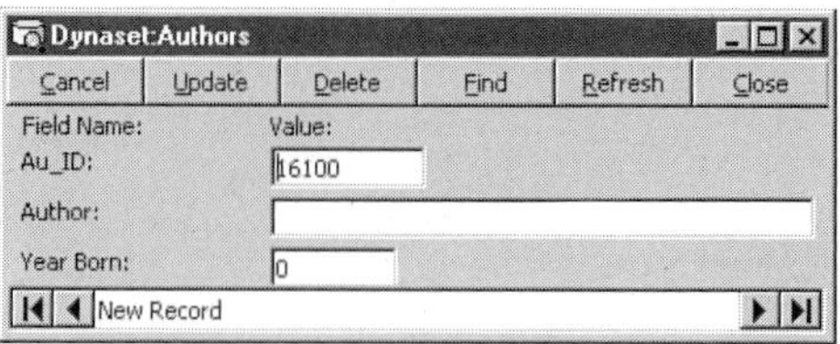

FIGURE 25.7.
Adding a new record.

When you finish making changes to the table, click the Update button to commit the changes to the database. This simply means that you're satisfied with the changes you've made to the table and want to make them permanent. Clicking Update will bring up a confirmation box like the one shown in Figure 25.8. Click Yes to commit the changes or No to cancel the changes.

FIGURE 25.8.
The Commit Changes? confirmation box.

Clicking the Delete button brings up a confirmation box asking whether you want to delete the current record. Click Yes to delete the record or No to leave the record in the table.

Clicking Find brings up a dialog box asking you to enter a search expression, which can be any valid SQL WHERE clause for that table. Figure 25.9 shows a search expression entered into the text box. Click OK to have Visual Basic search for any records that match the expression. If a match is found, that record's data appears on the form. If a match isn't found, the form stays on the record it was on when you began the search. If for some reason your search expression has an error in it—perhaps because you misspelled a field name—a dialog box informs you of an error in the search expression.

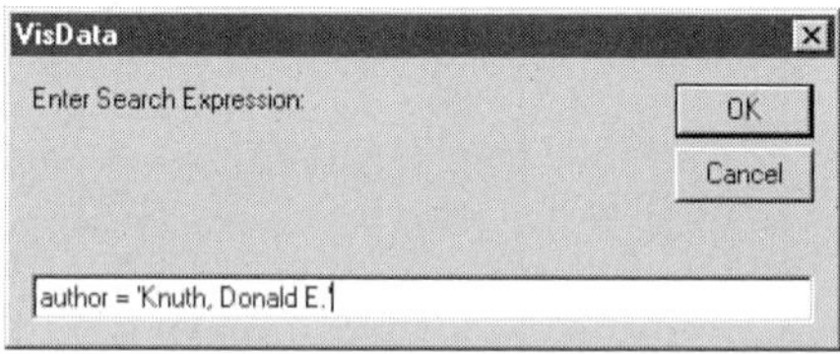

FIGURE 25.9.
The Enter Search Expression dialog box.

To see changes made in the table while you're using VisData, click the Refresh button. The table is regenerated to reflect any changes made to the table, and you're placed in the first record in the table.

Working with Table Designs

The commands on the Database Window's Design menu let you work with a table's structure. Right-click any entry in the Database Window for a pop-up menu with several choices. Choosing Design from the menu loads the Table Structure form, which has functions for

- Adding a field
- Removing a field
- Renaming a field
- Changing a field's ordinal position
- Allowing a field to be zero-length
- Designating a field as required
- Creating validation text for a field
- Creating a validation rule for a field
- Creating a default value for a field
- Adding an index
- Removing an index
- Renaming an index

Figure 25.10 shows the Table Structure form for the Authors table in the `Biblio` database.

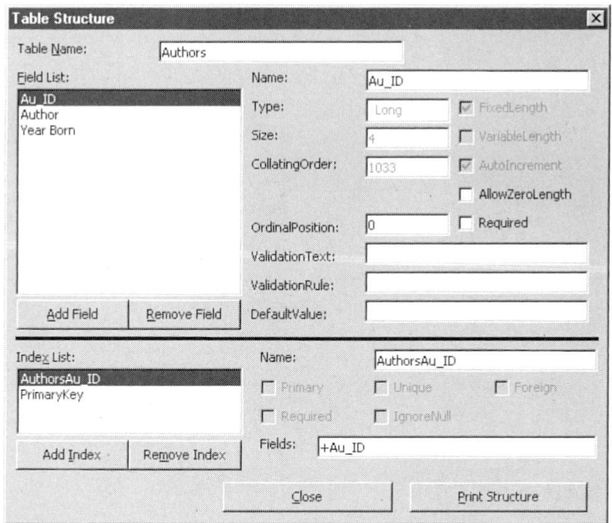

FIGURE 25.10.
The Table Structure form, displaying the Authors table.

The information for the first field listed in the table is displayed when the form is first loaded. To display the structure of another field, click a field in the Field List. Figure 25.11 shows the structure of the Year Born field.

FIGURE 25.11.
The Year Born field selected in the Table Structure form.

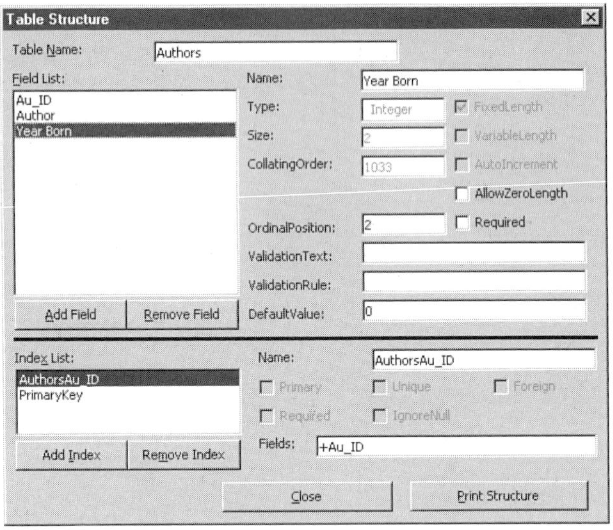

You can edit indexes the same way you edit fields. If you want to add an index to the table, click the Add Index button. The Add Index to Authors form will load, as shown in Figure 25.12.

FIGURE 25.12.
The Add Index to Authors form.

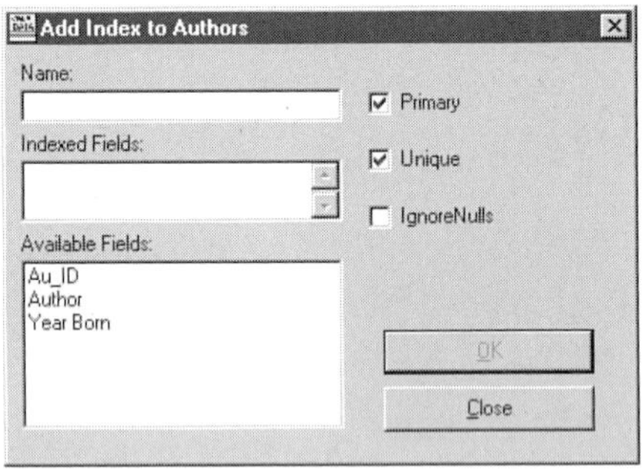

Enter a name, the fields to be indexed, whether the index is unique or primary, and whether the index should ignore null values. Click OK to add the index to the Index List. Click Close at any time if you decide not to create the new index.

When you finish editing the structure of the table, you can print the structure or close the form.

Using Query Builder

For most experienced Visual Basic programmers, building database queries is second nature. However, for newer programmers and for those Visual Basic programmers who haven't done much database programming, creating database queries can be time consuming. SQL, the nonprocedural language that Query Builder is based on, is easy to use for simple queries but can become complex, especially when you're trying to pull information from more than one table.

Query Builder presents an interactive interface for you to create the equivalent of a SQL statement without actually writing SQL code. To do this, Query Builder provides prompts to fill in the necessary parameters for a query. You can use the Query Builder by selecting it from Visual Data Manager's Utility menu. Figure 25.13 shows the Query Builder form and its parameters.

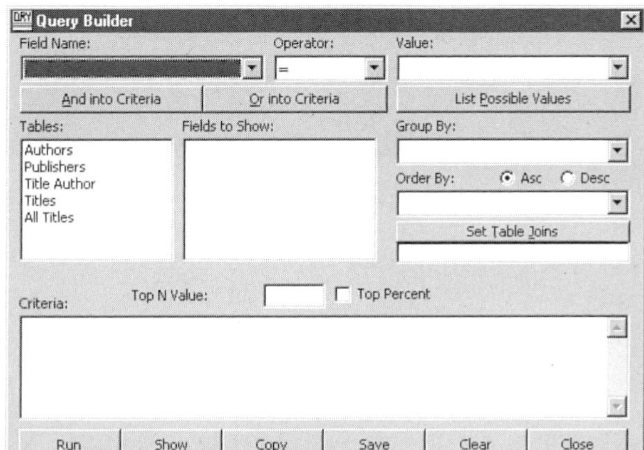

FIGURE 25.13.
The Query Builder form.

Building a Query in Query Builder

When the Query Builder form is first loaded, all the parameters are blank except the Operator parameter, which defaults to =. To build a query, the first thing you need to do is select a table to query. Selecting a table in the Tables list will fill in the first field from the table in the Field Name combo box. Also, all the fields from the table will be displayed in the Fields to Show list box (see Figure 25.14).

With Field Name and Operator filled in, the only parameter missing to have a complete query is Value. Figure 25.15 shows a query built to determine whether the famous algorithmist Donald Knuth is among the authors in the Authors table. The field name Author from the Authors table is selected in the Field Name box, the default = (equals) operator is used in the Operator box, and the name "Knuth, Donald E." is entered in the Value box.

FIGURE 25.14.
Querying the Authors table.

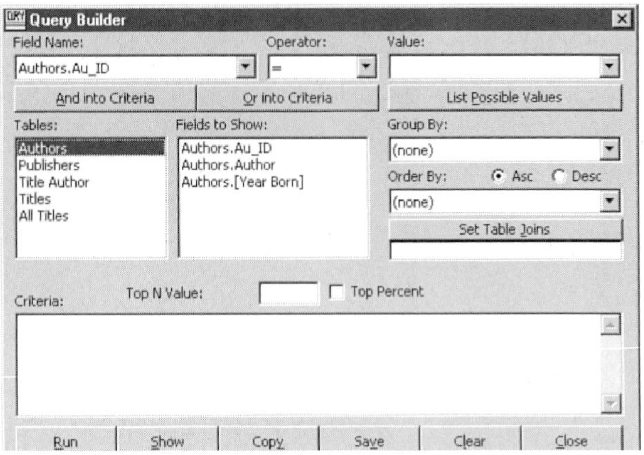

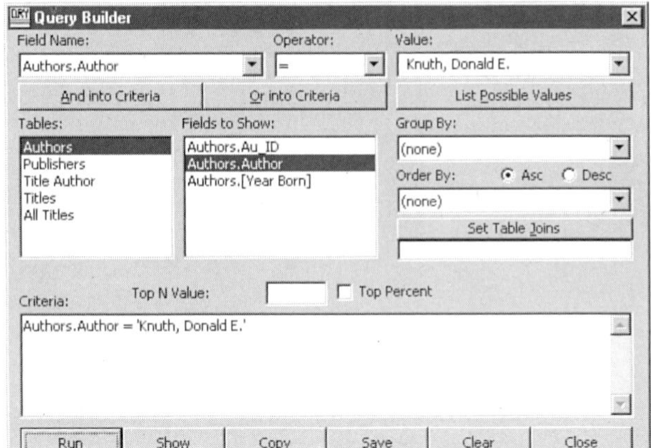

FIGURE 25.15.
A complete Query Builder query.

Running Query Builder Queries

When you're finished entering the query parameters, click the And into Criteria button. This will add the query to the Criteria box at the bottom of the Query Builder form. You can define and add one or more queries to the Criteria box and specify what the logic will be when multiple queries are used together. By adding a query with the And into Criteria button, you are specifying that the parameters of your query must be satisified if a record is to be included in the result recordset. If you add a query with the Or into Criteria button, you are specifying that either your query's parameters or those of a previously added query can be satisfied if a record is to be included in the result recordset. For the first query that you add, it doesn't matter whether you use the And into Criteria button or the Or into Criteria button because it is a single query and cannot yet be logically linked with another query.

To run the query, click the Run button at the bottom of the form. A dialog box appears, asking you whether this is a SQL *passthrough query* (a SQL-specific query that you use to send commands directly to a SQL database server). Click No, and a SQL Statement window will be displayed with the results of the query (see Figure 25.16).

FIGURE 25.16.
Results from the Query Builder query.

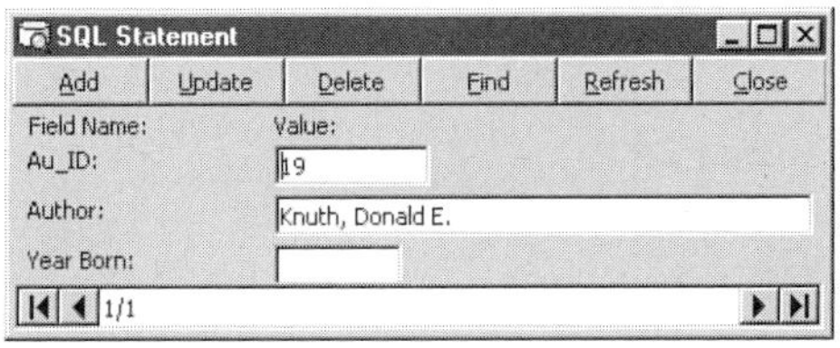

The Au_ID, Author, and Year Born fields are displayed. Also, the data control displays `1/1` as its caption, which means that the SQL Statement window is displaying number 1 of 1 record. Notice, too, that from this window you can perform all the same functions that were available to you when you viewed the Authors table earlier: Add, Edit, Delete, Sort, Filter, Move, and Find. To hide the SQL Statement window, click Close.

Another button at the bottom of the Query Builder form is Show. Clicking this button shows the entire SQL statement that was generated from Query Builder. Figure 25.17 displays the SQL statement for the query just created.

SQL Query
Select Authors.Au_ID,Authors.Author,Authors.[Year Born] From Authors Where (Authors.Author = 'Knuth, Donald E.')
OK

FIGURE 25.17.
The SQL statement generated from Query Builder.

TIP

The Show command is especially helpful if you're still learning SQL. I've known several people who became decent SQL programmers primarily from studying the SQL statements generated from an automated query builder.

If you select a single field name in the Fields to Show box, you can group the results of the query by that field. Simply select the field name in the Group By box. For example, if you specify that the Publishers.Name field should be equal to SAMS or NEW RIDERS and then choose the Publishers.Address field in both the Fields to Show and Group By boxes, the result of the query will show only the Publishers.Address field for those two publishers.

When defining a query, you can also specify that the results be sorted by a certain field in either ascending or descending order. Use the Order By radio buttons and combo box to specify the sort order and field.

Finally, you can add joins to the query by clicking on the Set Table Joins button. Of course, you must have two tables selected before adding a join. A dialog box will prompt you to select the tables and the field to join.

Testing SQL Statements

Located next to the Database Window on the VisData form is the SQL Statement form, from which you can write and test SQL statements to see whether they return the value(s) you're looking for. This feature is one of the best improvements of VisData over the Visual Basic 4 Data Manager. Before Visual Basic 5, if you wanted to test a SQL statement before you added it to your code, you had to leave the Visual Basic IDE and run the SQL code from the database environment. Now you can write the SQL statement and test it without leaving Visual Basic.

The SQL Statement form couldn't be easier to use. Just click in the SQL Statement form, type your SQL statement, and click Execute. Figure 25.18 shows the SQL Statement form.

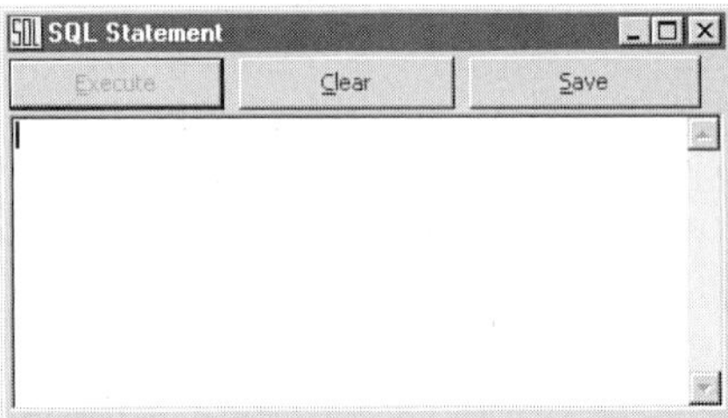

FIGURE 25.18.
The SQL Statement form.

The SQL Statement form has three buttons:

- *Execute,* which runs your SQL statement after you enter it into the form
- *Clear,* which erases any text that has been entered into the form
- *Save,* which saves the SQL statement as a `QueryDef` object that you can later reference in your code

Nothing is simpler than using the SQL Statement form—unless, of course, you don't know how to write SQL statements. To use the form, enter a SQL statement and click the Execute button. Figure 25.19 shows a SQL statement that again looks for Donald Knuth in the Authors table.

When you click Execute, a dialog box will ask whether the statement is a SQL passthrough query. Unless it is, click No, and the SQL code will execute. Figure 25.20 shows the results of executing the SQL statement. The results, as expected, are the same as with the Query Builder example.

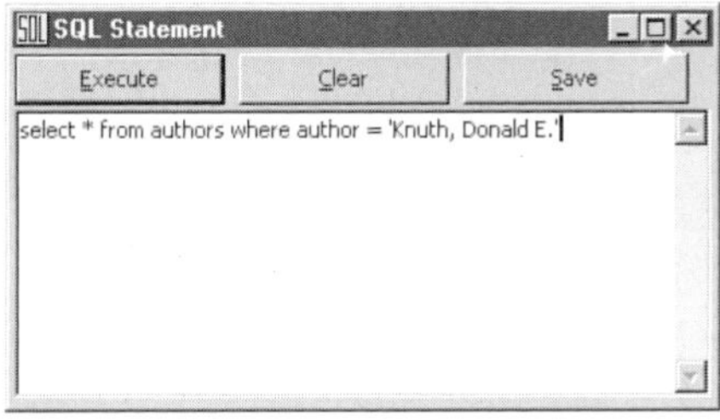

FIGURE 25.19.
A SQL statement ready to execute.

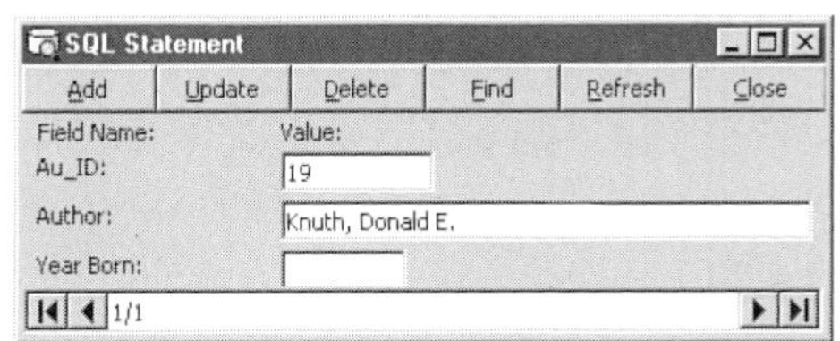

FIGURE 25.20.
Results of SQL statement execution.

If you misspell something or use the wrong field name in the SQL statement, VisData will generate an error message. The error message will display an error number and an explanation of what VisData interprets as the cause of the error. Suppose that you type the following SQL statement into the form:

```
select * from author where author = 'Knuth, Donald E.'
```

When this statement is executed, the error message in Figure 25.21 is generated. The error message asks whether you want to display the Data Access Objects error collection. If you click Yes, the Errors form will display the error number, the object name, and an explanation of the error.

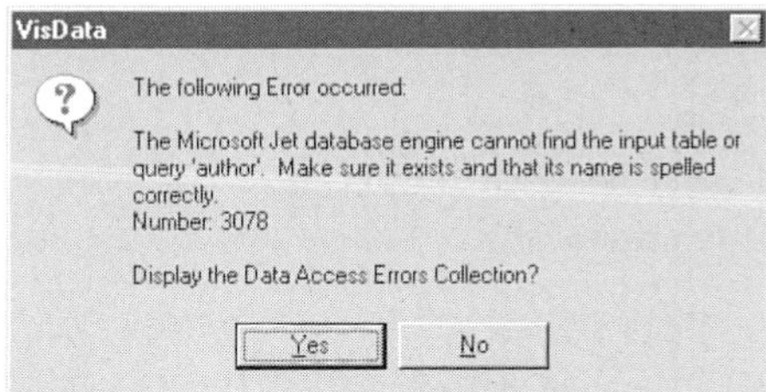

FIGURE 25.21.
A VisData error message.

Finally, you can enter any legal SQL statement in the SQL Statement form. You've seen a simple `select` query, but you can execute everything from inner and outer joins to crosstab queries in the SQL Statement form.

Creating a New Database in VisData

You can use VisData to create a new database and the tables that make up the database. You can create the following types of databases:

- Microsoft Access 2.0 and 7.0
- dBASE III, IV, and 5.0
- FoxPro 2.0, 2.5, 2.6, and 3.0
- Paradox 3.*x*, 4.*x*, and 5.*x*
- ODBC
- Text files

To create a new database, choose File | New | Microsoft Access | Version 7.0 MDB... from the VisData menu. Here, you'll use Access 7.0 because you're using 32-bit Visual Basic.

VisData displays a dialog box prompting you for the name of the database file. Enter **`Clients`** and click the Save button. The Database Window and SQL Statement forms appear.

In the Database Window, right-click Properties. One selection that will appear is New Table. Select New Table to display the Table Structure form (see Figure 25.22).

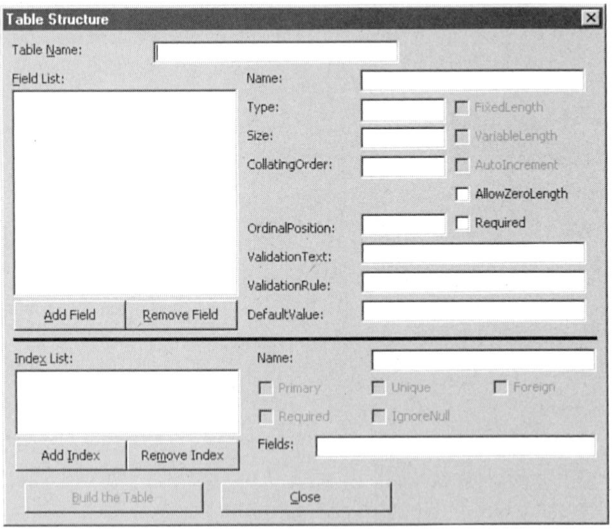

FIGURE 25.22.
The Table Structure form.

This form, which you've seen before when editing a table's structure, is used to create a table and its structure. The first field to fill in is the Table Name field. Here, you're creating a table of client names and addresses, so type **`Client Info`** in the text box.

The next step is to create the fields that will make up the table. Click the Add Field button to display the Add Field form (see Figure 25.23).

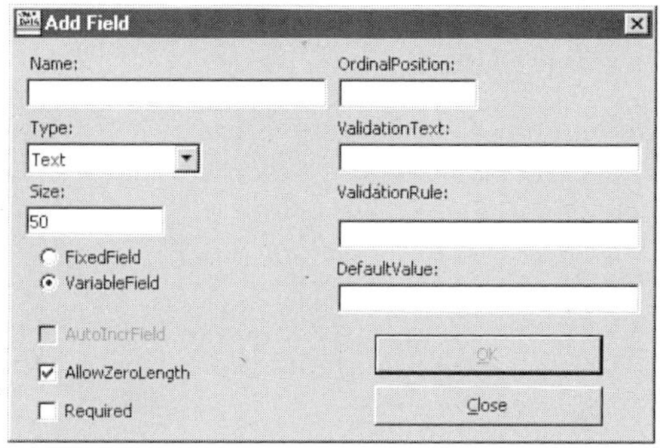

FIGURE 25.23.
The Add Field form.

Type a name into the text box and press Tab to go to the Type field. The following field types are allowed:

Boolean	Double
Byte	Date/Time
Integer	Text
Long	Binary
Currency	Memo
Single	

The next field is Size. Select a size that's long enough to hold the longest name but not so long that you end up wasting a lot of space.

Next is a selection for whether you want the field to be fixed length or variable length. Because you don't know the exact size of each client name, select a variable field length.

The next selection is a grayed-out check box for AutoIncrement. An AutoIncrement is one that automatically increments its value by 1 every time a record is added. Because a text field can't do that, the field is disabled.

Following AutoIncrement is AllowZeroLength. Many text fields need to be allowed to have a zero length because they might not always be storing any data. However, because you're entering the Name field, you don't want any blank names, so don't allow this to be a zero-length field.

Select the next check box, Required, if you want a field to be a required entry every time a new record is entered into the table. For this table, the name is definitely required, so select Required.

Following Required is OrdinalPosition. You can assign a position to each field in the table by putting values in this text box. You aren't really interested in OrdinalPosition for this example, so leave it blank.

Next you're prompted to enter information into the ValidationText text box. This text will appear if you enter a validation rule in the ValidationRule text box, explained in the following paragraph. For example, if the validation rule says that the text can't be longer than 20 characters and users try to enter a field longer than 20 characters, the text in the ValidationText text box will be displayed.

If you want to limit what the user can enter for this field, enter a rule in the ValidationRule text box. An example might be that a number has to be within a range of numbers, as in `Between 10 and 20`.

Finally, the DefaultValue text box lets you enter a default value for the field. This value is placed in the field if users choose not to enter their own value.

After you fill out the information for a field, click OK. You can then continue defining more fields, or click the Close button to finish adding fields. When you've entered all the fields for the table, click Build the Table. VisData will build the table and then you can use it like any other Access database table.

Summary

This chapter showed you how to use the VisData Visual Data Manager to add, delete, and edit records in an existing database table. VisData can also be used to create new tables and to create, edit, and test SQL expressions.

Although you can use all VisData features without actually using VisData, you'll find that using VisData makes connecting your applications to databases easier and more efficient. Thus, VisData is a worthwhile addition to your Visual Basic toolkit.

CHAPTER 26

Reporting Magic with Crystal Reports

IN THIS CHAPTER

Inputting, storing, and retrieving data are important functions for most computer applications, and Visual Basic provides many tools and utilities for working with these functions. Another function, reporting, is often the most important function of an application because communicating the data stored and manipulated in an application is always the end goal of application development. Many application designs begin with deciding on the content and layout of the reports the application will produce.

Beginning with Visual Basic 3.0, the Professional Edition (and the Enterprise Edition for Visual Basic 4) has provided the Crystal Reports report writer for an easy way to create professional-looking reports. As users of older versions of Visual Basic and BASIC will attest, designing reports was often the hardest and most-disliked part of application development. Crystal Reports makes report creation easy and, for the most part, fun.

This chapter discusses using Crystal Reports as a design tool for creating and managing high-level reports. In this chapter, you'll run Crystal Reports from inside the Visual Basic IDE, although you can run it as a standalone program by choosing it from the Visual Basic 5 Program Manager group.

Designing Reports with Crystal Reports: An Overview

Crystal Reports provides you with the tools to completely design the look and grouping of a report. Designing the look of a report involves the following:

- Laying out the group headings
- Laying out the column headings
- Choosing font styles

Designing the grouping of a report involves deciding which group of data causes a break in a report. A good sample database you can use to design a report around is the `Biblio` database included with VB. This database includes several tables that present data on books, the authors of the books, and the publishers of the books. For example, by using `Biblio`'s Titles table, you might design a report that has a break in it every time a new publisher comes up in the report. This report might have a report title of "Titles by Publisher" and a group heading of "Titles by:", where the specific publisher is filled in after the colon.

You can add subtotals to these groupings, either for adding columns of numbers or for creating a count of the items of a group. By using the preceding example, you can create a row heading called "Number of Books Published:" that's printed for each publisher group, along with the number of books published. At the end of the report, you can have another row heading, "Total Books Published:", for all the books published by all the publishers. These kinds of decisions go into creating a Crystal Reports report.

Using Crystal Reports

Crystal Reports is located on Visual Basic's Add-Ins menu as the option Report Designer. Selecting it brings up the Crystal Reports Pro form, as shown in Figure 26.1.

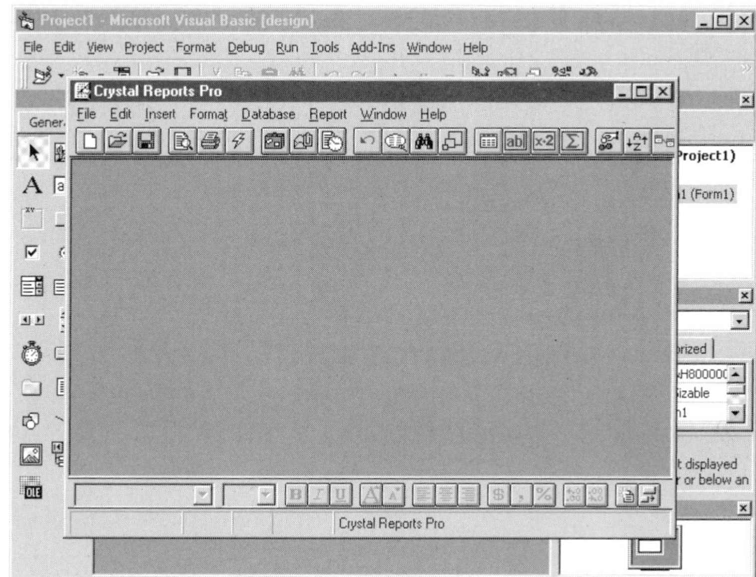

FIGURE 26.1.
The Crystal Reports Pro form.

The Pro form has several different menu selections and a toolbar across the top. You examine the menu selections in more detail later; the toolbar consists of the following choices, in order from left to right:

- Create a new report
- Open an existing report
- Save the report
- Preview report in a window
- Print report to a printer
- Discard saved data and reprint report in previous window
- Export report to a file, to mail,…
- Mail a report
- Launch report to Crystal Reports Server
- Undo last change
- Select fields

- Search for a particular value in report
- Zoom report (fit to window, fit to width, full size)
- Insert a database field
- Insert a text field
- Insert a formula field
- Insert a summary (sum, maximum, count...) for selected field
- Select records to be used in report
- Set record or group sort order
- Visually link tables in report using Experts

Creating a New Report

To create a new report, choose File | New or click the New icon from the toolbar. Crystal Reports has a set of *Experts*, report templates that you can pattern your report after. The different report Experts are shown in the Report Gallery in Figure 26.2.

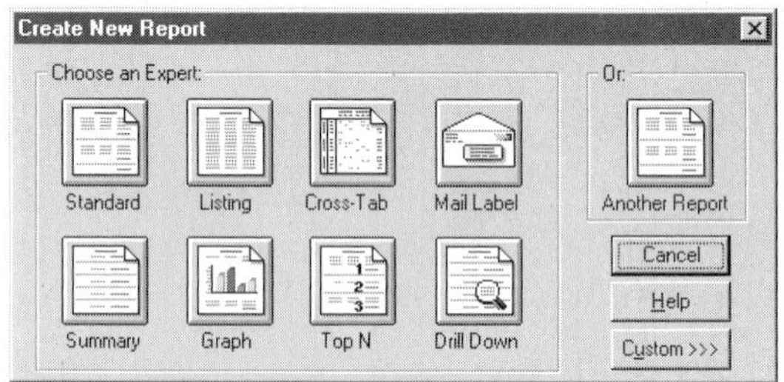

FIGURE 26.2.
The Report Gallery.

Besides the eight standard report Experts, if you've defined another type of Expert, you can select it with the Another Report button. You can create your own report Expert by clicking the Custom button.

The report Experts in the Report Gallery are used to create the following types of reports:

- *Standard*—A report that uses a tabular format and allows data groupings, subheadings, and subtotals
- *Listing*—A tabular report that lists all data without any groupings, subheadings, or subtotals
- *Cross-Tab*—A report that presents the data in a row-oriented format, like a spreadsheet
- *Mail Label*—A report used to print mail labels or the data in a mail-label format
- *Summary*—A report that prints only subtotal and total data
- *Graph*—A report that prints data in a graphic format

- *Top N*—A report that prints the top items based on user-selected criteria
- *Drill Down*—A report that prints subheading data and the detail data that's part of the subheading

For a standard report, click the Standard button. The Create Report Expert form is loaded (see Figure 26.3). This form has tabs, or pages, that represent the steps that are taken to create a report. The first page you see is Tables, which is discussed in the following section.

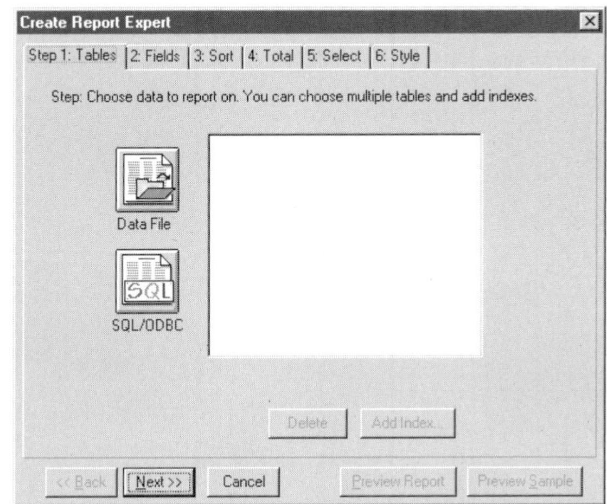

FIGURE 26.3.
The Create Report Expert form.

At the bottom of the Create Report Expert form are two navigation buttons (Back and Next), a Cancel button, a Preview Report button, and a Preview Sample button. The Back button returns you to previous steps in the Create Report Expert, and the Next button takes you to the next step. The Cancel button, of course, cancels the creation of the report. The Preview Report button prints a preview of the report based on how you've defined the layout (if you aren't far enough along in the creation process to print a preview, the button will be disabled). The Preview Sample button prints a sample report of the type you've selected (it's also disabled if you haven't entered enough information for Crystal Reports to generate a report).

The Tables Page

The first step in creating a new report is to select a data file on which the report will be based. The two choices are Data File and SQL/ODBC. Choose Data File if you're building a report based on a desktop database file such as Microsoft Access, dBASE, Paradox, and so on. Choose SQL/ODBC if you're building a report based on a relational database system such as SQL Server, Oracle, and so on. For this example, choose Data File.

When you click Data File, a file directory dialog box appears. For this example, you're working with the `Biblio` database, so choose `BIBLIO.MDB` from the File Name list box by double-clicking its name or by clicking it once and then clicking the Add button after you find the correct path to the database. At this point, you could select more databases to be used if your report required them. For this sample, we'll use only the `Biblio` database, so click the Done button.

If you did opt to select more than one database, there may be cases where one database has table names that are the same as those in another database. When this happens, Crystal Reports will prompt you to provide alias names for any tables that share the same name as a previously loaded table. You will also be asked to specify alias names for all the tables in a database if Crystal Reports' Use Default Alias option has been turned off. Figure 26.4 shows an Alias Name dialog box.

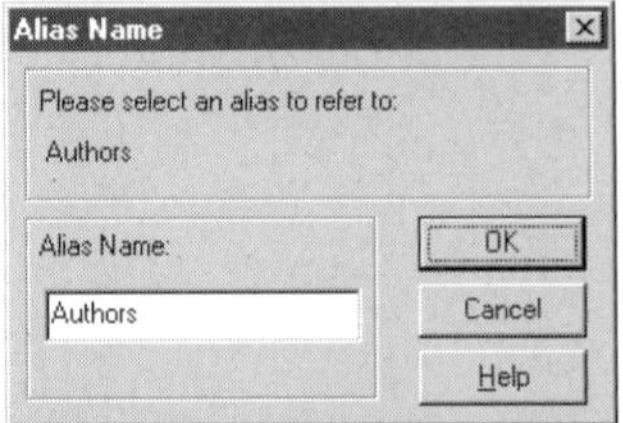

FIGURE 26.4.
The Alias Name dialog box.

> **NOTE**
>
> An *alias* is used to have more than one name that refers to a database table. For different reasons, database administrators and others who control the design and maintenance of databases change table names. This doesn't present a problem unless there are specific formulas or references to the old table name. Then, of course, programs, queries, and so on won't work properly because the wrong table name will be used in the queries, formulas, and other references to the old table. The answer to this problem is to use an alias that points to the actual table, regardless of its name.

The original table name appears in the text box under Alias Name. If you want to use an alias, type it here; otherwise, leave it the same. Click OK if you're changing the name, or click Cancel if you're leaving it the same.

If Crystal Reports' Use Default Alias option is turned off, you will be prompted for alias names for each table in the `Biblio` database. If so, click Done when you've gone through the series of Alias Name dialog boxes. You're then taken to Step 2.

The Links Page

Step 2, Links, presents the database schema that identifies the links between different tables. Figure 26.5 shows the partial schema diagram for the `Biblio` database presented in Step 2.

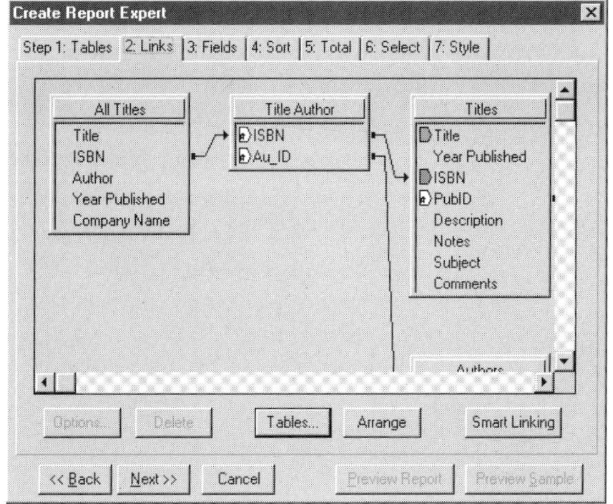

FIGURE 26.5.
The `Biblio` *database schema.*

Figure 26.5 is a partial view of the schema only because the whole schema won't fit on the form. You can use the scrollbars along the right side and bottom of the page to view the parts of the diagram not shown.

If you want, you can rearrange the table boxes by dragging them to different positions on the form. Figure 26.6 shows all the table boxes brought into view by rearranging them.

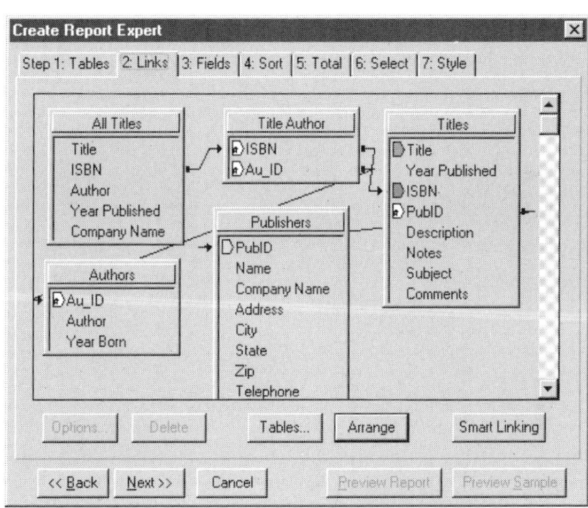

FIGURE 26.6.
The `Biblio` *database schema, rearranged.*

Notice that the arrows indicating the links between tables are redrawn to follow the tables to their new locations. If, after trying to rearrange the schema, you find your arrangement more confusing than the system's original arrangement, you can click the Arrange button to have Crystal Reports Basic put the schema back in its original form.

At the bottom of the Create Report Expert form during Step 2 are three enabled buttons: Tables, Arrange, and Smart Linking. These options, and others, are also available from a floating menu accessed by right-clicking a blank spot of the form. Figure 26.7 shows the Links floating menu.

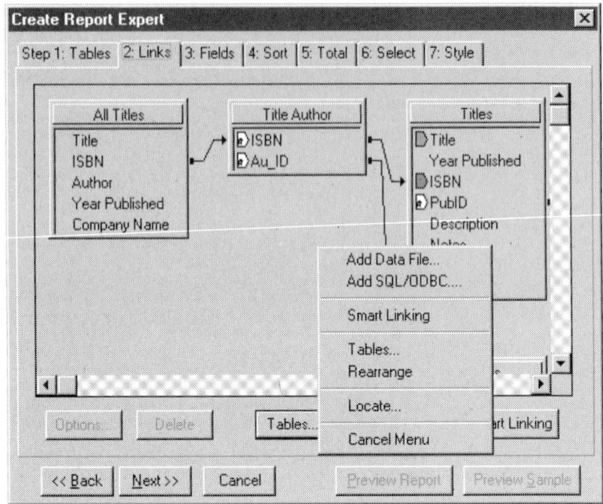

FIGURE 26.7.
The Links floating menu.

The Links floating menu contains the commands for the buttons at the bottom of the form, plus several more menu commands:

- *Add Data File*—Adds a data file from a desktop database
- *Add SQL/ODBC*—Adds a data file or a table view from a relational database
- *Locate*—Finds a table in the schema and centers it on the form
- *Cancel Menu*—Hides the floating menu from view

The links shown in the schema diagram are the links you or someone else set up when designing the database. You usually don't want to change them. If, for some reason, you want the report to be based on different links, you can change them during the Link step. Right-clicking a link brings up another floating menu, as shown in Figure 26.8.

Choosing Options from the floating menu brings up the Link Options form (see Figure 26.9). From this form you can make the following changes:

- The order of the link (which table is the From table and which table is the To table)
- Which, if any, index to use
- The fields in the index
- Whether to allow partial matches
- What kind of link to use when linking to two files from one file
- The SQL join type to use (the default is =)

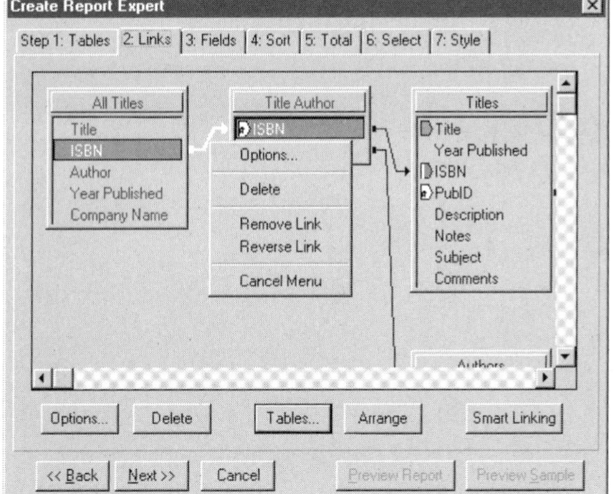

FIGURE 26.8.
Floating-menu selections for changing a link.

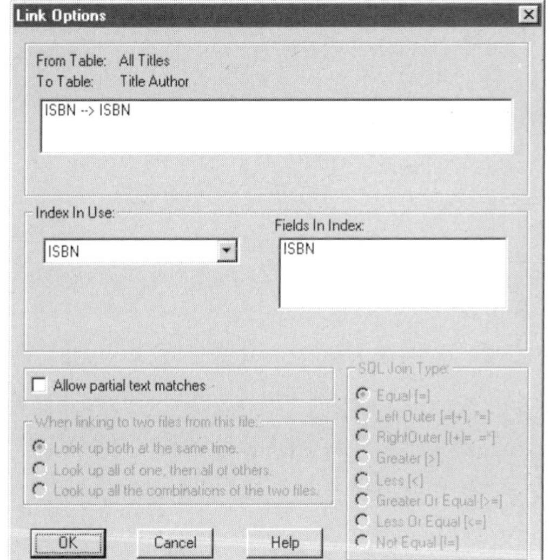

FIGURE 26.9.
The Link Options form.

The other menu selections on the floating menu include the following:

- Delete and Remove Link both delete the link.
- Reverse Link makes the From table the To table and makes the To table the From table.
- Cancel Menu hides the floating menu.

For this example, don't change any of the links; move on to Step 3.

The Fields Page

Step 3, Fields, defines the database fields that will make up your report. The Fields page is shown in Figure 26.10. This page displays two list boxes (Database Fields on the left and Report Fields on the right), an Add button that allows you to move fields from the left list to the right list, a Remove button to move the fields back to the left column, and two All buttons to move all the fields either way.

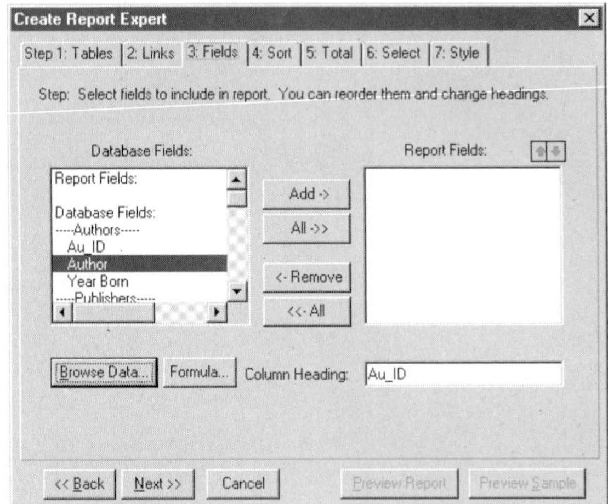

FIGURE 26.10.
The Fields page.

A field can be moved in two ways:

- You can highlight a field with the mouse and click Add to move it to the right column.
- You also can double-click a field to move it from one column to the other, depending on where it starts from.

Below the two columns are the Browse Data and Formula buttons. If you highlight a field and click Browse Data, a list box appears showing the selected field's data. Figure 26.11 shows the Browse Data form displaying data from the Author field of the Authors table.

For this example, you'll create a report listing book authors and their titles for the Macmillan Computer Publishing company, along with a description of each book. The fields you need for this report are Company Name from the Publishers table, Author from the Authors table, and Title and Description from the Titles table. Add them to the report by double-clicking them in the Database Fields list box.

Order is important, and although you can reorder the fields later, go ahead and put the fields in order as you add them to the report. To do this, simply select the field you want to go in the leftmost column of the report first, the field you want to go in the second column next, and so on. Figure 26.12 shows the finished Fields page.

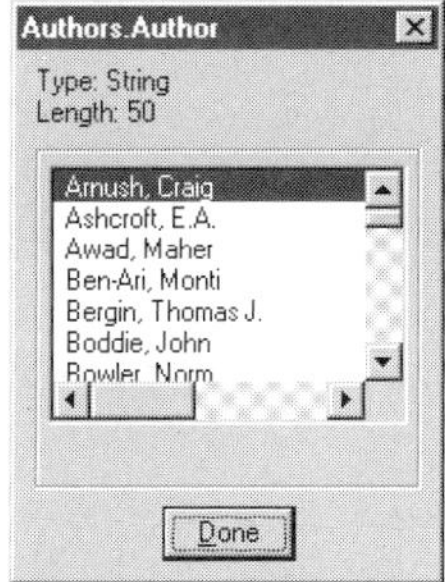

FIGURE 26.11.
The Author field's data.

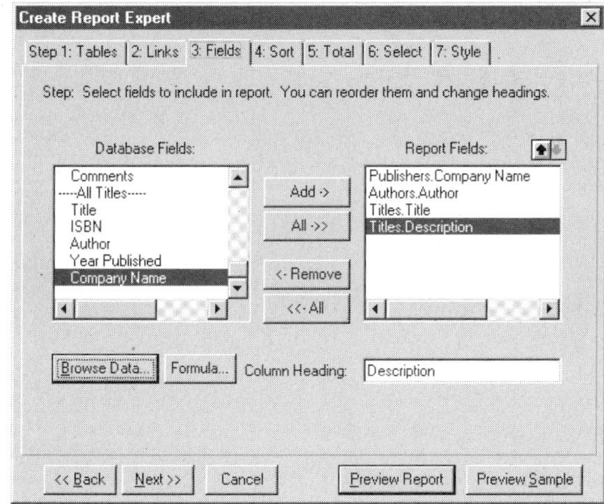

FIGURE 26.12.
The selected fields in the Fields page.

Another way to change the order of the fields is to use the up- and down-arrow buttons located above the upper-right corner of the Report Fields list box. To move a field up in the order, for example, highlight the field and click the up-arrow button; the field exchanges places with the field before it. To move a field down in the order, highlight a field and click the down-arrow button; the field exchanges places with the field after it.

During this step, you can also specify the names of the column headings in the report by typing in a new name in the Column Heading text box. By default, the column headings are assigned the names of the fields. This works out well for the sample report because the field names are descriptive. But in some cases, you may need to change the column headings to something more appropriate.

After you have the fields in the order you want, you're ready to move to Step 4, Sort.

The Sort Page

This sample report is a list of all the titles, with author names and descriptions, of the books published by Macmillan Computer Publishing. Step 4 asks you to choose the fields you want to sort and group by, giving the report a logical ordering. For example, for this report, you probably want all the books written by the same author to be grouped together. So choose Author as the field to sort and group together by selecting its name in the Database Fields list box and then clicking the Add button to move it to the Report Fields list box (see Figure 26.13).

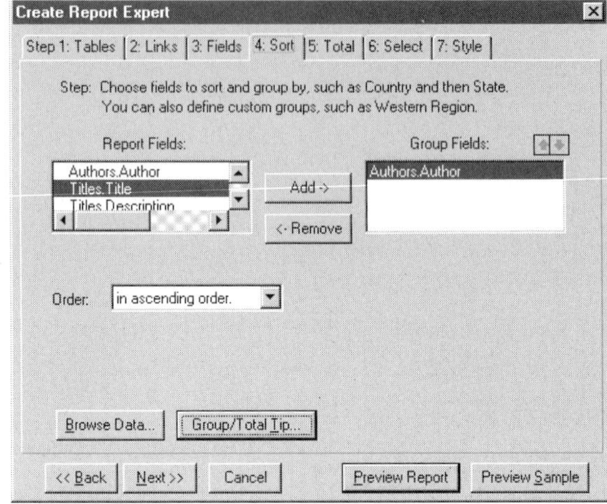

FIGURE 26.13.
The Sort page selection with the Author field selected.

The order that the field is sorted in can also be specified. The Order combo box lists four order choices:

- Ascending order
- Descending order
- Specified order
- Original order

We want the Author field to be sorted in ascending order. Because that is the default sort option, there's no need to change it.

Below the Order combo box are two buttons: Browse Data and Group/Total Tip. The Browse Data button lets you look at the data for each field listed in the Report Fields list box. The Group/Total Tip button provides some online help for hints on creating the proper sorting and grouping for your data.

This example requires only one sort field, Author, so you're ready to move on to Step 5, Total.

The Total Page

Step 5 allows you to add subtotals and counts to your fields. In the example, you want to know how many books are written by a particular author, so make the Author field a Total field by selecting its name in the Report Fields list box and then clicking the Add button (see Figure 26.14).

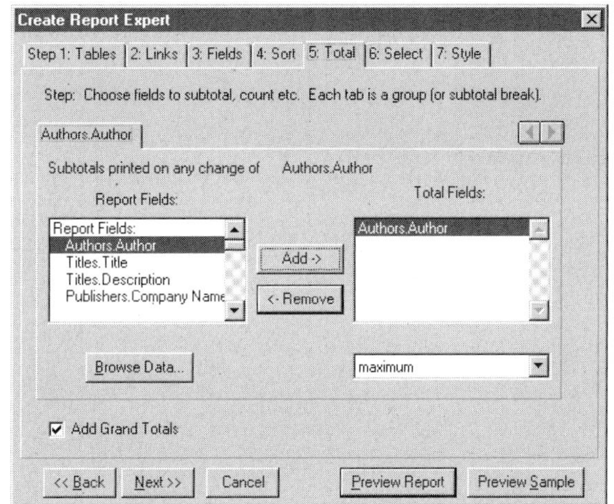

FIGURE 26.14.
Choosing the Author field to be subtotaled.

You can base the subtotal on one of four criteria listed in the combo box below the Total Fields list box:

- Maximum identifies the highest value in the group.
- Minimum identifies the lowest value in the group.
- Count counts all the records in the group.
- Distinct Count counts only distinct records in the group.

At the bottom of the page is the Add Grand Totals check box. If you check this box, each totaled field will have a grand total at the end of the report.

Under the Report Fields list box is the Browse Data button, which allows you to look at the data in a field to help you choose the right fields for subtotaling.

You've selected the only field needed to subtotal on for this example, so you can move to Step 6, Select.

The Select Page

The Select step is used to create a filter for the records that will appear in the report. If you're familiar with SQL, this filter is like SQL's `Where` clause. In this example, you're reporting on book titles published by Macmillan Computer Publishing, so you need to create a filter that allows only records that match Macmillan Computer Publishing as the publisher to be part of the report.

To create the filter, select a field from the Report Fields list box. For this step, the list box is divided into two separate lists of fields: the fields that have been selected for the report and the fields that are part of the database tables. You aren't limited to using just the fields selected for the report in creating a filter; any field from the database you're working with will work. However, in this example, the field you want to create a filter on is in the list of fields on the report (Publishers.Company Name).

To make the Publishers.Company Name field the filtered field, highlight it in the Report Fields list box and click the Add button to move it to the Select Fields list box.

When a field is selected to be the filtered field, two combo boxes are loaded and displayed below the Report Fields list box. These combo boxes allow you to select the operator used to filter the field you've selected (see Figure 26.15).

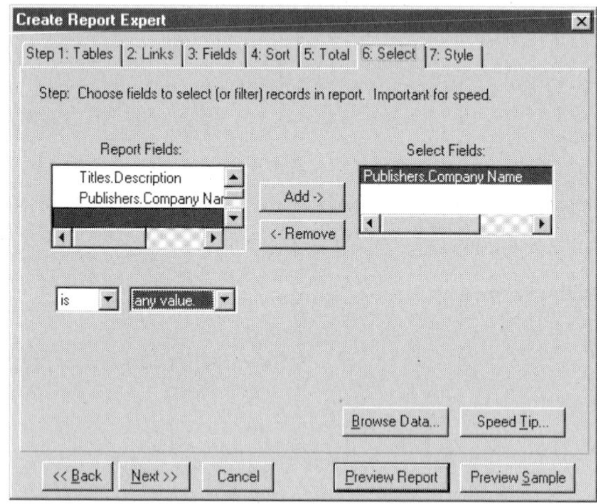

FIGURE 26.15.
The Select page's operator combo boxes.

The combo boxes are used together to create a logical operator for the filter. The first combo box presents only one or two choices: `is` and `is not`. The second combo box presents a list of choices for creating the filter. By clicking the combo box, the following logical operators are presented:

```
any value           between
equal to            starting with
one of              like
less than           formula:
greater than
```

If you're a SQL programmer, you're familiar with these choices. Even if you've never used SQL before, each choice is fairly self-descriptive. For example, `between` is used to select fields that are between one value and another value, as in the following SQL code:

```
Select * Where Publisher.Company Name between "Macmillan Computer Publishing" _
    and "Sams"
```

This code prints the data from all the fields where the company name of the publisher falls alphabetically between Macmillan Computer Publishing and Sams.

For the example, you want to filter out all the records except those that match Sams Publishing, so you will select `is` and `equal to` from the two combo boxes.

A third combo box appears after you select the logical operator. This combo box lists possible data values from the field you've selected for your filter, taken directly from the database.

Select Sams by scrolling down the list until you find it. Click it, and Sams will be highlighted in the combo box (see Figure 26.16).

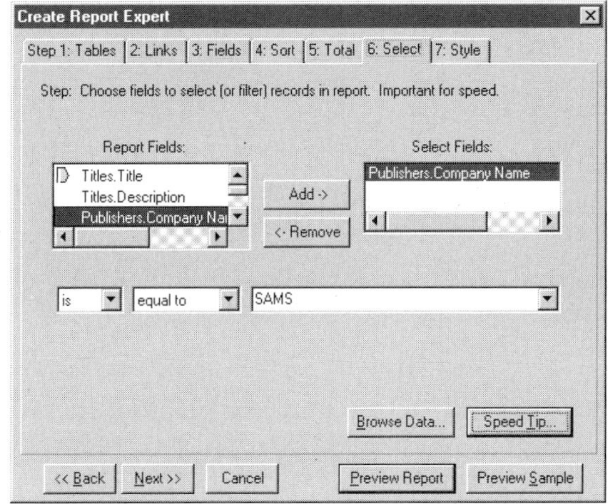

FIGURE 26.16.
The Publishers table's company names for the Select filter.

Toward the bottom of the page are two buttons, Browse Data and Speed Tip. The Browse Data button, as on the other pages, allows you to browse the data in the field highlighted in the Report Fields list box. The Speed Tip button provides some hints on how to make the filter you create select records faster.

You're finished with the Select page, so you can move to the final step, Style.

The Style Page

You use the Style page to give the report a title and to select a style for the report. The styles you can choose from include

Standard	Executive, Leading Break
Leading Break	Executive, Trailing Break
Trailing Break	Shading
Table	Red/Blue Border
Drop Table	Maroon/Teal Box

The styles are presented in a list box with a graphic representation of the style. Figure 26.17 shows the Table style selected (Table) and its graphic representation, as well as the title for the report you're creating in this example ("Authors and Book Titles for Macmillan Computer Publishing").

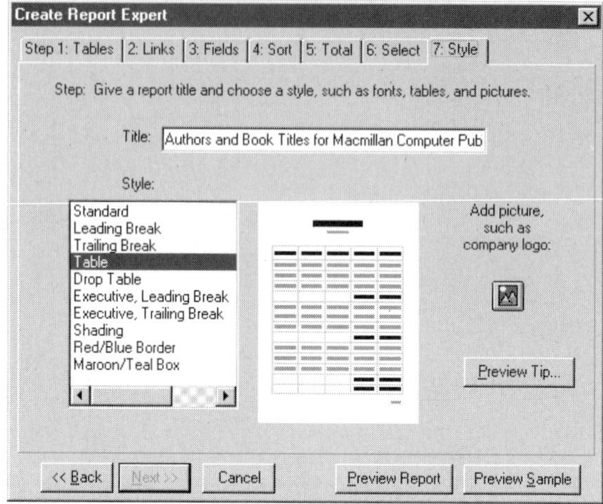

FIGURE 26.17.
The Style page selections.

On the right side of the Style page is a button that you can click if you have a picture to add to the report. A dialog box will appear to help you browse to find the picture file you want to use. When you select the file, click OK to add the picture to your report.

Below the Add Picture button is the Preview Tip button. When clicked, this button provides some tips on how to use the Preview Report or Preview Sample buttons to make changes to your report after you complete these initial steps.

You're finished with the initial design of the report and can now preview it to see how it looks. To do this, click the Preview Sample button at the bottom of the Style page.

Previewing Your Report

When you click the Preview Sample button, a dialog box appears, asking whether you want to preview the report with all the records from the database or a specific number of records (the default is 100). Figure 26.18 shows this dialog box.

You probably won't want to select all the records for the Preview Sample, especially if you know that the report is going to select a lot of records. Instead, select the first *x* records, where *x* is the number you think will be enough to let you see the full layout of the report. In other words, the number selected needs to be enough to generate subgroups, subtotals, and so on if you've selected these options for your report. Because you've selected a table format for this sample report, you don't need to view too many records, so select 10 for the Preview Sample.

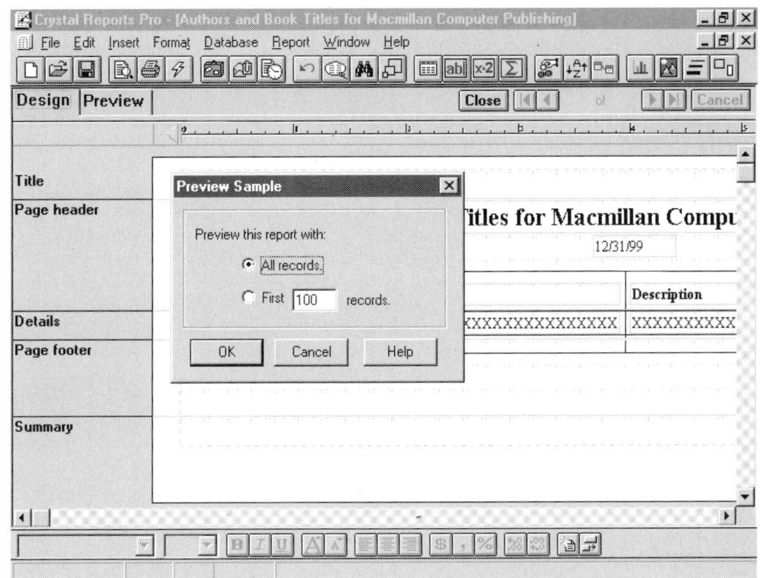

FIGURE 26.18.
The Preview Sample dialog box.

Click OK to have Crystal Reports generate the sample report. It can take a while for the sample to be created, depending on how many records are in the database (on my desktop system, it took about a minute).

When Crystal Reports is finished generating the report, a preview screenshot of the report appears (see Figure 26.19). The report is displayed on a tabbed page labeled Preview.

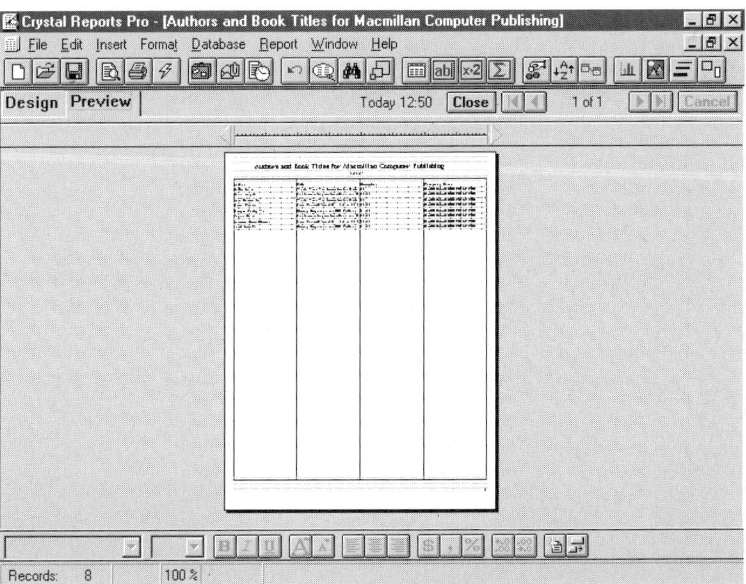

FIGURE 26.19.
The sample Preview report.

To get a better view of the data on the report, use the zoom button on the toolbar (the button with the three hollow boxes). Click it to have the report fill the whole screen (see Figure 26.20).

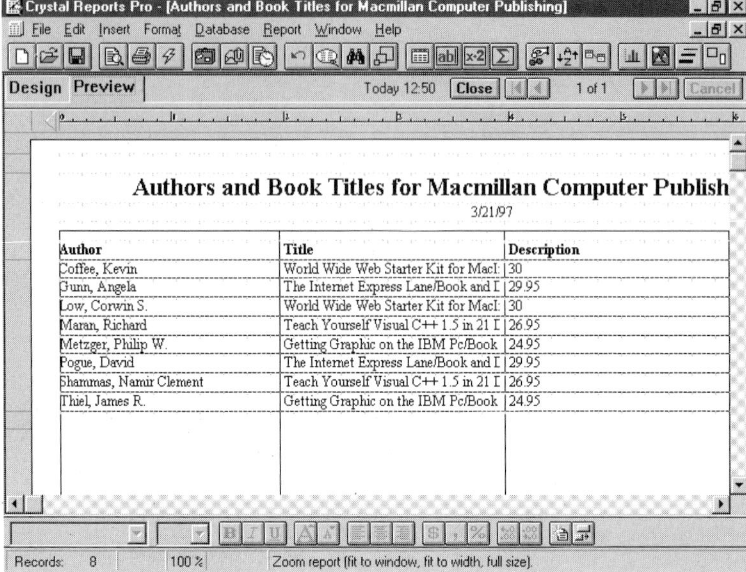

FIGURE 26.20.
The sample Preview report, filling the screen.

When the report is enlarged to full-screen size, you won't be able to see all the columns without scrolling. Use the scrollbar at the bottom of the form to scroll left or right. If the number of records chosen for the preview create more rows than will fit onscreen, use the scrollbar on the right for scrolling up or down.

Below the left/right scrollbar are two buttons on the right part of the Font toolbar. The button on the left, when clicked, displays the Report Style Expert to allow you to change the report style if you want to. The button to the right displays the Auto Arrange form, which asks whether you want to auto-arrange the fields and lines in the report. If you've changed the style of the report by adding text boxes, lines, or other elements, this form will arrange them into the style you've selected.

Right-clicking anywhere on the Preview Sample will bring up a floating menu (see Figure 26.21). Many of the items are checked because these are the default settings for Preview Sample. Besides the settings you can toggle on and off, you can change several other settings from this menu, including Page Margins, Set Report Title, and Set Print Date.

If you right-click inside one of the text boxes holding data, a different floating menu appears (see Figure 26.22). When you bring up this floating menu, all the records in the column are highlighted. The changes you make from this menu, then, affect all the records highlighted. To see an example of how this works, right-click one of the records in the Title column and choose Change Font. The familiar Font dialog box then appears. For this example, just change the font from regular to bold by selecting Bold in the Font style list box and clicking OK. Figure 26.23 shows the new Preview Sample.

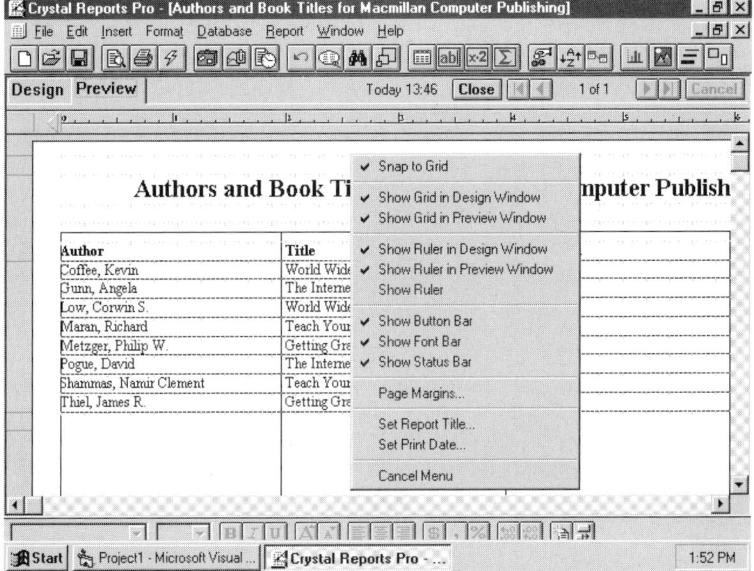

FIGURE 26.21.
The Preview Sample floating menu.

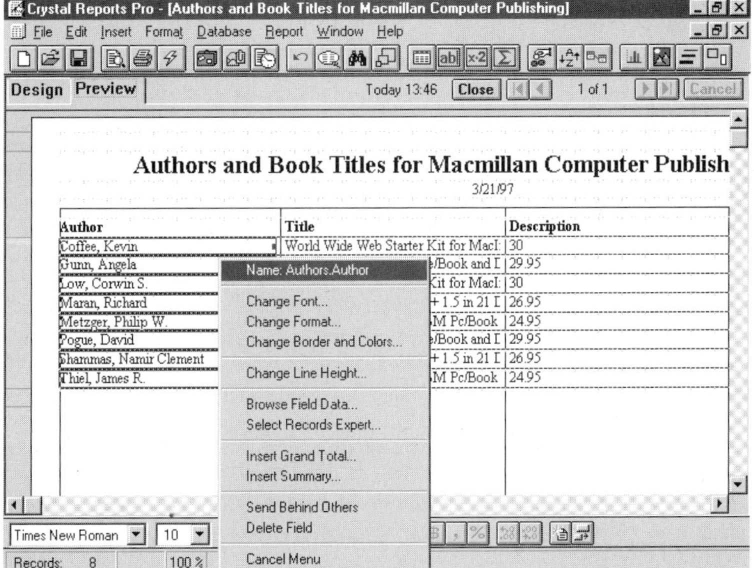

FIGURE 26.22.
The Field Data floating menu.

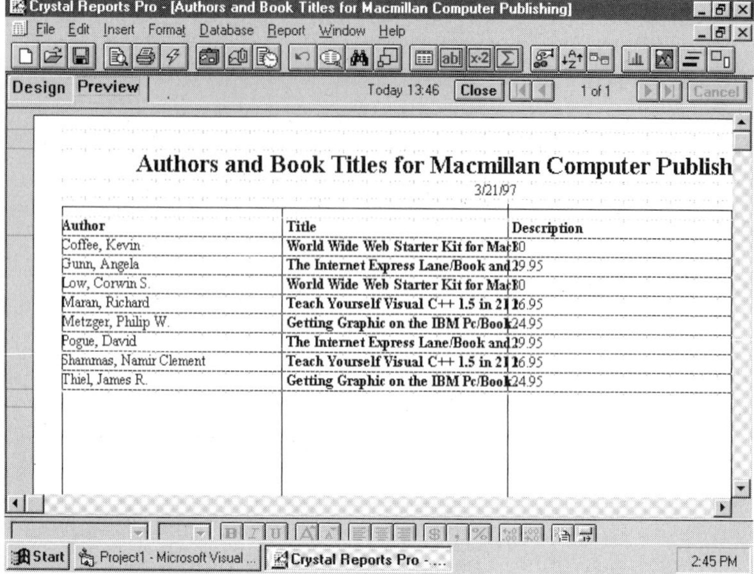

FIGURE 26.23.
Changing the Title column to a bold font.

Saving Your Report

When you're finished generating your report, you need to save it. Click the disk icon on the toolbar; the File Save As dialog box appears. Crystal Report reports are saved with an `.RPT` extension. Type a name into the File Name text box and click OK to save the report. You can open this report later to make changes or to print it when you need to.

Summary

The report designer built into the Visual Basic IDE provides you with the full reporting capabilities of Crystal Reports Version 4.0. The report designer helps you attach to a database, lay out your report, choose the right fields, create groups and subtotals for the records of the report, filter out records you don't want in the report, and make changes to the report after the basic design is created.

CHAPTER 27

SQL and the T-SQL Debugger

IN THIS CHAPTER

This chapter serves two distinct purposes. It begins with an overview of Structured Query Language (SQL), describing what it is and how it works from an ANSI perspective. The first section provides many tables and examples to illustrate the syntax used for communicating with a database engine, as well as a general discussion of the different ways you can handle the data you retrieve. The second half of the chapter deals with Microsoft's T-SQL Debugger (short for "Transact-SQL Debugger"), a tool for debugging stored procedures on SQL Server. You get a walk-through of the debugger, and examples and options are pointed out to give you a thorough understanding of how it simplifies further communication with the server.

Working with Standard SQL

Structured Query Language (SQL) has quickly become the standard relational database language. SQL gives you a way to impose standards when you use a relational database. Some relational databases still don't support SQL, but the vast majority of them do. Here are some of the relational databases that support SQL:

SQL Server	Informix
Access	SQLBase
Sybase	Ingres
Oracle	

NOTE

This chapter covers some of the basics of SQL language—that is, the American National Standards Institute (ANSI) SQL. It's not database-specific, which means that certain database engines can have a slightly different syntax. This also means that some of the code presented might not work correctly for a given database engine. Consult the documentation for your specific database engine to be sure.

You can use this SQL standard in a client/server environment or in a standalone environment. Either way, SQL is the language used to query the database engine. A *database engine* is the heart of the database; it's the way the database vendor decides how the database operates and functions, how data is stored, how syntax is used, and how processing occurs.

You can actually use SQL to do more than construct queries. Using SQL implies that you're querying the database to get data returned from it. In fact, there's much more to it than this. You use SQL to insert new data, update existing data, and even control the parameters of the database engine.

You can send SQL to a database engine by many means. The database engine comes with an interactive tool for sending SQL statements to get a result. This is sometimes referred to as *Interactive Structured Query Language (ISQL).*

This chapter deals with SQL as a whole. SQL can be, and has been, the subject of entire books. This chapter can't cover every aspect of SQL, but it covers the basics. The chapter also doesn't discuss specific database engines. Certain things are common in all SQL databases. These basic commonalties are the subject of the rest of this chapter. However, for the examples, the following sample data is used. The data is broken up into four tables, shown in Tables 27.1 through 27.4.

Table 27.1. The `INVENTORY` table.

Product ID	*Description*	*Supplier ID*	*Quantity*
MS001	Visual Basic	M001	45
MS002	Word for Windows	M001	100
MS003	Excel	M001	10
SO001	OCX-10 Home Automation/VB Interface	S002	145

Table 27.2. The `SALES` table.

Product ID	*Staff ID*	*Date Sold*	*Quantity Sold*
MS001	D001	8/26/96	5
SO001	M001	8/26/96	5

Table 27.3. The `STAFF` table.

Staff ID	*Last Name*	*First Name*
D001	Duck	Donald
M001	Mann	Anthony
M002	Mouse	Mickey

Table 27.4. The `SUPPLIER` table.

Supplier ID	*Supplier*
B001	Borland
I001	Intuit
M001	Microsoft
S001	Sams Publishing
S002	SoftHouse

The tables give you an idea of the structure of a database and how the fields relate to each other. Designing databases isn't the topic of this chapter; however, it's important to see how the data relates so that the examples presented later make sense.

By looking at Tables 27.1 through 27.4, you can see that the `INVENTORY` table contains a list of all items a company can stock. The table also contains a field for the quantity in stock and the product ID used to identify when a sale is made in the `SALES` table. Listing the description of the product every time a sale occurs is inefficient. Also, a supplier ID field identifies the company that supplies the product from the `SUPPLIER` table.

The `SALES` table relates to the tables discussed in the preceding paragraph, but also has a field for the staff ID (the person selling the item). The name of the person selling the item is looked up in the `STAFF` table, based on the staff ID.

That's how the four tables relate to each other. Each table contains simple data. However, if the database is designed correctly, it makes no difference how much data is in the tables.

Retrieving Data

By far the most common SQL statement is the `SELECT` statement. This statement is used to retrieve rows of data from a table as well as for many other purposes (which are presented in the rest of this chapter). To use this statement, you must know the names of the columns in the table you're trying to receive, or you can use an asterisk to specify all columns. The `SELECT` statement for Microsoft Jet SQL has the following general syntax:

```
SELECT [ALL¦DISTINCT] [TOP xx [PERCENT]] select_list
FROM table_names
[WHERE {search_criteria¦join_criteria}
[{AND¦OR search_criteria}]]
[GROUP BY [ALL]aggregate_free_expression [,aggregate_free_expression...]]
[HAVING search_conditions]
[ORDER BY {field_list} [ASC¦DESC]]
```

where

- `ALL` specifies that every row is returned, including duplicates. (This is the default and doesn't need to be used.)
- `DISTINCT` specifies that only non-duplicate rows are to be returned.
- `TOP` specifies that you want only the top *xx* number of records returned. You can also specify the `PERCENT` keyword after the number *xx* to return only the top *xx* percentage of the total records to be returned. (See the later section "Limiting the Selection" for more information.)
- *`select_list`* is the list of column names in the tables to return, separated by commas.
- *`table_names`* is the list of tables that return data.
- *`search_criteria`* is the list of column names in the tables to return.

- `join_criteria` is the list of column names in one table that joins to other column names in a different table.
- `aggregate_free_expression` is an expression that doesn't include an aggregate. See Table 27.6 later in this chapter for a list of aggregate functions that can't be included in this expression.
- `field_list` is a list of the columns the data is sorted on.
- `ASC` specifies that the sort order is ascending. (This is the default and doesn't need to be used.)
- `DESC` specifies that the sort order is descending.

If you're not intimately familiar with SQL, the preceding information can seem pretty confusing. Let me simplify it by providing examples from Tables 27.1 through 27.4.

NOTE

The keywords throughout this chapter, such as `SELECT`, `FROM`, and so on, aren't case-sensitive. They're listed here in uppercase to set them apart from the regular text, but you can type them in lowercase.

Selecting Records

To use the `SELECT` statement, you must know what you want to select and from what. In other words, you need to know the column names and the table names you're trying to select. If you don't know the column names, you must use an asterisk to select all columns in the tables. For example, if you want to select all values from the `Supplier` column in the `SUPPLIER` table, you use this statement:

```
SELECT Supplier
FROM SUPPLIER
```

Or you could use this:

```
SELECT *
FROM SUPPLIER
```

NOTE

Even though the keywords aren't case-sensitive, some databases have case-sensitive column names and table names. For this example, the table names have been designated in uppercase, whereas the column names have been designated in lowercase. Columns are sometimes referred to as *fields* and column names as *field names*. They're synonymous.

NOTE

Even though a SQL statement can consist of many lines of text, it's actually one statement. To help you understand this concept, as a general rule a statement consists of all lines of SQL text between two SELECT keywords.

Also, even though these SQL text lines are shown on separate lines, they actually can be put on one line. They're generally constructed on multiple lines because they're easier to read. The SQL standard calls for the database engine (whichever one is used) to ignore the carriage return between SQL keywords in the statement.

The preceding SQL statement produces a complete list of the suppliers in the SUPPLIER table, but the order returned is the order in which they're entered into the table. If you want to sort the list alphabetically, you can use this statement:

```
SELECT Supplier
FROM SUPPLIER
ORDER BY Supplier
```

The ORDER BY keyword (sometimes referred to as the ORDER BY *clause*) needs a column name to know which column to sort on. This ensures that the data is ordered by the Supplier column. By default, the data is ordered in ascending order. To sort in descending order, use this statement:

```
SELECT Supplier
FROM SUPPLIER
ORDER BY Supplier DESC
```

If you want to select multiple columns, use the following statement:

```
SELECT Supplier,Supplier_ID
FROM SUPPLIER
ORDER BY Supplier
```

This statement selects the Supplier column first, followed by the Supplier_ID column. All values in the table are returned because you didn't limit the search. Two columns are selected in the preceding statement (which, coincidentally, is the total number of columns in the SUPPLIER table). However, if you have a table with 100 columns and you want to select all the columns, you don't have to type the names of all 100 columns. You can select all columns in a table with a statement like this:

```
SELECT *
FROM SUPPLIER
ORDER BY Supplier
```

The asterisk indicates that all columns are selected from the SUPPLIER table. The table is still sorted by the Supplier column in ascending order.

Limiting the Selection

You don't have to return all data from a table; you can limit the number of rows returned by using the WHERE keyword. Suppose that you want to find out what the supplier ID is for SoftHouse. You want to limit the number of rows in the SUPPLIER table to all rows where the supplier is equal to "SoftHouse". You can do this with the following code:

```
SELECT *
FROM SUPPLIER
WHERE Supplier = "SoftHouse"
ORDER BY Supplier
```

The data returned is only the data that matches the WHERE keyword (also referred to as the WHERE clause). If no supplier is named SoftHouse, no rows are returned.

NOTE

The string literal in the WHERE clause is case-sensitive. Therefore, "SoftHouse" isn't the same as "SOFTHOUSE".

Also, some implementations of SQL require the use of single quotation marks (apostrophes) rather than double quotation marks.

The ORDER BY clause isn't necessary in the preceding statement, but it doesn't hurt it either. By design, each supplier appears in the SUPPLIER table only once. Because you're looking for only one supplier, the order is irrelevant. However, if you're looking for more than one supplier, it becomes relevant. Suppose that you're looking for "SoftHouse" or "Microsoft". Use this SQL statement:

```
SELECT *
FROM SUPPLIER
WHERE Supplier = "SoftHouse" OR Supplier = "Microsoft"
ORDER BY Supplier
```

In this case, two rows are returned: first the "Microsoft" row and then the "SoftHouse" row, thanks to the ORDER BY clause.

Another way to write the preceding statement is to use the IN keyword, which lets you list a range of values to test for. The values are separated by a comma. The preceding statement is rewritten as this:

```
SELECT *
FROM SUPPLIER
WHERE Supplier IN ("SoftHouse","Microsoft")
ORDER BY Supplier
```

Using the IN keyword can generally save a lot of typing because the column name doesn't have to be repeated. Table 27.5 lists additional keywords that you can use in the WHERE clause.

Table 27.5. Keywords that you can use in a WHERE clause.

Keyword	Purpose
IN	Tests for values in a specified range
NOT IN	Tests for values not in a specified range
LIKE	Tests for values that are like a specified value
NOT LIKE	Tests for values that aren't like a specified value
IS NULL	Tests for null values
IS NOT NULL	Tests for non-null values
AND	Tests for multiple conditions
OR	Tests for either specified condition
BETWEEN	Tests for values between a set of specified values
NOT BETWEEN	Tests for values not between a set of specified values
EXISTS	Tests for existing values
NOT EXISTS	Tests for nonexisting values
ANY	Tests for any values
ALL	Tests for all values

A common necessity is to return values that, for example, start with a certain letter, such as *S*. You can do this by using the `LIKE` keyword. If you want to return all rows from the `SUPPLIER` table for a supplier starting with an *S*, use this statement:

```
SELECT *
FROM SUPPLIER
WHERE Supplier LIKE "S%"
ORDER BY Supplier
```

This statement returns rows containing the suppliers `"SAMS Publishing"` and `"SoftHouse"`. The following is the syntax for using the `LIKE` keyword, where you might have a percent sign before the *`constant`*, after the *`constant`*, or both:

```
LIKE "[%]constant[%]"
```

The *`constant`* is the value for which you're testing. The percent signs are wildcard symbols, just like asterisks in DOS. If you're looking for any supplier with an *S* in its name, use this statement:

```
SELECT *
FROM SUPPLIER
WHERE Supplier LIKE "%S%"
ORDER BY Supplier
```

NOTE

Microsoft Access uses an asterisk (*) wildcard symbol in place of the percent sign (%) when accessed through DAO. The percent sign applies to SQL Server and other client/server databases, as well as Access via ODBC. The rest of the syntax is the same. Also, the expression placed between wildcard symbols is case-sensitive.

NOTE

You must use at least one percent sign in a LIKE clause. If you don't, no rows are returned.

Because the SELECT keyword is used to return values, you can even go so far as to return a value that's not part of the database. This is referred to as a *calculated column*. For example, you can return a percentage of the quantity in the INVENTORY table. Instead of the following SQL statement, which returns the quantity that's actually in the database,

```
SELECT Quantity
FROM INVENTORY
```

you can use this SQL statement to return 10 percent of the quantities:

```
SELECT Quantity * .10
FROM INVENTORY
```

This works only for a numeric data type. You certainly can't do this if Quantity is a string.

Another way to limit the number of records returned is to use the TOP keyword. Suppose that you want to test a SQL statement to determine whether you've used the correct syntax. However, you don't want to return potentially millions of rows of data for a test. You can use the optional TOP keyword to limit the number of rows.

The TOP keyword without a following PERCENT keyword returns only the first *xx* number of records of the total recordset. For example, the following will return only the first 10 records from the SUPPLIER table:

```
SELECT TOP 10 *
FROM SUPPLIER
ORDER BY Supplier
```

If 250 records were in the table, only the first 10 would be returned. Likewise, this example will return the first 10 percent of the total records from the SUPPLIER table:

```
SELECT TOP 10 PERCENT *
FROM SUPPLIER
ORDER BY Supplier
```

Again, if 250 records were in the table, only the first 25 would be returned.

Setting Up Joins

A *join* is a way to return data from two tables. The key to doing this is that you must join or link the columns of data between the two tables so that the database engine knows how to look it up. You create the join in the `WHERE` clause. If you want to select all items in the `INVENTORY` table but also with the company that supplied the item, you have to do a join between the `INVENTORY` and `SUPPLIER` tables. This is because a column (`Supplier_ID`) is common to both tables, and this column is what the join is based on. This is also called a *common key*, which is a "key" field used as a join. For the `SUPPLIER` table, it's the primary key, which means that this column is used to access a row in the table. It's not the primary key in the `INVENTORY` table because it isn't used to access a row in this table; the `Product_ID` column is the primary key in that table. Again, how to determine primary keys and database design isn't the purpose of this chapter.

To perform the join mentioned here, use this code:

```
SELECT Supplier, Description, Quantity
FROM SUPPLIER s, INVENTORY i
WHERE i.Supplier_ID = s.Supplier_ID
ORDER BY Supplier
```

This statement selects the `Supplier`, `Description`, and `Quantity` columns from the `SUPPLIER` and `INVENTORY` tables. For every occurrence of a supplier ID in the `INVENTORY` table, the supplier is looked up by using the same `Supplier_ID` column, and the values are assigned to be equal.

The individual letters `s` and `i` you see in the preceding code are *aliases*. You use these to identify a column in a table that has the same name in another table you're trying to access. If you don't specify this alias, you receive an error telling you that the column name is ambiguous. This alias gives the database engine a way to decipher which column you're referring to. The alias name goes after the table names in the `FROM` clause. The name can be any unique value (treated as a string without quotes) as long as it isn't the name of a table you're trying to access.

After the alias is established in the `FROM` clause, you can reference it by using this format, where *`alias`* is the name of the alias defined and *`column`* is the name of the column in the aliased table:

```
alias.column
```

For example, consider the `WHERE` clause in the previous statement:

```
WHERE i.Supplier_ID = s.Supplier_ID
```

It follows the syntax of *`alias.column`* on each side of the `=` sign. After the alias is established, you can use it in any of the SQL clauses that are part of that same statement.

If you're trying to select (return) columns in different tables, you must also reference the alias to avoid any ambiguity. Even if you aren't selecting columns with the same name, you may still use the alias. For example, the following isn't incorrect:

```
SELECT s.Supplier, i.Description, i.Quantity
FROM SUPPLIER s, INVENTORY i
WHERE i.Supplier_ID = s.Supplier_ID
ORDER BY s.Supplier
```

It performs the same function. However, it does introduce a possible element of error. At least one field in the ORDER BY clause needs to be in the SELECT clause. If you change the last line to the following, you receive an error because the Supplier column doesn't exist in the INVENTORY table:

```
ORDER BY i.Supplier
```

You can create even more complex joins. Suppose that you want to select the supplier, product description, and quantity, but return only the rows in the INVENTORY table where the supplier is "Microsoft". You have to do a join again to the SUPPLIER table because the only reference to SUPPLIER in the INVENTORY table is an ID, Supplier_ID, which is used as a lookup key in the SUPPLIER table. You can do the join with this statement:

```
SELECT s.Supplier, i.Description, i.Quantity
FROM SUPPLIER s, INVENTORY i
WHERE i.Supplier_ID = s.Supplier_ID
AND s.Supplier = "Microsoft"
ORDER BY s.Supplier
```

Again, the ORDER BY clause isn't absolutely necessary because only one row can be in the SUPPLIER table with the name "Microsoft".

You can use the techniques and topics discussed here to join multiple tables in your application. However, remember that the more joins you do, the longer it takes the database engine to come back with the results.

Working with Aggregates

An *aggregate* is a mathematical SQL function. Table 27.6 lists the types of SQL aggregates available.

Table 27.6. SQL aggregates.

Aggregate	*Purpose*
COUNT()	Counts the number of rows returned
SUM()	Sums the number of rows returned
AVG()	Averages the number of rows returned
MAX()	Finds the maximum value in the rows returned
MIN()	Finds the minimum value in the rows returned

In each aggregate listed in Table 27.6, an expression (typically a column name) is expected in the parentheses. However, the expression can be any valid SQL expression.

If you want to find out how many rows are returned from this statement,

```
SELECT s.Supplier, i.Description, i.Quantity
FROM SUPPLIER s, INVENTORY i
WHERE i.Supplier_ID = s.Supplier_ID
ORDER BY s.Supplier
```

you can use this statement instead:

```
SELECT COUNT(*), s.Supplier, i.Description, i.Quantity
FROM SUPPLIER s, INVENTORY i
WHERE i.Supplier_ID = s.Supplier_ID
ORDER BY s.Supplier
```

This statement returns four columns, the count of the number of rows returned, the supplier, the description, and the quantity. The joins in the statement were discussed earlier in the "Setting Up Joins" section.

When using an aggregate function, you can use a `GROUP BY` clause to tell the database engine how to do the calculation. For example, if you want to sum the number of items stocked for each supplier, you must use a `GROUP BY` clause. If you don't, how does the database engine know how to return the sum? Refer to Table 27.1 to follow this example. Would the database engine sum the quantities for each `Product_ID`, `Description`, `Supplier_ID`, or a combination of the three? That's where the `GROUP BY` clause comes in. In this scenario, you can perform the necessary function by using this statement:

```
SELECT SUM(Quantity)
FROM SUPPLIER s, INVENTORY i
WHERE i.Supplier_ID = s.Supplier_ID
GROUP BY s.Supplier
ORDER BY s.Supplier
```

This means that for every new supplier, the `Quantity` is summed. If the `GROUP BY` clause is omitted, only one row is returned, and it's the sum of all quantities.

Inserting Data

Without inserting data, there would never be the need to perform any `UPDATE`, `DELETE`, or `SELECT` statements. Inserting rows (or records) into a table requires an `INSERT` statement. The syntax of the `INSERT` statement is

```
INSERT [INTO] table[(column_list)]
VALUES{(insert_values)}¦sql_select_statement
```

where

- *`table`* is the name of the table to insert into.
- *`column_list`* is a listing of columns that have data inserted, separated by commas.
- *`insert_values`* is the list of values to be inserted into the columns in *`column_list`*. The same number of values must be in the *`insert_values`* list as in the *`column_list`* list.

- *sql_select_statement* is an alternative way to insert values into a table. You can select values of another table to be inserted. In this case, you don't use the VALUES keyword. You must make sure that the number of columns you're returning in your SQL statement is the same number as in the *column_list* list.

NOTE

Microsoft Access requires the INTO keyword; SQL Server doesn't.

To use the INSERT statement to insert a new supplier into the SUPPLIER table, you can use this statement:

```
INSERT SUPPLIER(Supplier_ID,Supplier)
VALUES ("C001","Crystal Services")
```

The row is simply inserted into the table. Here are some considerations, however:

- Does the primary key field already exist?
- Are you concerned about case sensitivity?
- Are you inserting values with the correct data type?

These questions are important. Except for the case-sensitivity question, the questions presented here can result in errors if they aren't addressed properly. For example, the following will result in error:

```
INSERT SUPPLIER(Supplier_ID,Supplier)
VALUES (1,"Crystal Services")
```

The Supplier_ID column doesn't expect a numeric data type; it expects a string data type. If you aren't going to include any characters, you must construct the SQL statement this way:

```
INSERT SUPPLIER(Supplier_ID,Supplier)
VALUES ("1","Crystal Services")
```

Rather than insert into a table by hard-coding the values, you can insert by selecting the values from another table. Suppose that you have a table, MASTER, which also has Supplier_ID and Supplier columns from which you'll select values. You can insert all items from the MASTER table like this:

```
INSERT SUPPLIER(Supplier_ID,Supplier)
SELECT Supplier_ID,Supplier
FROM MASTER
```

On the other hand, if you wanted to insert based only on a certain value from the MASTER table, you could construct your SQL SELECT statement based on any valid SQL rule. You could do this:

```
INSERT SUPPLIER(Supplier_ID,Supplier)
SELECT Supplier_ID,Supplier
FROM MASTER
WHERE Supplier="Crystal Services"
```

As presented in the "Retrieving Data" section earlier in the chapter, the WHERE clause limits the number of rows returned.

Deleting Data

Deleting rows (or records) from a table requires a DELETE statement. The syntax of the DELETE statement is

```
DELETE FROM table
[WHERE search_conditions]
```

where *table* is the name of the table to delete from, and *search_conditions* are any valid SQL expressions to limit the number of rows deleted.

The DELETE statement deletes an entire row or rows in the database. You can't delete only one column.

You can use the DELETE statement to delete all rows in the SUPPLIER table by using this statement:

```
DELETE FROM SUPPLIER
```

CAUTION

You don't receive a confirmation when you use the DELETE statement. If the statement is executed, the rows are deleted. It's that simple. Be very careful when you use the DELETE statement.

If you want to delete the rows only where the supplier is a certain value, you do it like this:

```
DELETE FROM SUPPLIER
WHERE Supplier = "Borland"
```

This statement deletes all values in the SUPPLIER table where the Supplier is "Borland".

NOTE

Be careful when you delete (or update) a row in a table in case a value relates to a value in a different table. If it does, you might possibly orphan a row of data in the other table. Creating an *orphan* means that the value related to data in the table from which you deleted now has no way of being referenced and that the row in the second table is just taking up space.

There are ways around this that aren't within the scope of this chapter, as stated earlier. When you design the database, you can place a trigger on the column so that orphaning doesn't happen inadvertently.

Updating Data

Updating rows (or records) in a table requires an UPDATE statement. The syntax of the UPDATE statement is

```
UPDATE table
SET assignment_list
[WHERE search_conditions]
```

where

- *table* is the name of the table to insert into.
- *assignment_list* is a listing of all updates that will take place.
- *search_conditions* are any valid SQL expressions to limit the number of rows updated.

If you want to update the Supplier_ID column of the SUPPLIER table, you can use the UPDATE statement:

```
UPDATE SUPPLIER
SET Supplier_ID="XXX"
```

All rows in the Supplier_ID column are updated to "XXX". To prevent the rows from being updated, you need to limit the search by using a WHERE clause with any valid SQL expression. You can limit the updating, as described earlier, to only where the Supplier is equal to "Borland". You do this as follows:

```
UPDATE SUPPLIER
SET Supplier_ID="XXX"
WHERE Supplier = "Borland"
```

CAUTION

You don't receive a confirmation when you use the UPDATE statement. If the statement is executed, the rows are updated. It's that simple. Be very careful when you use the UPDATE statement.

On the other hand, if you want to update based only on a certain value from another table, you can use any valid SQL SELECT statement in place of *assignment_list* in the syntax presented earlier. Suppose that you have a table, MASTER, that also has Supplier_ID and Supplier columns out of which you'll select values. You can insert an item from the MASTER table to update a record in the SUPPLIER table like this:

```
UPDATE SUPPLIER
SET Supplier_ID = (SELECT Supplier_ID
FROM MASTER
WHERE Supplier = "SoftHouse")
WHERE Supplier = "SoftHouse"
```

The last two lines of the preceding statement look as though they're repeated, but they really aren't. The parentheses around the statement between the second and fourth lines indicate a query within a query. The inner query selects from the `MASTER` table the supplier ID where the supplier is `"SoftHouse"`. The outer query, the `UPDATE` statement, updates the `Supplier_ID` column to the value returned from the inner query but limits the rows for which this applies to where the supplier is equal to `"SoftHouse"`. If the last line isn't present, all rows in the `Supplier_ID` column are updated.

The query-within-a-query concept (called *nested queries*) opens up more possibilities for you when you use SQL. As you develop more advanced applications that retrieve data, you'll find that understanding SQL is vital.

Grouping SQL Statements into Transactions

A transaction is an important part of proper database design. A *transaction* provides a way to group a series of critical SQL statements. That way, if something fails, you can revert the database to the state it was in before the statements were issued. The following three statements handle transactions:

- `BEGINTRANS` marks the beginning of a transaction.
- `COMMITTRANS` marks the end of a transaction.
- `ROLLBACK` rolls the transaction back to the state the database was in before `BEGINTRANS` was issued.

You indicate the beginning of the group of statements with the `BEGINTRANS` keyword. If there are no errors, the transaction ends with the `COMMITTRANS` keyword, which commits all statements executed since `BEGINTRANS` was issued. However, any errors must be handled in an error handler, which must tell the database not to issue any of the statements executed since the `BEGINTRANS` was issued. This is done with the `ROLLBACK` keyword.

The database can do this because it stores the data in a transaction log. The transaction log stores the data in the state that it was at the time the `BEGINTRANS` was issued. Therefore, the data can be rolled back by using the transaction log.

A good example of when you might use transactions is in an order entry/accounting application. In one transaction, with one order, you want to do the following things:

- Let the shipping department know about the items to be shipped
- Update the customer's record
- Decrease inventory

All these items need to be handled at once. If any of them fail, all need to fail. For example, if the SQL statement to decrease the inventory fails and you don't force the customer's record and the shipping department transactions to fail, there's no integrity between the sets of data. The customer's record would say that an item was ordered, the shipping department would ship the item, but the inventory wouldn't be decreased. As this situation continues, the inventory database would show a large number of items, but these items wouldn't actually exist because the shipping department keeps receiving orders to ship them out. The code fragment in Listing 27.1 illustrates how to use transactions with your SQL statements.

Listing 27.1. Multiple SQL statements wrapped in a transaction.

```
'Handle Error
On Error Goto SaveError
'Begin the transaction
BeginTrans
'Instruct the shipping department to ship the item
sCmd = "INSERT INTO Shipping(Cust_ID, Stock_Num, Qty) "
sCmd = sCmd + "VALUES (101, '119945A', 2) "
'issue statement
dbMain.Workspaces(0).Execute sCmd

'Update the customer's record
sCmd = "INSERT INTO Order(Cust_ID, Stock_Num, Qty, Price, Date) "
sCmd = sCmd + "VALUES (101, '19945A', 2, 19.95, '12/15/96') "
'issue statement
dbMain.Workspaces(0).Execute sCmd

'Update inventory
sCmd = "UPDATE Inventory "
sCmd = sCmd + "SET On_Hand = On_Hand - 2 "
sCmd = sCmd + "WHERE Stock_Num = '19945A' "
'issue statement
dbMain.Workspaces(0).Execute sCmd

'there were no errors, commit
CommitTrans
Exit Sub

'error handler
SaveError:
    MsgBox Error$
    Rollback
    Exit Sub
```

Altering the Database Structure with Data Definition Statements

You can use data definition statements to create or alter the database structure itself. You can use them to do the following:

- Create tables
- Add columns to tables
- Add indexes on tables
- Delete tables and indexes

These statements are issued from Visual Basic just as any other statement would be issued—by using the EXECUTE method of the database object.

Creating Tables

To create a table, you use the CREATE TABLE keywords, which use the syntax

```
CREATE TABLE table (field1 type [(size)] [index1] [, field2 type [(size)]
➥[index2] [, ...]][, multifieldindex [, ...]])
```

where

- *table* is the name of the table to be created.
- *field1*, *field2*... are the names of fields to be created in the new table. (At least one field must be created at this time.)
- *type* is the data type of the new field.
- *size* is the field size in characters for a text field.
- *index1*, *index2*... specifies a CONSTRAINT clause defining a single-field index.
- *multifieldindex* specifies a CONSTRAINT clause defining a multiple-field index.

Suppose that you wanted to create a table named Orders. This table would have five columns: Cust_ID, Stock_Num, Qty, Price, and OrderDate. Also, there would be a primary key index on the Cust_ID column:

```
CREATE TABLE Orders (Cust_ID Double CONSTRAINT PKey PRIMARY KEY, Stock_Num
➥TEXT(10), Qty Integer, Price CURRENCY, OrderDate DATE)
```

If you want to make the Cust_ID, Stock_Num, and OrderDate the primary key, you would do so like this:

```
CREATE TABLE Orders (Cust_ID Double, Stock_Num TEXT(10), Qty Integer,
➥Price CURRENCY, OrderDate DATE, CONSTRAINT PKey PRIMARY KEY(Cust_ID,
➥Stock_Num, OrderDate))
```

Adding or Deleting Columns and Indexes

To alter a table, use the ALTER TABLE keywords with the following syntax:

```
ALTER TABLE table {ADD {[COLUMN] field type[(size)] [CONSTRAINT index] I
CONSTRAINT multifieldindex} ¦
DROP {[COLUMN] field I CONSTRAINT indexname} }
```

where

- *table* is the name of the table to be altered.
- *field* is the name of the field to be added to or deleted from the table.
- *type* is the data type of the field.
- *size* is the field size in characters for text fields.
- *index* is the index for the field.
- *multifieldindex* is the definition of a multiple-field index to be added to table.
- *indexname* is the name of the multiple-field index to be removed.

Suppose that you wanted to add a `Ship_Date` column to the previous example. You could do that like this:

```
ALTER TABLE Orders
ADD COLUMN Ship_Date DATE
```

If you then wanted to delete a column, you could do that like this:

```
ALTER TABLE Orders
DROP COLUMN Ship_Date
```

You can use this same general syntax to add or delete indexes. The only difference is that you must follow the rules for the `CONSTRAINT` clause, which follows one of two basic syntaxes. The first is for a single field index, which follows this basic syntax:


```
CONSTRAINT name {PRIMARY KEY ¦ UNIQUE ¦
REFERENCES foreigntable [(foreignfield)]}
```

where

- *name* is the name of the index to be created.
- *foreigntable* is the name of the foreign table containing the field or fields specified by *foreignfield1*, *foreignfield2*, and so on.
- *foreignfield1*, *foreignfield2*... are the names of the fields in *foreigntable* specified by *ref1* and *ref2*. You can omit this field if the referenced field is the primary key of *foreigntable*.

The second is for a multiple field index, which follows this basic syntax:

```
CONSTRAINT name
{PRIMARY KEY (primary1[, primary2 [, ...]]) ¦
UNIQUE (unique1[, unique2 [, ...]]) ¦
FOREIGN KEY (ref1[, ref2 [, ...]]) REFERENCES foreigntable [(foreignfield1 [,
➥foreignfield2 [, ...]])]}
```

where

- *name* is the name of the index to be created.
- *primary1*, *primary2*... are the names of the fields to be designated as the primary key.
- *unique1*, *unique2*... are the names of the fields to be designated as a unique key.
- *ref1*, *ref2*... are the names of foreign key fields that refer to fields in another table.
- *foreigntable* is the name of the foreign table containing the field or fields specified by *foreignfield1*, *foreignfield2*, and so on.
- *foreignfield1*, *foreignfield2*... are the names of the fields in *foreigntable* specified by *ref1* and *ref2*. You can omit this field if the referenced field is the primary key of *foreigntable*.

Deleting Tables and Indexes

Deleting tables or indexes requires a simple SQL statement that uses the DROP keyword. Of course, you know the name of the table to delete, but it can be difficult to know the name of an index. If you created it, you would know the naming conventions you've used. For example, a primary key index could be called Pkey. However, if you've used some other tool to create the tables and indexes, you might not know the name. One thing you could do is cycle through the Indexes collection to determine all index names.

The DROP keyword is used with this general syntax:

```
DROP {TABLE table | INDEX index ON table}
```

where *table* is the name of the table to delete or the name of the index to delete that resides in a table, and *index* is the name of the index to delete.

If you wanted to delete the table Orders, you would do so like this:

```
DROP TABLE Orders
```

You'll receive no confirmation prompt before the table or index is deleted. Issuing the statement will perform the action.

NOTE

Client/server databases, such as SQL Server, also allow you to DROP databases, provided that you have the appropriate permissions to do so.

Using the T-SQL Debugger

Microsoft has included a new feature in the Enterprise Edition of Visual Basic 5, called the Transact-SQL Debugger (or T-SQL Debugger, for short). It isn't compatible with any other version of Visual Basic. Before the T-SQL Debugger existed, debugging stored procedures on SQL Server was very difficult. You had to raise errors under certain circumstances to know what was going on within the stored procedure. In other words, you had to devise a custom method of debugging stored procedures. The T-SQL Debugger changes all that by providing a way to debug stored procedures from within Visual Basic.

Installing the T-SQL Debugger

To install the T-SQL Debugger, you need to know a few things. First, there are a client-side setup and a server-side setup. The client-side setup is installed automatically when you choose the Typical installation option. If you choose the Custom installation option, you must select the SQL Debugging option under Enterprise Features.

NOTE

The process of installing the T-SQL Debugger is documented in the `README.TXT` file located in `VB5.0\TOOLS\TSQL\SRVSETUP` on the VB5 Enterprise Edition CD-ROM. The location of the file on your CD might be slightly different if you are using a different implementation of Visual Basic.

The server-side setup is a little more complicated:

1. Although Service Pack 2 for Windows NT 4.0 is included on the Visual Basic 5.0 CD-ROM, it is recommended that you download the newer Service Pack 3 from Microsoft's Web site and install that instead. Make sure that you reboot your system after the Service Pack has been installed.
2. Make sure that SQL Server 6.5 or greater is installed, as well as SQL Server Service Pack 2 (SP2). On the Visual Basic 5.0 CD-ROM, the SP2 is located in the `\TOOLS\TSQL\SQL65.SP2` subdirectory. If your copy of VB resides on a different CD (such as Visual Studio), the location of the Service Pack may be different. In any case, install the Service Pack and reboot when prompted.

CAUTION

Make sure that no errors occur when you install SQL Server 6.5 Service Pack 2 because installing the Service Pack alters the database by issuing scripts that are necessary for you to continue. If any errors occur, your database won't be updated. Also, make sure that you reboot each time you're prompted. If you don't, this could affect the overall installation process.

3. Set up the actual T-SQL Debugger by running the `SDI_NT4.EXE` program on Visual Basic 5.0's CD-ROM in the `\TOOLS\TSQL\SRVSETUP` subdirectory.

Even though you're set up to debug your stored procedures, you should consider a few points before continuing:

- Make sure that the MSSQLServer service is *not* set up to log on as a system account. Make sure that it's set to log on as a local account (see Figure 27.1).
- If you're using TCP/IP as a protocol, make sure that the machines communicate with each other by typing **`PING`** at the server's command prompt, followed by the name of the computer you're trying to connect with. For example, Figure 27.2 shows the results of the `PING` command with a computer named `NOTEBOOK`.

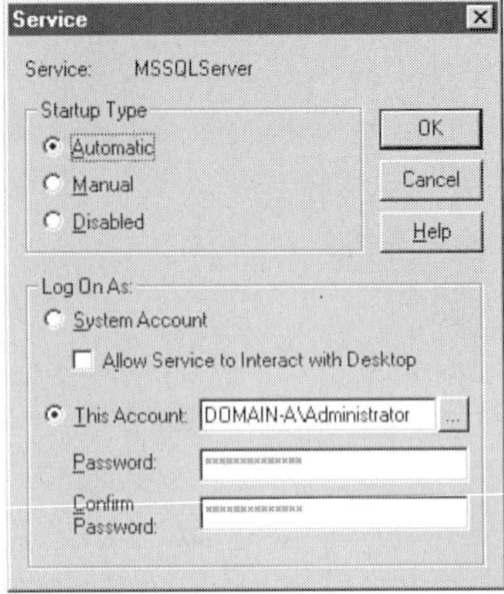

FIGURE 27.1.
MSSQLServer service startup parameters.

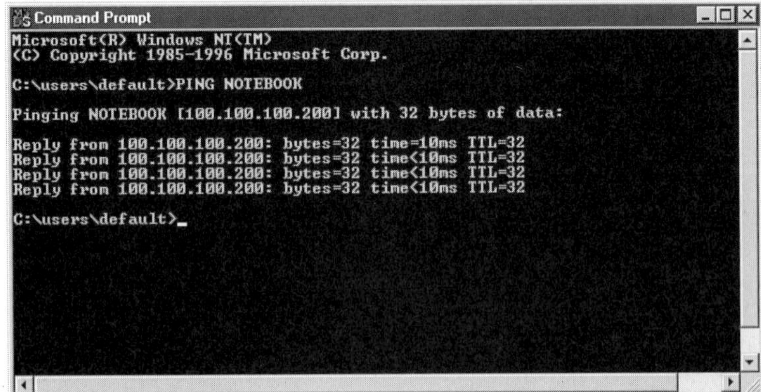

FIGURE 27.2.
Using the `PING` *command.*

- Make sure that you have Remote Data Objects 2.0 or later installed on the client computer.
- Make sure that the RPC Services (Remote Procedure Call and Remote Procedure Locator) are running on the Windows NT server.

If you have problems, the system will tell you to look in the client and server logs but won't tell you where the logs are located. The server log is actually the Windows NT `Application` event log. The client log, `AUTMGR32.LOG`, is on the client machine in the `\WINDOWS\SYSTEM` subdirectory. This is a cumulative log, with the most recent entries at the bottom.

NOTE

If everything looks fine but you can't figure out why stored procedures aren't debugging, it's best to first reboot the client machine. If that doesn't work, try rebooting the server.

Using the T-SQL Debugger

As an add-in, the T-SQL Debugger must be selected for use. Choose Add-Ins | Add-In Manager from the Visual Basic menu. Make sure that a check mark is next to the VB T-SQL Debugger option (see Figure 27.3).

FIGURE 27.3.
Selecting the T-SQL Debugger for use.

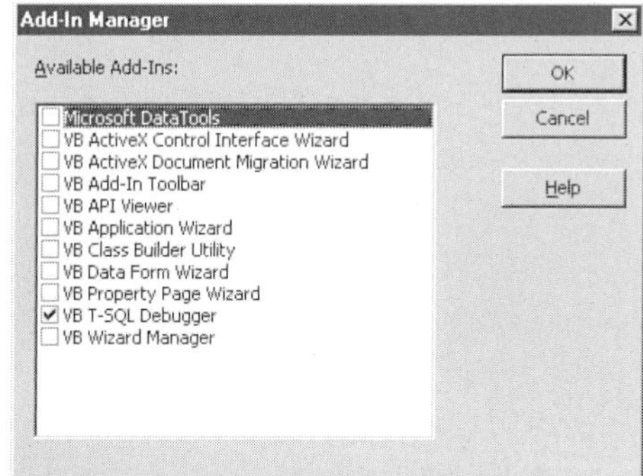

After you select it, notice that the Automation Manager is running. The Automation Manager runs because it's necessary to coordinate Remote Procedure Calls (RPC) with the server. Next, choose Add-Ins | T-SQL Debugger from the menu to start the debugger.

NOTE

You might notice that the T-SQL Debugger is actually offscreen. Apparently, Microsoft didn't take into account the resolution of the add-in. Simply move it to the center of the screen for use.

Creating Queries

When you invoke the T-SQL Debugger, notice a dialog box with three tabbed pages. You must fill in the first page, Settings, to establish an ODBC connection with SQL Server before you can continue. The following fields are required:

- DSN
- SQL Server
- UID
- Password (if any)

To begin, select a Data Source Name (DSN), a 32-bit data source registered with ODBC. If you don't have one on your machine, you can create one by clicking the Register DSN button and configuring a 32-bit DSN in the dialog box that appears.

Next, select or enter the name of the server where SQL Server is installed. For example, you might name your server `SERVER-A`. After you successfully log on, this server will be conveniently added to the drop-down list for future use.

Enter the database. If you leave the Database field blank, the default database (usually `Master`) is used. For example, type **pubs**.

UID is the user ID registered with SQL Server. Type a valid user ID, such as **sa** (the default administrator logon). Also type the password, if one exists.

Although they aren't necessary to change for you to continue, the following RDO (Remote Data Objects) options are available:

- Lock Type specifies the type of RDO locking that will occur. The possible values are `rdConcurReadOnly`, `rdConcurValues`, `rdConcurLock`, `rdConcurRowver`, and `rdConcurBatch`.
- Result Set specifies the type of RDO resultset that will be returned. The possible values are `rdOpenKeyset`, `rdOpenForwardOnly`, `rdOpenStatic`, and `rdOpenDynamic`.
- Options specifies miscellaneous options for how queries are executed. The possible values are `rdNone` and `rdExecDirect`.

Figure 27.4 shows how the Settings page looks when configured properly.

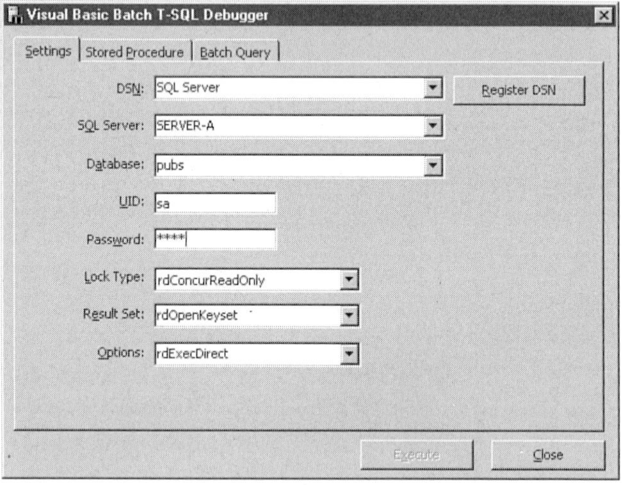

FIGURE 27.4.
The Settings page of the T-SQL Debugger.

After the required fields are filled in, notice that the Stored Procedure and Batch Query tabs are enabled. Click the Stored Procedure tab to establish an RDO connection with the server. You'll see a list of stored procedures contained within the database (`pubs`) you selected in the earlier example. You'll see these possible stored procedures:

- `byroyalty`
- `reptq1`
- `reptq2`
- `reptq3`

Select a stored procedure to run (for example, the `byroyalty` stored procedure). Figure 27.5 shows what the Stored Procedure page now looks like.

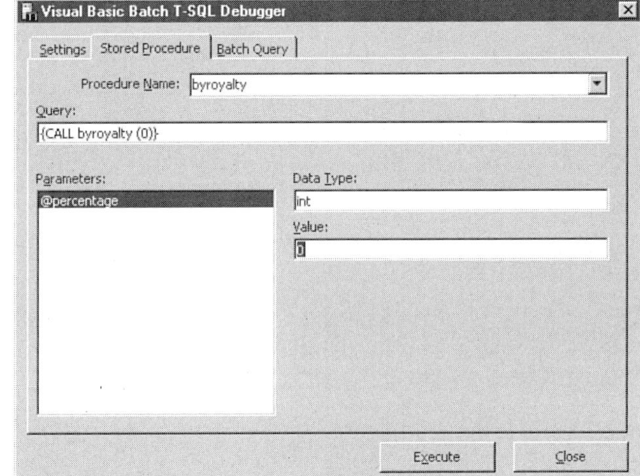

FIGURE 27.5.
The Stored Procedure page of the T-SQL Debugger.

Notice at the bottom of the dialog box that the Execute button becomes enabled. This is because the T-SQL Debugger is ready to debug the stored procedure.

Alternatively, you can traverse the list of parameters shown on the left and set values for them in the Value text box. That way, you can try different values to debug the stored procedures. However, as you'll see shortly, you can actually change the value in the debugger, just as you would in the Visual Basic debugger. As you change the values, notice that the Query text box changes to reflect the new values. This is the actual query that will be sent to the server.

NOTE

Although you can actually change the value in the Query text box, it's not recommended because the Value text box doesn't reflect a change in this case.

If you want to execute the query at this time, see the next section, "Executing Queries."

You use the Batch Query page to place text that will be used in a batch query. A *batch query* is a series of SQL statements transmitted to the server, one after another, in a group. Figure 27.6 shows a sample batch query. Each item in the batch must be separated by the keyword `GO`.

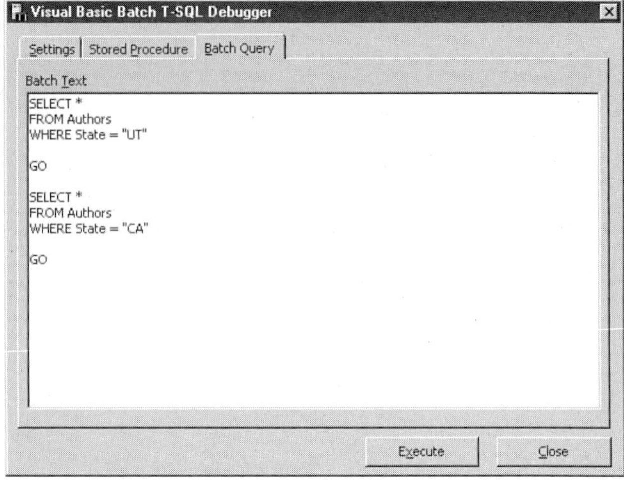

FIGURE 27.6.
The Batch Query page of the T-SQL Debugger.

Executing Queries

To execute the query, simply click the Execute button. Doing so establishes another connection with the server and places the query in the debugger window (see Figure 27.7, showing the `byroyalty` stored procedure).

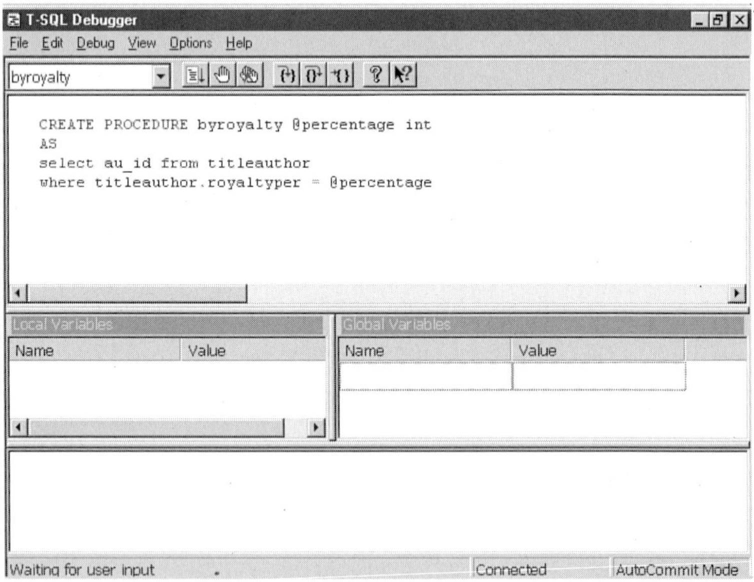

FIGURE 27.7.
The T-SQL Debugger with a stored procedure to execute.

T-SQL Debugger
File Edit Debug View Options Help
byroyalty

```
CREATE PROCEDURE byroyalty @percentage int
AS
select au_id from titleauthor
where titleauthor.royaltyper = @percentage
```

Local Variables
Name Value
Global Variables
Name Value
Waiting for user input Connected AutoCommit Mode

The debugger window has four panes:

- The top unlabeled pane contains the actual stored procedure text.
- The Local Variables pane lists the local variables in the stored procedure.
- The Global Variables pane lists global variables within SQL Server 6.5.
- The bottom unlabeled pane is the results window.

To execute the query, click the Go toolbar button, press the F5 key, or choose Debug|Go from the menu.

If you receive the error message shown in Figure 27.8, refer to the steps listed earlier in the "Installing the T-SQL Debugger" section or refer to the online help. If you don't receive an error, the stored procedure is executed (see Figure 27.9).

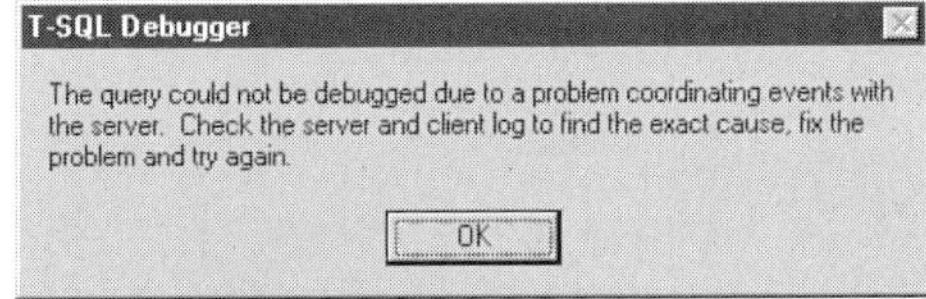

FIGURE 27.8.
A T-SQL Debugger server error.

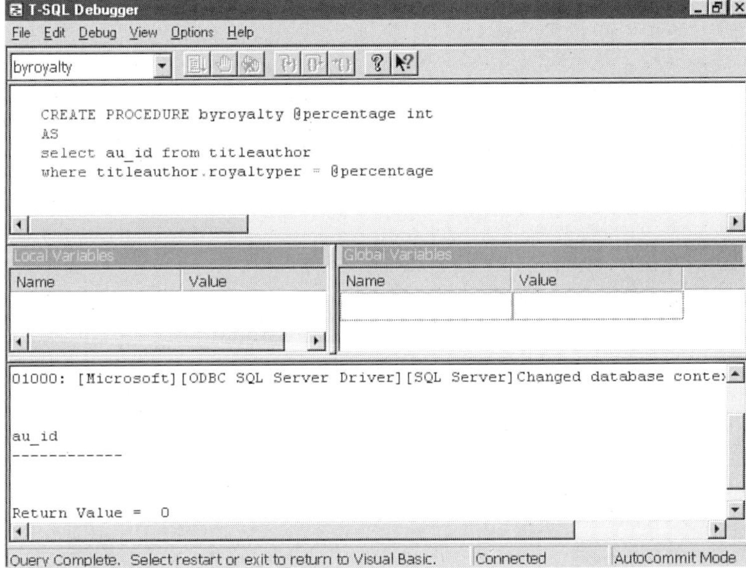

FIGURE 27.9.
The T-SQL Debugger after a stored procedure is executed.

After you execute a query, notice that the Go toolbar button becomes disabled. To enable it, choose Debug|Restart from the menu or press Shift+F5. Now you can execute the query as before.

Debugging Queries

Debugging a query with the T-SQL Debugger is similar to debugging a query in Visual Basic. A *breakpoint* tells the debugger to pause execution when it reaches the code line containing the breakpoint. That way, you can check the values of variables at a specific point. You can set breakpoints by clicking a line of text in the query and then clicking the Set/Remove Breakpoint toolbar button, pressing the F9 key, or choosing Edit | Set Breakpoint from the menu. A red dot appears in the margin of the line containing the breakpoint.

After you set a breakpoint, you can step through the code as you would in Visual Basic. You have the following options:

- Step Into
- Step Over
- Run To Cursor

To activate the Step Into option, click the Step Into toolbar button, press the F8 key, or choose Debug | Step from the menu. Step Into executes every line of code. If the code calls a label or another procedure, Step Into steps through each line in that code as well. As each line is executed, the system pauses after each line of code. It's useful to set a breakpoint at a specific point in the code where you suspect a problem to be located, allowing the program to pause execution. Then stepping through the code to watch program execution helps find errors in code.

Activate the Step Over option by clicking the Step Over toolbar button (Step Over has no hotkey or menu option). The Step Over option executes each line in the current procedure but not every line of code of a called procedure. The code is executed, but not every line is shown.

The Run To Cursor option lets you determine which line of code is executed next. To use it, place the cursor on the line you want to execute. Then click the Run To Cursor toolbar button or choose Debug | Run To Cursor from the menu (no hotkey is available). All lines of code between where the cursor was and where the cursor currently is will be skipped.

While you're debugging code (by setting breakpoints), you can query or set the values of variables to test different scenarios without having to rerun your query externally. Figure 27.10 shows the code stopped at a breakpoint, with the values of all local variables.

Notice in the Local Variables pane that the value of the `@percentage` variable is 0. Another way to tell the value of your variables is to place the mouse pointer over the variable to see the value in a ToolTip.

To change the value, simply click the Value field in the Local Variables pane and manually change the value. After you change it, press Enter. Notice that placing the cursor over the variable changes it immediately. You then can step through the rest of the procedure and view the results. Change the percentage to 25 to view the results as shown in Figure 27.11. Two author IDs are returned at 25 percent.

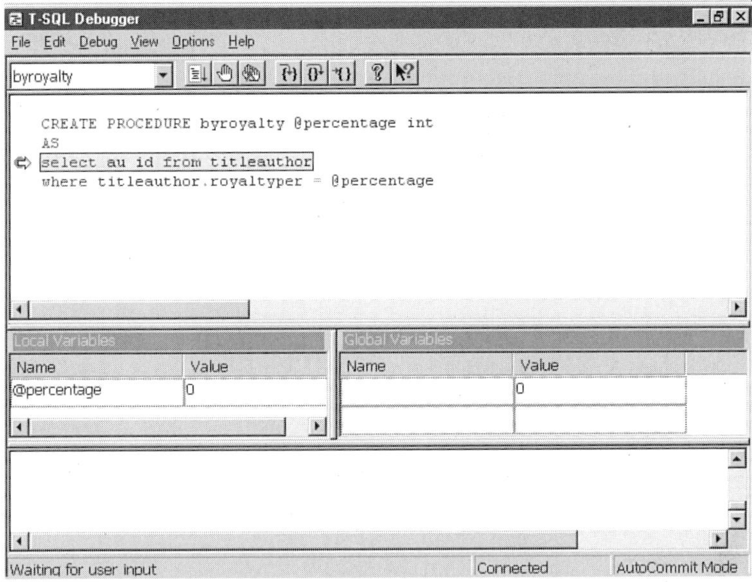

FIGURE 27.10.
The T-SQL Debugger stopped at a breakpoint.

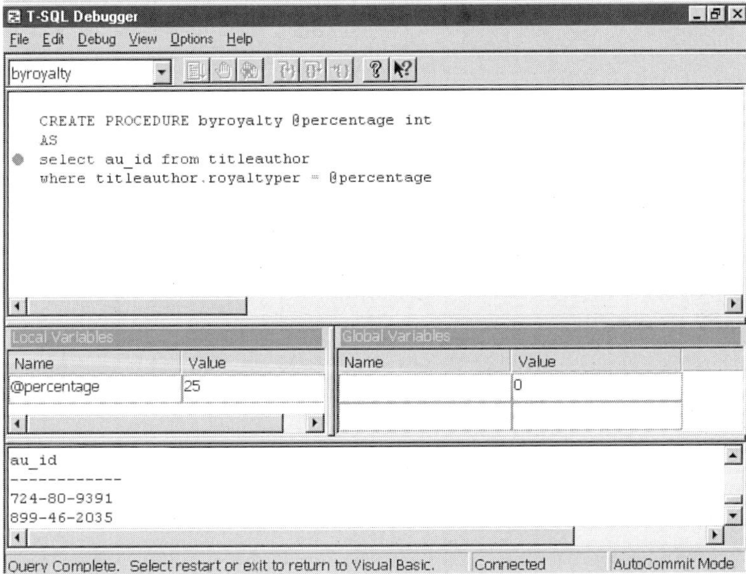

FIGURE 27.11.
The T-SQL Debugger after a variable value is changed.

You use the Global Variables pane to query or set the values of global variables. These global variables, stored within SQL Server, are available to all stored procedures and queries. Again, only while debugging can you query or set the value of these options. For example, stop a query at a breakpoint and type the global variable **`@@OPTIONS`**, which stores different options within

SQL Server. (All global variables begin with `@@`.) Press Enter to see the value of the global variable. This value might not be included in the stored procedure. Figure 27.12 shows what this pane looks like.

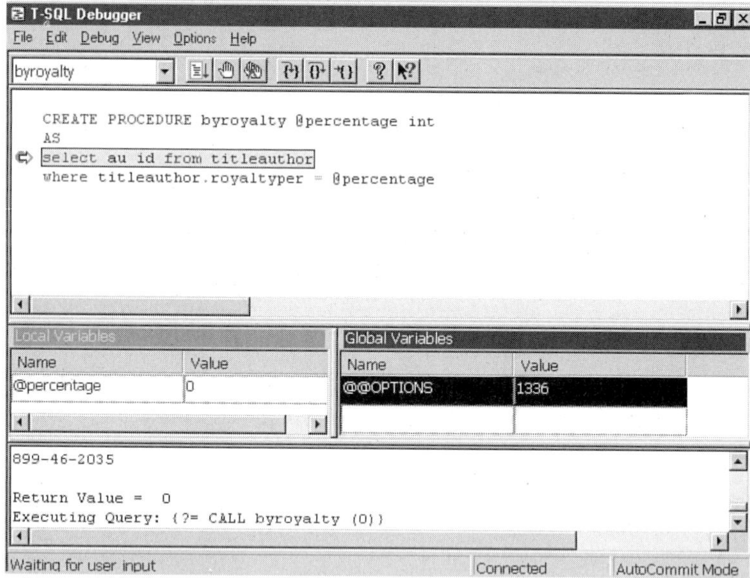

FIGURE 27.12. *The T-SQL Debugger after a global variable is entered.*

T-SQL Debugger Options

You can set two options while using the debugger. One is to view the call stack. If one stored procedure calls another, you'll have more than one query in the call stack. To view this stack, choose View | Call Stack from the menu. Figure 27.13 shows this window.

The other option is the mode that the debugger is in. You can choose between Auto Commit and Auto Rollback. With Auto Rollback, a query is automatically rolled back if it's not committed in code. With Auto Commit, every complete transaction is automatically committed when it's executed.

You can toggle between these two modes by choosing Options | Safe (Auto Rollback) Mode from the menu. If a check mark is next to this item, the debugger is in Auto Rollback mode; if there isn't a check mark, the debugger is in Auto Commit mode.

You can also add a watch to a global variable, just as you can add a watch in Visual Basic. A *watch* shows the value of specified variables. To add a watch, select Edit | Add Watch from the menu to place the watch in the Global Variables pane. To remove the watch, simply click it and press Delete.

Another nice feature is the ability to view the contents of a temporary table. To view the contents, simply choose View | Temp Table Dump from the menu. At the prompt, type the name of the temporary table. You then can view the results of the table.

FIGURE 27.13.
The T-SQL Debugger call stack.

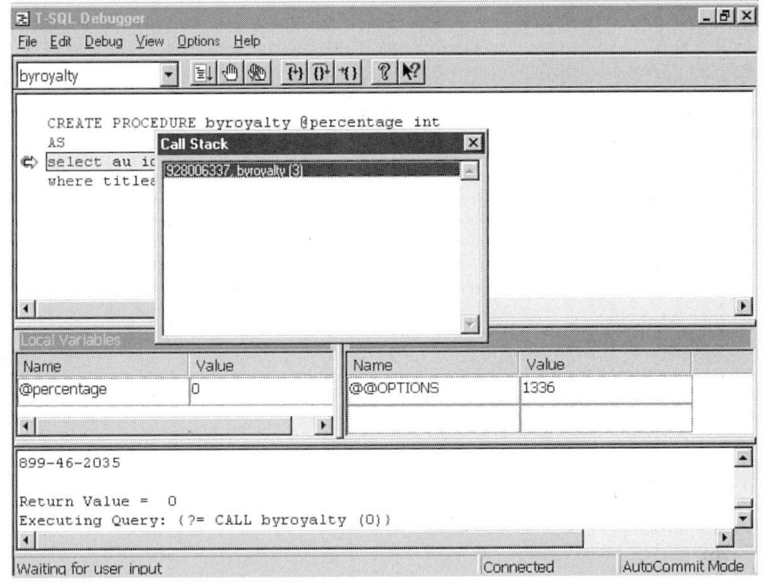

You can view the results of your stored procedures or any messages in the Output window. You can toggle the Output window on and off by choosing View | Output Window. If a check mark is next to the option, the Output window will be shown.

In addition to these stated options, you can choose your own colors for items in the debug window by choosing Options | Colors. The following items can have colors assigned:

Comment	Keyword
Constant	Number
Datatype	Operator
Function	String
Identifier	Execution Indicator

You can also choose the font for the text in the debugger by choosing Options | Font from the menu.

NOTE

You can also debug a stored procedure from within Visual Basic in break mode via the `UserConnection` object. You can right-click the object to see an option labeled Debug Stored Procedure. This will begin the debugging session listed throughout this chapter.

Summary

SQL is important because it has become the standard language of most databases. SQL varies slightly among different databases, but the core components discussed in this chapter are common to most databases, except where noted. This chapter gives a good insight into SQL and how it's used. Please use this chapter as an ongoing reference for your database projects.

Microsoft's introduction of the T-SQL Debugger into the Enterprise Edition of Visual Basic 5 is a tremendous improvement. Until now, debugging stored procedures was difficult, if not impossible. You had to devise your own schemes for returning values and error codes from stored procedures, a cumbersome task because the stored procedures had to be recompiled after these schemes were put in place.

The T-SQL Debugger makes it easy to debug stored procedures. It allows you to step through your stored procedures, as well as query and set the value of variables. Using the T-SQL Debugger saves countless hours of tedious work. This chapter showed you how to use the T-SQL Debugger.

Getting Connected with the UserConnection Designer

IN THIS CHAPTER

With the introduction of Visual Basic 5.0, you have a new tool with which to create sophisticated client/server applications. The UserConnection designer is a design-time tool and a runtime object that provides you with an easy way to manage all your database processing from one central location.

The `UserConnection` object allows you, as a database developer, to place all your database queries, whether they're simple SQL statements or complex stored procedures, in the `UserConnection` object at design time. You can then reference these queries and stored procedures much as you do methods of an object. This gives you the benefit of having the parameters to the queries and stored procedures displayed in the editor and also provides an easy way to encapsulate all your database logic in one central location.

In this chapter, you learn how to set up the `UserConnection` object, create a new `UserConnection` object, create queries for the `UserConnection` object, and then execute these queries from the Visual Basic Code Editor.

Setting Up the `UserConnection` Object

Although the `UserConnection` object is installed with Visual Basic, it's not automatically available to use in your applications. You have to turn on the UserConnection designer manually so that you can use it in your applications.

To set up the UserConnection designer for use in your applications, follow these steps:

1. Choose Project | Components from Visual Basic's menu bar.
2. In the Components dialog box, click the Designers tab to see the list of component designers available within Visual Basic.
3. Select the UserConnection designer by marking the check box beside the listing for the object. Your dialog box should look something like the one pictured in Figure 28.1.

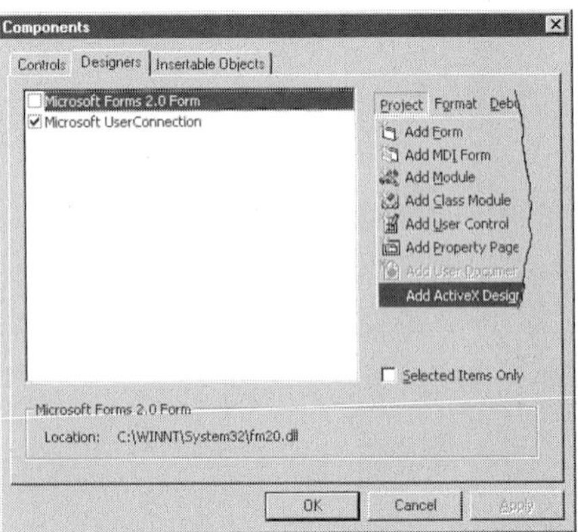

FIGURE 28.1.
Selecting the UserConnection designer.

After you set up the UserConnection object designer, you can begin using the object in your applications. To add the object to your application, choose Project | Add ActiveX Designer | Microsoft UserConnection from the menu. This creates the `UserConnection` object and places it in the Designers group in the Project Explorer. It also displays the UserConnection Properties dialog box to allow you to set the initial properties for the object, such as how to connect to the database, the username and password, as well as which cursor library to use.

You can create multiple `UserConnection` objects to provide various functionality, including the capability to access multiple data sources, such as accessing a SQL database and an Access `.MDB` file. You can also add multiple objects to partition your application into various modules. You could have an object that contains the queries and stored procedures for each department or have one object for queries and one object for stored procedures.

The nice feature about the `UserConnection` object is that it lets you focus more on solving a business problem rather than a programming problem. The `UserConnection` object is a seamless way to simplify your database programming within Visual Basic.

Using the `UserConnection` Object

Now that you have the `UserConnection` object set up and ready to insert into your application, you can begin using the `UserConnection` object in your applications.

When you add the `UserConnection` object to your application by choosing the option from the menu, you're initially presented with the dialog box shown in Figure 28.2.

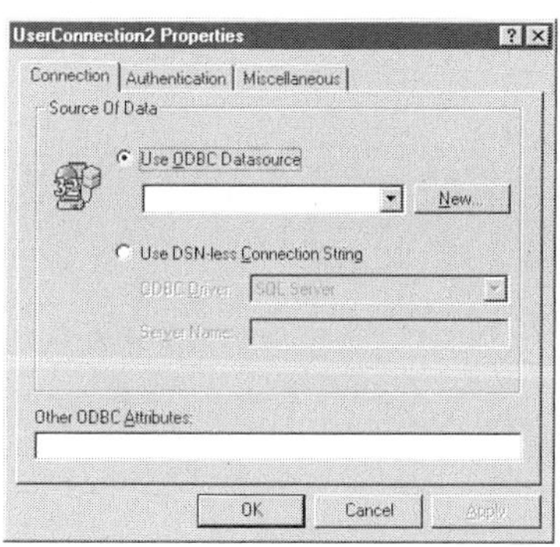

FIGURE 28.2.
The `UserConnection` *object's initial dialog box.*

As you can see, you can specify the connection information here in the object's Properties dialog box. The `UserConnection` object lets you connect to a data source by using an ODBC data source name or by using a DSN-less connection by specifying the ODBC driver that you'll be using and the database server to which you'll be connecting.

The Authentication page in the Properties dialog box lets you specify the authentication information for the object. You can specify a username and a password that the object will use when it connects to the database specified on the Connection page of the Properties dialog box.

On the Authentication page, you also can specify whether to display an ODBC prompt to users. You can choose to always display the prompt, never display the prompt, or display only when needed. Depending on your situation, you may want to choose to always display the prompt if you're deploying a client/server application and want your users to validate themselves to the database.

TIP

I have found that, as a general rule for server applications, it's best to never display the prompt; for client applications, it's best to set the prompt to display only as needed.

The Miscellaneous page lets you specify various information for the object, such as the login timeout, query timeout, and the cursor library that should be used.

CAUTION

In my applications, I have discovered that Microsoft SQL Server stored procedures don't work well in a Server Cursor environment. They seem to return errors complaining about more than a `Select` statement being in the stored procedure. If you plan to use Microsoft SQL Server as your database and plan to use stored procedures, I recommend that you use a library other than Server Cursor.

Connecting to a Database

At design time, you can specify all the connection information needed to connect to a database. In your code, you need to call the `EstablishConnection` method to actually connect to the database by using the information in the `UserConnection` object. The syntax for the `EstablishConnection` object is as follows:

```
object.EstablishConnection prompt, [readonly, ]options
```

The `EstablishConnection` method can take three optional arguments:

- *`prompt`* lets you specify whether to display the ODBC prompt to users or use the information contained in the object to make a connection. The default is to not display the prompt unless `to DSN` is specified.
- The second argument is the `readonly` parameter, which lets you specify whether the connection will enable updates or be a read-only connection to the database.

TIP

A read-only connection is useful in reporting applications where you don't want users to be able to update the data they're reading.

- You can use the *options* parameter to pass any options that you want the object to use. The only current available option is the `rdAsyncEnable` option, which lets you make query execution optional.

Listing 28.1 shows how to create a `UserConnection` object in code and then connect to the database by using the `EstablishConnection` method.

Listing 28.1. The `EstablishConnection` method.

```
Option Explicit
Private uConn as New UserConnection1

Private Sub DBConnect ()

    UConn.EstablishConnection

End Sub
```


Using UserConnection Object Events

The `UserConnection` object provides eight events that you can use to handle events generated by the object. These events are accessed directly from the `UserConnection` object designer window by clicking the View Code button in the designer's toolbar.

Table 28.1 lists the `UserConnection` object events and a short description of their purpose and how to use them.

Table 28.1. `UserConnection` object events.

Event	*Description*
`BeforeConnect`	Lets you process or display information directly before a call is made to connect to the database.
`Connect`	Fired after a connection is made to the database. You can use this event to check for any errors that occurred in connecting to the database.
`Disconnect`	Fired after the object disconnects from the database.
`Initialize`	Fired when an instance of the object is created.

continues

Table 28.1. continued

Event	*Description*
`QueryComplete`	Occurs after a query is executed, allowing you to check whether the query was executed successfully.
`QueryTimeout`	Fired when an executing query takes longer than the specified query timeout value. You can use this event to determine whether you'll continue waiting for the query to complete or terminate the running query.
`Terminate`	Fired if a connection to the database is terminated.
`WillExecute`	Occurs before a query is executed, allowing you to cancel execution of the query or perform special processing before the query is sent to the database to be executed.

Adding a New Query

The main purpose of the `UserConnection` object is to allow you to place all your database queries and stored procedures into a central location where they can be maintained and modified. In the following steps, you'll add a query to the `UserConnection` object and then write some code to execute the query and get the resultset returned from the database.

This query will return a listing of all records from a table named `Users`. This simple query is used only to illustrate how to use the `UserConnection` object; I hope your real-world queries are more involved than this SQL statement. Follow these steps to create a new query in the `UserConnection` object:

1. Open the UserConnection designer by double-clicking the object in the Project Explorer.
2. When the designer is open, you can add a new query by clicking the Insert Query toolbar button at the top of the designer.
3. When you click the Insert Query toolbar button, a Properties dialog box appears, allowing you to enter various information about the query. For this example, set the Query Name field to be `TestQuery1`.
4. Select the Based on User-Defined SQL option at the bottom of the dialog box and enter the following SQL statement:

   ```
   Select * From Users
   ```

5. After you enter all information, your dialog box should look like the one in Figure 28.3. When you've entered all information correctly, you can click OK to return to the object designer.

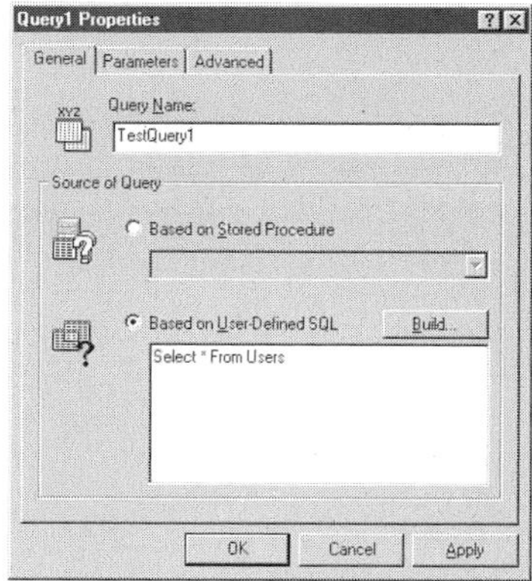

FIGURE 28.3.
The query properties dialog box.

You've now created a query method in the `UserConnection` object. To actually use that query, you need to write some code behind it. One nice thing about the `UserConnection` object is that the query you just created becomes a visible method of the object. You don't have to specify a query from a collection or select the query from a list; you can call the query directly as though it were a member of the object. Listing 28.2 shows how you execute the query and get the results returned from the query.

Listing 28.2. The execute query method.

```
Option Explicit
Private uConn as New UserConnection1

Private Sub Execute ()

    Dim rs as rdoResultSet

    uConn.EstablishConnection
    uConn.TestQuery1
    Set rs = uConn.LastQueryResults

End Sub
```

Notice that you call the `LastQueryResults` method of the `UserConnection` object. This method is what you use to get the resultset returned by the executed query. The resultset isn't returned by the query method as you might expect but is stored internally in the `UserConnection` object until you call the `LastQueryResults` method to obtain the resultset.

Adding Parameterized Queries and Stored Procedures

In addition to executing standard queries, you can create queries and stored procedures that take arguments or parameters. For a stored procedure, the parameters are automatically given the correct names and data types. For your own parameterized queries, you need to specify the name of the argument, but the designer will usually assign the correct data type to your parameter, based on the column it's being compared against.

I'll forgo an example that uses stored procedures because the object handles naming the parameters and setting the data types. Instead, let's modify the query used in the previous example to find records from the `Users` table that match a given parameter.

TIP

To get the return value from a stored procedure, get the return value of the stored procedure method. If the stored procedure returns a value of `10`, the stored procedure method of the `UserConnection` object returns a value of `10`.

You find records from the `Users` tables only where the LastName column is equal to a specified value. Follow these steps to create a parameterized query for execution in your code:

1. Create a new query as outlined in the previous example and name it `TestQuery2`.
2. In the SQL statement block, enter the following SQL statement:

```
Select * From Users Where LastName = ?
```

3. Click the Parameters tab of the properties dialog box (see Figure 28.4). Change the Name to Lastname, the ODBC Binding Data Type to be a VarChar, and the Visual Basic Data Type to be a String.
4. After you enter all information for the parameter, click OK and exit the UserConnection object designer.

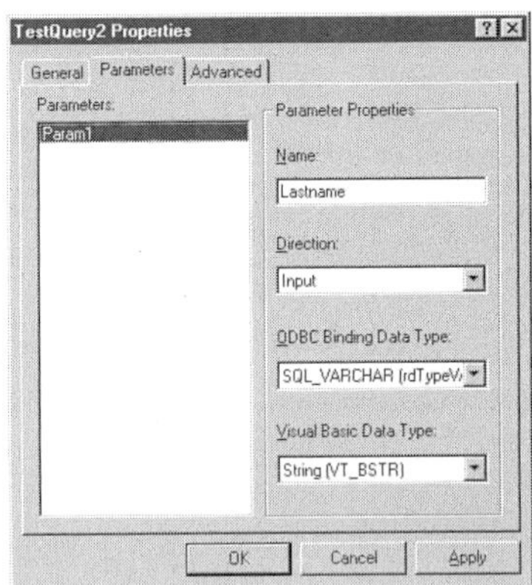

FIGURE 28.4.
The Parameters page of the query properties dialog box.

Now execute the query, passing in the value of `Smith` as the parameter for LastName. Listing 28.3 shows how to execute the query, passing a parameter and then obtaining the resultset returned by the query.

Listing 28.3. Parameterized queries.

```
Option Explicit
Private uConn As New UserConnection1

Private Sub Method()

    Dim rs As rdoResultset

    uConn.EstablishConnection
    uConn.TestQuery2 'Smith'

    Set rs = uConn.LastQueryResults

End Sub
```

The `UserConnection` object is useful because it lets you use Visual Basic's features to view information about the SQL query. Figure 28.5 displays the code window and what you see when writing code to execute the query. Notice that Visual Basic displays the name of the parameter and the data type required by the parameter.

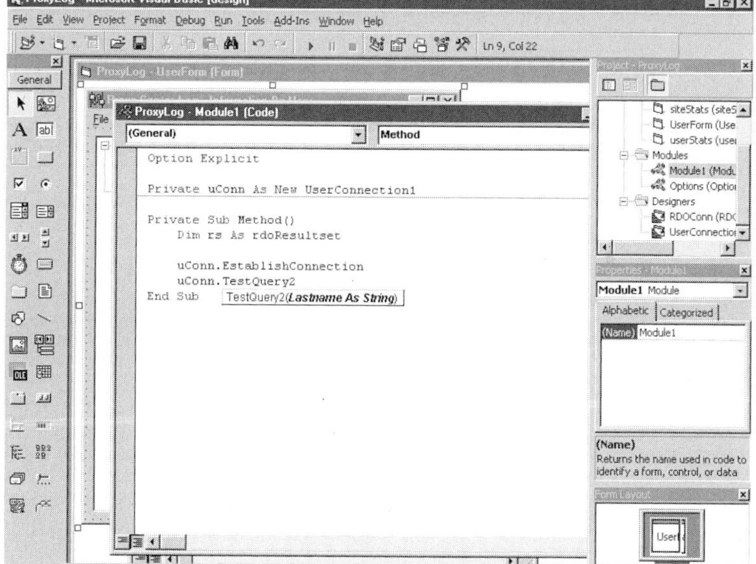

FIGURE 28.5.
Coding parameterized queries.

Summary

In this chapter, you've learned how to use the `UserConnection` object provided in Visual Basic to simplify the creation of database applications. Whether you're creating application servers or client/server applications, the `UserConnection` object can simplify your database development by providing a single location to place all database-related information and by also making query execution almost transparent.

Because of its capability to treat a database query as a method, the `UserConnection` object simplifies the coding of database applications. You no longer have to assign each parameter for a query or a stored procedure to a specific collection item. You can specify the parameters as arguments to a method, which means that you have more time for solving business problems and can spend less time learning how to execute a query in Visual Basic.

ODBC Fundamentals

IN THIS CHAPTER

When you develop Visual Basic applications, you have two ways of accessing information stored in a database. Included in Visual Basic is a component called the Jet engine, which becomes a part of your database application. As you issue commands to retrieve information from the database, the commands are interpreted by the Jet engine, but the processing of these commands is done locally on your PC. This is true whether the database resides on your PC or is located on a file server somewhere else on the network.

In the client/server world, databases are usually too large to be located on a single PC. Also, many users probably require access to the information stored there. For these reasons, database servers are used to process any application request for data. Your application would issue a request for information, usually in the form of a SQL statement. This request is then passed to the database server, which processes it and returns a recordset containing the resulting data for the request. In this way, the actual processing of the recordsets is done by the server, not by your PC.

This chapter explores how to connect your database by using a method called ODBC, or Open Database Connectivity. Visual Basic and other PC-based data-access tools and programming languages use ODBC to communicate with most databases. That way, the application can reference an ODBC data source rather than the actual path and filename of the database. This really means that the database can reside anywhere on the network. ODBC is a component of Microsoft's Windows Open System Architecture (WOSA).

ODBC provides a set of application program interface (API) functions, which makes it easier for you to connect to a wide variety of database systems. Because of the use of ODBC standards, you can use the same set of functions and commands to access information in SQL Server, Oracle, or Interbase, even though the actual data-storage systems are quite different. Even a number of PC databases can be accessed with ODBC functions. Because of these standards, you don't have to learn different access languages for each database you want to use. The ODBC standard allows you to write standard SQL program code that's translated and then passed to the database in use.

Understanding ODBC Drivers

ODBC drivers are the DLL files containing the functions that connect to various databases. There are separate sets of drivers for each database system. For many standard databases, such as PC databases and SQL Server, these drivers are provided with Visual Basic. For other databases, you can obtain the ODBC driver from the manufacturer of that database.

ODBC drivers are divided into two types: single-tier or multiple-tier. A *single-tier* driver is used to connect to PC-based database systems that may reside on either the local machine or a file server. Multiple-tier drivers are used to connect to client/server databases where the SQL statement is processed by the server, not the local machine.

Each ODBC driver that you encounter must contain the following basic set of functions, known as the *core-level capabilities*:

- Provide database connections
- Prepare and execute SQL statements
- Process transactions
- Return result sets
- Notify the application of errors

To use an ODBC driver in your application, you need to install the ODBC driver on your PC and then create the ODBC definition for your database by using the ODBC Administrator.

Using the ODBC Administrator

Before you can use ODBC to connect to your database, you must have the ODBC drivers installed on your PC and set up the ODBC data source. You can do both by using the ODBC Administrator, an application that's installed when you install Visual Basic 5. Most ODBC suppliers also include the administrator application with their ODBC drivers.

NOTE

As with any software, several versions of the ODBC administrator are in use. This chapter discusses the version that comes with Visual Basic 5.

After you install the drivers on your PC, you can set up an ODBC data source reference for the related database that you want to use.

Accessing ODBC

To set up ODBC access on your system, you need to use the ODBC Administrator application. You'll find this in the Control Panel (see Figure 29.1), which is accessible by choosing Start | Settings | Control Panel.

When the ODBC Administrator is started, you'll see a Windows 95–style tabbed dialog box (see Figure 29.2). The initial tab is the User DSN definition page, which displays User or Local data source definitions.

You can define three types of ODBC data sources with the ODBC Administrator:

- *User*—Data sources that are local to a computer for the current user.
- *System*—Data sources that any user can access on the computer.
- *File*—Definition file containing the ODBC connect information.

FIGURE 29.1.
The ODBC Administrator is located in the Control Panel of Windows 95.

ODBC Administrator

FIGURE 29.2.
Local ODBC data sources are displayed and maintained on the User DSN page.

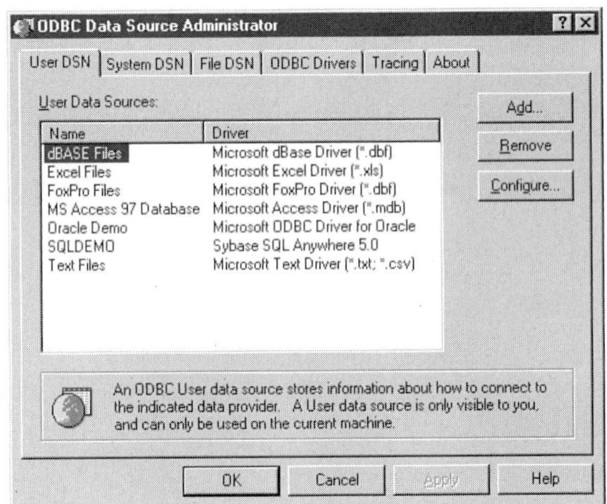

Each of these is used for specific reasons within a standalone or network environment. Generally, if you're developing a Visual Basic application that will be using an ODBC database, you define a User data source to access the database. Before you can add a data source definition, you need to make sure that the needed ODBC drivers are installed on your PC. To do this, click the ODBC Drivers tab (see Figure 29.3) for a list of the ODBC drivers already on your PC.

If you experience any problems when using an ODBC connection, first check to make sure that you're using the correct version of the driver. The ODBC Drivers page displays information about the current drivers installed on your PC. When checking versions, pay close attention to the company that supplied it and the date and time when it was created. The company becomes important when more than one ODBC driver is available for a database; the date and time can be useful if the company doesn't change the version number every time it makes a fix to the driver and redistributes it.

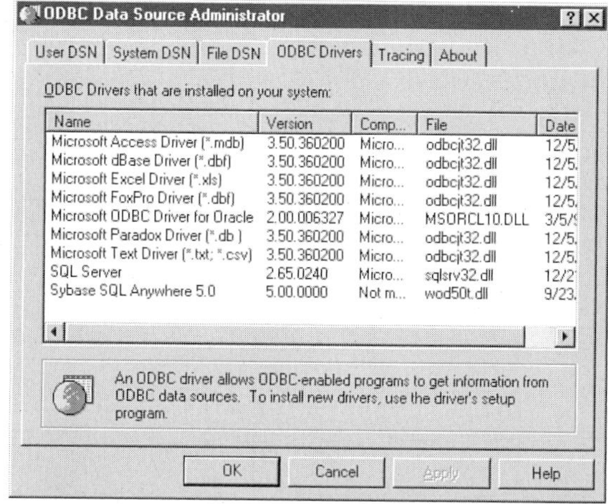

FIGURE 29.3.
With the ODBC Drivers page, you can obtain all the version information you might need about a driver.

> **NOTE**
>
> ODBC drivers from different companies usually support different options for a particular database. Check to make sure that the driver you're using supports the functions you need on the database.

The Administrator application no longer controls the installation and deletion of ODBC drivers. These functions are now done by the setup program supplied with the drivers. After you determine that you have the ODBC drivers you need, you can define the data sources that your application will use to access the database.

Defining an ODBC Data Source

The first step in defining a data source for your application is to determine the type of data source you'll need. Each of the three data source types addresses specific application requirements for connecting to and accessing database information. For most single-use applications, the User DSN is the correct definition to use. However, using the System DSN definition is a good idea if you think the application might be used in a client/server environment. By using the System DSN definition, any user logged in to the PC can access the data source through this ODBC definition.

Defining a data source is the same for all the different types of DSN data sources. To add a new data source, click the Add button on the User DSN page (refer to Figure 29.2) to display the Create New Data Source dialog box (see Figure 29.4). This dialog box lists all the available ODBC drivers. Select the appropriate driver for the database you'll be using and click the Finish button.

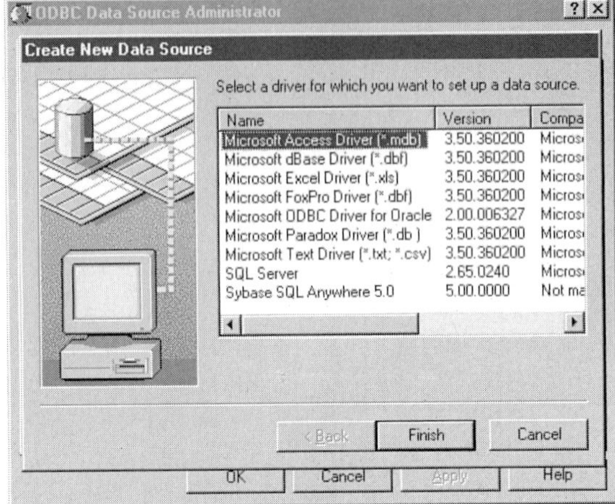

FIGURE 29.4.
Selecting the ODBC driver is the first step to setting up a data source.

The next dialog box displayed depends on the database you're using. Each available database requires its own set of information to perform correctly. Figure 29.5 shows the dialog box for a Microsoft Access database.

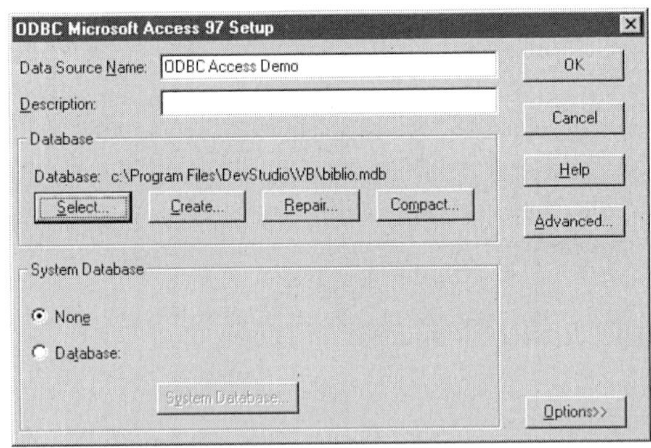

FIGURE 29.5.
A Setup dialog box allows you to specify the information necessary to connect to an ODBC data source.

In the Data Source Name text box, enter the name that you'll use in your applications to refer to the data source. You also might want to include a description of the data source. After entering the name, choose the actual database that you want to access with your program by clicking the Select button. An open-file dialog box appears. If this Access database is new, you can choose to create the database file from this dialog box. However, you still will need to add the table and column definitions to the file, using either Access or the Visual Data Manager. You also can perform maintenance such as repairing and compacting the file on the Access database. After selecting your database and specifying a data source name, click OK to complete the definition process.

NOTE

You can define as many different data sources as you might need by using the same ODBC driver.

Although the dialog boxes for other databases are different from the one just described, you would specify both a data source name to be used by your applications and the connection information for the database that you'll access. Figures 29.6 and 29.7 show the dialog boxes for a server-based Oracle database and a PC-based SQL Anywhere database, respectively.

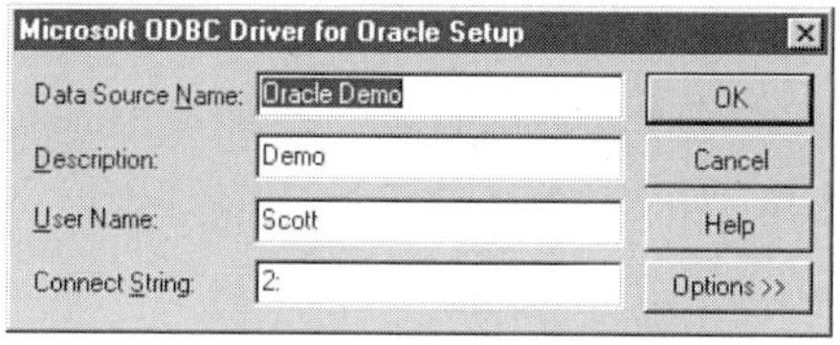

FIGURE 29.6.
The Oracle dialog box requires you to enter a database user ID, password, and network connection string, in addition to the data source name.

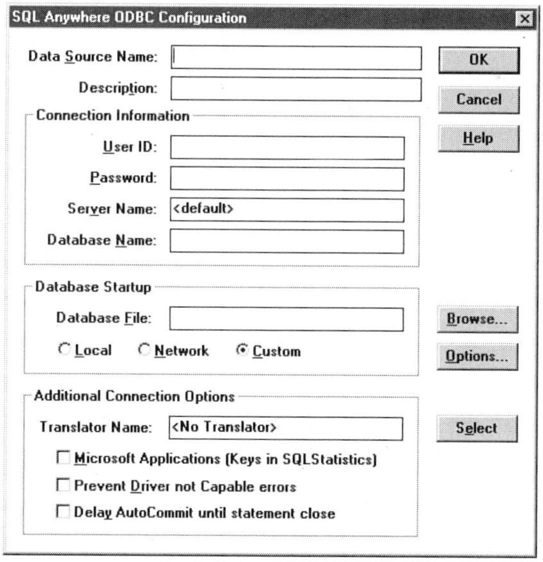

FIGURE 29.7.
The SQL Anywhere dialog box requires you to specify the database user ID, password, and full database name on the PC.

The DSN pages also allow you to modify or delete ODBC sources. To modify a data source, select the data source and click the Configure button, as shown earlier in Figure 29.2. This displays the same dialog box that you used to create the data source. To delete a data source, select it and click the Remove button. Now that you have the data source defined for your database, you're ready to start using it in a Visual Basic application.

Referencing ODBC in a Visual Basic Application

Before the advent of remote data objects in Visual Basic, it was much more difficult to use ODBC databases in your programs. To use ODBC, you had to declare and make calls directly to the ODBC API functions in your program. Remote data objects have changed this by providing an interface to the ODBC API that uses the familiar Visual Basic Data control operations of setting properties and calling methods. Because properties and methods are used in all Visual Basic programs, accessing ODBC databases is now much easier for developers to understand and accomplish with minimal effort. As you'll see, except for the way you open the ODBC data source, everything else that you'll do in your application is exactly as though you were using the standard Data controls.

Visual Basic has two methods of accessing databases:

- Using the Data controls to bind the data source directly to the controls on a Visual Basic form
- Programming the access directly in the application, using the Data Access Objects to connect to the data source

When you use ODBC data sources, Visual Basic provides a second set of tools that are used instead of the standard Data controls and Data Access Objects, which are primarily used to access local databases that use the Microsoft Jet engine. The Remote Data Control and Remote Data Objects are designed to be used with ODBC data sources.

Using the Remote Data Control

The fastest way to create applications with ODBC data sources is by using the Remote Data Control (RDC). The RDC lets you set a few properties of the control and then handles all the tasks of making the connections to the ODBC data source for you. This way, the RDC automates the methods of the remote data objects in the same way that the Data control automates the methods of the Data Access Objects. To use the RDC, you must add the control to your application. By using the Components dialog box (see Figure 29.8), which you access from the Project menu, you can add the control. Simply check the box next to Microsoft Remote Data Control and then click OK.

After you add the control to your project, notice a new control in the toolbox (see Figure 29.9). After you include the control in your project, you then add it to the forms that require access to the data source.

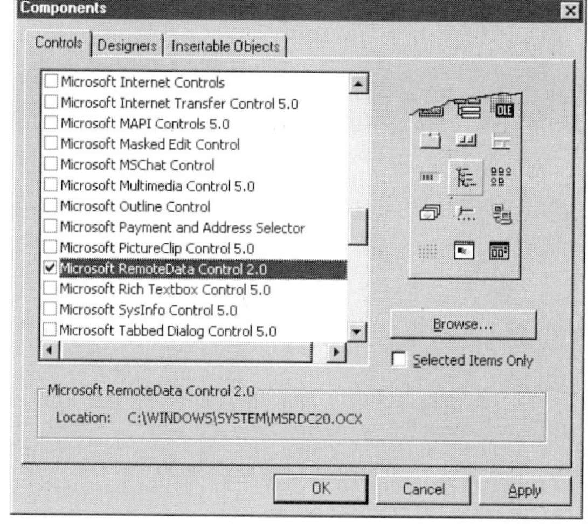

FIGURE 29.8.
Using the Remote Data Control is easy after the control is added to your project.

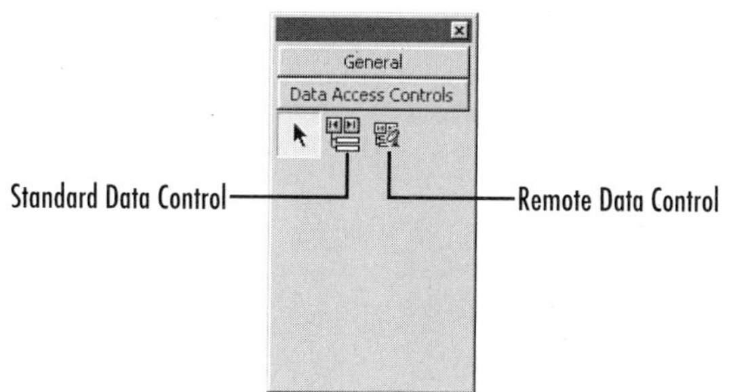

FIGURE 29.9.
The Remote Data Control uses a slightly different icon to distinguish itself from the standard Data control.

After putting the RDC on a form, you need to set the control's properties to identify which ODBC data source you want to access. The Property Pages for the control prompts you for the ODBC data source name (see Figure 29.10).You also need to enter a username and password for the database. Finally, at the bottom of the dialog box, the Remote Data Control requires you to enter a SQL statement. As with the standard Data control, you can change this SQL statement in the form's load routine.

After setting up the Remote Data Control, you can use any bound control that you have to display and edit information in the resultset created by the Data control. The bound controls are set up the same way they would be for use with the Data control, except that now the `DataSource` property of the bound controls points to a Remote Data Control. When set up, the bound controls are updated with new information each time a new row is accessed by the Remote Data Control.

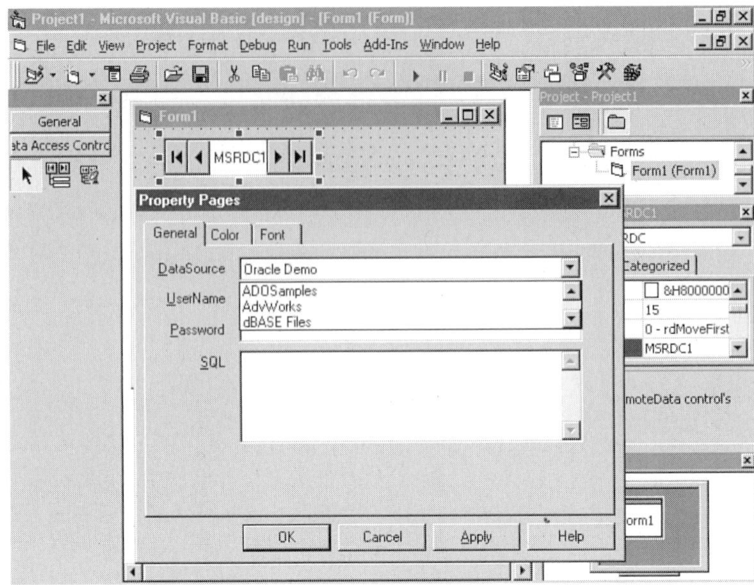

FIGURE 29.10.
Setting the properties for the Remote Data Control in the Property Pages dialog box.

Accessing a Database with RDO

If the Remote Data Control is too restrictive for what you need to do in your application, you can choose to access the data source through program code. The Remote Data Object (RDO) is designed to help you do just that. Again, the differences between the standard Data Access Object (DAO) and the Remote Data Object is in the way you'll connect to the data source and the command set that you'll use. To illustrate the similarities between the RDO and DAO models, Listings 29.1 and 29.2 both issue a SQL request to an Access database. The difference between the two listings is simply the objects and methods used to create the recordset to be used. When the recordset or resultset is established, all other statements are the same.

Listing 29.1. Accessing information in an ODBC data source by using the RDO methods.

```
Dim ws As rdoEnvironment
Dim db As rdoConnection
Dim rs As rdoResultset
Dim SQLSel As String
SQLSel = "Select * From Authors"
Set ws = rdoEngine.rdoEnvironments(0)
Set db = ws.OpenConnection("ODBC Access Demo")
Set rs = db.OpenResultset(SQLSel,rdOpenKeyset)
rs.MoveFirst
txtName.Text = rs("Author")
rs.Close
db.Close
```

Listing 29.2. Accessing the same information by using the DAO methods.

```
Dim ws As WorkSpace
Dim db As Database
Dim rs As Recordset
Dim SQLSel As String
SQLSel = "Select * From Authors"
Set ws = DBEngine.Workspaces(0)
Set db = ws.OpenDatabase("C:\Program Files\Devstudio\VB\Biblio.Mdb")
Set rs = db.OpenRecordset(SQLSel,rdOpenDynaset)
rs.MoveFirst
txtName.Text = rs("Author")
rs.Close
db.Close
```

Debugging ODBC Problems

When using ODBC to access your databases, sometimes you'll experience problems. When this happens, you need some information about the ODBC driver and what it's doing when a problem occurs. You can obtain this information from the ODBC Drivers page in the ODBC Administrator. The other information about what the driver is doing is a little more difficult to get. Two methods are available to you with Visual Basic and the ODBC Administrator that allow you to capture what's being done by the ODBC driver you're using. The ODBC Administrator provides a utility to trace all calls made to an ODBC driver from any program (see Figure 29.11).

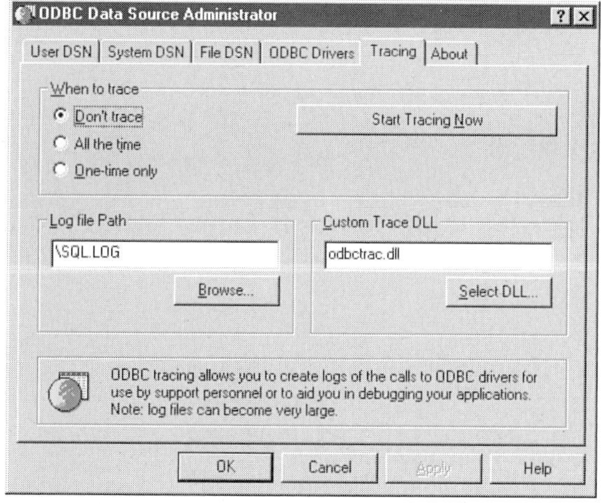

FIGURE 29.11.
Using the Trace utility provided with the ODBC Administrator.

The other way to capture information about the ODBC calls is to use a utility that comes with Visual Basic 5 called ODBC Spy (see Figure 29.12).

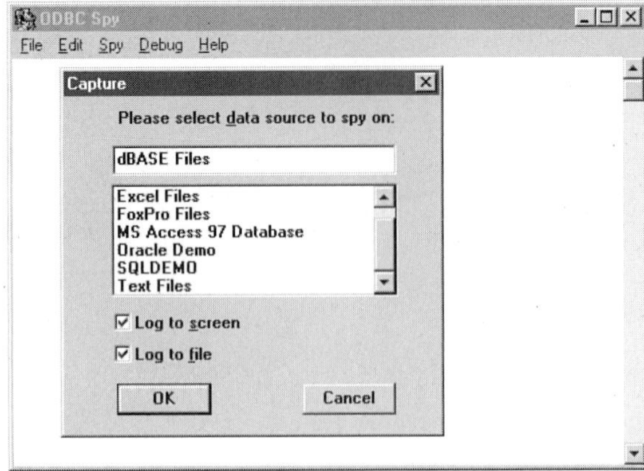

FIGURE 29.12.
Tracing ODBC calls by using the ODBC Spy utility.

NOTE

The ODBC Spy utility isn't installed with Visual Basic 5. It can be found on Visual Basic's CD-ROM in the `\TOOLS\ODBCSPY` directory. The `README.TXT` located in that directory gives more information about how to install ODBC Spy.

Each method will capture what the ODBC driver is doing; however, the level of detail varies. The ODBC Spy utility captures just enough of the calls to show what's happening and whether a call was successful or there was an error, as shown in the following:

```
SQLAllocEnv
    0x01000000
    SQL_SUCCESS
SQLAllocConnect
    0x01000000
    0x01010000
    SQL_SUCCESS
SQLGetInfo
    0x01010000
    SQL_DRIVER_ODBC_VER
    [5]02.50
    6
    5
    SQL_SUCCESS
SQLSetConnectOption
    0x01010000
    SQL_LOGIN_TIMEOUT
    0x0F000000
    SQL_ERROR
SQLDriverConnect
    0x01010000
    0x780C0000
    [36]DSN=Oracle Demo;UID=scott;PWD=tiger;
    SQL_NTS
```

```
[53]DSN=Oracle Demo;UID=scott;PWD=tiger;ConnectString=2:;
255
53
SQL_DRIVER_COMPLETE_REQUIRED
SQL_SUCCESS
```

As you can tell from just this small section of the log, understanding what these entries mean can take some time. The ODBC log shows each individual call to the database and its resulting status code. If you remove all the internal notations, however, the log is a little easier to follow:

```
SQLAllocEnv
    SQL_SUCCESS
SQLAllocConnect
    SQL_SUCCESS
SQLGetInfo
    SQL_SUCCESS
SQLSetConnectOption
    SQL_ERROR
SQLDriverConnect
    SQL_DRIVER_COMPLETE_REQUIRED
    SQL_SUCCESS
```

The ODBC Administrator Trace utility captures much more detail for the same function. The section of the Trace log shown next is for the same ODBC calls as the ODBC Spy log shown previously. You can see that the Trace log contains not only what the call was, but also the program that made the call and other detailed information about the call:

```
VB5             fffa3dd9:fffaf711     ENTER SQLAllocEnv
        HENV *                  0x236a7a98

VB5             fffa3dd9:fffaf711     EXIT  SQLAllocEnv
➥  with return code 0 (SQL_SUCCESS)
        HENV *                  0x236a7a98 ( 0x0178255c)

VB5             fffa3dd9:fffaf711     ENTER SQLAllocConnect
        HENV                    0x0178255c
        HDBC *                  0x02460e60

VB5             fffa3dd9:fffaf711     EXIT  SQLAllocConnect
➥  with return code 0 (SQL_SUCCESS)
        HENV                    0x0178255c
        HDBC *                  0x02460e60 ( 0x017839a4)

VB5             fffa3dd9:fffaf711     ENTER SQLSetConnectOption
        HDBC                    0x017839a4
        UWORD                          103
        UDWORD                        15

VB5             fffa3dd9:fffaf711     EXIT  SQLSetConnectOption
➥  with return code 0 (SQL_SUCCESS)
        HDBC                    0x017839a4
        UWORD                          103
        UDWORD                        15

VB5             fffa3dd9:fffaf711     ENTER SQLSetConnectOption
        HDBC                    0x017839a4
        UWORD                          110
        UDWORD                        0
```

```
VB5             fffa3dd9:fffaf711    EXIT  SQLSetConnectOption
➥  with return code 0 (SQL_SUCCESS)
        HDBC                    0x017839a4
        UWORD                          110
        UDWORD                         0

VB5             fffa3dd9:fffaf711    ENTER SQLDriverConnectW
        HDBC                    0x017839a4
        HWND                    0x00000598
        WCHAR *                 0x0178289c [       -3]
➥  "DSN=Oracle Demo;UID=scott;PWD=tiger;"
        SWORD                           -3
        WCHAR *                 0x01783a70
        SWORD                          510
        SWORD *                 0x007ff4ce
        UWORD                            3 <SQL_DRIVER_COMPLETE_REQUIRED>

VB5             fffa3dd9:fffaf711    EXIT  SQLDriverConnectW
➥  with return code 1 (SQL_SUCCESS_WITH_INFO)
        HDBC                    0x017839a4
        HWND                    0x00000598
        WCHAR *                 0x0178289c [       -3]
➥  "DSN=Oracle Demo;UID=scott;PWD=tiger;"
        SWORD                           -3
        WCHAR *                 0x01783a70 [      106]
➥  "DSN=Oracle Demo;UID=scott;PWD=tiger;ConnectString=2:;"
        SWORD                          510
        SWORD *                 0x007ff4ce (106)
        UWORD                            3 <SQL_DRIVER_COMPLETE_REQUIRED>
```

It takes knowledge to understand the calls that the ODBC drivers make when you access a data source. However, if you spend the time learning how to read the logs, you can solve some of the problems that might crop up when using the ODBC drivers. For more information on ODBC drivers and database programming with VB, check out *Teach Yourself Database Programming with Visual Basic 5* or *Visual Basic 5 Database Developer's Guide*, both from Sams Publishing.

Summary

In this chapter, you took a quick look into what ODBC database connections really are and how they can be used within a Visual Basic application. As you've seen, in addition to the way you'll open the database connection, the rest of the program access for an ODBC database is the same as using the Visual Basic Jet engine to access the information. This chapter also explored how to use the ODBC Administrator to create and modify the ODBC data source definitions that you'll use. Finally, if you have a problem with the ODBC access, you learned how to trace the calls to the ODBC driver, using the ODBC Trace utility that comes with the Administrator.

CHAPTER

Using Microsoft Visual Data Tools

IN THIS CHAPTER

Visual Basic comes with some utilities not automatically installed in Visual Basic. You can install these utilities manually from the Visual Basic CD-ROM. The Microsoft Visual Data Tools are great to install and use in creating and managing physical database objects. They provide features not offered by other database managers.

NOTE

The Visual Data Tools are not included with the Learning or Professional Editions of Visual Basic. They do come with Visual Basic Enterprise Edition, Visual Studio 97, and Visual InterDev.

Installing the Visual Data Tools

Installing the Visual Data Tools is straightforward. You can find the tools in the `VB\TOOLS\DATATOOL` directory on the Visual Basic CD-ROM or on disk 1 of Microsoft Visual Studio. The Visual Data Tools are also available with the purchase of Microsoft Visual InterDev. You can install the program by running the Setup program in the `DATATOOL` directory, but make sure that you've installed the SQL Server 6.5 Service Pack 2 first. See the `README.WRI` file in that directory for notes about installing and using Visual Data Tools.

Looking at the Database Features

The Visual Data Tools, in addition to being great tools for developing Web applications, also are great for creating and managing databases.

One of the most difficult parts about creating an application is getting the database portion correct. How many of you have had to recode because of a change to the database structure? Changes to the database probably cause more applications and components to require updating than any other source.

The Visual Data Tools don't replace good design techniques or database design tools such as ERwin or PowerDesigner, which help you better design a database. The Visual Data Tools allow you to create a database but provide only limited features for creating entity relationship models, as do the aforementioned database design tools. The Visual Data Tools database features also allow you to manage a database that's already created.

TIP

For more information about ERwin, visit the Logic Works Web site at `http://www.logicworks.com/`. For more information about PowerDesigner, visit Powersoft's site at `http://www.powersoft.com/`.

The following sections cover some examples of how to use the database features provided by the Visual Data Tools with Microsoft SQL Server. Most features described here work with other databases, but some features are specific to Oracle, and other features are specific only to Microsoft SQL Server.

Creating and Changing Database Tables

The Visual Data Tools provide a way to create new database tables and provide some advanced features when you're creating new tables and making changes to existing tables. By using these tools, you can create new tables within the database by using a data diagram. The Visual Data Tools let you add tables and columns, and specify advanced column properties such as column data type, user-defined data types, identity information, default values, and other properties.

The Visual Data Tools also offer a dream feature for database administrators. You can actually change the data type of a column within a table and then have the Visual Data Tools make the change on the table, even if it already contains data. If you've ever had to make table changes while preserving data, you know this is a real time-saver. Previously, you would have had to back up the data within the table, drop the table, create the new table, and then move the data back into the new table.

The following steps show how to create a database table by using the database tools in the Visual Data Tools. You'll use the database diagrams available in the Visual Data Tools to create the table.

1. Make sure that you have an open database project. When you're in the project, right-click the Database Diagram and choose to create a new diagram.

> **TIP**
>
> To create a new database project, choose File | New and then select the Database Project Wizard from the Projects dialog box. The wizard then guides you through creating a project and connecting it to your database.

2. After the empty diagram is created, right-click anywhere in it and choose New Table. A dialog box appears, asking for the name of the new table.
3. After you specify the name of the table you want to create, you see a grid in which you can specify the columns you want in the table. Table 30.1 lists the properties that you can modify with the new table grid; Figure 30.1 shows the new table grid.
4. After you specify all the columns that you want in the table and the properties for all the columns, close the new table grid and save the structure of the database.

Table 30.1. Column properties for the example table.

Property	*Description*
`Column Name`	The name of the column and how it will be referenced from your queries and stored procedures.
`Data Type`	The data type that the column will use. You can use any standard data types provided by the database or any user-defined data types that you've created.
`Length`	Some data types let you specify a length that determines the amount of data allowed within the data type.
`Precision`	The precision of numeric columns. *Precision* indicates how many digits will be displayed for a number.
`Scale`	The scale of a numeric column. *Scale* is the number of digits allowed after the decimal point.
`Allow Nulls`	A selection box that determines whether the column will allow null values to be entered.
`Default Value`	The default value placed in the column if no value is specified when a new record is inserted.
`Identity Column`	A selection box that determines whether the column will be an identity key. An *identity key* is a column that's automatically populated with an increasing numeric value. Useful as a primary key of a table.
`Identity Seed`	The initial value for the identity column when a record is first inserted.
`Identity Increment`	The increment value added to new records that are defined as identity columns.

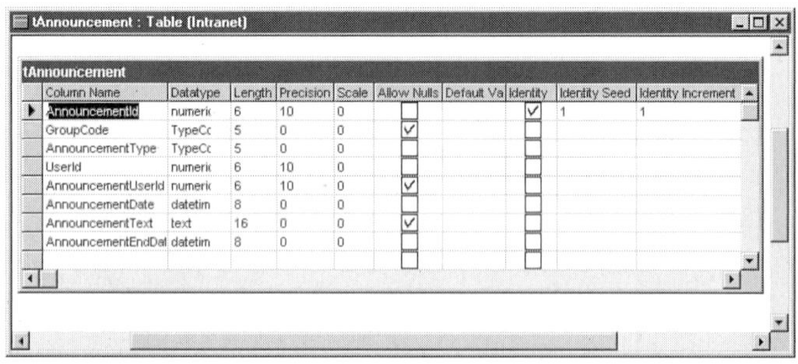

FIGURE 30.1.
Creating a new table.

From the column grid, you can add a primary key to the table by highlighting the column or columns that you want to be the primary key for the table and then clicking the Primary Key toolbar button (which has a key icon).

Viewing Data in Database Tables

By using the Visual Data Tools, you can add, delete, and modify data stored in the database table. You can edit the information in a grid, which is easier and quicker than using SQL Insert and Update statements, although the Visual Data Tools still allow you to create queries to manage data.

To view the data stored in a table, select the table that you want to view data for and then double-click the table or right-click it and choose Open. The Visual Data Tools then display all the data for table in a grid format for you to view, modify, or insert new rows.

Creating Database Diagrams

One of the most useful features of the database tools provided by the Visual Data Tools is the capability to create database diagrams for tables in your table. Other products let you view tables in a diagram format, but the Visual Data Tools let you create multiple diagrams for your database, so you can have a database diagram for individual departments within your organization or for separate functions of your application.

The benefit of having separate diagrams is so that administrators and users can view tables related only to the work they're doing. That way, your administrators can work only on tables they're responsible for, thus making managing easier because they don't see the tables from other sections of the database.

Another benefit of using the Visual Data Tools database diagrams is that because they're saved in the database (in the `dtProperties` table), they can be modified by anyone with access to the Visual Data Tools and the database where the diagrams are stored. Unlike other tools that store the diagrams in proprietary files, the Visual Data Tools store the diagrams on the database for everyone to access.

To create a new diagram, right-click the Database Diagrams option in Data Explorer and then choose New Diagram. When a blank diagram appears, you can drag and drop tables from the Data Explorer to the new diagram. The diagram will display all the relationships between the tables contained on it. Figure 30.2 shows a database diagram with several tables on it. Notice the relationships pictured on the diagram between the various tables.

Creating Stored Procedures

The Visual Data Tools also provide you with tools for creating stored procedures and triggers.

NOTE

The capability to create stored procedures and triggers is available only on the Oracle and Microsoft SQL Server databases.

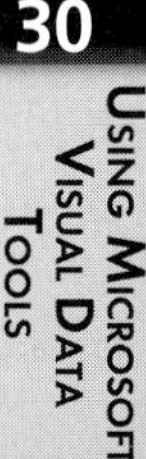

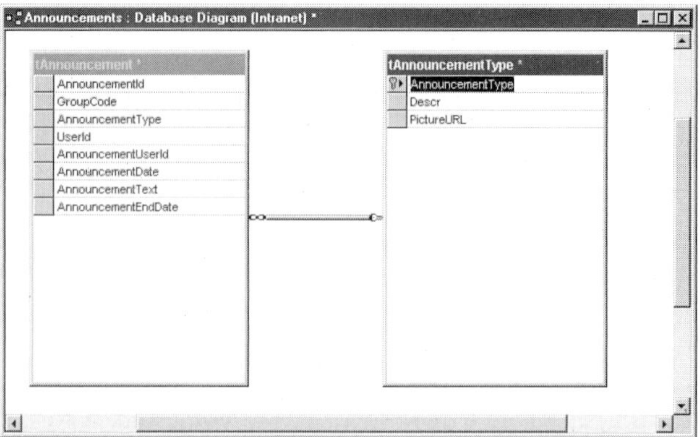

FIGURE 30.2.
The database diagram.

Creating stored procedures can sometimes be difficult unless you have the database client tools installed. But why should you have to install database-specific tools to create stored procedures? For all relational databases that I've worked with, the full text of the stored procedures is stored in the system tables for the database. The Visual Data Tools use the system tables to let you create new stored procedures or modify current stored procedures.

The Visual Data Tools also provide more information about your stored procedures than most other development tools. The tools let you view all the parameters and return values that your stored procedures use. Knowing the parameter names passed to the stored procedure is helpful when you want to pass only certain parameters and need to assign parameter values to parameter names. Figure 30.3 shows a sample stored procedure in the database editor window. Notice the parameters listed for the stored procedure on the left in the database explorer window.

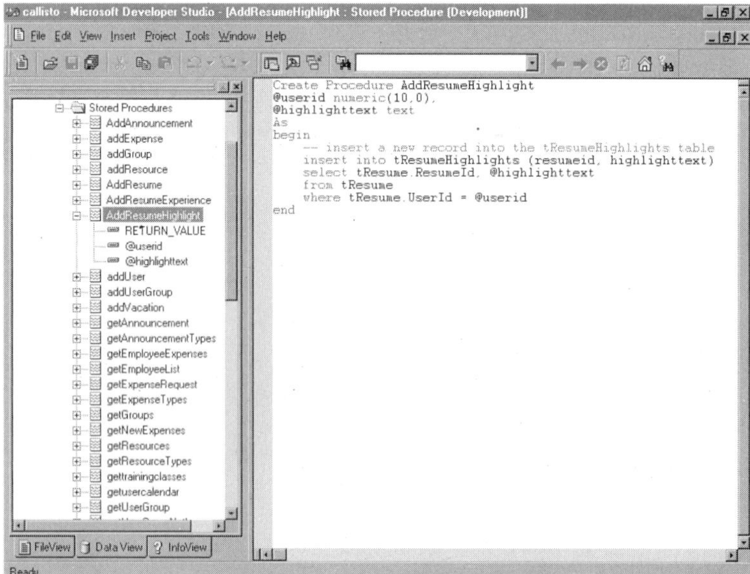

FIGURE 30.3.
The stored procedure editor.

Summary

The Microsoft Visual Data Tools provide an easy and powerful way to create and manage your database. With the capability to add stored procedures, triggers, and views, the tools provide features beyond those of most other tools available.

The tools also provide you with detailed information about stored procedures and tables, going as far as to provide a listing of the parameters that should be passed to a stored procedure. The Visual Data Tools also let you change a column's data type or length without requiring that you drop the constraints on the table, drop the table, create the new table, and then add the data back into the table. This in itself is worth the price of the tools. However, because the tools come as freebies with Visual Basic or Visual Studio, there's really no reason for you not to use them.

CHAPTER 31

Adding and Controlling Remote Data Objects

IN THIS CHAPTER

In creating database applications, you sometimes have to link the data returned from a database to the editing controls located on a form. To this end, Visual Basic 5 provides the Remote Data Control (RDC) to facilitate the development of database applications.

With the Remote Data Control, you can link a resultset returned from a SQL `Select` statement or a stored procedure to various data-aware controls on a Visual Basic form. That way, you can control multiple controls with one object because moving the record position in the Data control displays new information in all the controls linked to the control.

Adding the Remote Data Control to Your Project

The Remote Data Control object isn't placed on the object list by default; you have to add the control manually. Follow these steps to place the control in the object list:

1. Choose Project | Components from the menu.
2. In the Components dialog box, select the Microsoft Remote Data Control from the list (see Figure 31.1).
3. Close the dialog box and then add the control to your project by dragging it from the object list to your form.

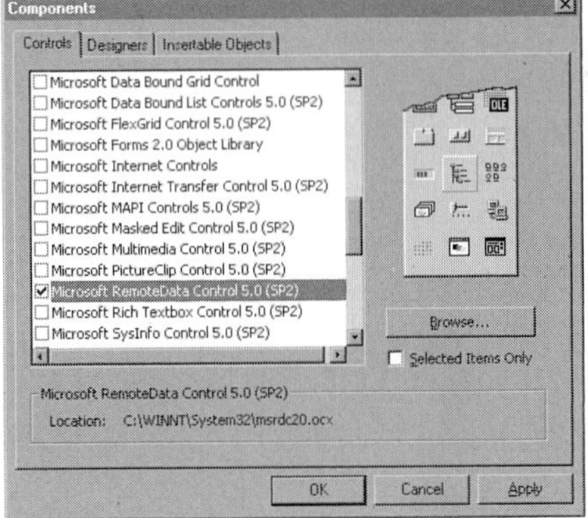

FIGURE 31.1.
The Components dialog box.

Using the Remote Data Control

After you add the RDC to your form, you need to specify the control's properties by using the Property Explorer or the control's custom property page. I generally recommend the property page because it gives you a more well-defined view of the properties that you can edit. Figure 31.2 shows the custom property page for the Remote Data Control.

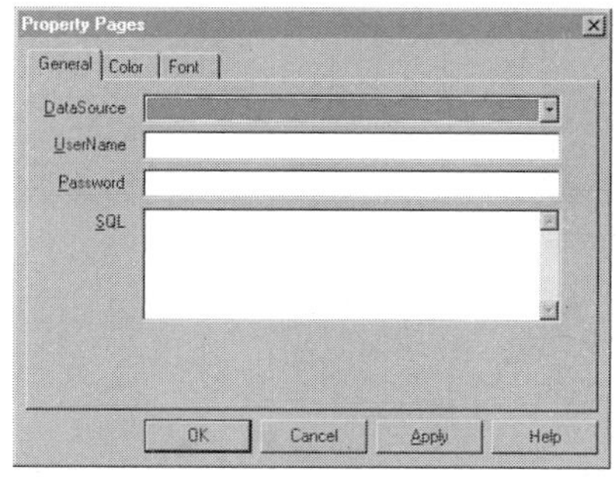

FIGURE 31.2.
The custom property page for the RDC object.

The most important properties that you can edit on the property page are the data source to use, the username and password to connect to the database, and the SQL statement to use to provide records to the control:

- The data source to use determines which database or database file is used to retrieve information. The data source can be any valid ODBC data source declared for the current computer.
- The username is the login name required to connect to the specified data source.
- The SQL statement for the RDC determines the resultset returned to the data control. You can specify any valid SQL `Select` statement or a stored procedure that returns a resultset to the data control.

Remote Data Control Properties

The Remote Data Control provides many properties similar to the ones provided by the `rdoResultSet` object. The following sections cover some of the more important properties provided by the RDC. Some properties, such as `Font`, aren't covered because they are self-explanatory.

The `BOFAction` and `EOFAction` Properties

The `BOFAction` property allows you to move to specified locations in the resultset. Use the `rdMoveFirst` constant to tell the control to move to the first record in the resultset. You also can use the `rdBOF` constant to move to a position before the first record in the resultset.

The `EOFAction` property lets you specify positions at the end of the file to move to. `EOFAction` provides three constants for positioning within the control:

- Use `rdMoveLast` to move to the last record.
- Use `rdEOF` to move to a position after the last record.
- Use `rdAddNew` to add a new record at the end of the current resultset and set it to be the current record.

The Connect Property

The Connect property lets you specify the connect string that will be passed to the remote database. The string can consist of one or more parameters and their values. Each parameter is separated by a semicolon.

The four most commonly used parameters for the connect string are DSN (the data source name), UID (the name of a registered user for logging into the database), PWD (the user's password), and DATABASE (the default database to use once connected). For example, to connect to a database named TestBase from a data source named TestSource with the username JDoe and the password test, you might use the following code:

```
RemoteData1.Connect = "DSN=TestSource;UID=JDoe;PWD=test;DATABASE=TestBase;"
```

The connect string can also specify the driver description (DRIVER), the name of the remote server (SERVER), the workstation ID (WSID), and the application name (APP). Some ODBC drivers may allow or require other parameters as well.

You can change the Connect property to be any string required by your applications. In many applications, it's common to save the connect information in the Registry or in an .INI file and then set the connect information to the values obtained in the Registry.

The CursorDriver Property

You can change the cursor driver used in retrieving information from the database. Table 31.1 lists the various cursor driver settings that you can use. The type of cursor driver that you use determines how the records are retrieved from the database.

Table 31.1. CursorDriver property settings.

Driver Setting	Description
rdUseIfNeeded	The control chooses an appropriate driver to use. If possible, a server-side cursor driver is chosen.
rdUseOdbc	The control uses the ODBC driver library.
rdUseServer	The control uses the server-side cursor driver.
rdUseClientBatch	The control uses an optimistic batch cursor driver library.
rdUseNone	The control doesn't use a cursor.

The various cursor drivers offer different options. Using some cursor drivers will prevent you from accessing the number of records in the resultset but will provide speed improvements over other drivers.

The Options Property

The `Options` property provides only two different options that can be specified but allows you to specify that a query is to be executed asynchronously. Executing a query in this manner allows execution to be returned to the application while the query is executing on the database. Asynchronous queries can benefit your applications by allowing you to cancel a query being executed or by giving control back to users while a long query is executing on the database server.

The following code line changes the `Option` property of a control named `rdcEmployees` so that it executes queries asynchronously:

```
rdcEmployees.Options = rdAsyncEnable
```

If you want to use the ODBC `SQLExecDirect` API function to execture the query, you can set the `Options` property to `rdExecDirect` as follows:

```
rdcEmployees.Options = rdExecDirect
```

The Prompt Property

The `Prompt` property allows you to determine what type of prompt users are presented with. A prompt is used to obtain connection information from users. For applications where users have separate login information, you probably want to show a prompt every time the application starts to obtain user-specific information. For other types of applications, you might want to never display the login prompt, such as an application that runs as a Windows NT service or an application that runs on a server such as an application server or an Internet component.

Table 31.2 lists the various constants that can be provided to the `Prompt` property.

Table 31.2. `Prompt` property settings.

Property	*Description*
`rdDriverPrompt`	The control displays the ODBC Data Sources dialog box to users.
`rdDriverNoPrompt`	The control uses information provided to it. If incorrect information is supplied, the control returns an error.
`rdDriverComplete`	The control uses the information provided to it. If incorrect information is supplied, the prompt is displayed as in the `rdDriverPrompt` setting.
`rdDriverCompleteRequired`	This setting behaves like `rdDriverComplete` but disables the control for information not required.

The ReadOnly Property

The ReadOnly property allows you to specify whether users should be allowed to edit the control's resultset. If the property is set to TRUE, users can't update the information contained in the control. If the value is set to FALSE, users can edit the information in the control normally.

NOTE

ReadOnly information is associated mostly with reporting.

The ResultSet Property

The ResultSet property of the Remote Data Control is where the information returned from the database is stored. This property is a standard rdoResultSet object and provides all the properties and method provided by the rdoResultSet object.

You can set the ResultSet property to the value of another rdoResultSet object. This way, you can use other methods to obtain a resultset and then use the RDC to provide the capability to link controls on the form with the data in the custom resultset. This feature is used commonly with the UserConnection object. By using the UserConnection object, you can create resultsets and then assign them to the Remote Data Control to provide linking capabilities to the edit controls on your forms. This way, you can centralize all database logic while still providing an easy way to populate edit controls on your forms.

Assigning a new rdoResultSet object is as easy as declaring a new object, opening a resultset from the database, and then setting the property value to the rdoResultSet object as in the following code:

```
Dim conn as new UserConnection1
Dim rs as rdoResultSet

' Establish connection
conn.EstablishConnection

' Call method and get resultset
conn.Query1
Set rs = conn.LastQueryResult

' Set remote data control (rdcEmployees) resultset
Set rdcEmployees.ResultSet = rs
```

Remote Data Control Events

The Remote Data Control provides several events over the standard mouse and drag events that you should be aware of. These events provide you with a means to handle errors and user responses, as well as provide you with the ability to perform some processing after an asynchronous query completes and returns from the server.

The following sections cover four events: `Error`, `QueryCompleted`, `Reposition`, and `Validate`. All these events are available from the code editor for the Remote Data Control object located on your form.

The Error Event

The `Error` event allows you to handle errors that occur in the Remote Data Control while none of your code is executing. Because the Remote Data Control automatically retrieves the resultset of a specified SQL statement after the `Form_Load` event, you have no code running to intercept any errors that occur during this process. The `Error` event lets you capture these errors and perform any processing required by your application.

The `Error` event provides many arguments that you can use to determine the nature of the error. It also provides a return argument that you can use to tell the control whether it should display the error message to users. The `CancelDisplay` argument allows you to stop the control from displaying the standard database error message and to display a custom message depending on your application's needs. You can set the value to `TRUE` or to the predefined constant of `rdDataErrContinue` to prevent the standard error message from being displayed. The default for the argument is `FALSE` or the constant `rdDataErrDisplay`, which will display the error message to users. You can return nothing or not code for the event if you want the control to generate the error message and display it to users.

The QueryCompleted Event

The `QueryCompleted` event is simply a blank method for you to perform any processing required after an asynchronous query finishes processing. When you set the control to execute queries asynchronously, the control executes the query on the database and then returns control back to the application while the query is executed. The `QueryCompleted` event provides you with a way to handle any special processing after the results return from the database for the query.

This event can be useful for queries that require large amounts of time to process. A useful feature is to execute a query and then allow users to continue with another process in the application. When the query is completed, you can display a message to tell users that the query is complete and that they can now view the results, or you can perform any other processing after query results are returned from the database.

The Reposition Event

The `Reposition` event occurs whenever the current row position changes in the control. If you use any of the `Move` methods or any other method that changes the current row position, this event is fired. In this event, you can provide custom processing such as updating the current form to represent the data now displayed in the new row.

The Validate Event

The `Validate` event allows you to handle any processing that you want to occur before a SQL statement is processed and sent to the database. This event occurs before a new row becomes the current row; before the `Update` method is invoked; and before the `Delete`, `UnLoad`, and `Close` actions occur. `Validate` allows you to stop the current action from happening or to change the action to a different action.

By using the `Action` argument, you can change the requested action to some other action by passing back the appropriate setting. Changing the action might be useful if users have edited information on the current row and are requesting to move to a different row. You might ask users if they want to save the information they just edited before moving and choose to cancel the action or invoke an edit or update action in place of their move action. Table 31.3 lists all the available action constants that can be used for the `Action` argument.

Table 31.3. `Action` argument settings.

Setting	*Description*
`rdActionCancel`	Cancels the requested operation
`rdActionMoveFirst`	Executes the `MoveFirst` action
`rdMovePrevious`	Executes the `MovePrevious` action
`rdActionMoveNext`	Executes the `MoveNext` action
`rdActionMoveLast`	Executes the `MoveLast` action
`rdActionAddNew`	Executes the `AddNew` action
`rdActionUpdate`	Executes the `Update` action
`rdActionDelete`	Executes the `Delete` action
`rdActionFind`	Executes the `Find` action
`rdActionBookmark`	Executes the `Bookmark` action
`rdActionClose`	Executes the `Close` action
`rdActionUnload`	Executes the `Unload` action
`rdActionUpdateAddNew`	Inserts a new row into the control
`rdActionUpdateModified`	Changes the current row
`rdActionRefresh`	Executes the `Refresh` action
`rdActionCancelUpdate`	Cancels the `Update` action
`rdActionBeginTransact`	Begins a transaction in the control
`rdActionCommitTransact`	Commits a transaction in the control
`rdActionRollbackTransact`	Rolls back a transaction in the control
`rdActionNewParameters`	Informs the control that the parameters or columns for the resultset have changed
`rdActionNewSQL`	Informs the control that the SQL statement for the control has changed

Remote Data Control Methods

The Remote Data Control provides many of the same methods provided by the `rdoConnection` object, but the following sections cover some of the more important methods. The RDC provides various methods for transaction handling, canceling execution of a query, and updating the contents of the control's resultset.

The `BeginTrans` Method

The `BeginTrans` method lets you start a new transaction within the control. This new transaction can later be committed or rolled back, depending on the error status of the query's execution.

If you don't begin a transaction before executing SQL statements, these SQL statements are executed automatically against the database and take effect immediately. By using the `BeginTrans` method, you can wait until all transactions are completed before applying them to the database.

To use the `BeginTrans` method for a Remote Data Control named `rdcEmployees`, use the following syntax:

```
rdcEmployees.BeginTrans
```

This code would begin a transaction on the database and proceed to log executed SQL statements until a `CommitTrans` or `RollBackTrans` method is called.

The `CommitTrans` Method

The `CommitTrans` method is the successful way to end a `BeginTrans` action. `CommitTrans` informs the database that no errors were encountered and that all query executions requested within the transaction can be applied to the database.

If you fail to commit a transaction, the transaction could remain open and keep database resources locked. This can lead to dead locking when others request resources that you've locked, and you begin to request resources they have locked. Keep your transactions together and do not allow user response within a transaction.

The following code begins a transaction with a Remote Data Control object named `rdcEmployees` and then commits the transaction after several SQL statements by using the `CommitTrans` method:

```
rdcEmployees.BeginTrans
  .
  .
  .
' SQL Statements
  .
  .
  .
rdcEmployees.CommitTrans
```

This code commits the transaction to the database, thereby making any changes permanent.

The RollBackTrans Method

The `RollBackTrans` method is your way of telling the database that an error occurred somewhere within the transaction and that all queries executed within the transaction should be disregarded. This prevents the database from becoming out of whack with incomplete data in the database.

If you didn't use a transaction and were adding a user record with an accompanying user phone record and the user record insertion succeeded but the phone record insertion didn't, you would have a user in the database without a phone record. When someone looks at this user record, she would assume that the user has no phone number or that it's not known. Because users of your application shouldn't assume, it's better to have either none of the information or all the information.

The following code snippet begins a transaction, executes several SQL statements, and then rolls back the transaction, restoring the database to its state before the execution of the SQL statements:

```
rdcEmployees.BeginTrans
  .
  .
  .
' SQL Statements
  .
  .
  .
rdcEmployees.RollbackTrans
```

The Cancel Method

The `Cancel` method is your way to stop the execution of a currently running asynchronous query. You can use this method to stop the processing of a query executed by the control.

To call the `Cancel` method, use the following syntax:

```
rdcEmployees.Cancel
```

> **CAUTION**
>
> Stopping an executing query can have unpredictable results, and some queries can't be stopped after they're started. Use the `Cancel` method carefully because it can produce undesirable results.

The UpdateControls Method

The `UpdateControls` method allows you to, in essence, refresh the controls bound to the particular Remote Data Control. The RDC will redisplay in all bound controls the original data that was available, overwriting any modifications made to the data but not saved by users. This method can be helpful if you change your mind about new data and want to revert to original data values.

The syntax for calling the `UpdateControls` method is as follows:

```
rdcEmployees.UpdateControls
```

The UpdateRow Method

The `UpdateRow` method does just what it says—updates the current row and saves its data values to the database. Before allowing users to move to another row in the result set, you should prompt them to see whether they want to save their data. If they choose to save, call the `UpdateRow` method before moving to the new row.

The syntax for calling the `UpdateRow` method is as follows:

```
rdcEmployees.UpdateRow
```

Summary

The Remote Data Control is simple to use and provides more functionality and features than its cousin, the Data control. It allows you to use all the functionality of RDO without sacrificing the linking of the Data control.

Use the Remote Data Control in any application where you're using RDO and want to display results returned from a database to the user to be edited. The Remote Data Control's real strength is its capability to make data available for editing. The `rdoResultSet` and `rdoConnection` objects offer the same database functionality that the Remote Data Control offers, but the RDC lets you make the database results visually presentable.

CHAPTER 32

ActiveX Data Objects

IN THIS CHAPTER

One of the most constantly changing aspects of Visual Basic development is database access. There are many different ways to implement database connectivity in your VB programs, including Data Access Objects (DAO), the Open Database Connectivity (ODBC) API, OLE databases (OLE DB), and Remote Data Objects (RDO) to name just a few.

Microsoft's newest technology for database access is ActiveX Data Objects, or ADO. ADO is likely to become the new standard for database connectivity, at least according to Microsoft. It has become something of a buzzword, though many are unsure of the role that ADO plays (or will play) when it comes to Visual Basic development.

Programmers familiar with other database access methods will also be wondering about ADO's strengths and weaknesses, and whether they should consider adopting ADO as a new way of programming database applications. Will it be worth the effort of learning to use this new technology, or can you afford to ignore it and continue using the older standards?

This chapter will likely answer many of your questions and will explain how ADO fits into the scheme of things for VB developers. It will also show some sample ADO code so that you can compare it to the database access techniques you are used to.

An Overview of ADO

ADO (ActiveX Data Objects) is Microsoft's new entry in the area of database connectivity. It is based on OLE DB, also a relatively new technology designed by Microsoft to facilitate multiplatform database access and destined to become the successor to ODBC. In fact, ADO is nothing more than a "wrapper" for OLE DB, which was previously unavailable to Visual Basic programmers. ADO encapsulates OLE DB's functionality into a single ActiveX server library. If you are familiar with RDO (Remote Data Objects), you know that VB's Remote Data Control acts as a wrapper for ODBC. ADO works in a similar way, only with OLE DB. Also, ADO is not implemented as an ActiveX control but as an ActiveX server library.

Because Microsoft has announced plans to replace ODBC with OLE DB, ADO certainly sounds like the way to go for accessing multiplatform databases. Of course, the transition will be gradual, taking place over the course of the next few years, but looking at ADO and considering its merits is a step that should be taken now.

ADO is based on the COM (Component Object Model) standard, which is also the basis for all ActiveX objects. Because COM is implemented on other platforms, ADO can therefore also be ported to platforms other than Windows. This is why Microsoft is moving away from ODBC and is touting OLE DB/ADO as the new standard for database access.

Because ADO is based on COM, it can also be used with online applications that access databases over an intranet or the Internet. Best of all, it provides a standard interface to databases of all kinds, whether they be local or server-based. This means that you can use ADO to access a FoxPro database or an Oracle database without having to know the differences between the two.

You would think that the advantages of ADO come at a cost in terms of difficulty of use, but they don't. ADO is relatively easy to use, about the same as DAO (Data Access Objects). If you've mastered DAO programming, you should have little or no problem with ADO.

ADO combines DAO's complete support of the Jet database engine with ODBC and RDO's open and flexible support for other database formats. That combination is hard to beat no matter how you look at it.

So what are the disadvantages? For one thing, ADO is new technology, and therefore comes with all the baggage that newness typically brings. Its initial implementation is somewhat limited, and it has not yet been widely adopted as an industry standard. But every new technology has to start somewhere, and ADO definitely has a lot of potential.

The current implementation of ADO (version 1.5) is missing some features that will be important to serious database programmers. For example, it is unable to efficiently connect or run queries asynchronously because it lacks an event model. An ADO database connection's status has to be constantly checked to determine whether an asynchronous process has completed.

In terms of functionality, RDO has ADO beat. But this is likely to change. Microsoft has announced that the next version of ADO will be significantly beefed up to support a much wider range of database operations.

For Visual Basic programmers, this means that ADO cannot be ignored—at least not forever. If you're involved in any aspects of ODBC database connectivity, ADO is more than likely your future. You may not want to jump into ADO development just yet, but it behooves you to know more about it.

The Nuts and Bolts of ADO

ADO uses two primary object types to facilitate database access: `Connection` and `Recordset`. Of course, it uses a variety of other object types as well, such as `Command`, `Field`, `Error`, and `Parameter`. Those will be discussed later.

Appropriately, the `Connection` object is used to establish a session between a database and an application. For example, the following code

```
Dim conn As ADODB.Connection
Set conn = CreateObject("ADODB.Connection")
conn.Open "DSN=DBServ;SERVER=Oracle;UID=test;PWD=test"
```

could be used to open a new database connection to a database server.

The `Recordset` object contains a set of records from the base table or the result of a query and is the main interface to the data in a database. For example

```
Set rs = conn.Execute("SELECT * FROM Customers")
```

uses the `Execute` method of the `Connection` object to assign the results of a query to a `Recordset` object.

If you're only opening a single `Recordset` object, you don't need to use the `Connection` object to establish a database connection. Instead, you can use the `Open` method of the `Recordset`:

```
Dim rs As New ADODB.Recordset
rs.Open("SELECT * FROM Customers")
```

In the preceding example, a `Connection` object is created, but it isn't assigned to an object variable. This is all seamless to the programmer, of course, and makes for an easier way to access databases.

The `Field` object and the `Fields` collection are used with the `Recordset` object to store the columns of data in a table. Each `Field` in turn has its own `Properties` collection, which contains information about the field, such as size and type.

ADO also uses several other object types and collections. The `Error` object and the `Errors` collection, for example, are used to hold any database errors that might occur. The `Command` object defines a specific command that is to be executed on a data source, such as a SQL statement or a stored procedure. The `Parameter` object and the `Parameters` collection are associated with a `Command` object and represent the parameters for the command to be executed.

Trying It Out

Before you can start using ADO, you have to make sure that it is available on your system. ADO was not included on the VB5 CD-ROM because it was not yet available when that product was released. However, ADO is included with Microsoft Internet Information Server 3.0 and higher.

You can also download ADO from Microsoft's ADO Web page at `http://www.microsoft.com/data/ado/`. Choose the "Updated Microsoft Data Access Components" option. The ADO Web site also has additional documentation about how to use the ADO library in Visual Basic.

To add the ADO library to your Visual Basic projects, choose Project | References from VB's menu. Put a check mark next to Microsoft ActiveX Data Objects 1.5 Library and then click OK.

To get started with ADO, look at Listing 32.1. It shows a simple Sub procedure that connects to a database, issues a SQL statement, and adds fields from the resulting `Recordset` to a ListBox control.

Listing 32.1. A sample procedure that uses the ADO library to access a database. (Note that the connect properties will have to be changed if you want to use this program on your system.)

```
Private Sub ADORead()

' Create a new Recordset object and call the Open method
' to connect to a database.
Set rs = CreateObject("ADODB.Recordset")
rs.Open "SELECT * FROM custname", _
```

```
    "DATABASE=cust;UID=test;PWD=test;DSN=Customers"

' Loop through the Recordset and add fields to the
' List1 ListBox.
Do Until rs.EOF
    List1.AddItem rs.Fields(0).Value
    rs.MoveNext
Loop

End Sub
```

The database connect parameters in Listing 32.1 are based on a theoretical database and will need to be changed to reflect a database on your system before the program will work properly. You also need to change the SQL statement to reflect a field in your database's table.

Summary

Although it is somewhat limited in its current implementation, ActiveX Data Objects promise to be the new standard for multiplatform database access. Microsoft plans to phase out ODBC in favor of ADO.

ADO holds a great deal of potential as an all-purpose database connectivity tool. It combines ODBC's cross-platform database support with all of DAO's Jet database support. Because it is based on the COM model, ADO can also be easily ported to other development platforms.

It may not be time to jump on the ADO bandwagon just yet because the technology is still in its infancy. But a move towards ADO should be anticipated and planned for because it's likely that the current version of ODBC will be the last released by Microsoft.

This chapter presented the major advantages and disadvantages of ADO and discussed some of the nuts and bolts of how ADO is used. It should serve as a primer for developers who want to learn more about this new method of database access.

VI

PART

IN THIS PART

Advanced Programming Topics and Techniques

CHAPTER 33

Mail Enable Your Applications with MAPI

IN THIS CHAPTER

As the use of intranets and the Internet becomes more common, application programmers must learn to tap into the power of this new technology. In the past, standalone programs were the norm, but the next generation of applications will require the capability to communicate on a global scale. For example, a few years ago it was sufficient to design a program to monitor machines in a factory and produce reports concerning their efficiency. Today, that same program might be expected to send those reports automatically to the factory foreman or to other management personnel thousands of miles away. The easiest way to do that is through electronic mail (email). And that's where MAPI comes in.

In a nutshell, MAPI (Mail Application Programming Interface) is a specification that defines a complete messaging subsystem. Primarily, it defines common interfaces by which mail-related components can interact. These components include service providers such as *message store providers* that can create, submit, and store mail messages; *address book providers* that can maintain a database of message recipients; and *transport providers* that handle the actual transmission of messages. It may sound complicated, but it's not. This chapter provides you with a better understanding of what MAPI is and how it works. This chapter also shows how you can use MAPI to add electronic messaging functionality to your Visual Basic programs.

Understanding the MAPI Specification

Microsoft created MAPI to establish a common interface for various mail-related components, including those developed by other vendors. Primarily, it allows client applications (such as ones written in Visual Basic) to interact with service providers. In this context, *service providers* are programs that perform mail-related tasks. Three principal types of service providers are defined under MAPI: address book providers, message store providers, and transport providers. These provider types are discussed in more detail later, along with another important part of the MAPI system—the MAPI Spooler.

The MAPI specification uses a layered model (see Figure 33.1). At the top of the model are the client applications, which sometimes provide an interface that simplifies the use of email messaging for end users. In other types of client applications, the messaging might be transparent to users.

The bottom layer of the model is the various service providers that furnish MAPI-compliant message services. It doesn't matter which programming language these components are written in as long as they "speak MAPI." Microsoft Exchange is a good example of a MAPI-compliant component because it acts as an address book provider and as a message store provider.

NOTE

It's the job of the transport provider to translate messages into the different messaging system formats such as SMTP. These messaging systems are actually the lowest level in the

MAPI model. But because this translation process is transparent to the MAPI programmer, it isn't discussed in this chapter.

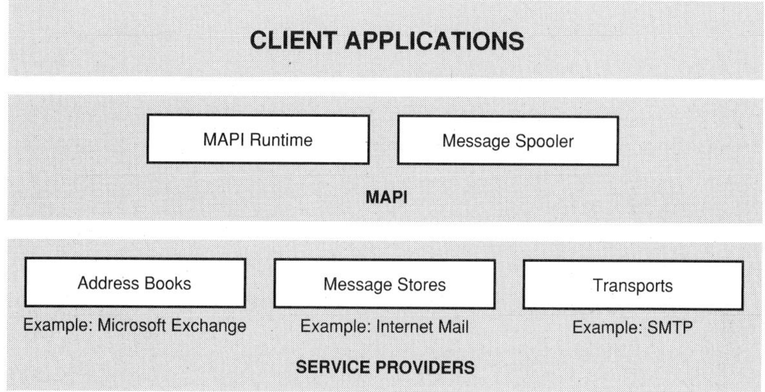

FIGURE 33.1.
The MAPI specification uses a layered model, with MAPI providing an interface between client applications and various service providers.

Tying together the top and bottom layers of the model is MAPI itself, which consists of the MAPI runtime system (DLLs) and the Message Spooler. MAPI provides interfaces to the client applications and the service providers, acting as a middleman or interpreter so that the two can "talk together."

At a basic level, MAPI functions resemble the print spooler built into Windows 95 and Windows NT. When you're writing an application that prints a report, you don't have to worry about who manufactured the printer that will receive the report. That task is left to the Windows print spooler, which translates the report so that it will look fundamentally the same no matter what printer is being used. MAPI works the same way: It enables your application to send and receive email messages no matter what transport provider your system uses (as long as the transport provider is MAPI-compliant). It also enables you to use the services of MAPI-compliant address book and message store providers.

NOTE

As an experienced Visual Basic programmer, you might be a little confused that MAPI stands for *Mail Application Programming Interface* because it doesn't function like the APIs you're used to. Under normal circumstances, an API consists of a related set of functions that can be called from within a VB program. Microsoft's first implementation of MAPI worked that way (that implementation is now referred to as *Simple MAPI*). Extended MAPI,

continues

continued

which is used in VB5, doesn't work that way; instead, all MAPI services are accessed with two ActiveX controls (or COM objects). Like other ActiveX controls, they have events, methods, and properties. By responding to events, calling methods, and setting properties, much of MAPI's functionality is available to VB programmers.

MAPI Service Providers

MAPI service providers do the bulk of the work in the MAPI system. They also shield client application programmers from a great deal of additional coding, as you'll see later.

Although most programmers choose to use existing MAPI service providers such as Microsoft Exchange, it's possible to create your own custom service providers—doing so, though, can be difficult and requires a lower-level language such as C++. If you're interested in learning more about service provider creation, I recommend *Inside MAPI* by Microsoft Press.

Address Book Providers

Address book providers contain databases of addressing information for message recipients. These databases are organized into hierarchies, using *containers* that hold information for various recipients.

When a new message is created, it might be given an email address such as `jdoe@xyzco.com` as its recipient. In that case, the address book provider is sidestepped, and the message is sent to its destination. If a literal name such as John Doe is given as the message's recipient, however, that name must be translated into a valid email address. In that case, you use the address book provider to look up the literal name. If the name is found, the message is assigned an email address, and it can continue on to the message store provider for delivery. If the name isn't found, a dialog box might appear that allows a user to add the name (and a corresponding email address) to her personal address book for later use.

Among other functions that improve the efficiency of email messaging for end users, address books are also useful for creating distribution lists. A *distribution list* consists of one or more related email addresses lumped together under a single name. When a message is addressed to that name, a copy is sent to each person in the distribution list. For example, business owners might want to send copies of their promotional newsletters to 100 different subscribers each month. Rather than send 100 messages individually (a time-consuming chore), they can send the newsletter to a single address created as a distribution list. The address book provider does all the work and sends a copy of the message to each person on the list. By providing this kind of functionality, address book providers can be an important part of the MAPI system.

Note that on any given computer, more than one address book provider might be in use. MAPI merges all them together, however, so that they appear as a single provider to the client application.

Message Store Providers

Message store providers maintain email messages in some sort of database system, typically organized as a hierarchy that uses folders to group messages pertaining to a particular user or subject. Although the message store provider's code (in most cases, a DLL or OCX) is actually executed on the same machine as the client application that's using it, the message database itself can reside locally or on a network.

Message store providers also have another important function. They handle the transmission and receipt of email messages, working closely with the system's transport provider. The following section discusses this in more detail, but keep in mind that it's through the message store provider that your client application will send outgoing messages and receive incoming messages.

Examples of message store providers include Microsoft Exchange, Lotus's cc:Mail, and Hewlett-Packard's OpenMAIL, although many more are available. Some message store providers, such as Exchange, can function as address book providers as well.

Transport Providers

Several underlying messaging protocols have become de facto standards, such as SMTP and X.400. Other protocols might be proprietary in nature. Regardless of which protocol is being used to send messages to and from the Internet or an intranet, it's the transport provider's job to translate those messages to work with the given protocol. Here's how it works:

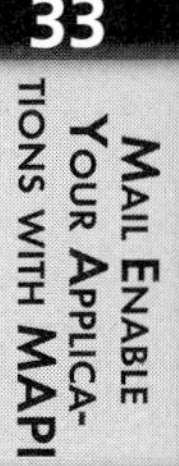

1. Outbound messages (sent *from* the client application) are sent to the message store provider.
2. The message store provider hands the message over to the MAPI Spooler, which sends it to the transport provider.
3. The transport provider converts the message into a stream of bytes compatible with the messaging protocol being used.

Inbound messages work the same way, only in reverse:

1. The transport protocol receives a byte stream and converts it into a MAPI message.
2. The message is sent to the Spooler, which places it into a receive folder furnished by the message store provider.
3. The client application now has access to the new message and can retrieve it from the message store provider.

Because the message store providers and the MAPI Spooler handle transmission and receipt of messages, your client applications probably won't deal with transport providers at all. It helps, though, to know the role that these components play within the MAPI system.

The MAPI Spooler

Like transport providers, your client applications can't deal directly with the MAPI Spooler. But you should be aware of how the Spooler works.

The MAPI Spooler runs in a completely separate process from the client application, just as the Windows print spooler runs in its own process. Even if more than one client application is running, a single instance of the MAPI Spooler is used. When inbound messages are received, the Spooler must determine to which message store provider they should be delivered. Outgoing messages from different message store providers are sorted by submission order, placed into a common queue, and then sent to the appropriate transport providers one by one.

Using the MAPI Controls: MAPISession and MAPIMessages

All the MAPI functionality in Visual Basic 5 is provided by two powerful ActiveX controls: MAPISession and MAPIMessages. The MAPISession control is the simplest of the two and is used only to begin and end MAPI sessions. The MAPIMessages control, on the other hand, provides all the message-related services available under MAPI. Both are invisible controls—they aren't displayed on the form when the program is in run mode.

The sequence of events for a typical MAPI application is as follows:

- Set properties for the MAPISession control that will affect the way in which a MAPI session will be started.
- Call the MAPISession control's `SignOn` method, which begins a new MAPI session.
- Use one or more MAPI services by setting properties or calling methods provided by the MAPIMessages control.
- Call the MAPISession control's `SignOff` method to terminate the MAPI session.

The MAPIMessages control allows you to retrieve messages from the mail server's inbox, perform operations on retrieved messages, and create new messages. It works closely with the mail server, which provides several dialog boxes related to many of the MAPI services. For example, when you create a new message with the MAPIMessages control's `Compose` and `Send` methods, a dialog box appears that facilitates the composition of a new message, saving you from an incredible amount of programming.

The way in which you use the MAPIMessages control might seem a little strange at first; I admit that it was a bit hard for me to get used to. But when you understand how the various properties and methods of the MAPIMessages control work together, you'll master MAPI programming very quickly. The two sample applications created later in this chapter give you a good introduction to how MAPI works in Visual Basic, so relax if you don't yet fully understand how the MAPI controls function. When you see them in action, they'll be much easier to comprehend.

Tables 33.1 and 33.2 list the unique methods and properties available for each control. Note that neither control has events and that "standard" properties, such as `Name` and `Index`, are excluded.

Table 33.1. Methods and properties for the MAPISession control.

Name	Description
	Methods
`SignOff`	Ends a MAPI session.
`SignOn`	Starts a MAPI session.
	Properties
`Action`	Starts or ends a MAPI session. This property should no longer be used but is included to provide backward compatibility with a previous version of MAPI.
`DownloadMail`	Specifies whether new mail should be downloaded from the mail server after beginning a MAPI session.
`LogonUI`	Specifies whether a dialog box should appear when a MAPI session is started.
`NewSession`	Specifies whether a new MAPI session should be started if a valid MAPI session already exists.
`Password`	Specifies the password for the account associated with the `UserName` property.
`SessionID`	Returns the handle for the current MAPI session. This value is set when the `SignOn` method is called.
`UserName`	Specifies the user or profile name to be used when starting a MAPI session.

Table 33.2. Methods and properties for the MAPIMessages control.

Name	Description
	Methods
`Compose`	Clears all components of the compose buffer.
`Copy`	Copies the currently indexed message to the compose buffer so that it can be edited.
`Delete`	Deletes a message, a recipient, or an attachment.

continues

Table 33.2. continued

Name	Description
	Methods
`Fetch`	Creates a message set from messages in the inbox. You can specify the type of messages included in the set by using the `FetchMsgType` and `FetchUnreadOnly` properties. The message set can also be sorted by first setting the `FetchSorted` property.
`Forward`	Copies the currently indexed message into the compose buffer so that it can be sent (forwarded) to another email address.
`Reply`	Copies the currently indexed message into the compose buffer so that a reply can be sent to the originator of the message.
`ReplyAll`	Sends copies of the reply to all recipients of the currently indexed message; it's similar to the `Reply` method.
`ResolveName`	Searches the address book for the currently indexed recipient of a message and returns an error if it's not found. If the `AddressResolveUI` property is `True`, a dialog box for address resolution is displayed rather than an error.
`Save`	Saves the message in the compose buffer.
`Send`	Sends the message in the compose buffer to the mail server for delivery.
`Show`	Displays the Address Book dialog box.
	Properties
`Action`	Performs a number of message-related functions. This property is no longer used but is included to provide backward compatibility with a previous version of MAPI.
`AddressCaption`	Specifies the caption that appears at the top of the Address Book dialog box.
`AddressEditFieldCount`	Specifies which editing controls are displayed in the Address Book dialog box.
`AddressLabel`	Specifies the caption on the To: button in the Address Book dialog box.
`AddressModifiable`	Specifies whether users can modify the address book.
`AddressResolveUI`	Specifies whether a dialog box should be displayed when the `ResolveName` method is called.
`AttachmentCount`	Returns the number of attachments for the currently indexed message.

Name	Description
	Properties
`AttachmentIndex`	Sets or returns the pointer to the currently indexed attachment of a message.
`AttachmentName`	Specifies the filename of the currently indexed attachment.
`AttachmentPathName`	Specifies the full path to the currently indexed attachment.
`AttachmentPosition`	Specifies the position of the currently indexed attachment within the body of the message (in characters).
`AttachmentType`	Specifies the type of the currently indexed attachment (data file, embedded OLE object, or static OLE object).
`FetchMsgType`	Specifies the type of messages to be included in the message set when the `Fetch` method is called.
`FetchSorted`	Specifies the order in which the messages in the message set are sorted when the `Fetch` method is called.
`FetchUnreadOnly`	Specifies that only unread messages should be retrieved from the inbox when the `Fetch` method is called.
`MsgConversationID`	Identifies that the currently indexed message is part of a message thread.
`MsgCount`	Returns the total number of messages included in the current message set.
`MsgDateReceived`	Returns the date on which the currently indexed message was received.
`MsgID`	Returns the ID number of the currently indexed message. This number is generated internally by the MAPI subsystem and should be unique for each message in the message set.
`MsgIndex`	Sets or returns the pointer to the currently indexed message.
`MsgNoteText`	Specifies the body of the currently indexed message.
`MsgOrigAddress`	Returns the address of the originator (sender) of the currently indexed message.
`MsgOrigDisplayName`	Returns the name of the originator (sender) of the currently indexed message.
`MsgRead`	Returns a value indicating whether the currently indexed message has been read.
`MsgReceiptRequested`	Specifies whether a return receipt has been requested for the currently indexed message.

continues

Table 33.2. continued

Name	Description
	Methods
`MsgSent`	Specifies a value indicating whether the currently indexed message has been sent to the mail server for delivery.
`MsgSubject`	Specifies the short subject description of the currently indexed message.
`MsgType`	Specifies the type of the currently indexed message.
`RecipAddress`	Specifies the email address for the recipient of the currently indexed message.
`RecipCount`	Returns the total number of recipients for the currently indexed message.
`RecipDisplayName`	Specifies the name of the currently indexed message recipient.
`RecipIndex`	Sets or returns the pointer to the currently indexed message recipient.
`RecipType`	Specifies the type of the currently indexed message recipient.
`SessionID`	Returns the handle to the current MAPI session.

As you can see, there is quite a bit to these two controls, especially MAPIMessages. Don't worry; I'll go through just about all of it in this chapter.

Creating MAPI Programs with Visual Basic

You're almost ready to start creating some sample MAPI programs with Visual Basic. Before you do, I'd like to briefly explain the three different types of MAPI applications: mail-enabled, electronic mail (email), and mail-aware. Each provides a different level of email functionality:

- *Mail-enabled applications* are applications whose main function isn't specifically email-related but contain some email messaging services, often transparently to users. The example given earlier in this chapter of a program that monitors machines in a factory and emails information regarding their efficiency is a mail-enabled application. The first sample program that follows this section is also an example of a mail-enabled application.
- *Electronic mail,* or *email applications,* provide electronic messaging services as their main function. These programs typically have a user interface that simplifies the creation and handling of email messages by end users. Microsoft's Internet Mail is just one example of an email application.

- *Mail-aware applications* are similar to email applications, but their main function might not be messaging-related. A word processor, for example, might allow you to compose a document and email it to another person. In that way, it functions like an email application. However, the capability to send the document is more a bonus than the main function of the program. Microsoft Word 97 allows you to email its documents, so it's an example of a mail-aware application.

As time goes on, more and more programs will feature some degree of electronic messaging functionality. Most of these applications will be mail-enabled or mail-aware, incorporating email services into their basic design as just another basic feature demanded by end users.

CAUTION

Before you begin creating MAPI client applications in Visual Basic, you must have a properly configured MAPI-compliant mail server on your system. A standalone or network computer running Windows 95 or Windows NT might use Microsoft Exchange, which is included with those operating systems. Not having the necessary components installed can result in unpredictable errors and the inability of the following sample applications to work properly. If you're unsure of whether your system has a mail server installed, consult the online help system or your network administrator.

Creating Mail-Enabled Applications

You first will create a mail-enabled program because such an application provides a good introduction to how MAPI works with Visual Basic without going into too much too soon. Later, you'll create a more robust program that covers many more of the services provided by MAPI.

This program is a simple login/logout interface that might be used to track employee activity of some kind. Perhaps it could be a front end to another application. When employees begin to use the application, they log in with their username and password. When finished, they log out, and someone else can use the application.

When three employees have logged in and out, an activity report with all six transactions (three logins and three logouts) is automatically generated and sent to a manager or supervisor for review. To make testing of the program easier, a button has been added so that the activity report can be sent immediately instead of waiting until all six transactions take place.

The program interface will look like the one shown in Figure 33.2. Notice that there are places for employees to enter their username and password. There are also Log In and Log Out buttons, as well as a button to immediately generate and send the activity report.

To create the program interface, add the various controls to the form; then use Table 33.3 to change the properties of the controls.

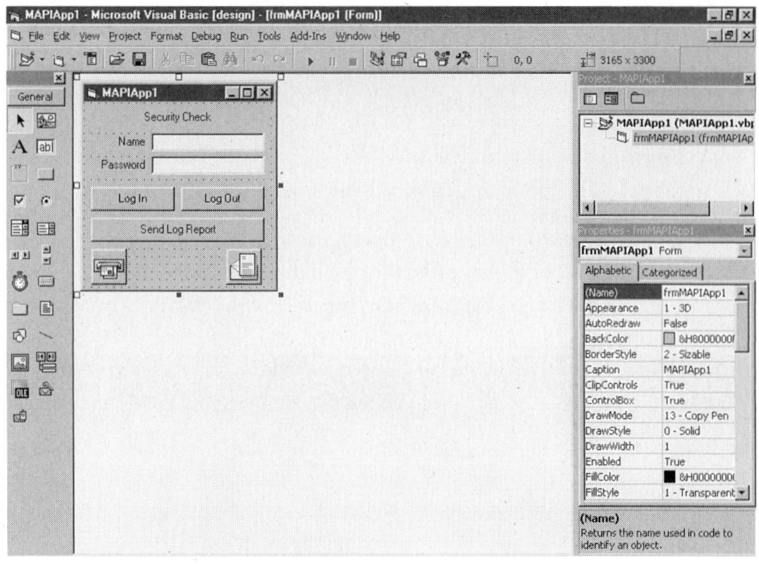

FIGURE 33.2.
The interface for the employee login/logout program.

Table 33.3. Control properties for the employee login/logout program.

Control	*Property*	*Setting*
Form	`Name`	`frmMAPIApp1`
	`Height`	`2895`
	`Left`	`60`
	`Top`	`345`
	`Width`	`3045`
Label	`Name`	`lblTitle`
	`Alignment`	`2 - Center`
	`Caption`	`Security Check`
	`Height`	`255`
	`Left`	`120`
	`Top`	`120`
	`Width`	`2775`
Label	`Name`	`lblName`
	`Alignment`	`1 - Right Justify`
	`Caption`	`Name`
	`Height`	`255`
	`Left`	`120`
	`Top`	`510`
	`Width`	`855`
Label	`Name`	`lblPassword`
	`Alignment`	`1 - Right Justify`

Control	Property	Setting
	Caption	Password
	Height	255
	Left	120
	Top	870
	Width	855
TextBox	Name	txtName
	Height	285
	Left	1080
	Top	480
	Width	1815
TextBox	Name	txtPassword
	Height	285
	Left	1080
	PasswordChar	*
	Top	840
	Width	1815
CommandButton	Name	cmdLogIn
	Caption	Log In
	Height	375
	Left	120
	Top	1320
	Width	1335
CommandButton	Name	cmdLogOut
	Caption	Log Out
	Height	375
	Left	1560
	Top	1320
	Width	1335
CommandButton	Name	cmdSendLog
	Caption	Send Log Report
	Height	375
	Left	120
	Top	1800
	Width	2775
MAPISession	Name	mpsSession
	Left	120
	Top	2280
MAPIMessages	Name	mpmSendLog
	Left	2280
	Top	2280

NOTE

If the two MAPI ActiveX controls (MAPISession and MAPIMessages) aren't already in your toolbox, press Ctrl+T or choose Project | Components. In the Components dialog box, double-click Microsoft MAPI Controls 5.0 so that its box is checked; then click OK to add the two controls to your toolbox.

After you create the form, it's time to do some coding. This program uses only four subroutines, and only one actually uses the MAPI controls. I'll save that subroutine for last so that I can discuss it in more detail.

Before you start coding these four subroutines, you need to add two module-level variables to the General Declarations section. These two variables will be used throughout the rest of the program:

```
Dim mintLogCount As Integer
Dim mstrLogActivity(6) As String
```

NOTE

When naming objects and variables in Visual Basic, I prefer using Microsoft's coding conventions. Notice that a three-character mnemonic precedes every object and variable name to indicate its type (`frm` for Forms, `cmd` for Command Buttons, `int` for integers, and so on). You also can precede variable names with a one-character scope indicator (`g` for global or `m` for module-level). I have found these coding conventions useful, and I advise you to consider adopting their use.

The first subroutine is for the Log In button's `Click` event (see Listing 33.1). When the event is triggered, the program verifies that users have typed something in the Name and Password text boxes. (Of course, the verification process would be much more involved if this were more than just a simple test program, with all names and passwords being looked up in an employee database. In the interest of keeping it simple, I'll ease up on the security a bit.)

Listing 33.1. Code for `cmdLogIn`'s `Click` event.

```
Private Sub cmdLogIn_Click()

    ' Make sure that both a name and a password have been
    ' entered.
    If txtName.Text = "" Or txtPassword.Text = "" Then
        MsgBox "Please enter your name and password."
        Exit Sub
    End If

    ' If this were a real application, code for checking the
    ' user's login information would go here.
```

```
    cmdLogIn.Enabled = False    ' Disable LogIn button and...
    cmdLogOut.Enabled = True    ' ...enable LogOut button.

    txtName.Enabled = False
    txtPassword.Text = ""
    txtPassword.Enabled = False

    ' Add this login to the activity log.
    mintLogCount = mintLogCount + 1
    mstrLogActivity(mintLogCount) = "User " _
        & UCase$(txtName.Text) & " logged IN at " _
        & Time$ & " on " & Date$

End Sub
```

When an employee logs in, a transaction line with the username and the login date and time is added to the `mstrLogActivity` array. Later, this array is used to generate the activity report emailed to a supervisor.

The next section of code is for the Log Out button's `Click` event (see Listing 33.2). Like the routine in Listing 33.1, it adds a transaction line to the `mstrLogActivity` array. If the array has six transactions, the `SendActivityLog` subroutine is called. That's the subroutine that actually uses the two MAPI controls, which I'll discuss in just a moment.

Listing 33.2. Code for `cmdLogOut`'s `Click` event.

```
Private Sub cmdLogOut_Click()

    ' Add this logout to the activity log.
    mintLogCount = mintLogCount + 1
    mstrLogActivity(mintLogCount) = "User " _
        & UCase$(txtName.Text) & " logged OUT at " _
        & Time$ & " on " & Date$

    ' If the activity log is "full", then send it out via
    ' e-mail.
    If mintLogCount = 6 Then
        SendActivityLog
    End If

    txtName.Text = ""
    txtName.Enabled = True
    txtPassword.Enabled = True

    cmdLogIn.Enabled = True
    cmdLogOut.Enabled = False

End Sub
```

Next, you have yet another `Click` event, this time for the Send Log Now button (see Listing 33.3). It also calls the `SendActivityLog` subroutine to email the login/logout report.

Listing 33.3. Code for `cmdSendLogNow`'s `Click` event.

```
Private Sub cmdSendLog_Click()

' Check to see if there's actually anything in the activity
' log before sending it.
If mintLogCount = 0 Then
    MsgBox "Activity log empty - nothing to send!"
    Exit Sub
End If

SendActivityLog

End Sub
```

Now that you've taken care of the overhead, it's time to get down to business. Listing 33.4 shows the `SendActivityLog` subroutine.

Listing 33.4. The `SendActivityLog` subroutine, which handles all the MAPI services used by the login/logout program.

```
Public Sub SendActivityLog()

    Dim intMsgLoop As Integer
    Dim strMsgBuffer As String

    On Error GoTo SendActivityLogError

    ' Establish a MAPI session.
    mpsSession.UserName = "security"
    mpsSession.Password = "test"
    mpsSession.DownLoadMail = False
    mpsSession.LogonUI = False
    mpsSession.SignOn
    mpmSendLog.SessionID = mpsSession.SessionID

    ' Create the body of the message in a temporary buffer.
    strMsgBuffer = ""
    For intMsgLoop = 0 To mintLogCount
        strMsgBuffer = strMsgBuffer _
            & mstrLogActivity(intMsgLoop) & Chr$(13) & Chr$(10)
    Next intMsgLoop

    ' Compose and send the message.
    mpmSendLog.Compose
    mpmSendLog.RecipAddress = "schief@mapiland.com"
    mpmSendLog.RecipDisplayName = "Security Chief"

    mpmSendLog.MsgSubject = "Activity Log - " & Date$ _
        & "/" & Time$
    mpmSendLog.MsgNoteText = strMsgBuffer
    mpmSendLog.Send
```

```
    ' Set the activity log's index to zero, effectively
    ' "clearing out" the log.
    mintLogCount = 0

    mpsSession.SignOff

    Exit Sub

SendActivityLogError:
    MsgBox Error$, vbCritical, "Critical Error: " & Str(Err)
    End

End Sub
```

Because this routine does most of the work in the program and contains all the MAPI-related code, look at it in more detail.

To begin with, notice that an error handler has been implemented. Whenever you're working with the MAPI controls, it's always a good idea to set up some kind of error handling. Many things can go wrong if you're not careful in your coding. In fact, the MAPI specification defines 36 different error conditions that can arise when using the MAPI controls. Under normal circumstances, you'll probably want to implement a much more robust error-handling routine that traps for specific errors or offers the users options when an error occurs. But in the interest of simplicity, you'll display only the error description and its value and then end the program. If you have the necessary 32-bit MAPI DLLs installed properly on your system, you won't run into any problems.

Because the subroutine in Listing 33.4 contains all the MAPI-related action in the program, I'll go through it section by section and discuss each part in more detail.

Establishing the MAPI Session

The following code segment establishes a MAPI session by using the MAPISession control (`mpsSession`):

```
' Establish a MAPI session.
mpsSession.UserName = "security"
mpsSession.Password = "test"
mpsSession.DownLoadMail = False
mpsSession.LogonUI = False
mpsSession.SignOn
mpmSendLog.SessionID = mpsSession.SessionID
```

The `UserName` and `Password` properties are changed to reflect the login information you want to use (in this case, a username of `security` and a password of `test`). If you want to run this program on your system, you'll have to change these two properties to something that works with your mail server—your own name and password, for example.

NOTE

You don't need to specify a password at all if you use a profile name rather than a username. Most MAPI-compliant mail servers (including Microsoft Exchange) allow you to set up different profiles. A discussion of profiles and how Windows Messaging works is beyond the scope of this chapter. However, you can use the Windows help system to learn more on those topics.

The `DownLoadMail` property is set to `False`, specifying that any new messages shouldn't be retrieved when the user has signed on. Because this program's only function is to send an employee activity report to the appropriate party, it's not set up to receive mail.

The `LogonUI` property is also set to `False`. If it's set to `True`, a dialog box will appear that prompts for the username and password to log on to the service provider. Because you don't want the dialog box to appear, you set this property to `False`, and no user intervention is required. If you use invalid values for the `UserName` and `Password` properties, the dialog box appears whether the `LogonUI` property is `True` or `False`. On the other hand, if you assign valid `UserName` and `Password` property values, the dialog box still won't appear, even if the `LogonUI` property is set to `True`.

After all the necessary properties are set, the MAPISession control's `SignOn` method is called. When a MAPI session is started, it's assigned a Session ID number. In the preceding code segment, that number is placed into `mpsSession`'s `SessionID` property. You must copy that value so that the MAPIMessages control knows which MAPI session to use when its own methods are called. Note that when a MAPI session has been initiated, the MAPISession control isn't used again until the MAPI session is to be terminated (by using the `SignOff` method).

Adding Elements to a Temporary String Used to Hold the Message Body

The following code segment loops through the `mstrLogActivity` array and adds its elements to a temporary string (`strMsgBuffer`) used to hold the body of the email message.

```
' Create the body of the message in a temporary buffer.
strMsgBuffer = ""
For intMsgLoop = 0 To mintLogCount
    strMsgBuffer = strMsgBuffer _
        & mstrLogActivity(intMsgLoop) & Chr$(13) & Chr$(10)
Next intMsgLoop
```

A carriage return and linefeed are added to the end of each element so that the information isn't lumped into one long line of text.

Addressing and Sending the Message

Now you need to address and send the message. First, you call the MAPIMessages control's `Compose` method to clear all the components in the compose buffer, which is used to create new messages (or to edit and resend existing messages, as you'll see later):

```
' Compose and send the message.
mpmSendLog.Compose
mpmSendLog.RecipAddress = "manager@mapiland.com"
mpmSendLog.RecipDisplayName = "Mr. Manager"
mpmSendLog.MsgSubject = "Activity Log - " & Date$ _
    & "/" & Time$
mpmSendLog.MsgNoteText = strMsgBuffer
mpmSendLog.Send
```

The `RecipAddress` property is assigned the email address of the person receiving the message, and the `RecipDisplayName` property gets the name of the recipient. In the example, I've used a fabricated email address and name; you might want to change these two properties to a valid email address that you can use to test the program.

Next, you give the message a subject, using the `MsgSubject` property, and assign the temporary string you created earlier to the message body (the `MsgNoteText` property). Now you're ready to send it. To do so, the MAPIMessages control's `Send` method is called. This sends the message to the mail server, which in turn relays it to the recipient specified by the `RecipAddress` property.

Resetting the Activity Log

After the activity log is sent, it should be reset or "cleared out" so that it can be used again. By setting the log's counter back to zero, you can record more employee activity in the log:

```
' Set the activity log's index to zero, effectively
' "clearing out" the log.
mintLogCount = 0

mpsSession.SignOff
```

Finally, you close your MAPI session by calling the MAPISession control's `SignOff` method. You don't have to tell the MAPIMessages control that the session is over, but you can no longer use that control's methods until a new session is started. Calling any of its methods without having a MAPI session in progress results in an error.

Saving the Project

Save the project as `CH3301.VBP` and the form as `CH3301.FRM`; then compile and run the program. If you aren't on a network with an email gateway or have to use dial-up networking to connect to the Internet, make sure that you've established a connection to the Internet first.

When the program runs, type a username and password—anything will do because you don't perform any validation on what's entered. Click the Log In button. The password will disappear, and text boxes are disabled until you click the Log Out button, so do that now. Then enter another name and password, if you want, and log in and out. Now click the Send Log Report button to send the activity log. All this work is transparent to the user, so it might not seem like anything has happened. But if you check the mailbox for the recipient assigned to the message, you'll see some new mail.

Before moving on to the next MAPI application, try a few things. Exit the program and change the line in the `SendActivityLog` subroutine from

```
mpmSendLog.Send
```

to

```
mpmSendLog.Send True
```

and run the program again. When you click the button to send the activity log, you'll see a window similar to the one shown in Figure 33.3.

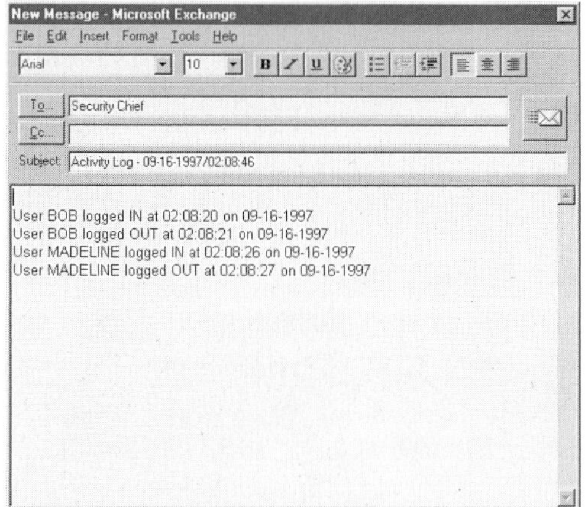

FIGURE 33.3.
The window displayed when the `Send` *method is called with a* `True` *argument.*

The mail server displays this window, so it might look different on your system if you're not using Microsoft Exchange. You'll see more of this window when you create the next application. For now, exit the program and remove the `True` argument from the line of code you just changed.

Now try adding an attachment to the message sent by the login/logout application. Suppose that along with the employee activity log, you want to include another log file created by the application that the employees are using. This file is a simple ASCII text file named `USE.LOG` and is located in the `C:\APP` directory (for testing purposes; feel free to change the filename and path to indicate a file that exists on your system). To add the attachment to the message, modify the section of code in the `SendActivityLog` subroutine so that it looks like Listing 33.5.

Listing 33.5. The modified code segment in the `SendActivityLog` subroutine so that an attachment is added to the message being sent out.

```
' Compose and send the message.
mpmSendLog.Compose
mpmSendLog.RecipAddress = "manager@mapiland.com"
mpmSendLog.RecipDisplayName = "Mr. Manager"
mpmSendLog.MsgSubject = "Activity Log - " & Date$ _
    & "/" & Time$
```

```
mpmSendLog.MsgNoteText = strMsgBuffer
mpmSendLog.AttachmentType = mapData
mpmSendLog.AttachmentName = "Program Use Log"
mpmSendLog.AttachmentPathName = "C:\App\Use.log"
mpmSendLog.AttachmentPosition = Len(mpmSendLog.MsgNoteText)
mpmSendLog.Send
```

As you can see, four new lines have been added to `SendActivityLog`. All of them set properties of the `mpmSendLog` control:

- The `AttachmentName` property specifies a descriptive name for the attachment.
- The `AttachmentPathName` property specifies its full path and filename. To test the use of attachments, you have to change the `AttachmentPathName` property to reflect a file that exists somewhere on your system.
- The `AttachmentType` property indicates what kind of object the attachment is. It can be a data file (`mapData`), an embedded OLE object (`mapEOLE`), or a static OLE object (`mapSOLE`). In the example, the attachment is a regular data file, so the `mapData` constant is used.
- The `AttachmentPosition` property specifies where in the message body the attachment will be positioned. If you want it to appear after the third character, this property is set to 3. Often, attachments are placed at the end of the message. This is the case in the sample code, so the `AttachmentPosition` property is set to the length of the entire message body.

That just about wraps it up for the login/logout application. In the next section, you create a simple email program that demonstrates how to use many more of the MAPI services in Visual Basic.

Creating Email Applications

In the preceding section, you created an application that sends email transparently—users weren't involved in the process of sending the messages. Now you'll create an application that relies totally on users: a simple email program displaying messages read in from the mail server and allowing users to create and send new messages as well as perform various services on existing messages. Although it's a primitive and simple program, it provides an example of an email application.

The program consists of three main sections. At the top is a ListBox containing the subjects of all messages read in from the mail server. In the middle is a Label displaying header information for the currently selected message. The last section is a TextBox displaying the body of the currently selected message.

When users click one of the message subjects in the ListBox, the name of the sender, the subject, and the date the message was received appear in the Label. The body of the message appears in the TextBox.

When a message is selected, users can click any of the following command buttons that perform message services: Reply, Reply All, Forward, Copy, and Delete. If users click the New button, they can compose and send a new message. Last but not least, users can view the address book by clicking the appropriately named Address Book button.

You might think that even a simple program like this would take quite a bit of coding. If so, you'll be pleasantly surprised. Because MAPI does most of the work for you, the amount of program code is minimal.

Begin by assembling the program's interface. By using Table 33.4 as a guide, add the various components and change their properties so that your form looks like the one shown in Figure 33.4.

Table 33.4. Control properties for the simple email application.

Control	*Property*	*Setting*
Form	Name	frmMAPIApp2
	Caption	MAPIApp2
	Height	6465
	Left	60
	Top	345
	Width	6615
Label	Name	lblTitle
	Alignment	2 - Center
	Caption	Simple E-Mail Application
	Font	MS Sans Serif 12pt
	Height	375
	Left	1320
	Top	120
	Width	3975
CommandButton	Name	cmdMsgNew
	Caption	New
	Height	255
	Left	120
	Top	600
	Width	975
CommandButton	Name	cmdMsgReply
	Caption	Reply
	Height	255
	Left	1200
	Top	600
	Width	975

Control	Property	Setting
CommandButton	Name	cmdMsgReplyAll
	Caption	ReplyAll
	Height	255
	Left	2280
	Top	600
	Width	975
CommandButton	Name	cmdMsgForward
	Caption	Forward
	Height	255
	Left	3360
	Top	600
	Width	975
CommandButton	Name	cmdMsgCopy
	Caption	Copy
	Height	255
	Left	5520
	Top	600
	Width	975
CommandButton	Name	cmdMsgDelete
	Caption	Delete
	Height	255
	Left	5520
	Top	600
	Width	975
ListBox	Name	lstMessages
	Height	1035
	Left	120
	Top	1080
	Width	6375
Label	Name	lblMsgInfo
	BorderStyle	1 - Fixed Single
	Font	MS LineDraw 8pt
	Height	735
	Left	120
	Top	2280
	Width	6375

continues

Table 33.4. continued

Control	*Property*	*Setting*
TextBox	`Name`	`txtMsgBody`
	`Height`	`2775`
	`Left`	`120`
	`MultiLine`	`True`
	`ScrollBars`	`2 - Vertical`
	`Top`	`3000`
	`Width`	`6375`
CommandButton	`Name`	`cmdAddrBook`
	`Caption`	`Address Book`
	`Height`	`255`
	`Left`	`3120`
	`Top`	`6120`
	`Width`	`1575`
CommandButton	`Name`	`cmdExit`
	`Caption`	`Exit Program`
	`Height`	`255`
	`Left`	`4800`
	`Top`	`6120`
	`Width`	`1695`
MAPISession	`Name`	`mpsSession`
	`Left`	`120`
	`Top`	`5880`
MAPIMessages	`Name`	`mpmMessages`
	`Left`	`720`
	`Top`	`5880`

When your form design is complete, you can begin adding the program's code. I'll take the sections one by one so that I can explain each part in more detail.

Listing 33.6 shows the code for the form's `Load` event. There's really nothing new here. When the program starts, it first displays itself and then establishes a MAPI session. When a session is started, the `FetchMessages` subroutine is called. As you'll see in just a moment, that routine reads in the messages from the mail server and displays their subjects onscreen.

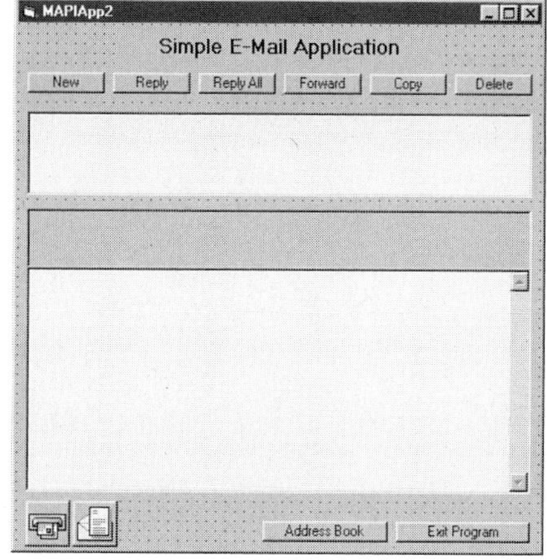

FIGURE 33.4. *The interface for the simple email application.*

Listing 33.6. Code for the form's Load event.

```
Private Sub Form_Load()

    On Error GoTo ErrHandler

    ' Show the form so it shows up behind the login
    ' dialog box.
    Me.Show

    ' Start a new MAPI session.
    mpsSession.DownLoadMail = True
    mpsSession.LogonUI = True
    mpsSession.SignOn
    mpmMessages.SessionID = mpsSession.SessionID

    ' Read messages from the message server's InBox.
    FetchMessages

    ' If there are messages, display the first one.
    If lstMessages.ListCount > 0 Then
        lstMessages.ListIndex = 0
        lstMessages_Click
    End If

    Exit Sub

ErrHandler:
    CriticalError

End Sub
```

Note that I've added error handling to this code. In fact, I've done so in all the routines and events that perform some sort of MAPI function. Any error that arises will be handled by the `CriticalError` routine (see Listing 33.7). If an error does occur—and let's hope it doesn't—this routine displays a message box with the error number and description. It also terminates the MAPI session if it has already been started.

Listing 33.7. The `CriticalError` routine, which handles any errors that may occur throughout the program's various subroutines and events.

```
Public Sub CriticalError()

    ' An error has occurred. Inform the user and exit
    ' the program.
    MsgBox Error$, vbCritical, "Critical Error: " & Str(Err)
    If mpsSession.SessionID Then
        mpsSession.SignOff
    End If
    End

End Sub
```

The next code section (see Listing 33.8) is for the `FetchMessages` routine mentioned earlier. Its job is to retrieve all the messages in the mail server's inbox.

Listing 33.8. The `FetchMessages` routine, which retrieves messages from the mail server.

```
Public Sub FetchMessages()

    Dim intMsgIndex As Integer

    On Error GoTo ErrHandler

    ' Read all messages (read and unread) from the server,
    ' and sort as specified by the user's inbox.
    mpmMessages.FetchSorted = True
    mpmMessages.FetchUnreadOnly = False
    mpmMessages.Fetch

    ' Clear the ListBox and add to it all of the
    ' messages just read.
    lstMessages.Clear
    intMsgIndex = 0
    If mpmMessages.MsgCount > 0 Then
        Do
            mpmMessages.MsgIndex = intMsgIndex
            lstMessages.AddItem mpmMessages.MsgSubject
            intMsgIndex = intMsgIndex + 1
        Loop Until (intMsgIndex = mpmMessages.MsgCount)
    End If
    Exit Sub

ErrHandler:
    CriticalError

End Sub
```

The first thing the routine in Listing 33.8 does is set some of the properties for the MAPIMessages control's `Fetch` method. The `FetchSorted` property is set to `True`, specifying that the messages should be retrieved in whichever order they are in the mail server's inbox. If the default value (`False`) was used, the messages would be retrieved in the same order in which they were received.

The `FetchUnreadOnly` property is also set here. By assigning it to `False`, it specifies that all messages should be retrieved, not just the unread ones. The default value for this property is `True` (retrieve unread messages only).

Next, the `Fetch` method is called. It sends all the messages in the mail server's inbox to your application and stores them in a message set. You can think of the *message set* as a kind of array because you can access messages in the set individually, just as you can access elements of an array individually. To index a message, you simply change the MAPIMessages control's `MsgIndex` property to point to the message you want to access. You can then read other properties that apply to the message, such as `MsgSubject`, `MsgNoteText`, or `MsgDateReceived`. You also can call methods that perform some sort of function on the currently indexed message. For example, if you wanted to forward the current message, you would call the `Forward` method. It might sound a little strange, and it does take a little getting used to, but using the MAPI controls is really a snap.

Okay, back to the `FetchMessages` routine. Now that you have all the messages in the mail server's inbox stored in the message set, you need to list them onscreen somehow. This is where the ListBox control (`lstMessages`) comes in. The next piece of code adds all the message subjects in the message set to `lstMessages` (after clearing whatever was in there before).

First, you need to tell just how many messages were read in when the `Fetch` method was called. This is stored in the MAPIMessages control's `MsgCount` property. If it's more than zero, you know that at least one message has been retrieved and is stored in the message set. In that case, you use a `Do...Loop Until` structure to loop through the message set and add each message subject to the ListBox. Note that you have to set `msmMessages`'s `MsgIndex` property to point to a different message each time the loop is performed.

Listing 33.9 shows the `Click` event for the New button, which allows users to create a new mail message and send it to the mail server for delivery. Only two lines of this code actually perform that function, and they both call methods of `mpmMessages`, the MAPIMessages control. The `Compose` method is called first. It clears all components of the compose buffer. Next, the `Send` method is called. Use the `True` argument to indicate that a dialog box should be displayed so that users can add the various elements of the message (subject, body, and so on). The dialog box appears when the `Send` method is provided by the mail server, so it might be different from machine to machine.

Listing 33.9. Code for the New CommandButton's `Click` event.

```
Private Sub cmdMsgNew_Click()

    On Error GoTo ErrHandler

    ' Create a new message.
    mpmMessages.Compose
    mpmMessages.Send True

    lstMessages.SetFocus
    Exit Sub

ErrHandler:
    CriticalError

End Sub
```

If you're delighted to find out that it takes only two lines of code to create and send a new message with the MAPI controls, you'll be glad to know that all the other message services are just as easy.

NOTE

After the `Send` method is complete, the program focus is set to the `lstMessages` control. I added this line so that the focus would be taken off the New button—more of a cosmetic touch than anything else. I've also done the same in all the other CommandButton `Click` events, as you'll see.

Now start adding the code for the other buttons' `Click` events. They're all similar. Listing 33.10 shows the first, `cmdMsgReply_Click`.

Listing 33.10. Code for the Reply button's `Click` event.

```
Private Sub cmdMsgReply_Click()

    On Error GoTo ErrHandler

    ' Reply to currently indexed message.
    mpmMessages.MsgIndex = lstMessages.ListIndex
    mpmMessages.Reply
    mpmMessages.Send True

    lstMessages.SetFocus
    Exit Sub

ErrHandler:
    CriticalError

End Sub
```

As promised, the code is short and simple. The MAPIMessages control's `MsgIndex` property is set to reflect the message number selected in the ListBox (`lstMessages`). This makes that message the currently indexed message. Next, `mpmMessages`'s `Reply` method is called, which copies the current message to the compose buffer and adds `RE:` at the beginning of its Subject line. Finally, the `Send` method is called, and the message dialog box is displayed.

As you can see, the code for the Reply All button's `Click` event (see Listing 33.11) is almost identical to Reply's `Click` event. The only difference is that rather than the `Reply` method being called, the `ReplyAll` method is used.

Listing 33.11. Code for the Reply All button's `Click` event.

```
Private Sub cmdMsgReplyAll_Click()

    On Error GoTo ErrHandler

    ' Reply to all recipients of the currently indexed
    ' message.
    mpmMessages.MsgIndex = lstMessages.ListIndex
    mpmMessages.ReplyAll
    mpmMessages.Send True

    lstMessages.SetFocus
    Exit Sub

ErrHandler:
    CriticalError

End Sub
```


These two buttons do have slightly different functions. The Reply button sends a reply message only to the originator (sender) of the message. The Reply All button, however, sends a copy of the reply message to all the recipients of the original message.

Moving on, you have the Forward button's `Click` event (see Listing 33.12). Again, it's similar to the last two code listings. The `Forward` method copies the currently indexed message to the compose buffer. The message is then edited in the dialog box displayed when the `Send` method is called. The Subject line in the dialog box is prefixed with `FW:` when the `Forward` method is used.

Listing 33.12. Code for the Forward button's `Click` event.

```
Private Sub cmdMsgForward_Click()

    On Error GoTo ErrHandler

    ' Forward the currently indexed message.
    mpmMessages.MsgIndex = lstMessages.ListIndex
    mpmMessages.Forward
    mpmMessages.Send True
```

continues

Listing 33.12. continued

```
    lstMessages.SetFocus
    Exit Sub

ErrHandler:
    CriticalError

End Sub
```

Listing 33.13 shows the code for the Copy button's `Click` event. The `Copy` method simply copies the currently indexed message into the compose buffer. It doesn't alter the Subject line like some of the previously discussed methods.

Listing 33.13. Code for the Copy button's `Click` event.

```
Private Sub cmdMsgCopy_Click()

    On Error GoTo ErrHandler

    ' Copy the currently indexed message.
    mpmMessages.MsgIndex = lstMessages.ListIndex
    mpmMessages.Copy
    mpmMessages.Send True

    lstMessages.SetFocus
    Exit Sub

ErrHandler:
    CriticalError

End Sub
```

The last of the message services' code is for the Delete button (see Listing 33.14). It's different from the rest of the listings thus far because it doesn't call the `Send` method. After pointing to the current message, the `Delete` method is called, and the message's subject is removed from the ListBox control.

Listing 33.14. Code for the Delete button's `Click` event.

```
Private Sub cmdMsgDelete_Click()

    On Error GoTo ErrHandler

    ' Delete the currently indexed message and remove its
    ' subject from the ListBox.
    mpmMessages.MsgIndex = lstMessages.ListIndex
    mpmMessages.Delete
    lstMessages.RemoveItem lstMessages.ListIndex

    ' Some odds and ends to take care of.
    If lstMessages.ListCount > 0 Then
        lstMessages.ListIndex = 0
```

```
    Else
        lblMsgInfo = ""
        txtMsgBody = ""
    End If

    lstMessages.SetFocus
    Exit Sub

ErrHandler:
    CriticalError

End Sub
```

This routine also does a bit of housekeeping when a message is deleted. If no message subjects are left in the ListBox control, it blanks out any message currently onscreen. If some message subjects still remain in the ListBox control, it changes the ListBox pointer to highlight the first message in the list.

When users click one of the message subjects in the ListBox control, you want the corresponding message to be displayed. The code in Listing 33.15 displays the message's originator (sender), subject, and date received in the `lblMsgInfo` Label control and the body of the message in the `txtMsgBody` TextBox control.

Listing 33.15. `lstMessages`'s `Click` event, displaying a message when users click a message subject.

```
Private Sub lstMessages_Click()

    ' When the user clicks on a message's subject, display
    ' the info (From, Subject, and Date) in the lblMsgInfo
    ' box and the message body in txtMsgBody.
    mpmMessages.MsgIndex = lstMessages.ListIndex
    lblMsgInfo = "From: " + mpmMessages.MsgOrigDisplayName + Chr$(13) _
        + "Subj: " + mpmMessages.MsgSubject + Chr$(13) _
        + "Date: " + mpmMessages.MsgDateReceived
    txtMsgBody = mpmMessages.MsgNoteText

End Sub
```

A single MAPIMessages method, `Show`, allows you to display an Address Book dialog box provided by the mail server. Listing 33.16 shows the code that displays the dialog box when the Address Book button is clicked.

Listing 33.16. Code for the Address Book button's `Click` event.

```
Private Sub cmdAddrBook_Click()

    On Error GoTo ErrHandler

    ' Show the Address Book dialog box.
    mpmMessages.Show
```

continues

Listing 33.16. continued

```
    lstMessages.SetFocus
    Exit Sub

ErrHandler:
    CriticalError

End Sub
```

You're almost finished—only a few more subroutines to go! The `Click` event for the Exit button (see Listing 33.17) verifies that the users want to exit the program. It then terminates the current MAPI session and ends the program if users decide to proceed with the exit.

Listing 33.17. Code for the Exit button's `Click` event.

```
Private Sub cmdExit_Click()

    Dim intExit As Integer

    ' Make sure the user really wants to exit the
    ' program.
    intExit = MsgBox("Exit the program?", vbYesNo, _
        "Exit Program")
    If intExit = vbYes Then
        mpsSession.SignOff
        End
    End If

    lstMessages.SetFocus

End Sub
```

The last thing to add to the program is the bit of code shown in Listing 33.18. It prevents users from typing anything into the TextBox control (`txtMsgBody`), which contains the body of the currently selected message.

Listing 33.18. Code for `txtMsgBody`'s `KeyPress` events, preventing users from typing anything into the text box used to display the message body.

```
Private Sub txtMsgBody_KeyPress(KeyAscii As Integer)

    ' Prevent users from typing into the text box that
    ' contains the message body.
    KeyAscii = 0

End Sub
```

Finally, you're ready to try out the program. Save the project as `CH3302.VBP` and the form as `CH3302.FRM`; compile and run the program. The first thing you'll see is a dialog box similar to the one shown in Figure 33.5 (again, yours might look different if you're using a mail server other than Microsoft Exchange).

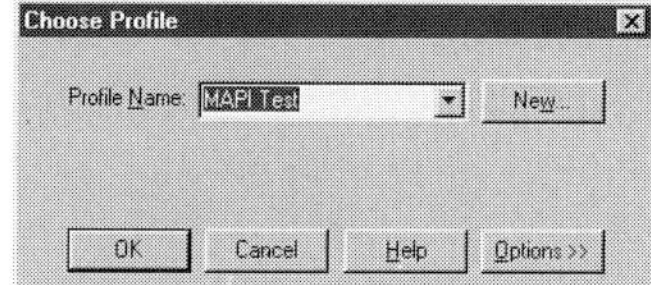

FIGURE 33.5.
When the program is run, the mail server requests a profile name.

After establishing a MAPI connection, the program receives messages from the mail server's inbox. It might take a few moments after the MAPI session is established, but you'll then see a dialog box telling you that the program is checking for messages (see Figure 33.6).

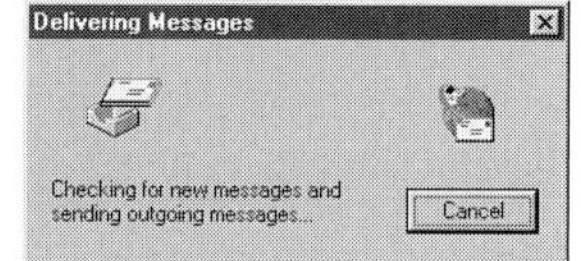

FIGURE 33.6.
The program retrieves messages from the mail server's inbox.

When mail retrieval is completed, you'll see a list of the messages (if any) that were in the mail server's inbox. Try sending a new message by clicking the New button. When you do, a window pops up like the one shown in Figure 33.7. (Again, yours might be different, based on the kind of mail server you're using.)

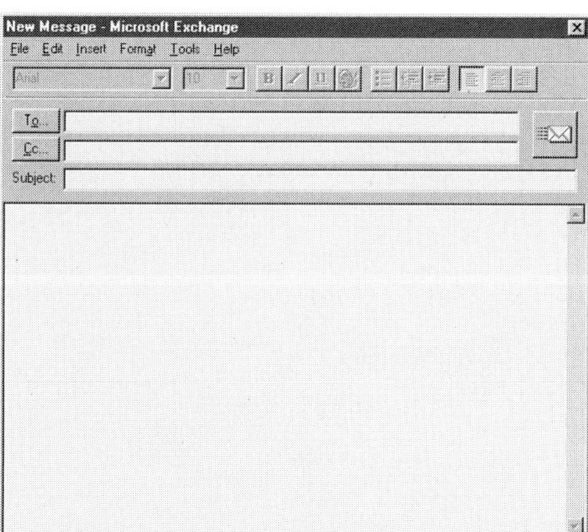

FIGURE 33.7.
When sending a new message, the mail server provides a window where you can compose and send the message.

Don't forget to click the Send button when you're finished composing your message. For the dialog box provided by Microsoft Exchange, the button to send the message is located to the right of the To and Cc lines.

Try using some of the other message services in the program. Then click the Address Book button to display the Address Book dialog box (see Figure 33.8). In the Address Book dialog box, you can add new entries to your personal address book. You can also delete entries, create distribution lists, and perform several other operations.

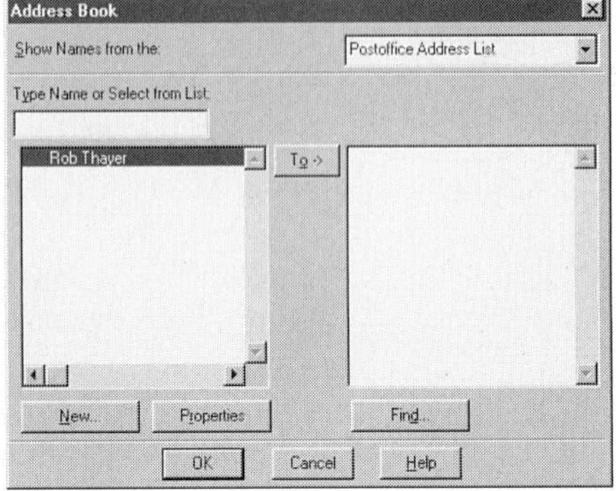

FIGURE 33.8.
The Address Book dialog box lets you change your personal address book.

That's it for the tour of the simple email application. True to its name, the application is simple and does lack in some areas. For instance, the application doesn't support message attachments, but it does show almost all the services supported under MAPI.

Summary

This chapter introduces the creation of MAPI applications with Visual Basic. The chapter first discusses the MAPI specification and its various components. You learned that MAPI acts as a standard interface between electronic messaging client applications and service providers.

You also learned about the two powerful MAPI ActiveX controls, MAPISession and MAPIMessages. The MAPISession control is used to start and end MAPI sessions, and the MAPIMessages control provides all the MAPI message services.

The sample applications using the two ActiveX controls illustrate how easily you can implement MAPI in Visual Basic. These sample applications provide an introduction to MAPI programming.

CHAPTER 34

Creating Telephony Applications with TAPI

IN THIS CHAPTER

TAPI stands for Telephony Applications Programmer Interface, and it is a library of functions that can be used to provide programs with telephony support. So what is telephony? In a nutshell, *telephony* is a term that refers to the merging of computers and the telephone system.

"The telephone system" is a broad category and can include many different communication mediums. The most common is POTS, which stands for Plain Old Telephone System. POTS is the phone system that has existed for years, and we use it every day. More recent communication protocols include ISDN (Integrated Services Digital Network) and T1, which were designed to be faster and handle a greater volume of data than POTS.

The protocol used for data and voice communication is inconsequential with TAPI. It allows your programs to work with different phone systems through a standard interface.

As stated earlier, telephony (and therefore TAPI) is a merging of computers and telephones. This goes far beyond voice communications. You can use TAPI to perform operations directly with the phone system, such as obtaining Caller ID information, recording and playing back audio through voice phone lines, or monitoring for digits pressed by a caller. With TAPI, you can create a complete voice mail system as well as many other telephone-based applications.

TAPI is extremely versatile. Unfortunately, there is a price to be paid. TAPI is somewhat difficult to work with because it is implemented as a library of functions rather than as an ActiveX control (like MAPI, the Messaging API). The number of TAPI functions is high—well over 100 in TAPI version 2.1. What's worse, little information is currently available for Visual Basic programmers who want to utilize the TAPI library. In-depth use of the TAPI functions in VB requires an investment in time and patience as well as a certain amount of skill in using C functions.

The good news is that many third-party components are now on the market that make TAPI development much easier. Several are listed in Chapter 50, "Third-Party Controls." It's recommended that you at least consider purchasing one of these products if you plan to do any serious TAPI development.

This chapter will introduce you to the basics of using the TAPI library directly. A sample application that initiates a TAPI-based phone call will be created so that you can see exactly how a TAPI session can be constructed in Visual Basic.

How It Works

The TAPI library acts as a layer between an application and the physical telephone line, be it POTS, ISDN, T1, or PBX, analog or digital. In fact, TAPI can communicate with multiple telephone lines (called *line devices*) simultaneously and can merge two. For example, a voice line can be merged with a fax line to create fax-on-demand services through a voice mail system.

TAPI can also communicate with *phone devices*, which are telephones emulated by PCs. The Windows Phone Dialer is an example of a simple phone device because it emulates a telephone and can be used with physical phone lines attached to the system.

At times, other components are also used by TAPI. For example, call managers are programs that actually establish a connection with a line device and also communicate with TAPI to provide that service to other applications. In addition to being a phone device, the Windows Phone Dialer can also be used as a call manager.

TAPI has various levels of service, depending on the type of telephony operations required and the type of communication medium being used. *Basic Telephony* provides only a minimum of functions that can be used on POTS lines. *Supplementary Telephony* includes more advanced services, such as call holding, transferring, and conferencing. Finally, *Extended Telephony* are extensions to the TAPI library and are particular to a specific TAPI service provider.

There are many different levels to TAPI, and many different aspects of how it communicates with devices and applications. A more detailed description is beyond the scope of this chapter. However, you can find several resources on the Internet and on Microsoft's Web site that discuss how the TAPI system works.

NOTE

As of this writing, the current working version of TAPI was 2.1. However, TAPI 3.0 will be included with Windows NT 5. For more information about the new version, see Microsoft's Web site at `http://www.microsoft.com/communications/tapilearn30.htm`.

Types of TAPI Applications

There are basically two types of TAPI applications: Full Telephony and Assisted Telephony. Full Telephony applications do not require additional components (other than the TAPI library) to utilize TAPI services. This is because Full Telephony applications operate at a lower level and have to call more basic TAPI functions to establish and manage TAPI sessions.

Assisted Telephony applications require components or programs such as call managers in order to use TAPI services. These applications work at a higher level and are easier to program because there isn't as much overhead required for managing TAPI sessions.

To illustrate the difference between a Full Telephony and an Assisted Telephony application, consider the steps each needs to take to establish a TAPI session and make a phone call. A Full Telephony application would have to do the following:

- Call the `lineInitialize` function to start the TAPI session.
- Call the `lineNegotiateAPIVersion` function to establish that the correct TAPI services are installed and are being used.
- Call the `lineOpen` to connect to the appropriate line device.
- Set up the necessary calling parameters in the `LINECALLPARAMS` structure.
- Call the `lineMakeCall` function to dial a phone number.

In addition to the preceding steps, you would also have to write a callback function to be used with the `lineInitialize` function.

In an Assisted Telephony application, you need only pass four arguments to the `tapiRequestMakeCall` function. The call manager (a separate program) does everything else for you. The sample program shows how to create an Assisted Telephony application using `tapiRequestMakeCall`.

Creating a TAPI Application

In this section, you'll build an Assisted Telephony application in Visual Basic that will start a TAPI session by dialing a given phone number. The dialing will actually be done by another program, the Windows Phone Dialer utility. The VB program will also end the session. You can then "fill in the blanks" and use other TAPI functions during the session.

Before you can begin building the program, you'll need to make sure that you have the necessary components. Read the following section to see whether you have everything you need or need to download something that is missing.

What You'll Need

In Windows 95 and certain versions of Windows NT, the TAPI library is not included. However, it can be downloaded from Microsoft's Web site for free. The file, `TAPI21.EXE`, can be found at `http://www.microsoft.com/communications/telephony.htm`.

`TAPI21.EXE` is a self-extracting archive. When you run it, it will ask you the name of the directory to which its files will be extracted. When the file extraction is finished, the directory will contain additional executable programs that install the TAPI library on different operating system platforms. For example, the file `TAPI2195.EXE` is the TAPI implementation for Windows 95, and `TAPI21NT.EXE` is TAPI for Windows NT. Install whichever one is appropriate for your system, but first consult the `README.TXT` file in the same directory. It will give you specific information on how to install TAPI.

If you'll be using TAPI through an ordinary modem, you may also need to download Unimodem, a driver that converts TAPI functions to standard AT modem commands. It also functions as a TAPI service provider. You can find it at `http://www.microsoft.com/hwdev/devdes/modemddk.htm`.

For the example included in this chapter, you'll also need the Windows Phone Dialer utility. This is included with Windows 95 and should be found in the Accessories group.

A Sample Program

Now that you're sure that you have all the necessary components, you can start building the sample program. Invoke Visual Basic and start a new project (Standard EXE).

The first thing you need to do to build the sample TAPI session is to design a user interface. Use Figure 34.1 and Table 34.1 as a guide for adding the controls to the form and changing their properties.

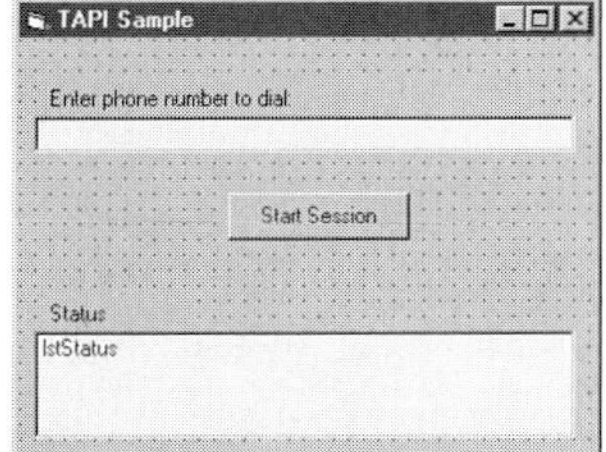

FIGURE 34.1.
The user interface for the sample TAPI application.

Table 34.1. The controls and their properties for the sample TAPI application's user interface.

Control Type	*Property*	*Value*
Form	`Name`	`frmTAPITest`
	`Caption`	`TAPI Sample`
	`Height`	`3210`
	`StartUpPosition`	`2 - Center Screen`
	`Width`	`4605`
Label	`Name`	`lblEnterPhone`
	`Caption`	`Enter phone number to dial:`
	`Height`	`255`
	`Left`	`240`
	`Top`	`360`
	`Width`	`3855`
TextBox	`Name`	`txtPhoneNum`
	`Height`	`285`
	`Left`	`120`
	`Top`	`600`
	`Width`	`4335`

continues

Table 34.1. continued

Control Type	Property	Value
CommandButton	Name	cmdStartSession
	Caption	Start Session
	Height	375
	Left	1680
	Top	1200
	Width	1455
Label	Name	lblStatus
	Height	255
	Left	240
	Top	2040
	Width	1095
ListBox	Name	lstStatus
	Height	840
	Left	120
	Top	2280
	Width	4335

After the user interface has been designed, a module needs to be added to the project so that the TAPI functions can be declared. Add a module to the project; then add the code in Listing 34.1 to the module.

Listing 34.1. The function declaration for `tapiRequestMakeCall`, plus some global error constants—to be placed into a module.

```
Declare Function tapiRequestMakeCall Lib "tapi32" _
    (ByVal lpszDestAddress As String, _
     ByVal lpszAppName As String, _
     ByVal lpszCalledParty As String, _
     ByVal lpszComment As String) As Long

Global Const TAPIERR_CONNECTED = 0&
Global Const TAPIERR_DROPPED = -1&
Global Const TAPIERR_NOREQUESTRECIPIENT = -2&
Global Const TAPIERR_REQUESTQUEUEFULL = -3&
Global Const TAPIERR_INVALDESTADDRESS = -4&
Global Const TAPIERR_INVALWINDOWHANDLE = -5&
Global Const TAPIERR_INVALDEVICECLASS = -6&
Global Const TAPIERR_INVALDEVICEID = -7&
Global Const TAPIERR_DEVICECLASSUNAVAIL = -8&
```

```
Global Const TAPIERR_DEVICEIDUNAVAIL = -9&
Global Const TAPIERR_DEVICEINUSE = -10&
Global Const TAPIERR_DESTBUSY = -11&
Global Const TAPIERR_DESTNOANSWER = -12&
Global Const TAPIERR_DESTUNAVAIL = -13&
Global Const TAPIERR_UNKNOWNWINHANDLE = -14&
Global Const TAPIERR_UNKNOWNREQUESTID = -15&
Global Const TAPIERR_REQUESTFAILED = -16&
Global Const TAPIERR_REQUESTCANCELLED = -17&
Global Const TAPIERR_INVALPOINTER = -18&
```

The code in the module also includes several global constants for the TAPI error conditions. Many of these won't be used in the sample program, but you'll want to add them anyway. If you start experimenting with other TAPI functions, it will help to know exactly the error that is being returned. A `Sub` procedure that will be added later will use these constants to display the TAPI error that occurred.

The next section of code to add is for the `cmdStartSession` CommandButton's `Click` event (see Listing 34.2). This is where the TAPI session will be started, and where the `tapiRequestMakeCall` function will be called.

Listing 34.2. The code for the TAPI sample program. When the Start Session button is clicked, the `tapiRequestMakeCall` function is called.

```
Private Sub cmdStartSession_Click()

Dim lonTAPIStatus As Long

' Check to see if a phone number was entered.
If RTrim(txtPhoneNum.Text) = "" Then
    lstStatus.AddItem "Err: No Phone Number Entered"
    Exit Sub
Else
    strPhoneNum = RTrim(txtPhoneNum.Text)
End If

' Initiate the TAPI session with the
' tapiRequestMakeCall function.
lonTAPIStatus = tapiRequestMakeCall(strPhoneNum, _
    "TAPI Sample", strPhoneNum, "")

' Report the status.
Call TAPIStatus(lonTAPIStatus)

End Sub
```

Note that after the `tapiRequestMakeCall` function is called, another routine named `TAPIStatus` (see Listing 34.3) is also called. This is used to sort out the different TAPI error codes and report back (in the `lblStatus` ListBox) a readable error message. This routine will be handy if you go farther with TAPI and start using the other TAPI functions.

Listing 34.3. The TAPIStatus Sub procedure, which is used to report the status of a TAPI function call.

```
Private Sub TAPIStatus(lonStatCode As Long)

' Based on the TAPI status code (passed to this
' procedure in lonStatCode), add an appropriate message
' to the lstStatus ListBox.
Select Case lonStatCode
    Case TAPIERR_CONNECTED
        lstStatus.AddItem "Ok"
    Case TAPIERR_DROPPED
        lstStatus.AddItem "Dropped"
    Case TAPIERR_NOREQUESTRECIPIENT
        lstStatus.AddItem "Err: No Request Recipient"
    Case TAPIERR_REQUESTQUEUEFULL
        lstStatus.AddItem "Err: Request Queue Full"
    Case TAPIERR_INVALDESTADDRESS
        lstStatus.AddItem "Err: Destination Address Invalid"
    Case TAPIERR_INVALWINDOWHANDLE
        lstStatus.AddItem "Err: Window Handle Invalid"
    Case TAPIERR_INVALDEVICECLASS
        lstStatus.AddItem "Err: Device Class Invalid"
    Case TAPIERR_INVALDEVICEID
        lstStatus.AddItem "Err: Device Class ID"
    Case TAPIERR_DEVICECLASSUNAVAIL
        lstStatus.AddItem "Err: Device Class Unavailable"
    Case TAPIERR_DEVICEIDUNAVAIL
        lstStatus.AddItem "Err: Device ID Unavailable"
    Case TAPIERR_DESTBUSY
        lstStatus.AddItem "Destination Busy"
    Case TAPIERR_DESTUNAVAIL
        lstStatus.AddItem "Destination Unavailable"
    Case TAPIERR_UNKNOWNWINHANDLE
        lstStatus.AddItem "Err: Unknown Windows Handle"
    Case TAPIERR_UNKNOWNREQUESTID
        lstStatus.AddItem "Err: Unknown Request ID"
    Case TAPIERR_REQUESTFAILED
        lstStatus.AddItem "Err: Request Failed"
    Case TAPIERR_REQUESTCANCELLED
        lstStatus.AddItem "Err: Request Cancelled"
    Case TAPIERR_INVALPOINTER
        lstStatus.AddItem "Err: Invalid Pointer"
End Select

End Sub
```

Before you run the program, make sure that you load in the Windows Phone Dialer utility (look for it in Windows's Accessories group). That program will act as the call manager and will handle the dialing of the phone number that is passed to the `tapiRequestMakeCall` function.

Running the program will invoke the call manager, which dials the number entered in the `txtPhoneNum` TextBox. Figure 34.2 shows the TAPI sample program and the Windows Phone Dialer.

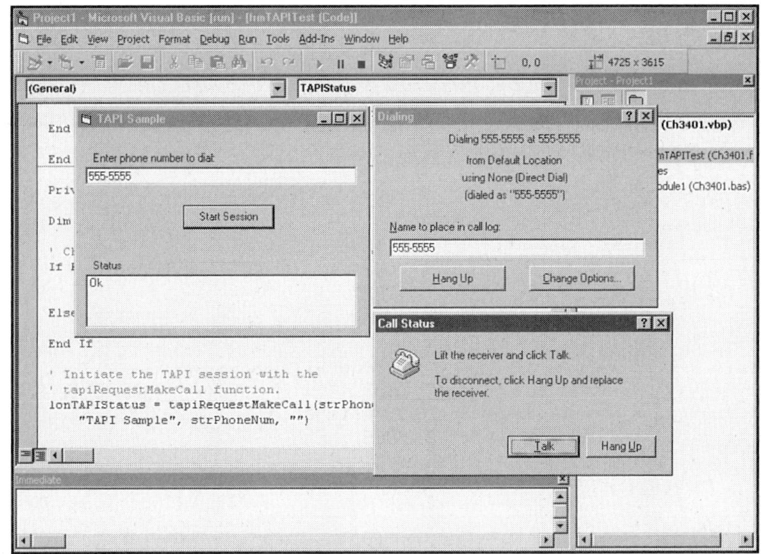

FIGURE 34.2.
The TAPI sample program in action, using the Windows Phone Dialer as a call manager.

The sample program gets you started with using the TAPI library. You can now use the other TAPI functions to start building more complex telephony applications.

Other TAPI Functions

The `tapiRequestMakeCall` function used in the sample program is just one of the more than 100 functions in the TAPI library. Although it does establish a TAPI connection, it cannot be used to access media streams. Instead, the `tapiRequestMediaCall` function should be used. The function definition for `tapiRequestMediaCall` is as follows:

```
Declare Function tapiRequestMediaCall Lib "tapi" _
    (ByVal hWnd As Long, ByVal wRequestID As Long, _
    ByVal lpszDeviceClass As String, _
    ByVal lpDeviceID As String, ByVal dwSize As String, _
    ByVal dwSecure As Long, ByVal lpszDestAddress As String, _
    ByVal lpszAppName As String, _
    ByVal lpszCalledParty As String, _
    ByVal lpszComment As String) As Long
```

There are many more functions in the TAPI library. If you want to learn more about how TAPI works, access Microsoft's Web site and search for "TAPI." Another good reference source is the *MAPI, SAPI, & TAPI Developer's Guide*, also published by Sams Publishing.

Summary

Telephony has become a buzzword in the last few years. As communication media improve and newer and faster protocols are devised, the marriage between the computer and the telephone will become more commonplace.

Microsoft's TAPI library allows PC developers to take advantage of some impressive telephony operations. However, in its current implementation, TAPI is not very easy to use for Visual Basic programmers. Third-party vendors offer controls that will ease the TAPI development process and should be strongly considered.

This chapter introduced TAPI and showed how to create an Assisted Telephony application that uses a call manager to dial a phone number. This simple application can act as a starting point for anyone who wants to further explore the TAPI library.

CHAPTER 35

Visual Basic and Office 97

IN THIS CHAPTER

Although Visual Basic is a powerful language, there are times when the components that you need already exist in another application. Instead of having to recode such components, it is sometimes possible to "borrow" them from another application.

All the applications in the Microsoft Office suite are based on object libraries that contain many external components. For example, Microsoft Excel makes available object types such as Worksheets and Charts. You can use these object types in your Visual Basic programs using the OLE container control or OLE automation.

The OLE container control can be used to link or embed objects directly into your programs. For instance, you can have a Microsoft Word document displayed in a window on a form. The document can be edited by double-clicking on the window. This allows you to implement the full functionality of the complex Word application with little or no coding.

OLE automation gives you access to the hundreds of object classes that were used to build the Microsoft Office applications. You can use these classes just as you would the classes that you create yourself.

This chapter introduces you to the OLE control and OLE automation. With even a basic understanding of how OLE objects can be used, you will be able to utilize an extraordinary number of new program components and object classes.

OLE

OLE is a cornerstone of both the Windows operating system and Visual Basic. It provides a way for applications to communicate with one another and to share each other's components. For example, you can add the functionality of the various Office 97 applications (for example,Word and Excel) right into your own Visual Basic programs. This is easily accomplished by using OLE technology.

OLE used to be short for "Object Linking and Embedding," and that is a large part of what OLE does—it allows objects (documents) to be linked to or embedded into applications. It also does much more than that (which is why OLE no longer stands for the restrictive "Object Linking and Embedding" description), but those are the functions that will be discussed in this chapter. From a programmer's point of view, linking and embedding allow you to add an object, such as a Word document or an Excel spreadsheet, into your application without having to do a lot of extra coding to support it. In fact, an OLE object can be completely self-sufficient and not require a single line of code, as you'll see by following some of the examples given in this chapter.

Although linking and embedding both allow the functionality of one application (the *server*) to be added to another application (the *container*), they each go about it differently. When an object is linked, the container application is given a *reference* to the object rather than the object itself. This way, the data can be shared simultaneously with more than one application. If a change is made to the data in one application, any other applications that share the same data will also show the change. On the other side of the coin, embedded objects (and their data) actually exist within the container application. If the data is changed, any other applications that contain copies of the same data will not show the change. You'll see examples of both linked and embedded objects later in this chapter.

This may sound like cutting edge technology, but OLE is nothing new. In fact, its beginnings go all the way back to 1991. Over the years, OLE has been refined and enhanced, resulting in the current version (2.0). In addition to linking and embedding documents within applications, OLE now deals with many more issues, such as object storage and reuse. The ActiveX controls in VB's Toolbox are based on OLE technology. In fact, the `.OCX` extension given to ActiveX components stands for "OLE Custom Control" because they communicate via 32-bit OLE interfaces. Controls in previous versions of Visual Basic (VBXes) were not based on OLE and used the Windows messaging services for communication.

Although it is not discussed in this chapter, there is another way for objects to communicate with each other. DDE, which stands for Dynamic Data Exchange, also provides a way for data and functions to be shared between applications. However, DDE, an older technology, is far more limited than OLE and should not be used unless OLE is for some reason not supported.

In Visual Basic, OLE objects can be used in two different ways. The first is through the OLE control, which allows an object to be embedded (or linked) into a Visual Basic program. The other way is through OLE automation, which accesses objects directly and lets you manipulate them from within your VB programs. Both the OLE control and OLE automation will be covered in this chapter.

The OLE Control

Visual Basic supports OLE linking and embedding via its OLE control. Using this control, you can add the functionality of complex programs, such as Word and Excel, directly into your programs with a minimum of effort. The best way to understand how the OLE control works is to see it in action, so the first thing you'll do is create a program that contains linked and embedded objects.

This example will embed a Microsoft Word document into a Visual Basic program. For the program to work, you must have Microsoft Word installed on your system. Although OLE allows you to "borrow" the functionality of other applications (servers) and use it in your own programs (containers), the server application must be present on the system on which you are running the container program.

NOTE

If you don't have Microsoft Word, you can substitute any other kind of linkable object available on your system. This will be discussed in just a moment.

To create the sample program, start a new project (Standard EXE). Use Table 35.1 as a guide for placing the controls on the form and building the program.

Table 35.1. The controls (and their property values) that make up the OLE test project.

Control Type	*Property*	*Value*
Form	`Name`	`frmOLETest`
	`Caption`	`OLE Test`
	`Height`	`6030`
	`StartUpPosition`	`2 - Center Screen`
	`Width`	`7215`
CommandButton	`Name`	`cmdSave`
	`Caption`	`Save`
	`Height`	`495`
	`Left`	`3000`
	`Top`	`4680`
	`Width`	`1215`
OLE	`Name`	`oleObject`
	`Height`	`4185`
	`Left`	`390`
	`Top`	`240`
	`Width`	`6435`

Note that when you place the OLE control on the form, you will see the Insert Object dialog box, shown in Figure 35.1.

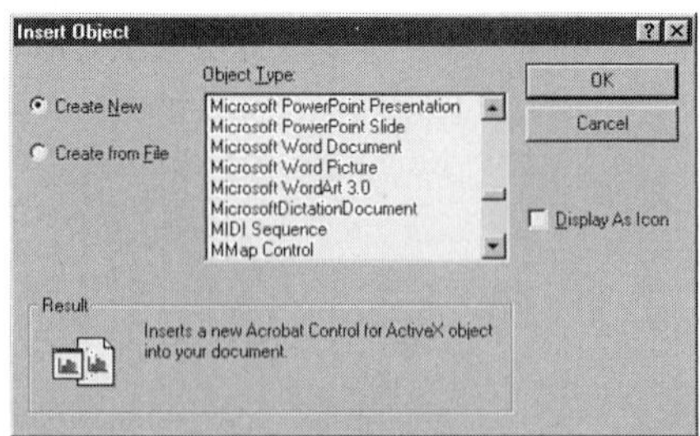

FIGURE 35.1.
The Insert Object dialog box, which appears automatically whenever an OLE control is added to a form.

The Insert Object dialog box provides a list of all object types available on your system (your list will most likely be different from the one shown in Figure 35.1). You are also given two options for inserting the object: Create New or Create from File. If you select the Create New option, an object with no data (a new object) will be embedded into your application. If you select the Create from File option, a specific object will be inserted. For this example, select Create from File.

When you select the Create from File option, the list of embeddable objects disappears, and you are asked to specify a filename. You can use any file you want, but for this example, the Microsoft Word document `OLETEST.DOC`, which can be found on the CD that accompanies this book, will be used.

After you specify the file to be used, click the Insert button. You will be returned to the Insert Object dialog box. For now, leave the Display As Icon option unchecked. You'll learn more about it in just a moment. Click OK to insert the object.

You should then see a copy of the object (`OLETEST.DOC` or whatever file you specified) inside the OLE control (see Figure 35.2). You can now finish changing the OLE control's properties as shown in Table 35.1.

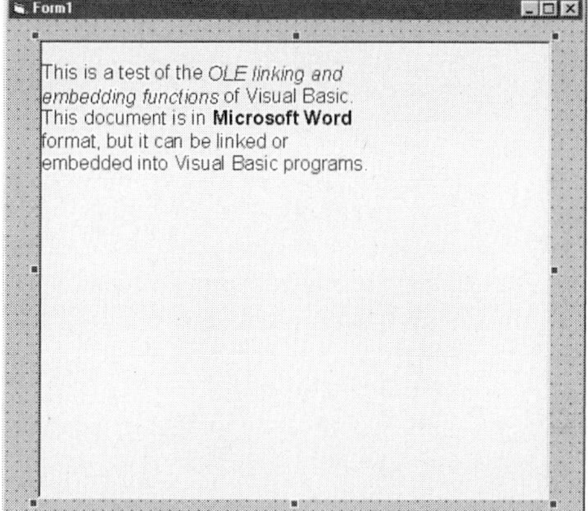

FIGURE 35.2.
An embedded object (Microsoft Word file `OLETEST.DOC`*) inside an OLE control.*

Go ahead and run the program. The object still appears in the OLE control, no surprise there. But double-click on the OLE control and see what happens. You are allowed to edit the object (in this case, a Word document) right from within your application. Essentially, you've embedded a copy of the object, along with the server application that it belongs to, in your own application (see Figure 35.3).

Notice also that after the document has been activated (by double-clicking on it), your application is provided with a menu bar, which it did not have before. These menu options are taken directly from Word and can be used to make changes to the document, just as they would if you had loaded the document into Word and edited that way.

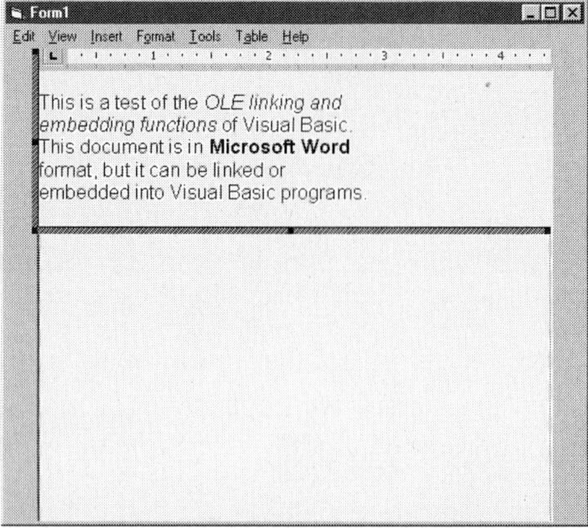

FIGURE 35.3.
Editing the embedded object from within the running VB application.

NOTE

If your application already has a menu bar and an embedded object is activated, it will merge its menu options with those of your application.

You can make as many changes as you want to the embedded document, but you'll find that there is no way to save them because Word's File menu is missing. Why is that?

When you embed an object in Visual Basic, you have to use VB code to save changes to the object. This is accomplished using the OLE control's SaveToFile method.

Exit the program and then add the code in Listing 35.1 to the `cmdSave` CommandButton's `Click` event.

Listing 35.1. The `cmdSave_Click` event, which saves the data of the `oleObject` OLE container control.

```
Private Sub cmdSave_Click()

Dim intFileNum As Integer

' Get the next available file number.
intFileNum = FreeFile

' Open a binary file with the name of the embedded
' object (oleObject.SourceDoc) and write out the
' object's data to that file using the OLE control's
' SaveToFile method.
If oleObject.OLEType = vbOLEEmbedded Then
   Open oleObject.SourceDoc For Binary As #intFileNum
   oleObject.SaveToFile intFileNum
   Close #intFileNum
End If

End Sub
```

In the preceding code, the `SaveToFile` method is used only if the object is embedded rather than linked (`oleObject.OLEType = vb.OLEEmbedded`). `SaveToFile` works with linked objects too (`oleObject.OLEtype = vb.OLELinked`), but it doesn't save the object's data. Instead, it saves the link information and an image of the data to the file.

To save the object's data to a file, you need to open a binary file, call the `SaveToFile` method, and then close the file. The filename used in the preceding procedure comes from the OLE control's `SourceDoc` property, which contains the name of the file specified in the Insert Object dialog box.

NOTE

If you want to save the object in OLE version 1.0 format, use the `SaveToOle1File` method in place of `SaveToFile`.

If you run the program again, make some changes to the embedded object, and then click the Save button, the object's data will be saved. You can verify this by stopping the program and running it again. When the object data is loaded in, it should include the changes that you made.

To try some other variations of embedded objects, stop the program and then right-click the `oleObject` OLE control. You will see a pop-up menu of options. Choose Insert Object and the Insert Object dialog box opens.

Once again, choose the Create from File option and specify the `OLETEST.DOC` file (or any other object). Then make sure that the Link option is checked. Click OK, and you should see a message that asks you whether you want to delete the current embedded object (see Figure 35.4). Choose Yes.

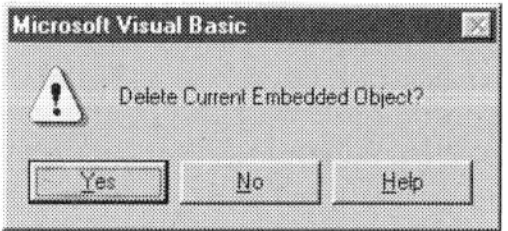

FIGURE 35.4.
After selecting a new object from the Insert Object dialog box, you are asked whether you want to delete the current embedded object.

You now have a linked object contained in your application. It may look the same as an embedded object, but as you'll soon see, it acts differently.

Run the program; then double-click the object. Instead of being able to edit the object within your application, the object's server application (in this case, Microsoft Word) is invoked. The object can then be edited and saved within the server application. When the file is saved, it is automatically updated in your application.

Stop the program; then go back to the Insert Object dialog box by right-clicking the `oleObject` control and choosing Insert Object from the pop-up menu. Choose the Create from File option; then specify the same file you've been working with. This time, leave the Link option unchecked, but check the Display As Icon option. Click OK to accept your choices.

You'll get another prompt, but this time it asks whether you want to delete the current link. Remember, a linked object is only a reference to an object and not the object itself. The last object that was inserted into the application was linked, not embedded. So you are asked whether you want to delete the link rather than the embedded object. Choose Yes.

Because you selected the Display As Icon option, you'll see an icon rather than the object's data (see Figure 35.5). If you run the program and double-click the icon, the object's server application will again be invoked, and the object can be edited (and saved). The Display As Icon option is useful if you don't want to actually display an object's data but still want the user to be able to edit it indirectly through your program.

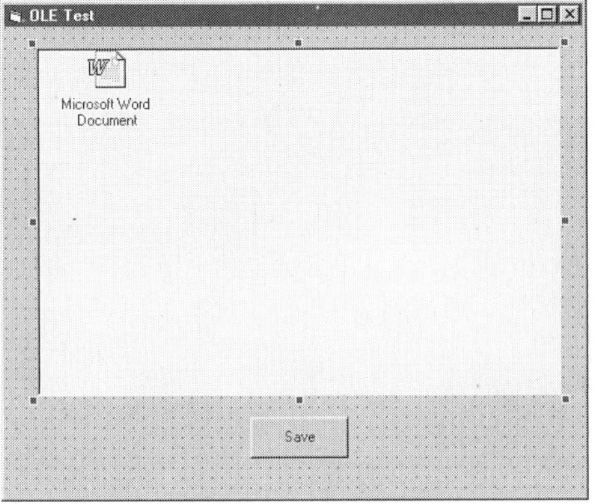

FIGURE 35.5.
An embedded Word document with the Display As Icon option selected.

If you don't want to embed an existing object, you can use the Create New option on the Insert Object dialog box. This will embed a blank object in the OLE container control. It's basically the same as using the Create from File option, but because it's a new file, there isn't any data associated with it. Figure 35.6 shows an embedded Microsoft Excel Chart object.

Along with the chart is a toolbar that allows you to specify how the chart will look. For example, you can choose the type of chart displayed by using the Chart Type pull-down icon. When the program is run, the toolbar will disappear. It reappears when the user double-clicks the embedded object to make it active.

There are probably dozens of different embeddable object types available on your system. You can use any of them in your programs, but keep in mind that the object's server application must be present on each user's system if you plan to distribute your programs. So if you choose to use Microsoft Excel charts in your application, you must be sure that anyone who uses the application also has Microsoft Excel installed on her system.

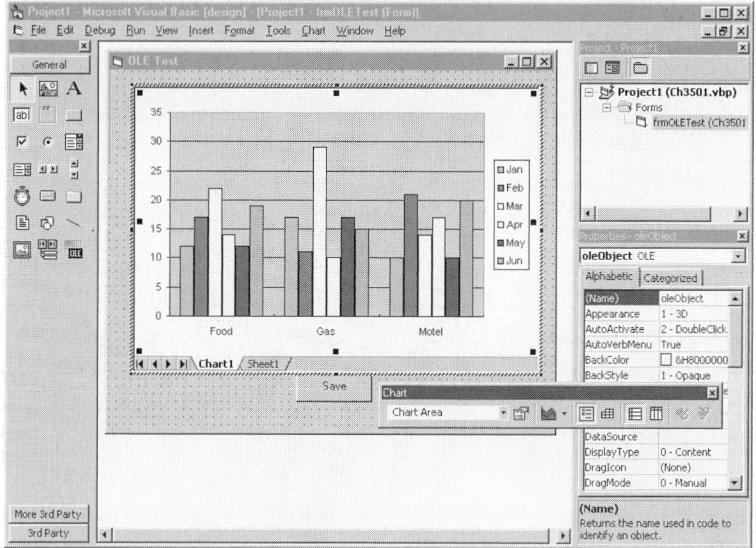

FIGURE 35.6.
An embedded Microsoft Excel Chart object.

OLE Control Properties and Methods

Like any other ActiveX control, the OLE container control has properties that can be used to specify how it looks and acts. It also has a few methods that can be called to accomplish certain tasks. This section gives brief descriptions of some of the more important properties and methods of the OLE container control.

Objects often have many operations that can be performed on them. These are called *verbs*. If you right-click an embedded object at runtime, the pop-up menu that appears will show all the valid verbs for the object. For example, if you run the program with the embedded Microsoft Excel Chart object and right-click the object, the pop-up menu contains two options (verbs): Open and Edit. The Open verb opens the object's server application (in this case, Microsoft Excel) and displays the object's data. The Edit verb allows the chart to be edited within the OLE container control, just as if you had double-clicked the object. You can disable the pop-up verb menu by setting the `AutoVerbMenu` property to `False`. A setting of `True` enables the pop-up menu (the default).

You can obtain a list of all of an object's valid verbs using the `ObjectVerbs` and `ObjectVerbsCount` properties. `ObjectVerbs` is a zero-based string array that contains all the supported verbs for the object, and `ObjectVerbsCount` specifies the number of elements in the `ObjectVerbs` array (minus one). The default verb for the object is always contained in `ObjectVerbs(0)`. The `ObjectVerbFlags` property can be used to determine the menu state of a verb when passed its element number in the `ObjectVerbs` array. Possible values are `vbOLEFlagChecked (&H0008)`, `vbOLEFlagDisabled (&H0002)`, `vbOLEFlagEnabled (&H0000)`, `vbOLEFlagGrayed (&H0001)`, and `vbOLEFlagSeparator (&H0800)`. To update the list of verbs that an object supports, call the `FetchVerbs` method.

If you want to cause an object to perform the operation associated with one of its supported verbs, you can use the `DoVerb` method. The `DoVerb` method takes only one argument, and that is a numeric value that indicates the verb to be performed. Possible values for the argument are: `vbOLEShow (-1)`, `vbOLEOpen (-2)`, `vbOLEHide (-3)`, `vbOLEUIActivate (-4)`, `vbOLEInPlaceActivate (-5)`, and `vbOLEDiscardUndoState (-6)`. If you want to perform the operation for the object's default verb, either call the `DoVerb` method without an argument or use the value `vbOLEPrimary (0)`.

The `AutoActivate` property specifies how an object can become activated. The default value is `vbOLEActivateDoubleclick (2)`, which means that the user needs to double-click the object to activate it. However, you can change this property to `vbOLEActivateManual (0)`, which means that you must call the `DoVerb` method to activate the object; `vbOLEActivateGetFocus (1)`, which activates an object when it receives the focus (by single-clicking on it); or `vbOLEActiveAuto (3)`, which activates an object when it gets the focus or when it is double clicked.

If you want to check to see whether an object's server application is running, then examine the value of the `AppIsRunning` property. A value of `True` indicates that the server application is running. The `AppIsRunning` property is only available at runtime.

To specify how the object appears within the OLE container control, use the `SizeMode` property. The default value (`vbOLESizeClip, 0`) indicates that the object is displayed actual size. If the OLE control is too small to display all the data, the data is clipped. You can change this property to `vbOLESizeStretch (1)`, which resizes the object so that it will fit within the OLE control; `vbOLESizeAutoSize (2)`, which resizes the OLE control automatically to fit all of the object; and `vbOLESizeZoom (3)`, which resizes the object to fit the container control the best it can while still maintaining the object's original proportions.

As you saw earlier in this chapter, a linked object is updated whenever it is changed by its server application. The `UpdateOptions` property can be used to change when and how linked data gets updated. The default is `vbOLEAutomatic (0)`, which means that the object is updated whenever its data changes. Other possible values are `vbOLEFrozen (1)`, which indicates that the data should only be updated when its linked data is saved by the server application; or `vbOLEManual (2)`, which indicates that the data should only be updated when the OLE control's `Update` method is called. Keep in mind that the `UpdateOptions` property only works for linked objects, not embedded objects.

If you only want to display a specific section of an object's data rather than all the data, you can use the `SourceItem` property. For example, if you only wanted the OLE control to contain a range of cells for an Excel spreadsheet, you might set the `SourceItem` property to `R1C1:R5C5`. This would display only the cells in rows 1 through 5 and columns 1 through 5. Of course, the type of information that you use with the `SourceItem` property depends on the type of object you are dealing with.

Finally, if you want to display the Insert Object dialog box, call the OLE control's `InsertObjDlg` method. This will allow the user to specify the type of object that should be contained by the OLE control.

OLE Automation

Another way to integrate Microsoft Office and other applications' components into your own programs is by using OLE automation. OLE automation does not require that you use the OLE control. Instead, you define objects of different classes in your code.

Before you can use OLE automation, you need to know the class of the object that you want to use. The easiest way to list available classes on your system is to use the References dialog box (see Figure 35.7). Choose Project | References from VB's menu. You will be shown a list of object libraries available on your system. Simply check the ones you want to use; then click OK.

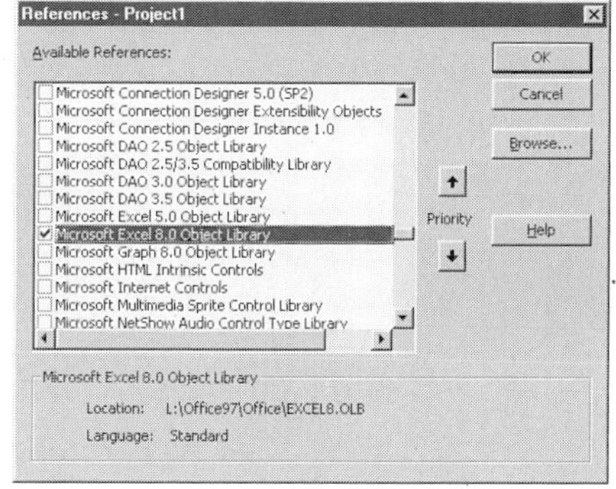

FIGURE 35.7.
The References dialog box, which lists available OLE object libraries on your system.

In this example, the Microsoft Excel 8.0 object library will be used. This object library contains a number of Excel-specific objects that can be used by the VB programmer.

To see the objects now available to you, use VB's Object Browser (see Figure 35.8). Press F2 to display the Object Browser.

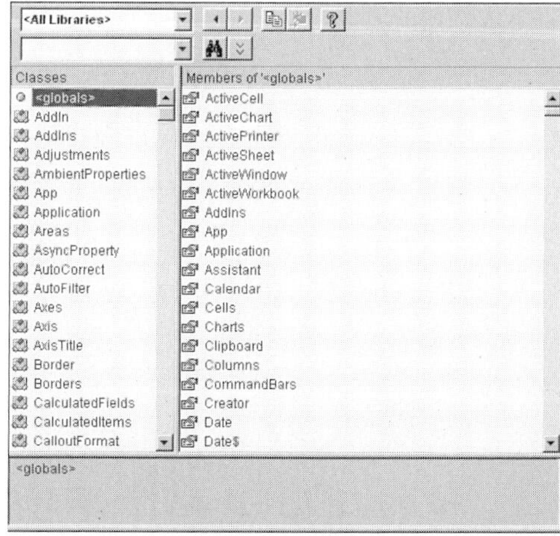

FIGURE 35.8.
The Object Browser, which can be used to display the objects available in all referenced object libraries.

By default, the Object Browser shows all the objects in all the object libraries referenced by your project. This can be a little confusing because you only want to see the objects available from the Excel 8.0 object library. Use the Object Browser's top list box to select Excel so that only the Excel objects will be shown.

You should now have a list of objects in the Excel 8.0 object library (see Figure 35.9). As you can see, quite a few objects are still available to you just from this one library. These are the object classes that the Excel application uses. The classes are defined as public, so they are exposed to outside applications, such as your Visual Basic programs.

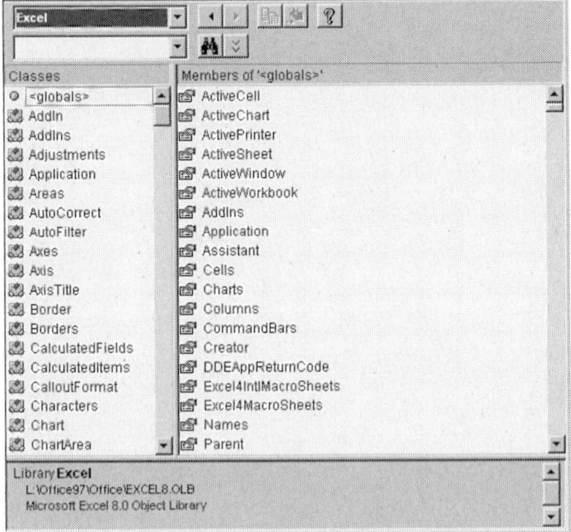

FIGURE 35.9.
The Object Browser, showing only the objects exposed by the Excel 8.0 object library.

If you select one of the object classes, such as `Worksheet`, you will see the list of properties, methods, and events for that class. After you look at some of the object classes in an object library, it becomes obvious that OLE automation can provide your programs with an incredible number of complex prewritten software components. However, keep in mind that you cannot use these classes in your programs if your users do not also have the object library installed on their systems (that is, if they do not have Microsoft Excel on their systems).

So how do you use these object classes in your programs? Simple: Declare an object variable of a particular class just as you would any other object. For example, the following line of code

```
Dim objSpread As New Worksheet
```

declares the variable `objSpread` to be of class type `Worksheet`, which was one of the object classes exposed in the Excel 8.0 object library. You must have established a reference to the object library you will be using before using any classes from that library. We established a reference to the Excel library earlier by using the References dialog box.

Declaring an object this way is known as *early binding* because the compiler knows the type of object that the variable will hold when the program is compiled. Objects can also be declared using *late binding*, where the variable is declared as type `Object`, but the actual class is not specified. For example, the Excel `Worksheet` object (`objSpread`) declared previously could also be declared by using the following code:

```
Dim objSpread As Object
Set objSpread = CreateObject("Excel.Worksheet")
```

The variable is declared to be of type `Object` and then is assigned an actual object type by using the `CreateObject` statement. Late binding is appropriate if you don't know an object's class when the variable that holds it is declared. However, you should try to use early binding whenever possible because it is more efficient.

After an object has been declared by using either early or late binding, you may want to load some existing data into the object. This is accomplished using the `GetObject` statement. For example, to declare an object to be of Microsoft Word's `Document` class and to load in the `OLETEST.DOC` document used in earlier examples, the following code might be used:

```
Dim objDocument As New Word.Document
Set objDocument = GetObject("OLETest.doc")
```

The `GetObject` statement can also be used to define the class of the object while also specifying its data, such as:

```
Dim objDocument As Object
Set objDocument = GetObject("OLETest.doc", Word.Document)
```

After you've defined an object, you can use its properties, methods, and events to specify how it should look and what it should do. Because of the complexity of the Microsoft Office object libraries and their many object classes, a discussion of how to use individual components is beyond the scope of this chapter. Because the Office components are used the same way through OLE automation as they are in VBA, a comprehensive book on VBA is recommended for more information.

When you are finished using an object, you should close it (using a `Quit` or `Close` method works for some objects) and set the object to `Nothing`. This will free up any system resources that the object may have been using.

Using OLE Automation

To illustrate how OLE automation works, the following sample program can be constructed. It uses two objects, one of the `Word.Application` class and one of the `Word.Document` class. Together, they are used to display an instance of the Word application and a new document. The application will be displayed on the screen, and the document will be given some text. Command buttons in the sample program will allow the document's data to be saved and the application to be closed.

Start a new project (Standard EXE) and add a new module. In the module's General Declarations section, add the following lines of code:

```
Public objWordApp As New Word.Application
Public objWordDoc As Object
```

This will declare the two objects that will be used in the program. One (`objWordApp`) will be early bound, and one (`objWordDoc`) will be late bound.

To build the program's user interface, go back to the project's form and use Table 35.2 and Figure 35.10 as a guide for adding the various components and changing their properties.

Table 35.2. The components that make up the OLE automation sample program.

Control Type	*Property*	*Value*
Form	`Name`	`frmOLEAuto`
	`Caption`	`OLE Automation`
	`ControlBox`	`False`
	`Height`	`2805`
	`StartUpPosition`	`2 - CenterScreen`
	`Width`	`1560`
CommandButton	`Name`	`cmdLaunch`
	`Caption`	`Launch App`
	`Height`	`495`
	`Left`	`180`
	`Top`	`165`
	`Width`	`1215`
CommandButton	`Name`	`cmdSaveDoc`
	`Caption`	`Save Doc`
	`Height`	`495`
	`Left`	`180`
	`Top`	`795`
	`Width`	`1215`
CommandButton	`Name`	`cmdCloseApp`
	`Caption`	`Close App`
	`Height`	`495`
	`Left`	`180`
	`Top`	`1425`
	`Width`	`1215`
CommandButton	`Name`	`cmdExit`
	`Caption`	`Exit`
	`Height`	`495`

Control Type	Property	Value
	Left	180
	Top	2070
	Width	1215

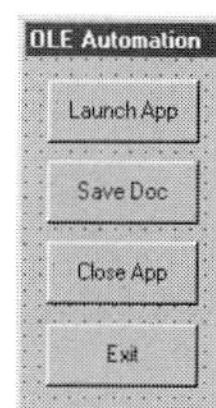

FIGURE 35.10.
The OLE automation sample program's user interface.

After the program's user interface has been created, some code needs to be added. The first section of code (see Listing 35.2) is for the first command button, which launches the Word application.

Listing 35.2. The code for the `cmdLaunch_Click` event, which launches the Word application using OLE automation.

```
Private Sub cmdLaunch_Click()

' Check to see if application has already been
' launched.
If Not (objWordDoc Is Nothing) Then
    MsgBox "Application already launched!"
    Exit Sub
End If

' Set up the size of the Word application window and
' make the app visible.
objWordApp.Width = 300
objWordApp.Height = 200
objWordApp.Left = 0
objWordApp.Top = 0
objWordApp.Visible = True

' Add a document to the Word application.
Set objWordDoc = objWordApp.Documents.Add()

' Give the document some text.
objWordDoc.Content = "This is a test"

End Sub
```

This event procedure first checks to see whether the application has already been launched. It does this by evaluating the `objWordDoc` object to see whether it is `Nothing`. If it is `Nothing`, that means it hasn't yet been assigned an object class and, consequently, that the application hasn't been launched. Note that the `objWordApp` object cannot be compared to `Nothing` because it was assigned an object type (`Word.Application`) when it was declared.

Next, the size of the Word application window and its position (upper-left corner of the screen) are specified using the `objWordApp` object's `Top`, `Left`, `Height`, and `Width` properties. Then the application is revealed by setting its `Visible` property to `True`.

A document is added to the newly launched Word application by using the `Add` method for the application's `Documents` collection (`objWordApp.Documents.Add`). This new document is represented by the `objWordDoc` object. Some content is added to the document using the `Content` property.

The rest of the command buttons' `Click` events are shown in Listing 35.3.

Listing 35.3. The `Click` events for the rest of the command buttons in the OLE automation sample program.

```
Private Sub cmdSaveDoc_Click()

' Check to see if objWordDoc is Nothing. If it is,
' then the app hasn't been launched, so nothing can be
' saved. Otherwise, use objWordDoc's Save method to
' save the document.
If objWordDoc Is Nothing Then
    MsgBox "Application not launched!"
Else
    objWordDoc.Save
End If

End Sub


Private Sub cmdCloseApp_Click()

' Check to see if objWordDoc in nothing. If it is,
' then the app cannot be closed because it hasn't yet
' been launched. Otherwise, quit the app and assign
' objWordApp and objWordDoc to Nothing to free up
' resources.
If objWordDoc Is Nothing Then
    MsgBox "Application not launched!"
Else
    objWordApp.Quit
    Set objWordDoc = Nothing
    Set objWordApp = Nothing
End If

End Sub
```

```
Private Sub cmdExit_Click()

' Check to see if objWordDoc is Nothing. If it is,
' then exit the program. Otherwise, notify the user
' that the app must be closed first.
If objWordDoc Is Nothing Then
    End
Else
    MsgBox "Close application first!"
End If

End Sub
```

In all the `Click` events, the `objWordDoc` object is checked to see whether it is `Nothing` before the rest of the procedure is executed. In the `cmdSaveDoc_Click` event, the document cannot be saved if the application has not been launched. In the `cmdCloseApp_Click` event, the application cannot be closed if it hasn't been launched. And in the `cmdExit_Click` event, the program can only be exited if the `objWordDoc` is equal to `Nothing` (indicating that the application either hasn't been launched or has been closed).

The `cmdSaveDoc_Click` event is triggered when the Save Doc command button is clicked. It uses the `objWordDoc` object's `Save` method to save the document.

The `cmdCloseApp_Click` event closes the application and is triggered when the Close App button is clicked. To close the application, the `objWordApp` object's `Quit` method is called. Then the `objWordApp` and `objWordDoc` objects are both set to `Nothing` to free up any system resources they were using.

Finally, the `cmdExit_Click` event ends the program. By the time the program ends, the application must have already been closed (if it was launched in the first place).

When you run this sample program, you should see a small form with four buttons on it. Clicking the Launch App button will launch the Word application, create a new document, and add some text to it (see Figure 35.11).

If you click the Save Doc button, you'll be asked to provide the filename of the document. If you click Cancel, the program will give you an error. That's because the program returns an error that you can trap for if the user chooses not to save the document. Otherwise, you wouldn't be able to tell whether the document was actually saved. The sample program doesn't trap for the error, so an error condition results.

The Close App button will quit the application. If the document hasn't been saved since it was last changed, you will be prompted if you want to save the document before exiting. Choose No to close the application. Click the Exit button to exit the program.

Admittedly, the sample program doesn't do much. But it does show how OLE automation can be used with Microsoft Office components (or any components, for that matter) to add extra functionality to your programs.

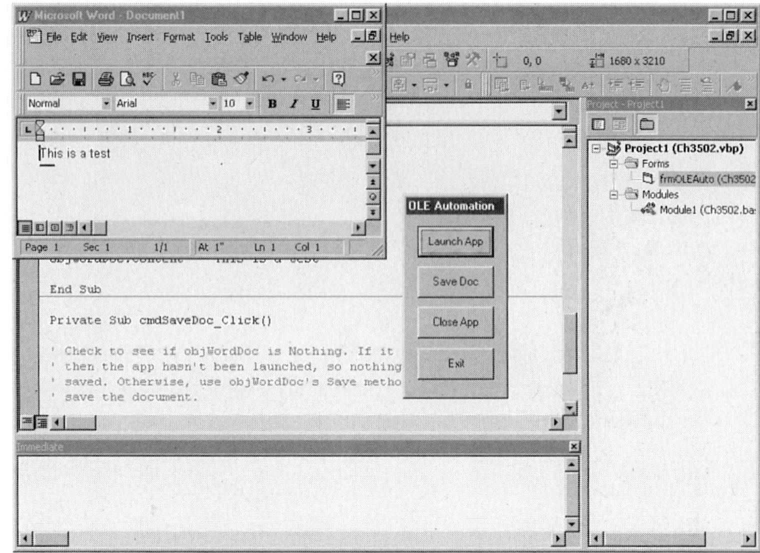

FIGURE 35.11.
The OLE automation sample program can launch the Microsoft Word application.

Summary

The Windows operating system has a built-in way of allowing components from one application to be used in another application. OLE allows an application's objects to be linked or embedded into other programs. In Visual Basic, the OLE control is used to implement linking and embedding of objects.

Another way of using an application's exposed classes (object types) is through OLE automation. OLE automation lets you use component types from applications like Microsoft Word and Excel right in your VB programs.

36

The Basics of Multimedia Programming

IN THIS CHAPTER

Now that computers are faster, they can efficiently handle the intense calculations required for multimedia. These days, mass-market programs and applications are considered to be of poor quality if they don't have flashy graphics, animation, and video. Even programs that traditionally don't use multimedia, such as Intuit's Quicken personal finance software, have been updated to include spoken help files and videos to introduce you to their many features.

Implementing multimedia—music, sound, animation, and video—into programs was quite a chore only a short time ago. Visual Basic's MMControl changed all that. This flexible and useful control makes it easy to add all kinds of multimedia to your programs.

This chapter introduces you to the MMControl object. It also shows you how to build a complete Multimedia Player application that uses MMControl to play CD audio, MIDI files, WAV files, and AVI video files.

The MMControl Object

Many different multimedia functions are provided through VB's MMControl object (an ActiveX control). Although simple to use, MMControl does many things.

The control (shown in Figure 36.1) displays several buttons that can be used to control playback and (in some cases) recording of several different multimedia file formats, including CD audio, WAV, MIDI, and AVI video. The control can also be used invisibly, with its properties, methods, and events providing all the functionality you need to play and control multimedia files.

FIGURE 36.1.
The MMControl, which allows you to play CD audio, WAV files, MIDI files, and AVI video files.

> **NOTE**
>
> If the MMControl is not in your Toolbox, then choose Project|Components from VB's menu. Scroll down until you see Microsoft Multimedia Control 5.0 and click its check box to select it. Click OK and the control will appear in your Toolbox.

If you want to try out the MMControl object, simply place it on a form. Then add the following lines of code to the `Form_Load` event:

```
MMControl1.Mode = "CDAudio"
MMControl1.Command = "Open"
MMControl1.Command = "Play"
```

You've just written a CD player application! It's that easy. Just make sure that you have an audio CD in your CD-ROM drive before you run the program. The controls on the MMControl object will let you skip tracks, pause or stop playback, and even eject the CD tray.

MMControl Object Properties

Basically, all of MMControl's functionality is accessed by setting properties. The first property set in the preceding lines of code (`Mode`) specifies the type of device that will be used, in this case `CDAudio`. Other possible values are `WaveAudio` for WAV files, `Sequencer` for MIDI files, and `AVIVideo` for AVI video files. However, many other device types are supported, such as `Scanner`, `MMMovie`, and `Videodisc`, to name a few.

When dealing with file-based multimedia, such as MIDI and WAV files, the `FileName` property needs to be set to the file's full path. For example, to play the `BACH.MID` file in the directory `C:\MUSIC`, you would use the following line of code:

```
MMControl1.Filename = "C:\Music\Bach.Mid"
```

The next property that needs to be discussed is the `Command` property. By setting `Command` to different values, you tell the MMControl object to perform certain functions. For example, to play the file, you set `Command` to `Play`. To eject the CD tray, you set `Command` to `Eject` (you must have set the `DeviceType` property to `CDAudio` first).

Clearly, `Command` is a useful property. It accepts many different values, including:

`Open`	Opens a device
`Close`	Closes a device
`Play`	Begins playback
`Pause`	Pauses playback
`Stop`	Stops playback
`Back`	Steps backward in the file
`Step`	Steps forward in the file
`Prev`	Skips to the previous track
`Next`	Skips to the next track
`Seek`	Seeks to a certain position in the file
`Record`	Records to the device
`Eject`	Ejects media
`Sound`	Plays a sound
`Save`	Saves an open file

Some commands are not valid with certain types of devices. For example, you cannot use `Eject` with a WAV file.

The easiest way to use MMControl, obviously, is to utilize its built-in buttons to control playback of files. All you need to do is set the control's `DeviceType` and `Filename` properties and then send an `Open` value to the `Command` property to open the playback device. The buttons can do everything else except close the device (you must set the `Command` property to `Close` to do that). However, you can ignore MMControl's interface entirely and devise your own interface. The sample program in this chapter will show you how.

Building a Multimedia Player

To illustrate how to use MMControl to play CD audio, MIDI files, WAV files, and AVI video files, a Multimedia Player program will be constructed that can handle all those file types. Although the program will use the buttons built into the MMControl to control playback and other functions, it will also have a pull-down menu so that you can see how the MMControl can be used both directly and indirectly.

The program will be built step by step, with code being discussed as it is added. The first section of code will handle the playback of CD audio files.

Building the Multimedia Player's User Interface

Before any code can be added, however, the program's user interface must be created (see Figure 36.2). The interface contains a large Picture control that will be used for playing back AVI video files. Although that feature won't be implemented until later in this chapter, the Picture control will be added to the interface now to make things easier.

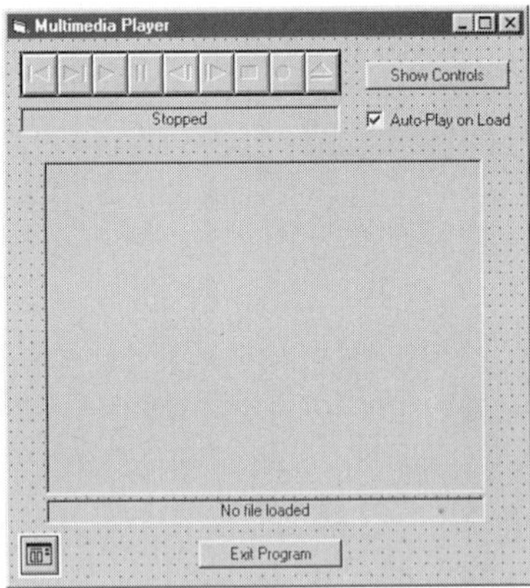

FIGURE 36.2.
How the Multimedia Player's user interface should look.

Figure 36.2 and Table 36.1 can be used as guides for building the program's user interface.

Table 36.1. The controls and their property settings for the Multimedia Player (CH3601) program.

Control Type	*Property*	*Value*
Form	`Name`	`frmCh3601`
	`Caption`	`Multimedia Player`
	`Height`	`5835`
	`Left`	`165`
	`StartupPosition`	`2 - Center Screen`
	`Top`	`450`
	`Width`	`5685`
MMControl	`Name`	`mmmControls`
	`Height`	`495`
	`Left`	`135`
	`Top`	`120`
	`Visible`	`False`
	`Width`	`3540`
Label	`Name`	`lblStatus`
	`Alignment`	`2 - Center`
	`BorderStyle`	`1 - Fixed Single`
	`Caption`	`Stopped`
	`Height`	`285`
	`Left`	`135`
	`Top`	`720`
	`Width`	`3525`
CommandButton	`Name`	`cmdShowHideControls`
	`Caption`	`Show Controls`
	`Height`	`300`
	`Left`	`3945`
	`Top`	`255`
	`Width`	`1575`
CheckBox	`Name`	`chkAutoPlay`
	`Caption`	`Auto-Play on Load`
	`Height`	`240`
	`Left`	`3945`

continues

Table 36.1. continued

Control Type	*Property*	*Value*
	`Top`	`765`
	`Value`	`1 - Checked`
	`Width`	`1605`
PictureBox	`Name`	`picVideo`
	`Height`	`3585`
	`Left`	`390`
	`Top`	`1305`
	`Width`	`4830`
Label	`Name`	`lblFileName`
	`Alignment`	`2 - Center`
	`BorderStyle`	`1 - Fixed Single`
	`Caption`	`No file loaded`
	`Height`	`270`
	`Left`	`390`
	`Top`	`4935`
	`Width`	`4830`
CommonDialog	`Name`	`dlgLoadFile`
	`Left`	`75`
	`Top`	`5295`
CommandButton	`Name`	`cmdExit`
	`Caption`	`Exit Program`
	`Height`	`300`
	`Left`	`2070`
	`Top`	`5385`
	`Width`	`1575`

Adding Menu Items

The next step in building the Multimedia Player is to add the menu items. Most of these menu items will not be implemented until later in this chapter. To make things easier, they will all be added now. Use Table 36.2 as a guide for adding the menu items with VB's Menu Editor (choose Tools | Menu Editor).

Table 36.2. The menu items to be added to the Multimedia Player with VB's Menu Editor.

Caption	*Name*	*Enabled?*
&CD	`mnuCD`	Yes
Play	`mnuCDPlay`	Yes
Previous Track	`mnuCDPrevTrack`	No
Next Track	`mnuCDNextTrack`	No
Pause	`mnuCDPause`	No
Stop	`mnuCDStop`	No
-	`mnuCDDivider`	Yes
Eject	`mnuCDEject`	No
&WAV	`mnuWav`	Yes
Load WAV File	`mnuWavLoad`	Yes
-	`mnuWavDivider`	Yes
Play	`mnuWavPlay`	No
Pause	`mnuWavPause`	No
Stop	`mnuWavStop`	No
&MIDI	`mnuMIDI`	Yes
Load MIDI File	`mnuMIDILoad`	Yes
-	`mnuMIDIDivider`	Yes
Play	`mnuMIDIPlay`	No
Pause	`mnuMIDIPause`	No
Stop	`mnuMIDIStop`	No
&Video	`mnuVideo`	Yes
Load AVI File	`mnuVideoLoad`	Yes
-	`mnuVideoDivider`	Yes
Play	`mnuVideoPlay`	No
Pause	`mnuVideoPause`	No
Stop	`mnuVideoStop`	No
E&xit	`mnuExit`	Yes

Adding Code: Playing CD Audio

Now that the program's user interface has been completed, it's time to start adding code. Again, the CD Audio functions will be implemented first.

The first thing that should be added to the code is the `SendMMCommand` procedure (see Listing 36.1), which takes a multimedia command such as `Play` or `Stop` and sends it to the MMControl object, `mmmControls`. Of course, commands can be sent directly to `mmmControls` by simply setting its `Command` property, but the `SendMMCommand` procedure serves two major purposes. It makes sure that invalid commands are not sent to `mmmControls`, and it sets `mmmControls`' `Notify` and `Wait` properties to the appropriate values before sending the command. This can save a great deal of coding later.

Listing 36.1. The `SendMMCommand` procedure, which is used to send multimedia commands to the `mmmControls` object.

```
Private Sub SendMMCommand(strCmd As String)

Dim booGoodCmd As Boolean

' Test to see if the command specified by the strCmd
' argument is recognized. If it is, set mmmControls'
' Notify and Wait properties to the appropriate values.
booGoodCmd = True
Select Case strCmd
    Case "Open"
        mmmControls.Notify = False
        mmmControls.Wait = True
    Case "Close"
        mmmControls.Notify = False
        mmmControls.Wait = True
    Case "Play"
        mmmControls.Notify = True
        mmmControls.Wait = False
    Case "Pause"
        mmmControls.Notify = False
        mmmControls.Wait = True
    Case "Stop"
        mmmControls.Notify = False
        mmmControls.Wait = True
    Case "Prev"
        mmmControls.Notify = False
        mmmControls.Wait = True
    Case "Next"
        mmmControls.Notify = False
        mmmControls.Wait = True
    Case "Eject"
        mmmControls.Notify = False
        mmmControls.Wait = True
    Case Else
        booGoodCmd = False
End Select

' Only send the command to the MMControl if it
' is something that was recognized.
If booGoodCmd = True Then
    mmmControls.Command = strCmd
End If

End Sub
```

Another procedure, the CDOkay function (see Listing 36.2), checks to see whether an audio CD is in the drive and is ready to play. It will be used in several places in the program to obtain the CD's status.

Listing 36.2. The CDOkay function, which checks to see whether an audio CD is in the CD player and is ready to play.

```
Private Function CDOkay() As Boolean

' Check the CD audio device to make sure a CD is
' ready to play. This function returns a True value if
' the CD is ready, False if it is not.
mmmControls.DeviceType = "CDAudio"
SendMMCommand "Open"
If mmmControls.CanPlay Then
    CDOkay = True
Else
    SendMMCommand "Close"
    CDOkay = False
End If

End Function
```

To test a CD's readiness, the mmmControls object is used. First, its DeviceType is set to CDAudio. Then the Open command is sent to open the device. If the CanPlay property indicates that the CD can be played, the device remains open and is ready to go. Otherwise, the device is closed. The CDOkay function returns a True value if the device is ready and a False value if it is not.

When commands are issued to control the playback of certain devices, it is helpful to know whether another device is already playing. After all, you wouldn't want to play two devices at once. To keep track of when a device is playing and when it is not, a Boolean variable will be used. When a device begins to play, the variable will be set to True. When a device stops, the variable will be set to False. Add the following line to the General Declarations section to declare the Boolean variable booPlaying:

```
Public booPlaying As Boolean
```

This variable has to be initially set to False because nothing should be playing when the program begins. To give it its initial value, add the following line to the Form_Load event:

```
booPlaying = False
```

The next procedure to be added to the program (see Listing 36.3) contains the code that will actually handle the different commands, such as Play, Stop, and Eject. Later, similar procedures will be added to control the WAV, MIDI, and Video menu options.

Listing 36.3. The `CDOptions` procedure, which handles all the CD audio device's functionality.

```
Private Sub CDOptions(strOption As String)

Select Case strOption
    Case "Play"
        ' If something else is playing, then stop it.
        If (mmmControls.DeviceType <> "CDAudio") And _
           (booPlaying = True) Then
              SendMMCommand "Stop"
              SendMMCommand "Close"
        End If
        ' If there is no CD available, notify the user;
        ' otherwise, play the CD only if it is stopped.
        If CDOkay = True Then
            If booPlaying = True Then
                lblStatus = "Playing CD"
                SendMMCommand "Play"
            Else
                lblStatus = "Playing CD"
                SendMMCommand "Play"
                booPlaying = True
                CDMenuToggle (True)
            End If
        Else
            lblStatus = "CD not ready!"
        End If
    Case "Next"
        ' If the CD is playing or is stopped, skip to
        ' the next track.
        If (mmmControls.Mode = mciModePlay) Or _
           (mmmControls.Mode = mciModeStop) Then
              lblStatus = "Playing CD"
              SendMMCommand "Next"
        End If
    Case "Prev"
        ' If the CD is playing or is stopped, skip to
        ' the previous track.
        If (mmmControls.Mode = mciModePlay) Or _
           (mmmControls.Mode = mciModeStop) Then
              lblStatus = "Playing CD"
              SendMMCommand "Prev"
        End If
    Case "Pause"
        ' If the CD is playing, pause it; if the CD is
        ' stopped, play it.
        If mmmControls.Mode = mciModePlay Then
            lblStatus = "Paused"
            SendMMCommand "Pause"
        ElseIf mmmControls.Mode = mciModeStop Then
            lblStatus = "Playing CD"
            SendMMCommand "Play"
        End If
    Case "Stop"
        ' Make sure CD is playing or is paused before
        ' stopping it.
        If (mmmControls.Mode = mciModePlay) Or _
           (mmmControls.Mode = mciModeStop) Then
```

```
                lblStatus = "Stopped"
                SendMMCommand "Stop"
                SendMMCommand "Close"
                booPlaying = False
                CDMenuToggle (False)
        End If
    Case "Eject"
        ' If the CD is available, eject it. First, stop
        ' it if it is currently playing.
        If (mmmControls.Mode = mciModePlay) Then
            SendMMCommand "Stop"
            booPlaying = False
            CDMenuToggle (False)
        End If
        ' If the CD device is not open, open it.
        If mmmControls.Mode = mciModeNotOpen Then
            mmmControls.DeviceType = "CDAudio"
            SendMMCommand "Open"
        End If
        ' If the CD tray can be ejected, then eject it.
        If mmmControls.CanEject Then
            lblStatus = "Ejecting CD"
            SendMMCommand "Eject"
        Else
            lblStatus = "Cannot eject CD"
        End If
        SendMMCommand "Close"
End Select

End Sub
```

The `CDOptions` procedure is passed a single argument (`strOption`) that specifies which operation is to be performed. Possible values are `Play`, to start playing a CD; `Prev`, to skip to the previous track; `Next`, to skip to the next track; `Pause`, to pause playing; `Stop`, to stop play of the CD; and `Eject`, to eject the CD tray.

Each option tests certain conditions before the appropriate command is passed to the `mmmControls` object. For example, when a request is made to `Play` the CD, a test is made to see whether some other device type is already playing. If it is, then the device is stopped and closed. Next, the `CDOkay` function is used to determine whether the CD can be played. If it can't, then the user is notified with a message in the status label (`lblStatus`). If the CD can be played, then the `Play` command is issued to the `mmmControls` object, and the CD begins to play.

After a CD begins to play, the CD menu items (that is, Next Track and Previous Track) should be enabled. When playback stops, the CD menu items (other than Play) should be disabled. Also, after a CD starts to play, the items on the other menus (WAV, MIDI, and Video) should also be disabled. This is all accomplished by four procedures (see Listing 36.4) that are each passed a Boolean value that specifies whether the menu items should be enabled or disabled. If a value of `True` is passed, it means that the menu items should be enabled, and the other menus' items should be disabled.

Listing 36.4. The menu-toggling procedures, which toggle the Enabled properties of a menu's items and, in some cases, disable other menus' items.

```
Private Sub CDMenuToggle(booValue)

' Toggle the Enabled properties of the CD menu items.
' If the properties are to be enabled, then disable all
' of the other menus (Wav, MIDI, and Video).
mnuCDStop.Enabled = booValue
mnuCDPause.Enabled = booValue
mnuCDEject.Enabled = booValue
mnuCDNextTrack.Enabled = booValue
mnuCDPrevTrack.Enabled = booValue

If booValue = True Then
    WavMenuToggle (False)
    MIDIMenuToggle (False)
    VideoMenuToggle (False)
End If

End Sub


Private Sub WavMenuToggle(booValue)

' Toggle the Enabled properties of the Wav menu items.
' If the properties are to be enabled, then disable all
' of the other menus (CD, MIDI, and Video).
mnuWavPlay.Enabled = booValue
mnuWavStop.Enabled = booValue
mnuWavPause.Enabled = booValue

If booValue = True Then
    CDMenuToggle (False)
    MIDIMenuToggle (False)
    VideoMenuToggle (False)
End If

End Sub


Private Sub MIDIMenuToggle(booValue)

' Toggle the Enabled properties of the MIDI menu items.
' If the properties are to be enabled, then disable all
' of the other menus (CD, Wav, and Video).
mnuMIDIPlay.Enabled = booValue
mnuMIDIStop.Enabled = booValue
mnuMIDIPause.Enabled = booValue

If booValue = True Then
    CDMenuToggle (False)
    WavMenuToggle (False)
    VideoMenuToggle (False)
End If

End Sub
```

```
Private Sub VideoMenuToggle(booValue)

' Toggle the Enabled properties of the Video menu items.
' If the properties are to be enabled, then disable all
' of the other menus (CD, Wav, and MIDI).
mnuVideoPlay.Enabled = booValue
mnuVideoStop.Enabled = booValue
mnuVideoPause.Enabled = booValue

If booValue = True Then
    CDMenuToggle (False)
    WavMenuToggle (False)
    MIDIMenuToggle (False)
End If

End Sub
```

The next procedure to be added, `ExitProgram`, closes any open device and ends the program. Listing 36.5 shows the `EndProgram` procedure.

Listing 36.5. The `ExitProgram` procedure, which closes any open device and ends the program.

```
Private Sub ExitProgram()

' Issue a Stop command if a device is playing. Then,
' test to see if a device is open. If it is, close it.
' Then end the program.
If booPlaying = True Then
    SendMMCommand ("Stop")
End If
If mmmControls.Mode <> mciModeNotOpen Then
    SendMMCommand ("Close")
End If
End

End Sub
```

The `ExitProgram` procedure should be called when the Exit menu item is selected, or if the Exit Program button (`cmdExit`) is clicked. Therefore, add the following line of code to both the `mnuExit_Click` event and the `cmdExit_Click` event:

```
ExitProgram
```

Only one more bit of code needs to be added to the program before it can be tested. As the program currently exists, the menu items don't actually do anything. They need to pass a value to the `CDOptions` procedure to tell it what to do. Listing 36.6 contains the contents of the `Click` events for the CD menu items.

Listing 36.6. The `Click` events for the CD menu items. Each issues a command to the `CDOptions` procedure.

```
Private Sub mnuCDEject_Click()

CDOptions ("Eject")

End Sub


Private Sub mnuCDNextTrack_Click()

CDOptions ("Next")

End Sub


Private Sub mnuCDPause_Click()

CDOptions ("Pause")

End Sub


Private Sub mnuCDPlay_Click()

CDOptions ("Play")

End Sub


Private Sub mnuCDPrevTrack_Click()

CDOptions ("Prev")

End Sub


Private Sub mnuCDStop_Click()

CDOptions ("Stop")

End Sub
```

Before running the program, it would be a good idea to save it. Save the project as `CH3601.VBP` and the form as `CH3601.FRM`. Then run the program.

You'll notice that the multimedia controls are not visible on the form. Also, the Show Controls button does not do anything yet. This is so that you only use the pull-down menu items. Try playing an audio CD and moving from track to track using the Next Track and Previous Track options. Pause playback; then choose Pause or Play to start it up again. Finally, click the Stop button to stop playback. When you're finished, exit the program.

Adding Code: Playing WAV Files

To continue building the program, we'll add the code necessary to handle WAV files. `WavOptions`, a procedure similar to the `CDOptions` routine added earlier, will be used to process the WAV playback commands. Listing 36.7 shows the `WavOptions` procedure.

Listing 36.7. The `WavOptions` procedure, which processes the commands for WAV file playback.

```
Private Sub WavOptions(strOption As String)

Select Case strOption
    Case "Load"
        ' Show the "Load WAV File" dialog box.
        dlgLoadFile.DialogTitle = "Load WAV File"
        dlgLoadFile.Filter = "*.wav"
        dlgLoadFile.filename = "*.wav"
        dlgLoadFile.ShowOpen
        ' Get a filename. If the filename is the same as
        ' the filter, no file was selected.
        If dlgLoadFile.filename = dlgLoadFile.Filter Then
            lblFileName = "No file selected"
        Else
            lblFileName = dlgLoadFile.filename
            ' If something else is playing, stop it.
            If booPlaying = True Then
                SendMMCommand "Stop"
                SendMMCommand "Close"
                booPlaying = False
                WavMenuToggle (False)
            End If
            ' If the file should be automatically
            ' played when loaded, then play it.
            If chkAutoPlay.Value = 1 Then
                lblStatus = "Playing WAV File"
                mmmControls.filename = dlgLoadFile.filename
                mmmControls.DeviceType = "WaveAudio"
                SendMMCommand "Open"
                If mmmControls.CanPlay Then
                    SendMMCommand "Play"
                    booPlaying = True
                    WavMenuToggle (True)
                Else
                    SendMMCommand "Close"
                    lblStatus = "Cannot play WAV file"
                End If
            End If
        End If
    Case "Play"
        ' If something else is playing, then stop it.
        If (mmmControls.DeviceType <> "WaveAudio") And _
           (booPlaying = True) Then
              SendMMCommand "Stop"
              SendMMCommand "Close"
              booPlaying = False
              WavMenuToggle (False)
        End If
```

continues

Listing 36.7. continued

```
        ' If the playback is stopped, then start it.
        If mmmControls.Mode = mciModeStop Then
            lblStatus = "Playing WAV file"
            SendMMCommand "Play"
            booPlaying = True
            WavMenuToggle (True)
        ' If the playback is paused, start it up again.
        ElseIf mmmControls.Mode = mciModePause Then
            lblStatus = "Playing WAV file"
            SendMMCommand "Play"
        ' If the device is not open, open it and play
        ' the selected file.
        ElseIf mmmControls.Mode = mciModeNotOpen Then
            lblStatus = "Playing WAV file"
            mmmControls.filename = dlgLoadFile.filename
            mmmControls.DeviceType = "WaveAudio"
            SendMMCommand "Open"
            If mmmControls.CanPlay Then
                SendMMCommand "Play"
                booPlaying = True
                WavMenuToggle (True)
            Else
                SendMMCommand "Close"
                lblStatus = "Cannot play WAV file"
            End If
        End If
    Case "Pause"
        ' If the file is paused, play it; if it's
        ' playing, pause it.
        If mmmControls.Mode = mciModePlay Then
            lblStatus = "Paused"
            SendMMCommand "Pause"
        ElseIf mmmControls.Mode = mciModePause Then
            lblStatus = "Playing WAV File"
            SendMMCommand "Play"
        End If
    Case "Stop"
        ' If the file is playing or is paused, stop it.
        If (mmmControls.Mode = mciModePlay) Or _
           (mmmControls.Mode = mciModePause) Then
              lblStatus = "Stopped"
              SendMMCommand "Stop"
              SendMMCommand "Close"
              booPlaying = False
              WavMenuToggle (True)
        End If
End Select

End Sub
```

One of the biggest differences between the `WavOptions` procedure and the `CDOptions` procedure is the multimedia commands processed in each. The `WavOptions` procedure does not process the `Prev` (Previous Track), `Next` (Next Track), or `Eject` commands because they don't apply to WAV file playback. However, a new command (`Load`) has been added. This command uses the CommonDialog control (dlgLoadFile) to display a Load WAV File dialog box where the user can select a WAV file for playback. If the Auto-Play on Load CheckBox (chkAutoPlay) is checked, then the file will be automatically played as soon as it has been loaded.

Before you can try out the program with WAV files, you need to add code to the WAV menu items' Click events to pass a command to the WavOptions procedure. Listing 36.8 shows the code that needs to be added.

Listing 36.8. The Click events for the WAV menu items. Each issues a command to the WavOptions procedure.

```
Private Sub mnuWavLoad_Click()

WavOptions ("Load")

End Sub


Private Sub mnuWavPause_Click()

WavOptions ("Pause")

End Sub


Private Sub mnuWavPlay_Click()

WavOptions ("Play")

End Sub


Private Sub mnuWavStop_Click()

WavOptions ("Stop")

End Sub
```

You can now try out the program to see how it works with WAV files. Of course, it's always a good idea to save it first.

Adding Code: Playing MIDI Files and AVI Videos

To add the capability to play back MIDI files and AVI Video files, two more procedures need to be added. As you might have guessed, they are MIDIOptions and VideoOptions, and they are similar to the WavOptions procedure you just added. The biggest differences are in how the Load and Play commands are processed. The first procedure, MIDIOptions, is shown in Listing 36.9.

Listing 36.9. The MIDIOptions procedure, which handles the commands for playback of MIDI files.

```
Private Sub MIDIOptions(strOption As String)

Select Case strOption
    Case "Load"
        ' Show the "Load MIDI File" dialog box.
        dlgLoadFile.DialogTitle = "Load MIDI File"
        dlgLoadFile.Filter = "*.mid"
        dlgLoadFile.filename = "*.mid"
        dlgLoadFile.ShowOpen
        ' Get a filename. If the filename is the same as
        ' the filter, no file was selected.
        If dlgLoadFile.filename = dlgLoadFile.Filter Then
            lblFileName = "No file selected"
        Else
            lblFileName = dlgLoadFile.filename
            ' If something else is playing, stop it.
            If booPlaying = True Then
                SendMMCommand "Stop"
                SendMMCommand "Close"
                booPlaying = False
                MIDIMenuToggle (False)
            End If
            ' If the file should be automatically
            ' played when loaded, then play it.
            If chkAutoPlay.Value = 1 Then
                lblStatus = "Playing MIDI File"
                mmmControls.filename = dlgLoadFile.filename
                mmmControls.DeviceType = "Sequencer"
                SendMMCommand "Open"
                If mmmControls.CanPlay Then
                    SendMMCommand "Play"
                    booPlaying = True
                    MIDIMenuToggle (True)
                Else
                    SendMMCommand "Close"
                    lblStatus = "Cannot play MIDI file"
                End If
            End If
        End If
    Case "Play"
        ' If something else is playing, then stop it.
        If (mmmControls.DeviceType <> "Sequencer") And _
           (booPlaying = True) Then
              SendMMCommand "Stop"
              SendMMCommand "Close"
              booPlaying = False
              MIDIMenuToggle (False)
        End If
        ' If the playback is stopped, then start it.
        If mmmControls.Mode = mciModeStop Then
            lblStatus = "Playing MIDI file"
            SendMMCommand "Play"
            booPlaying = True
            MIDIMenuToggle (True)
        ' If the playback is paused, start it up again.
        ElseIf mmmControls.Mode = mciModePause Then
```

```
            lblStatus = "Playing MIDI file"
            SendMMCommand "Play"
        ' If the device is not open, open it and play
        ' the selected file.
        ElseIf mmmControls.Mode = mciModeNotOpen Then
            lblStatus = "Playing MIDI file"
            mmmControls.filename = dlgLoadFile.filename
            mmmControls.DeviceType = "Sequencer"
            SendMMCommand "Open"
            If mmmControls.CanPlay Then
                SendMMCommand "Play"
                booPlaying = True
                MIDIMenuToggle (True)
            Else
                SendMMCommand "Close"
                lblStatus = "Cannot play MIDI file"
            End If
        End If
    Case "Pause"
        ' If the file is paused, play it; if it's
        ' playing, pause it.
        If mmmControls.Mode = mciModePlay Then
            lblStatus = "Paused"
            SendMMCommand "Pause"
        ElseIf mmmControls.Mode = mciModePause Then
            lblStatus = "Playing MIDI File"
            SendMMCommand "Play"
        End If
    Case "Stop"
        ' If the file is playing or is paused, stop it.
        If (mmmControls.Mode = mciModePlay) Or _
           (mmmControls.Mode = mciModePause) Then
              lblStatus = "Stopped"
              SendMMCommand "Stop"
              SendMMCommand "Close"
              booPlaying = False
              MIDIMenuToggle (True)
        End If
End Select

End Sub
```

There are some minor differences (such as the `MIDIMenuToggle` procedure being called rather than the `WavMenuToggle` procedure) between the `MIDIOptions` routine and the `WavOptions` routine. Other differences include the way files are loaded and played. When displaying the Load File dialog box, different file filters are used to indicate MIDI file extensions rather than WAV file extensions. Also, the `Sequencer` device is used for playback rather than the `WavAudio` device.

Before the `MIDIOptions` procedure can be used, the MIDI menu items need to be able to pass commands to the procedure. Listing 36.10 shows the `Click` events for the MIDI menu items.

Listing 36.10. The `Click` events for the MIDI menu items. Each issues a command to the `MIDIOptions` procedure.

```
Private Sub mnuMIDILoad_Click()

MIDIOptions ("Load")

End Sub

Private Sub mnuMIDIPause_Click()

MIDIOptions ("Pause")

End Sub

Private Sub mnuMIDIPlay_Click()

MIDIOptions ("Play")

End Sub

Private Sub mnuMIDIStop_Click()

MIDIOptions ("Stop")

End Sub
```

The `VideoOptions` procedure (see Listing 36.11) is the next one to be added to the program. Although it is much like the `WavOptions` and `MIDIOptions` procedures, it has one small difference.

Listing 36.11. The `VideoOptions` procedure, which handles the commands for playback of AVI video files.

```
Private Sub VideoOptions(strOption As String)

Select Case strOption
    Case "Load"
        ' Show the "Load MIDI File" dialog box.
        dlgLoadFile.DialogTitle = "Load Video File"
        dlgLoadFile.Filter = "*.avi"
        dlgLoadFile.filename = "*.avi"
        dlgLoadFile.ShowOpen
        ' Get a filename. If the filename is the same as
        ' the filter, no file was selected.
        If dlgLoadFile.filename = dlgLoadFile.Filter Then
            lblFileName = "No file selected"
        Else
            lblFileName = dlgLoadFile.filename
            ' If something else is playing, stop it.
            If booPlaying = True Then
                SendMMCommand "Stop"
                SendMMCommand "Close"
```

```
            booPlaying = False
            VideoMenuToggle (False)
        End If
        ' If the file should be automatically
        ' played when loaded, then play it.
        If chkAutoPlay.Value = 1 Then
            lblStatus = "Playing Video"
            mmmControls.filename = dlgLoadFile.filename
            mmmControls.DeviceType = "AVIVideo"
            mmmControls.hWndDisplay = picVideo.hWnd
            SendMMCommand "Open"
            If mmmControls.CanPlay Then
                SendMMCommand "Play"
                booPlaying = True
                VideoMenuToggle (True)
            Else
                SendMMCommand "Close"
                lblStatus = "Cannot play MIDI file"
            End If
        End If
    End If
Case "Play"
    ' If something else is playing, then stop it.
    If (mmmControls.DeviceType <> "AVIVideo") And _
       (booPlaying = True) Then
          SendMMCommand "Stop"
          SendMMCommand "Close"
          booPlaying = False
          VideoMenuToggle (False)
    End If
    ' If the playback is stopped, then start it.
    If mmmControls.Mode = mciModeStop Then
        lblStatus = "Playing Video"
        SendMMCommand "Play"
        booPlaying = True
        VideoMenuToggle (True)
    ' If the playback is paused, start it up again.
    ElseIf mmmControls.Mode = mciModePause Then
        lblStatus = "Playing Video"
        SendMMCommand "Play"
    ' If the device is not open, open it and play
    ' the selected file.
    ElseIf mmmControls.Mode = mciModeNotOpen Then
        lblStatus = "Playing Video"
        mmmControls.filename = dlgLoadFile.filename
        mmmControls.DeviceType = "AVIVideo"
        SendMMCommand "Open"
        If mmmControls.CanPlay Then
            SendMMCommand "Play"
            booPlaying = True
            VideoMenuToggle (True)
        Else
            SendMMCommand "Close"
            lblStatus = "Cannot play Video file"
        End If
    End If
```

continues

Listing 36.11. continued

```
    Case "Pause"
        ' If the file is paused, play it; if it's
        ' playing, pause it.
        If mmmControls.Mode = mciModePlay Then
            lblStatus = "Paused"
            SendMMCommand "Pause"
        ElseIf mmmControls.Mode = mciModePause Then
            lblStatus = "Playing Video"
            SendMMCommand "Play"
        End If
    Case "Stop"
        ' If the file is playing or is paused, stop it.
        If (mmmControls.Mode = mciModePlay) Or _
           (mmmControls.Mode = mciModePause) Then
              lblStatus = "Stopped"
              SendMMCommand "Stop"
              SendMMCommand "Close"
              booPlaying = False
              VideoMenuToggle (True)
        End If
End Select

End Sub
```

For the AVI video to be displayed, the MMControl object must know the handle of the PictureBox control that will be used for video playback. Therefore, the handle of the `picVideo` control (`PICVIDEO.HWND`) is assigned to MMControl's `hWndDisplay` property.

Once again, it is necessary to add code to the menu options. This time, it is for the Video menu items. Listing 36.12 shows the events that need to be coded.

Listing 36.12. The `Click` events for the Video menu items. Each issues a command to the `VideoOptions` procedure.

```
Private Sub mnuVideoLoad_Click()

VideoOptions ("Load")

End Sub


Private Sub mnuVideoPause_Click()

VideoOptions ("Pause")

End Sub


Private Sub mnuVideoPlay_Click()

VideoOptions ("Play")

End Sub
```

```
Private Sub mnuVideoStop_Click()

VideoOptions ("Stop")

End Sub
```

Now that the CD audio, WAV, MIDI, and AVI video support has been added to the program, it's almost finished. There are only a few odds and ends to take care of.

The first thing is the `mmmControls` object. The way the program is set up now, the `mmmControls` object is not visible on the screen. To enable it to be displayed when the Show Controls button (`cmdShowHideControls`) is clicked, add the code in Listing 36.13 to the `cmdShowHideControls_Click` event.

Listing 36.13. The `cmdShowHideControls_Click` event, which toggles the display of the `mmmControls` object.

```
Private Sub cmdShowHideControls_Click()

' If the multimedia controls are visible, then hide
' them. Otherwise, show them. Change the button caption
' to reflect a new choice.
If mmmControls.Visible = True Then
    mmmControls.Visible = False
    cmdShowHideControls.Caption = "Show Controls"
Else
    mmmControls.Visible = True
    cmdShowHideControls.Caption = "Hide Controls"
End If

End Sub
```

Also, the program has one problem that you might not be aware of yet. When a file is finished playing, the status display should read `Stopped`. It doesn't do that, because the program doesn't know when the file has stopped and when it is still playing.

To sense when a file is finished playing, the `mmmControls` object's `Done` event can be used to indicate such status. The `Done` event is triggered when a command is completed that was sent to the `mmmControls` object with the `Notify` property set to `True`. If you recall back to the `SendMMCommand` procedure, you'll see that the `Notify` property is set to `True` for the Play command only. Listing 36.14 shows code that can be added to that event to handle a file that has finished.

Listing 36.14. The `mmmControls_Done` event, which is used to indicate when a file has finished playing.

```
Private Sub mmmControls_Done(NotifyCode As Integer)

' Stop and close the current device.
lblStatus = "Stopped"
SendMMCommand "Stop"
SendMMCommand "Close"
booPlaying = False
' Toggle off the menu items for the current device.
Select Case mmmControls.DeviceType
    Case "CDAudio"
        CDMenuToggle (False)
    Case "WaveAudio"
        WavMenuToggle (False)
    Case "Sequencer"
        MIDIMenuToggle (False)
    Case "AVIVideo"
        VideoMenuToggle (False)
End Select

End Sub
```

You should now have a complete multimedia program that will play CD audio, WAV files, MIDI files, and AVI videos. Figure 36.3 shows the program in action, playing a video from the Windows 95 CD-ROM.

FIGURE 36.3.
The Multimedia Player in action, playing an AVI file of Weezer's "Buddy Holly" music video (located on the Windows 95 CD-ROM).

The program is a good start, but it can be enhanced in several ways. For example, there are no provisions for recording WAV files. Also, the controls on the `mmmControls` object do not react the same way as the pull-down menu items. For one thing, they do not cause the status display to be updated when they are clicked. They also don't enable and disable the pull-down menu items when files are played or stopped. If you want to get some hands-on experience with using the MMControl object, then dive right in and see whether you can modify the Multimedia Player program to your liking.

Summary

Multimedia is here to stay. If you are producing mass-market software or even shareware, then adding multimedia to your programs will give them a professional edge. The best part is that it's easy to do. VB's MMControl can be used to play back audio files, CDs, videos, and a host of other device types. This chapter showed you how to use the MMControl object.

CHAPTER 37

Navigating the Registry

IN THIS CHAPTER

The *Registry* replaces the old Windows 3.*x* `.INI` files as the place where the operating system and application programs store system-specific information. When you install an application on your computer, the installation process puts information in the Registry that, in effect, tells your operating system about the application being installed.

The Registry, unlike the `.INI` files it replaces, is a hierarchical database that stores information in an organized format. `.INI` files, on the other hand, stored information in ASCII text files that anyone could read and change.

This chapter discusses the structure of the Registry, how to use the RegEdit utility program to view and edit the Registry, and—most important—how to access the Registry with Visual Basic to add information specific to the applications you've designed. In particular, you'll learn how to use four built-in VB functions for retrieving, setting, and deleting Registry values.

CAUTION

Making a mistake while editing the Registry can lead to serious—even fatal—problems with your operating system. Before you do any work with the Registry, back it up and store it in a safe place. If you do make a mistake in the Registry, a backup could be the only way to save yourself the hassle and inconvenience of rebuilding your operating system.

The System Registry is stored in the file `SYSTEM.DAT`, which is typically found in the Windows directory. However, it is hidden and marked as read-only in its attributes. There is also a `SYSTEM.DA0` file (also hidden and read-only), which is an automatic backup copy that is made of the Registry file whenever you restart Windows.

Touring the Registry

I'll begin this tour of the Registry by identifying the Windows tool I will use to conduct the tour: RegEdit. RegEdit is a program that can be found in the Windows directory. Figure 37.1 shows the RegEdit icon on my desktop.

FIGURE 37.1.
The RegEdit icon.

To run RegEdit, either type **`regedit`** in the Start | Run... dialog box and click OK, or create a shortcut on your desktop for it. The latter is a good idea if you plan to browse or edit the Registry regularly.

When you run the RegEdit program, you'll see that it is divided into two window panes (see Figure 37.2). The pane on the left shows the Registry hierarchy, and the pane on the right is used to display values.

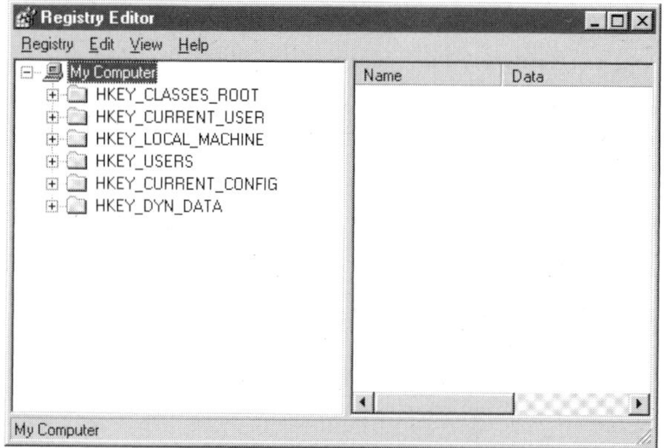

FIGURE 37.2.
The Registry's top-level keys.

As I mentioned in this chapter's introduction, the Registry is a hierarchical database. It's made up of six levels, called *keys*, that are broken down into subkeys and key settings. Each top-level (or root) key stores information about specific hardware or software settings. The top-level keys of the Registry (shown in the left window pane of the RegEdit program) are as follows:

- `HKEY_CLASSES_ROOT` stores information about OLE (object linking and embedding), DDE (dynamic data exchange), and shell integration.
- `HKEY_CURRENT_USER` contains information about the currently logged-in user, mostly software data pertaining to applications to which the user has access.
- `HKEY_LOCAL_MACHINE` stores information regarding hardware configuration on the user's PC, software installed on the user's PC, peripheral devices installed on the user's PC, and information about the Windows environment.
- `HKEY_USERS` contains information about all users with access to the computer system.
- `HKEY_CURRENT_CONFIG` stores information on multiple hardware configurations on the user's system.
- `HKEY_DYN_DATA` contains information about Plug and Play devices, performance statistics, and virtual device drivers for the user's computer system.

To look at the subkeys within a top-level Registry key, open the key's folder by double-clicking its name or clicking the key's + icon. Figure 37.3 shows the subkeys for `HKEY_CURRENT_USER`.

As stated earlier, the Registry window is divided into two panes: on the left are the Registry's keys and subkeys, and on the right are the selected subkey's settings. You can discover a subkey's setting names and data values by double-clicking the subkey's folder just as you clicked the key's folder to get to the subkeys.

Before you can get to a setting's name and value, however, you might have to navigate through more than one level of subkeys. Remember that the Registry is a hierarchical database, meaning that it has several layers of keys and subkeys. To get a better feel for how the Registry is organized, open and look at one of the `HKEY_CURRENT_USER` subkeys—`SOFTWARE` (see Figure 37.4).

This subkey is used by some software vendors and contains information about applications created by those vendors that are installed on my computer system. (I actually have more software installed than just Microsoft and Netscape packages; these two are the ones that use this subkey to store information.)

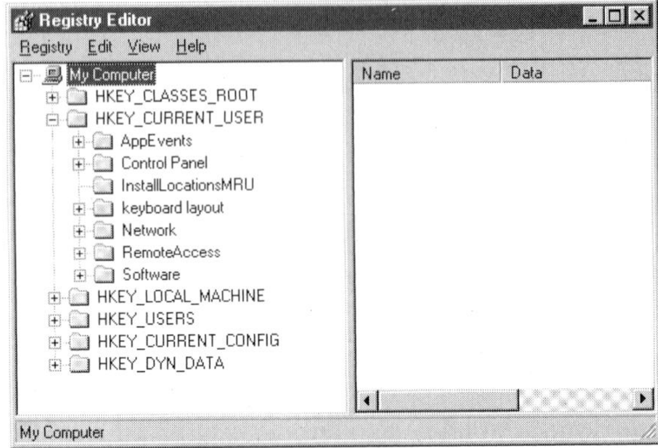

FIGURE 37.3.
The subkeys of `HKEY_CURRENT_USER`.

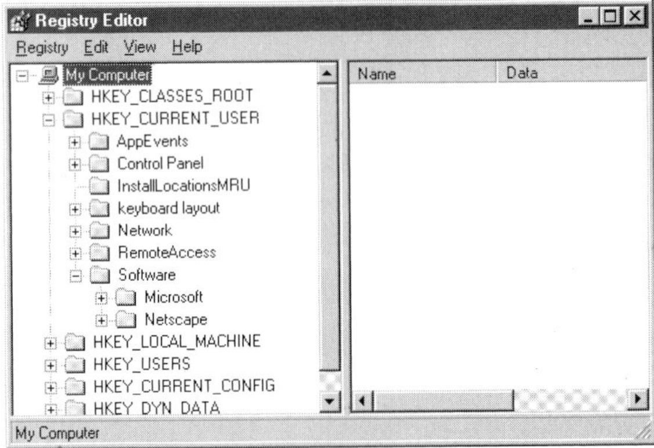

FIGURE 37.4.
The `Microsoft` *and* `Netscape` *subkeys of* `HKEY_CURRENT_USER\Software`.

To continue this exploration of the Registry, expand the `HKEY_CURRENT_USER\Software\Microsoft` subkey to see what actual system information is being stored. Double-clicking the subkey displays more subkeys in RegEdit's left pane (see Figure 37.5).

NOTE

As you delve deeper into the Registry hierarchy, it can be difficult to remember the various keys and subkeys that led you to your current location. Luckily, the RegEdit program displays the "path" for the current subkey at the bottom of its window. Simply click once on a key's name so that it is highlighted, and the path will appear.

FIGURE 37.5.
The subkeys of `HKEY_CURRENT_USER\Software\Microsoft`.

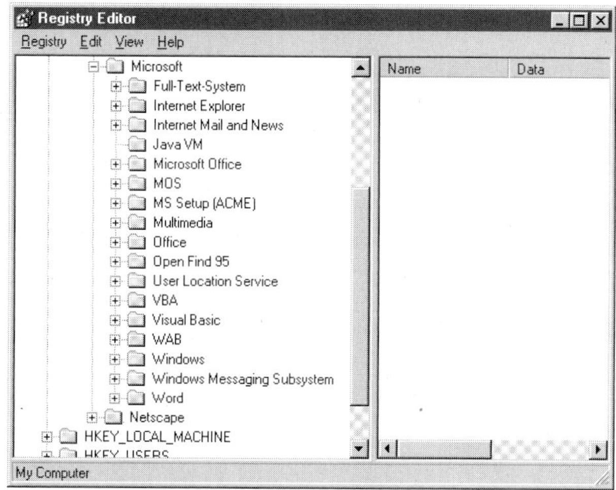

To finally see some actual Registry data settings, double-click the Visual Basic subkey and then the 5.0 subkey below that. In the right pane is a group of settings for Visual Basic 5.0 (Figure 37.6 shows RegEdit with the right pane pulled all the way to the left, hiding almost all the left pane).

FIGURE 37.6.
Registry settings for Visual Basic 5.0.

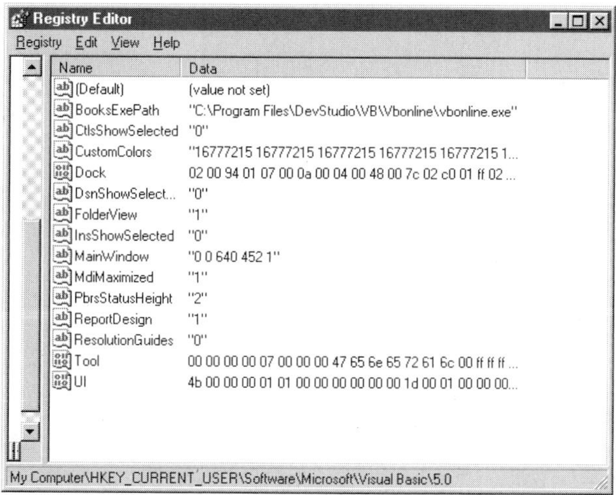

In the right pane are two columns: Name and Data. The Name column holds the name of the setting; the Data column holds the value of the setting. For example, the `BooksExePath` setting in Figure 37.6 is the setting VB uses to find the Books OnLine application. The value for this setting is `C:\PROGRAM FILES\DEVSTUDIO\VB\VBONLINE\VBONLINE.EXE`. Whenever a user wants to load the Books OnLine application, Visual Basic knows to follow this path to find the program.

As you've probably noticed by looking at Figure 37.6, there appear to be two types of values that can be stored in Registry settings: strings and binary numbers. Although many more data types are possible, you run across these two types the most often.

You can tell whether the Registry setting accepts string or binary data by looking at the icon displayed to the left of the setting's name. The two icons in Figure 37.6 are a torn piece of paper with the letters ab on it (representing string data) and a torn piece of paper with 0s and 1s on it (representing binary data). Although you should always be able to determine the type of data stored in a Registry setting just by looking at it, you can use the icon as a guide.

You've now seen how to navigate through the Registry to get from the top-level keys to individual settings. Before you learn how to work with the Registry in Visual Basic, however, you need to understand how to set and change Registry settings.

Backing Up the Registry

The program that you've been using to examine Registry settings can also be used to set and edit Registry values. But before you learn how to edit the Registry, you need to learn how to back it up in case of problems.

Because of the nature of the Registry's data, if you accidentally change or delete a key or setting in the Registry that's needed by the operating system, your whole system can become unusable. Therefore, always make a backup of the Registry before you make any changes to it.

You can back up the Registry in several ways:

- Use a utility program called the Microsoft Configuration Backup (MCB), which is located on the Windows 95 CD-ROM. MCB allows you to back up the Registry up to nine times. The program keeps track of which backup is which so that you can tell MCB which backup copy you want to use should you ever need to restore your Registry.
- Export it to an ASCII file. In RegEdit, choose Registry | Export Registry File. In the dialog box that appears (see Figure 37.7), enter a new name for the Registry file in the File Name text box and click OK. RegEdit creates an ASCII file with the filename you entered.

NOTE

When you export the Registry, make sure that you have the top-level My Computer key selected and none of the subkeys open. By default, if a subkey is selected when you export the Registry, only that "branch" of the Registry is used. Check the Export Range section at the bottom of the Export Registry File dialog box to see what is being exported. Select the All button if you want to export the entire Registry.

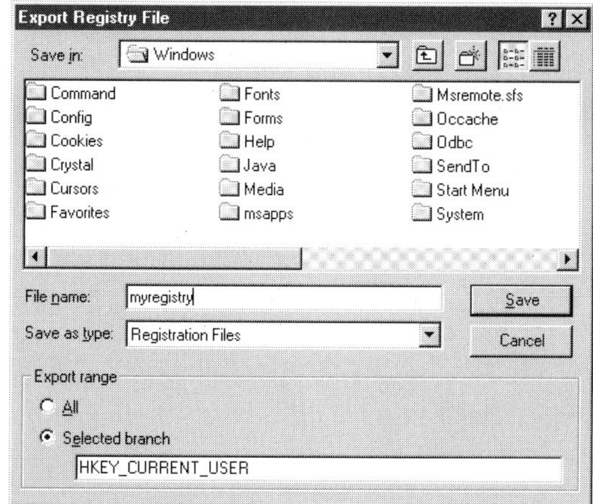

FIGURE 37.7.
Exporting the Registry file.

Figure 37.8 shows part of the exported Registry file. You can examine this text file with any word processing program or editor that can display ASCII text. If you export the whole Registry, however, you can't examine the exported file with Notepad; the file is too large for Notepad to display. A full Registry contains literally thousands of keys, subkeys, and settings similar to those shown in Figure 37.8.

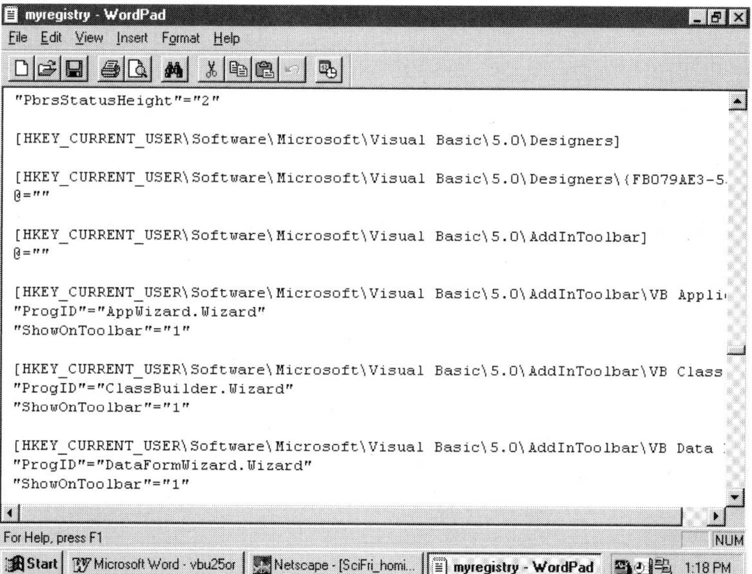

FIGURE 37.8.
A portion of the exported Registry.

If you do somehow manage to damage your Registry during editing, you can import the exported file back into your system by choosing Registry | Import Registry File from the menu in RegEdit. In the dialog box that appears, enter the name of the previously exported Registry file, and the file's keys, subkeys, and settings are imported back into the Registry. The Registry then will be in the same state it was when you exported it.

Now that you know how to back up the Registry, you're ready to use RegEdit to change Registry settings.

Setting and Editing Registry Values with RegEdit

Editing a key is simple:

1. Double-click the Registry setting. A dialog box appears, asking you for a new value for the setting (see Figure 37.9).
2. To change the value of the setting, simply delete the highlighted data and enter new data.

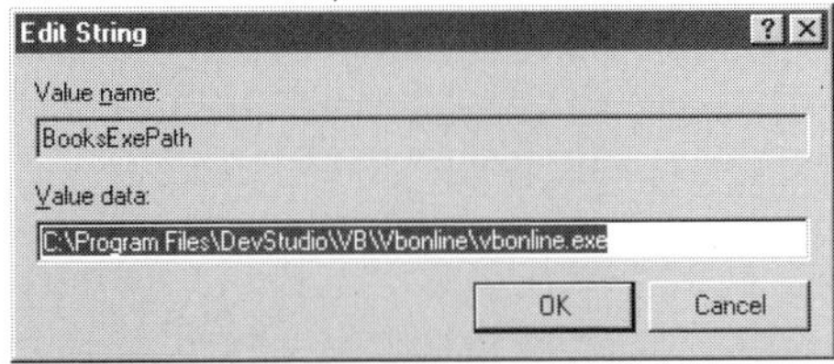

FIGURE 37.9.
Editing a Registry setting value.

> **CAUTION**
>
> Editing the Registry can create serious system problems if you enter wrong information in a Registry setting. For example, if the data in Figure 37.9 is changed to a nonexistent file path, the Books OnLine application will be unusable until the data is corrected.

To use RegEdit to add new settings to the Registry, follow these steps:

1. Right-click the Registry key under which you want to put the data. When the pop-up menu appears, choose New and then Key. A new subkey is created, titled Default (see Figure 37.10).
2. Type a name for the subkey. It appears in the tree immediately below the key you right-clicked.
3. From here, you can create more subkeys and actually add data to them. To create a setting and assign it a value, move to the right pane after you create the subkey. In Figure 37.11, for example, a Registry subkey for `Screen Settings` has been created under the `MyProg Settings` key. In that example, you would right-click the `Screen Settings` key, select New, and then select String Value.

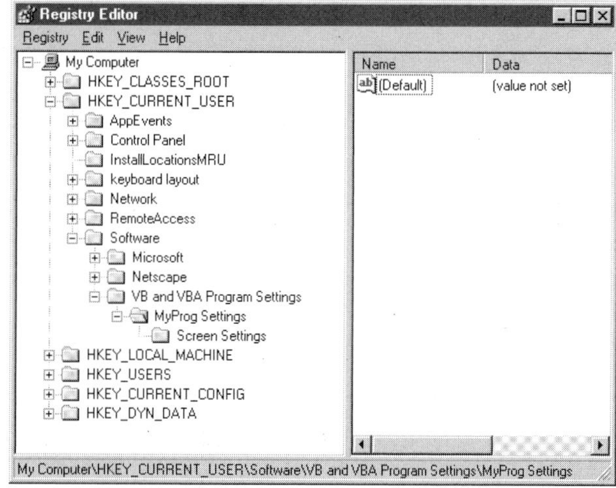

FIGURE 37.10.
Creating a new key with RegEdit.

4. A new string value icon is created; at the prompt, enter a name for the setting. Figure 37.11 shows a new setting named `Display Type`.

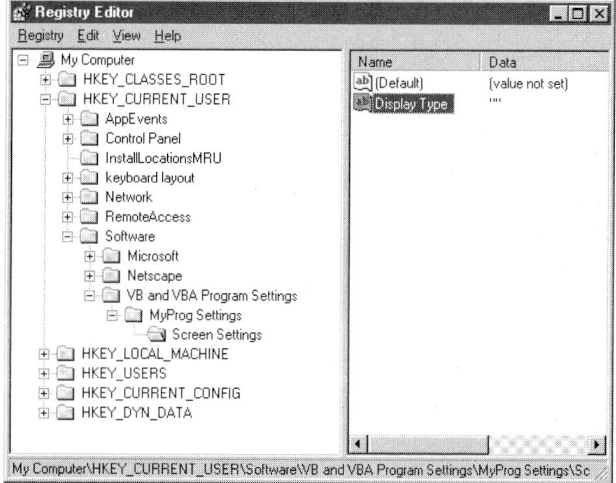

FIGURE 37.11.
A new Registry setting for `Display Type`.

5. To add a value for the setting, double-click `Display Type`. A dialog box like the one shown in Figure 37.12 will appear. Enter a value for the setting.

You now have a new Registry setting with a value.

With this overview of the Registry, you're now ready to see how to use Visual Basic to make changes to the Registry.

FIGURE 37.12.
Adding a value to the `Display Type` *setting.*

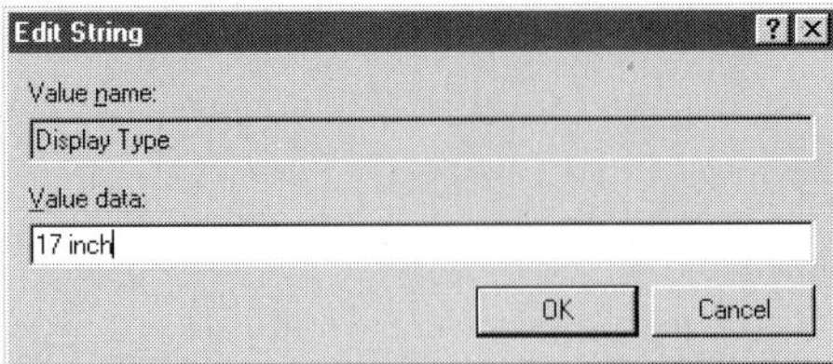

Changing the Registry with Visual Basic

Visual Basic provides a key in the Registry for storing information about applications created in VB:

```
HKEY_CURRENT_USER\Software\VB and VBA Program Settings\
```

Within this Registry key, you'll have to provide the name of your application, the section of the application (hardware, user information, and so on), and the subkey itself.

> **NOTE**
>
> On some systems, the Registry key used for saving application information may be different from the one shown earlier. One alternate key is
>
> `HKEY_USERS\.Default\Software\VB and VBA Program Settings\`

You can use two VB functions and two VB statements to create and edit your Registry settings:

- The `SaveSetting` statement creates or saves Registry settings.
- The `GetSetting` function retrieves Registry settings.
- The `GetAllSettings` function returns an array of Registry settings.
- The `DeleteSetting` statement deletes Registry settings.

The following sections describe how to use these functions and statements in your VB code to work with the Registry.

The SaveSetting Statement

To create a Registry setting, use the `SaveSetting` statement, which takes four arguments:

- *`AppName`* is the name of the application in the Registry.
- *`Section`* is the section of the setting under *`AppName`*.
- *`Key`* is the name of the key setting under which the setting will be saved.
- *`Setting`* is the value of the Registry setting.

Figure 37.13 shows a simple VB form that can set and change Registry settings. To build the form, use Table 37.1 as a guide for adding controls and changing their names and properties. When you're finished, save the form as `CH3701.FRM` and the project as `CH3701.PRJ`.

Table 37.1. The controls and their property values for the sample Registry editing program.

Control Type	*Property*	*Value*
Form	`Name`	`frmRegSample`
	`Caption`	`Navigating the Registry`
	`Height`	`3705`
	`Left`	`60`
	`Top`	`345`
	`Width`	`4680`
Label	`Name`	`lblAppName`
	`Caption`	`App Name:`
	`Height`	`255`
	`Left`	`240`
	`Top`	`690`
	`Width`	`1140`
Label	`Name`	`lblSection`
	`Caption`	`Section:`
	`Height`	`255`
	`Left`	`240`
	`Top`	`1200`
	`Width`	`1140`
Label	`Name`	`lblKeyName`
	`Caption`	`Key:`
	`Height`	`255`
	`Left`	`240`
	`Top`	`1710`
	`Width`	`1140`
Label	`Name`	`lblKeyValue`
	`Caption`	`Registry Value:`
	`Height`	`255`

continues

Table 37.1. continued

Control Type	*Property*	*Value*
	Left	240
	Top	2205
	Width	1140
TextBox	Name	txtAppName
	Height	345
	Left	1560
	Top	660
	Width	2865
TextBox	Name	txtRegSection
	Height	345
	Left	1560
	Top	1155
	Width	2865
TextBox	Name	txtKeyName
	Height	345
	Left	1560
	Top	1665
	Width	2865
TextBox	Name	txtKeyValue
	Height	345
	Left	1560
	Top	2160
	Width	2865
CommandButton	Name	cmdCreateRegSetting
	Caption	Create Registry Setting
	Height	360
	Left	270
	Top	2835
	Width	1905

Control Type	Property	Value
CommandButton	Name	cmdGetRegSetting
	Caption	Get Registry Setting
	Height	360
	Left	2505
	Top	2835
	Width	1905

The code for creating a new Registry setting is found in the `cmdCreateRegSetting` CommandButton's `Click` event:

```
Private Sub cmdCreateRegSetting()

    Dim strAppName As String
    Dim strSection As String
    Dim strKey As String
    Dim strRegValue As String

    strAppName = Trim(txtAppName.Text)
    strSection = Trim(txtRegSection.Text)
    strKey = Trim(txtKeyName.Text)
    strRegValue = Trim(txtKeyValue.Text)
    SaveSetting strAppName, strSection, strKey, strRegValue

End Sub
```

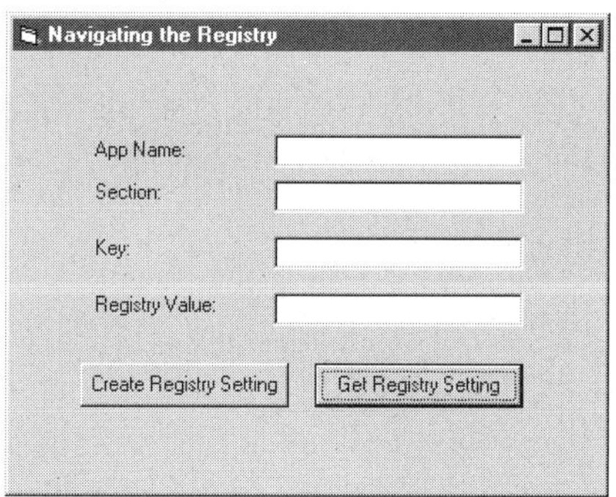

FIGURE 37.13.
A VB form for creating and editing Registry settings.

The code for the `SaveSetting` statement is straightforward. The application name, section name, key setting name, and key setting value are entered in the text boxes. These strings are then given to the `SaveSetting` statement; when the statement is executed, the Registry setting is created.

You can also use the SaveSetting statement to change a Registry setting. Just change the value of the *Value* argument in the SaveSetting statement, and a new value is entered for the Registry setting. Figure 37.14 shows what will have to be entered to change the Display Type value from 17 inch to 21 inch.

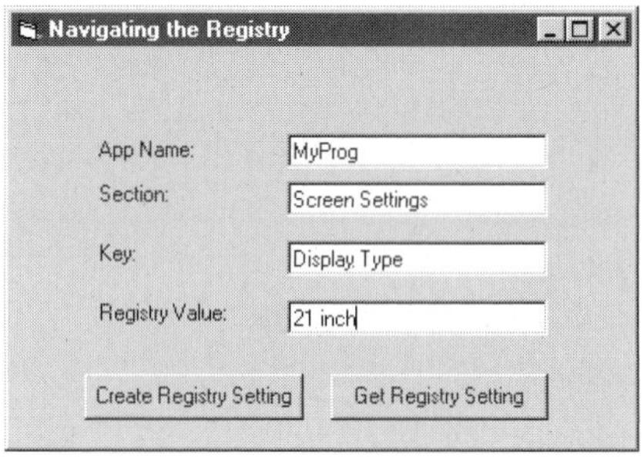

FIGURE 37.14.
Changing a Registry setting with SaveSetting.

The GetSetting Function

To retrieve a Registry value, use the GetSetting function. The GetSetting function takes the following arguments:

- *AppName* is the name of the application in the Registry.
- *Section* is the section of the setting under *AppName*.
- *Key* is the name of the key setting that will be retrieved.
- *Default* is the default value to retrieve if there's no Registry value.

The code for using the GetSetting function is also straightforward:

```
Private Sub cmdGetSetting_Click()

    Dim strAppName As String
    Dim strSection As String
    Dim strKey As String
    Dim strRegEntry As String

    strAppName = Trim(txtAppName.Text)
    strSection = Trim(txtRegSection.Text)
    strKey = Trim(txtKeyName.Text)
    strRegEntry = GetSetting(strAppName, strSection, strKey, "No value")
    txtKeyValue.Text = strRegEntry

End Sub
```

The first three arguments are entered in the text boxes, and the default setting value ("No value") is added to the end of the function arguments. The last line of this code takes the value retrieved by the function and puts it into the txtKeyValue TextBox control. Figure 37.15 shows the results of running the GetSetting function. If there hadn't been a value for this Registry setting, the last text box would have displayed the message No value.

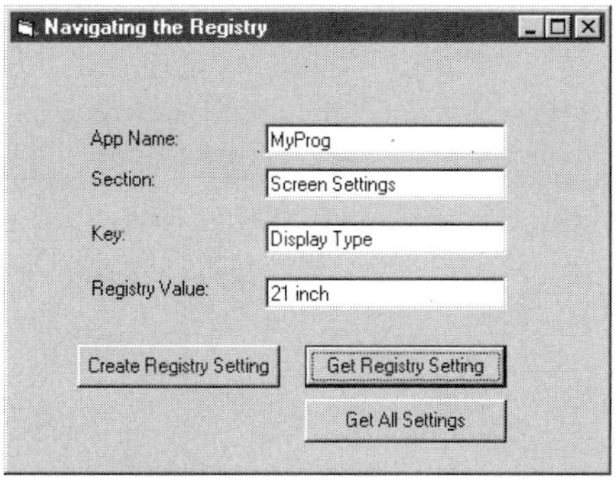

FIGURE 37.15.
Retrieving a Registry key setting value with the `GetSetting` *function.*

Navigating the Registry
App Name: MyProg
Section: Screen Settings
Key: Display Type
Registry Value: 21 inch
Create Registry Setting
Get Registry Setting
Get All Settings

The GetAllSettings Function

To retrieve all the Registry settings for an application section, the `GetAllSettings` function is used. This function takes just two arguments—the application name and the section name—and returns all the key settings and their values in an array.

To illustrate the use of the `GetAllSettings` function, add a ListBox, a Label, and another CommandButton to the sample program's form. Also change the `Height` and `Width` properties of the form to accommodate the extra controls. Use Table 37.2 as a guide for adding the new controls and changing their properties.

Table 37.2. The controls and their property values for the sample Registry editing program.

Control Type	*Property*	*Value*
Form	`Name`	`frmRegSample`
	`Height`	`4005`
	`Width`	`6885`
Label	`Name`	`lblAllSettings`
	`Alignment`	`2 - Center`
	`Caption`	`All Registry Settings`
	`Height`	`225`
	`Left`	`4635`
	`Top`	`705`
	`Width`	`2010`
ListBox	`Name`	`lstRegKeys`
	`Height`	`2790`
	`Left`	`4575`

continues

Table 37.2. continued

Control Type	*Property*	*Value*
	`Top`	`1005`
	`Width`	`2100`
CommandButton	`Name`	`cmdGetAllSettings`
	`Caption`	`Get All Settings`
	`Height`	`360`
	`Left`	`2505`
	`Top`	`3390`
	`Width`	`1905`

Add the code to return all the Registry settings for a given key in the `Click` event of the `cmdGetAllSettings` control:

```
Private Sub cmdGetAllSettings_Click()

    Dim strAppName As String
    Dim strSection As String
    Dim varSettings As Variant
    dim intLoop As Integer

    strAppName = Trim(txtAppName.Text)
    strSection = Trim(txtRegSection.Text)
    varSettings = GetAllSettings(strAppName, strSection)
    For intLoop = 0 To UBound(varSettings, 1)
       lstRegKeys.AddItem varSettings(intLoop, 0) & " " & varSettings(intLoop, 1)
    Next intLoop

End Sub
```

As with the other examples in this section, this code is straightforward. It resembles the other examples, except where the contents of the array are displayed in the `lstRegKeys` ListBox by using a `For...Next` loop. Figure 37.16 shows the results of running this code with the sample program you've been using.

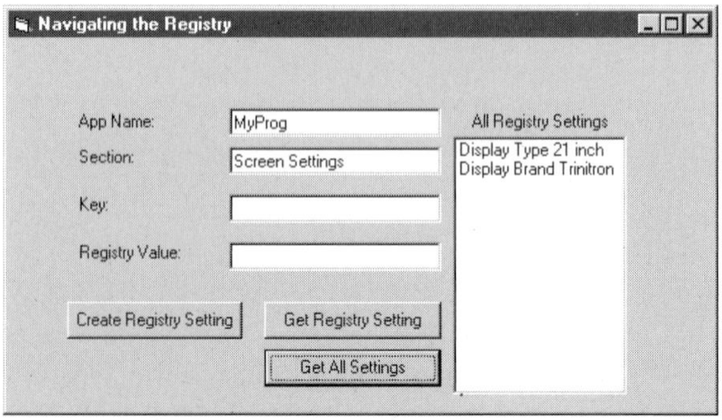

FIGURE 37.16.
Displaying all Registry settings in a list box.

The DeleteSettings Statement

To delete a Registry key setting and its value, use the `DeleteSettings` statement. This statement takes the regular arguments—application name, section name, and key setting name—and deletes the given setting and its value. If you want to delete all the settings for the application, you just use the `DeleteSettings` statement with the application name; if you want to delete all the settings within a section of an application's Registry settings, use the `DeleteSettings` statement with the application name and the setting. For example, to delete the `Display Type` Registry setting, use the following line of code:

```
DeleteSetting "MyProg", "Screen Settings", "Display Type"
```

To delete the key settings under the `Screen Settings` section, use this line of code:

```
DeleteSetting "MyProg", "Screen Settings"
```

Finally, to delete a whole application, use the following line of code:

```
DeleteSetting "MyProg"
```


Summary

The Registry provides a structured, hierarchical database for storing information about your applications and your user's computer systems. Unlike `.INI` files, which were used in previous versions of the Windows operating system, the Registry stores its information in a proprietary format and can't simply be edited like a text file. This chapter explained how the Registry is structured, how to edit the Registry, and how to use Visual Basic functions and statements to store, retrieve, and delete information in the Registry.

CHAPTER

Understanding the Extensibility Model

IN THIS CHAPTER

The key principle behind extensibility is that you can extend some object beyond its core base of behavior. You might say that one attribute of a good system is that its users can effectively extend it without jeopardizing the primary engine that drives it.

Visual Basic 5 is such a system. The core VB development environment is a robust beast. But even this great system needs tweaking from time to time, especially where repetitious development chore patterns emerge. For instance, when you're building a huge SQL string, you must break up the string into repetitious lines of code, such as the following:

```
Dim strSQL As String
strSQL = strSQL & "SELECT SomeColumn FROM SomeTable "
strSQL = strSQL & "WHERE SomeIndex = '"  & strAnotherString
...
```

By implementing some clever extensible behavior to Visual Basic, you can automate the process of building large SQL strings so that all you need to do is add the column name(s), values, and `WHERE` clause constraints.

Assessing the Extensibility Object Model

To implement extensibility features, Visual Basic offers the powerful Extensibility Object Model (EOM). Through the EOM, many core objects in Visual Basic itself are available to you at no extra charge (except for the cost of this book, perhaps). Of course, just because the EOM is a powerful interface into the rich world of the VB engine doesn't mean that it's easy to learn, much less to implement. If it were that easy, you could probably just as easily develop your own Visual Basic compiler.

The EOM consists of six loosely coupled packages of objects with methods that implement key services of the Visual Basic development environment. (*Package* is an object-oriented term that refers to a group of related but distinct objects that carry out a common subsystem behavior.) These six object packages in the EOM are

- Core Objects
- Form Manipulation
- Event Response
- Add-in Management
- Project and Component Manipulation
- Code Manipulation

Understanding the Core Objects Package

The Core Objects package contains the bread and butter of Visual Basic extensibility. In a loose sense, it has the same importance as the MFC (Microsoft Foundation Classes) has in Visual C++. Its objects include the following:

- The root object
- The `IDTExtensibility` Interface object
- The Visual Basic instance variable

The Root Object

Just as `CObject` is the base class of the MFC in Visual C++, so is the VBE (Visual Basic Environment) object to the extensibility services of Visual Basic. The VBE object is also known as the root object of the extensibility model. It's the base object for every extensibility object and collection in Visual Basic. Each object and collection owns a reference to the VBE object via a VBE property. The collections owned by the VBE object include the following:

- `VBProjects`
- `Windows`
- `CodePanes`
- `CommandBars`

The `VBProjects` Collection

The `VBProjects` collection allows you to access a set of Visual Basic properties. This feature can be helpful if your development environment has an established process for developing software—that is, you could easily audit projects quickly to make sure that they're on track. You also could use this facility to rapidly and automatically add enterprise-wide classes or frameworks, or to complete subsystems into a set of projects before a developer adds the first line of new code.

Table 38.1 shows some of the more important properties and methods for the `VBProjects` collection. It also provides brief descriptions of each.

Table 38.1. Some of the properties and methods of the `VBProjects` collection.

Name	*Type*	*Description*
`Filename`	Property	Returns the full pathname of the group project file.
`StartProject`	Property	Returns or sets the project that will start when users choose Start from the Run menu, click the Run button, or press the F5 key.

continues

Table 38.1. continued

Name	*Type*	*Description*
`AddFromFile`	Method	Allows you to add or open a project or group project. Its only required argument is the string representing the path of the file you want to add. Also, an optional Boolean argument, if set to `True` when the file being added isn't a group project file, closes the existing group project; subsequently, the new project is created as the only open project. If it's set to `True` when the file being added is a group project file, the current group project is replaced by the one you're adding. If it's set to `False` when the file being added is a group project file, each project in the corresponding group project is inserted into the current group project. The `AddFromFile` method returns a reference to the `VBNewProjects` collection.
`AddFromTemplate`	Method	Allows you to add project templates into the `VBProjects` collection. Its only required argument is the string representing the path of the file you want to use as a template. This method is similar to `AddFromFile`, except that you're dealing with project templates rather than project files.

The `Windows` Collection

With the `Windows` collection, you can access windows such as the Project and Properties windows. Also, this collection allows you to access a group of all currently open code windows and designer windows. VB adds a window to this collection each time you open a code or designer window. Similarly, each window you close is removed from this collection. With each window in the collection, for instance, you can show, hide, or position windows.

Invoking the `Close` method has different implementations for different types of windows. For instance, if you invoke `Close` on a code or designer window in the collection, that window is simply closed and removed from the collection. However, if you invoke it on a window that's a linked window frame, the window isn't closed, but rather unlinked from the other windows. If you invoke the `Close` method on a Project or Properties window, the object's `Visible` property is set to `False`, but it remains in the collection.

Table 38.2 shows some of the properties and methods for `Window` objects in the `Windows` collection, as well as brief descriptions of each.

Table 38.2. Some of the properties and methods of `Window` objects (in the `Windows` collection).

Name	*Type*	*Description*
`LinkedWindowFrame`	Property	A read-only property that returns the `Window` object representing the frame that contains the window. With this property, you can access the object representing the *linked window frame*. A linked window frame is a window frame (a listview style area) containing links to more than one window. The Project and Properties windows in VB5 are examples of window frames. The linked window frame has properties distinct from the window(s) it contains. If the window has no links with other windows in the frame, the `LinkedWindowFrame` property returns `Nothing`. An example of such a linked window frame would be the Project and Properties windows that are linked by default when you run Visual Basic 5.
`CreateToolWindow`	Method	Creates a new Tool window containing a reference to the *`DocObj`* object you pass in as the fifth argument. See more about the `CreateToolWindow` method in the following paragraph.

The `CreateToolWindow` method mentioned in Table 38.1 has the following syntax:

```
object.CreateToolWindow(AddInInst, ProgId, Caption, GuidPosition, DocObj) _
  As Window
```

The first argument, *`AddInInst`*, is an object instance of an add-in from the development environment you pass in. The *`ProgId`* argument is of the `String` data type and represents the program identifier of the ActiveX `Document` object. The *`Caption`* argument is also a `String` that contains text you want displayed as the caption for the window. The *`GuidPosition`* argument is a `String` that holds a unique identifier for the window.

The DocObj argument in the preceding code is an object that represents an ActiveX Document object. When you call this method, the DocObj argument you pass in will be set to an actual ActiveX Document object.

Collections of the Windows Collection

The Windows collection uses the CodePanes and CommandBars collections.

The CodePanes collection allows you to access the collection of code panes now open in your Visual Basic project.

The CommandBars collection allows you to access the collection of command bars. Each command bar object is a menu-style toolbar, combining the best of the menus and toolbars that users have come to expect. Each command bar object in the collection can itself contain other command bar objects, given the type of command bar you implement. The different types of command bars are

- Pop-up
- ComboBox
- Button

The VBE object has a CommandBarEvents property that, when accessed, returns the current CommandBarEvents object. Also, the user of your command bar can actually move to another area inside a menu or toolbar. Programmatically speaking, you shouldn't hard-code its actual position.

Referencing an object within the CommandBars collection can be straightforward. To reference the Add-Ins menu object, you would declare a command bar object variable and instantiate it as follows:

```
Set objCmdBar = VBInstance.CommandBars("Add-Ins")
```

With this approach, you don't have to memorize the object's ordinal position.

TIP

Because some built-in attributes of the CommandBars collection and each command bar object might change with subsequent versions of Visual Basic, you might consider creating your own classes to encapsulate its methods and properties. That way, the other classes and modules in your system will refer to your class, which in turn delegates its methods and property assignments to the CommandBars collection, the command bar object, or both.

This is useful especially in those cases where the software manufacturer changes the name of a method or property in a new version of its software, yet you had already implemented the previous version in numerous systems across your enterprise. Then you can carefully implement the new version of that software with later versions of your own.

Suppose that you have a third-party component with a class `BankAccount` in it, and that class had an attribute (property) called `AccountNum`. That's the current version, and you use that component in ten systems within your company (and each system, in turn, uses the component in 20 subsystems). When the new version comes out, the software company changed the attribute name to `AccountNumber`. You can see how much work that would be if you didn't encapsulate that component into a class (interface class). With an interface class, all enterprise systems would refer to it, and in turn this class would delegate its members to the component. When the component changes, only the interface class is affected; all other classes can stay in production.

You use the `Events` object to access properties that allow add-ins to connect to all events in Visual Basic for Applications. The properties of the `Events` object return objects of the same type as the property name. For example, the `CommandBarEvents` property returns the `CommandBarEvents` object.

You can use the `SelectedVBComponent` property to return the active component. (The *active component* is the component being tracked in the Project window.) If the selected item in the Project window isn't a component, `SelectedVBComponent` returns `Nothing`.

The IDTExtensibility Interface Object

The `IDTExtensibility` Interface object exposes the public methods and properties of the extensibility model. By *expose*, I mean that because you don't directly use the services (methods) and properties of the underlying extensibility model, you need to invoke the methods of the model's agent, so to speak. You can think of interfaces as public agents for the private implementation of an extensibility model object you instantiate.

To use the `IDTExtensibility` object, you have to add a reference to it in your project. To do this, choose Project | References from VB's menu. When the References dialog box appears, find the Microsoft Visual Basic 5.0 Extensibility object and put a check mark next to it. Then click OK.

Before you use the `IDTExtensibility` Interface object, you also need to designate a class to implement it. To implement this interface, insert the following line in the General Declarations section of your class module:

```
Implements IDTExtensibility
```

This line causes a new entry to appear under the Class item in the left-hand drop-down box (object list) of your class module. You'll insert your implementation code in the methods and properties associated with `IDTExtensibility`.

The four methods for add-in servicing (for managing your add-ins) are shown in Table 38.3. These methods define the Add-Ins interface with Visual Basic and are called by the VB IDE at specific times. For example, the `IDTExtensibility_OnConnection` method is called when VB starts (and the add-in is part of the current project), when the add-in is selected via the Add-In Manager, or when the add-in is selected by the user from VB's Add-In menu.

Table 38.3. The four methods that define an Add-Ins interface with Visual Basic.

Method Name	*Function*
`IDTExtensibility_OnConnection`	Called when the add-in is being connected to the VB IDE.
`IDTExtensibility_OnDisconnection`	Called when the add-in is no longer being used by the VB IDE.
`IDTExtensibility_OnStartupComplete`	Called when the add-in has been connected to the VB IDE, though it is only used when the add-in has been connected when Visual Basic starts.
`IDTExtensibility_OnAddInsUpdate`	Called whenever the `VBADDIN.INI` file has been modified.

If you noticed, the methods listed in Table 38.3 have names similar to those of events. When an actual event occurs, these methods (known as *add-in event handlers*) are fired. The class in your code that implements `IDTExtensibility` must implement these four event-handling methods, even if that means you put a `Rem` comment command or a comment character (`'`) in the interface method.

The Visual Basic Instance Variable

The Visual Basic instance variable (also known as a *dynamic identification variable*) identifies a particular instance of your Visual Basic session. This instance identifier allows you to have separately identifiable running instances of Visual Basic in memory.

The instance variable is of the type `VBIDE.VBE`. To use this variable, declare it in a class module or general module (also known as a *class utility* in MS Visual Modeler, a software design tool now available for Visual Basic 5). Therefore, if you declared it in a class module as private, the declaration would look like the following:

```
Private mVBInst As VBIDE.VBE
```

The prefix `m` identifies the variable as a module-level variable.

NOTE

The `VBIDE.VBE` object will not be accessible by your programs unless you have a reference to the `IDTExtensibility` object. See "The `IDTExtensibility` Interface Object" section earlier in the chapter.

Understanding the Form Manipulation Package

The objects and object collections within the Form Manipulation package offer methods (or services) to allow you to automate common development tasks that are particular to forms in your Visual Basic projects. That is, you can iterate through all the forms (each of type `VBForm`) in a project, much the way you're probably accustomed to doing by using the `Forms` collection. Along the same lines, you can manipulate all the controls on a `VBForm` object by using the `VBForm`'s public collection, `VBControls`.

Within the Form Manipulation package are several objects, including `CommandBar` and `CodePane`.

The CommandBar Object

The `CommandBar` object allows you to work with menus and toolbars. Visual Basic lets you create and delete command bars as well as modify their attributes, such as size, location on the form, and their icons. You also can handle the events associated with command bars by using the `Events.CommandBarEvents` collection of the current instance of VB (`VBInst`).

The CodePane Object

The `CodePane` object allows you to display the lines of code you may have in a given object. This object is a public member of the `CodeModule` object. You refer to a `CodePane` object by using a syntax similar to this:

```
Set MyCodePane = MyVBComponent.CodeModule.CodePane
```

Understanding the Event Response Package

Obviously, when you extend Visual Basic with the EOM, you require some mechanism for processing every action VB users carry out. The EOM provides the capability to respond to such events. The source of events can be an object or a collection of objects. Now, you can process events for the VBA object, as well as collections such as `VBProjects`, `VBComponents`, `VBControls`, and `References`. Typical events you might want to process could include

- Starting a new project
- Ending an existing project
- Adding a member to a project or deleting one (that is, forms, components, classes, and so on)

- Adding an object to a collection or removing one (that is, forms, components, classes, projects, and so on)
- Adding a reference to a project or deleting one

You can probably find many more uses for Event Response objects. The idea is that you can better manage the methodology and process of developing Visual Basic software systems by using the capability to respond to events in the Visual Basic development environment.

Understanding the Add-In Management Package

Managing add-ins is essential to using the EOM. Visual Basic provides you with the `AddIns` collection and the `AddIn` object for working with add-ins. By using each `AddIn` object, you can connect and disconnect add-ins, as well as use objects exposed within them.

Understanding the Project and Component Manipulation Package

Visual Basic's Extensibility Object Model allows you to manipulate one or more projects and components within corresponding project or component collections. Remember that a project is the development environment entity containing all components that make up your current software-development effort. A component, in turn, is a member of that project and can be a form, code module, control, or whatever member is necessary to implement your project.

The object types for project objects are `VBProject` (a single object) and `VBProjects` (a collection of `VBProject` objects). The object types for component objects are `VBComponent` (a single object) and `VBComponents` (a collection of `VBComponent` objects). When you add a new `VBProject` to the `VBProjects` collection, the `VBProjects` collection returns a reference to the newly added `VBProject` object after it's finished adding the object to the collection. The same pattern applies to `VBComponent` and `VBComponents` as well.

Understanding the Code Manipulation Package

At the center of the Code Manipulation package is the `CodeModule` object. Unlike the `CodePane` object, which allows only read-only access to code, the `CodeModule` object allows you to alter code. In turn, unlike the `CodePane` object, the `CodeModule` object doesn't let you view the code. Therefore, if you want to view and alter code, you need the services of the `CodePane` object in the Form Manipulation package. This combined use of services would loosely couple the Code Manipulation and Form Manipulation packages.

In saying that you can alter the code, I mean that you can add, delete, or replace blocks of code. So if you decided to create your own version of Visual Modeler (Microsoft's object-oriented modeling tool for VB5), you could use the `CodeModule` object to automatically create the code from your models.

The CodeModule object is useful, particularly for software development managers, system architects, and the like. You can use the CodeModule object, for instance, to count the number of lines of code in a component's module. The CodeModule property for the line count is CountOfLines. CodeModule would be a public object within a VBComponent object.

With the CountOfLines property, you could use the CodeModule's Line property to refer to a particular line of code (represented as a string). Therefore, by using the CountOfLines and Lines properties, you could grab all the text in a module by using syntax similar to the following:

```
For lonCurrentLineNumber = 1 To MyVBComponent.CodeModule.CountOfLines
    strAllCodeText = strAllCodeText & _
    MyVBComponent.CodeModule.Lines(lonCurrentLineNumber, 1) & vbCrLf
Next lonCurrentLineNumber
```

where lonCurrentLineNumber is the number representing the current line of code, MyVBComponent is an arbitrary project component you specify (that is, form, class, and so on), and strAllCodeText is the string value that represents all the lines of code you just accumulated.

Implementing the Extensibility Model in a Practical Way

Now that you know a little more about the Extensibility Model, it would be a good idea to exercise that knowledge by creating a sample add-in. In this section, you'll build a sample Visual Basic add-in that will count the number of lines of code for a given program component.

To begin creating the sample add-in, start a new project. Choose the AddIn project type (see Figure 38.1).

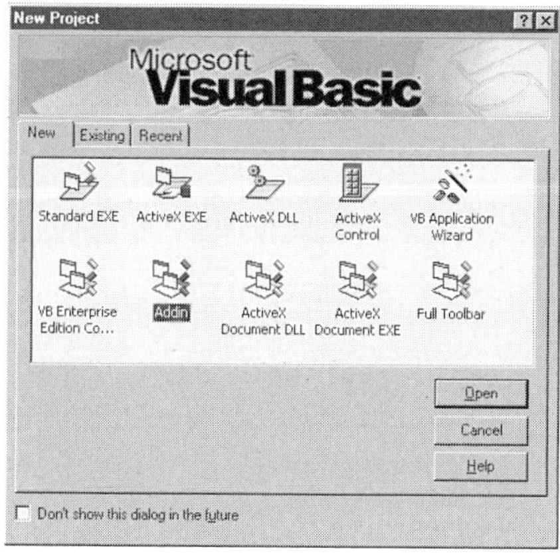

FIGURE 38.1.
To create the sample add-in, first start a new project of the AddIn *type.*

The `AddIn` project type includes many components necessary for creating Visual Basic add-ins. There is a form (`frmAddIn`) that you can modify to provide a user interface for your add-in. There's also a class module (`Connect`) that contains the four methods (`IDTExtensibility_OnConnection`, `IDTExtensibility_OnDisconnection`, `IDTExtensibility_OnAddInsUpdate`, and `IDTExtensibility_OnStartupComplete`) that are needed for the add-in's interface to Visual Basic. Finally, the project also has a code module (`AddIn`) that contains a short procedure (`AddToINI`) that can be used to modify the `VBADDIN.INI` file to include the add-in.

In this sample, you won't have to worry about any of the project's components except the form and the `Connect` module. You'll change it so that the user can enter the name of a component (and the project that it belongs to) that will have its number of code lines counted.

Display the form on the screen. It should look like the one shown in Figure 38.2.

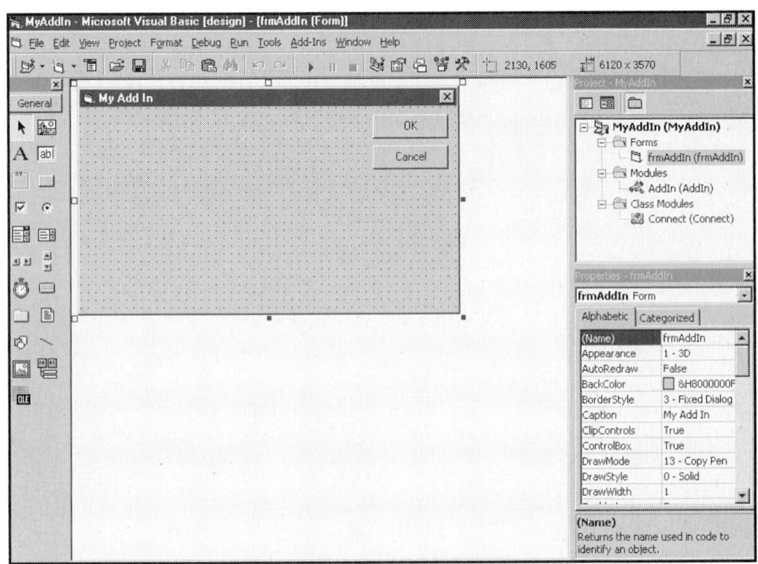

FIGURE 38.2.
The form for the `AddIn` *project before it is modified to fit the purposes of the sample add-in.*

Notice that two CommandButton controls are included on the form for you. We won't be using them, so go ahead and remove them from the form.

To build the add-in's user interface, use Figure 38.3 and Table 38.4 as a guide for adding the different controls and changing their properties.

Table 38.4. The controls and their properties that make up the sample add-in's user interface.

Control Type	*Property*	*Value*
Form	`Name`	`frmAddIn`
	`Caption`	`Code Line Counter`
	`Height`	`3480`
	`StartUpPosition`	`2 - Center Screen`
	`Width`	`3825`
Label	`Name`	`lblProject`
	`Caption`	`Project`
	`Height`	`255`
	`Left`	`360`
	`Top`	`240`
	`Width`	`1695`
TextBox	`Name`	`txtProject`
	`Height`	`315`
	`Left`	`240`
	`Text`	(Nothing)
	`Top`	`480`
	`Width`	`3135`
Label	`Name`	`lblComponent`
	`Caption`	`Component`
	`Height`	`255`
	`Left`	`360`
	`Top`	`1080`
	`Width`	`1695`
TextBox	`Name`	`txtComponent`
	`Height`	`315`
	`Left`	`240`
	`Text`	(Nothing)
	`Top`	`1320`
	`Width`	`3135`

continues

Table 38.4. continued

Control Type	*Property*	*Value*
CommandButton	`Name`	`cmdCountCodeLines`
	`Caption`	`Count Code Lines`
	`Height`	`375`
	`Left`	`240`
	`Top`	`2040`
	`Width`	`1695`
CommandButton	`Name`	`cmdDone`
	`Caption`	`Done`
	`Height`	`375`
	`Left`	`240`
	`Top`	`2520`
	`Width`	`1695`
Label	`Name`	`lblCodeLines`
	`Alignment`	`2 - Center`
	`Caption`	`Code Lines`
	`Height`	`255`
	`Left`	`2400`
	`Top`	`2280`
	`Width`	`855`
TextBox	`Name`	`txtCodeLines`
	`Alignment`	`2 - Center`
	`Enabled`	`False`
	`Height`	`405`
	`Left`	`2400`
	`Text`	(Nothing)
	`Top`	`2520`
	`Width`	`855`

Next, you need to add a few short event procedures to `frmAddIn`. Listing 38.1 shows these procedures.

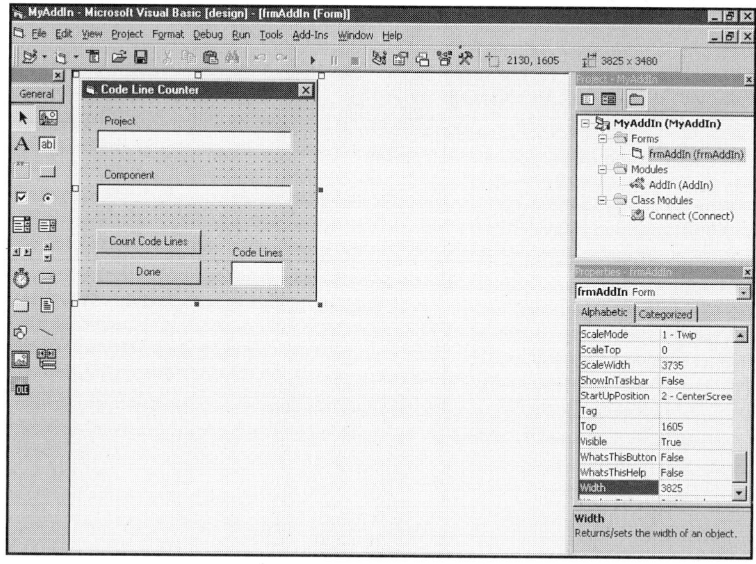

FIGURE 38.3.
The user interface (`frmAddIn`) for the sample add-in.

Listing 38.1. The code procedures for the sample add-in, which should be added to the `frmAddIn` form.

```
Private Sub cmdCountCodeLines_Click()

Dim strVBProject As String
Dim strVBComponent As String
Dim objVBComponent As VBComponent

' Get the Project name and Component name from the
' form's two TextBox controls.
strVBProject = txtProject.Text
strVBComponent = txtComponent.Text

' Set objVBComponent to the program component suggested
' by strVBProject and strVBComponent.
Set objVBComponent = _
VBInstance.VBProjects.Item(strVBProject).VBComponents.Item(strVBComponent)

' Assign the number of lines of code (CountOfLines) of the
' component objVBComponent to the txtCodeLines TextBox.
txtCodeLines.Text = Str(objVBComponent.CodeModule.CountOfLines)

End Sub


Private Sub cmdDone_Click()

' Hide the Add-In window.
Connect.Hide

End Sub
```

Before going any farther, let's take a closer look at the two event procedures you just added. The first, cmdCountCodeLines_Click, is triggered when the user clicks on the Count Code Lines button. It uses the project and component names that were typed into the form's TextBox controls (txtProject and txtComponent) to assign that component to the objVBComponent object. Note the hierarchy used to obtain a component item in the following line of code:

```
Set objVBComponent = _
VBInstance.VBProjects.Item(strVBProject).VBComponents.Item(strVBComponent)
```

First the VBInstance object is referenced and then its VBProjects collection. The string value strVBProject included in the first set of parentheses indicates the project name, which is used as the key argument for the VBProjects collection's Item method.

After the project has been referenced from the VBProjects collection, that project's VBComponents collection is accessed by using the strVBComponent string as a key argument for the collection's Item method. This long sequence of referencing ultimately assigns the specified component (strVBComponent) that is part of the specified project (strVBProject) to the objVBComponent object.

The next line of code

```
txtCodeLines.Text = Str(objVBComponent.CodeModule.CountOfLines)
```

is used to access the CodeModule of the newly assigned objVBComponent object. The CountOfLines property of the CodeModule object contains the number of lines of code in that particular component. This number is assigned to the txtCodeLines TextBox so that the user can see the results.

The second event procedure that was added is the cmdDone_Click event. This contains only a single line of code that calls the Connect object's Hide method, hiding the add-in's user interface. The Connect object is an instance of the Connect class, which, as you may remember, is a part of the AddIn project. It is defined in the form's General Declarations section.

You can remove the Click events for the CancelButton and OKButton objects because they were deleted earlier. These event procedures are no longer valid because they will never be triggered.

You only need to make one small change, and the project will be finished. Bring up the code in the Connect class module. In the IDTExtensibility_OnConnection procedure, there is a line of code that looks like this:

```
Set mcbMenuCommandBar = AddToAddInCommandBar("My AddIn")
```

Change "My AddIn" to "Code Line Counter". If you don't, then the add-in will appear on VB's Add-In menu as "My AddIn," which isn't very descriptive.

That's all there is to the sample add-in. However, you need to do something before you save the project. Choose Project | MyAddIn Properties from the menu. Change the project name from "MyAddIn" to something more appropriate, such as "CodeLineCounter". Then click OK. Now you can save the project. Save the form as CLCFORM.FRM, the module as CLCMODULE.BAS, the class as CLCCONNECT.CLS, and the project as CODELINECOUNTER.VBP.

Compile the add-in by choosing File | Make CodeLineCounter.exe from the menu. When the Make Project dialog box appears, be sure to specify that the executable file be placed in the same directory as Visual Basic. You'll want VB to have access to the add-in later.

Before you can use the add-in, you'll have to make a change to the `VBADDIN.INI` file so that Visual Basic will know that the add-in is available. You'll find that file in your `Windows` directory, and you can edit it with any text editor (Notepad works fine). Add the following line to the end of the file:

```
CodeLineCounter.Connect=0
```

Save the file; then get back into Visual Basic. Open any project that you might happen to have handy. Then choose Add-In | Add-In Manager from the menu. You should see a list similar to the one shown in Figure 38.4, though the items on your screen may be different.

FIGURE 38.4.
Visual Basic's Add-In Manager.

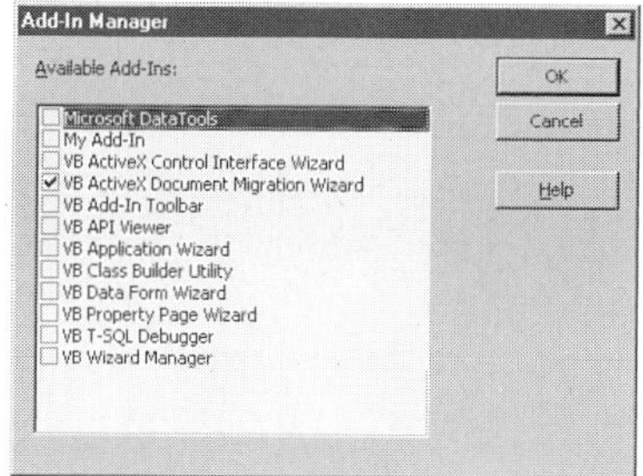

Notice that you now have an option for My Add-In. Put a check mark in its box by clicking on it; then click OK.

As soon as the add-in loads, it will be added to VB's Add-In menu. Invoke it by choosing it from that menu, and you'll see its user interface. Enter the name of a project currently loaded into Visual Basic and then the name of one of its components. For example, if you have a project named `Project1` which contains a form named `Form1`, then enter those names in the appropriate text boxes. Then click on the Count Code Lines button. You should then see the number of lines of code in the Code Lines text box. Try it with other components if you want. When you're finished, click the Done button.

NOTE

If you go back to make changes to the sample add-in, make sure that you remove it from the Add-Ins menu using the Add-In Manager. Otherwise, you won't be able to recompile the project.

Admittedly, this is a simple add-in. It could use some work. For example, instead of having the user enter the project and component names into text boxes, you might want to use combo boxes that contain the names of all available projects and components so that the user need only select the ones he wants. But it does serve as an example of how to use the Extensibility Object Model in Visual Basic and should provide a starting point for further explorations into this area of programming.

Summary

In this chapter, you learned about the Extensibility Object Model and its members. The EOM is a useful service for extending Visual Basic's behavior. It facilitates a better way to manage the Visual Basic development process by allowing you to manage and manipulate each project programmatically.

This capability to extend Visual Basic more than compensates for Visual Basic's lack of pure inheritance capabilities (as some would argue) by allowing you to automate the software reuse process. System auditors can easily audit projects to ensure compliance with company policy (is this a benefit or a threat to ingenuity?). If you have a favorite application-design tool that doesn't generate code for Visual Basic, you can bridge this compatibility gap with the EOM. If your company has a motto that must be placed on every application's main form, and this motto changes every month for some new marketing campaign, you could automate the process of adding the latest motto to every main form by using the EOM.

Visual Basic's extensibility features make it a top contender for the favorite software-development tool of corporate America. After reading this chapter, you should have some sense of Visual Basic's new stature.

39

Tuning and Optimizing Your Application

IN THIS CHAPTER

Visual Basic has evolved into an extremely powerful programming language. Visual Basic 5 has added many new language features as well as increased the performance of common tasks such as form displaying. Many tips and tricks required in earlier versions of Visual Basic are no longer required; however, with the many different application scenarios available to the Visual Basic 5.0 programmer, such as building ActiveX Internet components or distributed applications, optimizing and tuning is as important as ever.

In this chapter, you learn how to optimize and tune Visual Basic applications and components. This chapter shows you how to use several different utilities, such as the Visual Basic Code Profiler, to analyze existing applications. You also learn how to use various optimizing techniques and tricks and how to create and use a form template to perform simple code benchmarking.

Optimizing and Tuning with Visual Basic 5

Visual Basic 5 presents many new features and opportunities for optimizing and tuning applications and components. Visual Basic 5 is the first version of Visual Basic to exist only in a 32-bit form and include a native code compiler to speed up application execution times. Because Visual Basic 5 exists only in a 32-bit platform, you're dealing with an advanced 32-bit operating system such as Windows 95 or Windows NT, which offer improved performance and resource usage over Windows 3.x. This immediately raises the following questions:

- Do I still need to optimize and tune?
- Should I still worry about using up resources?

The answer to both questions is a resounding *yes*, and in this chapter you learn that optimizing and tuning Visual Basic 5 applications is more than telling end users to buy faster machines with more memory. Before getting into the finer points of optimizing and tuning Visual Basic applications, let's quickly review what optimizing and tuning is all about.

Understanding the Art of Optimizing and Tuning

Optimizing and tuning an application means one or more of the following:

- Increasing the execution speed of the application
- Effectively managing limited resources
- Decreasing the application size
- Increasing the display speed of an application
- Increasing the perceived speed of an application

You can tune an application for one or more of these definitions; however, it's difficult to tune an application for all of them because several of these definitions work against each other. For example, optimizing for speed often increases the size of the program; likewise, optimizing for size often decreases the speed of the application.

I've read many different books and articles and listened to several speakers at Visual Basic conferences refer to optimizing and tuning as an art form. I don't think of optimizing and tuning as an art form used excessively by Visual Basic gurus; rather, I think of it as part of the software development cycle and obtainable by all programmers willing to put in a little extra time and effort. Consider some important optimizing and tuning points as you develop your application.

Using Proper Software Designs When Creating Applications

Back in the old days (that is, before Visual Basic), programming environments often required programmers and programming teams to use different methodologies to map out the application's functional and detail design specifications and data dictionaries before a line of code was even written. Today, many C++ programmers use more modern object-oriented methodologies to generate program specifications before they ever sit down and write a line of code. Unfortunately, my experience has been that when working with many different clients, programming teams, and programmers, the Visual Basic community doesn't follow the same design methodologies. All too often applications are prototyped and then quickly modified into the end product. These prototyped applications would benefit from a quick design session with object-oriented methodology or just some simple diagrams and brainstorming.

The first important lesson of optimizing and tuning is that they start in the design phase (for example, when you're selecting the proper algorithms and defining the data structures and objects used by your application). Select the faster, more efficient algorithms or plan on benchmarking a few. When defining your data structures, avoid slow and inefficient data types (such as variants) in favor of faster data types (such as integers and strings).

Testing on the Designated Platform or Environment

Too often developers test and develop on machines or in environments far superior to their application's actual production platform or environment. During the initial design phase, make sure that you take into account the production environment or platform in which your application will reside. For example, take into account platform parameters such as memory, disk space, and processor power. If the platform is a 486 with 8 MB of RAM, you don't want to deliver an application that uses Word 97 and Excel 97 via OLE Automation. The platform won't be able to support such functionality in a reasonable amount of time.

During the development phase, periodically test the application in the production environment to identify possible bottlenecks. By detecting bottlenecks early in the development cycle, you can resolve them before the application goes live and becomes critical. You should always have the requirements of the program written down so that you can refer back to them during testing to ensure that those requirements are being met. A well thought out plan for testing is also imperative.

Knowing What to Optimize

An important part of learning to tune and optimize Visual Basic applications is to understand what can be optimized, where to optimize, and what can't be optimized. You can optimize Visual Basic code, algorithms, and data access methods. You can't do anything to speed up your application if it's accessing files on a network, which is extremely slow.

A good example of knowing what to optimize—and where—is a client/server application that uses Microsoft SQL Server on the back end. The application is very fast except for one particular form that loads and displays very slowly. How should you approach optimizing and tuning for this application? There's no point tuning the forms that load quickly because you're happy with their performance. Instead, focus on the one form that loads and displays slowly. You can examine the data-access method used, although this probably isn't the problem because the other forms also use the same data-access method but run fine. You can optimize and tune the form display time by trying to limit the number of repaints, but after you optimize the form display, the form is still slow. What now?

You've already determined that the data-access methods are the same as on all the other forms and that you've done all you can to optimize the form display. At this point, it's time to stop trying to optimize the Visual Basic application and look more closely at the query used to populate the form. Is the query using indexes? Are the tables involved substantially larger than the tables used for the other forms?

It's the complexity of knowing what and where to optimize that has lead many to call optimizing and tuning an art. Optimize and tune things that you can change, such as Visual Basic code, algorithms, and display speed. Spend your time optimizing and tuning the poorly performing parts of your application, not the parts that are already running fast. Understand the big picture of your application's environment and any outside resources your application interacts with, such as the network, the database, and other components.

Testing Compiled Versions

When performing benchmark testing, test with compiled versions of Visual Basic. After all, you'll be distributing compiled versions, and you take out the oddities and overhead of testing in the Visual Basic development environment.

Optimizing and Tuning During the Entire Life Cycle

As stated earlier, optimizing and tuning is part of the development life cycle, not something you do at the end. Tune and optimize your code throughout the development life cycle. Especially when completing an ActiveX component or a frequently used function, make optimizing and tuning part of the debugging and initial test phases.

Avoiding Over-Optimizing

Avoid spending several hours rewriting code that works fine and isn't a bottleneck. For instance, avoid writing the fast sort routine when your current bubble sort routine works fine and you call the routine only once to sort 20 items. It's an entirely different story, however, if you're sorting many items, and the sort routine is called in a recursive routine and is now a bottleneck. Don't go crazy trying to optimize and tune each and every line. Write good, efficient code and spend your time fixing slow routines and bottlenecks.

Commenting Your Code Like a Maintenance Programmer

Too often, I have looked at well-written code from other consultants that performed well, but the consultants had failed to add a single line of comments! Comments *don't* increase the size of the application or hinder your application's performance. *Comment your code!* Comments are used to help you, as well as other programmers, maintain and enhance your application in the future. Programmers forced to maintain and enhance existing systems (for example, maintenance programmers) know all too well the difficulty of working with poorly commented code, and they learn not to be part of the problem by adding lots of comments. Make sure that you comment your code so that you, as well as individuals who may inherit your applications in the future, can easily determine what the code is doing and why.

Creating and Using Templates to Perform Code Benchmarking

What if you're busy developing an application and reach a critical coding point? Maybe you're about to create several forms that populate combo boxes from a database, and you're wondering what will be the fastest database access method to use or what's the fastest recordset type. You want to begin using the proper methods from the start so that you don't have to go back later and change the code to take advantage of a faster method. What do you do? What else but write some code and perform some benchmark testing?

Visual Basic 5 offers a feature that lets you quickly create benchmarking programs by using a form template. Included on the CD-ROM accompanying this book you'll find a Visual Basic form called `FRMTIMER.FRM`. Place this form in your Visual Basic home directory's `\TEMPLATE\FORMS` subdirectory. When you want to create a quick test program to benchmark some code, start a new Visual Basic project and select Project | Add Form from the main Visual Basic menu. The Add Form dialog box appears (see Figure 39.1).

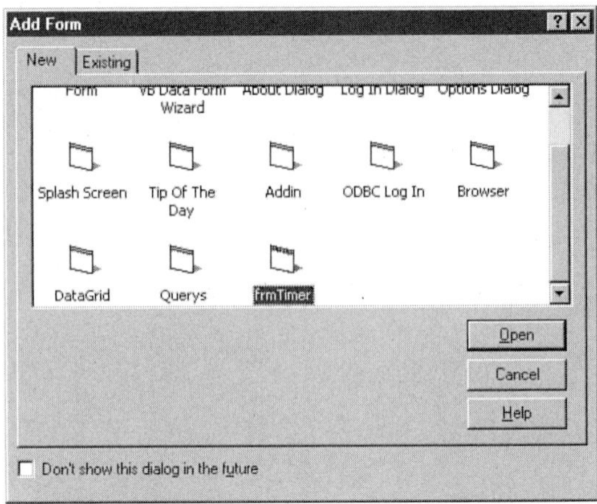

FIGURE 39.1. *The Add Form dialog box.*

Select the `frmTimer` form shown in Figure 39.1. The `frmTimer` template includes skeleton code to quickly test two different coding algorithms and compare them. Add the code you want to test to the command button click event. Compile and execute the program by using the radio buttons to determine which algorithm you're testing. The amount of time required to execute each algorithm is displayed in a label control. Two label controls are used on the form, so after both tests are executed, you can easily compare the amount of time required to execute the algorithms. Listing 39.1 shows the code in `frmTimer`.

Listing 39.1. Benchmarking skeleton code.

```
Private Sub cmdTest_Click()

    Dim Start, Finish, TotalTime

    If Option1.Value = True Then
        Start = Timer

        'Put the code you wish to time
        'here!

        'End of Code time test
        Finish = Timer
    Else
        'Option 2 selected
        Start = Timer

        'Put the code you wish to time
        'here!

        'End of Code time test
        Finish = Timer

    End If
```

```
    TotalTime = Finish - Start  ' Calculate total time.

    '
    'Set up display results
    '
    If Option1.Value = True Then
        'Option 1
        lblOpt1.Caption = "Total time to execute " & _
                          Option1.Caption & ": " & _
                          TotalTime
    Else
        'Option 2
        lblOpt2.Caption = "Total time to execute " & _
                          Option2.Caption & ": " & _
                          TotalTime

    End If

End Sub
```

The Visual Basic `Timer` function is used to perform benchmarking timing. Let's use the form template to benchmark a Visual Basic DAO performance tip. When you're modifying and adding database records with DAO, using the DAO object model methods (such as `Edit`, `AddNew`, and `Update`) is a common DAO programming practice. When you use these DAO methods to modify many records, performance can become an issue. A faster way to modify records when working with DAO is to replace the DAO methods with SQL statements and the DAO `Execute` method (for example, `AddNew` is replaced with a SQL `Insert` statement, the `Update` method is replaced with a SQL `Update` statement, and the `Delete` method is replaced with a SQL `Delete` statement). You can further increase the performance by placing the entire operation within a transaction. The code in Listing 39.2 demonstrates this performance tip. The benchmarking form is shown in Figure 39.2.

39 TUNING AND OPTIMIZING YOUR APPLICATION

Listing 39.2. DAO performance-timing code.

```
Private Sub cmdTest_Click()

    Dim Start, Finish, TotalTime          'Timer Variables
    Dim rstPublishers As DAO.Recordset    'Holds the recordset used by Option 2
    Dim strSQL As String                  'Update string for Option 2

    'With this timing example we just want to measure
    'the update time. All connections and recordsets
    'will be established prior to the timers starting.

    'Open the recordset for Option 1
    If Option1.Value = True Then
        'Open the Recordset object for the update
        'Only retrieve records from the state of CA
        '
        Set rstPublishers = _
            gdbBiblio.OpenRecordset("SELECT * FROM Publishers", _
            dbOpenDynaset)
```

continues

Listing 39.2. continued

```
Else
    strSQL = "UPDATE Publishers Set Comments = "
    strSQL = strSQL & "'Buy VB Development Unleashed'"

End If

'Begin the timing operation
If Option1.Value = True Then
    Start = Timer

    'DAO Update Timing Test - Note this is POOR
    'Performance - DO NOT UPDATE Several DATABASE
    'Records this way!
    With rstPublishers
        While Not .BOF And Not .EOF
            'Update the recordset comment field
            .Edit rstPublishers("Comments") = "Buy VB Development Unleashed"
            .Update

            'Move to the next record
            .MoveNext
        Wend
    End With

    'End of Code time test
    Finish = Timer

    'Clean up
    rstPublishers.Close
    Set rstPublishers = Nothing
Else
    'Option 2 selected - SQL Updates and Transactions
    Start = Timer

    'Note: The following code performs much faster!
    'When updating, adding or deleting records using DAO
    'use transactions to speed up the operation.
    'When modifying or deleting a large number of records
    'use SQL statements
    gwksTest.BeginTrans
    gdbBiblio.Execute strSQL
    gwksTest.CommitTrans
    'End of Code time test
    Finish = Timer

End If

TotalTime = Finish - Start  ' Calculate total time.

'
'Set up display results
'
If Option1.Value = True Then
    'Option 1
    lblOpt1.Caption = "Total time to execute " & _
```

```
                                Option1.Caption & ": " & _
                                TotalTime
    Else
        'Option 2
        lblOpt2.Caption = "Total time to execute " & _
                                Option2.Caption & ": " & _
                                TotalTime
    End If

End Sub
```

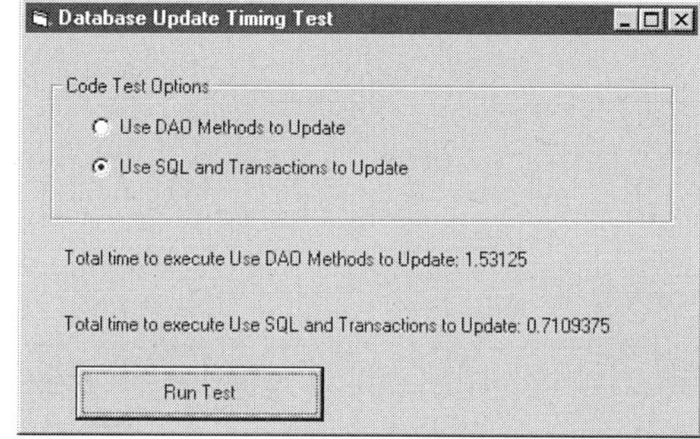

FIGURE 39.2.
The `frmTimer` *benchmarking record updating with DAO methods rather than SQL.*

> **NOTE**
>
> The code in Listing 39.2 uses the Visual Basic Microsoft Access database that ships with Visual Basic, `BIBLIO.MDB`. The code assumes that the database is in the same directory as the benchmarking application. Make the changes as necessary for your machine.

Reviewing Performance Tips and Tricks

Let's review some common Visual Basic 5.0 optimization and tuning tricks.

Using the Visual Basic Compiler to Tune and Optimize

Visual Basic 5 is the first version of Visual Basic to include a native compiler as well as the p-code compiler available in previous versions. P-code is compiled to pseudocode that's interpreted to machine code at runtime. Native compiled code is compiled to machine code, so no interpretation is required at runtime. Native compiled code is typically faster than p-code applications; however, p-code applications are smaller than the same native compiled program. Again, there's the paradox of tuning for speed versus size, and vice versa. The native code compiler included with Visual Basic includes advanced tuning options to further optimize your compiled application (for example, you can select options such as ignoring overflow checks with integers).

Keep in mind that native code isn't the final answer to optimizing your applications. Native code improves performance greatly with mathematical code, complex algorithms, and looping code (see Table 39.1). If your application relies on graphical displays or database access, you might not notice huge performance gains between the native compiled code and the applications generated by p-code. Table 39.1 shows the benchmarks obtained by an application compiled with p-code, native, and native with all the advanced options selected.

Table 39.1. Compiled application benchmark test (time in seconds).

Test	*P-Code*	*Native*	*Native with Options*
Graphics	3.84	3.84	4.01
Variant Counter	12.85	10.77	10.38
Long Counter	2.74	.44	.05
Double Counter	4.95	1.98	1.60
Splash Screen	1.32	1.27	1.26
String Copy	.28	.27	.27

NOTE

The application used to obtain the various benchmark tests in Table 39.1 is the `OPTIMIZE.VBP` project that ships with Visual Basic 5 in the `\SAMPLES\PGUIDE\OPTIMIZE` subdirectory. The Optimizing application (see Figure 39.3) contains many good examples of common Visual Basic 5 performance and optimization tips.

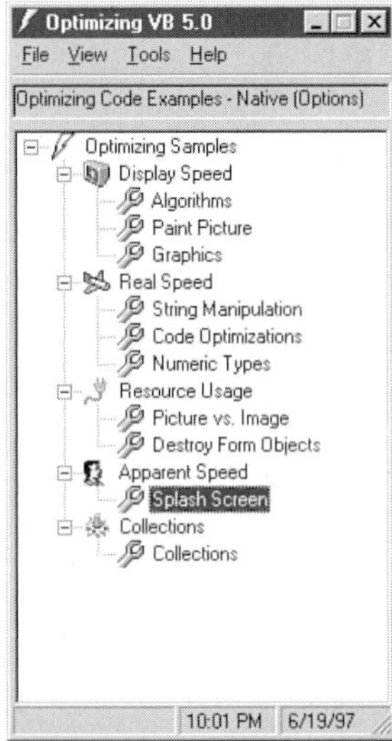

FIGURE 39.3.
The Visual Basic 5.0 Optimizing application.

NOTE

The compiled versions of the Optimizing application used to generate Table 39.3 are slightly larger than the application generated by p-code. The sizes of each compiled application are as follows:

- P-code: 481 KB
- Native: 534 KB
- Native with options: 532 KB

Sorting Strings with a List Box

If you need to sort some data quickly and don't have a sort routine already written, use a Visual Basic ListBox control to sort the data. It makes no sense to spend time writing and optimizing a sort routine to sort a couple of items when you can use a Visual Basic list box control to perform the sort. Set the list box control's `Sorted` property to `True` and use the `AddItem` method to add each item to the list box. You can then read the items from the list box in sorted order. This trick might not provide you with the fastest possible sort routine, but it's not slow and will help you meet your project deadlines.

If using a ListBox to sort items is not feasible, you'll find some sorting algorithms in Chapter 54, "Algorithms For VB Programmers." That chapter also contains code for an efficient Quick Sort routine.

Using the Windows API

For years, Visual Basic programmers have been taking advantage of the Windows API to improve application performance and add functionality that can't be accomplished by using Visual Basic alone. Entire books have been written about using the Windows API. You can use the API for simple speed-enhancing tricks, such as quickly finding a string in a list box, or for more complex tricks such as creating a thread from a Visual Basic application with the Windows API. The Windows API is a great way to increase your application's performance. Wrap your favorite API calls into a Visual Basic class module to make them easier to use and modify.

Using Data Controls to Conserve SQL Server User Connections

Using bound data controls to populate a combo box or fill text boxes in a form is a great way to rapidly put together fully functional data-entry forms. Sometimes, several data controls are used on a single form to retrieve data and fill combo boxes. In a Microsoft or Sybase SQL Server environment, each data control uses a database connection (referred to as a *user connection*). A connection for each data control surprises many programmers when they learn that their simple data-entry form uses five simultaneous connections, they have only a ten-user license, and seven users need to use the application. Of course, you could resort to writing code to query the database and populate the combo boxes or form; however, you lose the speed and ease of use provided by the data control.

When populating combo boxes and list boxes with static-type recordsets, use code methods so that you don't waste several user connections populating list and combo boxes. The code in Listing 39.3 shows how to use a data control to easily populate a data-bound grid or form while using only a single-connection global SQL Server connection.

Listing 39.3. Using a data control to populate a grid or form with only one global SQL Server connection.

```
Dim gTest As New RDO.rdoConnection    'Global RDO connection used by all the forms

Private Sub Form_Load()

Dim rsTest As RDO.rdoResultset        'Define a local RDO Resultset

'Set up the RDO connection parameters. These
'Will vary from one SQL Server to another.
With gTest
    .Connect = "uid=sa;pwd=;DSN=PubsDB;"
    .CursorDriver = rdUseOdbc
    .EstablishConnection rdDriverNoPrompt
End With

'Fill combo box
Set rsTest = gTest.OpenResultset("Select au_id from pubs..authors", rdOpenStatic)

'Open the recordset using the global connection
Set rsTest = gTest.OpenResultset("Select * from pubs..authors", rdOpenStatic)

'Set the data control resultset
'This data control could be bound to a grid or
'other controls, however it will not use a new
'user connection. Instead it will use the global connection.
Set MSRDC1.Resultset = rsTest

End Sub
```

NOTE

The code in Listing 39.3 uses RDO (Remote Data Objects), which is distributed only with the Enterprise Edition of Visual Basic and designed specifically for client/server databases such as Microsoft SQL Server and Oracle.

TIP

If the same set of static data is fetched from a remote database and is being used repeatedly throughout the application, you can boost performance by caching the recordset in a string array or other suitable data type. Subsequent access to the data is blazingly fast because the information is already in RAM and doesn't require a trip to the database to retrieve the resultset. As always, use caution when dealing with clients with low memory (8-12 MB) and do not cache extremely large resultsets, as they will use up large amounts of memory.

Understanding Visual Basic Limitations

Not only is it important to know what tips and tricks can be used to help tune and optimize your code, but it's also important to know that Visual Basic has some limitations and what those limitations are before you create an application that exceeds those limitations. Some Visual Basic limitations are as follows:

- Only 254 control names can be used per form (control arrays count once).
- A line of Visual Basic code can't exceed 1,023 bytes.
- A Visual Basic form, class, or module can't load more than 65,534 lines of code.
- The code in a module can't exceed 64 KB.
- The maximum number of items a list box can store is 32 KB.

Reducing the Dots When Using Objects

I recently helped a programmer use the Microsoft Excel `WorkSheets` object to read information from a Lotus Notes database and an RDBMS (relational database management system) database into an Excel spreadsheet by using a Visual Basic application. The routine took more than five minutes to complete. I looked at the code to try to speed up the process, and the first change I made to the code reduced the time to around 40 seconds. What was the change? I reduced the number of dots when referencing the Excel objects used in the code. For instance, Excel has a complex object module, and often programmers write code that references several objects to get to the object they want to use. The following code illustrates this example:

```
oApplication.oWorkbooks(0).WorkSheets(0)
```

Each dot used requires multiple calls to the object and OLE services; by reducing the number of dots, you greatly reduce the number of calls. To reduce the number of dots, get a reference to the object you want to use; this technique, called *aliasing*, can be used with ActiveX objects as well as objects created within your project.

The following example assigns the Excel `WorkSheets` object to a variable. The variable can then be used to execute the methods and properties of the worksheet object without the references to the application or `Workbook` object, thus reducing the number of dots used:

```
Set oWorkSheet = oApplication.oWorkbooks(0).WorkSheets(0)
```

Using Method Parameters with Out-of-Process or Distributed Components

When calling out-of-process or distributed components, it's faster to pass parameters through a method call than to set several object properties and then invoke a method that uses the properties. Expensive cross-process calls are required for each property that's set, as well as for the method invoked. By using parameters with a method, the cross-process calls can be reduced to the method call. As an alternative, you can create a local object, set parameters on the local object, and then pass an object reference as a parameter to the remote object.

Increasing Perceived Speed with Splash Screens and Progress Indicators

If your application takes a long time to load, use a *splash screen* to give users something to look at during the load process. Splash screens improve the users' perception of the application's load time. If your application performs operations that take more than 5–7 seconds, display a progress indicator to aid the users' speed perception as well as indicate that the program is still functioning (users have a terrible habit of giving up and hitting Ctrl+Alt+Delete).

Using Early Object Binding Versus Late Binding

If you know the object type when using objects, use early binding. *Early binding* is when you declare the type of object that is to use the variable in your code. The following example declares a variable as an `Excel Application` object:

```
Dim oXl As Excel.Application
```

Early binding allows the compiler to check your code to make sure that the object actually supports the methods and properties you're using during compile time, as opposed to you finding out at runtime. Visual Basic lets you use early binding for objects by selecting a reference to the object through Visual Basic's main menu (choose Project | References). Early binding is also much faster than *late binding*, when you declare objects as follows:

```
Dim oXl as Object
```

Use late binding only when the type of object you'll be using is unknown at runtime.

Optimizing Display Speed

The key to optimizing display speed is to try to minimize the number of repaints and the amount of memory consumed by graphics. Some standard optimization and performance tips are as follows:

- If you don't use graphical methods, turn off the `ClipControls` property (forms and picture box control).
- For displaying images and bitmaps, use the image control rather than the picture box control. The image control uses substantially fewer resources than the picture box control.
- If you have many controls on a form, place them in a picture box control. When all the controls are set with the proper data, set the picture box control's `Visible` property to `False` while you load the controls on the form. Make the picture box visible to display the loaded form, thus reducing the number of repaints.

Optimizing Data Types

The following are useful tips when working with Visual Basic data types:

- Avoid variants.
- Use `long` integers or integers where possible.
- Never use floating-point data types (`single`, `double`, `currency`, and so on) for loop counters.

Optimizing File I/O Operations

To speed up file I/O, read file information into arrays. Also, rather than write a line at a time to a file, cache the information in a memory buffer (for example, a string variable) and then write the cache memory buffer to the file.

Optimizing Memory

Here are some useful tips to help you reduce the amount of memory used by your application:

- Avoid variants, unless they have to be used, such as for certain aspects of OLE automation.
- Release memory used by objects (including forms) when you're done with them by setting them to `Nothing`.
- Unload unused forms.

Avoiding Calling Functions and Procedures in Different Modules

Visual Basic modules are loaded into memory on demand, not on application startup, which means that a module isn't loaded until a function or procedure in the module is called. During application startup, refrain from calling functions or procedures in many different modules. This slows application startup as each module is loaded into memory. Try to keep functions and procedures with similar functionality in the same module.

Selecting the Proper Component Type

Visual Basic 5 lets you create in-process (DLL) or out-of-process (EXE) ActiveX code components. Further complicating the type of component to create is the thread model you should select. Visual Basic 5 lets you mark components as thread safe and generate components that support multiple threads or single threads.

For your applications, should you create an in-process (DLL) or out-of-process (EXE)? That depends on the application or service you're providing. An in-process component is faster when it's used on the same machine because it loads in the same address space as the application using the component. With DLLs, costly cross-process calls are avoided. In a distributed environment, however, out-of-process components deserve a second look because they provide asynchronous callback capabilities. By using asynchronous callbacks, a client can invoke a component method without *blocking* (that is, waiting for the component to finish). When the component completes the method, the client is notified. The Internet has been *the* hot technology area of the past year; take a closer look at creating components for Web-based applications.

Optimizing Web-Based Components

You can use Microsoft's Web browser, Internet Explorer, to download ActiveX components and use them on a client machine. When creating ActiveX components to execute in a browser, create in-process components (DLLs) for the best performance. ActiveX components can also be used on the Web server side by Microsoft's Internet Information Server (IIS) and the Active Server Page framework. When creating Web-based server ActiveX components, create the component as an in-process component (that is, an ActiveX DLL).

Generating an ActiveX DLL provides better performance than out-of-process components because an in-process component runs in the same process space as the application that uses the component (that is, Internet Information Server). As such, the application can reference the component's properties and methods without making the costly cross-process calls required in out-of-process components. Out-of-process components do have some positive features not available to in-process components that can be used in a distributed computing or client/server environment, such as asynchronous callbacks or asynchronous notification events. In a Web-based environment, stick to using ActiveX DLLs.

Multithreaded or Single-Threaded Components

You can't spawn a new thread with a Visual Basic application or component without using the Windows API from within your Visual Basic application to do so. However, multithreaded clients such as Internet Information Server can take advantage of multithreaded ActiveX components by spawning multiple threads of objects when creating objects from multithreaded components.

A *thread* is executing code; every application in a Windows environment has at least a single thread of execution. An application or component is said to be multithreaded if the application can create more than one thread of execution. Suppose that you have a financial database application and a computation that executes for a long time. If your application is multithreaded, you can start your computation by creating a thread to perform the computation and, while the computation thread is executing, begin to edit a database table by using another thread. Preemptive multitasking operating systems, such as Windows NT and Windows 95, allocate separate time slices for each thread that's to execute (that is, the computation thread and the edit table thread), giving the appearance of performing both tasks simultaneously.

When creating ActiveX components used in a Web or distributed environment, create multithreaded ActiveX components. Multithreaded ActiveX components are created at compile time by selecting the project option Unattended Execution. When the ActiveX DLL is compiled with the Unattended Execution check box selected, a DLL that supports multithreading is generated.

When creating multithreaded ActiveX components, keep in mind how Visual Basic DLLs use apartment-model threading. Remember also that ActiveX component automation uses serialization of requests to prevent multiple threads from executing a new operation before previous operations have completed.

Keeping component serialization intact is important because Visual Basic ActiveX components aren't re-entrant. *Re-entrancy* is the code's capability to be executed by a thread. Before the thread completes, it yields control of the processor to another thread to process the same code. When the second thread yields processor control, the variables and stack pointer are restored to the exact state before the processor yielded control to another thread. Because Visual Basic ActiveX components aren't re-entrant, when you create ActiveX components, don't do any of the following in your component, which may cause the processor to yield to another thread before completing the current operation:

- Call `DoEvents`
- Raise an event handled by an object on another thread or process
- Invoke a method or property of an object in another thread or process

NOTE

Multithreaded applications don't always equate to a faster application. In many cases, multithreaded applications let you manage the perception that an application is executing faster by not locking up the user interface during a lengthy process. Multithreaded applications and components make more sense when developing for server-side processing. Also keep in mind that Visual Basic doesn't currently support debugging multithreaded applications.

Using the Visual Basic Code Profiler

Visual Basic ships with a code-analyzing tool called the Visual Basic Code Profiler to help you optimize and tune your applications. You can use the Code Profiler to determine how many times a code line or function has been executed. This form of profiling is called *code coverage* and is useful for finding *dead code* (code that's never executed) in your programs. By pointing out what code is executed the most, code coverage is helpful in determining which functions or lines of code you may want to re-examine and tune.

The Code Profiler also can be used for performance optimizing by timing how long each line of code or function takes to execute. Using the Code Profiler for optimizing application performance is useful in helping you determine which functions or lines of code are possible application bottlenecks, as well as what parts of your application you may need to optimize.

Installing the Visual Basic Code Profiler

The Visual Basic Code Profiler isn't part of the Visual Basic installation. You can find the profiler on the Visual Basic CD-ROM in the `\TOOLS\UNSUPPRT\VBCP` directory. To install the code profiler, follow these steps:

1. Copy the `VBCP.DLL` file located on the Visual Basic 5 CD-ROM directory, `\TOOLS\UNSUPPRT\VBCP`, to a directory on your computer's hard drive (for example, the Visual Basic default directory).
2. To register the Code Profiler, use the Windows 95 or Windows NT 4.0 Explorer and the Registry utility, `REGSVR32.EXE`. Start the Explorer and locate `REGSVR32.EXE` on the Visual Basic CD-ROM in the `\TOOLS\REGUTILS` directory.
3. Start another copy of Explorer. Locate the `VBCP.DLL` file on you computer's hard drive. With the mouse, select `VBCP.DLL`, drag the file onto `REGSRV32.EXE`, and release. The Registry utility will register the Code Profiler DLL and display the successful Registry dialog box (see Figure 39.4).

FIGURE 39.4.
A successful Registry dialog box.

4. The following code is required in the Visual Basic Add-In initialization file, `VBADDIN.INI`, and is located in the Windows directory. Add the code if it doesn't exist:

```
[Add-Ins32]
VBCP.VBCPClass=0
```

5. From the Visual Basic Main Menu, select Add-Ins | Add-In Manager. The Add-In Manager dialog box appears (see Figure 39.5).
6. Check the VB Code Profiler and then click OK. The Visual Basic Code Profiler is now installed and ready to use.

FIGURE 39.5.
The Add-In Manager dialog box.

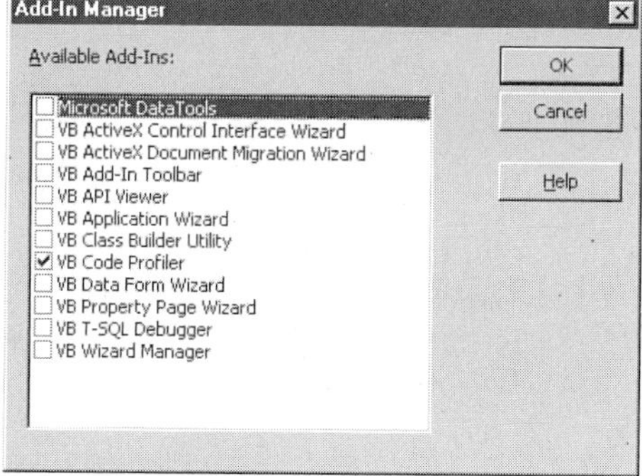

Using the Visual Basic Code Profiler

Using the Visual Basic Code Profiler is simple; before you open the project you want to profile, start the Code Profiler by selecting it from Visual Basic's Add-Ins menu. The Code Profiler dialog box appears (see Figure 39.6).

NOTE

The Code Profiler adds code to the project being analyzed and creates temporary files in your Visual Basic project. It's a good idea to back up your existing Visual Basic project before using the Code Profiler.

FIGURE 39.6.
The Visual Basic Code Profiler dialog box.

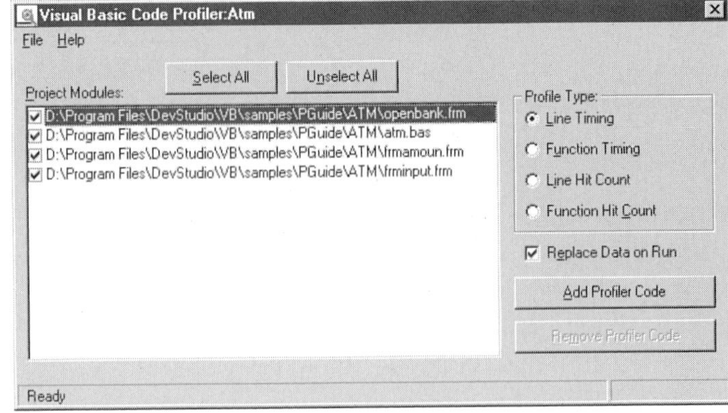

Follow these steps to profile your application:

1. In the Profile Type section, select the type of profile you want to run. The selections are as follows:

Line Timing	Amount of time required to execute each code line
Function Timing	Amount of time required to execute a function
Line Hit Count	Number of times a code line was executed during a run
Function Hit Count	Number of times a function was executed during a run

2. Mark the Replace Data on Run check box if you don't want to accumulate statistics from a previous test run. This cleans out the code profiler database and shows statistics for the current run.

   You should mark this check box if you want to select a different type of profile. Mixing statistical information from different profile runs isn't recommended because the old data may not be valid with the newly selected profile.

3. Click the Add Profiler Code button.

TIP

If you see an error message that says `The Project or Component is dirty. Please save and try again`, you need to save the current Visual Basic project and then reopen it.

This step adds lines of code to your application used by the profiler and creates temporary Visual Basic files. Listing 39.4 shows an example of code the profiler adds during this step.

Listing 39.4. Example of Visual Basic code with code profiler lines added.

```
Select Case DoFlag
        Case True
  VBCP_Update 1, "cmdStartStop_Click", 2
            cmdStartStop.Caption = "Start Demo"
  VBCP_Update 1, "cmdStartStop_Click", 3
            DoFlag = False
  VBCP_Update 1, "cmdStartStop_Click", 4
            mnuOption.Enabled = True
  VBCP_Update 1, "cmdStartStop_Click", 5
            If mnuCtlMoveDemo.Checked = True And _
               VBCP_UpdateIf(1, "cmdStartStop_Click", 6) Then
                ' Hide bouncing graphic again.
                picBall.Visible = False
  VBCP_Update 1, "cmdStartStop_Click", 7
            ElseIf mnuLineDemo.Checked = True And _
               VBCP_UpdateIf(1, "cmdStartStop_Click", 8) Then
                ' Remove lines from the form.
                Cls
```

NOTE

The profiler code is designated with `VBCP_`.

4. Run the Visual Basic project you're profiling. The Code Profiler collects statistics while you're using the application.
5. After you test all your application features, you can review the statistics collected by the Code Profiler by selecting one of the following menu options located under the Code Profiler's File menu:
   - *View Results*—Shows the results of the selected test profile
   - *Export Results*—Exports the results to be used in other applications, such as Microsoft Excel
   - *Project Statistics*—Provides statistical information on the project being profiled
6. Choose File | View Results, and the Analysis window appears (see Figure 39.7).

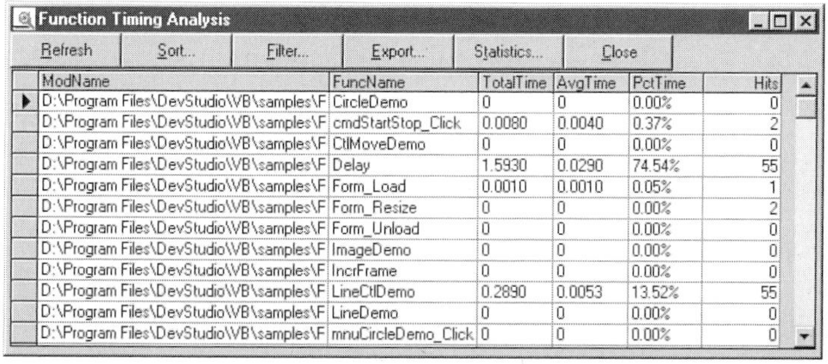

FIGURE 39.7.
The Visual Basic Code Profiler Analysis window.

Function Timing Analysis

Refresh | Sort... | Filter... | Export... | Statistics... | Close

ModName	FuncName	TotalTime	AvgTime	PctTime	Hits
D:\Program Files\DevStudio\VB\samples\F	CircleDemo	0	0	0.00%	0
D:\Program Files\DevStudio\VB\samples\F	cmdStartStop_Click	0.0080	0.0040	0.37%	2
D:\Program Files\DevStudio\VB\samples\F	CtlMoveDemo	0	0	0.00%	0
D:\Program Files\DevStudio\VB\samples\F	Delay	1.5930	0.0290	74.54%	55
D:\Program Files\DevStudio\VB\samples\F	Form_Load	0.0010	0.0010	0.05%	1
D:\Program Files\DevStudio\VB\samples\F	Form_Resize	0	0	0.00%	2
D:\Program Files\DevStudio\VB\samples\F	Form_Unload	0	0	0.00%	0
D:\Program Files\DevStudio\VB\samples\F	ImageDemo	0	0	0.00%	0
D:\Program Files\DevStudio\VB\samples\F	IncrFrame	0	0	0.00%	0
D:\Program Files\DevStudio\VB\samples\F	LineCtlDemo	0.2890	0.0053	13.52%	55
D:\Program Files\DevStudio\VB\samples\F	LineDemo	0	0	0.00%	0
D:\Program Files\DevStudio\VB\samples\F	mnuCircleDemo_Click	0	0	0.00%	0

The title bar of the Analysis window reflects the test performed. For Figure 39.7, the Function Timing profile was selected. For the Function Timing profile, the Analysis window displays the module name, the name of the function called, the total time spent executing the function, the average time for each execution of the function, and the number of times the function was executed (that is, hits). If lines are being profiled instead of functions, the line number is displayed in the Analysis window as well as the line of text being profiled instead of the function name. You can perform other functions with the Analysis window, such as apply filters to the results, export the results, or sort the results, as shown in the Visual Basic Code Profiler Sort dialog box in Figure 39.8.

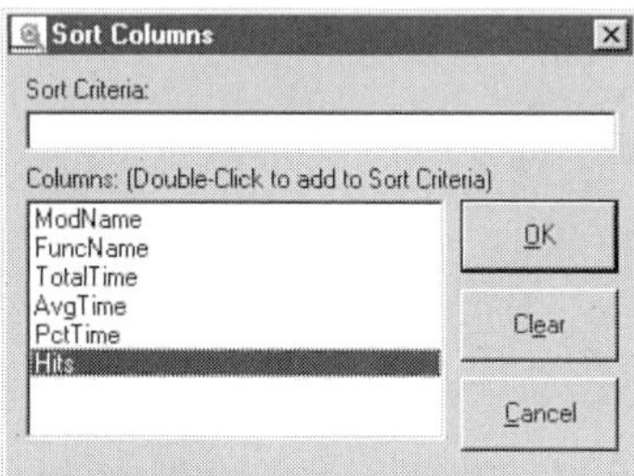

FIGURE 39.8.
The Visual Basic Code Profiler Sort dialog box.

The Sort dialog box lets you sort by a specific column. This feature is useful when profiling a large project. For example, you can sort by the number of hits to quickly find the most used routines, or you can sort on the TotalTime, PctTime, or AvgTime to quickly locate possible bottlenecks.

NOTE

Setting the sort order requires double-clicking one of the columns to display another dialog box, which lets you sort the results in ascending or descending order.

Another feature of the Visual Basic Code Profiler is the project statistics information. Figure 39.9 shows a dialog box of project statistical information, such as the number of lines of code and functions in a project.

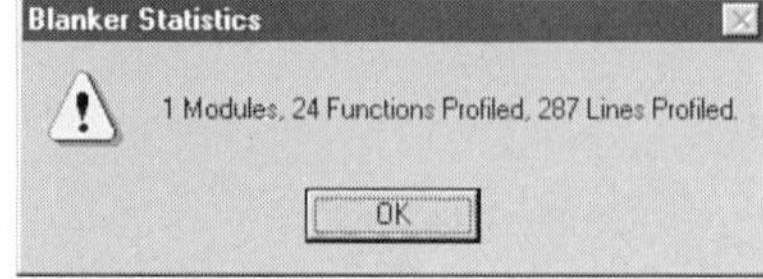

FIGURE 39.9.
The Visual Basic Code Profiler Statistics dialog box.

NOTE

When you're finished profiling your project, don't forget to remove the profiling code that the Visual Basic Code Profiler adds. To remove the profiler code, click the Remove Profiler Code button shown in Figure 39.6.

Summary

In this chapter, you learned the many different factors and parameters you need to take into consideration to properly optimize and tune your Visual Basic applications. You learned some of the standard optimizing and tuning tricks, such as using `long` integers rather than `variants` whenever possible. Different tips and tricks were given to help you decide what to optimize and what not to optimize. The Visual Basic Code Profiler was discussed in detail as a tool to help you find dead code and to quickly locate functions and lines of code that require optimizing and tuning.

VII
PART

IN THIS PART

Reference

CHAPTER 40

Commands Syntax

IN THIS CHAPTER

Visual Basic provides more than 200 built-in statements and functions. Some are used frequently; some are seldom used at all. Even experienced programmers sometimes happen upon a statement or function they didn't know about.

This chapter can be considered a quick-reference guide to all of VB's built-in statements and functions. It offers the syntax for each, as well as a brief description of what it does and how its arguments (if any) are used. This is by no means a complete reference. Microsoft's *Visual Basic 5.0 Language Reference* is probably the best source for in-depth information on VB's statements and functions. If you have any questions about syntax or use of a particular statement or function, then you are strongly urged to consult that reference to obtain additional information.

Functions and Statements

Abs Function

`Abs(number)`

Returns the absolute value of *number*. The data type returned is the same as the data type of the *number* argument.

AppActivate Statement

`AppActivate title[,wait]`

Activates the application window that has the string *title* in its title bar or, alternatively, the task ID specified by *title*. The optional *wait* argument (`Boolean`) can be used to specify whether the calling application should wait until it has the focus before the application window is activated.

Array Function

`Array(arglist)`

Returns a `Variant` data item that contains an array. *arglist* refers to a comma-delimited list of values that make up the elements of the array, with the first value corresponding to the first element of the array, the second value corresponding to the second element of the array, and so on.

Asc Function

`Asc(string)`

Returns an `Integer` value that represents the ASCII code for the first character in the *string*.

Atn Function

`Atn(number)`

Returns a `Double` value that is the arctangent of *number*.

Beep Statement

```
Beep
```

Sounds a tone through the PC's speaker. Frequency and duration of the tone may vary from system to system.

Call Statement

```
[Call] name [argumentlist]
```

Executes a sub, function, or DLL procedure. The *name* argument specifies the name of the procedure to call, and *argumentlist* is an optional list of arguments that will be passed to the called procedure. The `Call` keyword is optional, but if it is included, then at least one or more arguments for *argumentlist* must also be included.

CBool Function

```
CBool(expression)
```

Converts the value of *expression* to a `Boolean` data type. The argument *expression* can be any valid string or numeric expression.

CByte Function

```
CByte(expression)
```

Converts the value of *expression* to a `Byte` data type. The argument *expression* must be a numeric value between 0 and 255.

CCur Function

```
CCur(expression)
```

Converts the value of *expression* to a `Currency` data type. The argument *expression* must be a numeric value between –922,337,203,685,477.5808 and 922,337,203,685,477.5807.

CDate Function

```
CDate(expression)
```

Converts the value of *expression* to a `Date` data type. The argument *expression* must be a valid date expression.

CDbl Function

```
CDbl(expression)
```

Converts the value of *expression* to a `Double` data type. The argument *expression* must be a numeric value between –1.79769313486232E308 and –4.94065645841247E-324 for negative values, or between 4.94065645841247E-324 and 1.79769313486232E308 for positive values.

`CDec` Function

`CDec(`*`expression`*`)`

Converts the value of *`expression`* to a `Decimal` data type. The argument *`expression`* must be a numeric value of +/–79,228,162,514,264,337,593,543,950,335 for zero-scaled numbers (numbers with no decimal places), or +/–7.9228162514264337593543950335 for numbers with 28 decimal places.

`ChDir` Statement

`ChDir` *`path`*

Changes the current directory to the one specified by the *`path`* argument. Note that although `ChDir` changes the default directory, it does not change the default drive as well.

`ChDrive` Statement

`ChDrive` *`drive`*

Changes the current drive to the one specified by the *`drive`* argument.

`Choose` Function

`Choose(`*`index`*`, `*`choice-1`*`[, `*`choice-2`*`, ... [, `*`choice-n`*`]])`

Returns a value from a list of choices (specified by the arguments *`choice-1`* through *`choice-n`*) based on the value of the *`index`* argument. If *`index`* is 1, then the value returned by the `Choose` function will be the value represented by *`choice-1`*; if *`index`* is 2, then the value returned will be that of *`choice-2`*; and so on.

`Chr` Function

`Chr(`*`charcode`*`)`

Returns a one-character `String` value that represents the ASCII character of the number specified by the *`charcode`* argument.

`CInt` Function

`CInt(`*`expression`*`)`

Converts the value of *`expression`* to an `Integer` data type. The argument *`expression`* must be a numeric value from –32,768 to 32,767. Fractions are rounded.

`CLng` Function

`CLng(`*`expression`*`)`

Converts the value of *`expression`* to a `Long` data type. The argument *`expression`* must be a numeric value from –2,147,483,648 to 2,147,483,647. Fractions are rounded.

Close Statement

```
Close [filenumberlist]
```

Closes any files opened with the `Open` statement that correspond to the file numbers specified by *`filenumberlist`*. The *`filenumberlist`* argument can contain a single file number (for example, #1) or multiple file numbers (for example, #1, #4, #5). If the *`filenumberlist`* argument is omitted, all open files will be closed.

Command Function

```
Command
```

Returns any command-line arguments specified when launching Visual Basic. For compiled programs, `Command` returns the command-line arguments specified when the program was launched.

Const Statement

```
[Public ¦ Private] Const constname [As type] = expression
```

Declares a constant with the name *`constname`* and the value represented by *`expression`*. The `Public` and `Private` keywords define the constant's scope, and the optional `As` *`type`* specifies the constant's data type. If the `As` *`type`* is omitted, the constant will be declared as the data type most appropriate for *`expression`*.

Cos Function

```
Cos(number)
```

Returns a `Double` value that is the cosine of the angle specified by the *`number`* argument.

CreateObject Function

```
CreateObject(class)
```

Creates and returns a reference to an ActiveX object of type *`class`*. The *`class`* argument should use the syntax *`appname.objecttype`*, where *`appname`* is the name of the application providing the object, and *`objecttype`* is the class of the object to be created.

CSng Function

```
CSng(expression)
```

Converts the value of *`expression`* to a `Single` data type. The argument *`expression`* must be a numeric value from –3.402823E38 to –1.401298E-45 for negative values, or from 1.401298E-45 to 3.402823E38 for positive values.

CStr Function

`CStr(expression)`

Converts the value of *expression* to a `String` data type. The string that `CStr` returns depends on the data type of the *expression* argument: For `Booleans`, `CStr` returns either `True` or `False`; for `Dates`, `CStr` returns a date based on the short date format on your system; for `Errors`, `CStr` returns the word `Error` followed by the error number. *expression* values that are `Empty` return a zero-length string, and numeric *expression* values return a string containing the number. A `Null` *expression* value will cause a runtime error.

CurDir Function

`CurDir[(drive)]`

Returns a `String` value that represents the full path of the current directory. If the *drive* argument is given, then `CurDir` returns the directory path of the current directory for that drive.

CVar Function

`CVar(expression)`

Converts the value of *expression* to a `Variant` data type. The argument *expression* can be either numeric or a string.

CVErr Function

`CVErr(errornumber)`

Returns a `Variant` of subtype `Error` that contains the error number specified by the *errornumber* argument.

Date Function

`Date`

Returns a `Variant` of subtype `Date` that contains the current system date.

Date Statement

`Date = date`

Sets the current system date as specified by the *date* argument. For Windows 95 systems, *date* must be a valid date between January 1, 1980 and December 31, 2099. For Windows NT systems, *date* must be a valid date between January 1, 1980 and December 31, 2079.

DateAdd Function

```
DateAdd(interval, number, date)
```

Returns a `Variant` of subtype `Date` calculated by taking the date specified by the *`date`* argument and adding or subtracting the amount of time specified by *`interval`* and *`time`*. The *`interval`* argument contains a code that represents a unit of time (for example, *yyyy* for years, *m* for months, *d* for days), and *`number`* is the number of units to be added to *`date`*.

DateDiff Function

```
DateDiff(interval, date1, date2[,firstdayofweek[,firstweekofyear]])
```

Returns a `Variant` of subtype `Long` that represents the number of time units between two dates (*`date1`* and *`date2`*). The *`interval`* argument contains a code that represents the unit of time (for example, *yyyy* for years) that will be returned by the function. The optional *`firstdayofweek`* and *`firstweekofyear`* arguments are used to specify how the time difference should be calculated when certain codes are used for *`interval`*.

DatePart Function

```
DatePart(interval, date[,firstdayofweek[,firstweekofyear]])
```

Returns a `Variant` of subtype `Integer` that contains the part of *`date`* specified by *`interval`*. The *`interval`* argument contains a code that represents the unit of time (for example, *ww* for weeks) that will be returned by the function. The optional *`firstdayofweek`* and *`firstweekofyear`* arguments are used to specify how the date should be calculated when certain *`interval`* codes are used.

DateSerial Function

```
DateSerial(year, month, day)
```

Returns a `Variant` of subtype `Date` that represents a date as specified by the *`year`*, *`month`*, and *`day`* arguments.

DateValue Function

```
DateValue(date)
```

Returns a `Variant` of subtype `Date` that is derived from the date value specified by the *`date`* argument.

Day Function

```
Day(date)
```

Returns a `Variant` of subtype `Integer` that represents the day of the month (1–31) for the date value specified by the *`date`* argument.

DDB Function

```
DDB(cost, salvage, life, period[, factor])
```

Returns a `Double` value that represents the depreciation of an asset for a specified amount of time using a given method of depreciation. The *cost* argument represents the initial cost of the asset, *salvage* represents the value of the asset at the end of its working lifetime, *life* represents the lifetime of the asset, and *period* represents the period (in months) for which the depreciation is calculated. The optional *factor* argument specifies the rate at which the balance declines. If it is omitted, then the double-declining depreciation method is used.

Declare Statement

```
[Public ¦ Private] Declare Sub name Lib "libname" [Alias "aliasname"][([arglist])]
```

or

```
[Public ¦ Private] Declare Function name Lib "libname"
[Alias "aliasname"][([arglist])][As type]
```

Declares references to `Sub` or `Function` procedures in an external DLL (dynamic-link library). The optional `Public` and `Private` keywords define the procedure's scope. The *name* argument is the name of the procedure, and the *libname* argument specifies the DLL that contains the procedure. The optional *aliasname* argument specifies an alternate name for the procedure in the DLL. *arglist* is a list of arguments passed to the procedure. For `Function` procedures, the `As` *type* specifies the data type of the value returned by the `Function`. `Declare` statements can only be used at module level.

DefBool Statement

```
DefBool letterrange[, letterrange]...
```

Specifies that all variables and function return values that begin with the letters specified by the *letterrange* arguments are automatically defined to be of the `Boolean` data type. The *letterrange* arguments should be constructed as *letter1*[-*letter2*], where *letter1* is the first (or only) letter in the range, and *letter2* is the last letter in the range. `DefBool` can only be used at module level.

DefByte Statement

```
DefByte letterrange[, letterrange]...
```

Specifies that all variables and function return values that begin with the letters specified by the *letterrange* arguments are automatically defined to be of the `Byte` data type. The *letterrange* arguments should be constructed as *letter1*[-*letter2*], where *letter1* is the first (or only) letter in the range, and *letter2* is the last letter in the range. `DefByte` can only be used at module level.

DefCur Statement

`DefCur letterrange[, letterrange]...`

Specifies that all variables and function return values that begin with the letters specified by the *letterrange* arguments are automatically defined to be of the Currency data type. The *letterrange* arguments should be constructed as *letter1*[-*letter2*], where *letter1* is the first (or only) letter in the range, and *letter2* is the last letter in the range. DefCur can only be used at module level.

DefDate Statement

`DefDate letterrange[, letterrange]...`

Specifies that all variables and function return values that begin with the letters specified by the *letterrange* arguments are automatically defined to be of the Date data type. The *letterrange* arguments should be constructed as *letter1*[-*letter2*], where *letter1* is the first (or only) letter in the range, and *letter2* is the last letter in the range. DefDate can only be used at module level.

DefDbl Statement

`DefDbl letterrange[, letterrange]...`

Specifies that all variables and function return values that begin with the letters specified by the *letterrange* arguments are automatically defined to be of the Double data type. The *letterrange* arguments should be constructed as *letter1*[-*letter2*], where *letter1* is the first (or only) letter in the range, and *letter2* is the last letter in the range. DefDbl can only be used at module level.

DefDec Statement

`DefDec letterrange[, letterrange]...`

Specifies that all variables and function return values that begin with the letters specified by the *letterrange* arguments are automatically defined to be of the Decimal data type. The *letterrange* arguments should be constructed as *letter1*[-*letter2*], where *letter1* is the first (or only) letter in the range, and *letter2* is the last letter in the range. DefDec can only be used at module level.

DefInt Statement

`DefInt letterrange[, letterrange]...`

Specifies that all variables and function return values that begin with the letters specified by the *letterrange* arguments are automatically defined to be of the Integer data type. The *letterrange* arguments should be constructed as *letter1*[-*letter2*], where *letter1* is the first (or only) letter in the range, and *letter2* is the last letter in the range. DefInt can only be used at module level.

DefLng Statement

`DefLng letterrange[, letterrange]...`

Specifies that all variables and function return values that begin with the letters specified by the *letterrange* arguments are automatically defined to be of the `Long` data type. The *letterrange* arguments should be constructed as *letter1*[-*letter2*], where *letter1* is the first (or only) letter in the range, and *letter2* is the last letter in the range. `DefLng` can only be used at module level.

DefObj Statement

`DefObj letterrange[, letterrange]...`

Specifies that all variables and function return values that begin with the letters specified by the *letterrange* arguments are automatically defined to be of the `Object` data type. The *letterrange* arguments should be constructed as *letter1*[-*letter2*], where *letter1* is the first (or only) letter in the range, and *letter2* is the last letter in the range. `DefObj` can only be used at module level.

DefSng Statement

`DefSng letterrange[, letterrange]...`

Specifies that all variables and function return values that begin with the letters specified by the *letterrange* arguments are automatically defined to be of the `Single` data type. The *letterrange* arguments should be constructed as *letter1*[-*letter2*], where *letter1* is the first (or only) letter in the range, and *letter2* is the last letter in the range. `DefSng` can only be used at module level.

DefStr Statement

`DefStr letterrange[, letterrange]...`

Specifies that all variables and function return values that begin with the letters specified by the *letterrange* arguments are automatically defined to be of the `String` data type. The *letterrange* arguments should be constructed as *letter1*[-*letter2*], where *letter1* is the first (or only) letter in the range, and *letter2* is the last letter in the range. `DefStr` can only be used at module level.

DefVar Statement

`DefVar letterrange[, letterrange]...`

Specifies that all variables and function return values that begin with the letters specified by the *letterrange* arguments are automatically defined to be of the `Variant` data type. The *letterrange* arguments should be constructed as *letter1*[-*letter2*], where *letter1* is the first (or only) letter in the range, and *letter2* is the last letter in the range. `DefVar` can only be used at module level.

DeleteSetting Statement

```
DeleteSetting appname, section[, key]
```

Deletes an application's section or key setting entries from the System Registry. The `appname` argument specifies the name of the application, and `section` is the name of the section to be deleted. If the optional `key` argument is used, then only that key (and not the whole section) will be deleted.

Dim Statement

```
Dim [WithEvents] varname[([subscripts])] [As [New] type] [,[WithEvents]
varname[([subscripts])] [As [New] type]]...
```

Declares one or more variables or objects. The `varname` argument is the name of the variable, and the optional `As [New] type` indicates its data type. If the `New` keyword is used, then an implicit creation of the object is made. The optional `WithEvents` keyword (valid only when the `Dim` statement is used in class modules) indicates that `varname` is an object variable as is used to respond to events triggered by an ActiveX object. The optional `subscripts` are the dimensions of an array variable.

Dir Function

```
Dir[(pathname[, attributes])]
```

Returns a `String` value containing the name of a file, directory, or folder that matches a pattern (specified in the `pathname` argument) and/or a file attribute (specified in `attributes`). The first time the `Dir` function is called, it returns the name of a file based on the `pathname` and `attributes` arguments. If the function is called again and no arguments are given, then it returns the second file name for the given `pathname` and `attributes`, and so on.

Do...Loop Statement

```
Do [{While ¦ Until} condition]
   [statements]
   [Exit Do]
   [statements]
Loop
```

or

```
Do
   [statements]
   [Exit Do]
   [statements]
Loop [{While ¦ Until} condition]
```

Repeats one or more `statements` while a `condition` is `True` or until a `condition` becomes `True`. The optional `Exit Do` keywords pass control to the line of code immediately following the `Do...Loop` structure.

DoEvents Function

```
DoEvents( )
```

Temporarily gives control to the operating system so that it can process other events. The `DoEvents` function is typically used inside loops so that a program does not tie up system resources for a long period of time.

End Statement

```
End
End Function
End If
End Property
End Select
End Sub
End Type
End With
```

Ends a program (`End`), procedure (`End Function`, `End Property`, or `End Sub`), type structure (`End Type`), or program block (`End If`, `End Select`, or `End With`).

Enum Statement

```
[Public ¦ Private] Enum name
    membername [= constantexpression]
    membername [= constantexpression]
      ...
End Enum
```

Declares an enumeration type named *`name`* that is composed of one or more members specified by *`membername`*. Members can be assigned values using *`constantexpression`*. The optional `Public` and `Private` keywords define the enumeration's scope.

Environ Function

```
Environ({envstring ¦ number})
```

Returns the `String` value of the operating system variable specified by *`envstring`* or, alternatively, the numeric order of the environment string in the environment-string table specified by *`number`*.

EOF Function

```
EOF(filenumber)
```

Returns a `True` or `False` value (`Integer`) that indicates whether the end of file marker has been reached for the `Random` or `Input` file associated with the *`filenumber`* argument.

Erase Statement

```
Erase arraylist
```

Reinitializes the elements in one or more fixed-size array and frees up the dynamic-array storage space that was taken up by the array(s). The *arraylist* argument is one or more comma-delimited array names.

Error Function

```
Error[(errornumber)]
```

Returns a `String` value that contains the error message that corresponds to the *errornumber* argument.

Error Statement

```
Error errornumber
```

Causes an error to occur. The *errornumber* argument indicates the type of error that should occur.

Event Statement

```
[Public] Event procedurename [(arglist)]
```

Declares a user-defined event with the name *procedurename*. The optional `Public` keyword indicates that the `Event` should be visible throughout the project, even though that is the default. The optional argument list (*arglist*) should contain one or more arguments defined using the syntax:

```
[ByVal ¦ ByRef] varname[()] [As type]
```

where *varname* is the name of the argument, `As` *type* indicates the data type of the argument, and the optional `ByRef` or `ByVal` keywords specify whether the argument should be passed by reference (`ByRef`) or by value (`ByVal`). If `ByRef` and `ByVal` are not specified, then the argument will be passed by reference.

Exit Statement

```
Exit Do
Exit For
Exit Function
Exit Property
Exit Sub
```

Exits a procedure (`Exit Function`, `Exit Property`, or `Exit Sub`) or looping structure (`Exit Do` or `Exit For`).

Exp Function

`Exp(number)`

Returns a `Double` value that is `e` (the base of natural logarithms) raised to the power specified by *`number`*.

FileAttr Function

`FileAttr(filenumber, returntype)`

Returns a `Long` value that indicates the file mode for a file opened using the `Open` statement. The argument *`filenumber`* is the file number for the open file, and *`returntype`* indicates the type of information to be returned. Although *`returntype`* can be set to 2 to return the operating system file handle for the open file, it only works on 16-bit systems and should be avoided in VB5. Instead, use a value of 1 for *`returntype`* to return the open file type. The possible values returned by the `FileAttr` function for indicating file type are 1 for `Input`, 2 for `Output`, 4 for `Random`, 8 for `Append`, and 32 for `Binary`.

FileCopy Statement

`FileCopy source, destination`

Copies the filename and path specified by the *`source`* argument to the filename and path specified by the *`destination`* argument.

FileDateTime Function

`FileDateTime(pathname)`

Returns a `Variant` of subtype `Date` that indicates the date and time when the file specified by the *`pathname`* argument was last modified.

FileLen Function

`FileLen(pathname)`

Returns a `Long` value that contains the file size (in bytes) of the file specified by the *`pathname`* argument.

Fix Function

`Fix(number)`

Returns the integer portion of the number specified by the *`number`* argument. If *`number`* is negative, then `Fix` returns the first negative integer greater than or equal to *`number`*.

For Each...Next Statement

```
For Each element In group
    [statements]
    [Exit For]
    [statements]
Next [element]
```

Executes one or more `statements` for each `element` in the array or collection specified by `group`. The optional `Exit For` can be used to immediately exit the looping structure.

For...Next Statement

```
For counter = start To end [Step step]
    [statements]
    [Exit For]
    [statements]
Next [counter]
```

Executes one or more `statements` a specified number of times. The `counter` argument is a variable used to increment from `start` to `end`. By default, `counter` is incremented by 1 each time the loop is executed, although the optional `step` argument can be used to specify a different increment. The optional `Exit For` can be used to immediately exit the looping structure.

Format Function

```
Format(expression[, format[, firstdayofweek[, firstweekofyear]]])
```

Returns a `Variant` of subtype `String` that contains the value specified by `expression` using a format defined by the `format` argument. The `format` argument uses codes (for example, `d` for days or `#` for numbers) to determine how `expression` will be formatted. The optional `firstdayofweek` and `firstweekofyear` arguments are used when formatting certain values.

FreeFile Function

```
FreeFile[(rangenumber)]
```

Returns an `Integer` value the represents the next file number available for use with the `Open` statement. The optional `rangenumber` argument can be used to specify which range of file numbers should be used: 0 (the default) for file numbers in the range of 1–255, or 1 for file numbers in the range of 256–511.

Function Statement

```
[Public | Private | Friend] [Static] Function name [(arglist)] [As type]
    [statements]
    [name = expression]
    [Exit Function]
    [statements]
    [name = expression]
End Function
```

Declares the various parts of a `Function` procedure. The optional `Public`, `Private`, and `Friend` keywords can be used to define the `Function`'s scope, and the optional `Static` keyword indicates that the procedure's local variables are preserved between calls to the `Function`. The *name* argument specifies the name of the `Function` procedure and can be assigned a value (*name = expression*) that will be returned by the procedure. The data type of the return value can be specified using the `As` *type* clause. The optional `Exit Function` can be used to exit the `Function` procedure immediately.

The optional list of arguments (*arglist*) defines the arguments that will be passed to the procedure. The arguments should use the following syntax:

```
[Optional] [ByVal | ByRef] [ParamArray] varname[()] [As type] [= default value]
```

where the `Optional` keyword can be used to specify that the argument is not required (*default value* assigns the argument's default value), `ByVal` and `ByRef` determine whether the argument should be passed by value or by reference (the default), and the `ParamArray` keyword specifies that the argument is an `Optional` array of `Variant` elements. `ParamArray` can only be used with the last argument in the argument list.

FV Function

```
FV(rate, nper, pmt[, pv[, type]])
```

Returns a `Double` value that indicates the future value of an annuity based on a number (*nper*) of periodic fixed payment amounts (*pmt*) and a fixed interest rate (*rate*). The optional *pv* argument specifies a present value or lump sum of a series of future payments, and the optional *type* argument specifies when payments are due (0 for end of the payment period, the default; 1 for beginning of the payment period).

Get Statement

```
Get [#]filenumber,[ recnumber,] varname
```

Reads data from the open disk file corresponding to the *filenumber* argument into a variable (*varname*). `Get` works with files open as `Random` or `Binary`, and a record number (*recnumber*) can be specified when retrieving data from a `Random` file. When using `Binary` files, *recnumber* can alternatively be used to specify the byte position from which the data is to be read.

GetAllSettings Function

```
GetAllSettings(appname, section)
```

Returns a list of key settings and their values from a specific application (*appname*) entry and section (*section*) in the System Registry.

GetAttr Function

```
GetAttr(pathname)
```

Returns an `Integer` value that represents the attributes for the file, directory, or folder specified by the *pathname* argument. The value returned can be compared bitwise with several VB constants (`vbNormal`, `vbReadOnly`, `vbHidden`, `vbSystem`, `vbDirectory`, and `vbArchive`) to determine which attributes are set.

GetAutoServerSettings Function

```
object.GetAutoServerSettings([progid], [clsid])
```

Returns a `Variant` array that contains information concerning the state of an ActiveX *object*'s registration. The optional *progid* and *clsid* can be included to specify the object's ProgID and CLSID, respectively. The values of the elements of the `Variant` array that is returned by `GetAutoServerSettings` are, in order: local/remote registration of object (True if the object is registered remotely), the remote machine name, the RPC network protocol name, and the RPC authentication level.

GetObject Function

```
GetObject([pathname] [,class])
```

Returns a reference to an object of type *class*. The *pathname* argument can be included to specify the path and filename from which the object should be retrieved; however, if it is omitted, then the *class* name must be specified.

GetSetting Function

```
GetSetting(appname, section, key[, default])
```

Returns a single key setting value from a specific application (*appname*) entry and section (*section*) in the System Registry. If no value is set for the key setting specified, then the optional *default* value can be returned. If default is omitted, then the default value returned will be a zero-length string.

GoSub...Return Statement

```
GoSub line
    ...
    line
    ...
Return
```

Transfers program control to the subroutine indicated by the line label or line number *line* until the `Return` statement is reached; then returns control to the line of code immediately following the `GoSub` statement.

GoTo Statement

```
GoTo line
```

Transfers program control to the line of code specified by the line label or line number *line*. The line must be inside the procedure that contains the `GoTo` statement.

Hex Function

```
Hex(number)
```

Returns a `String` value that represents the hexadecimal value of the argument *number*.

Hour Function

```
Hour(time)
```

Returns a `Variant` of subtype `Integer` that represents the hour (0–23) of the time value specified by the *time* argument.

If...Then...Else Statement

```
If condition Then [statements] [Else elsestatements]
```

or

```
If condition Then
    [statements]
[ElseIf condition-n Then
    [elseifstatements] ...
[Else
    [elsestatements]]
End If
```

Conditionally executes one or more *statements* if the value expressed by *condition* is `True`. One or more `ElseIf` clauses can be included to test other conditions and execute other statements (*elseifstatements*) if the preceding condition is `False`. An `Else` clause can also be included to execute other statements (*elsestatements*) if none of the preceding conditions are `True`.

IIf Function

```
IIf(expression, truepart, falsepart)
```

Returns one of two values based on whether *expression* evaluates to `True` or `False`. If `True`, then `IIf` returns the *truepart* value; if `False`, then the *falsepart* value is returned.

IMEStatus Function

```
IMEStatus
```

Returns an `Integer` value that represents Windows' current Input Method Editor (IME) mode. `IMEStatus` is only available in Far East versions.

Implements Statement

```
Implements [interfacename ¦ class]
```

Specifies an interface (*interfacename*) or class (*class*) that will be implemented in the class module in which the `Implements` statement is used.

Input # Statement

```
Input #filenumber, varlist
```

Reads data from the open file associated with the *filenumber* argument and places it in the variables in the *varlist* argument. The *varlist* argument should contain one or more comma-delimited variables.

Input Function

```
Input(number, [#]filenumber)
```

Returns a `String` value containing characters read in from the open file that corresponds to the *filenumber* argument. The number of characters to be read in are specified by the *number* argument.

InputBox Function

```
InputBox(prompt[, title][, default][, xpos][, ypos][,helpfile, context])
```

Displays a dialog box and waits for the user to enter text or click a button; then returns what the user entered in a `String` value. The *prompt* argument specifies the message to be displayed in the dialog box, *title* specifies an optional caption for the dialog box's title bar, and *default* specifies the optional default value returned by the `InputBox` function if no value is entered by the user. The optional *xpos* and *ypos* arguments specify (in twips) the horizontal and vertical position of the dialog box on the screen. The optional *helpfile* and *context* arguments are used to provide context-sensitive Help for the dialog box.

InStr Function

```
InStr([start, ]string1, string2[, compare])
```

Returns a `Variant` of subtype `Long` that specifies the starting position of the first occurrence of a substring (*string2*) within another string (*string1*). The optional *start* argument specifies from which character in *string2* to start searching; the default is 1 (first character). The optional *compare* argument specifies the type of string comparison that will be made (0 for binary or 1 for textual noncase-sensitive).

Int Function

`Int(number)`

Returns the integer portion of the number specified by the *number* argument. If *number* is negative, then `Int` returns the first negative integer less than or equal to *number*.

IPmt Function

`IPmt(rate, per, nper, pv[, fv[, type]])`

Returns a `Double` value that indicates the interest payment for a fixed-period annuity based on a number (*nper*) of periodic fixed payments (*per*) and a fixed interest rate (*rate*). The *pv* argument specifies the present value of a series of payments or receipts. The optional *fv* argument specifies the future value or cash balance left after the final payment. The optional *type* argument specifies when payments are due (0 for end of the payment period, the default; 1 for beginning of the payment period).

IRR Function

`IRR(values()[, guess])`

Returns a `Double` value indicating the internal rate of return for an array of *values* that represent cash flow. The *values()* array must contain at least one negative value (payment) and one positive value (receipt). The optional *guess* argument specifies an estimate value to be returned by `IRR` (default estimate is .1).

IsArray Function

`IsArray(varname)`

Returns a `Boolean` value that indicates whether the variable specified by *varname* is an array.

IsDate Function

`IsDate(expression)`

Returns a `Boolean` value that indicates whether *expression* is capable of being converted to a date value.

IsEmpty Function

`IsEmpty(expression)`

Returns a `Boolean` value that indicates whether a numeric or string *expression* has been initialized.

IsError Function

`IsError(expression)`

Returns a `Boolean` value that indicates whether a given *`expression`* is an error value.

IsMissing Function

`IsMissing(argname)`

Returns a `Boolean` value that indicates whether an optional `Variant` argument (*`argname`*) has been passed to a procedure. `IsMissing` returns `True` if no value has been provided for the specified argument.

IsNull Function

`IsNull(expression)`

Returns a `Boolean` value that indicates whether a given *`expression`* contains no data and is `Null`.

IsNumeric Function

`IsNumeric(expression)`

Returns a `Boolean` value that indicates whether a given *`expression`* can be evaluated as a numeric value.

IsObject Function

`IsObject(identifier)`

Returns a `Boolean` value that indicates whether a given *`identifier`* represents an object variable.

Kill Statement

`Kill pathname`

Deletes the file(s) or directory represented by the *`pathname`* argument. Filenames in the *`pathname`* argument can contain wildcards, allowing multiple files to be deleted.

LBound Function

`LBound(arrayname[, dimension])`

Returns a `Long` value that represents the smallest subscript for a dimensioned array (*`arrayname`*). For multidimensional arrays, the *`dimension`* argument can be included to specify which dimension should be used.

LCase Function

`LCase(string)`

Converts a *string* to all lowercase characters and returns a new `String` value.

Left Function

`Left(string, length)`

Returns a `String` value *length* characters long that is taken from the left side of a given *string*.

Len Function

`Len(string ¦ varname)`

Returns a `Long` value that indicates the number of characters in a *string* or, alternatively, the number of bytes required to store a particular variable (*varname*).

Let Statement

`[Let] varname = expression`

Assigns the value of an *expression* to a variable (*varname*). The `Let` keyword is usually omitted and is assumed by Visual Basic.

Line Input # Statement

`Line Input #filenumber, varname`

Reads a line of data (ending with a carriage return or carriage return-linefeed) from an open disk file corresponding to the *filenumber* argument. The data is placed in the `String` or `Variant` variable specified by *varname*.

Load Statement

`Load object`

Loads an *object*, such as a form or control, into memory.

LoadPicture Function

`LoadPicture([stringexpression])`

Loads the image specified by the *stringexpression* argument and returns it. This allows pictures to be loaded in and assigned to a Form's `Picture` property, a PictureBox control, or an Image control. If no *stringexpression* argument is given, then `LoadPicture` returns an empty picture.

LoadResData Function

```
LoadResData(index, format)
```

Loads data from the resource (.RES) file with the identifier of the *index* argument. The *format* argument specifies the format of the data (1 for cursors, 2 for bitmaps, 3 for icons, 4 for menus, 5 for dialog boxes, 6 for strings, 7 for font directories, 8 for fonts, 9 for accelerator tables, 10 for user-defined resources, 12 for group cursors, and 14 for group icons). The data returned by the LoadResData function can be assigned to a variable or object of the appropriate type.

LoadResPicture Function

```
LoadResPicture(index, format)
```

Loads a bitmap, icon, or cursor from the resource (.RES) file with the identifier of the *index* argument. The *format* argument specifies the format of the data (0 for bitmaps, 1 for icons, and 2 for cursors). The data returned by the LoadResPicture function can be assigned to an object of the appropriate type.

LoadResString Function

```
LoadResString(index)
```

Loads a string from the resource (.RES) file with the identifier of the *index* argument. The string that is returned can be assigned to a variable of String or Variant data type.

Loc Function

```
Loc(filenumber)
```

Returns a Long value that indicates the current byte position within the open file that corresponds to the *filenumber* argument.

Lock Statement

```
Lock [#]filenumber[, recordrange]
```

Prevents another process from accessing all or part of the open file that corresponds to the *filenumber* argument. The *recordrange* argument refers to a range of records (or bytes) that are to be locked and should use the syntax:

```
recnumber ¦ [start] To end
```

where *recnumber* is the record number (for Random files) or byte position (for Binary files) where locking should begin. Alternatively, the starting and ending record numbers or bytes to be locked can be specified using the *start* and *end* arguments.

LOF Function

`LOF(filenumber)`

Returns a `Boolean` value that represents the byte size of the open file that corresponds to the *`filenumber`* argument.

Log Function

`Log(number)`

Returns a `Double` value that represents the natural logarithm of a specified *`number`*.

LSet Statement

`LSet stringvar = string`

or

`LSet varname1 = varname2`

In the first syntax, `LSet` assigns a *`string`* value to a `String` variable (*`stringvar`*), left-aligning the string to the `String` variable. In the second syntax, `LSet` copies a variable (*`varname2`*) from one user-defined type to a variable (*`varname1`*) in another user-defined type.

LTrim Function

`LTrim(string)`

Returns a `Variant` of subtype `String` that contains a copy of a given *`string`* with any leading spaces removed.

Mid Function

`Mid(string, start[, length])`

Returns a `String` value of one or more characters, taken from the `String` variable specified by the *`string`* argument. The *`start`* argument specifies the character position within *`string`* where the new `String` is to be obtained, and the optional *`length`* argument specifies how many characters are to be taken from *`string`*. If no *`length`* is specified, then all the characters in *`string`* (starting at the position given in the *`start`* argument) are used.

Mid Statement

`Mid(stringvar, start[, length]) = string`

Replaces one or more characters in a `String` variable (*`stringvar`*) with another *`string`*. The *`start`* argument specifies the character position within *`stringvar`* to place the new *`string`*, and the optional *`length`* argument specifies how many characters of *`string`* should be used. If *`length`* is omitted, then the entire *`string`* is used.

Minute Function

`Minute(time)`

Returns a `Variant` of subtype `Integer` that represents the minute (0–59) of the time value specified by the *time* argument.

MIRR Function

`MIRR(values(), financerate, reinvestrate)`

Returns a `Double` value that represents the modified internal rate of return for an array of *values* that represent cash flow. The *values()* array must contain at least one negative value (payment) and one positive value (receipt). The *financerate* argument specifies the interest rate paid as a cost of financing, and the *reinvestrate* argument specifies the interest rate received on gains from cash reinvestment.

MkDir Statement

`MkDir path`

Creates the new directory or folder specified by the *path* argument.

Month Function

`Month(date)`

Returns a `Variant` of subtype `Integer` that represents the month (1–12) for the date value specified by the *date* argument.

MsgBox Function

`MsgBox(prompt[, buttons][, title][, helpfile, context]`

Displays a message in a dialog box with one or more buttons and waits for the user to respond. `MsgBox` then returns an `Integer` value that represents the button that was clicked. The *prompt* argument specifies the message to be displayed in the dialog box, and *title* specifies an optional caption for the dialog box's title bar. The optional *buttons* argument specifies which buttons will be displayed. The optional *helpfile* and *context* arguments are used to provide context-sensitive Help for the dialog box.

Name Statement

`Name oldpathname As newpathname`

Renames the file, directory, or folder specified by the *oldpathname* argument to the name specified by *newpathname*.

Now Function

`Now`

Returns a `Variant` of subtype `Date` that contains the current system date and time.

NPer Function

`NPer(rate, pmt, pv[, fv[, type]])`

Returns a `Double` value that indicates the number of periods for an annuity based on periodic fixed payments (*pmt*) and a fixed interest rate (*rate*). The *pv* argument specifies the present value of a series of payments or receipts. The optional *fv* argument specifies the future value or cash balance left after the final payment. The optional *type* argument specifies when payments are due (0 for end of the payment period, the default; 1 for beginning of the payment period).

NPV Function

`NPV(rate, values())`

Returns a `Double` value that represents the present value of an investment based on a discount rate (*rate*) and an array of *values* that represent cash flow. The *values*`()` array must contain at least one negative value (payment) and one positive value (receipt).

Oct Function

`Oct(number)`

Returns a `String` value that represents the octal value of the argument *number*.

On Error Statement

```
On Error GoTo line
On Error Resume Next
On Error GoTo 0
```

Enables or disables the use of an error-handling routine. The `On Error` statement can specify a line label or line number (specified by the *line* argument) to branch to when an error occurs, allowing error-handling to be enabled. Alternatively, using `On Error Resume Next` causes program control to be transferred to the line of code immediately following the line of code that causes an error. Finally, On `Error GoTo 0` disables all error-handling.

On...GoSub Statement

`On expression GoSub destinationlist`

Evaluates a given *expression* and, depending on its value, transfers program control to a certain subroutine. The possible subroutines are contained in the *destinationlist* argument, which contains one or more comma-delimited line labels or line numbers. If *expression* evaluates to

1, then the first subroutine in the *destinationlist* is used; if it evaluates to 2, then the second subroutine in the *destinationlist* is used; and so on. Control is transferred to the line of code immediately following the `On...GoSub` line when a `Return` statement is encountered.

On...GoTo Statement

```
On expression GoTo destinationlist
```

Evaluates a given *expression* and, depending on its value, transfers program control to a certain line label or line number. The possible transfer points are contained in the *destinationlist* argument, which contains one or more comma-delimited line labels or line numbers. If *expression* evaluates to 1, then the first line label in the *destinationlist* is used; if it evaluates to 2, then the second line label in the *destinationlist* is used; and so on.

Open Statement

```
Open pathname For mode [Access access] [lock] As [#]filenumber [Len=reclength]
```

Opens a file for input/output and assigns it to the given *filenumber*. The *pathname* argument specifies the name of the file to open, and *mode* indicates the file mode (`Append`, `Binary`, `Input`, `Output`, or `Random`). The optional `Access` clause can be used to specify permissions for the file (Read, Write, or Read Write). The optional *lock* argument can specify the operations that can be performed on the file by other processes (`Shared`, `Lock Read`, `Lock Write`, or `Lock Read Write`). The *reclength* argument can be used to specify the record size for random files or the buffer size for sequential files.

Option Base Statement

```
Option Base [0 | 1]
```

Declares the default lower bound of array subscripts. `Option Base` can only be used at module level.

Option Compare Statement

```
Option Compare [Binary | Text | Database]
```

Declares the default method used for string comparisons. `Option Compare` can only be used at module level.

Option Explicit Statement

```
Option Explicit
```

Forces explicit declaration of all variables in a module. If `Option Explicit` is not used, undeclared variables are automatically typed as `Variants`. `Option Explicit` can only be used at module level.

Option Private Statement

```
Option Private Module
```

Prevents a module's contents (that is, variables and objects) from being used outside its project. `Option Private` is only necessary when working with host applications that allow variables and objects to be referenced across multiple projects.

Partition Function

```
Partition(number, start, stop, interval)
```

Returns a `Variant` of subtype `String` that describes a range of numbers in which the *`number`* argument falls. The *`start`* and *`stop`* arguments specify the overall range of numbers, which is split up into smaller ranges as specified by the *`interval`* argument. The `Partition` function returns a string representation of the smaller range in which the number can be found, such as "1: 10" for a *`number`* that falls in the range of 1 to 10.

Pmt Function

```
Pmt(rate, nper, pv[, fv[, type]])
```

Returns a `Double` value that indicates the payment for an annuity based on a number (*`nper`*) of periodic fixed payments and a fixed interest rate (*`rate`*). The *`pv`* argument specifies the present value of a series of payments or receipts. The optional *`fv`* argument specifies the future value or cash balance left after the final payment. The optional *`type`* argument specifies when payments are due (0 for end of the payment period, the default; 1 for beginning of the payment period).

PPmt Function

```
PPmt(rate, per, nper, pv[, fv[, type]])
```

Returns a `Double` value that indicates the principle payment for a given period (*`per`*) of an annuity based on a number (*`nper`*) of periodic fixed payments and a fixed interest rate (*`rate`*). The *`pv`* argument specifies the present value of a series of payments or receipts. The optional *`fv`* argument specifies the future value or cash balance left after the final payment. The optional *`type`* argument specifies when payments are due (0 for end of the payment period, the default; 1 for beginning of the payment period).

Print # Statement

```
Print #filenumber, [outputlist]
```

Writes data to the open sequential file that corresponds to *`filenumber`*. The optional *`outputlist`* argument can consist of one or more comma-delimited expressions to be written and should use the following syntax:

```
[{Spc(n) ¦ Tab[(n)]}] [expression][charpos]
```

where Spc is optionally used to write *n* spaces, and Tab is optionally used to advance to the *n*th column number. The *expression* argument can specify the data to be written, and the *charpos* argument can specify the insertion point for the next character. If *charpos* is omitted, the next character will be written on the next line. If it is a semicolon, the next character will be written immediately following the last character.

Private Statement

```
Private [WithEvents] varname[([subscripts])] [As [New] type][,[WithEvents]
varname[([subscripts])]      [As [New] type]]...
```

Declares one or more private variables. The *varname* argument specifies the name of the variable being declared, and *subscripts* are the dimensions for an array variable. The optional As [New] *type* clause can be used to specify the variable's data type, with the New keyword enabling implicit creation of an object. The optional WithEvents keyword specifies that the variable being declared is an object variable used to respond to events triggered by an ActiveX object. The Private statement can only be used at module level, and variables declared with it cannot be used outside their own module.

Property Get Statement

```
[Public ¦ Private ¦ Friend] [Static] Property Get name [(arglist)] [As type]
    [statements]
    [name = expression]
    [Exit Property]
    [statements]
    [name = expression]
End Property
```

Declares the various parts of a Property Get procedure, which is used to obtain the value of a property. The optional Public, Private, and Friend keywords can be used to define the procedure's scope, and the optional Static keyword indicates that the procedure's local variables are preserved between calls to the procedure. The *name* argument specifies the name of the property to be retrieved and can be assigned a value (*name = expression*) that will be returned as the property's value. The data type of the property can be specified using the As *type* clause. The optional Exit Property can be used to exit the Property Get procedure immediately.

The optional list of arguments (*arglist*) defines the arguments that will be passed to the procedure. The arguments should use the following syntax:

```
[Optional] [ByVal ¦ ByRef] [ParamArray] varname[()]     [As type] [= default value]
```

where the Optional keyword can be used to specify that the argument is not required (*default value* assigns the argument's default value), ByVal and ByRef determine whether the argument should be passed by value or by reference (the default), and the ParamArray keyword specifies that the argument is an Optional array of Variant elements. ParamArray can only be used with the last argument in the argument list.

Property Let Statement

```
[Public ¦ Private ¦ Friend] [Static] Property Let name ([arglist,] value)
    [statements]
    [Exit Property]
    [statements]
End Property
```

Declares the various parts of a `Property Let` procedure, which is used to assign a value to a property. The optional `Public`, `Private`, and `Friend` keywords can be used to define the procedure's scope, and the optional `Static` keyword indicates that the procedure's local variables are preserved between calls to the procedure. The *`name`* argument specifies the name of the property being referenced, and *`value`* indicates the value to be assigned to the property. The optional `Exit Property` can be used to exit the `Property Let` procedure immediately.

The optional list of arguments (*`arglist`*) defines the arguments that will be passed to the procedure. The arguments should use the following syntax:

```
[Optional] [ByVal ¦ ByRef] [ParamArray] varname[()]     [As type] [= default value]
```

where the `Optional` keyword can be used to specify that the argument is not required (*`default value`* assigns the argument's default value), `ByVal` and `ByRef` determine whether the argument should be passed by value or by reference (the default), and the `ParamArray` keyword specifies that the argument is an `Optional` array of `Variant` elements. `ParamArray` can only be used with the last argument in the argument list.

Property Set Statement

```
[Public ¦ Private ¦ Friend] [Static] Property Set name ([arglist,] reference)
    [statements]
    [Exit Property]
    [statements]
End Property
```

Declares the various parts of a `Property Set` procedure, which is used to set a reference to an object. The optional `Public`, `Private`, and `Friend` keywords can be used to define the procedure's scope, and the optional `Static` keyword indicates that the procedure's local variables are preserved between calls to the procedure. The *`name`* argument specifies the name of the property being used, and *`reference`* indicates the object reference to be set to the property. The optional `Exit Property` can be used to exit the `Property Set` procedure immediately.

The optional list of arguments (*`arglist`*) defines the arguments that will be passed to the procedure. The arguments should use the following syntax:

```
[Optional] [ByVal ¦ ByRef] [ParamArray] varname[()] [As type] [= default value]
```

where the `Optional` keyword can be used to specify that the argument is not required (*`default value`* assigns the argument's default value), `ByVal` and `ByRef` determine whether the argument should be passed by value or by reference (the default), and the `ParamArray` keyword specifies that the argument is an `Optional` array of `Variant` elements. `ParamArray` can only be used with the last argument in the argument list.

Public Statement

```
Public [WithEvents] varname[([subscripts])] [As [New] type][,[WithEvents]
varname[([subscripts])] [As [New] type]]...
```

Declares one or more public variables. The `varname` argument specifies the name of the variable being declared, and `subscripts` are the dimensions for an array variable. The optional `As [New] type` clause can be used to specify the variable's data type, with the `New` keyword enabling implicit creation of an object. The optional `WithEvents` keyword specifies that the variable being declared is an object variable used to respond to events triggered by an ActiveX object. The `Public` statement can only be used at module level, and variables declared with it can be used outside their own module.

Put Statement

```
Put [#]filenumber, [recnumber], varname
```

Writes data to the open disk file corresponding to the `filenumber` argument from a variable (`varname`). `Put` works with files open as `Random` or `Binary`, and a record number (`recnumber`) can be specified when writing data to a `Random` file. When using `Binary` files, `recnumber` can alternatively be used to specify the byte position at which the data is to be written.

PV Function

```
PV(rate, nper, pmt[, fv[, type]])
```

Returns a `Double` value that indicates the present value of an annuity based on a number (`nper`) of periodic fixed payments (`pmt`) and a fixed interest rate (`rate`). The optional `fv` argument specifies the future value or cash balance left after the final payment. The optional `type` argument specifies when payments are due (0 for end of the payment period, the default; 1 for beginning of the payment period).

QBColor Function

```
QBColor(color)
```

Returns a `Long` value that represents the RGB color code that corresponds to a given color `number` (0–15) of the color palette used in Microsoft QuickBasic.

RaiseEvent Function

```
RaiseEvent eventname [(argumentlist)]
```

Triggers an event. The optional `argumentlist` specifies one or more comma-delimited arguments to be passed to the event procedure. The event procedure must be declared in the same module as the `RaiseEvent` function or an error will occur.

Randomize Statement

```
Randomize [number]
```

Initializes the random number generator, using the optional *number* argument as a seed value.

Rate Function

```
Rate(nper, pmt, pv[, fv[, type[, guess]]])
```

Returns a `Double` value that indicates the fixed interest rate per period for an annuity based on a number (*nper*) of periodic fixed payments (*pmt*). The optional *fv* argument specifies the future value or cash balance left after the final payment. The optional *type* argument specifies when payments are due (0 for end of the payment period, the default; 1 for beginning of the payment period). The optional *guess* argument specifies an estimate value to be returned by `Rate` (default estimate is .1).

ReDim Statement

```
ReDim [Preserve] varname(subscripts) [As type] [, varname(subscripts) [As type]]...
```

Redimensions one or more dynamic array variables and reallocates their storage space. The optional `Preserve` keyword can be used to keep the contents of the array intact when it is being redimensioned. The *varname* argument is the name of the variable, and the optional `As` *type* clause indicates its data type. The *subscripts* are the dimensions of the array variable.

Rem Statement

```
Rem comments
```

Allows *comments* to be added to a program. Everything on the line after the `Rem` statement is ignored by Visual Basic. An apostrophe (`'`) can also be used in lieu of the `Rem` statement.

Reset Statement

```
Reset
```

Closes all files opened with the `Open` statement and writes any file buffer contents to disk.

Resume Statement

```
Resume [0]
Resume Next
Resume line
```

Resumes execution of a program when an error-handling routine is finished. `Resume` by itself causes execution to resume with the statement that caused the error or, if the error occurred in a called procedure, the statement that last called out of the error-handling procedure. `Resume Next` causes execution to resume with the statement immediately following the one that caused the error. `Resume` *line* transfers control to the line label or line number specified by the *line* argument.

RGB Function

`RGB(red, green, blue)`

Returns a `Long` value that represents an RGB color value as specified by the *red*, *green*, and *blue* color components passed to the `RGB` function. All color components should be `Integers` in the 0–255 range.

Right Function

`Right(string, length)`

Returns a `String` value *length* characters long that is taken from the right side of a given *string*.

RmDir Statement

`RmDir path`

Removes the directory or folder specified by the *path* argument.

Rnd Function

`Rnd[(number)]`

Returns a `Single` value that contains a randomly generated number less than 1 but greater than or equal to zero. The optional *number* argument can be used to determine how `Rnd` generates the random number.

RSet Statement

`RSet stringvar = string`

Assigns a *string* value to a `String` variable (*stringvar*), right-aligning the string to the `String` variable.

RTrim Function

`RTrim(string)`

Returns a `Variant` of subtype `String` that contains a copy of a given *string* with any trailing spaces removed.

SavePicture Statement

`SavePicture picture, stringexpression`

Saves an graphic image from an object's `Picture` or `Image` property to a file. The *picture* argument specifies the control from which the graphics file is to be created (`Picture` or `Image`), and *stringexpression* specifies the path and filename to which the image is saved.

SaveSetting Statement

```
SaveSetting appname, section, key, setting
```

Saves or creates an application (`appname`) entry, section (`section`), key setting (`key`), and value (`setting`) in the System Registry.

Second Function

```
Second(time)
```

Returns a `Variant` of subtype `Integer` that represents the second (0–59) of the time value specified by the *time* argument.

Seek Function

```
Seek(filenumber)
```

Returns a `Long` value that specifies the current record or byte position for the open file associated with `filenumber`. When dealing with `Random` files, `Seek` returns the number of the next record to be read or written. For all other file types, `Seek` returns a byte position.

Seek Statement

```
Seek [#]filenumber, position
```

Sets the record or byte `position` of the open file associated with `filenumber`.

Select Case Statement

```
Select Case testexpression
    [Case expressionlist-n
        [statements-n]] ...
    [Case Else
        [elsestatements]]
End Select
```

Evaluates an expression (`testexpression`) and, depending on the result, executes one or more statements (`statements-n`) that correspond to the expression's value (`expressionlist-n`). In other words, the value of `testexpression` is compared with one or more other values (`expressionlistn`), and whichever matches gets its statements (`statements-n`) executed. If there are no matches, an optional `Case Else` set of statements (`elsestatements`) is executed.

SendKeys Statement

Generates one or more keystrokes as if they came from the keyboard. The `string` argument determines which keystrokes to send, and the optional `Wait` argument (`Boolean`) specifies whether keystrokes must be processed before control is returned to the procedure. `False`, the default value, means that control is returned to the procedure immediately after the keystrokes are sent.

Set Statement

`Set objectvar = {[New] objectexpression ¦ Nothing}`

Assigns an object reference (*objectexpression*) to a variable or property (*objectvar*). The optional `New` keyword can be used to indicate that the object should be created implicitly. To disassociate *objectvar* with a specific object and free up the resources it is using, assign it the `Nothing` keyword.

SetAttr Statement

`SetAttr pathname, attributes`

Sets attributes for the file or directory specified by the *pathname* argument. The *attributes* argument can use several VB constants (`vbNormal`, `vbReadOnly`, `vbHidden`, `vbSystem`, `vbDirectory`, and `vbArchive`) that can be combined bitwise to determine which attributes are set.

Sgn Function

`Sgn(number)`

Returns a `Variant` of subtype `Integer` that represents the sign of a given *number*.

Shell Function

`Shell(pathname[, windowstyle])`

Runs the executable program specified by the *pathname* argument and returns a `Variant` of subtype `Double` that represents the program's task ID. If `Shell` is unsuccessful, it returns zero. The optional *windowstyle* argument determines the style of the window in which the shelled program runs.

Sin Function

`Sin(number)`

Returns a `Double` value that represents the sine of a given angle (as specified by the *number* argument).

SLN Function

`SLN(cost, salvage, life)`

Returns a `Double` value that represents the straight-line depreciation of an asset when given its initial *cost*, *salvage* value at the end of its useful life, and *life* span.

Space Function

```
Space(number)
```

Returns a `Variant` of subtype `String` that contains a *`number`* of spaces.

Spc Function

```
Spc(n)
```

Inserts a specified number of spaces (*n*) when writing or displaying text using the `Print #` statement or the `Print` method.

Sqr Function

```
Sqr(number)
```

Returns a `Double` value that represents the square root of a given *`number`*.

Static Statement

```
Static varname[([subscripts])] [As [New] type] [, varname[([subscripts])]
[As [New] type] ...
```

Declares one or more static variables, which retain their values as long as the program is running. The *`varname`* argument is the name of the variable, and the optional `As [New]` *`type`* indicates its data type. If the `New` keyword is used, then an implicit creation of the object is made. The optional *`subscripts`* are the dimensions of an array variable.

Stop Statement

```
Stop
```

Suspends program execution.

Str Function

```
Str(number)
```

Returns a `Variant` of subtype `String` that is a representation of a given *`number`*.

StrComp Function

```
StrComp(string1, string2[, compare])
```

Returns a `Variant` of subtype `Integer` that indicates the result of a comparison between two strings (*`string1`* and *`string2`*). The optional *`compare`* argument specifies how strings are to be compared, with 0 for a binary comparison and 1 for a noncase-sensitive textual comparison.

StrConv Function

```
StrConv(string, conversion)
```

Returns a Variant of subtype String that has been converted from an original *string* as specified by the *conversion* argument. The *conversion* argument can use several VB constants to specify the type of conversion, such as vbUpperCase, vbLowerCase, and vbProperCase.

String Function

```
String(number, character)
```

Returns a Variant of subtype String that is of the length specified by *number* and is filled with a given *character*.

Sub Statement

```
[Public ¦ Private ¦ Friend] [Static] Sub name [(arglist)]
    [statements]
    [Exit Sub]
    [statements]
End Sub
```

Declares the various parts of a Sub procedure. The optional Public, Private, and Friend keywords can be used to define the Sub's scope, and the optional Static keyword indicates that the procedure's local variables are preserved between calls to the Sub. The *name* argument specifies the name of the Sub procedure. The optional Exit Sub can be used to exit the Sub procedure immediately.

The optional list of arguments (*arglist*) defines the arguments that will be passed to the procedure. The arguments should use the following syntax:

```
[Optional] [ByVal ¦ ByRef] [ParamArray] varname[()] [As type] [= default value]
```

where the Optional keyword can be used to specify that the argument is not required (*default value* assigns the argument's default value), ByVal and ByRef determine whether the argument should be passed by value or by reference (the default), and the ParamArray keyword specifies that the argument is an Optional array of Variant elements. ParamArray can only be used with the last argument in the argument list.

Switch Function

```
Switch(expr-1, value-1[, expr-2, value-2 ... [, expr-n, value-n]])
```

Evaluates a list of expressions (*expr-1*, *expr-2...expr-n*) and returns a Variant value that corresponds to the first expression that evaluates as True. If *expr-1* is True, then Switch returns the value indicated by *value-1*; if *expr-2* is True, then Switch returns the value indicated by *value-2*; and so on.

SYD Function

`SYD(cost, salvage, life, period)`

Returns a `Double` value that represents the sum-of-years' digits depreciation of an asset when given its initial *cost*, *salvage* value at the end of its useful life, *life* span, and *period* for which depreciation is calculated.

Tab Function

`Tab(n)`

Positions output to a given column (*n*) when writing or displaying text using the `Print #` statement or the `Print` method.

Tan Function

`Tan(number)`

Returns a `Double` value that represents the tangent of a given angle (specified by the *number* argument).

Time Function

`Time`

Returns a `Variant` of subtype `Date` that contains the current system time.

Time Statement

`Time = time`

Sets the system time to the time specified by the *time* argument.

Timer Function

`Timer`

Returns a `Single` value that represents the number of seconds that have elapsed since midnight.

TimeSerial Function

`TimeSerial(hour, minute, second)`

Returns a `Variant` of subtype `Date` that represents a time as specified by the *hour*, *minute*, and *second* arguments.

TimeValue Function

`TimeValue(time)`

Returns a `Variant` of subtype `Date` that is derived from the time value specified by the *time* argument.

Trim Function

```
Trim(string)
```

Returns a `Variant` of subtype `String` that contains a copy of a given *`string`* with any leading and trailing spaces removed.

Type Statement

```
[Private ¦ Public] Type varname
    elementname [([subscripts])] As type
    [elementname [([subscripts])] As type]
    ...
End Type
```

Defines a user-defined type (UDT) structure that contains one or more elements (*`elementname`*). The optional `Public` and `Private` keywords specify the UDT's scope, and *`varname`* specifies the UDT's name. Elements can be arrays (by specifying *`subscripts`*), and their data type must be defined using the `As` *`type`* clause. The `Type` statement can only be used at module level.

TypeName Function

```
TypeName(varname)
```

Returns a `String` value that indicates the data type of a given variable (*`varname`*). Possible return values are `Byte`, `Integer`, `Long`, `Single`, `Double`, `Currency`, `Decimal`, `Date`, `String`, `Boolean`, `Error`, `Empty`, `Null`, `Object`, `Unknown`, `Nothing`, or an object type.

UBound Function

```
UBound(arrayname[, dimension])
```

Returns a `Long` value that represents the largest subscript for a dimensioned array (*`arrayname`*). For multidimensional arrays, the *`dimension`* argument can be included to specify which dimension should be used.

UCase Function

```
UCase(string)
```

Converts a *`string`* to all uppercase characters and returns a new `String` value.

Unload Statement

```
Unload object
```

Unloads an *`object`* (such as a form or control) from memory and frees up any resources being used by the object.

Unlock Statement

```
Unlock [#]filenumber[, recordrange]
```

Removes locking that prevents another process from accessing all or part of the open file that corresponds to the `filenumber` argument. The `recordrange` argument refers to a range of records (or bytes) that are to be unlocked and should use the syntax:

```
recnumber | [start] To end
```

where `recnumber` is the record number (for `Random` files) or byte position (for `Binary` files) where unlocking should begin. Alternatively, the starting and ending record numbers or bytes to be unlocked can be specified using the `start` and `end` arguments.

Val Function

```
Val(string)
```

Returns the numeric value of a `string`. The data type that is returned by `Val` depends on the kind of numeric value the string contains. If the string does not contain a numeric value, then `Val` returns zero.

VarType Function

```
VarType(varname)
```

Returns an `Integer` value that represents the subtype of the variable specified by `varname`. Several VB constants are used to define the data type values returned by the `VarType` function, including: `vbEmpty`, `vbNull`, `vbInteger`, `vbLong`, `vbSingle`, `vbDouble`, `vbCurrency`, `vbDate`, `vbString`, `vbObject`, `vbError`, `vbBoolean`, `vbVariant`, `vbDataObject`, `vbDecimal`, `vbByte`, and `vbArray`.

Weekday Function

```
Weekday(date, [firstdayofweek])
```

Returns a `Variant` of subtype `Integer` that represents the day of the week for a given `date`. `Weekday` returns a 1 for Sunday, 2 for Monday, and so on. The optional `firstdayofweek` argument can be used to specify the first day of the week. If `firstdayofweek` is not specified, then Sunday (1) is assumed.

While...Wend Statement

```
While condition
    [statements]
Wend
```

Repeats one or more `statements` while a `condition` remains `True`. When the `condition` becomes `False`, then control is passed to the line of code immediately following the `While...Wend` structure.

Width # Statement

```
Width #filenumber, width
```

Assigns an output line `width` (in characters) for the open file associated with `filenumber`.

With Statement

```
With object
    [statements]
End With
```

Executes one or more `statements` on a single `object` or user-defined type.

Write # Statement

```
Write #filenumber, [outputlist]
```

Writes data to the open sequential file associated with the `filenumber` argument. The `outputlist` argument should contain one or more comma-delimited variables that contain the data to be written to the file.

Year Function

```
Year(date)
```

Returns a `Variant` that represents the year for the date value specified by the `date` argument.

Summary

This chapter is designed to be a quick-reference for all of VB's built-in functions and statements, providing syntax and a brief description for each. For more information about particular functions and statements, consult Visual Basic's online Help system or Microsoft's *Visual Basic 5.0 Language Reference.*

CHAPTER 41

Controls Syntax: Properties, Events, and Methods

IN THIS CHAPTER

Visual Basic relies heavily on components such as ActiveX controls and objects. Each component often has dozens of properties, events, and methods by which it can be modified or manipulated. It's often difficult to remember the details of a control or object's interface, especially if it is an object that is seldom used.

This chapter provides a quick reference to the properties, events, and methods of Visual Basic's many components. Not only are all the ActiveX controls detailed here, other important objects (such as `Screen`, `Printer`, and `UserControl`) are also included. Although this is not meant to be a complete reference, it may prove useful because it allows you to see all the properties, events, and methods for a control within the space of a page or two. It also provides pertinent information about each, such as the data types of properties, the syntax of methods, and the arguments of events. If you require a more in-depth source of information, Microsoft's *Visual Basic 5.0 Language Reference* and *Visual Basic 5.0 ActiveX Controls Reference* are highly recommended.

Each control or object in this chapter shows the full list of properties, events, and methods. A few notes about the way the information is presented are listed here:

- Properties, events, and methods that are common to many controls or objects are detailed at the beginning of this chapter. Any applicable common properties, events, and methods are also listed for each control and object in the chapter, but they are not detailed.
- Property listings give the data types, or the appropriate object type, collection name, or enumeration name for each property. Properties with an asterisk to the left of their names are read only at runtime.
- Event listings show the arguments returned by the events, as well as each argument's data or object type.
- Method listings show the arguments that may be passed to the method, but they do not show the arguments' data or object type. Optional arguments are enclosed in brackets.
- In some cases, a control will utilize an object that has its own set of properties, events, and methods. The object's interface elements are not included in this reference.

Common Properties, Events, and Methods

Many properties, events, and methods are common to many controls. For example, the `BorderStyle` property is used in several different controls. In some, it is implemented as an `Integer` value. Others use the `BorderStyleConstants` enumeration type.

This section lists many common properties, events, and methods used in Visual Basic. The information here portrays the most commonly used formats. However, some controls may use slightly different implementations. For example, an event may return different arguments, or a method may have a different syntax.

Common Properties

The following list includes properties that are common to several different controls.

*Appearance	Integer
BackColor	Long
*BorderStyle	Integer or BorderStyleConstants Enum
Container	Object
DataBindings	DataBindings Collection
DataChanged	Boolean
DataField	String
DragIcon	IPictureDisp Object
DragMode	Integer
Enabled	Boolean
Font	StdFont Object or IFontDisp Object
FontBold	Boolean
FontItalic	Boolean
FontName	String
FontSize	Single
FontStrikethru	Boolean
FontTransparent	Boolean
FontUnderline	Boolean
ForeColor	Long
*hDC	Long
Height	Single
HelpContextID	Long
*hWnd	Long
*Index	Integer
Left	Single
LinkItem	String
LinkMode	Integer
LinkTopic	String
LinkTimeout	Integer
MouseIcon	IPictureDisp Object
MousePointer	Integer

*Name	String
*Object	Object
OLEDragMode	Integer
OLEDropMode	Integer
*Parent	Form Object or Object
RightToLeft	Boolean
ScaleHeight	Single
ScaleLeft	Single
ScaleMode	Integer
ScaleTop	Single
ScaleWidth	Single
TabIndex	Integer
TabStop	Boolean
Tag	String
ToolTipText	String
Top	Single
Visible	Boolean
WhatsThisHelpID	Long
Width	Single

Common Events

The following list includes events that are common to several different controls.

```
Click()
DblClick()
DragDrop(source As Control, x As Single, y As Single)
DragOver(source As Control, x As Single, y As Single, state As Integer)
GotFocus()
KeyDown(keycode As Integer, shift As Integer)
KeyPress(keyascii As Integer)
KeyUp(keycode As Integer, shift As Integer)
LinkClose()
LinkError(linkerr As Integer)
```

LinkExecute(*cmdstr* As String, *cancel* As Integer)

LinkNotify([*index* As Integer])

LinkOpen(*cancel* As Integer)

LostFocus()

MouseDown(*button* As Integer, *shift* As Integer, *x* As Single, *y* As Single)

MouseMove(*button* As Integer, *shift* As Integer, *x* As Single, *y* As Single)

MouseUp(*button* As Integer, *shift* As Integer, *x* As Single, *y* As Single)

OLECompleteDrag(*effect* As Long)

OLEDragDrop(*data* As DataObject, *effect* As Long, *button* As Integer, *shift* As Integer, *x* As Single, *y* As Single)

OLEDragOver(*data* As DataObject, *effect* As Long, *button* As Integer, *shift* As Integer, *x* As Single, *y* As Single, *state* As Integer)

OLEGiveFeedback(*effect* As Long, *defaultcursors* As Boolean)

OLESetData(*data* As DataObject, *dataFormat* As Integer)

OLEStartDrag(*data* As DataObject, *allowedeffects* As Long)

Common Methods

The following list includes methods that are common to several different controls.

Drag	*object*.Drag(*action*)
LinkExecute	*object*.LinkExecute(*cmdstr*, *cancel*)
LinkPoke	*object*.LinkPoke
LinkRequest	*object*.LinkRequest
LinkSend	*object*.LinkSend
Move	*object*.Move(*rows*, *start*)
OLEDrag	*object*.OLEDrag
Refresh	*object*.Refresh
Scale	*object*.Scale(*x1*, *y1*)-(*x2*, *y2*)
ScaleX	object.ScaleX(width, fromscale, toscale)
ScaleY	object.ScaleY(height, fromscale, toscale)
SetFocus	*object*.SetFocus
ShowWhatsThis	*object*.ShowWhatsThis
ZOrder	*object*.ZOrder(*position*)

Animation

Properties

Common Properties: BackColor, Container, DragIcon, DragMode, Enabled, Height, HelpContextID, hWnd, Index, Left, Name, Object, OLEDropMode, Parent, TabIndex, TabStop, Tag, ToolTipText, Top, Visible, WhatsThisHelpID, Width

AutoPlay	Boolean
BackStyle	Integer
Center	Boolean

Events

Common Events: Click, DblClick, DragDrop, DragOver, GotFocus, LostFocus, MouseDown, MouseMove, MouseUp, OLECompleteDrag, OLEDragDrop, OLEGiveFeedback, OLESetData, OLEStartDrag

Methods

Common Methods: Drag, Move, OLEDrag, SetFocus, ShowWhatsThis, ZOrder

Close	*object*.Close
Open	*object*.Open (*file*)
Play	*object*.Play ([*repeatcount*], [*startframe*], [*endframe*])
Stop	*object*.Stop

CheckBox

Properties

Common Properties: Appearance, BackColor, Container, DataChanged, DataField, DragIcon, DragMode, Enabled, Font, FontBold, FontItalic, FontName, FontSize, FontStrikethru, FontUnderline, ForeColor, Height, HelpContextID, hWnd, Index, Left, MouseIcon, MousePointer, Name, OLEDropMode, Parent, RightToLeft, TabIndex, TabStop, Tag, ToolTipText, Top, Visible, WhatsThisHelpID, Width

*Alignment	Integer
Caption	String
DisabledPicture	IPictureDisp Object
DownPicture	IPictureDisp Object
MaskColor	Long

Picture	IPictureDisp Object
*Style	Integer
UseMaskColor	Boolean
Value	Integer

Events

Common Events: Click, DragDrop, DragOver, GotFocus, KeyDown, KeyPress, KeyUp, LostFocus, MouseDown, MouseMove, MouseUp, OLECompleteDrag, OLEDragDrop, OLEDragOver, OLEGiveFeedback, OLESetData, OLEStartDrag

Methods

Common Methods: Drag, Move, OLEDrag, Refresh, SetFocus, ShowWhatsThis, ZOrder

ComboBox

Properties

Common Properties: Appearance, BackColor, Container, DataChanged, DataField, DragIcon, DragMode, Enabled, Font, FontBold, FontItalic, FontName, FontSize, FontStrikethru, FontUnderline, ForeColor, Height, HelpContextID, hWnd, Index, Left, MouseIcon, MousePointer, Name, OLEDragMode, OLEDropMode, Parent, RightToLeft, TabIndex, TabStop, Tag, ToolTipText, Top, Visible, WhatsThisHelpID, Width

*IntegralHeight	Boolean
ItemData	Long Array
List	String Array
*ListCount	Integer
ListIndex	Integer
Locked	Boolean
*NewIndex	Integer
SelLength	Long
SelStart	Long
SelText	String
*Sorted	Boolean
*Style	Integer
Text	String
TopIndex	Integer

Events

Common Events: Click, DblClick, DragDrop, DragOver, GotFocus, KeyDown, KeyPress, KeyUp, LostFocus, OLECompleteDrag, OLEDragDrop, OLEDragOver, OLEGiveFeedback, OLESetData, OLEStartDrag

Change()

DropDown()

Scroll()

Methods

Common Methods: Drag, Move, OLEDrag, Refresh, SetFocus, ShowWhatsThis, ZOrder

AddItem	*object*.AddItem(*item* [, *index*])
Clear	*object*.Clear
RemoveItem	*object*.RemoveItem(*index*)

CommandButton

Properties

Common Properties: Appearance, BackColor, Container, DragIcon, DragMode, Enabled, Font, FontBold, FontItalic, FontName, FontSize, FontStrikethru, FontUnderline, Height, HelpContextID, hWnd, Index, Left, MouseIcon, MousePointer, Name, OLEDropMode, Parent, RightToLeft, TabIndex, TabStop, Tag, ToolTipText, Top, Visible, WhatsThisHelpID, Width

Cancel	Boolean
Caption	String
Default	Boolean
DisabledPicture	IPictureDisp Object
DownPicture	IPictureDisp Object
MaskColor	Long
Picture	IPictureDisp Object
*Style	Integer
UseMaskColor	Boolean
Value	Boolean

Events

Common Events: Click, DragDrop, DragOver, GotFocus, KeyDown, KeyPress, KeyUp, LostFocus, MouseDown, MouseMove, MouseUp, OLECompleteDrag, OLEDragDrop, OLEDragOver, OLEGiveFeedback, OLESetData, OLEStartDrag

Methods

Common Methods: Drag, Move, OLEDrag, Refresh, SetFocus, ShowWhatsThis, ZOrder

Common Dialog

Properties

Common Properties: FontBold, FontItalic, FontName, FontSize, FontStrikethru, FontUnderline, hDC, Index, Name, Object, Parent, Tag

Action	Integer
CancelError	Boolean
Color	OLE_COLOR
Copies	Integer
DefaultExt	String
DialogTitle	String
FileName	String
FileTitle	String
Filter	String
FilterIndex	Integer
Flags	Long
HelpCommand	Integer
HelpContext	Long
HelpFile	String
HelpKey	String
InitDir	String
Max	Integer
MaxFileSize	Integer
Min	Integer
PrinterDefault	Boolean
ToPage	Integer

Events

No events

Methods

ShowColor	*object*.ShowColor
ShowFont	*object*.ShowFont
ShowHelp	*object*.ShowHelp
ShowOpen	*object*.ShowOpen
ShowPrinter	*object*.ShowPrinter
ShowSave	*object*.ShowSave

Data

Properties

Common Properties: Appearance, BackColor, DragIcon, DragMode, Enabled, Font, FontBold, FontItalic, FontName, FontSize, FontStrikethru, FontUnderline, ForeColor, Height, Index, Left, MouseIcon, MousePointer, Name, OLEDropMode, Parent, RightToLeft, Tag, ToolTipText, Top, Visible, WhatsThisHelpID, Width

Align	Integer
BOFAction	Integer
Caption	String
Connect	String
*Database	Database Object
DatabaseName	String
DefaultCursorType	Integer
DefaultType	Integer
*EditMode	Integer
EOFAction	Integer
Exclusive	Boolean
Options	Integer
ReadOnly	Boolean
Recordset	Recordset Object
RecordsetType	Integer
RecordSource	String

Events

Common Events: DragDrop, DragOver, MouseDown, MouseMove, MouseUp, OLECompleteDrag, OLEDragDrop, OLEGiveFeedback, OLESetData, OLEStartDrag, Resize

Error(*dataerr* As Integer, *response* As Integer)

Reposition()

Validate(*action* As Integer, *save* As Integer)

Methods

Common Methods: Drag, Move, OLEDrag, Refresh, ShowWhatsThis, ZOrder

UpdateControls	*object*.UpdateControls
UpdateRecord	*object*.UpdateRecord

DBCombo

Properties

Common Properties: Appearance, BackColor, Container, DataBindings, DataChanged, DataField, DragIcon, DragMode, Enabled, Font, ForeColor, Height, HelpContextID, hWnd, Index, Left, MouseIcon, MousePointer, Name, Object, OLEDragMode, OLEDropMode, Parent, RightToLeft, TabIndex, TabStop, Tag, Text, ToolTipText, Top, Visible, WhatsThisHelpID, Width

BoundColumn	String
BoundText	String
IntegralHeight	Boolean
ListField	String
Locked	Boolean
*MatchedWithList	Boolean
MatchEntry	MatchEntryConstants Enum
RowSource	IRowCursor Object
*SelectedItem	Variant
SelLength	Long
SelStart	Long
SelText	String
Style	StyleConstants Enum
*VisibleCount	Integer
*VisibleItems	Variant Array

Events

Common Events: Click, DblClick, DragDrop, DragOver, GotFocus, KeyDown, KeyPress, KeyUp, LostFocus, MouseDown, MouseMove, MouseUp, OLECompleteDrag, OLEDragDrop, OLEDragOver, OLEGiveFeedback, OLESetData, OLEStartDrag

Change()

Methods

Common Methods: Drag, Move, OLEDrag, Refresh, SetFocus, ShowWhatsThis, ZOrder

ReFill	*object*.ReFill

DBGrid

Properties

Common Properties: Appearance, BackColor, BorderStyle, Container, DataBindings, DataChanged, DragIcon, DragMode, Enabled, Font, ForeColor, Height, HelpContextID, hWnd, Index, Left, Name, Object, Parent, TabIndex, TabStop, Tag, ToolTipText, Top, Visible, WhatsThisHelpID, Width

AddNewMode	*enum*AddNewModeConstants Enum
Align	Integer
AllowAddNew	Boolean
AllowArrows	Boolean
AllowDelete	Boolean
AllowRowSizing	Boolean
AllowUpdate	Boolean
ApproxCount	Long
Bookmark	Variant
Caption	String
Col	Integer
ColumnHeaders	Boolean
*Columns	Object Array
CurrentCellModified	Boolean
CurrentCellVisible	Boolean
DataMode	enumDataModeConstants Enum
DataSource	ICursor Object
DefColWidth	Single

EditActive	Boolean
ErrorText	String
FirstRow	Variant
HeadFont	IFontDisp Object
HeadLines	Single
hWndEditor	OLE_HANDLE Object
LeftCol	Integer
MarqueeStyle	enumMarqueeStyleConstants Enum
MarqueeUnique	Boolean
RecordSelectors	Boolean
Row	Integer
RowDividerStyle	enumDividerStyleConstants Enum
RowHeight	Single
ScrollBars	enumScrollBarConstants Enum
*SelBookmarks	Variant Array
SelEndCol	Integer
SelLength	Long
SelStart	Long
SelStartCol	Integer
SelText	String
Split	Integer
Splits	Object Array
TabAcrossSplits	Boolean
TabAction	enumTabActionConstants Enum
Text	String
VisibleCols	Integer
VisibleRows	Integer
WrapCellPointer	Boolean

Events

Common Events: Click, DblClick, DragDrop, DragOver, GotFocus, KeyDown, KeyPress, KeyUp, LostFocus, MouseDown, MouseMove, MouseUp

AfterColEdit([*index* As Integer,] ByVal *colindex* As Integer)

AfterColUpdate([*index* As Integer,] *colindex* As Integer)

```
AfterDelete([index As Integer,] colindex As Integer)
AfterInsert(index As Integer)
AfterUpdate(index As Integer)
BeforeColEdit([index As Integer,] ByVal colindex As Integer,
          ByVal keyascii As Integer, cancel As Integer)
BeforeColUpdate([index As Integer,] colindex As Integer,
          oldvalue As Variant, cancel As Integer)
BeforeDelete([index As Integer,] cancel As Integer)
BeforeInsert([index As Integer,] cancel As Integer)
BeforeUpdate([index As Integer,] cancel As Integer)
ButtonClick([index As Integer,] ByVal colindex As Integer)
Change([index As Integer])
ColEdit([index As Integer,] ByVal colindex As Integer)
ColResize([index As Integer,] colindex As Integer,
          cancel As Integer)
Error([index As Integer,] ByVal dataerror As Integer,
          response As Integer)
HeadClick([index As Integer,] colindex As Integer)
OnAddNew([index As Integer])
RowColChange([index As Integer, lastrow As String,
          lastcol As Integer])
RowResize([index As Integer,] cancel As Integer)
Scroll([cancel As Integer])
SelChange([index As Integer,] cancel As Integer)
SplitChange([index As Integer])
UnboundAddData(rowbuf As RowBuffer, newrowbookmark As Variant)
UnboundDeleteRow(bookmark As Variant)
UnboundGetRelativeBookmark([index As Integer,]
          startlocation As Variant, ByVal offset As Long,
          newlocation As Variant, approximateposition As Long)
UnboundReadData(rowbuf As RowBuffer, startlocation As Variant,
          readpriorrows As Boolean)
UnboundWriteData(rowbuf As RowBuffer, writelocation As Variant)
```

Methods

Common Methods: Drag, Move, Refresh, ZOrder

AboutBox	*object*.AboutBox
CaptureImage	*object*.CaptureImage
ClearFields	*object*.ClearFields
ClearSelCols	*object*.ClearSelCols
ColContaining	*object*.ColContaining (*coordinate*)
GetBookmark	*object*.GetBookmark (*value*)
HoldFields	*object*.HoldFields
ReBind	*object*.Rebind
RowBookmark	*object*.RowBookmark (*value*)
RowContaining	*object*.RowContaining (*coordinate*)
RowTop	*object*.RowTop (*value*)
Scroll	*object*.Scroll (*colvalue*, *rowvalue*)

DBList

Properties

Common Properties: Appearance, BackColor, Container, DataBindings, DataChanged, DataField, DragIcon, DragMode, Enabled, Font, ForeColor, Height, HelpContextID, hWnd, Index, Left, MouseIcon, MousePointer, Name, Object, OLEDragMode, OLEDropMode, Parent, RightToLeft, TabIndex, TabStop, Tag, ToolTipText, Top, Visible, WhatsThisHelpID, Width

BoundColumn	String
BoundText	String
IntegralHeight	Boolean
ListField	String
Locked	Boolean
*MatchedWithList	Boolean
RowSource	IRowCursor Object
*SelectedItems	Variant
Text	String
*VisibleCount	Integer
*VisibleItems	Variant Array

Events

Common Events: Click, DblClick, DragDrop, DragOver, GotFocus, KeyDown, KeyPress, KeyUp, LostFocus, MouseDown, MouseMove, MouseUp, OLECompleteDrag, OLEDragDrop, OLEDragOver, OLEGiveFeedback, OLESetData, OLEStartDrag

Methods

Common Methods: Drag, Move, OLEDrag, Refresh, SetFocus, ShowWhatsThis, ZOrder

ReFill	*object*.ReFill

DirListBox

Properties

Common Properties: Appearance, BackColor, Container, DragIcon, DragMode, Enabled, Font, FontBold, FontItalic, FontName, FontSize, FontStrikethru, FontUnderline, ForeColor, Height, HelpContextID, hWnd, Index, Left, MouseIcon, MousePointer, Name, OLEDragMode, OLEDropMode, Parent, TabIndex, TabStop, Tag, ToolTipText, Top, Visible, WhatsThisHelpID, Width

*List	String Array
*ListCount	Integer
ListIndex	Integer
Path	String
TopIndex	Integer

Events

Common Events: Click, DragDrop, DragOver, GotFocus, KeyDown, KeyPress, KeyUp, LostFocus, MouseDown, MouseMove, MouseUp, OLECompleteDrag, OLEDragDrop, OLEDragOver, OLEGiveFeedback, OLESetData, OLEStartDrag

Change([*index* As Integer])

Scroll()

Methods

Common Methods: Drag, Move, OLEDrag, Refresh, SetFocus, ShowWhatsThis, ZOrder

DriveListBox

Properties

Common Properties: Appearance, BackColor, Container, DragIcon, DragMode, Enabled, Font, FontBold, FontItalic, FontName, FontSize, FontStrikethru, FontUnderline, ForeColor, Height,

HelpContextID, hWnd, Index, Left, MouseIcon, MousePointer, Name, OLEDropMode, Parent, TabIndex, TabStop, Tag, ToolTipText, Top, Visible, WhatsThisHelpID, Width

Drive	String
*List	String Array
*ListCount	Integer
ListIndex	Integer
TopIndex	Integer

Events

Common Events: DragDrop, DragOver, GotFocus, KeyDown, KeyPress, KeyUp, LostFocus, OLECompleteDrag, OLEDragDrop, OLEDragOver, OLEGiveFeedback, OLESetData, OLEStartDrag

Change([*index* As Integer])

Scroll()

Methods

Common Methods: Drag, Move, OLEDrag, Refresh, SetFocus, ShowWhatsThis, ZOrder

FileListBox

Properties

Common Properties: Appearance, BackColor, Container, DragIcon, DragMode, Enabled, Font, FontBold, FontItalic, FontName, FontSize, FontStrikethru, FontUnderline, ForeColor, Height, HelpContextID, hWnd, Index, Left, MouseIcon, MousePointer, Name, OLEDragMode, OLEDropMode, Parent, TabIndex, TabStop, Tag, ToolTipText, Top, Visible, WhatsThisHelpID, Width

Archive	Boolean
FileName	String
Hidden	Boolean
*List	String Array
*ListCount	Integer
ListIndex	Integer
*MultiSelect	Integer
Normal	Boolean
Path	String
Pattern	String
ReadOnly	Boolean
Selected	Boolean Array

System	Boolean
TopIndex	Integer

Events

Common Events: Click, DblClick, DragOver, GotFocus, KeyDown, KeyPress, KeyUp, LostFocus, MouseDown, MouseMove, MouseUp, OLECompleteDrag, OLEDragOver, OLEGiveFeedback, OLESetData, OLEStartDrag

PathChange([*index* As Integer])

PatternChange([*index* As Integer])

Scroll()

Methods

Common Methods: Drag, Move, OLEDrag, Refresh, SetFocus, ShowWhatsThis, ZOrder

Form

Properties

Common Properties: Appearance, BackColor, Enabled, Font, FontBold, FontItalic, FontName, FontSize, FontStrikethru, FontTransparent, FontUnderline, ForeColor, hDC, Height, HelpContextID, hWnd, Left, LinkMode, LinkTopic, MouseIcon, MousePointer, Name, OLEDropMode, RightToLeft, ScaleHeight, ScaleLeft, ScaleMode, ScaleTop, ScaleWidth, Tag, Top, Visible, Width

*ActiveControl	Control Object
AutoRedraw	Boolean
*BorderStyle	Integer
Caption	String
*ClipControls	Boolean
*ControlBox	Boolean
*Controls	Object
*Count	Integer
CurrentX	Single
CurrentY	Single
DrawMode	Integer
DrawStyle	Integer
DrawWidth	Integer
FillColor	Long

FillStyle	Integer
Icon	IPictureDisp Object
*Image	IPictureDisp Object
KeyPreview	Boolean
*MaxButton	Boolean
*MDIChild	Boolean
*MinButton	Boolean
*Moveable	Boolean
Palette	IPictureDisp Object
PaletteMode	Integer
Picture	IPictureDisp Object
*ShowInTaskbar	Boolean
*StartUpPosition	Integer
*WhatsThisButton	Boolean
*WhatsThisHelp	Boolean
WindowState	Integer

Events

Common Events: Click, DblClick, DragDrop, DragOver, GotFocus, KeyDown, KeyPress, KeyUp, LinkClose, LinkError, LinkExecute, LinkOpen, LostFocus, MouseDown, MouseMove, MouseUp, OLECompleteDrag, OLEDragDrop, OLEDragOver, OLEGiveFeedback, OLESetData, OLEStartDrag

```
Activate()
Deactivate()
Initialize()
Load()
Paint()
QueryUnload(cancel As Integer, unloadmode As Integer)
Resize()
Terminate()
Unload(cancel As Integer)
```

Methods

Common Methods: Move, OLEDrag, Refresh, Scale, ScaleX, ScaleY, SetFocus, ZOrder

Circle	*object*.Circle [Step] (*x*, *y*), [*color*, *start*, *end*, *aspect*]

Cls	*object*.Cls
Hide	*object*.Hide
Line	*object*.Line [Step] (*x1*, *y1*) [Step] (*x2*, *y2*), [*color*], [B][F]
PaintPicture	*object*.PaintPicture(*picture*, *x1*, *y1*, *width1*, *height1*, *x2*, *y2*, *width2*, *height2*, *opcode*)
Point	*object*.Point(*x*, *y*)
PopupMenu	*object*.PopupMenu(*menuname*, *flags*, *x*, *y*, *boldcommand*)
PrintForm	*object*.PrintForm
PSet	*object*.PSet [Step] (*x*, *y*), [*color*]
Show	*object*.Show(*style*, *ownerform*)
TextHeight	*object*.TextHeight(*string*)
TextWidth	*object*.TextWidth(*string*)
WhatsThisMode	*object*.WhatsThisMode

Frame

Properties

Common Properties: Appearance, BackColor, BorderStyle, Container, DragIcon, DragMode, Enabled, Font, FontBold, FontItalic, FontName, FontSize, FontStrikethru, FontUnderline, ForeColor, Height, HelpContextID, hWnd, Index, Left, MouseIcon, MousePointer, Name, OLEDropMode, Parent, RightToLeft, TabIndex, Tag, ToolTipText, Top, Visible, WhatsThisHelpID, Width

Caption	String
*ClipControls	Boolean

Events

Common Events: Click, DblClick, DragOver, MouseDown, MouseUp, OLECompleteDrag, OLEDragDrop, OLEDragOver, OLEGiveFeedback, OLESetData, OLEStartDrag

Methods

Common Methods: Drag, Move, OLEDrag, Refresh, ShowWhatsThis, ZOrder

HScrollBar

Properties

Common Properties: Container, DragIcon, DragMode, Enabled, Height, HelpContextID, hWnd, Index, Left, MouseIcon, MousePointer, Name, Parent, RightToLeft, TabIndex, TabStop, Tag, Top, Visible, WhatsThisHelpID, Width

LargeChange	Integer
Max	Integer
Min	Integer
SmallChange	Integer
Value	Integer

Events

Common Events: DragDrop, DragOver, GotFocus, KeyDown, KeyPress, KeyUp, LostFocus

Change([*index* As Integer])

Scroll()

Methods

Common Methods: Drag, Move, Refresh, SetFocus, ShowWhatsThis, ZOrder

Image

Properties

Common Properties: Appearance, BorderStyle, Container, DragIcon, DragMode, Enabled, Height, Index, Left, MouseIcon, MousePointer, Name, OLEDragMode, OLEDropMode, Parent, Tag, ToolTipText, Top, Visible, WhatsThisHelpID, Width

DataChanged	Boolean
DataField	String
Picture	IPictureDisp Object
Stretch	Boolean

Events

Common Events: Click, DblClick, DragDrop, DragOver, MouseDown, MouseMove, MouseUp, OLECompleteDrag, OLEDragDrop, OLEDragOver, OLEGiveFeedback, OLESetData, OLEStartDrag

Methods

Common Methods: Drag, Move, OLEDrag, Refresh, ShowWhatsThis, ZOrder

ImageList

Properties

Common Properties: BackColor, Index, Name, Object, Parent, Tag

hImageList	OLE_HANDLE Object
ImageHeight	Integer
ImageWidth	Integer
ListImages	ListImages Collection
MaskColor	OLE_COLOR Object
UseMaskColor	Boolean

Events

No events

Methods

Overlay	*object*.Overlay(*key1*, *key2*) As IPictureDisp

Internet Transfer (Inet)

Properties

Common Properties: Index, Name, Object, Parent, Tag

AccessType	AccessConstants Enum
Document	String
*hInternet	Long
Password	String
Protocol	ProtocolConstants Enum
Proxy	String
RemoteHost	String
RemotePort	Integer
RequestTimeout	Long
*ResponseCode	Long
*ResponseInfo	String

*StillExecuting	Boolean
URL	String
UserName	String

Events

StateChanged(ByVal *state* As Integer)

Methods

Cancel	*object*.Cancel
Execute	*object*.Execute(*url*, *operation*, *data*, *requestheaders*)
GetChunk	*object*.GetChunk(*size* [, *datatype*])
GetHeader	*object*.GetHeader(*hrdname*)
OpenURL	*object*.OpenURL(*url* [, *datatype*])

Label

Properties

Common Properties: Appearance, BackColor, BorderStyle, Container, DataChanged, DataField, DragIcon, DragMode, Enabled, Font, FontBold, FontItalic, FontName, FontSize, FontStrikethru, FontUnderline, ForeColor, Height, Index, Left, LinkItem, LinkMode, LinkTimeout, LinkTopic, MouseIcon, MousePointer, Name, OLEDropMode, Parent, RightToLeft, TabIndex, Tag, ToolTipText, Top, Visible, WhatsThisHelpID, Width

Alignment	Integer
AutoSize	Boolean
BackStyle	Integer
Caption	String
UseMnemonic	Boolean
WordWrap	Boolean

Events

Common Events: Click, DblClick, DragDrop, DragOver, LinkClose, LinkError, LinkNotify, LinkOpen, MouseDown, MouseMove, MouseUp, OLECompleteDrag, OLEDragDrop, OLEDragOver, OLEGiveFeedback, OLESetData, OLEStartDrag

Change()

Methods

Common Methods: Drag, LinkExecute, LinkPoke, LinkRequest, LinkSend, Move, OLEDrag, Refresh, ShowWhatsThis, ZOrder

Line

Properties

Common Properties: BorderStyle, Container, Index, Name, Parent, Tag, Visible

BorderColor	Long
BorderWidth	Integer
DrawMode	Integer
X1	Single
X2	Single
Y1	Single
Y2	Single

Events

No events

Methods

Common Methods: Refresh, ZOrder

ListBox

Properties

Common Properties: Appearance, BackColor, Container, DataChanged, DataField, DragIcon, DragMode, Enabled, Font, FontBold, FontItalic, FontName, FontSize, FontStrikethru, FontUnderline, ForeColor, Height, HelpContextID, hWnd, Index, Left, MouseIcon, MousePointer, Name, OLEDragMode, Parent, RightToLeft, TabIndex, TabStop, Tag, ToolTipText, Top, Visible, WhatsThisHelpID, Width

Columns	Integer
*IntegralHeight	Boolean
ItemData	Long Array
List	String Array
*ListCount	Integer
ListIndex	Integer

*MultiSelect	Integer
*NewIndex	Integer
*SelCount	Integer
Selected	Boolean Array
*Sorted	Boolean
*Style	Integer
Text	String
TopIndex	Integer

Events

Common Events: Click, DblClick, DragDrop, DragOver, GotFocus, KeyDown, KeyPress, KeyUp, LostFocus, MouseDown, MouseMove, MouseUp, OLECompleteDrag, OLEDragDrop, OLEDragOver, OLEGiveFeedback, OLESetData, OLEStartDrag

ItemCheck(*item* As Integer)

Scroll()

Methods

Common Methods: Drag, Move, OLEDrag, Refresh, SetFocus, ShowWhatsThis, ZOrder

AddItem	*object*.AddItem(*item* [, *index*])
Clear	*object*.Clear
RemoveItem	*object*.RemoveItem(*index*)

ListView

Properties

Common Properties: Appearance, BackColor, BorderStyle, Container, DragIcon, DragMode, Enabled, Font, ForeColor, Height, HelpContextID, hWnd, Index, Left, MouseIcon, MousePointer, Name, Object, OLEDragMode, OLEDropMode, Parent, TabIndex, TabStop, Tag, ToolTipText, Top, Visible, WhatsThisHelpID, Width

Arrange	ListArrangeConstants
ColumnHeaders	ColumnHeaders Collection
DropHighlight	ListItem Object
HideColumnHeader	Boolean
HideSelection	Boolean
Icons	Object

`LabelEdit`	`ListLabelEditConstants`
`LabelWrap`	`Boolean`
`ListItems`	`ListItems` Collection
`MultiSelect`	`Boolean`
`SelectedItem`	`ListItem` Object
`SmallIcons`	`Object`
`Sorted`	`Boolean`
`SortKey`	`Integer`
`SortOrder`	`ListSortOrderConstants`
`View`	`ListViewConstants`

Events

Common Events: `Click`, `DblClick`, `DragDrop`, `DragOver`, `GotFocus`, `KeyDown`, `KeyPress`, `KeyUp`, `LostFocus`, `MouseDown`, `MouseMove`, `MouseUp`, `OLECompleteDrag`, `OLEDragDrop`, `OLEDragOver`, `OLEGiveFeedback`, `OLESetData`, `OLEStartDrag`

`AfterLabelEdit(`*`cancel`*` As Integer, `*`newstring`*` As String)`

`BeforeLabelEdit(`*`cancel`*` As Integer)`

`ColumnClick(`*`colheader`*` As ColumnHeader)`

`ItemClick(`*`item`*` As ListItem)`

Methods

Common Methods: `Drag`, `Move`, `OLEDrag`, `Refresh`, `SetFocus`, `ShowWhatsThis`, `ZOrder`

`FindItem`	*`object`*`.FindItem (`*`string`*`, [`*`value`*`], [`*`index`*`], [`*`match`*`]) As ListItem`
`GetFirstVisible`	*`object`*`.GetFirstVisible() As ListItem`
`HitTest`	*`object`*`.HitTest (`*`x`*`, `*`y`*`) As ListItem`
`StartLabelEdit`	*`object`*`.StartLabelEdit`

MAPIMessages

Properties

Common Properties: `Index`, `Name`, `Object`, `Parent`, `Tag`

`Action`	`Integer`
`AddressCaption`	`String`

AddressEditFieldCount	Integer
AddressLabel	String
AddressModifiable	Boolean
AddressResolveUI	Boolean
AttachmentCount	Long
AttachmentIndex	Long
AttachmentName	String
AttachmentPathName	String
AttachmentPosition	Long
AttachmentType	Integer
FetchMsgType	String
FetchSorted	Boolean
FetchUnreadOnly	Boolean
MsgConversationID	String
MsgCount	Long
MsgDateReceived	String
MsgID	String
MsgIndex	Long
MsgNoteText	String
MsgOrigAddress	String
MsgOrigDisplayName	String
MsgRead	Boolean
MsgReceiptRequested	Boolean
MsgSent	Boolean
MsgSubject	String
MsgType	String
RecipAddress	String
RecipCount	Long
RecipDisplayName	String
RecipIndex	Long
RecipType	Integer
SessionID	Long

Events

No events

Methods

`Compose`	*object*.`Compose`
`Copy`	*object*.`Copy`
`Delete`	*object*.`Delete ([`*value*`])`
`Fetch`	*object*.`Fetch`
`Forward`	*object*.`Forward`
`Reply`	*object*.`Reply`
`ReplyAll`	*object*.`ReplyAll`
`ResolveName`	*object*.`ResolveName`
`Save`	*object*.`Save`
`Send`	*object*.`Send ([`*value*`])`
`Show`	*object*.`Show ([`*value*`])`

MAPISession

Properties

Common Properties: `Index`, `Name`, `Object`, `Parent`, `Tag`

`Action`	`Integer`
`DownloadMail`	`Boolean`
`LogonUI`	`Boolean`
`NewSession`	`Boolean`
`Password`	`String`
`SessionID`	`Long`
`UserName`	`String`

Events

No events

Methods

`SignOff`	*object*.`SignOff`
`SignOn`	*object*.`SignOn`

Masked Edit (MaskEdBox)

Properties

Common Properties: Appearance, BackColor, BorderStyle, Container, DataBindings, DataChanged, DataField, DragIcon, DragMode, Enabled, Font, ForeColor, Height, HelpContextID, hWnd, Index, Left, MouseIcon, MousePointer, Name, Object, OLEDragMode, OLEDropMode, Parent, TabIndex, TabStop, Tag, ToolTipText, Top, Visible, WhatsThisHelpID, Width

AllowPrompt	Boolean
AutoTab	Boolean
ClipMode	ClipModeConstants
ClipText	String
Format	String
FormattedText	String
Mask	String
MaxLength	Integer
PromptChar	String
PromptInclude	Boolean
SelLength	Long
SelStart	Long
SelText	Long
Text	String

Events

Common Events: DragDrop, GotFocus, KeyDown, KeyPress, KeyUp, LostFocus, OLECompleteDrag, OLEDragDrop, OLEDragOver, OLEGiveFeedback, OLESetData, OLEStartDrag

Change()

ValidationError(*invalidtext* As String, *startpos* As Integer)

Methods

Common Methods: Drag, Move, OLEDrag, Refresh, SetFocus, ShowWhatsThis, ZOrder

MDIForm

Properties

Common Properties: Appearance, BackColor, Enabled, Height, HelpContextID, hWnd, Left, LinkMode, LinkTopic, MouseIcon, MousePointer, Name, OLEDropMode, RightToLeft, ScaleHeight, ScaleWidth, Tag, Top, Visible, Width

*ActiveControl	Control Object
*ActiveForm	Object
AutoShowChildren	Boolean
Caption	String
*Controls	Object Collection
*Count	Integer
Icon	IPictureDisp Object
*Moveable	Boolean
Picture	IPictureDisp Object
*ScrollBars	Boolean
StartUpPosition	Integer
*WhatsThisHelp	Boolean
WindowState	Integer

Events

Common Events: Click, DblClick, DragDrop, DragOver, LinkClose, LinkError, LinkExecute, LinkOpen, MouseDown, MouseMove, MouseUp, OLECompleteDrag, OLEDragDrop, OLEDragOver, OLEGiveFeedback, OLESetData, OLEStartDrag

Activate()

Deactivate()

Initialize()

Load()

QueryUnload(*cancel* As Integer, *unloadmode* As Integer)

Resize()

Terminate()

Unload(*cancel* As Integer)

Methods

Common Methods: Move, OLEDrag, SetFocus, ZOrder

Arrange	*object*.Arrange(*arrangement*)
Hide	*object*.Hide
PopupMenu	*object*.PopupMenu(*menu*, [*flags*], [*x*], [*y*], [*defaultmenu*])
Show	*object*.Show([*modal*], [*ownerform*])
WhatsThisMode	*object*.WhatsThisMode

Microsoft Tabbed Dialog (SSTab)

Properties

Common Properties: BackColor, Container, DataBindings, DragIcon, DragMode, Enabled, Font, ForeColor, Height, HelpContextID, hWnd, Index, Left, MouseIcon, MousePointer, Name, Object, OLEDropMode, Parent, TabIndex, TabStop, Tag, ToolTipText, Top, Visible, WhatsThisHelpID, Width

Caption	String
Rows	Integer
ShowFocusRect	Boolean
Style	StyleConstants
Tab	Integer
TabCaption	String Array
TabEnabled	Boolean Array
TabHeight	Single
TabMaxWidth	Single
TabOrientation	TabOrientationConstants
TabPicture	IPictureDisp Array
Tabs	Integer
TabsPerRow	Integer
TabVisible	Boolean Array
WordWrap	Boolean

Events

Common Events: Click, DblClick, DragDrop, DragOver, GotFocus, KeyDown, KeyPress, KeyUp, LostFocus, MouseDown, MouseMove, MouseUp, OLECompleteDrag, OLEDragDrop, OLEDragOver, OLEGiveFeedback, OLESetData, OLEStartDrag

Methods

Common Methods: Drag, Move, OLEDrag, SetFocus, ShowWhatsThis, ZOrder

MSChart

Properties

Common Properties: BorderStyle, Container, DataBindings, DragIcon, DragMode, Enabled, Height, HelpContextID, hWnd, Index, Left, Name, MousePointer, Object, Parent, TabIndex, TabStop, Tag, ToolTipText, Top, Visible, WhatsThisHelpID, Width

*ActiveSeriesCount	Integer
AllowDithering	Boolean
AllowDynamicRotation	Boolean
AllowSelections	Boolean
AllowSeriesSelection	Boolean
AutoIncrement	Boolean
*BackDrop	Backdrop Object
BorderStyle	VtBorderStyle Enum
*Chart3d	Boolean
ChartData	Variant
ChartType	VtChChartType Enum
Column	Integer
ColumnCount	Integer
ColumnLabel	String
ColumnLabelCount	Integer
ColumnLabelIndex	Integer
Data	String
*DataGrid	DataGrid Object
DoSetCursor	Boolean
DrawMode	VtChDrawMode Enum
*Footnote	Footnote Object
FootnoteText	String
*Legend	Legend Object
*Plot	Plot Object
RandomFill	Boolean

Repaint	Boolean
Row	Integer
RowCount	Integer
RowLabel	String
RowLabelCount	Integer
RowLabelIndex	Integer
SeriesColumn	Integer
SeriesType	VtChSeriesType Enum
ShowLegend	Boolean
Stacking	Boolean
TextLengthType	VtTextLengthType Enum
*Title	Title Object
TitleText	String

Events

Common Events: Click, DblClick, DragDrop, DragOver, GotFocus, KeyDown, KeyPress, KeyUp, LostFocus, MouseDown, MouseMove, MouseUp

AxisActivated(*axisid* As Integer, *axisindex* As Integer, *mouseflag* As Integer, *cancel* As Integer)

AxisLabelActivated(*axisid* As Integer, *axisindex* As Integer, *labelsetindex* As Integer, *labelindex* As Integer, *mouseflag* As Integer, *cancel* As Integer)

AxisLabelSelected(*axisid* As Integer, *axisindex* As Integer, *labelsetindex* As Integer, *labelindex* As Integer, *mouseflag* As Integer, *cancel* As Integer)

AxisLabelUpdated(*axisid* As Integer, *axisindex* As Integer, *labelsetindex* As Integer, *labelindex* As Integer, *updateflags* As Integer)

AxisSelected(*axisid* As Integer, *axisindex* As Integer, *mouseflag* As Integer, *cancel* As Integer)

AxisTitleActivated(*axisid* As Integer, *axisindex* As Integer, *mouseflag* As Integer, *cancel* As Integer)

AxisTitleSelected(*axisid* As Integer, *axisindex* As Integer, *mouseflag* As Integer, *cancel* As Integer)

AxisTitleUpdated(*axisid* As Integer, *axisindex* As Integer, *updateflags* As Integer)

AxisUpdated(*axisid* As Integer, *axisindex* As Integer, *updateflags* As Integer)

ChartActivated(*mouseflag* As Integer, *cancel* As Integer)

ChartSelected(*mouseflag* As Integer, *cancel* As Integer)

```
ChartUpdated(updateflags As Integer)
DataUpdated(row As Integer, column As Integer, labelrow As Integer,
labelcolumn As Integer, labelsetindex As Integer, updateflags As Integer)
DonePainting()
FootnoteActivated(mouseflag As Integer, cancel As Integer)
FootnoteSelected(mouseflag As Integer, cancel As Integer)
FootnoteUpdated(updateflags As Integer)
LegendActivated(mouseflag As Integer, cancel As Integer)
LegendSelected(mouseflag As Integer, cancel As Integer)
LegendUpdated(updateflags As Integer)
PlotActivated(mouseflag As Integer, cancel As Integer)
PlotSelected(mouseflag As Integer, cancel As Integer)
PlotUpdated(updateflags As Integer)
PointActivated(series As Integer, datapoint As Integer, mouseflag As Integer,
cancel As Integer)
PointLabelActivated(series As Integer, datapoint As Integer, mouseflag As
Integer, cancel As Integer)
PointLabelSelected(series As Integer, datapoint As Integer, mouseflag As
Integer, cancel As Integer)
PointLabelUpdated(series As Integer, datapoint As Integer, updateflags As
Integer)
PointSelected(series As Integer, datapoint As Integer, mouseflag As Integer,
cancel As Integer)
PointUpdated(series As Integer, datapoint As Integer, updateflags As Integer)
SeriesActivated(series As Integer, mouseflag As Integer, cancel As Integer)
SeriesSelected(series As Integer, mouseflag As Integer, cancel As Integer)
SeriesUpdated(series As Integer, updateflags As Integer)
TitleActivated(mouseflag As Integer, cancel As Integer)
TitleSelected(mouseflag As Integer, cancel As Integer)
TitleUpdated(updateflags As Integer)
```

Methods

Common Methods: Drag, Move, Refresh, SetFocus, ShowWhatsThis, ZOrder

AboutBox	*object*.AboutBox
EditCopy	*object*.EditCopy

EditPaste	*object*.EditPaste
GetSelectedPart	*object*.GetSelectedPart (*part*, *index1*, *index2*, *index3*, *index4*)
Layout	*object*.Layout
SelectPart	*object*.SelectPart (*part*, *index1*, *index2*, *index3*, *index4*)
ToDefaults	*object*.ToDefaults
TwipsToChartPart	*object*.TwipsToChartPart (*xval*, *yval*, *part*, *index1*, *index2*, *index3*, *index4*)

MSComm

Properties

Common Properties: Index, Name, Object, Parent, Tag

Break	Boolean
CDHolding	Boolean
CommEvent	Integer
CommID	Long
CommPort	Integer
CTSHolding	Boolean
DSRHolding	Boolean
DTREnable	Boolean
EOFEnable	Boolean
Handshaking	HandshakeConstants Enum
InBufferCount	Integer
InBufferSize	Integer
Input	Variant
InputLen	Integer
InputMode	InputModeConstants Enum
NullDiscard	Boolean
OutBufferCount	Integer
OutBufferSize	Integer
Output	Variant
ParityReplace	String
PortOpen	Boolean

RThreshold	Integer
RTSEnable	Boolean
Settings	String
SThreshold	Integer

Events

OnComm()

Methods

No methods

MSFlexGrid

Properties

Common Properties: Appearance, BackColor, BorderStyle, Container, DataBindings, DragIcon, DragMode, Enabled, Font, ForeColor, Height, HelpContextID, hWnd, Index, Left, MouseIcon, MousePointer, Name, Object, OLEDropMode, Parent, RightToLeft, TabIndex, TabStop, Tag, ToolTipText, Top, Visible, WhatsThisHelpID, Width

AllowBigSelection	Boolean
AllowUserResizing	AllowUserResizingSettings Enum
BackColorBkg	OLE_COLOR Object
BackColorFixed	OLE_COLOR Object
BackColorSel	OLE_COLOR Object
CellAlignment	Integer
CellBackColor	OLE_COLOR Object
CellFontBold	Boolean
CellFontItalic	Boolean
CellFontName	String
CellFontSize	Single
CellFontStrikeThrough	Boolean
CellFontUnderline	Boolean
CellFontWidth	Single
CellForeColor	OLE_COLOR Object
*CellHeight	Long
*CellLeft	Long

`CellPicture`	`IPictureDisp` Object
`CellPictureAlignment`	`Integer`
`CellTextStyle`	`TextStyleSettings` Enum
`*CellTop`	`Long`
`*CellWidth`	`Long`
`Clip`	`String`
`Col`	`Long`
`ColAlignment`	`Integer` Array
`ColData`	`Long` Array
`ColIsVisible`	`Boolean` Array
`ColPos`	`Long` Array
`ColPosition`	`Long` Array
`Cols`	`Long`
`ColSel`	`Long`
`ColWidth`	`Long` Array
`DataSource`	`IRowCursor` Object
`FillStyle`	`FillStyleSettings` Enum
`FixedAlignment`	`Integer` Array
`FixedCols`	`Long`
`FixedRows`	`Long`
`FocusRect`	`FocusRectSettings` Enum
`FontWidth`	`Single`
`ForeColorFixed`	`OLE_COLOR` Object
`ForeColorSel`	`OLE_COLOR` Object
`FormatString`	`String`
`GridColor`	`OLE_COLOR` Object
`GridColorFixed`	`OLE_COLOR` Object
`GridLines`	`GridLineSettings` Enum
`GridLinesFixed`	`GridLineSettings` Enum
`GridLineWidth`	`Integer`
`HighLight`	`HighLightSettings` Enum
`LeftCol`	`Long`
`MergeCells`	`MergeCellsSettings` Enum
`MergeCol`	`Boolean` Array

MergeRow	Boolean Array
*MouseCol	Long
*MouseRow	Long
*Picture	IPictureDisp Object
PictureType	PictureTypeSettings Enum
Redraw	Boolean
Row	Long
RowData	Long Array
RowHeight	Long Array
RowHeightMin	Long
*RowIsVisible	Boolean Array
*RowPos	Long Array
RowPosition	Long Array
Rows	Long
RowSel	Long
ScrollBars	ScrollBarsSettings Enum
ScrollTrack	Boolean
SelectionMode	SelectionModeSettings Enum
Sort	Integer
Text	String
TextArray	String Array
TextMatrix	String Array
TextStyle	TextStyleSettings Enum
TextStyleFixed	TextStyleSettings Enum
TopRow	Long
*Version	Integer
WordWrap	Boolean

Events

Common Events: Click, DblClick, DragDrop, DragOver, GotFocus, KeyDown, KeyPress, KeyUp, LostFocus, MouseDown, MouseMove, MouseUp, OLECompleteDrag, OLEDragDrop, OLEDragOver, OLEGiveFeedback, OLESetData, OLEStartDrag

Compare(*row1* As Integer, *row2* As Integer, *cmp* As Integer)

EnterCell()

LeaveCell()

RowColChange()

Scroll()

SelChange()

Methods

Common Methods: Drag, Move, OLEDrag, Refresh, SetFocus, ShowWhatsThis, ZOrder

AddItem	*object*.AddItem (*item*, [*index*])
Clear	*object*.Clear
RemoveItem	*object*.RemoveItem (*index*)

MSRDC (Remote Data Control)

Properties

Common Properties: Appearance, BackColor, Container, DragIcon, DragMode, Enabled, Font, ForeColor, Height, Index, Left, Name, Parent, Tag, ToolTipText, Top, Visible, WhatsThisHelpID, Width

Align	Integer
*BatchCollisionCount	Long
*BatchCollisionRows	Variant
BatchSize	Long
BOFAction	BOFActionConstants Enum
Caption	String
Connect	String
Connection	rdoConnection Object
CursorDriver	CursorDriverConstants Enum
DataSourceName	String
EditMode	Integer
Environment	rdoEnvironment Object
EOFAction	EOFActionConstants Enum
ErrorThreshold	Long
KeysetSize	Long
LockType	LockTypeConstants Enum
LoginTimeout	Long

LogMessages	String
MaxRows	Long
*Object	Object
Options	Integer
Password	String
Prompt	PromptConstants Enum
QueryTimeout	Long
ReadOnly	Boolean
Resultset	rdoResultSet Object
ResultsetType	ResultsetTypeConstants Enum
RowsetSize	Long
SQL	String
UpdateCriteria	Integer
UpdateOperation	Integer
UserName	String
*Version	String

Events

Common Events: DragDrop, DragOver, MouseDown, MouseMove, MouseUp

Error(*number* As Long, *description* As String, *scode* As Long, *source* As String, *helpfile* As String, *helpcontext* As Long, *canceldisplay* As Boolean)

QueryCompleted()

Reposition()

Validate(*action* As Integer, *reserved* As Integer)

Methods

Common Methods: Drag, Move, Refresh, ShowWhatsThis, ZOrder

BeginTrans	*object*.BeginTrans
Cancel	*object*.Cancel
CommitTrans	*object*.CommitTrans
RollbackTrans	*object*.RollbackTrans
UpdateControls	*object*.UpdateControls
UpdateRow	*object*.UpdateRow

Multimedia (MMControl)

Properties

Common Properties: BorderStyle, Container, DataBindings, DragIcon, DragMode, Enabled, Height, HelpContextID, hWnd, Index, Left, MouseIcon, MousePointer, Name, Object, OLEDropMode, Parent, TabIndex, TabStop, Tag, ToolTipText, Top, Visible, WhatsThisHelpID, Width

AutoEnable	Boolean
BackEnabled	Boolean
BackVisible	Boolean
CanEject	Boolean
CanPlay	Boolean
CanRecord	Boolean
CanStep	Boolean
Command	String
DeviceID	Integer
DeviceType	String
EjectEnabled	Boolean
EjectVisible	Boolean
Error	Integer
ErrorMessage	String
FileName	String
Frames	Long
From	Long
hWndDisplay	Long
Length	Long
Mode	Long
NextEnabled	Boolean
NextVisible	Boolean
Notify	Boolean
NotifyMessage	String
NotifyValue	Integer
Orientation	OrientationConstants Enum
PauseEnabled	Boolean
PauseVisible	Boolean

`PlayEnabled`	`Boolean`
`PlayVisible`	`Boolean`
`Position`	`Long`
`PrevEnabled`	`Boolean`
`PrevVisible`	`Boolean`
`RecordEnabled`	`Boolean`
`RecordMode`	`RecordModeConstants` Enum
`RecordVisible`	`Boolean`
`Shareable`	`Boolean`
`Silent`	`Boolean`
`Start`	`Long`
`StepEnabled`	`Boolean`
`StepVisible`	`Boolean`
`StopEnabled`	`Boolean`
`StopVisible`	`Boolean`
`TimeFormat`	`Long`
`To`	`Long`
`Track`	`Long`
`TrackLength`	`Long`
`TrackPosition`	`Long`
`Tracks`	`Long`
`UpdateInterval`	`Integer`
`UsesWindows`	`Boolean`
`Wait`	`Boolean`

Events

Common Events: `DragDrop`, `DragOver`, `GotFocus`, `LostFocus`, `OLECompleteDrag`, `OLEDragOver`, `OLEGiveFeedback`, `OLESetData`, `OLEStartDrag`

`BackClick(`*`cancel`*` As Integer)`

`BackCompleted(`*`errcode`*` As Long)`

`BackGotFocus()`

`BackLostFocus()`

`Done(`*`notifycode`*` As Integer)`

```
EjectClick(cancel As Integer)
EjectCompleted(errcode As Long)
EjectGotFocus()
EjectLostFocus()
NextClick(cancel As Integer)
NextCompleted(errcode As Long)
NextGotFocus()
NextLostFocus()
PauseClick(cancel As Integer)
PauseCompleted(errcode As Long)
PauseGotFocus()
PauseLostFocus()
PlayClick(cancel As Integer)
PlayCompleted(errcode As Long)
PlayGotFocus()
PlayLostFocus()
PrevClick(cancel As Integer)
PrevCompleted(errcode As Long)
PrevGotFocus()
PrevLostFocus()
RecordClick(cancel As Integer)
RecordCompleted(errcode As Long)
RecordGotFocus()
RecordLostFocus()
StatusUpdate()
StepClick(cancel As Integer)
StepCompleted(errcode As Long)
StepGotFocus()
StepLostFocus()
StopClick(cancel As Integer)
StopCompleted(errcode As Long)
StopGotFocus()
StopLostFocus()
```

Methods

Common Methods: Drag, Move, OLEDrag, Refresh, SetFocus, ShowWhatsThis, ZOrder

OLE

Properties

Common Properties: Appearance, BackColor, BorderStyle, Container, DragIcon, DragMode, Enabled, Height, HelpContextID, hWnd, Index, Left, MouseIcon, MousePointer, Name, Object, TabIndex, TabStop, Tag, Top, Visible, WhatsThisHelpID, Width

Action	Integer
AppIsRunning	Boolean
AutoActivate	Integer
AutoVerbMenu	Boolean
BackStyle	Integer
Class	String
Data	Long
DataChanged	Boolean
DataField	String
DataText	String
DisplayType	Integer
FileNumber	Integer
Format	String
HostName	String
*LpOleObject	Long
MiscFlags	Integer
*ObjectAcceptFormats	String Array
*ObjectAcceptFormatsCount	Integer
*ObjectGetFormats	String Array
*ObjectGetFormatsCount	Integer
*ObjectVerbFlags	Long Array
*ObjectVerbs	String Array
*ObjectVerbsCount	Integer
OLEDropAllowed	Boolean

*OLEType	Integer
OLETypeAllowed	Integer
*PasteOK	Boolean
*Picture	IPictureDisp Object
SizeMode	Integer
SourceDoc	String
SourceItem	String
UpdateOptions	Integer
Verb	Integer

Events

Common Events: Click, DblClick, DragDrop, DragOver, GotFocus, KeyDown, KeyPress, KeyUp, LostFocus, MouseDown, MouseMove, MouseUp

ObjectMove(*left* As Single, *top* As Single, *width* As Single, *height* As Single)

Resize(*newheight* As Single, *newwidth* As Single)

Updated(*code* As Integer)

Methods

Common Methods: Drag, Move, Refresh, SetFocus, ShowWhatsThis, ZOrder

Close	*object*.Close()
Copy	*object*.Copy()
CreateEmbed	*object*.CreateEmbed(*sourcedoc*, [*class*])
CreateLink	*object*.CreateLink(*sourcedoc*, [*sourceitem*])
Delete	*object*.Delete()
DoVerb	*object*.DoVerb([*verb*])
FetchVerbs	*object*.FetchVerbs()
InsertObjDlg	*object*.InsertObjDlg()
Paste	*object*.Paste()
PasteSpecialDlg	*object*.PasteSpecialDlg()
ReadFromFile	*object*.ReadFromFile(*filenum*)
SaveToFile	*object*.SaveToFile(*filenum*)
SaveToOle1File	*object*.SaveToOle1File(*filenum*)
Update	*object*.Update()

OptionButton

Properties

Common Properties: Appearance, BackColor, Container, DragIcon, DragMode, Enabled, Font, FontBold, FontItalic, FontName, FontSize, FontStrikethru, FontUnderline, ForeColor, Height, HelpContextID, hWnd, Index, Left, MouseIcon, MousePointer, Name, Parent, RightToLeft, TabIndex, TabStop, Tag, ToolTipText, Top, Visible, WhatsThisHelpID, Width

*Alignment	Integer
Caption	String
DisabledPicture	IPictureDisp Object
DownPicture	IPictureDisp Object
MaskColor	Long
Picture	IPictureDisp Object
*Style	Integer
UseMaskColor	Boolean
Value	Boolean

Events

Common Events: Click, DblClick, DragDrop, DragOver, GotFocus, KeyDown, KeyPress, KeyUp, LostFocus, MouseDown, MouseMove, MouseUp, OLECompleteDrag, OLEDragDrop, OLEDragOver, OLEGiveFeedback, OLESetData, OLEStartDrag

Methods

Common Methods: Drag, Move, OLEDrag, Refresh, SetFocus, ShowWhatsThis, ZOrder

PictureBox

Properties

Common Properties: Appearance, BackColor, BorderStyle, Container, DataChanged, DataField, DragIcon, DragMode, Enabled, Font, FontBold, FontItalic, FontName, FontSize, FontStrikethru, FontTransparent, FontUnderline, ForeColor, hDC, Height, HelpContextID, hWnd, Index, Left, LinkItem, LinkMode, LinkTimeout, LinkTopic, MouseIcon, MousePointer, Name, OLEDragMode, OLEDropMode, Parent, RightToLeft, ScaleHeight, ScaleLeft, ScaleMode, ScaleTop, ScaleWidth, TabIndex, TabStop, Tag, ToolTipText, Top, Visible, WhatsThisHelpID, Width

Align	Integer
AutoRedraw	Boolean

AutoSize	Boolean
*ClipControls	Boolean
CurrentX	Single
CurrentY	Single
DrawMode	Integer
DrawStyle	Integer
DrawWidth	Integer
FillColor	Long
FillStyle	Integer
*Image	IPictureDisp Object
Picture	IPictureDisp Object

Events

Common Events: Click, DblClick, DragDrop, DragOver, GotFocus, KeyDown, KeyPress, KeyUp, LinkClose, LinkError, LinkNotify, LinkOpen, LostFocus, MouseDown, MouseMove, MouseUp, OLECompleteDrag, OLEDragDrop, OLEDragOver, OLEGiveFeedback, OLESetData, OLEStartDrag

Change()

Paint()

Resize()

Methods

Common Methods: Drag, LinkExecute, LinkPoke, LinkRequest, LinkSend, Move, OLEDrag, Refresh, Scale, ScaleX, ScaleY, SetFocus, ShowWhatsThis, ZOrder

Circle	*object*.Circle(*step*, *x*, *y*, *radius*, *color*, *start*, *end*, *aspect*)
Cls	*object*.Cls
Line	*object*.Line(*flags*, *x1*, *y1*, *x2*, *y2*, *color*)
PaintPicture	*object*.PaintPicture(*picture*, *x1*, *y1*, [*width1*], [*height1*], [*x2*], [*y2*], [*width2*], [*height2*], [*opcode*])
Point	*object*.Point(*x*, *y*) As Long
PSet	*object*.PSet(*step*, *x*, *y*, *color*)
TextHeight	*object*.TextHeight(*str*) As Single
TextWidth	*object*.TextWidth(*str*) As Single

PictureClip

Properties

Common Properties: Height, hWnd, Index, Name, Object, Parent, Tag, Width

CellHeight	Integer
CellWidth	Integer
Clip	IPictureDisp Object
ClipHeight	Integer
ClipWidth	Integer
ClipX	Integer
ClipY	Integer
Cols	Integer
GraphicCell	IPictureDisp Object Array
Picture	IPictureDisp Object
Rows	Integer
StretchX	Integer
StretchY	Integer

Events

No events

Methods

No methods

Printer

Properties

Common Properties: Font, FontBold, FontItalic, FontName, FontSize, FontStrikethru, FontTransparent, FontUnderline, ForeColor, hDC, Height, RightToLeft, ScaleHeight, ScaleLeft, ScaleMode, ScaleTop, ScaleWidth, Width

ColorMode	Integer
Copies	Integer
CurrentX	Single
CurrentY	Single

*DeviceName	String
DrawMode	Integer
DrawStyle	Integer
DrawWidth	Integer
*DriverName	String
Duplex	Integer
FillColor	Long
FillStyle	Integer
*FontCount	Integer
*Fonts	String Array
Orientation	Integer
*Page	Integer
PaperBin	Integer
PaperSize	Integer
*Port	String
PrintQuality	Integer
TrackDefault	Boolean
*TwipsPerPixelX	Single
*TwipsPerPixelY	Single
Zoom	Long

Events

No events

Methods

Common Methods: Scale, ScaleX, ScaleY

Circle	*object*.Circle(*step*, *x*, *y*, *radius*, *color*, *start*, *end*, *aspect*)
EndDoc	*object*.EndDoc
KillDoc	*object*.KillDoc
Line	*object*.Line(*flags*, *x1*, *y1*, *x2*, *y2*, *color*)
NewPage	*object*.NewPage
PaintPicture	*object*.PaintPicture(*picture*, *x1*, *y1*, [*width1*], [*height1*], [*x2*], [*y2*], [*width2*], [*height2*], [*opcode*])

PSet	*object*.PSet(*step*, *x*, *y*, *color*)
TextHeight	*object*.TextHeight(*str*) As Single
TextWidth	*object*.TextWidth(*str*) As Single

ProgressBar

Properties

Common Properties: Appearance, BorderStyle, Container, DragIcon, DragMode, Enabled, Height, hWnd, Index, Left, MouseIcon, MousePointer, Name, Object, OLEDropMode, Parent, TabIndex, Tag, ToolTipText, Top, Visible, WhatsThisHelpID, Width

Align	Integer
Max	Single
Min	Single
Value	Single

Events

Common Events: Click, DragDrop, DragOver, MouseDown, MouseMove, MouseUp, OLECompleteDrag, OLEDragDrop, OLEDragOver, OLEGiveFeedback, OLESetData, OLEStartDrag

Methods

Common Methods: Drag, Move, OLEDrag, ShowWhatsThis, ZOrder

Property Page

Properties

Common Properties: Appearance, BackColor, Font, FontBold, FontItalic, FontName, FontSize, FontStrikethru, FontTransparent, FontUnderline, ForeColor, hDC, Height, HelpContextID, hWnd, MouseIcon, MousePointer, Name, OLEDropMode, RightToLeft, ScaleHeight, ScaleLeft, ScaleMode, ScaleTop, ScaleWidth, Tag, Width

*ActiveControl	Control Object
AutoRedraw	Boolean
Caption	String
Changed	Boolean
*ClipControls	Boolean
*Controls	Object Collection
*Count	Integer
CurrentX	Single

CurrentY	Single
DrawMode	Integer
DrawStyle	Integer
DrawWidth	Integer
FillColor	Long
FillStyle	Integer
*Image	IPictureDisp Object
KeyPreview	Boolean
Palette	IPictureDisp Object
PaletteMode	Integer
Picture	IPictureDisp Object
*SelectedControls	SelectedControls Collection

Events

Common Events: Click, DblClick, DragDrop, DragOver, GotFocus, KeyDown, KeyPress, KeyUp, LostFocus, MouseDown, MouseMove, MouseUp, OLECompleteDrag, OLEDragDrop, OLEDragOver, OLEGiveFeedback, OLESetData, OLEStartDrag

ApplyChanges()

EditProperty(*propertyname* As String)

Initialize()

Paint()

SelectionChanged()

Terminate()

Methods

Common Methods: OLEDrag, Refresh, Scale, ScaleX, ScaleY, SetFocus

Circle	*object*.Circle(*step*, *x*, *y*, *radius*, *color*, *start*, *end*, *aspect*)
Cls	*object*.Cls
Line	*object*.Line(*flags*, *x1*, *y1*, *x2*, *y2*, *color*)
PaintPicture	*object*.PaintPicture(*picture*, *x1*, *y1*, [*width1*], [*height1*], [*x2*], [*y2*], [*width2*], [*height2*], [*opcode*])
Point	*object*.Point(*x*, *y*) As Long
PopupMenu	*object*.PopupMenu(*menu*, [*flags*], [*x*], [*y*], [*defaultmenu*])

PSet	*object*.PSet(*step*, *x*, *y*, *color*)
TextHeight	*object*.TextHeight(*str*) As Single
TextWidth	*object*.TextWidth(*str*) As Single

RichTextBox

Properties

Common Properties: Appearance, BackColor, BorderStyle, Container, DataBindings, DataChanged, DataField, DragIcon, DragMode, Enabled, Font, Height, HelpContextID, hWnd, Index, Left, MouseIcon, MousePointer, Name, Object, OLEDragMode, OLEDropMode, Parent, TabIndex, TabStop, Tag, ToolTipText, Top, Visible, WhatsThisHelpID, Width

AutoVerbMenu	Boolean
BulletIndent	Single
DisableNoScroll	Boolean
FileName	String
HideSelection	Boolean
Locked	Boolean
MaxLength	Long
MultiLine	Boolean
*OLEObjects	OLEObjects Collection
RightMargin	Single
ScrollBars	ScrollBarsConstants Enum
SelAlignment	Variant
SelBold	Variant
SelBullet	Variant
SelCharOffset	Variant
SelColor	Variant
SelFontName	Variant
SelFontSize	Variant
SelHangingIndent	Variant
SelIndent	Variant
SelItalic	Variant
SelLength	Long
SelProtected	Variant
SelRightIndent	Variant

SelRTF	String
SelStart	Long
SelStrikethru	Variant
SelTabCount	Variant
SelTabs	Variant Array
SelText	String
SelUnderline	Variant
Text	String
TextRTF	String

Events

Common Events: Click, DblClick, DragDrop, DragOver, GotFocus, KeyDown, KeyPress, KeyUp, LostFocus, MouseDown, MouseMove, MouseUp, OLECompleteDrag, OLEDragDrop, OLEDragOver, OLEGiveFeedback, OLESetData, OLEStartDrag

Change()

SelChange()

Methods

Common Methods: Drag, Move, OLEDrag, Refresh, SetFocus, ShowWhatsThis, ZOrder

Find	*object*.Find(*string*, [*start*], [*end*], [*options*])
GetLineFromChar	*object*.GetLineFromChar(*charpos*)
LoadFile	*object*.LoadFile(*pathname*, [*flags*])
SaveFile	*object*.SaveFile(*pathname*, [*flags*])
SelPrint	*object*.SelPrint(*hdc*)
Span	*object*.Span(*characterset*, [*forward*], [*negate*])
UpTo	*object*.UpTo(*characterset*, [*forward*], [*negate*])

Screen

Properties

Common Properties: Height, MouseIcon, MousePointer, Width

*ActiveControl	Control Object
*ActiveForm	Form Object

*FontCount	Integer
*Fonts	String Array
*TwipsPerPixelX	Single
*TwipsPerPixelY	Single

Events

No events

Methods

No methods

Shape

Properties

Common Properties: BackColor, BorderStyle, Container, Height, Index, Left, Name, Parent, Tag, Top, Visible, Width

BackStyle	Integer
BorderColor	Long
BorderWidth	Integer
DrawMode	Integer
FillColor	Long
FillStyle	Integer
Shape	Integer

Events

No events

Methods

Common Methods: Move, Refresh, ZOrder

Slider

Properties

Common Properties: BorderStyle, Container, DataBindings, DragIcon, DragMode, Enabled, Height, HelpContextID, hWnd, Index, Left, MouseIcon, MousePointer, Name, Object, OLEDropMode, Parent, TabIndex, TabStop, Tag, ToolTipText, Top, Visible, WhatsThisHelpID, Width

*GetNumTicks	Long
LargeChange	Long
Max	Long
Min	Long
Orientation	OrientationConstants Enum
SelectRange	Boolean
SelLength	Long
SelStart	Long
SmallChange	Long
TickFrequency	Long
TickStyle	TickStyleConstants Enum
Value	Long

Events

Common Events: Click, DragDrop, DragOver, GotFocus, KeyDown, KeyPress, KeyUp, LostFocus, MouseDown, MouseMove, MouseUp, OLECompleteDrag, OLEDragDrop, OLEDragOver, OLEGiveFeedback, OLESetData, OLEStartDrag

Change()

Scroll()

Methods

Common Methods: Drag, Move, OLEDrag, Refresh, SetFocus, ShowWhatsThis, ZOrder

ClearSel	*object*.ClearSel

StatusBar

Properties

Common Properties: Container, DragIcon, DragMode, Enabled, Font, Height, hWnd, Index, Left, MouseIcon, MousePointer, Name, Object, OLEDropMode, Parent, TabIndex, Tag, ToolTipText, Top, Visible, WhatsThisHelpID, Width

Align	Integer
Panels	Panels Collection
ShowTips	Boolean
SimpleText	String
Style	SbarStyleConstants Enum

Events

Common Events: Click, DblClick, DragDrop, DragOver, MouseDown, MouseMove, MouseUp, OLECompleteDrag, OLEDragDrop, OLEDragOver, OLEGiveFeedback, OLESetData, OLEStartDrag

PanelClick(*panel* As Panel)

PanelDblClick(*panel* As Panel)

Methods

Common Methods: Drag, Move, OLEDrag, Refresh, ShowWhatsThis, ZOrder

Sysinfo

Properties

Common Properties: Index, Name, Object, Parent, Tag

*ACStatus	Integer
*BatteryFullTime	Long
*BatteryLifePercent	Integer
*BatteryLifeTime	Long
*BatteryStatus	Integer
*OSBuild	Integer
*OSPlatform	Integer
*OSVersion	Single
*ScrollBarSize	Single
*WorkAreaHeight	Single
*WorkAreaLeft	Single
*WorkAreaTop	Single
*WorkAreaWidth	Single

Events

Common Events: None

ConfigChangeCancelled()

ConfigChanged(*oldconfignum* As Long, *newconfignum* As Long)

DeviceArrival(*devicetype* As Long, *deviceid* As Long, *devicename* As String, *devicedata* As Long)

DeviceOtherEvent(*devicetype* As Long, *eventname* As String, *datapointer* As Long)

DeviceQueryRemove(*devicetype* As Long, *deviceid* As Long, *devicename* As String, *devicedata* As Long, *cancel* As Boolean)

DeviceQueryRemoveFailed(*devicetype* As Long, *deviceid* As Long, *devicename* As String, *devicedata* As Long)

DeviceRemoveComplete(*devicetype* As Long, *deviceid* As Long, *devicename* As String, *devicedata* As Long)

DeviceRemovePending(*devicetype* As Long, *deviceid* As Long, *devicename* As String, *devicedata* As Long)

DevModeChanged()

DisplayChanged()

PowerQuerySuspend(*cancel* As Boolean)

PowerResume()

PowerStatusChanged()

PowerSuspend()

QueryChangeConfig(*cancel* As Boolean)

SettingChanged(*item* As Integer)

SysColorsChanged()

TimeChanged()

Methods

No methods

TabStrip

Properties

Common Properties: Container, DataBindings, DragIcon, DragMode, Enabled, Font, Height, HelpContextID, hWnd, Index, Left, MouseIcon, MousePointer, Name, Object, OLEDropMode, Parent, TabIndex, TabStop, Tag, ToolTipText, Top, Visible, WhatsThisHelpID, Width

ClientHeight	Single
ClientLeft	Single
ClientTop	Single
ClientWidth	Single
ImageList	Object
MultiRow	Boolean
SelectedItem	Tab Object

ShowTips	Boolean
Style	TabStyleConstants Enum
TabFixedHeight	Integer
TabFixedWidth	Integer
Tabs	Tabs Collection
TabWidthStyle	TabWidthStyleConstants Enum

Events

Common Events: Click, DragDrop, DragOver, GotFocus, KeyDown, KeyPress, KeyUp, LostFocus, MouseDown, MouseMove, MouseUp, OLECompleteDrag, OLEDragDrop, OLEDragOver, OLEGiveFeedback, OLESetData, OLEStartDrag

BeforeClick(*cancel* As Integer)

Methods

Common Methods: Drag, Move, OLEDrag, Refresh, SetFocus, ShowWhatsThis, ZOrder

TextBox

Properties

Common Properties: Appearance, BackColor, BorderStyle, Container, DataChanged, DataField, DragIcon, DragMode, Enabled, Font, FontBold, FontItalic, FontName, FontSize, FontStrikethru, FontUnderline, ForeColor, Height, HelpContextID, hWnd, Index, Left, LinkItem, LinkMode, LinkTimeout, LinkTopic, MouseIcon, MousePointer, Name, OLEDragMode, OLEDropMode, Parent, RightToLeft, TabStop, Tag, ToolTipText, Top, Visible, WhatsThisHelpID, Width

Alignment	Integer
*HideSelection	Boolean
Locked	Boolean
MaxLength	Long
*MultiLine	Boolean
PasswordChar	String
*ScrollBars	Integer
SelLength	Long
SelStart	Long
SelText	String
Text	String

Events

Common Events: Click, DblClick, DragDrop, DragOver, GotFocus, KeyDown, KeyPress, KeyUp, LinkClose, LinkError, LinkNotify, LinkOpen, LostFocus, MouseDown, MouseMove, MouseUp, OLECompleteDrag, OLEDragDrop, OLEDragOver, OLEGiveFeedback, OLESetData, OLEStartDrag

Change()

Methods

Common Methods: Drag, LinkExecute, LinkPoke, LinkRequest, LinkSend, Move, OLEDrag, Refresh, SetFocus, ShowWhatsThis, ZOrder

Timer

Properties

Common Properties: Enabled, Index, Name, Parent, Tag

Interval	Long

Events

Common Events: None

Timer()

Methods

No methods

Toolbar

Properties

Common Properties: Appearance, BorderStyle, Container, DataBindings, DragIcon, DragMode, Enabled, Height, HelpContextID, hWnd, Index, Left, MouseIcon, MousePointer, Name, Object, OLEDropMode, Parent, TabIndex, Tag, ToolTipText, Top, Visible, WhatsThisHelpID, Width

Align	Integer
AllowCustomize	Boolean
ButtonHeight	Single
Buttons	Buttons Collection
ButtonWidth	Single
*Controls	Controls Collection

`HelpFile`	`String`
`ImageList`	`Object`
`ShowTips`	`Boolean`
`Wrappable`	`Boolean`

Events

Common Events: Click, DblClick, DragDrop, DragOver, MouseDown, MouseMove, MouseUp, OLECompleteDrag, OLEDragDrop, OLEDragOver, OLEGiveFeedback, OLESetData, OLEStartDrag

`ButtonClick(`*`button`*` As Button)`

`Change()`

Methods

Common Methods: Drag, Move, OLEDrag, Refresh, ShowWhatsThis, ZOrder

`Customize`	*`object`*`.Customize`
`RestoreToolbar`	*`object`*`.RestoreToolbar(`*`key`*`, `*`subkey`*`, `*`value`*`)`
`SaveToolbar`	*`object`*`.SaveToolbar(`*`key`*`, `*`subkey`*`, `*`value`*`)`

TreeView

Properties

Common Properties: Appearance, BorderStyle, Container, DragIcon, DragMode, Enabled, Font, Height, HelpContextID, hWnd, Index, Left, MouseIcon, MousePointer, Name, Object, OLEDragMode, OLEDropMode, Parent, TabIndex, TabStop, Tag, ToolTipText, Top, Visible, WhatsThisHelpID, Width

`DropHighlight`	`Node` Object
`HideSelection`	`Boolean`
`ImageList`	`Object`
`Indentation`	`Single`
`LabelEdit`	`LabelEditConstants` Enum
`LineStyle`	`TreeLineStyleConstants` Enum
`Nodes`	`Nodes` Collection
`PathSeparator`	`String`
`SelectedItem`	`Node` Object
`Sorted`	`Boolean`
`Style`	`TreeStyleConstants` Enum

Events

Common Events: Click, DragDrop, DragOver, GotFocus, KeyDown, KeyPress, KeyUp, LostFocus, MouseDown, MouseMove, MouseUp, OLECompleteDrag, OLEDragDrop, OLEDragOver, OLEGiveFeedback, OLESetData, OLEStartDrag

```
AfterLabelEdit(cancel As Integer, newstring As String)
BeforeLabelEdit(cancel As Integer)
Expand(node As Node)
NodeClick(node As Node)
```

Methods

Common Methods: Drag, Move, OLEDrag, Refresh, SetFocus, ShowWhatsThis, ZOrder

GetVisibleCount	*object*.GetVisibleCount() As Long
HitTest	*object*.HitTest(*x*, *y*) As Node
StartLabelEdit	*object*.StartLabelEdit

UpDown

Properties

Common Properties: Container, DragIcon, DragMode, Enabled, Height, HelpContextID, hWnd, Index, Left, Name, Object, Parent, TabIndex, TabStop, Tag, ToolTipText, Top, Visible, WhatsThisHelpID, Width

Alignment	AlignmentConstants Enum
AutoBuddy	Boolean
BuddyControl	Variant
BuddyProperty	Variant
Increment	Long
Max	Long
Min	Long
OLEDropMode	OLEDropConstants Enum
Orientation	OrientationConstants Enum
SyncBuddy	Boolean
Value	Long
Wrap	Boolean

Events

Common Events: DragDrop, DragOver, GotFocus, LostFocus, MouseDown, MouseMove, MouseUp, OLECompleteDrag, OLEDragDrop, OLEDragOver, OLEGiveFeedback, OLESetData, OLEStartDrag

Change()

DownClick()

UpClick()

Methods

Common Methods: Drag, Move, OLEDrag, SetFocus, ShowWhatsThis, ZOrder

UserControl

Properties

Common Properties: Appearance, BackColor, BorderStyle, Enabled, Font, FontBold, FontItalic, FontName, FontSize, FontStrikethru, FontTransparent, FontUnderline, ForeColor, hDC, Height, hWnd, MouseIcon, MousePointer, Name, OLEDropMode, Parent, RightToLeft, ScaleHeight, ScaleLeft, ScaleMode, ScaleTop, ScaleWidth, Tag, Width

AccessKeys	String
*ActiveControl	Control Object
*Ambient	AmbientProperties Object
AutoRedraw	Boolean
BackStyle	Long
*ClipControls	Boolean
*ContainedControls	ContainedControls Collection
*Controls	Object Collection
*Count	Integer
CurrentX	Single
CurrentY	Single
DrawMode	Integer
DrawStyle	Integer
DrawWidth	Integer
*EventsFrozen	Boolean
*Extender	Object
FillColor	Long
FillStyle	Integer

*Hyperlink	Hyperlink Object
*Image	IPictureDisp Object
KeyPreview	Boolean
MaskColor	Long
MaskPicture	IPictureDisp Object
Palette	IPictureDisp Object
PaletteMode	Integer
ParentControls	ParentControls Collection
Picture	IPictureDisp Object
PropertyPages	String Array

Events

Common Events: Click, DblClick, DragDrop, DragOver, GotFocus, KeyDown, KeyPress, KeyUp, LostFocus, MouseDown, MouseMove, MouseUp, OLECompleteDrag, OLEDragDrop, OLEDragOver, OLEGiveFeedback, OLESetData, OLEStartDrag

AccessKeyPress(*keyascii* As Integer)

AmbientChanged(*propertyname* As String)

AsyncReadComplete(*asyncprop* As AsyncProperty)

EnterFocus()

ExitFocus()

Hide()

Initialize()

InitProperties()

Paint()

ReadProperties(*propbag* As PropertyBag)

Resize()

Show()

Terminate()

WriteProperties(*propbag* As PropertyBag)

Methods

Common Methods: OLEDrag, Refresh, Scale, ScaleX, ScaleY, SetFocus

AsyncRead	*object*.AsyncRead(*target*, *asynctype*, [*propertyname*])
CancelAsyncRead	*object*.CancelAsyncRead([*property*])

CanPropertyChange	*object*.CanPropertyChange(*propname*) As Boolean
Circle	*object*.Circle(*step*, *x*, *y*, *radius*, *color*, *start*, *end*, *aspect*)
Cls	*object*.Cls
Line	*object*.Line(*flags*, *x1*, *y1*, *x2*, *y2*, *color*)
PaintPicture	*object*.PaintPicture(*picture*, *x1*, *y1*, [*width1*], [*height1*], [*x2*], [*y2*], [*width2*], [*height2*], [opcode])
Point	*object*.Point(*x*, *y*) As Long
PopupMenu	*object*.PopupMenu(*menu*, [*flags*], [*x*], [*y*], [*defaultmenu*])
PropertyChanged	*object*.PropertyChanged([*propname*])
PSet	*object*.PSet(*step*, *x*, *y*, *color*)
Size	*object*.Size(*width*, *height*)
TextHeight	*object*.TextHeight(*str*) As Single
TextWidth	*object*.TextWidth(*str*) As Single

UserDocument

Properties

Common Properties: Appearance, BackColor, Font, FontBold, FontItalic, FontName, FontSize, FontStrikethru, FontTransparent, FontUnderline, ForeColor, hDC, Height, hWnd, MouseIcon, MousePointer, Name, OLEDropMode, Parent, RightToLeft, ScaleHeight, ScaleLeft, ScaleMode, ScaleTop, ScaleWidth, Tag, Width

*ActiveControl	Control Array
AutoRedraw	Boolean
*ClipControls	Boolean
ContinuousScroll	Boolean
*Controls	Object Collection
*Count	Integer
CurrentX	Single
CurrentY	Single
DrawMode	Integer
DrawStyle	Integer
DrawWidth	Integer

FillColor	Long
FillStyle	Integer
HScrollSmallChange	Single
*Hyperlink	Hyperlink Object
*Image	IPictureDisp Object
KeyPreview	Boolean
MinHeight	Single
MinWidth	Single
Palette	IPictureDisp Object
PaletteMode	Integer
Picture	IPictureDisp Object
ScrollBars	Integer
*ViewportHeight	Single
ViewportLeft	Single
ViewportTop	Single
*ViewportWidth	Single
VScrollSmallChange	Single

Events

Common Events: Click, DblClick, DragDrop, DragOver, GotFocus, KeyDown, KeyPress, KeyUp, LostFocus, MouseDown, MouseMove, MouseUp, OLECompleteDrag, OLEDragDrop, OLEDragOver, OLEGiveFeedback, OLESetData, OLEStartDrag

AsyncReadComplete(*asyncprop* As AsyncProperty)

EnterFocus()

ExitFocus()

Hide()

Initialize()

InitProperties()

Paint()

ReadProperties(*propbag* As PropertyBag)

Resize()

Scroll()

Show()

Terminate()

WriteProperties(*propbag* As PropertyBag)

Methods

Common Methods: OLEDrag, Refresh, Scale, ScaleX, ScaleY, SetFocus

AsyncRead	*object*.AsyncRead(*target*, *asynctype*, [*propertyname*])
CancelAsyncRead	*object*.CancelAsyncRead([*property*])
Circle	*object*.Circle(*step*, *x*, *y*, *radius*, *color*, *start*, *end*, *aspect*)
Cls	*object*.Cls
Line	*object*.Line(*flags*, *x1*, *y1*, *x2*, *y2*, *color*)
PaintPicture	*object*.PaintPicture(*picture*, *x1*, *y1*, [*width1*], [*height1*], [*x2*], [*y2*], [*width2*], [*height2*], [opcode])
Point	*object*.Point(*x*, *y*) As Long
PopupMenu	*object*.PopupMenu(*menu*, [*flags*], [*x*], [*y*], [*defaultmenu*])
PrintForm	*object*.PrintForm
PropertyChanged	*object*.PropertyChanged([*propname*])
PSet	*object*.PSet(*step*, *x*, *y*, *color*)
SetViewport	*object*.SetViewport(*left*, *top*)
TextHeight	*object*.TextHeight(*str*) As Single
TextWidth	*object*.TextWidth(*str*) As Single

VScrollBar

Properties

Common Properties: Container, DragIcon, DragMode, Enabled, Height, HelpContextID, hWnd, Index, Left, MouseIcon, MousePointer, Name, Parent, RightToLeft, TabIndex, TabStop, Tag, Top, Visible, WhatsThisHelpID, Width

LargeChange	Integer
Max	Integer
Min	Integer
SmallChange	Integer
Value	Integer

Events

Common Events: DragDrop, DragOver, GotFocus, KeyDown, KeyPress, KeyUp, LostFocus

```
Change()
Scroll()
```

Methods

Common Methods: Drag, Move, Refresh, SetFocus, ShowWhatsThis, ZOrder

Winsock

Properties

Common Properties: Index, Name, Object, Parent, Tag

*BytesReceived	Long
*LocalHostName	String
*LocalIP	String
LocalPort	Long
Protocol	ProtocolConstants Enum
RemoteHost	String
*RemoteHostIP	String
RemotePort	Long
*SocketHandle	Long
*State	Integer

Events

Common Events: None

Close()

Connect()

ConnectionRequest(*requestid* As Long)

DataArrival(*totalbytes* As Long)

Error(*number* As Integer, *description* As String, *scode* As Long, *source* As String, *helpfile* As String, *helpcontext* As Long, *canceldisplay* As Boolean)

SendComplete()

SendProgress(*bytessent* As Long, *bytesleft* As Long)

Methods

Common Methods: None

Accept	*object*.Accept(*requestid*)
Bind	*object*.Bind([*localport*], [*localid*])
Close	*object*.Close
Connect	*object*.Connect([*remotehost*], [*remoteport*])
GetData	*object*.GetData(*data*, [*type*], [*maxLen*])
Listen	*object*.Listen
PeekData	*object*.PeekData(*data*, [*type*], [*maxLen*])
SendData	*object*.SendData(*data*)

Summary

This chapter provides a quick reference for many objects commonly used in Visual Basic, including all the standard and professional controls plus objects such as Screen and Printer. For each object, the chapter lists all its properties, methods, and events. Other information, such as the data type of properties, the syntax of methods, and the arguments of events, is also provided.

CHAPTER 42

Variable Types in Visual Basic

IN THIS CHAPTER

Although integers and strings are the most commonly used data types in Visual Basic, there are many more available to the VB programmer. Choosing the correct data type for a given purpose is essential for efficient programming. This chapter briefly discusses the different data types available in Visual Basic as well as some of their more common uses.

VB Data Types

Table 42.1 lists the data types available to Visual Basic. It also shows the amount of storage required for each type, as well as the possible values they can store.

Table 42.1. The data types available in Visual Basic and the possible values they can store.

Data Type	*Storage Size*	*Data Range*
`Boolean`	2 bytes	0 or 1
`Byte`	1 byte	0 to 255
`Currency`	8 bytes	–922,337,203,685,477.5808 to +922,337,203,685,477.5807
`Date`	8 bytes	1 January 100 to 31 December 9999 (Date) 00:00:00 to 23:59:59 (Time)
`Decimal`	12 bytes	–79,228,162,514,264,337,593,543,950,335 to +79,228,162,514,264,337,593,543,950,335
`Double`	8 bytes	–1.79769313486232E308 to –4.94065645841247E-324 (Negative values) +4.94065645841247E-324 to +1.79769313486232E308 (Positive values)
`Integer`	2 bytes	–32,768 to +32,767
`Long`	4 bytes	–2,147,483,648 to +2,147,483,647
`Single`	4 bytes	–3.402823E38 to –1.401298E-45 (Negatives) +1.401298E-45 to +3.402823E38 (Positives)
`String`	See later section	
User-Defined Types	See later section	
`Variant`	See later section	

Boolean

Although `Boolean` data types take two bytes of storage space, they can only store one of two values: True (`-1`) or False (`0`). Many property values are of type `Boolean` because they are used to specify a True/False state.

Byte

`Byte` data types can only store values from 0 to 255, such as those that make up the ASCII character set. This data type is commonly used to store single characters or binary data.

Currency

Variables of the `Currency` data type are unique in that they always display numbers with exactly four decimal positions (four digits to the right of the decimal point) and up to 15 integer positions. The values in `Currency` data values are actually stored as integer numbers that are scaled by 10,000 to give a fixed-point number. For example, the value 1,005,894.32 would be stored in a `Currency` variable as 10058943200. When the value is accessed, it is automatically divided by 10,000 to give 1005894.3200. This conversion process is transparent to the programmer.

As indicated by their name, `Currency` data types are commonly used to store monetary values. Using the `Single` or `Double` data type to store and calculate monetary values is often unpredictable, so the `Currency` data type should always be used for such purposes.

Date

`Date` data types can store date and time values simultaneously. Because the range of dates this data type can store goes all the way up to December 31, 9999, it is not affected by the Year 2000 (Y2K) bug.

Date and time values can also be stored in `Variant` data types, but using the `Date` data type to store dates and times is recommended.

Double

Variables of the `Double` data type can store extremely large floating-point numbers. You should only use this data type if you require a high degree of accuracy when storing numbers with a fractional amount. If the number to be stored is a large whole number, use the `Long` data type instead. If the number is a monetary value, use the `Currency` data value.

Integer

The `Integer` data type is one of the most efficient of all of Visual Basic's data types because it does not store floating-point numbers and it uses only two bytes of storage. `Integer` variables are commonly used in loops or to represent enumerated values (as in an `Enum...End Enum` structure).

Long

Like `Integer` the `Long` data type is efficient because it stores only whole numbers (integers). Whereas the `Integer` data type is limited to storing relatively small values, `Long` has a much greater range of possible values. `Long`s are often used as arguments for 32-bit API functions.

Single

Although the `Single` data type does not store fractional numbers as precisely as the `Double` data type, it will often suffice unless an unusual amount of decimal-place precision is required. Do not use `Single` data types to store and calculate monetary values or you may get unexpected results. For monetary values, always use the `Currency` data type.

String

The `String` data type is used to store a sequence (string) of ASCII character values. Actually, the ASCII sequence is stored elsewhere in memory and the `String` data type stores a pointer to the sequence's memory location.

`String` variables can be declared as either fixed-length or variable-length. Fixed-length `Strings` can be from 1 to 65,536 (64KB) characters long. Variable-length `Strings` are far more flexible and can be over 2 billion characters in length.

User-Defined Types

User-Defined Types, or UDTs, are data types that are created by the programmer using a `Type...End Type` construct. The UDT consists of one or more components that are defined as other data types, but together form a unique new data type. Chapter 10, "Data Structures, Collections, and Enumerations," discusses the creation and use of User-Defined Types.

Variant

The `Variant` data type is without a doubt the most flexible data type in Visual Basic, but its use should be avoided whenever possible because its flexibility also makes it very inefficient.

`Variants` can store the same values as any of VB's other data types, with the exception of fixed-length `Strings` and user-defined types. If you do not declare a variable used in your program as a specific data type, Visual Basic automatically assumes that it is a `Variant` (unless the `Option Explicit` statement is included in the program, in which case an error condition will occur).

`Variants` can also store two other values, `Empty` and `Null`. An `Empty` value indicates that the `Variant` has not yet been assigned a value; that is, no number or string has been assigned to the `Variant`. A `Null` value indicates that the `Variant` has intentionally been assigned no value.

Summary

Selecting the proper data type to store information in your program is crucial to efficient programming. Some programmers choose not to define their variables as specific data types, allowing Visual Basic to auto-define them as `Variants`. This makes for poor coding and slow programs. You should always use the data type that uses the least amount of storage but can still store the information in question. Use this chapter as a guide for determining the proper data type when declaring variables in your VB programs.

CHAPTER 43

Sequences of Events

IN THIS CHAPTER

Visual Basic is an event-driven language; that is, rather than execute in a top-down manner like programs created with earlier development tools, VB programs react to certain events. For example, if a user clicks a `CommandButton` control, that control's `Click` event is raised. The programmer has the ability to add code to such event procedures so the program can respond accordingly. It's safe to say that events are one of the cornerstones of Visual Basic programming.

As important as events are, even experienced programmers may be unaware of the exact order in which some events occur. Clicking a `CommandButton` control raises its `Click` event—that's easy, if not obvious. But which events are raised when a form loads, and in what sequence? The answer to that question may not be quite so obvious!

This chapter details the sequences of events that commonly occur in Visual Basic programs.

Common Event Sequences

Forms, `UserControl` objects, `UserDocument` objects, and classes are building blocks in Visual Basic. It is from them that we start creating many of our projects. Although we may work with these objects time and time again, it's often difficult to know or remember exactly what happens "behind the scenes" when they are created and destroyed. The following sections detail some of the sequences of events that occur during the lifetime of these objects.

Form Events

Most Visual Basic programs utilize forms. When each form is loaded into memory and displayed, a specific sequence of events occurs. The sequence is, in order:

`Load`

`Initialize`

`Resize`

`Activate`

`Paint`

When a form is unloaded, the following events are raised:

`QueryUnload`

`Unload`

`Terminate` (if the form is the only one in the program)

`UserControl` Events

When creating ActiveX controls using the `UserControl` object, it is essential that you understand which events the `UserControl` object raises, and in which order. This is not always cut and dry; a `UserControl` object operates differently at design time and at runtime. In this section, we'll only cover the events that occur for runtime instances of `UserControl` objects. Chapter 19, "Advanced ActiveX Control Creation," discusses in greater detail the sequence of events for `UserControl` objects both at design-time and at runtime.

The events that are raised when a runtime instance of a `UserControl` object (that is, an ActiveX control produced in Visual Basic) is first created on a form are as follows:

`Initialize`

`ReadProperties`

`Resize` or `Paint`

The `Paint` event is only raised if the control is a user-drawn control; otherwise, the `Resize` event is raised.

When the instance of the control is destroyed, only the `Terminate` event is raised.

ActiveX controls behave a little differently when instances of them are created on Web pages. Since there is no form from which they can read property settings, the `ReadProperties` event is replaced with the `InitProperties` event, making the sequence of events as follows:

`Initialize`

`InitProperties`

`Resize` or `Paint`

Again, when the instance of the control is destroyed, the `Terminate` event is raised.

`UserDocument` Events

The UserDocument object, the base for ActiveX documents created in Visual Basic, raises several events when it is initially loaded into a container application such as Internet Explorer. The sequence of events is as follows:

`Initialize`

`InitProperties`

`Resize`

`Show`

`EnterFocus`

`Paint`

When the ActiveX document is replaced with a Web page, the document still exists in memory. In that case, the following events are raised:

`ExitFocus`

`Hide`

When the document is returned to (by pressing Internet Explorer's Back button, for example), the following events occur:

```
Show
EnterFocus
Paint
```

Class Module Events

Class modules don't have a sequence of events that occur when they are initialized or when they are terminated. In fact, they only have two events: `Initialize` and `Terminate`. It doesn't take a rocket scientist to determine when each event occurs!

Summary

Because Visual Basic programs are event-driven, it is essential to know when events occur, and in what order. This chapter presented some of the common sequences of events that occur when some of the base objects in Visual Basic (forms, `UserControl` objects, `UserDocument` objects, and classes) are created and destroyed.

CHAPTER 44

Object and Variable Naming Conventions

IN THIS CHAPTER

Before Visual Basic came along, program code was a little more straightforward. There were different variable types (such as long integer and string), but that was about it. In such languages as C, you had to declare variables before you used them in your program, so there was always some form of documentation as to the type of each variable. Other languages such as QuickBasic didn't require that you declare your variables (although you could if you wanted to), but you had to tack on an identifier to the end of a variable name to specify its type (`$` for string, `%` for integer, and so on).

In Visual Basic, most programmers wisely choose to declare their variables before using them. Although this is a good idea, it does bring up a small problem: How does one determine a variable's type without having to refer to the variable declarations? This problem becomes bigger as the program increases in size and complexity and variables are declared not only at module-level, but also globally.

Microsoft has devised a practical and easy solution to this problem by suggesting that all variable names be preceded by a short mnemonic that indicates the variable's type. The first section of this chapter lists the various data types in Visual Basic and gives suggestions for their mnemonic identifiers.

Variables are not the only thing that may cause confusion in Visual Basic code. Unlike older top-down languages like C and QuickBasic, Visual Basic's event-driven design introduces objects such as CommandButtons and ListBoxes. Like variables, these objects are also assigned names. Without some kind of identifier, an object name can be very misleading. For example, does an object named `CustomerNames` refer to a ListBox, a Label, a TextBox, or some other kind of object?

The problem of object naming can also be easily solved by prefacing all object names with a short mnemonic. The second section of this chapter lists many of the common objects in Visual Basic and suggests identifying mnemonics.

The whole purpose of using mnemonic identifiers for variables and objects is to make code easier to read and understand. In order for it to work, however, you must adopt these standard naming conventions and use them religiously in all of your programs. You must also use the same identifiers each and every time. For example, don't preface a ListBox object with a "lbx" identifier in one program and "lst" in another—it will only lead to confusion. It may take some getting used to, but once you get into the habit of using the variable and object naming conventions set forth in this chapter, you'll be the better programmer for it.

Variable Naming Conventions

There are two schools of thought on variable naming conventions. One is that variables names should be prefaced by a one-character identifier, with two- or three-character identifiers used in only a few cases. The other is that all variables should have a three-character mnemonic identifier. Personally, I much prefer the latter. One-character identifiers do not make a variable's type as apparent as three-character identifiers, especially when it is referring to variable types like Byte (y) or Single (f).

Table 44.1 lists the variable types in Visual Basic. For each, a long identifier (three-character) and a short identifier (one- to three-character) mnemonic is given. These mnemonics are nothing more than suggestions. You can adopt the use of these identifiers in your coding, or you can devise your own list of mnemonic identifiers. The choice is yours. The only real trick is to maintain consistency in their use.

Table 44.1. Suggested variable naming conventions.

Variable Type	*Long Identifier*	*Short Identifier*
Boolean	bln or boo	b
Byte	byt	y
Currency	cur	c
Date (Time)	dtm	dt
Double	dbl	d
Error	err	e
Integer	int	i
Long	lng or lon	l
Single	sng	f
String	str	s
User-defined type	udt	udt
Variant	vnt	vnt

Indicating Variable Scope

Some variables are declared inside functions or subroutines; their scope is restricted to the procedure in which they are declared. However, other variables may be declared elsewhere in a form or module. If they are declared as Public, their scope is global and they can be used anywhere in the program. If they are declared as Private their scope is module-level, meaning that they can only be used in the module or form that contains the variable declaration.

For global and module-level variables, it's a good idea to add a one-character prefix to their names to indicate their scope. Prefix global variables with "g" and module-level variables with "m." Leave off the scope prefix indicator altogether for procedure-level variables.

Object Naming Conventions

The issue of naming conventions for objects is a little more complicated than that for variables. While there are only a limited number of variable types, the number of object types (including controls and data access objects) is much larger. Indeed, Visual Basic can support an unlimited number of objects with the addition of third-party controls.

This section suggests mnemonic identifiers for most of the more commonly used controls and objects in Visual Basic. Again, these identifiers are only suggestions. You should use whatever you feel is appropriate.

Controls

The Professional and Enterprise Editions of Visual Basic ship with over 50 different ActiveX controls. Table 44.2 lists most of those controls and provides suggested mnemonic identifiers.

Table 44.2. Suggested object naming conventions.

Object Type	*Identifier*	*Object Type*	*Identifier*
Animation	ani	Menu	mnu
CheckBox	chk	MSChart	mch
ComboBox	cbo	MSComm	mcm
CommandButton	cmd	MSFlexGrid	msg
CommonDialog	dlg	MSTab (SSTab)	mst
Data	dat	Multimedia MCI	mmm
DBCombo	dbc	OLE	ole
DBGrid	dbg	OptionButton	opt
DBList	dbl	PictureBox	pic
DirListBox	dir	PictureClip	pcl
DriveListBox	drv	ProgressBar	prg
FileListBox	fil	Remote Data Control	rdc
Form	frm	RichTextBox	rtf
Frame	fra	Shape	shp
Gauge	gau	Slider	sld
HScrollBar	hsb	Spin	spn
Image	img	StatusBar	sta
ImageList	ils	SysInfo	sys
InternetTransfer (Inet)	net	TabStrip	tab
Label	lbl	TextBox	txt
Line	lin	Timer	tmr
ListBox	lst	Toolbar	tlb
ListView	lvw	TreeView	tre
MAPIMessages	mpm	UpDown	upd
MAPISession	mps	VScroll	vsc
MaskEdBox	msk	Winsock	wsk
MDI Child Form	mdi		

Data Access Objects

When dealing with databases, several different object types may be used (such as Recordsets, Fields, and Query Definitions). These objects should also be prefixed with a mnemonic identifier. Table 44.3 lists the various data access objects and provides a suggested mnemonic for each.

Table 44.3. Suggested object naming conventions for data access objects.

Object Type	*Identifier*	*Object Type*	*Identifier*
Container	con	Parameter	prm
Database	db	QueryDef	qry
DBEngine	dbe	Recordset	rec
Document	doc	Relation	rel
Field	fld	TableDef	tbd
Group	grp	User	usr
Index	idx	Workspace	wsp

Menu Objects

When naming menu objects, it's a good idea to use the "mnu" mnemonic followed by the top-level menu item name and then the name of the menu item itself. For example, if a menu consists of three top-level items (File, View, and Help) and each top-level item contains other menu items, the menu item names might be similar to those shown in Table 44.4.

Table 44.4. A sample list of menu items, illustrating the menu item naming conventions.

Menu	*Menu Item*	*Name*
File		mnuFile
	Open File	mnuFileOpenFile
	Close File	mnuFileCloseFile
	Import	mnuFileImport
	Export	mnuFileExport
	Exit	mnuFileExit
View		mnuView
	Full Screen	mnuViewFullScreen
	Split Screen	mnuViewSplitScreen
Help		mnuHelp
	Index	mnuHelpIndex
	Topics	mnuHelpTopics
	Contents	mnuHelpContents

In the preceding table, notice how all of the menu items are prefixed with the "mnu" object identifier. Notice also how the name of the top-level menu item follows the identifier—all items contained within the top-level "File" menu item have the top-level name ("File") followed by their own names ("OpenFile," "CloseFile," and so on).

Following these naming conventions for menu items will allow you to tell at a glance where in the menu hierarchy a given menu item is located.

Summary

By adding short mnemonic identifiers to your variable and object names, your programs will be much easier to understand. You will be able to tell at a glance exactly what type of variable or object you are dealing with without having to refer back to where the variable or object was originally defined. By adding a single character to variable names where appropriate to indicate the variable's scope, you'll instantly be able to determine whether the variable was declared as global, module-level, or procedure-level.

This chapter presented suggested mnemonic identifiers for many of the variable and object types available in Visual Basic. You may decide to use these identifiers in your own programs, or you may prefer to create your own list of identifiers. The choice is yours, but you should always be consistent and use the same identifiers again and again.

CHAPTER 45

VB5 Project Types

IN THIS CHAPTER

In early versions of Visual Basic, the programmer was given few options (if any) as to the kind of project that was to be created. You either created standard programs (EXEs, which were actually just pseudocode) or nothing. In the past, VB had one purpose and one purpose only: application development. It's no wonder that VB has had a bad reputation as a "toy" language!

Visual Basic has come a long way, however, and now offers a wealth of options for developers. Of course, the "Standard EXE" option is still available and is the cornerstone of development in VB. But several new project options have been added into the mix. VB programmers can now create ActiveX controls, ActiveX documents, add-ins, and other component and object types. This chapter will introduce you to the many project types that are now available to you as a Visual Basic developer.

Which Project Type Is for You?

When you first start Visual Basic, you are presented with a dialog box that asks you to select a project type (or template) from which to begin working on a new project (see Figure 45.1). You're probably already familiar with the Standard EXE option, but you may be unaware of some of the other project types.

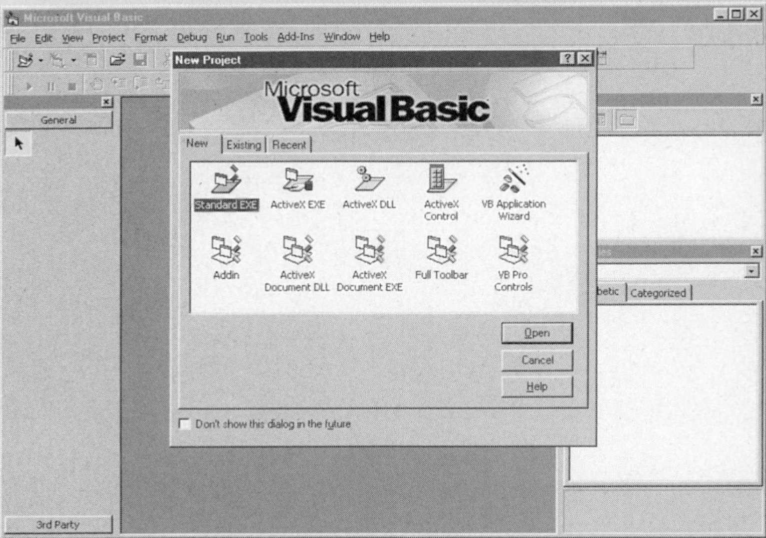

FIGURE 45.1.
When Visual Basic starts, it displays a dialog box that asks you to specify a project type if you are starting a new project.

You can see that a number of the project types deal with ActiveX in some way (ActiveX EXE, ActiveX DLL, and so on). You may know or have an idea about what an ActiveX control is, but what are ActiveX Document DLLs, ActiveX EXEs, and some of the other project types? Let's take a look at them one by one.

Standard EXE

That old stand-by, the Standard EXE project, hasn't changed much since Visual Basic was first conceived. Sure, there are new compiler options, newer and better controls, and a long list of other features that have been introduced in the years since VB's conception, but the concept is still the same. You start with a single VB form and end up with an executable file. Even novice VB programmers have a pretty good idea of what a Standard EXE project is, so we'll move on.

ActiveX EXE

Now we may be getting into unfamiliar territory. The first question that comes to mind is, "What's the difference between a Standard EXE project and an ActiveX EXE?" A good question, and it deserves a good answer.

ActiveX EXEs bear little resemblance to Standard EXEs, and they serve an entirely different purpose. Whereas Standard EXEs are used primarily to create executable applications, ActiveX EXEs are used to create out-of-process components.

In-process components are those that run in the same address space of an application (also called a *client*). In-process components can be thought of as parts of the application itself, even though they may actually exist in a separate file or library. For example, if your Visual Basic program calls a function that exists in a Dynamic Link Library (DLL), that function is linked to your application when the application is executed. It becomes a part of the application (its client) and runs in the same address space; thus it is an in-process component.

Out-of-process components, on the other hand, do not run in the same address space of their client but instead run in their own address space. An application (a client) can use out-of-process components the same way they use in-process components. However, out-of-process components offer an important benefit. Since they run in their own address space, the code for the out-of-process component can execute simultaneously with its client. Therefore, a client can tell an out-of-process component to do something without having to wait for it to finish. When the component's task is done it can notify its client by using *asynchronous notification*, a way of passing messages back to the client.

As mentioned earlier, ActiveX EXEs contain one or more out-of-process components in the form of class modules. You can create reusable components and compile them into an ActiveX EXE and use them in your Visual Basic applications. To create a project type like this, you should be familiar with creating and using class modules as well as how to implement asynchronous notification.

ActiveX DLL

As you might suspect, ActiveX DLLs differ from ActiveX EXEs in that they are in-process components instead of out-of-process components. Like ActiveX EXEs, ActiveX DLLs contain reusable components in the form of class modules. However, they are linked to their client applications when the application is executed and they run in the client's address space.

When a client application asks an in-process component to perform a task, control of the program is given to the component. The client application has to wait until the component is done performing the task before it can continue with its own processing.

ActiveX Control

Of all of the new features incorporated into Visual Basic 5, the capability to create ActiveX controls is probably the most talked about. Microsoft's free VB5 Control Creation Edition revolves around the ActiveX control project.

ActiveX controls (OCX files) are basically the same things as the OLE controls that have existed in Visual Basic for years, though the ActiveX denomination typically indicates that the control is 32-bit. The reusable objects in VB's Toolbox are all ActiveX controls.

By adding the capability to create custom ActiveX controls in VB5, Microsoft has greatly increased the power of Visual Basic. It used to be that you would have to use C++ or some other lower-level language to create such components. Now, it's just about as easy as creating a VB application.

ActiveX control projects are based on the UserControl object, which can act either as a container for other objects (constituent controls) or as a platform for creating unique new controls. By using constituent controls, you can easily assemble a new control from existing components, such as the objects in VB's Toolbox. The other option is to create new ActiveX controls without using any other controls. These are referred to as user-drawn controls because you have to create (draw) the control from scratch. For example, if you were creating a gauge control, it would probably be a user-drawn control because you couldn't assemble it using other existing objects.

Part IV of this book, "Energizing Your Applications with ActiveX," explains the design and creation of ActiveX controls.

VB Application Wizard

The VB Application Wizard is not a project type, but an easy way to create applications (Standard EXEs). By asking you several questions about the features that will be included in your program, the VB Application Wizard can create a skeleton application for you. You'll still have to "fill in the blanks" so to speak, but it alleviates some of the more mundane chores involved with applications programming.

ActiveX Document EXE

Before getting into the uses of this project type, an explanation of ActiveX documents is necessary. Simply said, ActiveX documents are reusable applications.

When you think of documents, you probably think of Microsoft Word files or something similar. And, in some ways, ActiveX documents are like Word documents. In fact, the common analogy for explaining ActiveX documents is to compare them to Word documents.

Word documents can be loaded and viewed by using a *container* application, such as Microsoft Word. Likewise, ActiveX documents can be loaded, viewed, and used within a container application, such as Internet Explorer. What this means is that you can create a completely separate and self-contained application and have it loaded into a Web browser (or some other such container) where it can be used just as if it were a self-running program.

In Visual Basic, the creation of ActiveX documents is based on the UserDocument object. The UserDocument object is very similar to a form; you can place controls on it and add code to it the same way. You can also add forms, class modules, and other objects to an ActiveX document project. When the project is compiled (either as a DLL or an EXE), a `.vbd` (Visual Basic Document) file is created. This is the main file for ActiveX documents created in Visual Basic, and will be the one that is accessed by the document's container application. You'll also need the compiled DLL or EXE file to use the ActiveX document, but the `.vbd` file acts as the starting point, just as a `.vbp` file is used to indicate the components of a VB project so Visual Basic knows what to include when the project is loaded in.

Like ActiveX EXEs, ActiveX documents are out-of-process components. When an ActiveX Document EXE is used in a container application, it runs in its own address space. This can cause some problems. If two instances of Internet Explorer (the container application) are both using the same ActiveX document, only one copy of the ActiveX document is actually loaded into memory (in its own address space). Since there is only one set of global variables for the ActiveX document, one container application may cause the variables to be set in such a way that would affect the other container application using the ActiveX document. Therefore, ActiveX Document DLLs are safer and faster to use.

ActiveX Document DLL

ActiveX Document DLLs are the same as ActiveX Document EXEs except that they run in-process with their client (a container application) instead of out-of-process. Although they can take up more resources than their EXE counterparts if multiple instances of the same ActiveX document are being used by different container applications, ActiveX Document DLLs are safer to use and execute slightly faster than ActiveX Document EXEs.

AddIn

Add-ins are extensions to Visual Basic's IDE (Interactive Development Environment). Microsoft includes several add-ins with Visual Basic itself, including the Visual Data Manager and the Report Designer. You can also purchase add-ins from third-party vendors. Chapter 51, "Third-Party Add-Ins," lists some of the more popular products currently available.

When you choose the AddIn project type, VB provides you with a form (`frmAddIn`), a basic code module (`AddIn.bas`), and a class (`Connect`). You can then use and build on these components to create the add-in.

Summary

Visual Basic 5 offers many more options for developers than simply creating applications. VB programmers can now create ActiveX controls, ActiveX documents, ActiveX component libraries, and even their own add-ins to extend VB's IDE. As Visual Basic evolves, the necessity to look to other development tools is minimized. Visual Basic is fast becoming a "one-stop shop" for developers, and the latest version has made incredible strides towards that end.

CHAPTER

The VB5 Support Files

IN THIS CHAPTER

Although VB5 has made some strides toward making Visual Basic truly standalone, it does fall short of the mark. When the product was initially released, there was some confusion as to whether VB would create standalone executables. Yes, some explained, there is a native code compiler now built in, and that will do it. Unfortunately, that is not the case. The compiler built into VB5 was taken from Microsoft's Visual C++ product, and it does indeed compile into native code rather than the pseudo-code or P-code that experienced Visual Basic programmers are familiar with. In many cases, this makes for faster executables and better code optimization. However, it does not make for standalone programs. Even when Visual Basic programs are compiled into native code, they still require runtime support files.

This chapter will help you sort out which support files are needed for your Visual Basic programs. In addition to listing the runtime files required by every VB program, it also lists the support files needed when various ActiveX components are added to your forms.

Program Support Files

Unfortunately, Visual Basic programs do not compile into completely self-contained executables. Instead, they require runtime files and libraries that must be present on a user's system before the program can be executed.

The good news is that only one runtime file is really specific to Visual Basic programs (`MSVBVM50.DLL`)—the VB5 Virtual Machine file, which contains the code for all the functions and statements built into Visual Basic. Prior versions of Visual Basic had similar files, such as `VBRUN400.DLL`.

The other runtime files are, most likely, already present on the user's system and may have been distributed with Windows. These files include

```
ASYCFILT.DLL
COMCAT.DLL
CTL3D.DLL
OLEAUT32.DLL
OLEPRO32.DLL
STDOLE2.TLB
```

Additional Support Files

If you use ActiveX controls in your program, the user must have the appropriate `.OCX` files registered on her system as well as the support files mentioned in the previous section. Table 46.1 lists the ActiveX controls included in Visual Basic 5 and their corresponding `.OCX` files.

Table 46.1. The ActiveX controls in VB5 and their corresponding .OCX files.

ActiveX Control	.OCX *File*
Animation	COMCT232.OCX
CommonDialog	COMDLG32.OCX
Crystal Reports	CRYSTL32.OCX
DBCombo	DBLIST32.OCX
DBGrid	DBGRID32.OCX
DBList	DBLIST32.OCX
ImageList	DBLIST32.OCX
InternetTransfer	MSINET.OCX
ListView	COMCTL32.OCX
MAPIMessages	MSMAPI32.OCX
MAPISession	MSMAPI32.OCX
MaskEdBox	MSMASK32.OCX
MSChart	MSCHART.OCX
MSComm	MSCOMM32.OCX
MSFlexGrid	MSFLXGRD.OCX
MSTab (SSTab)	TABCTL32.OCX
Multimedia MCI	MCI32.OCX
PictureClip	PICCLP32.OCX
ProgressBar	COMCTL32.OCX
Remote Data Control	MSRDC20.OCX
RichTextBox	RICHTX32.OCX
Slider	COMCTL32.OCX
StatusBar	COMCTL32.OCX
SysInfo	SYSINFO.OCX
TabStrip	COMCTL32.OCX
Toolbar	COMCTL32.OCX
TreeView	COMCTL32.OCX
UpDown	COMCT232.OCX
Winsock	MSWINSCK.OCX

Note that the standard ActiveX controls (TextBox, CommandButton, Label, and so on) are not included in the preceding list. Those controls are contained within the VB Virtual Machine runtime file.

In addition to their `.OCX` file, some of the more complex ActiveX controls require several library files. Crystal Reports requires a number of DLLs, such as

CO2C40EN.DLL	CRPE32.DLL	CRXLAT32.DLL	IMPLODE.DLL
P2BBND.DLL	P2BDAO.DLL	P2CTDAO.DLL	P2IRDAO.DLL
P2SODBC.DLL	PG32.DLL	U2DDISK.DLL	U2DMAPI.DLL
U2FCR.DLL	U2FDIF.DLL	U2FHTML.DLL	U2FREC.DLL
U2FRTF.DLL	U2FSEPV.DLL	U2FTEXT.DLL	U2FWKS.DLL
U2FWORDW.DLL	U2FXLS.DLL		

Programs that use databases may also require additional support files and libraries. The Jet database engine uses the following DLLs:

MSJET35.DLL	MSJTER35.DLL	MSRD2X35.DLL	MSREPL35.DLL
ODBCJI32.DLL	ODBCJT32.DLL	ODBCTL32.DLL	VB5DB.DLL
VBAJET32.DLL			

Other database interfaces, such as Remote Data Objects (RDO), also require additional support files:

ADME.DLL	DTCCM.DLL	DTCTRACE.DLL	DTCUTIL.DLL
MSDTCPRX.DLL	MSRDO20.DLL	RDOCURS.DLL	XOLEHLP.DLL

Summary

Visual Basic programs are never standalone; they always require runtime support files. In addition to the standard runtime files such as `MSVBVM50.DLL`, other files may be necessary. Using ActiveX controls in a program sometimes requires that the `.OCX` files for the controls also be distributed with the program. Other application features such as database access also require their own array of support `.DLL` files. This chapter helps decipher which files are needed and when.

CHAPTER 47

Differences Between the Learning, Professional, and Enterprise Editions

IN THIS CHAPTER

With the latest version of Visual Basic, Microsoft has released a total of four separate editions of the product. Each edition is targeted for a certain type of VB programmer and contains different tools and features. This chapter points out the major differences between the editions of VB5.

The Four Editions of Visual Basic

There are four different editions of Visual Basic 5 available. The Control Creation Edition is free and can be downloaded from Microsoft's Web site. Although it is fully functional in many ways, it should be considered a "demo" because it cannot create compiled applications.

As for the retail versions, the Learning Edition is primarily for beginners. The Professional and Enterprise Editions are for more advanced programmers.

To choose which version is best for you requires some knowledge of the features included in each edition. The following sections list many of the major differences between the four editions of Visual Basic. The prices of the retail products are also given, but you can usually find them discounted through a mail-order house or even your local software store. Students can often get products at a substantial discount through their school, too.

NOTE

For a complete list of the specific features that are available in each edition of Visual Basic, check out the product information sheet available at Microsoft's Web site, `http://www.microsoft.com/vbasic/prodinfo/newinvb5/byedition.htm`.

The Control Creation Edition

For the first time ever, Microsoft has released a free version of Visual Basic. Dubbed the Control Creation Edition, this version was actually available *before* the retail editions could be purchased. It is still available for free download from Microsoft's Web site.

The VB5 Control Creation Edition (or CCE) is useful for one function and one function only: to create ActiveX controls. You cannot create compiled Visual Basic applications with the CCE, not even simple ones. You can, however, create programs that can be run inside of Visual Basic.

The whole impetus behind releasing this free version of VB5 was to garner support for ActiveX technology (and, no doubt, increase the number of Internet Explorer users at the same time). By giving people a free tool with which they could easily create ActiveX controls, the CCE did a fair job of putting ActiveX technology in the spotlight. As of this writing, use of ActiveX controls on the World Wide Web still hasn't really "caught on," but it's likely that they will in the near future.

For those who have never used Visual Basic before, the CCE offers a good look at what VB programming is all about. Creating ActiveX controls is not too different from creating applications, so people can see whether or not visual programming is for them. No doubt many of the people who started out with the CCE later purchased one of the retail editions of Visual Basic.

The Learning Edition

Suggested Retail Price: $99.95

Targeted primarily at students and hobbyists, the Learning Edition of Visual Basic 5 offers a full-featured development environment with a low price tag.

The Learning Edition uses the same Integrated Development Environment (IDE) as the more advanced versions of Visual Basic. It does lack in other areas, however. For example, a limited number of controls are available in the Learning Edition's toolbox. Also, this edition of VB does not support add-ins.

The `Data` control is included, so Access databases can be utilized. But more advanced database options like ODBC are missing.

The code compiler that drives the Learning Edition is not as sophisticated as the one used in the Professional and Enterprise Editions. It cannot compile into native code, only p-code.

The project types in the Learning Edition are also somewhat limited. ActiveX document and ActiveX Server component project types are not available in this edition of Visual Basic.

Because the Learning Edition is targeted at beginning programmers, it includes something the other editions of VB don't: the *Learn Visual Basic Now* CD-ROM. It provides interactive lessons that allow novices to learn at their own pace.

The Professional Edition

Suggested Retail Prices: $499.00 Full version, $249.00 Upgrade version

Many of those who make their living developing Visual Basic applications will choose the Professional Edition. Moderately priced, it is the absolute minimum for serious development.

The Professional Edition takes over where the Learning Edition left off. It adds more controls (`FlexGrid`, `DBGrid`, `MSChart`, `MSComm`, and eight others), more project types (including ActiveX documents and ActiveX Server components), and more wizards.

This edition of Visual Basic also supports add-ins, and includes the Visual Basic Wizard Manager. The Microsoft Repository is also included. It provides a standard way of describing software tools, like objects.

The Enterprise Edition

Suggested Retail Prices: $1,199.00 Full version, $699.00 Upgrade version

Professional programmers who develop advanced client/server applications are the most likely to use the Enterprise Edition of VB5. Because the Enterprise Edition comes with Microsoft's SourceSafe utility, this version will also appeal to those who are involved in group projects where more than one programmer is involved.

The Enterprise Edition also adds other features and tools, such as the Microsoft Transaction Server, Remote Data Objects (RDO), the T-SQL Debugger, the Developer Edition of Microsoft SQL Server, the Application Performance Explorer, and Microsoft Visual Database Tools.

Summary

The four editions of Visual Basic (Control Creation, Learning, Professional, and Enterprise) are very different in the features that they include. Before purchasing (or upgrading to) a new edition, you should be sure that it has the functionality that you desire. This chapter lists many of the differences between the four versions so you can determine which one is for you.

CHAPTER 48

Comparing VB with Other Development Environments

IN THIS CHAPTER

With every new version, Visual Basic becomes more powerful and can be used in more ways. For example, the creation of ActiveX controls and ActiveX documents was not supported in the previous version of VB.

Unfortunately, Visual Basic still has limitations. There are simply things that it cannot do, or at least cannot do efficiently. When that is the case, another development environment needs to be considered.

This chapter points out some of the differences between Visual Basic and other development environments, such as Microsoft's Visual C++ and Visual J++. It will help you determine when a switch to another programming language is warranted, and why.

Also discussed are some of VB's competitors, including Borland's Delphi and Powersoft's PowerBuilder. You'll learn a little more about these development environments and how they compare to Visual Basic.

Alternative Development Environments

Dozens of development environments are available to programmers, but those in the Microsoft Visual Studio family are by far the most popular. Therefore, Visual Basic will be briefly compared here to two of the products in that family, Visual C++ and Visual J++. Each has its particular strengths and weaknesses. Although you should always carefully consider which language is right for whatever project you need done, this section will give you a general idea of when a language other than Visual Basic may be necessary.

Microsoft Visual C++

When it comes to flexibility, C++ is without a doubt the king of all development languages. You would be hard pressed to come up with a program or component that can't be implemented using C++. However, all this flexibility comes at a price. C++ is difficult to use and requires an investment in learning a complex language.

Some things that you might need C++ for include cross-platform development and support for OLE DB databases. The capability to write function libraries (DLLs) and tight, fast ActiveX controls (without the overhead of VB5 ActiveX controls) are also some of C++'s strong points.

Visual C++ is almost always the target for newly introduced technology. For example, the TAPI (Telephony Application Programmer Interface) library of functions does not lend itself well to Visual Basic. Instead, it is best implemented in Visual C++.

Visual C++, the most popular implementation of C++ on the Windows platform, does not offer the same kinds of high-level application building tools present in Visual Basic. Forms cannot be created and populated with controls nearly as quickly as they can in Visual Basic. It's safe to say that a moderate programmer may take twice the amount of time to create an application in Visual C++ as he would in Visual Basic.

As a language, C++ is based on the principles of object-oriented programming. Although Visual Basic uses objects and supports some of the tenets of object-oriented design, it cannot be called a true OOP language. For the total OOP package, Visual C++ (or Visual J++, which is discussed next) are better choices.

The gap between Visual Basic and Visual C++ is always narrowing. As Visual Basic gets more powerful, there are fewer reasons for using Visual C++ for development. However, if the capability to create programs and components without much overhead is a requirement for a project, Visual C++ is definitely the way to go.

Microsoft Visual J++

Java has become a popular language in the last few years as the Internet has also risen in popularity. Java's main strength is its capability to create binary code that can be immediately ported to any platform that supports the Java Virtual Machine (JVM) runtime environment. This means that a compiled Java program written using Visual J++ will work on many different platforms.

As a language, Java is somewhat easy to understand and use but not nearly as easy as Visual Basic. It is also far more limited than VB and does not support SQL Server or embedded OCXes (due to portability issues). Data access support is also limited with Java.

Microsoft's Visual J++, on the other hand, extends the capabilities of the Java language in several ways. It adds support for ActiveX controls and databases.`However, this added flexibility may prevent some Visual J++ applets from running on certain platforms, and the extra functionality has to be weighed with the issue of portability.

Like C++, Java produces fast and tight executable code. Visual J++'s JIT compiler comes close to matching the speed of Visual C++'s native code compiler.

When developing small applications for implementation on many different platforms, Visual J++ may well be the tool of choice. The popularity of Java suggests that it will probably be around for a while, though only time will tell whether Java lives up to its reputation as a viable cross-platform development tool.

Competing Products

Visual Basic is the undisputed leader when it comes to GUI-based development environments. However, it does have some competitors. Each has its strong points and cannot be ignored as viable alternatives to programming VB.

Borland's Delphi and Powersoft's PowerBuilder are two such competing products. These are the underdogs, and as such it is unlikely that they will ever enjoy the incredible popularity that Visual Basic has seen. As more people climb on the VB bandwagon, it makes it more difficult for these products to compete. People like to stay with a winner, and that goes double for programmers. After all, investing years in refining skills in a certain programming language is serious stuff. VB developers can be reasonably secure in their choice of expertise. But those who adopt products that are out of the mainstream need to consider the fact that their skills may not be as viable if the product loses favor or is no longer supported.

Borland Delphi

Borland's Delphi has been competing with Visual Basic for years, and many heated arguments have occurred between VB and Delphi programmers who insist that their development environment of choice is better than the other. In many ways, they are both right.

The biggest problems with Delphi are that it always seems to be one step behind Visual Basic, and that it does not have nearly the industry support that VB enjoys. It shares much of the same flexibility as VB and even offers some options over and above those provided by Visual Basic. For example, Delphi not only supports the use of ActiveX controls, it also supports its own proprietary format (VCL components).

So why aren't we all using Delphi rather than Visual Basic? That's a good question, though not easily answered. It's true that Delphi has many perks over VB, such as its capability to produce full-featured programs with a minimal amount of code. But going up against a giant like Microsoft is never easy, and Delphi has struggled to gain user support in the face of Visual Basic.

The current version of Delphi (version 3) has made some big strides in increasing the functionality of Delphi as an easy-to-use development environment. For example, ActiveX controls and ActiveForm objects can now be created in Delphi. Also, several wizards have been added that make code generation easier.

Delphi is, and has always been, the closest competitor to Visual Basic. But its use of proprietary technologies make it a tough choice for developers who like to stay in the mainstream.

Powersoft PowerBuilder

Although it has been around for several years, PowerBuilder recently has enjoyed a surge in popularity. Its impressive database and cross-platform support has made it an enticing development environment for creating complex client/server applications.

PowerBuilder's DataWindow is the star of the show and is more flexible and easier to use than the data access methods available in Visual Basic. However, this may change as newer versions of the ActiveX Data Objects (ADO) library become available for VB.

Current versions of PowerBuilder are also supported on platforms other than 32-bit Windows, unlike VB5. PowerBuilder is available for Windows, Mac, and UNIX platforms.

Some of the major weakness of PowerBuilder are the speed of the code it produces and its limited adoption by developers. Visual Basic excels in the speed of its compiled code and also edges out PowerBuilder when it comes to ease of development.

Summary

Visual Basic is a great development environment, and perhaps it is the best. But it still has limitations. This chapter explored some of the options available to VB programmers who are thinking about using other development environments, be they different languages or competing products. The chapter discussed the particular strengths and weaknesses of four different products, two from Microsoft and two from other vendors.

CHAPTER 49

Hidden Tools: The VB5 CD

IN THIS CHAPTER

You may not know it, but quite a few development tools, utilities, and sample projects are included on the Visual Basic 5 CD-ROM. Because many are unsupported by Microsoft, they are not automatically installed with Visual Basic. In fact, Microsoft makes no mention of them in the VB5 documentation or in the online Help system. They're hidden on the CD, just waiting for an enterprising programmer to happen on them and take them for a spin. You may find some so handy that you'll wonder what you did without them!

This chapter describes some of the more interesting but largely unknown goodies included on the VB5 CD. This is not meant to be an in-depth guide that details how to fully use the various utilities. Instead, it should be considered a starting point that will make you aware of what is available. If something sounds interesting, by all means try it out. You might just find a new tool that will greatly ease your VB development efforts.

Tools

The VB5 CD-ROM contains a wide array of extra tools and utilities. Some of these tools are simple; others are much more sophisticated. All are worth mentioning, and you should definitely take a closer look at any of them that sound like they might help you.

Component Registration Utilities

Location: `\TOOLS\REGUTILS`

The three registration utilities contained in this directory (REGSVR32, REGOCX32, and REGIT) are used to add in-process server components (DLLs and OCXs) to the System Registry. REGSVR32 can also be used to unregister server components from the Registry.

REGSVR32 is a Windows utility that both registers and unregisters in-process ActiveX server components in the System Registry. To register a server, use the following syntax:

```
RegSvr32 servername
```

The *servername* argument specifies the name of the server component to be registered and should be an ActiveX `.DLL` or `.OCX` file. To unregister a component, use the `/u` switch:

```
RegSvr32 /u servername
```

The REGOCX32 utility provides the same server registration function as REGSVR32 but is used primarily by Setup programs because it does not provide any dialog boxes. It is used just like the REGSVR32 utility:

```
RegOCX32 servername
```

The command-line REGIT utility also registers in-process servers and can accept wildcards, so multiple server components can be registered at one time. The syntax for REGIT is

```
REGIT servername
```

If you want to register all the .DLL files in a directory, you can use a wildcard, such as

```
REGIT *.dll
```

Help Workshop

Location: \TOOLS\HCW

Help Workshop is a program that can be used to assist in the process of creating Help files. It also allows you to edit content files for your Help system's Contents page and Help project files. Finally, it features a compiler that ties together all the components of a Help system into a single .HLP file that can be distributed with an application.

Chapter CD2, "Giving Your Users Help," explains how to use the Help Workshop program. That chapter also discusses how Help systems work.

ID Generators

Location: \TOOLS\IDGEN

This directory contains two simple utilities, GUIDGEN and UUIDGEN. Both are used to generate 128-bit globally unique identifiers (GUIDs) that can be used as class identifiers (CLSIDs) or interface identifiers (IIDs).

The GUIDGEN utility creates a random GUID that can be copied to the Clipboard in any of four different formats, most of which will appeal primarily to C programmers. However, the Registry format can be used by VB programmers when adding new ActiveX controls to the System Registry or a Web page.

The UUIDGEN utility creates system-unique GUIDs. Options include the capability to generate the GUID in Interface Description Language (IDL) format or in a C struct format.

ImageEdit

Location: \TOOLS\IMAGEDIT

ImageEdit is a no-frills image editor that can be used for creating and editing icons, bitmaps, and cursors for use in Visual Basic. It only supports images up to 256 by 256 pixels and bitmaps that use 16 colors or less. As you can imagine, ImageEdit's use is limited, but it is handy as a simple image-manipulation tool when designing simple graphics elements such as cursors and icons.

License Package Authoring Tool

Location: \TOOLS\LPK_TOOL

When you implement ActiveX controls on Web pages, you often have to include the appropriate licenses for those controls before they can be used. The License Package Authoring Tool allows you to bundle together all the licenses necessary for the ActiveX controls used on a single HTML page into an .LPK file. The .LPK file can be downloaded along with the ActiveX controls.

Chapter CD3, "License Packaging Authoring Tool," discusses how to use this utility. There is also a `README.TXT` file in this directory that provides a brief explanation of how to use the License Package Authoring Tool.

Migration Wizard

Location: `\TOOLS\UNSUPPRT\MIGRWIZ`

The Migration Wizard is actually a third-party VB4 product that seems to have been updated at the last minute to support Visual Basic 5. Created by Crescent Software, the actual name of this utility is "Upgrade Wizard," but it is referred to as the Migration Wizard.

The wizard's function is straightforward. Given the project name (`.MAK` or `.VBP`) of a 16-bit program, it scans the code looking for `Declare` and `Call` statements to Windows API and third-party functions. When found, it will either make any necessary changes to update the code for VB5 use or add a `TODO:` comment that explains what needs to be done to update the code. Although not overwhelming in its complexity, the Migration Wizard can save you some time when updating 16-bit programs to work with VB5, especially if the programs are large or have many function calls.

To use the Migration Wizard, you need to copy the contents of the CD directory to a hard drive and then run the `CSWIZ32.EXE` program. The wizard provides step-by-step instructions, so using it is a snap.

ODBC Spy

Location: `\TOOLS\ODBCSPY`

When accessing remote databases using ODBC drivers, it is often difficult to track down the cause of problems. The ODBC Spy utility can assist in the development process by logging all the ODBC API calls produced by your VB application. The log can be written to the screen or to a file, and generally provides more information than logs produced by the ODBC driver manager.

A `README.TXT` file in this directory explains how to install ODBC Spy on Windows 95 and Windows NT systems. The ODBC Spy utility is also discussed in Chapter 29, "ODBC Fundamentals."

OLE Messaging

Location: `\TOOLS\OLEMSG`

This directory contains information about the OLE Messaging library. A Help file (`OLEMSG2.HLP`) provides the documentation, and an Excel spreadsheet (`OLEMSG.XLS`) contains all the sample source code in the Help file. Using a spreadsheet to hold source code is a little strange, but it does work.

Also included here is a complete OLE Messaging sample application called TIMECARD that is written in Visual Basic. The project is stored in the `TIMECARD.CLI` subdirectory.

OLE Tools

Location: `\TOOLS\OLETOOLS`

This directory contains five tools geared towards working with OLE applications. Most of them require that MFC version 4.2 be installed on your system before they will run properly. Table 49.1 describes the OLE tools found here.

Table 49.1. The OLE tools included on the Visual Basic 5 CD-ROM.

Program Name	*Description*
DFVIEW	DocFile Viewer—Displays the contents of an OLE DocFile.
DOBJVIEW	Data Object Viewer—Displays objects that support the IDataObject interface.
IROTVIEW	Running Object Table Viewer—Displays the contents of OLE's running object table.
OLE2VW32	OLE 2.0 Object Viewer—Shows you what is happening with OLE objects on your system.
OLEVIEW	Another OLE 2.0 object viewer, this one shows objects in a hierarchy format.

Process Viewer

Location: `\TOOLS\PVIEW`

Process Viewer is a simple application that shows all the processes currently running on a system and some information about them. Process ID, base priority, number of threads, type (16-bit/32-bit), and the full pathname of the process are all shown.

Click on a process name, and you'll see its Thread ID (TID), Owning Process ID (PID), and thread priority. You can also kill a process after it has been selected.

There are two versions of this utility. `PVIEW.EXE` runs under Windows NT, and `PVIEW95.EXE` runs under Windows 95.

PSpy

Location: `\TOOLS\PSPY`

PSpy is a tool for determining just exactly what is going on with a running process. It shows you all the DLLs that the process is using and where they are loaded from. It also provides information on the Working Set of the process.

The Working Set is the physical RAM being used by a program. Because the Windows virtual memory manager automatically pages out the memory given to a program when it is not in use, it can be helpful to see exactly what memory a process is using.

If desired, a process's Working Set can be "flushed" by PSpy, which assigns the process no physical memory whatsoever. The process can run with no memory as long as it is idle. After some operation is performed, however, the memory manager will automatically provide it with any necessary physical memory space. By flushing a Working Set and then performing an operation, you can use PSpy to tell how much memory that operation requires.

Resource Compiler

Location: `\TOOLS\RESOURCE`

The Resource Compiler (RC) is used to create `.RES` files that contain program resources such as strings and bitmaps. Among other things, resource files are useful when building applications that support multiple languages, such as English and Spanish. With the strings stored in resource files instead of hard-coded into the program, only one version of the application needs to be maintained.

Chapter CD6, "Creating Resources Using the Resource Compiler," discusses how to use this utility in more detail.

Spy++

Location: `\TOOLS\SPY`

Spy++ (`SPYXX.EXE`) provides you with a graphical view of all the processes, threads, windows, and window messages on a system at any given time. This gives you the most complete picture of what's going on in Windows, right down to the slightest details.

Displaying information on processes and threads is handy, but other utilities like PSpy and Process Viewer give you just about the same thing. Spy++'s strengths lie in the way it provides data on windows and window messages.

Spy++ gives extensive information on all open windows, right down to the window's styles and extended styles it uses. You can also select specific windows to spy on by dragging Spy++'s Finder tool onto a window.

Using Spy++ to view the messages generated by Windows is interesting. You can choose to have the messages displayed in a list box, spooled out to a log file, or both. You can specify that only the message types that you want are shown or choose certain message groups.

Spy++ is a useful utility, but only hard-core programmers will really be able to exploit its power. However, even novices may find it interesting to use Spy++ to see what is going on inside Windows.

Template Manager

Location: `\TOOLS\UNSUPPRT\TMPLMGR`

The Template Manager is a VB add-in that allows you to easily import predefined control sets and menus into your Visual Basic projects. This add-in is discussed in more detail in Chapter 11, "Reusing and Sharing Components Using the Template Manager."

A newer version of the Template Manager can be downloaded for free from the Visual Basic Owner's Area of Microsoft's Web site. The URL is `http://www.microsoft.com/vbasic/owners/`.

VB Code Profiler

Location: `\TOOLS\UNSUPPRT\VBCP`

The VB Code Profiler is a VB add-in that is used to provide statistics about the way an application runs, which can be used to determine the areas where it can stand to be optimized or improved. Using it is simple.

After you load in a project, you bring up the Code Profiler window from VB's Add-Ins menu. Next, add Profiler code to your project, which Code Profiler does with a click of a button (it can also remove the code just as easily). After the code is in place, the program should be executed and put through its paces. The Profiler will gather data and statistics while the program is being used. Four profile options are available: Line Timing, Function Timing, Line Hit Count, and Function Hit Count. The option you choose will determine the kinds of statistics that the Code Profiler generates. When the program ends, you can call up the Profiler again and ask it to show you the results.

To install the Code Profiler, see the instructions in the `README.TXT` file that can be found in this directory.

Working Set Viewer

Location: `\TOOLS\UNSUPPRT\WSVIEW`

The Working Set Viewer allows you to view the Working Sets used by currently running processes. It allows you more control over the display and handling of Working Sets than the PSpy utility discussed earlier.

Source Code

Although a number of sample projects can be installed right along with Visual Basic, several more are hidden in other areas of the VB5 CD. These include two ActiveX control projects, a screen saver project, a Web browser project, and samples of using the Microsoft Repository. For the most part, these sample projects have been labeled "unsupported" and are included on the CD as extra educational materials.

By taking a close look at some of the unsupported sample projects, you can get a good idea of how VB5's more advanced features are actually implemented. For example, the HTTP Explorer will show you how a simple Web browser can be created in Visual Basic. You can in turn use some of the techniques you find in the sample project's source code and use them in your own programs.

This section describes some of the sample projects that can be found on the VB5 CD. It does not include the projects that can be installed during the Visual Basic installation process.

Calendar Control Project

Location: `\TOOLS\UNSUPPRT\CALENDAR`

This project centers around an ActiveX control called Calendar. As can be expected, the control displays a month in standard calendar format. It has built-in controls so that a specific month or year can be entered, as well as buttons that let the user flip to the next or previous month.

The control uses custom property pages, resource files, and class modules, so it's an excellent project for anyone interested in seeing how a sophisticated ActiveX control works. A test form is also included that allows several control properties to be set at runtime. The test form also shows any events triggered for the control.

HTTP Explorer Project

Location: `\TOOLS\UNSUPPRT\HTTPEXPL`

HTTP Explorer is a simple Web browser. Basically, it allows the user to specify the URL of an HTML page and then displays the page. There's really not much more to it than that, but it can be useful to anyone designing a program that needs to view Web pages.

IconHandler Project

Location: `\TOOLS\UNSUPPRT\IHANDLER`

IconHandler is an in-process ActiveX Server (DLL) that can be used to return the name of the file that contains the icon for an object when given the object's GUID. The Server is implemented as a simple class module. A test program is also included so that you can see how the Server is actually used after it has been compiled into a DLL.

Repository Sample Projects

Location: `\TOOLS\REPOSTRY`

This directory contains two Visual Basic projects that demonstrate how to write code that uses the repository. The first project, Browser, uses the repository to display VB5 project information. The second project, FileSys, shows how to customize the repository to support objects defined by the programmer. The `README.WRI` file that can be found in this directory provides more information about the sample projects.

Screen Saver Project

Location: `\TOOLS\UNSUPPRT\SSAVER`

This project illustrates how a screen saver can be created using Visual Basic. When executed, it displays floating animated graphics or *sprites*. A setup form is also included in the screen saver so that the sprite animation rate, size, speed, and number can be specified by the user.

SysTray Control Project

Location: `\TOOLS\UNSUPPRT\SYSTRAY`

SysTray is another ActiveX control created using Visual Basic. When placed on a form, it allows an icon to be placed in the Windows system tray. There's not much to this project, but it does provide another example of how ActiveX controls can be implemented in VB. Note that there is no premade test form, so you'll have to either compile SysTray or use multiple projects within Visual Basic to see how the control works.

Updates and Service Packs

Microsoft has included several product updates and Service Packs on the Visual Basic 5 CD. Unless they are applied, you may have difficulty getting certain aspects of VB5 to work properly. For example, if you do not have version 4.2 of the Microsoft Foundation Class library installed on your system, you may receive error messages when you try to use some of VB's ActiveX controls. Luckily, an updated version of the MFC library is included on the Visual Basic CD, so you don't have to go hunting for it on the Internet.

DCOM for Windows 95 and Service Packs for Windows NT 3.51 and Windows NT 4.0 are also included on the CD. Of course, you don't have to install any of them if you don't want to, but it's always wise to have the most current version of any piece of software, especially when it comes to operating systems.

DCOM For Windows 95

Location: `\TOOLS\DCOM95`

This patch adds Distributed COM (DCOM) support to Windows 95 systems. For more information on DCOM, see Microsoft's OLE Development Web site, `http://www.microsoft.com/oledev`.

MFC 4.2

Location: `\TOOLS\MFC42`

According to the `README.TXT` file found in this directory, some tools on the VB5 CD require MFC (Microsoft Foundation Class) 4.2. If you don't already have MFC 4.2 installed on your system, you may receive error messages such as

```
A required DLL file, MFC42.DLL, was not found.
```

If that is the case, you'll have to copy the `.DLL` files in this directory to your Windows `SYSTEM` directory.

NT 3.51 Service Pack 5

Location: `\TOOLS\NT351SP5.A`

If you are running Windows NT 3.51, you may want to apply this Service Pack. Only the Intel version of the Service Pack is included on the VB5 CD, so you'll have to download a different version from the Internet if you are running Windows NT 3.51 on a MIPS, Alpha, or PowerPC system.

NT 4.0 Service Pack 2

Location: `\TOOLS\NT40.SP2`

This Service Pack is for those running Windows NT 4.0. Again, only the Intel version is included on the CD, so if you are using a different development platform, you will have to download the appropriate Service Pack version from the Internet. Also, this Service Pack is now outdated. You should download Service Pack 3 from Microsoft's Web site.

Miscellaneous

The VB5 CD contains miscellaneous other items that are of value. These include a demo of Microsoft's *Mastering* series of training software, compressed CABs for VB support files, a version of Internet Explorer, international versions of the Setup Wizard, and additional Visual Basic documentation.

Component CABs

Location: `\TOOLS\CABINETS`

If you will be using ActiveX controls on a Web page, you may also find it necessary to distribute support files. In most cases, you would point to Microsoft's Web site for these support files because you would then be assured that the newest versions of the files would be installed. However, if you are implementing the controls over an intranet, you may want to have the support files downloaded from your own server.

This directory contains all of VB's support files, including the `MSVBVM50.DLL` library required when using any VB-created ActiveX controls. Each ActiveX control included with Visual Basic has its own compressed `.CAB` file, which includes all the support files (DLLs and OCXs) needed for that particular control.

Component Objects and Companion Products Catalog

Location: `\TOOLS\CATALOG`

This is an HTML version of Microsoft's Visual Basic Companion Products catalog, which lists many third-party controls and add-ins available for VB. Of course, the catalog is now seriously outdated and should not be relied on for accurate product information.

If you want to view the catalog anyway, you'll have to use a Web browser such as Internet Explorer or Netscape Navigator. There is an `INDEX.HTM` file in this directory that should be used as a starting point, and all other pages in the catalog can be accessed directly or indirectly from there.

Internet Explorer

Location: `\TOOLS\MSIE`

Microsoft's Internet Explorer 3.01 has been included on the VB5 CD, but it is already outdated. If you need a Web browser for viewing documents on the Internet, upgrading to a newer version is recommended. IE4 is now widely available for free download and for purchase. Those still using IE3 should download Internet Explorer 3.02 from Microsoft's Web site.

If all you want is a container application in which to test your VB5-created ActiveX controls, this version of Internet Explorer will do just fine. However, note that this version does not run on systems using Windows NT 3.51.

Mastering Series Training Sampler

Location: `\TOOLS\MSD`

This is a demo of Microsoft's *Mastering* series of products. It shows samples of six titles in the series: *Mastering Visual Basic 4.0*, *Mastering Access Programming*, *Mastering Visual C++*, *Mastering Exchange Development*, *Mastering Internet Development*, and *Mastering Microsoft Office Development*. An overview, a sample chapter, and sample lab exercises are provided for each title. Most of these titles are outdated, but you will get an idea of how the *Mastering* programs work so that you can see whether they're right for you.

The Sampler will run directly from the CD without having to be installed first. Simply run the `MSD.EXE` program that can be found in this directory. If you want to install the Sampler to your hard drive, run the `SETUP.EXE` program.

MCIWindX Documentation

Location: `\TOOLS\UNSUPPRT\MCIWINDX`

This directory contains a single Word document that details how to use the MCIWindX ActiveX control. The MCIWindX control is a wrapper around Windows' MCIWnd multimedia window class.

Setup Toolkit

Location: \TOOLS\STOOLKIT

If you're going to distribute your applications in countries where English is not the primary language, you may want to use different versions of the Setup program. This directory contains several Setup programs that use languages other than English, including Chinese, German, Japanese, and Korean. To use them, simply replace the SETUP.EXE file used with the Application Setup Wizard with the appropriate language version.

VB4 Controls

Location: \TOOLS\CONTROLS

Several ActiveX controls shipped with the Professional and Enterprise Editions of VB4 but are not included with VB5: ANIBTN32.OCX, GAUGE32.OCX, GRAPH32.OCX, GRID32.OCX, KEYSTA32.OCX, MSOUTL32.OCX, SPIN32.OCX, and THREED32.OCX. To maintain backward compatibility with VB4, these controls are included on the VB5 CD. However, they are not installed with Visual Basic 5.

If you already have VB4 on your system, you should already have these controls installed. However, if you find yourself having to work on a program created in VB4 that uses one of these controls, you'll have to install the control manually using the RegSvr32 and RegEdit utilities. See the README.TXT file in this directory for more information.

VB5 Documentation

Location: \TOOLS\DOCS

Quite a bit of documentation is included on the VB5 CD, including complete books such as the *VB5 Programmer's Guide*. All documentation is in Microsoft Word format and separated chapter by chapter.

The manuals that can be found on the CD include: *Guide To Building Client/Server Applications with Visual Basic*, *Component Tools Guide*, *Guide To Data Access Objects*, and the aforementioned *VB5 Programmer's Guide*. There is also a complete manual for using Crystal Reports, as well as documents that explain component downloading via the Internet and how to develop DLLs for use with Visual Basic.

Summary

Although the VB5 CD-ROM contains a wealth of helpful tools and utilities as well as other interesting items, many programmers don't even know about them. This chapter described some of the more useful tools that can be found on the CD.

CHAPTER

Third-Party Controls

IN THIS CHAPTER

Although Visual Basic comes with a decent selection of ActiveX controls in its Toolbox, it can't possibly cover all the bases. Sometimes you need a control that does something out of the ordinary. Or you may want to stray from the standard VB tools to create applications that really stand out. No matter what kind of functionality you're looking for, there's probably a third-party control that provides it.

The number of third-party controls now available is staggering. There are literally thousands of them. Some cost only a few dollars, whereas others are in the four- and five-figure range. It all depends on the kinds of features they provide.

The controls listed in this chapter are, for the most part, not too expensive and are in the range of the professional developer. Although the retail price for each product is listed, it's always a good idea to visit the company's Web site to see whether the price has changed and to obtain more information about the product you are interested in. Many companies also offer free evaluation versions of their products, which can be downloaded from their Web sites.

Many products listed here either come with both 32-bit and 16-bit versions of their controls, or have 16-bit versions available separately. If you are still using VB3 or VB4 for development, contact the vendors of the products you are interested in for more information.

The descriptions provided with each product are not designed to be reviews. Instead, they are meant to provide you with a brief overview of the product so that you can decide whether it is right for you. Again, it's always wise to check the company's Web site for more information in case the products contain features that have been mistakenly or purposely omitted here.

General-Purpose Controls

The controls described in this section are mostly control "suites" that include a variety of different controls. Many are designed for everyday use, and, once purchased, will be standard additions to your VB Toolbox.

Active CheckList

Component Café
P.O. Box 542269
Houston, TX 77254

Sales:	(800) 780-7645 or (714) 360-1773
Email:	`sales@componentcafe.com`
Web Site:	`http://www.componentcafe.com/`

Retail Price: $99.00

Component Café's Active CheckList actually includes three controls: Active CheckList, Active Button, and Active Spinner. All three are enhanced versions of controls included with Visual Basic. As can be expected, they provide more flexibility than their VB counterparts.

Active Button is a CommandButton-type control that lets you choose from eight different "button down" effects. It also allows more control over the button's appearance, with options for bevel, shadow, and border width; caption alignment; and the capability to add images.

Active Spinner is similar to VB's Spin control. However, it provides more flexibility in controlling its appearance than Spin.

Active CheckList (see Figure 50.1) is a ListBox-type control that can include check boxes for each item in the list. You often see this kind of control in setup programs, where you can select or deselect items in a scrolling list box. Of the three controls included in this product, I found Active CheckList to be the most interesting.

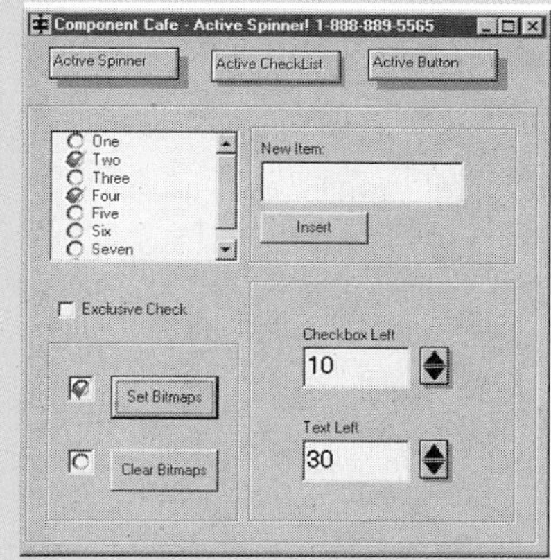

FIGURE 50.1.
The Active CheckList control, which is a combination of VB's CheckBox and ListBox controls. The Active Button and Active Spinner controls are also used in this sample program.

ActiveListBar

Sheridan Software Systems, Inc.
35 Pinelawn Road, Suite 206E
Melville, NY 11747

Sales:	(800) 823-4732 or (516) 753-0985
Tech Support:	(516) 753-0985
Fax:	(516) 753-3661
Email:	`sales@shersoft.com`
Web Site:	`http://www.shersoft.com/`

Retail Price: $139.00

Basically, ActiveListBar is a variation of Visual Basic's ListView control (see Figure 50.2). It allows you to present a list of several items, each with an accompanying graphic image. Items can be organized into groups, with the names of the groups being displayed as separate buttons within the ActiveListBar control. When the user clicks on the button for another group, it "slides" into place and the items in that group are displayed in the ActiveListBar control.

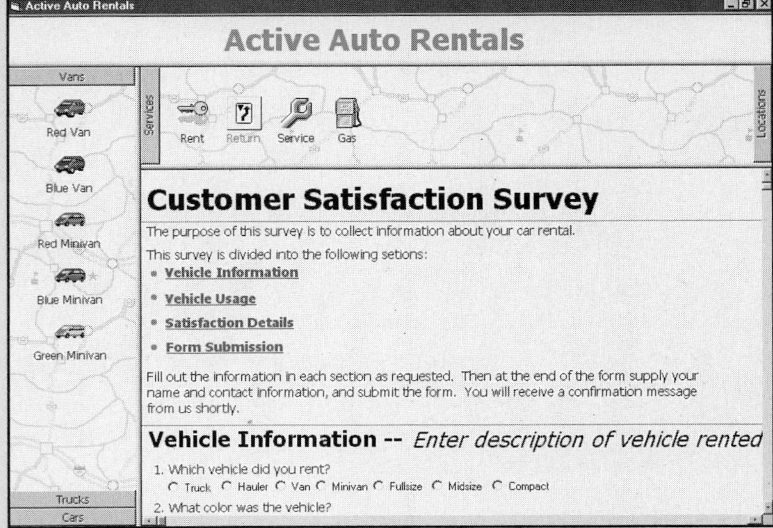

FIGURE 50.2.
In this application, two of Sheridan's ActiveListBar controls are used. One is displayed horizontally and one is displayed vertically.

Some of the ActiveListBar control's more noticeable features include:

The control (and the items it contains) can be displayed horizontally or vertically.

You don't need to use an ImageList control in conjunction with the ActiveListBar control. You can specify the images an ActiveListBar control will use via its property pages. Images can be exported to PNG-compressed files directly from the ActiveListBar control's property page.

When using the control on a Web page, the images are transferred asynchronously. Therefore, the application can start running without having to wait for the graphics to be downloaded.

You can easily add sound effects when events are triggered using the control's `PlaySoundFile` method. Sound files are also transferred asynchronously when the control is used on a Web page.

You can specify background graphics for the control. In fact, you can use different background graphics for separate groups within the same ActiveListBar control.

Items in an ActiveListBar control have their borders highlighted when the mouse cursor is moved over them.

ActiveThreed

Sheridan Software Systems, Inc.

35 Pinelawn Road, Suite 206E

Melville, NY 11747

Sales: (800) 823-4732 or (516) 753-0985

Tech Support: (516) 753-0985

Fax: (516) 753-3661

Email: `sales@shersoft.com`

Web Site: `http://www.shersoft.com/`

Retail Price: $139.00

Sheridan's ActiveThreed (see Figure 50.3) is a collection of seven 3D-style controls designed to replace the 3D controls included with Visual Basic. Actually, four of the controls (SSCheck, SSCommand, SSFrame, and SSOption) can be considered replacements; the other three controls (SSPanel, SSRibbon, and SSSplitter) are new. With the exception of the SSSplitter control, all the controls in this package add the following new features:

- Sound effects (via the `PlaySoundFile` method)
- Animated backgrounds, which can be easily assembled by adding bitmaps via the control's custom property pages
- Multiline captions
- Marquee-style captions, with the capability to have text scroll, slide, bounce, and blink
- OLE DragDrop support

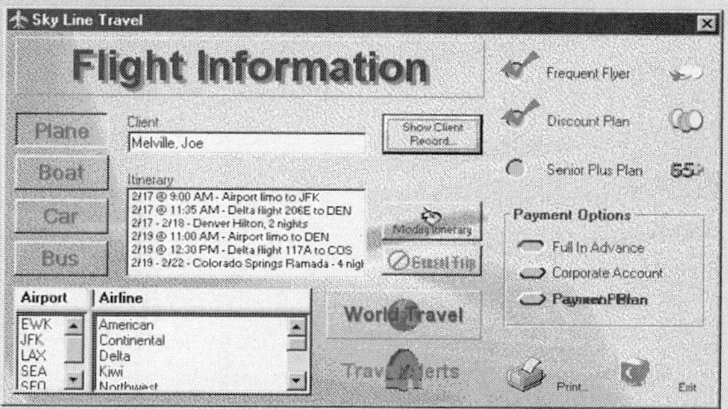

FIGURE 50.3.
A sample application created with several of the controls included in Sheridan's ActiveThreed package.

The SSPanel control is a container control, similar to a frame, that appears to be raised. You can group other controls onto an SSPanel for a nice 3D effect. You can also use a background image for the control and have it automatically resized to fit.

The SSRibbon control is a pushbutton that acts similar to an OptionButton control. By grouping together multiple SSRibbon controls, you can create a toolbar where the user can select one or more options. You can also add animated image sequences to an SSRibbon control both for its selected and unselected states.

The SSSplitter control displays multiple resizable frames similar to the frames sometimes used on Web pages. The panes of the SSSplitter control can be adjusted at design time and at runtime, and each pane contains a separate child control.

ActiveTreeView

Sheridan Software Systems, Inc.
35 Pinelawn Road, Suite 206E
Melville, NY 11747

Sales:	(800) 823-4732 or (516) 753-0985
Tech Support:	(516) 753-0985
Fax:	(516) 753-3661
Email:	`sales@shersoft.com`
Web Site:	`http://www.shersoft.com/`

Retail Price: $195.00

Sheridan's replacement for VB's TreeView control brings some important features that make for a much better user interface. It offers a better visual display and some other interesting options.

The display has been enhanced to support pictures, different fonts, and colors rather than the standard text offered by the TreeView control. This makes for a much more appealing user interface.

Aside from the improved and more flexible display, one new feature that stands out is ActiveTreeView's "Virtual Mode." When dealing with long scrolling lists of data, only the data currently displayed is actually loaded into memory. New data is swapped in and out of memory as necessary. This allows you to deal with huge lists without worrying about the control hogging up large amounts of memory.

Other new features include a MultiSelect option, where users can select more than one item from the tree; ToolTips, pop-up labels that show a node's full text when the cursor is placed on it; MultiColumns, allowing you to better organize data in columns; and ScrollBarTips, a location indicator that pops up when the user scrolls through a list of nodes, making for more intelligent scrolling.

In many situations, VB's TreeView control will fit the bill when you need to display a hierarchy list. But if you're looking to give your applications that extra edge, you might want to consider using Sheridan's ActiveTreeView instead.

ActiveX Gallimaufry

Desaware
1100 E. Hamilton Ave., Suite #4
Campbell, CA 95008

Sales:	(408) 377-4770
Fax:	(408) 371-3530

Email: `support@desaware.com`

Web Site: `http://www.desaware.com/`desaware/

Retail Price: $79.00

This collection of ActiveX controls with a strange name is actually a low-price package of "neat-o" controls that will enhance any programmer's library. *Gallimaufry* means "hodge-podge," and that's an apt description of this product.

There are six controls in the Gallimaufry. Table 50.1 lists them and provides a brief description of each.

Table 50.1. The ActiveX controls included in Desaware's ActiveX Gallimaufry.

Control	*Description*
Banner	A scrolling marquee that can be either opaque or transparent
HexEdit	A mini hex-editor that can view files smaller than 50 KB
dwPerspectiveList	A scrolling text display that makes lines of text disappear into the distance, just like in the opening scene of *Star Wars*
dwTaskBar	Adds a taskbar to an MDI application
RotatePic	Rotates bitmap images
SpiralBox	Draws spiral patterns similar to those created by a Spirograph toy

To be honest, most of the controls in the Gallimaufry will probably be used infrequently because few programs would require their functionality. After all, how many applications would benefit from having text that scrolls out to infinity (see Figure 50.4)?

Limited functionality aside, the Gallimaufry has one quality that makes it well worth purchasing: the source code for all the controls is included. If you want to look behind the scenes and see how ActiveX controls are created in Visual Basic, then the Gallimaufry provides several excellent examples.

Calendar Widgets

Sheridan Software Systems, Inc.

35 Pinelawn Road, Suite 206E

Melville, NY 11747

Sales: (800) 823-4732 or (516) 753-0985

Tech Support: (516) 753-0985

Fax: (516) 753-3661

Email: sales@shersoft.com

Web Site: http://www.shersoft.com/

Retail Price: $139.00

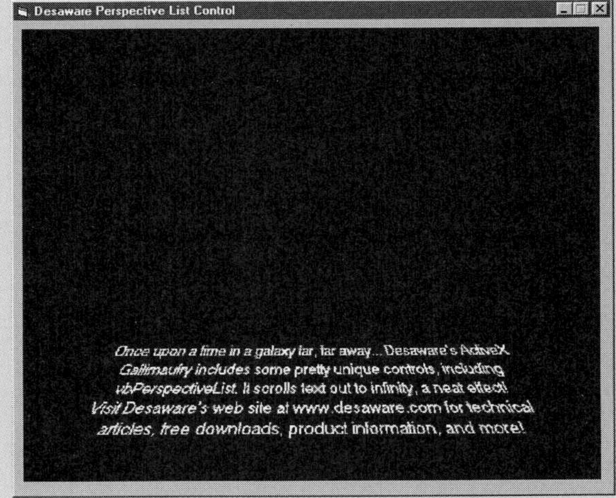

FIGURE 50.4. *The ActiveX Gallimaufry's dwPerspectiveList control, which provides neat* Star Wars*-type text scrolling.*

If you're creating scheduling software, time management applications, or any kind of program that accepts dates or times as user input, then Calendar Widgets might be just what you're looking for. A total of four ActiveX controls make working with times and dates a snap while giving your programs a truly professional look and feel.

Calendars can be shown in three different views, each accomplished with a separate ActiveX control (DayView, MonthView, and YearView). Figure 50.5 shows an instance of the DayView control in action, with a MonthView control partially visible behind it.

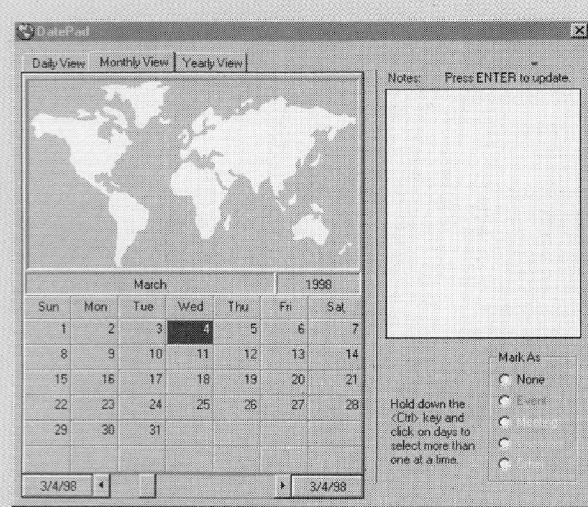

FIGURE 50.5. *The Calendar Widgets' DayView control, which shows a day planner-type time display. MonthView and YearView controls are also included with the Calendar Widgets product.*

There is also a calendar ComboBox (`DateCombo`) that lets users enter dates manually or by using the drop-down month display. This last control can be used in any program that accepts dates, and it really adds a nice, easy-to-use interface for date entry.

CaptiveX

NCompass Labs, Inc.
Third Floor Hudson House
321 Water St.
Vancouver, BC, Canada V6B 1B8

Sales:	(604) 606-0950
Fax:	(604) 606-0970
Email:	`ncompass@ncompasslabs.com`
Web Site:	`http://www.ncompasslabs.com/`

Retail Price: $199.00

CaptiveX is a collection of six unique ActiveX controls specifically designed for use on Web pages. Of course, they can also be used in VB programs. The controls included with this product are Cube, LightBoard, BillBoard, PowerPanels, PowerLabels, and Message Morph.

Cube allows you to map images to the six sides of a cube. The cube can rotate, and it can grow or shrink in size. This makes for a neat effect, though it's not something that you can use every day.

LightBoard is a take on the standard "marquee" control, where messages appear on a scrolling message display. This is one of the better implementations of a marquee control, however, and it allows for multiple messages with many possible transition effects (for example, Scroll Left, Drop, and Shake) and colors.

Message Morph is similar to LightBoard in that it displays messages. However, this control morphs a sequence of messages, one after another. This makes for an interesting effect.

BillBoard is a kind of image slide show where you can display a list of images in sequence. Like the LightBoard control, BillBoard allows you to use different transition effects when images are changed, such as Dissolve and Plummet.

PowerPanels is another image presentation tool, displaying a series of images on a 3D tile set. Again, a variety of transition effects are available.

PowerLabels makes text appear to "rush" towards the viewer in a three-dimensional configuration. It can also spin on an axis.

If you're looking for some unique ActiveX controls to enhance your VB Toolbox, and you want something that will really catch your user's eye, then CaptiveX might be perfect for you. If you're planning on using the controls on a Web site, then that's even more reason to consider this product because all the controls have been designed specifically for use on a Web page.

Component Toolbox Suite

DB Technologies, Inc.
203-2989 Pembina Highway
Winnipeg, MB
Canada R3T 2H5
Sales: (204) 985-5770
Tech Support: (204) 985-5770
Fax: (204) 275-5466
Email: dbitech@dbi-tech.com
Web Site: http://www.dbi-tech.com/

Retail Price: $399.00

The Component Toolbox Suite is actually a combination of four other DB Technologies products: Component Toolbox OCX (General Interface Controls), Solutions::PIM (Personal Information Management Controls), Solutions::Schedule (Employee/Resource Management Controls), and ctListBar. Altogether, 51 ActiveX controls are included in this package. They are listed in Table 50.2.

Table 50.2. The ActiveX controls included in the Component Toolbox Suite.

Control	*General Description*
ctAlarm	Alarm/Notification control
ctBanner	Animated Text/Picture Banner control
ctCalc	Calculator control
ctCheck	Enhanced CheckBox control
ctClip	Picture Clip control
ctClock	Digital/Analog Clock control
ctColor	Color Selection Dialog control
ctCPik	Color Picker control
ctData	Data Navigation Button control
ctDate	Monthly Calendar control
ctDays	Day-View control
ctDEdit	Date/Time Edit control
ctDial	Stereo Dial control
ctFile	File Selection Dialog control
ctFill	Fill Meter control

Control	General Description
ctFold	Tabbed File Folder control
ctFont	Font Dialog control
ctFormFX	Form Effects control
ctFrame	Frame control
ctGauge	Gauge control
ctGroup	Group Box control
ctLBar	List Bar control
ctMEdit	Masked Edit control
ctMenu	Menu Notification control
ctMeter	Status Meter control
ctMonth	Monthly Day-Timer control
ctMove	Animated Button control
ctNEdit	Numeric Masked Edit control
ctPaper	Lined Paper Text control
ctPrint	Printer Control Dialog control
ctPush	Picture/Toggle Button control
ctRadio	Radio Button control
ctRotate	Rotating Text control
ctRuler	Ruler control
ctSchd	Scheduling Bars control
ctSchedule	Multi-Resource Scheduling control
ctScroll	Scroll Bar control
ctSize	Resize Container control
ctSlider	Slider control
ctSpin	Spin Button control
ctSpiral	Spiral Ring Tab Binder control
ctSplit	Splitter Bar control
ctTabs	Page Tabs control
ctText	Text Label control
ctTips	Popup Help Tips control
ctTray	Tray Icon control
ctTree	Hierarchy Tree control

continues

Table 50.2. continued

Control	*General Description*
ctVList	Virtual ListBox control
ctWave	WAV File Player control
ctWeek	Weekly Planner control
ctYear	Year-View Calendar control

Many controls included in the Component Toolbox Suite are enhanced versions of standard VB controls. Several controls duplicate the functions of VB's CommonDialog control. But there are still plenty of other unique controls included in this product that make it well worth purchasing. For example, the ctSpiral control allows you to add a notebook-like container to your program (see Figure 50.6). There's a lot of functionality in this package, and it will certainly enhance any VB programmer's Toolbox.

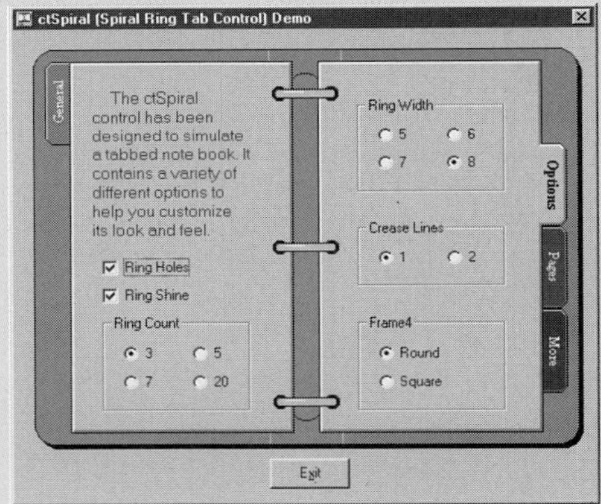

FIGURE 50.6.
The ctSpiral control, just one of the many controls included in the Component Toolbox Suite.

Designer Widgets 2.0

Sheridan Software Systems, Inc.
35 Pinelawn Road, Suite 206E
Melville, NY 11747

Sales: (800) 823-4732 or (516) 753-0985
Tech Support: (516) 753-0985
Fax: (516) 753-3661
Email: `sales@shersoft.com`
Web Site: `http://www.shersoft.com/`

Retail Price: $139.00

Designer Widgets consists of ActiveX controls that can be used to add some fancy features to your applications. Dockable Toolbar, FormFX, Notebook, and Index Tab are the four controls included.

The Dockable Toolbar lets you add floating toolbar palettes to your programs that can be "docked" to the top, bottom, or sides of a form. You can have multiple groups of buttons on each toolbar, and you can even put other controls on a toolbar.

FormFX gives you greater control over how your forms look. For example, with FormFX you can give form captions a 3D look, add bitmaps or icons to the caption area, or use multiple lines of text for your captions. There are many more ways that FormFX lets you control your forms, such as keeping them on top so that they never go behind any other windows.

The Notebook control displays an open notebook, where each "page" functions as a container for other controls. Both portrait and landscape modes are supported, and each page can be tabbed so that it can be accessed with a single mouse click.

The Index Tab control emulates a stack of index cards with tabs, similar to VB's Tabbed Dialog control. Of course, Index Tab is more flexible and allows you to do much more than VB's version. For example, each tab can consist of multiple pages that can be "earmarked" to make flipping through pages easier.

GreenTree ActiveX Components Suite

GreenTree Technologies, Inc.

33 Walt Whitman Road

Huntington Station, NY 11746

Sales:	(800) 257-7708
Tech Support:	(516) 271-6995
Fax:	(516) 271-8067
Email:	`sales@green-tree.com`
Web Site:	`http://www.green-tree.com/`

Retail Price: $399.00

GreenTree Technologies' ActiveX Components Suite is a conglomeration of six of the company's popular products: XGrid, DataMask, DataTree, DataList, DataView, and XShaper. Because each of these is in itself a distinct product (and can also be purchased separately), they'll all be discussed individually.

XGrid provides a full-featured spreadsheet with a single ActiveX control. It supports more than 100 Excel-compatible functions and can be data bound. Built-in cell types include Droplist, ComboBox, CheckBox, and MaskedEdit.

DataMask is a collection of three ActiveX controls that provide input masking of data. Just about any kind of input format can be achieved using the controls, and they all support international settings for date, time, and currency.

DataTree combines two ActiveX controls (Tree and ComboTree) that are take-offs on VB's TreeView control and display data in a hierarchy or "tree" format. The nodes on the tree can be expanded or collapsed, and the way the data is displayed is completely customizable.

DataList is also a combination of two ActiveX controls. One is similar to VB's ListView control, and the other is similar to VB's ComboBox control. Both can be data bound, and they offer a greater degree of display flexibility than their VB counterparts.

The DataView control provides complete data entry forms that can be used to enter or view data in a database without a single line of code. Simply place the ActiveX control on the form, set a few properties, and you have a complete data entry system (of course, you can customize the input fields if necessary). Also included with DataView is DataNavigator, which gives your programs database management and navigational controls on a single toolbar.

XShaper is unique in that it lets you create non-rectangular forms. You can design forms of almost any shape using the Shape Designer tool that provides design-time WYSIWYG editing of a window's shape.

GridWiz

McRae Software International, Inc.
17180 Creighton Drive
Chagrin Falls, OH 44023

Sales:	(216) 543-9242
Fax:	(216) 543-9242
Email:	`gridwiz@mcraesoft.com`
Web Site:	`http://www.mcraesoft.com/`

Retail Price: $149.00

Although GridWiz exists as a single ActiveX control, it actually functions like three controls in one. With GridWiz (see Figure 50.7), you can create grids, multicolumn list boxes, and tree grids. If desired, you can bind the control to any ODBC or DAO data source. Grid cells can be any of more than a dozen different types, including Edit Box, DropDownList, ComboBox, Button, and CheckBox. Input masking and formatting are also supported.

Although easy to use, GridWiz is a complex control. It has more than 200 properties, methods, and events that allow you to specify every detail of how the control is to be displayed. The Grid Workshop utility, included with GridWiz, can be used to create complex grids and workbooks. The Workshop uses a WYSIWYG editor, making it easy to specify how you want GridWiz to look and act.

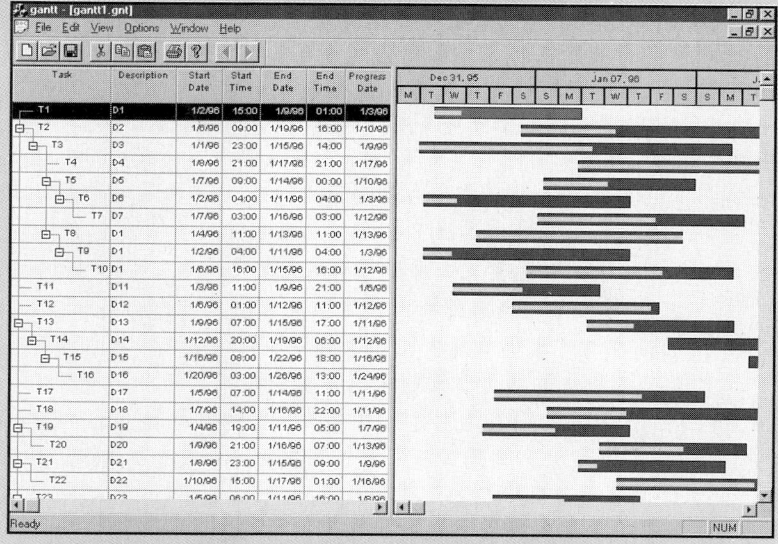

FIGURE 50.7.
A sample application created using the GridWiz control.

Instrumentation ActiveX Library (IAL)

Global Majic Software, Inc.

P.O. Box 322

Madison, AL 35758

Sales: (205) 864-0278

Fax: (205) 864-0708

Email: `gms@globalmajic.com`

Web Site: `http://www.globalmajic.com/`

Retail Price: $350.00

This collection of 11 ActiveX controls will probably be used primarily by those involved in creating manufacturing or simulation applications, though many other uses are certainly possible. The controls included in this package can be divided into three broad categories: those that act as gauges, those that accept information from users, and those that display information (often in interesting and unique formats).

One of the best things about the controls in Instrumentation ActiveX Library is that they are all extremely flexible. Many of them have more than 100 properties, which goes to show just how many of the controls' traits can be modified by the programmer. All the controls, with the exception of Odometer, Percent, and Toggle, are data-aware, so they can be used to display information pulled from a database.

The gauge controls bundled in the IAL include `Angular Gauge`, which is kind of like an analog tachometer (see Figure 50.8); `Linear Gauge`, a more flexible version of VB's Slider that can also be used as a meter or some other analog control; and Odometer, which can be used to indicate changing numeric values just like a car's odometer.

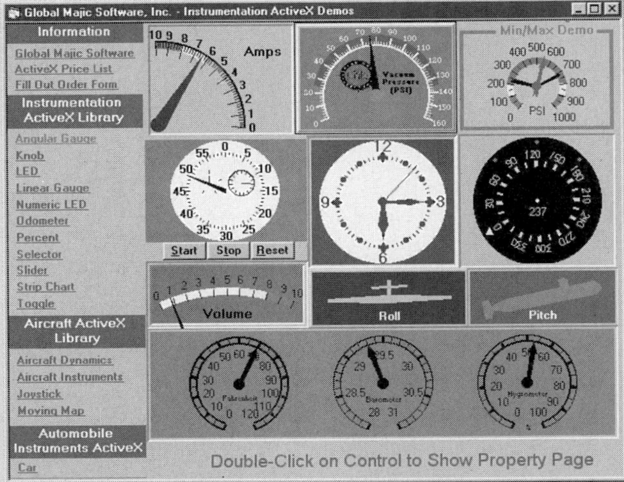

FIGURE 50.8.
A Global Majic Software demo program that shows several instances of their highly flexible Angular Gauge control. Note how different multiple instances of the same control can be.

The controls that accept user information include Knob, a kind of tuning knob; Selector Knob, a switching mechanism with a knob-like interface; Slider, another highly configurable version of VB's Slider control; and Toggle, a two-position switch.

Controls that display information include AlphaNumeric LED, an LED control implementation that can display numbers, the letters A through F, signs (+ or -), and a decimal point; LED, which emulates a light-emitting diode that can change in shape and color; Percent, a flexible version of the standard percentage bar control; and Strip Chart, a dynamic two-dimensional charting control.

Global Majic Software has become the major vendor of instrumentation controls, and for good reason. All their controls are fast, flexible, accurate, and uniquely designed.

List Pro

Far Point Technologies, Inc.
133 Southcenter Court, Suite 1000
Morrisville, NC 27560

Sales:	(800) 645-5913 or (919) 460-4551
Tech Support:	(919) 460-1887

Fax: (919) 460-7606
Email: `farpoint@fpoint.com`
Web Site: `http://www.fpoint.com/`

Retail Price: $245.00

List Pro contains more sophisticated versions of VB's ListBox and ComboBox controls called `fpList` and `fpCombo`. How much more sophisticated? Both controls break the 64 KB boundary and support up to 2 billion list items, single or multiple columns, embedding of bitmap images in columns and rows, and more than 200 properties for customizing the display. Not a bad start!

Support for headers has also been enhanced. The List Pro controls let you create multiple levels of group headers or column and group headers. You can also assign headers to parent groups and merge column or row cells that contain identical text.

The controls also support sort and search. Column data can be sorted in ascending or descending order, and list items can be searched by single character or multiple characters.

The `fpList` and `fpCombo` controls can also be data bound, with the capability to bind individual columns to different fields. Large data files can be quickly populated and displayed using the Virtual Data Manager.

If you need more flexibility than the ListBox and ComboBox controls provide, or if you're up against the 64 KB data boundary for those controls, then List Pro might be just the right product for you.

Mega Pack 2

Mabry Software, Inc.
P.O. Box 31926
Seattle, WA 98103-1926
Sales: (800) 996-2279 or (206) 634-1443
Fax: (206) 632-0272
Email: `mabry@mabry.com`
Web Site: `http://www.mabry.com/`

Retail Price: $179.00 without source code, $399.00 with source code

When it comes to third-party control suites, Mabry's Mega Pack 2 offers one of the largest collection of general-purpose ActiveX controls bundled into a single product. A total of 25 different controls are included in the Mega Pack 2, but five of them (MenuEv, MSlot, MSStat, Probe, and Ver) are only implemented in 16-bit VBXes, making them unusable in VB 5. Table 50.3 lists Mega Pack 2's 32-bit controls and provides a brief description of their function.

Table 50.3. The many controls included in Mabry's Mega Pack 2.

Control	*Description*
Alarm	Similar to VB's Timer control, but allows you to specify times (for example, 9:30 am) when it will fire. You can also specify that the control should fire every hour, every five minutes, and so on.
BarCod	One of the most useful controls in the Mega Pack 2, BarCod displays 19 different barcode formats, including Code 3 of 9 and PostNet.
BmpLst	Similar to VB's ListView control.
DFInfo	Provides detailed information about disk volumes and files.
FLabel	A greatly enhanced version of VB's Label control that offers extensive text formatting options.
FMDrop	Notifies your program when a file has been dragged and dropped from the Windows File Manager.
HiTime	A version of VB's Timer control that offers a much higher resolution. HiTime can have timer events trigger roughly every millisecond (by comparison, VB's Timer control can only trigger events every 55 milliseconds).
IniCon	Facilitates `INI` file access.
JoyStk	Provides information about joystick devices. Supports one or two normal joysticks, one four-button joystick, or one 3D joystick.
LED	Emulates a simple light-emitting diode.
MouseWheel	Provides support for Microsoft's IntelliMouse, which allows users to scroll and select data without taking their hands off the mouse.
PerCnt	An enhanced version of VB's ProgressBar control that can also display a percentage value to indicate the status of a given operation.
PicBtn	A version of VB's CommandButton that allows multiline captions and the addition of an image above, below, to the right, or to the left of the text.
RoText	A rotatable version of VB's Label control. Text can be rotated at any angle or degree of rotation.

Control	Description
SoundX	Provides Soundex and Metaphone algorithms; that is, it converts words or names into codes that represent how they sound when pronounced. SoundX can be used in database applications so that users can search for names that "sound like" the name they want to retrieve.
Tips	Displays Microsoft-style ToolTips or "help balloons" when the mouse cursor is moved over an instance of a control. Although most VB controls now have a `ToolTipText` property that accomplishes basically the same thing, the Tips control gives you more control over how the ToolTip is formatted and displayed.
Tray/X	Allows your application to display an icon (with ToolTips) in the system tray.
Validate	Facilitates data validation by allowing you to centralize all the data validation code for a form into a single event procedure.
Wave	Allows you to easily play and record WAV-format sound files from within your applications.
ZipInf	Provides information about the contents of a compressed `.ZIP` file, though it does not allow you to compress or decompress files.

Objective Grid/CCE

Stingray Software

9001 Aerial Center, Suite 110

Morrisville, NC 27560

Sales:	(800) 924-4223 or (919) 461-0672
Tech Support:	(919) 461-0672
Fax:	(919) 461-9811
Email:	`sales@stingray.com`
Web Site:	`http://www.stingray.com/`

Retail Price: $895.00

Joining the ranks of full-featured grid controls is Stingray Software's Objective Grid. This is one grid that has just about everything. Of course, it can be fully or partially data bound, but that's just the beginning.

To start, there is extensive formula support: more than 200 functions are supported, including mathematical, statistical, financial, string, date/time, matrix operations, interpolation, and much more. The control has an isolated design, so you don't have additional overhead if your application doesn't use formulas.

Objective Grid also supports a large variety of cell objects, from bitmaps to other ActiveX controls. Masked editing and input formatting is another option. The list of features for this control goes on and on.

Objective Grid is so sophisticated, it comes with a separate utility (Grid Designer) to create grids that exploit the full power of the control. Needless to say, the same thing can be accomplished by setting control properties, but the Grid Designer makes it much easier to get the grid you want set up fast.

OLETools

BeCubed Software, Inc.
1750 Marietta Hwy., Suite 240
Canton, GA 30114

Sales:	(770) 720-1077 or (888) 232-8233
Tech Support:	(770) 720-2278
Fax:	(770) 720-1078
Email:	`cs@bcubed.com`
Web Site:	`http://www.becubed.com/`

Retail Price: $229.00

OLETools is a huge collection of more than 50 general-purpose ActiveX controls. It's an eclectic mix, with a little bit of everything thrown in for good measure. Many are enhanced versions of the controls that come with Visual Basic. Table 50.4 lists all the controls and provides a brief description for each.

Table 50.4. The 50+ ActiveX controls that come with BeCubed Software's OLETools.

Control	*Description*
Mh3d	An enhanced version of VB's Label control
Mh3dButn	An enhanced version of VB's CommandButton control
Mh3dCalendar	Used to display and select dates from a monthly calendar
Mh3dCheck	An enhanced version of VB's CheckBox control
Mh3dCombo	An enhanced version of VB's ComboBox control
Mh3dCommand	An enhanced version of VB's CommandButton control
Mh3dDir	An enhanced version of VB's DirListBox control

Control	Description
Mh3dDrive	An enhanced version of VB's DriveListBox control
Mh3dFile	An enhanced version of VB's FileListBox control
Mh3dFrame	An enhanced version of VB's Frame control
Mh3dGauge	Displays linear, needle, or bitmap-style gauges
Mh3dGroup	Combines the functionality of a CommandButton control with that of an OptionButton control
Mh3dKeyStat	A CommandButton-like control used to monitor PC keyboard states (Caps Lock, Num Lock, Scroll Lock, and Insert)
Mh3dLabel	An enhanced version of VB's Label control
Mh3dList	An enhanced version of VB's ListBox control
Mh3dMultiLabel	An enhanced version of VB's Label control
Mh3dOption	An enhanced version of VB's OptionButton control
Mh3dText	An enhanced version of VB's TextBox control
MhAlarm	An audio-visual "attention getter"
MhAnimate	Displays a sequence of bitmap images
MhAVI	Displays `.AVI` (animation) files
MhCard	Displays playing cards from a standard 52-card deck
MhClock	Displays clocks in analog and digital formats
MhCommand	An enhanced version of VB's CommandButton control
MhCommonDialog	An enhanced version of VB's CommonDialog control
MhDateInput	A version of the TextBox control designed for entering dates
MhDial	A "volume control" type of dial
MhDice	Displays 3D dice
MhFileDisplay	A file viewer that allows you to browse ASCII text files of any size
MhFileList	An enhanced version of VB's FileListBox control
MhHistograph	Displays information as if it were being drawn on a plotter
MhImage	Displays images in a variety of formats
MhIni	Adds, retrieves, and modifies information in `.INI` files and the System Registry
MhInput	An enhanced version of VB's TextBox control
MhIntInput	A version of the TextBox control designed for entering numeric data

continues

Table 50.4. continued

Control	*Description*
MhInvisible	Lets you create a control that can be used to generate events for portions of a form or another control
MhMarque	Shows a moving banner of text, with or without bitmap images
MhMaskInput	A version of the TextBox control that lets you define your own edit masks
MhMulti	A version of the CommandButton control that lets you display five different bitmaps depending on the button's state
MhNetwork	Provides access to standard Windows network dialog boxes and functionality
MhOddPic	Displays images that are not rectangular in shape
MhOutBox	A picture control that gives you device-independent output capabilities
MhRealInput	A version of the TextBox control designed for entering real numbers and currency values
MhRollUp	A container control that operates like a drop-down combo box
MhSlide	A scrollbar-like control that displays a custom scale and buttons
MhSplitter	An elastic container control
MhStretch	Lets the user size other controls or mark a rectangular area of the display
MhSubClass	Provides access to subclassing services
MhTab	Similar to VB's TabStrip control
MhTimeInput	A version of the TextBox control designed for entering times
MhTimer	An enhanced version of VB's Timer control
MhTip	Provides pop-up captions when the mouse is moved over other controls
MhTree	Similar to VB's TreeView control
MhWave	Stores and plays `.WAV` files

As you can see, OLETools can add many new controls to VB's Toolbox. Most of the controls are flexible, providing increased functionality over those included with Visual Basic.

ProtoView ActiveX Component Suite

ProtoView Development Corporation
2540 Route 130
Cranbury, NJ 08512

Sales:	(800) 231-8588 or (609) 655-5000
Fax:	(609) 655-5353
Email:	`info@protoview.com`
Web Site:	`http://www.protoview.com/`

Retail Price: $299.00

This suite of ActiveX controls is actually a merger of three products that can also be purchased separately: Data Explorer, DataTable, and the WinX Component Library. Because they are separate products, each will be discussed here individually.

Data Explorer is an ActiveX control that combines elements of VB's TreeView and ListView controls. It provides an interface similar to that of Windows Explorer, with the display divided into a left and right pane. The left pane contains a hierarchy tree of nodes that the user can select. The right pane displays the data for a node that has been selected. The control is robust and can handle unlimited amounts of data per node.

DataTable is a database grid component that is both flexible and quick. It supports more than 32 predefined data types and can display queries and multidimensional arrays with up to 250 columns and 2 billion rows. Large grids use a virtual memory manager, so even huge amounts of data can be handled efficiently. DataTable also provides the programmer with great control over the way data is displayed, with built-in support for data formatting, color, 3D effects, and column sorting.

The WinX Component Library consists of 17 ActiveX controls that provide various general-purpose services. Table 50.5 lists the controls included in the WinX library. They are used primarily for data entry and to enhance a program's user interface.

Table 50.5. The controls included in the WinX library, which is one part of ProtoView's ActiveX Component Suite.

Control	*Description*
Button	An enhanced version of VB's standard CommandButton control
Calendar	Displays calendars in one-month, three-month, six-month, and one-year formats

continues

Table 50.5. continued

Control	*Description*
Currency	Allows entry and display of currency values in several international formats
Data Edit	Allows date entry in all international formats, complete with a drop-down calendar
Dial	A "stereo volume knob" that can be used as a replacement for a scrollbar
Font Selection	Two combo boxes that let a user easily select a font and size
Line 3D	A version of VB's Line control
Marquee	Displays streaming text and graphics
Mask Edit	Edits text input according to a predefined format
Multi-Directional	Four directional buttons combined into a Buttons single control, useful for directing scrolling or panning functions
Numeric Edit	Provides numeric data entry in a variety of formats
Percent Bar	Shows a graphic "percent complete" progress bar
Picture	Displays bitmaps, icons, and metafiles in a 3D frame
Shape 3D	A version of VB's Shape control
Text 3D	Displays text with a variety of three-dimensional effects
Time Edit	Allows entry and display of time values
Tree View	A version of VB's TreeView control

QuickPak VB/J++

Crescent Division of Progress Software
14 Oak Park
Bedford, MA 01730-9913

Sales:	(800) 352-2742 or (781) 280-3000
Tech Support:	(781) 280-3000
Fax:	(781) 280-4025
Email:	`crescent@progress.com`
Web Site:	`http://crescent.progress.com/`

Retail Price: $249.00

QuickPak VB/J++ contains several DLLs that can be used with either Visual Basic or Visual J++. No ActiveX controls are included in this package, so applying QuickPak's functionality is not as cut and dried as simply dropping controls onto a form. The product documentation is implemented completely through a set of local HTML pages, and no printed documentation is provided. Advanced programmers will likely have no problem using QuickPak's DLLs, but those with less experience might have a bit of a learning curve before they can start using QuickPak.

The functions included in the QuickPak product can be divided into eight general categories: array handling, file and directory handling, IIS/Personal Web Server management, Internet Core Messaging Protocol Network, string handling, system configuration, utility/memory routines, and Windows NT 4.0 security. There are far too many to list here; in all, QuickPak provides more than 300 preprogrammed routines.

After you install QuickPak, you'll have access to an instant library of functions that might have taken several years to put together if you had to code all the routines yourself—if you had the knowledge to do so, that is. Programmers who like to get into the hard-core aspects of VB coding will find the QuickPak library invaluable. Those who program in both Visual Basic and Visual J++ will also love the fact that they're actually getting two tools in one because QuickPak can be applied to either development environment.

StorageTools

Desaware
1100 E. Hamilton Ave., Suite #4
Campbell, CA 95008

Sales:	(408) 377-4770
Fax:	(408) 371-3530
Email:	`support@desaware.com`
Web Site:	`http://www.desaware.com/desaware/`

Retail Price: $129.00

StorageTools contains three ActiveX controls, Storage, Stream, and Registry. The first two allow you to create and read compound document files, and the latter lets you access the System Registry.

The Storage and Stream controls let you work with compound documents, a form of OLE structured storage. Compound documents have two primary structures, storages and streams. Storages act like directories, and streams act like files; each type has its own buffering. StorageTools' Storage and Stream controls allow you to easily read and create storages and streams as if they were regular files, using familiar Visual Basic commands.

The Registry control gives you complete command of the System Registry. Although several statements are built into Visual Basic for accessing the Registry, StorageTools' Registry control takes Registry access a step farther. It allows you to register filename extensions for documents used by your program so that the program will be launched when the document type is accessed. The Registry control also lets you create user- and machine-specific configuration settings in the Registry, as well as save and retrieve other bits and pieces of program information.

Also included with StorageTools is a standalone program called Storage Browser which, by using the Storage and Stream controls, lets you take a look inside compound documents to see how they are organized. The source code for the Storage Browser program is also included.

Desaware has a habit of creating unique products not duplicated by other third-party vendors. StorageTools is no exception, and you'd be hard pressed to find another product that offers its kind of functionality.

TX Text Control Collection

DBS GmbH
Kohlhökerstrasse 61
D-28203 Bremen
Germany

Sales:	0421 33591-0
Fax:	0421 33591-80
Email:	`sales@dbs-imaging.com`
Web Site:	`http://www.dbs-imaging.com/`

Retail Price: $749.00 DM

Though the name is a bit misleading, this product contains only one ActiveX control, TX Text. Two utilities that were built using the TX Text control are also included, a desktop publishing application called TX Publisher and TX Info Artist, which allows you to create hypertext documents that can be mass-distributed.

As mentioned previously, the TX Text control is the core component of this product. It provides a full-featured word processor that can be integrated directly into your VB applications. Four file formats are supported by TX Text, including RTF (Rich Text Format), HTML, ASCII, and a format native to the control.

Button bars, status bars, and rulers are represented by separate icons in VB's Toolbox, so you can selectively position and use these items with the TX Text control as you see fit. Some of the more interesting word processing features supported by TX Text include:

Placement of images within documents

Text that flows around images

Zoom in and out

Page Setup and Print dialog boxes

Text search and replace

Selective foreground and background colors

Lines and frames around text

The TX Text Control Collection includes two standalone applications created using the TX Text control. The first is TX Publisher, a relatively sophisticated desktop publishing application. Features include:

Multiple text frames

Exact positioning of text frames

Definable text flow from frame to frame

Multipage display

Positioning rulers

Text that flows around images

The other application included in the TX Text Control Collection is a software design tool called TX Info Artist. TX Info Artist actually consists of two separate programs, Designer and Viewer. The Designer is a text processor that lets you create hypertext documents such as catalogs and program documentation. The documents created by the Designer program can be displayed with the Viewer program. You can mass-distribute the documents and the Viewer on CD-ROM or whatever format you find acceptable.

The features of the TX Text ActiveX control are also implemented in a DLL file, which is also included with this product. The TX Text Control Collection comes with manuals that explain how to use both the ActiveX control and the DLL.

VSVIEW

VideoSoft

5900-T Hollis Street

Emeryville, California 94608

Sales:	(888) 228-4839 or (510) 595-2400
Tech Support:	(510) 595-2400
Fax:	(510) 595-2424
Web Site:	`http://www.videosoft.com/`

Retail Price: $249.00

VSVIEW is a collection of four unrelated ActiveX controls. The main control is vsPrinter, which is a significantly more flexible version of VB's `Printer` object. It allows a far greater degree of control over how documents are printed from within Visual Basic. Word wrap, headers and footers, graphics, and multicolumn printing are just a few of the features provided by vsPrinter. Best of all, you can allow your users to preview documents in your programs before they are printed using vsPrinter's built-in preview capability (see Figure 50.9). Zooming and panning are fully supported during print preview.

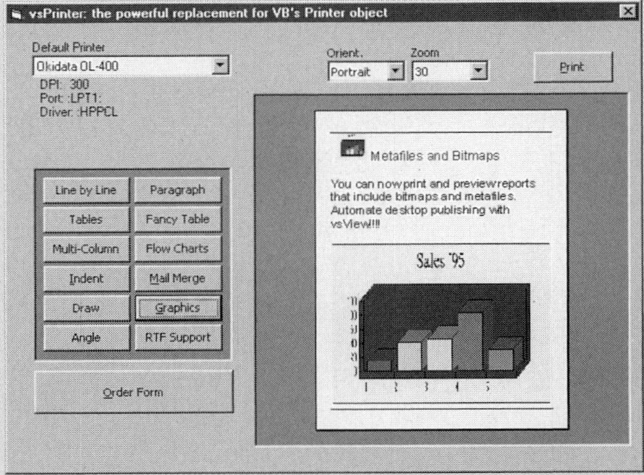

FIGURE 50.9.
VSVIEW's vsPrinter object allows previewing of documents before they are printed.

The other controls included in the VSVIEW package are vsViewPort, which provides an extremely useful scrollable container; vsDraw, a drawing control that lets you create complex line art; and vsInForm, which allows you to easily customize several attributes of a container.

VSVIEW also includes VideoSoft's DataReporter, an object that can be called from within a VB program to provide a fully functional report designer. Users can drag and drop data fields into the DataReport to easily create data-aware reports.

VS-OCX

VideoSoft
5900-T Hollis Street
Emeryville, California 94608

Sales:	(888) 228-4839 or (510) 595-2400
Tech Support:	(510) 595-2400
Fax:	(510) 595-2424
Web Site:	`http://www.videosoft.com/`

Retail Price: $99.00

VideoSoft's VS-OCX is a collection of three general-purpose ActiveX controls that can come in handy for applications of all kinds. The controls included in the VS-OCX product are vsElastic, vsAwk, and vsIndexTab.

The vsElastic control is probably the most useful of the bunch. It can be used as a replacement for VB's Image, Label, CommandButton, Frame, and Progress controls. Its primary role is as a container for other objects. When objects are placed inside a vsElastic control, they can be automatically resized and repositioned when the form or the vsElastic control is resized. As you might imagine, this can save you from a lot of tedious coding. The vbElastic control can also add 3D borders to any of the controls placed inside it.

UNIX programmers might have an idea of what the vsAwk control does because it is based on the UNIX AWK command. vsAwk is a sophisticated string parser, allowing you to search files for words or strings. It can also be used to perform some data manipulation and string formatting tasks.

The vsIndexTab control is similar to VB's Tab control, providing a way to implement notebook-like tabbed pages that can be accessed individually. The vsIndexTab offers only slightly more functionality than the standard Tab control.

Database Controls

The products listed in this section provide some sort of database functionality. Some are designed as replacements for the standard controls that come with Visual Basic, whereas others offer unique new ways of accessing data.

Data Widgets 2.0

Sheridan Software Systems, Inc.

35 Pinelawn Road, Suite 206E

Melville, NY 11747

Sales:	(800) 823-4732 or (516) 753-0985
Tech Support:	(516) 753-0985
Fax:	(516) 753-3661
Email:	`sales@shersoft.com`
Web Site:	`http://www.shersoft.com/`

Retail Price: $295.00

This collection of ActiveX controls is perfect for anyone creating database front-end applications. All the controls have been designed specifically to facilitate database use.

The DataGrid control is similar to VB's DBGrid control. In fact, it is functionally and visually consistent with the VB version. But DataGrid adds many new features such as individual fonts and colors for columns, groups, rows, and cells. It also adds extra cell types such as check box, button, label, and combo box.

The DataCombo and DataDropDown controls are combo boxes that can be tied in directly to a database. The Data Option Set control allows data fields to be bound to option buttons, and the DataCommand control allows you to create command buttons that perform database operations such as Add, Delete, Refresh, Bookmark, and Auto-Position.

Also included with the Data Widgets is the Enhanced Data Control, which acts as a replacement for VB's Data control. It extends the VB version in several ways, such as support for bookmark storage and enhanced database navigation. You can even define pictures for each button on the control.

True DBGrid Pro 5.0

APEX Software Corporation
4516 Henry Street
Pittsburgh, PA 15213

Sales:	(800) 858-2739 or (412) 681-4343
Tech Support:	(412) 681-4738
Fax:	(412) 681-4384
Email:	`sales@apexsc.com`
Web Site:	`http://www.apexsc.com/`

Retail Price: $299.95

Unlike many of the other products listed in this chapter, True DBGrid Pro centers around one powerful ActiveX control. True DBGrid (see Figure 50.10) is a replacement for VB's DBGrid, extending the functionality of that control in many different ways. However, it still remains 100 percent compatible with DBGrid.

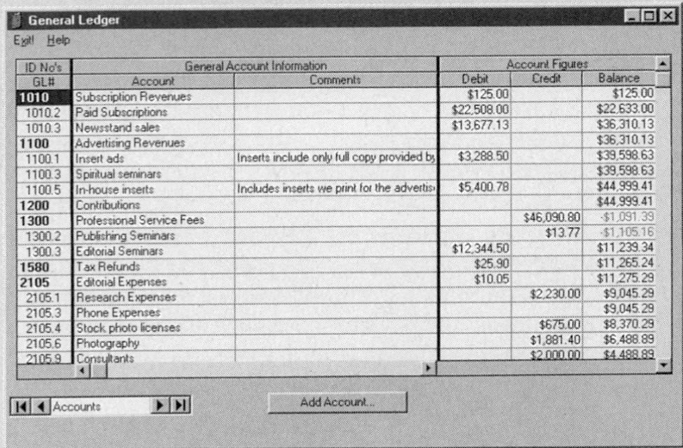

FIGURE 50.10.
A sample program created with True DBGrid.

Some of the more impressive features of True DBGrid are its Excel-like Splits, fixed non-scrolling columns, in-cell objects (including bitmaps, command buttons, check boxes, and radio buttons), enhanced drag and drop, data-sensitive display, and unbound columns. Database interactivity has also been improved, with database values being automatically translated into alternate text and graphics without having to code. Defining how grids will look with True DBGrid can be accomplished completely in design mode, without a single line of code.

Those familiar with a previous version of True DBGrid will find that some new features have been added, such as an array-based storage mode, reusable grid layouts, input masking, multiline displays, runtime CellTips, alternating row colors, and more.

True DBGrid also comes with a data-aware multicolumn control (True DBDropDown), which can be used inside True DBGrid's cells or by itself. Add-in migration utilities for converting projects that use previous versions of True DBGrid are also included.

Graphics Controls

The products listed in this section deal with graphics, commonly designed as replacements for VB's PictureBox and Image controls. They typically offer more flexibility and image processing options than their VB counterparts.

ImageKnife/OCX

Olympus Software Europe
Wendenstraße 14-16
Hamburg, Germany

Sales:	+49-40-23773-411
Fax:	+49-40-23773-644
Email:	`info@olympus-software.com`
Web Site:	`http://www.olympus-software.com/`

Retail Price: $549.00

The ImageKnife/OCX product contains a single OCX called PicBuf (short for "picture buffer"), which is similar to VB's Picture control. In fact, images assigned to a Picture control can be transferred to a PicBuf control and vice versa.

As might be expected, PicBuf controls are far more flexible than their Picture counterparts. For one thing, they support a much greater variety of image formats, including BMP, DIB, FIF, GIF, JPEG, Paintbrush OLE, PCX, PNG, Targa, and TIFF. Images can range from 1-bit (2 colors) to 24-bit (16.7 million colors).

After an image has been assigned to a PicBuf control, it can be processed and manipulated in many different ways. Some of its more interesting features include:

- Panning and zooming of an image
- Copying of full or partial images from one PicBuf control to another with image-scaling options
- Capability to add automatic scrollbars to images that are larger than the PicBuf control to which they are assigned
- Advanced palette processing options
- Various image processing methods, such as `Mirror`, `Soften`, `Sharpen`, `Rotate`, and `Blur`
- Enhanced methods for drawing lines and shapes directly onto a PicBuf control, including `Arc`, `Chord`, `Pie`, `Polygon`, `PolyLine`, `Rect`, and `RoundRect`

The manual that comes with the ImageKnife software is more than 200 pages long, most of which is used to describe the numerous properties, methods, and events of the PicBuf control. As you can imagine, this is one sophisticated image control.

The ImageKnife product was originally created and sold by Media Architects. It went out of business, and Olympus Software bought the rights to the product.

ImageMan ActiveX Suite

Data Techniques, Inc.
300 Pensacola Road
Burnsville, NC 28714

Sales:	(800) 955-8015 or (704) 682-4111
Tech Support:	(704) 682-0161
Fax:	(704) 682-0025
Email:	`custsvc@data-tech.com`
Web Site:	`http://www.data-tech.com/`

Retail Price: $495.00

The ImageMan ActiveX Suite consists of only two ActiveX controls, but each one does quite a bit. The first control, Image, provides support for a wide variety of raster and vector image formats, including BMP, DCX, DIB, DXF (AutoCAD), EPS, FMF, GIF, IMG, JPEG, PCX, PhotoCD, PNG, RLE, Targa, TIFF, WMF, and WPG. It also provides some interesting image processing options like high-speed rotation, but the number of options available is not as robust as some other graphics controls like ImageKnife.

The other control in the ImageMan ActiveX Suite is Scanner, which allows your applications to instantly support a number of TWAIN-compatible devices such as scanners, digital cameras, and frame grabbers. Using the Scanner control, you can determine which and how many scanners are available on a user's system, select a scanner (either through code or by letting the user select a device using a built-in dialog box), and actually scan one or more pages. The whole process is straightforward and should be implemented with little or no trouble.

One of the nicest things about Data Techniques' products is that tech support is free (if it's needed at all). Also, registered users of the ImageMan product can obtain the latest releases and documentation from Data Techniques' Web site. Things like that make an already excellent product even better.

Charting

The products listed in this section are used for drawing 2D and 3D charts and graphs. These are typically complex software components, offering a myriad of options for the graphic display of data.

Chart FX

Software FX, Inc.

7100 W. Camino Real, Suite 117

Boca Raton, FL 33433

Sales:	(800) 392-4278 or (561) 391-9494
Fax:	(561) 998-2383
Email:	`sales@softwarefx.com`
Web Site:	`http://www.softwarefx.com/`

Retail Price: $249.00

ChartFX is an intense charting control that gives you an incredible amount of precision over how charts and graphs are displayed. More than 35 different chart types are supported, and each can be tuned in many ways (see Figure 50.11).

In addition to a high degree of chart control, Chart FX has some other neat features. Charts can be displayed in real time, legends can be dockable, and zoom in/out capabilities are available. An end-user interface is also included, providing users with a toolbar of icons that can be used to perform many chart-related functions such as toggling 2D and 3D views, copying a chart to the Clipboard, printing a chart, changing the chart's rotation, and many others.

Another version of this product, Chart FX Internet Edition, includes server-side as well as client-side components for displayed database-aware charts and graphs via Windows NT-based Web servers. All browser types are supported by Chart FX Internet Edition.

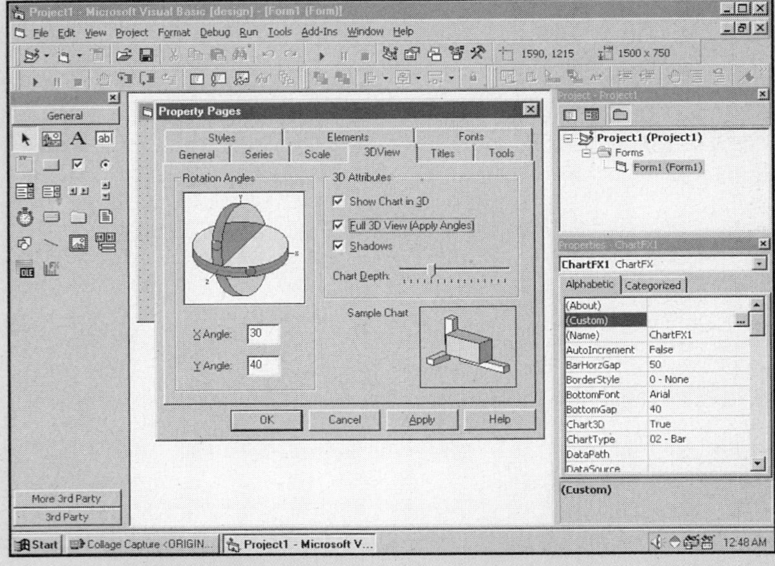

FIGURE 50.11.
ChartFX gives you a substantial amount of control over how its 35+ charts and graphs are displayed.

Graphics Server

Pinnacle Publishing, Inc.
P.O. Box 72255
Marietta, GA 30007-2255

Sales:	(800) 788-1900 or (770) 565-1763
Tech Support:	(206) 625-9436
Fax:	(770) 565-8232
Email:	custserv@pinpub.com
Web Site:	http://www.pinpub.com/

Retail Price: $349.00

When it comes to creating graphs and charts, Graphics Server is one serious product. With two dozen graph types (many available in both 2D and 3D formats), it offers a full range of options for anyone who needs to display information graphically.

In addition to having a healthy palette of graph and chart types (see Figure 50.12), Graphics Server also provides the programmer with a substantial amount of control over how the graphs are displayed. A "True3D" system allows graphs to be drawn as if viewed by any angle in a 3D space. Other features include "hot graphs" that return information when a user clicks on particular sections of a graph, data binding, printing options, and the capability to use custom graphics so that you can create your own graph types.

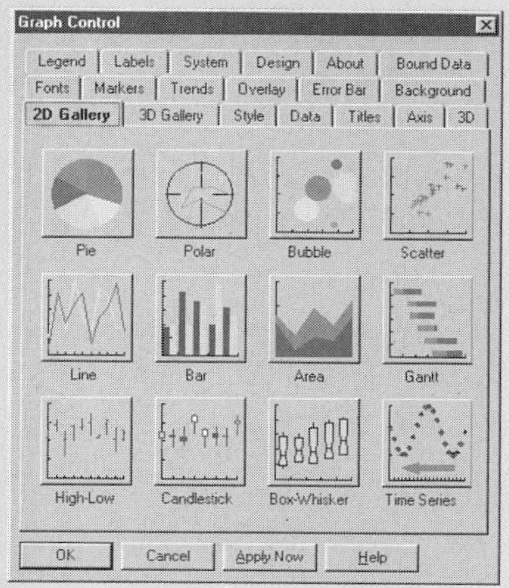

FIGURE 50.12.
Graphics Server provides two dozen different graph and chart types, with many available in both 2D and 3D versions.

The latest version of Graphics Server also provides extra functionality for those who want to display graphs over the Internet. Charts and graphs generated by Graphics Server can be exported to JPEG files, making them ready to implement into Web pages. No big deal there, but you can also have Graphics Server generate a client-side or server-side image map so that users can click on the elements of a graph and be forwarded to other Web pages. Another bonus for Internet developers is the inclusion of digitally signed `.CAB` files so that a runtime version of the ActiveX control can be easily distributed.

Graphics Server comes with both an ActiveX control (Graph) and a DLL, so that it can be used with just about any Windows development platform. VB programmers will likely prefer the ActiveX control because it is the easiest to use.

Compression/Decompression and Encryption

The products listed in this section are used to process data in some way. Data compression and decompression services, as well as encryption and decryption, are the focus of the controls here.

Active Delivery

Inner Media, Inc.
60 Plain Road
Hollis, NH 03049

Sales:	(800) 962-2949 or (603) 465-3216
Tech Support:	(603) 465-2696
Fax:	(603) 465-7195
Email:	`sales@innermedia.com`
Web Site:	`http://www.innermedia.com/`

Retail Price: $249.00

Active Delivery allows you to create sophisticated self-extracting file archives. Using an easy-to-use wizard, you can tell Active Delivery which files you want to include in the archive, as well as specific details about the extraction process itself. For example, you can specify which programs should run before or after the archive files have been extracted, which "splash screen" to show during extraction (if any), which OCX and DLL files to register in the System Registry, and several other options. All this information is stored in an AD Script file. What you'll end up with is a single `.EXE` that, when executed, will launch your AD Script and start the extraction process. No additional files or components are necessary on the user's system to run the executable file.

So far, Active Delivery probably sounds a lot like an enhanced version of VB's Application Setup Wizard. But here's where Active Delivery starts to differ. It includes an OCX file that can be used from within your Visual Basic applications so that you can create these same self-extracting install programs without using the wizard directly. If your programs need to create self-extracting archives with little or no user interaction, then Active Delivery can come in handy.

The Active Delivery package also contains DLL and VCL files, both of which duplicate the functionality of the OCX file. You can use these components with other development platforms such as C++ or Delphi.

Crusher! Data Compression Toolkit

DC Micro Development
P.O. Box 54588
Lexington, KY 40555

Sales:	(800) 775-1073
Tech Support:	(606) 245-4175
Fax:	(606) 245-9305
Email:	`info@dcmicro.com`
Web Site:	`http://www.dcmicro.com/`

Retail Price: $299.00

Unlike the other products in this section, the Crusher! Data Compression Toolkit does not use an ActiveX control. Instead, it consists of 45 functions that can be called to perform services such as buffer compression and decompression, file compression and decompression, encryption and decryption, and creation of self-extracting archives.

Although Crusher! lacks the ease of use inherent with ActiveX controls, it makes up for it in other ways. Its compression algorithm uses 32-bit CRC computations and is powerful, with typical compression ratios of 50 percent for binary data and 20 percent or better for text data. Data can be compressed buffer-to-buffer for the utmost in efficiency.

Also included with this product are standalone Windows and command-line utilities that can be used to produce regular and self-extracting archives. The source code is also included.

Because Crusher! uses a DLL to provide its services, it can be used by just about any Windows programming language, including C, C++, and Delphi (and of course Visual Basic). Versions of Crusher! are also available for platforms other than Windows, and the API is identical across all the platforms supported.

DynaZIP

Inner Media, Inc.
60 Plain Road
Hollis, NH 03049

Sales:	(800) 962-2949 or (603) 465-3216
Tech Support:	(603) 465-2696
Fax:	(603) 465-7195
Email:	`sales@innermedia.com`
Web Site:	`http://www.innermedia.com/`

If your programs need to compress and decompress files using a format compatible with PKWARE's PKZIP and PKUNZIP products, then DynaZIP may be the control for you. Actually, this product includes a total of three controls: Duzocx1, for decompressing files; Dzocx1, for compressing files; and Dstatocx, which can be used as an external progress monitor (percentage control). It also includes DLLs that can be used in lieu of the ActiveX controls.

A full range of features is included in DynaZIP, including:

- Retrieval of information from ZIP files about their contents
- Integrity testing of ZIP files
- Creation, addition, deletion, and updating of ZIP files
- Encryption and decryption
- Recursing of files into subdirectories
- Support for long filenames
- Reading and writing of comments in ZIP files
- Compression of items in memory directly to a ZIP file

In a nutshell, DynaZIP can do just about everything that PKZIP and PKUNZIP can do. However, those programs are not required for DynaZIP to work; all compression and decompression of files is performed by the OCXes included in this product.

HASHcipher/OCX and DEScipher/OCX

Bokler Software

P.O. Box 261

Huntsville, AL 35804

Sales:	(205) 539-9901
Fax:	(205) 882-7401
Email:	`info@bokler.com`
Web Site:	`http://www.bokler.com/`

Retail Price: $259.00

Bokler's HASHcipher/OCX and DEScipher/OCX are two products that are available together or separately. Both provide strong encryption services that are implemented with ActiveX controls. You can use them to secure email messages, protect sensitive data, or encrypt files and directories.

DEScipher/OCX allows you to encrypt or decrypt data streams using the U.S. government's DES (Data Encryption Standard) method of encryption. All modes of DES are supported, including Electronic Codebook, Cipher Block Chaining, Cipher Feedback, and Output Feedback.

To use DEScipher/OCX, you need only place the ActiveX control on your form, set a few properties, and then call one of the control's methods. No prior knowledge of data encryption is necessary, and the manual included with the product explains the encryption process completely.

HASHcipher/OCX also allows you to encrypt or decrypt data streams, but it uses the SHS (Secure Hash Standard) method of encryption. SHS offers one of the highest levels of security of any encryption method available outside the military. Using HASHcipher/OCX is a little more complicated than using DEScipher/OCX, but the process is still straightforward.

In this day and age, data security is often a primary concern. Encryption and decryption are hot topics, and VB programmers may find a real need to incorporate data encryption into their programs. Bokler's DEScipher/OCX and HASHcipher/OCX are two products that provide tried-and-true encryption services.

Communications

Many of the products listed in this section provide fax services. Others provide voice mail and telephony services, while still others offer controls to facilitate serial communications.

FaxMan

Data Techniques, Inc.
300 Pensacola Road
Burnsville, NC 28714

Sales:	(800) 955-8015 or (704) 682-4111
Tech Support:	(704) 682-0161
Fax:	(704) 682-0025
Email:	custsvc@data-tech.com
Web Site:	http://www.data-tech.com/

Retail Price: $495.00

Sending and receiving fax transmissions in Visual Basic is not the easiest thing to do. Luckily, FaxMan simplifies the process.

The entire FaxMan system revolves around the FaxMan server, which manages the transmission and receipt of faxes, all existing fax devices, and logging of fax events. The server component needs to be installed along with any VB applications that utilize the FaxMan system. It can be loaded into memory on demand, or it can be loaded at Windows startup so that it automatically handles fax events at all times.

Another essential part of the FaxMan system are the FaxMan print drivers. These drivers allow faxes to be sent by any application capable of sending output to a printer (provided that the printer is selectable).

The ActiveX control used within a Visual Basic program essentially communicates with the FaxMan server to accomplish certain tasks. It allows you to create a program that can monitor the progress of faxes, schedule faxes, and display send/receive logs.

In short, you can create an entire fax application using the components of the FaxMan system. The product includes up to 10,000 runtime licenses, so you can distribute the FaxMan system only so many times. Additional licenses can be purchased, of course, but it's important to note that FaxMan does not allow unlimited licensing.

PDQComm

Crescent Division of Progress Software
14 Oak Park
Bedford, MA 01730-9913

Sales:	(800) 352-2742 or (781) 280-3000
Tech Support:	(781) 280-3000
Fax:	(781) 280-4025

Email: crescent@progress.com

Web Site: http://crescent.progress.com/

Retail Price: $199.00

When it comes to third-party controls for serial communications, PDQComm is one of the best. PDQComm begins where VB's MSComm control leaves off. It provides various terminal emulation modes, including TTY, ANSI, VT-100, VT-52, and VT 220, as well as multiport access so that you can use more than one COM port simultaneously. Baud rates of up to 230,400 are possible using PDQComm and the appropriate Windows communications driver.

PDQComm also supports a wide variety of file transfer protocols, such as XModem-Checksum, XModem-CRC, XModem-1K, YModem-G, YModem-Batch, ZModem, CompuServe B+, and Kermit. The ZModem protocol features Automatic ZModem, so file transfers can start automatically without user intervention. File transfers occur in the background, so your program can perform other tasks during uploads and downloads. Transfers can be monitored by a built-in file transfer box that displays information such as bytes transmitted, elapsed time, and file size.

PDQComm is so powerful, a complete terminal program can be created simply by setting control properties—no code is necessary. With that kind of functionality, it's no wonder that this product has received so much praise!

Also included in the PDQComm package is PDQTapi, which allows you to implement telephony features into your programs without having to use the `TAPI32.DLL` functions directly. If you're developing telephony applications, PDQTapi alone is well worth the price of PDQComm.

Another freebie included with PDQComm is ModemWare, a collection of dialogs and routines that you can reuse in your programs. With ModemWare, you can perform functions such as accessing service networks like CompuServe or Dow Jones without having to reinvent the wheel. The code has already been written for you, so you can put PDQComm to work right away.

VBVoice

Pronexus, Inc.

112 John Cavanagh Road

Carp, Ontario

Canada K0A 1L0

Sales: (613) 839-0033

Fax: (613) 839-0035

Email: info@pronexus.com

Web Site: http://www.pronexus.com

Retail Price: $595 for one-line version (other versions available, contact vendor)

When it comes to creating telephony applications such as voice mail and info-on-demand systems, it simply doesn't get much easier than using Pronexus's VBVoice. This amazing product allows you to use even advanced telephony functions in your programs with a minimum of effort.

More than 25 ActiveX components are in the VBVoice toolbox. Each component provides a different service, and components can be "strung together" in a flowchart type of configuration. For example, to create a voice mail system, you would first use the LineGroup control, which waits for a call. Then you would add a PlayGreeting control, which plays a greeting message. Next, you might add a GetDigits control to determine which digits the caller punches in on his telephone keypad. Based on the digits entered, several other controls can be used to perform specific functions, such as playing messages, recording voice mail, or even sending a fax (a separate product, VBFax, is required for fax capabilities). Finally, you would use the OnHook control to terminate the call. By using these different controls and stringing them together, you create a "call flow" that dictates how your application will work.

Of course, each control can be completely customized to fit your needs. For example, the PlayGreeting control can play whatever sound file you specify, or it can seamlessly play back multiple sound files to create a longer greeting message. Although VBVoice provides everything you need to record your messages, you can also use preexisting sound files, such as WAVs and other formats.

After an application has been created using VBVoice's components, it can be tried out right from within Visual Basic without actually receiving a call. The VBVoice Test Mode utility simulates a call, even providing a telephone keypad so that you can enter digits for your application to respond to.

VBVoice supports speech recognition and Text-to-Speech synthesis, allowing you to create truly state-of-the-art telephony applications. It also supports multiple lines in a single application, with each channel streaming in its own thread. Different versions of VBVoice are available based on the number of lines you want to use, with up to 96 lines supported on a Quad T1. Inquire with Pronexus about the pricing for the different versions.

Visual Voice Pro 4.0

Artisoft, Inc.

Computer Telephony Product Group

5 Cambridge Center

Cambridge, MA 02142

Sales:	(800) 914-9985 or (617) 354-0600
Fax:	(617) 354-7744
Email:	`visualvoice@artisoft.com`
Web Site:	`http://www.artisoft.com/telephony`

Retail Price: $795 for two-line version (other versions available, contact vendor)

Artisoft's Visual Voice Pro is a collection of ActiveX controls that can be used to create sophisticated telephony applications. Utilities are also included that can help you test any applications you may create, even if your computer is not hooked up to a phone.

Visual Voice Pro supports a full range of telephony features, such as playback and recording of messages, touch-tone digit retrieval, Caller ID analyzation, and call conferencing. You can also integrate other Visual Voice products such as Visual Fax and Visual Voice Recognition (both sold separately) into your applications for extra functionality.

To make things easy, Visual Voice Pro includes a Code Wizard that will walk you through the process of creating a telephony application. You can create working programs in just a few minutes, and the Code Wizard will write all the code for you.

The standard edition of Visual Voice Pro is designed to work with Dialogic hardware only. However, another version, Visual Voice for TAPI, is also available. It will work with any modem that works through a TAPI driver. In any case, you don't need any special hardware during the development phase, so you can create applications that will run at other locations and be sure that they work properly before implementing them.

Internet

Many products are now available that make it easy to write Internet applications and to take advantage of Internet-related services such as electronic mail, FTP, and the World Wide Web. The products listed here typically contain a suite of controls that provide access to different Internet services. Other products, such as those by NCompass Labs, are not development tools per se but are designed to implement ActiveX operability via the Internet or an intranet.

Internet Pack

Mabry Software, Inc.
P.O. Box 31926
Seattle, WA 98103-1926

Sales:	(800) 996-2279 or (206) 634-1443
Fax:	(206) 632-0272
Email:	`mabry@mabry.com`
Web Site:	`http://www.mabry.com/`

Retail Price: $129.00 without source code, $359 with source code

Mabry's Internet Pack is a low-cost toolkit for anyone who wants to develop applications that utilize the various services of the Internet, such as FTP, Gopher, email, and newsgroups. Each of the 11 ActiveX controls included in this product accesses a different Internet service. Table 50.6 lists the controls and their specific purposes.

Table 50.6. The ActiveX controls included in Mabry's Internet Pack.

Control	*Description*
ASocket	Facilitates the development of unique TCP/IP and server software using sockets
Finger	Requests user information such as last date of logon, mail waiting status, and real name from an Internet host
FTP	Allows you to send and receive files and manage directories on an FTP server
FTP/X	A more enhanced version of the FTP control, FTP/X provides access to the complete FTP client protocol, including asynchronous and synchronous modes of operation
GetHst	Translates host names to IP addresses and vice versa
Gopher	Allows you to retrieve information from Gopher sites
Mail	Assists in managing email, supporting both Simple Mail Transfer Protocol (SMTP) and Post Office Protocol (POP) as well as UUENCODE/UUDECODE for attachments
News	Allows you to access Network News Transfer Protocol (NNTP) servers to read and post newsgroup messages
RAS	Provides access to the RAS subsystem
Time	Allows you to retrieve the Greenwich Mean Time from an Internet host
WhoIs	Retrieves information about a person or domain name that is registered with the InterNIC

Like all of Mabry's products, the controls in the Internet Pack are solid in their design while still providing the programmer with a large degree of flexibility. If you're interested in developing Internet applications, this is a good product to have.

Internet ToolPak

Crescent Division of Progress Software
14 Oak Park
Bedford, MA 01730-9913

Sales:	(800) 352-2742 or (781) 280-3000
Tech Support:	(781) 280-3000
Fax:	(781) 280-4025

Email: crescent@progress.com

Web Site: http://crescent.progress.com/

Retail Price: $295.00

Crescent also has a collection of ActiveX components for creating Internet applications. Like all the other Crescent products, its Internet ToolPak consists of several well-designed components that provide all the functionality you need to get the job done.

The controls included in the Internet ToolPak can be used to create applications that use just about any Internet service, such as FTP, HTTP (Web documents), and newsgroups. Electronic mail functions can also be accessed, with both MIME and UUENCODE/UUDECODE attachment formats supported. There is also direct support for TCP/IP, Remote Access Services (RAS), and Telnet.

Altogether, 16 ActiveX controls are in the Internet ToolPak. There is also a Telnet Form and an Internet Mail Wizard to get you started with your terminal emulation and electronic mail applications.

PowerTCP

Dart Communications

6647 Old Thompson Road

Syracuse, NY 13211

Sales: (315) 655-1024

Fax: (315) 431-1025

Email: info@dart.com

Web Site: http://www.dart.com/

Retail Price: $598.00

PowerTCP includes all the ActiveX controls you need to create Internet and network client/server applications. Just about all the bases are covered, from low-level TCP data stream communications to access of higher-level protocols such as FTP and POP3. The complete list of protocols supported by PowerTCP is shown in Table 50.7.

Table 50.7. Protocols supported by Dart Communications' PowerTCP.

Protocol	*Description*
TCP	Transmission Control Protocol, for data stream communications between networked devices
Telnet	Telecommunications Network Protocol, for terminal-based access to remote hosts

Protocol	Description
VT220	Full VT220, VT100, and VT52 terminal emulation
FTP	File Transfer Protocol, for storage and retrieval of files on remote hosts
SMTP	Simple Mail Transfer Protocol, sends electronic mail with support for UUENCODE and MIME attachments
POP3	Post Office Protocol, for retrieving mail and attachments from POP3 servers
UDP	User Datagram Protocol, for sending and receiving datagram packets
TFTP	Trivial File Transfer Protocol, a method of sending and receiving files similar to FTP
SNMP	Simple Network Management Protocol, for comprehensive network management capabilities with both manager and agent functionality

PowerTCP comes complete with a number of sample programs that illustrate how to use all the ActiveX controls included in the product. An end-user license and a royalty-free distribution license are also included, but you may have to purchase additional runtime licenses if you will be distributing programs written using PowerTCP's components. OEM licenses are available.

Socket Tools

Catalyst Development Corporation

56925 Yucca Trail, Suite 254

Yucca Valley, CA 92284

Sales: (760) 228-9653

Fax: (760) 369-1185

Email: `sales@catalyst.com`

Web Site: `http://www.catalyst.com/`

Retail Price: $247.00

Catalyst Development also offers a full complement of ActiveX controls for Internet application development with its Socket Tools. Table 50.8 lists some of the controls included in this product.

Table 50.8. Some of the controls included in Catalyst's Socket Tools.

Control	*Description*
Dialer	Establishes and monitors connections to a remote host when using Dial-Up Networking (RAS)
DnsClient	Queries a remote name server to resolve host names to IP addresses
FingerClient	Obtains user information from a Finger server
FtpClient	Sends and receives files to and from a host
GopherClient	Retrieves documents from a Gopher server
MailMessage	Creates and parses messages, with support for the MIME format
NewsClient	Used to scan, retrieve, and post messages on remote news servers
Ping	Pings a host to see whether it is reachable
PopClient	Retrieves electronic mail messages from a remote mail server
RemoteCmd	Allows commands to be executed on a remote UNIX host
SmtpClient	Sends electronic mail messages to a remote host
Socket	Provides access to the standard Windows Sockets library
TelnetClient	Interacts with a remote host using terminal emulation
Terminal	Provides ANSI terminal emulation
TimeClient	Retrieves current time and date information from a remote server
WebClient	Displays HTML documents and establishes a connection with Web servers
WhoIsClient	Returns information about a specific domain or user from a remote server

Two other ActiveX controls are also included with Socket Tools. Though they really don't have anything directly to do with building Internet applications, they can be used in conjunction with the WebClient control. The AudioPlayer control plays a variety of sound file formats, such as WAV, MIDI, AIFF, AU, and VOC. The Viewer control displays BMP, GIF, PCX, JPEG, and XBM images.

ScriptActive and DocActive

NCompass Labs, Inc.
Third Floor Hudson House
321 Water St.
Vancouver, BC, Canada V6B 1B8

Sales: (604) 606-0950

Fax: (604) 606-0970

Email: ncompass@ncompasslabs.com

Web Site: http://www.ncompasslabs.com/

Retail Price: Contact vendor

If you're developing ActiveX controls for use on the Internet or an intranet, you're no doubt aware that one of the major limitations in doing so is in the area of Web browser support. Only Microsoft's Internet Explorer supports technology such as ActiveX controls and documents, right? Well, yes and no. Two tools from NCompass Labs are bringing ActiveX functionality to Netscape browsers, giving you the freedom to develop ActiveX controls and documents that will work on either Microsoft *or* Netscape browsers.

The first product is ScriptActive. ScriptActive adds ActiveX and VBScript support to Netscape browsers (version 3 or 4.x, including Communicator). Web pages that use ActiveX controls and/or VBScript need to be converted using the ScriptActive HTML Conversion Utility, which converts ActiveX HTML to HTML that can be read by both Internet Explorer and Netscape with ScriptActive. However, before users can view the converted documents with a Netscape browser, they must have the NCompass plug-in. It should be noted that the plug-in does not work with documents that have not already been converted.

Another product from NCompass Labs is DocActive. DocActive is a browser plug-in that allows users to view Active Documents, such as Word, Excel, or PowerPoint documents, inline within a Netscape browser window. Of course, you can create Active Documents with Visual Basic, and DocActive should support those, too.

Products like ScriptActive and DocActive are helping to blur the line between Internet Explorer and Netscape Navigator. This is a boon to anyone who is actively involved in the development of online applications or interactive Web pages.

Visual Internet Toolkit

Distinct Corporation

12900 Saratoga Avenue

P.O. Box 3410

Saratoga, CA 95070-1410

Sales: (408) 366-8933

Fax: (408) 366-0153

Email: sales@distinct.com

Web Site: http://www.distinct.com/

Retail Price: $395.00

Last but not least in the Internet development category is Distinct's Visual Internet Toolkit. Like many of the other products already mentioned, the Visual Internet Toolkit provides support for many high- and low-level Internet protocols. But this product also has a few that the others don't.

In addition to ActiveX controls that support protocols such as HTTP, POP, SMTP, NNTP, MIME/UUENCODE, RAS, FTP Client/Server, TFTP, Telnet, VT220, Finger, WhoIs, and Windows Sockets, Visual Internet Toolkit also supports RCP (Remote Copy Protocol) and TCP Server. Plus, you can traverse firewalls with Visual Internet Toolkit's SOCKS5 support and access secured Web documents with the HTTP control's SSL support. A control for Rexec, Rshell, and Rlogin functions is also included for those accessing remote UNIX servers.

Here's another bonus: Several tools for debugging Internet applications are included with Visual Internet Toolkit. The Distinct Network Monitor, Distinct License Manager, and Distinct Floating License Manager all come with the product.

Distinct Corporation claims that Visual Internet Toolkit features more TCP/IP protocols than any other competing product. That may very well be true.

Miscellaneous

The products listed in this section provide unique services that don't fit into any of the preceding categories.

MIDI Pack

Mabry Software, Inc.
P.O. Box 31926
Seattle, WA 98103-1926

Sales:	(800) 996-2279 or (206) 634-1443
Fax:	(206) 632-0272
Email:	`mabry@mabry.com`
Web Site:	`http://www.mabry.com/`

Retail Price: $99.00 without source code, $299.00 with source code

If you want to do nothing more than play back MIDI files from within your programs, VB's MCI control will suffice. But if you need to tap into the full power of MIDI, then Mabry Software's MIDI Pack may be just what the doctor ordered. Using several ActiveX controls, it provides the means by which MIDI input and output can be more precisely controlled.

The MIDI Pack includes a total of eight ActiveX controls (see Table 50.9). Only three of them (MIDIFile, MIDIIN, and MIDIOUT) are used to control the playback and monitoring of MIDI streams and messages. The other five controls are gadgets that can be used to enhance

MIDI programs or create neat applications like audio mixers and music processing applications (see Figure 50.13).

Table 50.9. The ActiveX controls included in Mabry Software's MIDI Pack.

Control	*Description*
MIDIFile	Reads and writes format 0 (single track) and format 1 (multiple-track) MIDI files
MIDIIN	Retrieves messages from external MIDI devices
MIDIOUT	Controls the contents and timing of MIDI messages sent to internal or external MIDI devices
HIndic	Displays a horizontal meter (VU meter)
HSlide	A horizontal slider control for creating audio mixers
Knob	A round adjusting knob with four different styles
VIndic	Displays a vertical meter (VU meter)
VSlide	A vertical slider control for creating audio mixers

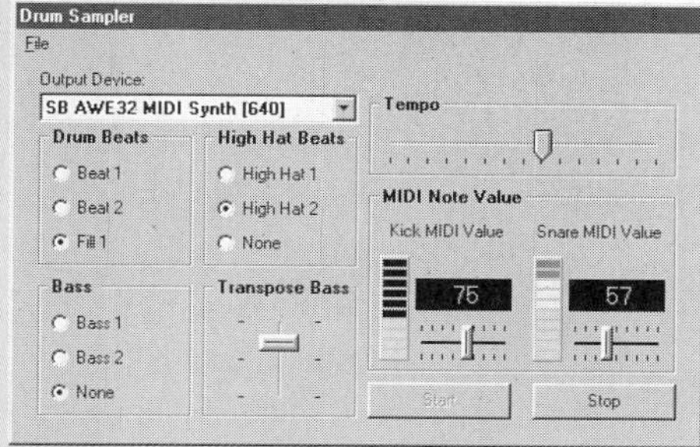

FIGURE 50.13.
A MIDI Drum Sampler created with some of the ActiveX controls in Mabry's MIDI Pack.

All in all, MIDI Pack provides a cool set of tools that can be used to create advanced MIDI-based applications. The inclusion of specialized tuning gadgets and meters makes MIDI Pack a must for serious MIDI developers.

Sax Basic Engine

Sax Software Corporation
950 Patterson Street
Eugene, OR 97401

Sales:	(800) 645-3729 or (541) 344-2235
Tech Support:	(541) 344-4761

Fax: (541) 344-2459
Email: info@saxsoft.com
Web Site: http://www.saxsoft.com/

Retail Price: $995/Enterprise Edition, $495/Professional Edition

If you're developing a sophisticated application that can be enhanced with a built-in macro language, you may be shy about programming in that kind of functionality because you know it will take a lot of extra work. Luckily, the Sax Basic Engine allows you to add a VBA-compatible macro language into your application with a minimum of effort. Simply add the SaxBasic ActiveX control to your form and you have a big head start.

The Sax Basic Engine gives your application a built-in editor and a complete IDE in which users can code their own macros. This includes support for Windows API function calls, OLE Automation, in-code creation of custom dialog boxes, and the use of BASIC subroutines and functions.

Although the Sax Basic Engine offers full support for modern BASIC source code, it can also be extended with your own variables and functions. This is as easy as adding `Property Get`, `Property Let`, `Sub`, and `Function` procedures.

One word of caution for those considering using this control: Because the Sax Basic Engine absolutely requires OLE Automation, it cannot be used with the Standard EXE project type. Instead, you have to use an ActiveX EXE project type.

Clearly, this product is not for everyone. Unless you are developing a truly complex application that would benefit from its own built-in macro language, the Sax Basic Engine won't do you much good. But if your program needs to be enhanced to allow user programmability, this product can save you an incredible amount of time.

TWAINWizard

Olympus Software Europe
Wendenstraße 14-16
Hamburg, Germany
Sales: +49-40-23773-411
Fax: +49-40-23773-644
Email: info@olympus-software.com
Web Site: http://www.olympus-software.com/

Retail Price: $129.00

TWAINWizard's name is a little misleading because it's not the kind of wizard you're used to dealing with (like the Setup Wizard). Instead, it's an ActiveX control (Twiz) that allows your programs to communicate with TWAIN-compatible input devices such as scanners and digital cameras.

TWAINWizard works by acting as a middleman between a container (a program) and a source (the input device). First, some properties are set that specify how the image will be acquired. Next, one of TWAINWizard's Acquire methods are invoked. At this point, TWAINWizard takes over and waits for the input device to finish sending its image. After the transfer is complete, TWAINWizard fires an event that lets the container know that the image has been received. If an error should occur during the transfer, a different event is fired to make the container aware of the error condition.

TWAINWizard was created to complement ImageKnife, another product by Olympus Software that can be used to process images. The two together are all the tools needed to create one heck of an image scanning and manipulation program.

VersionStamper

Desaware

1100 E. Hamilton Ave., Suite #4

Campbell, CA 95008

Sales:	(408) 377-4770
Fax:	(408) 371-3530
Email:	`support@desaware.com`
Web Site:	`http://www.desaware.com/desaware/`

Retail Price: $149.00

One of the biggest problems with the component-based programming model is that different versions of a particular component are difficult to keep track of. Compounding this problem is the fact that today's applications typically require a wide array of support components, such as OCXs and DLLs. When you distribute an application to end users, it's difficult to know whether their systems contain the support components you need. And if they do have them, you need to know whether they are the correct versions.

Of course, component version checking is often done when a program is installed on a user's system. But how do you know that another program won't install an older version of a DLL? And what if one or more components are mistakenly deleted from the user's system?

Desaware's VersionStamper was created to help solve the nightmare of dealing with program components. It embeds into a program's executable file a complete list of every DLL, OCX, and any other software component that the program requires. The necessary version number of each component is also embedded. When the program is run, it confirms that all the necessary components are present and accounted for, and that the version of each is current enough. VersionStamper gives you complete control over this process, and it can be modified easily.

If all the necessary software components are not present or are outdated, you can include a "rescue" program with your application that can compare the component requirements of the executable with the runtime enviroment. The executable program need not be loaded for the rescue program to work. Two sample rescue programs with full source code are included with VersionStamper.

You can also choose to add a feature where the missing or outdated components are automatically downloaded from an Internet site and updated on the user's system. Problems can also be reported to a specific email address, if desired.

All this version-checking functionality can be added to a program via the ActiveX control VersionStamper. Several forms and modules are also included that can be incorporated into your applications to handle the component checking process. VersionStamper also comes with several standalone programs and utilities that you can use externally from your application. Sample projects and source code are also included.

Summary

The number of third-party controls available for Visual Basic is incredible. Almost every kind of service you can think of has probably already been wrapped up into an OCX and is being sold by a software vendor somewhere. This chapter described some of the more popular control packages currently available.

Third-Party Add-Ins

IN THIS CHAPTER

One of Visual Basic's best qualities is that it is expandable. Microsoft knew that it could never incorporate all the features that programmers want, so it created VB with an open architecture. This includes the use of add-ins, which add extra functionality to the VB development environment itself.

Several third-party software companies offer products that enhance the Visual Basic environment directly. Other products are designed to be used with VB but are standalone and do not interact with Visual Basic. For example, InstallShield's Express2 is a replacement for VB's Setup Wizard. It was designed specifically to create installation programs for VB applications (and other platforms), but it is run as a standalone instead of inside Visual Basic.

This chapter describes some of the more popular products available as add-ins or utilities for Visual Basic. These are not reviews in the purest sense, only brief descriptions that will provide you with a basic overview of each product so that you can decide whether it is something that might be of benefit. Contact information is also given for each product to point you in the right direction for obtaining more information.

Visual Basic Add-Ins

Although many VB add-ins are on the market today, only one is described in this chapter. VBCommander is a true add-in in that it actually adds new features to the VB development environment.

VBCommander

BeCubed Software, Inc.

1750 Marietta Hwy., Suite 240

Canton, GA 30114

Sales:	(770) 720-1077 or (888) 232-8233
Tech Support:	(770) 720-2278
Fax:	(770) 720-1078
Email:	`cs@bcubed.com`
Web Site:	`http://www.becubed.com/`

Retail Price: $159.00

BeCubed Software's VBCommander is a general-purpose add-in that enhances Visual Basic's development environment by adding more than 100 new time-saving features. Many of these features are simple, but they alleviate a lot of mundane work that you probably hate to do. For example, if you want to add an error handler to a procedure, simply select all the code in the procedure and click VBCommander's Error Handling option. It will automatically add an `On Error Goto` line at the beginning of the procedure and a fully functional error handler at the end of the procedure. You can also add a module-level error handling routine just as easily.

VBCommander's functions can be accessed through a small floating toolbar (see Figure 51.1). The toolbar has three tabs, Desktop, Controls, and Utilities. Each tab has seven buttons, and each button can access two functions (right-click for one function, left-click for the other).

FIGURE 51.1.
VBCommander's floating toolbar, from which its 100+ functions can be accessed.

Some of the more useful features and functions provided by VBCommander are listed in Table 51.1.

Table 51.1. Some of the more useful features of the VBCommander add-in.

Feature	*Description*
Cloning	Clone controls, menus, procedures, and forms
Common Dialog Designer	Eases the use of Common Dialog forms
Control Array Handler	Easily builds control arrays
External Editor	Allows you to retrieve and edit code outside the VB IDE
Icon Clipper	Extracts icons from `.EXE` files
Input Box Designer	Designs and creates input boxes
Message Box Designer	Designs and creates message boxes
Project ToDo List	Maintains a to-do list for your projects
Property Prompter	Prompts for common properties when you drop a control onto a form
SQL Builder	Helps you build SQL commands
String Search	Searches for strings in a project and reports its findings, all in one pass

VBCommander adds many features that should have been incorporated into the VB IDE in the first place. These are great time-savers that will help alleviate some of the more mundane aspects of programming in Visual Basic.

Standalone Utilities

Some products do not work directly with the Visual Basic environment but are designed to complement it in some way. The products described in this section are standalone utilities that can be used to assist in different stages of the development process.

ERwin/ERX

Logic Works
111 Campus Dr.
Princeton, NJ 08540

Sales:	(609) 514-1177
Fax:	(609) 514-1175
Web Site:	`http://www.logicworks.com/`

Retail Price: About $3,500.00

When it comes to designing complex client/server database systems, Logic Works' ERwin/ERX makes things easy. It allows you to diagram database entities and their relationships graphically. Entity-relationship (ER) diagramming tools are nothing new, of course, and have been in use for years. Two standard diagramming methods, the Air Force's IDEF1X and the more popular Information Engineering (IE) notation, are both supported by ERwin. But ERwin is more than just a diagramming tool.

After a database system has been diagrammed logically (see Figure 51.2), ERwin can create it physically. All the database structures are built for you automatically based on the information in your model. This includes all its tables, indexes, views, stored procedures, and any other components you may have specified.

ERwin can do the same thing in reverse, too. Give it a physical database system to work with, and it will create a graphical diagram of the system's objects and their relationships. And if you don't keep your physical databases and their logical representations in sync, ERwin will do a complete compare and straighten things out for you.

ERwin is a great product; there's no doubt about that. But it's not for hobbyists. Its high price tag—although worth every cent—will put it out of reach for all but professional programmers.

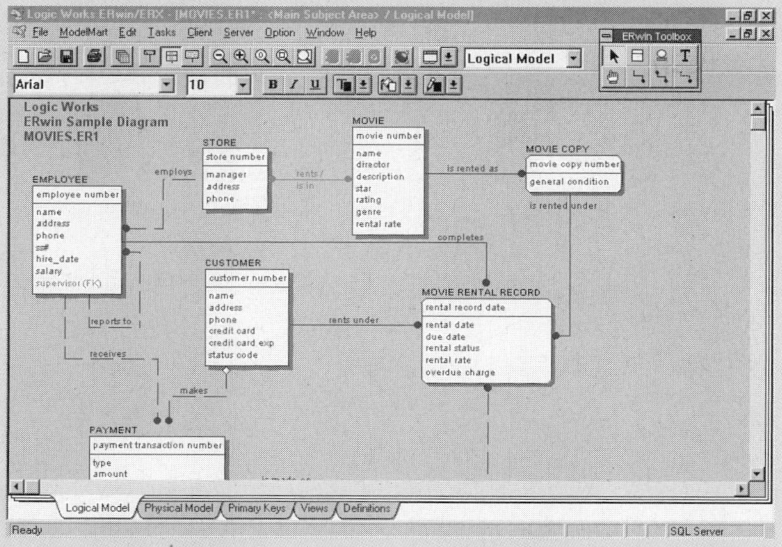

FIGURE 51.2.
After a database system has been logically diagrammed by using ERwin's design tool, a physical version can be created automatically.

InstallShield Express2

InstallShield Software Corporation
900 National Parkway, Suite 125
Schaumburg, IL 60173-5108

Sales:	(800) 374-4353 or (847) 240-9111
Tech Support:	(847) 413-2896
Fax:	(847) 240-9120
Email:	`sales@installshield.com`
Web Site:	`http://www.stirling.com/`

Retail Price: $245.00

When you're distributing applications, the installation process is often as important as the program itself. After all, if the program doesn't install smoothly and correctly, the program probably won't run in the first place. Worse yet, your users will lose confidence in your application before they even get a chance to try it out.

For many programmers, the Setup Wizard included with Visual Basic is enough to create installation programs for simple applications. But if you need more control over the install process, or if you want to give your installs more of a professional edge, a third-party product like InstallShield Express2 is a must.

InstallShield Express2 makes creating high-quality install programs a snap. Like the Setup Wizard, it walks you through the steps necessary to create the install program. It then provides you with a Setup Checklist (see Figure 51.3) that allows you to make big and small modifications to the install process. For example, you can specify that entries be made in the System Registry by clicking the "REG Files" option. You're then presented with a dialog box that lets you detail exactly the kind of entries that should be made, and where. This capability to fine-tune the install process is where InstallShield Express2 really shines.

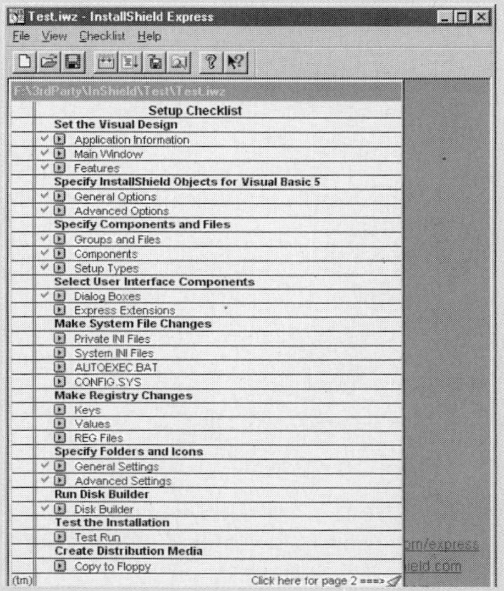

FIGURE 51.3.
After the install program has been created, it can be fine-tuned by modifying any of the items on the Setup Checklist.

InstallShield Express2 has much more going for it. It supports a variety of programming platforms other than VB, including Visual C++ 5.0 and Delphi 3.0. It can also create install programs in languages other than English, such as Italian, Spanish, Swedish, Dutch, and Finnish. The list of notable features goes on and on.

The InstallShield Software Corporation has always created premium installation products, and programmers all over the world swear by them. InstallShield Express2 is another high-quality product that deserves a place on any professional developer's software shelf.

VB HelpWriter Pro

TeleTech Systems
750 Birch Ridge Dr.
Roswell, GA 30076

Sales: (770) 433-6964 or (800) 606-5285

Email: `support@teletech-systems.com`

Web Site: `http://www.teletech-systems.com/`

Retail Price: $99.00

Although VB HelpWriter is not nearly as sophisticated as WinHelp Office, the other Help authoring tool included here, some may see its simplicity and low price as two of its better features. VB HelpWriter automates the process of creating Windows Help files, and it does it quite well.

To begin with, VB HelpWriter acts as a standalone program. Unlike other Help authoring products, it does not require that you use Microsoft Word to assist in creating your Help files. Everything can be done using VB HelpWriter and the Help compiler included with the Professional and Enterprise Editions of Visual Basic.

VB HelpWriter automates Help file creation by scanning your source code and creating a framework. All you need to do is add Help text (and graphics and special formatting, if you're so inclined), and you're done. VB HelpWriter adds source code to your program to add context-sensitive Help and can optionally create a dictionary of common terms in the Help file and a Glossary.

VB HelpWriter supports embedded bitmaps, sound, macros, and multiple windows within the Help files it creates. However, it does not support HTML Help, Microsoft's newest Help format.

WinHelp Office

Blue Sky Software

7777 Fay Avenue, Suite 201

La Jolla, CA 92037

Sales: (619) 459-6365 or (800) 793-0364

Tech Support: (619) 551-5680

Fax: (619) 459-6366

Email: `sales@blue-sky.com`

Web Site: `http://www.blue-sky.com/`

Retail Price: $699.00

The WinHelp Office suite is likely to be the most complete set of Help authoring tools on the market today. The core product in the suite is RoboHELP, which can also be purchased separately.

The files created by RoboHELP may use Microsoft's newest Help format, HTML Help. HTML Help allows many more formatting options and interactivity than the old WinHelp standard, and RoboHELP takes full advantage of it. RoboHELP makes it easy to build top-notch Help files and even add multimedia features.

Those who have to support old-style WinHelp 3.1 files will be glad to find that they have not been forgotten—backward compatibility has been completely maintained by WinHelp Office. WinHelp Office even includes several utilities to assist in dealing with old-style Help files. The WinHelp 3.1 Extension Pack allows you to add Windows 95-style Contents, Index, and Find tabs as well as book view, page view, and full text search to WinHelp 3.1 Help systems.

The WinHelp Office suite also includes a variety of different tools and utilities that assist in creating interesting and engaging Help files, such as

- The Help Video Kit, which allows you to "record" onscreen actions so that they can be played back as tutorials. You can even add narration.
- The PCHelpDesk utility lets you provide your users with access to your Knowledge Base or FAQ files, all from within your Help system.
- Debugging and managing Help files is made easier with tools like WinHelp Inspector, Keyword Reporter, and WinHelp BugHunter.
- Conversion tools that allow you to easily convert Help files to `.RTF`, `.HPJ`, and Microsoft Word formats. You can also convert existing WinHelp 3.1 Help systems to newer formats. Best of all, there's a Moving-to-HTML Kit that converts Help files to HTML to make instant Web pages.
- Graphics tools, including the Graphics Locator, which allows you to view and organize all the graphic images on your system, and ReSize, a handy tool for quickly resizing images and changing their resolution and graphics format. A gallery of royalty-free clip-art is also included.

The WinHelp Office suite comes complete with full documentation. Five different manuals are included with the product, covering all its tools and utilities.

Other Products

In some cases, a product is neither an add-in nor a standalone utility; instead it integrates with the Visual Basic development environment in some other way. The two products in this section, ARTEMIS and SpyWorks Professional, work with VB in different ways. ARTEMIS is a set of DLLs designed to replace the Jet database engine. SpyWorks Professional is a set of ActiveX controls and utilities that enhance Visual Basic in a number of ways.

ARTEMIS

Luxent Development Corp.
27349 Jefferson Avenue, Suite 110
Temecula, CA 92590

Sales:	(888) 458-9368 or (909) 699-9657
Fax:	(909) 695-5679
Email:	`tech@luxent.com`
Web Site:	`http://www.luxent.com/`

Retail Price: $199.00

In a nutshell, ARTEMIS is a database engine designed to replace the Microsoft Jet engine used with Visual Studio development products. Of course, there's no point in replacing something if you're not improving it at the same time. ARTEMIS does make some improvements over the Jet engine, but there's a lot of give and take involved.

For one thing, it should be noted that ARTEMIS is small—in some cases, the runtime files add up to less than 200 KB in size. That's the good news. The bad news is that ARTEMIS's small size means that something was given up. The number of database formats supported by ARTEMIS is far fewer than those supported by Jet; only Clipper and FoxPro databases are still on the list. However, ARTEMIS also adds its own proprietary format (HiPer-SIx) that is both compact and fast.

ARTEMIS uses an Xbase-like syntax, and all database operations are performed by calling functions. For example, if you want to create a new index file, you would have to call the `sx_Index` function. None of it is too difficult (especially for more advanced programmers), but if you're used to accessing databases through VB's Data control, you may have a bit of a learning curve.

ARTEMIS includes a Fast Text Search Indexing System, or FTS, which is implemented within a separate DLL. It provides the capability of quickly searching for string values within a field of a database table. It also supports "fuzzy searches" so that you can look for words that sound alike as well as exact matches.

Graphics images can be referenced within ARTEMIS databases by using the Light Lib Images ActiveX control, also included with this product. The images are actually bound to a memo field in a database table, not encoded into the database itself.

ARTEMIS is an interesting product, and it has some definite strong points. If you want a replacement for the Jet engine that has a small footprint and you aren't picky about the database format you use, it may be just the thing you're looking for.

SpyWorks Professional

Desaware
1100 E. Hamilton Ave., Suite #4
Campbell, CA 95008

Sales:	(408) 377-4770
Fax:	(408) 371-3530
Email:	`support@desaware.com`
Web Site:	`http://www.desaware.com/`

Retail Price: $249.00

SpyWorks is a collection of useful ActiveX components, classes, dynamic link libraries, and utilities that should have been included with Visual Basic but weren't. Advanced programmers will find that SpyWorks allows them to do much more than they thought was possible in VB.

Some of the more interesting features of SpyWorks include

- Dynamic Export Technology, which lets you create ActiveX DLLs with truly exportable functions (an ActiveX DLL created with Visual Basic will not let you have functions that are callable from other programs).
- An ActiveX control that lets you intercept keyboard entries before they are received by VB or other applications.
- A VB5-created DLL for subclassing, hooks, and management of custom windows.
- A Winsock library for accessing the Winsock API directly without the overhead of an ActiveX control.
- An ActiveX control that allows you to tap into the messages that are passed to Windows objects such as forms and controls.
- ActiveX extensions that let you override the behavior of interfaces that are part of your components and let you add new standard interfaces to your components.
- An ActiveX control containing a pool of function addresses that can be used as callback functions for Win32 API functions.

The preceding list contains only a few SpyWorks features. There are many more, all enhancing Visual Basic in unique ways. SpyWorks is definitely one of the most useful products on the market. Once you try it, you'll wonder how you got along without it.

Summary

A wide variety of third-party add-ins and utilities are available to Visual Basic developers. This chapter described just a few of the products currently available. Although some integrate directly with the VB environment, many are standalone programs designed to ease a certain stage of development.

CHAPTER 52

Differences Between VBA and VB5

IN THIS CHAPTER

Visual Basic for Applications, or VBA, has come into vogue in the past few years. When Microsoft started integrating VBA into its popular Office suite of applications, VBA came into the limelight as the new standard for macro languages. By including VBA with applications such as Word, Excel, and PowerPoint, Microsoft has combined the flexibility and ease of programming that Visual Basic offers with the power of the application that hosts it.

Microsoft has also begun licensing Visual Basic to other software developers, meaning that VBA will be used in more applications than just the ones created by Microsoft. Visio and AutoCAD are just two examples of companies that have licensed VBA for use in their own applications.

Even though VBA parallels Visual Basic in many ways, VB developers may still be unfamiliar with the intricacies of the macro language. Indeed, the first question a VB programmer is likely to ask before trying to use VBA is, "What's the difference between the version of Visual Basic that I'm familiar with and VBA?" This chapter will answer that important question.

An Overview of VBA

As a Visual Basic programmer, you are no doubt aware of the possibilities (and limitations) inherent with VB; that is, you know what Visual Basic can do and what it cannot do. You've worked with VB extensively and have come to know all its little perks and quirks.

At face value, VBA is much like Visual Basic. The two development environments, or IDEs, look similar at first glance. But after a closer look, you'll see some minor differences.

VBA also is a lot like Visual Basic on the inside, but once again, there are differences. VBA is not as full-featured as Visual Basic, but that stands to reason. After all, VBA is not a full-fledged development environment; it is a macro language. This brings up an important point. Before VBA can be exploited, the role that it plays must be understood.

What VBA Is and Is Not

The first thing that differentiates VBA from Visual Basic is the fact that VBA is designed to function as a macro language, whereas Visual Basic is designed as a way of creating applications and program components. VBA cannot create compiled executable code like Visual Basic can. VBA projects can only run within their host application. For example, if a VBA project is created to work with Excel (its host application), then it can only be executed within the Excel application.

So what can VBA do, and what is it used for? VBA is used to enhance or extend its host application in some way, such as adding new functions to Excel or changing Word's menu structure by adding new options or removing the ones you don't want to see. VBA can also be used to facilitate communication and interoperability between applications that support VBA. For example, you could use VBA to read an Access database and transfer that information to a Word document. The possibilities are endless.

The VBA Development Environment

One area of difference between VBA and Visual Basic is in the development environment, or IDE. Compare the IDE for VBA (see Figure 52.1) with that of Visual Basic (see Figure 52.2). You'll notice several things right away.

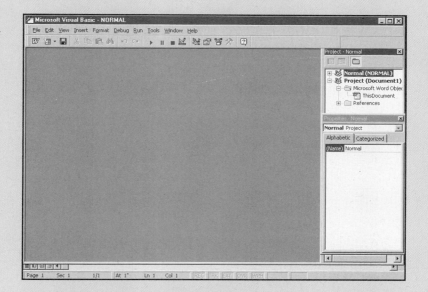

FIGURE 52.1.
The VBA development environment, or IDE.

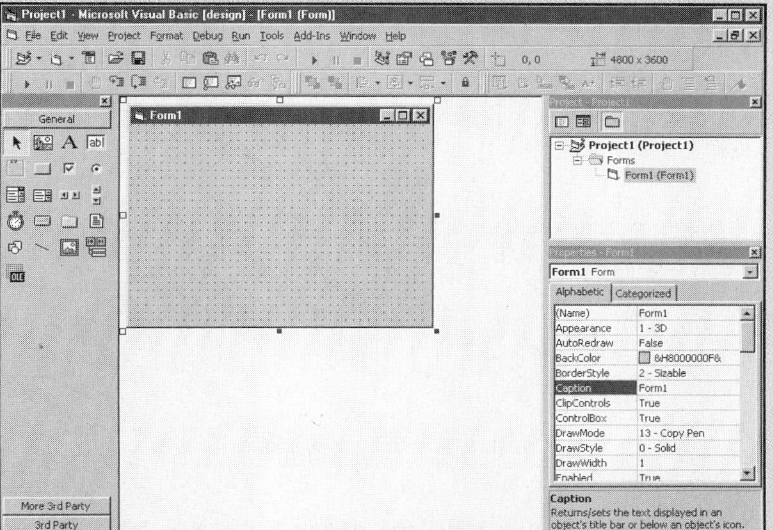

FIGURE 52.2.
VB5's development environment.

NOTE

The VBA environment depicted in Figure 52.1 and in the rest of this chapter shows the Project and Properties windows on the right side of the screen. However, when you use VBA for the first time, they may be on the left side of the screen. Like Visual Basic, VBA also allows you to determine where your windows will be placed. You can move them to the right side if that is more familiar to you.

For one thing, VBA does not provide a blank form or container object right away like most Visual Basic projects do. Instead, you have to add a `Form` yourself (although in VBA, forms are called `UserForms`, which will be discussed later).

Also, you'll notice that the Toolbox is missing. VBA does have a Toolbox (see Figure 52.3), but it does not appear until a `UserForm` object has been added to the project. VBA's Toolbox is not dockable, like VB's Toolbox is. Instead, it exists in a floating window.

FIGURE 52.3.
VBA's floating Toolbox, which is not visible until a `UserForm` *object has been added to the project.*

The controls included in VBA's Toolbox are different from those in Visual Basic, as you can see. The controls in the VBA Toolbox come from the Microsoft Forms 2.0 control library, which includes versions of many of VB's standard controls: Label, TextBox, ComboBox, ListBox, OptionButton, Frame, CommandButton, and Image. It also includes one of the VB Professional controls (TabStrip). The HScrollBar and VScrollBar controls used in Visual Basic have been combined into a single ScrollBar control, and the ToggleButton, Multipage, and SpinButton controls have been added.

Like in Visual Basic, VBA's Toolbox can be modified by adding and removing controls. However, VBA does not support all ActiveX controls.

Another difference between the development environments for VBA and Visual Basic is in their menu bars. VB's Project menu item has been replaced with the Insert menu item in VBA. Both provide similar services, allowing you to insert new objects such as forms (`UserForms` in VBA) and class modules into the current project. VB's Project menu has many more insertable objects than VBA, however.

Missing from VBA's menu bar is the Add-Ins menu item. There's a good reason for this: VBA does not support add-ins.

The VBA and VB menu bars differ in other ways, too. For example, VBA's File menu is quite different from the File menu in Visual Basic. VBA files and projects themselves cannot be saved or loaded, so there are no options to facilitate this. VBA projects are saved with their host document or document template and do not exist separately. The only way to share VBA forms and modules with other VBA projects is by importing and exporting them. Options for Import and Export are included in VBA's File menu.

The toolbars of Visual Basic and VBA are different, too. VBA adds a few new icons, such as the one that switches back to the host application. In Figure 52.1, this is the leftmost icon on the toolbar, which shows a Microsoft Word logo. Other icons are missing from VBA's Toolbar. For example, the Menu Editor icon is not on the VBA Toolbar because that tool is not included in VBA.

You can see that there are many differences between the Visual Basic and VBA design environments. Some are apparent right away, but others are hidden.

Programming Differences

Probably the best way to illustrate how Visual Basic and VBA differ in the way they are programmed is to create two separate but similar projects, one using Visual Basic and one using VBA. The first project will be created in Visual Basic. It will be so simple that you probably won't even want to try it out.

The VB program will use a TextBox control and a CommandButton control. When the CommandButton is clicked, the text in the TextBox will be parsed (separated into words) and reversed. For example, if the phrase "Let the fun begin" was entered, it would be changed to "begin fun the Let". Not the most useful program, to be sure, but it will serve to illustrate the differences between a VB and a VBA program.

NOTE

In this text, VBA projects are often referred to as *programs*. However, in VBA they are usually called *macros*. In this context, you can think of a macro and a program as being synonymous.

The interface for the VB program will look like the one in Figure 52.4 and as stated earlier it will use one TextBox control (`txtInputArea`) and one CommandButton control (`cmdReverse`). Listing 52.1 shows all the code for the program.

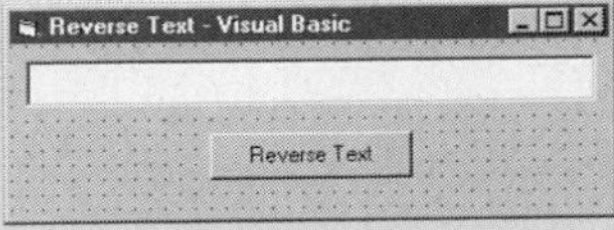

FIGURE 52.4.
The user interface for the Visual Basic version of the Reverse Text program.

Listing 52.1. The code for the Visual Basic version of the Reverse Text program.

```
Private Sub cmdReverse_Click()

Dim intSpacePos As Integer
Dim intLastPos As Integer
Dim strNewWord As String
Dim strNewText As String

' You can set this value depending on your preferences.
' If you want to have this routine strip out any non-
' alphanumeric characters (A-Z, a-z, 0-9, Space), then
' set it to True. Otherwise, set it to False.
booAlphanumericOnly = True

' If there's nothing in the text box, exit the routine.
If txtInputArea.Text = "" Then Exit Sub

' Add a space to the end of the text so it can parse
' the last word.
txtInputArea.Text = txtInputArea.Text & Chr(32)

' Parse the contents of the text box (txtInputArea).
Do
    intSpacePos = InStr(intLastPos + 1, _
        txtInputArea.Text, Chr(32))
    If intSpacePos Then
        strNewWord = Mid(txtInputArea.Text, _
            intLastPos + 1, intSpacePos - intLastPos)
        ' Strip out non-alphanumeric characters?
        If booAlphanumericOnly Then
            strNewWord = StripPunctuation(strNewWord)
        End If
        ' Add the new word to the front of the string,
        ' so the string of words becomes reversed.
        strNewText = strNewWord & strNewText
    End If
    intLastPos = intSpacePos
Loop Until (intSpacePos = 0)

' Assign the new string (which should be reversed) back
' to the text box.
txtInputArea.Text = strNewText

End Sub


Function StripPunctuation(strWordIn) As String

Dim bytChar As Byte
```

```
Dim intCharPos As Integer
Dim strNoPuncWord As String

strNoPuncWord = ""

' Loop through the current word and discard anything
' that isn't alphanumeric or a space.
For intCharPos = 1 To Len(strWordIn)
    bytChar = Asc(Mid(strWordIn, intCharPos, 1))
    Select Case bytChar
        Case 32:
            ' Add spaces (ASCII 32).
            strNoPuncWord = strNoPuncWord & Chr(32)
        Case 48 To 57:
            ' Add characters 0-9 (ASCII 48-57).
            strNoPuncWord = strNoPuncWord & Chr(bytChar)
        Case 65 To 90:
            ' Add characters A-Z (ASCII 65-90).
            strNoPuncWord = strNoPuncWord & Chr(bytChar)
        Case 97 To 122:
            ' Add characters a-z (ASCII 97-122).
            strNoPuncWord = strNoPuncWord & Chr(bytChar)
    End Select
Next intCharPos

StripPunctuation = strNoPuncWord

End Function
```


Although the code is somewhat lengthy, the program is still simple. It loops through the text in the text box (`txtInputArea`) looking for spaces (also known as *parsing*). When it finds a space, it extracts a word and adds it to the beginning of a string (`strNewText`). When the loop is done, `strNewText` contains all the words in the text box, except reversed.

A Boolean variable (`booAlphanumericOnly`) is used to determine whether nonalphanumeric characters should be stripped out of the string. If alphanumeric characters, such as punctuation, are left in, then the text string "This is a test." would be reversed to "test. a is This". Stripping out the nonalphanumeric characters fixes this and results in "test a is This". If `booAlphanumericOnly` is set to `True`, then the function `StripPunctuation` is called during the parsing loop. It does the work of stripping out any unwanted characters.

If you want to try out the Visual Basic program, go ahead. Just remember to call the TextBox control `txtInputArea` and the CommandButton control `cmdReverse`.

Next, a similar program will be created using VBA. Instead of using text entered into a TextBox, however, the VBA program will use any currently selected text. The host application will be Microsoft Word, so you can select any text you want reversed in a document and then invoke the program and have it do its thing.

To implement the reverse text processing code in VBA, start up the host application, which in this case will be Microsoft Word. Choose Tools | Macro and then select Macro from the pop-up window (or press the shortcut key, Alt+F8). This will display the Macros dialog box (see Figure 52.5), which lists all the macros available for the current document. Unless the document that you are using was generated from a template that included macros or you have been fooling around with VBA on your own, the list of macros should be empty.

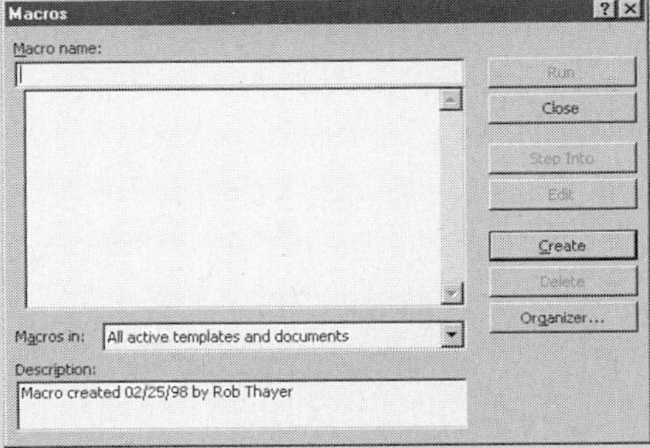

FIGURE 52.5.
The Macros dialog box, which lists all the macros available for the current document.

To create a new macro, type in a name (`ReverseText` is suggested) and click the Create button. After a few moments, Word will bring you directly to the VBA environment. It also provides you with an empty Sub procedure for your new macro as well as comment lines that indicate when the macro was created (see Figure 52.6).

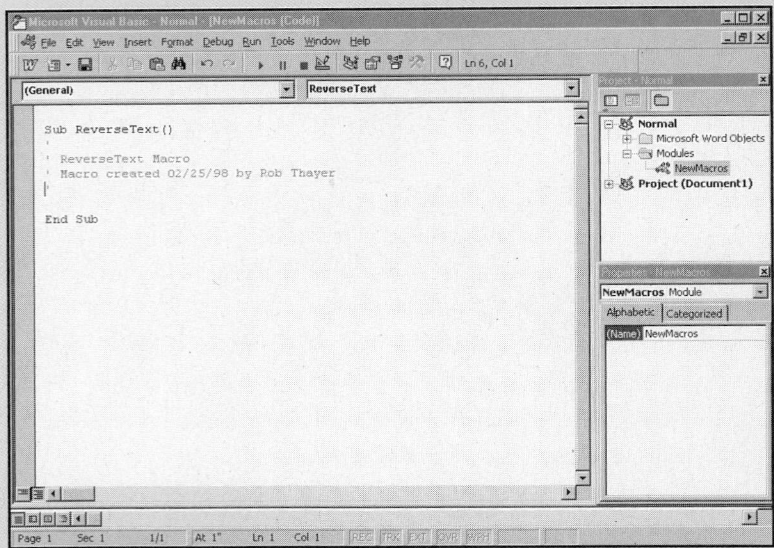

FIGURE 52.6.
When you add a new macro, the VBA environment is called up and an empty Sub procedure is added for you.

You can now add the code for the `ReverseText` Sub procedure (see Listing 52.2). This is essentially the same code that was used with the VB version of the program, but with a few minor—but important—changes.

Listing 52.2. The code for the `ReverseText` Sub procedure, a Microsoft Word macro.

```
Sub ReverseText()
'
' ReverseText Macro
' Macro created 02/25/98 by Rob Thayer
'
Dim intSpacePos As Integer
Dim intLastPos As Integer
Dim strNewWord As String
Dim strNewText As String
Dim strSelText As String

' You can set this value depending on your preferences.
' If you want to have this routine strip out any non-
' alphanumeric characters (A-Z, a-z, 0-9, Space), then
' set it to True. Otherwise, set it to False.
booAlphanumericOnly = True

' Add a space to the end of the selected text so it can parse
' the last word.
strSelText = Word.Selection & Chr(32)

' If there's nothing in the selection, exit the routine.
If RTrim(strSelText) = "" Then Exit Sub

' Parse the contents of the selection (strSelText).
Do
    intSpacePos = InStr(intLastPos + 1, _
        strSelText, Chr(32))
    If intSpacePos Then
        strNewWord = Mid(strSelText, _
            intLastPos + 1, intSpacePos - intLastPos)
        ' Strip out non-alphanumeric characters?
        If booAlphanumericOnly Then
            strNewWord = StripPunctuation(strNewWord)
        End If
        ' Add the new word to the front of the string,
        ' so the string of words becomes reversed.
        strNewText = strNewWord & strNewText
    End If
    intLastPos = intSpacePos
Loop Until (intSpacePos = 0)

' Assign the new string (which should be reversed) back
' to the selection.
Word.Selection = strNewText

End Sub
```

The biggest difference here is that the `txtInputArea` control is no longer used to provide the text to be processed. Instead, a new string (`strSelText`) is used. It gets its value from another object, `Word.Selection`. This is important, and it merits further discussion.

In VBA, you often utilize objects and classes from the host application (in this case, Word). All the Office 97 applications use a wide variety of different objects. In Word, there is a `Documents` collection, a `Document` object, an `ActiveDocument` object, and many others. There is also a `Selection` object, which is what is being used here. The `Selection` object contains any text currently selected.

The VBA macro we are constructing here is applied to the current selection. However, it could just as easily be applied to the entire document if, instead of assigning `strSelText` the value of `Word.Selection`, it was assigned the value of `Word.ActiveDocument.Content`, which refers to the entire content of the whichever document is active. Using the current selection makes more sense, however.

To become fluent in using VBA, you must be familiar with the various objects and classes implemented in the host application or applications for which you want to create macros. This is a key point. You wouldn't be able to use Visual Basic effectively if you did not have an understanding of VB's objects (forms, text boxes, command buttons, and so on). Likewise, you cannot use VBA effectively if you do not understand the objects available to it. A discussion of Office 97 objects and classes is beyond the scope of this chapter. Consult a book on VBA programming for more information (*Special Edition Using Visual Basic for Applications 5* by Que Publishing is recommended).

To continue with the VBA project, the `StripPunctuation` function needs to be added next (see Listing 52.3). This is identical to the function used in the Visual Basic project created earlier.

Listing 52.3. The `StripPunctuation` function, which is used by the `ReverseText` Sub procedure (a Word macro).

```
Function StripPunctuation(strWordIn) As String

Dim bytChar As Byte
Dim intCharPos As Integer
Dim strNoPuncWord As String

strNoPuncWord = ""

' Loop through the current word and discard anything
' that isn't alphanumeric or a space.
For intCharPos = 1 To Len(strWordIn)
    bytChar = Asc(Mid(strWordIn, intCharPos, 1))
    Select Case bytChar
        Case 32:
            ' Add spaces (ASCII 32).
            strNoPuncWord = strNoPuncWord & Chr(32)
        Case 48 To 57:
            ' Add characters 0-9 (ASCII 48-57).
            strNoPuncWord = strNoPuncWord & Chr(bytChar)
        Case 65 To 90:
            ' Add characters A-Z (ASCII 65-90).
            strNoPuncWord = strNoPuncWord & Chr(bytChar)
        Case 97 To 122:
```

```
            ' Add characters a-z (ASCII 97-122).
            strNoPuncWord = strNoPuncWord & Chr(bytChar)
    End Select
Next intCharPos

StripPunctuation = strNoPuncWord

End Function
```

To try out the macro, exit VBA (don't worry; you won't lose your work) and go back to the Word document. Type in some text and then select it (see Figure 52.7). Press Alt+F8 to display the Macros dialog box. Note that the ReverseText macro is now listed.

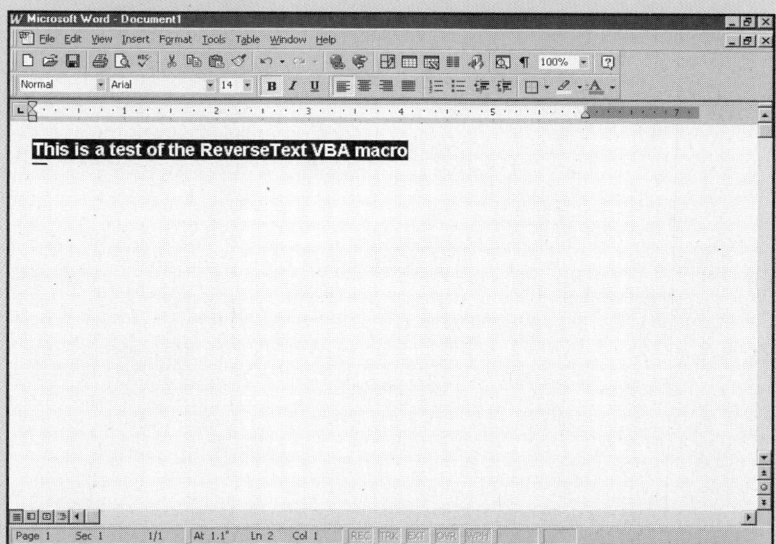

FIGURE 52.7.
Selected text in Microsoft Word, which will be processed by the ReverseText macro.

With the ReverseText macro selected, click the Run button. The `ReverseText` procedure will then be executed, and the selected text will be reversed (see Figure 52.8).

> **NOTE**
>
> The ReverseText macro is somewhat limited in that it is only designed to work with single lines of selected text. Modifications to facilitate the handling of multiple lines of text can be made relatively easily, but were not included originally in an attempt to keep the code as simple as possible.

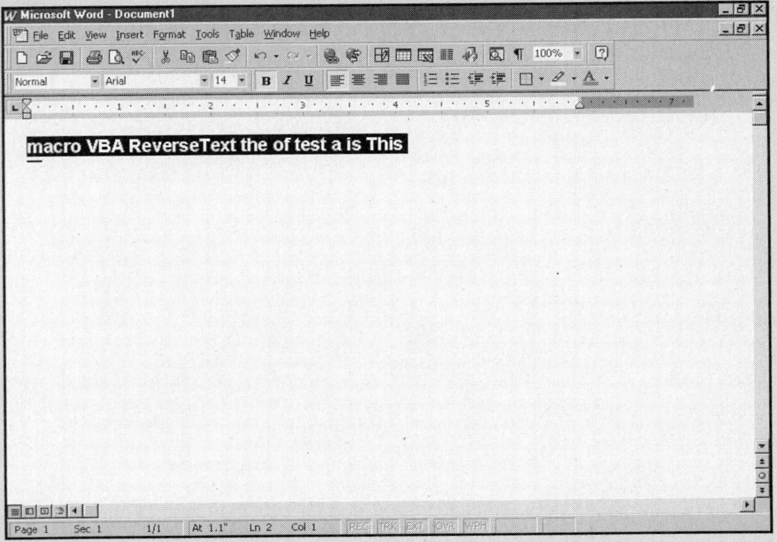

FIGURE 52.8.
The selected text is reversed using the ReverseText macro.

As you can see, the VBA macro and the VB program created earlier do basically the same thing; they are just implemented differently. To review, note the differences between the VB and VBA projects:

- The VB program used the contents of a TextBox control for the text to be processed. The VBA macro uses the Word object `Word.Selection`.
- In the VB program, the main processing code was contained in a command button's `Click` event. In the VBA macro, the code is contained in a Sub procedure.
- The VB program uses a form with controls for its user interface. The VBA macro will work from within its host application (Microsoft Word). Essentially, Word is utilized as its user interface.

Consider the last difference pointed out in the preceding list. The VBA macro has no user interface. Instead, it uses Microsoft Word and works "behind the scenes." Of course, this is not always the case. There may be times when you want a user interface to be displayed, perhaps to allow the user to select different options or customize the macro that will be performed. Because VBA works with a host application, a form is not automatically displayed by default like it is in a VB program. So how do you implement a form-like interface in VBA?

First, you design the form—that much is obvious. In VBA, a form is called a `UserForm`. To display it, you would use a line of code such as the following:

```
UserForm1.Show
```

This code would be placed in the Sub procedure of the macro. So if it were to display a form for the ReverseText macro, the `ReverseText` Sub might look like this:

```
Sub ReverseText()

    UserForm1.Show

End Sub
```

The form (`UserForm1`) could contain controls that in turn call other procedures or respond to events, just like they do in Visual Basic. Once forms are used, VBA becomes easier to understand to VB programmers.

As you get into VBA and start developing more complex macros, you'll find other differences from Visual Basic. But using what you've learned in this chapter, you should have an understanding of how VBA works. Your skills as a VB programmer will take you the rest of the way.

Summary

Visual Basic and VBA are development environments that are both similar and different. Because VBA is a macro language and relies on a host application (such as Microsoft Word or Excel), the concept of a standalone executable program is not feasible in VBA.

VBA has some differences that may at first be confusing to VB programmers. However, after a few sample VBA macros are constructed, Visual Basic developers should have no problem adapting to VBA.

This chapter was designed to introduce VB programmers to VBA. It presented two similar programs, one created in Visual Basic and the other as a VBA macro, to illustrate how the two environments differ.

CHAPTER

Useful API Functions

IN THIS CHAPTER

Visual Basic is a powerful language. It has literally hundreds of built-in functions and statements that can be used to accomplish many small miracles, such as determining how many days have elapsed between two dates or reading information from a disk file. Add to that functionality a full palette of ActiveX controls that can be used as building blocks for creating some extraordinary applications and you have one incredible development environment capable of doing just about anything. Well, almost anything.

Even with the power of VB's built-in library of functions and statements and its unlimited toolbox of external controls, there are still things that VB either cannot do or cannot do efficiently. For example, copying one section of memory—including video memory—to another is not directly supported in Visual Basic. You could probably write a routine that would accomplish this seemingly simple feat, but it would be painfully slow. Unfortunately, VB just is not equipped to handle things like that.

If you wanted to add some animation to your Visual Basic program, you might find that there is no efficient way to do so and surmise that VB simply is not the kind of development environment that supports animation. And, in a way, you would be right. But VB can tap into a huge library of functions that extend it in ways you may not have imagined. The best part is that the users of your VB program already have this library of functions built into their operating system, so you don't have to distribute any extra files or libraries if your program makes use of them.

So what is this library called? It's the Win32 API (Application Programmer's Interface), and it's built into every copy of Windows 95. Consisting of several DLLs (Dynamic Link Libraries), it contains thousands of functions that can be easily accessed from within Visual Basic or any other high-level language.

This chapter will detail some of the more important and useful functions accessible through the Win32 API. Of course, what is shown here is only a smattering of what is actually available. If you want to find out more about the API functions, I suggest you look at Dan Appleman's *Visual Basic 5.0 Programmer's Guide to the Win32 API*. It's the definitive guide to all the API functions, and it was written with the VB programmer in mind.

If you want to learn more about how to actually call API functions from within Visual Basic, see Chapter 5 of this book, "Using Windows API Functions." This chapter assumes that you have some knowledge of how to call API functions, so you will want to read Chapter 5 first if you are not already familiar with how to do so. You should also be aware of the `WIN32API.TXT` file, which contains all the declarations for the Win32 API functions as well as various constants and type structures used by the API functions. The `WIN32API.TXT` file is also covered in Chapter 5.

Graphics and Display Functions

One of the most useful aspects of the Win32 API is improving the performance of graphics. Even relatively simple graphics operations can require a great deal of calculation and memory manipulation. As a high-level language, Visual Basic is inadequate for performing such operations. For smooth animation and efficient graphic displays, Win32 API functions are often necessary.

Two of the most important API functions for graphics are `BitBlt` and `StretchBlt`, both of which copy bitmap images from one location to another. Among other uses, they can help create fast and smooth animation by quickly copying graphics images from one area of the screen to another.

Other graphics-related API functions include `RoundRect`, which can be used to draw rectangles with rounded corners; `CreateFontIndirect` and `SelectObject`, which can display text at any angle; and `FlashWindow`, which flashes a window's caption, perhaps in an attempt to get the user's attention. All these functions are detailed in this section.

Many more graphics functions are included in the Win32 API. Some provide services already covered by VB's built-in functions and statements, but others offer unique services that can only be accomplished through the API.

Copying Images: BitBlt& and StretchBlt&

Although you can copy one PictureBox image to another using a single line of code, there are times when you require more control over how the copy operation is performed. For example, you may want to copy only a portion of the source image to the destination image. For that, you'll need to use the Win32 API's `BitBlt&` function, which is declared as follows:

```
Declare Function BitBlt& Lib "gdi32" (ByVal hDescDC As Long, _
    ByVal x As Long, ByVal y As Long, ByVal nWidth As Long, _
    ByVal nHeight As Long, ByVal hSrcDC As Long, _
    ByVal xSrc As Long, ByVal ySrc As Long, ByVal dwRop As Long)
```

The arguments for the `BitBlt&` function are described in Table 53.1.

Table 53.1. The arguments of the BitBlt& API function.

Argument	*Description*
`hDescDC`	The device context of the destination image
`x`	The logical x (horizontal) coordinate of the destination image's upper-left corner
`y`	The logical y (vertical) coordinate of the destination image's upper-left corner
`nWidth`	The width of the destination image
`nHeight`	The height of the destination image
`hSrcDC`	The device context of the source image
`xSrc`	The logical x (horizontal) coordinate of the source image
`ySrc`	The logical y (vertical) coordinate of the source image
`dwRop`	The raster operation to be use during the memory transfer

Typically, the `BitBlt&` function is used to copy all or part of the contents of a PictureBox control to another PictureBox control. Because the arguments of the function deal in pixels, the `ScaleMode` property of each PictureBox control should always be set to 3 (Pixel). The `x` and `y` arguments specify the logical coordinates *within the destination device context*, which means that an x, y coordinate of 0, 0 would indicate the upper-left corner of the source image, not the upper-left corner of the video screen. The same is true of the `xSrc` and `ySrc` arguments, though they refer to the logical coordinates of the source device context. The `nWidth` and `nHeight` arguments specify how much of the source image to transfer to the destination image.

The `dwRop` argument specifies the type of raster operation that should be performed during the image transfer. In most cases, this argument will be set to `&HCC0020`, which indicates a straight copy should be performed. However, other `dwRop` values are shown in the following table. The mnemonic (that is—`SRCCOPY`) is the constant for the value as defined in the `WIN32API.TXT` file.

SRCCOPY	&HCC0020	Destination = Source
SRCPAINT	&HEE0086	Destination = Source OR Destination
SRCAND	&H8800C6	Destination = Source AND Destination
SRCINVERT	&H660046	Destination = Source XOR Destination
SRCERASE	&H440328	Destination = Source AND (NOT Destination)
NOTSRCCOPY	&H330008	Destination = NOT Source
NOTSRCERASE	&H1100A6	Destination = (NOT Source) AND (NOT Destination)
MERGECOPY	&HC000CA	Destination = Source AND Pattern
MERGEPAINT	&HBB0226	Destination = (NOT Source) OR Destination
PATCOPY	&HF00021	Destination = Pattern
PATINVERT	&H5A0049	Destination = Pattern XOR Destination
PATPAINT	&HFB0A09	Destination = (NOT Source) OR Pattern OR Destination
DSTINVERT	&H550009	Destination = NOT Destination
BLACKNESS	&H42	Destination = 0
WHITENESS	&HFF0053	Destination = All bits set to 1

NOTE

The preceding raster operation codes suggest that certain types of bit manipulation be performed on the destination image. This can result in some strange effects. You might want to try experimenting with them to see what results you come up with.

All this may sound a bit confusing, but it's actually pretty simple. Basically, you define a source image and a destination image (`hDescDC` and `hSrcDC`) by providing a device context for each, which can be easily obtained using the PictureBox's `hDC` property. You also define the coordinates for the point within the source image (`xSrc`, `ySrc`) where the copying should begin as well as the number of pixels across (`nWidth`) and down (`nHeight`). You also specify the coordinates within the destination image (`x`, `y`) where the copied image should be placed. Finally, the `dwRop` argument determines which raster operations should be performed during the image transfer.

Take the following example. Suppose that a form has two PictureBox controls, `picSource` and `picDest`. The `picSource` control is the larger of the two, about 100 pixels by 100 pixels square in size. `picDest` is only about 25 by 25 pixels square. If you wanted to copy a portion of the `picSource` image into `picDest`, the best way to do it would be to use the `BitBlt&` function, as shown in the following code:

```
Dim lonSrcX As Long
Dim lonSrcY As Long
Dim lonStatus As Long
Dim lonRasterOp As Long

' The ScaleMode property for the PictureBox controls
' must be set to 3 (Pixel).
picSource.ScaleMode = 3     ' Pixel
picDest.ScaleMode = 3       ' Pixel

' The lonSrcX and lonSrcY variables are used to specify
' the upper-left corner within the source image of where
' to start copying.
lonSrcX = 10
lonSrcY = 10

' Specify the raster operation to use during the image
' transfer. A straight copy is &HCC0020.
lonRasterOp = &HCC0020

lonStatus = BitBlt&(picDest.hDC, 0, 0, 25, 25, _
    picSource.hDC, lonSrcX, lonSrcY, lonRasterOp)
```

The preceding code will copy the source image (`picSource`), starting at 10 pixels left and 10 pixels down from its upper-left corner, to the destination image (`picDest`). The copy will be placed starting in the upper-left corner of `picDest` because 0, 0 have been specified for the `BitBlt&` function's `x` and `y` arguments. The `nHeight` and `nWidth` arguments are both set to 25, so a portion of the `picSource` image 25 pixels high and 25 pixels wide will be placed into `picDest` (which, coincidentally, is the same size as the `picDest` control). The `dwRop` argument is set at `&HCC0020`, which specifies that a straight copy with no image manipulation or raster operation should be performed.

If you try out the sample code, make sure that you declare the `BitBlt&` function in a code module and that an image is assigned to the `picSource` control. Otherwise, you may get unexpected results.

You may have already picked up on BitBlt&'s major limitation: it can only be used to copy images (or portions of images) directly and with no resizing or scaling. If, for example, you wanted to copy a source image 200 pixels wide by 200 pixels high into a destination image that is 50 pixels wide and 40 pixels high, you can't do it with BitBlt& because the source image would have to be scaled to fit the destination image. However, there is a slightly different version of BitBlt& that will accomplish this task: StretchBlt&.

```
Declare Function StretchBlt& Lib "gdi32" (ByVal hDC As Long, _
    ByVal x As Long, ByVal y As Long, ByVal nWidth As Long, _
    ByVal nHeight As Long, ByVal hSrcDC As Long, _
    ByVal xSrc As Long, ByVal ySrc As Long, ByVal nSrcWidth As Long, _
    ByVal nSrcHeight As Long, ByVal dwRop As Long)
```

The StretchBlt& function has the same arguments as BitBlt&, with the addition of nSrcWidth and nSrcHeight. The function works exactly the same way as BitBlt&, but you can now specify the height and width of the destination image, which BitBlt& assumed from the source image's height and width. If the source's height and width are different from the destination's height and width, the source image will be automatically reduced or enlarged to fit the parameters of the destination image.

Draw a Rectangle with Rounded Corners

Perhaps this isn't the most useful API function, but it can be used to create a more interesting program interface. With RoundRect&, you can draw rectangles with rounded corners. You can do the same thing with VB's Shape control, but RoundRec& can be used to draw rectangles inside other objects, such as PictureBox controls. The function is declared as follows:

```
Declare Function RoundRec& Lib "gdi32" (ByVal hDC As Long, _
    ByVal X1 As Long, ByVal Y1 As Long, ByVal X2 As Long, _
    ByVal Y2 As Long, ByVal X3 As Long, ByVal Y3 As Long)
```

The arguments of the RoundRect& function are detailed in Table 53.2.

Table 53.2. The arguments of the RoundRect& API function.

Argument	*Description*
hDC	The device context for the object on which the rectangle will be drawn.
X1, Y1	The logical coordinates for the upper-left corner of the rectangle.
X2, Y2	The logical coordinates for the lower-right corner of the rectangle.
X3	The width (in pixels) of the ellipse used to round the corners of the rectangle. Use zero for no rounding.
Y3	The height (in pixels) of the ellipse used to round the corners of the rectangle. Use zero for no rounding.

Using the `RoundRect&` function is straightforward. You need only specify the device context of the object on which the rectangle will be drawn (`hDC`), the upper-left coordinates of the rectangle within the device context (`X1`, `Y1`), the lower-left coordinates of the rectangle (`X2`, `Y2`), and the height and width of the ellipse used for the rounding effect (`X3` for the height, `Y3` for the width). If you don't want any rounding at all, use zero for both `X3` and `Y3`.

The `RoundRect&` function uses pixels for all its arguments, so you should always set the `ScaleMode` property of the object that is being used to 3 (Pixel). An example of how the `RoundRect&` function might be used follows. It draws a rectangle with rounded corners onto a PictureBox control called `picCommand`.

```
Dim lonDC As Long
Dim lonStatus As Long

picButton.ScaleMode = 3
lonDC = picButton.hDc

Status& = RoundRect&(lonDC, 5, 5, picButton.ScaleWidth - 5, _
    picButton.ScaleHeight - 5, 20, 20)
```

The rectangle starts 5 pixels left and 5 pixels down from `picButton`'s upper-left corner. The rectangle's lower-right corner will be 5 pixels right and 5 pixels up from `picButton`'s lower-right corner. An ellipse 20 pixels wide and 20 pixels high is used to round the corners.

Rotating Text

If you want to display text sideways or at any other degree of rotation, you'll need to use three Win32 API functions: `CreateFontIndirect&`, `SelectObject&`, and `DeleteObject&`.

The first function in this trio, `CreateFontIndirect&`, does the bulk of the work. It actually creates a new font, based on an existing TrueType font. The new font will be rotated at the correct degree of rotation, and you can display it on the screen just as you would any other font.

The `Declare` statement for the `CreateFontIndirect&` function should look like this:

```
Declare Function CreateFontIndirect& Lib "gdi32" _
    Alias "CreateFontIndirectA" (lpLogFont As LOGFONT)
```

It looks simple, and it is. Its single argument, `lpLogFont`, is a user-defined type called `LOGFONT` that contains specific information about the font to be created. The `LOGFONT` type (and the `LF_FACESIZE` constant that it uses) should be defined as follows:

```
Public Const LF_FACESIZE = 20

Public Type LOGFONT
    lfHeight        As Long
    lfWidth         As Long
    lfEscapement    As Long
    lfOrientation   As Long
    lfWeight        As Long
    lfItalic        As Byte
```

```
    lfUnderline       As Byte
    lfStrikeOut       As Byte
    lfCharSet         As Byte
    lfOutPrecision    As Byte
    lfClipPrecision   As Byte
    lfQuality         As Byte
    lfPitchAndFamily  As Byte
    lfFaceName        As String * LF_FACESIZE

End Type
```

To create a new font, you need only assign values to the various items of the `LOGFONT` type and then call the function. For example, to create a new font that is based on the Arial TrueType font and rotated at 45 degrees, you would assign the string "Arial" (terminated with a null character, ASCII 0, at the end) to the `lfFaceName` item, and the degree of rotation multiplied by ten (450) to the `lfEscapement` item.

Setting the height of the font is a little trickier. You must multiply the desired point size by -20 and then divide it by the `Screen` object's `TwipsPerPixelY` property. You'll see an example of this later in this section.

The `CreateFontIndirect&` function returns a zero if it is not successful. If that is the case, you can use `GetLastError&` to determine the nature of the error. If the function is successful, however, it will return the handle for the new font which, as you'll soon see, will be used with the `SelectObject&` function.

After the new font has been created, you have to select the new font to the device context in which it will be used with the `SelectObject&` function. For example, if you will be displaying the new font inside a PictureBox control, then you must use `SelectObject&` to specify that the new font's handle should be associated with the PictureBox control.

The `SelectObject&` function's `Declare` statement is as follows:

```
Declare Function SelectObject& Lib "gdi32" (ByVal hDC As Long, _
    ByVal hObject As Long)
```

The `hDC` argument specifies the device context of the object that will be using the new font. In the case of a PictureBox control, you can use its `hDC` property.

The `hObject` argument refers to the handle of the newly created font. This is the same value that was returned by the `CreateFontIndirect&` function.

If the `SelectObject&` function is successful, it will return a handle to the object previously assigned to the device context. So if you're assigning a font to an object with `SelectObject&`, it will return the handle of the font previously assigned to the object. If the function is unsuccessful, it will return zero.

After the font is created and assigned to an object, you can use the object's `CurrentX` and `CurrentY` properties to change the position at which the text will be displayed. You can then use the object's `Print` property to display the text.

When you're finished using the new font, it's a good idea to destroy it to free up system resources. This is done using the `DeleteObject&` function. It is declared as shown in the following line:

```
Declare Function DeleteObject& Lib "gdi32" (ByVal hObject As Long)
```

The only argument for this function is `hObject`, which should be the handle of the font.

If the `DeleteObject&` function is not successful, it returns zero. Otherwise, it will return a nonzero value.

The following code segment shows how the `CreateFontIndirect&`, `SelectObject&`, and `DeleteObject&` functions might be used to display text upside down inside a PictureBox named `picShowText`.

```
Dim udtLOGFONT As LOGFONT
Dim lonFontSize As Long
Dim lonFontHandle As Long
Dim lonLastFont As Long
Dim lonStatus As Long

lonFontSize = 20

' Set up the items in the udtLOGFONT type, which will
' determine what the new font will look like.
udtLOGFONT.lfEscapement = 1800                ' Degree of rotation * 10.
udtLOGFONT.lfFaceName = "Arial" & Chr$(0)     ' Font name.
udtLOGFONT.lfHeight = (lonFontSize * -20) / Screen.TwipsPerPixelY

' Create the new font and get its handle.
lonFontHandle = CreateFontIndirect&(udtLOGFONT)

' Assign the new font to the picShowText object, and
' get the handle of the previous font assigned to that object.
lonLastFont = SelectObject&(picShowText.hDC, lonFontHandle)

' Print some upside-down text.
picShowText.CurrentX = picShowText.Width - 300
picShowText.CurrentY = picShowText.Height - 300
picShowText.Print "This is upside-down!"

' Assign the last font used back to the picShowText object.
lonStatus = SelectObject&(picShowText.hDC, lonLastFont)

' Destroy the new font.
lonStatus = DeleteObject&(lonFontHandle)
```

Flash a Window's Caption

If you want to get your user's attention, one good way is to flash the caption of your form. To do that, you'll use the `FlashWindow&` API function.

The `Declare` statement for the `FlashWindow&` function is as follows:

```
Declare Function FlashWindow& Lib "user32" (ByVal hWnd As Long, _
    ByVal bInvert As Long)
```

The hWnd argument specifies the handle of the window that will have its caption flashed. If you want to flash the caption of a form, you can pass the form's hWnd property as the argument, as you'll see later.

The bInvert argument is either True or False and specifies the state of the window's caption. True makes the caption inverse, and False returns it back to its original state.

The FlashWindow& function returns a True value if the window was active before the function was called, and False if it was not active.

The best way to establish a steady flashing rhythm for the caption is to use a Timer control. The following example shows the Timer event for a Timer control called timFlashTimer. Every time the event is triggered, it calls the FlashWindow& function to flash Form1's caption. The static booState variable is used to determine whether the caption should be inverse or normal. The value of booState flip-flops every time the Timer event is executed.

```
Private Sub timFlashTimer_Timer()

Static booState As Boolean
Dim lonStatus As Long
Dim lonFormHandle As Long

' Get Form1's handle.
lonFormHandle = Form1.hWnd

' Call the FlashWindow& function.
lonStatus = FlashWindow&(lonFormHandle, booState)

' Flip-flop booState's value.
booState = Not booState

End Sub
```

If you were to use this event in a program, you would have to add some way of controlling timFlashTimer. By disabling and enabling the Timer, you can control when the form's caption is flashed. You can also change the Timer's Interval property to specify how quickly or how slowly the caption is flashed.

System Functions

Many functions provided by the Win32 API deal with core features of the Windows operating system. This section shows you how you can use some of the API's system functions to do things that Visual Basic doesn't let you do.

By dealing directly with the operating system through the API, you can gain more control over how child processes are handled within your programs. The API functions CreateProcess&, WaitForSingleObject&, and CloseHandle& can be used together to spawn child processes and wait until they are finished executing before continuing on with the processing of the application that started the new process.

Other API functions such as `SystemParametersInfo&` allow you to keep users from rebooting the system using Ctrl+Alt+Delete or switching applications with Ctrl+Tab. When you do want the system rebooted, the `ExitWindowsEx&` function lets you do it right from within your program.

You can also obtain information about the system by using API functions. For example, you can determine the locations of the Windows and Windows System directories using the API functions `GetWindowsDirectory&` and `GetSystemDirectory&`.

The system functions detailed here are just the tip of the iceberg, of course. Hundreds more are available in the Win32 API.

Wait for a Child Process

When you want to run another program from inside your Visual Basic program, you use VB's `Shell` command. But unfortunately, using `Shell` doesn't give you much control over the new process. If you want to wait until the process is finished before your program has control again, the `Shell` command leaves you in the lurch.

Fortunately, three API functions can be used together to allow you more control over the child processes that your programs start. The `CreateProcess&` function starts the process, the `WaitForSingleObject&` function is used to wait until the process is finished, and the `CloseHandle&` function destroys the process.

The `CreateProcess&` function is declared as follows:

```
Declare Function CreateProcess& Lib "kernel32" _
    Alias "CreateProcessA" (ByVal lpApplicationName As String, _
    ByVal lpCommandLine As String, _
    lpProcessAttributes As SECURITY_ATTRIBUTES, _
    lpThreadAttributes As SECURITY_ATTRIBUTES, _
    ByVal bInheritHandles As Long, ByVal dwCreationFlags As Long, _
    lpEnvironment As Any, ByVal lpCurrentDirectory As String, _
    lpStartupInfo As STARTUPINFO, _
    lpProcessInformation As PROCESS_INFORMATION)
```

That's a long `Declare` statement, but it's primarily because the `CreateProcess&` function gives you such control over the process that is created. The arguments for the function are detailed in Table 53.3.

Table 53.3. The arguments for the `CreateProcess&` API function.

Argument	*Description*
`lpApplicationName`	The name of the application that will be executed.
`lpCommandLine`	The command line to be executed.

continues

Table 53.3. continued

Argument	*Description*
`lpProcessAttributes`	Defines the security for the process. This argument can also be declared as `ByVal As Long` and passed as zero if the process does not allow inheritance.
`lpThreadAttributes`	Defines the security for the primary thread of the process. This argument can also be declared as `ByVal As Long` and passed as zero if the process does not allow inheritance.
`bInheritHandles`	Specifies whether the handles in the current process can be inherited by the child process. A value of `True` allows the handles to be inherited.
`dwCreationFlags`	Specifies how the process is run and what priority it is given.
`lpEnvironment`	A pointer to an environment block.
`lpCurrentDirectory`	The path of the directory to use for the new process, or `null` to specify the directory that is in use when the function is called.
`lpStartupInfo`	Various information about how to create the process.
`lpProcessInformation`	The process and thread identifiers of the new process and a new process and thread handle for the new process.

Several type structures are required for passing information to the `CreateProcess&` function. We'll take a look at them one by one.

The `SECURITY_ATTRIBUTES` structure is used by both the `lpProcessAttributes` and the `lpThreadAttributes` arguments. In both cases, you don't have to use the `SECURITY_ATTRIBUTES` structure if the process does not allow inheritance. Instead, declare the `lpProcessAttributes` and `lpThreadAttributes` as `ByVal As Long` and pass zero values for both arguments when the function is called.

When it is used, the `SECURITY_ATTRIBUTES` structure is declared as follows:

```
Type SECURITY_ATTRIBUTES
    nLength As Long
    lpSecurityDescriptor As Long
    bInheritHandle As Long
End Type
```

Because a discussion of inheritance and process security is beyond the scope of this brief explanation of the API functions, the `SECURITY_ATTRIBUTES` structure will not be used in the sample code at the end of this section.

Another type of structure used by the `CreateProcess&` function is `STARTUPINFO`, which contains information about how the process should be started. It is declared as follows:

```
Type STARTUPINFO
    cb As Long
    lpReserved As String
    lpDesktop As String
    lpTitle As String
    dwX As Long
    dwY As Long
    dwXSize As Long
    dwYSize As Long
    dwXCountChars As Long
    dwYCountChars As Long
    dwFillAttribute As Long
    dwFlags As Long
    wShowWindow As Integer
    cbReserved2 As Integer
    lpReserved2 As Byte
    hStdInput As Long
    hStdOutput As Long
    hStdError As Long
End Type
```


In many cases, the only item in the `STARTUPINFO` structure that you need to set is `cb`. The `cb` item specifies the length of the `STARTUPINFO` structure, and it should be set using a line of code such as:

```
udtStartupInfo.cb = Len(udtStartupInfo)
```

The rest of the items in the `STARTUPINFO` structure can be left alone. Of course, you can set them to obtain greater control over your child process. A detailed description of each item is beyond of the scope of this discussion, however.

The final type structure used by the `CreateProcess&` function is `PROCESS_INFORMATION`, which is defined as follows:

```
Type PROCESS_INFORMATION
    hProcess As Long
    hThread As Long
    dwProcessId As Long
    dwThreadId As Long
End Type
```

The `PROCESS_INFORMATION` structure is used to return the process and thread identifiers for the new process as well as its process and thread handle. The process handle will be used to specify which process to wait for when the `WaitForSingleObject&` function is called.

One argument of the `CreateProcess&` function requires a closer look. The `dwCreationFlags` argument is used to specify how the process will run and what priority it is given. This is done using constants that can be found in the `WIN32API.TXT` file. These constants are also shown in the following list along with their values.

`CREATE_SUSPENDED`	`&H4`	Suspends the new process immediately. The process will not start again until the `ResumeThread&` function is called.
`IDLE_PRIORITY_CLASS`	`&H40`	The process is given a very low priority.
`HIGH_PRIORITY_CLASS`	`&H80`	The process is given a very high priority.
`NORMAL_PRIORITY_CLASS`	`&H20`	The process is given a normal priority.

The `CreateProcess&` function returns a nonzero value if it is successful, and a zero value if it fails. In the case of an error, you can use `GetLastError&` to determine the problem.

After the process has been created, a second API function should be called to wait until the process has finished executing. The `WaitForSingleObject&` function does just that, and it is declared as follows:

```
Declare Function WaitForSingleObject& Lib "kernel32" _
    (ByVal hHandle As Long, ByVal dwMilliseconds As Long)
```

The `hHandle` argument specifies the handle of the process that should be waited on. The process handle is returned by the `CreateProcess&` function in the `PROCESS_INFORMATION` structure.

The `dwMilliseconds` argument specifies how long the function should wait for the process to finish, in milliseconds. If its value is zero, then the function will return immediately. If it is set to the constant `INFINITE (-1)`, then it will wait as long as it takes for the process to complete.

After the process is finished, it should be closed using the `CloseHandle&` function. The declaration for that function is as follows:

```
Declare Function CloseHandle& Lib "kernel32" (ByVal hObject As Long)
```

The only argument that needs to be passed to the `CloseHandle&` function is the handle of the process that will be closed. Again, the handle process is returned by the `CreateProcess&` function in the `PROCESS_INFORMATION` structure.

The following sample code begins printing the numbers from 1 to 100 to VB's Immediate window. When it gets to 50, it stops and creates a new process that runs Windows' Calculator application. As soon as the Calculator program is closed, the printing of numbers continues until 100 is reached. Note that because the `SECURITY_ATTRIBUTES` structures are not needed, the `CreateProcess&` function should be declared with the `lpProcessAttributes` and `lpThreadAttributes` arguments defined as `ByVal As Long`.

```
Dim intCount As Integer
Dim lonStatus As Long
Dim lonProcHandle As Long
```

```
Dim strCmdLine As String
Dim udtProcessInfo As PROCESS_INFORMATION
Dim udtStartupInfo As STARTUPINFO

strCmdLine = "c:\Win95\calc.exe"
udtStartupInfo.cb = Len(udtStartupInfo)

For intCount = 1 To 100
     Debug.Print intCount
     If intCount = 50 Then
          ' Create the process.
          lonStatus = CreateProcess&(vbNullString, strCmdLine, _
               0, 0, 1, &H40, 0&, vbNullString, udtStartupInfo, _
               udtProcessInfo)
          ' Determine the new process' handle.
          lonProcHandle = udtProcessInfo.hProcess
          ' Wait until the process is finished.
          lonStatus = WaitForSingleObject&(lonProcHandle, -1)
          ' Close the process.
          lonStatus = CloseHandle&(lonProcHandle)
     End If
Next intCount
```

Exit Windows

The `ExitWindowsEx&` function is simple in its implementation, but its effects are profound. It causes a shutdown of the Windows operating system.

The `Declare` statement for the `ExitWindowsEx&` function is as follows:

```
Declare Function ExitWindowsEx& Lib "user32" (ByVal uFlags As Long, _
    ByVal dwReserved As Long)
```

The only argument you have to worry about when calling `ExitWindowsEx&` is `uFlags`. The `dwReserved` argument is reserved by the operating system and should always be set to zero.

The `uFlags` argument specifies how the system should be shut down. Its possible values are shown in the following table. The mnemonic refers to the constant defined in the `WIN32API.TXT` file, and the number indicates the value assigned to the constant.

EWX_LOGOFF	0	Terminates all processes; then logs off.
EWX_FORCE	4	Terminates processes, including those that do not respond, and then logs off.
EWX_REBOOT	2	Reboots the system.
EWX_SHUTDOWN	1	Shuts down the system (ready for power off).

`ExitWindowsEx&` returns a nonzero value if it is successful and zero if an error occurs. Use `GetLastError` to determine the error.

The following sample code shows how the `ExitWindowsEx&` function can be used to reboot a system.

```
Dim lonStatus As Long
Dim lonShutdownFlags As Long

lonShutdownFlags = 2 ' Value of EWX_REBOOT.

' Reboot the system.
lonStatus = ExitWindowsEx&(lonShutdownFlags, 0)
```

Stop Ctrl+Alt+Delete and Ctrl+Tab

When your VB application is running, you may want to disable the user's ability to reboot the system using Ctrl+Alt+Delete or to switch applications using Ctrl+Tab. If that is the case, then you'll need to use the `SystemParametersInfo&` API function.

`SystemParametersInfo&` actually allows you to retrieve and set a wide variety of Windows system parameters. However, the only service of the function that will be discussed here is the disabling of the Ctrl+Alt+Delete and Ctrl+Tab keys.

The `Declare` statement for the `SystemParametersInfo&` function should be as follows:

```
Declare Function SystemParametersInfo& Lib "user32" _
    Alias "SystemParametersInfoA" (ByVal uAction As Long, _
    ByVal uParam As Long, lpvParam As Any, ByVal fuWinIni As Long)
```

The `uAction` argument specifies which system parameter should be set. There is a long list of possible parameters for this argument, but the one we're interested in is `SPI_SCREENSAVERRUNNING`, a constant defined in the `WIN32API.TXT` file. Its value is 97.

The second argument for the function is `uParam`. The possible values for the `uParam` argument depend on the system parameter specified by the `uAction` argument. For the `SPI_SCREENSAVERRUNNING` parameter, the possible values are `True` and `False`. A value of `True` will disable the Ctrl+Alt+Delete and Ctrl+Tab keys, whereas a value of `False` will enable them.

The `lpvParam` argument can have several uses depending on which system parameter is being used with the function. In some cases, it returns the value of the system parameter before it is changed. The `lpvParam` argument can be any kind of variable type, but it should match the variable type used by the `uParam` argument. Because the values of `uParam` are of type Boolean for the `SPI_SCREENSAVERRUNNING` system parameter, a Boolean variable should be declared and passed to the function as the `lpvParam` argument.

If the `lpvParam` argument is of type `Integer` or `Long` or is a data structure, it should be passed to the function by reference (`ByRef`). In all other cases, it should be passed by value (`ByVal`).

The final argument, `fuWinIni`, determines whether the system parameters being changed by the `SystemParametersInfo&` function should be stored in the `WIN.INI` file, the System Registry, or both. A value of zero prevents any updates.

An example of using the `SystemParametersInfo&` function to disable the Ctrl+Alt+Delete and Ctrl+Tab keys follows:

```
Dim booOldValue As Boolean
Dim lonStatus As Long
Dim lonSysParam As Long

lonSysParam = 97 ' Value for SPI_SCREENSAVERRUNNING

' Disable Ctrl+Alt+Del and Ctrl+Tab.
lonStatus = SystemParametersInfo&(lonSysParam, True, _
    booOldValue, 0)

' Enable Ctrl+Alt+Del and Ctrl+Tab.
lonStatus = SystemParametersInfo&(lonSysParam, False, _
    booOldValue, 0)
```

Find the Windows and System Directories

If you need to obtain the full path for a system's Windows directory or the `WINDOWS\SYSTEM` directory, you can use the API functions `GetWindowsDirectory&` and `GetSystemDirectory&`.

The `GetWindowsDirectory&` function should be declared using the following `Declare` statement:

```
Declare Function GetWindowsDirectory& Lib "kernel32" _
    Alias "GetWindowsDirectoryA" (ByVal lpBuffer As String, _
    ByVal nSize As Long)
```

The `Declare` statement for the `GetSystemDirectory&` function is

```
Declare Function GetSystemDirectory& Lib "kernel32" _
    Alias "GetSystemDirectoryA" (ByVal lpBuffer As String, _
    ByVal nSize As Long)
```


Both the `GetWindowsDirectory&` and the `GetSystemDirectory&` functions have two arguments, `lpBuffer` and `nSize`. The `lpBuffer` argument is a fixed-length string that will hold the directory path returned by either function. `nSize` indicates the size of the `lpBuffer` string. The functions always return the size of the path, regardless of whether the `lpBuffer` string is large enough to hold it. If the string is not large enough, then the return value should be used to resize the string to the proper size, and the function should be called again. If you define the string used for the `lpBuffer` argument as at least 255 characters, it is unlikely you will encounter a directory path that won't fit into the string.

The following section of code shows how the `GetWindowsDirectory&` and `GetSystemDirectory&` functions might be used in a program:

```
Dim strDirPath As String * 255
Dim lonStatus As Long

strDirPath = Space$(255)

lonStatus = GetWindowsDirectory&(strDirPath, 255)
Debug.Print strDirPath

lonStatus = GetSystemDirectory&(strDirPath, 255)
Debug.Print strDirPath
```

Summary

Visual Basic can let you do many things, but it won't let you do everything. Sometimes, you have to bypass VB and interact directly with the Windows operating system. This is accomplished through a huge library of functions called the Win32 API.

The Win32 API has hundreds of built-in functions. This chapter showed you how to use a few of them to accomplish tasks that would be impossible or inefficient in Visual Basic.

CHAPTER 54

Algorithms for VB Programmers

IN THIS CHAPTER

Although Visual Basic has evolved into a serious tool for software development, the more complicated aspects of data processing are often left to other languages, such as C++. The VB programmer who goes looking for information on how to perform complex algorithms often comes up empty handed.

There is no good reason for this. Perhaps a few years ago, when Visual Basic was more limited and was considered to be a "toy" language, it could have been ignored as a competitor with other "real" development tools. However, that is no longer the case. It stands to reason that there would be information available specifically for VB programmers who want to delve into more advanced processing methods such as sorting, encryption, and compression. Unfortunately, that is not the case.

This chapter will provide you, the VB programmer, with the basic knowledge you need to understand and use some of the data processing algorithms that have been reserved for other languages and development environments.

Algorithms

Most programs that you write in Visual Basic are simple. Few really need to manipulate data in ways that require complex algorithms. However, sometimes you may find yourself looking for just such an algorithm. You may need to sort data in some way, or encrypt it to secure it from prying eyes. Or, you may need to compress your data so that it will take up less space or so that it can be sent faster over a network connection.

Unfortunately, it may be difficult to find the algorithms you need to complete the task at hand. Don't worry, this chapter can help. It will introduce you to the basics of some of the more common algorithms in use today for sorting, data encryption, and data compression. It also provides you with sample code for each of those data processing tasks. You can adapt the code for your own use, or you can use the information provided about other algorithms as a start for learning more.

Sorting

One of the most common processing tasks that involves an algorithm is sorting. Many different algorithms have been devised to accomplish sorting. The Insertion, Bubble, Heap, Exchange, Shell, and Quick Sort methods are all viable ways of sorting items.

This section briefly describes these common sorting methods. It also provides an example Quick Sort routine, which is typically the fastest and most efficient of the different sorts.

The sort descriptions that follow operate on the premise that the data to be sorted is contained in an array. However, data can be sorted in formats other than arrays. For example, random files can be sorted just as easily as arrays, though the overhead of disk access will undoubtedly make the sorting less efficient.

Insertion Sort

The Insertion sort method loops through an array, evaluating each item in the array with all the preceding items. It then determines where the current item should be placed by moving backward through the array and inserts it into its new location. All the elements between the new location and the current item's old location are moved down to the next item to make space for the insertion.

Bubble Sort

The Bubble sort method is slightly more efficient than the Insertion sort. It loops through an array of items and compares adjacent items to see whether they are out of order. If they are, it switches them. It keeps looping through the array until no items are switched, indicating that the array has been sorted.

Heap Sort

The Heap sort method uses a binary tree (a "heap") to organize items in an array into nodes, with each parent node being greater in value than its child nodes. The heap is constantly being rebuilt and reorganized as the array is looped through and array items are moved up and down the tree.

Although the Heap sort is generally more efficient than the Insertion and Bubble sort methods, it is somewhat complicated and is not as efficient as other sort methods. The Exchange sort, for example, usually provides better results and is much easier to understand.

Exchange Sort

The Exchange sort method loops through each item in an array and compares it with the item that follows. If the following item is smaller than the current item, it is switched (exchanged) with the current item. The process then repeats for the next item in the array. When the last item in the array is reached, the array will have been sorted.

Shell Sort

The Shell sort method works similarly to the Bubble sort, but instead of comparing adjacent items in an array it initially compares items that are halfway between the first and last items in the array. If the values are out of order, it switches them. It then determines the halfway point again and repeats the process. This halving of the array and comparing items continues until adjacent items are being compared. By then, most of the items in the array will have been sorted. A final loop through the array works the same way as the Bubble sort and ensures that everything is in order.

Quick Sort

One of the fastest ways to sort items is by using the Quick Sort method. Quick Sort works by being passed a lower and upper boundary of an array of items. If the lower boundary is less than the upper boundary, then the boundaries are tested to see whether they are next to each other (upper boundary minus lower boundary equals one). If they are, and they are not in sorted order, then the two array items for the boundaries are switched. If the boundaries are not next to each other, then a random "pivot" item is selected that is somewhere between the lower and upper boundaries. The Quick Sort routine is called recursively with the new upper and lower boundaries representing each side of two the subdivisions created by the randomly selected pivot. This keeps happening until the array is sorted.

Because the Quick Sort routine is called recursively (that is, it calls itself within its own code), it can be difficult to grasp how it works. The QuickSort routine shown in Listing 54.1 should help you gain a better understanding of how such a sort might be coded.

Listing 54.1. The QuickSort routine, which sorts the items in the globally defined `strArray()` array.

```
Public Sub QuickSort(lonLower, lonUpper)

Dim lonRandomPivot As Long
Dim lonTempLower As Long
Dim lonTempUpper As Long
Dim strLastItem As String
Dim strTempItem As String

Randomize Timer

' Only sort if the lower boundary is lesser
' than the upper boundary.
If lonLower < lonUpper Then
    If lonUpper - lonLower = 1 Then
        ' Switch the upper and lower array items
        ' if the lower is greater than the upper.
        If strArray(lonLower) > strArray(lonUpper) Then
            strTempItem = strArray(lonUpper)
            strArray(lonUpper) = strArray(lonLower)
            strArray(lonLower) = strTempItem
        End If
    Else
        ' Pick a random "pivot" item.
        lonRandomPivot = Int(Rnd _
            * (lonUpper - lonLower + 1)) + lonLower
        ' Switch the upper array item with the
        ' pivot item.
        strTempItem = strArray(lonUpper)
        strArray(lonUpper) = strArray(lonRandomPivot)
        strArray(lonRandomPivot) = strTempItem
        ' Store the upper array item.
        strLastItem = strArray(lonUpper)
```

```
        Do
            ' Define the temporary upper and
            ' lower boundaries.
            lonTempUpper = lonUpper
            lonTempLower = lonLower
            ' Move down towards the pivot item,
            ' looping until the pivot item is greater
            ' than or equal to the temporary
            ' lower boundary.
            Do While (lonTempLower < lonTempUpper) And _
                (strArray(lonTempLower) <= strLastItem)
                    lonTempLower = lonTempLower + 1
            Loop
            ' Move up towards the pivot item, looping
            ' until the pivot item is less than
            ' or equal to the temporary upper
            ' boundary.
            Do While (lonTempUpper > lonTempLower) And _
                (strArray(lonTempUpper) >= strLastItem)
                    lonTempUpper = lonTempUpper - 1
            Loop
            ' If the pivot item hasn't been
            ' reached, then two of the items on
            ' either side of the pivot are out
            ' of order. If so, then switch them.
            If lonTempLower < lonTempUpper Then
                strTempItem = strArray(lonTempUpper)
                strArray(lonTempUpper) = strArray(lonTempLower)
                strArray(lonTempLower) = strTempItem
            End If
        Loop While (lonTempLower < lonTempUpper)
        ' Switch the temporary lower boundary
        ' item with the original upper boundary
        ' item.
        strTempItem = strArray(lonTempLower)
        strArray(lonTempLower) = strArray(lonUpper)
        strArray(lonUpper) = strTempItem
        ' Call the QuickSort routine again
        ' recursively, using new upper and
        ' lower boundaries.
        If (lonTempLower - lonLower) < (lonUpper - lonTempLower) Then
            QuickSort lonLower, lonTempLower - 1
            QuickSort lonTempLower + 1, lonUpper
        Else
            QuickSort lonTempLower + 1, lonUpper
            QuickSort lonLower, lonTempLower - 1
        End If
    End If
End If

End Sub
```

The routine shown in Listing 54.1 makes the assumption that a publicly defined array called `strArray` exists. It also assumes that the array is populated with data.

To try out the QuickSort procedure, you must define the strArray array in a code module. Another variable, lonArrayCount, should also be defined to keep track of the number of items in the array. The following code shows how strArray and lonArrayCount should be declared:

```
Public lonArrayCount As Long
Public strArray(1000) As String
```

Next, you must have a way of populating the array with data. The following subroutine can be used to read in the lines of a sequential file that will be stored in the array.

```
Public Sub ReadFile(strFileName As String)

Open strFileName For Input As #1
Do
    lonArrayCount = lonArrayCount + 1
    If (lonLineCount <= 1000) And (Not EOF(1)) Then
        Line Input #1, strArray(lonArrayCount)
    End If
Loop Until (EOF(1) Or lonArrayCount = 1000)
Close #1

End Sub
```

The argument that is passed to the ReadFile procedure, strFileName, should indicate the path and filename of a sequential file that contains data to be sorted. Note that a maximum of 1,000 lines of data will be read in because that is the number of elements that strArray can hold as it was defined.

After the array has been sorted, it should be written back out to another file. The following WriteFile routine can be used to accomplish that task. Again, the argument passed to the WriteFile routine should indicate the path and filename of the output file.

```
Public Sub WriteFile(strFileName As String)

Dim lonArrayPtr As Long

Open strFileName For Output As #1
For lonArrayPtr = 1 To lonArrayCount
    Print #1, strArray(lonArrayPtr)
Next lonArrayPtr
Close #1

End Sub
```

Finally, the ReadFile, QuickSort, and WriteFile routines should be called. You could add a CommandButton control to the form and put the following code in the control's Click event. Or, you could add it the Form_Load event so that it runs as soon as the program is executed.

```
ReadFile
QuickSort 1, lonArrayCount
WriteFile
```

Note that the initial values passed to the QuickSort routine are 1 and lonArrayCount, which represents the total number of items that have been read into strArray. These are the ultimate upper and lower boundaries of the items in the array. QuickSort will keep dividing the items between the upper and lower boundaries, determining new boundaries and calling itself recursively, until the array is sorted.

Data Encryption/Decryption

We are living in the Information Age. Computers thrive on information, with more and more data being obtained and processed every day. Data about you, your business, your bank account, your bills, and your credit is being processed every day. Information is a commodity that is sometimes valued more than gold and silver, and it's not likely to change any time soon.

Most information is freely accessible, available to anyone who wants it. The Internet is the world's largest source of information, an unlimited amount of data that is, for the most part, free for the asking.

But some information is not meant for public eyes and has to be secured lest it fall into the wrong hands. Details of military operations, financial information, medical records, and some forms of communication are all types of information that need to be kept secret. This is where data encryption (also known as cryptography) comes in.

Data encryption is nothing new. It goes back to ancient civilizations that used hieroglyphics to build messages. The Rosetta Stone, which dates to 196 B.C., contains a message that was encrypted using a combination of three different languages. But although data encryption has always been important, never has it been as necessary and widespread as it is today.

A wide range of encryption techniques have been devised. Some are simple, whereas others are incredibly complex. Obviously, the simpler the encryption technique, the easier it is to "crack." Also, as computers get faster and more efficient, they become more capable of cracking existing encryption techniques. Therefore, newer and better methods of encrypting data are constantly being invented.

This section discusses some of the more common methods of encryption in use today. It also illustrates a simple but effective encryption method that can be used in your own programs.

Data Encryption Standard (DES)

DES was developed by the U.S. National Bureau of Standards in 1975 in an attempt to devise an encryption method that could be used in government applications. It has become one of the the world's most used encryption techniques.

DES encrypts data in 63-bit blocks of text, using a 56-bit key. Later versions of DES, such as 3-Round DES (Triple DES) and 6-Round DES, encrypt data multiple times using the same encryption method but different keys.

International Data Encryption Algorithm (IDEA)

IDEA was devised in 1990 as the replacement for DES. Again, 63-bit blocks of text are used, but they are split into four 16-bit blocks and are encrypted separately. Also, a 128-bit key is used. A long sequence of calculations and bit operations are performed on the data and then the 16-bit blocks of encrypted data are combined together to once again form a 63-bit block.

IDEA is one of the most secure encryption methods ever devised, and it has not yet been broken. Of course, that may change in the near future as new methods of cryptoanalysis are created.

Pretty Good Privacy (PGP)

PGP has come into vogue in the past few years as a widely available method of data encryption. It uses a public/private key encryption strategy, where two different keys are used for encryption and decryption. One key is made public, and one is kept secret. The public key is used for encryption, so anyone can encrypt data with that key. To decrypt the data, however, requires the private key. The private key cannot be obtained in any way from the public key, and vice versa. So why use two keys? That way, data can be transferred over unsecure channels, such as the Internet. You can give someone a public key and have him encrypt messages or data for you without having to know your private key.

PGP has the capability of using large keys, up to 2,047 bits in size. Despite the fact that it is in widespread use by the masses instead of being used primarily by the government, PGP is one of the most secure methods of data encryption ever devised. That's probably why its creator, Phil Zimmermann, was for a time being closely investigated by the U.S. government as a possible violator of the International Traffic in Arms Regulations (ITAR).

PGP uses the IDEA method for its data encryption. It also uses elements of other encryption methods such as RSA (Rivest-Shamir-Adelman) and MD5 (Message Digest 5) to manage its keys as well as for data hashing and compression.

XOR Encryption

One simple way to encrypt and decrypt data is by using the XOR Encryption method. Basically, the characters in the data stream and those of a code key are XORed together to create an encrypted character. The process is exactly the same for data being encrypted as it is for data being decrypted.

The code key is a string made up of any alphanumeric characters you want to use. It can be any number of characters long, but the longer the key is the more secure the encryption.

XOR Encryption is not a tight method of encryption, meaning that it can be broken relatively easily. However, if you want to encrypt messages or documents so that they cannot be viewed with a text editor or browser, then XOR Encryption offers a simple way to do so.

Listing 54.2 shows a function called `XOREncryption` that can be used to both encrypt and decrypt data. You need only pass it the code key (a string) and the data to be encrypted or decrypted.

Listing 54.2. The XOREncryption routine, which both encrypts and decrypts data when provided with a code key and the data.

```
Public Function XOREncryption(strCodeKey As String, _
    strDataIn As String) As String

Dim lonDataPtr As Long
Dim intXORValue1 As Integer
Dim intXORValue2 As Integer
Dim strDataOut As String

For lonDataPtr = 1 To Len(strDataIn)
    ' The first value to XOR comes from the data to be
    ' encrypted.
    intXORValue1 = Asc(Mid$(strDataIn, lonDataPtr, 1))
    ' The second value to XOR comes from the code key.
    intXORValue2 = Asc(Mid$(strCodeKey, _
        ((lonDataPtr Mod Len(strCodeKey)) + 1), 1))
    ' The two values are XORed together to create a
    ' decrypted character.
    strDataOut = strDataOut + Chr(intXORValue1 Xor _
        intXORValue2)
Next lonDataPtr

' The XOREncryption function returns the encrypted (or
' decrypted) data.
XOREncryption = strDataOut

End Function
```

To try out the `XOREncryption` routine, you can add it to a form that has three TextBox controls (`Text1`, `Text2`, and `Text3`) and a CommandButton control. In the CommandButton's `Click` event, add the following code:

```
Dim strCodeKey As String
Dim strEncryptedText As String

strCodeKey = "Wxz19hgl3Kb2dSp"
strEncryptedText = XOREncryption(strCodeKey, Text1.Text)
Text2.Text = strEncryptedText
Text3.Text = XOREncryption(strCodeKey, strEncryptedText)
```

This will encrypt the contents of the `Text1` control using the code key stored in the `strCodeKey` variable. It then places the results in `Text2` and then decrypts the encrypted data and places it into `Text3`.

You may be wondering why the `strEncryptedText` string is used to store the encrypted data instead of just placing it in `Text2`. The encrypted data is likely to contain strange characters, including nulls. The TextBox will truncate the encrypted string if it encounters a null, so it cannot be relied on to hold the entire string of encrypted data.

Data Compression/Decompression

Years ago, data compression was important because computer resources (memory and disk space) were limited. The more that could be fit into the same space, the better. Data compression started to become commonplace. Installation disks almost always contained compressed files, and no computer hobbyist could do without a copy of the latest file compression utility. Even the data on hard disks was compressed using programs like Stacker or DoubleSpace.

Data compression is still important today, if perhaps for different reasons. Programs are now typically distributed on CD-ROM, and compression is often not really a major concern because the disk can hold so much data (though CD-ROMs that are nowhere near being full usually have their data compressed anyway). Multi-gigabyte hard disks are now common, so the number of systems that use drive-compression utilities is dwindling. These days, the importance of data compression is no longer so much a matter of storage space but of speed.

Telecommunications, in particular communication with the Internet, is more popular than ever before. And although efforts are being made to provide better and faster methods of telecommunications for the masses, many computers still connect to online services via dial-up connections that use relatively low-speed modems. This is where data compression becomes vitally important. Compressed data takes far less time to transfer than noncompressed data, meaning that accessing online services is faster. And the faster that information can be obtained, the better.

Data compression is still important; there's no doubt about that. Still, few programmers know how compression is achieved. There are two main reasons for this. The first is that there are several third-party controls and products that provide data compression and decompression services (see Chapter 50, "Third-Party Controls"), so the programmer doesn't have to worry about how compression works, only that it does work. The second reason is perhaps more obvious: it's complicated. Data compression and decompression algorithms can be difficult to understand.

So why would you want to even fool around with trying to do data compression yourself? For one thing, there may be times when you can't find an ActiveX control that will do exactly what you want it to do. Most controls that offer compression/decompression services apply only to files. You may need to compress a data stream instead. Or you may not want the overhead that comes with an ActiveX control. Whatever the reason, it helps to know a little about how data compression can be achieved. This section discusses some standard methods used for data compression and details one of the simpler compression algorithms.

Code Table Optimization

One of the easiest methods for compressing data is to use a technique known as Code Table Optimization. Basically, Code Table Optimization works on a simple premise: instead of using 8 bits to store a character, you use less than that, say 5 or 6 bits. Using 5 bits allows you to store values between 0 and 31; 6 bits gives you double the range, with values between 0 and 63.

The main drawback here is obvious: you can only store a limited number of ASCII characters using this method. However, it is relatively easy to code and gives you a 25 percent or 37.5 percent compression rate every time, depending on how many bits you use.

Huffman Compression

Huffman Compression uses a technique somewhat similar to Code Table Optimization. It also stores characters using a smaller number of bits, though it uses a more intelligent way of determining how the bits should be used. The Huffman Compression method scans a file (or data stream) and figures out which characters are used most often. This is usually accomplished using a binary tree, with the least-used characters being sifted to the bottom nodes of the tree. After each character's "weight," or number of times it occurs, has been established, it is assigned a binary code. The more common a character, the shorter the binary code. For example, the most frequently used characters might be assigned a two-digit (two-bit) binary code. The next most frequent characters would be assigned three-digit binary codes, and so on. The binary codes are combined and strung together, resulting in a compressed version of the original data. A table that defines the binary codes that were used is also included with the compressed data so that the seemingly random string of bits can be decoded and uncompressed.

Lempel-Ziv-Welch (LZW)

One of the more popular (and more efficient) compression methods is Lempel-Ziv-Welch or LZW Compression. LZW often provides the best results, but it is also more complicated than the other methods.

The LZW method creates a table of "shorthand" codes that stand for pieces of the data being compressed. The data is examined character by character. If a unique combination of characters is found, they are assigned a new code and are added to the shorthand table. When like character combinations are found, their shorthand code is written out instead of the characters themselves. This "tokenizing" of character phrases often results in a high compression rate.

Because LZW compression is so complicated, a more detailed discussion of how it works is beyond the scope of this chapter. Several documents on the Internet explain it, so do a few searches there for more information.

Run-Length Encoding (RLE)

Run-Length Encoding or RLE is a comparatively simple compression algorithm that yields high rates of compression for certain kinds of data, particularly graphics. RLE simply replaces subsequent characters that are repeated more than twice with two bytes: one to indicate how many times the character repeats (the "manager" byte), and one for the character itself. The manager byte is differentiated from other bytes because its uppermost bit is set. This allows the other seven bits of the byte to hold the number of characters that are repeated, a possible value of 0 through 127. Because no repeat character sequences of zero are possible, 1 can be added to the character count, giving an actual possible value range of 1 through 128.

If a character has its uppermost bit set, then it may be mistaken as a manager byte. To get around this, any character with its uppermost bit set is always assigned a manager byte that indicates a count of one.

This may be confusing, so let's look at an example. Take the following string of hexidecimal values that represent the string "AAABCCCCCCDDDD":

```
41h 41h 41h 42h 43h 43h 43h 43h 43h 43h 44h 44h 44h 44h
```

The first three bytes (41h 41h 41h) can be compressed down to two bytes, a manager byte indicating the count (3) and a byte for the character (41h). The result would be: 82h 41h. The 82h in binary is 10000010, a value (character count) of two with the uppermost bit set. Remember that the character count has 1 added to it, so a value of 2 actually represents 3. The compressed data (82h 41h) can be written out.

Moving along in the data, the next character (42h) only appears once. No compression can be done on that, so the character can be written out without modification.

Next in the data are six characters that have the same value, 43h. Again, this can be compressed down to two bytes, a manager byte and the character. The manager byte in this case will be 85h, which is 10000101 in binary. The last three bits (101) indicate that the count is 5, which will have 1 added to it, giving a count of 6. So the next two bytes written out are 85h 43h.

The next four characters are also repeats, so they too will get summed up in two bytes: 83h and 44h. This gives us a complete output of

```
82h 41h 42h 85h 43h 83h 44h
```

The original 14 bytes have been compressed down to 7, giving a 50 percent compression rate. Not too bad!

As mentioned eariler, if a character byte with its uppermost bit set is encountered, it gets assigned its own manager byte. Therefore, the character byte F5h would be written out as two bytes (80h and F5h). This is only if the character byte appears only once and is not repeated. If it is repeated, it gets counted just like any other character.

You may be wondering what happens when a character count is greater than 128, the largest value that can be stored in the manager byte. That's a good question but easily answered. The first 128 occurrences of the character get the manager byte and the character byte, as usual. The remainder of the characters are then treated as if the first 128 bytes weren't even processed. If there are enough characters to be assigned a manager byte, then that's what happens. Otherwise, the characters are written out as-is.

As you can imagine, Run-Length Encoding only works well on data that has many repeat character sequences. Text files seldom yield good results with RLE, but other data such as graphics usually do quite well.

To illustrate how the RLE Compression method can be coded, two sample functions have been included (see Listing 54.3). They each accept two arguments that specify the names of TextBox controls. The `RLECompress&` function compresses any data that is in the TextBox control indicated by its first argument and displays the compressed data in the TextBox indicated by its second argument. The `RLEUncompress&` function uncompresses the data in the TextBox indicated by its first argument and displays the uncompressed data in the TextBox indicated by its second argument.

Listing 54.3. The `RLECompress` and `RLEUncompress` routines, which both take two TextBox controls as arguments and compress or uncompress the contents of one TextBox and place the results in the other.

```
Public Sub RLECompress(txtDataIn As TextBox, _
    txtDataOut As TextBox)

Dim intCharCount As Integer
Dim intNewChar As Integer
Dim intLastChar As Integer
Dim intCharLoop As Integer
Dim lonCharPtr As Long
Dim lonCharStrLen As Long
Dim strCompressed As String
Dim bytMgrChar As Byte

intCharCount = -1
lonCharStrLen = Len(txtDataIn.Text)

' Loop through the contents of the TextBox
' character by character. The loop is executed
' an additional time to process the last
' character.
For lonCharPtr = 1 To (lonCharStrLen + 1)
    ' If this is not the last loop, then
    ' intNewChar is assigned the character that
    ' is read in. Otherwise, a -1 value indicates
    ' that it is the last loop.
    If lonCharPtr < lonCharStrLen + 1 Then
        intNewChar = Asc(Mid(txtDataIn.Text, _
            lonCharPtr, 1))
    Else
        intNewChar = -1
    End If
    ' Add one to the character count.
    intCharCount = intCharCount + 1
    If lonCharPtr > 1 Then
        ' Same character as last time?
        If intNewChar = intLastChar Then
            ' Is the character's high bit set?
            If intCharCount = 128 Then
                ' If high bit is set, then the
                ' character will get its own
                ' manager byte. Assign the count
                ' to zero (count is always one
                ' less than actual).
```

continues

Listing 54.3. continued

```
                bytMgrChar = 128
                bytMgrChar = bytMgrChar Or 127
                ' Add the manager byte and the
                ' character to the output string.
                strCompressed = strCompressed _
                    & Chr(bytMgrChar) & Chr(intLastChar)
                ' Set the character count to zero.
                intCharCount = 0
            End If
        Else
            ' The character read this time is
            ' different than the one read last time,
            ' so check to see if the character count
            ' is more than two.
            If intCharCount > 2 Then
                ' The character count is more than
                ' two, so this character sequence
                ' can get a manager byte. Set the
                ' count to one less than actual.
                bytMgrChar = 128
                bytMgrChar = bytMgrChar Or (intCharCount - 1)
                ' Add the manager byte and the
                ' character to the output string.
                strCompressed = strCompressed _
                    & Chr(bytMgrChar) & Chr(intLastChar)
            Else
                ' Two of the same characters have
                ' been encountered, but that's not
                ' enough to warrant a manager byte.
                ' Add the two characters to the
                ' output string.
                For intCharLoop = 1 To intCharCount
                    ' Check to see if the character
                    ' has its high bit set. If
                    ' it does, it'll have to have a
                    ' manager byte.
                    If bytLastChar > 127 Then
                        bytOutChar = 128
                        bytOutChar = bytOutChar Or (intCharCount - 1)
                        strCompressed = strCompressed _
                            & Chr(bytMgrChar) & Chr(intLastChar)
                    Else
                        ' The character does not have
                        ' its high bits set, so it
                        ' can be added to the output.
                        strCompressed = strCompressed _
                            & Chr(intLastChar)
                    End If
                Next intCharLoop
            End If
            ' Reset the character count.
            intCharCount = 0
        End If
    End If
    ' Make the most recently read character the
    ' last character so it can be checked in
    ' the next loop iteration.
```

```
    intLastChar = intNewChar
Next lonCharPtr

' Assign the compressed string to the output
' TextBox.
txtDataOut.Text = strCompressed

End Sub


Public Sub RLEUncompress(txtDataIn As TextBox, _
    txtDataOut As TextBox)

Dim bytNewChar As Byte
Dim intCharCount As Integer
Dim lonCharPtr As Long
Dim strUncompressed As String

lonCharPtr = 0
Do
    ' Increment the character pointer.
    lonCharPtr = lonCharPtr + 1
    ' Get the next character.
    bytNewChar = Asc(Mid(txtDataIn.Text, lonCharPtr, 1))
    ' Is the high bit set?
    If bytNewChar > 127 Then
        ' The high bit is set, so it must be a
        ' manager byte. Get the character count.
        intCharCount = (bytNewChar And 127) + 1
        ' Get the next character.
        lonCharPtr = lonCharPtr + 1
        bytNewChar = Asc(Mid(txtDataIn.Text, lonCharPtr, 1))
        ' Add the string of characters to the
        ' output string.
        strUncompressed = strUncompressed _
            & String(intCharCount, bytNewChar)
    Else
        ' This is a solo character (no manager
        ' byte), so add it to the output string.
        strUncompressed = strUncompressed _
            & Chr(bytNewChar)
    End If
' Keep looping until the last character has
' been processed.
Loop Until (lonCharPtr >= Len(txtDataIn.Text))

' Assign the uncompressed string to the output
' TextBox.
txtDataOut.Text = strUncompressed

End Sub
```

Of course, you can modify these routines to compress and uncompress things other than the contents of a TextBox. Also, if you're going to be reading in data from a disk file, you wouldn't want to read it in a byte at a time. Instead, you would want to read in large chunks of the file into memory and then process the chunks byte by byte using the preceding routines.

Summary

Visual Basic is often ignored as a serious development platform, so it is often difficult for VB programmers to find information about common data processing tasks in a language they can understand. This chapter discussed some of the more commonly used algorithms in the areas of sorting, data encryption, and data compression. It also provided sample code for implementing sorts, encryption, and compression into your own programs.

CHAPTER 55

Online Resources for VB Programmers

IN THIS CHAPTER

In the last few years, the art of programming has changed drastically. Everything is moving towards an object-oriented design philosophy, where objects and code libraries are reusable. We no longer have to reinvent the wheel every time we need program elements written. In many cases, it's likely that someone else has already invented a newer and better wheel and is willing to share his invention with whomever is interested.

The way that code and ideas are shared among programmers has also changed drastically in the last few years. It used to be that you might have a group of friends or colleagues with whom you could discuss programming topics. Today, you can interact with literally millions of programmers all over the world through the Internet. Many of them have created Web pages that contain volumes of information that can be accessed 24 hours a day. Some have even created reusable components or programs that they have made publicly available and can be downloaded for free.

The Internet is an excellent tool for programmers—that is certain. But it has one major drawback: it's too big! Finding what you're looking for is often a daunting chore, requiring you to look through numerous Web pages until you finally find the information you seek. For every great Web site, there are at least ten real stinkers.

To help you in your efforts of finding timely and reliable information on the Internet relating to Visual Basic programming, this chapter lists several excellent Web sites. Due to the volatile nature of the Web and the way that sites come and go without notice, it's possible that a few of them will no longer be accessible by the time this book goes to print. However, only those that are likely to be around for a while have been included, so your chances of finding that a site is still online are good.

Also included in this chapter is a list of Usenet newsgroups relating to Visual Basic or Windows programming. These are always excellent resources because you can post questions that will be read by thousands of programmers all over the world. It's likely that one of them will know the answer and will post a reply, usually within a few days.

World Wide Web Sites

Only a few years ago, Web sites for Visual Basic programmers were few and far between. Fortunately, as the number of Internet users shot up, so did the number of VB sites. Now there are thousands of them, from large-scale corporate endeavors to personal home pages of beginner programmers.

This section includes some of the better Web sites for obtaining Visual Basic information, finding free ActiveX controls and sample source code, posing questions, and learning online. Consider these starting points, though it's likely that you'll find the information you're looking for at one of these sites and will have to go no farther.

Some of the sites listed here include long lists of other VB-related Web sites. You can spend days or weeks exploring all of them. Of course, you don't want to get carried away, but it's always well worth taking the time to seek out new resources.

General VB Information

The Web sites listed here are of general interest and often contain a wide variety of features pertaining to Visual Basic programming. Some of them are so extensive that you would have a tough time seeing all that they have to offer.

Advanced Visual Basic

`http://vb.duke-net.com/`

A great site designed for more advanced programmers, *Advanced Visual Basic* contains developer news, a few how-to articles by Chris Duke, tuning and optimization tips, OLE troubleshooting information, a forum and chat area, and an excellent database of Windows errors. This site is a must-see.

Carl & Gary's Visual Basic Home Page

`http://www.apexsc.com/vb/`

Developed jointly by Carl Franklin and Gary Wisniewski, *Carl & Gary's* is the original Visual Basic Web site, and it's still one of the best. The amount of information found here is staggering, the result of years of building and consistently adding new features.

The Cobb Group's Developer's Channel

`http://www.cobb.com/devel.htm`

The Cobb Group, which publishes *Inside Visual Basic* and other development newsletters, has created this site for software developers. You can find some good articles and tips here. You can also sign up to receive a free issue of *Inside VB.*

The Development Exchange

`http://www.devx.com/home/devxhome.asp`

Sponsored by the *Visual Basic Programmer's Journal*, the most popular print magazine for VB programmers, *The Development Exchange* has tons of information on Windows development. Although VB definitely has its place at this site, there is also information for C++ and Java programmers. The only downside is that you have to be a member of the Premier Club to gain complete access ($20 a year). However, there is still a lot you can get to even without the club membership.

Focus On Visual Basic

`http://visualbasic.miningco.com/`

This site, which is only one part of the huge Mining Company mega-site, has a lot of information on Visual Basic in general. Pete Forde, the site's guide, does an excellent job of keeping it up-to-date and searching out resources that are not widely known.

The Game Programming MegaSite

`http://www.perplexed.com/GPMega/index.htm`

Although much of this site is geared towards C++ and Assembler programmers, it does include a VB section that has some interesting articles on developing games in Visual Basic. There is also an algorithm section that might be of help in determining how certain graphic effects are created.

Gary Beene's VB World

`http://web2.airmail.net/gbeene/welcome.html`

Gary Beene has assembled a great collection of links to VB-related sites, and he does a good job of keeping them updated. He's also started working on an online VB4 tutorial, but it still has a way to go before it's finished.

Joe Garrick's World of Visual Basic

`http://www.citilink.com/~jgarrick/vbasic/`

Joe Garrick has created a resource for both beginning and advanced VB programmers. His site contains a beginner's corner, database programming information, tips and tricks, a Q&A section, and downloads. There's even a humor page for when you're not in the mood for programming.

Macmillan Computer Publishing

`http://www.mcp.com/`

The MCP site includes some real gems for VB programmers. Of special note is the Resource Center, from which you can access the *Visual Basic Power Source*. Another nice feature is the Personal Bookshelf, where you get to select up to five fully searchable online versions of current MCP books.

Microsoft Site Builder Network

`http://www.microsoft.com/sitebuilder/`

For those developing ActiveX controls and using them on Web pages, obtaining membership in the Site Builder Network is a must. You can find tons of information and free software here, as well as a steady of stream of articles and other new features. Membership is free.

Microsoft Visual Basic Start Page

`http://www.microsoft.com/vbasic/`

If you're looking for information on Visual Basic, it pays to go directly to the source. Microsoft's site is an excellent resource for all kinds of VB info, especially product news and helpful articles. Register in the VB Owner's Area, and you can access a lot more stuff, including updated tools and utilities.

MSDN Online Library

http://premium.microsoft.com/msdn/library/

The Microsoft Developer's Network (MSDN) is the best source of information on Microsoft products anywhere. You'll have to register to obtain access to most of the good stuff, but it's free and well worth the time.

Object Magazine Online

http://www.sigs.com/omo/

Although it doesn't include any resources specific to Visual Basic, *Object Magazine Online* is still worth checking out, especially if you are interested in object-oriented programming techniques. Unfortunately, you cannot access the entire magazine online, but there's still a lot here.

VBQuery

http://www.advercast.com/vb/index.shtml

If you're looking for VB information, this is a good place to start. *VBQuery* is a searchable database of more than 1,000 VB-related Web sites. The search engine is fast, and the database is huge, so *VBQuery* can almost always assist you in finding the information you need.

VBxtras

http://www.vbxtras.com/

If you're looking for third-party controls or add-ins, then you might want to check out *VBxtras*. This online software catalog has hundreds of titles that can be purchased directly from the Internet. You can also find product demos, a *TechZine*, and even a JobNet for those seeking employment.

Visual Basic Online Magazine

http://206.171.105.131/vb-mag/

Visual Basic Online Magazine is just what its title suggests, a magazine for VB programmers that is completely online. Like any other magazine, it includes feature articles, regular columns, product reviews, and much more. New issues come out monthly.

The Visual Basic Resource Index

http://www.qns.com/~robinson/vb/vb1.html

This site is a huge categorized index of other Visual Basic sites. It also contains links directly to certain articles in Microsoft's VB Knowledge Base. Explore this index, and you're sure to find some interesting sources of VB information.

Q&A Sites

If you have a specific question about Visual Basic programming, the Web sites listed here might be able to help you out. They include forums where you can post your question and have it answered by the Web site's hosts or other programmers. An archive of previously answered questions is also available, so you might find the information you're looking for right away.

Ask the VB Pro

`http://www.inquiry.com/techtips/thevbpro/index.html`

One of the Web's oldest and largest Q&A sites, Inquiry.com's *Ask the Pros* (which was recently acquired by Fawcett Technical Publications) is an excellent resource for finding answers to programming questions of all kinds. Aside from the "Ask the VB Pro" page, there is also an "Ask the Java Pro" page, an "Ask the C++ Pro" page, and so on.

Help Talk Online's Visual Basic Support

`http://www.helptalk.com/vb/`

This question-and-answer forum is one of the better ones on the Web. Few questions are left unanswered, and answers come quickly. John Dunbar, the moderator of the forum, often answers many of the questions himself and interjects with comments of his own about hot news in the VB community, book reviews, and other things.

Free ActiveX Controls

When you need to add certain functionality to your programs, ActiveX controls are usually the best way to go. The Web sites listed here offer several ActiveX controls that can be downloaded and used for free.

B.E. Network

`http://www.blackthorne.com/`

Blackthorne Enterprises has developed a couple dozen ActiveX controls that they are distributing as freeware. Many of them are simple (for example, check to see whether a sound card is present), but their simplicity is often what makes them so handy.

COOL.STF

`http://www.coolstf.com/`

This site contains a small collection of free and shareware ActiveX controls, including `RASDial`, `EZFTP`, and a control for UU encoding and decoding. It also has some code samples and articles on VB programming.

Sample Code Repositories and Software Libraries

Sometimes, when you're unsure about how to code something, it's often helpful to see how other people have accomplished the same thing. To do that, however, you need to be able to find the code that you're looking for. The following Web sites contain archives of code and sample programs that can be downloaded for free.

Also included in some of these archives are shareware and freeware programming utilities for Visual Basic. Some also have demo versions of third-party products such as ActiveX controls so you can try them out before you buy them.

FreeCode

`http://www.freecode.com/`

FreeCode is a source code archive that focuses primarily on Internet programming, such as email and chat applications. The development languages represented in the archive include C++, Java, and Perl, but there is some VB code here and there, too.

Planet Source Code

`http://www.planet-source-code.com/vb/default.htm`

When it comes to libaries of source code, *Planet Source Code* has one of the biggest and best. Plus, the library is searchable so that you can easily find exactly what you're looking for. You'll want to bookmark this one.

Programmer's Heaven

`http://www.programmersheaven.com/`

Programmer's Heaven contains a sizable collection of files relating to Visual Basic and other development platforms. The files are a sampling of the contents of two CD-ROMs that can be purchased here. Aside from VB source code and utilities, *Programmer's Heaven* also contains links to other programming-related sites on the Web.

SoftSeek

`http://digitalwave.softseek.com/Programming/Visual_Basic/`

This searchable software archive has a decent collection of Visual Basic ActiveX controls, demos, and shareware utilities. Actually, the Programming section is only a small part of the entire archive, and you can find all kinds of other shareware and freeware products here, too.

Tutorials and Online Classes

If you want to learn about Visual Basic, one of the best ways to do so is through an online course. These courses are often inexpensive but do require that you purchase a specific book to follow along with the lesson plan of the class. One of the best perks of being enrolled in an online course is that you can interact with experienced instructors and other VB programmers.

The two online universities listed in this section offer continuing education units (CEUs) for any courses completed. You usually have to pay a few dollars extra to get the credits, but the cost is minimal.

eZone

`http://www.waite.com/ezone/`

Waite Group Press offers free online classes centered on its *Interactive Course* series of books, including the *Visual Basic 5 Interactive Course* and *Visual Basic 5 Web Database Interactive Course* titles. As you follow along in the books at your own pace, you can also ask questions of the class instructors or chat with other programmers who are also taking the course.

ZD University

`http://www.zdu.com/`

Ziff-Davis, publisher of magazines and books, has created an online university that offers classes on a wide range of computer-related subjects. Most classes last about two months. The tuition fee is a flat $4.95 per month, and you can enroll in as many classes as you can handle.

Newsgroups

One of the best ways to receive timely information about Visual Basic is to browse through the dozens of newsgroups dedicated to the subject. You can join in on the discussions or post a question that you would like answered. Responses are often quick, sometimes coming within hours, but usually taking a day or two.

To access newsgroups, you may need to install special client software. However, many Web browsers have newsgroup client applications included in their suite of programs. Both Netscape and later versions of Internet Explorer include support for newsgroups with their products, but you may have had to specify that the newsgroup client option be included when the software was installed.

To access newsgroups from within a Web browser, simply type **`news:`** and the name of the newsgroup in the same text box in which you would type a Web site URL. For example, to access the Usenet newsgroup `comp.lang.basic.visual`, you would type in:

```
news:comp.lang.basic.visual
```

Some newsgroups may not be accessible through your Internet service provider. If that is the case, you can either ask your ISP to start carrying the newsgroups you want, change ISPs, or connect to another news server.

Microsoft Public VB Newsgroups

Microsoft has created a number of public newsgroups for discussion of Visual Basic topics. As you can see by the following list, everything from third-party controls to the Setup Wizard is covered.

```
microsoft.public.access.modulesdaovba
microsoft.public.activex.programming.scripting.vbscript
microsoft.public.inetsdk.programming.scripting.vbscript
microsoft.public.vb.3rdparty
microsoft.public.vb.addins
microsoft.public.vb.bugs
microsoft.public.vb.controls
microsoft.public.vb.controls.creation
microsoft.public.vb.controls.internet
microsoft.public.vb.crystal
microsoft.public.vb.database
microsoft.public.vb.database.dao
microsoft.public.vb.database.odbc
microsoft.public.vb.database.rdo
microsoft.public.vb.dos
microsoft.public.vb.enterprise
microsoft.public.vb.general.discussion
microsoft.public.vb.installation
microsoft.public.vb.ole
microsoft.public.vb.ole.automation
microsoft.public.vb.ole.cdk
microsoft.public.vb.ole.servers
microsoft.public.vb.setupwiz
microsoft.public.vb.syntax
microsoft.public.vb.winapi
microsoft.public.vb.winapi.graphics
microsoft.public.vb.winapi.networks
microsoft.public.word.vba
```

Other VB Newsgroups

Several other newsgroups about Visual Basic are also available. Almost all news servers carry the `comp.lang` newsgroups, so you shouldn't have much trouble finding access to the newsgroups in the following list.

`alt.lang.vb5.rumors`

`comp.lang.basic.visual`

`comp.lang.basic.visual.3rdparty`

`comp.lang.basic.visual.announce`

`comp.lang.basic.visual.database`

`comp.lang.basic.visual.misc`

`comp.lang.visual.basic`

Non-English VB Newsgroups

For those who do not speak English as their primary language, there are several Visual Basic-related newsgroups for other languages such as Spanish, German, Japanese, French, and Italian.

`cz.comp.lang.basic.visual` (Czechoslovakian)

`es.comp.lenguajes.visual-basic` (Spanish)

`fido.ger.basic` (German)

`fido7.ru.visual.basic` (Russian)

`fj.lang.visualbasic` (Japanese)

`fr.comp.lang.basic` (French)

`it.comp.lang.visual-basic` (Italian)

`japan.comp.lang.visual-basic` (Japanese)

Summary

The Internet is a boon for Visual Basic developers because it offers an incredible amount of information and resources. In fact, often there is too much information, making it difficult to find exactly what you're looking for.

This chapter briefly discussed some of the best Visual Basic resources currently available on the Internet's World Wide Web. These Web sites can be used as starting points for locating the information you seek. Also included in this chapter was a list of newsgroups that focus on Visual Basic programming and related topics.

CHAPTER

VB5 Acronyms and Buzzwords

IN THIS CHAPTER

Technology changes so rapidly that it is often difficult to keep up. Visual Basic is no exception. Every new version of VB brings a host of new technologies and buzzwords that can confuse even the most advanced programmer.

The computer industry is particularly fond of acronyms. It seems that every new thing to come down the pike is immediately branded with an acronym. Take databases for example. You've got ODBC, JET, ADO, RDO, DAO, ISAM—and that's just to name a few!

If you find yourself lost in the world of acronymns and buzzwords, you can use this chapter as a guide for deciphering some of the more commonly used terms and acronyms. It will also introduce you to many of the new technologies implemented in this version of Visual Basic.

NOTE

The list of acronyms and buzzwords contained in this chapter is far from complete. If you want to find out the definitions of industry terms not listed here, you can try TechWeb's Tech Encyclopedia at `http://www.techweb.com/encylopedia`. It contains a searchable database of more than 10,000 definitions.

VB5 Acronyms

ADC—Advanced Data Connector

See RDS—Remote Data Services.

ADO—ActiveX Data Objects

A database interface that allows client applications to access and manipulate databases in a database server through a provider. ADO was originally used with Microsoft's Internet Information Server, but it can now be used in high-level languages like Visual Basic. ADO is the new database standard.

API—Application Program Interface

A library of functions that can be called within applications to communicate with an operating system or some other low-level system program. The Win32 API, for example, contains hundreds of functions that can be called from within a VB program. These functions are used to perform services that are built into the Windows operating system, such as copying memory or obtaining information about hardware connected to the system.

ASP—Active Server Pages

Web pages that contain embedded program code (typically VBScript or JScript) that is executed by the server. Active Server pages can be far more dynamic than static Web pages because they can interact with databases or perform other actions.

CASE—Computer-Aided Software Engineering

Software, such as a systems diagramming tool, used to assist in or simplify the development of applications.

CGI—Common Gateway Interface

The medium by which an HTML page interacts with a Web server. CGI scripts are short programs or "applets" that are written in a scripting language such as Perl and can perform some function and return the results via a Web page.

CLSID—Class ID

A globally unique identifier assigned to a class so that it can be differentiated from other components. Class IDs are sometimes referred to as UUIDs (Universally Unique Identifiers).

COM—Component Object Model

A software architecture designed by Microsoft that standardizes the way components are created and used, as well as facilitating communication between objects. ActiveX objects are built on the Component Object Model specification.

CORBA—Common Object Request Broker Architecture

A standard for communication between objects no matter where they reside on a network or in which language they were written. CORBA was designed by the Object Management Group (OMG) and is competing with Microsoft's DCOM for industry acceptance. However, DCOM-CORBA interoperability is supposedly in the works.

DAO—Data Access Object

An interface for accessing databases, implemented in Visual Basic as an ActiveX control. DAO allows applications to access databases using the JET engine. It can also be used for accessing ODBC databases by using ODBCDirect.

DBMS—DataBase Management System

Software that acts as an interface between a database and an application. It manages requests from the application and handles the physical organization, indexing, security, storage, and retrieval of data from the database.

DCOM—Distributed Component Object Model

Based on COM, DCOM facilitates the communication of objects across a network. DCOM is built into Windows NT 4.0 and is also available for Windows 95.

DHTML—Dynamic HyperText Markup Language

An enhanced version of HTML that allows Web pages to become more flexible, almost like mini applications. IE4.0 and Netscape Communicator both support DHTML, but each has its own version.

DLL—Dynamic Link Library

A library of functions that can be called from within an application. Although many programs may use the same DLL simultaneously, it usually exists in memory only once. The Win32 API consists of several DLLs that contain the hundreds of functions used by both the Windows operating system and other applications.

DNS—Domain Naming System

A way of allowing Internet host computers to have mnemonic host names, such as `http://www.microsoft.com`. DNS servers are equipped with software that looks up the host names in a database and returns their corresponding IP addresses.

FTP—File Transfer Protocol

A protocol used for transferring files over a TCP/IP network, such as the Internet.

GUI—Graphical User Interface

A way of communicating with users via graphics elements such as icons, pull-down menus, buttons, and windows. All Windows-based programs that interact with a user have some kind of GUI.

GUID—Globally Unique Identifier

A globally unique 128-bit number assigned to an object (such as an ActiveX control) so that it can be differentiated from other objects.

HTML—HyperText Markup Language

The language used to define Web pages. HTML consists of tags that are embedded into text files and specify how a page looks and how it responds to user actions.

HTTP—HyperText Transport Protocol

The data transfer protocol used to connect to servers on the World Wide Web.

IDE—Integrated Development Environment

A development tool that combines several elements of program design into a single environment. Visual Basic's user interface is referred to as the IDE because it combines an editor, compiler, debugger, and other tools into a single easy-to-use development environment.

IE—Internet Explorer

Microsoft's Web browser. Later versions of Internet Explorer are often referred to as IE3 or IE4.

IIS—Internet Information Server

Microsoft's Web server software. IIS runs under Windows NT only and supports Netscape's SSL security protocol.

ISAM—Indexed Sequential Access Method

A data storage method that stores data sequentially and maintains an index of key fields for all the records in the database so that they can be accessed directly.

ISAPI—Internet Server Application Programmer Interface

A programming interface for interacting with Microsoft's Internet Information Server (IIS). ISAPI functions can be called from within Web pages to perform services on the server such as accessing a database.

ISDN—Integrated Services Digital Network

A standard for delivering voice, data, and signaling information via end-to-end digital circuits. ISDN is an alternative to using analog modems for communications and offers enhanced data transmission speeds.

JET—Joint Engine Technology

The database engine used in Visual Basic, C++, and Microsoft Access. The JET engine can access a wide variety of database formats.

MAPI—Messaging Application Programming Interface

A set of functions that enable applications to implement electronic messaging features. In Visual Basic, MAPI can be utilized through two ActiveX controls, MAPISession and MAPIMessage.

MCI—Media Control Interface

Microsoft's API for the control of multimedia hardware. With MCI, you can play MIDI files, AVI videos, and audio CDs. You can also play and record WAV files.

MDI—Multiple Document Interface

The standard user-interface architecture for Windows applications that allows a user to work with more than one document at a time. An MDI application can have multiple child windows displayed within its main window.

MDO—Microsoft Development Objects

A tool information model (TIM) that VB5 uses to track Visual Basic projects and their contents in the Microsoft repository.

MSDN—Microsoft Developers Network

Microsoft's huge repository of information for software developers. This information can be obtained for free via the Internet or on CD-ROM (for a yearly subscription fee).

MTS—Microsoft Transaction Server

A component-based transaction processing system for creating and using Internet and intranet server applications. MTS defines a model for application development and provides the runtime infrastructure for deployment and management.

NSAPI—NetScape Application Programmer Interface

A library of functions that can be used to perform actions on Netscape's Web Server such as accessing data in a database.

ODBC—Open DataBase Connectivity

A standard interface protocol that allows applications to connect to external database servers or files. The Microsoft JET engine can be used to access external databases such as Microsoft SQL Server, or the ODBC API can be used directly without using JET.

ODBCDirect

A method for accessing ODBC data sources through RDO by using DAO features. Although DAO usually uses the JET database engine, JET is bypassed when using ODBCDirect.

OLE—Object Linking and Embedding

A specification that allows separate applications to share and integrate information with each other.

OLE DB

A method for accessing all data via a standard COM interface, regardless of where or how it is stored. This includes not only databases but also files, electronic mail, documents, and other forms of data.

OOP—Object-Oriented Programming

A method of program design that uses objects (modules and classes) that can be used again and again.

RDBMS—Relational DataBase Management System

A data access system that can link together two or more databases by a common field. By comparison, flat-file databases can only access one database at a time.

RDC—Remote Data Control

The ActiveX control in Visual Basic 5 Enterprise Edition that facilitates the use of RDO (Remote Data Objects).

RDO—Remote Data Objects

A way of accessing ODBC data sources without using a local query processor. RDO is actually a wrapper that simplifies use of the ODBC API.

RDS—Remote Data Services

Programming interfaces used to access databases on the Internet or an intranet using an ActiveX-enabled browser such as Internet Explorer. Before being integrated into ADO, RDS was called ADC (Advanced Data Connector).

SAPI—Speech API

A library of functions available from Microsoft that enable programs to provide services such as speech recognition and text-to-speech.

SDI—Single Document Interface

A user-interface architecture that allows a user to work with only one document at a time. MDI, Multiple Document Interface, is a more commonly used architecture and provides users more flexibility.

SDK—Software Development Kit

A set of code and utilities that can be used by developers to create software or implement special functionality in their programs. SDKs are usually geared for C++ developers.

SP2—Service Pack 2

In Visual Basic, SP2 commonly refers to the Service Pack that Microsoft released to fix bugs in VB. It also added some extra functionality to the language, such as support for threading. A third Service Pack was also released and is referred to as SP3.

SQL—Structured Query Language

A sub-language that can be used to interrogate and process data within a relational database system.

TAPI—Telephony Application Programmer Interface

A set of functions available from Microsoft that allows a program to interact directly with telephone systems. Telephony merges the computer and the telephone, allowing sophisticated communciations features like voice mail to be used from within applications.

TCP/IP—Transmission Control Protocol/Internet Protocol

A set of transport protocols most commonly used on the Internet. TCP is a connection-oriented data transfer protocol, and IP is connectionless.

TIM—Tool Information Model

A format for storing information about a software tool in a repository database.

UDP—User Datagram Protocol

A data transfer protocol used in place of TCP when transferring data that does not have to be delivered whole. For example, streaming audio and video are usually transferred via UDP because if data packets are lost, there is no time to retransmit them.

UDT—User-Defined Type

A data type created by the programmer using the `Type...End Type` structure. User-defined types typically consist of two or more separate items of data that together are considered a single data type.

URL—Universal Resource Locator

An address that points to the location of a file on the Internet. URLs can point to files on any kind of Internet service, including the World Wide Web, FTP, and newsgroups.

VB5CCE—Visual Basic 5 Control Creation Edition

The version of Visual Basic 5 that Microsoft has made available for free download from the Internet. The CCE is limited and can only be used to create ActiveX controls.

VBA—Visual Basic Applications Edition

A subset of Visual Basic that is typically integrated into applications such as word processors and spreadsheets and can be used to perform operations on the application's data. VBA is almost identical to Visual Basic, but programs created with it can be used only within the application that supports VBA.

XML—Extensible Markup Language

A subset of the SGML (Standard Generalized Markup Language) document language, designed for use on the World Wide Web. Instead of using a predefined set of tags like HTML, XML defines the tags that will be used within the document itself.

Y2K—Year 2000

The year in which some computer programs, especially older ones, will cease working properly because of the way dates are stored. Dates that allow only two digits to represent the year will have problems because the year will be stored as "00," which to the computer comes before "99," not after.

Technology Buzzwords

ActiveX

A set of technologies based on the Component Object Model (COM) that enable software components to interact with one another regardless of the language used to created them. ActiveX components can be used both locally and across networks, such as the Internet.

ActiveX Documents

Mini-applications that can be loaded into a container program, such as a Web browser, and executed. ActiveX documents can be developed in Visual Basic just like regular applications and can be distributed via the Internet or an intranet as easily as if they were Web pages.

BackOffice

An integrated family of server software built on the Windows NT operating system. Because BackOffice uses an open architecture, it can be expanded and integrated with other existing systems.

Client/Server

An architecture in which one computer (the client) requests information from another (the server). For example, a Web browser is a *client* application that requests a document from a Web *server*.

DirectX

A set of programming interfaces that provides applications with low-level access to multimedia hardware. This low-level access is used to improve performance.

In-Process

Code that runs within the address space of an application instead of in its own address space. A DLL file is an example of an in-process component because it runs in the same address space as the application that uses its functions.

N-Tier

Refers to a client/server environment that consists of an unspecified number of tiers. In a two-tier client/server system, a client application requests information from a single server directly.

In a three-tier client/server system, a user interface exists on the client, the application logic is executed on one or more servers, and the data may be stored in a separate database server.

Out-of-Process

Code that runs in its own address space instead of within the address space of another application. An ActiveX EXE is an example of an out-of-process component because it runs in its own address space.

Repository

A common place in which to store information about relationships between objects, providing a standard way in which to describe software tools.

Visual InterDev

A product available from Microsoft that integrates a variety of visual development tools that can be used to create and manage Web projects. Visual InterDev facilitates the development of Active Server pages as well as regular HTML pages.

Windows CE

A version of Windows designed to run on Handheld Personal Computers (HPCs). Although Windows CE-based applications can share data with Windows 95 applications because they share similar programming models, Windows CE supports only a subset of the Win32 API to minimize the amount of memory needed to run the operating system.

Summary

Although this short chapter cannot come close to defining the thousands of acronyms and buzzwords used within the computer industry, it does cover many of those often used by Visual Basic programmers. Nobody can be fluent in all the acronym-branded technologies introduced by Microsoft and other industry standard-setters, but it does help to have some idea of what the acronyms stand for and what the technology represents.

CHAPTER 57

VB5 Certification Requirements

IN THIS CHAPTER

As of late, Microsoft's Certification programs have garnered a lot of attention from professional Visual Basic programmers. By securing the credentials of "Certified Solution Developer" from Microsoft, the clients or potential employers of the programmer are offered some proof that an individual is well-versed in Visual Basic development. But does Microsoft certification really offer proof of a programmer's competence in a specific area of study? Yes and no.

To be sure, the exams given by Microsoft to those wishing to obtain certified status are not easy. Passing them requires a fair amount of knowledge in almost all aspects of Visual Basic programming. For example, if you are not well-versed in topics such as how to create and use ActiveX documents, your chances of scoring well on the exam are slim. Make no mistake—you need to know your stuff to be Microsoft certified.

Because of the large number of programmers who would like to become certified, several companies have created products that promise to help them along towards that goal. There are several software packages now available that emulate the Microsoft exams. There are also seminars being held that will teach you everything you need to know in order to pass the Microsoft exam of your choice.

Can attending a one- or two-week seminar or using a software package arm you with enough knowledge to pass the exam? In many cases, yes. But can doing those things make you a Visual Basic expert? Certainly not. Expertise comes from working with a product over a period of time and learning its intricacies, not from some kind of crash course.

Clients and employers who may be impressed by your certification status will most certainly expect you to back it up with a high level of knowledge and skill. Therefore, my advice for those seeking to become Microsoft certified in Visual Basic is to determine the topics covered on the certification exam that may cause you some trouble and set a proper course of study. If, for example, you are unfamiliar with the creation and use of ActiveX controls, learn as much as you can on that topic. Use books like this one to obtain an understanding of how it is done. Create and use several ActiveX controls until you have the process down cold. Only then will you be confident in your skills.

This chapter will provide you with an idea of the topics that are covered on the Microsoft exam. It is not meant to be the definitive guide to obtaining certification in Visual Basic applications development, but merely as a general overview of the skills needed for becoming certified.

Although this book was not specifically designed as a resource for those studying for certification, it does cover several of the topics included on the exam. Where relevant, you will be pointed to other chapters in this book that can help you brush up on each topic.

Topics Covered on the VB5 Certification Exam

Although there's no way to tell exactly which questions will be asked when you take Microsoft's certification exam, it is possible to generalize as to the topics that will be covered. The information contained here was taken from Microsoft's *Preparation Guide for Exam 70-165*, which lists the various skills that are required to pass the "Developing Applications with Microsoft Visual Basic 5.0" exam. It should give you an idea of the depth of the exam and how much knowledge is required to receive a passing score.

NOTE

The contents of Microsoft's certification exams and the topics they cover are liable to change at any time. The only real way of ensuring that you will pass the exam is to know Visual Basic inside and out. After all, that is what certification is meant to prove.

Events

You should know the purposes of the more common Visual Basic events and how and when to use them. For example, given a specific task to code, you should know whether to place the code in a Form's `Initialize` or `Load` event.

Chapter 43, "Sequences of Events," can help you in this area.

Forms

You should know how to design and create forms at design time, and how to add and delete forms at runtime. You should also know how to use the `Forms` collection.

Menus

Know how to add, modify, and delete menus manually at design time and dynamically at runtime. Also know how to add pop-up menus to your applications.

Controls

Several of the Windows Common Controls (`TreeView`, `ListView`, `ImageList`, `Toolbar`, and `StatusBar` are covered, so you should know how to use them. You should also know how to create and destroy controls dynamically (during runtime) and how to use control collections.

Chapter 12, "The ListView, TreeView, and ImageList Controls," gives examples of how to use those controls in your programs. Chapters 14, "Dynamic Control Creation and Indexing," and 10, "Data Structures, Collections, and Enumerations," can also help you learn about using controls.

Drag and Drop Operations

Questions related to coding for drag and drop operations may also be on the exam. You should also know how drag and drop works within the Microsoft Windows environment.

Chapter 15, "Implementing OLE Drag-and-Drop Capabilities into Controls," covers this topic.

Variables

When declaring variables, you should how (and why) to define their scope as Public, Private, or Static.

Subs and Functions

You should know how to write your own `Sub` and `Function` procedures and how to call them. Know how to define and pass arguments to your procedures, including arrays, named arguments, and optional arguments. Also know how to call `Sub` and `Function` procedures from outside of the module in which they are defined.

Using DLLs

Several questions concerning the use of DLLs with VB applications are also likely to be included in the exam. You should be able to declare and call DLL routines and identify when the Alias clause is necessary. You should be familiar with how to pass various argument types to DLL routines, including strings, null pointers, values by reference (ByRef) and by value (ByVal), and function pointers (using a callback function). Finally, you should be able to create a DLL routine that is passed string arguments and modifies them.

Error Handling

You should know how to code and implement error handlers in your programs and how to use the `Err` object. Knowledge of the error-handling options available in the VB development environment (Break on All Errors, Break in Class Module, and Break on Unhandled Errors) may also be necessary. Finally, you should know how to raise errors from a server object.

Chapter 3, "Handling Errors," discusses some aspects of error handling in Visual Basic. Chapter 4, "Debugging and Testing Techniques," also provides some information in this area.

Help

Implementing Help features in your applications is covered on the exam. You should know how to use the `HelpFile` property of controls as well as how to use the `CommonDialog` control to display Help files.

Chapter CD2, "Giving Your Users Help," covers the creation and use of Help files. For information on how to use the `CommonDialog` control, see Chapter 13, "Leveraging Windows: Using the Common Dialog Creation Control."

Class Modules

You should know how to create and use class modules, including how to determine whether the class should be public or private. You should be able to add properties and methods to your classes, and know how (and why) to declare properties and methods as Friends. Questions regarding the `Instancing` property, which specifies whether or not instances of a public class can be created outside of the project in which the class is defined, may also be asked.

ActiveX Controls

Thorough knowledge of building and using ActiveX controls is necessary. Raising events, creation and use of property pages, and storage and retrieval of persistent control properties may be covered. You should also know how to add an ActiveX control to a Web page.

Part IV of this book, "Energizing Your Applications with ActiveX," discusses the creation and use of ActiveX controls in detail.

ActiveX Documents

The creation and use of ActiveX documents is also covered in the exam, so you should be familiar with that subject. Be prepared to compare ActiveX documents to embedded objects, create new ActiveX document projects that use one or more `UserDocument` objects, know how to retain persistent data for ActiveX documents, and how to automate ActiveX documents. Finally, you should also know how to implement ActiveX documents into Web pages.

ActiveX Clients

Several questions regarding the creation and use of ActiveX clients are likely to be included in the exam. Know how to build ActiveX clients and how to use the `Dim` statement to reference objects as well as the `Set` statement to create an instance of an object. Also know how to use the `CreateObject` function.

Automation Servers

You should be familiar with the creation and use of Automation servers that expose objects, properties, methods, and events. You should also be able to create methods that display forms and multithreaded components. Definition of property procedures, the `App` object, and asynchronous calling of object servers using callback mechanisms are other areas that may be covered on the exam.

Database Access

Expect several questions pertaining to database access to be included in the exam. You should know how to bind controls to databases and how to effectively use the data controls, including (but not limited to) `DBList`, `DBCombo`, `ListBox`, `DBGrid`, and `MSFlexGrid`.

You should also know how to access databases through VB code and how to use `Recordset` objects. Prepare to be able to add, modify, and delete records in a `Recordset` as well as how to navigate through them. You should also be able to use the `Find` and `Seek` methods to search a `Recordset`.

Internet Access

Knowing how to create Internet-enabled applications is a must for scoring well on the exam. You should be familiar with the use of the `Hyperlink` object to access the Internet (or an intranet), and should know how to create applications that can connect to the Internet and browse HTML pages.

Compiler Options

Aside from knowing how to compile programs, you should have an understanding of the various compiler options and when using them would be appropriate. You should know the compiler options that are available when compiling to native code (new in VB5) as well the differences between compiling to p-code and native code.

Conditional Compilation

You should know how to use conditional compiler options, including the use of the `#If...#End If` and `#Const` directives. You should also know how to set the appropriate flags for conditional compilation.

Debugging Techniques

Obtaining a thorough understanding of debugging techniques is essential before taking the exam. Topics that may be covered include the following: setting watch expressions at runtime, defining the scope of watch variables, and monitoring and using the Immediate and Locals debugging windows. You should also know how to use multiple project groups to facilitate the debugging process, including how to debug DLLs in process and how to test and debug ActiveX controls in process.

Chapter 4 discusses many of the commonly used techniques for program debugging.

Using the Setup Wizard

You should know how to use VB's Setup Wizard to build setup programs and how to properly alter the SETUP.INF and VB5DEP.INI files that the Setup Wizard creates. Using the Wizard, you should also be able to create a setup program that installs and registers ActiveX controls.

Chapter CD1, "Using the Setup Wizard," provides instruction on how to effectively use the Setup Wizard.

The System Registry

Several questions may be asked concerning the use and management of the Windows system registry. You should know how to use the `SaveSetting` and `GetSetting` statements to save and retrieve application-specific information to and from the registry as well how to make changes to the registry manually using the RegEdit program. Registration of components may also be covered, including use of the Regsvr32 utility and the Remote Automation Connection Manager.

Chapter 37, "Navigating the Registry," discusses several aspects of system registry manipulation, both manually using RegEdit and through VB code.

Application and Control Distribution

You should know how to distribute ActiveX controls and applications over the Internet. A knowledge of CAB files and how they are used is also necessary.

I

INDEX

Symbols

A

D

G

H

J-K

L

M

N

O

P

S

V

W

X-Z

Sams' Teach Yourself Database Programming with Visual Basic 5 in 21 Days

Michael Amundsen & Curtis Smith

Visual Basic, the 32-bit programming language from Microsoft, is used by programmers to create Windows and Windows 95 applications. It can also be used to program applications for the Web. This book shows those programmers how to design, develop, and deploy Visual Basic applications for the World Wide Web.

Presented in a daily format with each week focusing on a different area of database development. Written by a Microsoft Certified Visual Basic Professional.

CD-ROM includes chapter examples, function libraries, Microsoft Access/JET 2.5 compatibility layer, and the WHAT6 Help Authoring Tool.

$45.00 US/$63.95 CDN *New - Casual - Advanced*
0-672-31018-X *1,080 pp.*

Visual Basic 5 Client/Server How-To

George Szabo, Noel Jerke, David Jung, & Don Kiely

Readers get thorough coverage of Visual Basic 5 in the popular "How-to" format. More that just a reference, this book answers more than 100 of the most common Visual Basic questions showing readers how to quickly fix their problem and move on to the work of creating stunning Visual Basic 5 applications. CD-ROM contains all the sample documents and source code from the book. Covers hot topics such as OOP, ODBC, OLE, RDO, distributed computing, and three-tier client/server development. Saves hundreds of hours of programming time by providing step-by-step solutions to more than 75 Visual Basic 5 client/server problems.

$49.99 US/$70.95 CDN *Intermediate - Advanced*
1-57169-078-6 *900 pp.*
Waite Group Press

Doing Objects in Microsoft Visual Basic

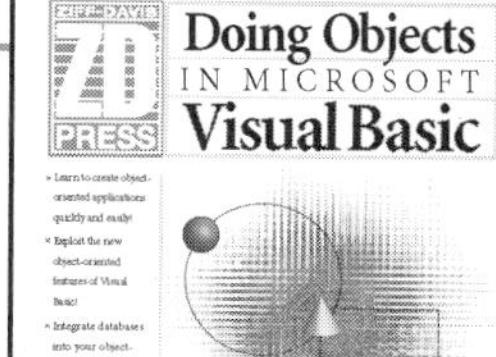
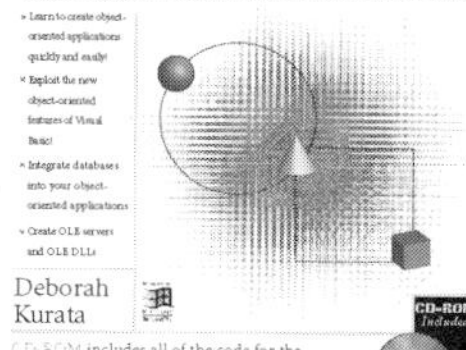

Deborah Kurata

Want to learn how to design and build Visual Basic applications, without relying on a lot of complicated tricks? This complete guide lays out the framework for development, providing a sturdy foundation for learning and success. Emphasizing architecture design and approach, this book examines project requirements, using the GUIDS methodology to design the framework and UI of the application, and builds the application using the object-oriented features of Visual Basic. Follows in the steps of a very successful and popular first edition. Written by a recognized author, programmer, and speaker. CD-ROM contains all of the code discussed in the book, project files, and sample chapters from *PC Magazine Visual Basic Programmer's Guide to the Win32 API.*

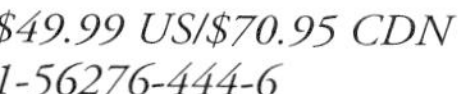

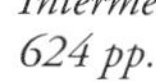

$49.99 US/$70.95 CDN *Intermediate - Advanced*
1-56276-444-6 *624 pp.*
Ziff-Davis Press

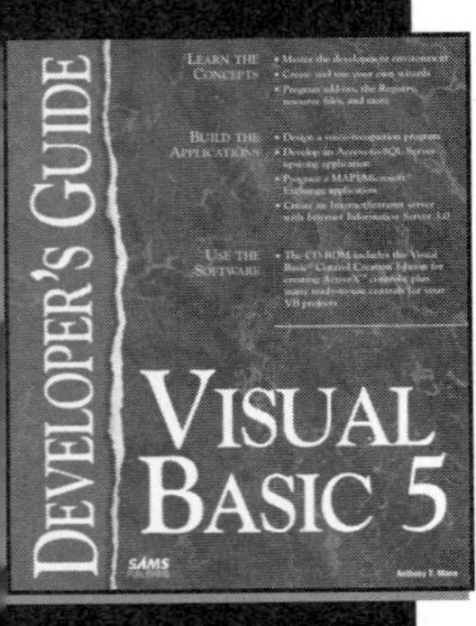

Visual Basic 5 Developer's Guide

Anthony T. Mann

Visual Basic 5 Developer's Guide takes the programmer with a basic knowledge of Visual Basic programming to a higher skill level. Readers learn how to exploit the new features of the latest version of Visual Basic, in addition to implementing Visual Basic in a network setting and in conjunction with other technologies and software. Learn expert programming techniques and strategies to create better applications.

Contains a full section of real-world examples readers can incorporate in their own applications. CD-ROM contains the complete source code for all of the programs in the book.

$49.99 US/$70.95 CDN *Accomplished - Expert*
0-672-31048-1 *1,032 pp.*

Special Edition Using Visual Basic 5, Second Edition

Mike McKelvy, Jeff Spotts, & Brian Siler

Special Edition Using Visual Basic 5, Second Edition takes a tutorial approach. It is assumed that the reader is new to Visual Basic. The book will teach programming with Visual Basic at a steady, consistent pace. Once the reader has been taught the Visual Basic programming language, the book will progress into more advanced topics. Such hot topics include an overview of COM, creating ActiveX controls, using Visual Basic with Active Server Pages, and more.

Special Edition Using Visual Basic 5, Second Edition builds on the success of the best-selling first edition. This new edition incorporates changes based on feedback from the readers of previous editions of *SE Using VB.* Based on this feedback, *Special Edition Using Visual Basic, Second Edition* provides a smoother, easier way to learn and exploit Visual Basic 5.0. *Special Edition Using Visual Basic 5, Second Edition* goes beyond most tutorials by providing expanded coverage of hot topics such as creating ActiveX controls, creating distributed applications, tapping into the Transaction Server, and more.

$39.99 US/$56.95 CDN *New - Casual*
0-7897-1288-1 *1,200 pp.*
Que

Dan Appleman's Visual Basic Programmer's Guide to the Win32 API

Daniel Appleman

No other book on the market can compete with this complete guide to WIN32 API. It is already being hailed as the definitive reference for Visual Basic programmers as it contains a wealth of background information on how Windows works. Includes API Toolkit and Desaware API Class Library. CD-ROM contains video annotations by the author in the full text, searchable edition of the book and source code examples.

$59.99 US/$84.95 CDN *Beginning - Advanced*
1-56276-446-2 *1,584 pp.*
Ziff-Davis Press

Dan Appleman's Developing ActiveX Components with Visual Basic

Daniel Appleman

This is the latest guide from the best-selling author of *Dan Appleman's Visual Basic Programmer's Guide to the Win32 API*. Dan Appleman's unique, no-holds-barred style of writing is perfect fo' VB programmers who want to learn how to create ActiveX components. Cuts to the chase, covering the most essential problems. Shows how to program around the bugs with techniques from Visual Basic masters. Explores how to avoid common pitfalls.

$49.99 US/$70.95 CDN   *Intermediate*
1-56276-510-8   *768 pp.*
Ziff-Davis Press

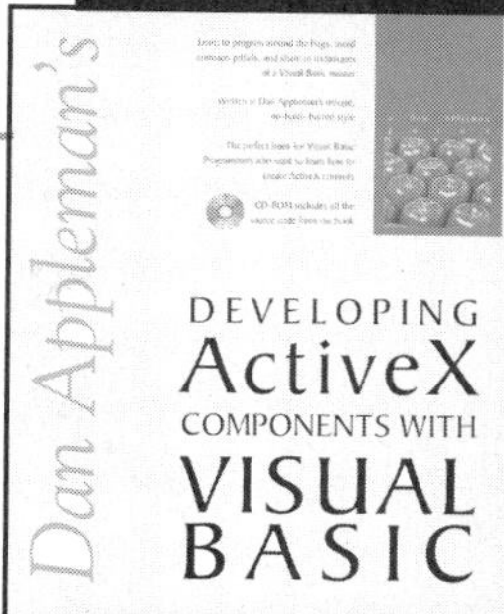

Platinum Edition Using Visual Basic 5

Loren D. Eidahl

Platinum Edition Using Visual Basic 5's unique approach provides an unparalleled reference and tutorial by assuming basic knowledge at the start and then progressing rapidly into more challenging issues. The two hottest and least understood topics in Visual Basic today are COM programming and distributed computing. *Platinum Editing Using Visual Basic 5* covers both topics in exhaustive depth, using clear examples and concise writing. The CD-ROMs provide the finishing touches with thousands of additional pages of Visual Basic coverage, a vast array of pre-built controls, a library of complete applications, and a comprehensive electronic index. Designed for the developer who wants in depth coverage of core topics and new technologies and features. Provides an unparalleled reference and tutorial by assuming basic knowledge at the start and then progressing rapidly into more challenging issues. Covers COM programming and distributed computing in exhaustive depth, using clear examples and concise writing.

$60.00 US/$84.95 CDN   *All User Levels*
0-7897-1412-4   *1,400 pp.*
Que

The Waite Group Visual Basic 5 SuperBible Set

Eric Winemiller, David Jung, Pierre Boutquin, John Harrington, Bill Heyman, Ryan Groom, Todd Bright, & Bill Potter

Visual Basic 5 SuperBible covers the fundamentals of the Visual Basic language, plus the new additions. Every Visual Basic object, property, method, event, and keyword is covered in detail. Includes coverage of Visual Basic 5 improvements: ActiveX controls, enumerated types, encapsulation and variable scoping, and the native-code compiler. Contains well-researched index, subject-oriented tables, and numerous internal cross-references guide the reader to the exact information they need.

$69.99 US/$98.95 CDN   *Intermediate - Advanced*
1-57169-102-2   *2,200 pp.*
Waite Group Press

Sams' Teach Yourself More Visual Basic 5 in 21 Days

Lowell Mauer

Using the formula of the best-selling Sams' Teach Yourself series, this comprehensive guide teaches readers everything they need to know about Visual Basic—quickly and easily. Using a logical, easy-to-follow format, users will be developing dynamic Visual Basic programs in no time. Explores the newest features of Visual Basic and advanced programming techniques-in detail. Workshops, Q&A sections, and Do's and Don'ts make learning easy and fun. The CD-ROM is loaded with all the source code from the book, third-party utilities, and sample scripts.

$29.99 US/$42.95 CDN *Casual - Accomplished - Expert*
0-672-31062-7 *1,000 pp.*
Sams Publishing

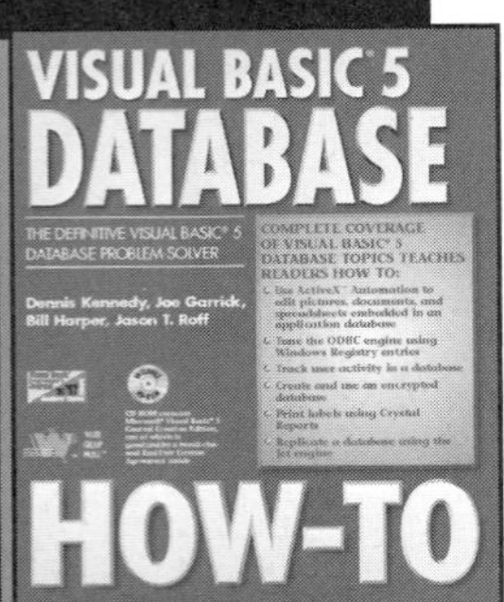

Visual Basic 5 Database How-To

Dennis Kennedy, Joe Garrick, Bill Harper, & Jason T. Roff

With the release of Visual Basic 5, database development in Visual Basic has moved to a new level of sophistication. With *Visual Basic 5 Database How-To*, readers can keep abreast of the new developments. The book contains more than 120 step-by-step solutions to challenging, real-world problems, presented in Waite Group Press's award-winning "How-To" format, tackling even the most complex issues with easily understood solutions. Readers will discover how to use the power of SQL Server in their own apps and learn how to use Open Database Connectivity to create powerful high-end programs quickly. The book teaches how to take command of Structured Query Language (SQL) to create recordset, build parameter queries, and even construct entire databases. Readers will learn to make use of popular database formats, such as Access, FoxPro, Paradox, dBase and Btreive, easily and effectively. And, with ActiveX technology, readers can create their own custom data access controls. The CD-ROM included contains complete source code for every solution provided in the book, so the reader can save hours of coding time and have a library of useful code on hand for any database programming situation. For Visual Basic developers, this complete, easy-to-use guide provides the information and resources needed to write high-quality database applications, no matter the database management system. Covers Visual Basic 5 Professional and Enterprise Editions. Spans a wide variety of database programming situations for intermediate and advanced Visual Basic developers. More than 120 practical step-by-step solutions to common Visual Basic database problems.

$49.99 US/$70.95 *Intermediate - Advanced*
1-57169-104-9 *1,008 pp.*
Waite Group Press

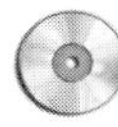

Web Development with Visual Basic 5

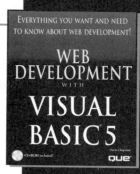

Davis Chapman

Web Development with Visual Basic 5 is a comprehensive tutorial and reference guide to the newest web development technologies. Developers will learn what these technologies are and when to use them. Tutorial—Developers can use this book to teach themselves the latest Web development technologies. Reference—Developers will discover it is an essential desk reference for clarification of difficult topics, troubleshooting, or debugging existing applications. Developers will benefit from the practical advice and real-world applications which demonstrate how to implement new technologies such as Active Server Pages. Learn to create multi-tier, distributed Web applications using Microsoft Transaction Server and COM objects. Unlock the secrets to Web Database access using Data Access Objects (DAO), Remote Data Objects (RDO), ActiveX Data Objects, and Visual InterDev. Covers all of the key ActiveX developer technologies, including ActiveX controls, Active Documents, Active Server Pages, Active Data controls, and more.

$49.99 US/$70.95 CDN   Accomplished - Expert
0-7897-0811-6   1,000 pp.   CD-ROM ICON
Que

Web Database Developer's Guide with Visual Basic 5

Mark Swank, Drew Kittel, & Mark Spenik

Written by developers for developers, this advanced guide shows users how to design, develop, and deploy secure client/server databases on the Internet and intranet Web sites using the latest version of Microsoft Visual Basic.

Includes real-world examples and applications throughout the book for users to implement on their sites.

CD-ROM is loaded with author's source code and a collection of Web and database tools.

Covers Databases
$59.99 USA/$83.95 CAN   Accomplished - Expert
1-57521-276-5   900 pp.
Databases
Sams.net

Book ISBN 0-672-31297-2

MISCELLANEOUS

If you acquired this product in the United States, this EULA is governed by the laws of the State of Washington.

If you acquired this product in Canada, this EULA is governed by the laws of the Province of Ontario, Canada. Each of the parties hereto irrevocably attorns to the jurisdiction of the courts of the Province of Ontario and further agrees to commence any litigation which may arise hereunder in the courts located in the Judicial District of York, Province of Ontario.

If this product was acquired outside the United States, then local law may apply.

Should you have any questions concerning this EULA, or if you desire to contact Microsoft for any reason, please contact the Microsoft subsidiary serving your country, or write: Microsoft Sales Information Center/One Microsoft Way/Redmond, WA 98052-6399.

LIMITED WARRANTY

NO WARRANTIES. Microsoft expressly disclaims any warranty for the SOFTWARE PRODUCT. The SOFTWARE PRODUCT and any related documentation is provided "as is" without warranty of any kind, either express or implied, including, without limitation, the implied warranties or merchantability, fitness for a particular purpose, or noninfringement. The entire risk arising out of use or performance of the SOFTWARE PRODUCT remains with you.

NO LIABILITY FOR DAMAGES. In no event shall Microsoft or its suppliers be liable for any damages whatsoever (including, without limitation, damages for loss of business profits, business interruption, loss of business information, or any other pecuniary loss) arising out of the use of or inability to use this Microsoft product, even if Microsoft has been advised of the possibility of such damages. Because some states/jurisdictions do not allow the exclusion or limitation of liability for consequential or incidental damages, the above limitation may not apply to you.

3. UPGRADES. If the SOFTWARE PRODUCT is labeled as an upgrade, you must be properly licensed to use a product identified by Microsoft as being eligible for the upgrade in order to use the SOFTWARE PRODUCT. A SOFTWARE PRODUCT labeled as an upgrade replaces and/or supplements the product that formed the basis for your eligibility for the upgrade. You may use the resulting upgraded product only in accordance with the terms of this EULA. If the SOFTWARE PRODUCT is an upgrade of a component of a package of software programs that you licensed as a single product, the SOFTWARE PRODUCT may be used and transferred only as part of that single product package and may not be separated for use on more than one computer.

4. COPYRIGHT. All title and copyrights in and to the SOFTWARE PRODUCT (including but not limited to any images, photographs, animations, video, audio, music, text, and "applets" incorporated into the SOFTWARE PRODUCT), the accompanying printed materials, and any copies of the SOFTWARE PRODUCT are owned by Microsoft or its suppliers. The SOFTWARE PRODUCT is protected by copyright laws and international treaty provisions. Therefore, you must treat the SOFTWARE PRODUCT like any other copyrighted material except that you may install the SOFTWARE PRODUCT on a single computer provided you keep the original solely for backup or archival purposes. You may not copy the printed materials accompanying the SOFTWARE PRODUCT.

5. DUAL-MEDIA SOFTWARE. You may receive the SOFTWARE PRODUCT in more than one medium. Regardless of the type or size of medium you receive, you may use only one medium that is appropriate for your single computer. You may not use or install the other medium on another computer. You may not loan, rent, lease, or otherwise transfer the other medium to another user, except as part of the permanent transfer (as provided above) of the SOFTWARE PRODUCT.

6. U.S. GOVERNMENT RESTRICTED RIGHTS. The SOFTWARE PRODUCT and documentation are provided with RESTRICTED RIGHTS. Use, duplication, or disclosure by the Government is subject to restrictions as set forth in subparagraph (c)(1)(ii) of the Rights in Technical Data and Computer Software clause at DFARS 252.227-7013 or subparagraphs (c)(1) and (2) of the Commercial Computer Software—Restricted Rights at 48 CFR 52.227-19, as applicable. Manufacturer is Microsoft Corporation/One Microsoft Way/ Redmond, WA 98052-6399.

7. EXPORT RESTRICTIONS. You agree that neither you nor your customers intend to or will, directly or indirectly, export or transmit (i) the SOFTWARE or related documentation and technical data or (ii) your software product as described in Section 1(b) of this License (or any part thereof), or process, or service that is the direct product of the SOFTWARE, to any country to which such export or transmission is restricted by any applicable U.S. regulation or statute, without the prior written consent, if required, of the Bureau of Export Administration of the U.S. Department of Commerce, or such other governmental entity as may have jurisdiction over such export or transmission.

terms of this EULA; and (2) you may permit your end users to reproduce and distribute the object code version of the files designated by ".ocx" file extensions ("Controls") only in conjunction with and as a part of an Application and/or Web page that adds significant and primary functionality to the Controls, and such end user complies with all other terms of this EULA.

2. DESCRIPTION OF OTHER RIGHTS AND LIMITATIONS.

a. **Not for Resale Software.** If the SOFTWARE PRODUCT is labeled "Not for Resale" or "NFR," then, notwithstanding other sections of this EULA, you may not resell, or otherwise transfer for value, the SOFTWARE PRODUCT.

b. **Limitations on Reverse Engineering, Decompilation, and Disassembly.** You may not reverse engineer, decompile, or disassemble the SOFTWARE PRODUCT, except and only to the extent that such activity is expressly permitted by applicable law notwithstanding this limitation.

c. **Separation of Components.** The SOFTWARE PRODUCT is licensed as a single product. Its component parts may not be separated for use by more than one user.

d. **Rental.** You may not rent, lease, or lend the SOFTWARE PRODUCT.

e. **Support Services.** Microsoft may provide you with support services related to the SOFTWARE PRODUCT ("Support Services"). Use of Support Services is governed by the Microsoft policies and programs described in the user manual, in "online" documentation, and/or in other Microsoft-provided materials. Any supplemental software code provided to you as part of the Support Services shall be considered part of the SOFTWARE PRODUCT and subject to the terms and conditions of this EULA. With respect to technical information you provide to Microsoft as part of the Support Services, Microsoft may use such information for its business purposes, including for product support and development. Microsoft will not utilize such technical information in a form that personally identifies you.

f. **Software Transfer.** You may permanently transfer all of your rights under this EULA, provided you retain no copies, you transfer all of the SOFTWARE PRODUCT (including all component parts, the media and printed materials, any upgrades, this EULA, and, if applicable, the Certificate of Authenticity), and the recipient agrees to the terms of this EULA. If the SOFTWARE PRODUCT is an upgrade, any transfer must include all prior versions of the SOFTWARE PRODUCT.

g. **Termination.** Without prejudice to any other rights, Microsoft may terminate this EULA if you fail to comply with the terms and conditions of this EULA. In such event, you must destroy all copies of the SOFTWARE PRODUCT and all of its component parts.

1. **GRANT OF LICENSE.** This EULA grants you the following rights:

a. **Software Product.** Microsoft grants to you as an individual, a personal, nonexclusive license to make and use copies of the SOFTWARE for the sole purposes of designing, developing, and testing your software product(s) that are designed to operate in conjunction with any Microsoft operating system product. You may install copies of the SOFTWARE on an unlimited number of computers provided that you are the only individual using the SOFTWARE. If you are an entity, Microsoft grants you the right to designate one individual within your organization to have the right to use the SOFTWARE in the manner provided above.

b. **Electronic Documents.** Solely with respect to electronic documents included with the SOFTWARE, you may make an unlimited number of copies (either in hardcopy or electronic form), provided that such copies shall be used only for internal purposes and are not republished or distributed to any third party.

c. **Redistributable Components.**

(I) **Sample Code.** In addition to the rights granted in Section 1, Microsoft grants you the right to use and modify the source code version of those portions of the SOFTWARE designated as "Sample Code" ("SAMPLE CODE") for the sole purposes of designing, developing, and testing your software product(s), and to reproduce and distribute the SAMPLE CODE, along with any modifications thereof, only in object code form provided that you comply with Section d(iii), below.

(ii) **Redistributable Components.** In addition to the rights granted in Section 1, Microsoft grants you a nonexclusive royalty-free right to reproduce and distribute the object code version of any portion of the SOFTWARE listed in the SOFTWARE file REDIST.TXT ("REDISTRIBUTABLE SOFTWARE"), provided you comply with Section d (iii), below.

(iii) **Redistribution Requirements.** If you redistribute the SAMPLE CODE or REDISTRIBUTABLE SOFTWARE (collectively, "REDISTRIBUTABLES"), you agree to: (A) distribute the REDISTRIBUTABLES in object code only in conjunction with and as a part of a software application product developed by you that adds significant and primary functionality to the SOFTWARE and that is developed to operate on the Windows or Windows NT environment ("Application"); (B) not use Microsoft's name, logo, or trademarks to market your software application product; (C) include a valid copyright notice on your software product; (D) indemnify, hold harmless, and defend Microsoft from and against any claims or lawsuits, including attorney's fees, that arise or result from the use or distribution of your software application product; (E) not permit further distribution of the REDISTRIBUTABLES by your end user. The following **exceptions** apply to subsection (iii) (E), above: (1) you may permit further redistribution of the REDISTRIBUTABLES by your distributors to your end-user customers if your distributors only distribute the REDISTRIBUTABLES in conjunction with, and as part of, your Application and you and your distributors comply with all other

By opening this package, you are agreeing to be bound by the following agreement:

Visual Basic Control Creation Edition was reproduced by Sams Publishing under a special arrangement with Microsoft Corporation. For this reason, Sams Publishing is responsible for the product warranty and for support. If your disk is defective, please return it to Sams Publishing, which will arrange for its replacement. PLEASE DO NOT RETURN IT TO MICROSOFT CORPORATION. Any product support will be provided, if at all, by Sams Publishing. PLEASE DO NOT CONTACT MICROSOFT CORPORATION FOR PRODUCT SUPPORT. End users of this Microsoft program shall not be considered "registered owners" of a Microsoft product and therefore shall not be eligible for upgrades, promotions or other benefits available to "registered owners" of Microsoft products.

You may not copy or redistribute the entire CD-ROM as a whole, Copying and redistribution of individual software programs on the CD-ROM is governed by terms set by individual copyright holders. The installer and code from the author is copyrighted by the publisher and the author, Individual programs and other items on the CD-ROM are copyrighted by their various authors or other copyright holders. This software is sold as-is without warranty of any kind, either expressed or implied, including but not limited to the implied warranties of merchantability and fitness for a particular purpose. Neither the publisher nor its dealers or distributors assumes any liability for any alleged or actual damages arising from the use of this program. (Some states do not allow for the exclusion of implied warranties, so the exclusion may not apply to you.)

NOTE: This CD-ROM uses long and mixed-case filenames requiring the use of a protected-mode CD-ROM Driver.

END-USER LICENSE AGREEMENT FOR MICROSOFT SOFTWARE

Microsoft Visual Basic , Control Creation Edition

IMPORTANT—READ CAREFULLY: This Microsoft End-User License Agreement ("EULA") is a legal agreement between you (either an individual or a single entity) and Microsoft Corporation for the Microsoft software product identified above, which includescomputer software and may include associated media, printed materials, and "online" or electronic documentation ("SOFTWARE PRODUCT"). By installing, copying, or otherwise using the SOFTWARE PRODUCT, you agree to be bound by the terms of this EULA. If you do not agree to the terms of this EULA, do not install or use the SOFTWARE PRODUCT; you may, however, return it to your place of purchase for a full refund.

Software PRODUCT LICENSE

The SOFTWARE PRODUCT is protected by copyright laws and international copyright treaties, as well as other intellectual property laws and treaties. The SOFTWARE PRODUCT is licensed, not sold.

The companion CD-ROM contains all of the authors' source code and sample from the book, as well as many third-party software products.

Windows 95/NT 4 Installation Instructions

1. Insert the CD-ROM into your CD-ROM drive.
2. From the Windows 95 desktop, double-click the My Computer icon.
3. Double-click the icon representing your CD-ROM drive.
4. Double-click the icon titled `SETUP.EXE` to run the installation program.
5. The installation program creates a program group with the book's name as the group name. This group contains icons to browse the CD-ROM.

NOTE

If Windows 95 is installed on your computer and you have the AutoPlay feature enabled, the `SETUP.EXE` program starts automatically when you insert the CD into your CD-ROM drive.

System Requirements

This CD-ROM contains the Microsoft Visual Basic Control Creation Edition. Some of the features of Visual Basic 5 discussed in this book may not be usable with the Control Creation Edition. The Control Creation Edition is provided to allow you to become familiar with the Visual Basic environment and to create your own ActiveX controls.

The following are the minimum system requirements for the Visual Basic® Control Creation Edition:

- A personal Computer with a 486 or higher processor
- Microsoft Windows 95 or Windows NT Workstation 4.0 or later
- 8 MB of memory (12 MB recommended) if running Windows NT Workstation
- The following hard disk space:

  Typical installation: 20 MB

  Minimum installation: 14 MB

  CD-ROM installation (tools run from the CD): 14 MB

  Total tools and information on the CD: 50 MB
- A CD-ROM drive
- A VGA or higher-resolution monitor (SVGA recommended)